Encyclopedia of the

NORTH
AMERICAN
COLONIES

Encyclopedia of the

NORTH AMERICAN COLONIES

EDITOR IN CHIEF
Jacob Ernest Cooke, *Lafayette College*

ASSOCIATE EDITORS
W. J. Eccles, *University of Toronto*
Ramón A. Gutiérrez, *University of California, San Diego*
Milton M. Klein, *University of Tennessee*
Gloria Lund Main, *University of Colorado*
Jackson Turner Main, *University of Colorado*
Alden Vaughan, *Columbia University*

SPECIAL CONSULTANTS
Mathé Allain, *University of Southwestern Louisiana*
Carl A. Brasseaux, *University of Southwestern Louisiana*
Charles T. Gehring, *New Netherland Project*
William C. Sturtevant, *Smithsonian Institution*

Volume I

CHARLES SCRIBNER'S SONS / NEW YORK
MAXWELL MACMILLAN CANADA / TORONTO
MAXWELL MACMILLAN INTERNATIONAL / NEW YORK   OXFORD   SINGAPORE   SYDNEY

Charles Scribner's Sons
Macmillan Publishing Company
866 Third Avenue
New York, NY 10022

Maxwell Macmillan Canada, Inc.
1200 Eglinton Avenue East
Suite 200
Don Mills, Ontario M3C 3N1

Library of Congress Cataloging-in-Publication Data

Encyclopedia of the North American colonies / editor in chief, Jacob Ernest Cooke; associate
editors, W. J. Eccles . . . [et al.]; special consultants, Mathé Allain . . . [et al].
    p. cm.
    Includes bibliographical references and index
    ISBN 0-684-19269-1 (set: alk. paper)
    1. Europe--Colonies--America--History--Encyclopedias.   2. North America--History--
Encyclopedias.   I. Cooke, Jacob Ernest, 1924–
E45.E53   1993   93-7609
940′.03--dc20   CIP

ISBN 0-684-19269-1   Set
ISBN 0-684-19609-3   Volume 1
ISBN 0-684-19610-7   Volume 2
ISBN 0-684-19611-5   Volume 3

3   4   5   6   7   8   9   10

Printed in the United States of America

The paper used in this publication meets the minimum requirements of American National
Standard for Information Sciences--Permanence of Paper for Printed Library Materials. ANSI
Z3948-1984. ⊗™

EDITORIAL STAFF

Managing Editors
DAVID L. BAIN
(1990–1992)

ANN LESLIE TUTTLE
(1993)

Copy Editors and Researchers
GRETCHEN GORDON   MICHAEL LEVINE

JONATHAN G. ARETAKIS   JERILYN FAMIGHETTI   EDWARD FERRARO
BARBARA IBRONYI   ALICE NASH   ELIZABETH I. WILSON

Proofreaders
CARL FLANDERS   STEPHEN FLANDERS
CAROL HOLMES

Cartography
ELLEN R. WHITE

Index
AEIOU, INC.

Publisher
KAREN DAY

CONTENTS

Volume I

CONTENTS

CONTENTS

CONTENTS

CONTENTS

CONTENTS

CONTENTS

Volume III

CONTENTS

CONTENTS

LIST OF MAPS

Volume I

Volume II

Volume III

CHRONOLOGY

Since the North American colonies did not win independence from imperial rule simultaneously, this chronology assumes the following terminal dates for each major imperial power's involvement: Scandinavia, 1655; Netherlands, 1664; Great Britain, 1776; Spain, 1821; France, 1867; and Russia, 1867.

985	The Norseman Eirik the Red settles a colony in western Greenland; the settlement lasts until the fourteenth or fifteenth century.
c. 1000	Leif Eiriksson, returning to Greenland from Norway, is driven onto the North American coast.
1444	Portuguese raid on the coasts of northwestern Africa begins maritime slave trade.
1478–1834	Spanish Crown officially sanctions the Spanish Inquisition.
1479–1516	Ferdinand and Isabella reign in Spain.
1483–1498	Charles VIII reigns in France.
1485–1509	Henry VII reigns in England.
1492	Christopher Columbus sails west in search of a new route to Asia and finds a "New World."
1494	Treaty of Tordesillas: Globe is divided between Spanish and Portuguese empires.
1497	Venetian navigator John Cabot and his son Sebastian, commissioned by Henry VII of England to discover a new trade route to Asia, reach the east coast of North America.
1498–1515	Louis XI reigns in France.
c. 1500	Norman and Breton fishermen visit Newfoundland coasts.
1502	Spanish introduce enslaved Africans to their "new" Caribbean colonies.
1503	Casa de Contratación (House of Trade) established in Seville to manage transatlantic trade for Spain.
1507	Martin Waldseemüller proposes that the New World be called "America" after the Florentine explorer Amerigo Vespucci, who made voyages to South America for Spain (1499–1500) and for Portugal (1501–1502)
1509–1547	Henry VIII reigns in England.
1513	Juan Ponce de León claims Florida for Spain.
1515–1547	Francis I reigns in France.
1516–1556	Charles I reigns in Spain.
1518	African slaves are brought to Hispaniola (Haiti) to work in gold mines.
1518–1521	Hernán Cortés captures the city of Tenochtitlán, ruled by Montezuma, and conquers the Aztec Empire in Mexico.
1519–1522	Spanish fleet commanded by Portuguese navigator Ferdinand Magellan; upon his death Juan del Lano completes the first circumnavigation of the globe.
1521	Juan Ponce de León tries unsuccessfully to colonize Florida.
1524	Charles V creates Council of the Indies to govern the New World.
	Giovanni da Verrazano, Florentine navigator in the service of Francis I, explores the coast of North America from Cape Fear to Cape Breton.
1531	Virgin of Guadalupe appears before an Indian and comes to symbolize the unification of Spanish and Native American causes.
1531–1550	New Spain expands to the north from Mexico, extending its conquests to New Mexico and Arizona.

CHRONOLOGY

1534   The Act of Supremacy establishes the king as head of the Church of England, voiding the authority of the pope, and formally launches the English Reformation.

Ignatius Loyola founds the Society of Jesus, known as the Jesuit order.

Jacques Cartier explores the Gulf of Saint Lawrence on his first voyage to North America.

1535–1536   Cartier sails up the Saint Lawrence River to Montreal and winters at Quebec.

1539–1543   Hernando de Soto explores southeastern North America from Florida to the Mississippi River.

1540–1542   Francisco Vásquez de Coronado explores the Southwest in search of gold; he meets Zuni people and reaches the Grand Canyon. His party includes Esteban, a Moor.

1541–1542   Cartier and Jean-François de la Rocque de Roberval try to establish a settlement at Quebec.

1542–1543   Juan Rodríguez Cabrillo conducts first European exploration of California coast north of Baja.

1547–1553   Edward VI reigns in England.

1547–1559   Henry II reigns in France.

c. 1550   Mohawk, Oneida, Onondaga, Cayuga, and Seneca peoples unite to form the Iroquois confederacy, also known as the Five Nations, in the sixteenth century.

1550   Juan Gines de Sepúlveda argues in a debate on slavery in Valladolid, Spain, that Indians are "slaves by nature" based on Aristotle, while Bartolomé de Las Casas argues that Indians are rational beings.

1553–1558   Mary I reigns in England.

1555   Abdication of Charles V, Holy Roman emperor and king of Spain (as Charles I), in favor of his son Philip and brother Ferdinand; Philip II inherits control over the Low Countries.

Tobacco is brought to Spain from America for the first time.

1556–1598   Philip II reigns in Spain.

1558–1603   Elizabeth I reigns in England.

1559–1560   Francis II reigns in France.

1560–1574   Charles IX reigns in France.

1562   Civil wars of religion are fought between French Protestants (Huguenots) and Catholics.

1562–1568   John Hawkins makes slave-trading voyages from Africa to the West Indies and the Spanish Main.

1564   France establishes Fort Caroline on Saint John's River in Florida, settlement quickly overrun by the Spanish.

1565   Pedro Menéndez de Avilés founds Saint Augustine in Florida.

1565–1574   Spain establishes *presidios* in an effort to colonize the area north of the Florida Peninsula to Virginia.

1566   First Jesuit missionaries arrive in Florida.

1572   Powhatan, a Pamunkey leader, unites two dozen Algonquian-speaking tribes in the Chesapeake region to form the Powhatan confederacy.

1573   Ordinances of Discovery: Ordinances establish procedures for settling Spain's American Empire.

1574–1589   Henry III reigns in France.

1579   Francis Drake drops anchor off the California coast and becomes the first Englishman to encounter the Native people of California.

1579–1584   Willem I, prince of Orange-Nassau, serves as the first stadtholder of the Netherlands after the Union of Utrecht unites seven northern provinces.

c. 1580   Moscovites move east across Siberia in search of "soft gold"—sables.

1582   Antonio de Espejo leads expedition to New Mexico.

1583   Sir Humphrey Gilbert leads expedition to Newfoundland.

1584–1586   Sir Walter Raleigh promotes a colony on Roanoke Island, off the coast of present-day North Carolina; artist John White and scholar Thomas Harriot prepare a detailed account of the people, flora, and fauna, which is published in 1588.

CHRONOLOGY

1584–1625	Prince Maurits of Orange-Nassau assumes the inherited stadtholdership.
1587	Recolonization of Roanoke Island; settlement disappears by 1590.
1588	The Spanish Armada is destroyed off the coast of England; England becomes the pre-emininent naval power in Europe.
1589	Richard Hakluyt's *Principall Navigations, Voyages, and Discoveries of the English Nation* is published in London.
1589–1610	Henry IV (Henry of Navarre) reigns in France.
1595	Philip II of Spain licenses Don Juan de Oñate to colonize the Kingdom of New Mexico.
1598	The Edict of Nantes marks the end of the Religious Wars; Huguenots are granted limited political rights in France.
	Juan de Oñate establishes the *Camino Real;* it eventually stretches for eighteen hundred miles (2,900 kilometers) and links Mexico City to Santa Fe, New Mexico.
1598–1599	The Acoma Pueblo defy Spanish authority in New Mexico.
1598–1621	Philip III reigns in Spain.
1602	Bartholomew Gosnold explores the Atlantic coast from southern Maine to Narragansett Bay; smallpox breaks out among his Indian trading partners.
	The United East India Company (Vereenigde Oostindische Compagnie, VOC) is chartered by the States General of the United Provinces.
1603	Samuel de Champlain founds a French settlement in Acadia.
1603–1625	James I (James VI of Scotland) reigns in England.
1604	Pierre de Gua, sieur de Monts and lieutenant general of Acadia, establishes Port Royal on the Saint Croix River.
1606	James I grants charters to the Virginia Company of London (Virginia Company) and the Virginia Company of Plymouth (Plymouth Company).
1606–1607	"Le Théâtre de Neptune en la Nouvelle-France," written by Marc Lescarbot, is performed at Port Royal.
1606–1608	The Plymouth Company establishes the short-lived Sagadahoc colony near the mouth of the Kennebec River (present-day Maine).
1607	Colonists found Jamestown—the first permanent English settlement—in Virginia. Captain John Smith emerges as leader but leaves in 1609.
	Massasoit becomes chief of the Wampanoag, a powerful New England tribe.
1608	Samuel de Champlain establishes a settlement at Quebec on the site of Stadacona, a recently deserted Iroquois village.
1609	Champlain accompanies a Huron-Algonquin war party against the Mohawk.
	Henry Hudson explores the Hudson River as far north as present-day Albany.
	Santa Fe is established.
1609–1613	Champlain explores fur-trade routes, traveling the Canadian interior as far as Georgian Bay with Algonquin and Huron guides.
1610–1643	Louis XIII reigns in France.
1612	New varieties of tobacco are planted in Virginia; tobacco boom in the Chesapeake region begins soon thereafter.
1613	Port Royal is destroyed by English forces under Samuel Argall.
1614	Captain John Smith explores the coast of northern "Virginia" and proposes it be called New England.
	Pocahontas, daughter of the Indian chief Powhatan, marries the English colonist John Rolfe at Jamestown.
	The States General grant the New Netherland Company a monopoly; Fort Nassau, a fur-trading post, is established on Castle Island—the present-day Port of Albany—and is replaced ten years later by Fort Orange (in present-day Albany).
1615	Four Recollet friars arrive in Quebec and begin formal missionary activity.

CHRONOLOGY

1616	The first African slaves brought to British America land in Bermuda.
1617	The first tobacco shipment from Virginia arrives in England.
1619	The first "negroes" in the mainland British colonies are brought to Virginia by the Dutch.
1620	Puritan Separatists (the Pilgrims) establish a colony at Plymouth on land that had been cleared of earlier Wampanoag inhabitants by an epidemic.
1621	The States General charter the West India Company (WIC).
1621–1665	Philip IV reigns in Spain.
1622	Opechancanough leads the Powhatan confederacy against the English in Virginia.
1624	Captain John Smith's *Generall Historie of Virginia, New-England and the Summer Isles* is published.
	Thirty Walloon families settle in New Netherland.
1625	Jesuits come to Quebec.
	Willem Verhulst arrives as director of New Netherland.
1625–1647	Prince Frederik Hendrik reigns as stadtholder.
1625–1649	Charles I reigns in England.
1626	Peter Minuit becomes director of New Netherland and serves until 1631; he buys land from the Manhattan Indians. The first African slaves arrive in New Amsterdam (New York City).
1627	New France grants charter to the Compagnie des Cent-Associes (Company of New France).
1628–1632	Acadia and Quebec come under English control but are returned to France in 1632.
1629	The Charter of Freedoms and Exemptions establishes the patroonship plan of colonization; approved by the West India Company.
	John Winthrop agrees to serve as governor of Massachusetts Bay colony's Puritan community.
	The Massachusetts Bay Company is chartered; its first outpost is established

	at Salem (Naumkeag). Sir Ferdinando Gorges and Captain John Mason claim lands in Maine and New Hampshire.
1630–1641	Puritans found a colony on Providence Island, off the coast of Nicaragua, but colony is ended by Spanish conquest.
1630–1642	The Great Migration; sixteen thousand settlers from England arrive in the Massachusetts Bay colony.
1631	Patroonships of Rensselaerswyck (upper Hudson), Pavonia (Jersey City), and Swaanendael (Lewes, Delaware) are founded in New Netherland.
1632	The colony of Maryland is granted to Cecilius Calvert, second lord Baltimore.
	Minuit is removed as director of New Netherland and replaced by Bastiaen Jansz Crol.
1632–1674	The *Jesuit Relations* give annual reports of missionary efforts in New France.
1633	The Collège de Québec is founded in Quebec City.
1633–1638	English colonists start to settle lands along the Connecticut River.
	Wouter van Twiller is director-general of New Netherland.
1636	Clergyman Roger Williams, banished from Massachusetts Bay because of his unorthodoxy, establishes a colony at Providence, Rhode Island.
	Harvard College is founded at Cambridge, Massachusetts.
1636–1637	The Pequot War: Conflict with English colonists in Connecticut leads to the virtual destruction of local Pequot inhabitants.
1636–1638	The Antinomian Crisis: Anne Hutchinson challenges the authority of clergymen by leading prayer meetings in her Boston home, is exiled with many of her followers, and settles in Rhode Island.
1638	The first printing press in Anglo-America is established in Cambridge, Massachusetts.
	Peter Minuit, working for the Swedish South Company, founds New Sweden on the Delaware River (Wilmington, Delaware).

1638 1647	Willem Kieft is director of New Netherland.	
1639	The Hôtel-Dieu, the first hospital in North America, is founded in Quebec.	
	WIC monopoly of the fur trade in New Netherland is ended.	
1641	*The Bay Psalm Book* is published in Boston; the first book printed in the colonies.	
1642	Massachusetts government requires parents to provide reading instruction to their children.	
	Montreal is founded as a base for French fur traders on the Saint Lawrence River.	
1642–1643	Kieft's War: The Dutch wage war against the Indians of the lower Hudson Valley.	
1642–1649	The English Civil War pits royalists against Parliamentarians (mostly Puritans).	
1642–1654	Johan Printz is governor of New Sweden.	
1643	Massachusetts Bay, Plymouth, Connecticut, and New Haven form the New England confederation to unite against Dutch, French, and Indian threats.	
	Roger Williams's book on southern New England Indian languages, *A Key into the Language of America,* is published in London.	
1643–1715	Louis XIV reigns in France.	
1646–1665	The Iroquois launch devastating raids against neighboring tribes such as the Algonquin, Huron, Nipissing, and Neutral; refugees from these groups move east to Quebec or inland to the Great Lakes region.	
1647	Peter Stuyvesant becomes director-general of New Netherland as well as Dutch islands in the Caribbean.	
1647–1650	Prince Willem II reigns as stadtholder.	
1649	Charles I is executed; England becomes a commonwealth.	
	Maryland passes a Toleration Act, granting religious freedom to all Trinitarians, which is repealed in 1654.	
	The Swedish ship, *Kattan (The Cat),* bringing much-needed supplies to New	

	Sweden, is lost off the coast of Puerto Rico.
1650	The Hartford Treaty settles the boundary dispute between New Netherland and New England.
	Poems by Anne Bradstreet, the first American poet, are printed in a London publication, *The Tenth Muse Lately Sprung Up in America.*
	The States General, opposing the authority of the house of Orange, assumes control over Dutch general policy.
1652	The Dutch establish almshouses in Beverswyck (Albany).
1652–1654	In the American phase of the First Anglo-Dutch War, New Netherland attempts to expel all English colonists.
1653	A defensive wall is built across Manhattan Island (Wall Street) in response to a threatened invasion from New England.
	Oliver Cromwell is installed as Lord Protector of the Commonwealth.
1654	The first Jews arrive in New Amsterdam.
	Swedish forces under Governor Johan Rising capture the Dutch post Fort Casimir on Trinity Sunday and rename it Fort Trefaltighet (Fort Trinity).
1655	Adriaen van der Donck's *Description of New Netherland* is published in the Netherlands with observations on the land, the flora, the fauna, and the culture of the Indians.
	The Peach War: A Manhattan Indian woman is killed while picking peaches in Governor Peter Stuyvesant's yard; Indians retaliate by attacking New Amsterdam.
	Stuyvesant conquers New Sweden in the Delaware Valley ending Scandinavia's jurisdiction in North America.
1658–1664	Hostilities with Esopus Indians end with the cession of the Esopus Valley to the Dutch.
1660	First Stuart Navigation Act orders that all goods imported to or exported from

English colonies must be carried by English ships.

1660–1685 Reign of Charles II of England marks restoration of Stuart monarchy. English ships.

1661 Massasoit, chief of the Wampanoag and a friend of the Pilgrims, dies.

1662–1683 Jean-Baptiste Colbert serves as controller general of finances in New France.

1663 Canada is declared to be a royal province with Quebec as its capital. To encourage settlement, Louis XIV gives dowries to young unmarried women who are willing to go to Canada in search of husbands.

Charles II of England grants Carolina (present-day North and South Carolina) to eight proprietors.

John Eliot's translation of the Bible into the Massachusett Indian language is published in Cambridge, Massachusetts.

1664 The Compagnie des Indes Occidentales is formed to control French trade in Canada, South America, West Africa, and West Indies.

In a surprise peacetime attack, an English naval force funded by James, the duke of York, captures New Netherland, which is renamed New York in his honor.

1665 Caleb Cheeshahteaumuck becomes the first North American Indian to earn a degree at Harvard.

France wages war against England and the Netherlands in Europe and against the Mohawk in Canada.

1665–1667 Second Anglo-Dutch War: Provoked by the English capture of New Netherland, the Dutch retaliate and are joined by French forces in 1666; Peace of Breda concludes war in 1667.

1665–1700 Charles II reigns in Spain.

1666–1667 Canadian forces invade the five Iroquois nations, who capitulate to French terms for peace.

1668 The British establish Charles Fort at the mouth of the Rupert River in southeastern James Bay (Rupert's Land).

1669 John Locke draws up the Fundamental Constitutions, which influence the later development of the Carolinas.

1670 Royal charter incorporates the Hudson's Bay Company and enables it to control the fur trade in the Hudson Bay region and establish Rupert's Land.

1672 The Royal African Company is granted a monopoly of the English slave trade to America and the West Indies.

1672–1674 Third Anglo-Dutch War: Dutch naval forces capture New York and restore it as a Dutch colony under the peace of Westminster.

1673 A regular mail route is established between New York and Boston.

The trader and explorer Louis Jolliet, accompanied by the Jesuit missionary Jacques Marquette, follows the Mississippi River to the mouth of the Arkansas River.

1674 François-Xavier de Laval becomes the first bishop of Quebec.

1675 Four Pueblo Indians in New Mexico are hanged; others are whipped and enslaved for practicing sorcery and killing seven Franciscans.

1675–1676 King Philip's War: Indians of southern New England, led by the Wampanoag Metacomet (King Philip), unite unsuccessfully to drive out the English. Many surviving Indians are killed or enslaved.

1676 Bacon's Rebellion in Virginia: Frontiersmen led by Nathaniel Bacon attack a group of Susquehannock, defy the government, and burn Jamestown; the rebellion collapses after Bacon's defeat.

Mohawk converts to Catholicism move to Caughnawaga in Canada.

1677 The Covenant Chain: A system of alliances between the English colonies and the Iroquois confederacy, is established at Albany.

1678 A Jewish burial ground is established in Newport, Rhode Island.

1680 Death of Kateri Tekakwitha, "The Lily of the Mohawks," a Catholic convert and the first Native American to be proposed for sainthood; beatified in 1980.

Pueblo Revolt: Pueblo Indians revolt and drive the Spanish from New Mexico.

Spain reaffirms the New Laws of 1542, which stated that Indians are human and should not be enslaved.

1681 The French initiate a *congé* (trading license) system in an effort to regulate the fur trade in New France.

The Pennsylvania Charter is granted to William Penn by Charles II.

1682 Franco-Iroquois wars; Anglo-American attack on Quebec.

The Narrative of the Captivity and Restoration of Mrs. Mary Rowlandson is published in Boston. The author's account of her capture by Wampanoag Indians in 1676 becomes a best-seller and initiates a new American literary genre, the captivity narrative.

René-Robert Cavalier de La Salle descends the Mississippi River to the Gulf of Mexico and claims the entire river valley for Louis XIV; he names the territory Louisiana.

1684 Anglo-French conflict in Hudson Bay; Franco-Iroquois hostilities recommence.

1685–1688 James II reigns in England.

1686–1688 Sir Edmund Andros is appointed to govern the Dominion of New England, a forced union of New England, New York, and New Jersey.

1687 Father Eusebio Francisco Kino arrives in Pimería Alta (modern Arizona) and accelerates the pace at which mission settlements are established.

Spain declares that any slaves who escape from English colonies will be welcomed as free people in Florida.

1688–1702 William III and (until 1694) Mary II reign in England.

1689–1691 The Glorious Revolution in America: Colonists revolt against the "Dominion of New England" and imprison royal governor Edmund Andros; Leisler's Rebellion occurs in New York, in which Dutch merchant Jacob Leisler names himself governor and is executed for treason in 1691.

1689–1697 War of the League of Augsburg, known as King William's War in the colonies, brings French and English colonies into conflict with their respective Indian allies.

1690 Anglo-American forces under Sir William Phipps are defeated at Quebec.

1690s–1720 Georgian-style houses begin to appear in New England and the South.

1692 The Crown suspends William Penn as governor of Pennsylvania and assigns New York Governor Benjamin Fletcher to take over; Penn is restored as governor in 1694.

1692–1693 Salem witchcraft trials result in twenty executions.

1693 The College of William and Mary is founded in Virginia.

1695 Jews begin public worship in New York City.

The *New England Primer* is compiled and published by Benjamin Harris, Boston. The *Primer* becomes a staple of elementary education for the next one hundred years.

1696 South Carolina adopts first codification of slave laws in the British mainland colonies.

Spain reconquers New Mexico.

1699 Pierre Lemoyne d'Iberville establishes a post at Biloxi and founds the first French colony in Louisiana.

A Sulpician mission is founded at Cahokia in the Illinois country.

1700 Samuel Sewall's *The Selling of Joseph,* the first published Anglo-American protest against slavery, is issued in Boston.

1700–1746 Philip V reigns in Spain.

1701 Anglicans establish the Society for the Propagation of the Gospel in Foreign Parts (SPG) to convert Indians and Africans.

Detroit is founded by Antoine de la Mothe Cadillac at the entrance from Lake Erie to Lake Huron to control trade in the Illinois country.

Franco-Iroquois peace treaty: The Iroquois confederacy agrees to remain neutral in future Anglo-French conflicts.

Yale College is founded in New Haven.

1702–1713 The War of Spanish Succession (known as Queen Anne's War in the colonies) again brings conflict to French and English colonists and their respective Indian allies.

1702–1714 Anne reigns in England (Great Britain after 1707).

1704 *The Boston News-Letter* begins publication; first regularly issued colonial newspaper.

1705 Britain offers bounties for naval stores (wood products including pitch, tar, hemp, and masts); pines are increasingly cut down from the coast of Acadia to New Jersey.

1706 Louis XIV receives at Versailles Nescambiouit, an Abenaki chief from Pigwacket (Maine).

1707 The Act of Union unites England and Scotland into the United Kingdom of Great Britain.

1708 Michel Sarrazin and Joseph Pitton de Tournefort compile a catalog of Canadian plants that identifies, classifies, and names over two hundred varieties.

1709 Intendant Jacques Raudot legalizes the ownership of African or Indian slaves in New France.

1710 Anglo-American assault on Canada fails.

British forces conquer Port Royal in Acadia and rename it Annapolis Royal.

1711–1713 Tuscarora War: North and South Carolina join with the Yamassee to defeat the Tuscarora; Tuscarora survivors migrate north and join the Iroquois nations.

1712 Slave uprising occurs in New York; insurrection quelled by militia.

1713 Treaty of Utrecht: France cedes Acadia, Newfoundland, and Hudson Bay to Great Britain. New France's Abenaki allies are not consulted about the disposition of their lands.

1714–1727 George I reigns in Great Britain.

1715–1728 Yamassee War: In response to abuses by the English, the Yamassee attack South Carolina and are defeated by a coalition of English and Cherokee forces.

1715–1774 Louis XV reigns in France.

1716/17 William Levingston, a Scottish merchant, builds a theater in Williamsburg and imports indentured actors and actresses.

1718 British Parliament passes Transportation Act that exiles convicts to the colonies as punishment for crimes.

New Orleans is founded by John Law's Compagnie de l'Occident (Company of the West or the Mississippi Company), which fails two years later.

1719–1729 Colonial discontent with proprietors ultimately leads to the creation of separate royal governments in North and South Carolina.

1720–1722 Spanish forces attempt to occupy Texas.

1721 First smallpox inoculation in North America made in Boston by Dr. Zabdiel Boyleston.

Regular postal service begins between London and New England.

Robert Walpole becomes Chancellor of the Exchequer and, as Prime Minister 1721–1747, follows a hands-off colonial policy.

1722–1727 Dummer's War: Abenaki try to push back the line of English settlement in northern New England.

1725 The *New York Gazette,* the first newspaper in New York City, begins publication.

1727–1760 George II reigns in Great Britain.

1728 John Bartram, the father of American botany, starts a garden near Philadelphia for his experiments in hybridization.

1729 Natchez Rebellion occurs in Louisiana.

1730 Great Wagon Road begun. It eventually stretches for eight hundred miles (1,280 kilometers) between Philadelphia and backcountry Georgia.

1731 Benjamin Franklin founds a subscription library in Philadelphia.

CHRONOLOGY

Forges de Saint-Maurice is established at Trois-Rivières in New France; bog iron is used to produce goods for local use.

1731–1743   Mark Catesby (1679?–1749), English naturalist and traveler, publishes *The Natural History of Carolina, Florida, and the Bahama Islands* in London.

1732   Benjamin Franklin publishes the first edition of *Poor Richard's Almanack* in Philadelphia.

1733   James Oglethorpe founds Georgia as refuge for English debtors.

Parliament passes the Molasses Act, levying a tax on the import of molasses from the French West Indies.

1734–1735   The clergyman Jonathan Edwards leads a religious revival in Northampton, Massachusetts.

1735   John Peter Zenger, German-born printer and publisher of the *New York Weekly Journal*, is acquitted of seditious libel in a landmark trial for freedom of the press.

1737   "Walking Purchase": Delaware Indians agree to sell Pennsylvania as much land as a man can walk in a day and half, which turns out to be sixty-four miles (102 kilometers)—the entire Lehigh Valley.

1738   The painter John Singleton Copley is born in Boston.

1738–1745   The Great Awakening: English evangelist George Whitefield stimulates religious revivals throughout the British colonies.

1739   Stono Rebellion: About one hundred slaves in South Carolina rebel in hopes of escaping to Spanish Florida; the uprising is thwarted by the militia.

1740s   Eliza Pinckney experiments with indigo cultivation in South Carolina; due to her efforts, indigo becomes a new staple crop.

1740–1748   War of the Austrian Succession: Spain and France ally against Austria and England.

1741   Rumors of a slave conspiracy in New York City create a panic; thirty-one slaves are executed, seventy are banished, and four whites are killed.

Russian explorers Vitus Bering and Aleksey Chirikov land on the American mainland and islands on the Gulf of Alaska. They contact natives and return with sea otter pelts.

1743   The American Philosophical Society is established in Philadelphia by Benjamin Franklin.

Reverend Eleazar Wheelock decides to admit Indians to Moor's Charity School in Lebanon, Connecticut; the school is moved to Hanover, New Hampshire, and renamed Dartmouth College in 1770.

1744–1748   King George's War: The North American phase of the War of the Austrian Succession leads to the destruction of Saratoga, New York, by Canadian and Indian forces; the Peace of Aix-la-Chapelle ends the war in 1748.

1746   College of New Jersey (later Princeton University) is founded.

1746–1759   Ferdinand VI reigns in Spain.

1747   Redwood Library in Newport, Rhode Island, is founded.

1748   Charleston Library Society is established.

Treaty of Aix-la-Chapelle ends the War of the Austrian Succession.

1748–1751   The Swedish naturalist Peter Kalm visits North America and collects scientific data for Carolus Linnaeus.

1752   The British Empire shifts from the Julian to the Gregorian Calendar.

1754   The British Crown charters King's College in New York City; renamed Columbia College in 1784.

New York Society Library established.

Seven Years' War starts when Virginia sends militia under Colonel George Washington to challenge French expansion in the Ohio Valley; Washington surrenders after being surrounded by the French.

Thomas Chippendale's pattern book for furniture, *The Gentleman and Cabinet-Maker's Director*, is published in London.

1755   French-speaking Acadians are deported from Acadia by the British; many migrate to Louisiana.

The painter Gilbert Charles Stuart is born in North Kingstown, Rhode Island.

Philadelphia Academy (later University of Pennsylvania) is chartered.

1757–1763   Anne Grant lives in Albany, New York, and gathers impressions for her later work, *Memoirs of an American Lady: With Sketches of Manners and Scenery in America, as They Existed Previous to the Revolution* published in London in 1808.

1759   The famed Indian clergyman and missionary Samson Occum becomes a fully ordained Presbyterian minister.

1759–1760   Under General James Wolfe, British forces capture Quebec; Wolfe and the French leader, Louis-Joseph de Montcalm die in battle. A year later, French forces capitulate at Montreal, surrendering Canada and its dependencies.

1759–1788   Charles III reigns in Spain.

1760–1820   George III reigns in Great Britain.

1762   Spain declares war on Great Britain.

1763   Treaty of Paris: Spain cedes Florida to Great Britain; France cedes Louisiana to Spain and cedes Acadia, Canada, and Cape Breton to Great Britain.

Britain issues Royal Proclamation forbidding colonists to settle west of the Appalachian Mountains until further land can be acquired from the Indians.

Touro Synagogue opens in Newport, Rhode Island.

1763–1764   Pennsylvania frontiersmen, known as the Paxton Boys, massacre Conestoga Indians and march toward Philadelphia to attack Indians in protective custody there; they are dissuaded by Benjamin Franklin and others.

1763–1766   The Ottawa chief Pontiac leads an alliance of Indians against British outposts in the Northwest; Pontiac signs peace treaty in 1766.

1764   Rhode Island College (later Brown University) is founded.

Sugar Act: Widespread colonial protest erupts when the British Parliament passes act that in effect gives Great Britain monopoly on Anglo-American sugar market; duty is lowered two years later, ending protest.

1764–1774   Britain enacts a series of measures intended to raise money from the colonies and assert British authority. American colonists resist and tensions escalate.

1765   The first American medical school is founded in Philadelphia.

The Stamp Act generates outrage in the colonies and is repealed in response to widespread colonial protest.

1766   In the Declaratory Act, Parliament asserts its "full power and authority over the colonies."

New York-to-Philadelphia stage coach route is established; the journey takes two days.

Queens College (later Rutgers University) is founded.

1767   The New York Assembly is suspended for refusing to provide quarters for troops as required by the 1765 Quartering Act.

The Jesuits are expelled from Spanish territories; Franciscans take over the western missions.

The Townshend Duties Act places customs duties on a number of items imported from England.

1768   The Massachusetts Assembly is dissolved for refusing to assist in the collection of taxes.

1769   Junípero Serra founds the first Spanish mission in California at San Diego.

Spain colonizes Alta California.

1770   The Boston Massacre: Three people are killed when British troops fire into a crowd.

1771   Permanent Moravian missions to Labrador Eskimos are founded.

1773   Boston Tea Party: Colonists protest the duty on tea by dumping a shipload into Boston Harbor.

A hospital for the insane is built in Williamsburg.

Poems on Various Subjects, Religious and Moral by Phillis Wheatley of Boston, a former slave taken from Senegal, is published in London.

The Quebec Act provides a permanent civil government and grants religious toleration to Catholics in Canada, angering American colonists.

1774   First Continental Congress meets at Philadelphia, with representatives of all colonies except Georgia; George Washington takes command of the Continental Army; battles of Lexington and Concord fought.

Lord Dunmore's War forces Shawnee Indians into a peace that facilitates the British settlement of Kentucky.

"Mother Ann Lee," founder of the Shakers, arrives in America from England.

1774–1793   Louis XIV reigns in France.

1775   Second Continental Congress assembles in Philadelphia, again without Georgia.

1775–1776   Americans mount an unsuccessful invasion of Quebec.

1776   Adam Smith's *An Inquiry into the Nature and Causes of the Wealth of Nations* is published in London; Thomas Paine's *Common Sense* is published in Philadelphia.

Declaration of Independence asserts separation of British mainland colonies from Great Britain.

Minister to the Indies José de Gálvez restructures and reforms the Spanish colonial administration with the creation of Provincias Internas.

1777   Bowing to military force, the Cherokee Indians cede lands to North and South Carolina.

Vermont declares its independence from New York and New Hampshire and adopts a constitution that prohibits slavery and allows all adult men to vote.

1778   Captain James Cook explores the Northwest Coast.

1779   Spain declares war on Britain and enters the American War for Independence.

1781   General George Washington and the marquis de Lafayette defeat British troops led by General Charles Cornwallis at Yorktown, Virginia.

1783   Treaty of Versailles: Great Britain recognizes independence of United States of America; Florida is returned to Spain.

1784   Province of New Brunswick established in British North America to accommodate Loyalists.

1786   Jean-François de Galaup, comte de La Pérouse, leads an expedition to the Pacific, exploring the coasts of Alaska and California before continuing west.

1788   Bread riots occur in France.

1788–1808   Charles IV reigns in Spain.

1789   French Revolution begins.

1789–1790   Spanish expedition under Alejandro Malaspina explores the West Coast from Prince William Sound (Alaska) to Monterey (California).

1789–1793   Alexander Mackenzie reaches the mouth of the Mackenzie River and then the Pacific Coast in two overland journeys from the east.

1791   Constitution Act: Britain divides the province of Quebec into Lower Conada (Quebec) and Upper Canada (Ontario).

1792   Captain George Vancouver explores the west coast of Canada.

Following slave revolts in the French Antilles, Louisiana prohibits the importation of slaves from French Caribbean colonies.

The Parliament of Upper Canada votes for the gradual abolition of slavery.

1794   Slavery is abolished in French colonies.

1795   Hearing rumors of Haitian independence and abolition in the French colonies, slaves in Pointe-Coupée (Spanish Louisiana) plan a revolt.

1799   The Russian-American Company is chartered and given a monopoly to conduct trade in Alaska.

CHRONOLOGY

1800	Spain returns Louisiana to France.
1802	Tlingit Indians capture and destroy the Russian town of New Archangel (Sitka) on Baranof Island.
1803	Louisiana Purchase: France sells Louisiana to the United States.
1805	Tlingit Indians destroy the Russian settlement at Yakutat.
1808–?	Joseph, Napoleon's brother, reigns as king of France.
1812	Red River settlement is founded in Manitoba.
	War of 1812 commences.
1812–1841	The Russian-American Company maintains a base at Fort Ross, in northern California.
1814	Treaty of Ghent ends War of 1812.
1814–1833	Ferdinand VII reigns in Spain.
1819	The United States buys Florida from Spain.
1820–1830	George IV reigns in Great Britain.
1821	Mexican independence is proclaimed by the Mexican Assembly.
	Spain cedes Florida to the United States ending Spanish presence in the Southeast.
1825	Father Ivan Veniaminov builds the first church in the Aleutian Islands.
1825–1832	Stephen F. Austin brings some eight thousand American colonists to Texas.
1830–1837	William IV reigns in Great Britain.
1833	Great Britain declares the end of slavery in its possessions, effective in 1834.
1837	Constitutional revolts in Lower and Upper Canada.
1837–1901	Victoria reigns in Great Britain.
1841	Act of Union reunites Upper and Lower Canada under one legislative assembly and establishes self-rule except on imperial policy.
1867	British North America Act creates a federal government in Canada, a milestone in the progress of colonial self-government, and establishes the Dominion of Canada.
	Russia sells its North American possessions to the United States for $7.2 million.

PREFACE

Some six decades ago, the distinguished historian Carl Becker contended that one should differentiate between past events that demonstrably occurred and our recollection, or "idealization," of them. "Facts" may be immutable, he wrote, but our memory of them is "always changing in response to the increase or refinement of knowledge." For this reason, he concluded that history "cannot be precisely the same for . . . one generation or for another."

Over recent decades, scholarship on the North American colonies has borne out Becker's argument. Studies focusing on once-peripheral subjects and revisionary approaches to familiar topics have altered our perception of this formative period. Commenting on the unevenness of scholarship that made new departures in historical writing desirable, Jack P. Greene and J. R. Pole observed in *Colonial British America: Essays in the New History of the Early Modern Era* (1984) that "We know vastly more, for instance, about New England and the Chesapeake than we do about other areas, about rural life than about urban, about religion than about secular culture, about external trade than about internal, about political ideology than about political process, about static wealth structures than about the dynamics of social development, about adult, white, independent males than about other elements in the population." The aim of the *Encyclopedia of the North American Colonies* is to provide a fuller understanding of our colonial heritage by incorporating recent literature on these previously neglected areas of colonial history.

The history of the North American colonies lasted from two to three hundred years, depending on the beginning date that one selects. Over these centuries there developed the recognizably distinct cultures of the North American continent, whose exploration and colonization is the subject of the present work. Chronologically, the *Encyclopedia* extends from the first Norse settlement in Newfoundland (tenth century) to the 1820s in New Mexico and the 1860s in Alaska. Geographically, the set traces the colonial history of what became the United States and Canada by encompassing Great Britain's North American colonies; the small but durable Russian settlements in the Pacific Northwest; New Netherland, Holland's short-lived but historically important New World outpost; New France, which expanded from settlements adjoining the Gulf of Saint Lawrence to include not only the lands along the Great Lakes but also the entire Mississippi Valley; and the Spanish Borderlands, which stretched from Florida across the Gulf of Mexico and fanned out from east Texas across New Mexico, Colorado, and Arizona, and up the coast to San Francisco Bay. The four principal imperial powers are represented on our cover by the following emblems: the fleur-de-lis for France, the lion for Great Britain, the Dutch West India Company's insignia for the Netherlands, and the shield of Castile and León for Spain.

PREFACE

The regions known today as Latin America and the West Indies are excluded for compelling intellectual and practical considerations. Historically intertwined with the borderlands north of the Rio Grande, Latin America has nonetheless become a distinct cultural region. Adequate treatment of so vast and complex a culture would have swollen the number of volumes of the present work far beyond feasible limits.

No other reference work similarly deals with the colonial history of the North American continent. Among United States historians, the thirteen British colonies have been the focus of intensive scholarly research that has produced an abundant and rich historical literature rivaling and often surpassing that on the infancy of any other nation. The same cannot be said of that part of the North American continent controlled by other powers, notably the Netherlands, France, and Spain. For example, the historical literature on New France, though comprehensive and scholarly, is sparse compared to that on the British colonies. Leaner yet are historical studies of the Spanish Borderlands.

This disparity has been illuminatingly explained by David J. Weber, the doyen of Spanish Borderland scholars. Our colonial past, he comments, has for the most part been recounted by the descendants of the victorious British who virtually ignore the fascinating and historically consequential history of the Spanish and French colonists. American history, Weber appositely concludes, is "usually seen . . . as the story of the expansion of English America rather than the stories of the diverse cultures that comprise our national heritage." Similarly Pauline Maier, an authority on British colonial history, has urged fellow scholars to abandon the traditional "confines of British Colonial America" in order to learn more "about the Spanish borderlands, French Canada, and Louisiana, whose development played so critical a role in the dynamics of imperial conflict." So also should historians pay more attention to New Netherland. That region's unique and important history has been demonstrated and enriched by the New Netherland Project (sponsored by the New York State Library) under the direction of Dr. Charles T. Gehring—who fortunately agreed to serve as a special consultant for the *Encyclopedia*. With the New Netherland Project's acquisition, translation, and annotation of relevant historical manuscripts, the field of Dutch-American studies has come of age, a development reflected in our many articles on New Netherland.

Designed to promote the broadest possible historical orientation, the *Encyclopedia of the North American Colonies* covers all the geopolitical regions and subjects referred to above. Our goal is both comprehensive coverage and a comparative analysis of settlements. In some instances it has been possible to treat subjects that pertain to each area in a single essay ("Colonial Political Culture" or "Philosophy"); in others, the absence of scholars qualified to discuss the comparative history of colonies precluded such an approach. For such topics (the majority), separate articles on the same subject were provided for the British colonies, New Netherland, the Spanish Borderlands, and New France. (Canada and Louisiana are treated sometimes together and separately.) The number of words allocated to each topic is largely based on our assessment of its importance in a region's history.

The very ambitiousness and originality of our approach created challenges. What, for example, was the comparative importance of Catholicism in the borderlands, New France, and the British colonies? When a development (such as religious pluralism, denominationalism, or revivalism) was significant in one area and of marginal importance in others, how much space should be allocated to each? Should the gauge of emphasis be retrospective or prospective importance? Most important of all: To what extent did the inevitable bias of students of the British colonies (a majority of our editorial board) becloud their view of the significance of developments in other areas, thus giving the *Encyclopedia* an Anglo-American slant?

The latter problem has been largely solved by the inclusion on our board of distinguished scholars on the history of New France and the Spanish Borderlands. William J. Eccles, the foremost authority on New France, is largely responsible for the many articles on that area. He delineated topics, selected authors, and critically appraised the quality of their contributions, on occasion providing such copious editorial comments that joint authorship might have been claimed. As to the Spanish Borderlands, whose inclusion is the most innovative feature of this *Encyclopedia,* Ramón A. Gutiérrez came as close to being indispensable as is possible in a collaborative reference work. As an academically recognized field of scholarly enquiry, the history of the borderlands is comparatively recent. By contrast to the history of the British and French colonies, the literature is relatively slender, and scholarly experts are as few in number as are universities that provide programs—much less departments—on the subject. All this rendered especially difficult the selection of qualified scholars to write articles often requiring independent archival research. (Only in the study of childhood and adolescence did we find the state of scholarship too undeveloped to satisfactorily treat the topic for the borderlands.) That Gutiérrez overcame such obstacles is demonstrated by the quality of many of the articles on the Spanish Borderlands included in this *Encyclopedia,* not least his own essays.

We also sought to provide comprehensive topical coverage. Traditionally, most books on American colonial history have focused on European discovery and the establishment of colonies; the relationship of colonial satellites to the parent country; their demographic complexion; political, social, and administrative organization; labor systems; trade and finance; the promotion of arts and technologies; religious life; intellectual and educational developments; and international rivalries and imperial wars. (For the Spanish Borderlands one might include such traditional themes as ranching and farming, Spanish-Indian relations, the church and the missions, military history and the *presidio.*) These subjects are also covered here, often with great fullness and interpretative originality. In the religion section, to give a single example, essays deal with the entire spectrum of religious belief and activity as they affected colonial life. Accordingly, chapters are devoted not only to the dominant churches, sects, and creeds but also to other aspects of the religious experience such as Native American worship and rival or complementary modes of belief like magic and witchcraft.

A major aim has been to incorporate recent changes of scholarly emphasis on the spatial, demographic, cultural, economic, and social aspects of the colonial past—subjects that would have been given scant coverage a half or even a quarter century ago. Particular attention is given, for example, to the cultures (pre- and post-European contact) of Native Americans, including religion, governance, trade and commerce, ecological and other results of Indian-colonist contact, detribalized and manumitted Indians, Native American families and life-styles, technologies, aesthetics, and languages. (As special consultant, William C. Sturtevant of the Smithsonian Institution not only helped formulate the volumes' contents but also shaped our editorial policy regarding the handling of Indian tribal and place names.) Similar attention is paid to African-American culture in several long articles devoted to the subject and, for example, in essays on interracial societies, hired labor, artisans, slave resistance, and the variant characteristics of slavery in the different imperial regions. The set also focuses on the history of the family, including childhood, adolescence, sexual mores and behavior, gender relations (emphasizing, appropriately, the role of women), and old age and death.

Also noteworthy is the *Encyclopedia*'s inclusion of essays on disease and medicine, urban problems, ethnicity, ecology, material culture, occupational structures, and secular social institutions. To give a final illustration of their distinctiveness, these volumes reflect the revived respect that recent scholars have accorded ideas and values as important historical determinants and their increasing use of statistics and quantification. In sum, the *Encyclopedia of the North American Colonies* makes available to a large audience (students, fellow scholars, and general readers) the best scholarship of our day and demonstrates the likely direction of historical interest and research.

The 193 contributors—distinguished historians of three generations—were drawn from all parts of the United States, Canada, Great Britain, and Western Europe, and represent a wide range of academic disciplines, including not only history but also cultural anthropology, sociology, folklore, historical geography, theology, archaeology, philosophy, the fine arts, and linguistics. With boundaries between disciplines becoming increasingly blurred, this multiplicity is appropriate, the more so since the work of nonhistorians has greatly enriched our understanding of the past.

The essays are not mere narratives of events but interpretations of sometimes-controversial subjects. The presuppositions and mindsets that govern these interpretations consequently differ from author to author. Some articles adhere to the familiar interpretations, while others challenge the traditional wisdom and offer more innovative viewpoints. Neither approach is superior to the other, both are factually plausible, and their juxtaposition demonstrates once again the spacious world of scholarship.

The *Encyclopedia* consists of 274 topical and thematic essays ranging in length from one thousand to fifteen thousand words. The purpose of our approach is to bring together in each essay information that in a dictionary-like arrangement would be scattered in various parts of the work. The articles, whether composite or comprehensive, offer thorough coverage of each topic and underscore its significance in the overall development of the economy, society, and culture of colonial North America. Cross-references, maps, extensive bibliographies (often annotated), a chronology, and a detailed index provide various means of access to the wealth of information contained in the essays.

This *Encyclopedia* is a timely reminder of not only the British but also the French, Spanish, Dutch, African, and Native American historical roots of present-day Canada and the United States. During the colonial centuries the pattern was set for development of our continent—its fundamental political principles, economic ideas and institutions, social and cultural practices, religious beliefs and activities, legal and philosophical systems, family life and folkways. So, too, was cast the mold that would shape the many deplorable features of our history: racism that did not disappear with the subsequent end of slavery; subjugation and discriminatory treatment of those Native Americans who escaped near-genocide; the unequal status of women; and the callous treatment accorded the modern equivalent of the colonial underclass. If remembrance of things

PREFACE

past can bring awareness of urgent issues of the present, familiarity with our colonial history may be imperative.

The editing of this work was a cooperative venture, and its merits are due to our special consultants and the distinguished historians who served on its editorial board. The contribution of a number of these were referred to above, but I would also like to acknowledge my debt to its other members.

The *Encyclopedia*'s articles on colonial regions, exploration, Puritanism, and African Americans bear the imprint of Alden Vaughan's scholarly expertness, just as many other essays and the map program benefited from his impressive knowledge of colonial America. Similarly, many of the most original essays—particularly those on gender relations, family life, and the colonial economy—were inspired and enriched by Gloria Main's editorial skill and archival knowledge. To students of Anglo-American colonial history, the name of Jackson Turner Main is synonymous with high standards of scholarship, a well-deserved repute of which this *Encyclopedia*—especially its essays on economic issues—has been the beneficiary. Personally, my greatest debt is to my longtime professional associate Milton M. Klein, who carefully read and commented on virtually every essay. When in doubt about the factual accuracy, interpretative plausibility, or requisite professional expository standards of articles submitted to the *Encyclopedia* I sought, cooperatively received, and usually followed his sage advice.

Administration was the responsibility of the publisher's full-time professional staff. Their many day-to-day decisions on administrative issues transformed seemingly procedural tasks into qualitative contributions. Charles Scribner, Jr., first broached the idea of a colonial reference work in 1985. Karen Day, publisher of Charles Scribner's Sons Reference Books, later selected its Editor in Chief, endorsed his choice of associates, and chose its Managing Editor and staff. More consequential yet, it was her decision to expand what was initially intended to be an encyclopedia of Great Britain's New World colonies to include the North American possessions of Europe's other imperial powers. As publisher, she hired Ann Leslie Tuttle to be Assistant Managing Editor, in which role her editorial abilities were matched by her persistence. Miss Tuttle became de facto director of the project following the premature death in December 1992 of its Managing Editor, David Bain.

The Encyclopedia of the North American Colonies is finally a tribute to David Bain's broad intellectual curiosity and interests, impressive knowledge, admirable administrative talent, and high professional standards. The range, depth of coverage, and quality of these volumes are in larger measure owing to him.

Encyclopedia of the

NORTH AMERICAN COLONIES

I

THE AMERICAN CONTEXT

The Natural Environment
The First Americans

THE NATURAL ENVIRONMENT

IN DISCUSSING THE settlement history of North America, the metaphor of the stage has often been used to evoke the natural environment, and Native Americans and European settlers alike have been described as actors upon that stage. The metaphor, though useful, fails to convey the dynamic quality of the natural world, nor does it suggest the role that humankind played in altering both the configuration and content of the landscape as the drama of habitation unfolded. No continent has undergone as rapid and as thorough a process of change over the past five hundred years as has North America. The scope of this transformation renders it difficult to appreciate both the natural worlds that existed prior to human occupation and the ecological contexts within which Indian societies functioned prior to European contact.

The natural environment per se is of less concern, however, than is the way in which native peoples perceived the environment in terms of their culturally defined needs. These needs selectively identified those aspects of nature with which societies could interact to provide support systems for their populations. The natural worlds depicted in map 1, therefore, are not the discrete physical regions that might be identified by modern science, but rather key elements of nature that could be recognized by preindustrial societies as indicators of settlement possibilities. These possibilities were acted upon through time to create the basic subsistence patterns that ex-

isted on the continent on the eve of European colonization (see map 2). These patterns, in turn, represent a long period of Indian adaptations to and transformations of North American environments.

CONTINENTAL ENVIRONMENTS

The most significant features of North America are its vast size and shape, its environmental diversity, and its topographic configuration. The continent stretches from 25°N in the Florida Keys to 83°N on Ellesmere Island in northern Canada, and (excluding Hawaii) from 53°W in southeastern Newfoundland to 168°W in Alaska's Seward Peninsula, which juts into the Bering Strait. The distance between the Atlantic and Pacific oceans along the forty-ninth parallel (49°N) is approximately three thousand miles (4,800 kilometers), while the distance along the hundredth meridian (100°W) from the Arctic islands to the lower Rio Grande is approximately thirty-six hundred miles (5,760 kilometers). These dimensions enclose a continental territory of almost 7.5 million square miles (19.5 million square kilometers).

The sheer scale of this continental structure assures an immense diversity of natural environments. In general, diversity decreases from south to north and from coast to interior, leaving the Arctic and Boreal regions, the Rocky Mountains, and the Dry Southwest as the areas of greatest challenge to human settlement. In contrast, North America contains between the Gulf of Mexico and the Great Lakes the most extensive area of mid-latitude environments amenable for human manipulation anywhere in the world. The physical diversity of the continent is the result of a complex combination of factors associated with geologic structure, surface topography and drainage, climate, vegetation, and soils.

Structurally, the oldest rocks in North America form the vast Laurentian Shield, which underlies northeastern Canada. The southern boundary of the shield is marked approximately by a line that can be drawn from the Saint Lawrence Valley and the Great Lakes northwest through the zone of lakes in western Canada to the Beaufort Sea in the Arctic. The remainder of the continent has been grafted onto, or superimposed upon, this ancient core to create its current surface topography.

Eastern North America comprises the three topographic regions of the Laurentian Uplands, which represent the surface expression of the shield, the Atlantic Coastal Plain to the south, and the Appalachian Highlands, which border the plain to the west and which represent the second oldest upland zone on the continent. The Laurentian Uplands present a range of hills and low mountains varying between one and three thousand feet (300 and 900 meters) along their southern edge, from which the rest of the landscape slopes down in a broad, saucer-shaped basin toward the lowlands bordering Hudson Bay.

The Atlantic Coastal Plain stretches southward from Cape Cod and Long Island in an ever-widening fashion toward Florida and the Gulf of Mexico, where it merges in the lower Mississippi valley with the continent's vast interior plains. Bordered by a depositional coastline of barrier islands, beaches, wetlands, and estuaries, the coastal plain meets the more resistant rocks of the Piedmont area of the Appalachians along a fall zone extending from southeastern Pennsylvania to central Alabama. The broadly rolling Piedmont is bordered to the west by a ridge of rounded mountains that runs from the Gaspé Peninsula bordering the southern Saint Lawrence Valley through northern New England and New York and southwestward to the Great

Smoky Mountains along the present North Carolina–Tennessee border. Reaching heights of three to four thousand feet (900 to 1,200 meters) through western Virginia, this Blue Ridge zone attains heights of over six thousand feet (1,800 meters) in the Great Smokies. Between this Blue Ridge and the Allegheny plateaus, which range south and west of New York and run between fifteen hundred and twenty-five hundred feet (450 and 750 meters) lies the Ridge and Valley province of narrow ridges and broad lowlands that provide important resource possibilities and routeways for human activity.

The Central Interior comprises an extensive system of lowlands stretching from the Great Lakes to the Gulf of Mexico and from the Allegheny plateaus across the Mississippi basin and the Great Plains to the eastern foothills of the Rocky Mountains. The Central Lowlands, which are drained by the Mississippi River system, represent the core of the continent's mid-latitude region. Most of these lowlands are of gently to broadly rolling terrain below six hundred feet (180 meters) in height. The Great Plains to the west rise from a discontinuously defined escarpment of fifteen hundred to two thousand feet (450 to 600 meters) in height to attain elevations of three to five thousand feet (900 to 1,500 meters) along the edge of the Rockies.

The Rocky Mountains, the youngest, highest, and most rugged upland feature on the continent, comprise two topographic zones. In the north, from Alaska to Wyoming, the mountain system comprises several ranges of ten-to-fourteen-thousand-feet (3,000 to 4,200 meters) elevation divided by deep, longitudinal valleys. In the south, the system divides into two. The eastern, more continuous, prong represents the main Rocky Mountain front, which reaches heights between nine thousand and fourteen thousand feet (2,700 and 4,200 meters) in Colorado and New Mexico. The western prong forms a somewhat lower, intermittent zone of mountains including the Cascades along the eastern border of Oregon and California and in the coast range of California. The southern Rocky Mountain system encloses a series of intermontane plateaus, from the Columbian Plateau in the north to the Colorado Plateau in the south, and a southern basin and range province of block-faulted mountains and valleys located in the continent's driest area. Along the central and northern Pacific coasts, in contrast, lies a hill and mountain region that provides a wetter, more rugged backdrop to a very narrow, discontinuous coastal plain.

Climatic Variations

Although the Rocky Mountain system poses the most formidable topographic barrier to human occupation of North America, the fact that the Rockies and the lower Appalachians in the east both generally parallel the coasts means that no physical barrier exists to impede the movement of air masses between the Arctic Ocean and the Gulf of Mexico. This results in dramatic shifts in temperature throughout the continent, leaving its northern half with a much more limited range of biotic resources than its southern half.

North America displays more climatic variation than any other continent except Asia; only a true tropical environment is absent. This variation contributes to a remarkable environmental diversity characterized by distinct patterns of variability, continentality, and seasonality. Variations in temperatures and precipitation are such that, east of the Rockies, the greatest temperature contrasts occur during the winter months in a south-to-north sequence, while the greatest variations in annual precipitation occur more generally in an east-to-west direction. The result is that areas located in the northerly heart of the continent experience greater annual temperature ranges and significantly less precipitation than southerly or coastal locations. At the eastern junction of the Boreal and Plains-Grasslands regions (Winnipeg area), for example, midwinter temperatures range from 0°F to −10°F because of the dominance of cold, polar air masses. The central Gulf coast (New Orleans area), on the other hand, experiences winter temperatures ranging between 50°F and 60°F, or some fifty to sixty degrees warmer. In mid summer, however, because of the northward penetration of maritime tropical air from the Gulf, the temperature range between the two locations is much reduced. The Gulf coast regularly produces temperatures in the low nineties, while west-central Canada is usually in the low-to-mid seventies with brief periods in the eighties not

uncommon. The long, severe winters of the northern and central areas of the continent, when the ground features a continuous cover of snow and the seas from the Bering Strait across northern Canada to the Saint Lawrence estuary are frozen, constitute the greatest single challenge to human and animal life on the continent. Farther south, however, in the lower Mississippi Valley, the southern Temperate Woodlands, the southern Plains, and the Dry Southwest, as well as along the coasts, winters tend to be mild to warm and spring and fall seasons are more prolonged, thus contributing to a greater array of resource possibilities.

Annual precipitation displays an equally varied continental pattern. Most of North America receives sufficient moisture to sustain some form of continuous plant cover except in the arid and semiarid Southwest. The wettest area is the Pacific Maritime region, where annual rainfall totals thirty to forty inches (about 1 liter) in the south, increasing to seventy to ninety inches in the north. East of the Rockies, precipitation decreases from the southeast toward the northwest. Thus the Gulf coast (New Orleans area) receives sixty-two to sixty-four inches annually, with low probability of either drought or snow, while in north-central Canada (Winnipeg area) the annual total is only eighteen to twenty inches (under 1 liter), with regular winter snows and irregular summer rains.

Although westerly winds originating in the Pacific Ocean prevail across most of the continent, the rainfall they bring falls largely along the mountainous Pacific coast and in the higher elevations of the Rockies. This leaves the southwestern interior, with two to five inches (50 to 125 millimeters) of precipitation, as the continent's driest region, and restricts precipitation on the western Plains-Grasslands region to a low and rather unpredictable ten to twelve inches (250 to 300 millimeters).

Throughout the eastern third of the continent south of the Boreal region, precipitation occurs primarily under unstable, cyclonic conditions that provide regular annual totals of from twenty-five to forty inches (625 to 1,000 millimeters) with slightly higher accumulations along the Atlantic coast. The northern Boreal and Arctic regions, dominated by cooler, more stable air masses, receive low annual levels of eight to twelve inches (200 to 300 millimeters) of precipitation, with much of it falling as winter snow.

Regional Diversity

The ecological consequences of these climatic patterns are far-reaching. They are reflected most clearly in the distribution of vegetation and soil types, and associated with variations in the frost-free season, the northern margins of crop cultivation, and the formation of edge habitats. Temperature lows determine annual growing seasons everywhere except in the Southwest, where drought is the limiting factor. The general decrease in annual temperatures and precipitation from the south toward the northern interior accounts for the land-cover variations that comprise the continent's principal ecological regions.

The Arctic, Boreal, and Rocky Mountain regions, with long periods of subjection to frosts (below 32°F), have short growing seasons (generally defined as the continuous period above 40°F) of less than ninety days, and thin, acidic, leached soils that support evergreen forests of spruce, larch, and fir species, or treeless tundra in the far north. These natural conditions render these regions unsuitable for agriculture. The critical northern limits of native farming, therefore, skirt the northern margins of the Saint Lawrence Valley, the northern shores of the Great Lakes, and the parkland zone along the Boreal–Plains-Grasslands border. Somewhat unpredictable rainfall conditions west of the hundredth meridian make the cultivation of crops on the western Plains-Grasslands region a risky endeavor, a risk that continues westward almost to the Pacific coast.

In the east, within the Temperate Woodlands regions, conditions encouraging greater land-cover diversity improve toward the south. Thus, the cooler, northern woodlands region, which has growing seasons ranging from 95 to 140 days, supports mixed evergreen and deciduous forests dominated by spruce, pine, hemlock, maple, and beech species on leached gray-brown soils suitable for some cultivated crops. Farther south, with growing seasons of 150 to 320 days, deciduous forests predominate, with oak-hickory associations and a wide variety of supplemental species supported by fertile brown forest soils.

Only in the southeast, where soil and drainage conditions encourage the growth of southern pine species, is the ubiquity of deciduous hardwoods challenged. No part of the continent is completely free of frost danger, but an almost year-round growing season can be found in the subtropical swamp conditions of southern Florida.

The forest-grassland border, which extends from coastal Texas through the central interior to the Boreal–Plains-Grasslands boundary, constitutes the principal zone of edge habitats in North America. Such habitats, or transition zones, create unusually diverse conditions for resource exploitation because they represent not only the meeting place of two contrasting ecological regions but also the subtleties of the changing transition zone between. From the perspective of human occupation they represent rich but challenging adaptive experiences. Thus in west-central Canada, the southern Boreal forest gives way to a parkland zone of aspen and oak groves before merging into tall-grass prairie dominated by wheatgrass species. Along the northwestern border with the Temperate Woodlands region, oak-hickory-maple woodlands diminish in favor of tall-grass prairie composed principally of bluestem species. Farther south, the forest–grassland transition consists of an oak-hickory-pine complex giving way more gradually to a mixed prairie-mesquite shrub cover. The tall-grass prairie subregion is underlain by rich, black-earth soils. But as rainfall decreases westward, lighter, calcareous, chestnut soils become more prominent and the prairie deteriorates into short-grass steppe in which less nutritious needle-grass and buffalo grass species predominate.

Edge habitats, however, occur wherever significant contrasts exist in land surface conditions or along seashores. The Dry Southwest region, for example, is replete with contrasts between plateau, block mountain, and basin formats conducive to ponderosa pine and juniper woodlands in higher elevations, sagebrush and saltbush steppes on plateaus, and creosote bush scrub in the drier southern basins. Similarly, along the floodplain of the lower Mississippi River, oak-hickory woodlands are replaced by cypress and tupelo species more adapted to high water-table conditions; in southern Florida, southern pine forests replace everglade swamp farther north;

and throughout the Boreal region, the presence of numerous freshwater lakes provides a variety of aquatic resources amid the evergreens.

HISTORIC INDIAN ENVIRONMENTS

The Indian worlds that the Spanish encountered during the sixteenth century, and that the English, French, Dutch, and Swedes experienced a century later, represented a twelve- to fourteen-thousand-year period of Indian adaptations to changing environments. The Asian peoples who crossed the Bering Strait land bridge into present-day Alaska and northwestern Canada had spread throughout the continent within two thousand years. They came initially as hunters and foragers at the end of the last continental glaciation, which covered the northern half of the continent as far south as the Missouri-Ohio line and eastward to Long Island. The Arctic, Boreal, and Cool Temperate Woodland regions were eroded severely and much of their topsoil was removed and deposited in the Missouri and Ohio valleys as the ice sheets melted. These hunters and gatherers, therefore, not only encountered new natural environments in North America but also had to adapt to changing ecological circumstances as temperatures became warmer, rainfall became more frequent, and forest and grassland distributions became more extensive. The consequence of this long period of environmental adjustment was that Indian societies created a considerably more varied and complex set of resource appraisals and food production systems than their ancestors had brought with them from Asia.

Until five thousand years ago, Indian subsistence patterns represented an elaboration and regionalization of nomadic hunting practices and intensive plant foraging. Within the Boreal region, caribou constituted the principal food source, supplemented by fishing and summer foraging. The bow and arrow probably evolved in this region and spread southward. In the Temperate Woodland regions, white-tailed deer were most prized, supplemented by smaller game, wildfowl, and fish where available. The Plains-Grasslands economy was dominated by the buffalo hunt, and in the Dry Southwest, jackrabbits and wild turkeys provided the subsistence base

together with foraging. Along the eastern and southwestern margins of the forest–grassland transition zone, however, Indian societies paid increasing attention to the systematic collection of wild plant foods, especially nuts, berries, acorns, and wild grass seeds, as well as to the hunting of small game, wildfowl, and fish. Increasing manipulation of local plant species led to the domestication of sumpweed and maygrass in the Mississippi Basin about forty-five hundred years ago, followed shortly by sunflower and goosefoot. In the Dry Southwest region, bottle gourd was introduced from Mexico, followed by varieties of beans and squashes that diffused gradually eastward.

Maize

The domestication of maize of Mesoamerican origin about three thousand years ago, and its diffusion throughout the southeastern part of the continent during the following thousand years, produced the most far-reaching modifications in Indian subsistence patterns and ecological relationships. Maize was a versatile and demanding grain that had a high food yield, provided a nutritious bread staple when ground, and combined with beans to create hominy. It was also a relatively deep-rooted plant with a high demand for soil nutrients that created rapid soil depletion. Societies that adopted maize were required to shift from nomadic or seminomadic settlement traditions to long-term or permanent sites where they could practice a variety of cultivation techniques. Two regional societies particularly flourished from this adoption, the Pueblo and Hohokam traditions of the Dry Southwest, and the Mississippian traditions of the lower Mississippi and Ohio valleys.

In the Southwest, eight-rowed flint maize and twelve-rowed dent maize formed the core of a sophisticated subsistence system that combined a maize-squash-gourd-bean complex with the hunting of jackrabbits and turkeys, the collection of pinyon nuts and juniper berries, and basketry and clay pottery technologies. In higher elevations, rainfall diversion techniques led to large, permanent settlements of multistoried, flat-roofed, dry-masonry houses. Along major river valleys, elaborate irrigation systems appeared in conjunction with occasionally terraced agriculture but more modest, wood-framed,

ECOLOGICAL REGIONS

Bering Strait

Beaufort Sea

Ellesmere Island

Pacific Maritime

Rocky Mountains

A r c t i c

B o r e a l

Gulf of Saint Lawrence

Pacific Ocean

Plains

Grasslands

Cool Temperate Woodland

Dry Southwest

Temperate Woodland

Atlantic Ocean

Gulf of Mexico

Subtropical Swamp

SUBSISTENCE REGIONS

b	buffalo
c	caribou
d	deer
f	fish
j	jackrabbit
m	moose
sm	sea mammals
s	shellfish

adobe house structures. All of these traditions flourished through the fourteenth century, but had declined by the time Spanish explorers reached the region in the mid sixteenth century.

In the Mississippi Basin, a more extensive cultural complex emerged based on flint and dent varieties of maize (with flint better adapted to the shorter growing seasons in the north), beans, squashes, gourd, sunflower, and Jerusalem artichoke, as well as meat from deer, wild turkey, waterfowl, and raccoon, fish and shellfish, and a variety of nuts, berries, fruits, and seeds. Agriculture was associated particularly with floodplain sites, with hoe and digging stick technology, and with shifting cultivation. Local societies created a variety of settlement locations, from short-term, special-purpose sites for hunting or plant collecting, to more permanent family homesteads in hamlets and villages, to large, ceremonial, mound towns of pole-and-thatch houses protected by earthworks. Riverine trade linked an extensive network of towns from the lower Mississippi to the southern Great Lakes. This is evident from the rich archaeological record of pottery remains, marine shells, copper, flint, and stone pipes, as well as from trade in furs, salt, and maize. The demise of this tradition is not well understood, but it reached its zenith during the thirteenth and fourteenth centuries and had largely disintegrated by the early seventeenth century. The Iroquois in northern New York were an offshoot of this tradition and represented one of the most developed economies on the eve of European contact.

CONTACT INDIAN ENVIRONMENTS

The worlds encountered by the first Europeans were neither "natural environments" nor "virgin lands." While Europeans described with both awe and disdain Indian ways of life as they perceived them, they often underestimated the natural challenges that the continent presented and minimized native economic achievements. The key aspect of Indian occupation of North America by the sixteenth and early seventeenth centuries was the harmony between ecological regions and the subsistence traditions of native cultures (see map 2).

Throughout the continent, hunting, foraging, and fishing had not been fully superseded

by agriculture as they had been in Europe. They remained integral elements of Indian livelihood even among societies committed to intensive farming. Hunting practices, whether providing almost the full complement of food items as in the Arctic, Boreal, Plains-Grasslands, and Rocky Mountain regions, or as a supplementary practice elsewhere, were an essential part of Native life and thought. Many Indian societies remained seminomadic because of their dependence on hunting, and even where agriculture was dominant, seasonal hunting camps were an essential feature of year-round livelihood patterns.

Agricultural practices, on the other hand, remained relatively unsophisticated and almost entirely crop-oriented. Perhaps the most striking aspect of Indian agricultural evolution was the absence of domesticated animals, with the exception of the dog and the turkey, and particularly the lack of herd animals as in European agriculture. This absence helps to account for the persistence of pedestrian hunting to supply a meat component to the diet and the persistence of hand tools in a farming system that lacked the technical modifications made possible with the use of draft animals, most notably the plow.

Subsistence regions across North America at contact time may be grouped into four categories based on dominant economic activities. Farming predominated throughout the eastern part of the continent as far north as the Ontario peninsula and upper Saint Lawrence Valley, as well as in permanent stream valleys in the Southwest. Hunting dominated activities almost everywhere else except in southern Florida, the Gulf coast, the southern California coast, and in the Pacific Northwest, where fishing was primary, and in the basin and range areas of the Dry Southwest, where gathering was relatively more important.

Farming
Farming patterns in the East varied in intensity. The most determined efforts occurred among the mid-Atlantic societies from southern New England to coastal Carolina. Along the southern Atlantic coast and in the interior from the Saint Lawrence Valley south almost to the Gulf of Mexico, Indian groups practiced similar farming traditions less intensively and hunting took on an

important supplementary role. In northern New England, the Michigan Peninsula, and in a broad transition zone stretching westward to the Missouri Valley and southward to northeastern Texas, farming was less widespread, more occasional, and remained supplementary to hunting. The triad of maize, beans, and squashes formed the basic elements of agricultural subsistence throughout the East. Land tenure was based on the collective needs of the community rather than on individual ownership, although among some native groups traditions of family gardens and family hunting territories had evolved.

Land clearance, which usually employed both men and women, involved girdling trees with axes about three feet above the ground, burning branches, trunks, and underbrush, and planting crops among the stumps, which would be removed gradually. The soil was broken up by hoe or spade-like implements and heaped into small hills in which maize kernels and bean seeds were planted, usually by women. In some areas, pumpkins were planted around the base of the hills and tobacco seeds planted in separate hills. Once crop yields began to decline, fields would lie fallow temporarily to renew fertility and new fields would be prepared. This collective, slash-and-burn, short-fallow cultivation system provided the basic dietary components for all eastern farming societies. The more intensive the farming, the more sedentary settlement patterns were likely to be. Along the mid-Atlantic coast, village and hamlet settlements were typically composed of arched pole-frame, bark-covered, multifamily houses that could be easily modified or rebuilt. Among groups with complex social organization, such as the Iroquois, such house construction could become quite elaborate, resulting in "long houses" extending up to two hundred feet to accommodate growing families.

Throughout eastern farming regions, crop production was supplemented by other food-producing activities in a complex annual system of activity cycles adapted to the region's seasonal harvests. Planting times for maize ranged from early April in the South to early June in the North, with staggered times for dent (early planting) and flint (later planting) varieties. Harvest time occurred in early September in the Saint Lawrence Valley but was a more protracted experience in the southeast, where harvesting could occur throughout September and into mid October. Most of this agricultural work was done by women and children. The gathering of nuts, fruits, berries, and seeds would be conducted between June and October and worked around the corn cycle. The fishing cycle varied depending upon the species caught. Freshwater lake species could be caught year round. In the upper reaches of major rivers, freshwater species were especially plentiful during the fall spawning season, while in tidal rivers and estuaries the spring spawning of ocean species was a particularly active fishing season. The hunting cycle, which generally involved a spring and early summer hunt for deer, small game, and waterfowl, and a larger hunt during the fall for deer and turkey, took most of the men and younger women away for lengthy periods, leaving half-deserted settlements populated mainly by married women and children. Only the winter period was a time of reduced activities and well-occupied towns and villages.

While fishing and gathering had relatively limited long-term environmental consequences, farming and hunting involved significant ecological changes. Shifting cultivation techniques created important, site-specific modifications by removing trees, creating new edge habitats, and encouraging new forms of plant succession in abandoned "old fields" that favored more abundant grass and brush species for browsing animals. The use of fire in hunting, whether to drive or trap game or to encourage more open browse cover for deer, had a more extensive impact. Regular burnings favored a succession of grass species and fire-resistant tree species, such as pines, that produced new edge habitats on a larger scale. Early European settlers described such fire practices and occasionally used them as well, but the extent of humanly induced open grasslands or parklands in eastern America remains a topic of debate.

Hunting, Fishing, and Gathering

Specialized hunting societies dominated the northern and central interior regions of the continent from Newfoundland west to the northern Rockies in Alaska, and from the Arctic shores to south Texas in regions either too cold or too dry for practical agriculture. These societies can be differentiated in terms of the principal game animals hunted and by the supplementary activities associated with hunting. Thus, deer remained the principal game animal along the northern Cool Temperate Woodlands region and in the northern Rocky Mountain region; moose was important in the eastern and southern parts of the Boreal region; caribou dominated hunting activity within the Boreal and sub-Arctic regions; sea mammals were the focus of Arctic life; and buffalo were the primary means of support in the Plains-Grasslands region and in the upper Mississippi Valley. Fishing supplemented game especially along the coasts and around interior lakes, while the gathering of seeds and wild rice was a distinctive characteristic of the Lake Superior area.

Hunting as a way of life, however, united all these regions in a shared world of techniques, nomadism, and animal-based cosmology. Game provided fresh meat, a surplus that was dried into beef jerky or compounded with animal fat and berries into pemmican for winter sustenance or trade, and skins and hides for clothing and shelters. Procurement and settlement practices varied with the types of game and their migratory habits. Plains-Grasslands buffalo hunters followed the herds along their northerly migration routes during the spring and summer and along their southerly trails in the fall. A common hunting technique was to engineer buffalo drives that stampeded animals between lines of stone piles to stumble over embankments or into palisaded traps where they could be killed with bows and arrows. Men did the hunting while women prepared the food and scraped the hides. Caribou hunting also required moving with the herds. In the Arctic and sub-Arctic this often involved considerable distances during the summer migrations, while in the Boreal region, woodland caribou generally were present throughout the year and made for especially efficient hunting during the fall rutting season. Moose are less of a large-herd animal except during mating season, so that spring and summer reliance on moose generally required supplemental food production through hunting hare and wildfowl and through fishing. Seasonal distinctions were most pronounced along the Arctic shores, where a brief spring and summer hunting season devoted to barren-ground caribou, hare, and

muskox gave way to a concentration on marine resources in the form of seal, walrus, whale, and fish during the long winter period. Winter in the Boreal and Cool Temperate Woodlands regions, however, was also the season for furbearing animals, particularly beaver, which were easily trapped for pelts that were used for winter clothing or for trade.

The nomadic traditions of North American hunting peoples created few sedentary settlements but did produce a wide variety of house forms. Portable structures were common, typically consisting of hide or bark tents wrapped around wood poles interlocked at the top to provide stability. During the more sedentary winter period, small earth-pit houses and larger rectangular, sod-covered earth lodges on wood frames were common sights in villages along the major rivers of the Plains-Grasslands region.

Along the northern Pacific Maritime coast, however, where economies were centered on intensive fishing and the hunting of sea mammals, settlements were larger and more permanent. Dependence on salmon fishing and the exploitation of halibut, herring, cod, shellfish, and seal created substantial villages and towns of large, wooden lodges made of cedar planking lashed to timber frames. Totem poles honoring revered ancestors stood as a distinctive feature at the entrance of many lodges. Temporary summer fishing camps employed a similar but more simplified design. The simplest house forms, however, were located in the basin and range areas of the Southwest. The struggle for subsistence in this semiarid region, based on extensive gathering of nuts and berries and the hunting of jackrabbits, was expressed in the simple pole-and-brush huts of this sparsely settled area of the West.

Native Populations
Calculating native population numbers and densities for the time of the eve of European contact is fraught with complications. Scholars traditionally have viewed the limited resource technologies of Native Americans as indicative of low population numbers of about one million people before 1500. It is now clear that Indian economies were capable of supporting a significantly larger population, although much less than the ten million or more natives projected for Me-

soamerica. The best current consensus is that there were about 3.25 million natives in the present continental United States and somewhat more than one million natives in Canada and Alaska. The highest population densities generally coincided with the farming and fishing societies of the Pacific and Atlantic coasts and the Southwest, and around the Great Lakes. Moderate densities were characteristic of the eastern Woodlands and the eastern Plains-Grasslands region, with low densities elsewhere and very sparse numbers in the Arctic, northern Boreal, Rocky Mountain, and desert Southwest regions.

The problem of population totals is compounded by the periodic and widespread native–European contacts that occurred during the sixteenth century, prior to sustained colonization. The "disease frontiers" induced by European-borne illnesses such as plague, smallpox, measles, scarlet fever, whooping cough, and influenza decimated substantial numbers of affected Indians and even depopulated some areas before European settlement. Such diseases were probably transferred by fishermen to Newfoundland and the Canadian Maritimes before the 1530s, and were recorded after Hernando de Soto's expedition to the Southeast during the late 1530s and early 1540s, after Jacques Cartier's visit to the Saint Lawrence Valley during the same decade, and after Francisco Vásquez de Coronado's explorations of the Southwest during the 1540s. Plague epidemics had reduced Indian societies along the coast of New England before 1620, and smallpox and measles spread through Iroquois and Huron settlements during the 1630s. It is clear, therefore, that exposed populations in the southern and eastern regions of the continent had been further reduced in numbers before the middle of the seventeenth century, although the actual totals involved can only be conjectured.

The decline in Indian populations and the places they occupied during the seventeenth and eighteenth centuries represented not only a series of retreating frontiers in the wake of European land acquisition and settlement but also a vanishing reservoir of geographical and natural knowledge about native North America that, indeed, had initially aided the newcomers in adapting to unfamiliar environments. European explorers and pioneers were helped by the natives'

vast knowledge of places and place-name terminology, of variations in terrain and drainage, of trails and canoes, of flora and fauna, including plant identification and utility and the habits of game animals, and also of land clearance and beef preservation. But above all, European proprietary claims were enhanced by the presentation of natural and native resources deemed to have commercial potential. Maize, tobacco, beaver furs, and buffalo hides provide much of the grist for the economic history of the colonial and immediate postcolonial eras. The principal exchanges induced by cultural contacts greatly benefited the newcomers but left the aborigines, in the words of Virginian Robert Beverley,

happy, I think, in their simple State of Nature, and in their enjoyment of Plenty, without the Curse of Labour. They have on several accounts reason to lament the arrival of the Europeans, by whose means they seem to have lost their Felicity, as well as their Innocence. The English have taken away great part of their Country, and consequently made every thing less plenty amongst them. . . . Afterwards I will treat of the present state of the English there, and the Alterations, I can't call them Improvements, they have made at this Day [1705]. (*The History and Present State of Virginia*, pp. 233, 156)

BIBLIOGRAPHY

Natural Environments

Hunt, Charles B. *Natural Regions of the United States and Canada.* San Francisco, 1967.

Pirkle, E. C., and W. H. Yoho. *Natural Regions of the United States.* Dubuque, Iowa, 1975.

Redfern, Ron. *The Makings of a Continent.* New York, 1983.

Shimer, John A. *This Sculptured Earth: The Landscape of America.* New York, 1959.

Trimble, Stanley W. "Nature's Continent." In *The Making of the American Landscape,* edited by Michael P. Conzen. Boston, 1990.

Wright, H. E., Jr., ed. *Late-Quaternary Environments of the United States.* 2 vols. Minneapolis, Minn., 1983.

Historic Environments

Butzer, Karl W. "The Indian Legacy in the American Landscape." In *The Making of the American Landscape,* edited by Michael P. Conzen. Boston, 1990.

Cohen, Mark Nathan, and George J. Armelagos, eds.

Paleopathology and the Origins of Agriculture. New York, 1984.

Ford, Richard I., ed. *Prehistoric Food Production in North America.* Ann Arbor, Mich., 1985.

Harris, R. Cole, ed. *Historical Atlas of Canada.* Vol. 1, *From the Beginning to 1800.* Toronto, Ontario, 1987.

Sturtevant, William C., ed., *Handbook of North American Indians.* 15 vols. Washington, D.C., 1978.

Ubelaker, Douglas H. "Prehistoric New World Population Size: Historical Review and Current Appraisal of North American Estimates." *American Journal of Physical Anthropology* 45 (November 1976):661–665.

West, Frederick H., "The Antiquity of Man in America." In *Late-Quaternary Environments of the United States.* Vol. 1, *The Late Pleistocene,* edited by Stephen C. Porter. Minneapolis, Minn., 1983.

Contact Environments

Albers, Patricia, and Jeanne Kay. "Sharing the Land: A Study in American Indian Territoriality." In *A Cultural Geography of North American Indians,* edited by Thomas E. Ross and Tyrel G. Moore. Boulder, Colo., 1987.

Axtell, James L. *The European and the Indian: Essays in the Ethnohistory of Colonial North America.* New York, 1981.

Beverley, Robert. *The History and Present State of Virginia.* Edited by Louis B. Wright. Chapel Hill, N.C., 1947; repr. 1968.

Conzen, Michael P., ed. *The Making of the American Landscape.* Boston, 1990.

Denevan, William M., ed. *Native Population of the Americas in 1492.* Madison, Wis., 1976.

Mitchell, Robert D., and Paul A. Groves, eds. *North America: The Historical Geography of a Changing Continent.* Totowa, N.J., 1987.

Peterson, Jacqueline, and John Anfinson. "The Indian and the Fur Trade: A Review of Recent Literature." In *Scholars and the Indian Experience: Critical Reviews of Recent Writing in the Social Sciences,* edited by W. R. Swagerty. Bloomington, Ind., 1984.

Sauer, Carl O. *Seventeenth Century North America.* Berkeley, Calif., 1980.

———. *Sixteenth Century North America: The Land and The People As Seen by the Europeans.* Berkeley and Los Angeles, 1971.

Robert D. Mitchell

See also **The Age of Reconnaissance; Ecological Consequences of Economic Development; The First American; and Native American Economies.**

THE FIRST AMERICANS

SINCE THE EARLIEST days of European settlement, scholars and others have puzzled over the origins of Native Americans. Where did these exotic peoples come from? Had they sailed across a vast ocean, or had they walked to their new homeland? How long had the Indians lived in the New World? Certainly, their origins were so ancient that no known American Indian oral tradition referred to them. And how did one explain the astounding diversity of Native American societies? There were small bands of hunters and fisherfolk, settled villages of farmers like the Virginia Indians, and complex and sophisticated civilizations like those of the Aztecs of Mexico and the Incas of Peru. Why did some early Americans create elaborate civilizations while others lived as simple farmers or survived off game or wild plant foods? Five centuries after Columbus, scholars are still grappling with these fundamental questions.

THE EARLIEST SETTLERS
(c. 15,000 years ago)

The scientific search for the first Native Americans has been conducted with passion and considerable acrimony for more than a century. This energetic quest has yielded no traces of archaic humans, of Neanderthals or other peoples from remote prehistory. Almost certainly, the first human inhabitants of the Americas were anatomically modern people, *Homo sapiens*. They were descendants of primordial modern human populations that evolved, probably in tropical Africa, well before one hundred thousand years ago. Such people were living in the Near East, and perhaps in Southeast Asia, by forty-five thousand years ago and had settled in the extremely cold northern latitudes of Europe and Asia by at least thirty-five thousand years ago. Sometime later, they crossed from Siberia into Alaska and peopled a virgin continent. The settlement of the Americas was part of a long-term colonization of the late Ice Age world by modern humans.

The Late Ice Age World

As recently as eighteen thousand years ago, the world was very different from our own, gripped by a prolonged period of intensely cold glacial conditions. This "Wisconsin" glaciation peaked about eighteen thousand to twenty thousand years ago. Only five thousand years later, the world's climate started to warm up rapidly, and the ensuing seven thousand years of global warming brought modern climatic conditions to all parts of the world.

During the late Wisconsin glaciation, the northern parts of North America were locked in a prolonged deep freeze. Two huge ice sheets covered much of Canada. The Laurentide ice sheet was centered east of Hudson Bay and extended west from Greenland to the Rocky Mountain foothills and south of the Great Lakes. The

Cordilleran sheet stretched from the Pacific coast over the mountains, from Alaska to Seattle. Continental North America was effectively isolated from the Arctic by impenetrable ice sheets. Throughout the world, sea levels were more than three hundred feet (90 meters) lower than they are today, so that Siberia was joined to Alaska by a low-lying, arid plain. A wide, rolling belt of treeless steppe and tundra extended across Central Europe and Eurasia into Siberia and Alaska. This region was the home of now-extinct cold-loving animals such as the mammoth, the steppe bison, and the woolly rhinoceros, as well as of some game species, such as the reindeer (caribou) and musk ox, that are still staples for northern hunters today.

Much of the colonization of the late Ice Age world by Homo sapiens took place during the Wisconsin maximum. To cross into the Americas required the ability to adapt to the extremely harsh conditions and long winters of the steppe-tundra. To survive these extreme conditions, late Ice Age peoples of twenty-five thousand years ago developed a sophisticated and highly portable technology based on antler, bone, and stone. Permanent settlement in areas like northern Eurasia and Alaska would have been impossible during the late Ice Age without such a technology. When people did settle the open plains, because the supply of game and other food resources was limited, human populations were extremely small and widely dispersed, gathering mainly in sheltered locales such as large river valleys, where game congregated for much of the year.

The Question of Ancestry

No one doubts that the ancestry of the first Americans lies among the ancient Siberians. The problem is to identify these ancestral populations with greater precision. Did Eurasian big-game hunting groups from west of Lake Baikal expand north and east toward the Bering Strait? Or did northern Chinese hunter-gatherers develop technologies that enabled them to move north into periglacial lands?

Dental morphology provides some of the best clues. All Native American teeth display characteristic features and cusp patterns identical to those found not in the teeth of prehistoric Europeans but in those of northeast Asians and northern Chinese. These traits may mean that populations ancestral to the Native Americans originated in northeast Asia over twenty thousand years ago. Furthermore, the dental similarities between northeast Siberians and Indians are so marked that the separation took place relatively recently, perhaps some fifteen thousand years ago. Dental morphology agrees with other genetic comparisons that show close and relatively recent biological relationships between Native American populations and Siberian peoples.

Unfortunately, the archaeology of northern China and northeast Siberia is still largely a mystery. But we do know that small populations of late Ice Age hunter-gatherers lived along the Middle Aldan River in Siberia as early as eighteen thousand years ago. Some of these Siberians may have been the ancestors of the first Americans.

The Bering Land Bridge

From about one hundred thousand to fifteen thousand years ago, Siberia and Alaska were joined by dry land. At times the two continents were linked by only a narrow strip of low-lying plain, but at others the Bering Land Bridge formed a broad corridor that covered the entire modern strait north into the Chuckchi Sea. The land bridge was windy steppe-tundra, dissected by numerous shallow river valleys. It was across this now-sunken plain that human beings came to the New World.

We know nothing of these people. We assume that they reached Alaska not as a deliberate act of exploration and settlement but as part of the natural dynamics of hunting and foraging that governed the entire late Ice Age population of the globe. Steppe-tundra peoples were constantly on the move, as families came together, split up, and hived off to form new groups. Their highly flexible way of life required large hunting territories and travel over long distances, natural movements that brought people onto the land bridge and, in time, into what is now Alaska.

Alaska and the Ice-Free Corridor

The earliest known archaeological sites in Alaska date to about 9500 B.C., some five millennia after the great warm-up at the end of the Ice Age began and undoubtedly a long time after first

16

settlement. Human settlement is well attested to along Alaskan coasts and in the interior after 8000 B.C. By this time, human beings had settled throughout the Americas, as far south as the Strait of Magellan.

It appears that sometime during the late Ice Age, perhaps as early as eighteen thousand to twenty thousand years ago, small numbers of hunters moved onto the land bridge, hunting big game and perhaps sea mammals. Some of these tiny bands may have pursued game onto higher ground in the east, into what is now Alaska. After fifteen thousand years, climatic conditions warmed up and sea levels rose, flooding the low-lying plains. At this point, some hunting bands may have settled permanently in Alaska and, in time, moved south into the heart of North America by a route that is the subject of much controversy.

For generations, conventional geological wisdom had it that there was a narrow ice-free corridor between the two great Wisconsin ice sheets that ran down the east side of the Rocky Mountains from southern Alaska to Alberta. Thus, humans could have moved south long before the end of the Ice Age. In 1989 Canadian geologists reported that the two ice sheets did in fact fuse into one along the length of the corridor. In any case, any ice-free landscape would have been devoid of game and vegetation and thus incapable of supporting humans. It would have been impossible for late Ice Age people to move south from Alaska overland throughout the late Wisconsin until the great ice sheets went into retreat.

If the first settlers did not come south by land, could they have paddled in canoes or skin boats along the frigid Alaskan and British Columbian coasts? In many parts of the Americas, the low sea levels of the Wisconsin glaciation exposed wide continental shelves, but this was not the case in the northwest, where coastal waters are deep. Had the first Americans come south along the coast, they would have had to have been expert seamen, capable of navigating Arctic, and often ice-strewn, seas in small canoes. At present, there is no evidence that late Ice Age peoples in such environments were capable of open water passages at all. They may have lacked the specialized technology to build skin boats and to survive the ravages of hypothermia in exposed Arctic waters.

Most likely, late Ice Age big-game hunters moved south from Alaska across rugged terrain as the great ice sheets began their retreat about fifteen thousand years ago.

The Earliest Settlement South of the Ice Sheets

Despite numerous, and often well-publicized, claims to the contrary, there is as yet no evidence for human settlement in continental North America before fifteen thousand years ago. Most claims for early occupation consist of small scatters of stone artifacts in the lowermost levels of caves and rock shelters in South America. For example, Boqueirao da Furada rock shelter in northeast Brazil is said to contain evidence of human occupation that extends back as early as forty-seven thousand years ago. The few stone tools from this remote site are far from convincing. The lowest levels of Pichimachay cave in highland Peru yielded what some experts believe to be chipped stones; in fact, the fragments may have fallen from the cave walls. An open site at Monte Verde in Chile with well-attested later occupation is thought by some to have prospered some thirty thousand years ago. The artifacts from these levels do not withstand the scrutiny of expert eyes. It is not sufficient to discover a single occurrence of very early settlement. What is needed are consistent patterns of human occupation, uncovered at many sites. So far these do not exist. The consensus of scholarly opinion places the first settlement of the Americas much later, at the very end of the Ice Age.

The earliest relatively well-dated human occupation comes from Meadowcroft Rockshelter in Pennsylvania, from a shelter occupied intermittently from as early as about 12,500 B.C. to about A.D. 1200. There are a few handfuls of stone tools from other caves and rock shelters such as Fort Rock in Oregon that date to 10,000 B.C. or slightly earlier. Then, after about 9500 B.C., the number of archaeological sites increases dramatically, as human populations rose sharply.

Almost certainly, then, the first settlement of North America was by a few families of late Ice Age hunters, who crossed from Siberia into Alaska, perhaps as early as fifteen thousand years ago. As the ice sheets retreated, their "Paleo-indian" successors moved south into the heart of a continent teeming with Ice Age game.

THE CLOVIS PEOPLE
(9500 to 9000 B.C.)

In about 9500 B.C. the Clovis culture, named after a site near the town of that name in New Mexico, appears. Most of what we know about the Clovis people comes from rare big-game kill sites on the Great Plains, places where Paleo-indian hunters attacked and killed lumbering mammoth or bison. At the end of the Ice Age and during the millennia that followed, the vast grasslands east of the Rockies became progressively drier, supporting now-extinct animals like the mammoth and large forms of bison. The same grasslands were home to scattered bands of Clovis people, who ranged over enormous hunting territories following migrating game and foraging for wild plant foods in season. Judging from the wide distribution of Clovis artifacts throughout North America as far north as Maine and Nova Scotia, the successors of the first settlers spread through the continent very rapidly, perhaps within as little as five centuries.

Most of our information about big-game hunting comes from the plains, where characteristic Clovis stone projectile points have been found among the bones of butchered bison and mammoth. Most plains kills lie on low ground, near creeks, springs, and ponds where the hunters could watch the prey for days on end while deciding on a strategy of attack. These were places where hunters armed only with stone-tipped spears could ambush large beasts as they stampeded into soft mud or swamps. Some Clovis hunters followed groups of female mammoths for weeks on end, observing the behavior of individual beasts with great care. Then they caught isolated animals off guard and culled the herd one by one at the same location over a period of many years. However many beasts were killed, the hunters and their families swarmed over the carcasses, dismembering the bones, removing the choice parts, and carefully preserving the hide. They camped nearby until they had consumed as much fresh meat as they could and dried such flesh as they could carry or cache for later use.

Normally, each Paleoindian band was anchored to a base camp or favored location where it wintered, then moved out during spring, summer, and fall. It was an isolated life, with minimal contacts with other people, except for a short period of the year when food was abundant. Then several bands would come together to exchange raw materials such as tool-making stone and perhaps to hunt together. It was then that marriages and initiation ceremonies took place and people exchanged visits and information before scattering for the long winter months.

As befitted people constantly on the move, the Clovis people used highly effective, lightweight tool kits. They based their hunting weaponry on beautifully made stone projectile points with carefully thinned bases. Clovis points were mounted on wooden staves, perhaps in wood or bone foreshafts that worked loose inside the wound once the head of the projectile was buried in its quarry. The hunters probably carried bundles of ready-mounted points and foreshafts that could be quickly inserted onto the end of a long spear, the prehistoric equivalent of the "snap-on" tool.

Clovis technology depended on points made of very fine-grained rock such as chalcedony, fine chert, and obsidian (volcanic rock). Such stone occurred at relatively few, widely separated locations. Some of the rock found with Clovis kills came from outcrops more than 180 miles (290 kilometers) away. When flaked, such rocks produce sharp edges that are ideal for cutting and shaping other vital raw materials like bone, hide, and antler. The stone workers obtained large lumps of suitable rock, which they shaped on both sides to form what archaeologists call "bifaces." These they carried around with them, knocking off carefully shaped large flakes that they turned into projectile points, knives, and other weapons.

In 9000 B.C. the population of North America probably totaled no more than a few thousand people living in every kind of local environment imaginable. It was at this point, soon after human settlers had adapted to a new and virgin continent, that the Clovis culture vanished, at the very moment that many species of familiar Ice

Age animals, large and small, vanished from the Americas.

This dramatic paleontological event was not confined to the Americas, for massive, even catastrophic extinctions of mammals occurred throughout the world by 9000 B.C. The North American casualties included the mammoth and the mastodon, the giant sloth, several forms of bison, and many camel species. All these animals were familiar prey, even staples, for Clovis bands wherever they lived. Biologist Paul Martin has argued that humans literally exploded into North America and beyond, into a continent populated by large herds of unsuspicious animals. The Clovis people expanded rapidly, he argues, their population rising sharply, especially at the frontier of human settlement, where game was most plentiful. Many of the species they preyed upon were slow-breeding species, soon exterminated through wasteful hunting. Inevitably, then, the game population passed into extinction, leaving humans starving or forced to adopt new ways of life.

Martin's critics argue that this explanation is too simplistic for such complex events. They believe that global warming at the end of the Ice Age proved lethal to big-game populations, especially cold-loving species. Drier climatic conditions over much of temperate North America as the great ice sheets retreated could have resulted in mass starvation of Ice Age species and caused their eventual extinction. During this process, according to this hypothesis, human populations were growing rapidly and hunting bands came into more frequent contact with one another, so that they cooperated in pursuing increasingly rare Ice Age animals. Perhaps, in time, Clovis bands helped drive many species of North American game animals into extinction.

With this catastrophic and still little understood event, the first chapter of North American prehistory ended.

THE HUNTER-GATHERERS
(9000 B.C. to Modern Times)

The Ice Age fauna vanished at a time when the North American continent was undergoing profound climatic and environmental change. Between 9000 and 4000 B.C. the climate became warmer and drier. Both the Cordilleran and the Laurentide ice sheets all but disappeared as world sea levels rose to their modern heights. Temperate woodlands spread northward across eastern North America and into southern Canada, while the plains became drier and the west increasingly arid. The changes in seacoasts, the appearance of the Great Lakes, and the flooding of river valleys all created new environmental opportunities for later Paleoindian groups and for the increasingly elaborate hunter-gatherer societies that followed them.

Undoubtedly, many Paleoindian bands perished as big game became scarce, but many others, opportunists like their remote ancestors, seized new opportunities and adapted to a great variety of challenging local environments. Some, on the Great Plains, remained big-game hunters right up to European contact many centuries later. Others adapted to harsh desert conditions in the arid western interior, living off seasonal plant foods and small game. Still others camped near marshes, lakes, and perennial streams or close to coasts and wide estuaries where relatively predictable fish, sea mammal, and waterfowl populations offered relatively easy food sources. Throughout the vast tracts of the eastern woodlands east of the Mississippi, people hunted deer and other game, relying heavily on plant foods and, later, on freshwater fish and mollusks.

Over a period of more than eleven thousand years, Native Americans developed an astounding diversity of hunter-gatherer societies. These diverse cultures unfolded, for the most part, in complete isolation. Only in the far north did biological and cultural contacts with Siberia continue. For thousands of years frequent canoe journeys across the Bering Strait brought immigrants, valued trade goods, or simply regular visitors. The harsh sub-Arctic latitudes of northern Canada effectively isolated the far north from the heart of the continent.

The remainder of prehistoric North America embarked on a trajectory of isolated, long-term cultural change that was to be cut off abruptly by European settlement after the fifteenth century A.D. No dramatic migrations set off major population movements, no wars of conquest pitted nation against nation. Rather, Native

American societies lived in every kind of landscape imaginable and adopted short- and long-term solutions to the most fundamental problem of all—survival.

For most of these eleven thousand years, the North Americans lived by hunting, by gathering wild plant foods and shellfish, and by fishing. They developed ingenious and highly effective adaptations to everything from subtropical coastlines to Arctic plains where it was winter for most of the year. Some of these environments were so harsh that conditions were too dry, or the growing season too short, for domesticated crops to propagate. In these regions, hunter-gatherers flourished and evolved into modern times, as the Eskimo, Aleut, Inuit, and Athabasca did in the far north. By the same token, hunter-gatherer bands lived in very arid conditions in the Great Basin and other parts of the western interior with only minor changes in subsistence and tool kits over more than ten millennia.

This long record of cultural continuity, of slowly evolving, and sometimes increasingly complex, hunter-gatherer societies is marked by three long-term trends that affected people living in every corner of North America. First, increasing specialization refined human tool kits, such as artifacts and weapons developed for ever more specific tasks. Second, the level of interdependence between close neighbors and between communities living at ever greater distances accelerated dramatically as time went on, especially after 2000 B.C. Lastly, Native American societies became more complex both socially and politically, especially in areas where food supplies were plentiful and predictable.

Hunter-Gatherers of the Far North (8000 B.C. to Modern Times)

In 8000 B.C. Alaska was still a cultural province of Siberia, as it had been in earlier times, occupied by peoples whose ultimate cultural roots lay to the west, in northeast Asia. As time went on, however, a much greater diversity of hunter-gatherer societies developed in Alaska, in the Aleutian Islands, in sub-Arctic regions, and in the Canadian Far North. For more than three thousand years, Paleo-Arctic peoples flourished over an enormous area of extreme northwestern North America. Many small groups lived on now submerged seacoasts, subsisting off fish and sea mammals. Most surviving Paleo-Arctic sites are inland hunting camps where only stone tools survive, so we know little of these peoples' lives. The distinctive stone spear barbs and fine knives made by Paleo-Arctic groups occur throughout Alaska and as far east as the western and southwestern Yukon Territory. Somewhat similar hunting artifacts were made on the Queen Charlotte Islands of British Columbia as early as 5000 B.C. Some of the most developed Paleo-Arctic cultures occur in the Aleutian Islands, where fishing and sea mammal hunting was well established at important sites like Anangula on Umnak Island as early as 6800 B.C. The Anangula people lived in semisubterranean houses entered through the roof, in a settlement atop a high cliff that was accessible only by boat.

At the time of European contact, Arctic peoples flourished across the Far North from Attu Island in the Aleutian chain to the eastern shores of Greenland, more than 6,800 miles (10,900 kilometers) away. There was considerable physical variation among these isolated populations, but they are generally considered to be the most Asian of all Native Americans. Linguistically, both Eskimo and Aleut belong within a single Eskimo-Aleut language stock that is related to Siberian speech stocks such as the Chuckchi and Ural-Altaic languages found widely in northeast Asia. How long ago, then, did Aleut and Eskimo appear in the Arctic? Some linguists and physical anthropologists believe that Paleo-Arctic people were Na-Dene speakers, hunter-gatherers who used light, barbed hunting weapons against game like the caribou and who arrived as the Ice Age ended, between fourteen thousand and twelve thousand years ago. They spread far to the south and east, into both the Pacific Northwest and the sub-Arctic, where they became the Athabasca. Later, some of them split off and moved south to become the modern-day Navajo and Apache. Then, goes this hypothesis, another migration about ten thousand to eleven thousand years ago brought maritime Aleut-Eskimo groups to Alaska, the ancestors of later Aleut and Eskimo. The Na-Dene/Aleut-Eskimo theory is highly controversial, for the issues are complex and data are in short supply. Did, for example, Aleut and Eskimo evolve separately from Na-Dene speakers, or were the latter a hybrid of

Paleoindian and Aleut and Eskimo? How long ago did Arctic maritime culture, the kind of adaptation associated with both Aleut and Eskimo, evolve? Were the Anangula people of Umnak Island ancestral Aleut, or did Aleut culture develop as a result of a blend between ancient Anangula traditions and cultural influences from later Eskimo cultures on the mainland? At present, all these questions remain unresolved.

By 2000 B.C. the Arctic Small Tool tradition appeared along the Alaska peninsula and along Bering Strait coasts. Arctic Small Tool people are thought to have crossed from Siberia, supplanting Paleo-Arctic groups, bringing the bow and arrow with them. This weapon was highly effective against caribou and waterfowl and spread rapidly through the Arctic and sub-Arctic and eventually throughout the Americas. At about the same time as these people appeared by the Bering Strait, they also moved along the shores of the Arctic Ocean into the Canadian Archipelago and along the Greenland coasts. They hunted musk ox and caribou, as well as fish and sea mammals in spring and summer, storing large caches of food for the winter, when trips to the outside were kept to a minimum due to subzero temperatures. Some Arctic Small Tool people moved nearly 750 miles (1,200 kilometers) further north than their distant relatives by the Bering Strait. Between 900 and 600 B.C. some of these Pre-Dorset groups lived on the islands of northern Hudson Bay, along the shores of Baffin Island, and in parts of Labrador. They exploited resident caribou herds, musk ox, and at least five seal species, as well as walrus, seal, and migrating waterfowl. These Pre-Dorset hunters were expert stalkers who used but the simplest of weapons in the chase. But over the centuries, they developed an increasingly sophisticated harpoon technology used to spear Arctic char and seal at winter breathing holes.

The Pre-Dorset people ventured a considerable distance inland, following caribou herds into areas around Hudson Bay that had lain under the vast Laurentide ice sheet. Once the ice started retreating, the thaw progressed rapidly, exposing the Great Lakes by 9000 B.C. and the last of the Labrador mountains by 3800 B.C. As the newly deglaciated land emerged from its mantle, tundra vegetation and animals migrated into the landscape and taiga (sub-Arctic forest) replaced

open country. Tiny hunter-gatherer populations followed game into the exposed lands, surmounting natural obstacles like ice-dammed lakes and flooded lowlands. One migration came from west of Hudson Bay, a later one from among peoples living around the Great Lakes, who spread along the Saint Lawrence Valley into the Quebec-Labrador peninsula.

Some time before 4000 B.C., several widespread "Archaic" traditions developed across the sub-Arctic. They include the Northern Archaic, centered on Alaska and the Yukon, and the Shield Archaic of the Hudson Bay and Barren Lands region. There was considerable cultural uniformity over a vast area, reflected in simple tool kits that varied little from one area to the next. For example, the Shield Archaic people of the Central Keewatin region camped along lakes and rivers, in a land of plentiful lichens, marshes, and shallow lakes, ambushing migrating caribou at key crossing points. These adaptations changed little over many centuries, so much so that Canadian archaeologists believe that the central and eastern Algonquian peoples of historic times are the direct descendants of Shield Archaic groups of 5000 B.C. or even earlier.

Further to the east, the Maritime Archaic represents a series of groups who flourished along the northern Maine and Labrador coasts, perhaps as early as 7000 B.C. These people exploited seacoasts in summer, fishing and hunting sea mammals, and hunted elk, moose, and other game in the interior the rest of the year. The Maritime Archaic reached its apogee during a period of unusually warm conditions after 4000 B.C., then waned when Pre-Dorset and later Arctic groups moved south in the first millennium B.C.

The Archaic cultures of the sub-Arctic slowly evolved into the Native American groups that occupied the region at European contact. They include the Beothuck of Newfoundland, the Cree and Ojibwa of the Hudson Bay lowlands, the Chipewyan west of the bay, and other Athapaskan-speaking groups to the northwest.

The Arctic Small Tool tradition gradually disappeared along the Bering Strait around 1500 B.C., to be replaced by a new maritime tradition that linked the entire strait region. Sea mammals and fish assumed ever greater importance in local life, as people on either side of the strait settled in larger, more permanent villages, culling the rich bounty of the ocean with an ever more elaborate hunting technology that now included composite harpoons, small kayaks, and large skin boats (*umiaks*). Whale hunting from such craft now assumed great importance in Arctic life, as expert teams of hunters pursued whales along narrow ice leads and in open water in spring and fall. Whaleboat captains became wealthy, influential leaders in their communities, often competing with their opposite numbers in nearby villages. Eventually, their increasingly elaborate culture developed into the Thule cultural tradition that developed around the Bering Strait by A.D. 900. Thule communities throughout the Bering Strait and along the Alaskan Peninsula and Siberian coast were in regular contact over enormous distances. And, after A.D. 1000, they spread rapidly eastward into the Canadian Arctic.

As these developments took hold in the west, the Dorset tradition emerged out of the Pre-Dorset culture in the east in about 500 B.C. The Dorset people were Arctic hunters without dog sleds or bows and arrows, who hunted game at close quarters with throwing spears and the simplest of weapons. Dorset people were, above all, sealers, who hunted all manner of sea mammals and many fish from shore. They lacked the elaborate boat technologies of the Bering Strait region. Dorset communities flourished over an enormous area of the eastern Arctic, marked by a remarkable art tradition—carvings in ivory, bone, soapstone, and other materials that depict animals and humans, often in minute detail. By A.D. 500 many communities may have participated in a vast cultural network in which shamans played a leading role in explaining and manipulating the forces of nature and the spiritual world. Five hundred years later, the Dorset tradition vanished in the face of Thule newcomers from the west.

Sometime around the beginning of the second millennium A.D., Thule people, perhaps speaking an archaic form of Inupiat language, began migrating to the east. By the thirteenth century, they had settled throughout the coasts of the Canadian Arctic and in Greenland. The Thule were far more efficient hunters than their predecessors, armed with elaborate weapons, skin boats and kayaks, and dog sleds. They were experts at hunting baleen whales, moving east during three centuries of warmer conditions between A.D. 900 and 1200 when retreating pack ice brought whale migration routes through the Canadian Archipelago. During the twelfth and thirteenth centuries, many Thule groups lived in large winter settlements, dwelling in stone, sod, and whalebone houses buried partially in the permafrost. Each community kept in touch with others, resulting in a standardization of culture over large areas as both exotic artifacts and ideas flowed along long-distance trade routes. The Thule were the Inuit peoples who came in contact with Norsemen from Greenland after A.D. 1000, trading furs, walrus ivory, and gyrfalcons for iron, copper, and other goods. In some areas, some descendants of Thule groups perpetuated various kinds of prehistoric hunter-gatherer ways of life into the twentieth century.

Complex Hunter-Gatherer Societies on the Pacific Coast (After 4000 B.C.)

The west coast of North America offers great environmental diversity, with rugged, forested coasts in southeast Alaska and the Pacific Northwest giving way to the highly varied coastal landscapes of California, with a generally Mediterranean climate. These shores supported some of the most elaborate hunter-gatherer societies of the prehistoric world.

Most human settlement along the Northwest Coast was concentrated on river banks or on the islands and shores of the coast. Here, an abundance of fish and sea mammals allowed relatively sedentary settlement. The earliest documented human settlement dates to about 8000 B.C., but many earlier sites lie below modern sea levels. Even as early as 1500 B.C., coastal communities were trading obsidian and other commodities with one another. By this time, too, fish and sea mammals were assuming ever greater importance in local life, and the woodworking skills for which Northwest peoples are famous were already in evidence. The widely dispersed populations of earlier times now moved into closer juxtaposition, as larger, more permanent settlements became the rule.

By 400 B.C. coastal populations were rising sharply. It was at this time that both bottom fishing for halibut and spring and fall salmon runs assumed great importance in Northwest life. So did the formal ownership of fishing and hunting territories, territories that were now managed by kin leaders with exceptional leadership powers. The power and authority of these individuals depended on their ability to attract followers and to retain their loyalty through the control, acquisition, and distribution of food and imported luxuries. The rich ceremonial life of the Northwest Coast people revolved around the need to manage predictable but ever fluctuating food supplies. The celebrated *potlatch,* a ceremonial feast where lavish gifts were exchanged, was, in the final analysis, a way of coping with fluctuations in the food supply and of ensuring the loyalty of one's followers.

The cultural roots of the Haida, Tlingit, Tsimshian, Kwakiutl, and other Northwest groups that existed at the time of settlement by Europeans go back many centuries. Along the north coast, increasing cultural elaboration appeared as early as 1000 B.C. There was intense warfare between some neighboring groups, as people competed for rich maritime resources, status, and wealth. Some early Tlingit sites in southeast Akaska were built on cliffs and other defensive locations, as were prehistoric Kwakiutl settlements in northern coastal British Columbia. Population densities fluctuated considerably over the centuries, perhaps reaching their height between A.D. 750 and 1400, but the causes of these changes and shifts in prehistoric settlement patterns are unclear. Large Haida villages on the Queen Charlotte Islands were similarly abandoned around A.D. 1450.

Between 400 B.C. and A.D. 400 the Marpole culture flourished over southern Vancouver Island, the Gulf and San Juan islands, and in the lower Fraser River valley. These were people who placed great emphasis on wealth and status, but the degree of social complexity fluctuated over time, in part because of changes in the distribution of critical food resources like salmon. The Marpole culture gave way to the historic Coast Salish culture by at least A.D. 1200, but details of the cultural transition are uncertain.

The Nootka of western Vancouver Island and the Makah of the Olympic Peninsula were famous, at the time of European contact, for their whale-hunting prowess. It is not known when whale hunting first began on the Northwest Coast, but it is of some antiquity. The famous Ozette site on Washington's Olympic Peninsula was partly buried by a catastrophic mudslide in about A.D. 1750. The waterlogged deposits have yielded richly decorated wooden boxes, clubs, whale harpoons, bows, and a magnificent cedarwood whale fin adorned with a mythical thunderbird outlined in sea otter teeth. Ozette lies at the back of a protected beach and was probably the most important sea mammal hunting site for hundreds of miles along the coast. The richness of its material culture testifies to the great elaboration of Northwest culture just before European contact and provides evidence for a flourishing Makah whale-hunting culture before A.D. 1200.

As late as the eighteenth century, some three hundred thousand Indians lived farther south, in what is now California, with densities as high as 10.5 people per square mile in resource-rich areas like the Santa Barbara Channel region of southern California. Local populations first reached significant levels about 6000 B.C., with a relatively rapid rise in coastal densities after 3500 B.C. This was the time when fishing and sea mammal hunting assumed much greater importance, as did the harvesting of acorns inland each fall. In the centuries that followed, the Channel people developed contacts with groups living up and down the coast, on the offshore islands, and far inland. They traded seashells, soapstone, beads, and other exotic goods as far east as the Southwest. Long-distance trade provided a way of compensating for food shortages and of acquiring essential nonlocal raw materials.

The Chumash peoples who inhabited the region at European contact were skilled navigators and expert fisherfolk, capable of paddling their planked canoes over long distances of open water. They lived in large villages of dome-shaped grass dwellings, some of them permanent settlements holding as many as one thousand people. The Chumash lived under hereditary chiefs, war leaders, and patrons of ceremonial feasts. They achieved a level of social complexity that represents about the limit of such complexity without adopting agriculture. Like other complex hunter-gatherer societies in the Midwest, the Northwest, and far southwest Florida, they were able to achieve this elaboration because

BERING LAND BRIDGE, ICE AGE

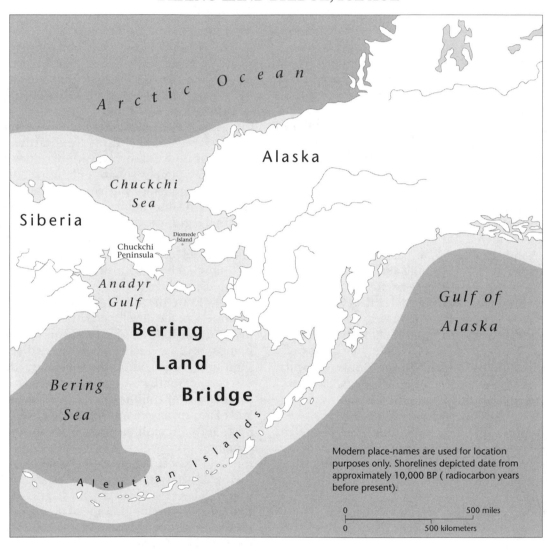

Arctic Ocean

Alaska

Chuckchi Sea

Siberia

Diomede Island

Chuckchi Peninsula

Anadyr Gulf

Bering Land Bridge

Gulf of Alaska

Bering Sea

Aleutian Islands

Modern place-names are used for location purposes only. Shorelines depicted date from approximately 10,000 BP (radiocarbon years before present).

0	500 miles
0	500 kilometers

SOME PRECONTACT ARCHAEOLOGICAL SITES

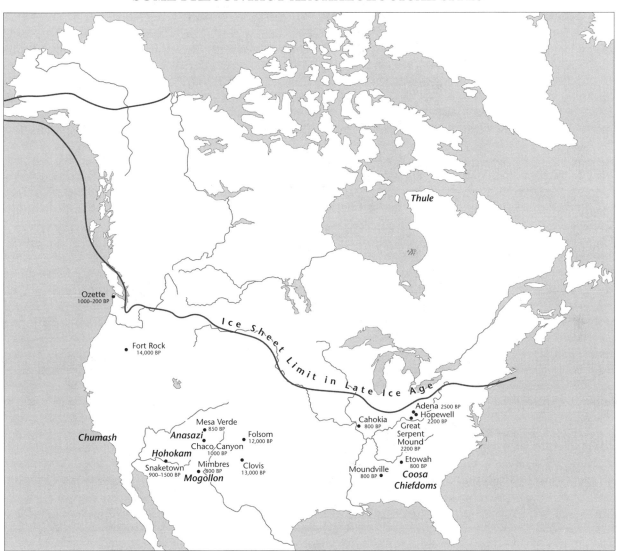

The sites depicted on this map are based on the author's discussion in the text. BP stands for radiocarbon years before present.

25

NORTHEAST CULTURE AREA

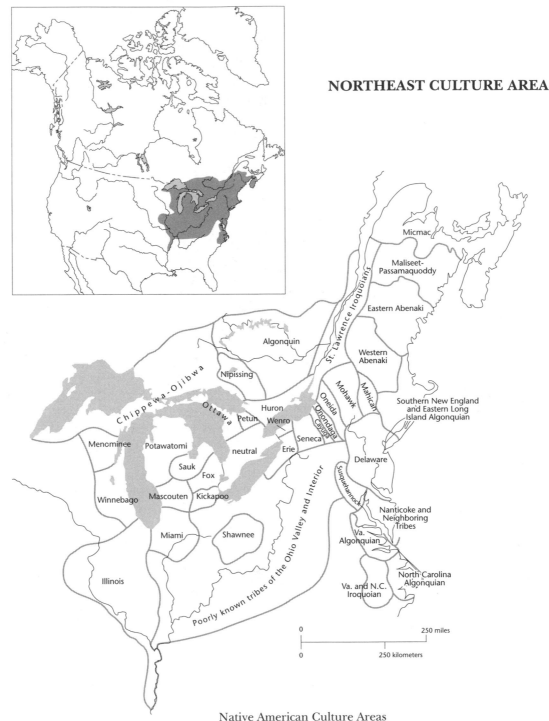

Native American Culture Areas

The maps in this series depict tribal territories at the earliest times for which evidence is available. Locations changed during the colonial period, especially in regions such as the Northeast and Southeast where Europeans displaced Native Americans. Post-colonial locations were often radically different. The maps are diagrammatic in that sharp boundaries are drawn, no territory is unassigned, and joint use or disputed areas are not identified. Maps are drawn from information supplied by William C. Sturtevant, and they are especially based on maps in the *Handbook of North American Indians*.

26

SOUTHEAST CULTURE AREA

Tutelo and Neighbors

Catawba and Neighbors

Yuchi

Cherokee

Chickasaw

Chakchiuma

Muskogee

Cusabo

Caddo

Tunica

Ofo

Alabama

Hitchiti

Yamasee

Choctaw

Tohome

Natchez

Houma

Biloxi

Chatot

Mobile

Apalachee

Atakapa

Chitimacha

Timucua

Tocobaga

Ais

Mocoço

Guacata
Jeaga

Calusa

Tekesta

Keys

0   250 miles

0   250 kilometers

27

PLAINS CULTURE AREA

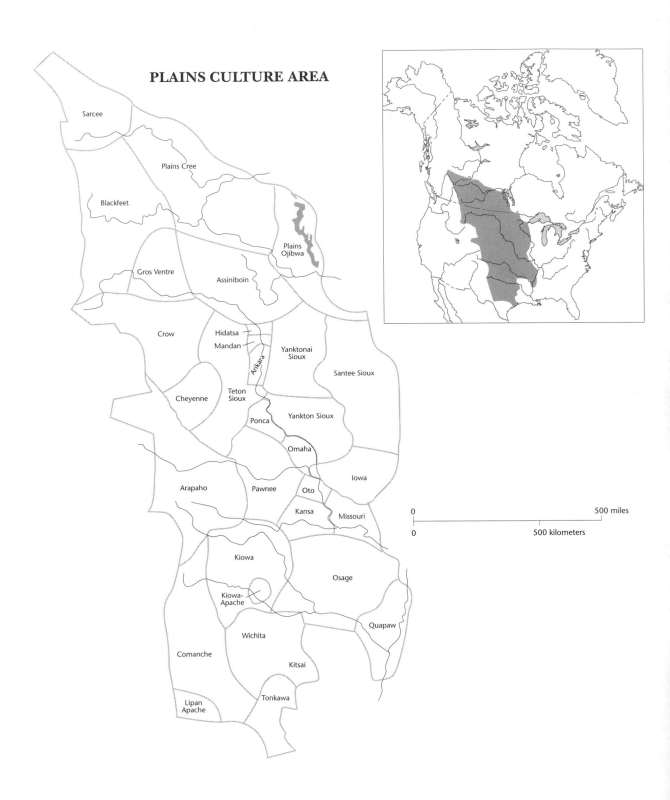

Sarcee

Plains Cree

Blackfeet

Plains Ojibwa

Gros Ventre

Assiniboin

Crow

Hidatsa

Mandan

Arikara

Yanktonai Sioux

Santee Sioux

Cheyenne

Teton Sioux

Yankton Sioux

Ponca

Omaha

Iowa

Arapaho

Pawnee

Oto

Kansa

Missouri

Kiowa

Osage

Kiowa-Apache

Quapaw

Wichita

Comanche

Kitsai

Lipan Apache

Tonkawa

0   500 miles

0   500 kilometers

SOUTHWEST CULTURE AREA

GREAT BASIN CULTURE AREA

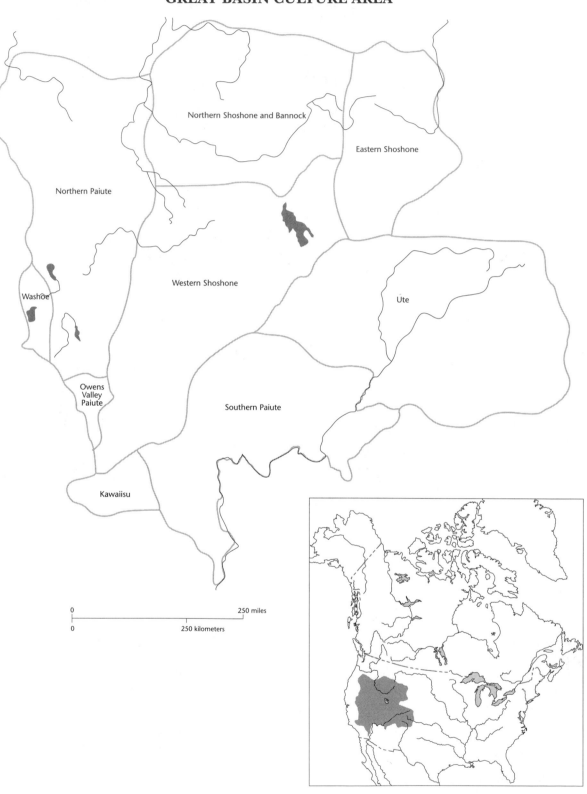

Northern Shoshone and Bannock

Eastern Shoshone

Northern Paiute

Western Shoshone

Washoe

Ute

Owens Valley Paiute

Southern Paiute

Kawaiisu

0   250 miles

0   250 kilometers

CALIFORNIA CULTURE AREA

Tolowa
Shasta
Yurok
Karok
Chilula
Whilkut
Hupa
Chimariko
Wiyot
Nongatl
Wintu
Mattole
Lassik
Sinkyone
Wailaki
Cahto
Yuki
Northern Pomo
Central Pomo
Southern Pomo
Kashaya
Coast Miwok
Achumawi
Atsugewi
Yana
Maidu
Nomlaki
Konkow
Northeastern Pomo
Eastern Pomo
Southeastern Pomo
Lake Miwok
Wappo
Patwin
Nisenan
Miwok
Costanoan
Northern Valley Yokuts
Esselen
Salinan
Monache
Foothill Yokuts
Tubatulabal
Southern Valley Yokuts
Northern Chumash
Central Chumash
Kitanemuk
Tataviam
Serrano
Island Chumash
Gabrielino
Cahuilla
Luiseño
Cupeño
Gabrielino
Diegueño

0   100 miles
0   100 kilometers

NORTHWEST CULTURE AREA

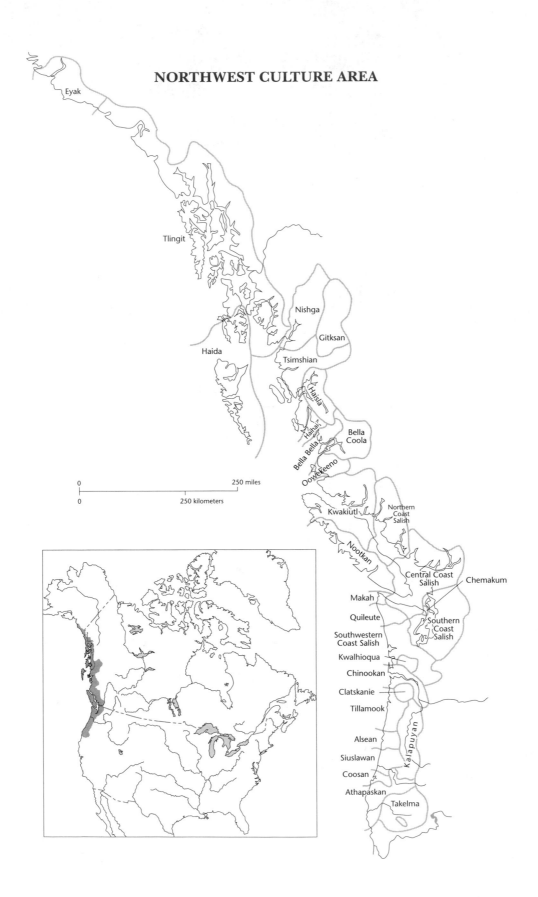

Eyak

Tlingit

Nishga

Gitksan

Haida

Tsimshian

Haisla

Hahai

Bella Bella

Bella Coola

Oowekeeno

Kwakiutl

Northern Coast Salish

Nootkan

Central Coast Salish

Chemakum

Makah

Southern Coast Salish

Quileute

Southwestern Coast Salish

Kwalhioqua

Chinookan

Clatskanie

Tillamook

Kalapuyan

Alsean

Siuslawan

Coosan

Athapaskan

Takelma

0   250 miles

0   250 kilometers

PLATEAU CULTURE AREA

Shuswap

Lillooet

Thompson

Nicola

Okanagan

Lake

Kutenai

Sanpoil

Columbia Salish

Kalispel

Spokane

Yakima

Klikitat

Coeur d'Alene

Wishram

Palus

Flathead

Umatilla

Walla Walla

Tenino

Cayuse

Nez Perce

Molala

Klamath

Modoc

0   100 miles

0   100 kilometers

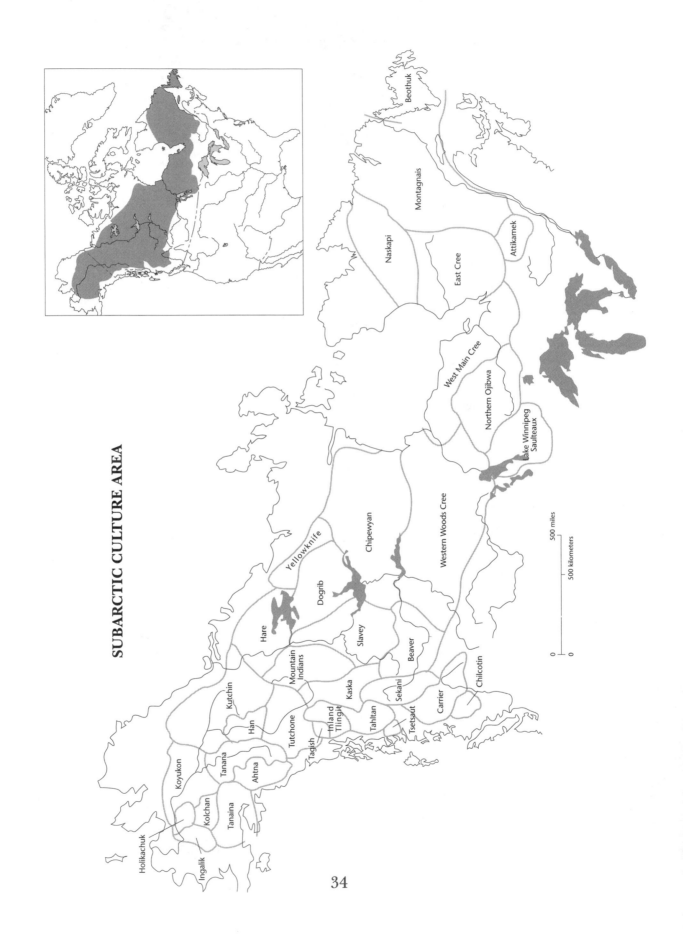

SUBARCTIC CULTURE AREA

Beothuk

Montagnais

Naskapi

East Cree

Attikamek

West Main Cree

Northern Ojibwa

Lake Winnipeg
Saulteaux

Yellowknife

Chipewyan

Dogrib

Hare

Slavey

Western Woods Cree

Mountain
Indians

Beaver

Kutchin

Kaska

Sekani

Carrier

Chilcotin

Han

Inland
Tlingit

Tahltan

Tsetsaut

Tutchone

Tagish

Koyukon

Tanana

Ahtna

Kolchan

Tanaina

Holikachuk

Ingalik

500 miles

500 kilometers

34

ARCTIC CULTURE AREA

East Greenland Eskimo

West Greenland Eskimo

Polar Eskimo

Baffinland Inuit

Igulik

Inuit of Quebec

Sallirmiut

Labrador Coast Inuit

Caribou Inuit

Netsilik

Copper Inuit

Mackenzie Delta Inuit

North Alaska Coast Inuit

Interior North Alaska Inuit

Kotzebue Sound Inuit

Bering Strait Inuit

Saint Lawrence Island Eskimo

Nunivak Eskimo

Mainland Southwest Alaska Eskimo

Pacific Eskimo

Aleut

500 miles

500 kilometers

0

0

35

of unusually favorable environmental circumstances. In other parts of North America, this emerging cultural and social complexity often foreshadowed more sedentary ways of life based on maize agriculture. However, along parts of the west coast the sheer bounty and diversity of the natural resource base made this subsistence strategy unnecessary.

Peoples of the River Bottoms (4000 to 1000 B.C.)

Many areas where more complex hunter-gatherer societies flourished lay by seacoasts, lakes, and rivers, especially after the Atlantic and the Pacific reached modern levels in about 4000 B.C. But the same high sea levels flooded large river valleys like the Mississippi, turning fast-moving streams and estuaries into slow, sluggish waterways meandering over swampy plains. Lush midwestern and southeastern river valleys and lake shores now offered great bounties of wild plant foods, deer, fish, and fowl. The inhabitants of these favored areas lived in large base camps for many months of the year, subsisting off rich fall nut harvests and other wild plant foods. In time, local population densities rose to the point that there was no room for expansion into virgin territory. Inevitably, territorial boundaries were drawn, and permanent settlements became more commonplace.

The famous Koster site in the Illinois River valley documents these long-term changes in great detail. Koster lies at the base of some 150-foot-high (450 meter) bluffs overlooking the river, a place close to ancient Clovis hunting grounds, for Clovis projectile points have been found close by. People started visiting this favored location about 7500 B.C. These seasonal settlements prospered, and the visitors stayed in larger numbers. By 5500 B.C. a one-and-three-quarter acre (about 1 hectare) village flourished near the bluffs. The inhabitants lived in substantial rectangular huts. By this time, the Illinois River flowed through a swampy floodplain with many shallow backwater lakes. Here the Koster people preyed on migrating ducks each fall. They speared and netted bullfish and other sluggish shallow water species year round. In late summer and early fall, they collected tens of thousands of hickory nuts and acorns, as well as harvesting starchy grasses. By 4000 B.C. the

Koster folk had developed an extremely effective hunting and gathering economy. Population densities were now such that there were occasional food shortages, and the hunter-gatherers augmented their supplies of wild grasses by cultivating such species as maygrass and sumpweed.

By this time, hunter-gatherer societies throughout the eastern woodlands lived in much more restricted territories, cherishing tenuous social and economic links that connected individual to individual, kin to kin, through valleys and entire drainages, over dozens, even thousands, of miles. These links were closely associated with long-distance exchange networks that carried Lake Superior native copper, hematite, Atlantic and Gulf Coast seashells, and fine-grained rocks from village to village. The farther some of these exotic materials were carried, the greater prestige they acquired. This may have led to a degree of social differentiation, to rankings between older and younger members of society, or perhaps to the emergence of one kin group as the "ranking" one. Judging from burial customs, these social rankings were commemorated in increasingly elaborate funerary rituals. Society was still basically egalitarian, but a few individuals achieved social prominence because of their outstanding qualities as traders and diplomats.

More intensive exploitation of food resources, even some cultivation of native plants, enhanced intervillage contacts and long-distance trade. The result was more permanent settlement, and greater ceremonialism.

ALGONQUIANS IN THE NORTHEAST (3000 B.C. to Modern Times)

Seventeenth-century sailors' accounts of the coastal peoples of the Northeast are a palimpsest of tantalizing and confusing impressions. These Algonquian folk were isolated from their western and northern neighbors by a block of Indians who spoke a variety of Iroquoian and other languages. The origins of the Algonquian is a mystery, but some form of their language goes back deep into prehistory, to a time between 4000 and 3000 B.C. when prehistoric cultures in the eastern woodlands shared many cultural and linguistic traits.

Most groups lived alongside rivers, seashores, or lakes. These permanent sources of water not only provided game, fish, mollusks, and plant foods but served as vital communication arteries between widely scattered bands. The higher ground between the river valleys served as boundary land, sometimes remote, sometimes traversed by narrow trails. They were buffers between different population concentrations. Historian Dean Snow has calculated that no more than 25,000 people lived in New England before 8000 B.C. and only between 158,000 and 191,000 in A.D. 1600. It was only in the last six centuries that the ancient barriers between different isolated populations began to break down. By this time, the introduction of new storage technologies and of maize agriculture had allowed high population densities in many parts of the eastern seaboard.

After 1650 B.C. the Algonquian-speaking populations of the Atlantic coast enjoyed a diverse and carefully scheduled annual routine that had them moving down to seashores and estuaries from spring to early fall, living off aquatic resources and plant foods, as well as game. As winter set in, they dispersed upstream into the interior, where they pursued forest game. This pattern persisted into historic times.

By 700 B.C. some of these hunter-gatherer groups were anchored to large base camps, some of them semipermanent settlements close to places where goosefoot and other native plants could be cultivated. Many of these communities received Adena and Hopewell cult objects from the interior. They buried their dead in closely packed cemeteries, depositing their prized possessions with them. Over the next seventeen centuries, a great variety of agricultural societies developed out of indigenous roots, with maize cultivation assuming increasing importance late in the first millennium A.D. Some of the coastal populations lived in substantial, semisubterranean dwellings, oval houses with sleeping benches around the walls and conical, tepee-like roofs.

In the Hudson Valley, Algonquian longhouses were up to one hundred feet (30 meters) long and twenty-five feet (8 meters) across, made of peeled hickory pole frames. Thick layers of bark covered these stout frameworks, creating warm and watertight dwellings that held as many

as eighteen families, or between 100 and 150 people. Like other Algonquian groups, these Native Americans enjoyed an elaborate ceremonial life, much of which revolved around powerful spirits associated with game, crops, and weather. All coastal Algonquian people, whether in the Northeast or in coastal North Carolina, where Elizabethan artist Thomas Harriot described their villages, enjoyed a rich and diverse culture with cultural, linguistic, and spiritual roots deep in prehistory.

IROQUOIANS
(Before 2000 B.C. to Modern Times)

The powerful Iroquoian confederacies dominated a large region from the Saint Lawrence Valley to New York at European contact. Fierce warriors, shrewd traders, and very sophisticated negotiators, the Iroquois were to play a dominant role in the Northeast to the very end of the colonial period and beyond.

The origins of the Iroquois go back before 2000 B.C. but are still little understood. Between A.D. 1000 and 1600, during the same favorable climatic conditions that brought the Thule to the Canadian Arctic and the Norse to Labrador, the Iroquois flourished in the upper Saint Lawrence River valley, where they cultivated maize at the extreme northern limit of its range. At first the new crop was a supplement to hunting and foraging, and the people lived in small settlements. By A.D. 1300 some Iroquois communities were much larger, the inhabitants dwelling in longhouses built close to one another inside stout wooden palisades. A century later, some of the largest Iroquois settlements numbered more than fifteen hundred people, placing great strain on society. Such large villages consumed great amounts of firewood and construction lumber, as well as agricultural land, so settlements were shifted more frequently as resources ran out.

This coming together in large settlements, perhaps for mutual protection, resulted in major social changes. Crowded together in congested villages, hitherto dispersed clans lived in an environment where quarreling and factionalism could rage out of control. It was then that the Iroquois developed formal village councils made up of representatives from each clan. These were often hereditary offices, and there may have been separate chiefs for peace and war. Warfare assumed great importance during the fourteenth century, perhaps as a result of cooler climatic conditions and greater competition for prime farming land and other strategic resources. War may also have been the way in which men proved themselves and achieved power and prestige, sacrificing their prisoners to the sun, the symbol of fertility and life.

Sometime before the end of the sixteenth century, neighboring Iroquois tribes in present-day Ontario and New York came together in loosely knit, larger associations—confederacies aimed at reducing blood feuding and warfare between close neighbors. The confederacy council of headmen from member tribes gathered regularly to adjudicate disputes and for ceremonial feasts. One such confederacy was the famous League of the Iroquois, or Iroquois confederacy, made up of the Five Nations: Seneca, Cayuga, Onondaga, Oneida, and Mohawk. This confederacy was an effective way of resolving disputes while allowing individual cultural identity in societies that placed a high premium on individual dignity, self-reliance, and social relationships. As later events were to show, these warlike and astute people were more than a match for the European fur traders and missionaries who settled among them.

The Huron, the northernmost of the Iroquoian-speaking peoples, farmers and traders who occupied the region between Lake Ontario and Lake Huron, were at first a match as well. They were robust, tall people, who lived in large, fortified settlements, mostly at the southeastern corner of Georgian Bay. Huron longhouses were generally about one hundred feet (30 meters) long and more than twenty feet (6 meters) wide. They housed several families, each with its own compartments. The Huron lived near the northern limits of maize cultivation but were able to grow sufficient surplus grain to be able to trade it for fish and furs from hunter-gatherer groups to the north. This gave them a unique place in the regional economy, for they provided vital commodities to people living many miles away and augmented their own economy at the same time. The Huron regarded trade as a reciprocal act, deeply embedded in their complex network of social relations. So they cultivated good relations with friendly neighbors, forming a confederacy of communities that protected their trade from outsiders. They were the conduits for fur trading over an enormous area and were well aware of the presence of Europeans long before they actually encountered any.

Excavations at the Draper site near Toronto show how the expanding European trade affected Huron life. The first Draper village was founded in about A.D. 1500, just as Europeans were penetrating the Saint Lawrence. During the next thirty-five to fifty years, the settlement expanded from a small village of about 550 people into a sizable town with more than 2,000 inhabitants. The Draper people added more longhouses as neighboring villages abandoned their old sites and joined the growing town. Part of this growth is attributable to endemic warfare, for hundreds of burned and broken human bones come from the excavations. At the same time, radical expansion of the fur trade had a profound effect on Huron life. Initially, the Huron treated the French as new, albeit powerful, trading partners. They thought it entirely logical to develop the same kind of trading alliance with the newcomers as they had enjoyed with their northern neighbors for centuries. At first their culture was enriched, but the inexorable effects of smallpox and other exotic diseases and an increasing dependence on European trade goods and French military protection made the Huron vulnerable to their Iroquois enemies. By 1650 this once-powerful group was decimated and dispersed in all directions.

SOUTHWESTERN PUEBLO SOCIETIES
(1500 B.C. to Modern Times)

When Columbus landed in the Indies, maize was the staff of life for American Indians living throughout the New World. Grown in association with beans and many minor crops, corn was a staple not only for small village communities but for great cities and civilizations, like those of the Aztecs and Incas. Corn had been domesticated in highland Central America by at least 5000 B.C. and was dominant in Mexican village farming economies by 3000 B.C. Maize first spread into what is now the southwestern United States much later, perhaps as early as 1500 B.C.

People had been growing maize and beans for centuries in northern Mexico before agriculture took hold farther north. In 1500 B.C. the sparse population of the Southwest lived by hunting and foraging, just as it had done for thousands of years. Southwesterners may have adopted corn as a supplement to familiar wild plant foods that were in short supply. Within a few centuries, maize, and later bean, cultivation became the basis of southwestern life.

By A.D. 200 corn sustained hundreds of small village communities, usually a few oval or circular houses dug partly into the ground to improve insulation. Eventually, the inhabitants needed more storage space, so they moved above ground and built combination dwellings and storage areas as multiroom adobe houses. In time, they constructed series of rooms abutting one another, forming pueblos. The compact, thick-walled construction of a pueblo was thermally very efficient in a climate with hot summers and cold winters.

Mogollon and Hohokam
(250 B.C. to A.D. 1500)

Two other southwestern cultural traditions flourished during the past two thousand years—Mogollon and Hohokam. The Mogollon people were highland folk who lived in the arid and sometimes mountainous country that is now eastern Arizona and southwestern New Mexico. Like their Anasazi neighbors, they dwelt in pueblos, but these were much smaller than those of Chaco Canyon or Mesa Verde. Mogollon women were accomplished potters, especially in the Mimbres Valley of New Mexico, where families buried their dead with elaborately painted clay bowls. These black-and-white and polychrome vessels depict humans engaged in different activities, insects and animals (such as the bighorn sheep), mythical beings, and legendary ancestors.

The Hohokam ("the vanished ones") of the southern deserts lived for the most part in small villages and are best known from a large settlement named Snaketown (after the Pima Indian name Skoaquik, "Place of Snakes") on the banks of the Gila River. In its heyday at the time the Anasazi prospered at Chaco, Snaketown was an untidy scatter of pit houses and aboveground pole and brush buildings. These houses lay outside a central plaza, itself surrounded by low

mounds up to fifty feet (15 meters) across and three feet (1 meter) high, capped with thick clay that turned them into platforms for large houses or shrines. Nearby lay two ball courts, about 130 feet by 100 feet (10 meters by 30 meters), excavated about 20 inches (50 centimeters) into the desert floor.

All these architectural features vaguely recall Mexican cities, with their much larger mounds, pyramids, and ball courts. This has prompted archaeologist Emil Haury and others to speculate that the Hohokam migrated into the Southwest from Mexico, bringing new ideas from the civilized lands to the south. Almost certainly, however, the architecture and the ideas behind them were indigenous. There are no signs of human sacrifice or of Mexican religious beliefs at Snaketown. The ball courts are smaller than those from Maya Copán, Chichén Itzá, and other Mesoamerican centers. The idea of a ball game may have come from Mexico, but the ceremonies associated with it were different. The courts may even have been arenas used for dances and other public ceremonies, even for markets. Nor is there any evidence that the Hohokam traded much farther afield than the Gulf of Mexico or the Pacific Coast.

Some pervasive cultural ideas may have drifted north from Mexico, but what is striking about the Anasazi, Mogollon, and Hohokam is that they were indigenous cultures, forged from local roots, adapted perfectly to an environment of climatic extremes and uncertain rainfall. This was not a region in which elaborate civilizations or great cities flourished, for the forces of nature required constant adjustments to cycles of drought and abundant rainfall.

The Anasazi
(A.D. 100 to 1300)

The Anasazi people, "the ancient ones," inhabited the high desert of the Four Corners region, the Colorado Plateau, and the San Juan Basin. This is a majestic land of flat-topped mesas, deep canyons, and wide open sagebrush plains. One major center of Anasazi culture lay in Chaco Canyon, New Mexico, a wide canyon with precipitous cliffs and rocky outcrops. Here, as early as A.D. 700 to 900, Anasazi communities built small pueblos, laid out in small arcs so that each room was equidistant from a central pit house that in later centuries became the kiva, the sacred place that was the center of pueblo ceremonial life and a symbolic representation of the primordial underworld from which humans emerged to people the earth.

The Chacoans tried to minimize the hazards of famine from crop failure by building three large, semicircular pueblos at the junctions of major drainages, where they could maximize floodwaters. The greatest of these towns was Pueblo Bonito, where more than eight hundred rooms surround an enormous semicircular plaza with many large kivas. Eventually, at least eleven major Chacoan "Great Houses" rose in the canyon during the eleventh century A.D., each a massive undertaking.

Even in good rain years, the soils of the canyon itself could support at most two thousand people. Yet the experts calculate that there were enough rooms in the canyon during the late eleventh century to support sixty-five hundred inhabitants. The only possible explanation for this imbalance is that large numbers of visitors converged on Chaco at certain times of the year, presumably for important ceremonies. In the 1980s aerial photographs and satellite images revealed a web of more than four hundred miles (640 kilometers) of unpaved prehistoric roadways that link Chaco to more than thirty outlying settlements. The Chacoans had no wheeled carts or draft animals, yet they constructed shallow tracks up to forty feet (12 meters) wide across the desert, some of them running straight for forty to sixty miles (64 to 96 kilometers). Stone-cut stairways link the road system to the bottom of the canyon. Most likely, the road network served many practical and symbolic functions and was used to transport logs and other heavy loads, to facilitate large-scale trading of turquoise from nearby Santa Fe, and to bring thousands of people to the canyon for major festivals.

What archaeologists call the Chaco Phenomenon encompassed an area of more than twenty-five thousand square miles (65,000 square kilometers) of the San Juan Basin and beyond. By A.D. 1115 at least seventy-five communities, dispersed over much of the Four Corners region, were linked through the social, economic, and ritual networks centered on Chaco Canyon. What is remarkable is that Chaco flourished in

such an unpredictable environment. Despite many good rain years, there must have been periodic food shortages and serious deforestation of the surrounding landscape. For example, at least twenty thousand pine beams went into the major pueblos, to say nothing of the firewood needed for cooking, heating, and making clay pots. Perhaps Chaco communities overextended themselves in the bounty of wet years and rendered themselves unusually vulnerable to the inevitable drought cycle that began about 1100. Stretched to its limits, the Chaco system collapsed, and the people moved to more productive areas, away from densely populated pueblos and into independent, widely dispersed hamlets.

Another major center of Anasazi population developed in the Mesa Verde and Montezuma Valley area of southern Colorado. The Anasazi first appeared at Mesa Verde around A.D. 600, living in small villages of pit houses with up to 150 residents. By the ninth century, these small hamlets coalesced into much larger villages, clustered around large pit houses that now became kivas. Two centuries later, as many as thirty thousand people lived in the nearby Montezuma Valley, some of them in pueblos of more than one thousand inhabitants. Nearby Mesa Verde's deep canyons were home to about twenty-five hundred people, who lived in compact, sometimes almost inaccessible, pueblos, in caves, and under convenient overhangs in the precipitous canyon walls.

The Mesa Verde farmers were experts at storing and conserving water. They built a system of collection ditches that diverted rainwater into an artificial reservoir capable of holding up to half a million gallons (two million liters). These water systems were so successful that relatively dense populations settled in some Mesa Verde canyons. Between 1150 and 1250, for example, some six hundred to eight hundred people lived in Cliff and Fewkes canyons, where they built 33 pueblos and a total of 550 rooms and 60 kivas huddled under high cliffs. The famous Cliff Palace was by far the largest pueblo, with 220 rooms and 23 kivas.

The canyon pueblos flourished for several generations. Then, in about 1300, the Anasazi abandoned Mesa Verde forever, and population densities fell sharply. Experts believe that the abandonment was the result of the same dry cycle that disrupted life in Chaco Canyon to the south. As they did at Chaco, the Anasazi moved away from Mesa Verde and scattered into smaller villages. Entire communities did not move away; rather individuals and families visited close kin, then shifted residence permanently, as the people of Chaco and Mesa Verde followed myriad paths into new, more dispersed settlements. In time, the Anasazi were absorbed into later southwestern society, leaving only their artifacts and great pueblos behind them.

THE MOUND BUILDERS
(1000 B.C. to European Contact)

Far to the east, along the Mississippi Valley and in the southern and southeastern United States, an entirely different and long-lived cultural tradition developed somewhat earlier than the Pueblo society of the Southwest and persisted until European contact and beyond. The woodland peoples of this region are famous for their elaborate burial rituals and for their magnificent earthworks—so extensive that some nineteenth-century archaeologists wondered if they had been built by long-forgotten civilizations from the Old World.

Adena and Hopewell
(1000 B.C. to A.D. 400)

About 2000 B.C., eastern North America was inhabited by hunter-gatherers who exploited every kind of temperate environment. The densest populations flourished in fertile river valley bottoms and near lakes, where plant foods and aquatic resources were abundant. Some of these communities buried their dead in low, natural ridges, overlooking strategic locations. To build even a modest burial mound required hundreds of basketfuls of earth, piled up not by individual families but by entire kin groups. From the very beginning, burial mounds from the western Appalachians to the Mississippi Valley and north into Michigan and Wisconsin were associated with different kin groups. They were places with strong links with mythical and human ancestors and were used for generations by people from nearby communities.

Between three hundred and five hundred "Adena" mounds have been found in the Ohio Valley alone. At first each kin group started with a small earthwork that covered the grave of a single individual. As more and more burials were added to the tumulus, it grew in size. Eventually, about the time of Christ, simple graves gave way to large burial chambers that contained one or two people, lying on or under circular houses. Perhaps the dead were exposed in these charnel houses before their bones were actually buried in the mound. The most important individuals were buried with masks, finely carved pipes, marine shells, copper ornaments, even sheets of mica. These artifacts proclaim them to have been shamans and kin leaders, the people who organized major rituals, controlled long-distance trade in exotic materials and ritual objects, and gathered people together to work on communal projects.

By 200 B.C. such leaders enjoyed great prestige and were buried with magnificent artifacts gathered from literally every corner of North America. Artisans used native copper and silver from the Lake Superior region and mica, quartz crystal, and chlorite from the southern Appalachians. These precious metals and finished cult objects such as mica ornaments, pipes, and masks passed along narrow trails that connected village after village all the way from the Great Lakes to Florida. Well-trodden paths brought chiefs calling on their neighbors with formal gifts of Gulf of Mexico seashells or sharp obsidian knives made of rock from as far away as the Yellowstone area of the Rocky Mountains. Months later, the recipient would reciprocate with a formal gift of his own to mark a kin relationship that sometimes endured for many generations.

These "Hopewell" people, named after an Ohio town, sometimes created entire mortuary landscapes of mounds and enclosures. They linked burial mounds with networks of circles, squares, and octagons joined by avenues. The average Hopewell burial mound is about thirty feet (10 meters) high and one hundred feet (30 meters) across, with a volume of about five hundred thousand cubic feet. Each would have taken about two hundred thousand hours of earthmoving with simple stone tools and baskets. Perhaps the most spectacular of all is the Great Serpent Mound in Ohio, modeled in the form of a snake

41

coiled along a low ridge with a burial mound between its jaws. Judging from the motifs that decorate ceremonial artifacts such as copper sheets and pipe bowls, there were close links between Hopewell kin groups, game animals, and birds of prey, perhaps the mythical ancestors of clans and lineages.

For all their elaborate burial customs, the Hopewell people lived in small villages and subsisted almost entirely on hunting and gathering. Their chiefs were important ritual leaders and expert traders whose authority came not from despotic rule but from their perceived spiritual and leadership powers.

It was not until the late first millennium A.D. that maize and beans spread into the Midwest and the Southeast across the plains from the Southwest. Not that the cultivation of plants was unknown, for eastern woodlands peoples had been growing native plants like goosefoot for thousands of years as a supplement to wild seeds. Maize and beans may have started off as supplements, but, grown on fertile river valley soils, they soon became the staples of the eastern North American diet.

The first millennium was a period of rapidly growing populations and, for all the bounty of wild foods, a time of periodic shortages. Hopewell people and their contemporaries lived in permanent settlements, anchored to their territories and stands of native plants. Households and communities coped with food shortages by helping one another, by sharing grain supplies and bartering food. Such cooperation required leadership and entrepreneurial skills and led to the appearance of important chiefs, men and women with highly developed ritual powers to intercede with the spiritual world for good crops and rain and an expertise in trading and diplomacy. Eastern North Americans now became even more dependent upon one another, living in a state of constant political flux. There was a multiplicity of chiefdoms large and small, as chiefs died and new people came into prominence.

Mississippian
(A.D. 900 to 1400 and Beyond)

By A.D. 1000 maize and bean agriculture had transformed the environment of eastern North America. Maize is a demanding crop that requires constant tending and widespread forest clearance to produce significant yields. Combined with game, migratory birds, fish, freshwater mollusks, and wild plants, it produced an abundance of food in fertile areas like the so-called American Bottom near Saint Louis. It was here, and in other exceptionally favored areas, that the most powerful "Mississippian" chiefdoms arose. At Cahokia (now in East Saint Louis, Illinois) the chief and his fellow nobles presided over the destinies of thousands of commoners, did not engage in agriculture, and lived off food given to them as tribute. They fulfilled their obligations to the community by carrying out sacrifices and other important ritual tasks only they could perform. In a sense, there was a form of ritual contract between the chief and his people, in which they supported him in exchange for spiritual guidance and ritual intercession.

The Mississippian was a patchwork of chiefdoms large and small, with the greatest of them based on great centers like Cahokia; Moundville, Alabama; and Etowah, Georgia. Nine centuries ago, Cahokia sprawled across more than five square miles (15 square kilometers) of the American Bottom, a tangle of thatched houses, earthen mounds, and small plazas dominated by an elaborate ceremonial precinct. The four terraces of one-hundred-foot-high (30 meter) Monk's Mound towered over a nearby plaza, platform mounds, charnel houses, and burial places. The central area was surrounded by a wooden palisade that effectively isolated the two-hundred-acre (80 hectare) precinct from the outside world. Cahokia's chiefs lived in the heart of the sprawling complex, but their identities are a mystery. One such important man was buried on a platform of twenty thousand shell beads, accompanied by three high-status men and women buried nearby. About eight hundred arrowheads and copper and mica sheets lay near these additional skeletons, perhaps those of close relatives sacrificed at the funeral. Nearby were the remains of four decapitated men with their hands lopped off. More than fifty young women lay in a pit close by, perhaps strangled to death as part of the mortuary rites.

The Mississippian culture in all its local manifestations extended from the Mississippi Valley far into Alabama, Georgia, and Florida and flourished from about A.D. 900 to European contact. To the south and east of Cahokia, another large and prosperous kingdom flourished at Moundville on the banks of the Black Warrior River near Tuscaloosa, Alabama. In A.D. 1000 Moundville was a small village. Between 1250 and 1400 it reached the height of its importance, having grown into a complex of mounds, plazas, and settlements covering more than 370 acres (148 hectares). The rectangular central plaza covered seventy-nine acres (32 hectares) and was surrounded by twenty large platform mounds where temples and the houses of the elite once stood. Moundville supported about three thousand people inside the bastioned palisade that protected the center on three sides. The fourth side opened to the river.

Judging from the Moundville burials, about 5 percent of the population constituted a hereditary, privileged group that was interred with great ceremony. It was they who lived in large residences atop platform mounds. When they died, their bones were stored in special charnel houses before eventual interment, resplendent with badges of privilege and rank and with fine shell ornaments, stone axes, masks, and other prestigious ritual objects. The rest of the population, the commoners, were buried outside the palisade in their own villages.

By the standards of great Mexican cities like Teotihuacan or Aztec Tenochtitlán, Cahokia, and Moundville were little more than medium-sized towns. The areas from which they collected tribute were small by Mayan standards; indeed, studies of the imports imply that tribute gathering was effective for only about nine miles (14 kilometers). Without large, organized caravans of porters or pack animals and a standing army for enforcing annual assessments, the chiefs of Moundville could compel tribute payment only from nearby communities. They did, however, draw some allegiance from local centers and villages up to forty-five miles (70 kilometers) away.

Trading and tribute were vital to the chiefs' survival. The magnificent artifacts of copper, mica, and shell they obtained from afar became potent symbols of their legitimacy, of their special relationship to the spiritual world. In the same vein, they used their control over the local

people to erect great earthworks clustered around imposing plazas as symbols of their world and of their authority. These were the settings in which they performed the important planting and harvest rituals that ensured the fertility of the land.

Mississippian religious beliefs are reflected in ceremonial artifacts found all over the Southeast, from the Atlantic and Gulf coasts as far inland as the lower Ohio Valley. They include finely made pottery, shell ornaments, and small copper ornaments depicting long-nosed gods that recall a mythological character who survived among such groups as the Winnebago of the upper Midwest. Engraved shell cups show male figures in ceremonial dress. Other pendants and ornaments depict woodpeckers, rattlesnakes, and birds of prey. Weeping eyes, circles, and crosses adorn sheet copper. There are axes with blade and shaft fashioned from a single piece of stone. Many motifs show a preoccupation with wind, fire, sun, and human sacrifice, merging one into the other in an ancient continuum that related to the rising sun, the morning star, and dawn or to stars in the northern night sky. These and other persistent motifs like weeping eyes, bilobed arrows, striped poles, and raccoon hindquarters have their origins in much earlier artistic traditions associated with Adena and Hopewell religious cults.

A basic cosmology was common to all Mississippian and southeastern communities, an ideology involving the sun and ancestor worship that supported the authority of chiefly nobles. Mississippian chiefs may have ruled as semidivine representatives of the sun. The great mounds they and their predecessors built may have served in part as burial places. They also functioned as the locations for shrines where chiefs would rekindle new fire during a ritual renewal of the world, perhaps during the ceremony honoring growing green corn in summer. Here, as in Mexico, it was believed that the sun died each evening and was reborn each morning—the heavenly body giving lifeblood to the world.

The Mississippian culture reached its apogee just as Columbus landed in the Indies, but Cahokia was long deserted when conquistador Hernando de Soto brought death and exotic disease to its ancient homeland in 1540. The powerful Coosa and Cherokee chiefdoms he encountered on his explorations soon dissolved in the face of smallpox and inexorable European expansion.

TRANSFORMATION OF INDIGENOUS CULTURES

For more than twelve thousand years, Native Americans adapted to North America's many environments with success. Their success is even more remarkable when one reflects that it all began when a virgin continent was settled by a few bands of Stone Age hunter-gatherers. Then came the disruptive, traumatic forces of Western civilization, which decimated and transformed the indigenous cultures of North America beyond recognition.

BIBLIOGRAPHY

General Works

Fagan, Brian M. *Ancient North America: The Archaeology of a Continent.* London, 1990. A broad-ranging synthesis of North American archaeology for general readers. Includes theories, culture history, and the archaeology of the centuries after 1492.

Sturtevant, W., ed. *Handbook of North American Indians.* Washington D.C., 1978–. A multivolume reference work that aims to document Native American societies north of the Rio Grande. About half the volumes have appeared in recent years, as follows:
Damas, David, ed. *Arctic.* Vol. 5, 1984.
D'Azevado, Warren, ed., *Great Basin.* Vol. 11, 1986.
Harris, Cole, and Geoffrey J. Matthews, editor and cartographer. *Historical Atlas of Canada.* Vol. 1. Toronto, Ontario, 1987. See especially plates 1–9.
Heizer, Robert F., ed. *California.* Vol. 8, 1978.
Helm, June, ed. *Subarctic.* Vol. 6, 1981.
Ortiz, A. A., ed. *Southwest.* Vol. 9, 1979; *Southwest.* Vol. 10, 1983.
Suttles, Wayne, ed. *Northwest Coast.* Vol. 7, 1990.
Trigger, Bruce, ed. *Northeast.* Vol. 15, 1978.
The references that follow either cover areas not yet published in the *Handbook* or offer more up-to-date material or interpretations.

The Earliest Settlers

Dillehay, Tom, and David Meltzer, eds. *The First Americans.* Clearwater, Fla., 1991. A set of essays that deals with major issues surrounding first settlement. For the more specialized reader.

Martin, Paul, and Richard Klein, eds. *A Pleistocene Revolution.* Tucson, Ariz., 1984.

Meltzer, David. "The Antiquity of Man and the Development of American Archaeology." *Advances in Archaeological Method and Theory* 6(1983):1–51. A detailed account of the nineteenth- and early-twentieth-century controversies surrounding the antiquity of humankind in the Americas.

Hunter-Gatherers

Dumond, Don. *Eskimos and Aleuts.* 2nd ed. London, 1987. A summary of Arctic archaeology which focuses on the origins of Eskimo and Aleut. Lavishly illustrated.

Frison, George C. *Prehistoric Hunters of the High Plains.* Orlando, Fla., 1978. A classic account of the evolution of big-game hunting in North America. Especially good on bison kills.

Maxwell, Moreau S. *Prehistory of the Eastern Arctic.* Orlando, Fla., 1985. A definitive account of the subject, which is especially strong on Thule settlement.

Moratto, Michael. *California Archaeology.* Orlando, Fla., 1985. Rich information on hunter-gatherers along the west coast and in the desert interior.

Price, T. Douglas, and James A. Brown, eds. *Prehistoric Hunter-Gatherers: The Emergence of Cultural Complexity.* Orlando, Fla., 1985. The essays in this volume range worldwide but are of critical importance for understanding hunter-gather societies in North America.

Snow, Dean. *Archaeology of New England.* Orlando, Fla., 1980. A broad but somewhat outdated summary of hunter-gatherer and other prehistory in the Northeast.

Southwestern Archaeology

Cordell, Linda. *The Prehistory of the Southwest.* Orlando, Fla., 1984. A definitive synthesis of the Southwest for the student and general reader. Strong theoretical orientation.

Ford, Richard, ed. *Early Food Production in North America.* Ann Arbor, Mich., 1984. Important articles on the origins of maize and other Native American crops.

Haury, Emil. *Hohokam, Desert Farmers and Craftsmen: Excavations at Snaketown.* Tucson, Ariz., 1976.

Le Blanc, Steven. *The Mimbres People.* London, 1983. A beautifully illustrated description of Mimbres life and culture, with special reference to their painted pottery.

The Mound Builders

Galloway, Patricia, ed. *The Southeastern Ceremonial Complex*. Lincoln, Nebr., 1989. The contributors discuss various aspects of the Southern Cult associated with the Mississippian Culture.

Silverberg, Robert. *The Mound Builders of Ancient America*. Greenwich, Conn., 1968. A wonderfully entertaining account of the Mound Builder controversies for the general reader.

Smith, Bruce D. "The Archaeology of the Southeastern United States: From Dalton to De Soto, 10,500–500 B.C." *Advances in World Archaeology* 5(1986):1–92. An important synthesis that deals with basic ecological and cultural developments.

Willey, Gordon R., and Jeremy A. Sabloff. *A History of American Archaeology*. 2nd ed. San Francisco, 1980. A general history that amplifies Silverberg.

Algonquian

Rountree, Helen. *The Powhatan Indians of Virginia*. Norman, Okla., 1989. A multidisciplinary study of the Indians encountered by English settlers in Virginia.

Wright, J. V. *Six Chapters of Canada's Prehistory*. Ottawa, 1976. A useful summary of Canadian archaeology.

Iroquois

Heidenreich, Conrad. *Huronia: A History and Geography of the Huron Indians*. Toronto, Ontario, 1971. A definitive account of the subject.

Trigger, Bruce G. *The Children of Aataentsic: A History of the Huron People to 1660*. 2 vols. Montreal, 1976. Trigger's brilliant monograph is the source on much of Iroquois archaeology and history. A superb melding of archaeological and historical evidence.

Brian Fagan

SEE ALSO **Indian Governance; Literature; Medical Practice; The Natural Environment; Recreations; The Slave Trade;** and **Technology;** and various essays in THE ARTS; ECONOMIC LIFE; RACIAL INTERACTION; RELIGION; THE SOCIAL FABRIC; and WAR AND DIPLOMACY.

II

OLD WORLD EXPANSION

THE AGE OF RECONNAISSANCE
EMERGENCE OF EMPIRES

THE AGE OF RECONNAISSANCE

THE AGE OF EUROPEAN reconnaissance of the ocean lying to the west, north, and south of the Continent began in the fourteenth century, but it had a background of travel and writing about travel in many parts of the Old World. The Crusades for centuries had also brought Europeans into touch with peoples of non-European culture and religion. Inside Europe, too, which may be defined roughly as the area within which Christianity was dominant, there was an Islamic element in the Iberian Peninsula, where from the eighth century a slow reconquest by Christians had taken place; by 1400 it was nearly complete. The exclusiveness of Christianity, especially of Catholic Christianity, meant that non-Christians were regarded as somewhat less than human, though there was a stubborn, if often overlaid, tradition that it was the function of Christian Europe to evangelize the non-Christian world. This was especially strong as the Christian Spanish kingdoms pushed their way gradually southward against Muslim Spain.

Fourteenth-century expansion was made possible by a number of factors: the example of the Mediterranean city-states Venice and Genoa, the former mainly with its galleys and the latter with its carracks, developed a seafaring trade involving the carrying of goods (Oriental and Mediterranean) to northern Europe, the Netherlands (the great mart at Bruges, in particular) and England and the bringing back of wool, cloth, tin, and such products. These city-states

established trading houses in many western and northern cities and provided capital to improve their struggling commerce of these cities and states to their own financial advantage.

The Italians also brought with them means which made outward expansion possible. They improved ships so that they—at least the carracks—could survive wilder seas; they brought the compass so that ships could have some effective control of the directions in which they were sailing; and their sailing routes, worked into charts from coastal observations, extended their range from the Mediterranean to the oceanic shores of Iberia, France, and the British Isles. Their maps soon included islands sighted, or believed to have been sighted, in the ocean, together with others culled from myths. Before 1400 such sea charts (portolans), despite their many imperfections, were laying the foundations for Atlantic navigation.

From the late thirteenth century, the Genoese were planning to circumnavigate Africa and reach Asia, though an expedition to do so in 1291 never returned. As the fourteenth century progressed, ships from Spain (not yet united) and Portugal made their way down the Moroccan coast and rediscovered the Canaries (known in classical times). Vessels returning from reconnoitering these islands had to sail out into the Atlantic, and this was probably one cause for the proliferation of islands on the increasing number of charts. Sightings of Madeira and many of the

MAJOR EUROPEAN VOYAGES OF DISCOVERY

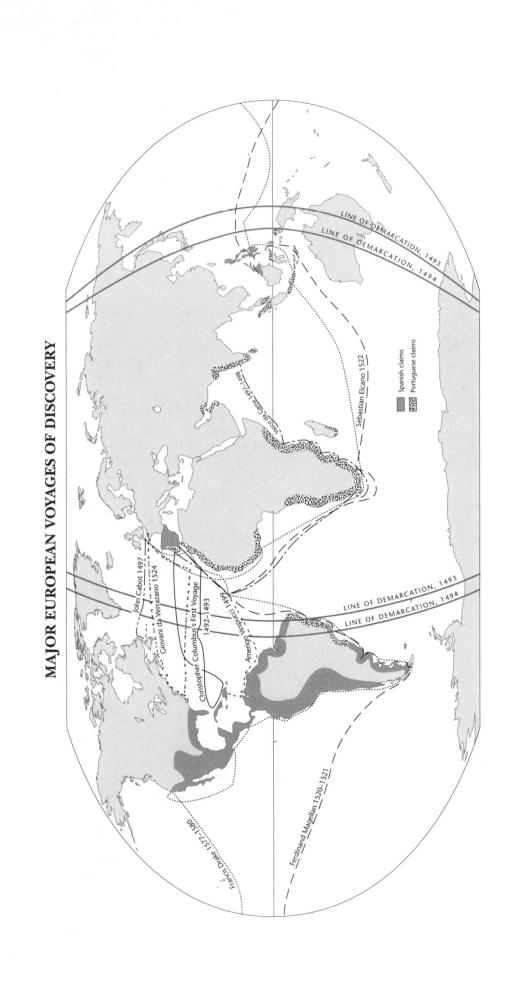

LINE OF DEMARCATION, 1493

LINE OF DEMARCATION, 1494

LINE OF DEMARCATION, 1493

LINE OF DEMARCATION, 1494

John Cabot 1497

Giovani da Verrazano 1524

Christopher Columbus's First Voyage 1492–1493

Amerigo Vespucci 1499

Vasco de Gama 1497–1498

Sebastian Elcano 1522

Francis Drake 1577–1580

Ferdinand Magellan 1520–1521

Spanish claims

Portuguese claims

Azores are thought to have been the result of such voyages, though their location on the charts was imprecise.

THE VIKINGS AND THE ENGLISH

Expeditions to North America came well toward the end of several successive phases of expansion in the ocean, except in regard to one precursor. This was the series of Norse voyages to "Vinland" in the opening years of the eleventh century. Norwegians had colonized Iceland in the later ninth century, and moved on in their seagoing craft to Greenland toward the end of the tenth, Eric the Red establishing two settlements on the then relatively fertile southwest of the great island of Greenland. Bjarni Herjolfsson, sailing to join Eric about 986, sighted land well to the west of Greenland and interested Eric sufficiently to inspire him to send his son Leif Eriksson to examine these shores about 1000. He did so, and named Baffin Island "Helluland" (Flat Stone Land), Labrador (and perhaps some land to the south) "Markland" (Treeland), and Newfoundland (or farther south) "Vinland."

These tales, and the subsequent story of the Vinland voyages, depend on sagas written some hundreds of years after the events, the facts in them open to many and often contradictory interpretations. The sagas say Leif returned in the spring, bearing vines with grapes on them from Vinland, though this seems unlikely for the season. Excavations made in 1961 indicate that the site at L'Anse aux Meadows, on the Newfoundland side of the Strait of Belle Isle, is the most likely location for the settlement where Leif wintered (Leifsbudir), though it was a long way from any grape-bearing area.

Subsequent voyages over about twenty years by members of Leif's extended family appear to have been based here, though there are indications of short-term occupation of a site to the north and possibly of another voyage, perhaps simply one of exploration, to someplace to the south, where grapes may have been gathered. An attempted settlement by Thorfinn Karlsefni, who had married into Eric's family, is said to have remained at the site for three years with a company, including women, before being driven off by attacks from Native Americans. The settlement was finally abandoned about

1020 for lack of profitable returns, and Greenland's only contact with America was maintained by occasional forays to Labrador to bring back timber. The Greenland colony died out in the fifteenth century, and the "Vinland" voyages remained unknown to the participants in the main European reconnaissance.

By the end of the fourteenth century, the English were fishing off the Icelandic coast. They were followed early in the fifteenth century by English East Coast traders, who in turn were followed by Bristol merchantmen from 1424. The English thus had, when their western reconnaissance got under way in the late fifteenth century, much experience of the stormy North Atlantic.

THE PORTUGUESE IN THE FIFTEENTH CENTURY

Portuguese expansion down the coast of Africa was the most continuous and significant expression of fifteenth-century reconnaissance. As such, it cannot be detached from the expansion of the Portuguese westward in latitudes similar to those of Portugal itself. The Portuguese took Ceuta from Morocco in 1415, beginning the attack on this Muslim state (never successfully completed), and it may well have been ships returning from Morocco which finally located Madeira about 1419. Dom Henrique (called Prince Henry the Navigator by English speakers since the mid nineteenth century) had much to do, as head of the Military Order of Christ, with the colonization of Madeira in 1439.

Significantly, it was the Genoese who supplied the plants and the techniques of the sugar industry, and also the vines from the eastern Mediterranean that first made colonization feasible outside the European mainland. A similar pattern occurred in the Azores, as the Portuguese reached out one thousand miles into the ocean from Portugal itself. Wheat, wine, and wood were among the products developed there, but some of the settlers in the Azores had to be found in the Netherlands. Again, Genoese capital was influential in setting these European advances westward.

It was, however, the separate attempts by Portuguese and Castilians who set foot on the more easterly of the Canary Islands early in the fifteenth century that began the long struggle against the native inhabitants, the Guanches, who were hard to pin down and massacre or enslave. The Iberian powers competed for authority in the Canaries down to the 1470s. By this time Portugal had advanced into the more profitable parts of West Africa and was obtaining some gold, malagueta pepper, and more slaves, especially after it had turned the shoulder of Africa, Sierra Leone, in the 1470s. By that time, too, the Portuguese had found and were colonizing the Cape Verde Islands, where they attempted the first experiments in plantation agriculture, using slaves to work under Portuguese masters.

The Portuguese were active on the Guinea Coast before 1480, and in 1482 established the first fortress-cum-trading post when they reached the gold-purchasing area. São Jorge da Mina became a rich center for trade in gold and slaves, and helped to finance the rapid progress of Portugal southward, so that Bartolomeu Dias was able to sail round the southern tip of Africa in 1488 and return to report that the sea route to the East was now open. This, and the subsequent voyage of Vasco da Gama to India in 1497–1498 were the high points of European expansion in the fifteenth century and overshadowed the discoveries of Columbus, and those of his successors, down to the conquest of Mexico.

Concentration on Africa did not divert Portugal entirely from westward ventures beyond the Azores. Indeed, the appearance of two great islands, Antilia (the Island of the Seven Cities) and Satanazes, on a sea chart as early as 1424 led them thereafter to be represented west of the Azores as if they were discoveries. However, in 1458 the Portuguese obtained from Venice a world map by Fra Mauro that convinced them that Africa could be rounded. In 1474 a letter came to an influential Portuguese gentleman from a Florentine physician and scholar, Paolo dal Pozzi Toscanelli. Presented to the king, it explained and illustrated on a map how a manuscript of Marco Polo's travels had convinced him that it was only some five thousand nautical miles (not the ten thousand or more that mathematicians had long before calculated) between Portugal and Cathay, while from Antilia, Cipangu (Japan) was only two thousand nautical miles. This prompted a charter to Fernão Telles in 1474, instructing him to locate Antilia as a starting point for further discoveries; a grant to Fernão Dulmo in 1486 told him to do likewise.

No result from these or other expeditions has been found. The return of Dias, with his news of a southeastern passage to the Orient, put Portugal out of competition for western discoveries, though João Vas Corte Real, governor of southern Terceira, is credited with having made voyages from Terceira. It was his sons who, in 1500–1503, made the first significant Portuguese discoveries on the North American coast.

COLUMBUS

Christopher Columbus (Cristoforo Colombo), a member of a Genoese family involved in cloth making, had gone as supercargo on at least one Genoese voyage to the mastic-producing island of Chios and had gained some expertise in seamanship. In 1476 he decided to attempt to get to northern Europe, but the Genoese fleet was attacked by corsairs off southern Portugal and he was cast ashore near Lagos in the Algarve. He was picked up from there, or from Lisbon, by a subsequent Genoese fleet in 1477 and brought to England. He then made his way to Bristol and sailed on a merchant vessel to Iceland. He may, though the sources are poor, have transferred to a fishing dogger and rounded the western end of the island, rejoining the Bristol ship at the trading mart south of Iceland and returning by way of Galway to Portugal, where he made his base with his chart-making brother, Bartolomeo.

This northern voyage probably had a partly mercantile basis—searching out new markets—but it also showed that his ambitions as an explorer had been aroused. Subsequently, Columbus settled in Madeira for a time and sailed at least once to Mina (1482–1483), all the while perfecting his nautical skills and learning to read in Latin texts and on all available charts what he could about the possibilities of further exploration to the west. By 1484 he had probably worked out his grand design. By juggling figures, he had convinced himself that Toscanelli's computations for the voyage to Asia should be greatly modified, so that within two thousand nautical miles from Gomera in the Canaries he would reach Cipangu.

By this time the eastern Atlantic was a well-traversed zone. Columbus's grand design was rejected by John II in Portugal in 1485, and he then turned to Ferdinand and Isabella. They put his request for help under consideration but sent him no reply, so that after Dias's return to Lisbon, Columbus turned with his brother to planning an expedition to Cipangu in the latitude of the British Isles, using a chart showing the Island of the Seven Cities roughly where Newfoundland is and the "island" of Brasil halfway across the ocean. Henry VII of England would not accept their plan in 1489, nor would the regent of France, Anne de Beaujeu.

Columbus was formally rejected by Spain in 1490 but returned to plead his case. In the euphoria following the capture of Granada in January 1492, Isabella relented and agreed in principle to support him. Money to fit out a small expedition was raised in part from an Aragonese official body and in part privately, by a Genoese merchant. In April, Columbus was granted paper privileges, if he succeeded, but the money promised was sufficient to supply him with only one substantial vessel, the *Santa Maria*, and two smaller craft, the *Pinta* and *Niña*. He assembled them at Palos and brought them to Gomera in September. He aimed to sail west along the twenty-eighth parallel, which would have brought him to Florida and made him the principal discoverer of North America. Instead, he turned southwest and on 12 October reached the island he named San Salvador, which he thought lay near Japan.

Watlings Island was identified as Columbus's landing place by a sufficient number of writers to have its name changed to San Salvador, but this as his place of arrival has not been formally accepted by all scholars. The surviving evidence, a truncated version of his *Journal* (*Diario*), is inadequate to provide certainty. Columbus's subsequent journey by way of a series of small islands similarly lacks identification, but he certainly reached northeastern Cuba by 29 October. This he regarded as being part of Asia. He perceived that the landmass he called Hispaniola was an island; on its north coast, after the *Santa Maria* ran aground, he established some of his men in a settlement called Navidad, having seen some

evidence of alluvial gold and much of cotton-growing.

Columbus returned safely to Europe in the *Niña,* arriving at Lisbon on 4 March 1493 (John II received his report kindly though, we suspect, with some skepticism). He sailed on to Palos and then traveled to Barcelona, where he reported his discovery of Asian land to the Catholic monarchs on 12 April. This was followed by a papal bull assigning the new land to Spain. Columbus's identification of the land as Asian was accepted, and this time the monarchy supplied him generously. Many ruthless and violent young men were available now that the Moorish war was over, and they formed the backbone of the initial colonizing force. Departing on 25 September 1493, Columbus brought the fleet of seventeen vessels to Hispaniola on 27 November, but found Navidad deserted. A new settlement was begun at once at Isabela, and the would-be colonists spread out looking for gold, finding just enough to whet their appetites and to begin their savage oppression of the inhabitants.

In April 1494 Columbus sailed west to investigate Cuba. Moving down the channel between Hispaniola and Cuba, he conducted a careful search along the south coast of Cuba, happening upon Jamaica on the way. Fifty miles (80 kilometers) from the western end of Cuba he gave up because his ships were failing. He made his men swear Cuba was part of the Asian mainland, though he was not confident that this was so. Thereafter Columbus was involved in the settlement of Hispaniola with the assistance of his brothers Bartolomeo and Diego; none of the three proved to be an effective administrator, and they allowed the genocide of the inhabitants to proceed. He was, however, able to send some alluvial gold back to Spain; in 1496, somewhat disconcerted at failing to find the riches of Cathay, he returned home, discouraged.

In late 1497 or early 1498 Columbus received news that English explorer John Cabot had just found an extensive mainland he believed to be Cathay, only some eighteen hundred miles (almost 2,900 kilometers) from Ireland. He then determined to sail again, but farther south this time. His 1498 voyage, as originally planned, would have brought him to northeastern Brazil, but he had to sail somewhat to the north, which brought him to the Caribbean shore of South

America. Columbus found Trinidad and then, in the Gulf of Paria, a mainland he reckoned to be the Earthly Paradise lying off southeast Asia, but much larger than he expected. He sailed on to southern Hispaniola, where a new city, Santo Domingo, was being built, but encountered many problems there.

A royal commissioner, Bobadilla, arrived in 1499 and was so furious at the maladministration he found that he packed Columbus and his brothers back to Spain in chains. Isabella took pity on Columbus and did not have him punished, though his privileges were greatly reduced. He was allowed to go on an exploring mission in 1502 with four small ships, and directed his search farther north, in the latitude of Honduras. Rounding the bulge of Honduras, he sailed against the wind south to Veragua. Columbus described himself as "completely broken in spirit" at having failed to find the passage between the Golden Chersonense (the Malay Strait) and farther Asia, though he could not give up the idea that he was still somewhere in the Orient. The two ships he had left began to fall to pieces on the way, so Columbus grounded the leaking hulks on Jamaica and remained there for more than a year, until help came in 1504 and he was able to return to Hispaniola. From there he was sent back to Spain for the last time.

Columbus's last years were wrapped in mystical meanderings, and he died in 1506 without being disillusioned about the validity of his grand design. More practical and ruthless men were left to carry on his explorations. Vasco de Balboa sighted the Pacific Ocean in 1513 spurring Hernando Cortés to begin his conquest of the Aztec Empire in 1519, which altered the whole character of the Spanish conquest. Ironically, a year after Columbus's death Martin Waldseemüller "invented" two continents between Europe and Asia, calling the southern one America for Amerigo Vespucci; the name America was added to the northern landmass by 1520.

ENGLAND AND PORTUGAL IN NORTH AMERICA

North America remained outside the effective sphere of Spain for some time after Columbus. If the English reached Newfoundland in 1481 or shortly after 1490, they left no effective traces on the map. Cabot's discovery, however, publicized the cod fishery; subsequent English voyages led to the exploitation of the inshore fishery, the first catches being brought to Bristol in 1502 and 1504. The exploration of the coast between Labrador and New England between 1498 and 1505, of which we have little detail, failed for lack of profitable trade; and Sebastian Cabot's attempt to round the newly recognized continental North America in 1508–1509 ended English activity there, except for the fishery.

At roughly the same time, the Portuguese reached North America. Gaspar Corte Real's voyages of 1500 and 1501 sent back knowledge of parts of Labrador, Newfoundland, and the Maritime Provinces, and his brother Miguel consolidated this knowledge in 1502. Both explorers, however, perished on the voyages. The cod fishery, both of the Grand Banks and inshore, was set in motion soon after. Owing to ignorance of longitude estimation, Spain, whose ships began to go to Newfoundland in the 1520s, regarded the Portuguese discoveries as being on the eastern side of the demarcation line of the Treaty of Tordesillas (1494) and accorded the Portuguese some theoretical rights in this region. French ships joined the fishery in 1504, and it soon became the main field for European enterprise in eastern North America, growing throughout the century.

An attempted Portuguese colony on Cape Breton Island about 1520 did not take root. English reconnaissances under John Rut in 1527, and under Richard Hore in 1536, left little impact, Rut losing one ship in an attempt to reach a Northwest Passage. Before 1540 the northeast was not further encroached upon by Europeans, though later in that decade the Spanish Basques established an important whale fishery, based on the southern shores of Labrador, that proved extremely profitable.

EARLY SPANISH EXPLORATION

For a long time Spain regarded North America as primarily a land boundary to the west of her main shipping route to Europe. Juan Ponce de León in 1513 made an unsuccessful attempt to colonize Florida. By that time expeditions around the Gulf of Mexico had outlined the shores between Mexico and Florida. Pedro de Quejo, sent by Lucas Vásquez de Ayllón in 1525, brought back slaves from what was to be South Carolina. The following year Ayllón headed what was intended to be the nucleus of a series of Spanish settlements from the original landing place as far north as the thirty-seventh parallel. Ayllón brought his expedition to what is now Winyah Bay in South Carolina, then moved his colony south to what is now considered to be the Sapelo River in Georgia. Here was planted the first Spanish town in North America, San Miguel del Gualdape. But Ayllón's death and divisions among the settlers soon brought it to an end with the loss of many of the would-be colonists.

Also in the 1520s, a series of attempts to settle on the Gulf Coast were made, the most important being that of Pánfilo de Narváez in 1527. Starting from Tampa Bay, he moved northward to a location near the site of modern Tallahassee. His westward march from there led to a settlement near the head of the Apalachicola River and subsequently one nearer its mouth. The colony fell to pieces when it was not reinforced, and its primitive boats, built so the settlers could escape, were gradually scattered and lost. The fate of the expedition came to light only when Alvar Nuñez Cabeza de Vaca emerged in California in 1536, having made the first traverse of the continent. The great expedition of Hernando de Soto in 1539 was intended to lay the foundations of a Spanish empire in North America. Instead, it became a random search for gold, progressing from Florida to North Carolina and westward to Arkansas. Much initiative and skill brought its one specific discovery, the great Mississippi River, and revealed the vast size of the North American South. Soto died in 1542, and Luis de Moscoso brought the survivors back to Mexico in 1543.

In contrast with these failures, the explorations undertaken from Mexico to the Pacific coast and the southwestern interior were conducted with more skill and planning, if they did not produce much more ultimate success in finding rich mineral resources. The appearance of Cabeza de Vaca in western Mexico in 1536 helped to stimulate exploration to the north. His tales of wealth in the interior led to the reconnais-sance by Marcos de Niza in 1539, who returned with the confident report that the mythical Seven Cities of Cíbola had been located far to the northeast. This was the spur to organize a major military expedition under Francisco Vásquez de Coronado, which worked its way to the Pueblo country on the Rio Grande in 1540 but found the "cities," relatively advanced in their Native culture, with nothing except accommodations (unwillingly given) and corn for the Spanish, apart from semiprecious turquoise. Coronado sent out useful reconnaissances, one of which came upon the Grand Canyon, but found no mineral deposits of any value. Another myth was sold to the expedition of the wonders of Quivira, far to the northeast. Coronado's subsequent expedition across the Great Plains to the Arkansas River (in modern Kansas) produced nothing of any value to Spain. Coronado knew when he had reached the limits of his capacity to explore, however, and he brought his expedition back to Mexico in 1542.

Between them, Soto's and Coronado's expeditions had exposed the enormous extent of the interior and were of great geographical (but little other) value. The California Peninsula meanwhile had been defined by several expeditions, so that an exploration of the west coast could be undertaken. Juan Rodríguez Cabrilho in 1542 brought his ships as far north as (probably) Monterey Bay, and after Cabrilho's death in 1543, Bartolomé Ferrelo continued to about the forty-first parallel; thus some conception of the western limits of the continent could, for the first time, be worked out. These great expeditions gave evidence of the power of Spain to carry European expansion across North America, if not to find means of exploiting and colonizing it.

INFLUENCE OF MAGELLAN AND THE VERRAZZANOS

The return of Sebastian Elcano in the *Victoria* in 1522, with news of Ferdinand Magellan's death as well as precious information on the Pacific Ocean, altered European perceptions of the world. It gave Spain and Portugal the chance to define the westward extension of their alleged monopoly rights (which they did not find easy to do). The publication of Maximilianus Transylvanus's account of the voyage, published at Cologne in 1523 (followed sometime later by Antonio Pigafetta's in Paris) turned the attention of other European powers to the character and limits of the North American continent and, especially, to the chances of finding a shorter route than the Strait of Magellan through or round it to the Pacific.

Francis I was earliest in the field. Silk merchants in France found him willing to support the voyage of Giovanni da Verrazzano to define the coastline and, if possible, find a passage in temperate latitudes. In 1524 Verrazzano made an effective reconnaissance of the shores of North America from modern Georgia to Newfoundland; he alleged that after crossing the Carolina Outer Banks, ships would rapidly reach the Pacific. He was unable, however, to find a passage directly through the landmass, though his indication of Penobscot Bay as a possible channel became influential.

Spain had been preparing a comparable expedition earlier under the Portuguese Estevão Gomes, but it did not sail until 1525. The Spanish already knew enough of the southeastern coast for him to pass quickly to about the thirty-seventh parallel and concentrate on the part that was hitherto uncharted—the mouth of the Hudson River, southern New England, Cape Cod with its dangerous shoals, and the territory to the north—but he was still unable to find a passage through to the western ocean. Maps by Gerolamo Verrazzano were made and circulated in several countries, one of them reaching Henry VIII. He, in turn, contemplated a parallel exploration and sent John Rut in 1527 to reconnoiter as much of the coast as possible. Rut did his job so well that he ended up, after a long voyage south, in the Caribbean, where the Spanish made it clear to him that North America belonged to Spain. He returned to report, but left us no map nor detailed narrative of the whole voyage.

Gomes made excellent charts (for the time) of the New England and Maritime shores, but they remained unpublished. In abbreviated form they were incorporated into the Spanish master chart almost unheeded, and they appeared in the official charts of 1527 and 1536, though in too low a latitude and with the Rio de las Gamas (Penobscot River) as their most prominent fea-

ture. The failure to follow up such reconnaissances left the profile of eastern North America, in maps of the subsequent period, dependent on what was believed of either the French or the Spanish version, or some conflation of the two.

THE FRENCH IN CANADA

The first major initiative in penetrating the interior of more northerly North America came through the exposure of the entrance to the Gulf of Saint Lawrence by French cod fishermen, leading in 1534 to Francis I sending Jacques Cartier to investigate what lay beyond the Strait of Belle Isle. In 1534 Cartier did an excellent survey of the Gulf of Saint Lawrence and brought home clear evidence of a great river entry to the west. This, in turn, led Francis to send Cartier in 1535 to proceed farther, settle over the winter, and to continue his searches for a channel through the continent. On his 1535 voyage Cartier explored the Saint Lawrence River, establishing a base near the later site of Quebec, and continued his exploration as far as Montreal. He was stopped there by evidence of falls on the river (the Lachine Rapids). At his base he survived, just, the first Canadian winter experienced by Europeans, and brought the remnant of his men back to France in 1536.

This initiative was not pursued at once, but in 1541 Cartier was again entrusted to found a base for a genuine colony of settlement, preparatory to a major colonization experiment under Jean-Francais de La Rocque de Roberval in 1542. He built a settlement at Cap Rouge, a good position somewhat to the west of Quebec, and wintered there, but his men would not stay so he returned to France in 1542.

Roberval, arriving in 1542, eventually found the prepared site and developed it further. His men, women, and children survived the winter, though with difficulty. He saw little hope of maintaining a permanent settlement, but an expedition from Francy Roi (as he called the settlement) followed Cartier's route to Montreal with similar results. Native Americans indicated that there was a route through North America, though they knew only of the Great Lakes, but Roberval could go no farther and returned home. His report to Francis I (the *Première relation*) led to a lack of enthusiasm for further ventures that even the publication of the narrative of Cartier's second voyage in 1545 (the *Brief recit*) could not revive. A number of fine manuscript maps made for royal patrons were equally ineffective. For the next several decades, French activities in the area seem to have amounted to no more than a few ships' making infrequent visits to the Saint Lawrence to trade in furs. The practice was regularized in 1580 and became the basis for further French encroachment in North America.

THE FRENCH AND SPANISH IN FLORIDA

In the late 1550s the Spanish became alarmed at the activities of French privateers off the coast of Florida and sent expeditions from the Gulf of Mexico and from the Atlantic to establish a Spanish post in Florida; both failed. However, in 1562 French Huguenots, anxious both to carry on the war against Spain, which had officially ended in 1559, and to create a place of refuge for themselves if conditions in France became intolerable, established a post in South Carolina on Port Royal Sound. Jean Ribault, who had returned to France for support, found his plans impeded by civil war. In England he succeeded in raising a flurry of excitement about the prospects of intervention for the first time in American settlement, in alliance with the Huguenots, largely through his boosting of the potentially rich produce of the region. In 1563 the commander of the planned English rescue force, Thomas Stukely, got an expedition to sea, but it was a fraud: he intended it merely for piracy off the coast of western Europe. English fervor for an American enterprise vanished as soon as it had arisen.

Finally, in 1564, Ribault obtained support from Charles IX to send René Laudonnière to Florida with a military expedition to establish a bridgehead for a colony on the Saint Johns River in Florida. The expedition's mixed history over the next year or so included some useful exploration of the interior of the Florida peninsula and of the coast as far north as Cape Fear. The group deteriorated, however, as parties from it engaged in piratical raids on the Caribbean. It was visited in 1565 by an English expedition under John Hawkins, whose men were able to see a little of the country for the first time.

The long-delayed colonizing expedition, under Ribault, arrived in August 1565. In fact, the Spanish, under Pedro Menéndez de Avilés, were already prepared to drive the French out. From Saint Augustine, Menéndez sent a force overland to destroy the nucleus of the French colony at Charlesfort. Ribault, unwisely, had mobilized all his resources and gone south to meet Menéndez at sea but had almost his whole fleet wrecked by a hurricane before encountering the Spanish. Charlesfort fell with scarcely a struggle, except for a few men who fled in smaller vessels left in the river. All the rest of the men, and some of the women, were killed. Then Menéndez moved southward, where he encountered shipwrecked, unarmed men who offered successive parties ambiguous terms for surrender. Menéndez slaughtered them, including Ribault himself. This first major clash of European forces on North American soil left a bitter legacy of hate on the part of the French, who retaliated by fresh attacks in the Caribbean and by a revenge mission in 1568 that claimed to have killed comparable numbers of Spanish at San Mateo (the former Charlesfort).

Saint Augustine became the first permanent European settlement in North America, but Menéndez's other elaborate ventures and plans all failed. The Spanish were able to hold Santa Elena on Port Royal Sound until 1586, when they were reduced to their Saint Augustine base with a few outposts a little to the north. Several small-scale expeditions into the interior produced no permanent results.

THE ENGLISH

English concern with North America developed only in the mid 1570s. First, it was directed to finding the Northwest Passage. In 1576 Martin Frobisher explored what is now Frobisher Bay. Some samples of ore brought home were diagnosed as gold-bearing, and this transformed the venture into a gold-mining experiment. In 1577 several hundred tons of rock were brought from an island at the mouth of Frobisher Bay (which, it was discovered, terminated not too far inland). Back in England, they were subjected to an elaborate refining process. A further mining fleet was sent out before results—entirely negative—were obtained. The ore brought back in 1578 had to be dumped, and much money and effort were wasted, but Frobisher's ship had, on the way out, been carried into Hudson Strait, and this opened the way to further exploration.

The surveying expeditions carried out by John Davis in 1585–1587 laid the foundations for future expeditions. His small vessels were unable to penetrate the great summer outflow of water and ice from Hudson Strait, but he put the coasts of western Greenland and eastern Baffin Island firmly on the map, and gave his name to Davis Strait.

Concurrently, plans developed for colonizing eastern North America in order to provide England with markets for cloth and other goods from the many small industries now springing up in England. Such plans, formulated with little or no regard to the Native American population, also surmised that settlers might prove able to live more profitable lives there than in England. Sir Humphrey Gilbert, who had planned colonies in Ireland, proposed to hand out American land, sight unseen, to investors and settlers. This would have produced a feudal principality for him and his family. But his first expedition of 1578 never reached America, and when, finally, in 1583 he set out to reconnoiter the coast southward from Newfoundland, with modern New England as his objective, he got only to Newfoundland. In Saint John's Harbour, he annexed the island formally to the English Crown and while he was there collected dues from foreign and English fishing vessels. After losing his flagship on Sable Island, he was obliged to sail for England and was lost off the Azores, his venture crashing to an end with only one vessel returning.

Gilbert's plan was taken up in 1584 by his half brother, Walter Raleigh, whose reconnaissance expedition was aimed much farther south. It landed on the Carolina Outer Banks and was well received by the local people, who invited the English to settle on Roanoke Island, in Croatan Sound. They attempted to do this in 1585, Sir Richard Grenville bringing out about one hundred men to settle on the island. Ralph Lane,

the governor, was no explorer; but Thomas Harriot and John White, sent to map the region and record all they could of aboriginal life, and also to assess the prospects of agriculture and other activities, did a remarkable job, making the first surveyed map, which extended to Chesapeake Bay, and keeping a very extensive record of what they saw.

Though the colony was taken home by Francis Drake in June 1586 (when supplies did not arrive), and White and Harriot lost much of their material in the hasty evacuation of the island, they brought enough back to England to reveal a small part of North America, its people, and its products to a European audience. A tract by Harriot, published in England in 1588, and a selection of drawings by White, engraved by Theodor de Bry as the first part of his *America* in 1590, provided invaluable and accessible information on part of eastern North America. This was followed in 1591 by Jacques Le Moyne de Morgues's narrative and illustrations of the French colony in Florida of 1564–1565.

Through these publications, good impressions of southeastern North America became widely available in Europe. Raleigh was discouraged by the failure of the first colony to find viable means of trade or production—or, indeed, to be free from Native American attacks. But in 1587 he allowed White and slightly more than one hundred men, women, and children to try their fortune at the City of Ralegh, to be constructed on or near Chesapeake Bay. They were never found, even though White searched for them in 1590. They apparently continued to live with the local Native Americans on the area north of the Great Dismal Swamp until about 1606, when they and their hosts were wiped out by Powhatan, who was engaged in expanding his hegemony over southern Virginia.

The arrival of more serious and better-backed English settlers in the Chesapeake in 1607 altered the whole picture of English exploration and settlement in North America. The exploration of the James River to the fall line and beyond, and the survey of Chesapeake Bay and its river system as a whole, changed the character of English activity in North America. John Smith's map, published in 1612, brought a further important section of North America to European view, thus adding a reasonably reliable picture to that provided by White and Le Moyne.

SPAIN: THE LATE SIXTEENTH CENTURY

The revival of Spanish exploration in the Southwest and the West followed the gradual penetration of northern Mexico for minerals. The first small expedition, under Antonio de Espejo in 1582, largely covered ground traversed by Coronado but penetrated somewhat farther to the west; its tales of mineral prospects led to an attempted colony by Gaspar de Sosa in 1590, which was a fiasco. These attempts stimulated the mounting of an official mission to New Mexico under Juan de Oñate in 1598. He promised his associates wealth, but in the Pueblo area the most they found was a bare subsistence: the few exploring expeditions to the west and northwest finding no mineral sources, though they were in fact there. While Oñate was following the Quivira myth, which brought him over a great stretch of the Great Plains to the Canadian River, from which he turned back unsatisfied, most of his colonists deserted and returned to Mexico. Oñate was recalled from New Mexico and replaced in 1609—under pressure from the Franciscans—by an official expedition under Pedro de Peralta, which went on to found a colony that formed an unsupported northern arm of the Spanish western empire.

Meantime, the English had shown their ability to attack the Spanish Pacific Ocean monopoly. Francis Drake in 1578–1579, after plundering many ports in Mexico and farther south, disappeared into the northwest. Eventually the Spanish learned that he had attempted to reach the western end of the Northwest Passage but had turned back. With help from the Miwok Indians somewhere about the thirty-eighth parallel, he had claimed the area for England as New Albion. It began to appear on the maps as such in 1595. In retaliation Sebastian Rodriguez Cermeño was sent north in 1595 to explore the coast and did so effectively up to about the forty-first parallel. But on his return, one of the ships was wrecked in the harbor behind Point Reyes (which many have seen as Drake's landing place) and he returned to Mexico with difficulty.

In 1600–1601 Sebastiano Viscaíno, entrusted with a more substantial force, was able to make a more intensive study of the California coast. He penetrated north to about the forty-fourth parallel and, most important, he brought back the first detailed charts of the coast, which helped to round off Spanish knowledge of western North America. The charts were not published, however, as there was no encouragement for further Spanish exploration for a long time to come.

THE SEVENTEENTH CENTURY

In the east the French, under Henry III, began to plan permanent settlement: the Marquis de La Roche failed to honor his commitments to explore the Saint Lawrence for this purpose (1583), though Samuel de Champlain did so in 1603, following Cartier's old route to Montreal but returning with new data. However, the known cold of the Saint Lawrence in winter promoted an attempt to find a base for the fur trade farther south. The Sieur de Monts (Pierre du Gua), with Champlain's help, explored the area from the head of the Bay of Fundy to the islands south of Cape Cod in the years 1604–1607; Champlain charted the coast in detail. The expedition's first base, at Sainte Croix, was rendered uninhabitable in the winter of 1604–1605, but an effective base was found at Port Royal, Nova Scotia. The furs in this eastern area did not prove profitable, however, and so efforts switched again to the Saint Lawrence in 1608. The establishment of the military and civilian trading post at Quebec in 1608 soon brought Champlain to explore the Richelieu River, to learn of the Hudson Valley, and to hear from Native sources about what lay beyond the rapids near Montreal. Thus the stage was set for a long program of exploration, largely for the benefit of the trade in beaver fur, in which the French were engaged. The map, published in 1613, covered the explorations of 1604–1611 and added a further segment to what was generally known as New France.

English activity in the east-northeast began in 1602. Expeditions in 1602, 1603, and 1605 brought back enough information to encourage the Virginia Company to establish a northern fur-trading settlement near the mouth of the Kennebec River (which Champlain had already explored) in 1607. It was not a success and was abandoned in 1608, leaving only small fishing settlements in New England before 1620. The Newfoundland fishery was now a great European enterprise, accounting for up to five hundred vessels each summer, but English colonies there, from 1611 on, failed to develop successfully.

The Dutch were just beginning to interest themselves in the North American continent at the opening of the seventeenth century and soon sent "sack ships" to purchase fish at Newfoundland and furs, if they could get them, in the Saint Lawrence. In 1609 Henry Hudson in the *Halve Maen* transformed their interest into activity on the mainland. Employed on one of the many Dutch voyages in search of a Northeast Passage, he found his way blocked by ice and made a dramatic voyage westward to North America. He concentrated on the somewhat neglected southern New England area and, sailing westward, entered the Narrows that had first been noted by Verrazzano in 1524 (but ignored subsequently). He was able to sail up the Hudson to where Albany later provided the first permanent fur-trading post in 1617; almost a decade after that (1625), construction of New Amsterdam on Manhattan Island began. Subsequent voyages brought the Dutch into the Delaware River. A handful of settlers was established on Governors Island in the 1630s, this leading to the later development of fur-trading on the river basin and much later to the building of a fort at Swanendael on the Delaware River.

The English, meantime, were again sending expeditions to the Davis Strait in the hope of finding the Northwest Passage. George Waymouth had no success in 1602, though interest grew in the following years, and when Henry Hudson returned to the English service in 1610, he was put in charge of the *Discovery*. In her he succeeded in passing through the strait later named after him and in working down the eastern shore of the great bay, to which he was also to give his name, to the end of James Bay, where he was forced to winter. Though survival was hard, Hudson proposed, after the winter was over, to attempt further discoveries. His men revolted and turned him and a few others adrift in a shallop, with no hope of survival. They brought the *Discovery* to Ireland with the report of the discovery and also Hudson's map of the bay, which led to further efforts in the North from 1612 and 1613. No passage was found, nor would one be until the nineteenth century. The map of 1611, published in 1612, added still more information on the coastal fringes of North America.

CONCLUSION

John Parry contemplates in *The Age of Reconnaissance:* "What was Columbus's contribution to the discovery of the sea? Chiefly that he set bounds to the Atlantic. The Ocean Sea . . . had seemed for practical purposes limitless. After Columbus it was finite: five weeks' sailing took one to the other side." The century that followed Columbus's death gradually revealed the outlines of one vital part of that "other side."

The Age of Reconnaissance had, by the early seventeenth century, totally transformed knowledge of large parts of the North American coast and inlets, but it had had only a peripheral effect on European exploration of North America. By 1610 only a handful of Europeans were established there—in Florida, Virginia, Canada, and New Mexico—but a great deal had been learned about eastern North America and a much more limited amount abut the interior and the Pacific coast. Yet the impetus for expansion of European activity and settlement was becoming substantial and was to expand by leaps and bounds in the half-century that followed, with dramatic effects on the Native American population and myriad openings for the new European intruders.

BIBLIOGRAPHY

Documentary Collections

Morison, Samuel Eliot, ed. and trans. *Journals and Other Documents on the Life and Voyages of Christopher Columbus.* New York, 1963.
Quinn, David B., Alison M. Quinn, and Susan Hillier. *New American World: A Documentary History of North America to 1612.* 5 vols. New York, 1979.

Basic Surveys

Fernández-Armesto, Felipe. *Columbus.* Oxford, 1991.

Jones, Gwyn. *The Norse Atlantic Saga.* 2nd ed. New York, 1986.

Morison, Samuel Eliot. *The European Discovery of America.* Vol. 1. *The Northern Voyages.* New York, 1974.

Parry, John H. *The Age of Reconnaissance.* London, 1963.

Penrose, Boies. *Travel and Discovery in the Renaissance.* Cambridge, Mass., 1955.

Quinn, David B. *North America from Earliest Discovery to First Settlements: The Norse Voyages to 1612.* New York, 1977.

Scammell, Geoffrey V. *The First Imperial Age: European Overseas Expansion c. 1475–1715.* Cambridge, England, 1981.

Special Topics

Andrews, Kenneth R. *Trade, Plunder, and Settlement: Maritime Enterprise and the Genesis of the British Empire, 1480–1630.* Cambridge, England, 1984.

Bolton, Herbert Eugene. *Coronado, Knight of the Pueblos and Plains.* 2nd ed. Albuquerque, N.Mex., 1964.

De Vorsey, Louis, Jr., and John Parker, eds. *In the Wake of Columbus: Islands and Controversy.* Detroit, Mich., 1985.

Fernández-Armesto, Felipe. *Before Columbus.* London, 1987.

Hoffman, Paul E. *A New Andalucia and a Way to the Orient: The American Southeast During the Sixteenth Century.* Baton Rouge, La., 1990.

Julien, Charles-André. *Les voyages de découverte et les premiers éstablissements.* Paris, 1948.

Morison, Samuel Eliot. *Admiral of the Ocean Sea.* 2 vols. Boston, 1942.

Quinn, David B. *Explorers and Colonies: America, 1500–1625.* London, 1990.

Ramos, Demetrio. *Audacia, negocios y política en los viajes españoles de descubrimiento y rascate.* Valladolid, Spain, 1981.

David B. Quinn

SEE ALSO **Emergence of Empires** and essays under COLONIAL SETTINGS.

EMERGENCE OF EMPIRES

SPAIN

THE SPANISH PRESENCE in the Southeast and the West of what became the United States goes back to the late fifteenth and early sixteenth centuries. Spaniards claimed and explored these lands very early in their imperial career but settled them only tenuously at first, concentrating on the densely populated areas in the Valley of Mexico and the Andean region of South America. Their colonies in southeastern North America were linked to settlements in the Caribbean islands and on the Gulf Coast of Mexico as part of a natural trading area. In the West, the Spanish Borderlands were not settled in earnest until the late seventeenth and eighteenth centuries. Much less developed than the long-settled colonies in New Spain (Mexico) and South America, they served as frontier outposts for continued exploration. Spanish expeditions eventually pushed as far as the western coast of what is today Canada, challenging not only British and French claims on those northern lands but Russian claims as well.

In United States history, the areas settled by Spain are called the Spanish Borderlands to denote their remoteness both from the English colonies in North America and from the heartland of the Spanish Empire. By the time the fledgling United States began to expand into the Spanish Borderlands, Spain had maintained a presence in North America for about 250 years. Strong traces of Spanish influence in the structures of government and culture continue to this day in the former borderlands, and throughout the United States as well.

In the late eighteenth century, the Spanish Empire contained fifteen to sixteen million people governed in several huge viceroyalties. The structure of government and society was defined by laws, administrative institutions, labor systems, commercial organization, art and architecture, literature, religion, and all of the other characteristics that define a civilization. Spanish colonial society had evolved through the amalgamation of European and American traits, and it was ruled by an elite of Spaniards, some born in Spain and others born in the colonies. The broader population included European, American, and African elements, varying according to the economic base of each region.

The creation of Spanish colonial society south of the Rio Grande cannot concern us here, but it is important to recognize that the roots of the Spanish Borderlands extended broadly in space and time, not only to the empire south of the Rio Grande but across the Atlantic to Iberia, and back in time to the Middle Ages and beyond. Without understanding that full context, it is impossible to understand the history of colonial North America.

EMERGENCE OF EMPIRES: SPAIN

MOTIVATIONS FOR SPANISH EXPLORATION

It was no accident that the voyages of Columbus had Spanish backing. Some of the motives that inspired Columbus were common to many Europeans, such as the desire to establish direct trade with Asia. In the Mediterranean world that produced Columbus, however, the Asian lure was particularly strong. Centuries of trade with the Middle East by Italian merchants and others had sustained the reputation of Asia as the home of wealth and luxury. In addition, centuries of struggle between Christianity and Islam around the Mediterranean had shaped a militant and millennarian Christianity that sought a route to Asia partly to find allies against the Muslims and to bring the Christian message to the peoples of Asia. Both of these impulses had great importance in Iberia, where they were woven into the fabric of the region's history and intellectual outlook.

The Iberian Peninsula forms the southwestern extreme of Europe, which is itself a peninsula of the vast Eurasian continent. Educated Europeans in the fifteenth century knew this, however incomplete their precise knowledge of the world as a whole. What Europeans knew about geography tended to follow from the trade goods they imported, and they had become fairly well informed about Asia by the fifteenth century. They were much less well informed about Africa for several reasons: the limited trade in products from sub-Saharan Africa; the belief that the region south of the equator, which they called the Torrid Zone, was too hot for human habitation; and Muslim zeal to prevent Christians from trading directly with Africa. The existence of two continents in the western ocean between Europe and Asia—North America and South America—lay completely outside the knowledge of even the best-educated Europeans in the fifteenth century.

Five hundred years before Columbus's first voyage, the Vikings had touched the shores of North America, but their voyages had little effect on the peoples living there or on the consciousness of Europeans. The great ocean to the west of Europe continued to lure adventurous European mariners, however. In the two centuries before Columbus's 1492 voyage, Europeans found and settled several groups of islands near the European and African coasts. Rumors of other islands inspired Columbus as he formulated his plans, and they inspired others as well. Nonetheless, islands occupied secondary importance in the dreams of Columbus and his contemporaries. Their longing for distant places focused on Asia.

Europeans gained their knowledge of Asia through contacts that began in ancient times and waxed and waned over the subsequent centuries. After the disintegration of the Roman Empire and its replacement by a collection of small kingdoms in the west and the Byzantine Empire in the east, direct contacts between western Europe and Asia largely disappeared. The closest indirect contacts were maintained through Spain, most of which in the early eighth century fell under the domination of the Muslims, who had previously expanded over the Middle East and the Mediterranean basin. The brilliant civilization of Muslim Spain served the rest of Europe as a small window on the riches of the Islamic world and Asia. Enclaves of Christian strength remained in mountainous northern Iberia, and from there Christian leaders mounted campaigns against the Muslim lands of the south. Their struggle became known as the *Reconquista*, or Reconquest, which involved parallel campaigns by Portuguese, Castilian, and Aragonese forces. By the mid 1080s, Christian forces had reached the center of the peninsula. Inspired by the Reconquest, legal scholars at the papal court in Rome developed the idea of the "just war," which validated warfare to regain lands that once had been in Christian hands. This doctrine clearly applied to the Iberian case, and it could easily be applied to Syria and Palestine as well, which had been ruled by Christians before the rise of Islam.

The Reconquest in Spain lasted from the early eighth to the late fifteenth century, but open hostility and warfare alternated with periods of what Spaniards call *convivencia* (living together). If it was not exactly peace, neither was it war. During the course of the Middle Ages, the Christian states grew in population and expanded southward when they could. When Muslim Spain was strong and unified, the Christian kingdoms made little headway, but they learned much and benefited economically from the more advanced Islamic civilization across their southern frontiers. When the Muslims were disunited, the Christian forces could advance, and over the course of several centuries Christian power extended slowly and inexorably southward. By the late fifteenth century, Portugal and Aragon had long since completed their reconquests, and the Kingdom of Granada in the far south was the last Muslim enclave in Iberia.

The experience of the Reconquest was instrumental in shaping several Iberian Christian notions about the world. One notion was that wealth could be gained from the armed conquest of alien peoples. Another was that the security of Christian society, and even its survival, depended upon unity and a militant defense of the faith. Nonetheless, it would be an error to assume that the typical Portuguese or Spaniard of the late Middle Ages was an armed professional warrior or minor nobleman. Instead, the social and occupational structure of the population was much like that in the rest of Europe.

Encouraged by the reconquest of their lands from the Muslims, the Spanish and Portuguese became fascinated by the possibility of establishing direct trade with Asia and with the ideal of a religious crusade against the Muslims in Africa and the Middle East. Other Europeans were developing similar ideas during the late Middle Ages.

THE CRUSADES

In 1095 the Byzantine emperor Alexios I Komnenos asked Pope Urban II for help in protecting Constantinople from the Muslim Seljuk Turks. The request struck a responsive chord in western Europe. By 1096 four major armies of experienced knights had formed, along with several mobs of inexperienced commoners. They set off for the Middle East to reclaim the birthplace of Christianity, and within five years Jerusalem was in their hands. This nearly spontaneous eruption of Christian militancy has come to be known as the First Crusade, and it would be followed by three other major crusades and several minor ones in the course of more than two centuries.

The Crusades owed their origins to a complex set of conditions in several cultural regions around the Mediterranean. Among the conditions were fears of the rising strength of the Seljuk Turks, whose territorial gains threatened access to trade routes and Christian holy places in the Middle East. The Crusades provided an outlet for the military exploits of warring knights in western Europe, as governments and religious leaders tried to divert them from destructive feuds and wars at home. Noble knights hoped to gain riches from the Crusades, to compensate for the increasingly limited opportunities for land and conquest they found at home.

Christian armies set up several enclaves in the Middle East, called the Crusader states, which provided a toehold for western Europeans at the gateway to Asia. The merchants and seamen of Italy's commercial cities were anxious to gain commercial privileges in the eastern Mediterranean, and the Crusades benefited them immensely.

Mercantile activities in the Middle East had a great impact on the growth of the western European economy in the later Middle Ages. Italian merchants and others used commercial bases in the Crusader states to expand their trading contacts throughout the eastern Mediterranean. They extended trading networks north to the Black Sea and south into Egypt, crossing religious frontiers in the process. One of the most profitable sectors of Italian business dealings in the Middle East was the provision of eastern European slaves to Egypt, a trade that continued into the fifteenth century.

THE GROWING TASTE FOR EXOTIC IMPORTS

Europeans learned a great deal from their exposure to the sophisticated Middle Eastern civilization. The wealthy embraced a more elaborate style of life, with more luxurious clothing, a more varied diet, increased consumption, and more sumptuous houses. Italians in the eastern Mediterranean catered to their demands, buying spices, rich cloth, slaves, and other luxuries from the Muslims to market in western Europe, and enriching themselves and their home cities in the process.

To take just one product as an example, sugarcane had been grown by the Muslims in the Middle East and the Mediterranean for centuries, but in the West it was a rare luxury, prized as a medicine and aphrodisiac, and sold in minuscule quantities at high prices. After the Crusades, sugar cultivation spread to many places in the Mediterranean. Sugar would later be introduced to the Atlantic islands by Spanish and Portuguese settlers in the fifteenth century, and to the Americas by Columbus, who took cane plants to Hispaniola on his second voyage.

The end of the Crusades by no means ended Europe's connection to the Middle East, and through it, to the farthest reaches of Asia. Many of the luxurious and exotic products prized by the European elite continued to arrive from Asia via the Middle East, but political and economic conditions over that vast landmass determined whether trade was profitable or even possible. During the eleventh and twelfth centuries, competing empires in Asia habitually disrupted trade. During the thirteenth and fourteenth centuries, however, the long overland routes from the Black Sea to China opened again, in the aftermath—ironically—of a terrifying series of conquests.

THE MONGOL EMPIRE

The conquerors and later peacemakers of Asia were the Mongols, a collection of nomadic tribes from the edge of the Gobi Desert, nearly a million strong in the thirteenth century. Their leader, Genghis Khan, initiated a career of conquest and pillage that spanned all of Asia. The Mongols were superb horsemen and mounted warriors whose armament included powerful bows, light armor, fine steel weapons, and siege tactics and explosives adopted from the Chinese.

Kublai Khan, grandson of Genghis, conquered all of China by 1276, though the Mongols had already begun to encounter resistance they could not overcome. For a period in the thirteenth and fourteenth centuries, however, a *pax mongolica* (Mongol peace) reigned throughout Asia, guaranteeing the safety of travelers along the overland routes spanning the Mongol Empire. The *pax mongolica* allowed contacts between Europe and Asia that were impossible previously, including visits to Asia by several European mis-

sionaries and merchants, among them the Venetian Marco Polo, who returned to tell their stories to Europeans fascinated by tales of faraway lands and untold riches.

THE DISRUPTION OF TRADE

Long-distance trade with Asia suffered a stunning blow after 1347, when bubonic plague arrived via the Asian caravan routes at the shores of the Black Sea. From there it spread like wildfire throughout Europe, where it was known as the Black Death, killing between one-quarter and one-third of the population in a few years. Partly as a result, the European economy experienced a steep depression that lasted a century. The epidemic also devastated the population of the Middle East and paralyzed long-distance commerce for a generation or more.

Political disruption added to the chaos. In the early fourteenth century the Ottoman Turks began to carve out an empire in Anatolia and the eastern Mediterranean. In China, the Mongols were pushed out of power in 1368 by a new dynasty, the Mings, who reversed the Mongol practice of welcoming outsiders and reestablished a traditional pattern of indifference to foreigners, their goods, and their ideas. In the Middle East a dissident Mongol tributary named Timur the Lame (whom Europeans called Tamerlane) carried out a series of brutal conquests from Persia to India during the late fourteenth century. The combination of plague and political disruption starting in the fourteenth century ended the golden age of trade and contact between Europe and Asia that had been protected by the Mongols.

While it lasted, the *pax mongolica* brought more Asian goods, and Asia itself, within the reach of Europeans. Mediterranean merchants explored the possibilities for direct trade with the markets of Asia, and missionaries considered ways of converting the huge Asian populations to Christianity. Popes and princes became aware that beyond the Islamic world there lived peoples who might be willing to form alliances against the Muslims of the Middle East. The more Europeans learned about the world east of Jerusalem, the more they searched for ways to travel there.

66

EUROPE'S REVIVAL IN THE FIFTEENTH CENTURY

By the late fifteenth century, population and trade in western Europe were recovering from the depression that marked the fourteenth and early fifteenth centuries. Nonetheless, the eastern Mediterranean and North Africa lay firmly in the hands of the Muslims, beyond the control of Christian leaders in Europe, and trade was subject to intermittent hostilities. In the Middle East, merchants from Italian cities such as Venice and Genoa reached an accommodation with the Muslims and purchased Asian and local goods for resale in Europe. In the western Mediterranean, despite centuries of reconquest and crusades and frequent attacks by Muslim pirates at sea, Christian merchants from southern Europe regularly traded in the ports of North Africa. The gold of West Africa supported Muslim rulers in several black African empires, as well as enriching trading cities south of the Sahara and in the Iberian Peninsula.

THE OTTOMAN CHALLENGE

In Iberia, although the Reconquest was nearly over, relations between the Christian kingdoms and Muslim Granada grew increasingly hostile in the late fifteenth century. The end of *convivencia* was largely due to the rise of a militant new force within Islam—the Ottoman Turks, who challenged the traditional Muslim rulers in the eastern Mediterranean and began a concerted campaign to extend the lands under Muslim control.

The Ottomans directed their main thrust in the fifteenth century against the Christian Byzantine Empire, which ruled extensive lands in southeastern Europe from its capital at Constantinople. After gradually encircling the city through conquests in the Balkans, the Ottomans took Constantinople in 1453, a bitter defeat for Christian Europe as a whole. For the Genoese and the Venetians, the expansion of the Ottoman Empire meant the loss of their commercial outposts in the Black Sea and the Aegean. By the late fifteenth century, the hostility between Islam and Christianity was an acknowledged fact, although Italians still traded in Muslim port cities and Christian pilgrimages to Jerusalem continued.

In earlier times, warriors, missionaries, and Crusaders had dreamed of recapturing the holy places of Christianity from Muslim control. In the fifteenth century the dream gained renewed fervor as the Ottomans advanced. Despite tensions within the Catholic church and the scandalous lives of some of the fifteenth-century popes, religion retained a powerful hold on the popular imagination. This was particularly true in Iberia, with its long history of defending Christianity against Islam.

EUROPE'S INTELLECTUAL LIFE

The intellectual horizons of Europe broadened greatly in the late medieval period, if only among the literate elite. The rediscovery of ancient works of law, literature, ethics, geography, science, medicine, and astronomy spurred the elite to learn more about distant cultures and languages. Even militant Christian missionaries recognized that they had to master the Arabic language and to learn more about Islam before they could hope to convert their Muslim enemies.

The dual concerns of Christian zeal and intellectual curiosity led to the intellectual current called humanism, which produced translations of works in Greek, Arabic, Hebrew, and Aramaic into Latin, the scholarly language of Christian Europe. The expanded market for books related to one development that would have profound repercussions far beyond the privileged elite. That development was the introduction into Europe of movable type sometime around 1450, which revolutionized the printing industry by enabling much faster and cheaper production of books.

The result of this intellectual activity was the richly textured culture of the Renaissance, spreading from the courts of the Italian city-states and the papal court at Avignon (and later Rome) to nearly every corner of Europe. Governmental and religious leaders immediately saw that printing could enhance the power and efficiency of their rule. They vied with each other to have the most distinguished scholars at their courts, for political as well as cultural reasons. Most of the rulers of the Italian city-states, as well as of emerging centralized monarchies such as Spain and England, had won their positions through warfare and guile rather than dynastic succession. By patronizing learning and culture, they helped to legitimize their rule and to silence would-be critics.

Printing allowed the classic works of ancient and modern learning to find a wider audience than ever before. Speculation and scholarly argument could be informed by citations from the ancient authorities of classical, Christian, Jewish, and Islamic civilizations. Learned scholars and laymen alike could study a wide range of opinion on topics such as geometry, geography, and cosmography—the shape of the known universe. The books in which Columbus found support for his ideas were readily available in Lisbon and Seville, as well as in the other major cities of Europe. Outside learned circles, by the late fifteenth century devotional works and the Bible began to find their way into quite humble homes. The earliest books printed by the new method reached an astonishing number for the time: as many as twenty million copies arrived on the European market before the end of the fifteenth century.

Perhaps the wider availability of learning stimulated the curiosity of Europeans to explore their world further. More likely, the printing press merely responded to a restless mentality that had already developed in the complex matrix of European culture. Europeans in the fifteenth century, recovering from the Black Death and newly embarked on a career of population increase and economic growth, were anxious to explore the farthest confines of the Old World— both in pursuit of wealth and in service to a militant Christianity. And the people of Portugal and Spain were perhaps the best suited to pursue those motives successfully. In both countries a newly centralized monarchy could give focus to the urge to explore, and a well-developed maritime technology could give it substance.

When Columbus sought support for a voyage westward toward Asia in the 1480s, he spoke to people at the courts of Portugal and Spain who were quite well informed about the rest of the world and anxious to exploit its commercial possibilities. For two centuries before Columbus, cartographers on the island of Majorca, a possession of the Crown of Aragon, had been producing detailed maps and atlases that depicted the Mediterranean and Europe with great accuracy and included some reliable information about Africa south of the Sahara. Marco Polo's late-thirteenth-century journey to China was certainly known in Spain, as were fanciful tales of make-believe travelers. Well-informed people in Iberia also knew of Francesco Pegolotti's fourteenth-century manual of commerce, *Pratica della mercatura*, with its description of Asian products and their origins. In the late fourteenth century, an anonymous Catalonian writer had produced a merchant's guide of his own that revealed some knowledge of China.

Both Portugal and Spain would establish empires in the fifteenth and sixteenth centuries. Portugal would lead the way, with enclaves in the Atlantic islands and down the African coast on the way to India. At first the Spanish Kingdom of Castile followed the same route, developing a strong rivalry with the Portuguese. Then the Treaty of Alcáçovas (1479) established spheres of influence that reserved African coastal exploration to Portugal. Thereafter, Castile concentrated on the Canary Islands and sponsored the voyage of Columbus westward toward Asia that unexpectedly revealed the existence of North America and South America. In the wake of Columbus, Spain would found an empire in the Americas whose borderlands would eventually be taken over by the United States. For that reason, the emergence of the Spanish Empire is more pertinent to the history of the United States than the emergence of the Portuguese Empire.

SPAIN ON THE EVE OF EMPIRE

Like several other European countries in the fifteenth century, Spain had a monarchical and bureaucratic form of government, a system of written law, and a well-organized Catholic church. Spanish monarchs were working to extend the legal authority of the Crown, as were their fellow monarchs elsewhere in western Europe. In this regard, two developments proceeded on parallel courses in Castile and Aragon, the principal Christian kingdoms in Spain during the fifteenth century. One was the growing dominance of Roman law. In the eleventh century the Italian legal scholar Irnerius had begun a serious study of the law code of the ancient Romans. In the next two centuries knowledge and application of Roman law spread widely in western Europe, in part because it tended to bolster central authority.

In the mid thirteenth century, Alfonso X of Castile produced a new legal code for his kingdom, known as the *Siete partidas*, which relied heavily on Roman law. Although it never fully replaced earlier law codes in Castile, the *Siete partidas* still had a significant influence on subsequent legislation in Spain and its empire. The second development was the gradual imposition of the Crown's legal authority throughout the kingdom, a process still incomplete in the late fifteenth century. As the power of the monarchy strengthened, so did the bureaucratic apparatus of councils and royal officials.

In the sophistication of its governmental structure, Aragon was probably ahead of Castile. After the marriage of Ferdinand of Aragon and Isabella of Castile in 1469, their two kingdoms remained legally separate. Nonetheless, Castile undoubtedly benefited from its closer association with Aragon and began to refine the bureaucracy that would later be introduced into the American colonies. The rule of law and a well-defined hierarchy of authority enabled Spain to establish royal control fairly soon after its early conquests in the Americas.

The Catholic church held a great deal of power in Spain, but in Europe as a whole the church had undergone major upheavals in the late medieval period. In the process of reestablishing its authority, the church hierarchy moved toward doctrinal uniformity and away from the relative toleration for unorthodox Christians and for non-Christians that had characterized earlier times. In the early thirteenth century the Fourth Lateran Council established restrictive measures for the Jews of Europe, requiring them to live in segregated residential quarters and to wear distinctive clothing to set them apart from the Christian majority. These measures were not enforced in Castile for nearly two centuries, but they affected Jews elsewhere immediately.

In the late thirteenth century England expelled Jews from its shores, and France did the same early in the fourteenth century. Spain also had a large number of Jewish residents and the only sizable Muslim minority in western Europe. During the fifteenth century, relations among the several religions worsened, influenced in part by fears engendered by the Black Death and the rise of the Ottomans. In 1492 Ferdinand and Isabella responded to public pressure and ordered the Jews to convert to Christianity or leave Spain. About half left, going mainly to North Africa or Portugal; the rest converted. The Muslims were given a similar choice in 1502. With few exceptions, all had to embrace Christianity or leave Spain; most chose to convert and remain.

The rising tide of religious intolerance that marked late medieval Europe created two large minority groups in Spain: the *conversos* ("New Christians" of Jewish origin) and the *moriscos* ("New Christians" of Muslim origin). Many "Old Christians" resented and feared the "New Christians," seeing their failure to observe Christian practices as an affront that could tempt God's wrath. A religious inquisition was founded in 1478 to enforce the orthodox behavior of all Christians, but primarily of those converted from other faiths. The growing militancy of Spanish Catholicism in the late fifteenth century shaped the response of Spanish conquerors to the native religions of the Americas. Their beliefs and religious practices would be rejected out of hand, and if peaceful persuasion failed to convert them to Christianity, many would be forcibly baptized.

THE SPANIARDS

Although we know little about Spanish population in the early medieval centuries, a safe guess for the total number in Spain's Christian kingdoms in the late fifteenth century would be roughly 5.3 million. About 82 percent of the population, and 76 percent of the land, came under the jurisdiction of Castile. Another 16 percent of the population and 22 percent of the land were in the Crown of Aragon, and the remaining 2 percent of the land and people were in Navarre. In the fifteenth century, Spaniards tended to identify with the region where they were born, calling themselves Castilians, Aragonese, Navarrese, Basque, and so on, rather than

EUROPEAN CLAIMS IN NORTH AMERICA BY 1648

Several European nations claimed far more territory than is actually shown here, but their realistic claims are roughly depicted in this map.

EUROPE IN 1648

Spaniards; regional identity remains strong even today. Nonetheless, it is useful here to deal with the country as a whole, because we are looking for general characteristics that shaped Spain's experience as an imperial power.

Like the rest of the preindustrial world, Spain required the labor of a large majority of its people simply to produce food. Roughly four out of every five Europeans worked on the land, but in Spain few of them lived on isolated farmsteads. Instead, they lived in hamlets, villages, and towns, traveling back and forth to work their land and tend their flocks and herds. They might call themselves farmers or livestock owners, but those terms described their occupations, not their dwelling place. For their residential status, they proudly identified themselves as citizens of the legal corporation of their hamlet, village, or town. Citizenship gave them a wide range of privileges and made them eligible for allotments of goods held in common for the use of all the citizens—for example, arable and grazing land, forest products, and water rights. The allocation and regulation of these common resources lay at the heart of local Spanish laws and customs and helped to bind the community together. Life for citizens in small towns differed greatly from conditions in large cities, many of whose inhabitants had lost their rural ties. Nonetheless, nearly all Spaniards shared the legal distinction of being part of an urban commune and defined themselves in those terms.

This pattern of settlement had developed in part because people needed to cluster around the sources of fresh water in the many dry areas of Spain. During the Reconquest, they also needed to cluster together for protection and mutual aid. The strong identification of Spaniards with a commune and its legal and social structures would be implanted in the Americas almost from the moment they arrived. Another ancient tradition was the importance of herding as a way to benefit from lands that were sparsely populated or unsuitable for farming. Livestock and ranching traditions would be carried across the Atlantic as well, shaping many areas in the empire, including the Spanish Borderlands.

The social and economic conditions under which individual Spaniards lived varied widely. Serfdom, which bound people to the land and forced them to make payments to an overlord, had never been widespread in Castile and, where it existed, it had been abolished by the end of the fifteenth century. Nonetheless, the population was hardly homogeneous in wealth or status. Some individuals owned or leased large farms and employed others to work for them. Others might own enough land to support a family, or own part of the necessary land and lease the rest. The land available for leasing was often owned by nobles or clerics who allowed others to use it for terms ranging from a year or two to virtual perpetuity. Large landowners were among those who earned their livelihood from the land in Spain, despite their social and economic distance from those who actually worked that land. The owner of a plow team, whether or not a landowner, was a cut above most others who worked the land because draft animals represented a considerable investment. The same argument could apply to other livestock owners. Those who owned neither land nor animals usually made a living by working for others, with no security in bad times. Some worked and were paid by the day. Others arranged labor contracts for a season or a year.

At the upper end of the social spectrum, urban and rural, was the nobility, whose ancestors had been given land and status in earlier centuries, usually for military service to the monarchy. The nobility was not a closed caste in Spain; movement into its ranks was common both before and after the fifteenth century, depending on the circumstances. Once a person was ennobled, that status was hereditary. All the children of a noble family were considered noble, not just the first-born child. Nonetheless, not all nobles were equal. The least prestigious and most numerous nobles were the hidalgos— loosely meaning "children of some distinction"— whose only advantages were a certain amount of local status and exemption from ordinary taxation. Above them were lords (señores) with small territorial possessions. At the top of the scale were the titulos or titled nobles, often called the grandes. Members of this exclusive group were defined by their wealth and power, both of which were growing in the fifteenth century.

The holdings of the grandes were scattered, and the greatest among them owned or controlled towns and lands in several provinces. While each titled noble typically had a favored stronghold and various other fortresses, he usually did not reside on his estates. Instead, the nobility, especially in Castile, tended to be urban, with their spheres of action in the major towns and cities of the realm. The greatest nobles followed the royal court. In the towns and cities nobles were able to dominate municipal governments and the judiciary by gaining supporters among lesser noble families through intermarriage and patronage. At the royal court they sought to establish hereditary control over important royal offices. They also exercised great influence on foreign commerce and over the administration of the *mesta*, the Crown-sponsored association of flock owners.

Another important source of wealth for the nobility came from political rewards, both for loyal service (particularly in time of war) and for promises of loyalty (particularly in time of political strife). This was just one way in which the political and economic positions of the nobility were closely linked. The monarchs had at their disposal a vast array of material rewards to grant as *mercedes* ("mercies," gifts or grants). Royal offices, both in the central government and in the provinces and cities, were lucrative gifts providing salaries and the potential for graft. Titles, most of them with more honorific than real value, were also bestowed as favors by the monarch. Grants of income based on royal taxes and customs revenues; outright monetary gifts and grants of vassals, towns, and villages; and the rights to found *mayorazgos* (entailed estates) were also bestowed on the nobility in return for their service and loyalty.

By inserting themselves into the highest levels of local and royal government, the Spanish nobility could secure and enhance their economic position as well as their social status. By the mid fifteenth century, about two dozen families belonged to what is usually called the high nobility. Through royal favor, marriage, and inheritance they had amassed great amounts of lands, titles, wealth, and political positions, and their position rested on control of the land and its bounty. Whether they raised wheat, wine grapes, or olives, or derived their wealth from wool, meat, and hides, their primary aim was to secure the greatest possible return from their agricultural and pastoral pursuits.

Nobles who lived along the coasts pursued profits from the fishing industry or from the export trade, either by controlling ports or by direct ownership of shipping. Nobles routinely engaged in business without losing either social status or their titles. One good example of a nobleman-capitalist was the Duke of Medina Sidonia in southern Spain. He was a shipowner in his own right, and negotiated directly with the city government of Genoa to sell the grain produced on his Andalusian estates. He also controlled the lucrative tuna fisheries of the Atlantic coast west of Cádiz, which earned him the popular nickname "The Tuna King."

Although very few of the Spanish high nobility migrated to America, they served as powerful role models for those who emigrated in search of increased wealth and status. Their military values, the way they dressed and spent their money, and their willingness to serve the Crown in anticipation of substantial rewards inspired Spanish conquerors and administrators in the New World.

Landless laborers and the nobility occupied the extreme lower and upper ends of the social spectrum. Between them was everyone else, with the members of the church forming a category all their own. Legally constituting a unified group with collective rights and privileges, the clergy actually mirrored all of society, with internal divisions and a well-defined hierarchy of wealth and status. In the late fifteenth century, the clergy as a whole represented some 2 to 5 percent of the population of the Christian kingdoms. Members of the secular clergy, those who ministered to the spiritual concerns of the laity, ranged from rich and worldly archbishops to bishops in smaller cities, canons of cathedrals and churches, and priests in local parishes.

The regular clergy lived in communities apart from secular society, governed by rules (*regula*) established by the founders of their particular monastic orders. They took vows to serve God through spiritual or charitable works, and in Spain the most important monastic orders included Benedictines, Cistercians, and the order founded by Thomas of Siena in the late fourteenth century to honor Saint Jerome. The Hieronymites, as they are known in English, had their headquarters at the monastery of Guadalupe in the hills west of Madrid—the heart of the area that produced many early venturers to America. Consequently, the Hieronymites and the Virgin of Guadalupe would have great influence in Spanish America. The orders of mendicant friars, the Franciscans and the Dominicans, flourished in the Spanish kingdoms as well. The strength of the Catholic church in Spain helps to explain why religion was not only a powerful motivator for the Spanish conquerors but also a major force in early colonizing efforts.

Related both to the nobility and to the clergy were several important religious-military orders, originally founded in the twelfth century to aid in the Reconquest. For their crucial contributions to winning and holding the frontier against the Muslims, the military orders had received huge land grants from successive rulers of Castile. The grand masters of the orders had jurisdiction over about one million people and enjoyed the privilege of bestowing nobility on some fifteen hundred individuals, the knights of the orders. These knights could be considered the middle ranks of the nobility. Along with the title of knight (*caballero*) often went jurisdiction over tracts of land belonging to the order. The lands so granted were called *encomiendas* (from the verb *encomendar*), because they were commended to the care and protection of the knight (*encomendero*). The military orders provided respected and influential positions for minor noble families and for the younger sons of great families. The pattern of granting *encomiendas* to hold newly conquered land was well established during the Reconquest, and variants of the institution were also used during the Castilian conquest of the Canary Islands, and later in the Americas.

Spaniards who were neither noble, nor members of the religious establishment, nor linked to the land surely did not exceed 5 percent of the total, and they were almost exclusively urban. In occupations they ranged from merchants, university-trained lawyers, notaries, and town councilors to dozens of varieties of artisans, shopkeepers, and peddlers, to servants and slaves. None of these urban groups has been studied very thoroughly, but as a whole they seem to have formed a substantial proportion of the men who first ventured across the Atlantic Ocean to found the Spanish Empire in America.

COMMERCIAL LIFE IN SPAIN

By the fifteenth century, Spanish commercial relations were highly developed, with merchant fairs such as the one at Medina del Campo integrating the interior and exterior trade of Castile.

In the late fifteenth century, Medina was the kingdom's financial center, and merchants from many parts of Europe met there to conduct business. The networks of trade developed by Aragon and Castile in the late Middle Ages encouraged Spanish interest in exploration and developed the commercial organization and business techniques that would be introduced in Spain's overseas empire. Even before the empire had taken hold bureaucratically, Spanish merchants would be able to establish regular trade to quite remote areas.

The foreign trade of Castile in the fifteenth century suggests the complexity of Europe's commercial networks, which had to be well developed or they could never have expanded to include the Americas. The Atlantic coastline defined one major circuit for Castilian merchants, a circuit that stretched from the Cantabrian ports to the Atlantic coast of France and to Flanders, the British Isles, and the North Sea.

The ability of Castilian merchants to supply wool and other goods to the French, Flemish, and English markets depended upon the development of maritime transport. Shipbuilders and mariners on Spain's northern coast had a well-deserved reputation for competence that was honed over the centuries. By the fifteenth century, Castile was one of western Europe's chief suppliers of high-quality wool. Because of this phenomenal growth, wool production and export became the single most important element in the Castilian economy before the establishment of the American colonies. Although the wool trade did not become part of Spain's transatlantic trade, the management and organizational skills required for international wool marketing would adapt well to Spain's American colonies.

SPAIN AND THE CANARY ISLANDS

Long before Columbus's fateful voyage, Spaniards were venturing into unknown portions of the Atlantic, and the first steps in Castilian overseas conquest had already been undertaken in Africa and the Canaries. Europeans first entered the uncharted portions of the Atlantic in the thirteenth and fourteenth centuries. Portuguese and Castilian ship captains initially visited the Canary Islands for easily obtainable items such as wood and the red dye called dragon's blood, the resin of the dragon tree (*Dracaena drago*). Some occasionally used the islands as pirate bases. In time, Castilians began to claim the Canaries as their own, and by the end of the fifteenth century, they firmly controlled the islands. Portugal established control over the Madeiras and the Azores.

Castilians developed a heightened interest in Africa after having established themselves in the Canaries, and their trade and commercial conflicts continued to involve both Africa and the Atlantic islands. Castile's monarchs also subsidized mariners to explore and exploit the coast of West Africa. By the mid fifteenth century there was a regular route from Senegal through the Canaries to Cádiz for the transport of slaves, ivory, and especially gold. In Cádiz most of the gold passed into the hands of the Genoese merchants who dominated financial activity in southern Spain. The Canaries provided several new products for the European economy, among them archil (dyer's moss), a lichen native to the area, which produced a red or violet dye for the textile industry. Demand for orchil increased greatly as dyes from the eastern Mediterranean became scarce and expensive as a result of Turkish expansion.

European settlers introduced sugarcane quite early to the Canaries, and from about 1455 sugar from the islands was shipped to Iberia for sale or reexport. Sugar production reached a peak early in the sixteenth century. Sugar was used as an alternative currency in those years, which indicates its importance in trade and in the local economy. Large plantations were worked by slave labor, first using native Canarians and later slaves imported from Africa. In 1526, near the peak of the Canarian sugar boom, there were twenty-nine mills in the islands, compared with sixteen in Portuguese Madeira. The Canaries served as a way station for the expansion of Spanish sugar production and refining. Cane cuttings and sugar processing techniques were taken from the Canaries to the newly discovered Caribbean islands and established there, beginning with Columbus's second voyage.

Just as the Canaries served as a link in the history of sugar, so experiences in the Canaries foreshadowed the relations between Europeans and native peoples in the Americas. The first would-be developers of the Canaries in the fourteenth and fifteenth centuries, armed with Castilian royal patents, found the islands inhabited by natives organized in tribes or bands. Scholars in the late twentieth century think they were related to the Berbers of northwest Africa. Because the native Canarians did not know how to work metal before the Europeans taught them, their culture has been classified as Neolithic. Most of them were primarily herders, although the people on Grand Canary Island had developed an agricultural economy.

In taking control of the Canaries, the Castilians made treaties with some of the bands and conquered others. Early on, the conquerors needed quick profits to pay for their expeditions, which were mainly financed on credit. The sale of slaves offered a quick and easy way to generate profits to repay the loans. According to medieval law, it was legal to enslave bands that resisted the Spanish incursion, through what was defined as a "just war." It was not legal to enslave bands that submitted voluntarily. However, members of allied bands who later rebelled or refused to carry out the terms of their treaties could be enslaved as "captives of a second war" (*de segunda guerra*). Conquerors and colonists often circumvented the laws, given the profits to be made in the slave trade. Nonetheless, law provided a structure to regulate relations between Europeans and other peoples and helped to establish royal control over the islands.

Enslaved Canarians could use lawsuits to try to win their freedom, but manumission was the most easily available path out of slavery. Everything depended on the inclination of the master. Most masters demanded payment before they would grant a slave's freedom. Others demanded the promise of future payments or future labor service. Many enslaved Canarians were sold in Spain or in Portuguese Madeira; others were kept in the islands and put to work, most frequently as household servants for European settlers.

For a variety of reasons, native workers never filled the labor needs of the colonial economy in the Canaries. The population of the Canaries was relatively small to begin with, and its numbers plummeted due to epidemic disease after the European incursion. Members of many native bands could not be enslaved legally, and those enslaved frequently attained manumission. In the early years of the sixteenth century, the Canarian slave trade to Europe ceased as the remaining islanders were increasingly assimilated into European culture and married colonists. Therefore, new sources of labor were necessary before the islands could be developed fully.

The labor problem was solved in several ways. Workers, both enslaved and free, including a number of free Castilian and Portuguese settlers, were brought to the Canaries. There was even a voluntary immigration of Muslims and *moriscos* from North Africa and Spain. Wealthier settlers brought slaves with them from the peninsula. Portuguese slave traders brought black slaves from West Africa, and Castilian slave traders raided the northern coast of Africa for captives to sell in the Canaries. In the Cape Verde Islands they could purchase African slaves directly from the Portuguese resident there. Less frequently, Castilians in the Canaries went directly to Senegambia and the Upper Guinea coast to acquire slaves. Many of the Africans, especially the North Africans, were freed soon after their arrival in the Canaries. Following the first Spanish contact with the Americas, a few American Indians were sold in the Canaries as well, but the Spanish Crown soon outlawed the slave trade in Indians. By the early sixteenth century, the Canary Islands had a labor force that was partly free and partly enslaved, varying with the labor needed for agriculture and other pursuits.

In the way Spaniards conquered, colonized, and organized the Canaries economically, they set many precedents that would later be repeated in the Americas. The initial search for quick profits under private entrepreneurs, followed by the establishment of royal control and an organized colonial economy, would characterize developments in both the Canaries and the Americas.

CONCLUSION

Spaniards in America replicated the customs and traditions that they had known at home: a town government as the basic political unit; written laws to mediate relations among Spaniards and between Spaniards and other peoples; loyalty to a monarchy as the source of law, administration, and patronage; agriculture, herding, mining, and industry as the bases of the economy; local and long-distance commerce to distribute the fruits of colonial production; militant Christianity; and territorial expansion as a way to acquire wealth and status. These deeply rooted traditions sprang from centuries of development related to the general evolution of European civilization and, in Iberia, related as well to centuries of confrontation with Islam. These traditions would shape every part of the empire, including the Spanish Borderlands.

BIBLIOGRAPHY

Aznar Vallejo, Eduardo. *La integración de las Islas Canarias en la corona de Castilla, 1478–1526.* Seville, Spain, 1983. How the Crown finally conquered the Canary Islands and established control over their administration.

Baer, Yitzhak. *A History of the Jews in Christian Spain.* Translated by Louis Schoffman. 2 vols. Philadelphia, 1961–1966. One of the classic works in the field.

Bisson, Thomas N. *The Medieval Crown of Aragon: A Short History.* Oxford, 1986. An excellent summary of Aragon in eastern Iberia, often neglected in favor of Castile, which dominated the center and the south.

Chaunu, Pierre. *European Expansion in the Later Middle Ages.* Translated by Kattarine Bertram. Amsterdam, 1979. A stimulating summary by an expert in transatlantic trade.

Contreras, Jaime, and Gustav Henningsen. "Forty-four Thousand Cases of the Spanish Inquisition (1540–1700): Analysis of a Historical Data Bank." In *The Inquisition in Early Modern Europe. Studies on Sources and Methods,* edited by Gustav Hennigsen, John Tedeschi, and Charles Amiel. De Kalb, Ill., 1986. Briefly presents extensive recent research on the Spanish Inquisition which places that institution in its legal and social context.

Diffie, Bailey W., and George D. Winius. *Foundations of the Portuguese Empire, 1415–1580.* Minneapolis, Minn., 1977. The best overview in English.

Domínguez Ortiz, Antonio, and Bernard Vincent. *Historia de los moriscos: Vida y tragedia de una minoría.* Madrid, 1978. Brief overview of the converted Muslims of Spain.

Fernández-Armesto, Felipe. *Before Columbus: Exploration and Colonization from the Mediterranean to the Atlantic, 1229–1492.* Philadelphia, 1987. Includes several chapters on the conquest of the Canary Islands.

Hillgarth, J. N. *The Spanish Kingdoms, 1250–1516.* 2 vols. Oxford, 1976–1978. Particularly strong on political and intellectual history.

Ladero Quesada, Miguel Angel. *España en 1492.* Madrid, 1978. The best extended analysis to date of the complex political, economic, and social matrix of late medieval Spain.

Lalinde Abadia, Jesús. *Iniciación histórica al derecho español.* Barcelona, Spain, 1970. An up-to-date summary of legal history in medieval Spain.

Lomax, Derek W. *Las órdenes militares en la Península Ibérica durante la edad media.* Salamanca, Spain, 1976. Analyzes the crusading orders of knights who spearheaded the medieval reconquest of Spain from the Muslims.

MacKay, Angus. *Spain in the Middle Ages: From Frontier to Empire, 1000–1500.* New York, 1977. Deals with the Reconquest as a shaping force for Spain's overseas exploration.

Martín Rodríguez, José Luis. *Economía y sociedad en los reinos hispánicos de la baja edad media.* 2 vols. Barcelona, Spain, 1983.

Mercer, John. *The Canary Islanders: Their Prehistory, Conquest, and Survival.* London, 1980. Good overview.

Nader, Helen. *Liberty in Absolutist Spain: The Habsburg Sale of Towns, 1516–1750.* Baltimore, Md., 1990. A stimulating analysis of the town's place in Castilian life.

O'Callaghan, Joseph F. *The Spanish Military Order of Calatrava and Its Affiliates.* London, 1975. Calatrava defended the south-central frontier of Castile against the Muslims during the Reconquest.

Phillips, J. R. S. *The Medieval Expansion of Europe.* Oxford and New York, 1988. Excellent analysis of exploration, trade, and missionary expeditions, largely toward Asia, in the centuries before Columbus.

Phillips, William D., Jr. *Enrique IV and the Crisis of Fifteenth-Century Castile, 1425–1480.* Cambridge, Mass., 1978. The political situation prior to the reign of Isabella of Castile.

———. *Slavery from Roman Times to the Early Transatlantic Trade.* Minneapolis, Minn., 1985. Discusses the legal and historical context of slavery in Europe, Africa, and the Middle East.

Phillips, William D., Jr., and Carla Rahn Phillips. *The Worlds of Christopher Columbus.* New York and Cambridge, 1991. The early chapters examine the historical background to Spanish exploration.

Van Kleffens, E. N. *Hispanic Law Until the End of the Middle Ages.* Edinburgh, 1968. Despite its age, a useful summary, and the only one in English.

Vassberg, David E. *Land and Society in Golden-Age Castile.* New York and Cambridge, 1984. Fundamental for the understanding of rural Spain, although the analysis deals mostly with the sixteenth century.

Carla Rahn Phillips

SEE ALSO **The Age of Reconnaissance; Mission Communities;** and **Settlements in the Spanish Borderlands;** the map accompanying this article.

FRANCE

DESPITE THE FACT THAT FRANCE was an Atlantic nation and the most populous in western Europe, it was the last, after Portugal, Spain, and England, to enter the running for a foothold in Asia. That was because throughout the entire fifteenth century its foreign policy was focused on the desire for preponderance in the Mediterranean. France lacked neither material resources nor navigators and with the Breton and Basque fishermen it knew well the route to Newfoundland. But fishing expeditions, carried on with no regard for politics or science, did not grant France any standing in the realm of knowledge of the wider world or any right of possession on the other side of the Atlantic.

THE COAST OF NEW FRANCE

In the wake of discoveries made by the Portuguese in the north and south Atlantic and by the Spanish in the west, the pope intervened in 1455 and then again in 1493–1494. He established a frontier from the North Pole to the South Pole, which reserved for Portugal all the territories found, or that would be found, to the east of the line, and Spain everything to the west. Thus, projecting west from a line 370 leagues (1,800 kilometers; 1,100 miles) from Cape Verde, anything up to the East Indies became part of the Spanish Empire; projecting east from that same line to the East Indies, everything could be claimed for Portugal. England, still Roman Catholic, carried on, ignoring both that demarcation line and the papal intervention.

France did the same. Its entry into the race was precipitated by the return of the *Vittoria,* the last surviving ship of Ferdinand Magellan's expedition. That explorer had discovered at the southern tip of America a strait that allowed ships to sail to Asia by the western route. The French expedition was made possible by the support of Italian bankers established at Lyons, which was at that time a commercial center for France, Italy, Spain, and Germany. These silent partners proposed to discover a shorter route than Magellan's, thereby assuring France a monopoly on Asian products. The enterprise was entrusted to Giovanni da Verrazano, a well-lettered Florentine, a Renaissance man, and an expert cosmographer.

Verrazano undertook to find a direct passage to Asia between Newfoundland to the north, where the English and Portuguese had already made landfalls, and the "Terra Florida," above the Gulf of Mexico, which the Spaniards had discovered. Between these two points remained an unknown world; no one knew whether they were connected or whether there was a way open between them that would allow navigation to Asia. France thus seemed to be offered one last chance to make up for the twenty-five-year delay in the international rivalry.

After a false start in 1523 Verrazano took to the sea the following year with the *Dauphine.* He proceeded directly to the northern end of the Florida Peninsula (around Cape Fear) and, setting a northward course, made an examination of the coastline. Suddenly there it seemed to be, the Sea of Asia, so ardently sought (as he wrote). He believed he had found it beyond an isthmus two hundred miles (320 kilometers) long, which unfortunately he could not cross. But that Sea of Asia, which cartographers would soon locate there, was actually North Carolina's Pamlico Sound.

Verrazano continued his exploration northward, past what would become Virginia and Chesapeake Bay, then New York and the Hudson River, which he ascended a short distance still seeking the elusive passage to Asia. He passed in front of the future New England, sailing perhaps as far as fifty degrees north along that continental barrier now over fifteen hundred miles (2,400 kilometers) long, still not finding the gap that would allow passage from the Atlantic to the Pacific.

Nevertheless he had proof that there was but one coastline between Florida and Newfoundland, and that this coastline, like the one of Central and South America as far as the Strait of Magellan, blocked direct access for ships to the Sea of Asia. It was at least another important step in current knowledge of the world's extent. Up to that time existing maps showed Newfoundland as a headland of Asia and attached South America to the Indian continent. Verrazano concluded that he had found a whole new continent, separate from Asia, something that had never previously been asserted.

As for France, it acquired by this voyage a foundation for its territorial claims along the entire length of the American coast. From Florida to Newfoundland, French place names now appeared on maps: for example, Annonciation in northern Florida, Arcadie in Virginia, Côte de Lorraine in Delaware and New Jersey, fleuve Vendôme for the Delaware River, and Angoulême in the New York region. And Verrazano gave a new name to the entire continent: Nouvelle-France (New France).

The Italian wars prevented Francis I from pursuing the promise of New France. Spain, however, which claimed everything west of the line of 1492, reacted without delay to the news of Verrazano's voyage. Spain sent Esteban Gomez to navigate the same coast in 1524–1525, and the French place-names were supplanted by Spanish ones. The Spaniard Lucas Vásquez de Ayllón did even more in 1526. Not only did he in his turn search along the coast for the passage to Asia, but he established a small colony in Chesapeake Bay; it, however, soon disappeared.

England, too, intervened along this same coastline. In 1527 John Rut arrived in Newfoundland, and from there, the two ships of his expedition traveled southward: one to New England, the other toward the Antilles. The last nation to arrive would make of this long coastline a definitively English colony.

THE VOYAGES OF CARTIER

Francis I, still interested in getting his share of the new discoveries, took up the North American enterprise again in 1532. The new French expedition of 1534, under the command of Jacques

Cartier from Saint-Malo, was the sequel, albeit tardy, to Verrazano's expedition. It took up the search where the earlier explorer had left off, but it had a second purpose, clearly stated: "to discover certain islands where it is said that there must be [a] great quantity of gold and other things to be found."

As he had been instructed, Cartier proceeded directly to Newfoundland, and—via the Baie des Châteaux (the Strait of Belle Isle)—entered an inland sea (the Gulf of Saint Lawrence). Cartier was the first European to navigate the gulf and to map it. As did Verrazano, he examined every opening that might lead to the Sea of Asia. On 3 July he visited Chaleur Bay, whose shape gave him hope that it was the passage he sought, but as he explored it further he realized that it was closing. This, he said, made him very angry. Another opening in the coast (Gaspé Bay) brought him no farther west but did at least give him the opportunity to make contact with natives from the interior of these lands. They were Iroquois from Stadacona (later Quebec). Cartier captured two of them to serve as guides. He eventually traveled north of Anticosti Island, but the approach of bad weather prevented him from sailing up the large opening that lay before him, the Saint Lawrence River.

This voyage of 1534 greatly facilitated the mapping of the Gulf of Saint Lawrence. But thanks to the Amerindians whom he took back to Europe, it placed a tantalizing hypothesis before Cartier: a waterway that led inland from the barrier of the North American coastline.

Francis I decided to verify this hypothesis. In 1535 he again sent Cartier with three ships. The native of Saint-Malo took up his exploration where he had left off. Open before him was a wide river that behaved like a sea, with its salt water and regular tides, a river into which significant waterways like the Saguenay emptied themselves. All this bolstered his hopes of getting to the Sea of Asia.

From the moment Cartier installed himself to pass the winter at Stadacona, in the heart of a small area that he called Canada (after the Iroquoian word for village), he wanted to know more about the region. Despite the opposition of the Iroquoians, he headed upstream. He visited what was to become Trois-Rivières, with its river (the Saint-Maurice) that had a wide mouth and strong current; a little inland sea (Saint Pierre Lake); and a river (the Richelieu) that he thought ran toward Florida. He got to Hochelaga (Montreal) where unfortunately the rapids barred his way. He thought he understood from the Iroquois who lived there that another great river flowed to that point from the west and might lead to a kingdom where gold and silver could be found. His two French-speaking guides having refused to go along on his voyage to Hochelaga, Cartier could learn no more than that, but he imagined all sorts of possibilities for a voyage farther west.

After a winter made extremely painful by the cold and scurvy, he returned to France in 1536 to report on his mission. Although he took back almost nothing in the way of gold, the expedition was profitable nonetheless. In addition to establishing relations—albeit fragile ones—with the natives and drawing up a map of the Saint Lawrence that would last almost a century, Cartier had opened up to France a major route for penetrating the interior of the continent.

In 1538 France began to prepare for another expedition. This one was to be very important, for besides continuing exploration, it was to found a settlement on the Saint Lawrence, the first French colony on American soil. In an attempt to calm the protestations of the Spaniards and Portuguese and to receive the support of the pope, it was necessary to proclaim solemnly that the purpose of the expedition was evangelization.

The expedition set off in 1541 under the command of Cartier, who was to set up a base while waiting for his superior, Jean-François de La Roque de Roberval, to arrive with all the necessary equipment. Cartier decided not to establish the base at the convergence of the Saint Lawrence and Saint Charles rivers, where it would have been too close to the Iroquois, who had become less reliable as allies. This time Cartier chose the western end of Cape Diamond at the mouth of the little Cap Rouge River. This place, which would be called Charlesbourg-Royal, was on the Saint Lawrence, which at that time was itself called France-Prime, no doubt after Francis I.

In 1542, believing that he had found an abundance of gold and diamonds, Cartier decided to return to France. In the Gulf of Saint Lawrence he met Roberval, who had finally arrived with his people. Roberval settled in the spot where Cartier had spent the winter, but the attempt to establish a colony failed immediately: the entire colony went back home in 1543.

The ostensibly precious minerals that Cartier brought back to France turned out to be nothing more than pyrite and quartz. Neither Cartier nor Roberval had progressed at all toward the interior of the continent between 1541 and 1543. Relations with the natives had deteriorated gravely. The French had to cope with a harsh winter climate, unlike the Spaniards to the south. Furthermore, France was entering a troubled period at home because of the Wars of Religion. In short, all this led to the abandonment of any permanent settlement in New France.

ATTEMPTS SOUTH AND NORTH

Yet the notion of a "New France" across the Atlantic was not completely relinquished. Brazil, a country rich in sugar and precious wood, was the next target. Because of those same Wars of Religion, a colony was founded as a refuge for the Huguenots. In 1555 both Protestants and Catholics went to settle in Guanabara Bay (today the bay of Rio de Janeiro), under the protection of Admiral Gaspard de Coligny and at the initiative of Nicholas Durand de Villegaignon. But the initial purpose soon foundered in dissension, and Portugal, worried by the presence of French people—and of the "reformed faith" to boot—in its territories, soon destroyed this heretical New France.

The Huguenots, who were becoming more and more active in France, did not renounce the plan of founding a refuge in America. Coligny wanted to try anew in Florida, very close to where Verrazano had begun his expedition in 1524. Jean Ribault and René Goulaine de Laudonnière arrived there at the end of April 1562. They explored the coasts with the same enthusiasm as had Verrazano and spread French toponymy the length of the shore. They decided to set up a stronghold, Charlesfort, in what is today the Beaufort Archipelago in South Carolina. The search for the fabulous riches that were traditionally said to exist in the New World soon imperiled the safety of the colony: Spain, which was just as opposed to the Huguenots and to competition as Portugal, destroyed it in 1564.

But the Huguenots continued their efforts at colonization. That same year, 1564, Ribault and Laudonnière traveled farther south and crossed the River Mai (Saint John's River). In 1565 Spain struck again: the Spaniard Pedro Menéndez de Avilés, who had founded Saint Augustine very close by, eliminated the new Huguenot colony. There would yet be Protestant monopolies in French America, but there would never again be a Protestant New France.

The long religious upheaval that shook France for a whole generation prevented any immediate political initiative to pursue the dream of a French empire in America. It was the fur trade that eventually brought the French back to Cartier's major route to the interior of the continent. Since the Saint Lawrence colony had been abandoned in 1543, small groups of French people had maintained cod fisheries and, above all, traffic in furs. The furs were at first brought back to Europe as an adjunct to the fish catch, but in the last quarter of the sixteenth century they became in themselves the purpose of an Atlantic voyage. Once peace had been restored at home, France would try again to establish a footing in North America.

In 1577 Henry III gave a marquis from Brittany, Troilus de La Roche de Mesgouez, viceroyalty over all the new lands. But the projected colony did not take shape until 1597 under Henry IV. La Roche chose Sable Island, about one hundred miles (160 kilometers) east of what is now Nova Scotia, as the center of his enterprise. There he had his people disembark, resupplying them each year through 1601. But when a new shipment arrived in 1603, the expedition found a devastated colony with only about ten survivors, who were sent back home.

The Huguenot Pierre de Chauvin de Tonnetuit owned the monopoly on the interior of the Saint Lawrence. In 1600–1601 he tried to establish a post at Tadoussac. It ended in failure around the same time as La Roche's.

CHAMPLAIN AT PORT ROYAL

Henry IV did not let go of the plans for a colony; he wanted the tax revenues from traders who would have monopolies in those areas. Despite the failures, 1603 marked an important stage in French colonization. That year the king granted a monopoly to a knight of the Order of Malta, Aymar de Chaste. François Gravé Du Pont and some merchants from Normandy became his partners. Losing no time, they sent a fleet to the Saint Lawrence. On board, officially as an observer only, was Samuel de Champlain, the geographer and draftsman from Saintonge.

The expedition undertook the first methodical inventory of the Saint Lawrence. In fact, not only did Champlain observe in minute detail the Montagnais that he met in Tadoussac, but he had enough free time to sail up the Saint Lawrence all the way to the island of Montreal. The ethnic landscape there had changed a great deal since the time of Cartier: the Iroquois had disappeared, leaving the land free for the Algonquin tribe, who had entered into an alliance with the French. Nevertheless, the Algonquin were constantly at war with the Iroquois from farther south, a rivalry that made fur trading a chancy business. This was one of the reasons why Pierre Du Gua de Monts, de Chaste's successor to the monopoly on trade on the Atlantic coast and in the Saint Lawrence area, chose to locate his base on the Atlantic coast of Acadia.

A temporary base was established first: on Saint Croix Island, at the mouth of the river of that name; later, Port Royal (Annapolis Royal) in what is now Nova Scotia. Then began a long search for a site that would combine all the optimal conditions for a French colony. The place had to be near the sea to facilitate contacts with France; it had to be near Native people with whom it was possible to engage in a lucrative trade in furs; hidden beneath the land had to be an abundance of minerals of all kinds; the soil had to be fertile; and a waterway had to give access to the Sea of Asia—for the traditional goal had not been forgotten.

Jean Biencourt de Poutrincourt et de Saint-Just (lieutenant to Du Gua de Monts) and Champlain (who did not yet have any official title) sailed up and down the Atlantic coast from 1604 to 1607, from the Bay of Fundy to Cape Cod, in search of this ideal spot. The fact that there was at that time no European occupying presence made this task easier.

The Micmac had been allies of the French from the first years. The French now added a group they called the Etchemin (Malecite) to their network of business contacts, but their land seemed no more profitable than that of the Micmac. In 1605 Du Gua de Monts sailed what would become the New England coast; at the same time as he found the climate pleasant, he found that access to the coast would probably be difficult, that the soil would not be rich enough, and that the Indians were not to be counted on.

In 1606 another examination was made of this coastline; this time the idea was to go south of Cape Cod, toward the "Refuge" (Rhode Island) that Verrazano had so highly touted, and toward Angoulême (the Hudson River), which would supposedly give onto the interior of the continent. But conflicts with the natives made it impossible to go beyond Cape Cod. The expedition returned to Port Royal for a winter made famous because of the *Théatre de Neptune,* a production put on by Marc Lescarbot (and believed to have been the first in America), and by the Order of Good Cheer, whose members took turns providing game and keeping spirits high.

A piece of bad news forced the temporary closure of Port Royal in 1607: Du Gua de Monts had just lost his monopoly, before having found the ideal site for a colony. In an irony of fate, the same year England sent settlers to two sites on the Atlantic coast: 45 colonists went to the mouth of the Kennebec River; another 105 people to Chesapeake Bay. From then on, England would occupy the areas along the Atlantic coast.

THE HABITATION AT QUEBEC

At that moment the French made a definitive choice in favor of the Saint Lawrence. Du Gua de Monts, who in 1608 had his monopoly extended, thought that he would be safe in that area from European competition and be able to take advantage of the bond formed with the natives in 1603; that the fur trade promised to be more rewarding there than in Acadia; and, finally, that the Saint Lawrence offered a greater possibility of getting to Asia. These were all reasons that Champlain had proposed.

Having chosen Champlain as his lieutenant, Du Gua de Monts sent him with the necessary funds to establish a habitation. Champlain chose a place where the river was no wider than a strait, which was called Quebec in Algonquian, meaning "narrowing". From there it was possible to control access to the interior of the continent.

For many years the settlement at Quebec would be no more than a trading post where the entire trading network of allied Native peoples would converge. To consolidate this network, Champlain chose to take sides against the Iroquois. In 1609 he made his way to confront the Iroquois on Lake Champlain, their attack route against the Saint Lawrence. Acting on the orders of his superior, Du Gua de Monts, he was doing no more than maintaining an alliance begun in 1603. This alliance with the Montagnais and the Algonquin and, shortly afterward, with the Huron, would enable him to spread his trading network all the way to the interior of the Great Lakes, where other trading routes culminated. The permanence of this alliance would be assured by interpreters who were sent to live among the natives.

The Saint Lawrence settlement remained precarious despite the advantages of this great trading network, for from 1609 on Du Gua de Monts had to cope with free competition in the Saint Lawrence itself. France reinstated the monopoly system in 1612, for the benefit of an influential prince, the count of Soissons. Champlain became the count's representative for New France. He was instructed to people it, to set up a proper government, and to pursue the search for a passage to Asia. Soissons died and was succeeded by his nephew, the prince of Condé, whose title was viceroy. To take advantage of his monopoly, he set up a company of merchants in Rouen and Saint-Malo. From then on the settlement of the Saint Lawrence seemed assured.

Meanwhile, the Port Royal settlement in Acadia, which had been reopened in 1610, was turning into a disaster. The settlement was plagued by internal dissension as much as by attacks from the English, who claimed the territory in the name of the Virginia Company.

THE COMPAGNIE DES CENT-ASSOCIÉS

In any event, the process of establishing a colony in the Saint Lawrence dragged on a long time. The merchants of Saint-Malo and Rouen wanted to have a certain number of their own people there, among them the Recollets, whom they sent in 1615 and supported financially. From the point of view of those who favored a systematic colonization, not enough progress was being made. In 1616, from Quebec, the Recollets proposed the first religious and political policy ever prepared in New France: a population program to allow the French (with the exception of the Huguenots) to come and accustom the natives to a settled life, a policy of independent investigation into the company that held the monopoly, and a program of missionary recruitment. Recollets Denis Jamet and Joseph Le Caron, Marc Lescarbot (with his *Histoire de la Nouvelle-France*), Biencourt de Poutrincourt, and even the Jesuit Pierre Biard (in his *Relation*): all appealed to the authorities and to the public for the adoption of these policies, asking them to create something in New France that "one day will bring useful things, honor and glory to all of old France."

The most important and substantial appeal came from Champlain in 1618. He drew up for the Chamber of Commerce and the king an inventory of what he hoped to get from the country in the way of fisheries, wood, mines, furs, farming, and animal husbandry, amounting to more than six million livres. And that was not all: there was also "that shortcut to China by way of the Saint Lawrence River." The river would become a great international route between Europe and Asia, from which the customs revenues to France would be ten times the tax revenues.

The king encouraged Champlain to carry on with his work but did not give him any help. He invited the merchants to cooperate but did not impose any conditions on them. The Recollets and the Jesuits took turns intervening. In 1626 Isaac de Razilly, of the religious and military Order of Malta, submitted a statement that seemed decisive in shaping France's attitude toward colonization. Cardinal Richelieu, first minister, had barely come to power when he took into his hands the fate of New France.

At that time two powerful commercial companies existed. One was the East India Company, founded in 1600 by the English; the other, the Vereenigde Oostindische Compagnie, established in 1602 by the Dutch. They were responsible for the colonial success of England and the Netherlands. A distinguishing feature of both companies was that each was the work of bourgeois businesses and not of the state, which was content to play the role of moderator. In France, by contrast, the great commercial companies were artificial creations of the government, which was setting its sights more toward increasing its political rather than economic power. It was in this spirit that Richelieu set up in 1627 a company to which he would give a huge colonial mission. Known as the Compagnie des Cent-Associés (Company of One Hundred Associates), the enterprise's official title was the Company of New France.

Each member was to invest three thousand livres. (The investments were permanent, and no interest payments were made for three years.) The company was assigned a more religious and charitable mission than it would have had if only merchants had been partners. Clergy and members of the aristocracy could thus join the partnership without demeaning themselves. In fact, 60 percent of the partners held high public office. The religious orientation was affirmed in the first article of the company, which stated the goal to lead the Amerindians "to the knowledge of the true God" and to gallicize them, and in the article that granted these American Indians the status of "natural French" people as soon as they had been baptized.

The king made the company seigneur to everything between Florida and the North Pole and from Newfoundland to the Great Lakes and "beyond, so far as they may be enabled to broadcast and make known His Majesty's Name." A good part of this domain, however, was already occupied by the English or the Dutch (Hudson Bay, Newfoundland, what was to become New York, and Virginia). Moreover, the part of New France that was settled was still insignificant, with its population of roughly a hundred people compared to the nearly three thousand of the other European colonies. Nevertheless, from then on France had a strongly built colonial entity: it enjoyed a well-organized trading network in the interior of the continent (which its European competitors did not yet have); and the interpreters and missionaries in place among the Amerindians assured the stability of its alliances. The New France of 1627 seemed to have all the elements necessary to realize its dreams of 1524.

BIBLIOGRAPHY

Quinn, David B. *North America from Earliest Discovery to First Settlement: The Norse Voyages to 1612.* New York, 1977.

Trudel, Marcel. *The Beginnings of New France, 1525–1663.* Toronto, Ontario, 1973. A translation of the first three volumes of Trudel's *Histoire de la Nouvelle-France.*

——. *Histoire de la Nouvelle-France. Les vaines tentatives, 1524–1603.* Vol. 1. Montreal, 1963.

——. *Histoire de la Nouvelle-France. Le comptoir, 1604–1627.* Vol. 2. Montreal, 1966.

——. *Histoire de la Nouvelle-France. La Seigneurie des Cent-Associés, 1627–1663.* Vol. 3, 2 vols. Montreal, 1979, 1983.

Marcel Trudel

SEE ALSO **The Age of Reconnaissance** and **French Settlements;** the map accompanying this article.

BRITAIN

ENGLAND IN THE LATE fifteenth century and throughout most of the sixteenth century was peculiarly isolated from continental Europe. The usurping Tudor dynasty was regarded for some time with hostility, followed by a period of scepticism about its stability. It was not until late in the reign of Henry VII (1485–1509) that the dynasty enjoyed a degree of acceptance. In the early part of his reign, Henry VIII (1509–1547) attempted to play a significant and dramatic part in continental affairs and had some success, thanks largely to the diplomatic skill and audacity of Lord Chancellor Thomas Wolsey. But the schismatic course Henry VIII embarked upon in 1534 cut him off to a great degree from European esteem and influence, and the rift deepened with the Protestant experiments during the short reign of Edward VI (1547–1553). Only in the brief reign of Mary (1553–1558), who married Philip of Spain, did England come back into the mainstream of continental politics, only to lose Calais, the last of her mainland territories.

Elizabeth embarked on an ecclesiastical policy very similar to that of her father, and she too was largely shut out from continental great-power politics. The subsequent isolation had some advantages in leaving her people with opportunities to pick and choose in their overseas experiments. On the other hand, there was much ignorance of what Spain, Portugal, and even France were doing outside Europe. England remained largely uninformed of these developments and even of the literature concerning them until the 1570s, when a wave of interest in overseas events and issues accompanied the awakening among her statesmen of something of an imperialist urge, though it would probably be going too far to call it an imperial policy.

The last twenty-five years of Elizabeth's reign, especially after the sea war with Spain began in 1585, brought some reversal of England's position in Europe. After the dispersal of the Great Armada in 1588, she could pose as the defender of non-Spanish Europe against the tyranny of Spain. Her closer links with the United Provinces, as they consolidated, and with France after the accession of Henry IV in 1589, enabled her to play a more significant part in continental affairs at the same time her subjects were indicating their resilience and ingenuity in harassing, if not seriously threatening, the combined Spanish-Portuguese Empire in the West and East.

Counterbalancing England's relative isolation from European affairs for much of the sixteenth century was the growth of a vigorous and uncompromising nationalism. The expression of national identity crystallized as early as 1558, when the sense of what it meant to be English was declared to be bound up with the existence of an independent national church. The expression "God is English" dates from that year. English churchmen claimed that the Church of England, as established by law in 1559, was the true representative of the universal church.

English nationalism was closely linked with the aggressiveness shown by her overseas adventurers, and this in spite of the limited financial and physical support they received from the state. It also explains many of the interesting and potentially important initiatives that were made overseas in the latter part of the century. One example was the impulse toward colonization in North America occasioned by the Catholic jibe that where their church was converting millions of non-Europeans to Christianity, the English church, despite its universalist claims, had converted none of the heathen (not even the Catholic Irish). Proponents of colonization in America, notably Richard Hakluyt, argued that colonization must be combined with missionary activity and this feature was stressed in a number of plans for colonization. The only instance where anything was done about it was when Thomas Harriot attempted to expound the Bible to the Carolina Algonquian in 1586, using their own tongue, but was chagrined to find that what they were prepared to venerate was the Bible itself, the "God in the Book," where his physical presence was presumed to reside.

THE PRELUDE TO EMPIRE

England's road to empire was more like a slow crawl than a triumphant progress. At the opening of the sixteenth century she was well placed, it seemed, to take part in the attempt to discover and penetrate lands to the west. By 1600, though, she had not progressed very far in that direction. She had completed the subjugation of Ireland at the death of Elizabeth I in 1603, but she had not a single colony or even trading post outside Europe at that date. Yet many of the tentative experiments of the late sixteenth century became the basis for substantial imperialist achievements in the seventeenth century.

The Iceland trading and fishing carried on over most of the fifteenth century made her a pioneer in North Atlantic seamanship. The Bristol merchants had begun to search the Atlantic immediately to the west of Iceland as early as 1480, and may well have found some signs of land, probably in 1481 or shortly after 1490. In 1496 John Cabot, a Venetian navigator, got the kind of encouragement from Henry VII, if not comparable financial support, that Columbus had received from Ferdinand and Isabella. His voyage of 1497 was important in that it disclosed a substantial landmass in latitudes comparable to those of England, even if it was not, as Cabot believed, the northern part of Cathay. The only tangible result of his voyages was the discovery and initial exploitation, from 1502 onward, of the inshore fishery at Newfoundland. It was soon to be exploited mainly by other nations. In the short run, the voyages undertaken in these years by John Cabot and his successors yielded no prospects of profitable trade with the inhabitants of the part of North America that had been discovered (now the Maritime provinces and New England). As a result, the Bristol voyages ceased in 1505.

Sebastian Cabot was the first to attempt to exploit the barely recognized fact that the North American continent stood as a barrier to Asia and to try to get around it by way of a northern passage. His expedition (1508–1509) may well have reached Hudson Strait, but on his return to England in May 1509 he was unable to induce the young Henry VIII to take the slightest interest in such a remote and probably barren prospect. Cabot, in turn, took himself into the Spanish service.

Obstacles to Overseas Expansion

For the greater part of the sixteenth century, the preoccupation of the London and provincial commercial elites was in the cloth trade. Unfinished woolen cloth, to be finished in the Netherlands, was exchanged at the port of Antwerp for products from the Mediterranean, Asia, and later from the new lands being exploited by Spain and Portugal. The cloth trade continued to be the growth industry of the first half of the sixteenth century, affecting the prosperity of all the developed parts of England. This, together with Henry VIII's other preoccupations at home, in Ireland, and on the European mainland meant that the promotion of exploration and discovery was of little interest to him. When Sebastian Cabot slipped back from Spain for a few months in 1521, he was quite unable to convince the London merchants that a cloth market of major dimensions might be developed with Asia by way of the supposed Northwest Passage. Intellectuals like Thomas More were excited by the new and enticing future opening up overseas, and a More connection, John Rastell, got two ships to sea in 1517 for a reconnaissance, with a view to an English colonial settlement in North America. However he got no farther than Ireland, as his crews would not brave the open ocean.

The Spanish conquests in the New World were surely much talked about at Henry's court. After hearing of French and Spanish reconnaissances of North American shores in 1524 and 1525, the king sent out John Rut with two ships in 1527 to do something similar, but one ship was lost approaching the ostensible Northwest Passage and the other coasted all the way south to the Spanish Caribbean islands. The latter ship returned in 1528, presumably making it clear (though we have no systematic record of the voyage) that no obvious advantages seemed to be derivable from coastal contacts with North American peoples and that, in any case, Spain, part of the great European empire of Charles V, whom Henry did not wish to antagonize, would resent the intrusion into the Americas of any other European state except, to a limited extent, Portugal. The fishery at Newfoundland did continue to attract some English ships, but there was no colonization. A few private trading voyages from Plymouth and Southampton were also made to Brazil in the 1530s and 1540s, to acquire brazilwood, but they had little wider effect.

A change in outlook and activity took place under the boy king, Edward VI. Sebastian Cabot returned from Spain to find a greater interest at court and among London merchants in overseas activities, an interest enhanced by the collapse of the Antwerp cloth market in 1550 owing to overproduction of finished cloth in the Netherlands. Merchants launched trading ventures to Morocco beginning in 1551 and to West Africa starting in 1553 to breach the Portuguese monopoly of trade there. In 1553 London merchants chose the Northeast Passage as the preferred route for a northerly approach to Asia. In that year Richard Chancellor made his way past the North Cape. Chancellor reached Saint Nicholas (Archangel), where he went on to Moscow to receive trading privileges from Ivan IV. Plans were also being made for an intrusion into the Amazon Basin while English vessels made ready for direct voyages, through the Mediterranean, to the Levant.

The accession of Mary and her marriage to Philip of Spain resulted in a cessation of officially sponsored African voyages (though it did not prevent their taking place); nor were any American ventures attempted. However, the Russian venture was heartily approved and the Muscovy Company chartered in 1555, opening up the possibility of diplomatic contacts with the czar. At the same time, Richard Eden, in 1553 and 1555, produced the first two books with effective translations from German and Spanish sources that brought tangible pictures of Spanish achievements in the New World before an English readership. He even had the audacity to propose that England should occupy parts of North America, though well outside the Spanish sphere.

ELIZABETHAN ENGLAND AND THE BEGINNINGS OF EXPANSION

With the accession of Elizabeth I in 1558, the prospects for English overseas expansion slowly improved. In the early years of her reign, Elizabeth could not afford seriously to offend Philip II of Spain. Nevertheless, she was willing to offer some cooperation to Huguenot elements that were reaching out to provide overseas refuges for their adherents in the event of a radical Catholic offensive against them at home. These Huguenots were also anxious to annoy Spain overseas and attack her possessions if opportunity offered. They were soon to sponsor piratical attacks by small vessels on Spanish commerce in the Caribbean, profitable sport in which many Catholics later participated and into which the English were gradually drawn.

In 1562 John Hawkins attempted to sneak into the slave trade between West Africa and the Spanish Indies, an effort that was a commercial success but a diplomatic failure, as Spain ordered him out of the Caribbean region forever. While he was away a plan was developed in England, with the queen's tolerance, for an English expedition to go to the aid of the first French pilot colony in "Florida" (actually in South Carolina). Thomas Stukely set out in command of the expedition in 1563, aided by a pamphlet by the French promoter Jean Ribault, but as it happened his ships made no attempt to reach America. In 1564 Hawkins tried again, this time by trading with Caribbean towns. On his way home in 1565, he called at the second French colony, this time on the Saint Johns River in Florida, which enabled a few Englishmen to see for themselves some of the more delectable features of that part of North America. By 1567 the queen was feeling more secure on her throne and allowed Hawkins to hire an old warship, the *Jesus of Lübeck*, as part of his squadron for a third venture to the Caribbean. This time he found the Spanish ports intimidated by the authorities into refusing his slaves and cloth, so

that he had to abandon most of his slaves on shore. Sailing westward, he had to put in at Vera Cruz to try to get the *Jesus* repaired, but the powerful treasure fleet from Spain caught him there. After a fierce fight he had to abandon the *Jesus,* but he took off most of her crew on the *Minion.*

The Rivalry Between Spain and England

This confrontation of England and Spain in the New World was a turning point in Anglo-Spanish overseas relations. Elizabeth let loose a number of pirates to prey on Spanish shipping and intercepted a cargo of bullion borrowed by Philip to pay his troops in the Netherlands. There the Spanish were pursuing a policy of severe repression of provincial liberties and Protestant beliefs, and the English queen had been indirectly assisting the rebels. Subsequent tensions did not lead immediately to open war, however, and in 1573 a truce was arranged, leading to the Treaty of Bristol in 1574. In the interim Francis Drake had been leading annual expeditions into the Caribbean, doing much minor damage to Spanish shipping and the smaller settlements. In 1573 he contrived, with some Huguenot aid, to capture an appreciable amount of the bullion being transported by mule train across the isthmus of Panama to Nombre de Dios for carriage to Spain. The queen profited by the transaction as did Drake, but Philip, though tempted to do so, was unable to take drastic reprisals. By this time, too, the Muscovy Company was an established institution. Ships were going intermittently to West Africa for gold and malaguetta pepper, and a number of vessels continued to reach Italian ports and proceed in a few cases directly to the Levant.

It was during the 1570s that England was awakened gradually to the prospects of more active intervention overseas. Spain's empire was shown to be vulnerable, and news filtering through suggested that contacts with supposedly Portuguese-dominated Asia might not prove unfruitful. Richard Eden was the pioneer in this field, but the real inspiration for a wider outlook and an effective commercial imperialism came from the lawyer Richard Hakluyt, who ran an information service to businessmen based on a carefully constructed network of correspondents ranging from India to Mexico. His mainstay was pointing out to merchants new markets and new sources of goods, but he gradually recognized that the installation of trading posts, followed by colonization by England of much of North America, was the best hope for long-term English prosperity. Hakluyt foresaw that settlements would provide new markets and sources of raw material and usefully employ the underemployed of the English towns.

The queen was gradually being made aware of the opportunities to be found in North America and that dominance in the western continent would enlarge and strengthen her power. Among the pamphlets that heralded the new approach to colonization, Hakluyt's *Divers voyages touching the discoverie of America* (1582) demonstrated how little could be found in English and continental printed sources on the New World. Still, it was valuable to promoters to get what was known into print, and from 1582 his younger cousin the Reverend Richard Hakluyt became (and was to remain) the primary propagandist for the new overseas objective.

The Early Irish Experiments

There was an Irish background to the growth of an English colonial and imperial policy. Garrisons were established in King's and Queen's counties in Mary's reign to protect the settled area around Dublin, and a few soldier-families settled near them. The soldiers were reinforced in 1563, but it was only after a northern rebellion (1565–1567) and a more serious one in Munster (1569–1573) that colonization became a prominent item in Irish affairs as seen from England. The queen regarded the lands of the former earldom of Ulster as somehow detachable from the Dublin administration, and under the prompting of Sir Thomas Smith, her secretary of state and a former associate of Richard Eden's, she agreed to invest his son with territorial rights in eastern Ulster. His attempt to colonize the Ards Peninsula began in 1572 but proved a failure after a little more than two years. However it set in train a larger project, attractive to many courtiers, to send the sixth earl of Essex to Antrim to expel intruding Scots and to establish a colony. Essex was militarily successful but the initiative ultimately failed.

As early as 1568, Sir Henry Sidney had recommended the confiscation and colonization of central and western Ulster to subdue the region and had sent young Humphrey Gilbert to urge the queen to undertake this as a state commitment. Wisely, the queen declined. Thereafter any parts of Ireland affected by local rebellions were slated for colonization to replace recalcitrant landowners. Both Gilbert and Richard Grenville were involved in the suppression of the uprising in Munster (1565–1573), and Gilbert drew up a series of plans for settling Englishmen from the southwest of England along the maritime fringes of southern Ireland, but to no effect whatever. Events in Ulster were suggesting caution in colonial investment. By 1577 all projects for Irish "plantations" seem to have been dropped; comparable plans now appeared for settling North America. For the time being, however, such plans were overshadowed by the Northwest Passage mirage and an abortive gold rush.

In 1576 two small vessels under Martin Frobisher sailed to about 63° north latitude and came to believe they had found a passage through the then ice-choked Frobisher Bay in Baffin Island. This aroused interest and also some scepticism in England. But a specimen of rock brought back from an island in the bay, analyzed in London as containing a high proportion of gold, turned exploration into a gold rush. Numerous ships and miners reached Baffin Island in 1577, excavated considerable quantities of hard metamorphic rock, and brought it back to England. The Company of Cathay was chartered and the queen even risked £1,350 in a 1578 venture. A fleet of fifteen vessels was engaged, most of which duly returned with some two hundred tons of rock. But by this time, enough of the earlier rock had been processed to discover that it contained mica and iron pyrites but no gold whatsoever. The whole project bankrupted many of those who had organized it. It also put gold hunting very low in the promotional literature for expansion.

Frobisher, driven south on his outward voyage, had discovered and entered Hudson Strait. This emboldened the remaining Northwest Passage enthusiasts to set further ventures going. John Davis made three important geographical exploratory voyages from 1585 to 1587. Though he was unable to enter Hudson Strait against the summer current of melting ice, he did discover that open water could be found as far as 73° north latitude. The whole area, bounded by what was soon known as Davis Strait, could now appear reasonably accurately on the map. No further ventures were made to the area until 1602.

Pamphlets describing the Frobisher voyages and a book with engraved depictions of Eskimo (Inuit) brought to England put her on the map as a would-be expansionist imperial power. But the Frobisher fiasco frightened off the big money of the London mercantile elite and the major aristocrats of the court, with the consequence that the earliest overseas colonizing efforts were starved of capital. At the same time, there was a good deal of money in smaller units to be gathered from courtiers and gentry who were accumulating cash by selling land. Some investment capital was also available in the outports like Southampton and Bristol, which were making a bid for survival and redevelopment in the face of the growing dominance of London commerce. Thus the propaganda offensive, which began after Sir Humphrey Gilbert gained his patent in 1578 to acquire land overseas and exploit it, played into the hands of the small expansionist group, headed by Sir Francis Walsingham, who had become secretary of state and was stoutly anti-Spanish and pro-expansion.

Gilbert's first expedition (1578) was underfinanced and held together by dubious piratical interests who saw in it an excuse to put their money into a venture that might benefit them rather than Gilbert. And so it turned out: the major part of Gilbert's fleet deserted him at the first opportunity. His own vessels failed to venture into the ocean (except for that commanded by the young Walter Raleigh, his half-brother). To recoup his fortunes, Gilbert turned to a share-pushing device which was well in advance of its time; namely, offering for sale large sections of land, sight unseen. Ignoring the existence of a settled society already in occupation, Gilbert was prepared to sell portions of eastern North America to any individual or group that put up a reasonable sum of money. Of these, many gentlemen, a few merchants—notably those of Southampton—and a large number of Catholic gentry were promised virtual autonomy in America if they subscribed.

But Gilbert was unlucky as well as unskillful. He failed to get to "Norumbega" (modern New England) in 1582 because of difficulties with his backers and adverse winds that prevented his ships from leaving the English Channel. In 1583 he did set out to survey the American coast from Newfoundland southward, and in August 1583 he formally annexed Newfoundland to the English Crown and proceeded to enact laws and sell fishing grounds to foreign shipmasters, a system he had no means of enforcing once he sailed away. On his forced return voyage, necessitated by the loss of his flagship, the *Delight*, he was lost at sea, and the *Golden Hind*, under Edward Hayes, alone returned to sing the praises of Newfoundland. The Catholic group, threatened by Spanish and Roman Catholic agents that they would be massacred if they intruded on Spanish-claimed territory, withdrew from the enterprise early in 1584. The first systematic plan for English intervention in North America came to an ignominious end.

Roanoke Island

It so happened that two major colonizing ventures were to follow almost immediately upon this setback. On the one hand, Walsingham backed Walter Raleigh's determination to carry out a plan comparable with that of Gilbert's but on a smaller scale. On the other hand, at about the same time Lord Burghley, the lord treasurer, was involved in planning a much wider scheme for English settlement in Munster. The individuals involved in them—in the case of Raleigh and Sir Richard Grenville in particular—were the same people, though the Munster plan, based on the confiscation of estates from those Irish and Old English landowners who had rebelled in 1579, proceeded at a much slower pace.

In April 1584 Raleigh got a reconnaissance expedition to sea. It was to locate a site for a colony in warmer territory, not too far to the north of the Spanish sphere, which was approximately modern Florida and South Carolina. Philip Amadas and Arthur Barlowe located the Carolina Outer Banks and eventually an island, Roanoke, in the sounds behind them. They considered it suitable for a settlement, especially as the inhabitants welcomed them and indicated they had no objection to their return with companions. It was a good location for a small survey party but a bad one for shipping, as there was no shelter on the Carolina Outer Banks and the sounds were too shallow for any sizable ships.

At the same time Richard Hakluyt, the younger, was sent to France as chaplain and secretary to the English ambassador to pick up French information on the New World. He was called back to England in the summer of 1584 and told to place before the queen all he had learned about North America as well as to set out the economic and strategic advantages to be gained by English colonization. The hope was that he could induce the queen to support further ventures by Raleigh. Hakluyt finished his "Discourse of Western Planting" by early autumn and presented it to Queen Elizabeth early in October. It was a private and confidential document, though a few copies were made for the principal associates in the North American venture. It brought only a very limited immediate response from the cautious queen: a knighthood for Raleigh, a royal ship, and some supplies, but no overall help or assumption of rights, except for the acceptance of the name Virginia for the colony to be.

Raleigh, a member of Parliament, contrived to get a committee of rich and influential members to consider a bill to enshrine his patent in a statute that the queen would not allow, any more than she would permit Raleigh himself to go to America. But it obtained for him the support of a group of wealthy and influential gentlemen, mainly from the west country, who put up much of the money for the expedition. This was planned for some five hundred colonists, an absurd number for settling Roanoke Island. Sir Richard Grenville, who led the expedition, arrived in July 1585 with little more than one hundred settlers, whom he placed in a hastily constructed strong point and village on the part of the island assigned to them by the local chief, Wingina. There were some gentlemen among the party who proved a drag on its activity, as well as a number of soldiers, among them the governor Ralph Lane. The significant people were Thomas Harriot, entrusted with investigating the inhabitants and executing a detailed map of the region, and John White, a skilled artist and cartographer, together with a metallurgist, Joachim Ganz from Prague.

Harriot and White carried out a boat and land survey of the coast and interior to the southern shore of Chesapeake Bay so as to locate a deep-water harbor, which they did, and also to find a location where a substantial colony might be accommodated without disturbing the local inhabitants. In the meantime, demands on the Indians for corn led to friction and ultimately open antagonism. When Lane tried to make an expedition into the interior via the Roanoke River in March 1586, he not only had to work his way against a river in spate but was also nearly starved out by the people he had antagonized. By June no relief had arrived, and the colony was in danger when Sir Francis Drake appeared from his major Caribbean raid and found the colonists only too willing to go home, which they did at the end of July. Grenville's relieving force arrived too late and left no colonists—just a small military holding party that was soon driven off by the Indians. From this point onward Walsingham's interest in the project weakened, and Raleigh, for the time being at least, confined himself to only a minor part in its subsequent development. The major part of the project's subsequent development was the work of John White and Thomas Harriot.

A group of small farmers and members of the lesser London companies with their families were brought together, incorporated as the City of Ralegh, and a first party was dispatched to Chesapeake Bay in the spring of 1587. Though White was governor, Simon Fernandes, a Portuguese pilot, took over control of the expedition. When it put in at Roanoke Island to pick up the men left by Grenville in 1586, they were nowhere to be found, and Fernandes refused to allow the settlers to continue in the ships to Chesapeake Bay. The main body was left to proceed overland, while a smaller party was stationed on Roanoke Island to await White, who had been persuaded against his better judgment to go home, return with supplies and reinforcements, and be guided by the people left at Roanoke to the colony's new site. Bad organization and harassment by pirates prevented White from returning to Roanoke Island in 1588 and, for some reason, no ships set out for the settlement in 1589. In 1590 a privateering squadron agreed to take White to Roanoke Island and to escort a supply ship to the colony after its Caribbean campaign was over. He reached the island but found it deserted, with indications that the holding party—probably scared away by a Spanish exploring party in 1588—had gone fifty miles

(80 kilometers) south to the village of the friendly chief, Manteo, leaving no indication of where the main body had settled. White could not persuade the privateer captains to convey him to this village, so he returned to England, having abandoned the colony. The lost colonists were presumed to be somewhere in Virginia. This enabled Raleigh to retain his patent, which was due to expire in 1591 unless a colony was in existence. Nothing was done for some years to attempt to make contact with it.

Its members, it is now known, had settled alongside the Chesapeake tribe in the fertile area in what is now southern Virginia, having no contact with England but mingling with their Indian neighbors, for some nineteen years. Then Powhatan, the ruler of the greater part of the Chesapeake Bay area, had them and their Indian hosts massacred about 1606 because he feared further English intervention. This was in fact to come in 1607, and had been heralded by one or two reconnaissance vessels that had entered the bay to trade in earlier years.

The importance of the Roanoke voyages can easily be exaggerated but they left a residue of experience that was not forgotten. Richard Hakluyt kept the achievements of the ventures alive in his *Principall Navigations, Voiages, and Discoveries of the English Nation* (1589). In its second edition of 1598–1600, it became a reference book for later enterprises. What had been saved by White and Harriot, though they lost most of their survey materials on hastily leaving Roanoke Island in 1586, enabled Harriot to complete his famous tract, *A Briefe and True Report of the New Found Land of Virginia,* in 1587. It was published in 1588, while White had preserved a portfolio of his drawings, a set of which he prepared for one of the important men of the time and which has fortunately survived together with other items that were copied in his family. Hakluyt was instrumental in getting Theodor de Bry, on a visit to England, to take the Harriot text and a group of the White drawings to Frankfurt, where he published them in four languages in 1590 as *America,* part I. This gave the venture a European currency and provided a groundwork for many later works on North America.

The Munster Plantation

At the same time the Roanoke venture struggled and foundered, the Munster plantation, in southern Ireland, was under way as the first state-organized colonial venture. The land confiscated was supposed to be cleared of Gaelic Irish and was divided up into substantial seignories, the holders of which were required to plant specified numbers of English farmers. Interspersed among them were estates of Old English landlords who had been innocent of rebellion and who retained Irish tenants on their lands, so no coherent network of seignories was established. In any event the technical resources of the state were not sufficient to lay out the seignories efficiently, though Raleigh was given more land than any other, and Grenville received a favorable location on Cork Harbor. Both men, working through agents, did their best to fulfill their obligations, and this diverted them from full attention to their transatlantic commitments. Raleigh eventually leased much of his land in blocks to London speculators who let their lands to Irish tenants. The latter soon appeared on even the best planted seignories and provided labor for construction and farming, since there were too few English to do so. The end result was that a few seignories flourished and passed muster when government inspectors visited them, while many others did not. So the Munster plantation remained a patchwork, even though at least five hundred to six hundred men and women were settled, an appreciable achievement.

In the end the plantation proved more vulnerable even than would the Virginia settlement at Jamestown. In 1598 a new wave of insurgency by both Irish and Old English swept away almost all the planters. Military action soon cleared many of the seignories, and reconstruction was well under way by 1603. But many landowners did not return, nor did their tenants. Raleigh, from 1598 onward, was concerned to rid himself of his commitments in Ireland and did so. Grenville was killed in 1591. The plantation was ambitious and came within sight of being a major success, but its failure to grow and stabilize revealed both the limited impulse of English people to emigrate, even to Ireland, and the limitations of state power to maintain and supervise a systematized colonial development even so close to England.

To treat the ventures of Gilbert and Raleigh before discussing Francis Drake's circumnavigation may seem inappropriate, but his expedition docs not fit easily into a purely chronological sequence. Drake equipped a small squadron, mainly from the enterprising southwestern mariners, and set off in 1577. He had some semi-official status in that he was supposed to explore for Walsingham and the rest of the expansionists to determine whether there was land in what is now Argentina and Chile, unoccupied by Spain, that might suit English settlers and traders. But all sorts of other objectives had been discussed. Was there a great unknown southern continent as yet untouched? Was there a western opening (as many printed maps showed) from the Northwest Passage?

Drake's own objective was to rob Spain's American Pacific shore and take revenge for his defeat of 1568. He surprised the Spanish after passing through the Strait of Magellan but was then blown far enough south to erase the idea of the southern continent from his own mind, if not from the minds of subsequent geographers. He also established that passage around what was to be named Cape Horn was practicable. He had cursorily examined the eastern and western regions of South America, as instructed, and dismissed them as unsuitable for English settlement. He collected a substantial amount of plunder along the coast but found the main treasure fleet at Callao still unladen. However, after a long chase he overcame the bullion-laden *Nuestra Señora de la Concepción* (alias *Cacafuego*) just north of the Equator. This gave him all the bullion he could carry in his two ships, though he lost one of them shortly after, which cut down his final haul.

Faced with the problem of returning to England, he made a foray northward in case an opening to the Passage appeared by the time he reached 48° north latitude. As it did not, he then turned eastwards to find a place to rest and re-equip on the California coast (Drake's Bay, behind Point Reyes, and San Francisco Bay are contested sites as his landing place). He found masses of seals and other sea mammals to store for food as well as helpful Native Americans, so that he was able to leave in six weeks. Before doing so he named the territory New Albion in case England needed an excuse to claim territory if ever a Northwest Passage voyage proved successful. He had Spanish charts for the Pacific Ocean and he made the crossing successfully though at some cost to his men. His progress through the Philip-

pines and the Indonesian islands was dramatic. He bought cloves at Ternate Island in the Moluccas and promised the ruler English aid against the Portuguese, while on the south coast of Java he got aid from an anti-Portuguese ruler, enabling him to make the incredibly long voyage to Sierra Leone and thence home in September 1580. Drake, knighted by the queen, became a popular hero.

His success led Thomas Cavendish to emulate him successfully in 1586–1588, his main prize being one of the Manila galleons that crossed annually from Asia to Mexico. After the Armada campaign, he eventually sailed up the Thames to great éclat and with substantial gains, though not comparable to those of Drake. Three subsequent attempts to follow the good fortunes of these two ventures, one of them, Cavendish's own, between 1589 and 1593, came each to a tragic and unsuccessful end. Spain's protective measures over her Pacific territories discouraged any further attempts. But Drake's circumnavigation, the first after Magellan's, deserves detailed treatment, as it was the first major blow to Spain's hitherto untouched, unchallenged dominance in the Pacific. Also alarming to Spain was news of Drake's contacts with anti-Portuguese islands in the Spice Island group. The voyage was the first indication that England might be able to mount a significant challenge to Spanish-Portuguese dominance of contacts with the extra-European world.

Open Conflict with Spain

The situation that moved England further toward direct conflict with Spain requires careful consideration. The Treaty of Bristol (1574) never worked effectively. English merchants were hampered by administrative restrictions on their trade with Spain and Portugal (conquered by Spain in 1580). The cloth trade had to abandon Antwerp but found new bases at Stade, Hamburg, and, eventually, at Middelburg through which the trade could be maintained, if at a lower level. On the other hand, the loss of the Antwerp trade (it finally fell into Spanish hands in 1584) meant that specialized exotic goods from overseas were not reaching England by their traditional Netherlands or Iberian routes. This, in turn, led English capitalists and shipowners—who were expanding the merchant marine—to seek the new markets and sources of supply in the Levant, West Africa, the Americas, and Asia. At the same time a growing wave of piracy in the Caribbean, accentuated by the expulsion of the Spanish ambassador in 1584 for plotting against the queen, led to growing exasperation in Spain, so that in May 1585 all English shipping in Iberian harbors was impounded.

England responded by releasing several hundred armed merchant ships to pillage Iberian vessels wherever they were to be found and, in particular, to raid the Caribbean in increasing numbers. Moreover, a revenge expedition under Drake was organized among the queen, London merchants, and aristocratic courtiers. In the autumn of 1585 it sacked Vigo in Spain, destroyed Santiago in the Cape Verdes, and overawed two of the main Spanish ports in the Caribbean, doing much damage and acquiring ransoms at Santo Domingo and Cartagena in response to threats of complete destruction. In neither case, however, were any major supplies of bullion found. Fever and problems with provisions thwarted plans to cross the Isthmus and take Panama and to attack the well-defended vital hub of Spanish commerce, Havana. And though he did not capture the garrison, Drake did proceed to destroy Saint Augustine. He went on to warn the Roanoke colonists of an impending Spanish attack and brought them home safely along with most of his original fleet.

This display of naval strength, only partly successful though it was, was sufficient to finalize Spanish plans for a Great Armada that, in cooperation with land forces from the southern Netherlands, would bring England to her knees. The fortunes of the Great Armada were mixed. It was harassed but not seriously damaged by English shipping which, however, held it off from the coast. At Calais it was scattered by English fireships, and in any event the Dutch were successfully impeding all attempts by the duke of Parma to join his land forces to the Spanish fleet. In fierce fighting in the North Sea the English had the tactical advantage but could not destroy any significant number of the major Spanish ships. When Medina Sidonia was forced to return round the north of Scotland, he was successful in bringing many of his major ships, though battered, back to Spain. But the shores of Ireland were littered with wrecks of most of the lighter vessels with heavy casualties to their crews. Spain was checked in her major objective, and though she never again got an attacking fleet into English waters, she showed great recuperative powers.

Her reinforcement of the Atlantic guardships protected her American treasure effectively on its way to Europe, but even fortification of her major ports in the Caribbean could not curb the irritating and persistent interruption of interisland commerce, which inflicted substantial but not crippling losses on Spanish-American trade. An attempt to do more brought Hawkins and Drake to lead a major attacking force to the Caribbean in 1595. However, it failed to capture Puerto Rico, where much gold was stored. Hawkins died a natural death soon after. The fleet then sailed on to Central America with the idea of renewing the attack across the Isthmus to Panama, but there Drake also died, again a natural death, and the fleet suffered badly from disease. Thomas Baskerville brought the remnants of the fleet home with some credit, but it was a major defeat for England. It was also the last major transatlantic attempt of any strength to be mounted with royal assistance.

The Last Stage of the Spanish Conflict

The earl of Cumberland captured and destroyed Puerto Rico in 1598, but there was no gold there at the time. Many other small ventures kept up the pressure in the years following. But as major merchants in London organized the privateering trade, it slowly changed its character, with much more emphasis on bringing home sugarcane, hides, and, ultimately, tobacco and doing some of this by trade rather than by theft. Raleigh's romantic venture into the Orinoco in 1595 in search of a mythical gold-rich "kingdom of El Dorado," produced some evidence of alluvial gold (which was to continue to tempt him down to his last voyage in 1617). It also opened the way to trade in tobacco both with Spanish Trinidad and with the inhabitants of the rivers of Guyana, a region so far almost untouched by Spain and where the first English Caribbean colony was to be attempted in 1604.

The privateering war encouraged the development of tough and durable merchant vessels that played their part in the commercial competition with the Dutch in the postwar years after 1604. It also led to new industries like sugar refining, which helped in the industrializing of the banks of the Thames, already marked by many blast furnaces and other industrial innovations. The precise degree of influence that privateering (piracy after 1604) had on the English economy is not easily quantifiable, but it was appreciable and contributed to the skill and daring of the early, better-capitalized overseas ventures at the beginning of the seventeenth century.

Pamphlets and books, reciting past achievements and providing incentives to new ones, had much to do with keeping the expansionist trend in motion. This was especially true of Richard Hakluyt's *Principall Navigations* in 1589 and even more, of his enlarged, three-volume edition published between 1598 to 1600, which expeditions voyaging overseas could carry with them as a guide over the next generation. But books had a good deal more specifically to do with inspiring the attempts to rival the Portuguese by trading directly to southeast Asia around the Cape of Good Hope. The riches of the few great Portuguese carracks captured during the war were influential, but an even more direct influence was the result of the Dutch voyages of 1595–1597, which had brought rich returns and, more specifically, the 1598 English edition of Jan Huyghen van Linschoten's great handbook to the Far East, the *Discours of Voyages into ye Easte & West Indies.*

The London merchant elite was at last stirred to put together capital adequate to mount a venture that had a good chance of success, the nucleus of what was to become the greatest imperial venture of the English mercantile community: the East India Company. Put together in 1599, it had to await its royal charter until 1600. Its first expedition to the East Indies put to sea in 1601 and was to prove, on its return in 1603 (after the queen's death), that a highly profitable trade could be carried on in this area.

The puny attempts made in 1597, 1602, and 1605 to renew contacts with North America, preliminary to settlement, could not compete with this new engine of empire. The Virginia Company of 1606, for all its seminal achievement in North America, was to remain small and relatively unimportant compared with the East India ventures, until English colonization in America effectively got under way in the latter years of the reign of James I. At least by 1603, though, imperialist thinking was powerful in England, whether it involved trade, peaceful or otherwise, with advanced societies in Asia or the injection of intruding English colonies into North America, with small regard to the societies already established there.

BIBLIOGRAPHY

Andrews, Kenneth R. *Elizabethan Privateering: English Privateering During the Spanish War, 1585–1603.* Cambridge, England, 1964.

———. *Trade, Plunder and Settlements: Maritime Enterprise and the Genesis of the British Empire, 1480–1630.* Cambridge, England, 1984.

Andrews, Kenneth R., and Paul E. H. Hair, eds. *The Westward Enterprise: English Activities in Ireland, the Atlantic and America, 1480–1650.* Liverpool, England, 1978.

Armada, 1588–1988: An International Exhibition to Commemorate the Spanish Armada—the Official Catalogue. London, 1988.

Axtel, James. *After Columbus: Essays in the Ethnohistory of Colonial North America.* New York, 1988.

Brown, George W., and Marcel Trudel, eds. *Dictionary of Canadian Biography.* Vol. 1, *1000–1700.* Toronto, Ontario, 1966.

Canny, Nicholas P. *Kingdom and Colony: Ireland in the Atlantic World, 1560–1800.* Baltimore, Md., 1988.

Hakluyt, Richard. *The Principall Navigations, Voiages, and Discoveries of the English Nations.* 12 vols. Glasgow, Scotland, 1903–1905.

Quinn, David B. *England and the Discovery of America, 1481–1620.* New York, 1974.

———. *Explorers and Colonists: America, 1500–1625.* London, 1990.

———. *North America from Earliest Discovery to First Settlements: The Norse Voyages to 1612.* New York, 1977.

———. *Set Fair for Roanoke.* Chapel Hill, N.C., 1985.

———. *Thomas Harriot and the Problem of America.* Oxford, 1992.

Quinn, David B., Alison Quinn, and Susan Hillier, eds. *New American World: A Documentary History of North America to 1612.* 5 vols. New York, 1979.

Quinn, David B., and Anthony R. Ryan. *England's Sea Empire, 1550–1642.* London, 1983.

Sauer, Carl Otwin. *Sixteenth Century North America: The Land and the People as Seen by Europeans.* Berkeley, Calif., 1971.

Thrower, Norman J. W. *Sir Francis Drake and the Famous Voyage, 1577–1580: Essays Commemorating the*

Quadricentennial of Drake's Circumnavigation of the Earth. Berkeley, Calif., 1984.

Waters, David W. *The Art of Navigation in Elizabethan and Early Stuart Times.* New Haven, Conn., 1958.

Willan, T. S. *The Early History of the Russia Company, 1553–1603.* Manchester, England, 1956.

———. *Studies in Elizabethan Foreign Trade.* Manchester, England, 1959.

Youings, Joyce, ed. *Ralegh in Exeter: Privateering and Colonization in the Reign of Elizabeth I.* Exeter, England, 1985.

David B. Quinn

SEE ALSO **The Age of Reconnaissance** and **British Settlements;** the map accompanying this article.

THE NETHERLANDS

THE PEOPLE OF THE United Netherlands were relative latecomers in the race for empire among Europe's maritime states. Lacking political unity the Netherlands failed to achieve nation-state status until late in the sixteenth century. Moreover in an age of religious zeal and global missionary activity, the Dutch Reformed church played a surprisingly small role in imperial matters. Nationalism arrived in the Netherlands in the guise of war against a foreign oppressor. Its handmaidens were commerce and state Calvinism, but in many ways the emergence of a Dutch seaborne empire was an accident of war, a by-product of rebellion. With its peculiar reliance on national joint-stock companies, its mercantile focus, and its lack of missionary impulse, the Dutch Empire is unique among the empires of Europe in the seventeenth century.

THE EIGHTY YEARS' WAR

The Eighty Years' War (1568–1648) gave birth to the United Netherlands. Part political rebellion and part religious crusade, the war created the Dutch national consciousness. The revolt against the Hapsburg dynasty forced an examination of the basis of nationhood, while the cruci-

ble of war fashioned a political union, the Union of Utrecht (1579), that recognized local autonomy and created a federalist state of seven independent provinces.

The war gave birth to the nation. Remembered in song and verse, preserved in monuments and folklore, it created a nationalism that drew its inspiration from a perceived sense of common history. In an epoch scarred with religion and saturated with the blood of religious martyrs, Calvinism played an important role as a unifying force. But it had not always been so.

In the beginning of the rebellion, Protestants were much less numerous in the provinces of Holland and Zeeland (the center of the northern revolt) than in the southern provinces. It was the war that forced a mass exodus of dissenters to the north and created a Calvinist state, but it was war and commerce that sustained the coalition of moderate merchant-oligarchs, the prince of Orange, and radical Calvinists.

The Eighty Years' War was not without interruption. After forty years of war, the longing for peace grew. In 1609 a truce was signed with Philip III of Spain, guaranteeing the independence of the Protestant northern provinces. The truce was not welcomed everywhere, especially in the case of hardline Calvinists, who believed any deal with the Spanish to be a bargain with the Antichrist. Nevertheless after months of negotiations and long debates in the States General, the truce was announced. For twelve years the peace held in Europe, but around the world the old enemies stalked each other and fought many engagements "beyond the line."

WAR AND COMMERCE

The commercial success of the United Provinces sustained the Eighty Years' War. Geographically the seven northern provinces straddled the mouths of several important rivers including the Scheldt, the Maas, and the Rhine, the last affording deep-water navigation into the heart of Europe. Lacking a strong agricultural base, the Dutch were forced to become traders of other peoples' products and to reclaim from the sea the very land they inhabited.

Crucial to the commercial success of the United Provinces was the development of the so-called "mother trade" (*moedercommercie*) between western Europe and the Baltic. By the end of the Eighty Years' War, the United Provinces dominated the Baltic trade, controlling nearly three-quarters of the traffic in grain, between half and three-quarters of the timber traffic, and almost half of the tonnage in Swedish metals. In the other direction, Dutch bottoms carried 75 percent of the salt and nearly all of the wines and spirits from France and Portugal. Over half the textiles imported to the Baltic were manufactured or finished in Holland.

The Baltic trade financed the rebellion and provided the seed capital for most of the colonial adventures of the seventeenth century. It was in the Baltic that young Dutchmen first learned the art of trade and first developed their reputation for parsimony and cunning. Although the trade suffered several setbacks during the Eighty Years' War, it remained the bulwark of the Dutch commercial system.

Amsterdam was at the center of this trade. It had become the boom town of northern Europe. Between 1585 and 1622, Amsterdam grew from a large market town of 30,000 to a commercial capital of 105,000. At least one-third of the population in 1622 consisted of emigrants from the southern provinces or their first-generation offspring. The emigrants, especially those from Antwerp, were key to the city's astounding economic success.

A tax assessment for the city of Amsterdam in 1631 revealed that 160 of the 685 wealthiest people in the city, just over 23 percent, were southerners of Flemish (Dutch-speaking) or Walloon (French-speaking Protestant) origin. Perhaps the best description of the role played by the southern exiles in the success of the northern provinces was penned by the great Dutch historian, Pieter Geyl. "Without the capital of the Antwerpers who had come north after the fall of the town, without their commercial knowledge and relations, Holland, small and in some respects still [a] backward area, could not possibly have risen to the opportunities that were offered her so suddenly."

The geography of the country also played an important role in determining the economy. In the first place, there was very little land available for farming and virtually none suitable for the baronial tastes of a landed gentry. Conse-

quently land prices were among the highest in Europe and so were Dutch land taxes. The result was that many people turned to buying shares in shipping, fishing, or trading voyages, thus providing a relatively stable base of capital drawn from people of moderate means.

The decentralized political system constituted another factor in the commercial rise of the United Provinces. The system had evolved during the rebellion to serve the needs of war and to protect the liberties of the individual towns and provinces. The States General handled foreign policy. By the Union of Utrecht (1579), the rebellious provinces had agreed to meet in a loosely constituted assembly at The Hague with the purpose of presenting a united front to the world. In point of fact, the States General was a league of nations. The seven provincial states were sovereign. In the province of Holland, for example, the states were composed of delegations of representatives nominated by the regents of the eighteen towns. A nineteenth delegation represented the province's nobility. The towns were free to send as large a delegation as they wished, but each delegation had one vote. In Zeeland much the same method was applied, but in Friesland the independent yeomanry controlled the states. In Gelderland the nobility dominated. Various other arrangements were found in the other provinces. Moreover the delegates sent to The Hague were held in check by the highly detailed instructions they received from the provincial states. Any decision of importance regarding the Union as a whole required a unanimous vote in the States General, virtually assuring that decisive action could come only after the attainment of political consensus.

In times of crisis, the States General proved to be ineffective in carrying out the national will or even, at times, in discerning it. On such occasions the province of Holland, which carried 58 percent of the government's financial burden, stepped in to provide leadership, although not always with the approval of its archrival, the province of Zeeland. The third player in the political game was the House of Orange.

The prince of Orange occupied an unusual position among the royalty of Europe. As stadholder (of one or more provinces), he was technically a servant of the merchant-oligarchs who controlled the provincial states and the States General. His position as commander-in-chief of the military made him the object of monarchist sentiment among the nobility. The lower classes, too, appeared to favor a prince of the blood over the distrusted merchant-oligarchs. The coalition was fragile, however. The prince of Orange could not act alone, but he had to act. This points up one of the unique features of the Dutch stadholderate: the stadholders were expected to lead and were therefore considered quasi-monarchs. Thomas Jefferson, searching for an appropriate term to describe the stadholders of the eighteenth century, called them "half-kings." And indeed they were.

When the *raadpensionaris* (chief advocate and highest official of the province of Holland) cooperated (as he did during the time of William I [1555–1584] and again in the days of William III [1672–1689]), the stadholder could act decisively and bring to heel both the States General and the provincial states. But when cooperation was not forthcoming, old feuds resumed.

The result was a coalition government that by its very refusal to define the locus of authority ensured that local autonomy at the provincial and municipal levels would be largely undisturbed. Commerce blossomed in this hothouse environment of war and cutthroat competition.

During the course of the Eighty Years' War, the seven Dutch-speaking, northern provinces succeeding in engulfing most of Europe's trade and a sizable portion of the carrying trade of Europe's empires. At the same time, the southern provinces that remained under Hapsburg control declined commercially, and Antwerp, once the greatest entrepôt of Europe, lay in economic ruins.

Since much of Dutch overseas trade involved poaching in the empires of other nations and outright piracy against the Spanish and Portuguese, the rise of the armed merchant marine meant an expansion of the already large navy. Indeed it was difficult to tell the difference between a Dutch merchant ship and a naval vessel. The former was generally privately owned, while the latter was commissioned with letters of marque or commanded by the admiralty. Both were invariably armed, and the men who sailed them were, if numerous foreign accounts can be trusted, a hard-bitten lot capable of the most daring feats at sea and the most shameful acts on land. But it was their numbers that changed the balance of power in Europe, southeast Asia, and for a while, the Caribbean.

One year before the truce of 1609, a report from the directors of the East India Company claimed that the honorable company had forty ships and five thousand men in Asia, four hundred men and twenty ships off the coast of West Africa, and one hundred ships and eighteen hundred men in the West Indies. Thirty-six years later a pamphleteer bragged that the United Provinces had over one thousand ships suitable as warships and another one thousand armed merchant ships on the high seas. Added to this were about six thousand herring-busses and small boats used on the inland waterways. At the end of the seventeenth century, the East India Company alone maintained over two hundred capital ships and thirty thousand employees, half of whom were sailors.

Dutch naval power was decisive in the rebellion against the Spanish Hapsburgs, and the unleashing of the East India Company's war fleet on the unprepared Portuguese in Asia literally marked the beginning of the eclipse of Portuguese power in the region.

NATIONAL JOINT-STOCK COMPANIES

Dutch colonialism was, from its inception, an activity conducted by the private joint-stock company rather than the state. The *voorcompagnieen* (literally, pre-companies) that sprang up in the wake of Dutch voyages of discovery were similar to English regulated partnerships, although they were based on a Dutch prototype known as the *rederij*, a highly flexible type of cooperative agreement in which a group of investors united to buy, build, charter, or freight a ship.

The New Netherland Company, chartered in 1614 by the States General to conduct trade along the North American coast, was one of these. Organized by Amsterdam merchants to exploit the region of Henry Hudson's discovery, it operated for several years until its charter expired and the West India Company took over the area. Similar *voorcompagnieen* had been organized as early as the late sixteenth century to trade for spices in southeast Asia, to collect salt from South America for the herring industry, to conduct whaling operations along the North American eastern seaboard, and to raid Spanish and Portuguese shipping in the Caribbean.

In the seventeenth century, a process of consolidation of overseas activities occurred as the numerous *voorcompagnieen* were supplanted by two national monopolies, each organized as a joint-stock company and each given the authority to conduct trade and war in the name of the national government. The first and most successful of the national joint-stock companies was the United East India Company, founded in 1602, some seven years before the conclusion of the truce with Spain. When the war with Spain resumed in 1621, becoming part of the Thirty Years' War, the second of the great national joint-stock companies, the West India Company, was founded. By the end of the Eighty Years' War in 1648, the East and West India companies had established a global empire for the Dutch.

The East India Company

The Vereenigde Oostindische Compagnie (VOC or United East India Company) had its origins in the events of the late sixteenth century. In 1585 an Iberian embargo of spices nearly destroyed the Amsterdam spice market, and the thought of another interruption spurred the merchant community to action.

Many Dutch mariners had sailed to Asia in the service of the Portuguese. One in particular, Jan Huighen van Linschoten, wrote about his adventures. He was employed by the Portuguese at Goa on the Malabar Coast of India, the main port of the pepper trade. He reported on the weak fortifications and poor management of the spice trade and urged his countrymen to take up the trade themselves.

Greed was not the only motive driving the Dutch to Asia in these years. Just fourteen years before in 1580, King Henry of Portugal, last monarch of the House of Aviz, died, and Philip II of Spain, Hapsburg monarch of the Netherlands, enforced his dynastic claim to the Portuguese throne (his mother had been a Portuguese princess) with armed force and bribes. The joining of the two crowns spelled renewed military activity in the Netherlands where Philip, enriched by the treasures of two empires, deter-

mined to test the strength of the recently signed Union of Utrecht. As the Dutch moved to the offensive in the Eighty Years' War at the end of the sixteenth century, the Portuguese rather than the Spanish colonial possessions suffered the most persistent attacks.

In 1594 nine merchants pooled their resources and founded a Company of Far Lands in Amsterdam. The company's purpose was to outfit two fleets to penetrate the Portuguese monopoly of the spice trade. Assisting in the planning was none other than Linschoten and Petrus Plancius, a Reformed minister and one of the greatest geographers of the age. Driven out of Flanders by the Spanish, he would play decisive roles in the history of the VOC, the West India Company (WIC), and New Netherland.

The first fleet set sail in 1595, consisting of four ships and 249 men. Two years later, after a harrowing adventure made more dangerous by inept leadership, three ships and eighty-nine men returned. Instead of cloves, nutmeg, and cinnamon (the more prized of the exotic spices), the ships carried pepper, the bulk spice of Asia. Nonetheless the sale of the cargo returned a profit to the merchant shareholders. In 1598 the docks of Amsterdam and other Dutch cities were scenes of mass activity as no less than twenty-two ships chartered by five different companies were readied for sea.

One expedition, commanded by Olivier van Noort, sailed west by the South American and Pacific route, making the first Dutch circumnavigation of the globe. Another, led by Jacob van Neck for the Company of Far Lands, returned with four ships laden with a fabulous cargo of spices. The shareholders received a 400 percent return on their investment.

In 1601 fourteen fleets with sixty-five ships sailed around the Cape of Good Hope. So many *voorcompagnieen* were in competition that they literally bumped into one another all over Asia. Eager skippers prowled the archipelago of southeast Asia bidding up prices and disrupting the inter-island spice trade. Their rich cargoes threatened to flood the market in Amsterdam. The situation was brought to the attention of the States General by concerned merchants as early as December 1597, and in January of the new year their "High Mightinesses" issued a call for the companies to merge.

Although unbridled competition was a disaster for the trade, the idea of monopoly did not set well in the national consciousness. Negotiations continued for months, led by Johan van Oldenbarnevelt, the *raadpensionaris* of the province of Holland. With a well-timed nudge from the prince of Orange, the States General approved the charter of the Vereenigde Oostindische Compagnie in 1602.

The VOC charter gave the directors extensive authority over half the globe. It is fair to say that the government of the United Provinces abdicated its sovereignty in agreeing to the charter of 1602. From the Cape of Good Hope east to the Straits of Magellan, the company exercised all the rights of a sovereign nation. It could conclude treaties with foreign leaders, build fortresses, punish criminals, and set economic policy. The charter also permitted the company to wage defensive war to protect its interests. It was in spirit and actuality a state within a state.

While some investors held back because of the war-making clauses in the charter, thousands came forth with their savings to gamble on the new company. The VOC gathered nearly 6.5 million florins (approximately $64.3 million in 1991 dollars) into its coffers.

The administrative structure of the VOC reflected the particularistic and competitive nature of Dutch maritime capitalism. The company was governed by a board of seventeen directors known as the Heeren XVII (Lords Seventeen). The Heeren XVII administered the affairs of the company and served as liaison to the government. They served, however, at the pleasure of six regional chambers located in the towns and regions of the *voorcompagnieen*.

Under the provisions of the charter, the magistrates of the towns in which the chambers were located had a large role in the appointment of chamber directors, and thus the VOC became almost immediately connected to the merchant-oligarchs of the maritime provinces. The merchant-oligarchs would be enriched by this connection, and they would become staunch defenders of the company monopoly in the years to come.

The Heeren XVII at first envisioned a purely mercantile empire, a system of "factories," or trading posts, strategically placed from the Cape of Good Hope to Indonesia as siphons tapped into the flank of Asia to draw off wealth. Accordingly the directors decided to secure a base for the fleet that would not be subject to arbitrary seizure by local authorities. Since they had already decided to enforce a spice monopoly in the Molucca Islands (part of the so-called Spice Islands) and a pepper monopoly everywhere else, the possession of naval and military bases was prerequisite. This strategy led the company to seize Jakarta in 1619. From there company fleets ravaged Portuguese interport trade, drove first the Portuguese and then the Spanish out of the Moluccas, and in 1641 captured the Portuguese stronghold of Malacca after a six-year blockade.

Malacca was the Singapore of the seventeenth century. Its command of the Malacca Straits, the passage between the Malay Peninsula and the island of Sumatra, through which passed the entire world's trade in cloves and nutmeg, had enabled the Portuguese to dominate the spice trade for 130 years. The fall of Malacca signaled a new order in southeast Asia. In a little less than forty years, the ships of the VOC commanded the seas from the Bay of Bengal to the Spice Islands.

Little attention was given by the Heeren XVII to the issue of settling Europeans in the tropics, the intention apparently being to maintain as small a contingent of employees as possible on station. The sense of color and race, which for cultural reasons may have been stronger among the Dutch and the English than among the Portuguese and Spanish, seemed to have precluded the possibility of a Creole empire in which European men married indigenous women. And while it is true that one governor-general and a few open-minded directors suggested a policy of intermarriage with native women, few others dared to risk the public outcry that an official policy might have created.

Policy or not, intermarriage occurred, and in 1613 the Heeren XVII directed the governor-general to allow pensioned married men and their families to remain in the East Indies as free burghers. The program was not without controversy, and in 1617 new regulations stated that free burghers could only marry native women who were Christian by baptism or conversion. Moreover the children of such marriages were to be brought up as Christians. Somewhat later the Heeren XVII required that native brides have a command of the Dutch language.

The former clerks, soldiers, sailors, and merchants who made up the majority of the free burghers lost many of their rights as Dutch citizens when they married native women. Free burghers and their Asian wives were not permitted to return to the fatherland (and even those who managed to marry a European woman were restricted to a single sea chest of clothing and personal belongings when returning). Such restrictions created a caste of second-class citizens defined by color and race in the second generation.

The lack of planning for settlement in Asia points up one of the persistent problems facing the directors of the VOC throughout its history: few Europeans wished to go, and those who did often represented the dregs of Dutch society. For the storming of a Malacca or for the cruel depredations visited on the peoples of the Spice Islands, such men were indispensable. They were less useful for transplanting Dutch culture to Asia.

The West India Company

The provincial states of Holland discussed plans for a West India Company as early as 1606. The promoter of the scheme was Willem Usselinx. The plan called for a chartered company with monopolistic rights to all trade west of the Cape of Good Hope and east of the Philippines.

Political considerations were crucial in defeating the plan in 1606. Negotiations for the truce with Spain were proceeding apace, and the founding of a West India Company threatened to destroy the hope for peace. Turning a deaf ear to the radical Calvinists who generally supported the idea of a company for the purpose of waging holy war against Philip II, Johan van Oldenbarnevelt, the political leader of Holland, succeeded in shelving the plan. When the debate surfaced again near the expiration of the truce in 1621, a religious dispute overtook it.

The dispute involved two theologians in the university at Leiden. Professor Jacobus Arminius maintained that man possessed free will, thus suggesting that good works were somehow effective in attaining grace. His opponent, Professor Franciscus Gomarus, took a staunchly Calvinist approach to the question, denying free will and arguing the doctrine of predestination. More was at stake than an issue of theology, however.

The Arminians were identified with Oldenbarnevelt and the merchant-oligarchs of the maritime provinces. The doctrine of free will appeared to some to be a theological version of the strict provincial independence advocated by Oldenbarnevelt's party. The stadholder, Prince Maurice, threw his support to the hardline Calvinists, not as a matter of principle but as a matter of politics. The prince's strategy was to turn the dispute over to a national synod scheduled to meet in the town of Dordrecht in November 1618.

The Synod of Dordrecht condemned the Arminian position as heresy and those who held such views as schismatics and teachers of false doctrines. Ministers and theologians who refused to accept the new orthodoxy were barred from any academic or clerical post. They were forbidden to teach children, give public lectures, hold public office, or conduct prayer. Meanwhile Oldenbarnevelt was tried and convicted on a charge of high treason. On 13 May 1619, the seventy-two-year-old statesman, architect of the Twelve Year Truce, was beheaded before a crowd estimated at five thousand in The Hague.

With Oldenbarnevelt out of the way, the plans for a West India Company were reconsidered. After much debate and compromise, the States General approved the charter of the West India Company in June 1621. A resolution was issued in the name of their High Mightinesses outlining the general points of the charter and warning all private merchants who were engaged in trade with the New World to cease and desist.

The West India Company's administration was modeled on that of the VOC. Capital was divided among five chambers: Amsterdam, Middleburg (for Zeeland), Rotterdam, Enkhuizen, and Groningen. The central administration was in the hands of the Heeren XIX, whose responsibilities paralleled those of the VOC's Heeren XVII. The individual chambers conducted most of the company's operations. Chambers were authorized to keep their own books, outfit their own fleets and trading expeditions, establish their own colonies (with approval of the Heeren XIX), and compete with every other chamber. The West India Company, like the VOC, was a compromise between the need to organize nationally and the fear among the provinces that the maritime states of Holland and Zeeland would engross the profits of the Americas and Africa. This decentralized administration, mirroring the jealousies and antagonisms of Dutch society, provided a great deal of independence for the chambers.

From the beginning the question that confronted the Heeren XIX as well as the directors of the chambers was what kind of empire to build. Some directors favored a factory system like that of the VOC that would involve only a minimum commitment of personnel. Others were enthused by the possibility of war in the Spanish main and the opportunity of capturing an enemy fleet laden with gold and silver. They wished to turn the company into an armed instrument for "singeing the king's beard." Still others had a different vision for the empire, favoring an agricultural empire based upon a plantation economy. In the context of the colony of New Netherland in North America it all boiled down to a choice of a factory system for acquiring peltries or a settlement policy for establishing plantations.

Peltries or Plantations for New Netherland.

In 1622, barely a year after the publication of the charter, the States General received a protest from Sir Dudley Carleton, English ambassador to The Hague, complaining about Dutch activities in North America. He revealed his government's concern by noting that "the King's government has lately been informed that the Hollanders have planted a colony in these regions, and renamed the ports and harbors, as is their fashion, and are of the intention to continue trafficking there." At the time the only activity in the area of Henry Hudson's discovery was the trading factories of the *voorcompagnieen*. Since the expiration of the charter of the New Netherland Company in 1618, the fur trade in New Netherland was wide open to the merchants of the fatherland. It is probable that several *voorcompagnieen* sent ships to the Hudson River area in the years 1618 to 1621. The first company vessel did not arrive until late 1623. In the meantime the challenge from the English government and the fear of a possible French plan to exploit the fur trade in the region convinced the directors of the Amsterdam chamber to settle European families in New Netherland.

The transport of some thirty Walloon families in 1624 and 1625 marked the beginning of New Netherland as a Dutch colony. The Walloons were both employees and subjects of the company. It was an awkward arrangement, and the Walloons soon proved to be more interested in their families and small plots of land than in the maintenance of the company's monopoly on furs. The company was in a difficult position as well. Most of its shareholders were impatient for dividends. A simple factory system appeared the less expensive way to extract profits. But issues of imperial jurisdiction were at stake, and the question of colonial claims had to be approached cautiously.

Since the Dutch were relative newcomers in the race for colonies, claims based on first discovery could not support a Dutch empire. Some members of the States General considered the possibility of a commercial alliance with English and French joint-stock companies to further the war with Spain in the New World. The discussion was serious enough to solicit a reply from the Heeren XIX in 1624. The directors informed "Their High Mightinesses" that the plan was not in the best interest of the United Provinces. Only occupation and effective use of a territory should be considered as a basis for a colonial claim. They were precise in their definition of occupation and use: "Any nation who for itself possesses such places, harbors, and rivers . . . and already occupies the same with colonists, cities or forts, containing at least 50 persons from the respective kingdoms and countries sent there, does possess and therefore has exclusive rights to said districts." This view may have been part of the reason for the relatively rapid deployment of Europeans in New Netherland.

Five years would elapse before the directors of the Amsterdam chamber reconsidered the question of peltries or plantations. This time they would experiment with a feudal manorial system. The plan envisioned several estates or patroonships. For settling at least fifty persons, the patroon was given extensive landholdings and the status of a feudal lord, with the right to hold court, punish criminals, grant honorary titles, and oversee the lives of his tenants. The system failed, although Rensselaerswyck, its one instance of success, would live on for centuries. In any case the company had made irreversible decisions. Once Europeans had been settled in New Netherland and once the company had decided to give away land as an incentive for their coming, the directors were committed to defend and govern them.

AUTUMN OF THE GOLDEN CENTURY

Historians have often played the "what if" game in their examination of Dutch history. What if all the Netherlands' provinces had been united, instead of just the seven northern ones? Might the rapid stages of economic development characteristic of eighteenth-century Britain have been possible there? What if the United Netherlands had greeted the nineteenth century with Belgian steel and coal and the water power of the Ardennes? Might Europe have witnessed an industrial revolution in the Netherlands to accompany the magnificent commercial revolution of the seventeenth century? Might the world have witnessed another golden age of Dutch art and culture, another age of Rembrandt? Could the commercial empire founded in the seventeenth century have become a territorial empire on which the sun never set? Such speculations are as hard to answer as they are to resist.

The Dutch Empire was a unique one in many respects. In Asia, where the goals of the VOC could be met by tapping into an existing maritime trade in spices, the Dutch succeeded as did few other Europeans. Along the coast of Africa, where the West India Company arrived late enough to benefit from Portuguese and Spanish experience, the Dutch merchants were highly successful in cornering the trade in slaves.

But in North America and elsewhere, where the contest for empire involved the transplanting and sustaining of large numbers of loyal Europeans for decades as they carved a colony from the wilderness, the Dutch were clearly less successful. Unlike England, whose tumultuous political and religious history encouraged a swarming of folk out of the realm, the prosperity of the Netherlands in the seventeenth century attracted people from all over Europe. Dutch colonies were always hard-pressed for settlers, and in North America far too few Hollanders migrated to New Netherland, compared to the English floodtide of colonists to Virginia and New England. Moreover the West India Company's policies often ran counter to the long-term needs of colonization. The directors were too concerned with the profits of trade to permit the type of local autonomy necessary to attract large numbers of loyal colonists. And finally, one might cite national will as a reason for the demise of Dutch colonial efforts in North America. In the final struggle against Great Britain, the Dutch proved willing to trade territory for commerce. Indeed they had always been willing to do so.

BIBLIOGRAPHY

Bachman, Van Cleaf. *Peltries or Plantations: The Economic Policies of the Dutch West India Company in New Netherland, 1623–1639.* Baltimore, Md., 1969.

Boxer, Charles R. *The Dutch in Brazil, 1624–1654.* Oxford, 1957.

——. *The Dutch Seaborne Empire, 1600–1800.* London, 1965.

——. *The Portuguese Seaborne Empire, 1415–1825.* London, 1969.

Davies, David W. *A Primer of Dutch Seventeenth-Century Trade.* The Hague, 1961.

Geyl, Pieter. *The Revolt of the Netherlands, 1555–1609.* London, 1932.

Motley, John Lathrop. *The Life and Death of John of Barneveld.* 2 vols. New York, 1874–1875.

Schama, Simon. *The Embarrassment of Riches: An Interpretation of Dutch Culture in the Golden Age.* New York, 1987.

Tex, Jan den. *Oldenbarnevelt.* 2 vols. Cambridge, England, 1973.

Oliver A. Rink

SEE ALSO **The Age of Reconnaissance** and **Dutch and Swedish Settlements;** the map accompanying this article.

III

COLONIAL SETTINGS

NORSE SETTLEMENTS

THE VIKING AGE SCANDINAVIANS had a lasting impact upon the peoples of western Europe. Their settlements, commercial ventures, and raids affected cultures from the Russian plains to the Irish Sea and from northernmost arctic Norway to the Mediterranean. During the Viking period (ca. A.D. 790–1100), Scandinavians also ventured across the North Atlantic, settling the Shetland and Faroe islands, Iceland, and Greenland and making a brief appearance on the shores of America. This North Atlantic arm of the Viking Age expansion connected the eastern and western hemispheres, and, for a few years at the end of the tenth century, a single language and culture reached from Kiev to the Gulf of Saint Lawrence.

VIKING EXPANSION ACROSS THE NORTH ATLANTIC

By the beginning of the Viking Age, most of Scandinavia was organized into a maze of local chieftainships. Chieftains were expected to be effective in protecting their clients and aggressive in pressing for every advantage for themselves and their supporters in their struggles with rival chieftains. Traditional law codes (which became increasingly formalized during the Viking period and were written down soon after) and the independence of farmer-clients served somewhat as a restraint on chiefly ambition, but warfare and

blood feuds were still commonplace. While Norway, Sweden, and Denmark were known as geographical terms, nothing resembling a nation-state (even by eighth-century standards) existed in pre-Viking Scandinavia.

As wealth from abroad entered Scandinavia, and as Scandinavian merchants, travelers, and mercenaries learned more of the kingdoms of the outside world, the combination of new resources and new ideas seems to have sparked increased competition among local chieftains and petty kings. Agriculture also prospered as a period of warm climate (now known as the Little Climatic Optimum) lengthened growing seasons in northwestern Europe. Population seems to have enlarged, which led to the settlement of the uplands and the extension of Norse farms into arctic Norway. The expansion of territorial boundaries during the Viking Age provided an outlet for this growing rural population and yielded new territory for the losers in the intensifying struggles among chieftains for dominance.

Ships and Seafaring
Neither a growing population nor competing chieftains would have produced the Viking expansion had the means for overseas travel, trade, and conquest been lacking. Through the efforts of maritime archaeologists, we know a good deal about Viking period ships and their construction. By the late eighth century, Scandinavian clinker-

built ships had reached a high level of perfection, combining lightness and shallow draft with great strength and sea-keeping ability. Viking ships could land on any beach, penetrate far up rivers, and survive North Atlantic storms on the open sea.

While strong and elegant, the clinker-built Viking ships had two significant limitations. They required a long run of high-quality timber (preferably oak) for the keel and naturally curved timbers for the stem and stern pieces. Since this quality timber was absent in the North Atlantic islands, settlers in Iceland and Greenland found it hard to replace oceangoing ships lost at sea. The Viking design also sharply limited cargo capacity—even the *knarrs* (trading vessels) could carry only a fraction of the cargo of the later carvel-built Hanseatic *cogs* that came to dominate European commerce in the later Middle Ages. Viking ships could reach distant points, but they could not carry enough passengers and supplies to ensure a viable transatlantic foothold. Population movement across the North Atlantic thus required a chain of settlements, each providing population and resources for successive ventures westward.

Colonization

Scandinavian North Atlantic settlement was a gradual process taking two hundred years to complete. Norse colonists settled the Shetlands and Orkneys around the year 800 and (according to tradition) Iceland around A.D. 874. Greenland was settled from Iceland by Eirik the Red around 985. Vinland was explored from Greenland and a settlement was attempted by the sons and daughter of Eirik around the year 1000.

Island chieftains who (like Eirik) had failed in local power struggles provided the ships and capital to sponsor further voyages of exploration and settlement. Unsuccessful farmers and dissatisfied younger siblings from successively filled island ecosystems provided the bulk of the personnel. The first settlers in a new land had the ritually important right to name the landscape and the economically vital right to claim the best pasture and hunting grounds. As prime grazing is often patchy and limited in the North Atlantic islands, this initial division of resources set the stage for increasing economic and social hierarchy in later generations.

Decline of the Colonies

During the eleventh and twelfth centuries, the Scandinavian North Atlantic enjoyed modest prosperity. Island populations seem to have stabilized at low levels; Iceland's population was probably between thirty thousand and sixty thousand, and Greenland's was six thousand at most. While state formation was taking place in the Scandinavian homelands, the more distant North Atlantic islands seem to have maintained a somewhat archaic chiefly oligarchy. Christianity had spread as far as Greenland by the year 1000, and most Scandinavians were at least nominally Christian by 1100. Chiefly competition was now conducted through the endowment of churches and monastic houses as well as by the traditional sheep stealing and house burning. In Iceland and probably Greenland, sagas and family histories were being composed, and poets and skalds from the North Atlantic were still in demand in continental courts.

Along with prosperity came the beginnings of decline. Iceland's chiefly dominance struggles had thrown up six great families whose escalating warfare increasingly exhausted local resources. Overgrazing in many areas triggered massive and irreversible soil erosion, turning whole districts into rocky wasteland. After 1250 volcanic eruptions coupled with the end of the favorable weather of the Little Climatic Optimum added to man-made disaster, and increasing numbers of North Atlantic farmers slipped from freeholder to tenant status.

After 1264 Iceland and Greenland became part of the Norwegian kingdom just as that kingdom was about to enter a long period of decline. Their local oceangoing ships long lost, the settlers of the western Atlantic depended upon continental merchants to carry their trade. Icelanders bitterly complained that the promised six ships per year seldom arrived, and it seems to have taken a papal letter five years to reach Greenland. The eastern Atlantic settlements in the Shetlands and northern Scotland were luckier, as they were becoming increasingly integrated into the stock fish trade through the Hanseatic League.

106

The late thirteenth and the fourteenth centuries saw accelerated decline in the western North Atlantic. The onset of the Little Ice Age (ca. 1250–1860 in the North Atlantic) crippled farming, and economic hardship in Norway affected transatlantic trade. Literature declined, and the populations of Iceland and Greenland became locked in a struggle for bare survival. By the later Middle Ages, the Norse North Atlantic was no longer the cutting edge of an expanding European population but a demoralized and isolated backwater.

THE EVIDENCE FOR A VINLAND SETTLEMENT

Yet for a brief period, the possibility existed for a European colonization of North America five hundred years before Columbus. In retrospect a successful settlement in temperate North America would have transformed the Norse North Atlantic by providing all the resources needed for ships, farms, and chiefly excess. Why did Vinland fail?

Documentary Sources

Two sagas, the *Greenlanders' Saga* and *Eirik the Red's Saga,* describe the attempted settlement. They are probably not independent, and the more colorful *Eirik's Saga* was compiled later and is less credible. The sagas have been overused as historical sources for some time—elaborate theories being built upon particular turns of phrase. It should be recalled that these sagas were written down nearly three hundred years after the events were recorded, and they probably compress events and certainly inflate the importance of characters (like Leif Eiriksson) whose ancestors numbered among the writer's patrons.

The sagas describe a series of voyages (initially led by Leif Eiriksson, and never using more than two ships) between Greenland and three localities—Helluland (Flat Stone Land), Markland (Forest Land), and Vinland (Grape Vine Land). Most scholars identify Helluland with Baffin Island in northernmost Canada and Markland with the coast of Labrador just to the south.

Vinland has been placed from Newfoundland to Virginia, but archaeological evidence favors the Newfoundland-to-Gulf-of-Saint-Lawrence region. During the Little Climatic Optimum, wild grapes may have grown along the southern shores of the Saint Lawrence and accounted for its name.

The prose narratives both mention contact with *skraeling,* who are described in various ways, but must be Native Americans. It has been suggested that the skraeling were maritime-adapted Indians rather than Dorset Inuit. Both Native groups were highly skilled marine hunters with long traditions of arctic adaptation. While some trade was mentioned in both sagas, all the encounters with the *skraeling* ended badly, with fatalities on both sides (including Thorvald Eiriksson, Leif's brother), causing the Norse to withdraw to Greenland.

A final settlement attempt, reported in both sagas, was ended by Freydis Eiriksdottir (Leif's sister). After a long winter of cabin fever, she killed all the other women in the settlement with her axe, and the party returned to Greenland.

Archaeological Evidence

Since the 1960s archaeological investigations at L'Anse aux Meadows in northernmost Newfoundland have uncovered the first, and thus far the only, traces of a Norse settlement in North America. Teams led by Helge and Anne Stine Ingstad and later by Birgitta Wallace for Parks Canada have excavated three house blocks and a smithy used in bog-iron extraction. In an article published in 1991 Wallace points to the absence of animal buildings and the abundance of woodworking debris as indications that the L'Anse aux Meadows site was a briefly occupied "gateway settlement" where boats could be repaired and refitted out of range of Indian intervention. Over one hundred radiocarbon dates from the site provide a cluster around the year 1000.

A single Norse coin has been recovered from the Goddard site, a long-occupied Native American hunting and fishing camp on Penobscot Bay in Maine. The site produced no other Norse finds but did contain quantities of chert (a stone used in tool making) from as far away as northern Labrador. The excavators note that the coin could have entered Native American trade networks at any point and does not necessarily reflect a Norse presence in Maine.

A Failed Attempt

While there is still a great deal we do not know about the Norse settlement of Vinland, we know that it failed. After decades of survey, no major Norse settlement on the scale of Greenland or Iceland has been discovered: the Old World plants, insects, and diseases that indelibly mark the post-Columbian contact are absent five hundred years before.

Many first colonization efforts fail, as the later history of North America bears ample witness. The Norse settlers of Vinland were few in number, had limited means, and were victims of some bad luck and some bad judgment. This could be the epitaph for a great number of colonial ventures, but in other cases initial failure was redeemed by persistence and eventual success. In Vinland the initial failure was decisive.

NORSE GREENLAND

Vinland's possibilities were limited by those of its neighbor settlement in Greenland. If Greenland had continued to produce surplus population, and wealth controlled by an elite determined on territorial expansion, later attempts to settle Vinland might have been successful. However Greenlandic population seems to have stabilized early, and its elites seem to have put their patronage into church architecture rather than further Vinland voyages.

Economic Organization

Norse Greenland was the most arctic of the North Atlantic settlements and was always beyond the limits of cereal agriculture. The permanent farms clustered in the two major pockets of vegetation that could support cattle, sheep, and goats. Settlers hunted caribou, birds, and sea mammals. Migratory harp and hooded seals were particularly important, and seal bones make up over 70 percent of some archaeological animal bone collections, and a quarter of the collections even from inland farms miles from the sea. Seals, sea birds, and caribou were probably taken in communal hunts with the carcasses shared among all settlers. This hunting and herding subsistence economy was limited to the restricted pockets of vegetation that provided grazing for the imported European animals. The Greenlandic population seems to have filled all possible farm sites over the course of two to three generations (ca. 1050–1075) and then stabilized. The smaller Western Settlement in the modern Nuuk district contained perhaps one thousand people, while the Eastern Settlement to the south (in the modern Qaqortoq and Narsaq districts) contained up to five thousand settlers.

While the settlements were small, the mixed subsistence economy provided a modest surplus during the Little Climatic Optimum. In 1127 the chieftains felt prosperous enough to trade the king of Norway a live polar bear for a bishop, and so Greenland became the westernmost episcopal see in Christendom. By the mid twelfth century, the settlement boasted a stone cathedral church at Gardar (modern Igaliku) equipped with imported bells and stained glass. The structure was approximately the size of the Icelandic episcopal cathedrals at Skalholt and Holar. Several other stone churches were constructed prior to 1300, as were a monastery and a nunnery. By the end of the thirteenth century, this smallest and most isolated Norse North Atlantic settlement possessed some of the most elaborate and impressive ecclesiastical buildings in the North Atlantic islands.

Economic Hierarchy

Current archaeological data (farm architecture, pasture size, and animal bone collections) indicate that later Norse Greenland was a sharply hierarchical little society with marked gradations in wealth and access to resources. A few large farms occupied the lusher pastures in the valley bottoms, and their inhabitants appear to have consumed quantities of cattle and caribou. A much larger number of very small farms occupied the poorer highlands, the concentration there apparently on seals, sheep, and goats. The bishop's manor at Gardar had space for 100 to 150 cattle, a prosperous second-rank farm might have thirty to fifty, and a typical small farm might have three to five. The effects of the initial division of land and resources in the first settlement period were clearly felt hundreds of years later, since bad seasons affected lowland and highland farms differently. Wealth and authority flowed downhill to accumulate in the hands of the few prosperous farmers, themselves often members of chiefly lineages.

Transatlantic Trade

In addition to a hunting and herding subsistence economy based in the fjords of the southwest, the Norse Greenlanders also carried on a remarkable long-distance hunt far to the north. This northern hunting ground (*Nordrsetur*), around modern Disko Bay, was nearly five hundred miles (800 kilometers) north of the northernmost farm, but it seems to have been visited annually by substantial numbers of Norse hunters. While the hunters took a variety of arctic species, the hunt seems to have focused upon the large walrus herds of the Disko region.

Greenland's major exports were walrus hide and walrus ivory. In 1327 the Norse Greenlanders contributed around 1,333 pounds (600 kilograms) of walrus ivory as a crusade tithe and "Peter's pence" (a tax for maintenance of the papal household). Fragments of the dense maxillary bone around the tusk roots are found on most excavated farms, and the small, peg-like, post-canine teeth were used extensively for amulets and handicrafts. The extracted walrus tusks themselves are virtually absent from Greenland, being too valuable as trade goods to be consumed at home. Unlike their relatives in the eastern North Atlantic, the Norse Greenlanders do not seem to have intensified and commercialized their fishing in the later Middle Ages; instead they continued an earlier pattern of low-volume trade in high-value arctic rarities.

Grain traded for beer, iron, wood, church bells, dyed cloth, and even churchmen were the major imports of Greenland. The last item may have caused more trouble than the first. All the bishops and bishops' stewards in Greenland were foreign-born, and some scholars believe that doctrinal conflicts may have arisen between the local chieftains and foreign clerics imbued with the assertive spirit of Pope Innocent III's reforms. The elaborate church construction programs that consumed so much scarce labor and materials in Greenland may thus have been the product of external conflicts as well as internal competition.

Inuit Contacts

Some time before 1170, Norse hunters in the Nordrsetur had a bloody encounter with Thule-culture Inuit migrating southward from Ellesmere Island in northernmost Canada. The Thule migration began at nearly the same time as the Norse expansion into the North Atlantic, moving in the opposite direction around the pole. These migrations from northern Alaska brought the ancestors of the modern Inuit into the eastern Arctic, replacing the earlier Dorset Paleo-eskimo in Canada. The Dorset had apparently become extinct in western Greenland shortly before the Norse arrived, and so the Norse inherited an empty landscape. The Thule people seem to have been as undaunted by the Norse Greenlanders as by the Dorset people, and their settlements rapidly spread down the coast of western Greenland. By the mid fourteenth century, their winter houses occupied the Norse sealing grounds in the Western Settlement. Norse documents and later Inuit legends record generally hostile but occasionally friendly relations; however few details of the interaction are known.

These Inuit hunters showed interest in the unfamiliar technology of the Norse, acquiring artifacts ranging from woolen cloth to bits of chain-mail armor. Norse artifacts were apparently passed back into arctic Canada, probably moving from hand to hand in small numbers. Inuit objects in Norse contexts are much rarer, and all seem to be nonessential curios. Despite a contact period lasting nearly 250 years, the Norse did not acquire Inuit fur clothing or skin boat technology. Instead they used tiny clinker-built boats lashed together with baleen (in place of scarce nails), and they dressed in homespun woolen imitations of the latest styles from Europe. The Norse also failed to acquire Inuit harpoons and seal-hunting methods, thus denying themselves access to the ringed seals that were to sustain many Inuit communities through the Little Ice Age. Some significant social barriers clearly were being maintained by the dominant portions of the Norse society against any sort of acculturation from the Inuit.

Decline and Extinction

Such conservatism exacted a heavy price. The cooling climate progressively worsened the stock-raising conditions in the two Norse settlement areas, and seal hunting in the communal Norse style probably became less effective. Tied to immobile pastures, farms, and stone churches, the Norse Greenlanders were unable to respond to shifting resources by moving their settlements, as did the Inuit.

The prized connection to Europe also began to fail in the fourteenth century. Fashion shifted away from ivory ornaments in Europe, and the competition of the Hanseatic League and the impact of the Black Death sent Norwegian commerce into decline. Around 1350 the smaller Western Settlement suddenly became extinct, possibly the victim of one last hard winter. After 1378 bishops of Gardar no longer took up their appointments in person. According to a fourteenth-century court case, the desperate Greenlanders were forcing weather-stranded sailors to buy their devalued trade goods. The last written document, dating from 1409, records both a properly observed Christian marriage ceremony and a burning for witchcraft in the Eastern Settlement.

Archaeological evidence indicates that at least some Norse Greenlanders survived to the end of the fifteenth century. The last members of the first European migration into the western hemisphere may have perished just as Columbus set out to begin the second.

COLUMBUS AND THE EIRIKSSONS

The historical contexts of the voyages of Eirik the Red and his children and those of the post-Columbian voyagers were different in several critical respects. The Norse explorers were petty chieftains without significant backing at home. If they succeeded, their ability to exploit success was limited. If they failed, no royal power or joint stock company would prop them up or rescue them. Their ships were small and few, their voyages were comparatively short, their economic resources were meager, and their North Atlantic bases were exceptionally vulnerable to climatic change. The Norse lacked firearms and cavalry and, more important, seem to have lacked the resistance to smallpox needed to prepare the way for their beachhead. When smallpox reached the Norse North Atlantic communities in the eighteenth century, it proved

as epidemic as among Native Americans, killing a quarter of the Icelandic population. The medieval Norse had few military or technological advantages over local Native Americans and (at least in Greenland) were probably less well adapted to local environmental conditions.

Perhaps as important, the Norse discoverers of Vinland held a different worldview than the later explorers. Unlike Columbus and his immediate successors, they were not surprised by a "New World" full of undreamed possibilities. Their cosmology saw a central sea ringed all around by islands and continents of different sizes occasionally connected to an outer ocean by channels of varied width. Vinland was thus just one more strange place around the rim; not a surprise but just one traveler's tale among many. Potential elite sponsors would have seen little adventure or profit in Vinland that could not have been had closer to home in Normandy, Northumbria, or perhaps Sicily, or Mikligard (Byzantium). In the early Middle Ages, the discovery of Vinland meant something quite different than did the discovery of the "Indes" five hundred years later. In a very real sense, Columbus *was* the first to discover the New World we know today.

BIBLIOGRAPHY

Bigelow, Gerald F., ed. "The Norse North Atlantic." *Acta Archaeologica* 62 (1991). Edited conference proceedings containing papers by most active North Atlantic archaeologists. The proceedings include a major new assessment by Birgitta Wallace of the L'Anse aux Meadows site and new theories concerning the Greenland colony.

Gad, Finn. *A History of Greenland*. 2 vols. London, 1970. Although the archaeological information is now rather dated, the first volume remains the most complete treatment of the documentary evidence in English. Volume two provides an excellent survey of Greenland under Danish colonial rule.

Ingstad, Anne Stine. *The Discovery of a Norse Settlement in America*. Oslo, 1977. The original publication of the first investigations at L'Anse aux Meadows. A solid monograph somewhat superseded by Wallace (in Bigelow, 1991).

Jones, Gwyn. *The Norse Atlantic Saga*. 2nd ed. Oxford, 1986. The most comprehensive and best written historical summary of the Norse North Atlantic expansion, including translations of major sagas and an extensive bibliography.

McGhee, Robert. "Contact Between Native North Americans and the Medieval Norse: A Review of the Evidence." *American Antiquity* 49, no. 1 (1984):4–26. An excellent survey of the Norse finds in North America, with an informed discussion of the Native American side of the contact.

McGovern, Thomas H. "The Archaeology of the Norse North Atlantic." *Annual Review of Anthropology* 19(1990):331–351. An overview of archaeological research in the region, with extensive bibliography.

———. "Management for Extinction in Norse Greenland." In *Historical Ecology,* edited by Carole Crumley. Santa Fe, N. Mex., 1994 . A discussion of Norse-Inuit contact and the Norse extinction from both ecological and cognitive perspectives.

Thomas Howatt McGovern

SEE ALSO The Age of Reconnaissance.

SETTLEMENTS IN THE SPANISH BORDERLANDS

SOUTHWEST

THE SPANISH PRESENCE in North America in the area north of the Rio Grande, in what is today the United States, is often divided into three discrete periods: discovery, conquest, and settlement. The period of American "discoveries" begins with the 1492 voyage of Christopher Columbus and ends in 1519, when Hernán Cortés marched into Tenochtitlán, the hub of the Aztec Empire in central Mexico. The defeat of the Aztecs in 1521 ushered in the second period, an era of conquests known for its violent military campaigns. In 1523, for example, Pedro Alvarado ventured south from central Mexico to conquer the Indians of Guatemala and from there, with Francisco Pizarro, staged the 1532 conquest of the Inca Empire in Peru. Hernando de Soto led an expedition to conquer Florida in 1539. And Francisco Vásquez de Coronado's expedition in 1540 vanquished the Pueblo Indians of New Mexico and eastern Arizona.

The epoch of conquest that began with Cortés effectively ended in 1548, when silver was discovered near Zacatecas in north-central Mexico. Energies formerly spent on pillage and rapine were now used to establish the mining

towns of northern New Spain's frontier: Guanajuato, Querétaro, San Luis Potosí, and Durango. From 1548 to the early 1580s, the fierce and nomadic Chichimec Indians who roamed beyond the silver mines effectively curtailed settlement farther north.

The third phase of the Spanish presence in North America was characterized by colonization and settlement. What differentiated this era from the two that had preceded it was the promulgation in 1573 of the Ordinances of Discovery. Prompted by royal concern over the massive decimation of America's Indians, the Ordinances outlawed brutal military expeditions of conquest such as those of Cortés, Vásquez de Coronado, and de Soto and set forth the procedures that would be used to settle Spain's vast American empire.

THE ROLE OF THE MISSION, *PRESIDIO*, AND TOWN

Throughout the Spanish Borderlands, three institutions were used to colonize and settle lands incorporated into the realm: missions, *presidios,* and towns. These usually developed sequentially because all three were controlled by the Spanish state and were used strategically to accomplish specific imperial aims. The missions were used by Spain's monarchs as their first, cheapest, and most highly disciplined line of assault in the pacification of newly acquired territories. Normally one thinks of the missions as fundamentally religious institutions, but in Spanish America this was only partially so. As the result of a 1486 treaty between Pope Innocent VIII and King Ferdinand and Queen Isabella of Spain, known generally as the *Real Patronato,* Spain became the patron of Roman Catholicism. In exchange for control over all church matters, Spain promised to tolerate no other religion in its realm. By virtue of the Patronato, the missions in America were always deemed quasi-military institutions, regulated by the Council of the Indies, and funded by the Ministry of War. They were staffed by priests and lay brothers who were disciplined, who solemnly vowed to obey superiors, who were morally committed to lives of poverty, and who were determined to serve God and king—if necessary, to the death. In every corner of Spanish America, Catholic priests became the vanguard of settlement after 1573, opening new missions that were intended to become Spanish towns.

Once the embryo of a mission community had been established, the religious usually requested military protection for their endeavors. The Crown would respond by sending a few soldiers to establish a military outpost near the mission. As the years passed and/or the particular defensive needs of a locality warranted more protection, these soldier-settler outposts would be expanded into full-blown armed garrisons, or *presidios.* Naturally when a *presidio* of from fifty to one hundred soldiers was established to protect a particular place, a whole range of support functions—food, clothing, manufactured goods—had to be provided. Civilian settlements quite often developed near mission/*presidio* complexes precisely to satisfy such needs. For when a *presidio* had to rely exclusively on supply trains and ships for its daily needs, its existence proved much more costly to the Crown and therefore much more precarious, and it was always shorter lived.

The missions of the Spanish Borderlands were organized primarily to Christianize America's Indians and only secondarily to "civilize" and Hispanicize them. Since Christianity was an urban religion that flourished best in towns and cities, the missionaries favored a developmental scheme that focused first on the conversion of organized Indian pueblos (towns), then on the congregation into towns of widely dispersed Indian settlements (*rancherías*), and finally on the gathering of nomadic Indian bands into settled villages (*congregaciones*).

Three mission types (of occupation, penetration, and liaison) corresponding to levels of urbanization were established throughout the Spanish Borderlands from Florida to California. For example the first *doctrinas* (Indian parishes) in New Mexico among the Pueblo Indians were missions of occupation established among the Tewa (San Juan de los Caballeros, Santa Clara, San Ildefonso) and the Keres Indians (Santo Domingo), whose densely populated towns dotted the Upper Rio Grande Valley. Once these groups were nominally converted, itinerant preachers pushed into pagan areas, forming missions of penetration by concentrating small, dispersed pueblos into larger towns. The missions of the Jémez area in New Mexico—San José de Guisewa and San Diego de la Congregación—were formed in this way, gathering twelve hamlets into two towns. From the missions of penetration, missions of liaison were launched on the remote frontier. If their work was successful, they would eventually become missions of penetration and finally missions of occupation.

The missions were relatively autonomous units that relied on Spanish colonists for their protection and only grudgingly, and at moments of great desperation, for provisions. Theoretically missions were chartered for a period of ten years. But in reality many of them had lives ten times that long. The Crown fully expected that at the end of ten years the Indians living in a mission would be ready for self-government and that, gradually, mission communities would become independent towns. Indeed this became the case when secularization occurred. The tragedy was that all too often the Indians had been ill-prepared for the transition, and their towns quickly lost their corporate identity and character.

Alongside the missions, close enough to offer protection but far enough removed to limit the corrupting influence of civilians on the Indians, were the *presidios,* or armed military garrisons. The *presidios*, often born as military outposts, consisted of anywhere from fifty to one hundred soldiers who enforced Spain's territorial claims, defended against marauding Indians, and often became the population nodes around which civilian settlements and towns eventually developed.

The establishment of a civilian settlement was usually the last step in the evolution of a particular place. In the seventeenth century, most settlements in the Spanish Borderlands were missions; San Agustín (Saint Augustine) in Florida and Santa Fe in New Mexico were the major exceptions. Towns and settlements founded or reoccupied after the 1680 Pueblo Revolt were usually situated closer to military outposts and *presidios* for protection. And particularly as a result of the Bourbon reforms instituted during the reign of King Charles III (1759–1788), which attempted to curb the power and privileges of the church, the missions became less important in the defense and pacification of new lands.

Civilian settlements in the Spanish Borderlands were categorized by size as *lugares* (villages), *villas* (towns), and *ciudades* (cities). A locality's size dictated the structure and nature of the municipal institutions that would be established and, to a large extent, the tenor of urban life. Royal charters of incorporation (*capitulaciones*) for the establishment of new settlements stipulated that once a site with a salubrious climate and an adequate water supply had been identified,

Let it be declared whether the place that is to be settled is to be a *ciudad, villa,* or *lugar* . . . if it be a *ciudad,* it shall have a judge with the title of *adelantado,* or a governor, or *alcalde mayor* [chief constable], or *corregidor* [local magistrate], or *alcalde ordinario* [constable] who shall have universal jurisdiction and together with the *regimiento* [municipal council] shall have the administration of the commonwealth. . . . For *villas* and *lugares* there shall be an *alcalde ordinario,* four *regidores* [municipal councillors], one *alguacil* [sheriff], one clerk of the council and public clerk and one *mayordomo*. (Charles Hackett, ed. *Historical Documents Relating to New Mexico.* Vol. 1, p. 267)

The two largest settlements in the Spanish Borderlands between 1598 and 1821 were Santa Fe and Albuquerque. The population in each never exceeded seven thousand souls. Consequently no settlement in the borderlands ever earned official designation as a *ciudad.* There were several *villas* and many more *lugares.*

All land in Spanish America, including subsoil rights, belonged to the king. The Crown held it in trust until possession was officially transferred to the church for the creation of a mission or to an individual or group of persons for the establishment of a civil settlement. The Crown's lands were known as *tierras realengas y baldías* (royal and vacant lands), and it was from this bank of lands that title to a particular plot was obtained. Spain's monarchs gave *mercedes reales* (royal land grants) to settlers on the borderlands so that the "land becomes their mother and as sons they love, honor, and defend her."

Land tenure in the Spanish Borderlands was organized around three types of *mercedes reales*: (1) community land grants given to a group of individuals who wanted to establish a settlement, (2) individual or private land grants, and (3) Indian or mission land grants that guaranteed Indian towns ownership over the lands they worked and occupied. During the seventeenth century, *mercedes* were given primarily to individuals and to Indian towns. As time passed, particularly during the eighteenth and early nineteenth centuries, grants to communities and to groups of landless and land-poor households became more common. As with the other spoils of conquest, what dictated the amount of land an individual gained as a *merced* was based on the laws of distributive justice that regulated the social body. Society was constituted of upper-, middle-, and lower-status persons, and it was to individuals of the highest estate that most land was given.

The 1573 Ordinances of Discovery and the 1681 *Recompilation of the Laws of the Indies* set forth very precise guidelines on how a budding town should be laid out and its terrain subdivided. Town land grants were at least four square leagues in size (one league was around 2.5 miles or 4 kilometers) and, depending on the specific geographical setting, either oblong or square in form. The first point that had to be established in a settlement was the *plaza mayor* (central square). From there *merced* plots were surveyed in a grid system with straight, parallel streets and rectangular blocks and lots. Though local variations abounded, in general the buildings that surrounded the central square were a church, the *casas reales* (royal buildings, including a residence for the local royal officers, residences for soldiers and their dependents, and a jail-house), a meeting place for the town council (*cabildo* or *ayuntamiento*), and the dwellings of the town's prominent citizens. After space for the public buildings devoted to religious, political, and military purposes had been marked off, the remaining land in a town *merced* was subdivided and distributed to *vecinos* (citizens by virtue of their right to land) as individual building lots ninety feet (30 meters) square.

The buildings that formed the core of a town occupied only a small fraction of the land in a *merced*. At the margins of every municipality were lands that belonged collectively to the town's settlers for their common use. These lands included tracts designated as *ejidos* (commons), as *dehesas* (pasture land), and as *propios* (municipal lands). Finally each *vecino* was entitled to a *suerte* (arable land) lot six hundred feet (180 meters) square for agricultural production.

The precise ways in which the missions, *presidios*, and towns developed and interacted in any one locale were dictated by several factors: the level of social organization of the indigenous population; the Crown's geopolitical motives for colonization; an area's ecological constraints; and the nature of historical interactions among missionaries, settlers, and Indians. Having explored the Spanish structures that established how settlements should be organized, the particularities of the settlement process in each area of the southwestern Spanish Borderlands can come into focus.

NEW MEXICO

The first attempts to settle what became the southwestern portion of the Spanish Borderlands, that area north of the Rio Grande and west of the Mississippi River under the administrative jurisdiction of New Spain's viceroy (as opposed to the southeastern borderlands, that area east of the Mississippi historically administered from Havana), began in the 1580s with several reconnoitering parties to the compact agricultural villages of the Pueblo Indians in the Upper Rio Grande Valley of New Mexico. These villages had been known since Coronado's expedition, but it was not until 1572, when the secularization of the Indian *doctrinas* (parishes) in central Mexico was well under way, that the Franciscan friars expressed a renewed interest in them. Two expeditions were sent to Pueblo country: one, in 1581, led by Fray Agustín Rodríguez, under the command of Francisco Sánchez Chamuscado; the other, in 1582, led by Antonio de Espejo, ostensibly to rescue two friars who had remained among the Pueblos in 1581.

Glowing reports of what existed in New Mexico reached King Philip II, and in 1595 he granted license to Don Juan de Oñate for the colonization of the Kingdom of New Mexico (a vague and extensive area that encompassed all of modern-day New Mexico and Arizona). Oñate's party, consisting of 129 soldiers and their dependents, reached the banks of the Rio Grande, near what is today El Paso, on 20 April 1598. Over the next ten months, Oñate and his soldiers demanded and obtained by force the submission and vassalage of the Pueblo Indian villagers. By February 1599 the colony was secure, though barely whimpering along, low on morale and provisions, repeatedly plagued by starvation, and constantly beset by bickering soldiers. In 1607 Oñate was removed as governor because of his personal and administrative excesses; he was replaced by Don Pedro de Peralta in 1609. One of Peralta's first official duties was to establish the city of Santa Fe, which he did in 1610.

During the first eighty years of Spanish presence in New Mexico, the area's settlement was largely defined by the Franciscan missionary project. Between 1598 and 1660, the Franciscans established about fifty missions to minister to the indigenous population. The New Mexican missions that functioned for more than a few years were: San Juan de los Caballeros (1598), San Gabriel (1598), San Ildefonso (1601), Santo Domingo (1604), Santa Cruz de Galisteo (1612), San Francisco de Nambé (1613), San Lázaro (1613), Nuestra Señora de la Asunción de Zía (1613), San Antonio de Isleta (1613), Natividad de Chililí (1614), San Francisco de Sandía (1617), Nuestra Señora de los Angeles de Pecos (1619), San Cristóbal (1621), San Felipe (1621), San Gregorio de Abó (1622), San Lorenzo de Picuries (ca. 1622), San Gerónimo de Taos (1622), San José de Guisewa (1622), San Diego de Jémez (1622), Nuestra Señora del Socorro (1626), Nuestra Señora de la Concepción de Cuarac (1628), Santa Clara (1628), San Isidro de Jumanas (1629), San Esteban de Acoma (1629), Nuestra Señora de la Purificación (1629), Nuestra Señora de la Candelaria (1629), San Bernardino Awátobi (1629), San Antonio de Senecú (1629), San Luis Obispo de Sevilleta (1629), San Miguel de Oraibi (1630), San Miguel de Tajique (1635), San Marcos (1638), San Bartolomé de Xongopovi (ca. 1641), Nuestra Señora de Guadalupe del Paso (1659), and Las Llagas de San Francisco de los Sumas (1660).

The only Spanish town established in New Mexico between 1598 and 1680 was Santa Fe. In 1610, when the town was founded, Santa Fe counted only sixty Spanish residents. Though at the colony's start the number of settlers totaled two hundred, when it was finally determined that the only mineral wealth that existed in New Mexico was salt, many settlers deserted the province and returned to central Mexico. They had gone to New Mexico seeking fame and fortune but found life on the frontier much too taxing. Those who decided to cast their fate with the budding colony were rugged soldiers—a few had brought their families—who quickly adapted to their new environment. By despoiling the Indians of food and clothing, these colonists "eat and drink and are happy and have no desire to abandon the said land; on the contrary, they want to . . . remain there for the rest of their lives," said Marcelo de Espinosa, a captain in the original colonizing party. The reason these settlers wanted to spend—and indeed spent— the rest of their lives in New Mexico, on the margins of the empire, was the privileges they enjoyed there.

All rights, privileges, and lands that existed in the realm were theoretically the property of Spain's monarchs. Whenever expeditions of conquest and colonization were dispatched to the various corners of Spain's empire, the sovereign spelled out in a *capitulación* (charter of incorporation) exactly what the colonists could expect in return for their labors.

Encomiendas

The soldier-settlers who entered New Mexico in 1598, as well as those who colonized Texas, the Pimería Alta (Arizona), and California in the eighteenth century, were promised lordship over the land by virtue of their subjugation of the Native population. As conquerors they became a dominating class whom the Crown rewarded with (1) *mercedes*—"building lots, pasture and farming lands, and ranches," (2) Indian vassalage in the form of *encomiendas* (tribute grants), and (3) aristocratic titles as "hidalgos of an established lineage, so that they might enjoy the same honors and privileges of hidalgos and caballeros in the kingdom of Castile." These benefits and honors were granted, the Crown stated, so "that a glorious memory may remain of the . . . original settlers."

Lordship over land went hand in hand with lordship over the Indians. The men who became lords on the Spanish Borderlands were "enemies of all kinds of work," said Fray Gerónimo de Zárate Salmerón in the mid 1620s. In this they were not unlike their compatriots in other areas of Mexico, for as Viceroy Luis Velasco stated in 1608, "No one comes to the Indies to plow and to sow, but only to eat and loaf." Given such disdain for physical labor and commerce, the settlers of the borderlands became dependent on Indians and on the tribute Indians were forced to pay for many of their basic needs. In Florida and in New Mexico, the original settlers were granted *encomiendas,* grants of Indian tribute that they received for providing the Franciscans with armed escorts into new missionary fields and for assisting in the conversion of the Indians. Theoretically the *encomienda* was abolished with the promulgation of the New Laws in 1542. But in Florida and New Mexico the institution was sanctioned until around 1693 as an incentive to draw Spanish colonists to these areas. Legal right to *encomienda* became a major determinant of wealth and status on the frontier. *Encomenderos* (persons who held an *encomienda*) not only forcibly extracted payments in foodstuffs and clothing from the Indian towns that had been "entrusted" to them but also illegally appropriated Indian labor and the use of Native lands. This differential access to the toil of tributary Indians distinguished *encomenderos* as a dominant class that exercised its hegemony in economics and politics.

The settlers (*vecinos*) of any town often consisted of *encomenderos* and *moradores*, individuals who did not enjoy rights to Indian tribute; the distinction resembled the Iberian medieval differentiation between *caballeros* (horsemen) and *peones* (foot soldiers). The *encomenderos* seized the best watered lands, the tribute of the most prosperous Indian villages, access to trading activities, and the spoils of administrative posts. Given the rude conditions of life on the frontier, one surmises that in the seventeenth century *moradores* lived from hand to mouth. Nonetheless they cherished the aristocratic status they had been granted as hidalgos, content with the precedence they enjoyed over the Indians and their ownership of land.

The Suppression of the Indians and Growth of Settlements

The yoke of Spanish lordship, which these legal rights ensured, was a particularly brutal one for the Pueblo Indians. From 1598 to 1680, their food reserves were depleted by the colonists, their lives were disrupted by Spanish labor demands, their religious images were desecrated by the friars, and their rituals were suppressed. Many saw their kin driven to the point of death; women were raped and children enslaved. In 1680 the Pueblo Indians formed a confederation and routed the Spanish from the area, a feat that reverberated throughout New Spain and spurred other Indians to similar action. When the fury of the Pueblo Revolt was over, 21 of 33 Franciscan friars were dead and 401 settlers had lost their lives. The 1,946 white survivors of the revolt fled south and regrouped near the Franciscan mission community of Nuestra Señora de Guadalupe, the site of the cathedral of what is now Ciudad Juárez, México, and the population node around which adjacent El Paso (Texas) developed.

Though the Franciscan friars had been catechizing among the nomadic Suma and Manso Indians and the semisedentary Jumano of the Lower Rio Grande drainage since the 1620s, the fruits of their labor had been slight. Indeed the branch and thatched straw huts they had originally constructed for shelter while they ministered to the Indians were not replaced by more permanent structures until 1668, when the grand church and convent complex at Nuestra Señora de Guadalupe was dedicated. In that decade Nuestra Señora de Guadalupe boasted an indigenous convert population of one thousand and a small number of Spanish settlers—probably no more than one hundred. Aside from its socioreligious functions, the Guadalupe mission served as a way station for travelers and as a depot for the supply caravans from Mexico City to New Mexico and from there back to points south.

The arrival of twenty-five hundred New Mexican refugees from the Pueblo Revolt late in 1680 rapidly transformed Mission Guadalupe into the embryo of modern El Paso. On 5 October 1680 three civilian campsites were established two leagues south of Guadalupe mission to house the refugees. The expectation was that these encampments would be temporary, the launching ground for the reconquest of New Mexico. But as time passed and a Spanish foray into New Mexico in 1681 was thwarted by the Pueblo rebels, the camps began to take on a more permanent look. In August 1683 a *presidio* with fifty armed soldiers was established to protect the settlers. By 1684 the Spanish and Indian population gathered in the El Paso area was organized into a mission, a *presidio*, and several municipalities. In these municipalities the New Mexican *vecinos* reestablished their town councils (*cabildos*), appointed municipal officers, and organized town life. By 13 October 1693, when a party of one hundred soldiers, seventy families, and eighteen friars—some eight hundred persons in all—departed El Paso under the command of Don Diego de Vargas to reconquer New Mexico, the *villa* of El Paso had firmly established roots.

Between 1693 and roughly 1700, Spanish authority was gradually reestablished over the rebellious Pueblo Indians of the Upper Rio Grande Valley. Though the struggling colony was racked by smaller revolts throughout these years, for all practical purposes the Native population had been subdued. The walled city of Santa Fe was reoccupied in late 1693 and a *presidio* with an armed garrison of one hundred soldiers was established there. On 21 April 1695, forty-four families left Santa Fe to found New Mexico's second town, Santa Cruz de la Cañada. And by 1706 the kingdom's third town had been established in Albuquerque. In the postrevolt period, only twenty-one missions were reestablished: Acoma, Cochiti, Galisteo, Isleta, Jémez, Laguna, Nambé, Pecos, Picuries, Pojoaque, Sandía, San Felipe, San Ildefonso, San Juan, Santa Ana, Santa Clara, Santo Domingo, Taos, Tesuque, Zía, and Zuni.

Throughout the eighteenth century, numerous censuses were conducted to chart the number of souls in the Christian fold and the growth in the ranks of the king's subjects. No full and accurate count of New Mexico's total population exists before 1746. Yet from impressionistic estimates one can approximate its total population in 1700 at around fourteen-thousand. Over the next century and a half, this population more than tripled, reaching 63,498 persons by 1842, through growth at an annual geometric rate of 1.61 percent. New Mexico's Spanish population totaled roughly eight hundred in 1693. Growing at a geometric rate of 2.66 percent annually, it numbered 4,353 by 1749, 9,742 by 1776, 16,358 by 1790, and 32,000 by 1830. The Pueblo Indian population of New Mexico was estimated in 1679 at seventeen thousand. By 1693 it had dropped to approximately nine thousand, a loss of roughly 47 percent. Between 1706 and 1860, the Pueblo population declined slowly, decreasing from about 9,000 to 6,500.

During the seventeenth century, Spain's presence in what became the United States was limited primarily to the mission settlements in Florida and New Mexico, with a healthy sprinkling of independent ranches here and there and a variety of incipient towns. The missions and towns that were established in these areas were of marginal importance to the empire. They were there primarily to lay claim to the land and to give vent to religious impulses in Spain and central Mexico. By the 1680s, after the successful Pueblo Revolt, different imperatives motivated Spain not only to reconquer New Mexico but also to colonize northern Mexico, thereby creating a defensive buffer for its silver-producing provinces further south. One-third of all the world's silver was being extracted from the mines in Mexico's north by the 1680s. The fortification of the northern frontier, first in Texas to check French advances into the Mississippi Valley, and later in California to curtail Anglo-American and Russian expansion, largely dictated the settlement policies Spain promoted in Mexico's far north.

TEXAS

While the Spanish were still smarting from their 1680 defeat by the Pueblo Indians in New Mexico and from defeats further south in the Tarahu-mara and the Altar Valley of Sonora, French and English explorers began to encroach on territory Spain claimed as its own. In 1682 Robert Cavelier, sieur de La Salle, led a French expedition from the Great Lakes down the Mississippi River to its mouth. On 9 April 1682 La Salle proclaimed the river, its delta, and adjacent lands possessions of King Louis XIV (they were later to be known as Louisiana), effectively dividing the Spanish frontier in half, into western and eastern parts.

The movement of the French into the Mississippi Valley had an immediate impact on the Spanish settlements of the Upper Rio Grande Valley. The growing presence of French colonists in Illinois and on the eastern edges of the Great Plains displaced the Comanche, Pawnee, Kansas, Wichita, and Osage Indians in a southwestern direction into Apache and Navajo hunting grounds. Enmities had existed between the Apache and Comanche for some time. Now, forced to compete for the same hunting and foraging grounds, pushed even further south by the southwestern migration of various Plains Indian groups, and hemmed in on the west by the Spanish towns and pueblos in New Mexico, the Apache began to raid the Rio Grande settlements with increasing regularity.

The Spanish responded to the French interlopers and to heightened levels of Indian depredations by expanding frontier defenses and fortifying those already in existence. Between 1687 and 1690, nine expeditions were dispatched to Texas to check French expansion westward from Louisiana. In 1690 Don Alonso de León, the governor of Coahuila, established San Francisco de los Neches, a small outpost in eastern Texas. This outpost was reinforced in 1691 with six missionaries and sixteen soldiers, but by 1693 the settlement had been abandoned. Twenty years passed before the Crown again expressed concern over Texas. In 1714, when a French trader from an outpost that had been established in Natchitoches (Louisiana) crossed into Coahuila, enough anxiety was aroused in Mexico City to prompt another campaign to colonize Texas.

Under the command of Captain Domingo Ramón, an expedition of some eighty persons—eleven Franciscan friars, twenty-five soldiers, and forty men, women, and children—was dispatched in 1716 to establish the missions of San Francisco de Los Tejas, Purísima Concepción de los Asinais, Nuestra Señora de Guadalupe de Nacogdoches, and San José de los Noachis, as well as the *presidio* of San Juan. In 1718 the *presidio* of San Antonio de Béjar and the mission of San Antonio de Valero were established. Near this mission and *presidio* the *villa* of San Fernando, the town that ultimately became San Antonio, was laid out on 2 July 1731 in accordance with the 1573 Ordinances of Discovery. On the following day, sixteen families of Canary Islanders who came to settle Texas were each given a house plot and agricultural fields. By 30 July 1731 these colonists had established a town council and appointed *regidores* (councilmen). Another *presidio*/mission complex was begun in 1721 near Espíritu Santo Bay at La Bahí. Though many other sites were established, abandoned, and temporarily reoccupied, only these three settlement nodes survived.

The Indian groups the Spaniards encountered in Texas in the vicinity of San Antonio and La Bahía were nomadic bands (Jaranames, Payaya, Toncahua, Carancahua) that subsisted by hunting, gathering, and fishing. The groups that surrounded the eastern Texas missions (Orcoquisa, Atacapa, Teja, Ai, Adai) were agriculturists who lived in dispersed settlements (*rancherías*) and supplemented their diet by hunting and foraging widely. The mobile way of life of these indigenous groups virtually guaranteed the failure of the Texas missions. No matter how hard the Franciscan missionaries labored, they made little headway in inducing nomads to accept Christianity and settle in permanent towns. Indeed lordship over America's Indian groups was much easier to establish when, as with the Pueblo Indians of New Mexico and Arizona, settled town life was a central feature of their culture. The mobile nature of the indigenous population in Texas also meant that tribute was never demanded of them and the *encomienda* was never established there.

No one knows how many Texas Indians were settled in missions and towns under Spanish control in the early 1700s. So few Indians were induced to abandon their nomadic existence for mission life that what numbers were reported are rather meaningless. In 1740, for example, the friars listed nine hundred Indians living in congregated mission communities. Sixty years later the number of such persons was only seven hundred. The nominally Spanish population, on the other hand, grew rapidly in the eighteenth century. In 1740 nine hundred "Spaniards," many of them from the Canary Islands, resided in Texas. By 1800 this population had grown to 3,550, representing an increase of 290 percent in sixty years, an average annual rate of growth of 0.44 percent. This population was gathered largely at San Antonio and at La Bahí del Espíritu Santo.

ARIZONA

During the colonial period, what is now Arizona was under the administrative jurisdiction of two provinces. The northern half of Arizona, specifically where the pueblos of the Hopi Indians sat, was governed from Santa Fe as part of the kingdom of New Mexico. The southern half of modern Arizona (roughly from Phoenix southward) was under the administrative control of Sonora and was referred to in the colonial period as the Pimería Alta. The Pimería Alta was first explored by Alvar Núñez Cabeza de Vaca in the 1530s and again in the 1540s by Francisco Vásquez de Coronado, who led an expedition into Mexico's far north. Shortly after New Mexico's colonization in 1598, Franciscan missionaries entered the Pimería Alta seeking Indian converts, and by 1642 or so they had established missions among the Opata Indians at Baseral-Bavispe, Guázabas-Oputo, Teuricachi-Cuquiárachi, Arispe-Banámichi, and Cucurpe-Opodepec. The Jesuits, who technically had control over this area, protested to viceregal authorities in Mexico City, and by 1651 the Franciscans had retreated. While some Jesuit missionary activity occurred in the Pimería Alta in the decades that followed, it was not until the 1680s, when a series of Native revolts disrupted Sonora, that renewed missionary vigor was displayed there.

The arrival of Jesuit Father Eusebio Francisco Kino in the Pimería Alta in 1687 accelerated the pace at which mission settlements were established. For the next twenty-four years, until his death in 1711, Father Kino worked among the natives of the province: the Pima, Papago, Sobaipuri, Yuma, Cocomaricopa, and Cocopa. With the exception of the Pima and Papago Indians, who practiced irrigation agriculture and lived in dense settlements, the rest of the Native groups Kino and his Jesuit brothers tried to Christianize and congregate into mission communities were nomadic hunters and gatherers and *ranchería* peoples.

The nomadic hunters and gatherers of the Pimería Alta, like those in Texas, proved quite difficult to Christianize because most of the material benefits that the acceptance of Christianity and settled life brought with it—seeds, livestock, tools, land rights—were of greater interest and utility to horticulturists than to hunters and gatherers. And, as in Texas, there were increased levels of Apache raiding throughout the northern borderlands, particularly after the 1680s. Thus, from the perspective of the Pimería Alta's nomads, settling in mission communities only made them targets for Apache wrath, European infectious diseases, and a sexually repressive regime. What little progress was made during the eighteenth century in the congregation and settlement of the Indian peoples of the Pimería Alta was short-lived, frequently ended in revolt, and was of limited importance for the area's development.

The indigenous population of the Pimería Alta in 1600 may have numbered around twenty thousand. By 1678 it numbered only 16,600. The real decimation of the Indian population that occurred later resulted from heightened levels of contact with Jesuit missionaries and Spanish civilians. A smallpox plague in 1719 and a measles epidemic in 1728 reduced the population to 7,100, a 65 percent drop from the original contact population in 1600. By 1800 the indigenous population numbered only 1,350. Throughout the eighteenth century, a few families of ostensibly Spanish, but actually of *mestizo* or mixed blood origin, entered the Pimería Alta, seeking mineral wealth. The constant level of Apache depredations kept the non-Indian population low. By 1831 the total population residing in the area's nominally Spanish towns—Tucson and Tubac—numbered around eight hundred. The towns, incidentally, had begun as *presidios*.

CALIFORNIA

The shoreline of Alta California was discovered and mapped by Juan Rodríguez Cabrilho in 1542, but despite this early interest in the area, more than two centuries passed before its colonization. Then it was nothing of inherent value in Alta California that prompted settlement. Rather, geopolitical concerns for the defense of the empire's northern fringe dictated the actions taken. Since the reconquest of New Mexico in 1693 and the establishment of settlements in Texas and the Pimería Alta in the early eighteenth century, the entire region of northern New Spain had been continually plagued by attacks from nomadic *indios bárbaros* ("barbarous" Indians). Mounted, armed, and now masters of equestrian hit-and-run tactics, these once foot-scampering nomads immersed northern New Spain in endless war. At a time when much of the world's silver was being extracted from the northern Mexican provinces of Nueva Galicia, Nueva Vizcaya, and Nuevo León, the Crown deemed it imperative to safeguard the unobstructed production of these mines. Marauding Indians were inhibiting orderly trade and communication between the northern provinces and central Mexico. Some solution to this problem had to be found.

Equally troubling, though undoubtedly less vexing, was the increasing penetration of New Spain's northern frontier by foreigners. Spain's xenophobia increased noticeably in 1763 when, at the end of the Seven Years' War, Spain acquired from France the trans-Mississippi West; England took everything east of the Mississippi, including Florida. Spain and England were now face to face in America. Already the French had armed the Comanche and had driven them south from Illinois into Apache hunting grounds, a movement that reverberated in Texas, New Mexico, and Arizona with heightened levels of Apache attacks. Meanwhile English merchants were clandestinely advancing toward Santa Fe with their wares, and Russian trappers from Alaska were hunting otter in Alta California.

To ascertain how best to deal with these problems, in 1765 King Charles III dispatched Cayetano María Pignatelli Rubí Corbera y San Climent (known simply as the Marqués de Rubí) and the Spanish Royal Corps of Engineers to review New Spain's frontier defenses, to map the area thoroughly, and to identify the mineral, agricultural, and hydraulic resources there. In 1768 Rubí and the Royal Corps of Engineers recommended, among other things, the refortification of the *presidios*, the establishment of intraprovincial east-west links between New Mexico, Arizona, and Alta California, and additional north-south links, such as one between Alta California and central Mexico.

As part of Spain's efforts to reexert its claim to Alta California, early in 1769 José de Gálvez, the *visitador general* of New Spain, ordered a joint land-sea expedition to establish settlements at San Diego and Monterey bays. Fray Junípero Serra, the father-president of the California missions, and Gaspar de Portolá, the governor of Baja California, traveled north by land, departing from the port of San Blas on the southwestern coast of New Spain in early January 1769. The plan was that the Serra-Portolá party would rendezvous at San Diego harbor with Vicente Vila, who had sailed north with sixty-two persons. The sailors reached San Diego on 29 April and were met by the land expedition on 1 July 1769. Two days later a *presidio* was established and, nearby, Mission San Diego de Alcalá. Bound by viceregal orders, on 14 July Portolá proceeded north toward Monterey with a few soldiers. After one failed attempt, which led to the inadvertent discovery of San Francisco Bay, the *presidio* of Monterey and Mission San Carlos Borromeo were dedicated on 3 June 1770.

In the decades that followed, the territory that separated San Diego and Monterey was filled gradually with missions, *presidios*, and towns. The Franciscans founded twenty-two missions between 1769 and 1823: San Diego de Alcalá (1769), San Carlos Borromeo (1770), San Antonio de Padua (1771), San Gabriel Arcángel (1771), San Luis Obispo (1772), Nuestra Señora de los Dolores (1776), San Juan Capistrano (1776), Santa Clara de Asís (1777), San Buenaventura (1782), Santa Bárbara (1786), La Purísima Concepción (1787), Santa Cruz (1791), Nuestra Señora de la Soledad (1791), San José (1797), San Juan Bautista (1797), San Miguel Arcángel (1797), San Fernando Rey (1797), San Luís Rey de Francia (1798), Santa Inés (1804), Santa Paula (1815), San Rafael Arcángel (1817), San Francisco de Solano (1823). *Presidios* were established at San Francisco in 1776 and at Santa Bárbara in 1786.

While civilian communities eventually developed around these missions and *presidios*, the only places officially begun as independent towns in Alta California were the pueblo of San José, the pueblo la Reina de los Angeles de Porciúncula (Los Angeles), and the *villa* of Branciforte. The town of San José de Guadalupe was officially founded by Governor Felipe de Neve on 29 November 1777, but it was not until 13 May 1783 that possession of the land by the town's settlers was duly certified. In full accordance with the Law of the Indies and the Ordinances of Discovery, first the town's plaza was marked off, then its streets, and finally the *solares* (town lots), *suertes*, *ejidos*, and *dehesas* were allotted to the town's *vecinos*.

Almost simultaneous with the founding of San José, Felipe de Neve set about laying the groundwork for the creation of the civilian settlement of Los Angeles. His intention was to create a food-producing settlement to provision the *presidios* in Alta California. On 4 September 1781 de Neve officially established the pueblo la Reina de los Angeles de Porciúncula, though conferral of actual title and possession of lands did not occur until 1786.

The *villa* of Branciforte (now Santa Cruz), named after New Spain's viceroy, Don Miguel de la Grúa Talamanca y Branciforte, was the last major town established in Alta California during the colonial period. Plans for it were originally drawn in 1797, spurred primarily by increasing levels of English, Russian, and American naval activity along the northern Alta California coast. Branciforte's settlement, though, proved much more difficult to accomplish than earlier communities. Colonists were hesitant to go there, and it was only by resorting to coercion that the governor finally was able to enlist a handful of persons for the project. Upon establishing Branciforte in December 1800, its settlers were quickly caught in cross fire between the governor and the Franciscans at nearby Mission Santa Cruz, who opposed the town's location so close to Native American neophytes. Branciforte sputtered along slowly but never really prospered. In 1803 there were 101 persons living there. By 1805 that number had dropped to thirty-one, and by the 1820s it was completely abandoned.

In his 1976 work Sherburne Cook estimated that on the eve of Spanish settlement in 1769, Alta California's indigenous population numbered some 64,500 individuals. By 1820 only

23,000 Indians remained, representing a 65 percent decline in the population—a demographic collapse similar in proportions to that witnessed in the Pimería Alta. In 1769 the population of Spanish origin in Alta California numbered 150, consisting primarily of missionaries and soldiers. With the arrival of additional families from Sonora in the 1770s, the area's population grew, reaching 3,400 by 1820. The pueblo of San José, for example, started with a settler population of 68 in 1777; by 1803, 217 persons of Spanish origin lived there. And Los Angeles, begun with 46 individuals in 1784, by 1810 had grown to 365. Between 1769 and 1820 the "Spanish" or non-Indian population of Alta California experienced an average annual growth rate of 0.65, a rate slightly higher than that in the Pimería Alta but considerably less than in New Mexico, where the constant influx of Apache and Comanche slaves into Hispano households, also, gradually swelled the ranks of those residing in Spanish towns.

CONCLUSION

The bulk of Spanish settlements founded during the colonial period in what is today the southwestern portion of the United States were placed there primarily to further Spain's geopolitical aims in the Americas. Missions, *presidios,* and towns, historically the three main Iberian institutions for frontier pacification, were chartered in New Mexico, Arizona, Texas, and California as specific imperial needs warranted. When buffer settlements were necessary to temper and check hostile nomadic Indian raiders in the Spanish Borderlands, first missionaries, then soldiers, and finally merchants and settlers were dispatched to peacefully, and when necessary, forcibly acculturate the Indians. When France, England, and Russia began expanding their vistas into what Spain considered its terrain at the beginning of the eighteenth century, colonists were granted charters for colonial towns, thereby giving meaning to the European adage, "to populate is to govern." And when the bulk of the silver extracted from America's mines was deemed in need of additional protection, the Crown relied on its time-tested institutions, again using New Spain's northern frontiers as a bulwark against undetectable advances.

The most successful and prosperous of these settlements was the kingdom of New Mexico. By 1821 it had a total population of roughly forty thousand, far outnumbering the thousand or so "Spanish" settlers that each had colonized Arizona, Texas, and California. The kingdom of New Mexico became a relatively prosperous colony, in comparison to the others in northern New Spain, primarily because the pre-Columbian indigenous population here—the Pueblo Indians—were sedentary horticulturalists who had developed the capacity to harvest abundant grains, and had established their towns near plentiful aquatic resources and densely stocked hunting grounds. In those areas where the pre-Columbian populations were primarily nomadic hunters, it proved much more difficult to get the Indians to become farmers or to get them willingly or speedily to conform to Spanish cultural patterns of comportment, settlement, and dress. Indeed, it was not until after the United States annexed Mexico's former northern territories at the end of the U.S.–Mexico War in 1848 that the nomadic raiders of the Southwest were finally pacified.

BIBLIOGRAPHY

Adams, Eleanor B., and Angélico Chávez, eds. and trans. *The Missions of New Mexico, 1776: A Description by Fray Atanasio Domínguez.* Albuquerque, N. Mex., 1956; 2nd ed. 1975.

Alessio Robles, Vito. *Coahuila y Texas en la época colonial.* Mexico City, 1938.

Bancroft, Hubert H. *History of Arizona and New Mexico, 1530–1885.* Albuquerque, N. Mex., 1962.

———. *History of California.* 7 vols. San Francisco, 1884–1890.

———. *History of the North Mexican States and Texas.* San Francisco, 1884–1889.

Bannon, John F. *The Mission Frontier in Sonora, 1620–1687.* New York, 1955.

Benavides, Alonso de. *Benavides' Memorial of 1630,* translated by Peter P. Forrestal. Washington, D.C., 1954.

Bolton, Herbert H. *Kino's Historical Memoir of Pimería Alta.* Cleveland, Ohio, 1919.

———. *Rim of Christendom: A Biography of Eusebio Francisco Kino, Pacific Coast Pioneer.* New York, 1960.

———. *The Spanish Borderlands: A Chronicle of Old Florida and the Southwest.* New Haven, Conn., 1921.

———. *Spanish Exploration in the Southwest, 1542–1706.* 1908; repr. New York, 1916.

Chapman, Charles E. *The Founding of Spanish California: The Northwest Expansion of New Spain, 1687–1783.* New York, 1916.

———. *A History of California: The Spanish Period.* New York, 1921.

Clark, Roger C. *The Beginning of Texas.* Austin, Tex., 1907.

Cook, Sherburne F. *The Conflict Between the California Indian and White Civilization.* Berkeley, Calif., 1976.

Crouch, Dora P., Daniel J. Garr, and Alex I. Mundigo. *Spanish City Planning in North America.* Cambridge, Mass., 1982.

Cruz, Gilberto R. *Let There Be Towns: Spanish Municipal Origins in the American Southwest, 1610–1810.* College Station, Tex., 1988.

Engelhardt, Zephyrin. *The Missions and Missionaries of California.* 4 vols. San Francisco, 1908–1915.

Espinosa, J. Manuel, ed. and trans. *First Expedition of Vargas into New Mexico, 1692.* Albuquerque, N. Mex., 1940.

García Icazbalceta, Joaquín, ed. *Codice franciscano.* Vol. 2 of *Nueva colección de documentos para la historia de México.* Mexico City, 1941.

Geiger, Maynard. *The Life and Times of Fray Junípero Serra. O. F. M.* 2 vols. Washington, D.C., 1959.

Hackett, Charles W., ed. and trans. *Historical Documents Relating to New Mexico, Nueva Vizcaya and Approaches Thereto, to 1773.* 3 vols. Washington, D.C., 1923–1937.

———. *Revolt of the Pueblo Indians of New Mexico and Otermin's Attempted Reconquest, 1680–1682.* 2 vols. Albuquerque, N. Mex., 1942.

Hammond, George P., and Agapito Rey. *Don Juan de Oñate: Colonizer of New Mexico, 1595–1628.* 2 vols. Albuquerque, N. Mex., 1953.

———. *The Rediscovery of New Mexico, 1580–1594: The Explorations of Chamuscado, Espejo Castaño de Sosa, Morlete, and Leyna de Bonilla and Humaña.* Albuquerque, N. Mex., 1966.

———, eds., and trans. *Narratives of the Coronado Expedition 1540–1542.* Albuquerque, N. Mex., 1940.

Hodge, Fredrick W., George P. Hammond, and Agapito Rey, eds. and trans. *Fray Alonso de Benavides' Revised Memorial of 1634.* Albuquerque, N. Mex., 1945.

Morfi, Juan Agustín. *History of Texas, 1673–1779.* 2 vols. Translated by Carlos Eduardo Castaneda. Albuquerque, N. Mex., 1935.

Nuttall, Zelia. "Royal Ordinances Concerning the Laying Out of New Towns." *Hispanic American Historical Review* 4, no. 4 (1921):743–753.

———. "Royal Ordinances Concerning the Laying Out of New Towns." *Hispanic American Historical Review* 5, no. 2 (1922):249–254.

"Ordenanzas sobre descubrimiento nuevo y población," Segovia, 13 July 1573. In vol. 8 of *Colección de documentos inéditos relativos al descubrimiento, conquista y organización de las antiguas posesiones españoles de América y Oceania sacados de los Archivos del Reino,* edited by Joaquín Franciso Pacheco, Francisco de Cardenas y Espeja, and Luís Torres de Mendoza. 42 vols. Madrid, 1854–1884.

O'Rourke, Thomas. *The Franciscan Missions in Texas, 1690–1793.* Washington, D.C., 1927.

Pérez de Villagra, Gaspar. *History of New Mexico, 1610.* Translated by Gilberto Espinosa. Los Angeles, 1933.

Richman, Irving B. *California Under Spain and Mexico, 1535–1847.* Boston, 1911.

Ramón A. Gutiérrez

SEE ALSO **The Age of Reconnaissance; Emergence of Empires; Indian-Colonist Contact;** and the map preceding **The French Settlements.**

SOUTHEAST

THE FIRST EUROPEAN COLONIZATION of the southeastern United States in the sixteenth century was an essentially Spanish venture. For more than three hundred years, from 1513 to 1821, the southern periphery of what is now the United States was occupied by a string of Spanish towns, missions, ranches, and *presidios.*

These settlements were a consequence of Spain's New World colonization venture, which began in 1493 with the settlement of Hispaniola by Christopher Columbus. The Spanish presence was concentrated in the Caribbean until about 1517, when the focus of colonial attention shifted to mainland Central and South America.

SPANISH EXPLORATIONS IN THE SOUTHEAST, 1513–1565

The first fifty years of Spanish activity in the Southeast were dominated by exploratory expeditions originating in the Caribbean. Even before the extension of Spanish exploration and settlement to Mexico and Central America, forays were regularly made to Florida in search of slaves and other resources. The earliest and best known of these ventures was that of Juan Ponce de León, who in 1513 claimed La Florida as a Spanish territory. The first successful effort to colonize the region, however, did not take place until 1565, when Pedro Menéndez de Avilés established the town of Saint Augustine.

Between the arrival of Ponce de León in 1513 and the founding of Saint Augustine in 1565, a number of other largely unsuccessful attempts were made to explore and colonize the southeastern United States. Explorations of the Gulf and Atlantic coasts of Florida were undertaken by Diego Miruelo in 1516, Francisco Hernández de Córdoba in 1517, and Alonso Alvarez de Piñeda in 1519. The southeastern Atlantic Coast was explored in 1521 by the Spanish slavers Pedro de Quexo and Francisco Gordillo, who also sailed up the Santee River in what is today South Carolina. Although none of these expeditions attempted to settle the area, they considerably enhanced Spanish knowledge of the coastal geography of the region.

The first attempt to establish a colony in the Southeast took place in 1526, near present-day Sapelo, Georgia. This was the settlement of San Miguel del Gualdape, established by Lucas Vásquez de Allyón with some six hundred Spanish and African settlers. The colony was abandoned after just three months because of Indian attacks, disease, hunger, and the death of Allyón himself. It is believed that many of the approximately one hundred African members of the expedition chose to remain behind with the Guale Indians.

A second major colonization effort took place in 1559, when Tristán de Luna y Arellano sailed with one thousand five hundred people and thirteen ships to northwest Florida in what is today Pensacola Bay. Unable to find sufficient food on the coast, the settlers were moved some forty leagues inland to live in a large deserted Indian village called Nanipacna. However, a hurricane sunk their still-laden supply ships. Many of the colonists rebelled and returned to New Spain, and the remaining ships and settlers were lost in a storm during an attempt to relocate the colony to the Atlantic Coast.

Between these abortive attempts to establish coastal settlements, the interior and coastal regions of the Southeast were explored by a series of expeditions, beginning with that of Pánfilo de Narváez in 1528. The four hundred-member party explored the Gulf Coast of Florida on foot and horseback from Tampa Bay to Apalachee Bay, where they built boats and took to the sea. Only four members of the expedition survived, arriving in Mexico after some eight years of wandering and captivity among Gulf Coast Indian groups.

The expedition of Hernando de Soto took place between 1539 and 1543 and covered a considerable amount of territory between Tampa Bay and the vicinity of Tampico, Mexico. The group of some five hundred people followed a route north through Florida, Georgia, and the Carolinas; west across the Appalachian Mountains to Tennessee; south to southern Alabama; and then westward through Mississippi to Arkansas, where the expedition spent much of 1541. De Soto died in 1542, and the 311 survivors took another year to build boats and sail down the Mississippi and along the Gulf Coast to Mexico.

Although unsuccessful in their mandate to locate riches and settle the area, these early expeditions provided a wealth of information about the native inhabitants of the Southeast on the eve of European colonization. They also undoubtedly introduced European pathogens that led to epidemics and Native population decline. Furthermore, Spanish military actions and slave raids encouraged attitudes of distrust and hostility toward Europeans among the people of La Florida, which affected the experiences of subsequent colonists in the region.

ESTABLISHMENT OF A SPANISH PRESENCE: THE SIXTEENTH CENTURY

In 1565, four years after the demise of the de Luna colony, Pedro Menéndez de Avilés founded Saint Augustine, which has persisted in its original location to the present day. Saint Augustine was established partly in response to the French attempts between 1562 and 1564 to found the Huguenot colonies of Charlesfort, at present day Parris Island, South Carolina, and Fort Caroline, near present-day Jacksonville, Florida. Charlesfort was abandoned by 1563, and Fort Caroline was destroyed by Pedro Menéndez in 1565. The French presence was a potential threat to the Spanish Caribbean Empire, and provided the impetus for the Spanish Crown's support for the Florida colony.

A more short-lived but nevertheless important colonization effort also took place under the auspices of Menéndez between 1566 and 1587 at Santa Elena, South Carolina, near the site of the ill-fated Charlesfort. Santa Elena was the capital of La Florida during its brief existence but was ultimately abandoned in 1587 because of Spanish failure to come to terms with the indigenous Guale inhabitants of the region. After that time Saint Augustine remained the only Spanish town in La Florida until the establishment of Santa Rosa Pensacola in 1698.

Throughout the sixteenth century La Florida, as claimed by Spain, was nearly synonymous with what is now considered to be the southeastern United States. It included not only present-day Florida but also the territory north to Virginia and west to the Mississippi. The early Spanish colonial presence, however, was concentrated primarily in the subtropical (northern) regions of the Florida peninsula, where agricultural productivity and Indian population densities were greatest. An unknown number of Indian inhabitants occupied the Florida peninsula when Europeans arrived, numbering in the tens of thousands.

The Spanish colonizers of the southeastern United States immediately introduced Catholic missions to the region, beginning in 1566, in an attempt to convert the Native inhabitants to Christianity, and to help secure and control a vast frontier. Jesuit missionaries operated in La Florida between 1566 and 1572, and established short-lived and unsuccessful missions in southeast Florida among the Tequesta Indians, in southwest Florida among the Calusa, and in Georgia and the Carolinas among the Guale and the Orista peoples. Those missions extended as far north as Chesapeake Bay, near the site of what is today Jamestown, Virginia. Indian rebellion and conflict caused the Jesuits to abandon Florida in 1572, and the Franciscan friars replaced them in 1573.

Through most of the sixteenth century La Florida had a minority European population of between three hundred and four hundred settlers, nearly all of whom were soldiers and their families. There were three principal military garrisons in La Florida during the sixteenth century: those at Saint Augustine and Santa Elena, and the garrison at San Mateo, established in 1565 near the site of Fort Caroline after its destruction. Each of the three was manned by a contingent of approximately 250 soldiers until the abandonment of Santa Elena in 1587. There were also smaller outposts, such as that of Fort Matanzas, built in 1569 on the inlet of that name, some twenty miles (32 kilometers) south of Saint Augustine.

With the death of Pedro Menéndez in 1574, La Florida reverted from a private-public partnership venture to a military Crown colony, supported and subsidized by the government. This economic arrangement was to persist (in a largely unsatisfactory manner) through the eighteenth century.

Both the Spanish and the Indian inhabitants of the young colony suffered a number of difficulties and disastrous setbacks during the sixteenth century. It was not until about 1580 that the Spaniards were able to make peace with the aggressive Timucua Indians of the Saint Augustine area, and this reconciliation was largely owing to the devastating decline of the Indian population through epidemics of European diseases. Epidemics of smallpox, measles, influenza, and cholera took place regularly, with alarming rates of fatalities for the Indian inhabitants of the Southeast. Major epidemics were recorded in 1570, 1587, and 1591, and those Indians who survived the sixteenth century were particularly hard hit by a terrible epidemic between 1613 and 1617 that was said to have killed half of the remaining Indians in La Florida.

Saint Augustine was attacked and burned to the ground in 1586 by British seaman Sir Francis Drake and his pirate fleet, and then almost completely destroyed again in 1599 by a hurricane and fire. By the beginning of the seventeenth century, the Spanish colony was reduced to about three hundred people concentrated in Saint Augustine, living in some 120 huts made of thatch, wood, and mud.

DEVELOPMENT OF THE SPANISH FRONTIER: THE SEVENTEENTH CENTURY

The abandonment of Santa Elena in 1587 and the settlement of Jamestown by the English in 1607 effectively impeded the reestablishment of Spanish settlements or missions in the Carolinas and northward after 1600. These events also marked both the withdrawal of Spanish presence into a more restricted area than during the sixteenth century and the beginning of the Spanish rivalry with other European powers in the region that was to shape the remainder of the colonial era.

Despite these developments, however, the Spanish occupation of the Florida hinterland frontier outside of Saint Augustine was more extensive during the seventeenth century than in any other period, before or after. A string of flourishing Franciscan missions had been established by the mid seventeenth century as far north as Saint Catherine's Island, Georgia, and as far west as the Apalachicola River in the Florida panhandle. In 1650 there were some fifty friars in forty missions serving more than twenty-six thousand Christian Indians, most of them in the Apalachee and Western Timucua regions of interior Florida.

In 1656, however, the Western Timucua mission Indians staged an eight-month-long rebellion against the Spaniards, resulting in the loss or abandonment of many of the towns and missions in the central Florida peninsula. Three years later a measles epidemic struck, killing by some estimates more than ten thousand Indians. In 1675 there were thirty-six missions in La Florida, serving some thirteen thousand Indians.

The missions were administered from Saint Augustine, which was still the only Spanish town in the Southeast. Throughout most of the seventeenth century, Saint Augustine was a military dominated, Crown-subsidized *presidio* settlement. Saint Augustine's population consisted of between five hundred and seven hundred people. Although most of the inhabitants were soldiers and their families employed by the *presidios,* a few of the more affluent settlers established cattle and wheat ranches in the Florida interior. A number of these ranches flourished for several decades.

The growing threats from English pirates and colonists to the north provoked an increase in Spanish defensive and military activity through the seventeenth century. Several outlying military posts were constructed and manned in the region during this period, many of them associated with the missions. Blockhouses or forts were built in the western territories at several locations: at the mission and town of San Luis in 1657 near present-day Tallahassee, at Apalachicola in western Georgia in 1689 to discourage trade between the English and the Apalachicola Indians, and at San Marcos de Apalache (ca. 1678 to ca. 1682) on the Gulf of Mexico to defend against English pirates.

Eastern forts included the blockhouse at San Mateo near the former site of the French Fort Caroline (although considerably reduced in size from its sixteenth-century status); another at Matanzas; and a smaller outpost farther south at Mosquito Inlet. Forts Picolata and San Francisco de Pupo faced one another across the Saint Johns River, protecting the road to San Mateo.

In 1668 Saint Augustine was attacked and sacked by English pirates led by Robert Searles. Two years later the English successfully penetrated the Carolinas and settled Charleston. These events provoked the Spanish authorities to recast La Florida from its role as an isolated dependency to that of an integral part of the Spanish defense of the Indies against other colonial powers.

The garrison at Saint Augustine was augmented, causing the Hispanic population of the colony to increase to about one thousand people. This was coupled with implementation of an ambitious defensive system, with the Castillo de San Marcos (built between 1672 and 1695) as its centerpiece. It was the first stone fortress to be built in La Florida, although it was the tenth fort in Saint Augustine. The previous nine forts had all been constructed of wood and were short-lived, owing to decay or enemy destruction. San Marcos, however, was never taken by an enemy, and it successfully protected Spanish interests in La Florida until the end of the Spanish occupation.

Spanish fears of English threats to La Florida, enhanced by the memory of pirate raids and the intensifying English presence in the Southeast, were not unfounded. Both before and after the founding of Charleston, problems were felt on the northern and northwestern frontiers, where English traders and slave catchers agitated the Indians and provoked them to attack the Spanish missions. In this provocation they were largely successful, and the Spanish missions to the Guale of the Georgia coast were abandoned by 1683, further retracting the geographical sphere of Spanish occupation in the Southeast.

Despite this retraction, however, Spaniards still claimed that the land between Charleston and the Saint Marys River (today a northern state boundary of Florida) was part of La Florida, while the English claimed the area for their own. This "debatable land" was to be a source of almost continuous Spanish-English conflict for the next century, from the establishment of Charleston in 1670 to the cession of Florida to the English in 1763.

Meanwhile, French activity in the Gulf of Mexico during the late seventeenth century provoked Spanish reaction and expansion. The landing of the La Salle expedition in 1685 at Matagorda Bay on the Texas coast awakened the first serious Spanish interest in the eastern Gulf Coast since the ill-fated de Luna expedition of 1559–1561. In 1698 a two-part expedition consisting of 407 men and 5 ships, led by Juan Jordán de Reina and Andrés de Arriola, established the Presidio Santa Maria de Galve on Pensacola Bay. This settlement, which lasted on that site until 1719, was the first of three Spanish *presidio* settlements in Pensacola. This first settlement of some 250 people was troubled by poor soil and lack of food, disciplinary problems caused by the large number of convict laborers in the colony, and repeated attacks by English-allied Indians.

It was established just in time, however. In 1699 a French fleet under Pierre Le Moyne d'Iberville sailed into the bay before sailing west to settle at what is today Biloxi, Mississippi. That settlement was to move twice before it settled permanently in 1711 on the site that is today Mobile, Alabama, creating a second foreign frontier for the Spaniards of La Florida.

FRONTIER RETRACTION AND THE GROWTH OF TOWN LIFE: 1700–1763

As the eighteenth century began, the Spanish presence in the southeastern United States was largely concentrated in the towns of Saint Augustine and Pensacola, and in the Apalachee missions of northwest Florida. The English threatened the colony's northern frontier, and the French were encroaching on the western frontier.

The English threat became a tangible reality after the death of Charles II in 1700, which provoked a French-Spanish alliance against the English in the War of the Spanish Succession. This was played out in the colonies as Queen Anne's War, and the English in Carolina wasted little time in attacking Spanish Florida. Carolina governor James Moore led an expedition against Saint Augustine in 1702, burning the outposts and missions between Charleston and Saint Augustine. Although he burned most of the town and held the Castillo under siege for nearly two months, Moore failed to take the Spanish settlement. Hoping to recoup some of the losses from that expedition, he led a series of devastating raids on the Spanish missions and ranches in the Apalachee region, which resulted in the virtual annihilation of those settlements by 1705. After that the only significant Spanish presence in the region was at Saint Augustine and at Pensacola.

Pensacola, meanwhile, withstood a series of attacks by the English and their Indian allies between 1702 and the end of Queen Anne's War in 1713. In 1719, however, the French from Mobile, after nearly two decades of amicable relations with their Spanish neighbors, captured Pensacola during the War of the Quadruple Alliance (1719–1721), in which France, England, Austria, and Holland went to war against Spain. Spain regained Pensacola after the conclusion of that war in 1722, and the settlement was rebuilt at a new site on Santa Rosa Island. Food and supplies remained a severe problem for the small settlement, however, and the Spaniards were forced to accept aid from their French neighbors at Mobile. The settlement of some two hundred people persisted on Santa Rosa

Island until it was destroyed by a hurricane in 1752 and relocated to the present site of Pensacola.

The precarious normality that resumed in eastern Florida after the end of Queen Anne's War was initially disrupted by the unsuccessful raid on Saint Augustine in 1728 by the Carolinian John Palmer. More profoundly it was interrupted by the English settlement of Georgia—the "debatable land" still claimed by Spain—in 1733.

Governor James Oglethorpe of Georgia soon embroiled the Spaniards of Florida in the international conflicts of 1739–1748, known variously as the War of Jenkins' Ear and King George's War in the colonies and the War of Austrian Succession in Europe. Saint Augustine was attacked but not taken in 1740, and the Spanish retaliated by unsuccessfully attacking Fort Frederica, located on Saint Simon's Island, Georgia, in 1741.

One of the factors in the intense Spanish-English colonial rivalry in the eighteenth-century Southeast was the issue of African slaves and freedmen. Africans had participated—either willingly or unwillingly—in the earliest exploratory and colonizing ventures of the Spaniards in the Southeast as soldiers, slaves, and settlers, and they seem to have quickly established cooperative relationships and alliances with Indians. Africans also intermarried with Spanish and Indian inhabitants of the colonies and played an important part, along with Spaniards and American Indians, in shaping Hispanic-American cultural patterns.

Beginning in 1687 the Spaniards made it known in the slave communities of the Carolinas that freedom would be granted to any slaves who successfully escaped to Florida and converted to Catholicism. Despite outraged English protest and measures by plantation owners to stop such escapes, more than one hundred African refugees had made the trip (often in the company of Indians) by the early eighteenth century. In 1738 a special regiment of these black Carolinian freedmen was formed, and a fort and town were built for them about two miles (about 3 kilometers) north of Castillo. This settlement, known as Gracia Real de Santa Teresa de Mose, served as the northernmost Spanish defense line against the English and was occupied by the community of free Africans until 1763 (with a hiatus from 1740–1752).

From the 1740s until 1763, Spanish Florida was relatively peaceful. The population of Saint Augustine increased to more than three thousand during that period, and naval stores industries began to develop in both Pensacola and Saint Augustine. This growth came to a halt, however, in 1763, when Spain ceded Florida to England in exchange for Cuba and acquired French Louisiana at the conclusion of the Seven Years' War (known in the colonies as the French and Indian Wars). At that time the Spanish presence consisted of the still-struggling settlement at Pensacola, a small garrison at the Fort of San Marcos de Apalache on the Gulf Coast, and Saint Augustine. Virtually all of the Spanish, African, and Indian residents of Florida evacuated the settlements en masse when the English took over.

THE SPANISH IN LOUISIANA

With the exchange of Florida and Louisiana, Spanish holdings in the borderlands were concentrated in a solid block from the Mississippi River to the Pacific and from the Gulf of Mexico northward indefinitely. Many French inhabitants of Louisiana and New Orleans chose to remain in the colony under Spanish rule.

Spain was not able to exploit the potential of this vast territory. Unable to populate it or to govern its exceptionally large number of Indian tribes, Spanish authorities abandoned the pattern of frontier control through missions that had been the mainstay of earlier borderland holdings. They instead adopted the trade-based relationship with the Indians that had been introduced to the region earlier by the French, with much of the trading activity conducted for them by French agents. Major posts for the control of Louisiana included Saint Louis, the Arkansas Post, and Natchitoches. Both on the frontier and in the major city of the region, New Orleans, French influence continued to be felt until the end of Spanish rule of Louisiana in 1800. In that year Spain sold Louisiana to France, permanently ending its presence there; France in turn sold it to the United States in 1803.

129

TERRITORIAL EXPANSION AND THE DECLINE OF SPANISH INFLUENCE, 1784–1821

Meanwhile, at the conclusion of the American War for Independence in 1783, Florida was returned to Spain, extending Spanish dominion completely across the southern rim of the North American Borderlands from that year until 1800. Following the pattern established during the previous two decades of British rule, Florida was divided into the two governmental districts of East Florida (from the Atlantic Ocean to the Apalachicola River) and West Florida, from the Apalachicola River to the Mississippi River. The Spanish, however, failed to regain dominance in the Florida colony. Saint Augustine, for example, was one of the most culturally diverse communities in North America during that period, with its population of between nine hundred and one thousand five hundred composed of Spaniards, English, Americans, Minorcans, Italians, Greeks, Swiss, Germans, Irish, Creek, Seminole, African Americans, Canary Islanders, and Scots. British and American settlers and economic interests were strongly entrenched in Florida and shaped the cultural orientation of the region during the late eighteenth and early nineteenth centuries. The colony never regained the predominantly Spanish cultural life that had characterized it in earlier periods.

There was a large emigration from the United States into Spanish Florida during this period, and the pressure for annexation to the United States was great. Such large numbers of United States citizens migrated to Florida that they in effect occupied the territory. This movement culminated in 1818 when Andrew Jackson captured and occupied Pensacola and West Florida, and in 1821 all of Florida was formally ceded to the United States, permanently ending the Spanish presence in the Southeast.

BIBLIOGRAPHY

Overviews and Bibliographies

Bannon, John Francis. *The Spanish Borderlands Frontier, 1513–1821.* New York, 1970. A classic.
Coker, William S., et al. "Research in the Spanish Borderlands." *Latin American Research Review* 7, no. 2 (1972):3–94. Contains a bibliography and five bibliographic essays dealing primarily with research in the post-1781 period.
George, Paul S., ed. *A Guide to the History of Florida.* New York, 1989. Chapters 1–6 include thorough bibliographic essays and bibliographies covering East and West Florida from the contact period to the end of the Spanish colonial period.
O'Donnell, James H. *Southeastern Frontiers: Europeans, Africans, and Americans, 1513–1840—A Critical Bibliography.* Bloomington, Ind., 1982.
Proctor, Samuel, ed. *Eighteenth-century Florida and its Borderlands.* Gainesville, Fla., 1976.
Service, James A. *A Bibliography of West Florida.* Vol. 1, *1535–1916.* Pensacola, Fla., 1984.
Thomas, David H., ed. *Columbian Consequences.* Vol. 2, *Archaeological and Historical Perspectives on the Spanish Borderlands East.* Washington, D.C., 1990. This comprehensive volume brings together the most recent information on Spanish exploration, sixteenth-century settlement, and missions in the southeastern borderlands, and it guides the reader to most of the relevant bibliographic materials.

Exploration and Contact

Hoffman, Paul E. *A New Andalucia and a Way to the Orient: The American Southeast During the Sixteenth Century.* Baton Rouge, La., 1990.
Lowery, Woodbury. *The Spanish Settlements Within the Present Limits of the United States, 1513–1561.* New York, 1901.
Quattlebaum, Paul. *The Land Called Chicora: The Carolinas Under Spanish Rule, with French Intrusions, 1520–1670.* Gainesville, Fla., 1956.
Weddle, Robert S. *Spanish Sea: The Gulf of Mexico in North American Discovery, 1500–1685.* College Station, Tex., 1985.

Spanish Florida, 1565–1763

Bushnell, Amy. *The King's Coffer: Proprietors of the Spanish Florida Treasury, 1565–1702.* Gainesville, Fla., 1982. One of the few social histories of the seventeenth-century Spanish southeastern borderlands.
Chatelain, Verne E. *The Defenses of Spanish Florida, 1565–1763.* Carnegie Institute of Washington Publication 511. Washington, D.C., 1941.
Deagan, Kathleen. *Spanish Saint Augustine: The Archeology of a Colonial Creole Community.* New York, 1983. Concerns the historical archaeology of eighteenth-century Spanish Florida.
———, ed. *America's Ancient City: Spanish Saint Augustine, 1565–1763.* Garland Sourcebooks on the Spanish Borderlands. New York, 1991.

Lyon, Eugene. *The Enterprise of Florida: Pedro Menéndez de Avilés and the Spanish Conquest of 1565–1568.* Gainesville, Fla., 1976. A basic source on the establishment of Florida in the sixteenth century.

McGovern, James, ed. *Colonial Pensacola.* Pensacola, Fla., 1974.

South, Stanley. *The Discovery of Santa Elena.* Institute of Archeology and Anthropology Research, Manuscript Series 165. Columbia, S.C., 1980.

TePaske, John. *The Governorship of Spanish Florida, 1700–1763.* Durham, N.C., 1964.

Waterbury, Jean Parker, ed. *The Oldest City: St. Augustine, Saga of Survival.* Saint Augustine, Fla., 1983.

The Spanish Floridas, 1784–1821

Coker, William, ed. *John Forbe's Description of the Spanish Floridas, 1804.* Pensacola, Fla., 1979.

Fretwell, Jacqueline, and Susan Parker, eds. *Clash Between Cultures: Spanish East Florida 1784–1821.* Saint Augustine, Fla., 1988.

Spanish Louisiana and the Mississippi Valley

Cox, Isaac J. *The West Florida Controversy, 1798–1813: A Study in American Diplomacy.* Baltimore, Md., 1918; repr. 1967.

Gardiner, C. Harvey. *The Spanish in the Mississippi Valley, 1762–1804.* Urbana, Ill., 1974.

Whitaker, Arthur P. *The Spanish-American Frontier, 1783–1795: The Westward Movement and the Spanish Retreat in the Mississippi Valley.* Boston, 1927.

Southeastern Spanish Missions

Gannon, Michael V. *The Cross in the Sand: The Early Catholic Church in Florida, 1513–1870.* Gainesville, Fla., 1965.

Geiger, Maynard J. *The Franciscan Conquest of Florida (1573–1618).* Studies in Hispanic-American History, vol. 1. Washington, D.C., 1937.

Lanning, John Tate. *The Spanish Missions of Georgia.* Chapel Hill, N.C., 1935.

Spanish-Indian Relations

Coker, William, and Thomas Watson. *Indian Traders of the Southeast Spanish Borderlands.* Pensacola, Fla., 1986. Deals primarily with the post-1763 period.

Hann, John H. *Apalachee: The Land Between the Rivers.* Gainesville, Fla., 1988.

Milanich, Jerald, and Samuel Proctor, eds. *Tacachale: Essays on the Indians of Florida and Southeastern Georgia During the Historic Period.* Gainesville, Fla., 1978.

Sturtevant, William C. "Spanish-Indian Relations in Southeastern North America." *Ethnohistory* 9, no. 1 (1962):41–94.

Swagerty, William R. "Spanish-Indian Relations, 1513–1821." In *Scholars and the Indian Experience: Critical Reviews of Recent Writing in the Social Sciences,* edited by William R. Swagerty. Bloomington, Ind., 1984.

Swanton, John R. *Early History of the Creek Indians and Their Neighbors.* Smithsonian Institution, Bureau of American Ethnology, Bulletin 73. Washington, D.C., 1922.

Kathleen Deagan

SEE ALSO **The Age of Reconnaissance; British Settlements, The Lower South; Emergence of Empires; Indian-Colonist Contact,** and the map preceding **The French Settlements.**

COLONIAL SETTLEMENTS AND OUTPOSTS

Bering Sea
Chukchi Peninsula
Saint Lawrence
Bering Strait

ALASKA
Kuskokwim
Kvikpak (Yukon)
Nushagak

Kodiak
Saint Paul's Harbor
Prince William Sound
Gulf of Alaska
Yakutat Bay

Sitka
Alexander Archipelago

Cook Inlet

Peace

Great Bear Lake

Great Slave Lake

Mackenzie

GREENLAND

Disko Bay

WESTERN SETTLEMENT
Godthåb (Nuuk)
Narssaq (Narsaq)
Julianehåb (Qaqortoq)
EASTERN SETTLEMENT

Baffin Island (Helluland)

Labrador (Markland)

VINLAND
L'Anse aux Meadows
Newfoundland

Lake Athabasca
Athabasca
Fraser
Vancouver Island
Columbia

Hudson Bay

York Fort
Fort Severn
Fort la Corne
Fort Paskoya
Saskatchewan
Fort la Jonquière
Lake Winnipeg
RUPERT'S LAND
Fort Albany
Moose Fort
Charles Fort
Tadoussac

Gulf of Saint Lawrence
Île Royale
Louisbourg

Red River Colony (Winnipeg)
Pembina

L. Superior

Fort Michilimackinac
Saint Paul

L. Michigan
L. Huron
Toronto
L. Ontario
Detroit
L. Erie
Fort Frontenac
Fort Presqu'isle
Fort Duquesne

Quebec
Trois-Rivières
Montreal
CANADA
Sagadahoc

Cobequid
Grand Pré
Annapolis Royal
ACADIA
Bay of Fundy

Portsmouth
NEW ENGLAND
Boston
Plymouth
Providence

Philadelphia
Lancaster
Baltimore
Annapolis
Saint Mary's
CHESAPEAKE
Jamestown
Edenton
Bath
New Bern

MIDDLE COLONIES
see inset

Cape Hatteras

Atlantic Ocean

Pacific Ocean

Bodega Bay
Fort Ross
San Francisco Bay
San Francisco
San Jose
Monterey Bay
Monterey
SOUTHWEST
ALTA CALIFORNIA
Santa Barbara
Los Angeles

San Diego

Colorado
Gila

NEW MEXICO
Albuquerque
Santa Fe

Tucson
Tubac
PIMERÍA ALTA
El Paso

Baja California

Rio Grande

Pecos

TEXAS
San Antonio

La Bahia
Galveston

ILLINOIS
Cahokia
Kaskaskia

Missouri
Ohio
Arkansas

Natchitoches
LOUISIANA
Arkansas Post
Red

SOUTHEAST
New Orleans
Fort Rosalie
Mobile
Pensacola
FLORIDA

Gulf of Mexico

LOWER SOUTH
Wilmington
Augusta
Charlestown
Savannah
Frederica
Saint Augustine
Savannah

Mississippi

Legend

- ▲ France, 1541–1840
- ● Great Britain, 1607–1776
- ◇ The Netherlands, 1614–1664
- ▫ Norse, c.985–c.1409
- ★ Russia, 1743–1867
- ■ Spain, 1492–1821
- ✿ Sweden, 1638–1655

Settlement
Outpost

0   250   500 miles
0 250 500 kilometers

Inset

Schenectady
Albany
Rensselaerswyck

Esopus (Kingston)
Fort Goede Hoop (Hartford)
Connecticut

Hudson

Pavonia
New Amsterdam
Newark
Heemstede
Breuckelen
Perth Amboy
Delaware

Philadelphia
Burlington
Fort Nassau

Fort Christina
Fort Casimir

0   100 miles
0 100 kilometers

Swanendael

FRENCH SETTLEMENTS

FOR FRANCE, THE SIXTEENTH CENTURY in America entailed a transition from the Old to the New World in space, in time, and in beliefs. This change did not occur smoothly, and it took nearly a century of abortive attempts before France settled, permanently and officially, beginning with Quebec.

Like other major European powers, France sought a quick route to China. Soon the successful Spanish conquests added the greed for American gold to the desire for a direct supply of spices as a motive for expansion. Excluded from the papal division of the New World of 1492–1493 and financially handicapped by war, France began its colonization of America relatively late. In 1524 the French Crown financed, in part, a voyage Giovanni da Verrazano had organized for Lyon shipowners. Ten years later it arranged a voyage of discovery under the leadership of Jacques Cartier. The voyage resulted in an unsuccessful attempt at colonization. Having lost hope for quick wealth, the French Crown lost interest in America for close to half a century.

THE ATLANTIC FISHERMEN

French colonization in America resulted from the development of the Atlantic fisheries. Whale hunting and cod fishing, at first along Newfoundland and then in the mouth of the Saint Lawrence River, played a far more important role than official undertakings in settling organized groups so as to exploit the wealth of the country.

Fishermen from Normandy and Brittany, from Saint-Malo and Dieppe, as well as from the Basque region, sailed the North American seas three decades before Jacques Cartier. Contracts indicate that they were there as early as 1504 or 1506. They came regularly and in large numbers. In 1527 the Englishman John Rut noted the presence of eleven Norman ships in Saint John's harbor. From the beginning of the sixteenth century, some 350 Newfoundland vessels with from 8,000 to 10,000 hands aboard fished annually off the banks of Newfoundland and in the mouth of the Saint Lawrence.

Fishing was done in two ways. Some fishermen drifted along the banks, salting the fish as they caught them and then returning across the Atlantic to their home port without having set foot ashore. Others came in larger vessels and settled on land as soon as they arrived. A dozen small boats went to the fishing grounds and returned daily, or every other day, with their catch. Ashore other members of the expeditions sun dried the cod. Spending several months on land, these latter came in contact with Indians and bartered with them.

In the mid sixteenth century, furs occasionally were added to the load of dried cod. Easily and plentifully obtainable from the Indians in exchange for small mirrors, combs, salt, hatchets, and other trade goods, they rapidly gained in importance. As early as 1581, merchants from Saint-Malo, Rouen, and Dieppe outfitted ships for purely commercial ventures. In 1583 a certain Étienne Bellenger brought back from the Gulf of Saint Lawrence furs worth ten times his investment. In 1584 Saint-Malo outfitted five ships exclusively for fur trading in the Saint Lawrence, doubling the number the following year. Later the fur trade became the monopoly of exclusive companies after private initiative finally attracted the attention of the Crown.

Fishing had brought the French to the Saint Lawrence, but it was fur trading that kept them there. However, that was not the only contribution made by the fishing fleet and its outfitters to French settlement in America. It was from them that the Crown found the pilots and seasoned crews it needed for its explorations and early colonizing efforts.

A FIRST ATTEMPT AT COLONIZATION

The first official attempt at settlement was spurred by information garnered from the Indians brought to France, who spoke of the great kingdom of Saguenay, thus reviving the greed for gold, and by the political and religious context of the times. During his second voyage to the new northern American lands in 1535, Jacques Cartier discovered a waterway, the Saint Lawrence River, that made it possible to sail into the heart of the continent. Back in France he sang the praises of his discovery and held out hope of eventual settlement and enrichment.

Hoping to find gold and a sea passage to the Indies, the king outfitted a third expedition, which was to be one of colonization and evangelization, and entrusted it to a minor Protestant noble, Jean-François de la Rocque de Roberval. Cartier was to serve under him. However, with the preparations dragging on, Cartier finally sailed alone in May 1541. He arrived in Quebec at the end of August with five ships and probably upward of fifteen hundred colonists, including some women. Distrusting the Iroquois, he set up camp a few leagues above Stadacona (Quebec) at the spot he called Charlesbourg Royal,

where the Cap Rouge River enters the Saint Lawrence.

Few details are known about this settlement attempt. Cartier described the place as quite beautiful. He erected two fortresses, one on top of the cliff there, the other at its foot. He had a few acres ploughed and in September explored as far as Hochelaga (Montreal) but could go no farther. It is known that during the winter of 1541–1542, the Indians displayed hostility toward the French settlement, but there is no indication that it turned into open war or even skirmishes. Nevertheless Cartier left as early as June 1542 with what he wrongly believed to be a load of gold, diamonds, and precious stones. It is not known whether he left some settlers or took them all back, though the latter is the most probable.

Roberval finally reached Quebec and met Cartier in the harbor of Saint John's, on Newfoundland, in June 1542. Cartier refused to turn back and sailed for France during the night. With two hundred men and three ships loaded with calves, cows, sheep, and horses, Roberval made his way to Charlesbourg Royal, renaming it France Royal. The winter was harsh and a quarter of the settlers died of disease. The severity of the climate and the small profit to be derived from trade did not encourage perseverance. As early as June 1543, it was decided to leave, and on 13 September, everyone was back in France. It was their only consolation, for the colonization attempt had failed; no wealth had been gained, nor had the passage to India been found. Disappointed and absorbed by the political and religious situation in Europe, the king lost interest in the New World.

During the half century following Cartier's explorations, France's attention toward pursuing North American ventures was diverted. A few private persons tried to create colonies for their Protestant co-religionists. The fishermen continued, tirelessly and almost anonymously, activities that were proving more and more lucrative and so more and more attractive to more and more people. The king showed little interest in North America, a region lacking gold, and so Crown-supported involvement remained limited, occasional, and ephemeral, motivated more by European political struggles than by the desire to build an empire. The Protestant venture is a case in point.

AN ATTEMPT AT PROTESTANT SETTLEMENT

Prompted by Nicolas Durand de Villegaignon and Admiral Gaspard de Coligny, some Protestants were interested in finding a place where they could live and practice their religion freely and safely. In 1555 Villegaignon left with six hundred settlers and landed on a small island off the coast of Brazil. Quarrels divided the little band, and some moved to the mainland. In March 1560 the Portuguese governor, warned by the Jesuits of this Protestant settlement, laid siege to the colony's fort and razed it.

Some of the survivors settled in Spanish Florida. During a first foray in 1562, Coligny left some thirty men who rebelled against their commanders and were finally brought home by an English ship. The fort there, too, was razed. In 1564 three hundred settlers arrived in Florida. But problems with the Indians and the pursuit of gold resulted in another failure. Several colonists accepted the offer of an English captain and returned home. The following year six hundred French people left for Florida. Hardly had they begun to establish themselves than a Spanish fleet arrived. The fort was attacked and destroyed, more than 130 settlers were killed, and the survivors returned to France. This failure signaled the end of French Protestant colonizing ventures.

MONOPOLISTIC VENTURES

During the last quarter of the sixteenth century, French ventures organized by private persons again were directed toward Newfoundland as well as the Gulf of Saint Lawrence and the Saint Lawrence River, which were being visited by more and more fishermen. Promoters were drawn by the natural wealth of the continent. Mesgouez de la Roche expressed the desire "to conquer some lands . . . wherefrom he hoped to draw many goods" for commerce. During his first expedition, in 1578, his main ship was taken by the English. His second attempt, in 1584, was no more successful; the vessel sank near French shores. Finally in 1598 he founded a settlement on Sable Island, east of Nova Scotia, where prisoners, vagabonds, and beggars managed to survive for five years by fishing and agriculture. In 1602 the leaders did not send supplies, and the settlement was greatly disrupted. The colonists were said to have rebelled and killed their leader. Some ran away while others simply dispersed, and so this attempt, too, ended in failure.

Meanwhile Pierre Chauvin de Tonnetuit in 1599 had been granted a trade monopoly in New France. His interest in fish and furs earned him the hostility of the Saint-Malo merchants who traded there. The next year he founded a small settlement at Tadoussac, at the mouth of the Saguenay, rather far inland. The sixteen men he left there suffered from a shortage of food and a harsh winter. A few died, and others sought refuge with the Indians. The French did not as yet know the continent well enough to live there permanently and safely.

KNOWLEDGE OF THE CONTINENT

The voyages of discovery, the exploitation of fisheries, and the attempts at colonization in the sixteenth century yielded much new information about the land and its inhabitants. But knowledge and adaptation are not identical, even when survival is at stake. The French who came to North America in the sixteenth century were competent primarily as sailors, as evidenced by the regular presence and the growing number of ships and seamen engaged in fishing, the travel accounts, and the maritime maps as well as by the lack of notable maritime disasters. The French had mastered the sea and its spaces. But the land and its Native populations were another matter. Though the French were beginning to recognize the potential of America, they still perceived the continent mainly as a barrier, or at best, as a strategic site on the way to India. They did not know how to exploit the flora and fauna, especially since they depended on the Indians for their fur supply. They were unable to draw year-round sustenance from the land and its bounty, and winter months took a heavy toll in the initial settlements.

French adaptation to the Native population was not much better. It is true that the fishermen bartered with the Indians for furs and established relatively good relations with them. But as soon as the French tried clumsily to impose their will, the Indians' initial warm welcome of the Europeans gave way to stubborn resistance. Faced with people who loved freedom, the French used force to bring some of them back to Europe. Everywhere the French tried to erect crosses as a sign of possession, a gesture that the Indians understood quite well, as their vehement protests demonstrate. Finally the French steadfastly sheltered themselves behind their fortified camps, displaying, as the Indians put it, their "war sticks." Jacques Cartier considered the Indians' staged demonstration of monsters and perils, intended to prevent the French ascent toward Hochelaga, to be disgraceful masquerades. He did not understand that his exploration was a violation of Indian territory, a denial of their rights, and aggression against their way of life.

In the seventeenth century, the recognition by other countries of a colony was bound up with actual occupation of the land, for purely maritime activity left no tangible mark on the landscape. This concept of colonization was fraught with significance, especially for France. Maritime powers such as England or Holland had other perspectives, but France's outlook was that of a continental kingdom with clearly delimited borders and concretely observable wealth. The settlement of New France proceeded from sea space to land space, one leading to the other. Even though sea-related activities were being increasingly pursued, they were not acknowledged as important because they did not result in anything tangible, such as architecture, landscape transformation, or writing.

Yet the conquest of North American space began from the sea. The Saint Lawrence became the main axis of the French colonies. It was the path for the explorer and the invader, the route for commerce, the sole means of communication among people and between continents. Colonization spread along the rivers and sprang from the confluences of the waterways. These places were points of attraction, and it was in them that regional specialization and settlement programs were. While Quebec looked to Europe for its livelihood, the settlement was oriented toward the hinterland and became involved in the fur trade, exploration, and evangelization. Then the state intervened to plan the occupation

of space, to extend it, and to ensure its use. The colonizing process became systematic and geopolitical in nature, but the settlers in turn transformed it to meet their needs and concerns.

QUEBEC: THE FIRST PERMANENT SETTLEMENT

In 1608 a French shipowner and merchant, Pierre Du Gua de Monts, founded Quebec, the first permanent French settlement in North America, with the help of Samuel de Champlain. The choice followed a period of trial and error in search of the best settlement site. From 1603 to 1608 Champlain explored the Atlantic coast, searching for the ideal location. In the summer of 1604, he and de Monts explored the east coast of Acadia, the Bays of Fundy and Annapolis Royal (then called French Bay and Port Royal, respectively). The winter spent on Saint Croix Island proved disastrous, and thirty-five settlers died of cold and scurvy. The following year, though, having explored the Atlantic shore as far as south of Boston and found no place to settle, he returned to Saint Croix and settled near Port Royal. In 1606 and 1607, exploration continued while ships went to Tadoussac to barter with the Indians for furs. In 1607 De Monts's monopoly was revoked and the settlers returned to France.

De Monts's monopoly was renewed the following year with the stipulation that he would settle in the interior because the king "thought it meet to continue the colony that his subjects might trade in pelts and other goods." Champlain settled at Quebec, a major event because it was the first accomplishment on land in the slow process that resulted in the creation of a colony. The site of Quebec offered several advantages: relatively easy access; location at the intersection of commercial axes; proximity to furs and fur-trading Indians; temperate climate; and location on a promontory that provided a certain security. In the longer term, the fertility of the surrounding lands would make it possible to feed a population, while the possible existence of mines refueled never-extinct dreams of wealth. Finally the narrowing of the Saint Lawrence suggested potential fulfillment of an old dream of controlling the China trade.

136

In Quebec, which would become the capital of New France, were defined the great challenges of colonization and the strategies for developing and organizing the territory. The early *Abitation*, a name given by Champlain, became a trading post, then a city with a deep-water harbor situated far inland, and finally the administrative center of New France. Quebec would become the crossroad for trade with the exterior, for liaison with the fatherland and for all administrative matters, and would be the principal center of population and services.

THE REGIONS OF NEW FRANCE

During the seventeenth century, the amount of occupied land grew constantly. As population grew, new centers replaced older ones and areas of activity multiplied. By the end of the century, French territory in North America occupied three-fourths of the continent. It stretched from Louisiana to Hudson's Bay, from Newfoundland to the as yet unexplored territories in the West, beyond the Great Lakes and Detroit.

The Atlantic Coast

The Atlantic coast, the banks of Newfoundland, and the mouth of the Saint Lawrence were still the domain of fishermen at the end of the seventeenth century. The precise number of French, Canadian, Newfoundlandian, and Acadian vessels that met there yearly is unknown, but it was more than three hundred ships with some five thousand hands. In the meantime settlements had begun along the shore. In Newfoundland, the French had scattered eight or nine agglomerations along the southern shore. In 1687 these did not have more than six hundred settlers. Except for Plaisance, where half the French-speaking population resided, these little settlements numbered a few dozen inhabitants huddled in the back of fish-rich bays. Furthermore, their existence was constantly threatened by the British from the east coast, so that frequent attacks prevented real growth.

In 1701 Acadia had a population of 1,450 souls distributed among a few settlements (including Beaubassin, Minas, and Cobequid) that were outposts of Port Royal. Soon population migrated to Île Royale (Cape Breton) and Île Saint-Jean (Prince Edward Island). Fishing was the main economic activity. In fact each year it attracted to Acadia's shore twice as many fishermen as there were settlers in the colony. The colony lived on fishing and agriculture, fertile lands having notably encouraged the raising of cattle.

Because of its twelve hundred miles (2,000 kilometers) of shoreline, the colony was easy to reach and hence was subject to devastating raids by rivals of France on a regular basis. In 1610 Biencourt de Poutrincourt replaced Champlain at Port Royal; three years later the colony was destroyed by a British expedition. After a retrocession to France in 1632, it was seized again by the English in 1654. Given back to the French in 1670, it was periodically besieged by Boston settlers until most of the territory was ceded to Britain in 1713.

Louisiana and the Mississippi Valley

French explorers from Canada went down the Mississippi River to the Gulf of Mexico. In 1700, however, the colony of Louisiana consisted of a single fortified outpost, and France was far from convinced that this new American venture, situated between Spanish and British America, was worthwhile. France already imported from the West Indies the tropical products that Louisiana could furnish. In 1713 the population in Louisiana and the Mississippi Valley (the Illinois country) did not exceed two hundred.

The colonies of Newfoundland, Acadia, and Louisiana did not have direct relations, and though theoretically they were all under the jurisdiction of the governor of New France, in fact they dealt directly with the home country. They and other French outposts in America were at a low level of economic development and depended on Canada, the most populated area of New France, for which they represented a sort of outreach, at least economically.

The Great Lakes Region

In the seventeenth century, the Great Lakes region included several outposts and forts. Since it was the area of New France richest in furs, it was a center of intense trading. It was the domain of the Indian hunter and the *coureurs de bois* (woods runners) but was also constantly traveled by explorers, missionaries, and soldiers who spent long periods in the region. The French, the British, and the Indian nations fought over its resources. An important Jesuit mission was established at Sainte Marie des Hurons, northwest of Georgian Bay after the peace of 1632. But Huronia was destroyed by the Iroquois between 1648 and 1652. From then on the French had to do their own trapping in the region. Also from that time they became more and more numerous in the area, although military and political factors influenced the number at any given time. In 1667 more than one thousand soldiers came to the region to put down the Iroquois, but during periods of peace, there were around five hundred *coureurs de bois*. From time to time, the regulations of the fur trade cut the number of voyageurs and fur traders down to one or two hundred. At the end of the seventeenth century, the region had been well explored and France had a firm, though disputed, hold over the area. On the other hand, except for missionary activities, there was no action in-depth resulting in agricultural occupation for the presence of families; in 1700 there was only a small beginning of a settlement at Detroit.

Canada

Canada constituted the center of French colonization in North America. From Tadoussac, probably the earliest gathering point of fishermen and fur traders, the population spread gradually upriver, and especially to the confluences of the principal tributaries at, successively, Quebec, Trois-Rivières, Montreal (first called Ville Marie), and Sorel. The population settled around three points. Quebec, chief port for arrivals of people and goods and exports, became the seat of government for New France, a religious center, and a focal point for services. Trois-Rivières, founded in 1634, long remained a stopover between the two larger settlements of Quebec and Montreal. Montreal, founded in 1642 by religious mystics, was at first a center of missionary activities. Fifteen years later it dominated the fur trade with the western regions.

Between these agglomerations, population increased to form rural areas of settlement filling the empty space between towns and spreading downriver from Quebec on the south bank. The Saint Lawrence provided the only means of communication between those settlements. Colonists

and officials quickly became aware of the prime importance of this waterway. At the end of the seventeenth century, the population was spread as a ribbon along the two banks of the river between Quebec and Montreal. Nearly 80 percent of the population lived from agriculture, between five hundred and one thousand men practiced the fur trade, and the towns numbered around three thousand inhabitants, a figure increased during the season of navigability by ship crews and returning *coureurs de bois*.

At the end of the seventeenth century, between fifteen thousand and sixteen thousand people lived on some twenty-seven hundred estates divided among eighty seigneuries along the Saint Lawrence between Quebec and Montreal. This population cultivated around 42,500 acres (17,000 hectares). The towns had some thirty-four hundred inhabitants: nineteen hundred in Quebec; thirteen hundred in Montreal, the stronghold of the fur trade; and a little over two hundred in the relay station of Trois-Rivières. This French-speaking population was increased by some fifteen hundred allied Indians gathered in reserves near Quebec and Montreal, allies whom church and state tried to convert to the virtues of Western civilization.

Unlike the British, who were restricted to the Atlantic coast by mountain chains, the French were able to claim a huge territorial empire covering three-quarters of the continent. But this immense size had a counterpart: fragility and lack of in-depth occupation. France took possession of territories without occupying, dominating, or even controlling them. France had to gain the friendship of and make trade alliances with the Indians, the earlier occupants. Faced by ever more numerous and more daring imperial rivals, France had to erect a chain of forts and outposts whose apparent strength was matched by the weakness of its links. As with land resources, the full potential wealth of New France's sea space remained untapped and unknown, as if the seasonal presence of thousands of fishermen did not meet the needs of colonization. Finally, with the densest population zone being in the Saint Lawrence Valley, a late seventeenth-century observer and cartographer noted that the landscape was still only an immense forest.

BIBLIOGRAPHY

Biggar, H. P. *A Collection of Documents Relating to Jacques Cartier and the Sieur de Roberval.* Public Archives of Canada Publications, vol. 14. Ottawa, 1930.

————. *The Early Trading Companies of New France.* Toronto, Ontario, 1901.

Brown, George W., David M. Hayne, and Francess G. Halpenny, eds. *Dictionary of Ontario, Biography.* Vols. 1–2. Toronto, Ontario, 1966, 1969.

Eccles, William J. *The Canadian Frontier, 1534–1760.* New York, 1969.

————. *France in America.* New York, 1972; rev. ed. 1990.

Julien, Charles-André. *Les voyages de découverte et les premiers établissements (XVe–XVIe siècles).* Brionne, France, 1979.

La Morandière, Charles de. *Histoire de la pêche française de la morue dans l'Amérique septentrionale (des origines à 1789).* 3 vols. Paris, 1962, 1966.

Mathieu, Jacques. *Les francophones en Amérique du Nord XVIe–XVIIIe siècles.* Paris, 1991.

Trudel, Marcel. *The Beginnings of New France, 1524–1663.* Translated by Patricia Claxton. Canadian Centenary Series, vol. 2. Toronto, Ontario, 1973.

*Jacques Mathieu**

SEE ALSO **The Age of Reconnaissance; British Settlements, The Lower South; The Conquest of Acadia; Emergence of Empires, France; The Fur Trade; and Indian-Colonist Contact;** and map preceding **French Settlements.**

* With the collaboration of Geneviève Pastolec.

DUTCH AND SWEDISH SETTLEMENTS

NEW NETHERLAND

WHEN HENRY HUDSON SAILED along the coast of North America from Delaware Bay to New York harbor in 1609, he was unaware that he was defining the limits of a Dutch colony in the New World. Hudson was sailing for the Dutch East India Company (VOC), a commercial stock company. Founded in 1602, it was turning profits for its investors by bringing back the exotic goods of the Far East, such as silks, porcelain, and spices.

Since the fall of Constantinople in 1453 to the Ottoman Turks, Europeans had sought alternate routes to the riches of the East: Columbus's famous voyage in 1492 being one of many unsuccessful attempts to circumvent the Turks. When the Portuguese explorer Vasco da Gama rounded the tip of Africa in 1499, he opened the East to European trade once again. The VOC had hired Hudson to find yet another route to the East, one that was possibly shorter and certainly safer than the route around the tip of Africa. Since 1568 the Dutch had been at war with Spain and, since 1580, with Portugal (after the Iberian crowns were united). Spanish and Portuguese interests in the Far East made the shipping lanes around the tip of Africa adventurous at best for the Dutch. Sailing in hostile waters was expensive; ships had to be heavily armed or to travel in convoy, and insurance premiums were high. All these costs ate into profits and reduced returns to the investors.

Hudson failed to find a northern passage to Cathay (China) but did succeed in opening an area of North America to the Dutch. Shortly after Hudson's explorations, various commercial operations in the Netherlands were licensed by the Dutch States General to trade with the natives along the major waterways from Maine to Virginia. By 1614 competition between traders had become so fierce and bloody that the Dutch government granted the New Netherland Company a trade monopoly in the region in order to stabilize the situation. The place name Nieuw Nederlant (New Netherland) first appears in a document of the States General dated 11 October 1614 concerning the licensing of traders. Under the terms of the Company's charter, trading cartels were permitted to finance four voyages within three years between the latitudes 40 and 45 degrees (between Barnegat Bay, New Jersey, and Eastport, Maine).

The main base of operations for the New Netherland Company became Fort Nassau on the upper Hudson, 150 miles (240 kilometers) north of Manhattan Island. The fort, built on Castle Island (now mostly occupied by the port of Albany), had interior dimensions of fifty-eight feet by fifty-eight feet (17 meters by 17 meters) and was surrounded by a moat eight-feet (2-meters) wide. The moat and breastworks protected a trading house that measured thirty-eight feet by twenty-eight feet (11 meters by 8 meters). Fort Nassau served as a focal point for fur trading activities that were to become the most lucrative in the Northeast.

Expeditions were sent from Fort Nassau into the interior in search of mineral deposits and other natural resources to exploit. One such expedition in 1614 turned near-disaster into a wealth of new and useful geographical information. Some time during the year a man named Kleyntie, accompanied by two compatriots, ventured westward into unexplored country, where the men were captured by Indians and held for ransom. The following year they were rescued in the Delaware River valley by the Dutch trader Cornelis Hendricksen. Their adventures from Fort Nassau to their point of capture, either along the Schoharie watershed or near the source of the Delaware River, and their eventual ransoming in the Delaware Valley gave Kleyntie insight into the configurations of the various waterways within New Netherland. The map upon which Kleyntie's expedition is reported shows awareness of the source of the Delaware River, extending far to the north into territory supplying furs to Fort Nassau. Dutch knowledge of the configuration of the various waterways within New Netherland is important for understanding their concerns regarding settlements on the three major river systems—the Hudson, the Connecticut, and the Delaware.

When the New Netherland Company's charter expired in 1618, the territory was once again opened to cutthroat trading activities. As if to define the moment, Fort Nassau was washed away by a spring freshet in the same year, forcing traders to operate seasonally from aboard ship or from makeshift shelters on shore. The chaotic situation was not resolved until 1621 when the West India Company (WIC) was chartered as a trading monopoly similar in organization to the VOC. The WIC's area of operations extended west from the west coast of Africa to the eastern reaches of the Indonesian archipelago. New Netherland was one of its many interests; others were the Gold Coast of Africa, Brazil, with its wealth of sugar and dyewood, and the salt-rich Caribbean islands. Although the WIC was founded in June 1621, it took almost two years for it to raise enough capital to finance its first attempt to take possession of its holdings in North America.

Peopling Three Satellite Trading Posts

It is unclear when the first settlers arrived in New Netherland. According to Catelyntie Trico, some did so as early as 1623. Trico's deposition, sworn out in 1688, states that she came over with Arien Jorissen Tienpont aboard the WIC ship *de Eendracht*, or *Unity*. Trico, who was from Paris, came over with a group of Walloons (French-speaking Belgians). She deposed that she and three other women married at sea. Upon arriving in New Netherland, hers was among eighteen families sent to Fort Orange in the upper Hudson River valley. Two families and six men were sent to a trading post in the Connecticut River valley, and two families and eight men were sent to High Island in the Delaware River valley. While sailing upriver, Trico's group stopped at Esopus (present-day Kingston, New York) to pick up some boats that had been left there the previous year by private traders. Trico also states that eight men were left behind at New York, most likely on *Noten* or Nut Island (present-day Governor's Island).

Although it can be argued that Trico's advanced age of eighty-three years may have clouded her memory for some details, her statement does accurately describe the early thinking of the WIC regarding settlements. It is evident from Trico's deposition that the first colonists were to be distributed among the three remote trading posts on the three major river systems in order to serve as agricultural support communities. Nut Island, off the tip of Manhattan, was to serve as a point of assembly for offloading coastal ships to large oceangoing ships, a role similar to that played by the island of Texel in the Netherlands.

Although Cornelis May should probably be considered the first director of New Netherland, historians rarely include his name on lists of the colony's leaders. However, he was the commander of the first group of colonists to come to New Netherland aboard the *Nieu Nederlandt* in 1624. It was his task to establish the new colonists at the three trading posts, located at the extremities of the colony, and to supervise company operations until his successor arrived the following year. The dispersed nature of the settlements probably made the cabin of Cornelis May's ship his council chamber and the center of the colony. Although May is not recorded in documentary sources as governor or director, Arien Jorissen Tienpont is twice referred to as governor by Trico. Again it may be the result of an aged memory that confused the two separate arrivals. However, if Trico did indeed arrive in 1623 aboard a ship skippered by Tienpont, then Tienpont must be considered the first director.

In 1625 May was replaced by Willem Verhulst, who came to serve as director of New Netherland, which, though settled the next year, was not to receive its charter until 1653. His instructions were to strengthen the trading posts and their related settlements, especially the post on High Island, which was intended to become the center of the colony. It is unclear why the directors were drawn to this island in the Delaware River (present-day Burlington Island, near Burlington, New Jersey). It is possible that they had been looking for a major trading center deep in Indian country but one that, unlike Fort Orange on the upper Hudson, was ice-free all year. The directors had apparently been misinformed about the Delaware River site. In fact, one winter it was reported that Indians coming from the west had been able to cross over the river on the ice to the Dutch trading post on the eastern shore. In the end, it was not the decision of poorly informed directors but an incident at Fort Orange that determined the location of the center of New Netherland.

Catelyntie Trico stated that she lived at Fort Orange for three years but in 1626 returned to Manhattan. She did not indicate her reason for leaving her new home in the north; however, it is known that the local commander, Daniel van Crieckenbeeck, became involved in a war between the Mohawk and Mahican in the spring of 1626. When he and six of his soldiers accompanied a Mahican war party for an attack on the Mohawk, they were ambushed a short distance from the fort and thoroughly defeated. In addition to many Mahican casualties, van Crieckenbeeck and three of his soldiers were killed. The Mohawk were outraged that the Dutch, who had instructions to remain neutral in such conflicts,

had betrayed them in this manner. Fortunately van Crieckenbeeck's indiscretion coincided with the arrival of Peter Minuit in 1626 as the new director of the colony.

Upon hearing the news, Minuit sailed immediately to Fort Orange. Minuit, who had been in the colony the previous year as a volunteer looking for precious metals and other marketable resources, knew the land and the various Native American peoples better than anyone else in the colony at that time. He saw the dangers in the situation and realized that the outlying support communities were in peril of destruction. Minuit resolved the problem by purchasing Manhattan Island for sixty guilders worth of trade goods and moving all the outlying families to this central location. Apparently the Mohawk agreed to allow trading personnel to remain at Fort Orange but insisted that the families be removed; or they may have indicated that they could no longer guarantee the settlers' safety. At this time the families from the trading posts on the Connecticut River and on High Island in the Delaware River valley were withdrawn. Instead of retaining a presence at the post on High Island, the colony established a new trading post on the eastern shore of the Delaware River at present-day Glouchester, New Jersey, which it christened Fort Nassau.

The initial experiment with satellite trading posts supported by agricultural communities on the three major river systems had failed. New Amsterdam at the southern tip of Manhattan Island had become the administrative center of the colony. The island had an excellent harbor, free of ice the year round, and was large enough to establish any number of support farms.

The Development of the Patroon System

For the first five years of its efforts at colonization, the West India Company had supplied New Netherland with only enough settlers to develop agricultural support farms at the various trading posts and, later, on Manhattan. Although there was a genuine fear among some directors that colonization would adversely affect company profits, it is also the case that the company was concentrating most of its attention on Africa and Brazil and therefore allowed the colonization effort to languish. In 1624, shortly after capitalization was attained, the WIC sent an expedition of twenty-six ships and thirty-three hundred men to conquer Bahia in Brazil; few resources were left for New Netherland. Initial gains by the Dutch in Bahia were reversed the following year by a Portuguese relief squadron; however, the market potential of Brazilian sugar remained the WIC's main interest in the New World. The euphoria following Piet Heyn's capture of the Spanish silver fleet in 1628 resulted in an even larger and more determined commitment to the capture of Brazil, again to the detriment of New Netherland.

Continued debate in the WIC concerning colonization resulted in a concession called the Charter of Freedoms and Exemption, passed in 1629; rather than expend WIC capital, the directors decided to privatize colonization through the creation of patroons. This plan of colonization allowed an investor or group of investors to negotiate with the natives for a tract of land upon which the purchaser was obligated to settle fifty colonists within four years at his own expense. In return, the patroon was granted the rights of high, middle, and low jurisdiction, which included the power of capital punishment, appealable to central council (along with cases involving more than £50), the right to appoint magistrates, and the right to possess all manorial privileges, such as those covering hunting, fishing, and fowling. The patroon held the land as perpetual fief of inheritance which could be disposed by last will and testament. The scheme was in many ways similar to the Portuguese system of land development in Brazil, in which the Crown granted to *donatários* (patroons) land called *capitanias* in return for colonizing and developing the region.

During Minuit's administration (1626–1631) furs began to flow back to the Netherlands through the warehouses of New Amsterdam. Minuit saw the need to encourage colonization in order to protect WIC interests from foreign encroachment. However, his promotion of the patroonships, especially Rensselaerswyck in the upper Hudson Valley, embroiled him in constant conflict with company personnel in New Netherland and eventually led to his dismissal by the antipatroon faction of the WIC. Minuit left a colony struggling for survival. The company's attention continued to be attracted to the potential of African gold, Brazilian sugar, and Caribbean salt, while New Netherland was starving for financial and human resources. The single bright spot was the patroonship of Rensselaerswyck, which was showing signs of success despite attempts by the antipatroon faction to sabotage all private interests in the colony.

Of all the patroonships registered from Sable Island near Nova Scotia to the island of Fernando do Noronho in the South Atlantic, only Rensselaerswyck experienced any degree of success; the rest either failed to be capitalized or were repurchased by the WIC. The antipatroon faction among the directors was so hostile and suspicious of the system that it had little chance of success. The survival and success of Rensselaerswyck is a tribute to both its founder and majority investor, Kiliaen van Rensselaer, and its ideal location. Ever since Hudson visited the area in 1609, the plain on the west bank of the Hudson River (commanded by Fort Orange since 1624) had been recognized as a critical location for the fur trade. The configuration of the Hudson and Mohawk rivers formed a natural conduit for trappers moving furs from the west through the Mohawk Valley to a point approximately where Schenectady now stands. From there trade followed an overland route to the southeast, avoiding the Cohoes Falls near the confluence of the Mohawk and Hudson rivers. At this point the furs were traded for merchandise stocked at Fort Orange and warehoused there until ships took them south to Manhattan for transshipment to Europe. A patroonship located in this region not only had the advantage of developing one of the most agriculturally productive regions in the Northeast but also had a WIC fort in its geographical center for protection. This situation, in which agricultural support was exchanged for protection, was the ideal situation envisioned by the pro-patroon faction among the WIC directors. Next to Manhattan, Rensselaerswyck and Beverswyck became the most important population center in the colony. Rensselaerswyck and Beverswyck (the upper Hudson region) had become as important as Manhattan by the mid 1650s.

The process of selecting a suitable location for a patroonship and negotiating with the Native owners for title to the land was left in the hands of an agent hired by the prospective patroon. In Kiliaen van Rensselaer's case, his agent, Bastiaen Jansz Crol (who succeeded Minuit in 1631 as director of the colony), not only had experience in New Netherland but had also served as commissary of Fort Orange for several years. Crol knew the region, its agricultural potential, and the natives with whom he had to negotiate. Thanks in part to his efforts, Rensselaerswyck eventually stretched along both sides of the Hudson River, with the WIC's trading post, Fort Orange, in its center on the western shore; the patroonship extended east and west as far as the situation with the natives would allow. By the mid 1650s there were over one thousand inhabitants in the Fort Orange/Rensselaerswyck area of New Netherland.

Much of the growth in the van Rensselaer patroonship occurred after the Charter of Freedoms and Exemptions was revised in 1639, opening the WIC's monopoly on the fur trade to everyone. Brant van Slichtenhorst, director of the patroonship from 1648 to 1652, boasted that during his tenure more than one hundred houses had been built. Not only had Fort Orange developed into the principal fur trading post in New Netherland, but the patroonship was also attracting numerous settlers to service the fur traders. Bakers, tailors, shoemakers, coopers, wheelwrights, blacksmiths, brewers, and carpenters all contributed to the operation of a growing community whose focus during July and August was on the fur trade but that was broadening into other areas. In addition to the various crafts and trades supporting the fur trade, other industries developed that took advantage of the abundance of waterpower from the many streams feeding into the Hudson. Gristmills for processing the increasing grain production, sawmills for exploiting the vast timber reserves, brickyards for producing building materials for the booming construction industry, and tanbark mills for servicing the tanneries were all creating a diversified economy that would allow the community to survive any interruption in the trade with the Indians.

The relationship between the WIC and the van Rensselaer patroonship was almost ideal. However, this relationship came to an end in April 1652 when everything within three thousand feet (1,000 meters) of Fort Orange was incorporated into the jurisdiction of the WIC. The newly formed village of Beverswyck, carved out of the middle of Rensselaerswyck, was the resolution of a long dispute between the patroon's director, Brandt van Slichtenhorst, and the WIC's

director, Peter Stuyvesant, over Stuyvesant's refusal to allow construction of any building within cannonshot of Fort Orange.

The establishment of Rensselaerswyck, for which Crol served both as agent and as signatory of the patent in his capacity as director of New Netherland, was the most memorable achievement of Crol's administration. Another patroonship established during Crol's administration was that of Swanendael on Delaware Bay near present-day Lewes, Delaware. The investors in this short-lived patroonship planned to profit from the whales that frequented the bay by establishing a whale oilworks in the patroonship. Unfortunately, the thirty-two men who were set ashore in 1631 to construct the necessary structures for the operation were all killed the following year because of a misunderstanding with the local Indians. The Dutch demanded punishment for an Indian who had stolen a metal boundary marker. When the Indians brought the culprit's head, the Dutch were upset by the harshness of the punishment. As a result of this reaction, the Indians decided that they could not deal with the Dutch. They surprised the Dutch in the fields during planting and killed them all. However, in the following century, the settlement at Swanendael did prevent Maryland from gaining control of the Delaware region and allowed the three lower counties to become the separate province of Delaware. Lord Baltimore's charter of 1632 gave him possession of all land not previously occupied by Christians. Since Swanendael was founded in 1631, Baltimore's claim did not legally include Delaware. In order to satisfy both Pennsylvania and Maryland, Delaware was created as a compromise.

Patterns of Settlement in New Netherland

Crol's short term as director was followed by that of the nephew of van Rensselaer, Wouter van Twiller (1632–1638). Van Twiller's tenure in office is distinguished by the almost complete stagnation in the colony. Much of the malaise can be attributed to the character of the director himself and part to the neglect of the WIC's directors, whose attention was almost completely focused on the conquest of Brazil. During van Twiller's administration there was little activity with regard to settlements within New Netherland. Michiel Pauw's patroonship of Pavonia

145

(centered at Ahasimus, present-day Jersey City) was bought out by the WIC. This agricultural settlement would grow rapidly, only to be devastated during the Indian wars of the 1640s and 1650s; a similar fate befell a settlement on Staten Island.

The year 1638 was a watershed for New Netherland. It saw the end of the administration of the weak and irresolute Wouter van Twiller and the advent of Willem Kieft (1638–1647) as director of the colony. It was also the final year of the WIC's monopoly on the fur trade and the end of a long period of peaceful relations with the Indians.

The WIC's concentration on maximizing profits had created an unattractive atmosphere for prospective colonists. The optimism sparked ten years earlier by plans to populate the colony with settlers working on large private estates owned by patroons had been diminished by suspicion and disaster. Now, just when the climate for colonization should have improved in the colony because of incentives related to the liberalized fur trade, Kieft became involved in a series of devastating wars with the Indians of the lower Hudson. Settlers from outlying regions fled to Manhattan for safety, and New Netherland soon became an unattractive choice for prospective settlers. Further, during the turmoil of Kieft's administration, New Englanders continued to encroach on WIC territory in the Connecticut River valley, and settlers and WIC personnel at the Dutch trading post of Fort Goede Hoop (Fort Good Hope, present-day Hartford, Connecticut) were harassed to the point that it was becoming impossible for them to remain there.

New Englanders were also crossing Long Island Sound to settle within the jurisdiction of New Netherland at Flushing, Gravesande (in present-day Brooklyn), and Heemstede (in present-day Nassau County). These settlers were a constant irritant to Kieft and later to Stuyvesant, who regarded them with deep suspicion, especially during the first Anglo-Dutch War (1652–1654). After the resolution of the Indian war during Kieft's administration, the settlements on Long Island grew so rapidly that the colony established local courts at Heemstede in 1644, Gravesande in 1645, Breuckelen in 1646, and Flushing in 1648. Other Dutch settlements besides that at Breuckelen were expanding on Long Island; however, it was not until Stuyvesant's

administration (1647–1664) that they were allowed to manage their own affairs through their own courts, established at Middelburgh in 1652, Amersfoort and Midwout in 1654, Rustdorp in 1656, and New Utrecht and Bushwyck in 1661.

It was also during Stuyvesant's administration that New Amsterdam, the settlement at the tip of Manhattan, officially became a city. The increase of population on Manhattan had placed such an administrative burden on Stuyvesant's council that New Amsterdam was granted the rights and privileges of a municipality in February 1653 and was allowed to administer its own affairs. In 1660 the settlement of Haerlem at the northern end of the island was granted a local court.

In addition to the growing settlements on Long Island and Manhattan, other settlements expanded as well. The settlement at Bergen, the former patroonship of Pavonia in New Jersey, was granted a court in 1661, as was Staten Island in 1664. Although Esopus (present-day Kingston), a halfway point between Manhattan and Fort Orange, had been attracting seamen, traders, and farmers since the early years of Dutch presence in the Hudson, it was not until 1661 that Wiltwyck (former Esopus) was granted its own court; until then it had fallen under the jurisdiction of the court at Beverswyck. (As a result of Indian attacks on remote farms during the 1655 Peach Tree War, Stuyvesant had ordered that scattered rural settlements, such as those in the Esopus region, consolidated into defensible communities. This consolidation in the Esopus region resulted in the formation of the village of Wiltwyck.) Farther to the north, Arent van Curler, a former official of Rensselaerswyck, petitioned Stuyvesant's council in 1661 for permission to form a settlement on the Mohawk River where the overland route to Fort Orange and Beverswyck began; he finally received permission in 1664 when the prospective settlers promised to devote themselves to agriculture and not become involved in the fur trade. The founding of this community (now Schenectady) completed the settlement pattern within New Netherland. In September 1664 the Dutch settlements fell to the English, beginning a long process of accommodation, adaptation, assimilation, and development into American communities.

It should be noted that the Dutch recaptured New Netherland during the third Anglo-Dutch

War in 1673, restoring their control over the former Dutch settlements. During this restoration period, which lasted from September 1673 until October 1674, several place names were changed to reflect contemporary political considerations: Beverswyck, which had become New Albany under the English, was renamed Willemstad; Fort Orange went from Fort Albany to Fort Nassau; Wiltwyck, from Kingston to Swanenburgh; New Amsterdam, from New York to New Orange; and Fort Amsterdam, from Fort James to Fort Willem Hendrick.

NEW SWEDEN AND THE SOUTH RIVER

In the mid 1600s Dutch and Swedish commercial and colonizing interests came into direct conflict in the Delaware Valley, the South (now Delaware) River region of New Netherland. Rather than being merely a conflict between two competing European powers, this dispute grew out of a century old relationship. The intellectual and financial forces of the two nations were so intertwined that their colonizing efforts in the New World reflect many common sources and influences.

Well before the Dutch revolt against Spanish rule in 1568, the Low Countries had served as a warehouse and transshipment point between southern Europe and the Baltic nations. Dutch ships brought to Baltic ports goods and merchandise from the Mediterranean and the Orient; in return they brought back, among other items, two of the most important products for the survival of the Low Countries—timber and grain. By the time of the revolt, this trade had become so lucrative to the Dutch economy that it was referred to as the "mother trade."

Dutch trading operations in the Baltic region not only brought merchants, financiers, skippers, and common seamen into direct contact with Swedes but also forged a relationship between the United Provinces of the Netherlands and the Crown of Sweden that affected events in the New World. According to Amandus Johnson,

Of foreign nations, except the immediate neighbors, Holland stood in closest connection with Sweden. From Holland, Sweden received many of its best and most useful citizens, capitalists, merchants and warriors. Dutch soldiers served in Swedish armies and Dutch captains and skippers commanded Swedish ships; Swedish students went to Holland to study commerce and Swedish scholars gained inspiration from Dutch teachers; Dutch money helped Sweden to support its armies and found its commercial companies, and from Holland came the first impulses of the transatlantic trade. (*The Swedish Settlements on the Delaware.* Vol. 1, pp. 12–13)

In addition to these bonds, the Dutch West India Company and the original Swedish South Company had common philosophical, financial, and personal ties that shaped the growth and development of both New Netherland and New Sweden.

As early as 1592 Willem Usselincx, an Antwerp merchant exiled in Amsterdam, had urged the Dutch government through pamphlet and public debate to inflict damage on Spain's holdings in the New World by forming a West India Company. According to Usselincx, a self-supporting Protestant colony in America would drain the financial resources of the Spaniards by competing profitably in New World markets and by forcing Spain to increase its military presence in the colonies. Some historians now believe that his ideas were more of a religious crusade against Spain than they were an organized plan worthy of consideration. In any case, he did become a focal point for discussion on the subject of the formation of a West India Company for several decades.

When the WIC was finally chartered in 1621 on terms unsatisfactory to Usselincx, he indicated his displeasure by taking his ideas elsewhere. In 1623 Usselincx offered a proposal for a trading company to Gustavus II Adolphus, king of Sweden. With a desire to acquire the trappings of a major world power, the king commissioned Usselincx to form an international trading company. In contrast to the Netherlands where his ideas foundered for philosophical reasons, in Sweden Usselincx's plans came to nought mainly because of the financial burden of the Thirty Years' War and the untimely death of the king. It took almost ten years for the proper circumstances to develop for a revived interest in a Swedish colony. In spite of Usselincx's lack of success, he had laid the groundwork for the two companies that would eventually confront one another in the New World.

Risky ventures such as the WIC and the Swedish South Company required more than zealous enthusiasm to succeed; strong financial support was necessary to ensure initial capitalization and resources adequate to survive the early lean years. The Dutch East India Company (VOC) had raised the necessary capital within six months. The success of private syndicates trading in the Far East had created such a get-rich-quick fever that everyone from barkeep to diamond merchant was prepared to risk disposable income on investment in overseas trading companies. The West India Company, on the other hand, required over two years to raise sufficient operating capital. The stock offering did not ignite the same enthusiasm as the earlier East India Company venture because of uncertainty caused by the resumption of war with Spain after expiration of the Twelve Years' Truce (1609–1621). The Spanish siege of Bergen-op-Zoom dampened investors' enthusiasm during most of 1622.

However, capitalization of a Swedish trading company more than a decade later proved to be much simpler, thanks to Samuel Blommaert, a director of the West India Company and a wealthy merchant, who was willing to organize a syndicate of Dutch investors that would finance 50 percent of the projected operating budget. Blommaert was disgruntled with the faction in the WIC that was opposed to colonization and generally upset with the management of affairs in New Netherland. With business interests in Sweden and friends in the Netherlands who served the Crown of Sweden, he was in the perfect position to assess the risks of a business opportunity and to persuade others to invest. All transactions between Blommaert and the Swedish Crown were kept confidential because of Blommaert's position in the WIC.

Originally the Swedes had sought a colony to serve as a market for Sweden's considerable copper production. Under consideration was Guinea on the west coast of Africa, where markets were to be developed to trade copper for gold and ivory. Then, during discussions in 1636 concerning the nature of the projected Swedish enterprise, a man appeared before Blommaert in Amsterdam and proposed a colony in the New World. He argued that opportunities were greater in the New World; profit was to be made with less risk and less cost. The man impressed Blommaert with his conviction, knowledge, and experience. After consultation with Swedish representatives in the Netherlands and with officials in Sweden, the decision was made to establish a colony in the New World. The man who had convinced Blommaert was Peter Minuit, former director of New Netherland from 1626 to 1631. Hired as director of the New Sweden Company for its initial voyage, Minuit knew exactly where to go in order to minimize risk and maximize profit.

These three men—Usselincx, Blommaert, and Minuit—all had one common bond: their interest in forming a colony in the New World. Usselincx dreamed of a Protestant colony that would compete with Spain in the New World, draining it of its financial resources. Such a colony would require a steady stream of Protestant colonists to make it viable. Usselincx's colony was to be populated by industrious freemen recruited from Germany and the Baltic region. In many ways Usselincx's views were ahead of their times. For example, he opposed slavery on both moral and economic grounds. Blommaert supported the long-term view among the directors of the WIC. This faction favored colonization and the development of a strong agricultural base and argued that the commercial interests of the West India Company would be strengthened by making the colony self-supporting and capable of defending itself from hostile interests. Minuit also subscribed to the long-term view, realizing that the colony's health depended on its agricultural base. Their opponents, on the other hand, viewed large-scale colonization as a threat to the WIC's commercial operations, maintaining that the colonists would become a drain on the company's profits through competition and smuggling.

Swedish Settlement on the Minquaes Kill

When Minuit crossed the Atlantic in 1638, he was heading for a tributary of the Delaware River called by the Dutch the Minquaes Kill. This waterway, which emptied into the river on the west side, was a perfect location for a settlement for several reasons. A major route into the interior, it was an important conduit for the fur trade. Because the Dutch trading post, Fort Nassau, was situated on the east side of the river, the

Swedish post would be in a favorable position to intercept any furs before they could cross the river to reach the Dutch; as the Dutch had not directly purchased this area from the Indians, any claim in protest by the WIC would be debatable. No value could be placed on Minuit's experience and knowledge of the region. As a volunteer to Willem Verhulst, his predecessor as director of New Netherland, he had explored the limits of the colony, giving him knowledge of the configurations of waterways and their access to the fur trade. As director of New Netherland in its early years, he thoroughly knew the colony's strengths and weaknesses and had arranged the purchase of Manhattan.

Although the Swedish expedition had been planned and commissioned by the Crown of Sweden, it had a distinctly Dutch character. Fifty percent of the operating capital came from Dutch investors, the largest share of all coming from Samuel Blommaert, who had organized the Dutch syndicate. Both ships, the *Kalmar Nyckel* and the *Fogel Grip,* had been built in Dutch shipyards; half of their crews had been recruited in the Netherlands. Both skippers were Dutch, and the bulk of the supplies had been shipped from Amsterdam to Sweden under Blommaert's watchful eye. Most important of all was the director of the expedition, Minuit, with his wealth of experience in New Netherland.

The Swedish colony on the Minquaes Kill had much in common with Rensselaerswyck on the Hudson. Both colonies had been inspired by Usselincx; both had the financial backing of Samuel Blommaert, who was the largest single investor in New Sweden and who held a one-fifth share in Rensselaerswyck; both colonies were located in areas that dominated the fur trade routes westward into the interior of the country. The selection of the location on the Minquaes Kill was the responsibility of Peter Minuit, who as director of New Netherland had signed and registered the purchase agreement for van Rensselaer's land on the west side of the Hudson River. As a result of his interest in the patroon system, Minuit's relationship to Kiliaen van Rensselaer—this strong proponent of the patroonship plan of colonization—was especially close. On the outward voyage as director of New Sweden, Minuit was forced into Texel for repairs. While his ships were being made

seaworthy for their crossing to the Delaware, he paid a visit to Amsterdam where by chance he met Kiliaen van Rensselaer. Although Minuit's mission was being kept secret because of the potentially controversial destination of his voyage, he agreed to ship supplies and personnel for the patroon to his colony on the Hudson. Among the six new Rensselaerswyck employees that Minuit transported to the New World was Arent van Curler, grandnephew of the patroon and future founder of Schenectady. There is no indication that Sweden's intentions were revealed to the WIC at this time, nor was it leaked that Samuel Blommaert, one of the WIC's directors, was actively involved in the venture. It apparently was strictly a business deal between two acquaintances with mutual interests, one hand washing the other.

Minuit moved quickly and efficiently upon his arrival at the site on the Delaware River where Wilmington, Delaware, now stands. He first investigated whether the Dutch had occupied the area since he had been in the New World and whether the English colony of Maryland had been extended eastward. He then began the process of gathering the "rightful owners" of the land to negotiate a transaction. Minuit's claim to the land would be based on legal purchase from the Native owners, in contrast to English and Dutch claims to the area that were based on prior discovery. Although the original Indian grants do not survive, it is apparent that Minuit was able to negotiate for two tracts; one extending north from the Minquaes Kill to the Schuyl Kill (the location of present-day Philadelphia) and the other south to Bombay Hook (a corruption of Dutch *Boomtjes Hoeck,* "Copse Point"). Minuit, who as director of New Netherland had registered the patroonship of the ill-fated Swanendael (of which Blommaert held a one-fifth share) on Delaware Bay for Samuel Godijn, was now careful not to interfere with any active claims maintained by the investors in this patroonship south of Bombay Hook.

RELATIONS BETWEEN DUTCH AND SWEDES

When Minuit arrived at the site along the Minquaes Kill, soon to be the location of Fort Christina, in 1638, Willem Kieft was in his first year as director of New Netherland. Unsure of his options and their possible international ramifications, Kieft adopted a cautious approach to this intrusion on the South River. Before any policy could be formed against the Swedish colony and win WIC approval, Kieft found himself embroiled in a protracted war with the Indians on the Manhattan rim. This disastrous war, which lasted from 1639 to 1645, left him with few resources and little energy to devote to the South River. Kieft was forced to adopt an attitude of accommodation with New Sweden, rather than confrontation. When English settlers from New Haven ventured to establish a colony along the Schuyl Kill in 1641, accommodation developed into cooperation: Dutch and Swedish forces teamed up to expel the intruders and burn their buildings. While the Dutch continued to be distracted by their Indian troubles around Manhattan, the Swedes consolidated their position; cargoes of furs and tobacco aboard the first Swedish ships to return from the New World encouraged the investors not only to continue but to expand their support for New Sweden.

As New Sweden successfully competed with the WIC in the fur and tobacco trade, the Dutch investors (including Blommaert) came under increasing pressure to dissolve their interests, and within three years of establishing its colony on the Delaware, the New Sweden Company had bought back all the shares held by Dutch investors. Although the New Sweden Company was ostensibly a private corporation, its financial support now came mostly from officials in the Swedish government. It had become in fact a commercial and colonizing arm of the Crown of Sweden. Unlike the WIC, the New Sweden Company was not answerable to a board of directors concerned with maximizing profits in order to satisfy and attract shareholders. In many ways it had become the colonial venture promoted by Willem Usselincx: a profitable colony of freemen with direct financial support from the home government.

Dutch and Swedish relations along the Delaware continued to be driven by the realization that accommodation and cooperation were necessary to oppose any further English incursions from New England and the tobacco colonies on the Chesapeake. New Sweden continued to strengthen its colony and its relations with the Indians, especially with the arrival in 1643 of Johan Printz as governor, accompanied by one hundred Swedish and Finnish settlers. The Dutch remained at a disadvantage in the Delaware because of the location of their sole trading post, Fort Nassau, on the east side of the river. Printz exploited his advantage by expanding his settlements and contacts with the Indian trade; only the lack of a steady supply of trade goods from Sweden kept him from dominating the Delaware fur trade completely.

When Peter Stuyvesant became director of New Netherland in 1647, relations between the Dutch and the Swedes along the Delaware changed dramatically. The passive laissez-faire policy of Kieft was replaced with an active, aggressive posture. Although Stuyvesant proceeded cautiously in order not to disrupt peaceful relations with the mother countries, he was determined to reestablish WIC authority over the Delaware. After an attempt to locate a trading post on the west side of the river along the Schuyl Kill failed, in 1651 Stuyvesant assembled a large military force that was to inaugurate a new strategy. The plan was to abandon Fort Nassau on the east side of the river and relocate it on the west side south of the Swedish stronghold at Fort Christina. The new Dutch post would not only be able to compete on equal terms for the fur trade but would also impede the movement of Swedish ships in and out of the river. Over one hundred men marched overland while a fleet of eleven ships sailed upriver, meeting at Fort Nassau. Stuyvesant could have done as he pleased in the Delaware; however, he was acting on his own initiative and contented himself with dismantling the fort and moving what he could to the new site. The location for his new stronghold, which Stuyvesant christened Fort Casimir, was a point of land just a few miles south of Fort Christina. *Sant Hoeck* (Sandy Point, as it was called by the Dutch) had a deep harbor, offered access to trade routes to the west, and commanded the river; surprisingly, it had never been occupied by either the Dutch or the Swedes. The Swedish governor, Printz, complained but did not have the power to counter Stuyvesant's actions.

It had been almost three years since Printz had received a relief ship from Sweden. The colonists needed supplies, the traders needed merchandise to satisfy the Indians, and Printz longed for his replacement so he could return home. The last ship, *Kattan* ("the Cat"), had run aground near Puerto Rico in 1649; the Spaniards had seized the ship and enslaved the passengers and crew. Toward the end of 1653, Printz decided that he could wait no longer. He traveled overland to New Amsterdam, accompanied by his family and twenty-five soldiers and colonists, all of whom boarded the first available ship to Europe. Printz promised his people on the Delaware that he would return or at least send a relief ship. He needed to do neither. By the spring of 1654 Stuyvesant had received instructions to permit resettlement of the inhabitants of New Sweden (about one hundred men, women, and children) within his jurisdiction. The WIC directors pointed out that population increase was necessary for the settlement to prosper and should be promoted by all means. WIC policy toward colonization had changed considerably since the opening of the fur trade in 1639.

Swedes Recapture Fort Casimir

On 30 May 1654 (Trinity Sunday) Printz's relief ship appeared before the Dutch Fort Casimir. The Swedish ship *Örn* ("the Eagle") was carrying Johan Rising, Printz's replacement as governor, much needed supplies and merchandise, and more than two hundred colonists. With a show of force and a good verbal bluff, the Swedish commander caused the Dutch garrison to surrender without firing a shot. Fort Casimir's defenses had been weakened in favor of strengthening Manhattan against a possible attack from New England during the first Anglo-Dutch War, and the remaining garrison amounted to a handful of men with no gunpowder to defend themselves. The Swedes renamed the fort *Trefaldighet* (Fort Trinity); the Delaware was once again a Swedish river. With the influx of these colonists, New Sweden's population swelled to over three hundred.

Although the loss of Fort Casimir and of control over the southern region of New Netherland was a blow and an embarrassment to the directors of the WIC and to Stuyvesant, two other events occurred during 1654 that were to reverse the fortunes of both colonies. First, in January the final capitulation of Dutch Brazil to the Portuguese was signed. As disastrous as this loss

was to the WIC, in the long run it meant that more human and financial resources could now be spared for the neglected colony in North America. As the loss of these South American possessions forced the WIC to modify its trade networks from Africa-Brazil-Caribbean islands to Africa-Caribbean islands-New Netherland, the population of New Netherland increased dramatically. Then, in July, Stuyvesant received word of the end of the first Anglo-Dutch War. After the construction of Fort Casimir the directors had cautioned Stuyvesant not to give any cause for complaint or dissatisfaction to the Swedes because the WIC did not want to add to its enemies, and fear of English intentions during the first Anglo-Dutch War had limited Stuyvesant's ability to act on the Delaware. Now that peace had been concluded with New Netherland's most dangerous adversary, the attitude toward New Sweden changed significantly. Upon hearing of the loss of Fort Casimir, the WIC directors instructed Stuyvesant not only to restore Dutch possessions on the Delaware to their former state but also to drive the Swedes from the river.

Capture of New Sweden

The final chapter in the history of relations between the Netherlands and Sweden along the Delaware was written in September 1655. With the support of a large warship on loan from the city of Amsterdam, Stuyvesant invaded New Sweden. His overwhelming assault quickly forced the surrender of all Swedish possessions and brought to a close the seventeen-year history of New Sweden. However, the end of New Sweden did not signify the end of Swedish presence on the Delaware. Although some soldiers and colonists did return to Sweden after the surrender, the majority of the Swedish and Finnish colonists remained as a cohesive group as the "Swedish nation" within New Netherland. Contrary to the directors' desires to remove them from the Delaware and scatter them among the Dutch population elsewhere, Stuyvesant allowed them to remain and to form villages. While administering the oath of allegiance to the people, he referred to them as "the Swedish nation, our good and faithful subjects, to whom we hereby assure and promise our favor and all possible assistance, as if they were our own nation." When the directors criticized Stuyvesant's handling of the Swedes, especially for allowing them to concentrate in their own settlements, he responded that he realized that the Swedes had little affection for the country and that the Dutch would feel the same if they were conquered. He thought it proper to govern them leniently in order "to win their hearts and divert their thoughts from a hard and tyrannical form of government." This was rather enlightened thinking in an age that usually witnessed the elimination of unwanted populations by either displacement or death.

The "Swedish nation" was still an entity when the English gained control of the Delaware in 1664. The English commander was given special instructions with regard to the former inhabitants of New Sweden: "To the Swedes you shall remonstrate their happy return under a monarchicall government and his Majesties good inclination to that nation." The only monarchy that the "Swedish nation" desired to be ruled by was the Crown of Sweden, a hope that was kept alive for many years but never realized.

After the seizure of New Sweden, this large concentration of Swedes and Finns was added to the growing multiethnic population of the colony. Recalling Willem Kieft's remark in 1642 that eighteen languages could be heard spoken in the Manhattan area, the colony continued to attract many non-Dutch settlers from all across Europe, from Norway to Croatia. Many were displaced persons from the Thirty Years' War, some were merely looking for an improvement in their way of life. It is estimated that about 50 percent of the population in the Manhattan area was non-Dutch. Included in this estimate are the many New Englanders who settled on Long Island within the jurisdiction of New Netherland. At Beverswyck and Rensselaerswyck along the upper Hudson the percentage of non-Dutch was lower because the patroon of Rensselaerswyck drew mostly on his own agricultural region in the Netherlands for settlers. In the early decades New Netherland attracted mostly young single males. As encouraging reports about the opportunities filtered back to Europe, families with children and servants began to make the Atlantic crossing. Although many were farmers and soldiers, practically every profession was represented among the craftsmen, from blacksmith to wheelwright. After the fall of Dutch Brazil in 1654 the North American colony began to attract those settlers who would otherwise have been sent to South America.

LAST YEARS OF NEW NETHERLAND

With the elimination of New Sweden and with the WIC's refocused attention after the loss of Brazil, the growth and development of New Netherland underwent some major changes. Not only did the colony in general experience an increased population growth in its last ten years of existence, but the action along the Delaware brought some new interests into the region. The city of Amsterdam's loan of its warship *De Waegh* ("the Balance") for the successful invasion of New Sweden was repaid by giving the city control over the Delaware region from Christina Kill (formerly Minquaes Kill) to Bombay Hook; eventually, the city was ceded control over the entire river. The colony of New Amstel, which developed in the area and was centered around Fort Casimir, became essentially a colony within a colony, as was Rensselaerswyck in the north. It hired its own administrative personnel and its own soldiers and solicited its own colonists. Colonization had once again been privatized, this time through municipal interests rather than through private investment.

This process ended in September 1664 when the English drive for hegemony along the coast of North America was completed with the conquest of New Netherland. The restoration of Dutch control over its former colony in 1673 during the third Anglo-Dutch War ended fourteen months later with the signing of the Treaty of Westminster under which the Netherlands received legitimate rights to its possession of Suriname, which it had seized from England during the second Anglo-Dutch War, in exchange for the return of New York to the English Crown.

BIBLIOGRAPHY

Bachman, Van Cleaf. *Peltries or Plantations: The Economic Policies of the Dutch West India Company in New Netherland, 1623–1639*. Baltimore, Md., 1969.
Boxer, C. R. *The Dutch Seaborne Empire 1600–1800*. London, 1965.

Burke, Thomas E., Jr. *Mohawk Frontier: The Dutch Community of Schenectady, New York, 1661–1710*. Ithaca, N.Y., 1992.

Cohen, David Stephen. "How Dutch Were the Dutch of New Netherland." *New York History* 62 (1981):43–60.

Dahlgren, Stellan, and Norman, Hans. *The Rise and Fall of New Sweden: Governor Johan Risingh's Journal in its Historical Context, 1654–1655*. Uppsala, Sweden, 1988.

Fernow, B. *Documents Relating to the Colonial History of the State of New York*. Vol. 12. Albany, N.Y., 1877.

Gehring, Charles T., trans. and ed. *Delaware Papers*. Vol. 18–21. New York Historical Manuscripts: Dutch. Baltimore, Md., 1978, 1981.

Johnson, Amandus. *The Swedish Settlements on the Delaware; Their History and Relation to the Indians, Dutch and English 1638–1664*. 2 vols. New York, 1911; repr. 1970.

Nissenson, Samuel G. *The Patroon's Domain*. New York, 1937.

O'Callaghan, Edmund B. *The Documentary History of the State of New York*. Vol. 3. Albany, N.Y., 1850.

Rink, Oliver A. *Holland on the Hudson: An Economic and Social History of Dutch New York*. Ithaca, N.Y. 1986.

———. "The People of New Netherland: Notes on Non-English Immigration to New York in the Seventeenth Century." *New York History* 62 (1981):5–42.

Shattuck, Martha D. "A Civil Society: Court and Community in Beverwijck, 1652–1664." Ph.D. diss., Boston University, 1993.

Van Laer, A. J. F., trans. and ed. *Documents Relating to New Netherland, 1624–1626, in the Henry E. Huntington Library*. San Marino, Calif., 1924.

———. *Van Rensselaer Bowier Manuscripts: Being the Letters of Kiliaen van Rensselaer, 1630–1643, and Other Documents Relating to the Colony of Rensselaerswiyck*. Albany, N.Y., 1908.

Weslager, C. A. *A Man and His Ship: Peter Minuit and the Kalmar Nyckel*. Wilmington, Del., 1989.

———. *New Sweden on the Delaware: 1638–1655*. Wilmington, Del., 1988.

———. *The Swedes and Dutch at New Castle*. Wilmington, Del., 1987.

Charles T. Gehring

SEE ALSO **The Age of Reconnaissance; British Settlements, The Middle Colonies; Emergence of Empires, The Fur Trade; Indian-Colonist Contact,** and the map preceding **The French Settlements.**

BRITISH SETTLEMENTS

NEW ENGLAND

NEARLY TWO DECADES before the *Mayflower* sailed into Plymouth harbor in 1620, French explorers surveyed the New England coast and rejected the area as a likely site for European settlement. The problem was not so much the interminable winters, rocky soil, and frozen harbors; after all, the French eagerly settled even less hospitable territory farther to the north. Rather, the explorers' brief encounters with the native inhabitants of the region led them to conclude that these Indians, unlike their counterparts in Canada, would not willingly participate in the fur trade that had become the raison d'être of French colonization in the New World. With so little prospect of a return on investment, the French retreated northward to consolidate their control over the lucrative trade along the Saint Lawrence.

Even as French interest waned, English curiosity about the region grew. Early in the seventeenth century, several Englishmen, including Benjamin Gosnold, Martin Pring, and George Waymouth, explored the New England coast and returned with glowing reports of seas teeming with fish, fertile soil awaiting English seeds, and large stands of timber ready for English axes. Although encounters with the natives had been less than amicable, it was assumed that Indian

captives brought back to England could be taught English ways, and then they could return to their homes and serve as cultural intermediaries to explain the beneficence of British rule to their neighbors.

Thus, more than a century after the voyage of John Cabot—the source of England's claim to the region—English joint-stock companies began to marshal men and resources for the purpose of settling New England. The first step was the formation of the Virginia Company of Plymouth (known as Plymouth Company) in 1606, created by the same charter that established the Virginia Company of London (Virginia Company), which later sponsored a settlement at Jamestown. The charter authorized the Plymouth Company, financed mainly by men from England's western counties, to begin settlements anywhere between the Potomac River and the present site of Bangor, Maine. With an enthusiasm fueled by their utter ignorance of what lay ahead, members of the company prepared to send a ship across the Atlantic in August 1606.

EARLIEST SETTLEMENT

Sagadahoc

That first expedition never even made it to New England. Blown off course, the company's vessel ended up in the Caribbean, where it was captured by the Spanish. Undaunted, the company sponsored two more ships, carrying 120 men (including two returning Indian captives), in the following year. This group planted itself at Sagadahoc, near the mouth of the Kennebec River. Although it was the first English settlement in New England, Sagadahoc's fate links it more closely to the Lost Colony at Roanoke Island (an attempt at settlement in what is now North Carolina, in 1587) than to the settlement begun at Jamestown in that same summer of 1607.

The colonists managed to build a fort, plant crops, and make overtures to local natives for purposes of trade, but in the end their efforts were in vain. A series of setbacks—a severe winter, a disastrous fire, the death of Sir John Popham (the Plymouth Company's most avid supporter at court), and the departure of the colony's resident leader, Raleigh Gilbert, to claim his English inheritance—plagued the ill-fated settlement in its first year. Equally devastating was the fact that the West Country merchants supporting the endeavor lacked the capital resources of the Londoners sponsoring the colony in Virginia. Desperate for a quick return on their investment, members of the Plymouth Company were disheartened when the Indians did not flock to Sagadahoc to bring furs and other commodities to the English traders. By 1608 the last of the settlers had returned to England. What remained of the company's assets fell to Sir Francis Popham, who used them to fund annual fishing expeditions to the region.

The legacy of Sagadahoc was a heightened skepticism about the wisdom of settlement in New England. For a while, it seemed that the region might become another Newfoundland, its coast dotted with seasonal fishing camps. But when John Smith visited New England in 1614, he not only gave the region its name, but also tried to spark renewed interest in permanent settlement. Smith acknowledged that fishing would likely be the mainstay of a colonial economy, but he argued as well—on the basis of his observations of Indian agriculture—that the land was indeed suitable for the transplantation of English families. Smith's vision would eventually be realized, but only under circumstances that he never anticipated, and which offered him no role in the process.

Plymouth Colony

In 1608, even as the last of the Sagadahoc settlers straggled back to England, other English people were deciding to leave their homeland. These emigrants were Separatists, who believed that the Church of England had become so irredeemably corrupt that the good of their souls demanded physical separation from its baneful influence. Their destination was Holland: first the city of Amsterdam, and then Leyden, where they lived and worshiped in peace for more than a decade.

Yet the exiles gradually grew disenchanted with their new home. Limited economic opportunities discouraged many settlers, while others feared that their children were losing touch with their English origins and succumbing to the worldliness of their Dutch neighbors. Still others saw little chance of advancing the gospel in Holland and wished to move to a more promising location for doing the Lord's work. After long and earnest debate, leaders of the group decided to move to the New World.

But where should they go? Some advocated moving to Guiana, on the northern coast of South America, but concern about the hot climate, diseases, and proximity to the hostile (and papist) Spanish effectively thwarted such plans. Soon another alternative appeared. The Virginia Company of London, fearing that bankruptcy would be its reward for managing the struggling settlements along the James River, offered incentives to any group of English folk who would agree to settle within its jurisdiction and pay their own way. Complex negotiations between the company and the leaders of the Leyden Separatists ensued, with the result being that a portion of the Leyden group agreed to pool resources and take the company up on its offer. Bidding farewell to their beloved pastor, John Robinson, and to friends and families who would remain behind, the emigrants left for England to prepare for their transatlantic voyage.

There they met up with a group of London Separatists and a number of "strangers"—people unknown to the Leyden emigrants and not sharing their religious views. The subsequent voyage to New England both began and ended inauspiciously. One of their two ships, the *Speedwell*, leaked so badly that it was forced to return to England. The sturdier *Mayflower* did make it to America after nearly eleven weeks at sea, only to drop anchor at a site some two hundred miles (320 kilometers) northeast of its intended destination. Because they were no longer within the jurisdiction described by their patent, some passengers concluded that the civil authority established by that document was no longer valid. To stave off this threat to order, which occurred even before the Pilgrims landed, their leaders drew up the Mayflower Compact. All of the free adult male passengers signed this agreement, promising to obey the government established by men of their own choosing and to accept the authority of the colony's first governor, John Carver.

The Pilgrims spent the next month searching for a suitable location for their settlement. Since it was already December, harsh weather made this task particularly urgent. They finally decided on the Plymouth site, attracted by the availability of fresh water and cleared ground, and the apparent absence of Indians. The colonists found the land vacant only because recent epidemics had devastated the local population—epidemics of European diseases unleashed by the Native Americans' chance encounters with European explorers. The depopulation of the Plymouth region had been so recent, and so swift, that the Indians' cornfields had not yet reverted to forest and the starving Pilgrims were saved by finding caches of corn buried by Native Americans who had not lived to use them. When Squanto appeared the next spring to show the Pilgrims how to plant corn and to help them communicate with the local tribes, the colonists could only marvel at the amazing providence of God in sending an English-speaking native to them. They did not realize that Squanto had been kidnapped some years earlier by an English sea captain, and had escaped to his homeland only to discover that he was the sole survivor of his Patuxet tribe.

That first winter in Plymouth was a harsh one for the Pilgrims; nearly half of them died of disease and exposure. Yet the colony managed to survive, and by the next autumn, the remaining inhabitants had laid in a supply of corn and beans, had cut timber for shipment back to England, and had begun trading for furs with local Indians. With relief and a profound sense of gratitude to God, they invited their Wampanoag neighbors to a harvest feast, an event that descendants would recognize as the first Thanksgiving. Within weeks of their celebration, however, the Pilgrims received a mixed blessing: the *Fortune* arrived with a new land patent from the Council

for New England (the reorganized Plymouth Company) and also brought thirty-five new settlers who, though welcome, severely strained the colony's food resources. In fact, Plymouth's "starving times" would not end until 1624, when the first cattle were imported from England to provide much-needed protein for the settlers' diet as well as manure and muscle power for more productive agriculture.

Plymouth colony's historical reputation far surpasses its relative importance in the development of early New England. Its population never exceeded seven thousand, and it was soon overshadowed by Massachusetts Bay colony, its more powerful and more populous neighbor to the north. Plymouth's legacy derives instead from the utopian vision that inspired its founding. Its settlers desired above all to establish pure churches of visible saints, gathered voluntarily to worship God according to His ordinances. This corporatist impulse likewise shaped the settlers' political life, as seen in the Mayflower Compact with its insistence that government properly rests in the consent of the governed. Their social and economic organization, at least initially, resembled a primitive experiment in communism—if for deferred capitalist ends. For seven years, the Pilgrims held all property—land, houses, livestock, and tools—in common and worked for the good of the company.

In the end this practice proved inefficient, and the common stock was divided up for private ownership in 1627. Moreover, as population grew, settlements multiplied, and some colonists even suggested abandoning the Plymouth site altogether. William Bradford, longtime governor of the colony and author of the remarkable *Of Plymouth Plantation, 1620–1647,* lamented this last development in particular as a departure from the colony's original communal ideal. Fortunately, Bradford did not live long enough to see his beloved colony absorbed by Massachusetts Bay in 1691.

Massachusetts Bay

As the Pilgrims struggled through their first years, other groups of English emigrants tried to establish settlements along the New England coast. Most failed because their foolhardy leaders antagonized local Indians, although in the case of Thomas Morton and his followers at Merrymount, the problem grew from the settlers' indulgence in behavior so licentious that in 1628 the Pilgrims sent a military expedition to expel them. One of these outposts, however, survived to become the nucleus of the Massachusetts Bay colony.

In 1623 a group calling themselves the Dorchester Adventurers received a patent from the Council for New England to set up a permanent camp at Cape Ann, where food would be raised to supply the annual fishing fleet sent out from England. But the rocky soil proved difficult to farm—or, perhaps, the fishermen were inept farmers—and the Adventurers went bankrupt in 1626. Some of the settlers, led by Roger Conant, chose not to return to England and instead moved to Naumkeag (later Salem). There they found a more promising site for agriculture and Conant, a devout Puritan, reported the fact to the Reverend John White of Dorchester, one of the former Adventurers. White, who hoped to found a religious colony in New England, convinced some of his former partners to join with several London merchants to form the New England Company and give colonization another try.

In 1628 the new company sent out some forty men under the leadership of John Endecott to take over the Naumkeag settlement from Conant. Concerned about the validity of its claim to land granted to the defunct Dorchester group, the New England Company approached Charles I for a new charter, which the king issued in 1629 to what was renamed the Massachusetts Bay Company. With its legal title secure, the company began to organize the largest exodus to date of English people to New England.

Like all commercial enterprises, the Massachusetts Bay Company hoped to make a profit from its New World investments. Many of its members, however, had an even more compelling reason for joining its ranks. Most of these men were Puritans, convinced that the Church of England was in dire need of reform. Unlike the Separatists who settled at Plymouth, the Puritans did not abandon the official church but rather hoped to "purify" it from within. But neither the king nor his archbishops appreciated the Puritan critique, and during the 1620s the prospects for ecclesiastical reform dimmed. At the same time, England's secular affairs took a turn for the worse, as the country experienced economic difficulties and increasing political divi-

sion—irrefutable signs, the Puritans believed, of God's displeasure. When Charles I suspended Parliament in 1629 (one week after confirming the Bay Company's charter), Puritans saw little hope for improvement. Those who were involved with the Massachusetts Bay Company proposed that their New England colony be a refuge from a corrupt England, a shelter from the divine retribution they believed was sure to come.

The man recruited to lead this Puritan colony was John Winthrop, a prosperous lawyer from Groton in Suffolk. Although Winthrop had turned to Puritanism in his youth, his decision to move to Massachusetts was not an easy one to make. But he came to believe that he could do more to serve the Lord's cause in New England than in England, and in 1629 he agreed to serve as the colony's first governor. The following spring, he boarded the *Arbella* and, in the company of six other ships, crossed the Atlantic.

By the time the so-called Great Migration ended in 1641 with the outbreak of the English Civil War, more than thirteen thousand men, women, and children had sailed to New England. This was largely a movement of family groups of middling economic status, many of whom forsook England's cities for a new life in what they typically called a "howling wilderness." Some of these colonists boasted that they came to New England to fish and not to pray, but most were Puritans who hoped to create a godly society where they could work and worship according to biblical precepts.

The Bay colony leaders enjoyed unusual autonomy in establishing their Puritan commonwealth. Normally, trading corporations involved in New World settlement maintained their headquarters in London, where their meetings and other activities could be monitored by royal officials. But because the Massachusetts Bay Company charter—whether through intention or oversight—dictated no location for its meetings, its leaders determined to hold them in America. The governor and the General Court of the company thus became, respectively, the governor and legislative assembly of the colony.

The utopian vision that infused this undertaking was most eloquently expressed by Governor Winthrop himself. In "A Modell of Christian Charity," a lay sermon he preached aboard the *Arbella* in the spring of 1630, the governor exhorted his fellow colonists to "be knitt together . . . as one man" in the work of creating a godly society. The Lord had made a special covenant with them, to bind them to Him for the performance of His will. Winthrop went on to warn that "wee shall be as a Citty vpon a Hill, the eies of all people are vppon us." The Puritans' success would forever rebound to the greater glory of God, but their failure would "open the mouthes of enemies to speake euill of the wayes of god." With this mingled promise and threat ringing in their ears, the emigrants set about trying to fulfill their part of the bargain with the Lord.

The covenant, in fact, became the model of both religious and social relations in the colony. Putting into practice the reforms they hoped the English church would eventually adopt, the colonists followed a congregational model of ecclesiastical organization. Each town was required to have its own church, gathered voluntarily from among the inhabitants, who drew up a covenant stating their intention to worship together in peace. The members had the authority to call and ordain—and, if necessary, dismiss—their minister. By the mid 1630s, Bay colony churches had devised a rigorous standard of membership. In order to "own the covenant," prospective members had not only to behave well and exhibit a thorough knowledge of basic Christian tenets, but also had to convince church members that they had felt the workings of God's grace in their souls—in other words, that they had had a conversion experience. In 1648 a group of prominent ministers outlined this "New England Way" of church government in the Cambridge Platform to guide future church founders.

For their town governments, colonists similarly devised covenants enjoining neighbors to live in harmony. Localities enjoyed remarkable freedom from interference by the central government. So long as none of their activities violated colony law, inhabitants could make whatever political arrangements they chose. Although this freedom initially spawned certain local variations, particularly as settlers attempted to reconcile their different English experiences, broad similarities soon emerged. Most towns were governed by an elected group of prominent men (usually called "selectmen") and a variety of lesser officials. The selectmen's duties varied from town to town, but often included resolving disputes, executing local ordinances, and keeping track of town finances. They also arranged for town meetings, usually held at least twice a year but more often when circumstances warranted. At one of these meetings each spring, inhabitants elected a representative to the General Court; otherwise, they addressed issues too important— or too potentially divisive—to leave to the selectmen's discretion.

One of the most important issues occupying townsmen was the division of land. The colony's General Court granted land to towns as corporate entities, and the inhabitants then divided it up among themselves. With few exceptions, lands were granted as freeholds—property the owners held outright and could sell or bequeath as they wished. In most cases, settlers initially divided up only a portion of the town's land, with people receiving unequal portions corresponding to their social standing and family size. The remainder was held in common by the town, to be divided up among the initial grantees (known as proprietors) when they needed it.

Officials at the colony level, like their local counterparts, were charged with maintaining order and harmony within Massachusetts. Their efforts, however, were complicated by the fact that they had first to translate the charter of a trading company into a workable plan of government. The charter vested governing power in the General Court, which consisted of the shareholders in the company. But these shareholders, also called freemen, comprised only a small proportion of the adult males in the colony. After the first meeting of the General Court in October 1630, attended by many men who technically had no political role, it was agreed to allow all adult males to become freemen. The court soon added one further proviso: freemanship would be restricted to church members.

With this change, freemanship may have been more widespread, but the freemen's political rights were still rather limited. Winthrop and his fellow magistrates insisted that freemen could not choose their governor but could only vote for the assistants, who then chose a governor and deputy governor from among themselves. Moreover, they concluded that the freemen had no legislative function, that power derived from consent by the freemen lay with the governor and assistants. Before long, a tax dispute led the freemen to dispute Winthrop's interpretation of their charter rights.

The problem began when Watertown's inhabitants initiated a protest on 17 February 1632 to a levy imposed by the assistants on all towns to defray the costs of building a palisade around Cambridge. Winthrop asserted that the assistants held the same taxing powers as Parliament, since both bodies were elected by the freemen. Unconvinced by this analogy, the freemen pressed for reform, and in 1632 the General Court ruled that henceforth the governor and the deputy governor would be elected by the freemen—although still from among the assistants. Each town would also choose two men to confer with the assistants about taxation.

This advisory group then asked to see the charter and realized that the document in fact gave full legislative power to the freemen. Not until May 1634, then, did the Bay colony acquire a bicameral legislature, with the freemen choosing members both for the lower house (known as the General Court) and for the upper house (known as the Court of Assistants). This body immediately assumed the right to make laws, levy taxes, and fulfill the other duties of a legislature. Since by this time the total number of freemen in the colony had grown too large to meet as a single body, the court also authorized each town to send two deputies to its sessions. Only at the annual election meeting would all freemen be allowed to vote.

The General Court's adoption of a system of representative government bore witness to the dramatic expansion of settlement in the colony. Population increase was matched by a corresponding growth in the number of towns. Members of the Winthrop fleet may have intended to settle together in one community, but upon landing they immediately scattered into seven towns. By 1650 Bay colonists had founded nearly forty towns, located along the Atlantic coast and as far inland as along the Connecticut Valley. This seemingly inexorable march of settlement also led to the formation of new colonies.

Bay Colony Offshoots: Connecticut and New Hampshire

As early as the mid 1630s, colonists from several Massachusetts towns complained of overcrowd-

ing—of cattle rather than of people, since they usually cited as evidence the shortage of pasture—and asked the General Court to give them new tracts of land. Many of the petitioners coveted the rich meadows of the Connecticut River valley. Although Bay colony officials opposed such a distant move, John Oldham, an Indian trader, nonetheless led a group of men in 1634 to establish a settlement at Pyquag (Wethersfield). This town soon had two neighbors, Windsor and Hartford, and by 1635 all three welcomed scores of emigrants from the Bay colony.

The exodus to Connecticut accelerated in 1636 when the eminent minister Thomas Hooker brought a portion of his Cambridge congregation to Hartford. Hooker had been driven from his English pulpit by Anglican authorities; he spent years in exile in Holland before arriving in Massachusetts in 1633, the same year that another Puritan luminary, John Cotton, settled in Boston. Hooker's decision to move to Connecticut may have been sparked by rivalry with Cotton. The two men differed on several doctrinal points (such as the extent to which an individual might prepare for the reception of divine grace); in addition, Hooker may have felt that Cotton, located in Boston, exerted a greater influence over Winthrop and other magistrates than he did.

Hooker and a few other Connecticut leaders (such as John Haynes and Roger Ludlow) may have moved because of religious or political dissatisfaction, but most other settlers, taking for granted the spread of Puritan influence in the valley, followed economic imperatives. Thus the character of the early Connecticut population differed somewhat from that of the Bay colony. Families did not at first predominate so heavily; there were relatively more single young men seeking to establish themselves on the land, and there were relatively fewer women. With time, however, the demographic configurations of the two colonies converged.

By the time of Hooker's departure, the Massachusetts General Court had reluctantly acceded to a process already under way, allowing the removal of settlers to Connecticut and claiming jurisdiction over the new settlements. The influx of Bay colonists into the region disturbed both the Dutch, who had earlier built a fort at the Hartford site, and Plymouth colony, which had likewise established a trading post near the river. The legitimacy of these new towns was further challenged late in 1635 when John Winthrop, Jr., arrived from England with a patent to Connecticut lands. A group of peers, including Lord Saye and Sele and Lord Brooke, had obtained the patent from the Council for New England and sent the younger Winthrop to establish their colony.

The clash of jurisdictional claims was initially resolved by compromise. In 1636 the General Court and John Winthrop, Jr., agreed to appoint a commission to govern the region, even as Winthrop arranged for the construction of a fort and new town at the mouth of the river, to be named Saybrook in honor of his employers. This compromise soon collapsed, however, when conflict with the Native Americans made the issue of political authority far more urgent.

The Pequot War began in 1636 as a blood feud in which the Indians killed a group of English traders in response to the traders' having murdered a native chief. The influx of settlers into Pequot territory and attempts by the younger Winthrop to assert his authority over the natives exacerbated tensions, until the Pequots launched a series of bloody raids on the river towns. The English and their Native American allies retaliated with even bloodier reprisals, which culminated in May 1637 with the massacre of a Pequot village on the Mystic River and the virtual extinction of the tribe.

The Connecticut settlers' desire for self-government emerged as representatives of the New England colonies organized their mutual defense and colonists in the river towns struggled to meet the fiscal and military demands of the conflict. The governing commission proved ineffectual, and the inhabitants replaced it with a general court of their own, made up of committees chosen by the towns and of magistrates selected in turn by the committees. In 1639 the court adopted Connecticut's first official frame of government, the Fundamental Orders. Modeled in part on the Massachusetts charter, the Fundamental Orders created a system for the election of a governor, magistracy, and representative assembly. Freemen were not required to be church members, although most probably were. The Fundamental Orders remained in

force until 1662, when the colony received a royal charter that ratified virtually all of its provisions.

Even though Connecticut had successfully removed itself from Massachusetts's authority, the colonies continued to bear close resemblance to one another. Patterns of land distribution, church organization, and local politics were highly similar. Both colonies likewise experienced significant geographical expansion. By 1675 town grants in Connecticut extended along the length of the river valley—linking up with the Bay colony's river towns—and also occupied the entire coastal region. Settlers had even crossed over to Long Island to establish towns, much to the consternation of the Dutch who claimed the island as theirs until 1664. Connecticut's royal charter included it within the colony's bounds, but Long Island would eventually be absorbed by New York.

To the north, New Hampshire was similarly populated by a spillover of colonists from Massachusetts. The Bay colony again claimed jurisdiction over these far-flung settlers, and again these claims did not go uncontested. Beginning in 1622—nearly a decade before the Winthrop fleet sailed—the Council for New England had divided up lands along the Piscataqua and Merrimack rivers, eventually extending the patents into Maine. Two prominent beneficiaries, Sir Ferdinando Gorges and Captain John Mason, were both members of the council who sought to establish fishing and trading posts in the area. In 1629 the two men agreed to divide the territory along the Piscataqua: Mason acquired the southern part, which he named New Hampshire, and Gorges retained Maine, which he hoped to turn into an Anglican colony.

Ten days after this division, however, Mason and Gorges received a charter for the Laconia Company, a venture aimed at wresting the local fur trade from the Dutch and the French. They sent over colonists who built three settlements without ever developing a profitable trade. By 1634 the Laconia Company was bankrupt, but two of its three settlements—at Strawberry Bank (later Portsmouth) and the Isles of Shoals—survived as the first New Hampshire towns. From this point on, however, the growth of New Hampshire depended on an influx of settlers from the Bay colony.

The Massachusetts émigrés moved north for both economic and religious reasons. The town of Hampton was begun by settlers who complained of straitened circumstances in their Bay colony homes but who otherwise had no quarrel with Massachusetts. Other arrivals, however, migrated precisely to escape Bay colony authorities. Some were Anglicans uncomfortable with Puritan rule, others were political enemies of Winthrop and his allies. Still others had been formally banished from the Bay colony during the Antinomian Controversy (discussed below). The most prominent of these involuntary exiles was the Reverend John Wheelwright, brother-in-law of Anne Hutchinson, who led a group of followers to found the town of Exeter.

Despite the desires of some of the settlers to escape Massachusetts, Bay colony officials claimed jurisdiction over large portions of New Hampshire and Maine. When the General Court created Norfolk County in May 1643, it deliberately included towns on both sides of the Merrimack River to make its point. As the seventeenth century progressed, New Hampshire communities grew to resemble their southern neighbors, although distance from Boston precluded meaningful oversight of local affairs by colony officials.

But the heirs of Mason and Gorges did not so readily accede to Massachusetts's appropriation of what they believed to be their rightful inheritance, and they sued the colony in English courts to recover their property. In 1677 English judges and the privy council rejected Massachusetts's defense but also refused to accept the plaintiffs' rather broad claims. The judges insisted that the power to govern New Hampshire lay with the Crown, not with the proprietors, and that conflicting issues of land ownership had to be settled in New England courts and not in London. Thus in 1679 New Hampshire became a royal colony with an appointed governor, and the Mason heirs reluctantly pursued their case in less-than-sympathetic colonial courts. Massachusetts managed to buy off the Gorges heirs and continued to claim Maine—a sparsely populated collection of fishing villages—as its own.

Religious Refuges: Rhode Island and New Haven

Two other colonies owed their origins more specifically to religious zeal, although the zealots occupied opposite ends of the religious spectrum. Because of their preoccupation with distinguishing the godly from the ungodly, Puritans (in England as well as New England) often divided over issues of membership and discipline. Rhode Island began as a cluster of villages founded by a variety of dissenters who questioned the purity of Bay colony churches, believing that church officials substituted mere formula for the true guidance of the spirit in choosing potential members. New Haven, on the contrary, originated in an attempt to bring to perfection the orthodoxy established by the Bay colony.

Rhode Island's most prominent dissenter was Roger Williams. Arriving at Salem in 1631, he served briefly as the town's pastor, moved to Plymouth for a few years, and then returned to Salem in 1633. During these peregrinations, Williams's religious views grew increasingly radical. A thoroughgoing Separatist, he urged the Massachusetts churches to reject completely the Church of England; he then questioned the extent to which Bay colony churches themselves contained only regenerate members. Williams went on to express opinions even more disturbing to the magistracy. He opposed governmental enforcement of the first four of the Ten Commandments, arguing, in effect, for a separation of church and state. He also attacked the validity of the Bay colony charter, claiming that the king had no authority to grant Indian lands to English settlers.

The General Court, fearing that his dangerous views would infect other inhabitants, tried Williams in the fall of 1635 and sentenced him to banishment. The authorities intended to send him back to England, but before they could do so, Williams (tipped off by none other than Governor Winthrop) fled through the wilderness to a site near the head of Narragansett Bay. Joined by a few followers from the Salem church, he established the village of Providence. Within a year, he would have new neighbors.

Soon after Williams's departure, Bay colony churches were once again embroiled in a religious dispute, known as the Antinomian Controversy. The central figure was Anne Hutchinson, who was devoted to the Reverend John Cotton but who took his teachings further than he intended. In his sermons, Cotton frequently emphasized the predestinarian doctrine of free grace, arguing that God ignored human effort in His choice of the elect. Hutchinson used this doctrine to chastise other Bay colony ministers, insisting that their practice of exhorting their congregations to avoid sin and to prepare their souls for the reception of divine grace violated this central principle of the Puritan faith. She began to hold meetings in her home to discuss these issues, and soon had a sizable group of followers, including the colony's governor, Sir Henry Vane.

Other members of the government, however, concluded that her opinions were every bit as pernicious as those of Roger Williams, and in 1638 Hutchinson was brought to trial. Her opponents characterized her beliefs as "antinomian"; that is, they reflected the heretical position that the elect, because of their dispensation of grace, were released from obeying the moral law. Hutchinson in fact never went to this extreme, but her claim during her trial that she had received divine revelations—a blasphemy to Puritans who believed that such revelations ceased in biblical times—sealed her fate. Sentenced to banishment, she left Massachusetts in March 1638 and sought refuge in Rhode Island.

More than eighty families, led by William Coddington, went with her. With Roger Williams's help, they obtained the island of Aquidneck from the Narragansett Indians and built the town of Portsmouth near its northern end. Hutchinson herself soon moved to Long Island and then to what is now Rye, New York, where she was killed in an Indian attack in 1643. Meanwhile, Portsmouth gradually prospered under Coddington's leadership, although the argumentative nature of many of its dissenter inhabitants precluded religious peace. In fact, quarrels over religious and other issues eventually induced Coddington to move away and found the town of Newport.

One of the most contentious of Portsmouth's inhabitants was Samuel Gorton, who settled there in 1639 and whose beliefs had made him persona non grata in both Plymouth and the Bay colony. Like Roger Williams, Gorton held certain religious views with disconcerting secular implications. For instance, his understanding of the essential divinity of all humans led him not only to reject the exclusiveness of Puritan church membership but the notion of social hierarchy itself. In the end, Gorton was too much even

for heterodox Portsmouth, and he was compelled to move on. He and a few friends bought land from the Narragansetts some twenty miles south of Providence, settled in the region in 1641, and established Warwick in 1643, the last of the original Rhode Island towns.

Known throughout the rest of the region as "the sewer of New England," this colony of dissenting outcasts lacked official sanction. Thus in 1644 Roger Williams returned to England to obtain a charter from a Puritan Parliament. But this document, which essentially authorized the union of the various existing settlements and provided for self-government, was rendered worthless by the restoration of Charles II in 1660. In 1663 a new charter specified the boundaries of the colony and prescribed a form of government, with an elected governor and bicameral legislature, like those of Massachusetts and Connecticut. The colony thus attained a measure of security, if not harmony.

New Haven, like Rhode Island, owed its origins to dissatisfaction with the Bay colony's religious ways, but in this case, the settlers objected that Massachusetts was insufficiently orthodox. Led by the Reverend John Davenport and Theophilus Eaton, a prominent London merchant, a group of emigrants arrived in Boston during the summer of 1637—precisely when that town was torn by the Antinomian Controversy. They had intended to settle in the Bay colony but, appalled by the religious turmoil and disturbed by rumors that Charles I might recall the Massachusetts charter, they decided to found their own colony.

Hearing that good land and—even more important to the merchants in the group—a natural harbor could be found at Quinnipiac on Long Island Sound, the settlers moved there in the spring of 1638. New Haven was to be the religious utopia that Massachusetts was not. For its frame of government, the colony's leaders chose a scheme devised by the Reverend John Cotton, in which Bay colony practices were perfected by additions from Scripture, especially the Mosiac code. Church government was equally rigorous. The colonists retained the tough membership standards adopted by Massachusetts and displayed even greater assiduousness in rooting out heterodoxy. Davenport himself labored over the town plan for New Haven, hoping that its topographical symmetry would symbolize a similarly harmonious political and religious climate.

Economic success, however, eluded the inhabitants. Connecticut resented New Haven's presence, and the leaders' hopes of expanding their commercial empire into the Delaware River valley upset Dutch and Swedish colonists in that area. The harbor was not as good as the merchants had been led to expect, and their Dutch neighbors imposed heavy regulations on trade with New Amsterdam (New York City), the nearest market. As a result, many merchants departed, and the remaining settlers faced a hardscrabble agricultural existence.

Even more disturbing than these economic disappointments were political challenges. Some settlers moved off to found new towns along the Sound and acknowledged New Haven's jurisdiction only when the Indians or the Dutch threatened war. Colony leaders, knowing that the lack of a charter rendered their claim to the region exceedingly weak, voted in 1644 to send an agent to Parliament to obtain one; a messenger conveying the application departed for England but was lost at sea in 1646. Nothing more was done until the Restoration, at which point New Haven's position was precarious indeed. Many of its strongest English supporters had been executed, and colony leaders had been notoriously reluctant to acknowledge Charles II's return to the throne. But the greatest threat came from closer to home: Connecticut had already taken over towns, including Guilford and Stamford, that had broken away from New Haven's control, and the rest of the colony was absorbed into Connecticut by the royal charter of 1662. New Haven's leaders contested this action for two more years, but to no avail.

Providence Island

Not all Puritan efforts at colonization were directed at the often forbidding territory along the northeast coast of North America. In 1630, even as the Great Migration to Massachusetts began, certain prominent Englishmen—including the earl of Warwick, Lord Brooke, Lord Saye and Sele, and the fiery parliamentarian John Pym—founded another Puritan colony on an island off the coast of Nicaragua. They named it Providence, and hoped that it would become a refuge for Puritans fleeing a troubled England as well as a magnet for emigrants who had already moved to New England.

This venture fused religious and political purposes, for its founders intended their strategically located colony to strike at the Spanish colonial empire. The Providence Island Company, unlike other such organizations, limited membership to aristocrats, who then sought colonists from among their dependents. Although it tried to recruit only godly families, the company had to supplement their numbers with emigrants of dubious spiritual estate. These problems of recruitment, as well as those engendered by the colony's dual mission, soon led to serious difficulties.

Almost from the start, the island's population split into factions. Because of its vulnerable location, the company sent governors with better military than religious credentials, whose peremptory assertions of authority antagonized the settlers. Economic distress created further divisions, for during the venture's short life the colonists never produced any staple crop capable of paying off the company's growing debts. Moreover, in its desire to control the colony's development, the company insisted that settlers occupy the land as tenants, not freeholders, and thus provoked massive dissatisfaction among colonists who knew that freehold land was available in other English colonies. Efforts to initiate privateering raids on Spanish settlements increased anxieties more than income.

Company leaders insisted that most of these problems could be solved by attracting more godly emigrants. Much to the dismay of Massachusetts authorities, the adventurers appealed to Bay colony settlers, enticing them with reports of the island's warm climate and rich soil. Only a few frostbitten New Englanders answered the call before the Spanish overran Providence Island and dispersed its settlers in 1641. Despite this disaster, the colony's founders never gave up hope of maintaining Protestant beachheads in the Caribbean to oppose the papist Spanish threat. But with the recall of Parliament in 1640, the return of Puritan gentlemen to national leadership, and the outbreak of civil war, their attention inevitably turned to securing the triumph of Protestantism in England itself.

THE ACHIEVEMENT OF STABILITY

The failure of the Providence Island colony contrasts sharply with the success of the mainland

New England settlements. As the seventeenth and eighteenth centuries progressed, the principal colonies of Massachusetts, Connecticut, Rhode Island, and New Hampshire achieved a degree of stability all the more remarkable for their occasionally tenuous beginnings. No better measure of such development exists than the region's demographic record. At the end of the Great Migration in 1640, the white population stood at approximately 13,500; by the end of the century, it had increased nearly sevenfold, to 91,000 settlers. On the eve of the revolution, there were more than half a million New England colonists. The average annual growth rate of about 2.4 percent meant that the population doubled every twenty-six years—and without significant immigration. Of the vast outflow of people from the British Isles and Europe to North America in this period, very few made their way to New England, daunted, perhaps, by the shrinking supply of unallocated land and the region's reputation for intolerance. Thus New England's remarkable growth rate was almost entirely sustained by natural increase, a demographic pattern that made the area unique among British colonial regions. By the outbreak of the Revolutionary War, only the upper reaches of the Connecticut Valley in New Hampshire and what would become Vermont, along with the interior of Maine, remained open for settlement.

The labors of this burgeoning population produced a thriving economy despite the region's limited natural-resource endowments. Lacking a lucrative fur trade or valuable staple crop, the inhabitants turned to a variety of endeavors in order to make a profit. The mother country had little use for New England's products, but the region's merchants found eager customers in Catholic Europe, the Wine Islands, and, most important of all, the West Indies. Fish proved the most valuable of New England's exports, followed by livestock and salted meat, virtually all of which went to the Caribbean market. Wood products, often shipped in the form of staves to be fashioned into casks for sugar, likewise found their way to the islands.

The natural concomitant to this commercial activity—particularly given New England's timber resources—was the development of shipbuilding and an extensive involvement in the carrying trade. These endeavors earned the region substantial income and credit; shipping, in fact, was probably the leading sector in the colonial economy. This trade, like the New England economy in general, lacked the specialized focus evident in other British colonies but was scarcely less prosperous for its diversity. Merchants usually shipped mixed cargoes in small vessels to a number of ports, valuing the flexibility that this practice allowed in responding to variable market demand. By the eve of the revolution, New Englanders had created a diversified commercial and agricultural economy far less susceptible to the cyclical fluctuations that plagued the staple-crop economies of the Chesapeake and West Indies.

New England's distinctive experience of economic development promoted social stability in other ways as well. Continuity, not change, characterized economic patterns for more than a century. The alliance of commerce, agriculture, and fishing first emerged in the 1640s as colonists struggled with an economic depression caused by the end of immigration, and their eighteenth-century descendants retained this formula for prosperity through diversification. The lack of a dominant staple crop limited the demand for labor; thus New Englanders turned to their families rather than to an international market for indentured servants and slaves, and avoided the problems associated with a heavy dependence upon unfree workers. And, finally, the general level of economic prosperity and gradually improving standard of living also minimized social strain. Most settlers attained a modest level of prosperity, while relatively few descended into poverty or enjoyed great wealth. This remarkable degree of social homogeneity, particularly in the first decades of settlement, helped to reinforce the exhortations toward cooperation and harmony that regularly issued from scores of Puritan pulpits.

CHALLENGES TO STABILITY

New England's stability was not achieved without cost. Several crises punctuated the region's early history, often instigated by precisely those processes of growth and development upon which New England's future depended. But if war, political upheaval, and religious controversy intermittently disrupted the colonists' lives, these challenges failed in the long run to undermine the foundations of New England society and culture.

King Philip's War

By far the most ominous event during the region's development occurred in 1675 with the outbreak of a conflict that threatened the very existence of New England. Fed up with the ceaseless encroachments of English settlers on their land, a confederation of Indians responded with violence. Led by Metacom, a Wampanoag chief whom the colonists called King Philip, the Indians attacked dozens of communities in several colonies. By the spring of 1676, they had completely destroyed twelve towns and killed nearly two thousand settlers. Such high casualties, considered as a proportion of the colonial population, made King Philip's War the deadliest conflict in American history.

The settlers retaliated with equal force, destroying Indian food supplies, burning villages, and killing hundreds of their enemies. After months of raids and counter-raids, the Indian confederation disintegrated. In August 1676 the English ambushed Metacom in his camp, and an Indian ally of the colonists shot and killed him as he tried to flee. His head was eventually carried back to the English fort at Plymouth. The end of the war signaled the final defeat of the region's Native peoples; never again would they pose so severe a threat to the colonists. From this point on, the expansion of English settlement, so abruptly halted in 1675, proceeded without hindrance from the land's original inhabitants.

The Dominion of New England

Within a decade of the war's end, however, another crisis loomed, this time emanating from the other side of the Atlantic. In 1685, James II succeeded his brother on the English throne. Obsessed with the idea of bringing order to the administration of England's overseas empire, the new king instituted a series of measures designed to bring the colonies under firmer royal control. The Lords of Trade—the governmental body responsible for colonial affairs—had complained for years about New Englanders' evasion of trade regulations, their recalcitrance in recognizing parliamentary authority, and their refusal—principally in Massachusetts—to permit Angli-

can worship. The king and his officials located the source of the trouble in the colonies' charters, which they believed fostered the settlers' excessive notions of autonomy. The first step at imperial reform, therefore, lay in annulling those charters; once this was accomplished, James planned to combine the New England colonies, along with New York and New Jersey, into one vast imperial unit called the Dominion of New England.

In December 1686, Sir Edmund Andros arrived in Boston as governor of the Dominion. A military man, Andros expected to see his orders obeyed, and he had little patience for the colonial protests that accompanied his every action. With their charter gone, Bay colonists lost their representative assembly and faced taxation without their consent. Merchants decried the rigorous enforcement of antismuggling laws. Property owners objected strenuously when Andros threatened to invalidate all land titles and reissue them only upon payment of substantial fees. Staunch Puritans were appalled when the governor took over the South Meeting House for Anglican worship. Such measures quickly earned Andros the hostility of most of the population.

Even as the New Englanders' discontent threatened to boil over into rebellion, news arrived in 1688 of the overthrow of James II, whose arbitrary policies in England (and rumored Catholicism) had stirred the English political classes to revolt. When Bostonians learned that James had been replaced on the throne by the Protestants William and Mary, they seized Andros, sent him back to England, and jailed his few prominent local supporters.

The aftermath of the Glorious Revolution nonetheless failed to bring about the complete restoration of pre-Dominion social and political arrangements. Connecticut and Rhode Island managed to retain their elective governorships because neither colony had surrendered its charter when called upon to do so. Massachusetts, however, received a new charter in 1691 that made it a royal colony, with a Crown-appointed governor. The new charter also eliminated church membership as a qualification for the franchise; voters needed only to be adult male property holders. Although the charter reaffirmed existing land titles, the General Court subsequently departed from its former practice of corporate land grants and increasingly allocated land to individuals or groups of proprietors, opening the door to speculation. And, finally, the charter confirmed Massachusetts's jurisdiction over Maine and its absorption of Plymouth colony.

However temporarily wrenching the Dominion crisis had been, New England emerged relatively unscathed. With their new charter, Massachusetts settlers saw the greatest changes, but not all of them were unwelcome. Many non–church members, for instance, approved of the new qualifications for the franchise. In fact, the charter of 1691 eventually became as much a political icon as its predecessor had been. In 1774, Bay colonists opposed its abrogation with a vehemence even more powerful than that directed against Andros almost ninety years earlier.

The Great Awakening

Religion, which usually served as a cohesive force in New England society, became the focus of the next challenge to stability. Though still recognizably Puritan, New England's religious climate had changed significantly by the first half of the eighteenth century, in large part because of sustained demographic growth. The exclusive nature of church membership favored by the founders left an increasing proportion of the population, who were unable to fulfill the stringent requirements, outside of the church. As early as 1662, ministers devised the Half-Way Covenant, which allowed church members' adult children—who had been baptized by virtue of their parents' membership but who had not yet given evidence of conversion and thus were not full members—to have their own offspring baptized. These second and third-generation colonists were thereby brought into the church as "halfway" members, unable to take communion or vote in church affairs until they too could demonstrate the workings of saving grace in their souls. Before long some ministers—most notably Solomon Stoddard—advocated full membership that would allow all pious Christians to participate in the sacraments, whether or not they could demonstrate that they had had a conversion experience.

Such changes aimed at improving settlers' access to religion. Yet people complained of "spiritual deadness" despite their performance of formal religious duties. Lay people, in fact, voiced the strongest opposition to the Half-Way Covenant, believing that it compromised the high standards of the founders. More than a few of them suspected that uninspired clerical leadership, rather than popular indifference, was at the root of New England's spiritual malaise. Thus a measure that had been intended to enhance ministerial control over the population instead encouraged popular anticlericalism. Then, beginning in the 1730s, a series of revivals shook the foundations of New England orthodoxy.

The first revivals occurred in the Northampton parish of Stoddard's grandson, Jonathan Edwards. These were soon submerged in a much larger movement. This Great Awakening received much of its impetus from the inspired preaching of the English evangelist George Whitefield, who traveled throughout the colonies during the 1740s. In town after town, he emphasized the emotional basis of religion, urging his audience to seek a "new birth" of faith. Soon dozens of itinerant evangelists were roaming the countryside, stirring congregations to what conservatives believed was an excess of enthusiasm.

Perhaps inevitably, the Great Awakening divided churches all over New England. Newly converted saints (called New Lights) complained that lenient admission practices had polluted church membership with sinners. Latent anticlerical sentiments blossomed as New Lights challenged the spiritual authority of their preachers, warning of the dangers of an unconverted ministry. All too often, the ministers' response seemed to fulfill their worst suspicions. Instead of nurturing this sudden outpouring of popular piety, many pastors rejected the calls for change and lobbied conservative legislators to pass laws against troublemaking itinerant preachers. Frustrated by this reaction, many New Lights left the churches to form new, purer congregations of their own.

The Great Awakening thus led to an unprecedented fragmentation of churches in New England. Never again would each town's population gather together every Sabbath to worship as a community. Even as congregational churches divided into factions, dissenting groups, such as the Baptists, gained new adherents. Yet for all this divisiveness, the Awakening also reanimated New England's religious life. The emotional message of Whitefield and the itinerants tapped a wellspring of popular piety and provided a potent antidote to the spiritual deadness that had once plagued worshipers. Religion resumed its place at the center of New England life.

The Last Colonial Wars

Even before the revivals had fully subsided in New England, the settlers found themselves embroiled in warfare. This time, their adversaries were the French and their Indian allies. Conflicts between the British and French in Europe had sparked colonial hostilities before—in King William's War (1689–1697) and Queen Anne's War (1701–1713). New Englanders' proximity to New France ensured their involvement in such conflicts, but up to this point their role had been limited. But beginning with King George's War (1744–1748) and its successor, the Seven Years' War—known in the colonies as the French and Indian War (1754–1763)—colonists found themselves drawn more fully than ever into the orbit of imperial affairs.

The climax of King George's War—so far as New Englanders were concerned—was the capture in 1745 of the French fortress at Louisbourg, by an expedition of New England volunteers under the command of General William Pepperell. Following on, and indeed drawing upon, the Great Awakening, this unprecedented victory renewed the colonists' conviction that they were indeed a chosen people. The return of Louisbourg to France under the terms of the treaty of Aix-la-Chapelle in 1748 thus astonished the erstwhile conquerors and raised doubts about British concerns for New England's interests.

Their suspicions did not prevent New Englanders from answering the call to arms once again when Britain and France resumed hostilities only a few years later. The Seven Years' War was a much bigger affair; it was the first world war, with battles raging from the backwoods of North America to the Native American subcontinent. Drawing upon their own cultural predispositions, New Englanders viewed the struggle with France not just in political, but in cosmic, terms. More than a third of Massachusetts's service-eligible men joined the army to help rid the continent of the papist minions of Satan. Serving alongside British regulars for the

first time, they eventually saw their exertions rewarded with the total defeat of France in the New World.

News of the victory was proclaimed throughout New England and colonists reveled in their membership in the great British Empire. Once again they construed the magnificent victory to be evidence of God's continued favor toward his chosen people. Many New Englanders believed that the outcome heralded the coming of the millennium. No one could have predicted that, within a decade, these same New Englanders would take the lead in rebelling against British authority.

Neither the British nor the colonists anticipated the consequences of such a great victory. Britain emerged from the conflict with a drained treasury and an enormous new empire to govern. Forced to address a variety of problems immediately, the British government took the unprecedented step of stationing ten thousand troops in the interior of North America. Parliament then passed a series of measures to tighten imperial administration and to raise taxes to refill the depleted treasury.

Much to the dismay of New Englanders, many of those taxes were aimed at the colonists, whom Parliament felt were the main beneficiaries of the defeat of France. Their contributions to the victory seemed to count for nothing, and British actions seemed aimed at turning the colonies into nothing more than a Protestant Ireland. Many colonists remembered the lessons of King George's War and wondered if British and American interests truly coincided. Some began to suspect that Satan had adopted a new guise to threaten God's covenanted people. New Englanders found themselves enmeshed in a web of imperial ties as never before, and would strain at them until at last the bonds gave way.

BIBLIOGRAPHY

Ammerman, David L., and Philip D. Morgan, compilers. *Books About Early America: 2001 Titles*. Williamsburg, Va., 1989. The most comprehensive bibliography of early American history, this volume contains a wealth of citations regarding New England, from the region's first settlement through the revolutionary era.

Anderson, Fred. *A People's Army: Massachusetts Soldiers*

and Society in the Seven Years' War. Chapel Hill, N.C., 1984.

Anderson, Virginia DeJohn. New England's Generation: The Great Migration and the Formation of Society and Culture in the Seventeenth Century. New York, 1991.

Andrews, Charles M. The Colonial Period of American History. 4 vols. New Haven, Conn., 1934–1938.

Bailyn, Bernard. The New England Merchants in the Seventeenth Century. New York, 1964.

Bradford, William. Of Plymouth Plantation, 1620–1647. Edited by Samuel W. Morison. Boston, 1952.

Bushman, Richard L. From Puritan to Yankee: Character and the Social Order in Connecticut, 1690–1765. Cambridge, Mass., 1967.

Calder, Isabel MacBeath. The New Haven Colony. New Haven, Conn., 1934.

Cronon, William. Changes in the Land: Indians, Colonists, and the Ecology of New England. New York, 1983.

Daniell, Jere R. Colonial New Hampshire: A History. Millwood, N.Y., 1981.

Gaustad, Edwin Scott. The Great Awakening in New England. New York, 1957.

Greene, Jack P. Pursuits of Happiness: The Social Development of Early Modern British Colonies and the Formation of American Culture. Chapel Hill, N.C., 1988

James, Sydney V. Colonial Rhode Island: A History. New York, 1975.

Kupperman, Karen Ordahl. "Errand to the Indies: Puritan Colonization from Providence Island Through the Western Design." William and Mary Quarterly, 3rd ser., 45, no. 1 (1988):70–99.

Labaree, Benjamin W. Colonial Massachusetts: A History. Millwood, N.Y., 1979.

Langdon, George D., Jr. Pilgrim Colony: A History of New Plymouth, 1620–1691. New Haven, Conn., 1966.

Leach, Douglas Edward. Flintlock and Tomahawk: New England in King Philip's War. New York, 1958.

Lockridge, Kenneth. A New England Town: The First Hundred Years. Dedham, Massachusetts, 1636–1736. New York, 1970.

Lovejoy, David S. The Glorious Revolution in America. New York, 1972.

McCusker, John J., and Russell R. Menard. The Economy of British America, 1607–1789. Chapel Hill, N.C., 1985.

McManis, Douglas R. European Impressions of the New England Coast, 1197–1620. University of Chicago Department of Geography. Research paper no. 139. Chicago, 1972.

Main, Jackson Turner. Society and Economy in Colonial Connecticut. Princeton, N.J., 1985.

Meinig, D. W. The Shaping of America: A Geographical Perspective on Five Hundred Years of History. Vol. 1, Atlantic America, 1492–1800. New Haven, Conn., 1986.

Morgan, Edmund S. The Puritan Dilemma: The Story of John Winthrop. Boston, 1958.

———. Visible Saints: The History of a Puritan Idea. New York, 1963.

Rutman, Darrett B. Winthrop's Boston: Portrait of a Puritan Town, 1630–1649. Chapel Hill, N.C., 1965.

Salisbury, Neal. Manitou and Providence: Indians, Europeans, and the Making of New England, 1500–1643. New York, 1982.

Taylor, Robert J. Colonial Connecticut: A History. Millwood, N.Y., 1979.

Vaughan, Alden T. The New England Frontier: Puritans and Indians, 1620–1675. Rev. ed. New York, 1979.

Winthrop Papers. 5 vols. Boston, 1929–1947.

Virginia DeJohn Anderson

SEE ALSO **Emergence of Empires; The Fur Trade; Indian-Colonist Contact;** and **Maritime Enterprises;** various essays in RELIGION; and the map preceding **French Settlements.**

THE MIDDLE COLONIES

THE MIDDLE COLONIES were born of paradoxical circumstances. They were products of an imperial initiative that began with the rapid expansion of English territorial claims in North America after the Stuart Restoration in 1660 but that increasingly emphasized efforts to integrate or centralize the administration of those claims. These tendencies had a linear logic in English politics, but to Americans they often appeared at odds with each other, and tensions between them permeated the late seventeenth century. Proprietary colonies—those owned by private parties under charter terms imposed by the Crown—seemed by 1700 to be obstacles to efforts to centralize colonial administration. But before 1680 they were useful instruments for expanding the scope of empire. They repaid debts to Stuart allies who supported royal interests while keeping new colonies in friendly hands at low cost to the Crown.

The first Restoration proprietor was James, duke of York, the brother of King Charles II and heir apparent to the throne. As lord high admiral, James had been an aggressive instrument of English anti-Dutch interests. In 1664 Charles gave him a charter for the lands claimed by the Dutch in North America between the Delaware and Connecticut rivers. An English fleet reached New Amsterdam in August and quickly compelled the surrender of the Dutch colony. The duke's first governor, Colonel Richard Nicolls, worked to implement the twin imperatives of Restoration colonial policy: expanded English settlement under tightened royal control. He sent commissioners to New England to examine colonial governance there and deployed troops to the Delaware River to proclaim the duke's authority over its Dutch and Swedish settlements, which had been ruled loosely from New Amsterdam.

Having displayed the duke's power at the edges of the latter's domain, Nicolls tried to consolidate control of the colony from its center at Manhattan. In 1665 he promulgated a legal code known as the Duke's Laws. This mixture of English and Dutch law established limited local self-government in English towns on Long Island, Westchester, and Staten Island and broad religious freedom for all Protestants. The code did not authorize a provincial assembly and was adopted without the consent of delegates from the colony's settlements. It was not immediately enforced in the Dutch towns of Manhattan or the Hudson River valley. Nicolls made Dutch colonists renew their land claims under titles from the duke, but he otherwise respected their property rights.

If the code's legal intent was to facilitate a gradual transition to English institutions, its social vision included a rapid influx of English colonists. In 1664 and 1665, Nicolls granted land to settlers migrating to the west of the Hudson River from Long Island. The Monmouth and Elizabethtown grants, between the Passaic River and Barnegat Bay, offered religious and political terms based on the Duke's Laws. They were part of Nicolls's effort to attract emigrants from the increasingly unsettled towns of New England. Nicolls considered the lands of Long Island and the Hudson River valley to be of poor quality and believed the area between the Hudson and Delaware rivers to be the "most improveable" part of James's new colony. He was shocked to

learn in 1665 that the Duke had granted this land to two English allies, Lord John Berkeley and Sir George Carteret, for the development of their own proprietary colony of New Jersey.

Nicolls spent his tenure in New York nurturing its fragile institutional life in a multiethnic setting. The Duke's Laws were slowly refined in English areas, whose inhabitants resented their authoritarian political elements, while in Dutch areas between Manhattan and Albany they were implemented only after 1670. Nicolls and his successor, Francis Lovelace, delicately grafted English goals to Dutch forms while trying to limit cultural conflict. When the Anglo-Dutch war resumed in 1672, a Dutch fleet seized the colony. The eagerness with which the Dutch populace embraced its "captors" showed how difficult cultural accommodation, much less Anglicization, would be. The unease of English colonists with authoritarian rule after New York was restored to the duke in 1674 suggested that, without popular political participation, mere institution building would not guarantee social stability.

Berkeley and Carteret found it no easier to establish a successful proprietary colony than had James. Their grant legally conveyed only the land between the Hudson and Delaware rivers and not political authority over the area, but they considered a government indispensable to profitable land tenure and were determined to establish one. In 1665 they named Philip Carteret, Sir George's cousin, governor of New Jersey. Carteret encouraged the Nicolls settlers and even purchased a share in the Elizabethtown patent. In 1666 he granted land at Newark to New Haven religious dissidents, who preferred the political risks of settlement under New Jersey landlords to submitting to Puritan "compromisers" in Connecticut. Those risks were reduced by constitutional terms embodied in the 1665 Concessions and Agreements offered to prospective migrants. That document defined the powers of the governor and his council, empowered an elective assembly to make laws, and guaranteed religious liberties as broad as those of New York.

Despite these provisions, the early public life of New Jersey was even more tumultuous than that of New York. The New England migrants embraced representative government with an alacrity that probably made James happy that he had denied an assembly to his own colonists. They questioned the powers of the proprietary governor, demanded guarantees of their "priveleges," resisted rent payments, claimed land titles by Indian rather than proprietary purchase, and in 1672 even overturned the government. This rebellion was crushed with the duke's support, but the Dutch recapture of the region in 1673 undermined the government's stability again.

In 1674 Berkeley sold his half of New Jersey to two Quakers, Edward Byllynge and John Fenwick, while James sent Edmund Andros to govern New York. The proprietors partitioned New Jersey into eastern and western divisions. Andros denied East Jersey's claim of exemption from New York customs duties and arrested Governor Carteret for his defiance. Carteret was freed, but in 1681 a dispute with his assembly sparked another revolt against proprietary rule. In West Jersey, Byllynge's bankruptcy delayed the colonization process. A group of Quakers led by William Penn arbitrated the case and became trustees for Byllynge. In 1676 they planned a Quaker colony on the east bank of the Delaware. They published the West Jersey Concessions, articles of government more liberal than those of East Jersey. These offered an assembly elected on broad suffrage, one in which the social characteristics of elected representatives closely resembled those of their constituents. The proprietary investment was divided into one hundred shares, a design that envisioned an equitable society of smallholding farmers with less social stratification than the one evolving in East Jersey.

The most important result of the West Jersey project was the involvement in colonial affairs of William Penn, who contributed more toward the development of regional life than any individual in the Restoration era. The focus of Penn's work rapidly shifted west of the Delaware, but his true arena remained the Middle Atlantic region as a whole. Penn's credibility among English Quakers and his friendship with the Stuarts made him peculiarly qualified to navigate the labyrinth of Restoration era colonial policy. His 1681 charter for Pennsylvania was the last broad proprietary grant before imperial policy shifted toward closer regulation of English overseas dependencies.

Pennsylvania was a more ambitious project than New Jersey. Penn's grant gave him a vast reservoir of land to sell and included the right to establish a government. These assets allowed him to exploit his ties in Quaker mercantile circles to raise capital. By mid 1682 he had sold almost five hundred thousand acres (200,000 hectares) of land, almost half of them to "First Purchasers" of five-thousand-acre (2,000 hectare) shares. In his appointments to public office, he linked investment closely to the distribution of power. And while his promotional rhetoric sincerely portrayed the colony as a "Holy Experiment," Penn also stressed its economic potential. He chartered a company, the Free Society of Traders, with important commercial privileges and monopolies and designed the port town from which the colony would grow squarely around the needs of trade.

These concessions were critical to capitalizing the colony and to recruiting leaders, but Penn also needed ordinary settlers to provide adequate returns on his investment. In 1682 and 1683 he drafted a system of government to attract immigrants. His initial plans suggested both his nostalgic attraction to an aristocratic social order and his visionary embrace of a politics as radical as Quaker social theory, but he finally settled on a system favoring the Quaker commercial elites who invested in his colony. His Frame of Government established an elective council with power to initiate laws and broad executive authority. The assembly had a brief annual term and a veto over proposed laws but few of the procedural immunities that were considered fundamental to the popular branch of an English constitutional system. Armed with forty "Laws Agreed Upon in England" to be submitted to the legislature and convinced that the council would be filled with wealthy Quakers committed to him and to his holy experiment, Penn sailed to America in 1682.

ECONOMIC AND POPULATION GROWTH, 1660–1720

The middle colonies, lying between New England and the South, had more fertile soil than the former and a healthier climate than the latter. Middle colonists were neither Puritans, laboring under injunctions to industry while harboring doubts about its material results, nor Cavaliers, averse to labor but willing to enjoy the fruits of expropriated toil. They were not modern profit maximizers, but they did embrace aggressively the opportunities the region offered them. By 1765 they had exploited these opportunities to create what John McCusker and Russell Menard have called "the best-balanced economies in colonial America."

This outcome did not seem likely in 1660. New York was a collection of subeconomies weakly tied to Manhattan. English towns on eastern Long Island maintained cultural and trade ties to New England. Dutch fur traders at Albany dealt with the Atlantic world through Boston more than New York. A Dutch and Swedish community in the Delaware Valley was attached loosely to New York but threatened by Maryland's claims in the Delaware Bay. The duke's governors tried to subordinate these subregions, but his own land policies gave away some of the most valuable of them.

New York's economy stagnated during the seventeenth century. Lacking an assembly to raise taxes, the duke's governors sought revenues, such as customs duties, that could be imposed by fiat. In the 1670s Governor Edmund Andros forced Long Island and the Delaware region to channel their trade through New York City. He gave the city's merchants control over grain and flour exports from the Hudson River valley and Albany control over the province's fur trade, but these policies brought no sustained economic growth. New York's fur production declined between 1660 and 1700. Andros's favoritism toward New York's Dutch merchants angered an assertive cohort of English merchants who began trading in the city in the 1670s. The growing contribution of grain products to New York's exports after 1680 offset the decline of furs. But New York trailed Pennsylvania in exploiting new food markets in the West Indies. The revenues the duke received from the colony always fell short of the expenses of governing and protecting it.

The changing relative importance of grain to furs, lagging revenues, and political needs led governors Thomas Dongan and Benjamin

Fletcher to exploit New York's most abundant resource, the land itself. During the 1680s Dongan granted large manors and nonmanorial tracts to his political allies. These stretched from Long Island to the upper Hudson Valley, and some included semifeudal legal privileges. During the next decade Fletcher granted manors and nonmanorial tracts totaling several million acres. Land distribution, however, proved to be as futile an economic development strategy as fur monopolies or regulated grain trade. In 1698 a new governor, Lord Bellomont, repudiated the factions Dongan and Fletcher had courted and reversed their land policy.

War and factional disorder extended New York's economic distress through the early 1700s. Its merchants were unable to exploit Atlantic markets, and Boston traders became the carriers of New York's produce to the Caribbean and imports from England. After peace was restored in 1713, the economy began expanding. Local merchants built their own shipping and entered the West Indian food markets and the direct colonial trade with Britain.

New York's economic development in this period was reflected in its population. An estimate for 1664 suggests that New York had 7,000 inhabitants when it became an English colony. By 1673 the population had grown by 50 percent to 10,500, and by 1689 it had doubled again to 20,000. But it fell to 18,000 in 1698 and only regained the 1689 level by 1703. As late as 1712, after a half century of economic stagnation, New York had only 22,600 people. The growth of trade after 1713 accompanied a surge in population. Fueled by emigration from a Europe that was at peace for the first time in a generation, New York's population had almost doubled to 40,500 by 1723.

Pennsylvania's early economic and demographic development contrasted with and affected New York's. About eight thousand settlers arrived between 1682 and 1686. They found a more open terrain and a better land distribution system than New York's. The Europeans living on the Delaware, while ethnically diverse, did not pose problems of cultural accommodation nearly as complex as those presented by the New York Dutch. The immigrants moved onto the land west of the Delaware, cleared small farms, and practiced mixed agriculture based on wheat production and animal husbandry. Pennsylvanians had to build a central urban place from the ground up, but this served as a multiplier rather than a retardant to growth by harnessing the capital brought by immigrants and the energies of craftsmen. Building Philadelphia also attracted established merchants and adventurers from adjacent colonies, who contributed energy to and took profits from the new colony.

This is not to say that Penn's plans proceeded more smoothly than the duke's. His settlers ignored his intention for them to live in compact villages in neatly spaced townships; instead they dispersed over the land in patterns that served their individual economic needs and small-group cultural affinities. Penn's urban and commercial ideas for Philadelphia were also unavailing. He planned a "greene countrie towne" stretching between the Delaware and Schuylkill rivers, but Philadelphians crowded near the Delaware and used the land as intensively as Londoners. The Free Society of Traders began to collapse almost before it began operating. Beaten to initial market opportunities by merchant interlopers from other colonies, the company went bankrupt in 1687.

Despite these problems the economic success of Pennsylvania was striking. Philadelphia merchants began exporting tobacco that had earlier been shipped through New York. They moved more quickly than New Yorkers to develop the Caribbean foodstuffs market. This stimulated the production of grains on Pennsylvania farms and hurt New York's ability to compensate for the decline in its fur trade. Penn also tried to annex the upper Susquehanna Valley in order to tap the flow of pelts through Albany to Atlantic markets. These developments embroiled Pennsylvania and New York in a broadening regional economic and political rivalry.

The resourcefulness of Pennsylvania's traders allowed its economy to grow, albeit unevenly in an era of Anglo-French wars. During the 1690s merchants used the disruptions of war to exploit their advantage over New York to supply West Indian food markets and undercut English merchants by shipping tobacco to Scotland. Their enterprise enraged their regional competitors, brought charges of complicity with pirates and trading with the enemy, and had political

consequences. Penn's efforts to protect his charter by enforcing the Navigation Acts, along with the renewal of Anglo-French war in 1702, plunged Pennsylvania into its first sustained economic downturn. The grain market collapsed and Atlantic privateering hurt the colony's shipping. The tobacco trade withered, and many Philadelphia merchants faced bankruptcy. Pennsylvania's commerce did not stabilize until 1710. After 1713 shipbuilding boomed, the grain market rebounded, and Pennsylvania broke New York's monopoly on the colonial fur trade to England.

Pennsylvania's population growth did not rigidly reflect its trade cycles. Surplus production for the market was still just a small part of what was basically a subsistence farming economy, and demographically the settlement of land was more crucial than trade. Penn's connections among western European Quakers, the effectiveness of his land distribution system, and Pennsylvania's open terrain gave it an advantage over New York. Starting from a base of about five hundred Europeans in 1681, the colony grew rapidly. In 1690 Penn's domain held about nine thousand settlers and by 1700 had reached twenty thousand. Pennsylvania gained fifteen thousand people (to thirty-five thousand) in the depressed decade after 1700 but only thirteen thousand (to forty-eight thousand) during the recovery of the 1710s.

New Jersey was dominated economically by its neighbors. It absorbed some migration from New England and New York, but its proprietors never mounted effective recruitment drives. It won legal skirmishes for exemption from New York customs duties but never developed ports competitive with New York or Philadelphia. East and West Jersey both had small farming economies beyond the subsistence level but short of significant market involvement. Settlement in East Jersey radiated southwest from the Newark and Raritan bays. In the "New England" towns, which accounted for two-thirds of the colony's six thousand persons in 1700, and in Dutch areas, farms ranged from one hundred to two hundred acres (40 to 80 hectares). Along the Raritan and Millstone rivers, some Scots proprietors held large estates that they tried to populate with tenants. In West Jersey about thirty-five hundred persons were spread in a thin band east of the

Delaware River by 1702. Small fishing settlements dotted the Atlantic coast, but the northwestern reaches of East Jersey and the central parts of West Jersey were unpopulated as late as 1720.

In both proprietary divisions, mixed farming prevailed, with small surpluses grown for local markets. Wheat was New Jersey's main crop, but the colony produced many specialized commodities such as fish, timber, fruits, cranberries, and peat. Products not used on family farms were sold in the coastal and West Indian markets. Each division had a town through which its trade was organized—Perth Amboy in the east and Burlington in the west—but these served mainly as gathering centers for New York and Philadelphia.

SOCIAL DEVELOPMENT, 1660–1720

The social structures of the middle colonies before 1720 reflected their open, competitive economic order. As much as they could within the constraints of their cultures, middle colonists built communities that facilitated their prosperity while softening the forces unleashed by economic competition. The cities of New York and Philadelphia were special crucibles of social change. They had more varied occupational structures and economic profiles than the towns and farms in their hinterlands. Their merchants mobilized small surpluses from many farms to organize the exports that sustained the region's wealth and supported its population growth and diversity.

In 1664 New Amsterdam had about 1,500 Europeans, mostly Dutch, and 375 African Americans, mostly slaves. By 1698 the city's population was almost 5,000, of whom about 700 were black. The proportion of Dutch in the white population had fallen to about half, while the English comprised one-third and the French one-tenth. Standard accounts of the period stress the imposition of English political control and extend this process to the colony of New York's society, economy, and culture under the rubric of Anglicization.

It is now clear, however, that something much more complex occurred. During an era in which New York became the bulwark of English power in America, its metropolis became a plural community of unusual resilience, if not stability. Most of the Dutch in New Amsterdam in 1664 stayed, and their children matured in an increasingly English polity. They preserved their cultural identity and economic power by marrying within their cohort and by exploiting the kinship networks that resulted. The conquest spurred English immigration but did not create a cohesive English community. Heavy population turnover and the diversity of the origins and economic roles of the English inhibited the development of English institutional life and of the type of kinship ties enjoyed by the Dutch.

National groups applied different strategies to the problems and opportunities presented by their interaction. The English exploited the transfer of political power to monopolize professional and administrative positions by 1695. The Dutch used kinship networks to control many of the city's craft occupations. These trends suggest downward mobility for the Dutch, but in 1695 the English, Dutch, and French communities held shares of the city's wealth nearly proportional to their population strength. However, this numerical equity did not produce an assimilated city. The Dutch and French communities used national churches as bases for mutual aid and solidarity. Evidence regarding education, language retention, marriage, and apprenticeship all indicate growing ethnic identity during the seventeenth century.

African Americans were distributed widely throughout Manhattan during the half century after 1660. Most were slaves living in the households of merchants and craftsmen. A small free black community in the seventeenth century diminished after 1700 because of growing English resistance to manumission. Some efforts were made by religious leaders to educate slaves and recruit them to subordinate roles in European institutional life. But blacks met mostly with the indifference or hostility of the dominant culture. They preserved a measure of cultural identity and rebelled against their enslavement in 1711.

After 1700 the Dutch and French communities were overwhelmed numerically by a stream of emigration from the British Isles. The newcomers tended to be unmarried merchants, craftsmen, and laborers; few were indentured servants, convicts, or married people with families. By 1730 the Dutch comprised less than 40 percent of the city's population, while the English cohort had reached almost 50 percent and the French community had fallen to about 8 percent. This trend did not, for the Dutch at least, produce cultural or economic decline. They continued to dominate the city's crafts and strengthened their grip on its mercantile life. The Dutch and French communities held disproportionate shares of the town's wealth. Dutch families continued to use kinship ties to preserve occupational niches and economic roles. Endogamous marriage, especially for men, remained an important tool for maintaining group identity. Thus as late as 1720 a growing English cohort held political power without social, cultural, or economic hegemony in the British Empire's third largest, and militarily most important, Atlantic seaport.

A different pattern prevailed in Philadelphia, where government was erected on a foundation of English cultural dominance from 1682. Pennsylvanians were a "mixed multitude," and by 1750 the colony had an even more pluralistic character than New York. But before 1720 no encounter between entrenched and interloping European groups comparable to New York's occurred. If New York's pluralism lacked, as Joyce Goodfriend put it, "an ideological backbone," the opposite was true of Philadelphia. Penn's injunctions to toleration echoed in a society where the need for its practice emerged more slowly in a climate of English, and especially Quaker, control.

This circumstance shaped Philadelphia's early development. The city more readily than New York assumed characteristics facilitating the private pursuit of economic gain. The population swelled from hundreds in 1682 to twenty-three hundred by 1700. Early settlers lived in caves, but by 1695 brick was common in the from five hundred to seven hundred houses dotting the town. Penn's plans for a dispersed townscape and his commercial design for a monopoly trading company collapsed as settlers rushed to exploit a fertile region. Philadelphia quickly developed or attracted a diverse community of traders who organized its expanding commerce.

They did so in ways that both enriched and divided the city. Philadelphia became as stratified by wealth within a decade of settlement as New York did in a generation of English control. The richest 10 percent of its citizens owned 46 percent of the town's assessed wealth in 1693 (compared with 45 percent for New York in 1695), while the poorest 30 percent held only 2 percent (compared with 3.6 percent for New York). Inhabitants between these brackets owned half of the town's taxable property in 1693. This stratum comprised an integrated cohort of small merchants, shopkeepers, and master artisans linking the farm surpluses of the regional hinterland with the mercantile enterprise of the elite. After 1700 inequality of wealth increased, in contrast to New York's experience of slightly decreasing material inequality between 1695 and 1730. By 1715 Philadelphia had a mercantile elite divided between Quakers and Anglicans but united by shared material possessions and public roles.

Slavery did not play as large a role in Philadelphia as in New York, but despite Quaker opposition to the institution, African Americans comprised 7 percent of the city's population in 1684. By 1720, according to Gary Nash, "almost every substantial merchant in the city . . . owned slaves." As in New York most slaves lived in merchant or artisan households and struggled to maintain private, communal, or institutional lives. The nonslave component of the city's lower social rungs also swelled after 1715, as a flood of immigration by free and indentured white laborers responded to the region's rapid economic development.

The rural Middle Atlantic, where most of the region's people lived in 1720, was a mosaic of social forms. These included several patterns of dispersed farm neighborhoods and a wide array of nucleated towns and villages. In New York fewer than a dozen enormous manors and nonmanorial estates lined the east bank of the Hudson River from Manhattan to Albany. These estates were still only thinly inhabited by tenants in 1720. Rensselaerswyck, surrounding Albany, had only 82 tenant families and 427 people in 1714. Nearby Livingston Manor had 33 tenant families and 170 inhabitants in 1716. Closer to New York City, population density increased, reflecting the commercial orientation of both landlords and tenants and the proximity of the urban markets. Philipsburgh Manor in Westchester County had 60 tenant families and 300

175

people in 1712. These tenants had terms ranging from verbal agreements severable at will to written leases for one or more "lifetimes." Some leases gave tenants an equitable interest in improvements to the land. Landlords collected modest rents and profited from milling, retail, and other services to the tenants. Most quasi-feudal rights of landlords had been purged from the system by 1720. But the retarding impact of the manors on New York's settlement is suggested by the fact that the counties in which they were located, often on the best land, had larger populations (consisting of freeholding farmers) outside of the manors than on them.

New Jersey had a different tenant system. The Scottish proprietors who joined Englishmen in 1682 to buy Carteret's interest in East Jersey sought to recreate in America the conservative social order of their homeland. They took land in large tracts in the Raritan Valley and Monmouth County and planned carefully for its development. They rejected as social models both the New England towns of East Jersey and the open farm settlements of West Jersey. By 1687 seven hundred Scots had taken up land under the proprietors. About half were indentured servants, many of whom came in family groups and worked on large proprietary estates. They were eligible to receive land on completing their terms, but many instead became tenants to their former employers. Scottish immigration slowed after 1690, but by 1720 the proprietors had created a band of Scots settlements between Sandy Hook and the Delaware River composed of loose clusters of farms that resembled neither the nucleated towns of New England nor the dispersed settlements of Pennsylvania.

By the eighteenth century, Pennsylvania and West Jersey had the least conservative rural social orders in the middle colonies. Settlers poured into Pennsylvania after 1681, fully populating the original counties of Philadelphia, Chester, and Bucks by 1730. They displayed some tendency toward ethnic or religious clustering, but this largely reflected fluctuations in the composition of the migration flow. Most took the best land they could find, settling in nuclear family units on large farms purchased on modest down payments, with quitrents due to Penn. In 1710 the average Chester County farm was 245 acres (98 hectares), but sizes were smaller near Philadelphia. Few in the first generation of settlers were servants, and there was little tenancy in rural areas before 1720. Families cleared part of their land and farmed mainly for domestic use, with small surpluses left over for sale. Economic inequality was not extreme. In Chester County, the most developed part of Philadelphia's hinterland, the poorest 30 percent of taxpayers owned more than 17 percent of the taxable wealth in 1693, and the richest 10 percent owned less than 24 percent. The remaining 73 percent between these extremes held almost 58 percent of the property in the county. By 1715 this stratification pattern had widened only marginally. The other rural counties in West Jersey and Pennsylvania probably had even flatter wealth profiles.

POLITICAL DEVELOPMENT, 1660–1720

The political development of the middle colonies both reflected the dynamic character imparted to the region by its rapid settlement, jurisdictional complexity, and economic competition and tempered that dynamic to foster stability by 1720. Early New York politics revolved around issues of ethnic relations and the royal prerogative. English traders in New York City and Long Island Puritans resented the duke of York's refusal to allow political liberty. In 1680 Governor Andros was recalled to England to account for his revenues. The colony's customs law expired in his absence, and the English merchants began a tax revolt against the proprietor. James, in political trouble in England because of his Catholicism, allowed an assembly on the condition that it approve a permanent revenue. The assembly drafted a "Charter of Libertyes and Priviledges" in 1683, codifying the rights New Yorkers claimed, and replaced the Duke's Laws with statutes. James II rejected the charter, and his accession to the Crown in 1685 precipitated a broad imperial assault on colonial autonomy. In 1688 New York was placed in a reorganized polity called the Dominion of New England.

When England's Glorious Revolution of 1688 drove James into exile, the Dominion dissolved into its constituent parts. New York, with no strong central institutions, fragmented into its geographic subregions. Dominion governor Edmund Andros was jailed in Boston, and a power vacuum in New York was filled by the colony's militia, led by Jacob Leisler, a German-born merchant. The revolt briefly united in interest English reformers who had compelled the charter of 1683 and Dutch colonists who distrusted both the struggle for English rights and James's rule. With Andros gone and English stability restored under William and Mary, this comity crumbled. Leisler, who saw the issue as a religious conflict between Protestants and "papists," used the 1683 laws to collect taxes but showed no respect for an assembly elected under his writs in 1690. The reformers concluded that he was a foe of English liberty. The ensuing struggle pitted English mercantile interests and some Anglicized Dutch traders against most of the colony's Dutch population and a few English foes of New York's political and economic establishment. The Crown sided with the establishment and in 1690 sent Henry Sloughter as the new governor to subdue Leisler and unify the colony during the war against France.

Leisler was hanged and the emergent Anglo-Dutch elite embraced Sloughter. New York was granted a permanent assembly as a result of Leisler's Rebellion, but it became a forum for factional contention between pro- and anti-Leislerian parties that convulsed the colony for two decades. A series of royal governors, who were themselves products of an unstable English party system, forged shifting alliances with these groups during the 1690s and 1710s. These alliances involved the distribution of patronage and land, granting of salaries and fees to the governors, and vitriolic political exchanges, but they produced little coherent policy and almost no legislative development. In 1710 Robert Hunter, a Scottish Whig, was appointed governor. After the stabilization of English politics under Whig hegemony in 1715 and the start of a generation of European peace in 1713, a new alignment emerged, pitting Hudson Valley landed gentry against New York City merchants. By judiciously yielding to the assembly elements of the prerogative that previous governors had unavailingly asserted, Hunter forged these groups by 1720 into a system of legislative competition that produced much conflict but little chaos until the end of the colonial period.

New Jersey's experience showed that formal guarantees of English rights did not preclude conflict over issues of political legitimacy. Politics were unsettled there after 1680 by doubts about the right of the proprietors to govern the colony. Its division into two parts, disputes between absentee and resident proprietors, and conflict between proprietors and representatives of the people all fostered political disorder. In 1685 the Scots proprietors living in East Jersey formed a board to manage their interests, and in 1688 the resident West Jersey Quaker proprietors organized for similar purposes. The boards tried unsuccessfully in 1687 to settle the boundary between their lands. Scottish and Quaker immigration had ebbed by 1690, and proprietary promotional efforts stagnated. New Jersey continued to receive dissident New Englanders and restless, landless New Yorkers. Proprietary weakness and fortuitous population growth further disordered New Jersey politics. Assemblies met irregularly at Perth Amboy and Burlington. They passed little legislation but served as a forum for disputes between the governors and assemblymen over land titles, quitrents, and taxes. The underlying issue in these disputes, the validity of the Nicolls patents of 1664 and 1665 versus the proprietors' reliance on preemptive titles from the duke of York, disturbed New Jersey politics until the revolution.

The brief incorporation of New Jersey into the Dominion of New England further weakened proprietary government. During the 1690s East Jersey's dispute with New York over the customs status of Perth Amboy's port, as well as Quaker West Jersey's indifference to defense efforts against France, strained a system that was too fractured to function even in peacetime. By 1698 government had collapsed and anarchy loomed in some towns, where residents rebuffed sheriffs and tax collectors. Under pressure from the Crown, the proprietors offered to surrender their rights to government. The agreement, finalized in 1702, created a unified royal colony with separate eastern and western divisions for the management of land rights, which remained with the proprietors.

Between 1702 and 1738 New Jersey shared a governor with New York. Governors lived in New York and managed New Jersey politics by manipulating the complex factions in its assembly and proprietary bodies. Lord Cornbury, New Jersey's first royal governor, favored the Puritan Nicolls patentees and the English nonresident East Jersey proprietors against the Scots-dominated resident Board of Proprietors. In the western division, he backed Anglicans against the Quaker-led resident Council of Proprietors. These constellations overlapped, with the Nicolls, English, and Anglican interests opposing the Scots and Quakers. Cornbury attacked the proprietary boards, and by 1706 both had disbanded. Salient political issues before 1720 included Anglican efforts to disenfranchise the Quakers, struggles over control of land and revenue, and the continuing efforts of the colony to control its own commerce. The arrival in 1710 of Robert Hunter had stabilizing effects in New Jersey as in New York.

In Pennsylvania neither the political institutions that James denied to New York nor the economic growth that eluded New Jersey brought political stability. The people's ability to participate in their own government made the colony as much a battleground as a holy experiment. His first assembly in 1682 rejected Penn's Frame of Government. Non-Quakers from the Lower Counties on the Delaware River resisted the Friends. After Penn returned to England in 1684, his appointees were challenged by Philadelphia merchants and country gentry who believed that his land and revenue policies restricted their opportunities. Penn's council president, Thomas Lloyd, led this assertive Quaker elite as the council assumed functions reserved by the charter to Penn. This elite faced a lower stratum of non-Quakers, small traders, substantial farmers, and residents of the lower Delaware who used the assembly to challenge the council. Penn, detained in England, in 1688 named John Blackwell, a Massachusetts Puritan, as deputy governor, but Quaker opposition toppled him a year later. The episode strengthened the assembly as a political institution and intensified the struggle among Pennsylvania's factions.

During the 1690s, war between England and France jeopardized the political position of Quakers. In 1692 the Crown suspended Penn's government and assigned New York governor Benjamin Fletcher temporarily to administer Pennsylvania. Its factions did not unite against Fletcher as they had against Blackwell. The established anti-proprietary Quaker elite opposed him, while many non-Quakers, lesser Philadelphia shopkeepers, and artisans supported him. Fletcher, like Blackwell, was unable to govern the Friends.

Penn was restored to power in 1694, and in 1699 he returned to Philadelphia to try to stabilize his colony. He was no more successful than Blackwell or Fletcher, but his efforts created a political structure that lasted until the revolution. Penn tried at first to enforce imperial trade laws and royal demands for military cooperation against France. The Quakers, fearing they would be brought permanently under royal rule, worked to make the assembly a bulwark against external control. When Parliament tried in 1700 to abolish American proprietary charters, Penn reversed himself and embraced his Quaker critics. In 1701 he returned to England to defend his province and reluctantly approved a new charter that strengthened the assembly and weakened his own power in all areas except land management.

For a decade after Penn's departure, Pennsylvania politics remained chaotic. The war between Britain and France devastated the colony's economy by cutting grain exports to the West Indies. Penn fought the confiscation of his government by lobbying Parliament and implying a willingness to sell it to the Crown with guarantees of Quaker religious liberty. This stance gained him the loyalty of the same Quaker mercantile and landowning elite that had resisted his powers before 1700. This faction dominated Penn's council, which was now appointive but without legislative functions. The opposition comprised a coalition of small farmers, poorer artisans, Lower County non-Quakers, and Anglicans, some of whom had supported Penn in the 1690s as a way of resisting the Quaker establishment. The coalition was led in the assembly by David Lloyd, a former Penn appointee whose rhetoric raised the political expectations of people who had previously been powerless. Militant Anglicans used Quaker pacifism as a weapon against Penn during an era of threatened French attacks.

In 1710 Penn's allies regained control of the political process. In assembly elections that year, all incumbents were defeated. Urban and rural Quaker gentry who had previously dominated the council took seats in the lower house, the colony's new center of political power. With the return of peace between England and France in 1713 and the resumption of Atlantic trade and economic prosperity, stability returned to Pennsylvania politics during the 1710s, as it did to New York and New Jersey.

ECONOMIC AND POPULATION GROWTH, 1720–1765

The economy of the middle colonies grew more steadily after 1720, although there were intraregional and temporal variations in this pattern. After 1713 New York entered what Michael Kammen has called "its first major period of concentrated commercial growth." It adapted to the shift from furs to grains and foodstuffs as export commodities, developed its own shipping, and seized control of its external trade from Boston. While its hinterland was smaller, New York City began to compete with Philadelphia in the West Indian provisions trade. By developing complex entrepôt functions, it earned enough credits to maintain a larger direct trade with Britain than did Philadelphia.

New York's trade balance with Britain remained negative, however, a circumstance that forced it to diversify economically. Attempts to produce naval stores by importing peasants from the German Palatine to work in the Hudson and Mohawk valley forests failed. The colony experienced painful recessions in the early 1720s, the 1730s, and the mid 1750s. Regional strains became less severe than those of the seventeenth century. But when eastern Long Island developed a whaling industry, its inhabitants tried to maintain their traditional ties to New England. And when Albany met the relative decline and westward shift of the fur trade by becoming a service center for upper Hudson Valley agriculture, it resisted Manhattan's interference in the provisions export trade. The Hudson Valley manors continued to lose their residual feudal legal privileges, and many historians believe that they offered some tenants avenues to capital accumulation and land ownership. But they became scenes of landlord-tenant conflict after 1750 and of a rebellion in 1766 that other historians attribute to the exploitative character of ten-

ancy. New York's land system and the political power of its landlords complicated efforts to populate and develop the colony after 1720.

For a generation after 1740, the vagaries of war and peace drove the provincial economy. Wars between England, Spain, and France in the 1740s brought small profits to New York traders provisioning expeditions against Canada and larger ones for Atlantic and Caribbean privateers. After a modest decline from 1748 to 1755, the Seven Years' War brought an even larger boom. The dispatch of regular British troops to America and naval fleets to American ports generated massive wartime profits. New York merchants received large supply contracts, and the multiplier effects of their commissions expanded the economy. Privateering brought £2 million to the colony during the war, and illegal trading with the French West Indies brought more. The boom had ended by 1760, however, as the fighting moved to the Caribbean, and the 1760s saw the worst depression in New York's colonial history. The imperial crisis leading to the American Revolution thus began in a climate of unemployment, inflation, and rising taxes.

New York's population grew more consistently after 1720 than before. Except for a slump in the war-ravaged 1740s, the colony's decennial increase ranged between 36 percent and 40 percent between 1720 and 1770. The population rose from about 36,000 in 1720 to 49,000 in 1730, 77,000 at mid century, and 168,000 in 1770. The proportion of African Americans, mostly slaves, peaked at 15 percent in the early 1720s and declined slowly to just under 12 percent by the eve of the revolution. But the area around New York City, including northeastern New Jersey, had the most entrenched slave economy north of the Chesapeake during the mid eighteenth century. Population became more decentralized during this period, from the metropolis up the Hudson River and into the Mohawk Valley, as the grain economy replaced the fur trade as New York's main inland industry.

If New York's economy solidified in the 1720s after two generations of stagnation, Pennsylvania's accelerated after one generation of strong initial growth. The decade began with a sharp recession precipitated by an English credit squeeze and by weak West Indian grain markets. The emission of paper money through government loans secured by land mortgages eased the crisis, and growth had resumed by mid decade. Exports of wheat, flour, and bread expanded rapidly during the 1730s. The West Indian market remained somewhat flat, but the islands continued to be the colony's main trade partner throughout the colonial period.

Pennsylvania merchants also found niches in other markets. They met relaxed trade restrictions with Ireland by sending grain, lumber, and flaxseed there in the 1730s. Philadelphia's direct trade with England remained smaller than New York's, but it grew during this period. The city did not challenge Boston's dominance of the coastal carrying trade, but it enlarged its share of that trade. The biggest change, however, was Philadelphia's entry into the southern European provisions markets.

The war-torn 1740s were generally prosperous years for Pennsylvania. Quaker merchants participated less in privateering than did their New York counterparts and reaped no profits on supply contracts for land expeditions mounted from New York. However, war stimulated demands for foodstuffs in the British West Indies and opportunities for illegal trading to the French West Indies. By 1750, though, the colony entered an interval of depressed trade that continued until the Seven Years' War brought relief after 1755. Food exports, especially to the Caribbean, remained profitable, but imports of English consumer goods glutted Philadelphia and produced a cycle of debt that bankrupted small city traders and plunged rural shopkeepers and farmers into hardship.

The initial economic impact of the Seven Years' War for Pennsylvania was deeper recession as frontier Indian raids cut harvests, British embargoes disrupted exports to the Caribbean, and military recruitment created unprecedented labor shortages. By 1758, however, the military tide turned in the continental colonies, and army supply contracts absorbed the slack from export losses. Philadelphia merchants responded quickly when West Indian demand increased in the late 1750s, and they embraced the corrupt "flag of truce" trade to the French West Indies to augment their legal wartime profits. Agricultural prosperity remained strong until 1763, but a mercantile recession beginning in 1760 hurt Philadelphia's trade. This presaged a broader slump in the provincial economy during the mid 1760s spurred by a postwar depression in England and a long-term decline in Caribbean markets. Changes in imperial policy after 1763 thus affected a colony facing its worst economic distress since 1725.

Reliable statistics on Pennsylvania's population during the half century after 1720 are scarce, and estimates vary widely. During this period the colony passed New York as the dominant population center in the mid Atlantic, reaching at least fifty thousand persons by 1730, more than one hundred thousand by 1750, and passing the two hundred thousand mark during the 1760s. This trend reflected the colony's economic growth, which, despite its cyclical trade pattern, remained impressive in absolute terms. Contributing heavily to this growth was the beginning, after 1713, of a tide of immigration from non-English countries, especially Germany and Ireland.

New Jersey's eighteenth-century economic history can only be sketched. It was an agrarian province, dependent on the capital and entrepreneurship of its neighbors until the revolution. With the help of those resources, it contributed significantly to the regional economy. Besides mixed grains and vegetables, its farms produced large amounts of pork and beef that were preserved—with salt made on the Atlantic coast—and shipped to the West Indies and the New England and southern colonies. New Jersey also had a variety of specialty industries that supported regional living standards. In the northern mountains, a charcoal iron industry developed after 1750. The southern counties produced smaller amounts of "bog iron" along with softwood lumber and glass products needed for the physical expansion of Philadelphia.

New Jersey's demographic history is almost as obscure as Pennsylvania's, with only three censuses and several estimates to rely on. Its population growth in the mid eighteenth century was somewhat faster than New York's but slower than Pennsylvania's. It rose from about twenty-six thousand people in 1720 to forty-seven thousand in 1737 and sixty-one thousand in 1745. There were no censuses between 1750 and the revolution, but the population probably neared seventy thousand by mid century and passed one hundred thousand by 1770. West Jersey's population passed East Jersey's before 1750, reflecting Pennsylvania's outpacing of New York in economic growth.

SOCIAL DEVELOPMENT, 1720–1765

Important themes in the social development of the middle colonies during this period include the growth, differentiation, and stratification of the region's metropolises, the intensive development of nearby rural areas, the emergence of secondary urban centers, and the evolution of slavery in the region.

New York City and Philadelphia grew impressively in this period: Philadelphia from fewer than five thousand persons in 1720 to more than twenty thousand in 1770 and New York City from about seven thousand to over twenty thousand. Philadelphia had matched New York's population by 1750, and both passed Boston during the next decade. Heavy immigration from England, Ireland, and Germany increased the region's pluralism. Pennsylvania received the largest share of these newcomers.

Immigration changed the urban labor structure. Between 1720 and 1755, seventy-five hundred servants were indentured in Philadelphia. Servants and slaves comprised more than one-fourth and often nearly two-fifths of the city's work force between the late 1720s and the early 1750s. Despite Quaker reservations about the institution, slavery expanded after 1720. The removal of import duties increased slave imports in the early 1730s. Later in the decade, the availability of poor white immigrants led colonists to use bound servants to meet their labor needs. But during the Seven Years' War, many servants enlisted in the British army, and the colony resumed buying slaves. Imports peaked in 1762 when perhaps five hundred slaves reached Philadelphia. The end of war and the recession of the 1760s shifted the pendulum back toward servants, and slavery began a slow decline in Pennsylvania. Slaves accounted for almost 9 percent of Philadelphia's population in 1767 but less than 4 percent by 1775. With fewer white indentured servants entering New York than Philadelphia, the former city had a broader involvement with slavery. Slaves comprised about 22 percent of adult males in 1723 and about 30 percent of the city's laborers by 1746. About one-fifth of the total city population during the 1750s was slave, and as late as 1771 the figure was almost 17 percent.

Increasing class stratification occurred in both cities, especially after the Seven Years' War. Between 1720 and 1750 both developed broad artisan and mechanic groups that benefited from upward and endured downward swings of the business cycle but found opportunities for material independence in the secular expansion of the colonial economy. The traumatic warfare of mid century enriched many of the merchants of both towns, while the postwar depression harmed many artisan trades. Many members of both groups thus reached the end of the colonial period committed to independence. But merchants viewed the crisis in terms of imperial regulation and the obstruction of Atlantic markets that they had helped to create and learned to manipulate and from which they derived much wealth and status. Artisans, on the other hand, saw themselves as being in a provincial world of increasingly insecure employment, rising taxes, and diminishing ability to transmit personal economic independence to the next generation.

Rural areas near the cities also changed during the mid eighteenth century. In Chester County, Pennsylvania, the modest degree of wealth stratification between 1693 and 1715 widened after 1720. In 1730 the poorest 30 percent of county taxpayers owned almost 10 percent of the wealth (down from 13 percent in 1715) and the richest tenth owned 28 percent. But by 1760 the wealth of the poorest 30 percent had fallen to 6.5 percent, while the share of the richest tenth had increased to about 30 percent. These aggregate figures obscure a complex social and occupational pattern in which most farmers pursued trades, a quarter of landholders were tenants, and many adults lived as "inmates" in the households of unrelated persons. Until the 1760s this flexible pattern of land ownership, tenancy, and craft trades sustained a growing grain-based farm export economy. In the decade before the revolution, however, tenancy declined, economic opportunity for non-landowners narrowed, and rural poverty and migration to the frontier increased.

In Westchester County, New York, just north of Manhattan, a different mosaic of tenancy and freeholding and of free and bound labor structured the agricultural economy. There in 1760 the Philipse family hosted 170 tenant families on their vast manor. The tenants lived on farms averaging 187 acres (about 75 hectares) each and paid rents of about £6 a year, more than on manors farther from New York City but below nonmanorial rates. They participated in a mid-century transition from wheat export farming to the production of meats and vegetables for city markets. They held oral leases at the will of the landlord but enjoyed stability of actual tenure. The improvements on their farms were treated as compensable equity if they left the manor. In 1775 the average Philipsburgh tenant owned more property than did typical freeholders in five neighboring Westchester County towns.

These examples only suggest the social complexity of the middle colonies in the mid eighteenth century. Another indicator is the proliferation of smaller urban centers. In Pennsylvania, forty-nine towns were founded between 1730 and 1765. Five of them were county seats, organized to provide government as well as market services to growing backcountry populations. Lancaster reflected the privatism and market-centered individualism that shaped Pennsylvania society from the beginning. It was founded in 1730 on land acquired by Andrew Hamilton, the colony's chief justice and an ally of the Penns, after the decision to establish a county seat was made. Hamilton donated lots for public functions and sold others, reserving an annual ground rent. The town had perhaps four hundred inhabitants by 1740, when it obtained borough status. In 1746 Lancaster had three hundred houses and about fifteen hundred residents. It had almost three thousand people by 1760, when growth stopped until the revolution. It was the largest inland settlement in America in the late colonial period, with German, English, and Scottish residents, members of five religious groups, and a complex occupational structure.

Bethlehem, by contrast, exhibited the deep communal impulse that kept Pennsylvania socially, if not always politically, stable in an environment of diversity and rapid economic growth. About fifty Moravian pilgrims came to the Lehigh River, 70 miles (112 kilometers) north of Philadelphia, in the winter of 1742. Bringing communal bonds and deep religious ties from Europe, they built temporary shelter and planned a permanent settlement. By 1745 they had constructed a community and a complex constellation of about fifty craft industries that sustained their own material needs and attracted the trade of nearby non-Moravian settlers. By 1750 Bethlehem had 400 residents and almost 700 acres (280 hectares) in agricultural production. The population swelled to 800 in 1756 with an influx of war refugees but began to decline from a peak of 660 in 1761. This downward cycle lasted into the nineteenth century. The Moravians had almost 5,000 acres (2,000 hectares) in cultivation and were an important commercial and industrial force in the region. After 1761 the sect dissolved its "General Economy" and replaced it with a more privatized, familial community model.

New York did not experience an eighteenth-century urban boom. Besides New York City, only Albany and perhaps Kingston reached threshold of scale to qualify as "urban" places before the revolution. The rest of the colony's settlements remained local service centers, albeit ones increasingly integrated by roads, rivers, and credit networks into a truly provincial economy. Albany underwent changes of character and role as well as scale. As the fur trade shifted west along the Mohawk River after 1730, Albany mobilized the growing wheat exports of the upper Hudson and Mohawk valleys and developed a more specialized merchant community. The wars of the 1740s and 1750s delayed this evolution but stimulated the city's diversity by bringing large detachments of British troops there. The growth of Albany was spurred by an infusion of army spending and the retirement of many soldiers there. After the Seven Years' War, migrating New Englanders also began settling in the city. These trends continued the slow dilution of Albany's historic Dutch character.

POLITICAL DEVELOPMENT, 1720–1765

Middle colony political dynamics during the mid eighteenth century were complex, but they comprised a coherent regional system. New York remained the most strategically important royal colony in North America, while Pennsylvania was the most prominent proprietary colony. New Jersey was both a royal colony sharing a governor with New York until 1738 and a landed proprietorship in which the Penns retained important interests. Between 1720 and 1765 politics were shaped by intervals of war and peace, by cycles of economic growth and stagnation, and by the intentions, ambitions, and abilities of a generation of English- and American-born officials.

New York politics produced a series of bilateral factional alignments of local leaders closely allied with royal governors. In 1720 Governor William Burnet inherited Robert Hunter's coalition of Hudson Valley landowners that dominated the colony's increasingly assertive assembly. His political skills did not match Hunter's, however, and during a peaceful and mostly prosperous decade, the landowners' faction—led by Lewis Morris—lost a series of elections and, by 1727, control of the assembly itself.

The Morrisites were replaced by urban merchants who tried to shift the provincial tax burden to New York's landed classes. Burnet's successor, John Montgomerie, supported the merchant group, as did William Cosby, who became governor in 1732. Cosby's arrival coincided with a recession in New York, and it caused the most violent political upheaval there between the Leisler era and the revolution. Morrisite leaders had fought with Montgomerie's allies but had refrained from attacking the governor himself. In 1733, however, they broke with Cosby. When Cosby suspended Lewis Morris as New York's chief justice, Morris went to England to seek the governor's recall.

Morris's allies set up a printer, John Peter Zenger, as the publisher of a newspaper to attack Cosby's regime. Zenger was arrested for seditious libel, but a New York jury acquitted him. The case did not, as popular accounts suggest, set precedents limiting the use of libel law, but it illustrated the politicization of the populace by disputes between members of the provincial elite. Morris failed to have Cosby removed, but Cosby's death in 1736 brought his and Morris's allies to the brink of violent conflict over the succession.

The politics of the 1740s and 1750s revolved more around war, and the costs and profits of mobilization for war, than around competing tax agendas. George Clinton, who served longer than any New York colonial governor (1743–

1753), tried to prepare the colony for King George's War against France (1744–1748). New Yorkers resisted the costs of mobilization, especially to their intermediary role in the fur trade between Albany and Montreal. Many preferred privateering and supplying expeditions of English troops to raising taxes and local forces to sustain those expeditions. James DeLancey, New York's chief justice, a former Cosby ally, and initially Clinton's chief advisor, led the opposition. Clinton allied with remnants of the old Morrisite coalition and, between 1748 and 1752, tried to build a party of followers in the assembly. He lost a series of elections during this period, and in 1753 left New York in defeat. DeLancey, whose patrons and relatives in England had secured his appointment as lieutenant governor, became the acting governor. He held the post during most of the 1750s, presiding over the government during much of the Seven Years' War.

It is difficult to discern clear patterns in the factional alignments surrounding Clinton and DeLancey in the 1740s and 1750s comparable to the merchant-landed split of the 1720s and 1730s. But the frequent elections that Clinton called in trying to defeat his foe had the same effect as the clashes of the Cosby years: the political energizing of previously inert layers of society. A brief but severe dispute over the religious character of King's College (Columbia University) in 1753 to 1754 reflected an emerging rivalry between Anglicans and Presbyterians with long-range political implications for the New York City area. DeLancey inherited many of the same problems (and limited solutions) of the Clinton era, such as securing reliable financial support for royal government from a jealous and penurious assembly and prosecuting New York's part in a long and draining war between Britain and France.

After 1760 a variant of the old landowner-merchant split reemerged in New York factional alignments. It revolved, however, more around the complex regional interests of New York City's mercantile community and the Hudson Valley's export industries than around old differences over whether to base the provincial tax burden on land or commerce. And it was complicated after 1765 by New York's long postwar depression, by rioting on many Hudson Valley manors over disputes between the landlords and land-hungry westward migrants from New England, and especially by England's aggressive reforms of imperial management.

Pennsylvania politics in the eighteenth century were shaped, like New York's, by the colony's social diversity and were driven by issues of war, land distribution, and economic growth. They differed, however, in important structural ways. Unlike New York's shifting factions built around the brief tenures of royal governors, Pennsylvania's proprietary structure fostered ongoing political organizations that can with caution be called parties. The appointees and supporters of the Penn governors formed a Proprietary party, while the assembly-based organization that dominated provincial politics until the eve of the revolution comprised what was known as the Quaker party.

The disputed ownership of the proprietorship after William Penn's death in 1718 led the assembly to expand its role in Pennsylvania government. Facing a severe depression between 1721 and 1723 and expecting the royalization of the government, the proprietary governor, Sir William Keith, worked with assembly leaders to issue the first paper money in the colony's history in 1722, to naturalize German aliens arriving in Philadelphia, and to involve poorer citizens in politics. This populist wave ebbed with the return of prosperity after 1726, and the wealthy, conservative Quaker establishment resumed control of the assembly.

In this case, however, the relative comity between Quaker and proprietary interests that had characterized earlier stable intervals did not resume. William Penn's heirs, John, Thomas, and Richard Penn, forsook their father's religion and his view of the colony as a holy experiment. They regarded Pennsylvania as a business and tried to increase their revenues. Thomas Penn came to America in 1732 and began collecting back rents and selling land at high prices. By mid century this policy had begun to enrich the Penns, but at a heavy political cost. The Quaker merchants, substantial farmers, and meeting elders who dominated the assembly party cast themselves as the true heirs of the founder's social vision, the defenders of the liberal charter of 1701, and the guarantors of the prosperity and liberty which that document promised. They

thereby avoided the risks to their hegemony inherent in Pennsylvania's increasingly plural, non-Quaker, and non-British social character. By using their decentralized meeting structure to coordinate political strategy, and through sensitivity to the popular desire for low taxes, peace, and minimal interference from proprietary agents, the Quakers controlled the assembly until the Seven Years' War.

Even after the "withdrawal" from politics in 1756 of pacifist Quakers who resisted the war measures that imperial authorities demanded, a coalition of moderate Quakers and their allies, coordinated by Benjamin Franklin, dominated provincial politics until 1764. The proprietors' supporters functioned as a patronage-dispensing network. They were so identified with the Penns' presumed greed and indifference to colonial liberties that they made few serious efforts to contest assembly elections for two decades after 1740. Through his agents Thomas Penn conducted a futile campaign to resist taxes on his Pennsylvania lands and to restore his power in prerogative matters such as the management of the legislative branch and the expenditure of public revenues.

These political arrangements were functional during two decades of relative peace and prosperity after 1720. They even served during the limited (for Pennsylvania) wars of the 1740s and the severer tests of the 1750s. They failed, however, to meet the challenges of the imperial crisis. In 1764 and 1765 the Quaker and Proprietary parties battled over Franklin's efforts to persuade the Crown to make Pennsylvania a royal colony. The Penns rebuffed this challenge in England, and their friends in Pennsylvania made some temporary political gains from the miscalculation of their foes. But neither side met effectively the challenges to colonial autonomy posed by Britain's imposition of a stamp tax in 1765 or its later efforts for imperial reform.

A different pattern characterized the political structure of New Jersey in the decades between the 1720s and the revolution. There a localized but cohesive gentry of substantial landholders, small merchants, and lawyers controlled politics by managing the assembly, dominating the council, and generally outmaneuvering a series of ineffective royal governors. After 1720 legislators were typically Quakers or Anglicans, wealthier than their neighbors, natives of the counties that they represented, and related to each other or to their predecessors. They wielded power by influencing the modest patronage at the disposal of the governors and by meeting the equally modest demands of their constituents. The need of an economy based on market agriculture and retail trade for a circulating currency made paper money the constant denominator of politics. That issue unified rather than divided the parochial county elites who controlled the assembly, and it explained their responsiveness to their constituents. The colony's largest landholders—the proprietors—opposed the circulation of paper money, especially in the 1740s and 1750s. But while they controlled the council and usually dominated the assembly, too, they were unable to compel the latter body to resist popular pressures for paper money. Indeed their obstruction on that issue caused the proprietors to forfeit the support of the assembly on the only issue that threatened provincial stability at mid century—rural disorders over the legitimacy of proprietary land titles—and the one on which they most needed and sought that support.

The land disputes faded after 1755, and the proprietary-led gentry resumed control of provincial politics during the 1760s. New Jersey, lacking great regional differences, a complex external trade, urban stratification, and severe conflicts among its religious and ethnic groups, did not approach the revolutionary crisis with the tumultuous disorders of the Hudson Valley manors, the class strife of New York City, or the destructive battles over royal government between Quakers and proprietors in Pennsylvania. Rather, its modestly wealthy elites governed the colony as long as they could in a climate of growing political disintegration, ignored the broader implications of the debate over independence, and quietly forfeited the legitimacy that they had exercised for almost a century.

THE ROAD TO REVOLUTION

We still have no really satisfactory account of how the specific social, economic, or even political structures and circumstances described above determined the timing and manner of the onset of the American Revolution in the middle colonies. Many of the overt facts are clear. The region's delegates to interprovincial councils after 1765 counseled strong but moderate Whiggish resistance to imperial reforms, but the delegations of New York, New Jersey, Pennsylvania, and Delaware formed the most serious bloc of resistance to Independence in Philadelphia in the late spring of 1776. The area between the Hudson and the Potomac valleys held relatively high concentrations of avowed Loyalists, and—south of the Raritan River, at least—still larger populations of religious Dissenters from war and even resistance to government. As the colonial resistance movement evolved toward armed defiance, British political planners viewed the Middle Atlantic as a potential buffer to the spread of "radical" New England notions to the rest of the continent. And as late as 1778, their military-strategist counterparts hoped to exploit "well affected" Americans in the same precincts as adjuncts to force in the restoration of imperial order. Radicals in the Continental Congress needed to encourage the only unequivocal "internal" revolution on the continent, in Pennsylvania, to secure the majority they needed for Independence, and New York was the last colony to authorize its delegates to approve its declaration.

But many interpretive generalizations that have been advanced to explain these facts now seem either inaccurate in the face of new knowledge, or mutually inconsistent from time to time and place to place. Relative prosperity may have retarded radicalization in Pennsylvania during the early 1770s, but not in New York in the late 1760s. The particular structure of their Atlantic commerce may have provided what Thomas Doerflinger has called a "logic of moderation" that impelled Philadelphia merchants to subordinate their generally Whiggish beliefs to their overall apolitical inclinations. But that same logic doubtless seemed perverse if not repugnant to the burgeoning cohort of poor, precariously situated laborers, whose increase Billy G. Smith has called "the most important shift in the city's occupational composition between 1756 and 1774." And the presence and the sentiments of the latter strata ensured that Pennsylvania's revolution, when it came, was anything but "moderate."

185

The highly factionalized structure of middle-colony politics may have fostered a fragile, wrangling "stability" that held revolution at bay even while encouraging domestic discord. But the same circumstance could be invoked to explain the eventual arrival of rebellion and its subsequent intensity. A sudden and belated emergence of a coherent and buoyant regional "consciousness" among middle-colony elites might justify the reluctance of their members to lead a revolution. But, again, it could also produce the opposite result, and, in any case, the burden of scholarship in the late twentieth century suggests that the emergence was anything but sudden or belated in the Middle Atlantic.

The most that it seems safe to venture at this point is that the actors who held substantial political power in New York, New Jersey, Pennsylvania, and Delaware during the late-colonial era *did* hesitate to lead their constituents very vigorously along the path of the logic of revolution—whether moderate or otherwise. The result would not have seemed perverse to either the Virginia gentry or the New England "fathers of the towns" who understood that to survive the violent dismemberment of the English empire they would have to direct it. Pennsylvania's colonial political development, and that of New York as well, according to John Murrin, did finally "seem to lead to a genuine crisis over who shall rule at home." The best of the last generation of scholarship on the region suggests that, in this as in other ways, politics was anything but "epiphenomenal." Rather it was the most visible form and logical manifestation of complex, but coherent and comprehensible, social and economic processes.

BIBLIOGRAPHY

Bibliographies

Greenberg, Douglas. "The Middle Colonies in Recent American Historiography." *William and Mary Quarterly*, 3rd ser., 36, no. 3 (1979):396–427. Remains the best starting place for bibliographic research.

Interpretive Essays

Bonomi, Patricia U. "The Middle Colonies: Embryo of the New Political Order." In *Perspectives on Early American History: Essays in Honor of Richard B. Morris*, edited by Alden T. Vaughn and George Athan Billias. New York, 1973.

Klein, Milton M. "Shaping the American Tradition: The Microcosm of Colonial New York." *New York History* 59, no. 1 (1978):173–197.

Zuckerman, Michael. "Introduction: Puritans, Cavaliers, and the Motley Middle." In *Friends and Neighbors: Group Life in America's First Plural Society*, edited by Michael Zuckerman. Philadelphia, 1982.

Surveys, Syntheses, and Overviews

Bonomi, Patricia U. *A Factious People: Politics and Society in Colonial New York*. New York, 1971.

Illick, Joseph. *Colonial Pennsylvania: A History*. New York, 1976.

Kammen, Michael. *Colonial New York: A History*. New York, 1975.

Kemmerer, Donald L. *Path to Freedom: The Struggle for Self-Government in Colonial New Jersey, 1703–1776*. Princeton, N.J., 1940.

Munroe, John A. *Colonial Delaware: A History*. Millwood, N.Y., 1978.

Nash, Gary B. *Quakers and Politics: Pennsylvania, 1681–1726*. Princeton, N.J., 1968.

Pomfret, John E. *Colonial New Jersey: A History*. New York, 1973.

———. *The Province of East New Jersey, 1609–1702: The Rebellious Proprietary*. Princeton, N.J., 1962.

———. *The Province of West New Jersey, 1609–1702: A History of the Origins of an American Colony*. Princeton, N.J., 1956.

Ritchie, Robert C. *The Duke's Province: A Study of New York Politics and Society, 1664–1691*. Chapel Hill, N.C., 1977.

Tully, Alan. *William Penn's Legacy: Politics and Social Structure in Provincial Pennsylvania, 1726–1755*. The Johns Hopkins University Studies in Historical and Political Science, 95th series, no. 2. Baltimore, Md., 1977.

Economic and Population Growth

Bining, Arthur C. *Pennsylvania Iron Manufacture in the Eighteenth Century*. Harrisburg, Pa., 1938. Outdated but still the standard account of a critically important regional industry.

Doerflinger, Thomas M. *A Vigorous Spirit of Enterprise: Merchants and Economic Development in Revolutionary Philadelphia*. Chapel Hill, N.C., 1986. Supersedes earlier work on the emergence and function of a group that helped to shape the regional economy of the Middle Atlantic from the late seventeenth century.

Kim, Sung Bok. *Landlord and Tenant in Colonial New York: Manorial Society, 1664–1775*. Chapel Hill, N.C., 1978. Challenges traditional accounts of the socially and economically regressive nature of the manorial land system in New York.

Klepp, Susan E., ed. *The Demographic History of the Philadelphia Region, 1600–1860.* Proceedings of the American Philosophical Society, vol. 133, no. 2. Philadelphia, 1989.

Lemon, James T. *The Best Poor Man's Country: A Geographical Study of Early Southeastern Pennsylvania.* Baltimore, Md., 1972. A model of how economic data and geographical methods can be combined to reshape the historical understanding of culture and society.

Levitt, James H. *For Want of Trade: Shipping and the New Jersey Ports, 1680–1783.* Newark, N.J., 1981. Shows the consequences for the colony of its inability to challenge New York City and Philadelphia's regional commercial hegemony.

McCusker, John J., and Russell R. Menard, eds. *The Economy of British America, 1607–1789.* Chapel Hill, N.C., 1985. Chapter 9 provides the best overview of the early Middle Atlantic economy.

Norton, Thomas Elliot. *The Fur Trade in Colonial New York, 1686–1776.* Madison, Wis., 1974. Traces the structure of a slowly declining but never unimportant industry.

Paskoff, Paul F. *Industrial Evolution: Organization, Structure, and Growth of the Pennsylvania Iron Industry, 1750–1850.* Baltimore, Md., 1983. Late colonial and beyond in focus, but better than Bining in theory and method.

Potter, J. "The Growth of Population in America, 1700–1860." In *Population in History,* edited by D. V. Glass and D. E. C. Eversley. London, 1965.

Schweitzer, Mary M. *Custom and Contract: Household, Government, and the Economy in Colonial Pennsylvania.* New York, 1987. Explores the complex boundary between individual economic behavior and early public policy.

Wacker, Peter O. *Land and People: A Cultural Geography of Preindustrial New Jersey, Origins and Settlement Patterns.* New Brunswick, N.J., 1975. Offers a foundation for understanding New Jersey's agricultural economy, but includes little hard economic data or analysis.

Wells, Robert V. *The Population of the British Colonies in America Before 1776: A Survey of Census Data.* Princeton, N.J., 1975. See Chapter 4.

Social Development

Archdeacon, Thomas J. *New York City, 1664–1710: Conquest and Change.* Ithaca, N.Y., 1976.

Goodfriend, Joyce D. *Before the Melting Pot: Society and Culture in Colonial New York City, 1664–1730.* Princeton, N.J., 1992.

Henretta, James A. "Families and Farms: *Mentalité* in Pre-Industrial America." *William and Mary Quarterly,* 3rd ser., 35, no. 1 (1978):3–32. Offers an important critique of Lemon's conclusions.

Kross, Jessica. *The Evolution of an American Town: Newtown, New York, 1642–1775.* Philadelphia, Pa., 1983. Applies to New York the methods that have been used to reconstruct New England towns.

Landsman, Ned C. *Scotland and Its First American Colony, 1683–1765.* Princeton, N.J., 1985. Offers an ingenious reconstruction of a little-known social order in rural New Jersey that differed from Lemon's in Pennsylvania and Kim's in New York.

Levy, Barry. *Quakers and the American Family: British Settlement in the Delaware Valley.* New York, 1988. Presents an important argument about the relationship between family structure and economic strategy among the Quakers of early Pennsylvania.

Merwick, Donna. *Possessing Albany, 1630–1710: The Dutch and English Experiences.* Cambridge, England, 1990. Approaches the evolution of urban space from an ethnocultural perspective.

Nash, Gary B. *Forging Freedom: The Formation of Philadelphia's Black Community, 1720–1840.* Cambridge, Mass., 1988. Reconstructs and interprets slavery and its aftermath in one urban context.

———. *The Urban Crucible: Social Change, Political Consciousness, and the Origins of the American Revolution.* Cambridge, Mass., 1979. An overview of urban social structure in the Middle Atlantic and a model of original synthesis.

Salinger, Sharon V. *"To Serve Well and Faithfully": Labor and Indentured Servants in Pennsylvania, 1682–1800.* Cambridge, England, and New York, 1987. Provides important data and insightful arguments about the evolution of an important economic and social institution.

Schwartz, Sally. *"A Mixed Multitude": The Struggle for Toleration in Colonial Pennsylvania.* New York, 1987. Offers a way of conceptualizing the broadest social implications of Pennsylvania's cultural pluralism.

Simler, Lucy. "Tenancy in Colonial Pennsylvania: The Case of Chester County." *William and Mary Quarterly,* 3rd ser., 43, no. 4 (1986):542–569.

———. "The Township: The Community of the Rural Pennsylvanian." *Pennsylvania Magazine of History and Biography* 106, no. 1 (1982):41–68.

Smaby, Beverly Prior. *The Transformation of Moravian Bethlehem: From Communal Mission to Family Economy.* Philadelphia, 1988. Shows the communal result of the convergence of sectarian and individualistic impulses in the Pennsylvania backcountry.

Smith, Billy G. *The "Lower Sort": Philadelphia's Laboring People, 1750–1800.* Ithaca, N.Y., 1990. Imaginatively explores working-class life in revolutionary Philadelphia.

Wolf, Stephanie Grauman. *Urban Village: Population, Community, and Family Structure in Germantown, Pennsylvania, 1683–1800.* Princeton, N.J., 1976. Anticipated Kross by a decade in appropriating the New England model for Middle Atlantic interpretive purposes.

Wood, Jerome H., Jr. *Conestoga Crossroads: Lancaster, Pennsylvania, 1730–1790.* Harrisburg, Pa., 1979. A biography of a Pennsylvania settlement created by the economic and social processes described by Lemon.

Political Development

Batinski, Michael C. *The New Jersey Assembly, 1738–1775: The Making of a Legislative Community.* Lanham, Md., 1987. Offers an interesting comparison with some of Purvis's interpretations of New Jersey political dynamics.

Countryman, Edward. *A People in Revolution: The American Revolution and Political Society in New York, 1760–1790.* The Johns Hopkins University Studies in Historical and Political Science, 99th series, no. 2. Baltimore, Md., 1981. Bridges New York colonial and state politics and revives some elements of the progressive-era class conflict interpretation that have vanished from historiography on the colonial period.

Head, John M. *A Time to Rend: An Essay on the Decision for American Independence.* Madison, Wis., 1968.

Hutson, James H. *Pennsylvania Politics, 1746–1770: The Movement for Royal Government and Its Consequences.* Princeton, N.J., 1972. Treats the efforts of the Penn family at mid century to challenge the Quaker establishment for control of Pennsylvania, the Quaker response, and the beginning of the revolutionary struggle.

Katz, Stanley N. *New Castle's New York: Anglo-American Politics, 1732–1753,* Cambridge, Mass., 1968. A pioneering study showing the importance of the imperial context for understanding New York politics in the mid eighteenth century.

Klein, Milton M. *The Politics of Diversity: Essays in the History of Colonial New York.* Port Washington, N.Y., 1974. A useful compilation of important articles, published widely, about the political implications of social and economic diversity in colonial New York.

Murrin, John M. "English Rights As Ethnic Aggression: The English Conquest, the Charter of Liberties of 1683, and Leisler's Rebellion in New York." In *Authority and Resistance in Early New York,* edited by William Pencak and Conrad Edick Wright. New York, 1988. Supplements, and in some respects challenges, Ritchie's account, *The Duke's Province,* of late-seventeenth-century New York politics.

———. "Political Development." In *Colonial British America: Essays in the New History of the Early Modern Era,* edited by Jack P. Greene and J. R. Pole. London and Baltimore, 1984.

Neuenschwander, John A. *The Middle Colonies and the Coming of the American Revolution.* Port Washington, N.Y., 1973.

Purvis, Thomas L. *Proprietors, Patronage, and Paper Money: Legislative Politics in New Jersey, 1703–1776.* New Brunswick, N.J., 1986. Delineates the main themes of provincial politics in New Jersey from the imposition of royal government to the American Revolution.

Sheridan, Eugene R. *Lewis Morris, 1671–1746: A Study in Early American Politics.* Syracuse, N.Y., 1981. Skillfully reconstructs the life and times of an influential pre-revolutionary New York and New Jersey politician.

Wayne Bodle

SEE ALSO **Dutch and Swedish Settlements; Emergence of Empires;** and **Indian-Colonist Contact;** various essays in RELIGION; and the map preceding **French Settlements.**

THE CHESAPEAKE COLONIES

THE CHESAPEAKE COLONIES of Virginia and Maryland were established respectively in 1607 and 1634. Within a few decades, the Chesapeake Bay and its tributaries were serving as links for a distinctive society of independent tobacco planters, indentured servants, and slaves, a society with world markets and a transatlantic culture. By the eve of American independence, the Chesapeake colonies accounted for a third of the population of British North America and annual exports valued above £1 million. Furthermore they had become a central component of the emerging nation's civic culture, political leadership, and social order.

THE CHESAPEAKE MARITIME ENVIRONMENT

An inland sea with 3,237 square miles (8,416 square kilometers) of surface and channels as deep as 156 feet (47 meters), the Chesapeake Bay drained an area of 64,900 square miles (168,740 square kilometers), equivalent to the six New England states. Twelve miles (19.2 kilometers) wide at the Atlantic Ocean between Cape Henry (36°55′41″ north latitude, 76°00′32″ west longitude) and Cape Charles (37° north latitude, 75° 30′ west longitude), the bay varied in width from a maximum of twenty-two miles (35 kilometers) at the mouth of the Potomac River to less than ten miles (16 kilometers) farther north. From Hampton Roads at the Virginia capes and the James River, the bay extended 195 miles (312 kilometers) north to the mouth of the Susquehanna River, which was unnavigable through most of the colonial era.

The Chesapeake and its forty-eight tributaries—including the James, York, Rappahannock, Potomac, and Patuxent rivers—offered 1,750 miles (2,800 kilometers) of navigable waterway and 4,600 miles (7,360 kilometers) of shoreline to colonial sailing vessels. Salty near the capes, its water was seasonally brackish inland and fresh in the upper reaches and tributaries. Salinity patterns defined a complex marine and wetland ecological system renowned for its marine life (including delectable oysters, crabs, and fish), although commercial fisheries were discouraged by British policies that limited the importation of sufficient quantities of salt. The bay's freshwater moorings protected wooden ships from barnacles and from the destructive shipworm *Teredo navalis* each June and July and, especially in eighteenth-century Maryland, supported a significant shipbuilding industry. "Ships of three hundred tuns sail near two hundred miles, and anchor in the fresh waters" of the Chesapeake colonies, a colonial governor boasted in 1663, "and by this means are not troubled with those Worms which endamage ships both in the Western Islands of America, and in the Mediterranean Sea." Estuaries that opened Virginia and Maryland's lush forests and rich land to exploration and settlement also brought ships to the planters' wharves and made London the chief metropolis for Chesapeake colonists throughout the colonial period, although the ports at Norfolk and Baltimore flourished after 1750.

Transportation between England and the Chesapeake was readily available; by 1700 some 160 ships made the annual voyage unless prevented by imperial wars. They came in huge fleets, moving to the seasonal demands of the tobacco trade; in the late seventeenth century, 80 percent of the tobacco ships entered the Chesapeake in autumn and winter and sailed home between March and June. During the imperial wars of the eighteenth century, however, the threat of French privateers encouraged the organization of summer tobacco convoys accompanied by royal men-of-war. By the 1740s the simultaneous rise of resident tobacco merchants, or factors, and of colonial inspection systems with government-operated warehouses enabled organized convoys to load quickly and return to Europe; 30 percent of the fleet left in May or June, while 43 percent waited for August and September, when the threat of worms had ended.

Before 1650 the voyage normally took three or four months along the southern route used by Columbus. Once clear of the English Channel, ships moved south between Portugal and the Madeira Islands to the tropic of Cancer and the Canaries and caught the trade winds for the three-thousand-mile (4,800-kilometer) westward reach. Replenishing their supplies in the West Indies, the ships followed the Gulf Stream north past the treacherous shoals and fogs of Cape Hatteras and at the thirty-seventh parallel (often in sight of land) awaited easterly winds to carry them into Chesapeake Bay. Christopher Newport's *Susan Constant, Godspeed,* and *Discovery* sailed this early southern route to Virginia in four months from 20 December 1606 to 26 April 1607. Leonard Calvert's *Ark* and *Dove* traversed the route to Maryland in four months from 22 November 1733 to 27 March 1734. Subsequently technological advances and growing English colonial populations north of the Chesapeake attracted convoys to more direct northern routes that averaged eleven weeks outbound to the Chesapeake and six or seven weeks on the return, speeded by the Gulf Stream and prevailing winds.

TOPOGRAPHY

The Chesapeake Bay separated the eastern and western shores of Virginia and Maryland. The former—also known as the Delmarva Peninsula because it embraces all of modern *Del*aware, much of *Mary*land, and two counties of *Vir*ginia—hung like a cluster of grapes between the bay and the Atlantic. On the western shore, an imaginary fall line running from Rockville, Maryland, through Fredericksburg and Richmond to Petersburg, Virginia, marked the boundary between tidewater and Piedmont. The region's coastal plain offered fertile valleys of alluvial soils, higher expanses of flat or rolling sandy brown loam over reddish clay subsoil, and many pockets of poorly drained white oak silt or swampy black and sandy loam. South of the bay lay coastal flatwoods drained by Albemarle and Pimlico sounds in North Carolina. Denied navigation to the Atlantic by the Outer Banks and the treacherous waters off Cape Hatteras, they remained a backwater of the colonial port of Norfolk.

Major rivers divided Virginia's tidewater into three peninsulas, or necks of land: the Northern Neck between the Potomac and Rappahannock; the Middle Peninsula between the Rappahannock and the York; and the Peninsula between the York and the James. Below the James a triangular region of tidewater and Piedmont sprawling west to the Blue Ridge and south to the Virginia–North Carolina line was known as the Southside.

West of the fall line, the red clay hills of the Piedmont rolled into the Blue Ridge Mountains, the easternmost range in the Allegheny Mountains and the first crests of the Appalachian system. Immediately west of the Blue Ridge lay the Shenandoah and other river valleys known collectively as the Valley of Virginia. Waters of the Shenandoah, James, and Roanoke rivers ran into the Atlantic, but the New, Kanawha, Clinch, and Holston rivers ran west and south into the Mississippi watershed via the Ohio and the Tennessee rivers. After explorers opened the Cumberland Gap to Kentucky, Chesapeake leaders and speculators envisaged canals carrying the produce of mid America through to foreign markets—dreams partially realized after independence by the Chesapeake and Ohio and the James River and Kanawha canals (and later by railroads to Baltimore, Norfolk, and Newport News).

BOUNDARIES AND TERRITORIAL CLAIMS

Colonial charters for the Chesapeake colonies shaped many subsequent events in North American history. On 10 April 1606, in the first charter of the two joint-stock enterprises comprising the Virginia Companies of London and of Plymouth, James I authorized two English colonies on the coast of North America: one between thirty-four degrees (Cape Fear River, North Carolina) and forty-one degrees (Long Island Sound) north latitude and the other between thirty-eight degrees (the Potomac) and forty-five degrees (Bangor, Maine) north latitude, provided the second colony was at least one hundred miles (160 kilometers) from the first. Reorganized in 1609 under its second charter (which encouraged public sale of its stock), the Virginia Company of London claimed all the territory from sea to sea "west and northwest" of a four-hundred-mile section of coast centered at Point Comfort (modern Hampton). Virginia's territory was confirmed by the company's third charter in 1612 (which also authorized lotteries to benefit the company); it embraced the entire continent north of a line from Wilmington, North Carolina, to Los Angeles and south of a line from Atlantic City to Anchorage.

On 30 June 1632 Charles I granted Cecilius Calvert, second lord Baltimore, a charter for a separate colony ("called Mariland in memory and honor of the Queene") within Virginia's partially settled 1609 boundaries. From Delaware Bay, Maryland's northern boundary at forty degrees north latitude ran as far west as the source of the Potomac, south across the Potomac and east along its south bank to Watkins Point, then across the bay to the Atlantic Ocean. Seventeenth-century Virginians violently contested Calvert's territory, and boundary quarrels with Pennsylvania ceased only after the Mason and Dixon line was drawn between 1763 and 1768, but Maryland basically retained the territory granted by Charles I in 1632.

Events altered Virginia's territorial claims. Twice Charles II gave lavish grants to his courtiers. The first, in 1663 and 1665, established the province of the Carolinas below Currituck Inlet at 35°30′ north latitude, from whence a 1728 expedition led by William Byrd II traced the present Virginia–North Carolina border 242 miles (387 kilometers) west to the Blue Ridge Mountains. Charles II's second gift did not alter Virginia's external boundaries, but his creation of the Northern Neck proprietary (confirmed in 1669) gave the Fairfax family title and rents to vast acres between the Potomac and Rappahannock rivers throughout the eighteenth century. The last colonial-era change in Virginia's boundaries occurred at the end of the Seven Years' War; the Treaty of Paris (1763) put the western limit of British North America at the Mississippi and recognized Spanish possession of New Orleans and the Louisiana territory.

After the Declaration of Independence, the new nation faced rivalries between states with claims to western lands (notably Virginia) and those without such claims (notably Maryland). To promote unity the Old Dominion ceded the territory between the Ohio and the Mississippi in 1781, whereupon Maryland ratified the Articles of Confederation and formally brought the national government into being. Five states were carved from this territory in accord with provisions of the Northwest Ordinance of 1787, and Virginia assumed its modern limits with the creation of Kentucky in 1792 and West Virginia in 1863.

NATIVE AMERICANS

When Europeans ventured into North America, the Native Americans of the lower Chesapeake enjoyed a complex society unified by Algonquian languages and religious beliefs associated with the deity Okee. They raised maize, beans, squash, sunflowers, and tobacco near permanent villages; fished and hunted with bow and arrow; and traded sheet mica from the Ohio River for copper from the Great Lakes. To the north the powerful Iroquoian-speaking Susquehannock were eight thousand strong at their fortified fur-trading capital near the head of the bay. Near the Potomac on southern Maryland's western shore, the Piscataway (or Conoy) led an Algonquian confederacy of some seven thousand persons, while across the bay the Nanticoke had a similar Algonquian network centered in modern Delaware. Less is known about Siouan tribes such as the Monacan west of modern Richmond or the Iroquoian Nottoway and Meherrin south of the James, whose aboriginal cultures had been disrupted before they had extensive contact with Europeans.

After conflict with Spanish Jesuits on a mission to the south bank of the York River in 1570 had brought deadly retaliation by Spanish troops in 1572, two dozen tidewater Algonquian tribes from the James to the Potomac rivers united under the Pamunkey leader Powhatan (or Wahunsonacock). The Powhatan confederacy (or Tsenacommacah) that greeted the *Susan Constant, Godspeed,* and *Discovery* embraced a nine-thousand-square-mile (23,000-square-kilometer) chiefdom comprised of twelve thousand inhabitants, including three thousand warriors.

ROANOKE ISLAND

Religious and national rivalries unleashed by the Protestant Reformation prompted sixteenth-century Englishmen to value the Chesapeake less for its "fruitfull and delightsome land" than for its strategic location as an imperial base. Treasure fleets laden with silver and gold from Mexico and South America financed Spain's hegemony in the Mediterranean as the European champion of Catholicism. English privateers roaming the Spanish Main—buccaneers such as Thomas Cavendish, Francis Drake, Martin Frobisher, and John Hawkins—were motivated by the desire to advance Protestantism and promote national defense as well as by personal profit, and a number of colonial leaders in the first half century of Chesapeake settlement were veterans of Protestant campaigns in the Low Countries.

In 1578, as England and the United Netherlands signed a defensive alliance against Spain, Elizabeth granted letters patent to Sir Humphrey Gilbert to plant a colony on North American shores. Bolstered by her promise that his colonists would enjoy "all the privileges of free denizens and persons native of England, in such ample manner as if they were born and personally resident in England," Gilbert twice ventured toward the New World, dying at sea in the second attempt. In March 1584 his half brother, Walter Raleigh, took over the charter and sent Philip Amadas and Arthur Barlowe to explore the present-day Outer Banks of North Carolina, where they explored Roanoke Island. They named the country Virginia in honor of the virgin queen.

Distant enough from Spanish Florida to escape surprise overland attack, Roanoke Island was intended as a self-sustaining military base for privateers preying upon Spanish shipping. In 1585 Richard Grenville and Ralph Lane led Raleigh's second Roanoke expedition, which included artist John White and scholar Thomas Hariot, whose invaluable reports and drawings gave Europeans their first accurate impressions of Virginia's Native population, flora, and fauna. After a difficult winter they left the island when Sir Francis Drake arrived and carried them home that spring. In 1587 Raleigh sent a third expedition, commanded by John White, that included families of men, women, and children intent upon re-creating landed English society in the New World as Elizabethan colonists were doing in northern Ireland. For inexplicable reasons White returned to England after establishing a colony at Roanoke Island. Raleigh was prevented from sending supplies back to the settlement by the Spanish Armada of 1588, which opened four years of Anglo-Spanish warfare.

When at last White did return, Roanoke was deserted. To this day the lost colony remains enshrouded in the mystery evoked by the word *Croatoan* found carved into a post at its abandoned stockade. Probably the Roanoke colonists abandoned the Outer Banks, moved north to the Elizabeth River (near modern Norfolk), and lived among the Chesapeake Indians, who were annihilated by Powhatan shortly before the Jamestown landing of 1607.

The failure at Roanoke interrupted English colonial ventures until Elizabeth I died in 1603 and her successor, James I, made peace with Spain. Raleigh's successors then planted the name Virginia on the shores of Chesapeake Bay and established at Jamestown the first permanent English colony in the New World.

JAMESTOWN AND THE MILITARY REGIME

The business objective of the Virginia Company of London was profit for its investors, but colonization of Virginia was also a national enterprise and godly mission to create, as Captain John Smith wrote: "a nurse[ry] for souldiers, a practise for marriners, a trade for marchants, a reward for the good, and that which is most of all, a businesse (most acceptable to God) to bring such poore infidels to the true knowledge of God and his holy Gospell." As business venture and religious mission, the Virginia Company fell short and went bankrupt in 1624; but the experiment in colonial organization on the banks of the Chesapeake taught Englishmen some lessons about human nature and government.

While the *Susan Constant, Godspeed,* and *Discovery* sailed to Virginia, Captain Christopher Newport exercised absolute command. When the 104 colonists touched land on 26 April 1607 and opened their sealed instructions, they learned that leadership had been vested in a seven-man council of state. Unfortunately, the designated councillors were already at odds. On 13 May 1607 the colonists anchored in the James River off a narrow isthmus and founded the capital they called Jamestown. Captain John Smith came ashore under arrest for conspiracy, but by September 1608 three councillors had returned to England and three had died, leaving him the only remaining one.

After a difficult summer Smith, a hero of battles against the Turks, enforced discipline in Virginia by his example and personality. He negotiated peace with Powhatan and compelled the colonists to labor for their survival. When a gunpowder accident forced his final departure from Virginia in October 1609, disaster soon followed. Governance by resident council collapsed into factionalism, and only some sixty-five colonists lived through the winter of 1609–1610 (known as the starving time). The survivors abandoned Jamestown that June, intent upon joining English fishing fleets off Newfoundland and hobbling home.

Sailing downriver, by sheerest chance the colonists encountered Thomas West, Lord De La Warr. Chosen from the circle of English officers with experience in Ireland and the Low Countries, De La Warr and his lieutenants, Sir Thomas Gates and Sir Thomas Dale, were sent out under the Virginia Company's new charter to replace the defunct seven-member council with a martial law regime under "one *able* and *absolute* governor." These soldier-governors brought garrison government to Virginia and stabilized the colony's day-to-day existence.

When the military regime ended in 1618, it left a cadre of militia leaders with both extensive civilian authority and economic power. In the meantime the marriage in 1614 of John Rolfe and Powhatan's daughter Pocahontas had cemented a truce between the colonists and the Powhatan confederacy; Rolfe's experiments with Caribbean tobacco that same year had given the colony a lucrative staple commodity just as eighty-one Virginia Company servants completed seven-year indentures and took private ownership of small tracts of land.

THE TOBACCO PROVINCE

Clinging to its dream of a colony producing commodities such as silk, flax, wheat, and glass—none of which could be produced in Virginia, transported across the Atlantic, and sold at a profit—the Virginia Company of London was mired in debt as it approached its 1616 deadline for paying the first joint-stock dividend to its investors. Its only tangible asset was Virginia land, so the company offered each shareholder fifty acres—indeed it offered fifty acres (20 hectares) in Virginia to anyone willing to pay £12 10s. Thus began a decade in which company projects for diversified commodities slid further toward bankruptcy while colonists on their own, as individuals and in groups, made remarkable profits on tobacco grown at private plantations such as Berkeley Hundred, Flowerdew Hundred, and Merchants Hope.

The tobacco boom had begun: exports skyrocketed from 2,300 pounds of tobacco in 1616 to 260,000 pounds a decade later. "All our riches for the present doe consiste in Tobacco," company official John Pory reported in 1619, "wherein one man by his own labour hath in one yeare, raised himselfe to the value of £200 sterling." Another planter cleared £1,000 in one crop "by the meanes of six servants," and labor was the key to prosperity. "Our principall wealth," Pory wrote, "consisteth in servants." That same year a wayward Dutch ship unloaded Virginia's earliest recorded African-American slaves. The "20. and odd Negroes" brought from the Caribbean to Point Comfort or Jamestown in 1619 presaged the region's future, but not until the decades after 1680 did enslaved blacks supplant white indentured servants as the Chesapeake's principal labor force.

Powhatan's successor, Opechancanough, saw proselytizing Englishmen such as George Thorpe and the intended missionary school at Henrico, near the falls of the James, as a serious cultural threat. The murder of Nemattanow, a prominent *werowance*, or commander, who claimed magical immunity to English bullets, provoked Opechancanough to launch a surprise attack in 1622 that left Thorpe and a quarter of the English population dead. The ensuing decade of Anglo-Powhatan warfare also forged a group of elite colonial leaders. Exploiting the combined powers of their civilian and military offices, three dozen councillor-commanders dominated the Chesapeake Bay, its Indian trading, and its internal and external commerce in tobacco, maize, and furs.

Tobacco remained a profitable staple commodity when peace returned in 1632, but the boom had ended. Prices dropped as production increased, and reduced profit margins in the 1630s precluded newcomers from replicating the councillor-commanders' mercantile success. Allying themselves with minor landholders and indentured servants (whose shares in the profits were smaller but real), Virginia's merchant-councillors imposed order in the colony while the failing Virginia Company put its final stamp on American history with reforms that undergirded a transition from regimented outpost to civilian province.

FROM CORPORATE TO ROYAL COLONY

On 18 November 1618 the Virginia Company of London instructed its new governor, Sir George Yeardley, "to lay a foundation whereon A flourishing State might in process of time by the blessing of Almighty God be raised." Led by outgoing treasurer Sir Thomas Smythe and his incoming rival Sir Edwin Sandys, the company sought to make its colony profitable by enlarging the population and expanding economic diversification. To attract immigrants, the company replaced martial law with English common law, reformed the land tenure system, and provided for local governments and a general assembly. By organizing the colony's existing plantations and hundreds (an ancient English unit of local government) into "cities or borroughs," the company initiated an evolution that led to monthly local courts in 1622, "shires" by

1634, and the creation of counties by legislation in June 1642. The first elected representative assembly in the New World met on 30 July 1619 at Jamestown for five days.

As did Maryland's fifteen years later, Virginia's first assembly resembled an early medieval parliament more than a modern legislature. The governor presided over a unicameral meeting of the council and twenty representatives (called burgesses like the members of the House of Commons from English boroughs) elected from ten localities. This first assembly followed parliamentary procedure under the guidance of Virginia's secretary, John Pory, a veteran of the House of Commons who organized the assembly's working papers for debate by several committees. After James I dissolved the bankrupt Virginia Company on 24 May 1624 and brought the colony under direct royal control, the legal fate of the General Assembly remained uncertain during fifteen years in which absolutism challenged representative government in England and throughout Europe. In the meantime the Virginia assembly, meeting almost annually, proved its utility.

In 1630 Charles I sent tactless and greedy Sir John Harvey to govern Virginia. Harvey soon alienated the leading Virginians (and their influential London business connections) with his claims of prerogative authority and his zeal to help rival and Catholic Maryland. The Virginia councillors placed Harvey under arrest in 1635 and sent him packing to the Commissioners for Plantations (forerunner of the Board of Trade) in London. Four years later, despite its role in deposing Harvey, Charles I's formal 1639 instructions to veteran governor Sir Francis Wyatt confirmed both the General Assembly's existence and the colonists' titles to lands granted by the defunct Virginia Company.

During the 1630s the regimented world run by Virginia's councillor-commander elite changed. As the population grew and spread west and north from Jamestown, earlier forms of local administration were eclipsed by well-defined counties. The end of Indian warfare in 1632 and passing of a generation of veteran militia leaders enhanced the significance of civilian offices in the council, assembly, and emerging counties. Behaving like civilian politicians, old councillor-commanders and rising merchant-

planters honored the legitimacy of these colonial institutions, while the commercial faction led by Samuel Mathews, Sr., and William Claiborne dominated the transatlantic tobacco and fur trades.

After a brief but ineffectual reprise by Harvey, Sir Francis Wyatt, governor from 1621 to 1626, resumed the post in 1639 and initiated a program of political and judicial reform completed by Sir William Berkeley, governor from 1642 to 1652 and again from 1660 to 1677. In March 1643 Virginia's burgesses organized themselves as the lower house of a bicameral assembly. Contemporaries such as John Ogilby, writing in 1671, compared the colony's government to England's traditional mixed constitution; laws, he observed, were enacted "by the Governor, with the consent of a General Assembly, which consists of two Houses, an Upper and a Lower; the first consists of the Council and the latter of the Burgesses chosen by the Freemen of the Countery." Less is known about the initial meeting of Maryland's assembly in 1635, but a Kent Island representative sought separate upper and lower houses in 1642 and Maryland's assembly became bicameral in 1650.

The underpinnings of Virginia's civilian polity stood revealed in a constitutional crisis of 1658. Repudiating a power grab by the Cromwellian governor and council after the death of the lord protector, Virginia's elected representatives threw them out of office and declared that political authority in Virginia was "resident only in the burgesses, representatives of the people, as is manifest by the records of the Assembly." Although happy to embrace Charles II and Governor Berkeley in 1660, colonial Virginians also had learned to hope "that what was their privilege now might be . . . their posterities hereafter." Despite religious tensions, Indian warfare, and civil war in England, the first half century of English settlement in the Chesapeake witnessed the emergence of a stable civilian public life in Virginia.

THE CALVERTS ESTABLISH MARYLAND

Influential Virginians had more at stake in the founding of Maryland by the Roman Catholic

Calverts than religion or land. As tobacco prices fell, fur-trading offered returns of as much as 3,000-percent profit as innovations in felt making and the expanding European market for hats created an enormous demand for prime North American beaver pelts at one pound each. The fur-trading Susquehannock did not welcome European settlers near their territory, however, and Virginia's entrepreneurs always kept a polite distance.

Location, not acreage, was critical to the lucrative beaver trade that Virginian William Claiborne and his English partners and investors developed in the northern bay. Claiborne's commercial empire depended upon two agriculturally insignificant sites: his trading ground on Palmer's Island (near the mouth of the Susquehanna River) and his base at Kent Island (near modern Annapolis), with its adjacent small islands for hogs. On a visit to Jamestown in 1628, Sir George Calvert, first lord Baltimore, had seen this commercial potential for the northern bay. Abandoning earlier efforts to colonize Newfoundland, Calvert shifted his attention to the land between Delaware Bay and the Potomac River that he had cleverly described as "not yet cultivated and planted." In creating Maryland, Charles I suddenly gave Claiborne's strategic outposts to a Roman Catholic courtier.

The *Ark* and the *Dove*

One hundred twenty-eight of Maryland's first settlers swore allegiance to Charles I and left London aboard the *Ark* and the *Dove* on 22 November 1633, and dozens of Catholics evading the oath by boarding in the English Channel swelled their number to "neere 200 people." After a stop in Virginia in March 1634, they entered the Potomac—"the sweetest and greatest river I have seene," one colonist wrote, "so that the Thames is but a little finger to it." Twenty-five miles (40 kilometers) from the bay, Governor Leonard Calvert raised a large cross and the English flag at Saint Clement's Island on 25 March and returned thanks for safe passage. Calvert and his deputies, after conferring with the Piscataway, decided to move toward the mouth of the Potomac and "upon the 27. day of march Anno Domini 1634, the Gouvernour tooke possession of the place, and named the Towne Saint Maries."

Maryland's population remained below five hundred until an influx of Puritan families arrived from Virginia in 1649, and early Maryland remained the frontier (and often the victim) of larger and more settled Virginia, which had more than ten thousand colonists by 1640. Virginia in 1644 easily survived a last surprise attack by the aging Opechancanough (who was captured by Governor Berkeley and treacherously murdered by a guard while awaiting trial) and in 1646 embarked on a new course of peaceful Indian-white relations under treaties of that year. Maryland's first two decades were more violent (often at the hands of Virginians bent on regaining the fur trade of the upper bay) and its existence tenuous. In 1645 with one ship and a few men Richard Ingle nearly destroyed Baltimore's colony. Maryland's "time of troubles"—the confused years of the 1640s—have defied clear narration ever since.

COMPARING THE COLONIES

By the end of the seventeenth century, modern historians agree, the Chesapeake colonies had come to resemble, in the hopeful title of John Hammond's 1656 contribution to the pamphlet controversy over Lord Baltimore's charter, *Leah and Rachel; or, The Two Fruitfull Sisters Virginia, and Maryland*. Modern recognition of the colonies' similarities—pioneered by Arthur Pierce Middleton's *Tobacco Coast* (1953)—defines many regional demographic, social, economic, and cultural characteristics that transcended local peculiarities in the eighteenth century. However, the Chesapeake's Leah and Rachel were not twins but sisters born thirty eventful years apart, and their seventeenth-century experiences with government, religion, and the Commonwealth and Protectorate diverged significantly.

Local Governments

The Virginia planters enjoyed administrative control of their colony from the dissolution of the Virginia Company of London in 1624 to Charles I's belated confirmation of colonial land titles and the General Assembly in 1639; fifteen years of royal indifference gave them time to fashion local institutions of government for themselves. The governor and council combined executive and judicial authority, and between 1619 and the accession of Charles II in 1660 Virginians elected burgesses in four out of every five years.

Beneath this provincial umbrella, local units based on militia organization were transformed between 1623 and 1641 into English-style counties with civilian justices of the peace, clerks, and courts that shared local administration with the Anglican parishes that were often led by the same men. Low-church Anglican or moderately Puritan in ecclesiastical practice, Virginia parishes functioned without interference from English diocesan or episcopal authorities until the 1690s. The General Assembly assigned many powers to the vestries—including full authority to select ministers and vestrymen—without regard for outside authority. Colonial Virginia's laity and gentry exercised as much control of their established church as did their New England counterparts, and the parishes, county courts, and House of Burgesses were the institutions by which the planters dominated their localities.

In Maryland the initial structure of the proprietary government was modeled on a legal anachronism, the medieval powers of the bishops of Durham. Empowered by his charter with virtually absolute legal authority over the laws, management, and defense of Maryland, Baltimore organized his decentralized and rural plantation colony as though it were an English baronial manor. Authority descended from the proprietor through his resident governor (his brother, Leonard Calvert) to lords of the manor (who exercised the authority of any two justices of the peace in England) and finally to their freeholders and tenants and lesser dependents. In practice, however, the absentee proprietor was often at odds with his leading colonists over religion, appointments, and fees, and courts of the manor had virtually disappeared by 1660— supplanted, as in Virginia, by institutions that, according to David W. Jordan, "corresponded more closely to those of contemporary rather than medieval England."

As in Virginia geographical expansion brought experiments with the ancient English hundred as a unit of local administration, but by 1658 Maryland's three thousand inhabitants lived in five counties. Lacking an established church, Maryland had no counterpart to Virginia's parishes until 1692, when the Anglican communion was imposed by the Protestants who had overthrown the proprietary government in the wake of the Glorious Revolution. Although Maryland's new parishes looked after their church buildings and worship, performed marriages, and kept vital records, its vestries had fewer administrative and political functions than Virginia's, and their insignificance led to their demise in 1776.

Religion

Under Elizabeth and James I, the English church included vigorous Protestants (including Virginia Company leaders George and Edwin Sandys). However, Charles I and Archbishop William Laud's enforcement of central ecclesiastical authority fueled political and constitutional strife over matters of faith and worship and drove some dissenters to seek refuge in the New World. Virginia's earliest lay-dominated Anglican local establishments attracted religiously motivated Protestant immigrants until about 1630, when Massachusetts Bay opened a more attractive New World venue for Puritan colonists.

The early ecclesiastical histories of Anglican Virginia, with its established church, and Maryland, with its toleration of Catholicism and diversity, reflected political realities in an age when religious differences often provoked social discord. Puritan-leaning English merchants who were allied with Claiborne and Mathews used the Calverts' support of Roman Catholicism to attack the Maryland charter, and local parishes in both colonies maintained communication with Puritans in England, New England, and the Caribbean.

After visiting England and witnessing Charles I's plight in the civil war, Governor Berkeley and the Virginia legislature began enforcing Anglican orthodoxy in the parishes by isolating and undermining politically active dissenting clergy. Pressured by the government, a group of Nansemond County Puritans led by Richard Bennett removed to Maryland in 1649 to establish the Providence settlement (renamed Annapolis in 1695) on the west bank of the bay near Kent Island. Maryland's celebrated toleration of lay Catholics, Puritans, and Jesuits (beginning well before its Toleration Act of 1649) enabled these newly arrived Puritan settlers to pose a serious challenge to Baltimore's authority through the 1650s. By the next decade, Quakers were present in both Chesapeake colonies, although far more numerous in Maryland, where they and Catholics comprised 25 percent of the population by the end of the century.

By law Virginia's Anglican parishes claimed public support through their enforcement of tithes and the performance of community functions associated with parochial authorities in England. Lay control of the vestries and parishes limited the power of the clergy (and the influence exercised by the bishop of London through his resident commissary from 1690). In addition to worship and the sacraments, Virginia's parishes participated in education, welfare, record keeping, the enforcement of public morality, and the annual processioning of lands throughout the colony—the seasonal protocol of walking the boundaries of all landholdings to maintain recognized property lines and enhance the peace by averting disputes.

Prior to 1662 some Virginia parishes sent burgesses to the General Assembly, and the vestries provided training grounds for aspiring local leaders, who were nominally required to be communing members of the Anglican church. Maryland's Catholic chapels and Quaker meetinghouses relied entirely upon voluntary support. With no religious restrictions barring Catholics or Quaker leaders from office until 1718, Marylanders of all Christian denominations were active in seventeenth-century local and provincial government. In a longer perspective, while the community functions of Virginia's parishes encouraged social and political stability during the early seventeenth century, the emergence of evangelical Presbyterians and Baptists in the mid eighteenth century caused greater disruption for Virginia's established Anglican church than for Maryland's voluntary congregations.

Surrendering to Parliament

The cataclysms of mid-seventeenth-century English history affected Virginia and Maryland in profoundly different ways; Baltimore's charter and colony were frequently under attack, and prominent Virginians were chief among the aggressors. The civil war, intrigues against Baltimore, and hostility from William Claiborne and his clique, supported by the Susquehannock, prolonged Maryland's time of troubles until the late 1650s.

Desperate for money after eleven years of personal rule, Charles I in 1640 convened what became the Long Parliament. Civil war began in 1642, and the executioner's axe fell on Archbishop Laud in 1645 and the king himself in 1649. No sooner had Parliament established a Commonwealth without king, bishops, or lords than Puritan merchants allied with Mathews and Claiborne wrote the Navigation Acts of 1650 and 1651 and sent a fleet and five commissioners to subdue Virginia, Maryland, and Barbados. Parliamentary commissioners Thomas Stegg (former speaker of the General Assembly and member of the Virginia Council) and Robert Dennis were lost at sea in the *John*, but the *Guinea* brought Richard Bennett, William Claiborne, and Edmund Curtis home. On 12 March 1652, after negotiations with governor Sir William Berkeley and the General Assembly, the commissioners concluded Virginia's peaceful surrender to the Commonwealth. Bennett became governor of Virginia, Claiborne resumed his old office as secretary of the council, and Berkeley retired to his Green Spring plantation.

Baltimore lobbied Parliament to deliver his colony from the hands of his enemies, but Article 4 of the surrender at Jamestown outlined Maryland's prospects at the hands of the commissioners: "That Virginia shall have and enioy the antient bounds and lymitts granted by the charter of the former Kings, And that we shall seek a new charter from the parliament to that purpose against any that have intrencht vpon the rights thereof." Meeting no armed resistance, Bennett and Claiborne entered Saint Mary's City on 29 March 1652 and replaced Baltimore's "Catholic tyrants" with a council of Virginia Protestants. Later that summer they negotiated a comprehensive treaty with the Susquehannock that excluded Marylanders from the fur trade, returned Kent and Palmer's Island to Claiborne, and freed the Susquehannock to attack their Iroquoian enemies to the north.

Virginia sent Samuel Mathews, Sr., to London to secure the repeal of Baltimore's charter. Meanwhile, in 1654, Maryland's Puritans revoked the Toleration Act, excluded Catholics from office, confiscated property, and moved their capital to Providence on the western shore.

197

Religious and political tensions between the colonies and within Maryland culminated in the March 1655 battle at the Severn River, where William Stone's proprietary force of 130 men suffered a catastrophic defeat and many casualties.

Restoration, Rebellion, and Revolution

Baltimore and the Virginia Puritans struck a compromise truce in 1658, while Oliver Cromwell's death that September and his son Richard's abdication the next spring opened the way for the restoration of Charles II in May 1660. Virginia's governor Samuel Mathews, Jr., died the same year. The task of naming a successor made the General Assembly uneasy about "offending a Supreme power which neither by present possession is soe, nor yet has a publiquely confessed politique capacity to be a Supreame power." Therefore, declaring themselves sovereign as representatives of the people, the burgesses in March 1660 risked inviting Berkeley out of retirement "until a Supreame settled power appeares." In October, Charles II affirmed Berkeley as royal governor of Virginia.

The Stuart Restoration enabled Baltimore to regain his Maryland proprietorship (although Claiborne pressed his claims to Kent Island until his death in 1677), but Charles II's return to the throne brought no reinstatement of his father's relaxed policies toward the Chesapeake. Over strong protests from Governor Berkeley and the Chesapeake tobacco planters, king and Parliament continued the anti-Dutch policies of 1650 and 1651 in the Navigation Act of 1660 and set the stage for a series of Anglo-Dutch wars. Then Charles II dashed mercantilist plans for diversified economic growth in the colony and undermined his colonial lieutenants with careless measures that sent per capita taxes soaring between 1671 and 1675. First, he gave away the Northern Neck to the Fairfax family and then gave away much of the remainder of Virginia to court favorites who had to be bought off. Second, heeding English shipping interests, he ordered an expensive but useless fort constructed at Point Comfort, where (as Virginians had predicted) it utterly failed to protect tobacco fleets from Dutch attack in 1667 and 1673.

Early in 1675 the northern Seneca forced the Chesapeake's former fur-trading allies, the Susquehannock, into refuge among the Piscataway near the Potomac, where members of both tribes were soon killed by irresponsible frontiersmen. Terror gripped the English colonies as roving bands of Susquehannock took revenge on isolated farmsteads. Berkeley opted for a measured response, but angry Virginians rallied to the Indian-baiting rhetoric of Giles Brent and Nathaniel Bacon, Jr. In the spring of 1676 Bacon and his armed followers marched to Jamestown to demand a commission from Berkeley to fight Indians. The seventy-year-old governor vacillated, first refusing Bacon a commission, then granting one, and then rescinding it. When Berkeley declared him a rebel, Bacon led his angry followers against the governor's "damned cowards," "wicked and pernicious councellors, confederates, aiders, and assisters against the commonality." His open rebellion brought civil war. Lacking a Baconian ringleader, Maryland initially was spared the worst while Jamestown burned. However, while in Virginia the mayhem ebbed quickly after Bacon died in October of "the bloody flux," in Maryland tensions unleashed by its neighbor's civil war inflamed events of the next decade.

After quiet resumed in the Chesapeake, the consequences of Bacon's Rebellion rippled through English public life. Financially dependent upon duties from Chesapeake tobacco, Charles II was hard-pressed by the disruption of an entire season's trade. Forced to turn to Parliament for revenue, Charles and his Catholic brother James, duke of York, clashed with the Protestant politicians who sought to exclude James from the royal succession. Charles II's death put the crown on a Catholic king, but it was the birth of James's son in June 1688 that threatened the future of the Protestant nation, which then welcomed William of Orange as its champion and king.

Virginians welcomed the Glorious Revolution calmly. Across the Potomac, however, John Coode's Protestant Association overthrew the proprietary government in August 1689 and petitioned William III to make Maryland a royal province. Baltimore's charter—already under scrutiny before news from Saint Mary's City reached England—was suspended in 1691. Although the Calverts retained their Maryland property, they never recovered political power even after the proprietorship was restored in 1716.

THE CHESAPEAKE'S SECOND CENTURY

As the eighteenth century began, Virginia and Maryland's similarities were enhanced by shared demographic change. In 1700 the population of Maryland was about thirty-two thousand, including forty-five hundred slaves; Virginia's was perhaps seventy-five thousand, including some ninety-five hundred slaves. The quadrupling of this regional population between 1700 and 1750 was accompanied by a major alteration in the character of immigration to Virginia and Maryland. About 1680, for complex local and international reasons, Chesapeake planters began importing slaves, rather than indentured servants, in large numbers. Sisters in law and practice, the Chesapeake colonies became a distinctive economic region whose staple economy was dominated by slave laborers (about 15 percent of the population in 1704) producing tobacco for export to British ports.

The new century also witnessed the expansion of settlement beyond the tidewater and across the Blue Ridge Mountains into the trans-Allegheny west. The 1716 expedition of Governor Alexander Spotswood and his Knights of the Golden Horseshoe beyond the area of settlement opened the Valley of Virginia to exploration and settlement. The Great Wagon Road welcomed German and Scotch-Irish from Pennsylvania, whose wheat and other grains made the small farms of the Valley of Virginia and western Maryland a prototype of the American Midwest. Tidewater families amassed huge Piedmont tobacco estates, and the leading men of both colonies speculated in vast tracts of unexplored land in the Ohio country through rival ventures such as the Ohio Company and the Loyal Land Company.

The 1730s saw the cultural flowering of the Chesapeake Anglophile gentry culture. Throughout Virginia and Maryland, the wealthier planters and townspeople replaced wooden residences with brick houses in the Georgian style to which their children added hyphens, or low connecting sections joining a main house with its flanking buildings, and wings in Palladian grandeur. William Parks brought printing to Annapolis in 1726 and to Williamsburg in 1730. Gentlemen who had circulated their belletristic and political writings to coterie circles in manuscript ventured into pseudonymous print in the *Maryland Gazette* (founded in 1727) and *Virginia Gazette* (founded in 1736). Planters emulated the sporting life of English country gentlemen, too; the first thoroughbred arrived in the Chesapeake in 1730, and a hundred more followed before independence.

When the Chesapeake frontiersmen met the Indian allies of New France, imperial rivalry between England and France found its North American arena. In 1754 Virginia's governor Robert Dinwiddie sent a small militia force commanded by George Washington to challenge French troops building Fort Duquesne at the forks of the Ohio River. Washington's militia failed, as did Edward Braddock's British regulars in 1755 at the onset of the Seven Years' War in America. The conflict's North American upshot was France's 1762 transferral of the Louisiana territory to Spain and the confirmation by the 1763 Treaty of Paris of the British conquest of Canada and the lands east of the Mississippi. Seeking to avoid conflict between the Chesapeake colonists and the Indians, Britain promptly closed the trans-Allegheny west to settlement by the Proclamation of 1763—and thereby raised a divisive issue in what became the movement toward American independence.

Faced with unprecedented public debt at the end of the Seven Years' War, Parliament imposed heavy taxes at home and tightened the administration of trade and navigation laws in the colonies. Chesapeake legislators had often objected to British intrusions in provincial affairs, but their reaction to the Stamp Act of 1765 opened a constitutional chasm as wide as the Atlantic. Relying on principles firmly articulated as early as the 1750s, rooted both in their history and in the civic republican tradition, the slaveholding planters of the tobacco coast allied themselves with Boston and New England in the American clamor against Parliament's claim of authority to tax the colonies. Marylanders overthrew the propriety government one final time, and from Williamsburg in 1774 came the call for what became known as the Continental Congress. In May 1776 Virginia instructed its delegation to introduce a resolution for independence, and on 2 July Congress passed Richard Henry Lee's motion that the colonies "were, and of right ought to be, free and independent states." Two days later Congress justified its decision to a candid world, and Leah and Rachel of the Chesapeake joined eleven sister states in the battles—military, constitutional, political, and social—that created the new republic.

BIBLIOGRAPHY

Bailyn, Bernard. "Politics and Social Structure in Virginia." In *Seventeenth-Century America: Essays in Colonial History,* edited by James Morton Smith. Chapel Hill, N.C., 1959.

Barbour, Philip L., ed. *The Complete Works of Captain John Smith (1580–1631).* 3 vols. Chapel Hill, N.C., 1986.

Billings, Warren M., ed. *The Old Dominion in the Seventeenth Century: A Documentary History of Virginia, 1606–1689.* Chapel Hill, N.C., 1975.

Billings, Warren M., John E. Selby, and Thad W. Tate. *Colonial Virginia: A History.* White Plains, N.Y., 1986.

Brugger, Robert J. *Maryland: A Middle Temperament, 1634–1980.* Baltimore, Md., 1988.

Carr, Lois Green. "The Foundations of Social Order: Local Government in Colonial Maryland." In *Town and Country: Essays on the Structure of Local Government in the American Colonies,* edited by Bruce E. Daniels. Middletown, Conn., 1978.

Carr, Lois Green, Philip D. Morgan, and Jean B. Russo, eds. *Colonial Chesapeake Society.* Chapel Hill, N.C., 1988.

Carr, Lois Green, Russell R. Menard, and Lorena S. Walsh. *Robert Cole's World: Agriculture and Society in Early Maryland.* Chapel Hill, N.C., 1991.

Clemens, Paul G. E. *The Atlantic Economy and Colonial Maryland's Eastern Shore: From Tobacco to Grain.* Ithaca, N.Y., 1980.

Craven, Wesley Frank. *Dissolution of the Virginia Company: The Failure of a Colonial Experiment.* New York, 1932.

———. *The Southern Colonies in the Seventeenth Century, 1607–1689.* Baton Rouge, La., 1949; rev. ed. 1970.

———. *White, Red, and Black: The Seventeenth-Century Virginian.* Charlottesville, Va., 1971.

Davis, Richard Beale. *Intellectual Life in the Colonial South, 1585–1763.* 3 vols. Knoxville, Tenn., 1978.

Fausz, J. Frederick. "Present at the 'Creation': The Chesapeake World That Greeted the Maryland Colonists." *Maryland Historical Magazine* 79 (1984):7–20.

Greene, Jack P. *Pursuits of Happiness: The Social Development of Early Modern British Colonies and the Formation of American Culture.* Chapel Hill, N.C., 1988.

Hall, Clayton Colman, ed. *Narratives of Early Maryland, 1633–1684.* New York, 1925.

Isaac, Rhys. *The Transformation of Virginia, 1740–1790.* Chapel Hill, N.C., 1982.

Jordan, David W. *Foundations of Representative Government in Maryland, 1632–1715.* New York, 1987.

Kukla, Jon. "Order and Chaos in Early America: Political and Social Stability in Pre-Restoration Virginia." *American Historical Review* 90, no. 2 (1985):275–298.

———. *Political Institutions in Virginia, 1619–1660.* New York, 1989.

Kupperman, Karen Ordahl. *Roanoke: The Abandoned Colony.* Totowa, N.J., 1984.

Land, Aubrey C. *Colonial Maryland: A History.* Millwood, N.Y., 1981.

Lebsock, Suzanne. *Virginia Women, 1600–1945: "A Share of Honour."* Richmond, Va., 1987.

Leonard, Sister Joan de Lourdes. "Operation Checkmate: The Birth and Death of a Virginia Blueprint for Progress, 1660–1676." *William and Mary Quarterly,* 3rd ser., 24, no. 1 (1967):44–74.

Main, Gloria L. *Tobacco Colony: Life in Early Maryland, 1650–1720.* Princeton, N.J., 1983.

Menard, Russell. "From Servants to Slaves: The Transformation of the Chesapeake Labor System." *Southern Studies* 16, no. 4 (1977):355–390.

Middleton, Arthur Pierce. *Tobacco Coast: A Maritime History of Chesapeake Bay in the Colonial Era.* Newport News, Va., 1953.

Morgan, Edmund S. *American Slavery, American Freedom: The Ordeal of Colonial Virginia.* New York, 1975.

Morgan, Edmund S., and Helen M. Morgan. *The Stamp Act Crisis: Prologue to Revolution.* Chapel Hill, N.C., 1953; rev. ed. New York, 1963.

Morton, Richard L. *Colonial Virginia.* Chapel Hill, N.C., 1960.

Perry, James R. *The Formation of a Society on Virginia's Eastern Shore, 1615–1655.* Chapel Hill, N.C., 1990.

Quinn, David B., ed. *Early Maryland in a Wider World.* Detroit, Mich., 1982.

Rutman, Anita H. "Still Planting the Seeds of Hope: The Recent Literature of the Early Chesapeake Region." *Virginia Magazine of History and Biography* 95, no. 1 (1987):3–24.

Rutman, Darrett B., and Anita H. Rutman. *A Place in Time: Middlesex County, Virginia, 1650–1750.* New York, 1984.

Salmon, Emily J., ed. *A Hornbook of Virginia History.* Richmond, Va., 1949; 3rd ed. 1983.

Sobel, Mechal. *The World They Made Together: Black and White Values in Eighteenth-Century Virginia.* Princeton, N.J., 1987.

Sydnor, Charles S. *Gentlemen Freeholders: Political Practices in Washington's Virginia.* Chapel Hill, N.C., 1952.

Tate, Thad W., and David L. Ammerman, eds. *The Chesapeake in the Seventeenth Century: Essays on Anglo-American Society.* Chapel Hill, N.C., 1979.

Vaughan, Alden. *American Genesis: Captain John Smith and the Founding of Virginia.* Boston, 1975.

Jon Kukla

SEE ALSO **British Settlements, The Lower South; Emergence of Empires; Indian-Colonist Contact; Internal Migration; Medical Practice, Health and Disease; Repeopling the Land;** and **Slavery;** the various essays in RELIGION; and the map preceding **French Settlements.**

THE LOWER SOUTH

NORTH CAROLINA, SOUTH CAROLINA, and Georgia constituted the lower southern colonies in British North America for most of the colonial period. Historians have therefore frequently treated them as a unit, without, however, always explaining why. Contiguousness was of course their most obvious link, but each colony had some unique characteristics. Moreover, northern North Carolina was in many respects more like Virginia than South Carolina, and Florida during the British period (1763–1783) resembled Georgia. Nevertheless, the two Carolinas and Georgia did exhibit significant similarities. Settlers from other colonies, rather than from Europe, were instrumental in establishing each of the three. More important, the tidewater area stretching from Cape Fear in North Carolina to the Altamaha River in southern Georgia had geographic features that suited the region to the large-scale production of rice; the plantation society, based on African-American slavery, that developed in the "greater Carolina" Low Country was unusual on the North American mainland in its resemblance to the culture of the West Indies, where blacks constituted a majority of the population.

IMPORTANT INFLUENCES: PHYSICAL GEOGRAPHY AND INDIANS

Despite the importance of the Low Country to the development of the lower southern colonies, it was only one element in the varied physical geography of the region. The outer banks of North Carolina constituted the eastern edge of an area of sand bars, inlets, shallow sounds, and marshy land that made both navigation and settlement difficult. Farther south, the sea islands of South Carolina and Georgia created a similar barrier but provided more arable land. On the mainland, the coastal plain stretched westward for 100 to 150 miles (160 to 240 kilometers). At the western margin of this plain, the fall line, a zone whose precise location varied with streamflow, marked the appearance of the first rapids. The eastern portion of the coastal plain was an area of swamps and rich alluvial soil, notable for high temperatures, high humidity, and billions of insects. It soon became notorious for its "pestilential fevers." White settlers therefore developed the convenient but not totally unfounded notion that they could not work in this environment and live.

Along the fall line, roughly parallel to the coast, a range of low-lying sand hills marked ancient shorelines from southern North Carolina to Georgia. Like George Washington, who traveled through the region on the road from Augusta, Georgia, to Charlotte, North Carolina, in 1791, would-be settlers considered this area a desolate pine barren and shunned it. West of the sand hills, rolling hills and hardwoods characterized the relatively fertile Piedmont that eventually merged with the Great Smoky Mountains of the southern Appalachian chain. At 6,684 feet (2,005 meters), Mount Mitchell in North Carolina is the highest mountain east of the Mississippi River, and the mountain chain of which it is a part constituted a substantial barrier to further western settlement. But as the land rose, mean temperatures declined, and colonists accordingly regarded the inland areas as the most healthful parts of their provinces.

Whether Native Americans thought similarly is unclear, but the largest and most powerful tribes tended to be located in the interior, and pre-Columbian population centers were often situated along the rivers near the fall line. Precisely how many Indians lived in southeastern North America when Europeans arrived will probably always be a matter of conjecture, because Native Americans lacked immunity to newly introduced European diseases and died by the thousands before anyone recorded their numbers. But later records are more complete, and the historian Peter Wood has been able to provide reasonably reliable estimates of the Native American population for the eighteenth century. In *Powhatan's Mantle* Wood suggests that in 1700, 7,200 Indians lived in the coastal plain and Piedmont of North Carolina, and perhaps 7,500 lived in South Carolina. By the end of the colonial period, these numbers had declined to approximately 500 in each of the colonies. The situation in Georgia, which was virtually unsettled by whites in 1700, is less clear, but the two largest groups in the Southeast—the Creek and the Cherokee—together probably numbered 25,000 in 1700 and perhaps 22,500 in 1775. These numbers conceal an almost 50 percent loss in the Cherokee population and a comparable gain in the number of Creek, who were farther from white settlements during the years in question. Some Indian tribes, like the Catawba, adapted and survived, but many others did not.

Even in their decline, however, Native Americans profoundly affected the development of these British colonies. They were not only partners in trade but also allies and adversaries in war. The attack by the Tuscarora (1711) on the settlement at New Bern was sufficiently serious that North Carolinians requested help from South Carolina. A combined force of whites and Yamassee Indians defeated the Tuscarora, who soon joined the Iroquois in New York and Pennsylvania. Four years later, the Yamassee themselves responded to repeated abuses by initiating an attack on South Carolina that eventually involved most of the southern tribes. The resulting Yamassee War (1715) depopulated the southern part of the province. Partly because the Cherokee remained neutral at first and then provided aid, Carolinians eventually defeated the Yamassee, who nevertheless continued to raid the colony from Florida for the next fifteen years. Then, during the Seven Years' War (1754–1763), the Cherokee attacked settlements all along the southern frontier. It took British troops and three military expeditions before the Cherokee agreed to peace terms in 1761. Fifteen years later, as the American Revolution began, most of the southern tribes except the Catawba sided with the British. The repeated result for the Indians was the surrender of tribal lands, but whites in the lower southern colonies also suffered losses of life and property. Recurrent hostilities made the Lower South a dangerous part of the world throughout much of the seventeenth and eighteenth centuries.

EUROPEAN EXPLORATION AND SETTLEMENT

The proximity of settlers from rival European powers in the early years of exploration increased the danger for all concerned. The Spanish were the first on the scene. Having established bases on Hispaniola and Cuba, Spaniards pushed north in search of gold, slaves, and perhaps the fountain of youth. Lucas Vásquez de Ayllón reached South Carolina in the 1520s but failed to establish a permanent settlement; some twenty years later, Hernando de Soto crossed the interior of Georgia and South Carolina, where he encountered an Indian chiefdom headed by a woman, Cofitachique, en route to his watery grave in the Mississippi River.

The French also became interested in the region; in 1524 the Italian explorer Giovanni da Verrazano, leading a French expedition, put into the mouth of the Cape Fear River before heading north along the outer banks. Nearly forty years later, Jean Ribaut built a small fort at Port Royal, South Carolina, which his men soon abandoned. René de Laudonnière then established another French post, Fort Caroline, near modern Jacksonville. All this French activity prompted a decisive Spanish response, and in 1565 Pedro Menéndez de Avilés destroyed the French settlement at Fort Caroline after founding what turned out to be the first permanent European settlement in North America, at Saint Augustine. Shortly thereafter, he established another post at Santa Elena (Port Royal), but in 1586 Sir Francis Drake's sack of Saint Augustine forced the Spanish to withdraw from Santa Elena. Still, for the next one hundred years, Spanish missions continued to exist on the coast of South Carolina and up the Chattahoochee River to the site of present-day Columbus, Georgia. Indeed, it was not until the Treaty of Madrid with England in 1670 that Spain recognized foreign claims in the area north of Saint Augustine.

The English were later to arrive but were more successful in establishing themselves when they did. Authorized to found colonies by Queen Elizabeth I, Sir Walter Raleigh sent Philip Amadas and Arthur Barlowe to explore the coast of North Carolina in 1584. They spent six weeks in the vicinity of Roanoke Island before returning to England with favorable reports. A second expedition sent by Raleigh under Richard Grenville and Ralph Lane in 1585 planted a colony on the island. But the garrison, fearing starvation and hostile Indians, returned to England in 1586 with Drake, who stopped by after burning Saint Augustine. A third expedition, this one led by John White, then established Raleigh's second colony on Roanoke Island during the summer of 1587. White returned to England for supplies; the attack of the Spanish Armada in 1588 delayed him there, and when he returned to Roanoke Island in 1590, the settlers were gone, perhaps to join the Croatan Indians on Okracoke Island. After Jamestown was founded in 1607, numerous Virginians explored the Albemarle Sound area, but their activities produced few recorded results.

In 1629 King Charles I of England granted "Carolana" (named for himself) to his attorney-general, Sir Robert Heath. This immense tract stretched from thirty-one degrees to thirty-six degrees north latitude and from sea to sea. Heath's tenure produced much negotiation and many legal complications but few settlers. However, on 24 March 1663, Charles II vacated Heath's claim and granted eight lord proprietors title to the same area. Modifications to the proprietors' charter two years later extended their claims southward to twenty-nine degrees (Saint Augustine) and northward to 36° 30′, which took in previously established settlements in the Albemarle Sound region. The eight proprietors were men of influence and some colonial experience. Anthony Ashley Cooper, later earl of Shaftesbury, owned a sugar plantation in Barbados; Sir John Colleton was a Barbadian planter; and William Berkeley served as governor of Virginia. His more influential brother, John, Lord Berkeley, and Sir George Carteret would become proprietors as well of New Jersey. George Monck, duke of Albemarle, William, Lord Craven, and Edward Hyde, earl of Clarendon rounded out the group. The proprietors, who hoped to colonize Carolina with settlers from the overcrowded island of Barbados as well as from other colonies, succeeded where others had failed.

After preliminary expeditions by William Hilton and Robert Sandford and two abortive attempts at colonization, Lord Shaftesbury organized the expedition that established the first permanent settlement. It sailed from England in August 1669, stopped in Ireland and Barbados, and, after the wreck of two of its vessels, reached Bull's Bay, South Carolina, on 15 March 1670. As instructed, the settlers proceeded southward to Port Royal Sound. That area, they soon concluded, was too close to the Spanish in Florida, so they accepted the suggestion of a local Indian, the Cacique of Kiawah, to move northward to the confluence of the Ashley and Cooper rivers. There, a few miles up the Ashley River at Albemarle Point, they established their settlement. In August, an attack by the Spanish from Saint Augustine failed. Nine years later, the proprietors directed the Carolinians to shift to the present site of Charleston (Charles Town until 1783, when the city was incorporated as Charleston).

White settlement of North Carolina proceeded somewhat differently. The first settlers were squatters from Virginia who, perhaps as early as 1653, moved into the area around Albemarle Sound adjacent to Virginia. The Carolina proprietors recognized their presence, created Albemarle County in the area, and commissioned William Drummond, a Scot who had lived in Virginia, as its governor. An early Barbadian outpost on the Cape Fear River was supposed to be the nucleus of a second county, Clarendon, but its failure meant that three hundred miles (480 kilometers) of wilderness separated the northern settlement from the main focus of proprietary interest on the Ashley River. The isolated outpost at Albemarle grew slowly, and the first town in North Carolina, Bath, on Pamlico Sound, was not established until 1706. North Carolina became a separate colony in 1712 in recognition of the fact that its isolation from the rest of Carolina made joint administration difficult. During the 1720s some settlers from South Carolina, as well as from elsewhere, moved into the lower Cape Fear area. Wilmington, begun about 1733, became the principal seaport of the colony.

Georgia, the last of the original thirteen colonies, was founded during the same period, and here too South Carolinians were involved. During Queen Anne's War (1702–1713), the southern frontier was an important military theater. The proprietary governor of South Carolina, James Moore, tried and failed to capture the Spanish fort at Saint Augustine in 1702; his second expedition two years later devastated the mission settlements in northern Florida. But the Tuscarora and Yamassee wars a decade later made the continued military vulnerability of the two Carolinas painfully apparent. In 1717 the proprietors therefore planned to grant the area south of the Savannah River to a Scot, Sir Robert Montgomery. As Margrave of Azilia, he would be in charge of a colony that could serve as a buffer against the Spanish in Florida. Several complications led to the collapse of that scheme, but during the 1720s, two influential South Carolinians, John Barnwell and Robert Johnson, continued to advocate alternative arrangements. One result of their proposals was the creation of a number of townships in South Carolina, located on the periphery of settlement. The inhabitants of these townships were to be immigrants who would receive governmental aid to establish themselves as yeoman farmers and, not incidentally, to become members of the militia.

The township envisioned for the area south of the Savannah River became Georgia when these plans fused with those of John Perceval,

earl of Egmont, and James Oglethorpe, who hoped to establish a new colony. Oglethorpe, who had been chairman of a parliamentary committee on jails, first intended to create a refuge for debtors who would otherwise have been imprisoned. But strategic considerations played a crucial part in the Crown's approval of the plan. On 9 June 1732, King George II granted the region between the Altamaha and Savannah rivers, from sea to sea, to twenty-one trustees, whose philanthropic venture was to last for twenty-one years. Their subsequent attempts to bar rum and slavery from the area had military as well as moral purposes, for both might have added to the vulnerability of the province by enervating the white populace and creating a potentially dangerous "domestic enemy."

Georgia became a successful colony, but not quite as planned. Oglethorpe led the first groups of settlers, who traveled by way of Charleston. Receiving assistance from South Carolinians, Oglethorpe arrived at the site of Savannah early in February 1733 and proceeded to lay out the city on a rectilinear plan, which still survives. His Indian diplomacy was equally prescient. Using John and Mary Musgrove (who was part Indian) as intermediaries, he negotiated agreements with Tomochichi of the Yamassee and, somewhat later, with leaders of the Creek, Cherokee, Chickasaw, and Choctaw Indians. These treaties fostered the economic life as well as the security of the province, but the Indian trade, though important, was never sufficient to produce general prosperity. Meanwhile, South Carolina appeared to be flourishing. The difference, a number of "Malcontents" among the Georgians concluded, was due to slavery. Under pressure, the trustees rescinded the prohibition on slavery in 1750; thereupon many South Carolinians, attracted by the abundance of potential ricelands, decided to become Georgians. By the 1760s Georgia was in many respects a newer South Carolina.

POLITICAL DEVELOPMENT

In the long run, governmental changes increased the resemblance among the three colonies, though at first the two Carolinas appeared to be moving apart. Under the 1663 charter, settlers in Carolina were to have the same rights as Englishmen, including a voice in lawmaking. The proprietors, however, received very broad powers, including the authority to create courts that might impose the death penalty; the proprietors could also punish rebellion, wage war, grant land, and establish new titles of nobility. To govern the distribution and exercise of these powers, Shaftesbury and the philosopher John Locke drew up the Fundamental Constitutions (1669). Perhaps influenced by James Harrington's *Commonwealth of Oceana* (1656), which advocated that political power be distributed in proportion to property holdings, this document provided that the aristocracy would collectively control two-fifths of the land, the people three-fifths. Landgraves and caciques—the two kinds of nobles to be created—would receive baronies totaling, respectively, forty-eight thousand acres and twenty-four thousand acres (19,200 and 9,600 hectares). Each of the proprietors was to head one of eight administrative courts; they and the subordinate members of these courts were to constitute the Grand Council, which was to propose legislation. A unicameral Parliament, composed of the proprietors, the nobility, and elected representatives of the freeholders, could only approve or disapprove these proposals.

This arrangement now appears anachronistic and topheavy, but it was designed to distribute and balance power so as to protect everyone. Not even the proprietors' power was sufficient, Shaftesbury claimed, to harm the humblest man. Moreover, the Constitutions included several extraordinarily liberal provisions, including the secret ballot and wide religious toleration.

The Fundamental Constitutions influenced the later development of the Carolinas, but it never became the law of the land. A governor appointed by the proprietors and council, to which a few elected representatives of the freeholders were added, governed from Charleston. This group promptly rejected the original version of the Fundamental Constitutions, because its members objected to some provisions; then they turned down revised versions on the grounds that so mutable a document could not truly be a fundamental constitution. By the 1690s the elected representatives began sitting separately and calling themselves the Commons House of Assembly.

North Carolinians went their separate but parallel ways from South Carolinians. Originally, the proprietors hoped that the colonists in the northern part of the colony would send representatives to the assembly at Charleston, but the Albemarle settlement was too distant for this to be feasible. By 1712 the proprietors accepted the inevitable and instructed the governor of South Carolina to appoint a deputy for North Carolina, thus dividing their holdings into two separate colonies. Different practices were already developing in the two colonies. In South Carolina, for example, counties eventually became little more than paper categories that designated the location of land grants under the headright system. The basic unit of local government was the parish, though most of the real power remained centered in Charleston. In North Carolina, on the other hand, counties were functional units of local government. Virginians who settled the Albemarle region, it is worth noting, were accustomed to the county system; the Barbadians in South Carolina were familiar with the parish.

Be that as it may, the political development of the two Carolinas exhibited similarities as well as differences. Politics in both colonies were turbulent and factional throughout the early years. During Culpepper's Rebellion in 1677, North Carolinians ousted their presiding official; in 1689 the assembly tried, convicted, and exiled the proprietary governor, Seth Sothel; and the following year a mini-insurrection unsuccessfully attempted to prevent his successor from taking office. Religious differences between adherents of the Anglican church and of the Society of Friends contributed to another abortive rebellion under Thomas Cary in 1711. In South Carolina, Barbadians who settled around a tributary of the Cooper River and thus became known as the "Goose Creek Men" frequently opposed the proprietors on religious and other issues. In 1690 South Carolina's Parliament overthrew and banished governor James Colleton (who was succeeded by Sothel). John Archdale, a proprietor and a Quaker who served as governor from 1695 to 1696, managed to bring a degree of political order and harmony. Nevertheless, political chicanery accompanied the act establishing the Anglican church in 1706.

More important, in 1719 the South Carolina assembly proclaimed itself to be a convention of the people, chose James Moore (son of the earlier proprietary governor, James Moore) as the executive in place of proprietary governor Robert Johnson, and requested that the Crown take over the provincial government. Numerous issues contributed to the revolt, but the central problem was the proprietors' inability to provide for the defense of the colony. Negotiations between the proprietors and the Crown followed, and in 1729 the Crown bought out seven of the eight proprietors, making both North and South Carolina royal colonies. The eighth proprietor, Sir John Carteret, retained title to what became known as the Granville District, or approximately the northern half of North Carolina, until the revolution.

Royal control led to increasing stability, especially in South Carolina, where Robert Johnson, the last of the proprietory governors, became the first permanent royal governor appointed by the Crown. Politically astute and popular, he implemented the township plan for settling the frontier and generally prepared the way for eventual settlement of long-standing factional disputes over land and paper currency. United by relative prosperity, the presence of slaves, and an ideology that condemned factionalism, South Carolinians developed a remarkably harmonious political life by the 1750s.

In comparison to their neighbors to the south, North Carolinians appeared to be less fortunate. Economic and demographic growth of the Cape Fear region increased sectional rivalry between the northern and southern areas of the colony, and the capital remained peripatetic until the 1760s, when the construction of Governor Tryon's palace at New Bern helped to fix its location. But comparative poverty mired North Carolina in political corruption, and local officials frequently continued to make politics and pelf (riches) closely related terms.

Georgia had a somewhat different political evolution under the trustees. Unwilling to appoint a governor or to pass laws locally (both of which would have required approval by the Crown), the trustees sought to govern the colony themselves. Although Oglethorpe acted as a de facto governor while there, none of the local officials appointed during the first decade had

primary responsibility over the whole colony. In 1743, however, the appointed president, William Stephens, and his council of assistants at Savannah received authority over a second county that had been established at Frederica. No local assembly met until 1751; resolutions adopted by the trustees in London served as laws.

Cumbersome governmental organization and acrimonious disputes involving both personalities and policies plagued the colony during its early years; and the trustees, disenchanted with their project, surrendered their trust to the Crown in 1752, one year before it expired. But royal control failed to produce much immediate improvement. The first royal governor, Captain John Reynolds, was an inept naval officer whose governing style smacked of the quarterdeck. His two successors were more effective. The last royal governor, James Wright, was particularly popular because of his success in acquiring more than two million acres (800,000 hectares) for the colony from the Creek and Cherokee Indians in 1773.

Differences in the political development of these three colonies, though conspicuous, were relatively minor compared with the basic similarities. All became royal colonies. As such, each had a governor and council appointed by the Crown, as well as an elected lower house. All went through periods of factional instability. But if decreasing turnover in the membership of the lower houses is a valid indication, each moved toward greater social and political stability. Despite the existence of property qualifications for voting in North Carolina and Georgia (but not in South Carolina), the representative bodies rested upon a relatively broad electoral base, and the increasing experience of many legislators augmented their self-confidence and competence. Modeling themselves on the British House of Commons, the representatives of the people used the power to tax and the force of precedent to enlarge their powers in other areas.

By the end of the colonial period, each of the lower houses had transformed itself from a subordinate body to the dominant, or near-dominant, force in government. This process had progressed farthest in South Carolina, which had an exceptionally powerful legislature in an unusually centralized system, and least in Georgia, where Parliament continued to underwrite some of the costs of government. But all of these colonies had the basis for effective self-government by the 1760s.

ECONOMIC AND SOCIAL DEVELOPMENT

The rise of the lower houses reflected economic and social changes in the respective colonies. Both the proprietors and the trustees of Georgia encouraged horticultural experiments, and local authorities continued to foster silk-making ventures and other novel enterprises throughout the colonial period. But none of these ventures proved to be very successful. Early settlers did perhaps best by sending provisions to the West Indies, and each of these colonies developed a significant open-range livestock industry. Supplying pirates—until local authorities captured and executed Blackbeard and others in 1718—brought some hard coin into the colonies. And the Indian trade, which in the late seventeenth and early eighteenth centuries involved the sale of captives as slaves as well as the exchange of deerskins and manufactured goods, proved lucrative for some individuals.

Development of Agricultural Resources

In the late 1690s, however, South Carolinians developed two products that provided more significant export earnings. One was naval stores; the other, rice. Dependent upon tar and pitch to keep both the merchant fleet and the Royal Navy afloat, Parliament encouraged the production of colonial naval stores by offering bounties, beginning in 1705. The two Carolinas responded with alacrity, and Charleston annually shipped nearly sixty thousand barrels of tar and pitch to England by the 1720s. But Parliament reduced the bounty on naval stores in 1729. North Carolinians, who lacked better alternatives, continued the industry to the point where their descendants would inhabit the "Tarheel State." During the 1760s, North Carolina accounted for 60 percent of the tar and pitch exported from the North American colonies.

Long before that time, however, many South Carolinians had shifted to the production of rice. Initially grown on dry land, as well as in inland swamps, rice became the most significant cash crop in the region in the 1690s. By the mid eighteenth century, production, which had come to be increasingly concentrated in the tidewater areas, had spread to the Cape Fear area of North Carolina and the coastal areas of Georgia. From 1768 to 1772 annual exports of rice from the lower South were worth £198,590, which placed rice fourth in value on the list of North American commodities.

The rice market had limitations, however, and colonials therefore tried various ways to overcome them. Parliament had enumerated the grain in 1705, which meant that colonials could not legally export it outside of the empire, though its major markets were in Europe. Transshipment through Great Britain, rice merchants complained, delayed the arrival of rice in Iberian ports past the Lenten season. Parliament accordingly permitted direct shipment of rice to this area after 1730. But problems persisted. The largest markets remained northern Germany and the Low Countries, and French threats to the rice ships produced a local depression during King George's War in the 1740s. Thereafter, matters improved. Peace returned in 1748, and the Royal Navy was able to provide better protection for merchant vessels during the next war. And after 1763, imperial authorities allowed the direct shipment of rice to foreign markets in Latin America and the Caribbean. Georgia and South Carolina were exporting record amounts by the early 1770s. Equally important, they had developed an alternative crop.

During the early 1740s, experiments by Eliza Lucas Pinckney and others led to the successful production of indigo in South Carolina. Because the dye was important to the British textile industry, British authorities sought to encourage its production by giving producers bounties as well as preference in the British market. Moreover, indigo complemented rice well, since it not only grew on dry land but also matured at a different time. As a result, planters in Georgia and, to a lesser extent, North Carolina, as well as South Carolina, began growing indigo. By the early 1770s, indigo was the sixth most valuable North American export, with shipments worth £111,864 per year.

As producers of agricultural products and, increasingly, as consumers of British manufactured goods, the colonies of the lower South fit the imperial system well. Confining most of their exports to the empire scarcely seemed a detriment to them. Indeed, the relative poverty of North Carolina appeared to result from an insufficient amount of such trade, while South Carolina and Georgia flourished on it. By the early 1770s the lower South was in fact the wealthiest area of British North America, and South Carolinians in the Charleston area were, on a per capita basis, by far the richest Americans.

Institution of Slavery

The dark side of this bright picture was the fact that much of the wealth within the region consisted of slaves. In an effort to attract substantial Barbadians to their colony, the Carolina proprietors made slavery legal from the beginning. But in the absence of a staple crop, slaves were comparatively few until the 1690s, when the cultivation of rice expanded dramatically. Then, ironically, with African Americans who had been familiar with the production of rice in their homelands probably providing the necessary expertise, the resulting profitability of rice produced a sharp increase in the demand for slaves. Although natural reproduction helped to increase the black population during part of the eighteenth century, imports of slaves accounted for most of the growth. Charleston became the leading terminus, and before the trade was finally ended in 1808, more than 80,000 Africans first gazed upon the New World in the harbor there. By 1710 slaves constituted a majority of the population in South Carolina, and they would remain so until the revolution. In the early 1770s approximately 107,000 blacks and 71,000 whites inhabited the province. More than 18,000 white Georgians, who received most of their slaves by way of South Carolina, held 15,000 blacks; and 197,000 white North Carolinians outnumbered 70,000 African Americans. In all of these provinces the slave population was concentrated on the coastal plantations.

The conditions under which these African Americans lived varied by time and place. During the early years in South Carolina, the relatively few slaves and their owners might work side by side, while black cowboys roamed the woods alone rounding up cattle. But thereafter the rap-

idly increasing number of Africans alarmed whites, who therefore imposed more restrictions. In 1696 South Carolinians adopted the first systematic slave code, designed to provide the legal basis for controlling African Americans. Both the act of 1696 and its successor of 1712 followed Barbadian models. In 1739, however, a slave named Jemmy led a revolt of perhaps as many as one hundred bondsmen who had just landed in the vicinity of Stono, South Carolina. They tried to fight their way to Saint Augustine, where the Spanish governor had offered freedom to blacks who escaped from Carolina. The Stono Rebellion failed, but the death of an untold number of slaves and more than twenty whites made it the most serious slave rebellion in any of the British North American colonies during the colonial period. The legislature responded with the slave code of 1740. Comprehensive and Draconian—slaves were subject to the summary jurisdiction of freeholders' court in which as few as three laymen, acting without a jury, could inflict the death penalty—this legislation served as the basic law of slavery in South Carolina until the Civil War. These events also influenced the slave codes of North Carolina and Georgia.

Conditions were harsh, but African Americans in the rice-producing areas of these colonies continued to enjoy a sometimes remarkable degree of autonomy. Unlike later cotton planters who organized their labor force in gangs, rice planters normally employed the task system. Drivers, who were themselves slaves, usually assigned the tasks and, in fact, sometimes acted as plantation overseers in all but name. Furthermore, laws designed to ensure the presence of white men on every plantation were often honored in the breach. Under these conditions, slaves developed cultural patterns resembling those of the West Indies.

Slaves frequently owned personal property, and African elements remained important in family relationships, religious practices, language, and other areas. But if the large plantations of the rice coast lay at one end of a spectrum of African-American acculturation in which the African elements were the most visible, the small tobacco plantations of northern North Carolina, where contact with whites was more constant, were probably at the other. The increasing number of slaves who worked the inland indigo plantations in South Carolina and Georgia doubtless experienced something in between. In short, slavery Americanized Africans from different backgrounds in different ways, and the results were scarcely more uniform than those of a similar process in free society.

Anglicization of Low Country Society

The white population was ethnically mixed in all of these colonies. Barbadians, with mostly English roots, dominated the first decade in South Carolina. But during the 1680s the proprietors made a successful attempt to attract English and French dissenters. The former settled the coastal parishes south of Charleston; the latter, who arrived in considerable numbers after King Louis XIV of France revoked the Edict of Nantes (1685), clustered around the Santee River to the north. Welsh settlers, who came by way of Delaware, also clustered in the northeastern part of the province, while Swiss Protestants eventually populated one of the townships, Purrysburg, on the Savannah River. Scotch-Irish settled some of the other townships; Germans congregated in the interior areas around Orangeburg and at the fork of the Broad and Saluda rivers. In North Carolina, another group of German-speaking Swiss and Palatines led by Baron Christopher von Graffenried founded New Bern in 1710; Highland Scottish Jacobites settled the Cross Creek area above Wilmington after their defeat at the Battle of Culloden (1746); Welsh settlers moved into the lower Cape Fear area as well as into other sections; and Moravians established a thriving community at Salem during the 1750s. Georgia was similarly mixed. Moravians came to the area but did not stay. German Lutherans founded a successful community at Ebenezer on the lower Savannah River, and highland Scots settled at Darien on the coast south of Savannah. A group of Puritans from New England, who had come to South Carolina in the 1690s, moved to Midway, Georgia, in the 1750s. Savannah, and later Charleston, contained small but significant Jewish populations. Lowland Scots frequently assimilated into the English populations. More easily identifiable, and most numerous among the non-English groups, were the Scotch-Irish who flooded into the backcountry of all three provinces during the last three decades of the colonial period. Historians dispute the precise composition of this mixed population, which varied somewhat in each of these colonies. But an educated guess would be that the proportions were approximately 5 percent French, 5 percent German, 10 percent Welsh, 10 percent Irish, 30 percent Scotch, and 30 to 40 percent English.

As these figures suggest, Dissenters undoubtedly outnumbered Anglicans, though the Church of England was the established church in all three colonies. These circumstances help to account for the considerable strength of the Great Awakening, the religious revival of the 1740s, in this area. Here, as elsewhere, George Whitefield was the catalyst. From Georgia, where he first landed in 1738 and where he eventually established a well-known orphanage, Whitefield traveled north. The impact of his preaching extended even to African Americans, especially in South Carolina, where the Bryan family of the Port Royal area sought to spread the Awakening to their slaves. But alarmed authorities imposed sanctions for such actions, and the specter of African Americans awakened to secular as well as to spiritual freedom chilled the revival in the Low Country. Most slaves remained outside the Christian fold until the end of the eighteenth century. But the Awakening continued to affect many of the Presbyterians and Separate Baptists in the backcountry. Divisive as some aspects of the Awakening were in these heterogeneous societies, it nevertheless strengthened the Protestant values common to most of the white population and thereby contributed to future unity.

The increasing Anglicization of these societies had a similar effect, for the elite that provided social and political leadership assiduously sought to model itself upon the English gentry. South Carolinians were, as contemporaries often remarked, excessively fond of English manners, and members of the elite increasingly sent their sons to school in England. By the end of the colonial period, South Carolinians constituted the largest group of Americans abroad for their education. And scattered throughout the towns and countryside in all of these colonies, men of property built commodious houses in the English manner. The Exchange building in Charleston was especially striking. Built during the 1760s and 1770s of stone imported from

England, it resembled its counterparts in Bristol and Liverpool. Intellectual activities exhibited a similar affinity for English models. The Charleston Library Society bought the latest British works, and some local figures aspired to membership in the Royal Society. Charleston—which had a population of about twelve thousand (half black and half white) in the early 1770s—and, to a lesser extent, the other cities of the lower South became, in the eyes of contemporaries, impressive exemplars of metropolitan culture.

INTERNATIONAL RIVALRY AND THE REVOLUTION

Problems during the Seven Years' War suggested that colonists considered themselves to be more English than British authorities were willing to concede. No major fighting occurred in Georgia. North Carolina contributed some troops for campaigns in Pennsylvania and New York as well as for local battles, but South Carolina was the main scene of action in the lower South. In 1759 various misunderstandings led to conflict with the Cherokee Indians, who raided the frontier from Virginia southward. Governor William Henry Lyttelton of South Carolina responded with a military demonstration that proved to be a fiasco. Not until 1761 were British and provincial units able to defeat the Indians. Meanwhile, conflicts between British and colonial officers over seniority and strategy produced serious friction. Nevertheless, South Carolinians and Georgians were especially pleased that the Peace of Paris in 1763 appeared to increase their security. Spain surrendered Florida to Britain and received Louisiana from France as compensation. Like other Americans, the inhabitants of the southern seaboard emerged from the war proud to be members of the British Empire and convinced that their efforts had helped to make it the greatest empire since antiquity.

There were, however, troubling aspects of the postwar period. The most important problem of local origin culminated, in the two Carolinas, in the Regulator upheavals of the 1760s, which, despite the similarity in name, were somewhat different in character. Both movements, to be sure, reflected the rapid growth of western settlements and their resultant underrepresenta-tion in the legislatures. Regulators in each province also armed and organized themselves in defiance of the authorities, and both groups used extralegal means to achieve their ends. Precisely what these ends were in North Carolina remains a matter of controversy among historians, though the immediate grievances were clear. Oppressive taxes, extortionate debt collection, and excessive court fees constituted obvious abuses, but the social composition and ideological component of the movement are more ambiguous. Whoever and whatever they were, the Regulators forced courts to close in several western counties. The response of North Carolina's governor and legislature was to organize a military expedition that met and defeated the Regulators in an engagement near Alamance Creek on 16 May 1771.

In South Carolina, matters never reached such a violent climax. Contemporaries as well as later historians, such as Rachel Klein, soon recognized that the South Carolina Regulators constituted a vigilante movement of rising planters who sought mainly to curb outlaw bands that had plagued the backcountry in the aftermath of the Cherokee War. Georgia, where the backcountry was still only sparsely settled by whites, did not have a Regulator movement.

More serious problems developed in the relationship between local inhabitants and imperial authorities during the 1760s. Glorying in the name of Briton, as they frequently said, Americans were convinced that they, as British subjects, were the freest people in the world. Their political culture, which derived many of its basic beliefs from writers of the British political opposition during the first half of the eighteenth century, rested on several assumptions about human nature and English history. Thanks to Adam and Eve, human beings were flawed and self-interested. To entrust anyone with unlimited power was therefore to invite exploitation and oppression, as the realities of slavery constantly reminded local inhabitants. The British constitution therefore limited the power of the government. In particular, because an individual's freedom depended upon the security of property, taxes were deemed to be voluntary, if necessary, gifts toward the support of government. To facilitate these gifts, propertyholders chose representatives whose control over the public purse gave them the means of checking the executive. The glorious history of successful parliamentary resistance to the tyranny of the Stuart kings during the seventeenth century demonstrated how the system should work in a crisis. Finally, Americans assumed that the local representative body, which in South Carolina and Georgia was termed a "Commons House," was their version of the British House of Commons. Most imperial authorities did not fully share this last assumption.

British measures after the Seven Years' War therefore came as a rude shock to Americans. To be sure, some steps that caused difficulty elsewhere did not trouble the inhabitants of the lower South very much. Legitimate trade was lucrative enough that the temptation to smuggle, for example, was minimal. Thus, Britain's decision to use the Royal Navy to interdict smuggling, to issue writs of assistance (general search warrants) to customs officers, and—initially at least—to enlarge the scope of the Vice-Admiralty Courts did not seriously aggrieve colonists in the lower South. During the late 1760s, however, customs officials sought to make a fraudulent case against a leading Charleston merchant, Henry Laurens, and the judge of the local Vice-Admiralty Court, who understood the situation, failed to protect him. Laurens's pamphlets attacking these abuses helped to popularize the issue and made him prominent throughout the colonies. Changes in policy governing the acquisition of land also produced a delayed reaction. The Proclamation of 1763, which limited colonial settlements to the eastern side of the Appalachian Mountains, still left enough open land for settlement to permit the rapid growth of these colonies. But the decision to stop granting lands under the headright system and sell it instead, announced in 1774, made colonists, as one royal governor observed, very restive. The change, however, came too late to have much effect on the pre-revolutionary controversy. Even the Currency Act of 1764, which prohibited the colonies from issuing legal-tender paper money, produced only relatively minor problems in South Carolina and Georgia. North Carolinians, on the other hand, found it to be disruptive, perhaps because their underdeveloped economy relied more on currency.

The major issues in all of these colonies concerned taxation and the closely related question of the assemblies' powers. Local leaders did not at first recognize that the Sugar Act of 1764 marked a change in policy; later, when they realized that Parliament intended the measure as a tax, all three legislatures protested it. Their reactions to the Stamp Act of 1765 were more forceful. Popular demonstrations in the ports of North and South Carolina impelled the stamp distributors to resign before they could implement the act. Armed men in the Cape Fear area of North Carolina even forced an officer of the Royal Navy to release two vessels that he had seized for sailing without stamped clearance papers. Alone among the thirteen colonies that later revolted, Georgia obeyed the Stamp Act, for a while. But South Carolinians threatened to reinforce local "Liberty Boys," and Georgia Governor James Wright eventually shipped the remaining stamps out of the colony.

Parliament defused the immediate crisis by repealing the Stamp Act in 1766 but accompanied this action with the Declaratory Act, which announced that Parliament had the right to legislate for the colonies "in all cases whatsoever." Clearly, British authorities had not accepted the colonial point of view. Christopher Gadsden, who led the Sons of Liberty in Charleston, was particularly wary of British intentions, but his warnings were lost in the general joy at repeal of the obnoxious tax. In 1767 imposition of the Townshend Duties proved how prescient Gadsden had been. Americans responded by organizing a nonimportation movement, in which American merchants refused to import British goods. A popular meeting held in Charleston in July 1769 pledged cooperation; a "convention" that was virtually a rump meeting of the North Carolina legislature followed suit a few months later. A mass meeting of Georgians adopted a similar nonimportation agreement; however, the agreement lacked sanctions against violators and therefore proved ineffective. Still, in 1770 Parliament responded to the disruption in trade with America by repealing all of the Townshend Duties except the tax on tea, which remained in force as the tangible equivalent of the Declaratory Act.

Meanwhile, the South Carolina legislature made a dramatic gesture. Acting in behalf of John Wilkes, a radical British politician, his political friends in Great Britain who had formed the

British Society of Gentlemen Supporters of the Bill of Rights solicited donations from leading Americans. The only official body to respond was the South Carolina Commons House, which sent £1,500 to London. Agitated imperial officials countered with instructions designed to prevent any repetition of so egregious a gesture. But because these instructions imposed restrictions on the wording of all bills designed to raise and appropriate money, South Carolinians became equally outraged. Dictating the form of a local tax bill from London—fully as much as the imposition of a direct tax on the colonies by Parliament—Americans were certain, would make their local representative bodies superfluous. And in that event, they would lose their first line of defense against a tyrannical executive. Rather than accept the instruction, the South Carolina legislature passed no tax act for the last five years of the colonial period. Subsidiary issues certainly influenced the revolutionary movement, but in these three colonies, at least, the most important disputes prior to 1774 involved the rights of the assemblies.

The Boston Tea Party (1773) and its aftermath widened the controversy. Demonstrations against the Stamp Act had reflected spontaneous popular involvement, especially among the artisans, and the organization of the Sons of Liberty served to channel and control popular enthusiasm for the rights of the colonies; during the nonimportation movement, enforcement committees had kept reluctant merchants in line with the threat of mob action. But the crisis over tea prompted a wider range of responses. In an attempt to prevent payment of the duties on tea, radicals at Boston dumped a cargo of it into the harbor on the night of 16 December 1773. While South Carolinians debated what to do about the tea sent to Charleston, royal authorities spirited it ashore, where it was kept in storage until it was sold to help finance the revolutionary effort. North Carolinians and Georgians escaped an immediate crisis because there were no tea consignees in either colony. But the Coercive (or Intolerable) Acts, which closed the port of Boston and drastically modified the Massachusetts charter, produced strong reactions. By the logic of these acts, a local minister declared, Charleston might be burned to the ground if someone urinated on the royal customs house. Eschewing such propagandistic hyperbole, fifty-one ladies met at Edenton, North Carolina, and firmly pledged to do everything they could to support the American cause. Popular meetings or provincial congresses held at New Bern and Charleston during the summer of 1774 elected delegates to the First Continental Congress. A similar gathering in Savannah decided not to participate in the Congress, but some parishes unsuccessfully attempted to send their own representatives.

Events moved rapidly during the next two years. Both Carolinas participated in the First Continental Congress; representatives from Georgia joined them at the Second Continental Congress after fighting had broken out in the spring of 1775. Rumors that British authorities planned to instigate Indian attacks and slave insurrections did much to unite the inhabitants, but the lower South contained a substantial number of loyalists. Nevertheless, battles in each of the southern colonies during late 1775 and early 1776, as well as a major but unsuccessful British attack on Charleston in June, prepared residents to accept independence. Yet even then, Henry Laurens (whose conflict with the customs service would eventually help to make him president of the Continental Congress upon the resignation of John Hancock) wept when he learned that the Declaration of Independence had been adopted. Nor was Laurens alone among otherwise staunch Americans.

CONCLUSION

As subjects of the English Crown, white inhabitants of the two Carolinas and Georgia had done very well indeed. Settling a remote and precarious coast during the seventeenth century, their predecessors had secured the area for England. The more idealistic dreams of the Carolina proprietors and the Georgia trustees foundered in the swampy lowlands, but the residents built communities that became, by many measures, increasingly stable, diverse, and prosperous. Political factionalism diminished; ethnic and religious heterogeneity increased; and prosperity—at least for those who owned rice and indigo plantations—reached unprecedented levels. But some individuals and groups paid a high price for these transformations.

Most Native Americans vacated the area or fell victim to European diseases; African Americans spent lifetimes laboring so that others might grow rich. Survivors in every sense of the word, these slaves managed to preserve many African cultural traits. Racially and sectionally divided societies were the result. In the coastal Low Country, as in the West Indies, a small minority of whites presided over a large black majority, while in the backcountry yeoman farmers as yet held few slaves. Within the three colonies, Eastern elites controlled the political process, often at the expense of more numerous inland residents. That, at the Constitutional Convention of 1787, the two Carolinas and Georgia would be the chief opponents of a ban on the African slave trade testifies to the social and political power of these elites, and, indeed, to the influence of the history of the region in shaping its unique social and political configuration.

BIBLIOGRAPHY

General Works and Bibliographies

Coleman, Kenneth. *Colonial Georgia: A History.* New York, 1976. A comprehensive survey, full of facts.

Crow, Jeffrey J., and Larry E. Tise, eds. *Writing North Carolina History.* Chapel Hill, N.C., 1979. Contains two essays that review writings on the colonial and revolutionary periods.

Lefler, Hugh Talmage, and William S. Powell. *Colonial North Carolina: A History.* New York, 1973. The standard survey.

O'Donnell, James H. *Southeastern Frontiers: Europeans, Africans, and American Indians, 1513–1840: A Critical Bibliography.* Bloomington, Ind., 1982. A balanced, remarkably full selection and discussion of works dealing with the major groups in the area.

Weir, Robert M. *Colonial South Carolina: A History.* Millwood, N.Y., 1983. Includes considerable social history and an extensive annotated bibliography.

Wright, J. Leitch, Jr. *The Only Land They Knew: The Tragic Story of the American Indians in the Old South.* New York, 1981. A readable survey, strongest on the Indians of the lower South in the eighteenth century.

Specialized Studies

Abbot, W. W. *The Royal Governors of Georgia, 1754–1775.* Chapel Hill, N.C., 1959. A concise, sophisticated, and readable political history.

Clowse, Converse D. *Economic Beginnings in Colonial South Carolina, 1670–1730.* Columbia, S.C., 1971. A detailed study of the early years when survival was problematical.

Coclanis, Peter A. *The Shadow of a Dream: Economic Life and Death in the South Carolina Low Country, 1670–1920.* New York, 1989. Argues that Carolina planters responded to market forces. Wide-ranging and stimulating.

Crane, Verner Winslow. *The Southern Frontier, 1670–1732.* Durham, N.C., 1928. A classic account of European competition for the land that became Georgia.

Crow, Jeffrey J., and Flora J. Hatley, eds. *Black Americans in North Carolina and the South.* Chapel Hill, N.C., 1984. A collection of essays, three of which deal with demography, historical archaeology, and historiography relevant to the colonial period.

Davis, Harold E. *The Fledgling Province: Social and Cultural Life in Colonial Georgia, 1733–1776.* Chapel Hill, N.C., 1976. Emphasizes everyday life.

Ekirch, A. Roger. *"Poor Carolina": Politics and Society in Colonial North Carolina, 1729–1776.* Chapel Hill, N.C., 1981. A persuasive discussion of the relationship between economic difficulties and corrupt politics.

Klein, Rachel N. *Unification of a Slave State: The Rise of the Planter Class in the South Carolina Backcountry, 1760–1808.* Chapel Hill, N.C., 1990. Includes a good discussion of life in the area during the 1760s.

Merrell, James Hart. *The Indians' New World: Catawbas and Their Neighbors from European Contact Through the Era of Removal.* Chapel Hill, N.C., 1989. A prize-winning study of how a small tribe in South Carolina accommodated and survived the European occupation.

Merrens, Harry Roy. *Colonial North Carolina in the Eighteenth Century: A Study in Historical Geography.* Chapel Hill, N.C., 1964. A well-written description and analysis of the changing geographies.

Morgan, Philip D. "Work and Culture: The Task System and the World of Lowcountry Blacks, 1700–1880." *William and Mary Quarterly* 39, no. 4 (October 1982):563–599. Argues that the relative autonomy of workers under the task system allowed slaves to become "protopeasants."

Sirmans, Marion Eugene. *Colonial South Carolina: A Political History, 1663–1763.* Chapel Hill, N.C., 1966. A detailed study of political development.

Spalding, Phinizy. *Oglethorpe in America.* Chicago, 1977. A very readable account of Oglethorpe's actions in Georgia.

Ver Steeg, Clarence Lester. *Origins of a Southern Mosaic: Studies of Early Carolina and Georgia.* Athens, Ga., 1975. Four essays emphasizing the heterogeneity of the region.

Wood, Betty. *Slavery in Colonial Georgia, 1730–1775.* Athens, Ga., 1984. A good discussion of how settlers rejected the trustee's plans for a nonslaveholding society.

Wood, Peter H. *Black Majority: Negroes in Colonial South Carolina from 1670 Through the Stono Rebellion.* New York, 1974. A readable, interdisciplinary treatment of black culture and resistance to slavery in the context of rising white paranoia.

Wood, Peter H., Gregory A. Waselkov, and M. Thomas Hatley, eds. *Powhatan's Mantle: Indians in the Colonial Southeast.* Lincoln, Nebr., 1989. An outstanding collection of diverse essays in ethnohistory. Topics covered include demography, trade, Indian cartography, communication routes, and symbolism.

Wright, J. Leitch. *Anglo-Spanish Rivalry in North America.* Athens, Ga., 1971. Traces Spanish reactions to English and American encroachments from the sixteenth century to the cession of Florida in 1821.

Robert M. Weir

SEE ALSO **Anglicanism; British Settlements, The Chesapeake Colonies; The Fur Trade; Indian-Colonist Contact; Medical Practice, Health and Disease; Settlements in the Spanish Borderlands, Southeast; Slavery;** various essays in OLD WORLD EXPANSION; and the map preceding **French Settlements.**

RUPERT'S LAND AND BRITISH COLUMBIA

THE OLD TERRITORY OF RUPERT'S LAND and the Province of British Columbia cover most of modern Canada. Yet they were distinct British colonies and never part of colonial Canada. Until its first four provinces—Ontario, Quebec, New Brunswick, and Nova Scotia—confederated on 1 July 1867, "Canada" still referred only to a relatively small region along the Saint Lawrence River, comprising present-day southern and central Ontario and Quebec. Rupert's Land was brought into Canada on 15 July 1870 as the new Province of Manitoba and the Northwestern Territories; British Columbia became a province in 1871.

THE ORIGINS OF RUPERT'S LAND

North and west of the Great Lakes watershed lies a huge, sparsely populated area of mainly subarctic climate. Heavily glaciated in recent geological time, it is largely underlaid by the Canadian Shield, whose Precambrian rocks are among the oldest in the world. The region attracted the attention of Europeans in the 1650s, as French fur traders—notably Médard Chouart, Sieur des Groseilliers, and Pierre Esprit Radisson—became aware that their best furs were coming through Indian middlemen from boreal Cree and Ojibwa trappers skilled in harvesting the beaver and other fur-bearing animals of that productive northern habitat. Des Groseilliers and Radisson began to conceive of a new fur-trade enterprise that would reach directly from Europe to the shores of Hudson Bay.

The authorities of New France, protective of their Saint Lawrence trade and at odds with Des Groseilliers and Radisson over trading licenses and tax payments, were not favorably inclined toward the traders' initiatives. Frustrated by their cool reception, the two pursued English support for undertaking voyages of trade and discovery to Hudson Bay. Their timing was opportune. England's military and trade rivalries with the French and the Dutch led members of the court of Charles II and of the London merchant community to take lively interest in new enterprises and trade routes that might also reveal the much-sought Northwest Passage to the Orient. Historian E. E. Rich noted that the traders' "weight of experience" and "their bizarre and forceful personalities" impressed both the king and such men as Anthony Ashley Cooper (later first earl of Shaftesbury) and Sir Peter Colleton.

Having already invested in the colonizing of Carolina and the Bahamas, to which they were granted charters in 1665 and 1670 respectively, Cooper and Colleton joined the king's cousin, Prince Rupert (in whose honor Rupert's Land was named), and others in financing the voyages of two small ships, the *Eaglet* and the *Nonsuch*, to Hudson Bay in June 1668. Storms caused the *Eaglet,* with Radisson aboard, to turn about and sail home; but Des Groseilliers and the *Nonsuch* wintered at the mouth of the Rupert River in southeastern James Bay, establishing Charles Fort as the first of numerous bayside posts and conducting a highly successful beaver trade with the Cree of the region.

These encouraging results led on 2 May 1670 to the granting of a royal charter to the "Governor and Company of Adventurers of England tradeing into Hudson's Bay," as the Hudson's Bay Company was first known. The eighteen recipients (who ventured their capital, not themselves; none actually visited the bay) received nominal rights to the "sole Trade and Commerce" of all shores and waterways lying beyond Hudson Strait excepting any lands already possessed by English subjects or "any other Christian Prince or State." In terms that vastly overstated the control they ever achieved over Rupert's Land, they were named "true and absolute Lordes and Proprietors" of a land quite different from their other chartered colonies or plantations and much larger than they realized.

The boundaries of Rupert's Land were poorly defined and often disputed. A watershed definition would encompass northern Quebec and most land north of the Great Lakes (which have a remarkably small drainage). Canada's major prairie rivers, the Red, Assiniboine, and Saskatchewan, whose waters reach Hudson Bay via Lake Winnipeg, drain an area extending into northern Minnesota and North and South Dakota as well as to the east slopes of the Rocky Mountains. Depending on one's interpretation of which other waterways were included, estimates of the size of Rupert's Land range between two and three million square miles (5,200,000 to 7,800,000 square kilometers).

When the new "proprietors" received their charter declaring the territory "one of our Plantacions or Colonyes in America," no provision existed for negotiations with the Algonquian, Athapaskan, Siouan, or Inuit peoples who occupied Rupert's Land; only recently have Indian claims questioned the significance of certain early "treaties" that Hudson's Bay men made with the Cree of Rupert River in the 1670s. From 1670 to 1713 the French were the challengers of Brit-

ish title around Hudson Bay. In 1686 they captured and held for a time the three Hudson's Bay Company forts in James Bay, and from 1697 to 1714 they occupied York Fort, renaming it Fort Bourbon. The 1697 Treaty of Ryswick would have granted James Bay to the French and York to the English but was never implemented in Hudson's Bay; the English retaking of the James Bay posts and the firm French hold on York outflanked the commissioners' intentions, although curiously the Hudson's Bay Company in 1700 and 1701 proposed compromise boundaries that would have left most of James Bay to the French.

The Treaty of Utrecht in 1713 declared Hudson Bay a British possession. But the inland boundaries of Rupert's Land were never finally fixed. Its southeastern watersheds encroached on areas that the French claimed. And the British themselves did not consistently claim the whole watershed; in 1719, while trying to settle details of the Utrecht treaty, their commissioners proposed the forty-ninth parallel, northern latitude, as the Rupert's Land border westward from Lake Mistassini in Quebec. The matter went unresolved, and for the next century, the realpolitik of the fur trade set the patterns of European activities and interactions in Rupert's Land.

A COLONY WITH A DIFFERENCE

Rupert's Land stood apart from other British colonies both geographically and in its character. Although it had a similar chartered origin, Rupert's Land provoked two centuries of controversy about its failure to develop like them. The Hudson's Bay Company was attacked for monopolizing trade without colonizing, civilizing, or Christianizing its enormous royal gift of territory. In 1749 parliamentary critics asserted that Hudson's Bay Company trading posts offered economic potentials similar to those of European cities and agricultural lands of equally high latitudes. Then and later, they argued unsuccessfully that the Hudson's Bay Company charter be canceled for nonfulfillment of its terms and the land opened to other more energetic entrepreneurs.

The fur trade was in fact the best base on which the company could build, given the environment and the resources and expertise that the Indians offered, and given Europe's market for beaver felt to make the hats that men of fashion demanded in the 1600s and 1700s. At that, the company scarcely cleared any profit in its first fifty years, as it struggled with the French and with its own inexperience. Besides problems in recruiting qualified employees (the solution after 1700 was mainly found in the hardy men of Scotland's Orkney Islands), its energies were consumed by building and provisioning subarctic posts and selecting trade goods of a type and quality to interest Indian traders. Relying on one or two ships per year to transport men, goods, and information through the pack ice of the Hudson Strait and weathering North Atlantic storms, it faced logistical problems little understood by colonialists in other climes.

Responding to this unique combination of environmental, business, and sociocultural conditions, the Hudson's Bay Company traders and their Indian counterparts forged adaptations that would have seemed foreign indeed to the English of Massachusetts or Virginia. The fur trade fostered a cross-cultural consensus about land use. The Indians intensified traditional hunting and processing occupations; both parties relied on those skills. The English of Hudson Bay claimed the land, but not for agriculture; their only "plantations" were small gardens of potatoes, turnips, and such around the posts. No settlers, white women, or clergy became residents until the founding of the Red River Colony (present-day Winnipeg, Manitoba) in 1812. The one exception proved and in fact generated the rule. In 1683 Governor Henry Sergeant arrived in James Bay with his wife, maidservant, and a clergyman. French attacks, the expense of installing Sergeant's domestic retinue, and other concerns led the company the next year to forbid repeating such experiments.

The company's London committee in its first century applied a quasi-military model to the building of its forts and the hierarchical ordering of its servants in Hudson Bay. But European forts were ill-suited to subarctic survival, and civilian employees—removed geographically and socially from "Their Honors," the shareholding directors in London—developed their own knowledge and views. They learned that both their lives and their trade success depended on the Swampy Cree, or "homeguard" (in Hudson's Bay Company vocabulary), Indians who resided nearest the posts. The Cree never enacted the military role the Hudson's Bay Company label implied. But Cree men trapped the beaver, muskrat, and other furs the English sought. Their goose hunts and other activities furnished the "country provisions" that Hudson's Bay Company men needed alongside their costly imported foods. Cree women processed the furs, furnished fish and small game to supplement the diet, and manufactured leather moccasins, snowshoes, and other accessories essential to subarctic life and travel.

Such interwoven economic relations meant that traders in Hudson Bay could not maintain the fortified isolates that their London committee prescribed. Native visitors seeking reliable trade ties expected appropriate hospitality; they and the Hudson's Bay Company factors gradually instituted rituals focusing upon Indian "trading captains," who led inland hunters downriver to the posts each spring with their furs. Surprised, too, that adult men would venture abroad without women's aid and company, Indians regularly promoted marital alliances that defied London rules against such relations. By the mid 1700s, unions "according to the custom of the country" were common. In years that followed, native wives and progeny acquired great importance in both the social fabric and the work life of company posts.

The London committee had limited control not only over its servants and their Indian trading partners but also over Rupert's Land itself. The company did not govern Native communities; they remained autonomous except for some homeguard groups drawn into close interdependence with the posts. Nor could it keep out the "Canadian pedlars" from Montreal. In the early to mid 1700s, French traders increasingly moved beyond Lake Superior, led by such explorers as the La Vérendrye family. In the decades after the British conquest of New France in 1763, several Scottish entrepreneurs (including Simon McTavish and Alexander Mackenzie) took over the Montreal fur trade. Building on French experience and voyageur labor, they posed still greater challenges to the Hudson's Bay Company. From their 1783 coalescence into the North West Company until that firm's merger with thc Hudson's Bay Company in 1821, the North-Westers stirred increasingly costly and violent trade rivalries as they reached ever farther into the Athabasca country (northern Alberta and beyond) and into British Columbia.

FUR TRADE AND COLONY

Trade rivalries were among several factors that led the Hudson's Bay Company to undertake the colonizing specified in its charter, 140 years after its granting. Thomas Douglas, the fifth earl of Selkirk, was both a substantial Hudson's Bay Company shareholder and a philanthropist eager to resettle Scottish highlanders hurt by land clearances and evictions. In 1811 the company granted him lands five times the size of Scotland, centering on the confluence of the Red and Assiniboine rivers (present-day Winnipeg) and extending into parts of Minnesota and North Dakota. In return, he was to recruit settlers (who were barred from fur trading) and to furnish lands to retiring Hudson's Bay Company servants and their native families. The company hoped these fertile plains would provide an agricultural base that would help in cutting the costs of trade provisioning.

The grant directly challenged the North-Westers. The buffalo herds of the region furnished meat that Indians and Métis (descendants of Canadian traders and Indian women) harvested for pemmican, the dried and pounded nourishment needed on the North-Westers' long transportation routes. Confrontations quickly developed over both pemmican and land, paralleling rising tensions in Athabasca and other areas where Hudson's Bay Company and North West Company traders had neighboring posts or overlapping travel routes. Only after the two companies merged in 1821 under the name of the Hudson's Bay Company and the firm control of Governor George Simpson could Red River be stabilized as a viable settlement.

Its agricultural potential, however, was never realized in its colonial phase. Floods, subarctic winters, and the lack of access to markets, of a wheat suited to the climate, and of steel plows, meant that buffalo hunting and trading of furs and other local and imported goods—increasingly along cart trails to Saint Paul (Minnesota) and elsewhere—remained of critical importance through the 1860s. Red River traders challenged the monopoly claimed by their colony's company creator. Métis and Scottish "halfbreed" fur-trade descendants constituted nine-tenths of the population by the 1860s. Their intimidation of Hudson's Bay Company officials in the trial of free trader Guillaume Sayer in 1849 loosened the company's hold on Red River, just as American and other entrepreneurs were challenging the Hudson's Bay Company's monopoly in all but the more-isolated northern areas of Rupert's Land.

When Canada confederated in 1867, the Hudson's Bay Company was already moving beyond the fur trade. In 1863 the London committee sold its controlling shares to the International Financial Society, a group of entrepreneurs who looked more to developing the southern parts of Rupert's Land than to northern furs. Concurrently, eastern Canadians, running short of prime farmland at home, promoted annexing Rupert's Land to facilitate their expansion and to protect against feared annexation by the United States. After extended negotiations, the Hudson's Bay Company agreed on 9 April 1869 "to surrender to Her Majesty all . . . Territorial rights in Rupert's Land, and in any other parts of British North America," in return for £300,000, one twentieth of the land to be opened to settlement, and retention of its existing posts.

Before the land transfer was completed, Canada's government in Ottawa appointed William McDougall to govern its new territory. The government's rush to begin new grid land surveys disturbed Red River inhabitants, as did the imminent arrival of a lieutenant governor and regime on which they had not been consulted. On 11 October 1869 Louis Riel and other Métis halted the surveyors' work. On 19 October the Métis barricaded the road from Pembina (North Dakota), notifying McDougall that his entry from that border point would not be allowed.

Riel then established a provisional government that secured the admission of Manitoba into the confederation in 1870 as a province, despite its small size and the handicap imposed by hostility between the largely francophone, Roman Catholic Métis and the incoming English Protestant Canadians. Many Métis moved out, some later joining Riel's ill-fated Northwest Rebellion of 1885 in Saskatchewan—the only military resistance that Canada encountered as its colonial history ended.

BRITISH COLUMBIA

The colonial phase of British Columbia history was brief and officially began only with the establishment of Vancouver Island as a colony in 1849. From the 1740s to 1811, dozens of Russian, British, Spanish, and American ships visited the Haida, Nootka, and other Pacific coastal Indians to trade for sea-otter pelts, which they then transported to China. Aside from the Russians in Alaska, none of these visitors established a lasting land base. The only Europeans to arrive overland from the east before 1805 were Alexander Mackenzie and his North West Company voyageurs, who reached the mouth of the Bella Coola River on 22 July 1793.

In 1805 and 1806 Meriwether Lewis and William Clark, sent on the initiative of President Thomas Jefferson—who had read Mackenzie's exploration narrative—wintered at the mouth of the Columbia River. The American acquisition in 1803 of the Louisiana Territory, which encompassed the Missouri River watershed and thus stretched north to the southern edge of Alberta by some definitions, had stirred new interest in regions lying beyond it, and the British and Americans became the prime contenders for the Pacific Northwest.

Early in 1811, a party sent by New York entrepreneur John Jacob Astor founded a trading post, Fort Astoria, at the mouth of the Columbia. In 1813, during the War of 1812, the North West Company peacefully negotiated to take over the fort, whose staff included a number of its former employees. Neither British nor Americans gained sovereignty, however; by a convention of 1818, lands claimed by either party west of the Rocky Mountains remained "free and open."

The Hudson's Bay–North West Company merger of 1821 initiated twenty-five years of land-based fur trading administered regionally by Chief Factor John McLoughlin, who was based first at Fort George (the old Astoria) and then at Fort Vancouver on the Columbia. The British government reaffirmed the company's "sole and exclusive privilege of trading with the Indians." The growing American settlement of the Oregon Territory in the 1830s, however, made monopoly increasingly untenable.

In 1841 several practical considerations led Governor Simpson to shift the Hudson's Bay Company's regional headquarters to a new base on Vancouver Island. Fort Victoria was begun in 1843, the same year that hundreds of American settlers traveled the new Oregon Trail. American expansionary pressures soon forced a boundary settlement; the Oregon Treaty of 1846 extended the border westward along the forty-ninth parallel, then southward, leaving Vancouver Island in British hands.

The Hudson's Bay Company secured proprietary rights to establish Vancouver Island as a colony in 1849. The British Colonial Office imported a new governor, who endured his Hudson's Bay Company–dominated constituency only a few months; his successor (1851–1864) was a senior Hudson's Bay Company officer, James Douglas. Fur traders still controlled affairs, although company activities diversified into timber, coal, gold, and other resources.

Gold changed the course of British Columbia's colonial history. In 1858 word of local gold discoveries brought an influx of some thirty thousand prospectors, mainly overflows from the California goldfields. The British government recognized the political implications and responded by creating the new mainland colony of British Columbia on 2 August 1858. In 1859 it took over from the Hudson's Bay Company the responsibility for governing Vancouver Island; James Douglas, however, held the governorship of both colonies until 1864.

The growing and diverse newcomer population spelled the end of Hudson's Bay Company dominance and the end of the synergetic (if sometimes difficult) relationships between fur traders and native peoples. In the early 1850s Governor Douglas made several treaties with Vancouver Island Indians over lands where Europeans wanted to settle; his successors overlooked such niceties. Gold rushes to the Cariboo country and elsewhere fueled immigration and pressures for rapid development and government expenditures.

In November 1866 the British Parliament combined the two colonies into one, British Columbia, with a mainland capital at New Westminster and a single legislative council. The new government faced debts of almost $1.3 million and a revenue crisis. Politicians contended over whether to remain British, join the growing American territories to the south, or seek membership in Canada's new confederation. The United States' purchase of Alaska in 1867 and its completion of a transcontinental railroad in 1869 sharpened British strategic concerns. By 1869 the Colonial Office was supporting the confederation option.

The British Columbians bargained hard over their terms of entry. Their central demand for a transcontinental transportation link received impetus from Ottawa's trouble with Louis Riel and the Métis in 1869 and 1870 in Manitoba. The Canadian government optimistically agreed to complete a rail link by 1881 (the last spike was actually driven in November 1885). British Columbia entered Canada on 20 July 1871 as its sixth province.

BIBLIOGRAPHY

Barman, Jean. *The West Beyond the West: A History of British Columbia.* Toronto, Ontario, 1991.

Brown, Jennifer S. H. *Strangers in Blood: Fur Trade Company Families in Indian Country.* Vancouver, British Columbia, 1980.

Fisher, Robin. *Contact and Conflict: Indian-European Relations in British Columbia, 1774–1890.* Vancouver, British Columbia, 1977.

Francis, Daniel, and Toby Morantz. *Partners in Furs: A History of the Fur Trade in Eastern James Bay, 1600–1870.* Kingston and Montreal, 1983.

Mancke, Elizabeth. *A Company of Businessmen: The Hudson's Bay Company and Long-Distance Trade, 1670–1730.* Winnipeg, Manitoba, 1988.

McNeil, Kent. *Native Rights and the Boundaries of Rupert's Land and the North-Western Territory.* Studies in Aboriginal Rights, no. 4. Saskatoon, Saskatchewan, 1982.

Rich, E. E. *The History of the Hudson's Bay Company, 1670–1870.* 2 vols. London, 1958–1959.

Jennifer S. H. Brown

SEE ALSO **The First Americans; French Settlements;** and **The Fur Trade;** various essays in OLD WORLD EXPANSION; and the map preceding **French Settlements.**

THE WEST INDIES
AND NORTH AMERICA

Antechamber to the New World for the European expansionists led by Spain, the West Indies were the focus of Spanish imperial interest only until larger and richer territories were discovered in Central and South America. Once other Europeans challenged the Spaniards and colonized the more northerly parts of the Americas, however—and to an even greater degree, once slave plantations were established—the West Indies assumed huge importance. The Caribbean became the cockpit of European rivalries as French, English, and Dutch developed island plantations while they were creating settlement colonies on the North American mainland and establishing trading stations for slaves in West Africa.

The close and reciprocal relationship between the mainland and the islands—subsequently obscured by the relative decline of the West Indies and the enormous expansion of the United States in the nineteenth century—can best be delineated in three main stages: (1) the role of the West Indies in the early phases of North American settlement and the establishment of trading patterns in the North Atlantic; (2) the indispensable connections between the North American mainland and Caribbean islands (and with Africa) at a time when European imperialism preferred plantation to settlement colonies; and (3) the part played by the West Indies during the early phases of commercial and territorial expansion by the United States, down to the establishment of the southern border at the Rio Grande in 1845 and the creation of the Canadian confederation in 1867.

EARLY SETTLEMENT AND TRADE

Spain

Once the pioneering Spaniards had established their base in Española (Hispaniola), the rapid depletion of local gold resources and the disastrous decline of the native population led them to fan outward to the neighboring islands and mainland in all directions, including northwest. The priority of Columbus's claim and the consequent allocation of the western half of the unknown world to Spain by the Spanish Pope Alexander VI had unwittingly given the Spaniards access to territory seventy-five times as large as Spain. The combined factors of the hugeness of this expanse and limited available manpower naturally led to a concentration on areas suitable for Spanish-type estates, with large malleable populations and, above all, large new sources of gold and silver; that is, to Mexico and Peru. Despite their teleological importance in the history of the United States, the Caribbean-based exploratory probes into the hinterland north of the Rio Grande by Juan Ponce de León, Pánfilo de Narváez, and Hernando de Soto were disappointing failures, as discouraging of permanent settlement as were the Spaniards' experiences in the Carib-defended islands of the Lesser Antilles and the disease-ridden tropical forests of the Spanish Main.

The later-coming powers of France, England,* and Holland never seriously threatened the centers of the Spanish American Empire, being able to claim and settle only those areas neglected by Spain, which they then developed in ways that were unsuitable and uncongenial to the Spanish imperial economy. The early rivalry with Spain and the location of some of the first settlements were to an extent conditioned by the Reformation: for nearly a century French, Dutch, and English *corsarios luteranos* ("Lutheran corsairs," as they were called by the Spaniards) carried out their depredations under the color of a Protestant crusade, while some of the early non-Iberian settlements were refuges for religious dissidents in the second phase of the Reformation.

A more important and lasting factor for the challenge to Spain (and Portugal, to which Spain was united between 1580 and 1640) was the emergence of state mercantilism among the non-Iberian powers. Learning from Spain's inability to move quickly or completely enough out of medieval to modern ways, France, Holland, and England each set their sights on preeminence in the world's collective balance of trade and accumulation of bullion, each government striving to expand both its overseas markets and its colonial production through the grant of monopolies to favored companies and individuals. The enthusiastic pursuit of exclusionary wealth and power led these nations from collaboration against Spain into a rising crescendo of wars between themselves, in time relegating Spain to the role of minor player, its empire more a commercial prize than a military threat.

France

Chronologically, it was France—a predominantly Catholic power—that led the challenge to Pope Alexander VI's division of the world between Portugal and Spain. Though at the fighting edge of expansion were Calvinist Huguenots supported by the minister Gaspard de Coligny, the French enterprise drew from a wide spectrum of national support, and it attempted settlements as far apart as the Saint Lawrence (1535–1542) and Rio de Janeiro (1555–1560). The Huguenots Jan Ribault and René de Laudonnière were the most adventurous of all, attempting settlement athwart the lifeline of the Spanish American Empire, at the Florida Strait (1562–1565).

All the initial French efforts failed; and that in Florida, along with the other activities of the "Lutheran corsairs," provoked drastic countermeasures organized by Pedro Menéndez de Avilés. Besides the eradication of the French settlements with exemplary savagery, these included the setting up of a system of convoys and *guarda costas* to protect Spanish trade and harass the traders of other nations; the creation of a chain of Caribbean fortress ports; and the delimitation of the northern frontier by the establishment of fortified posts centered on Saint Augustine, Florida.

It was only after the conclusion of its civil wars of religion, with the suppression of the Huguenots and the making of peace with Spain in 1598, that France reentered the arena, with the first permanent settlements in Canada and the Caribbean. These tended to be fragmented enterprises of different French regions and Atlantic ports until 1664, when the French control-

---

*In this essay we have tried to use names with historical accuracy, despite somewhat confusing variations that have occurred over time and place. The terms "England" and "English" are used up to the union with Scotland in 1707, when "Britain" and "British" become more accurate. "West Indies" is used for all those islands in a semicircle around the Caribbean Sea from Cuba to Aruba, along with the Atlantic islands of the Bermudian and Bahamian archipelagos; the almost-archipelagic coastal colonies of the Guianas and Belize are traditionally included with them. "The Caribbean" is the term used for the entire basin, including the Gulf of Mexico, though it impinges on North, Central, and South America. "Antilles" is used correctly for the Caribbean-fringing islands to the north and east, divided into (1) the four large islands of the Greater Antilles and (2) the Lesser Antilles, eastward of Puerto Rico. This latter term is used in preference to such classifications as the "British Leeward Islands," which are adjacent to the Dutch Windward Islands and hundreds of miles from the Dutch Leewards. The second-largest island in the Caribbean was called "Española" while it was under entirely Spanish control, after which it was divided into Spanish Santo Domingo and French Saint Domingue—which later became independent Haiti, taking the name of one of its aboriginal districts.

COLONIAL POSSESSIONS IN THE CARIBBEAN

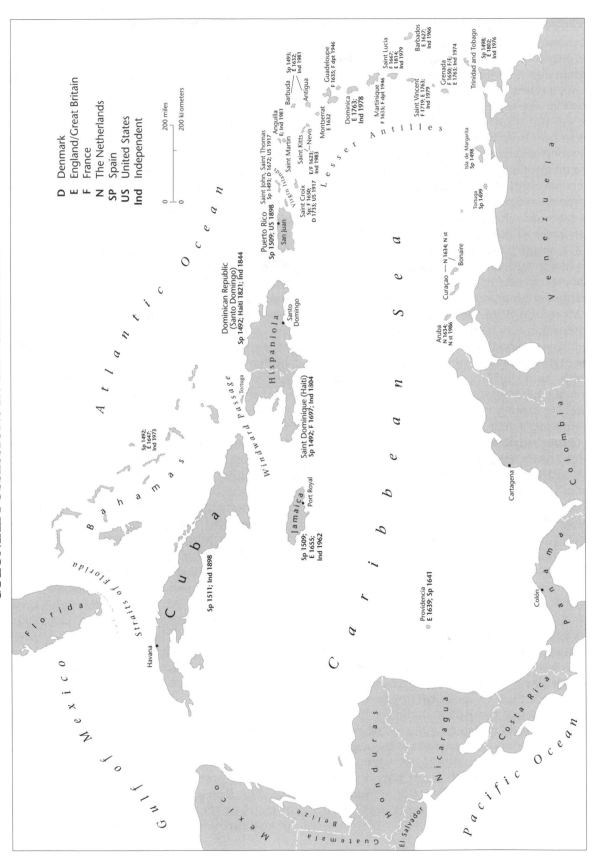

D Denmark
E England/Great Britain
F France
N The Netherlands
SP Spain
US United States
Ind Independent

200 miles
200 kilometers

Atlantic Ocean

Gulf of Mexico

Florida

Straits of Florida

Havana

Cuba
Sp 1511; Ind 1898

Bahamas
Sp 1492;
E 1647;
Ind 1973

Jamaica
Port Royal
Sp 1509;
E 1655;
Ind 1962

Windward Passage

Tortuga

Hispaniola

Santo Domingo

Dominican Republic
(Santo Domingo)
Sp 1492; Haiti 1821; Ind 1844

Saint Dominique (Haiti)
Sp 1492; F 1697; Ind 1804

Puerto Rico
Sp 1509; US 1898

San Juan

Saint John, Saint Thomas
Sp 1493; D 1672; US 1917

Anguilla
E; Ind 1981

Saint Martin

Saint Kitts
E/F 1623;
Ind 1983

Nevis

Saint Croix
Sp; F 1650;
D 1733; US 1917

Virgin Islands

Montserrat
E 1632

Barbuda
Sp 1493;
E 1632;
Ind 1981

Antigua

Guadeloupe
F 1635; F dpt 1946

Dominica
E 1763;
Ind 1978

Martinique
F 1635; F dpt 1946

Saint Lucia
F 1667;
E 1814;
Ind 1979

Saint Vincent
F 1719; E 1763;
Ind 1979

Grenada
F 1650; F/E;
E 1763; Ind 1974

Barbados
E 1627;
Ind 1966

Trinidad and Tobago
Sp 1498;
E 1802;
Ind 1976

Lesser Antilles

Caribbean Sea

Isla de Margarita
Sp 1498

Tortuga
Sp 1499

Curaçao — N 1634; N st

Bonaire

Aruba
N 1634;
N st 1986

Providencia
E 1639; Sp 1641

Cartagena

Colón

Panama

Pacific Ocean

Honduras

Nicaragua

Costa Rica

Venezuela

Colombia

Mexico

Belize

Guatemala

El Salvador

ler general Jean Baptiste Colbert attempted to weld them into a coherent imperial policy under the control of the royal Compagnie des Indes Occidentales. This policy visualized settlements and plantations dedicated to the economic advantage of the metropole through the development of fur trading, fisheries, tropical staple production, and a West African trade to provide slave labor, without any local self-determination and with minimal interconnections on the periphery. As with Spain's colonial policy, royal authority remained paramount, and the Catholic church became closely involved, mainly through the activities of missionary friars.

The gradual success of the French colonies, though, was largely self-generated, with considerable cross-recruitment in personnel and some intercolonial commerce in fish, cereals, and lumber. Moreover, once the explorers Louis Jolliet and Rene-Robert Cavelier de La Salle had penetrated from the Saint Lawrence to the mouth of the Mississippi—during the period from 1673 to 1682—and the French had expanded from the small islands of Martinique and Guadeloupe to take over from Spain and establish plantations in the western half of Española, there was at least the potential, around 1700, of an integrated empire that would give France hegemony in North America. That French supremacy was never achieved was due, in the simplest terms, to the economic and geopolitical advantages enjoyed by Holland and Britain, to their more rational or pragmatic imperial policies, and—down to 1763 at least—to the narrow superiority of the British military and naval forces.

Holland

The conception of an effectively integrated imperial system of the North Atlantic—in which the interrelationship of North American and West Indian colonies and the tapping of West Africa for slaves were almost as vital as the connections with the European metropole—was as much the work of the Dutch as the English. Although England's greater resources of people and Holland's early preference for a worldwide empire of commerce, as much as England's victory in three Anglo-Dutch naval wars between 1652 and 1674, gave England a predominance that ended only with the American War of Independence.

With the energies generated from its successful war of independence from Spain, the Calvinist, capitalist, mercantilist, republican, and federal Netherlands pursued an overseas empire in the same areas and in similar ways. But the Dutch had even more vigor than the English, whose initial expansion was complicated and delayed by the conflict between a centralizing monarchy and an emergent bourgeoisie, not resolved until after the civil wars.

At first the Dutch and English enterprises overlapped and reinforced each other. Not only did freebooters from both nations (as well as French *flibustiers*) combine against Spain and Portugal, but Henry Hudson worked alternately for English and Dutch (providing the latter with their title to New Netherland); the Pilgrim fathers found refuge and financial support in Holland before they departed for Massachusetts; and Dutch finance, expertise, and maritime resources were vital in the establishment of West Indian colonies, especially Barbados. The first settlement of that island was largely the work of the Anglo-Dutch Courteen company (based in Leyden and London). Its development as a sugar monoculture depended on emulating Dutch models in Pernambuco, Brazil; on obtaining capital, machinery, and slaves from Dutch merchants; and on shipping sugar to European markets in Dutch vessels. At the same time, the Dutch were heavily involved in the financing, shipping, and European sales of Virginian tobacco.

By the 1640s, the Dutch American empire was centered on sugar plantations in northeast Brazil and the Guianas, supplied with slaves from fortified factories in Guinea, and with at least the potential of provisions and lumber from the mainland colony of New Netherland. To these possessions the Dutch added islands in the Caribbean not already taken by the English and French, which if too small for profitable plantations would be ideal as trading posts. The very similarity of Dutch and English ventures, however, meant that rivalry and conflict were inevitable, which, when coupled with the continued enmity of the Catholic powers, meant that Holland was overextended.

The Dutch were expelled from Brazil (and Angola) by the Luso-Brazilians, and as a result of the exclusionist English Navigation Acts of

1651 and the consequent Anglo-Dutch wars—reluctantly initiated by the Commonwealth under Oliver Cromwell but continued by the more cynical Charles II—they were forced to concede the North American component of their Atlantic empire, New Netherland, in exchange for Surinam. Over the same period, Holland lost its primacy in West Africa and gave up the Virgin Islands and Tobago—subsequently shared among the English, Danes, and sundry minor European powers—retaining in the West Indies only the islands of Curaçao, Aruba, and Bonaire off the coast of Spanish Venezuela and the islets of Statia (Saint Eustatius), Saba, and Saint Martin in the northeast Antilles, which were to serve as important neutral entrepôts in the subsequent Anglo-French wars.

Similar minor victims of England's dominance in the late seventeenth and early eighteenth centuries were several Baltic powers. Sweden for a time had colonies or forts on Saint Barthélemy, the Delaware River, and the Gold Coast of Africa before being restricted to its tiny West Indian colony. Denmark never had a North American mainland colony to add to the Faeroes, Iceland, and Greenland but possessed the important Virgin Islands of Saint Thomas, Saint John, and Saint Croix, which it supplied with slaves from its own posts in Guinea. The German Brandenburgers and the subjects of the grand duke of Courland tried but failed to establish a similar system, involving small slave plantations in Tobago.

England

Though English colonization was initiated unsystematically by individuals, companies, and the state, and the method of developing colonies was likewise tripartite, involving chartered companies, quasi-feudal proprietors, and the Crown, it was at first an undifferentiated operation, finding suitable locations by chance and succeeding through sore trials and many errors. Those who read history backward can trace policies and institutions to their flimsiest taproots and claim that all later developments were destined; but it was a half century before the various parts of the mainland and the West Indies became clearly differentiated in purpose and personnel. Not until its second century would England's American empire resolve itself into a rational imperial system—and even then it retained pragmatic variations, unevenly and inefficiently run and, in the end, impermanent.

The protean English colonial promoter Walter Raleigh, besides being long involved in the "plantation" of Ireland and innumerable privateering ventures, was successively concerned in the Newfoundland fisheries and mining projects in Labrador, the settlement of the huge coastline he christened Virginia, and visionary schemes to discover El Dorado and take over the Spanish Main with the help of the natives. Despite Raleigh's failures, each of his enterprises had its successors during the reigns of the first two Stuarts. Mixed fortunes in Amazonia and the Guianas (not given up until 1664) led to more permanent success on the generally less populated, healthier, and more defensible small islands of the Lesser Antilles. Such success included Thomas Warner's descent upon Saint Kitts in 1624 and the settlement of Barbados by the Courteens and the proprietary James Hay, earl of Carlisle, in competition between 1625 and 1627, leading to an expansion into Nevis, Antigua, and Montserrat from 1628 to 1632. The quest for gold mines in Labrador was likewise given up in favor of a fairly effective claim to control the fishing of the Newfoundland and New England banks; while Virginia was parceled into more manageable swaths, and the first permanent settlements were established, after terrible difficulties, by a company on the Chesapeake (1607–1625) and by groups of Puritan refugees in Massachusetts (1620–1630).

The perspective of early English colonization is clearer when it is remembered that tiny Bermuda had more settlers than Virginia until 1620 and that the white population of the English West Indies kept pace with the mainland colonies for another fifty years. Bermuda, indeed, was almost the linchpin in these initial phases, retaining vital connections with all mainland colonies and being involved in the settlement, supply, and trade of the colonies in the West Indies before settling into lesser but still-important roles of shipbuilding, intercolonial trade, privateering, and the provision of salt for the cod fisheries from the Turks and the Caicos Islands.

The close interaction between all early enterprises and their gradual diversification, however, is epitomized by the history of the failed English colony on the island of Providencia off the coast of Nicaragua (1630–1641). Organized by a joint stock company in which Puritans such as the earl of Warwick and John Pym were prominent, the Providence Island Colony was promoted as a godly (if profit-oriented) venture and, for this reason, obtained vital support from Puritan adventurers in New England and Bermuda. Plantations and trade with the Indians were initiated; but since Providencia was on the direct route of the Spanish silver convoys from the Isthmus, the Spaniards—probably correctly—saw it chiefly as a base for privateers and expelled the English at a second attempt. Had it survived, the Providence Island Colony might well have developed as a sugar colony about the size and with the importance of Nevis; for the original smallholdings were already being consolidated and cultivated by a work force of black slaves as numerous as the white settlers. But the very fact that most of the slaves had been stolen from the Spaniards' ships or plantations added force to Spanish opposition.

PLANTATION ECONOMIES

The draconian extinction of the Providence Island Colony fueled the feelings of revenge against the Spaniards that contributed to the takeover of Jamaica during the Cromwellian Interregnum (1655). But a more general factor was the success of the sugar revolution in the Lesser Antilles, which began in Barbados in the 1640s and spread to the English Leeward Islands in the 1660s. As the Dutch had demonstrated, sugar was so valuable a commodity (producing five times the value of provisions per acre) that monoculture was inevitable wherever the land was suitable. But sugar plantations were highly capital-, land-, and labor-intensive, leading to the squeezing out of smallholders, the creation of an oligarchic plantocracy, and the substitution for white indentured laborers of a huge slave work force—provided first by a series of monopolistic companies, of which the Royal African Company (1672) was the last and greatest, and then, after 1698, by legally sanctioned independent slave traders. Jamaica was seen at first as a location for displaced small settlers but was

quickly monopolized by would-be planters. Between 1730 and 1770 it displaced Barbados as "the jewel in the English Crown"—with eight hundred sugar plantations and a slave work force eventually outnumbering all whites by ten to one.

One inevitable result of the establishment of plantation colonies was the phasing out of the international anti-Spanish brotherhood of the buccaneers—symbolized in most books by the destruction of their main base, Port Royal, Jamaica, by the earthquake of 1692. In fact, the buccaneers had already been outlawed—declared to be pirates or international sea robbers rather than loosely commissioned privateers—as a result of those treaties by which the Spanish had acknowledged the rights of the English, French, and Dutch to the colonies they had already effectively settled and planted. Expelled from their second main base on the island of Tortuga off northern Hispaniola in the 1690s, the desperate remnant of the buccaneers set themselves up in the Bahamas and North Carolina, taking advantage of the inefficiency of the proprietary government.

As Marcus Rediker has shown, the actual heyday of the pirates was the short period of peace and of colonial and commercial expansion after the end of Queen Anne's War with the French in 1713, beginning with the demobilization of the imperial navies and ending with the establishment of effective royal government in the Bahamas and Carolinas around 1725. Piracy continued a dreaded hazard for legitimate trade in the Caribbean for at least another century, though the activities of naval patrols and colonial admiralty courts (particularly the British) restricted the pirates to fugitive crews of unromantic desperadoes, lurking in the remoter and least policed harbors of southern Cuba and the Spanish Main.

Meanwhile, motive forces similar to those which established sugar plantations in the Caribbean had led to the first settlement of South Carolina by ambitious Barbadian planters with their slaves in 1670 (initially under a Bermudian governor), opening up a long-lasting connection. Slaves became increasingly available to the mainland colonies through the development of the African trade to the West Indies, and plantations rapidly expanded from the Chesapeake southward. Nonetheless, the very different commodities grown on mainland plantations (tobacco, cotton, and rice, brought in from South America, the West Indies, and Africa respectively), the different climate, and the much greater opportunities for smallholding settlers determined that no mainland colony would ever develop either the degree of monoculture or the overwhelming proportion of slaves found in the West Indies, except in a few localities such as the South Carolina low country and the Georgia Sea Islands.

Some black slaves were imported into all mainland colonies because they became so freely available, but the socioeconomic divergence of New England and the middle colonies from the colonies of the plantation sphere, especially the West Indies, was inevitable. This, and the reciprocal relationship between northeastern colonies and the West Indies, was encapsulated by John Winthrop of Massachusetts as early as 1647:

It pleased the Lord to open to us a trade with Barbados and other islands in the West Indies, which as it proved gainful, so the commodities we had in exchange there for our cattle and provisions, as sugar, cotton, tobacco and indigo, were a good help to discharge our engagements in England.

Richard Pares, in *Yankees and Creoles* goes so far as to claim that without reciprocal trade "the sugar colonies could not have existed and the North American colonies could not have developed." Once the English had established their monopoly of the coastline from Florida to Maine and their constellation of sugar colonies in the West Indies, it was realized that

the colonies north of the Mason-Dixon line had few staples of any value in the European markets but a permanent surplus of food and lumber; the West Indies, just the contrary; and the hybrid colonies from Maryland to Carolina produced both staple crops and a less important surplus of other kinds of food. (p. 2)

Unlike the French West Indian colonies, which could depend for supplies on a metropolitan country that was not only overwhelmingly agricultural but also several times the size of Great Britain, the English sugar islands became dependent on the wide range of essential supplies that could be delivered from North America in sufficient quantities and far more cheaply than those carried across the Atlantic.

From Boston and the many smaller ports of New England, and from New York, Baltimore, and Philadelphia, came dried and salted fish; pickled beef and pork; lard, butter, and cheese; peas, beans, and onions; corn, flour, and bread; cattle, horses, hogs, sheep, and poultry; oak and pine boards; "shook" (that is, broken-down) barrels; iron hoops, bricks, and leather. The southern ports of Wilmington, Charleston, and Savannah exported mainly rice and dry vegetables, pine tar, and all kinds of lumber—especially pine boards, staves, and shingles. In all, by 1770, 63 percent of all New England's dried fish was exported to the West Indies. From the middle (or "bread") colonies some four hundred thousand pounds (180,000 kilograms) of wheat, flour, and bread were shipped to the West Indies each year, half of which came from Pennsylvania and almost a third from New York. Only 19 percent of the rice produced by the mainland plantations went to the West Indies, but this amounted to more than 140,000 hundredweight per year.

To an extent, the North American shippers took payment in cash and in credits that were good in England for redressing the imbalance of their trade with the metropolis. But the majority of their exports to the West Indies were paid for in West Indian produce. Sugar, cotton, indigo, and later coffee were taken for North American and European markets, but the most favored commodity was the sugar by-product molasses, the raw material for rum production. By 1770 there were at least 25 sugar refineries and 127 rum distilleries in the middle and New England colonies, of which Boston boasted 7 of the former and 36 of the latter. The cities of Newport (Rhode Island), Philadelphia, and New York accounted for many of the rest of both.

By 1700 hundreds of vessels of from 15 to 150 tons (9 to 135 metric tons) were engaged in a commerce that was as often speculative and opportunistic as it was regular and by arrangement, amounting in combination to at least a quarter of the value of Britain's transatlantic traffic. This pattern of trade, with mainland vessels normally sailing out by the eastern Antilles or through the Windward Passage (through the Bahamas and between Cuba and Hispaniola), westward through the Caribbean, and back by the Straits of Florida, was an ever-increasing though minimally recognized component of a North Atlantic network of British imperial trade.

The North American–West Indian trade constituted a fourth side to what British historians have commonly misnamed the North Atlantic triangle, consisting of the traffic to and from Britain, Africa, and the West Indies. The pattern of trade was in fact more of a cat's cradle once the North Americans developed their own trade with West Africa (confusingly also termed the North Atlantic triangle by some American scholars), in which slaves for the mainland, British West Indian, and foreign markets were purchased very largely with North American rum—a disreputable traffic in which Rhode Island merchants predominated.

The mercantile connections between the thirteen colonies and the West Indies involved some interchange among people—Lawrence Washington sailing to Barbados for his health (accompanied by his half-brother George) and Alexander Hamilton traveling from Nevis to New York for his education are two famous examples. But, in general, North Americans were committed to making a life on the mainland, while the ideal of every white West Indian seems to have been to become a planter and then an absentee in England. West Indians opting to migrate to the thirteen colonies were even rarer than North American absentees living in England. This demographic feature was consonant with the growing incompatibility of British imperial policy and the North American economy once the French threat on the mainland declined and the ever-expanding North America–West Indies trade pressed on the large but finite opportunities offered by the British West Indies.

The burgeoning success of trade between the British thirteen colonies and the West Indies contrasted with the comparative failure of the commercial connection between the French colonies in Canada and the Antilles. The French ministry of the navy from Colbert's day down to the mid-eighteenth century made great efforts to develop this trade. Canada was to export timber, barrel staves, flour, peas, and salted fish—they also tried to ship horses but few of them survived the voyage—with the ships returning with cargoes of sugar, molasses, and a potent form of rum called *guildive*. Unfortunately, everything that Canada could supply, New England could provide at far lower cost, thanks to lower costs of production, a much shorter voyage, a longer shipping season, and lower insurance rates. Besides, Canada, with its minuscule population, was a limited market for sugar products. Consequently, Canadian ships all too often had to return to Quebec in ballast. Some French merchants trading to Quebec had much the same problem; their captains had to return by way of Saint Domingue (Haiti) or Martinique to get a return cargo that made the voyage worthwhile.

Besides these commercial considerations there was the even more potent question of relative military and naval power. The French role in North America and the West Indies was challenged and contained in the wars that ended in 1713 and 1748, but a far more important conflict was the so-called Seven Years' War, which ended in 1763. This was a widespread (even worldwide) struggle, with land fighting undertaken by the British against the French and their Indian allies from the Saint Lawrence to the Ohio-Mississippi frontier. But the critical confrontations were increasingly naval, so that much hinged on Britain's conquests of Louisbourg in 1759 and Havana in 1762. Britain had not even had a permanent naval force in the Caribbean before 1740; but after 1763, though it gave back Havana and did not develop Louisbourg as a naval station, it possessed a strong network of naval bases in the west—with Antigua and Jamaica dominating the eastern and central Caribbean, Bermuda in the mid Atlantic, and Halifax, Nova Scotia (held since 1713), serving not only as a base from which to defend the Saint Lawrence and northern mainland but also as an invaluable refuge from the Caribbean summer and hurricane seasons.

Up until the end of the Seven Years' War, the Anglo-Americans had, broadly, been prepared to accept such restrictive legislation as the Molasses Act of 1733 for the benefits of naval and military protection, particularly as long as their more or less clandestine trade with the foreign West Indies continued to be only loosely policed by Britain. The Treaty of Paris in 1763 formalized the French exclusion from the North American mainland; but far from capitalizing on wartime successes by retaining all conquered colonies, Britain actually seems to have encouraged the prosperity of those French and Spanish colonies, the trade of which so attracted the Americans. The French did give up the underdeveloped "neutral islands" of Dominica, Saint Vincent, Grenada, and Tobago; but because the powerful British West India lobby feared overproduction within its protected system, the French were allowed to retain Martinique and Guadeloupe, as well as to develop Saint Domingue, already poised to become the most profitable and productive slave-plantation colony in history.

Even more significant was the settlement made with Spain, which regained both Cuba and Louisiana while giving up East and West Florida to Britain. Following some relaxation of Spanish mercantilism, Cuba began to exhibit its potential as a plantation colony, while regarding Louisiana almost as a dependency of Havana. For the Americans, however, both Louisiana and Cuba offered prospects for at least commercial expansion, already encouraged by the extension of the mainland colonies into the Florida peninsula and panhandle—which at that time reached almost to the Mississippi.

New British sugar plantations were developed in the ceded islands of the Lesser Antilles, and some relaxation of mercantilism occurred with the Free Port Acts after 1765. Despite this, the restrictions on North American trade with the West Indies through the ever expanding code of Navigation Laws—and their implementation by a revitalized customs service and colonial vice-admiralty courts—contributed almost as much as taxation without representation, British attempts to close off the western frontier, occupation by the military, and the imbalance of colonial debts to provoke the majority of mainland colonials into a war for independence.

Quite apart from the probably specious argument that Britain was not absolutely wholehearted in retaining political control over the thirteen colonies because of the greater valuation it placed on the West Indies, the American War of Independence had a West Indian dimension in at least two respects. The timely arrival of Admiral François Joseph Paul de Grasse with the French West Indian fleet ensured the surrender of General Charles Cornwallis at Yorktown in 1781, essentially ending the war on land. Conversely, George Rodney's defeat of the same French admiral off Guadeloupe in the following year completely redressed the balance of the naval war, enabling Britain to sustain its imperial system in the West Indies for a further generation.

ANGLO-AMERICA AND THE BORDERLANDS AFTER 1783

Though the American War of Independence is usually cited as one of the first causes of the decline of the British West Indian plantation colonies, connections between the West Indies as a whole and those parts of North America that remained colonial dependencies continued to be of vital importance to both. Though the British North American colonies of Newfoundland, Nova Scotia, New Brunswick, and Lower Canada were unable to make up the shortfall in trade caused by the exclusion of U.S. traders from the West Indies, the attempt to do so provided a boost for their infant economies. Over the same period, the gradual expansion of the United States toward the Rio Grande was as much conditioned by changes in the European imperial system and by revolutionary changes in the Caribbean and the rest of Latin America as by forces generated within the new republic.

In 1800 Spain contracted to sell Louisiana back to the French, but Napoleon's grandiose plans to revive the French Caribbean Empire by the reconquest of Saint Domingue and the development of Louisiana were scotched by the catastrophic defeat of General Charles Victor Emmanuel Leclerc by the Haitian blacks and yellow fever, which led to the declaration of Haitian independence in 1804. In 1803 the United States was able to purchase Louisiana from the French (a tacit bargain in return for ending trade with Haiti), just as Napoleon was about to turn to the takeover of Spain itself.

The French invasion of Spain in 1808 not only encouraged the now isolated *criollos* of Hispanic America in their quest for independence but also made Spain, as Britain's new ally, the natural antagonist of the United States. The idealist anticolonialism of the Americans was severely qualified both by their ambitions to take over the adjacent Spanish territories and by the desire to compete with the British in monopolizing the huge potential Latin American markets under cloak of support for the independence movements there. Such concerns contributed to the assertion by Congress that Florida could never be transferred except to the United States, the outbreak of war with Britain and Spain in 1812, the acquisition of Florida from Spain in 1821, and the extension of the no-transfer principle throughout the western hemisphere by the Monroe Doctrine of 1823.

Contrary to the mythology that has grown around that famous dictum, it was originally made in conjunction with the British with the tacit approval of the French. As late as 1850 British trade to Latin America remained twice that of the United States, with political influence in proportion. Though the British, French, Dutch, and Danish colonies in the region steadily declined, from the ending of the slave trade in 1807 to the emancipation of the slaves between 1834 and 1863, the Americans were effectively unable to penetrate them economically during the rest of the nineteenth century—let alone prize them free from their imperial masters.

Nor were United States ambitions concerning the Hispanic territories easily or quickly fulfilled. As early as 1807, Thomas Jefferson had suggested to James Madison that after the destined acquisition of the Floridas, the southwestern boundary of the United States might be pushed back as the reward for helping the Mexicans achieve their independence, while Cuba might naturally come under American economic if not political sway. Despite American help for Hidalgo and Iturbide, British and even French competition, as well as Mexican national pride and distrust, kept the United States at bay and determined that the coastline from the Mississippi to the Rio Grande and the huge interior province of Texas would become one of the United States only through a process of steady infiltration, shady dealing, and an indirect war. In the Caribbean, though Santo Domingo eventually became independent (without notable help from the United States) in 1865, Cuba and Puerto Rico remained Spanish colonies for another three decades. Indeed, many proud nationalists in the former resisted a destiny manifested by a gradual monopolization of trade and by a rising tide of American investment under the paradoxical banner of *la lealissima colonia*.

Few maritimers in British North America would have continued to express loyalism in such grandiloquent terms. The imperial connection was of limited direct value once the structure of British mercantilism had been dismantled— first by the opening of West Indian ports during the last French war and, more slowly, once international rivalries over the Caribbean no longer threatened war, by the gradual abrogation of the Navigation Acts. Yet during the ensuing age of free trade the general West Indian connection did grow in importance for the British maritime colonies. Maritimers now traded their fish, provisions, and lumber, along with some manufactures, to British and foreign West Indies alike, taking in return unrefined sugar, molasses, and tobacco for processing and distribution. Moreover, the growing sophistication and volume of transactions between British North American ports and the West Indies, along with the imbalance of visible trade, was already laying the basis for the involvement in West India banking and insurance. This special relationship between the British maritime colonies and the West Indies, and the fear (somewhat exaggerated it must be admitted) of losing their primacy and of being economically diluted through a federated Canada, contributed to the maritimers' initial reluctance to engage in the plans for Canadian confederation in the 1860s.

BIBLIOGRAPHY

No single work comprehensively covers this huge geographical area and historical span. The literature from which more detailed information must be sought is immense, and the relevant works vary greatly in approach, sharpness of focus, and quality. Important gaps also remain, to frustrate explorations or encourage new research and writing. The following is a selection of the best and most recent relevant works, most of which include valuable specialist bibliographies. It can be augmented, of course, by the standard works on different regions and cognate topics cited elsewhere in the Encyclopedia.

Andrews, Charles M. *The Colonial Period of American History.* 4 vols. New Haven, Conn., 1934–1938.
Andrews, Kenneth R. *Trade, Plunder, and Settlement: Maritime Enterprise and the Genesis of the British Empire, 1480–1630.* Cambridge, England, 1984.

Bachman, Van Cleaf. *Peltries or Plantations: The Economic Policies of the Dutch West India Company in New Netherland, 1623–1639.* Baltimore, Md., 1969.

Barbier, Jacques A., and Allan J. Kuethe, eds. *The North American Role in the Spanish Imperial Economy, 1760–1819.* Manchester, England, 1984.

Blackburn, Robin. *The Overthrow of Colonial Slavery, 1776–1848.* London, 1988.

Bosher, J. F. *The Canada Merchants, 1713–1763.* Oxford, 1987.

Boxer, Charles R. *The Dutch Seaborne Empire, 1600–1800.* New York, 1965.

Cappon, Lester J., et al., eds. *Atlas of Early American History: The Revolutionary Era, 1760–1790.* Princeton, N.J., 1976.

Carrington, Selwyn H. H. *The British West Indies in the American Revolution.* Dordrecht, The Netherlands, 1988.

Curtin, Philip D. *The Atlantic Slave Trade: A Census.* Madison, Wis., 1969.

Davies, Kenneth G. *The North Atlantic World in the Seventeenth Century.* Minneapolis, Minn., 1974.

Davis, Ralph. *The Rise of the Atlantic Economies.* Ithaca, N.Y., 1973.

Eccles, W. J. *France in America.* New ed. Toronto, Ontario, 1990.

Eltis, David. *Economic Growth and the Ending of the Transatlantic Slave Trade.* New York, 1987.

Gipson, Lawrence Henry. *The British Empire Before the American Revolution.* 13 vols. New York, 1948–1968.

Giraud, Marcel. *A History of French Louisiana.* Vol. 1, *The Reign of Louis XIV, 1698–1715.* Baton Rouge, La., 1974.

Innis, Harold A. *The Cod Fisheries: The History of an International Economy.* Rev. ed. Toronto, Ontario, 1954.

Knight, Franklin W. *The Caribbean: Genesis of a Fragmented Nationalism.* 2nd ed. Oxford, 1990.

Liss, Peggy K. *Atlantic Empires: The Network of Trade and Revolution, 1713–1826.* Baltimore, Md., 1983.

McNeill, John Robert. *Atlantic Empires of France and Spain: Louisbourg and Havana, 1700–1763.* Chapel Hill, N.C., 1985.

Makinson, David H. *Barbados: A Study of North American–West Indian Relations, 1739–1789.* The Hague, 1964.

Mathieu, Jacques. *Le commerce entre la Nouvelle France et les Antilles au XVIIIe siècle.* Paris, 1981.

Meinig, Donald W. *The Shaping of America: A Geographical Perspective on Five Hundred Years of History.* Vol. 1, *Atlantic America, 1492–1800.* New Haven, Conn., 1986.

Mims, Stewart L. *Colbert's West India Policy.* New Haven, Conn., 1912.

Newton, Arthur Percival. *The Colonising Activities of the English Puritans: The Last Phase of the Elizabethan Struggle with Spain.* New Haven, Conn., 1914.

———. *The European Nations in the West Indies, 1493–1688.* London, 1933.

Pares, Richard. *Merchants and Planters.* Cambridge, England, 1960.

———. *War and Trade in the West Indies, 1739–1763.* Oxford, 1936.

———. *Yankees and Creoles: The Trade Between North America and the West Indies Before the American Revolution.* London, 1956.

Parkinson, C. Northcote, ed. *The Trade Winds: A Study of British Overseas Trade During the French Wars, 1793–1815.* London, 1948.

Price, Jacob M. *Capital and Credit in British Overseas Trade: The View from the Chesapeake, 1700–1776.* Cambridge, Mass., 1980.

Rediker, Marcus. *Between the Devil and the Deep Blue Sea: Merchant Seamen, Pirates, and the Anglo-American Maritime World, 1700–1750.* Cambridge, England, 1987.

Steele, Ian K. *The English Atlantic, 1675–1740.* New York, 1986.

Surrey, N. M. Miller. *The Commerce of Louisiana During the French Régime, 1699–1763.* New York, 1916; repr. 1968.

Tebeau, Charlton W. *A History of Florida.* Miami, Fla., 1971.

Walton, Gary M., and James F. Shepherd. *The Economic Rise of Early America.* Cambridge, England, 1979.

Williams, Eric E. *Capitalism and Slavery.* London, 1964.

Michael Craton

SEE ALSO **The Colonial Merchant; Maritime Enterprises; Slavery; The Slave Trade;** and **Trade and Commerce.**

THE RUSSIAN SETTLEMENTS

INTRODUCTION

THAT NORTH AMERICA was colonized not only from the east and south by Norse, Spanish, French, English, and other nationalities but also from the west by Russians is frequently neglected, and sometimes completely ignored. This disregard results partly from the late arrival of the tsar's subjects: their first permanent settlement was not founded until the eve of the American Revolution. Further, the number of Russians in Alaska never exceeded 1,000 and averaged only 550, and their tenure was brief; the Russian-American Company, chartered in 1799 to monopolize the administration and exploitation of Russia's sole overseas territory, sold its colony to the United States only sixty-eight years later. Moreover, the primary historical sources have been inaccessible.

Nevertheless, for a century and a quarter Russian explorers did probe the uncharted expanse of the North Pacific and the unmapped interior of the North American mainland. Russian *promyshlenniks* (hunters and trappers) pursued the sea otters and fur seals of the coastal waters from the westernmost Aleutians to Baja California. Russian officials managed and inspected the half-dozen far-flung "counters" (districts) of Russian America between the Bering Strait and the Golden Gate. Russian Orthodox missionaries proselytized and instructed the native Aleuts, Eskimos, Tlingits, and Pomos. Rus-

sian shipmasters plied the Pacific trade lanes as far as Hawaii and Chile. Lastly, Russian scientists investigated the indigenous peoples, plants, animals, minerals, soils, and climates of the Pacific Slope.

Expansion to Alaska was simply an extension of the Muscovy eastward advance across Siberia that was launched in the 1580s in search of "soft gold"—sable fur. The east was the only feasible direction for Moscow's imperial ambitions once the "gathering of the Russian lands" (the traditional homelands of the Eastern Slavs) had been achieved by Ivan III (the Great) earlier in that century. The west was blocked by other powers, such as Lithuania, Poland, and Sweden, and the south by formidable steppe nomads like the Crimean Tatars and their Ottoman Turkish allies. To the north lay the Arctic Ocean, whose chilly waters offered little more than abundant fish, yet here did the local Pomoryans, the largely Russian inhabitants of the White Sea coastland, spearhead the push into Siberia. (Their descendants would loom large in the occupation of Eastern Siberia and Alaska.)

The removal of the three roadblocks of the Kazan, Astrakhan, and Western Siberia Tatar khanates by Ivan IV (the Terrible) between 1552 and 1583 cleared the way for the fur rush across Siberia. The Siberian region had a virtual monopoly on sable, then the most valuable fur on the world market, as well as a dense network of navigable waterways; the aborigines—few in number, low in technology, and disunited—offered only weak resistance. Neither the Chinese nor the Japanese seriously opposed the eastward drive, in both cases because of ethnocentrism and self-imposed isolationism. Thus the Russians soon spanned the vast Siberian habitat of the fur bearers, founding forts at river junctions, on portages, and at Native villages, exacting fur tribute from the Native peoples of one river basin and hunting and trapping it out before proceeding to the next. By 1639, less than sixty years after starting across the Urals, Russians had reached the shores of what they logically called the Eastern Ocean.

Before entering the North Pacific, however, the Russians were momentarily distracted by the Amur Country, or Amuria, the basin of the Amur River. According to aboriginal rumor, it abounded in sable, precious metals, and grain, and it also afforded a convenient water route to the Pacific from the Siberian interior. From the mid 1600s, while Siberia's peasants concentrated on the fertile wooded steppe and steppe margins of Western Siberia and Prebaikalia, its *promyshlenniks* focused their attention on Transbaikalia and Amuria—the rugged, virgin frontier territory between Lake Baikal on the west, the Pacific Ocean on the east, the Yablonovy-Stanovoy Ranges on the north, and the Greater and Lesser Khingan Ranges on the south. It was not long, however, before the new (1644) Ching (Manchu) rulers of China, alarmed at what they regarded as Russian encroachment on the northern periphery of their Manchurian homeland, counterattacked in strength. Overmatched and far from home, Russia was forced in 1689 to sign the Treaty of Nerchinsk, the first pact between China and a European state. Under the terms Russia was granted trade with China at the frontier post of Kyakhta, south of Lake Baikal, but had to withdraw completely from the Amur basin to a point behind the mountain wall that separated Siberia from the Far East and the Pacific.

DISCOVERY IN THE NORTH PACIFIC AND NORTH AMERICA

Having been expelled from the Amur basin, Siberia's mountain men turned their attention to the sole remaining area of much promise, the far northeast. At the end of the 1600s, Kamchatka, known to the Russians since mid century, was conquered for its prime sable and fox. This large peninsula (twice the size of Florida), jutting 750 miles (1,200 kilometers) into the Pacific from the Siberian mainland, was to serve as a convenient springboard for Russian expansion to Alaska, inasmuch as its southern end approached the Aleutian causeway; its Avacha Bay afforded a deep, spacious, and sheltered harbor at Petropavlovsk; and its comparatively moderate climate was conducive to agricultural settlement.

Kamchatka was certainly a better springboard than the Chukchi Peninsula, even though the latter was separated from Alaska by only the fifty-mile-wide (80-kilometer) Bering Strait rather than by the fifteen-hundred-mile-wide (2,400-kilometer) Bering Sea. However, the Chukchi Peninsula was too remote and too harsh to serve as a land bridge—indeed, the natives kept the Russians at bay until 1869. And in 1716 to 1717 the lengthy and hazardous land route through the far northeast to Kamchatka from Yakutsk in Eastern Siberia was replaced by the shorter, safer, and cheaper sea route from Okhotsk, which would remain Russia's chief Pacific port until supplanted by Petropavlovsk and then Vladivostok in the last half of the nineteenth century.

It did not take long for the rapacious *promyshlenniks* to deplete Kamchatka of its furs. New sources had to be found both for themselves and the state, which benefited from the exaction of fur tribute from the natives, as well as from the enlargement of the empire by new lands and subjects, the tithe of the private catch, and the imposition up to 25 percent of duty on fur exports and Chinese imports at Kyakhta.

Peter the Great (reigned 1689–1725) authorized probes from Okhotsk to the Shantar and Kurile islands in 1709–1710 and from Kamchatka toward the North American mainland in 1719, but realized little success. At the end of his reign Peter, anxious to see his country accepted as a modern European nation in every respect but needing to enrich the treasury to subsidize this costly modernization program, dispatched the First (1725–1729)—and inspired the Second (1733–1742)—Kamchatka expeditions under Vitus Bering and Aleksey Chirikov. Intended to, in Peter the Great's words, "find glory for the state through art and science," the expeditions in fact extended to the New World the Russian eastward drive of and exploration cum settlement and exploitation. The purpose was not to determine whether Asia and North America were connected; Peter knew they were separate, an awareness stemming from Semyon Dezhnev's eastward voyage in 1648 around what he termed "the great rocky point" (either the entire Chukchi Peninsula or just Cape Chukotka) in 1648 from the west. Dezhnev's report was buried in the archives, but his exploit was common knowledge in Eastern Siberia. Western geographers remained uninformed, however, and the tsar exploited their ignorance in order to disguise the Bering-Chirikov voyages as attempts to sail between the two continents. Furthermore, Saint Petersburg did not want to prod rival European colonial powers into beating Russia to North America's Pacific Coast, so these expeditions and their successors were declared "secret." Indeed, when Spain finally learned of the Russian thrust in 1761, it pushed northward from New Spain's San Blas to preempt tsarist designs on the coast, claiming Alta California and founding San Diego in 1769.

The Russian explorers Ivan Fyodorov and Mikhail Ghozdev initially sighted the American mainland in 1732, but because of foul weather they did not disembark. The Russians had known since the early 1710s that a "great land" lay very close to the Chukchi Peninsula, so close that Chukchi-Eskimo contacts across the Bering Strait were not unusual. Bering and Chirikov decided to search much farther south, where the climate promised to be milder and the Native population larger. Their second expedition was successful, although Bering himself died on the return voyage. They landed in July 1741 on the American mainland and on islands of the Gulf of Alaska, where they discovered aborigines and located fur bearers but saw no sign of Europeans. They returned to Kamchatka with from fifteen hundred to eighteen hundred sea otter pelts, worth as much as one hundred silver rubles apiece at Kyakhta, or two to three times their Kamchatka value. The dark, soft, glossy fur of what the Russians called "Kamchatka beaver" or "sea beaver" proved even more valuable than sable, especially in the large North China market, where it was particularly prized as elegant trim. Little wonder that a "fur rush" along the Aleutian and Kurile island chains ensued within two years of Chiri-

kov's return. This rush would take the Russians rapidly across the Aleutians to "Alakshak" (whence derived "Alaska"), their initial name for the Alaska Peninsula, along the islands and around the coast of the Gulf of Alaska (reaching Kodiak Island in 1763), and down the Northwest Coast as far as Bodega Bay (1812), a day's ride north of the Spanish *presidio* of San Francisco.

EARLY VOYAGES TO NORTH AMERICA

1743–1755

From 1743 to 1800 as much as ten million rubles worth of furs—mainly sea otter (as many as 190,000 pelts) but also fur seal—were taken by 101 Russian voyages made by at least 42 private companies to the "eastern islands." The companies commonly realized profits of from 100 percent to 200 percent and sometimes even in the 500 percent to 700 percent range. There was virtually no state participation in these ventures, since it was cheaper for the government to encourage them and thereby gain tribute, taxes and duties, and imperial territory.

The voyages were organized and financed by small, short-lived trading companies formed by merchant families from the towns of northern and central European Russia and Siberia. These "principal partners" held shares in a company, which was named after the largest shareholder who was considered the company's head. The voyages themselves were manned by Kamchadals, natives of the Kamchatka Peninsula who were proficient and economical hunters and composed up to a half of the crews, along with Russian peasants and townsmen from Eastern Siberia. Most of the latter originally came from Pomorye on the White Sea, where there were well-developed traditions of fishing and sea-mammal hunting, trading, and coastal sailing—all of which lent themselves to the maritime fur trade of the far North Pacific rim. The crewmen were paid either wages or half-shares. They were inadequately trained, equipped (no compasses or charts), supplied, and housed. They were also harshly treated, and their working life was hard and short. Generally from a quarter to a third of the crews perished from disease, accident, or warfare; shipwrecks were common, with most vessels making no more than three voyages before being sunk, spent, or sold.

From 1743 through 1755 there were twenty-two trading and hunting voyages; most of these lasted one or two years, whereupon the companies were disbanded. They returned pelts worth an average of fifty thousand rubles per voyage. The majority of these voyages did not go far beyond Kamchatka, tapping primarily the Commander and Near Aleutian Islands. The flimsy ships were only forty-two to fifty-six feet (13 to 17 meters) in length, and clumsy, with high sides, short and heavy masts, narrow sails, and long rudders. Crudely built of local green timber, usually in Kamchatka, they were called *shitiks* (literally, "sewn ones") because their boards were secured with whalebone, rawhide thongs, or willow osiers.

The forty to fifty crewmen did not take many provisions; rather, they wintered in the Commanders, where they killed North Pacific (Steller's) sea cows (discovered by Bering and Chirikov) for food and sea lions and hair seals for hide, as well as sea otters for furs. During the summer they sailed to the Near Aleutians, where they would land on a sandy beach and erect *barabaras* (makeshift semisubterranean shelters). There they took Aleut islanders hostage in order to make them hunt sea otters and trap foxes in small parties under Russian *peredovshchiks* (foremen). Half of the crewmen hunted in *baidaras* (large, open boats made from the hides of sea cows and holding from six to eight people—the equivalent of Eskimo umiaks). The rest guarded the camps and ships and collected and prepared food. But the Russians never matched the boating and hunting skills of the Aleuts with their *baidarkas* (kayaks) and harpoons. The Aleuts were so essential to the success of Russian occupation that they were made virtual serfs. After gathering a full cargo, a ship returned to Kamchatka or Okhotsk, where the furs were inspected and taxed before being divided among the shareholders in kind or cash. Half went to the investors and half to the crewmen. The latter sold them to local wholesalers, who in turn marketed them at Kyakhta for at least twice what they had paid.

1756–1780

During the next period, fifty-six voyages were made, mostly to the rest of the Aleutians, the Alaska Peninsula, the Shumagins, and Kodiak Island, as well as the Kuriles. Because the trips probed farther, they lasted longer—from three to four years or more. These ventures returned cargo worth an average of 71,000 rubles per voyage—more both in total and on average than earlier, stemming from a number of improvements. The companies were more stable and the *promyshlenniks* more numerous; by the late 1770s, the members of Captain James Cook's third voyage reported as many as five hundred Russians and Kamchadals on the Aleutians, including eighty at Captain's Harbor (Illiuliuk) on Unalaska Island, the first permanent settlement. Participation in the fur traffic had no doubt been stimulated by the yielding of the government monopoly on the Kyakhta trade to private merchants in 1762, as well as by the abolition in 1773 of the "tenth" tax on fur imports to Siberia. Apprentice navigators had also made their appearance. And, in order to sail farther, the ships had to be better built as well as better manned. In 1757 *shitiks* began to be replaced by *gvozdenniks* ("nailed ones"), whose ribs were secured with pegs or nails. After the late 1760s, most of them were constructed and outfitted at Okhotsk rather than in Kamchatka because by 1768 the Stellar's sea cow, a key source of food for the voyagers, was extinct. As a result the ventures became more dependent upon grain, that—like other requirements such as nails, anchors, and rigging—was cheaper at Okhotsk, it being only half as far as Kamchatka from the supply point of Yakutsk. Moreover, a smallpox epidemic reduced Kamchatka's Native population from about 10,000 in 1768 to 3,800 in 1769, and two-thirds of the remainder were killed by yellow fever in 1799. As a result, more shipbuilders and seafarers had to be recruited from Okhotsk. Finally, on the Aleutian Islands themselves the *promyshlenniks* substituted *yurts* (driftwood huts) for their *barabaras* and even founded a permanent settlement.

CONSOLIDATION: 1780–1800

The receding range and declining population of the unprolific sea otter necessitated remoter voyages and longer sojourns. This, in turn, meant higher costs and greater risks. Sea otters had already disappeared from the Kamchatka coast by 1750 and from the Kurile Islands by 1780; by 1789 they were rarely seen around the Aleutians. That left the inshore waters of the Alaska Peninsula, the Gulf of Alaska, and the Northwest Coast as far south as Baja California as the only remaining sources of sea otters, and the Russians advanced quickly to tap them. They occupied Kodiak Island by the middle 1780s, Cook Inlet by the late 1780s, and Prince William Sound by the early 1790s. Ten years later they settled the Alexander Archipelago. There New Archangel, or Sitka, was founded in 1799; in 1808 it succeeded Saint Paul's Harbor on Kodiak as the colonial capital. By then, however, the Russians were encountering imperial competitors in the form of Spanish navy frigates (from 1774) checking tsarist penetration of the Spanish colonial northern frontier and hoping (like Captain Cook) to find a Northwest Passage. More important, the Russians were also meeting American and British coasters (from 1785) that had been alerted to the sea otter wealth of Vancouver Island's Nootka Sound by the published accounts of Cook's last voyage. Boston shipowners in particular successfully challenged the Russian *promyshlenniks* on the coast, trading better goods, such as iron, copper, firearms, textiles, provisions, and liquor, at lower prices to the Northwest Coast Indians for the "black skins" of sea otters. They then exchanged these at Canton for teas, fabrics, and porcelain for their European and North American customers. Russia's eastward drive was thus finally halted in the international arena of the Alaska panhandle, where Tlingit, Tsimshian, and Haida aborigines and Russian, British, and American interlopers jockeyed for commercial and political supremacy.

During this period the Russians undertook twenty-two fur trading voyages that went farther—to the Gulf of Alaska and even the Alexander Archipelago, as well as the Fur Seal (Pribilof) Islands—and took longer (from six to ten years) than those of the previous period. They returned furs worth as much as three million rubles, a smaller total than in the earlier years. But the average of 136,000 rubles per voyage was twice the previous average because there were only half as many voyages and the skins were scarcer and hence dearer. Fewer merchants could afford to ply the trade because ships had to sail farther and stay longer to fill their holds, requiring larger

investments of capital and longer waits for returns. In the 1780s half as many merchants as during the 1770s outfitted three-quarters as many ventures, which returned one-seventh more peltry. Only five merchant partnerships remained by the beginning of the 1780s, and only three by 1795: those of Grigory Shelikhov, Pavel Lebedev-Lastochkin, and the brothers F. and M. Kiselev. In 1797 there were 650 *promyshlenniks* in Russian America.

The Aleuts suffered even more from the longer voyages than did the *promyshlenniks* because they had to be deployed farther from home and stay away longer, thus their provisioning and procreating roles were even more disrupted. Half of all Aleut males between the ages of eighteen and fifty were obliged to hunt sea otters for their Russian overlords, who took hostages to ensure compliance. This reality, plus the toll taken by warfare (with the Russians and other Native groups, as well as among themselves), by new diseases like smallpox and syphilis, and by new habits (smoking, drinking), devastated the Aleut population that probably had totaled from eight thousand to ten thousand when the Russians arrived in the mid 1740s; fifty years later it had been reduced by two-thirds. So the Russians turned increasingly to the Kodiak Eskimos (Konyagas or Kodiaks), whose skill with kayaks and harpoons was second only to that of the Aleuts—and whose demographic fate was therefore to be the same.

This period was dominated by Grigory Shelikhov, the "Russian Columbus," who for most of the 1780–1800 period operated in partnership with Ivan and Mikhail Golikov. He and his partners accounted for half of the value of the period's entire take of furs. His success is explained by several factors. He assiduously cultivated influential officials, including governors-general of Siberia and royal favorites. (He even had his daughter marry future imperial chamberlain Nikolay Rezanov.) He realized that in order to continue the fur trade, voyages had to be financed not by the usual temporary partnerships lasting for only one voyage but rather by permanent companies. Such companies would raise capital by selling shares to investors, with the capital divided into a working fund, a rewards fund, and a reserve fund. He knew that longer and costlier voyages necessitated more stability, so he proposed establishing permanent settlements, developing farming and mining, regulating hunting and trapping, hiring and training natives, and making annual voyages between Siberia and Alaska to bring supplies and return furs. He insisted upon traveling himself to Okhotsk every year to oversee the unloading and embarking of company vessels, and he persistently and successfully petitioned the Crown for state assistance in the form of missionaries, artisans, and peasants.

Shelikhov also began to shift the base of his operations to the American mainland from the islands, which he felt were more vulnerable to foreign rivals. Shelikhov intended to found the capital of his colonial empire, Slavorossiya (literally, "Glory of Russia") on the mainland. It was, in fact, founded on Yakutat Bay in 1795, the year of his death, but its intended role was to be filled in the next phase by New Archangel (present-day Sitka), which was better situated with respect to the sea otter resource and international shipping. Finally, Shelikhov tried before his death to secure a commercial monopoly on the entire Russian maritime fur trade in the belief that such an organization could compete more vigorously against foreign rivals. However, the Enlightenment Empress Catherine II (the Great; reigned 1762–1796) believed in free competition; she refused, saying that "this request would create a monopoly and exclusive trade, which are against my principles." (By contrast, Peter the Great had urged Russian merchants to organize "East India–type companies.") But her son and successor, Paul I (reigned 1796–1801), who had both hated and feared his mother, valued different if inconsistent policies. The increasingly violent competition among the Russian companies for ever scarcer resources, as well as prospective international entanglements, alarmed Saint Petersburg. In 1799 the few remaining concerns amalgamated as the Russian-American Company, whose twenty-year charter gave it a monopoly on the administration and exploitation of Alaska under the watchful eye of the government. Its shareholders included the tsar himself and other high officials.

The company's formation may have been a natural outgrowth of the practices of the Russian merchants engaged in the maritime fur trade of the North Pacific and the legacy of the most successful of their number, Grigory Sheli-

khov. Alternatively, it may have represented a deliberate plan to create order out of the chaos arising from merchant rivalry in Irkutsk following Shelikhov's death in 1795 and to widen rather than limit merchant participation in the North Pacific fur trade. Or it could have been an attempt by the government to create a powerful, state-controlled, monopolistic company that would strengthen and expand Russian tenure in the North Pacific and counter foreign encroachment.

Whatever the motive, the restructuring reduced the number of Russians in Alaska to 225, including fewer than two hundred *promyshlenniks*. Most were state (non-serf) peasants and townsmen from Pomorye and Siberia who were scattered among a dozen and a half settlements, ranging from *zimovyes* (winter camps) and *odinochkas* (one-man outposts) to redoubts and *ostrogs* (forts). The latter were commonly situated atop rocky promontories (*kekury*) at the mouths of rivers or heads of bays in accordance with the requirements of maritime hunting and defense against native or foreign attack.

THE RUSSIAN-AMERICAN COMPANY

The First Charter, 1799–1819

Just as the previous period might be termed the Shelikhov phase, so this period might be called the Baranov phase, after Alexander Baranov, Shelikhov's lieutenant and the Russian-American Company's first colonial governor. He was the last of the old-style, rough-hewn, self-made, freewheeling merchant managers—"a rough, rugged, hospitable, hard-drinking old Russian; somewhat of a soldier; somewhat of a trader; above all, a boon companion of the old roystering school, with a strong cross of the bear," in the words of Washington Irving.

His regime was highlighted by expansion as far southward as Alta (Upper) California and even the Sandwich (Hawaiian) Islands, despite stronger Native opposition and keener foreign competition. The first major step in this direction was the founding of New Archangel on Baranof Island in the "straits" (tidal channels) of the Alexander Archipelago in an effort to counter the trade between the "Boston men" (Yankee shipmasters) and the unruly Tlingits. The site offered abundant sea otters and plentiful timber, along with favorable tides. In 1810 the town contained 621 residents, including 411 Konyagas, 199 Russians, and 11 Tlingit hostages, making it the largest settlement on the Pacific Coast north of the Mexican isthmus.

The second step was the establishment of Russian California. In 1812 Fort Ross was founded just north of San Francisco Bay. Eventually Port Rumyantsev on Bodega Bay, several ranchos (farms) along the coast, and an artel (hunting party) on the Farallon Islands off the Golden Gate were also established on the coast of what Francis Drake had dubbed New Albion. This exclave, which was intended to serve as a farming and hunting base, was to become the second most important "counter" (higher-ranking colonial subdivision) in Russian America. Leading economic activities were the hunting of sea otters, fur seals, and sea lions (the California subspecies of these three were nearly untapped), grain growing, stock raising, truck gardening, shipbuilding, brickmaking, and tanning, as well as trading with the neighboring Californios (Hispanics).

From 1815 to 1817 the Russians also tried to entrench themselves on Kauai Island, but were unsuccessful. The tragicomic attempt was made unilaterally by an egotistical and ambitious employee, Dr. Georg Schaffer, without company support or imperial consent, and more important, without the approval of the Hawaiian archipelago's hegemonic and powerful monarch, Kamehameha I.

Russian America's population was becoming more numerous, more widespread, and more diverse. In 1817, besides its headquarters in Saint Petersburg and its branches and agencies in ten cities in the motherland (primarily Siberia), the Russian-American Company had sixteen posts in its colony with between 450 and 500 *promyshlenniks* and 26 sailors. Two years later the colony numbered 8,385 natives (Aleuts, Kodiaks, and Indians), 391 Russians (378 males and 13 females), and 244 Creoles (mixed bloods). Most of the Russians were Siberian lower- to middle-class townsmen and peasants; peasant colonization, however, was hampered by the bonds of serfdom (not abolished until 1861), and the thousands of runaway serfs could find better farm-

land in the steppes of New Russia (the southernmost Ukraine), the North Caucasus, and Western Siberia than in faraway Alaska. Little wonder that the problem of supply, and especially of food, bedeviled Russian America.

The Creoles (an official term used by the Russians for offspring of Russian fathers and Native mothers) were both a racial and a social class. Like the Métis of New France and the mestizos of New Spain, they were the offspring of Native mothers and alien fathers. The Creoles were members of the burgher class of their fathers and were therefore exempted from taxation and from state and military service; like the Aleuts and Tlingits, they were allowed to use their own language in church and school. In view of the chronic shortage of Russian personnel, the Creoles, some of whom were very skilled, formed a vital contingent of the company's labor force. They numbered as many as nineteen hundred by the early 1860s.

Most company employees, whatever their ethnicity or class, labored hard and long (fifteen-year terms for Creoles from 1841), usually outdoors in a dank climate, on a spare diet consisting mostly of fish, and for meager pay. Both morbidity and mortality rates were high, and accidents were frequent; for example, scurvy was commonplace, and of the twenty-eight ships purchased or constructed by the company from 1799 through 1820, sixteen were wrecked and five were in disuse. The colonial capital of "barbarous, desolate Sitka," where according to one official, it was "always autumn" and "never rainless," amounted to little more than a muddy hodgepodge of wooden buildings overrun by rats, so much so that it was dubbed Ratville by the locals. The most common maladies were rheumatism and catarrh, arising from the variable weather and the heavy drinking.

This period was also characterized by much more of both Native opposition and foreign competition. The Koloshes, as the Russians called the Tlingits, stoutly resisted encroachment by the Russians, who made the double mistake of occupying their village sites and desecrating their mortuary poles. The Tlingits were more numerous and more cohesive than the Aleuts, thanks to their bountiful environment (rich in fish and timber, in particular) and tightly-knit clan system (which united different clans against a common enemy). The Tlingits were also much more aggressive than the Aleuts, especially after the Tlingit began from the mid 1790s to obtain rum and guns, including even cannon, from American and British coasters in exchange for sea otter skins. The formidable Tlingits even captured and destroyed New Archangel in 1802 (not reestablished until two years later with the help of a Russian naval ship, the *Neva*, which with the flagship *Nadezhda* accomplished the first Russian circumnavigation in the years 1803–1806), and as late as 1855 the Tlingits besieged the colonial capital.

Yankee shipmasters outcompeted the Russians, offering better goods and higher prices for Tlingit, Tsimshian, and Haida furs. Governor Baranov estimated that in the decade of the 1790s alone American and British traders had deprived the Russians of at least a hundred thousand sea otter skins worth four and one-half million rubles gross and three million rubles net. But the "Bostonians" also brought trade goods, primarily provisions, to the Russians, who came to rely upon Yankee supplies, for which they bartered mostly fur seal skins for the China market. The Russians and Americans also collaborated in joint hunting ventures on the coast of the Californias between 1803 and 1813, using the company's Aleuts and Konyagas with kayaks and the Americans' ships and evenly dividing the sea otter catch.

The Second Charter, 1819–1840

This penultimate, or halcyon, phase was delimited by the second twenty-year charter of the Russian-American Company. It was distinguished by corporate reorganization, a reorientation of settlement and exploitation northward and landward, less native hostility, and more regulated foreign competition. The colony had been inspected and found wanting in 1818 by the Russian navy Captain Vasily Golovnin, who was particularly critical of Baranov's style of management. The old trader was unceremoniously replaced that year; thenceforth every governor would be a naval officer rather than a merchant, and therefore more dutiful and more cautious. The company was becoming less and less a business venture and more and more a politicized, militarized, and bureaucratized agency of the

government. (Already in 1811 the Head Office had been put under the control of the Ministry of Internal Affairs.) Now, too, employees were paid salaries rather than shares; this provided more income security but less work incentive. But their overall welfare improved with the building of infirmaries, schools, and churches and with the posting of doctors, teachers, and clerics, including, most notably, Father Ivan Veniaminov, whose relatively enlightened missionization of the Aleuts and Tlingits, as well as his scholarly investigation of their cultures, was to earn him the Russian Orthodox Church's highest rank of Metropolitan of Moscow and Kolomna and, posthumously, sainthood.

The shift of exploitation and settlement to the north and the interior was prompted by the depletion of sea otters, the company's mainstay, which by the late 1810s had become scarce even at the southeasternmost extreme of their range along the shores of the Californias. International rivalry for sea otters was more intense on the Northwest Coast than anywhere else, so much so that this competition lasted barely a quarter of a century before peaking prior to the War of 1812. Thereafter, just as American coasters perforce took more and more land furs in lieu of sea otter skins, so too did the Russians turn inland for more and more beaver, land otter, fox, lynx, and other land pelts. These new resources emerged from a number of probes along the Bering Sea coast and into the Nushagak, Kuskokwim, and Kvikpak (Yukon) Rivers, culminating in Lieutenant Lavrenty Zagoskin's eighteen-month, three-thousand-mile (4,800-kilometer) overland expedition into the Alaskan interior in 1842–1844; new posts were founded at the mouths and on the lower courses of these waterways. The company even considered shifting its colonial capital northwestward to either the Kenai Peninsula or Kodiak Island.

This reorientation entailed more employees as well as more settlements. By 1833 Russian America comprised seven counters and districts, with 9,120 natives, 991 Creoles, and 627 Russians. The population now included more trained sailors and some Finns (Finland had become a grand duchy of the Russian Empire in 1809), who usually provided skilled labor. New Archangel, the governor's seat and the colony's entrepôt, was the dominant city, with 789 residents (including 309 Russians) in 1825. With a sheltered and ice-free harbor, it was the hub of colonial shipping, as well as a fishing and lumbering center. Kodiak Island boasted a more diversified economy of stock raising, truck gardening, brickmaking, fishing, and trapping; it was the colony's principal source of "colonial products" such as *yukola* (dried fish), *sarana* (the dried bulb of the yellow lily), *burduk* (sour rye flour soup), cowberries, and blubber. Saint Paul's Harbor was the largest settlement on the island, with forty-one Creoles, thirty-six Aleuts, and twenty-six Russians in 1825. The Pribilof Islands in the Bering Sea produced most of Russian America's fur seal skins (as many as three million fur seals were killed on the islands from 1786 through 1827), sea lion rawhides, *kamleikas* (waterproof capes made from sea mammal intestines), whalebone, whale oil, whale blubber, salted fur seal, and sea lion meat. (These last three items were staples of the company's Aleut and Creole employees.)

Russian California was the colony's materially most comfortable (thanks to warmer weather and better food) and economically most diversified subdivision, with activities including sea otter, fur seal, and sea lion hunting, grain growing, stock raising, truck gardening, shipbuilding, lumbering, brickmaking, tanning, and trading. Several new farms were established in the 1830s in an unsuccessful attempt to boost agricultural output. In 1830 the counter contained 112 Aleuts (in fact, probably Konyagas), 53 Creoles, and 37 Russians, plus an unspecified number of seasonal Pomo Indian laborers.

This period saw a stabilization of Russian America's foreign economic relations. New Spain gained its independence (as Mexico) in 1821 and opened its Californian ports to foreign trade; thereafter Russian-American Company ships embarked grain and beef annually at San Francisco and Monterey, despite periodic crop failures (caused by drought) and even the secularization of the productive Californian missions in the mid 1830s, whereupon the Russians turned to the private ranchos. Relations with the United States and Great Britain were formalized and regulated by treaties in the mid 1820s. On 15 September 1821 Tsar Alexander I, in an attempt to protect the sparsely settled, undersupplied, and weakly defended colony against American

poaching and smuggling, had unilaterally decreed that no foreign ships were to approach within one hundred miles (160 kilometers) of the coast north of 51° north latitude. But Russia soon had to relent in the face of superior American and British power on the faraway Northwest Coast and the continuing need for American supplies in the colony. By the terms of conventions in 1824 and 1825, respectively, American and British vessels were readmitted for ten years to the shores and ports of Russian America. Neither convention was renewed because by the mid 1830s the Americans were abandoning the coast trade in the wake of the depletion of fur bearers and the disaffection of fur buyers (who were switching from felt hats to silk hats) and were instead pursuing more lucrative prospects, like California's hide and tallow trade and North Pacific whaling.

The Russian-British convention was eventually replaced by a very different form of agreement. After its absorption of the rival North West Company in 1821 and under the astute management of Governor George Simpson, the Hudson's Bay Company had reentered the coast trade in earnest in the mid 1820s in order to block the increasing diversion of land furs from its interior posts to Russian and American ships on the coast. British trading posts were founded on the coast (Fort Vancouver in 1825, Fort Langley in 1827, Fort Simpson in 1831, and Forts McLoughlin and Nisqually in 1833), and British trading vessels were deployed in coastal waters. Colluding to oust their efficient American rivals from the coast trade, the British and Russian monopolies in 1839 signed a ten-year pact whereby the latter agreed to lease (for an annual payment in land otters) the mainland panhandle of Alaska to the former, which in turn agreed to deliver manufactures from England (by means of the annual supply ship from London) and provisions from its Columbia Department farms (at Forts Vancouver, Nisqually, and Langley) to New Archangel at moderate prices. This accord finally secured a reliable source of supplies for the Russian-American Company and enabled it to sell Russian California (which had been exhausted of sea otters and fur seals and had proved unfavorable for agriculture) to John Sutter in 1841, and to end trade with Mexican California; the agreement also allowed the company to stop buying supplies from American Nor'west-men who, deprived of the profitable Sitka market, completely withdrew from the coastal trade, leaving it more or less entirely in the hands of the Hudson's Bay Company, which now had an outlet for its surplus Columbian "country produce."

The higher quality and the lower prices of the British supplies helped to slow but not stop Russian America's ebbing profitability. Between 1824 and 1838, revenues rose by 13 percent but expenses grew by 91 percent, as a result of declining fur returns (especially from sea otter skins, the most valuable of all) and increasing outlays for the building of inland posts, the raising of employees' salaries, and the boosting of social services. Yet another cost was the smallpox epidemic of 1835–1838, which killed one-third of Kodiak's Eskimos (who had replaced the dwindling Aleuts as the company's sea otter hunters) and one-third, too, of the northern coast's Tlingits, Haidas, and Tsimshians (who sold not only furs but also potatoes, venison, halibut, wildfowl, berries, and eggs to the Russians). The disease broke the back of Tlingit resistance to Russian acculturation. Older (and hence more traditional and more influential) Indians succumbed disproportionately and in the process lost faith in their shamans, who failed to cure them, while becoming convinced of the superiority of the Russians, who successfully vaccinated themselves. Thereafter the Tlingits were less hostile and more tractable, accepting conversion more readily and even employment as stevedores and sailors.

The Final Phase, 1841–1867

This last, or waning, phase of Russian occupation was marked by retrenchment, diversification, deterioration, and ultimately abandonment. The Russian-American Company's charter was renewed in 1841 and in effect until 1867. The company was subordinated even further to the government; in 1844 the Board of Directors was enlarged to five members, only one of whom was a merchant, and after 1856 none of the directors was a member of the merchant class. In the colony employees wore uniforms; also, the company's own flag was displayed and its own currency (scrip) circulated. Despite some able governors like Ferdinand von Wrangell (1830–

1835), Adolph Etholen (1840–1845), and Mikhail Tebenkov (1845–1850), years of monopolistic insulation and bureaucratic management had made the company a cautious, overstaffed, and inefficient concern.

Retrenchment and diversification were necessitated by the decline of the fur trade. Although the company had undertaken some conservation measures, fur bearers—especially sea otters and fur seals—had been hunted to the verge of extinction. And fur markets had shrunk in response both to changing fashion in the West and to internal discord in China. Russian America exported only 778,440 sea otter, fur seal, beaver, land otter, fox, marten, and lynx pelts (the principal furs) in 1842–1862, compared with 1,480,608 pelts in 1797–1821—a decrease of nearly 40 percent on an annual basis. Although this contraction helped to lead to the relinquishing of Russian California and the Alaska panhandle, it was offset by expansion on the Asiatic side of the North Pacific, where the company reopened its Kamchatka agency in the mid 1840s and helped the state to explore and develop the Amur River basin from 1851 (and to administer Sakhalin from 1853)—all foreshadowing Russia's complete withdrawal from the American side in 1867 and its concentration on the Far East.

The company soon found alternatives to furs as sources of profit. In 1848 it began taking advantage of the collapse of Manchu China's resistance to foreign commercial penetration by buying tea directly from Shanghai, where it was cheaper than at Kyakhta, and shipping it more cheaply by sea than by land to Russia, where it was a popular beverage; as early as 1843 the company had been profiting more from tea sales than from fur sales. By means of periodic contracts with the American-Russian Commercial Company of San Francisco, the Russian-American Company began in 1852 to sell as much as five thousand tons of Kodiak and Sitka lake ice annually in the booming California market (in competition with Boston merchants, who had to ship all the way around Cape Horn). In addition, fish and timber were marketed in California and Hawaii. Coal mining at English Bay on the Kenai Peninsula and whaling in the North Pacific, mainly in the Okhotsk Sea, were also attempted, but much less successfully.

This diversification was reflected in colonial settlement. By 1862 Russian America's population totaled 10,156 (7,681 natives, 1,892 Creoles, 577 Russians, and 6 foreigners) in six subdivisions. Since 1833 the number of Russians had slightly declined but the number of Creoles had doubled, reflecting the increasing number of mixed liaisons and marriages and the company's growing reliance on Creole labor. Most of the Russians were still Siberian commoners who, in one governor's opinion, were the "best men" in the colony in spite of their "unruly" character. New Archangel, now usually called Sitka, remained the colonial metropolis, although the Hudson's Bay Company's Governor Simpson described it in 1841 as "preeminently the most wretched and most dirty" place he had ever seen. That year it contained 983 residents (including 493 Creoles and 401 Russians) occupying sixty-seven dwellings. In 1860 a naval officer counted more than one hundred wooden houses, three churches (one for Orthodox Russians, one for Lutheran Finns, and one for Christianized Tlingits), two schools (one for boys and one for girls), two mills (a sawmill and a shingle mill), and two warehouses. Another official found the capital well fortified by batteries and palisades. It was being defended against the Tlingits, not foreigners, and in 1855 the former attacked New Archangel (despite the presence of a Siberian battalion of one hundred men during the Crimean War of 1853–1855) and destroyed a nearby redoubt.

The company's new ventures, plus higher prices for scarcer furs (and an increase in the company's markup on colonial imports to 77 percent), helped raise yearly dividends on company shares from fifteen rubles in the mid 1840s to twenty rubles in the late 1850s. These returns, however, were still well below the dividends of thirty-three to thirty-four rubles of the late 1820s and early 1830s (and far below that of forty-three to forty-four rubles in 1802–1803). By the early 1860s the diversification program was faltering. The Crimean War, meanwhile, had revealed the indefensibility of the remote colony in the face of superior British sea power (a point stressed by Tsar Alexander II's brother, the Grand Duke Constantine, who headed the naval ministry, which was supposed to protect the colony). The burgeoning United States seemed destined to annex all of North America, including Russian America, especially in the event of a gold rush; an American Alaska would serve as a buffer between Russian Siberia and British North America and, moreover, secure American friendship. Russia wanted the United States as an ally to help Russia attain its foreign policy goals (such as access to the straits between the Black and Mediterannean Seas), particularly vis-à-vis Great Britain. Finally, the Amur Country, annexed by Russia in the 1850s in the wake of Manchu China's decline, seemed to offer greater agricultural and commercial promise much closer to the motherland. These considerations, nurtured by the climate of reform in Russia following its ignominious defeat in the Crimea, led to the sale of Russia's sole overseas colony to the United States for $7.2 million in 1867—the same year that saw the birth of the Dominion of Canada and the death of the notion of the United States' being manifestly destined to possess all of North America.

BIBLIOGRAPHY

Andreev, A. I., ed. *Russian Discoveries in the Pacific and in North America in the Eighteenth and Nineteenth Centuries,* translated by Carl Ginsburg. Ann Arbor, Mich., 1952.

Craig, Robert D., ed. *Russian America: The Forgotten Frontier,* special issue of *Pacifica* 2, no. 2 (1990):1–188.

Dmytryshyn, Basil, E.A.P. Crownhart-Vaughan, and Thomas Vaughan, eds. and trans. *The Russian-American Colonies, 1798–1867: A Documentary Record.* Portland, Oreg., 1989.

———, eds., *Russian Penetration of the North Pacific Ocean, 1700–1799: A Documentary Record.* Portland, Oreg., 1988.

Fedorova, Svetlana G. *The Russian Population in Alaska and California, Late 18th Century–1867.* Edited and translated by Richard A. Pierce and Alton S. Donnelly. Kingston, Ontario, 1973.

Fisher, Raymond H. *Bering's Voyages: Whither and Why.* Seattle, 1977.

Gibson, James R. *Feeding the Russian Fur Trade: Provisionment of the Okhotsk Seaboard and the Kamchatka Peninsula, 1639–1856.* Madison, Wis., 1969.

———. *Imperial Russia in Frontier America: The Chang-*

ing Geography of Supply of Russian America, 1784–1867. New York, 1976.

———. *Otter Skins, Boston Ships, and China Goods: The Maritime Fur Trade of the Northwest Coast, 1785–1841.* Montreal, 1992.

Golovin, Pavel Nikolaevitch. *The End of Russian America: Captain P. N. Golovin's Last Report, 1862.* Edited and translated by Basil Dmytryshyn and E.A.P. Crownhart-Vaughan. Portland, Oreg., 1979.

Khlebnikov, K. T. *Baranov, Chief Manager of the Russian Colonies in America.* Edited by Richard A. Pierce, translated by Colin Bearne. Kingston, Ontario, 1973.

———. *Colonial Russian America: Kyrill T. Khlebnikov's Reports, 1817–1832.* Translated by Basil Dmytryshyn and E.A.P. Crownhart-Vaughan. Portland, Oreg., 1976.

Makarova, Raisa V. *Russians on the Pacific, 1743–1799.* Edited and translated by Richard A. Pierce and Alton S. Donnelly. Kingston, Ontario, 1975.

Okun, S. B. *The Russian-American Company.* Edited by B. D. Grekov, translated by Carl Ginsburg. Cambridge, Mass., 1951.

Pierce, Richard A., ed. *Russia in North America: Proceedings of the 2nd International Conference on Russian America—Sitka, Alaska, August 19–22, 1987.* Kingston, Ontario, 1990.

Smith, Barbara Sweetland, and Redmond J. Barnett, eds. *Russian America: The Forgotten Frontier.* Tacoma, Wash., 1990.

Starr, S. Frederick, ed. *Russia's American Colony.* Durham, N.C., 1987.

Tikhmenev, P. A. *A History of the Russian-American Company.* Edited and translated by Richard A. Pierce and Alton S. Donnelly. 2 vols. Seattle, 1978.

Zagoskin, Lavrentii Alekseyevich. *Lieutenant Zagoskin's Travels in Russian America, 1842–1844: The First Ethnographic and Geographic Investigations in the Yukon and Kuskokwim Valleys of Alaska.* Edited by Henry Michael. Translated by Penelope Rainey. Toronto, Ontario, 1967.

James R. Gibson

SEE ALSO **The Fur Trade; Settlements in the Spanish Borderlands, Southwest;** and the map preceding **The French Settlements.**

IV

GOVERNMENT AND LAW

COLONIAL POLITICAL THOUGHT

INTRODUCTION

THE EUROPEAN COLONIZATION of America occurred during an era of extraordinary intellectual ferment in western Europe. Stimulated by the profound changes brought about by the rediscovery of the wisdom of antiquity, the expansion of trade and learning, the Reformation, the emergence of new nation-states, the development of print culture, the encounter with previously unknown places and peoples in America, the intensification of contact with Africans and Asians, and the extension of European cultures across the oceans European thinkers, from the Renaissance through the Enlightenment, produced a rich literature that subjected all areas of human endeavor, from the spiritual to the most mundane, to a thorough and often rigorous analysis. Indeed in the realm of political thought, the three hundred years from 1500 to 1800 were probably the most productive and the richest in modern history.

Political thought, one of two key concepts in the title of this essay, connotes analysis relating to the complex problems of the origins, purpose, organization, and functioning of governments and other political units. In Europe the debate over these and a variety of subordinate matters—a conflict between absolutists and constitutionalists, between Protestants and Catholics, between those who located the origins of government in the divine will and those who saw it as arising out of more mundane human needs, between those who emphasized order and stability and those who stressed the protection of individual liberties—was conducted within a broad intellectual forum that flowed across national boundaries. Themselves all heirs of the same classical and Christian traditions of political thought, scholars from all over Europe—Italy, Spain, France, England, the Netherlands, and the German states—contributed to a burgeoning corpus of political writing and participated in the general expansion of political consciousness that those writings represented.

Yet notwithstanding their involvement in this international enterprise, writers from every major national political culture in western Europe tended to produce a distinctive body of political thought. Their writings invariably reflected the particular political situations in which they found themselves and the specific temporal or situational concerns that engaged the attention of the polities to which they were attached at the time they wrote. At one and the same time, thus, they contributed to the unfolding of Western political thought in general and to the emergence of a peculiar national—Spanish or French or English—tradition of political ideas.

Two implications of the term colonial, the second major concept in the title of this article, also need to be spelled out. First, colonial refers to those populations that lived within the confines of the European-dominated political entities called colonies. It does not refer to those aboriginal societies that lived adjacent to or in association with or opposition to those entities. Second, it implies a specific kind of dependent relationship on the part of those entities with an independent metropolitan political society on the eastern side of the Atlantic, a dependence that had a cultural as well as a political and economic dimension to it. As extensions in many highly significant ways of the metropolitan cultures to which they were attached, all colonies displayed a strong tendency to exhibit and operate within patterns of political thought that were heavily derivative from their particular metropolis.

Its derivative character notwithstanding, colonial political thought was highly selective. Rather than adopting metropolitan political ideas wholesale, colonial political thinkers tended to pick and choose from among the available stock of political concepts those that seemed most relevant to the much simpler societies and the specific situations in which they found themselves.

The development of colonial polities in America also raised important new theoretical issues. Specifically, those settlements presented both colonists and European colonial administrators with two sets of issues for which there were no clear precedents in the immediate experience of older, established, independent polities of the sort that conventionally concerned European political writers. First was the relationship of colonies to the older polities under whose authority they had been founded. Second were the grounds on which European states and their colonists might claim title to American territory or jurisdiction over the aboriginal peoples who lived there.

If colonial political thought had concerns peculiar to itself, it was often also considerably less elaborate and much less well advanced than in Europe. The private learning, individual leisure, institutional matrices, and arenas of public discourse that encouraged political thought in the complex societies of Europe simply did not exist in many of the simple and underpopulated polities established in America. Throughout colonial North America—in Spanish Florida and New Mexico; in French Acadia (Nova Scotia), Canada, and Louisiana; in Dutch New Nether-

land (New York); and in most of the English colonies during their earliest years of settlement before they had achieved much sociocultural development—political thought tended to remain implicit and for the most part was not expressed formally but rather through the underlying imperatives and values that governed political relations and practices. In general the larger and more complex a colonial society, the more elaborate and the more explicit were its expressions of political thought.

Yet not even the rapidly growing British colonies, the places in colonial North America where during the eighteenth century traditions of political thought were most fully evolved and most often in contest, produced any great political thinkers or any major political treatises during the colonial era. Rather, even in those colonies political thought was manifest very largely in a scattered if increasingly rich body of occasional literature, including speeches, pamphlets, newspaper essays, histories, legal briefs, and sermons. This literature demonstrated both the colonists' continuing indebtedness to the Western and specifically British political traditions that were such an important part of their inheritance and their preoccupation with the particular local problems and issues which that literature sought to confront.

The failure of the colonies to produce any major political thinkers and the undeveloped and implicit nature of colonial political thought in all areas of colonial North America, except for seventeenth-century New England and the eighteenth-century British colonies, explains the neglect of this subject by historians. They have produced no systematic or serious studies for any of the non-English colonies at any point during their history or, with the notable exception of New England, for any of the English colonies before the last years of the seventeenth century. Even the study of English colonial political thought is still at a relatively primitive stage.

The absence of a prolific literature on this subject has dictated the particular strategy for this essay. Rather than focusing on colonial political thought per se, it consists largely of discussions of the separate metropolitan traditions of the states that were involved in the colonization of North America. Each is followed by briefer and, in the case of the non-English colonies, necessarily highly speculative analyses of the ways those traditions may have found expression in colonial settings of the sort that existed in North America before the third quarter of the eighteenth century.

HISPANIC COLONIAL POLITICAL THOUGHT

Paralleling the rapid spread of Spanish sovereignty over much of the Americas, the century beginning about 1525 was the golden age of Spanish political thought. In considerable part this development grew out of the lectures of Francisco de Vitoria (ca. 1485–1546), a Dominican who studied in Paris and occupied the main chair of theology at the University of Salamanca between 1526 and 1546. Although Vitoria never published his lectures, and their content is known only through manuscript *relectiones,* or summaries, he inspired two further generations of political theorists who achieved international standing as some of the principal and most effective contributors to the revival and reinterpretation of the political theories of Saint Thomas Aquinas.

Among the central Spanish figures in this movement was the Dominican Domingo De Soto (1494–1560), Vitoria's colleague at Salamanca. De Soto's principal work, *Ten Books on Justice and Law,* appeared in 1553–1557. Other key figures were the Jesuits Luis de Molina (1535–1600), who taught arts and theology at the University of Évora and published his *Six Books on Justice and Law* in 1593 to 1609 and, most important of all, Francisco Suárez (1548–1617), who taught at the University of Coimbra. Suárez's main contributions to political thought, *The Laws of God the Law-giver* and *A Defense of the Catholic and Apostolic Faith,* both published in Madrid in 1612, provided the fullest statement of the current state of Thomist Counter-Reformation political thought.

Along with such other thinkers as Cardinal Robert Bellarmine (1542–1621), the Italian Jesuit, these Spanish Counter-Reformation thinkers were principally concerned to contest two sets of modern social and political ideas. The first regarded those generated by the Protestant Reformation, in particular the doctrine that God directly ordained the establishment of political society. The second involved the reason-of-state philosophy associated with the writings of Niccolò Machiavelli (1469–1527), especially the notion that a prince could take any steps necessary to perpetuate his rule. Following and elaborating upon Aquinas, they used natural law theory to argue that men were capable of using their reason to construct the moral basis of political life. The thinkers, building upon Aquinas's conception of a universe ruled by a hierarchy of laws descending downward from the eternal law through divine law, natural law, and human law, contended both that God imprinted natural law in men's minds and that human law had to be compatible with the principles of natural justice that it contained. In this way they sought to use natural law to provide a moral foundation for the operation of human law.

By emphasizing the capacity of all men to understand the law of nature, these theorists hoped to establish the claim that all secular commonwealths were initially founded by their own citizens with the design of accomplishing their worldly goals. The authority thereby derived was complete in itself and was not subject to the jurisdiction of religious authorities, the pope in particular.

The basic theory was that man had originally lived in a condition of freedom, equality, and independence. It held that civil societies had come into being when collectivities of people contracted together to establish over themselves a new species of power that gave rulers authority to make laws and distribute justice. By this act these collectivities not only transferred but abrogated their original sovereignty, thereby elevating the ruler above themselves and even putting him beyond the bounds of the laws of the community over which he ruled. By this theory Suárez and other Spanish thinkers managed to buttress the doctrine, claimed by Spanish monarchs, of the independence of the secular state from papal authority. It also enabled them to reconcile the political climate of late-sixteenth-century Spain, which increasingly stressed the absolute powers of the Crown, with the natural law theory of the state, with its emphasis on the original freedom of the people.

These doctrines underlay the theory of political life that informed and rationalized the organization and operation of the Hispanic-American Empire, but the acquisition of that empire raised new questions involving the legitimacy of Spanish conquests in the New World. Debate on this subject turned around the question of the rationality of the Indians. Advocates for the Spanish settlers, the most important of whom was Juan Ginés de Sepúlveda (1490–1573), argued that the Indians fell into the category, derived from Aristotle, of "slaves by nature." These were people who lacked reason and could therefore legally and morally be enslaved. Indeed, they postulated that the obligation to evangelize the Indians required their enslavement.

In opposition, thinkers such as Vitoria and Bartolomé de las Casas (1474–1566), the famous defender of the rights of the Indians who opposed Sepúlveda in a special debate at Valladolid in 1550, applied conventional Counter-Reformation theory. They contended that Indians were rational beings, who, like all other people, could comprehend the law of nature and were therefore capable of establishing a legitimate political society. This group argued that since the Indians possessed genuine dominion in public and private affairs the Spaniards had no grounds to dispossess them of their lands, property, and freedom. According to these thinkers, Spanish dominion over the Indians derived from two sources: first, their duty to take charge over and evangelize a poorly educated and childlike people; and second, their long-term jurisdiction.

Widely circulated throughout the Hispanic-American Empire, these ideas received much explicit expression in the dense settler societies of Mexico and Peru. But among the smaller settler populations of the two Spanish colonies established within the present boundaries of the United States—Florida, founded in the 1560s, and New Mexico, begun in the 1590s—their use seems to have been far less evident on the surface of public life and probably also far less extensive. Even in these peripheral outposts of empire, however, royal officials seem to have used the natural rights philosophy of the Thomists to justify a patriarchal system of political authority that left nominal power in the hands of Crown officials in Spain or the colonies and placed the clergy clearly under the jurisdiction of secular authorities. In addition the metropolitan debate over the status of the Indians provided the basis for recurrent exchanges among local royal officials, members of the missionary orders, and settlers. The discussions examined their relative roles toward the large populations of Christian Indians among whom they lived and over whose self-governing "republics" the Spanish Crown claimed jurisdiction.

FRENCH COLONIAL POLITICAL THOUGHT

From the early sixteenth century through the early eighteenth century, French political thought exhibited a powerful drift towards absolutism, the concentration of authority in the hands of the monarch. Not that this drift went unopposed. Indeed at the beginning of the sixteenth century, Claude de Seyssel (1450–1520) in *The Monarchy of France* (1515), represented the predominant political philosophy. *The Monarchy of France* emphasized the extent to which the monarch's authority was limited by his obligation both to uphold his subjects' customary rights and to seek advice from other constituent members of the French polity through councils and assemblages of notables representing towns and regions.

Étienne Pasquier (1529–1615), who began publishing his massive *Researches on France* in 1565, and Jean Bodin (1530–1596), whose *Method for the Easy Comprehension of History* was issued in 1566, revived these ideas and sought to ground them in French historical traditions. Nearly a century later, so did leaders of the Fronde, a broad but uncoordinated effort between 1648 and 1653 to place constitutional limits on royal power. Writing from a Calvinist perspective, Huguenot political theorists, including Theodore Beza (1519–1605) in *Law of Magistrates* (1580), François Hotman (1524–1590) in *Franco-Gallia* (1573), and the anonymous writer of *A Defense of Liberty Against Tyrants* (1579), used a combination of historical arguments, scriptural contentions, and natural law contract theory to oppose absolutist doctrine and justify resistance to monarchs who violated the principles of religion and justice and the customary rights associated with the ancient French constitution.

But these efforts did not represent the mainstream of early modern French political thought. Already by the middle decades of the eighteenth century, works such as *Commentary on the Royal Constitutions and Ordinances* (1549), by Pierre Rebuffi (1487–1557), had begun to depict the king less as the presiding head of a feudal hierarchy than as an absolute ruler whose authority was limited only by his paternal role as the father of his people. Appalled by the disorder provoked by the Huguenot revolution, Bodin, in *Six Books of a Commonweal* (1576), thought by many scholars to be the most important work of political theory published in the sixteenth century, abandoned his earlier constitutionalism. Employing a rationalist approach, he championed a strong monarchy as the only way to restore unity and peace. To this end Bodin formulated a conception of sovereignty that virtually eliminated the possibility of any legal opposition to the ruler.

Over the next century, another group of works, culminating in the 1670s and 1680s with the extensive writings of Jacques-Bénigne Bossuet (1627–1704), including his *Discourse on Universal History* (1681), defended the sanctity of royal authority from a providentialist perspective. Those who wrote from this outlook dismissed the notion of natural law theorists that political society derived from the voluntary coming together of people in an act of self-preservation. Rather, they asserted, government had been imposed upon the people by a sovereign authority who was thereby at once carrying out the will of God and acting in the people's best interest. According to this view, kings thus were those elevated persons whom God had singled out to do his work on earth, and they occupied the same position in their kingdoms that God did in the universe. Like God, the all-powerful monarch had no interest in oppressing his people. His interests and the common good were one. For that reason absolute monarchy was the best form of government to preserve the liberty of subjects, liberty being defined in terms not of the individual possession of reserved rights or participation in government but of the paternalistic protection of citizens by agents of the king against oppression and exploitation from any source.

Such absolutist thought informed the French colonies in North America. During the sixteenth century, the French were active in the gulf and valley of the Saint Lawrence in both fishing and the fur trade. During the early seventeenth century, the French, under the auspices of joint stock companies, managed to establish some small settlements in Acadia and in Canada. But effective colonization only began in 1663, when the French Crown took these areas directly under its control. The designers of New France, established at the very moment when absolutist theory was at its zenith under Louis XIV, intended for it and later settlements established in Louisiana and the upper Mississippi Valley to be a perfect expression of that theory.

Theoretically, at least, the French colonies were to be paternal polities in which authority flowed downward from the king through his representatives in the colonies to the settlers. Composed only of orthodox Catholics living in families, the church and the family were to function as instruments of social control in a coherent and hierarchical, seigneurial regime. The broader settler population had no agencies of corporate expression in this region. Potential abuses of seigneurial power were to be prevented by the careful vigilance of royal intendants operating through royal courts. In many respects the relationship of these distant polities to the metropolitan government of France resembled that of the several subordinate jurisdictions that comprised France. In justifying their title to American lands, the French accepted the by then conventional European view that any land not occupied by a settled population was wasteland available for the taking. With few arenas for public discourse outside the small circles of the governing councils and little access to later political literature associated with the French Enlightenment, alternatives to or variations on this body of theory did not develop before the French relinquished their North American colonies to the British and Spanish in 1763.

DUTCH COLONIAL POLITICAL THOUGHT

From the time the Dutch began to be heavily involved in overseas expansion during the 1560s, Dutch political thought mostly ran in a very different direction from that of either the Spanish or French. Conditioned by their Protestantism and their long struggle for independence from Spain between 1568 and 1648, the United Provinces of the Netherlands, a loose confederation of semirepublican states presided over by a weak stadtholder, proved uncongenial to any political philosophy that glorified kingship and counseled nonresistance to all-powerful monarchs.

Among fifteenth-century contemporaries Hugo Grotius was the most famous Dutch political thinker. His *De Jure Belli ac Pacis* (1625) was the first statement of a strong rights theory to emanate from Protestant Europe. According to Grotius, men in the state of nature freely united in political society primarily for the purpose of achieving social peace, the principal requirement of which was respect for one another's rights and property. His view explained that men acquired property simply by taking possession of or altering or defining unclaimed or unoccupied land, resources, or goods, a theory that provided a useful rationale for competition over land and resources in the non-European world. Grotius detested the contemporary adulation of princes, who, he thought, should exist for the state and not vice versa. Their authority, as in the case of the United Provinces, was restricted by the terms of the original contract between the rulers and the ruled and by their obligation to protect the property, which included the personal liberty, of individual members of the societies they served. Nevertheless, he acknowledged that natural men were free to alienate their original liberty to a single ruler and might thereby subject themselves and their progeny to a state of enslavement to an absolute monarch.

A second line of Dutch political thought drew heavily upon and emphasized the classical republican tradition, especially as it had been reformulated in Renaissance Italy by the Florentines Niccoló Machiavelli (*The Prince* [1513] and *Discourses on the First Ten Books of Livy* [1517]), Donato Giannoti (1492–1573; *Libro de la Republica de Venitiani* [1540]), the Venetian Gasparo Contarini (1484–1542; *The Commonwealth and Government of Venice* [1543]), and Francisco Guicciardini (1483–1540; *The History of Italy* [1561–1564]). Focusing on the utility and inutility of monarchy, these writers, including Dirk Graswinckel (1600–1664) in *Venetian Liberties* (1634), Johan de la Court (1622–1660) and Pieter de la Court (1618–1685) in *Political Balance* (1662) and *Political Discourse* (1662), Johan de Witt (1625–1672) in *The True Interest and Political Maxims of the Republic of Holland* (1669), and Baruch

de Spinoza (1632–1677) in *Tractatus Theologico-Politicus* (1670), espoused a political theory in which state power was limited, government was the guardian of individual privileges, and the church was subordinate to the state. This theory emphasized the autonomy of citizens, excluded dependent people from citizenship, and championed religious toleration. It had no use for a nobility of blood and located sovereignty in the hands of the citizenry. These writers viewed the best form of government as one in which citizens ruled through a participatory assembly.

Governed for most of its short history through a company form of government, New Netherland provided little scope for the articulation and use of these ideas, many of which derived from works that appeared after the colony had been conquered by the English in 1664. Although Grotius's ideas of property provided a Dutch rationale for the occupation of the Hudson and Delaware River valleys, company efforts to restrict popular participation in the government of the colony in favor of a system of company guardianship meant that political exchange in the colony revolved mostly around demands from citizens for the extension of traditional Dutch municipal government to the colony and from settlers arriving from New England for traditional English-style municipal government.

BRITISH COLONIAL POLITICAL THOUGHT

The primitive state of political thought in New Netherland, New France, Acadia, Louisiana, Florida, and New Mexico during the colonial era stands in stark contrast to the situation in the English colonies. The latter had a political system characterized by vigorous representative institutions, popular elections, participatory local governments; a large and prosperous population that included a sizable independent and increasingly well-educated elite; and growing communication resources, including newspapers, publishers, private and public libraries, and educational institutions. These led early both to a deep familiarity with the rich political literature not just of England but of much of the rest of Europe and to the explicit and widespread use of that literature in competitive communities of political discourse. The result was the gradual development of a rich and complex stock of political ideas that underlay and informed the outpouring of an extensive polemical literature throughout the middle decades of the eighteenth century and beyond the colonial era. These ideas can best be approached through a discussion of six distinguishable but overlapping intellectual traditions: the jurisprudential tradition; the civic humanist tradition; the liberal tradition; the literature of political economy and improvement; the Scottish moral and historical tradition; and the literature of the continental Enlightenment.

The Jurisprudential Tradition

In the colonies the English jurisprudential tradition was earlier and more widely and persistently invoked than any of the other major sets of political ideas. This tradition emphasized the role of law as a restraint upon the power of the Crown. By law the exponents of this tradition meant not only statutory law as formulated by Parliament, but more especially the common law, that complex bundle of customs and judicial decisions that was the result of centuries of workings of the English legal system. Presumably embodying the collective wisdom of the ages, the common law was thought to be the chief guarantee of the Englishman's proud right to security of life, liberty, and property through devices such as trial by jury, habeas corpus, and representative government. Rooted in such older writings as *De Legibus et Consuetudinibus Angliae* (1569) by Henry Bracton (d. 1268) and *De Laudibus Legum Angliae* (1573) by Sir John Fortescue (ca. 1394–ca. 1476), this tradition was fully elaborated during the early seventeenth century in a series of works by several of the most prominent judges and legal thinkers of the era.

The most important figure in this effort was Chief Justice Sir Edward Coke (1522–1634). His *Institutes of the Laws of England*, published in four parts between 1628 and 1644 and frequently reissued thereafter, became the principal foundation for the English jurisprudential tradition as it reached the colonies. But several other judges among Coke's contemporaries also made important contributions, including Sir Henry Finch (ca. 1560–1625), Sir John Davies (1569–1634), and Nathaniel Bacon (1593–1660).

These writers lived in an age when, except for the Netherlands, every other major European state was slipping into absolutism and England's first two Stuart kings, James I and Charles I, were thought to be trying to extend the prerogatives of the Crown and perhaps even do away with Parliament in England. Therefore, they were all anxious to erect legal and constitutional barriers to ensure security of liberty and property against such exertions of royal power. Accordingly, they searched the records of both Parliament and courts for evidence of an ancient constitution.

Antecedent even to the common law itself and finding expression through that law, an ancient constitution could be appealed to by public leaders as both justification for an expanded governmental role by Parliament as protector of the rights of the people and for security against arbitrary government by the Crown. Despite the fact that monarchs had frequently violated or ignored it since the Norman Conquest, this ancient constitution, Coke and his colleagues contended, provided the context for legal government in England. Composed of a variety of maxims, precedents, and principles that these writers traced back through the Magna Charta to the ancient Saxon era and that included freedom from arbitrary imprisonment and taxation without consent, this ancient constitution was at once said to serve as the foundation of all governmental authority in England; to confine the scope of the discretion, or will, of the Crown within the limits specified by the higher, fundamental, or natural laws it expressed; and, in particular, to prevent the Crown from governing without Parliament.

This view was not without its contemporary critics. Royalist antiquarians like Sir Henry Spelman (ca. 1564–1641), Robert Brady (ca. 1625–1700), and Thomas Madox (1666–1727) attacked the whole idea of an ancient constitution as a myth manufactured by the legal writers. In a variety of works, these historians demonstrated that, far from being immemorial like the common law, Parliament was a relatively recent institution, created by the Crown during the twelfth and thirteenth centuries, when England was a feudal lordship, and thus owing its existence to the royal will. These works showed that when the common law writers had been unable to find clear evidence for the existence of an ancient constitution, they either had seized upon insubstantial and often ambiguous evidence or had simply invented precedents to support their case.

Notwithstanding its historical authenticity, however, this view was immediately challenged by a number of Whig writers in a barrage of late-seventeenth-century works that reaffirmed the existence of an ancient constitution. These included legal treatises by chief justices Sir John Vaughan (1603–1674) and Sir Mathew Hale (1609–1676); works of history, such as *The Ancient Right of the Commons of England Asserted* (1680) by William Petyt (1636–1707); and statements of Whig principles, such as *English Liberties* (1682) by Henry Care (1646–1688).

Because they advocated an expanded role for Parliament, a view that was congenial to Whig opponents of the later Stuart kings and, following the Glorious Revolution in 1688, to supporters of the revolutionary settlement of 1688–1715, these writers carried the day. The works of Spelman, Brady, and Madox fell into disuse during the early eighteenth century and rarely found their way into American libraries. But the Scottish philosopher and historian David Hume (1711–1776) provided powerful support for their view in his extraordinarily widely read *History of England* (1754–1761). With his customary skepticism, Hume challenged the concept of the ancient constitution. He argued that the eighteenth-century British constitution was, in fact, largely the modern product of the struggles between Crown and Parliament during the seventeenth century. Notwithstanding its allegedly Tory sentiments, Hume's *History* was bought by Americans in large numbers.

But Hume's view was not shared by his contemporaries in the English legal establishment. The principal eighteenth-century works in the English jurisprudential tradition, culminating in Sir William Blackstone's four-volume *Commentaries on the Laws of England* (1765–1769), all subscribed and gave what was seen as authoritative support to the idea of an ancient constitution and emphasized the common law and parliamentary government as barriers to the exercise of arbitrary power by the Crown.

Mostly settled contemporaneously with the great constitutional struggles of the seventeenth century and at a time when the jurisprudential tradition was being elaborated and refined in England itself, England's colonies thus inherited the ideas of limited government and consent. Accordingly, colonial leaders early developed the view that English people had a right to migrate to a new country, take their property and their constitutional rights as Englishmen with them into the new polities they founded overseas, and establish local institutions and adopt local customs to secure those rights to themselves and their posterity.

From the colonists' point of view, the Crown seemed to have recognized the legitimacy of this view by granting them royal charters that not only empowered them to establish governments over a specific territory but also confirmed their entitlement to all the traditional rights of Englishmen. They did not, however, regard these charters as the principal components of their constitutions but, as in the case of Magna Charta itself, as mere legal confirmations of their entitlement to rights they already possessed by virtue of their birthright as English people.

Notwithstanding the provisions in the early charters, English officials were never willing to admit in their fullest extent the colonists' claims to enjoy all the rights of the English constitution. For that reason the exact nature of the colonial constitutions and of the empire as a whole became the main points of contention between Crown and colonies. The many contests that everywhere developed over these issues revolved around two principal questions: whether the colonists were entitled to the benefits of the laws of England and whether the representative assemblies begun early in the history of every colony enjoyed the same status in the colonial constitutions as the House of Commons did in the English constitution. Neither of these questions was explicitly resolved during the colonial period.

The Civic Humanist Tradition

For hundreds of years before the seventeenth century, most social and political thinkers had conceived of society as an organic entity in which the social order was organized hierarchically in a series of separate ranks and statuses and authority flowed from the top downward through the hierarchy. English jurisprudential thought was fully compatible with this traditional model of political society and informed political attitudes in all the English colonies throughout the colonial era. In the seventeenth century, however, it received special emphasis and was most fully developed by the Puritan leaders of Massachusetts and Connecticut.

Puritan political theory revolved around the idea of the calling. According to that idea, God called all individuals to a particular station in life, occupation, and role in the polity, and they were obliged for the good order of society to remain and do well in their callings. For Puritans this doctrine justified placing power in the hands of people of wealth and eminence to whom the rest of the population owed deference and obedience. Although Puritans believed in a strict separation of church and state, they also believed that rulers should be chosen from among the godly and that the clergy should be handmaidens of rulers in maintaining social and political order. Underlying and reinforcing these ideas among New England Puritans was the idea of the covenant, according to which the members of a political society covenanted with God to live by his commands and covenanted with their rulers—who, having been called by God, had the sanction of his authority—to obey the rulers' commands. These particular political ideas were largely confined to those colonies controlled by Puritans, and even there they gradually lost force during the eighteenth century.

A far more powerful and pervasive set of political ideas that emphasized social order and hierarchy evolved out of the civic humanist or classical republican tradition. To some small extent, this tradition looked across the English Channel to the republican government of the Netherlands, which had been described for English readers by Sir William Temple (1628–1699) in his *Observations upon the United Provinces* (1673), and by Dutch writers like the Courts and de Witt. Like those Dutch writers, however, the civic humanist tradition drew primarily upon the writings of Machiavelli and other Renaissance Italians.

During the late seventeenth century, this tradition had been introduced into English political discourse by several republican writers, principally James Harrington (1611–1677) in *Oceana* (1656), John Milton (1608–1674) in *The Ready and Easy Way to Establish a Free Commonwealth*

(1660), and Algernon Sydney (1622–1683) in his posthumously published *Discourses Concerning Government* (1698). Following the Glorious Revolution, the civic humanist tradition flourished in three related groups of writings, all of which were profoundly critical of the new Whig political and economic order. First were the works of radical commonwealthmen, the most direct heirs of Harrington, Milton, and Sydney. They included Andrew Fletcher of Saltoun (1655–1716), Robert Molesworth (1656–1725), John Toland (1660–1724), John Trenchard (1662–1723), Walter Moyle (1672–1721), and Thomas Gordon (1690–1750). Trenchard and Gordon's *Cato's Letters* (1724) was the most influential work published by these authors. Second were the writings of a succession of radical Whig historians, who examined the history of the great events of the seventeenth century in England from a Whig perspective. The most significant of these works was the fifteen-volume *History of England* (1726–1731) by the French Huguenot exile Paul de Rapin-Thoyras (1661–1725). Third were the writings of Tory critics of the new Whig political and commercial order. The most important of these were the works of Henry St. John, viscount Bolingbroke (1678–1751), including *A Dissertation upon Parties* (1735), *A Letter on the Spirit of Patriotism* (1749), and *The Idea of a Patriot King* (1749). Alexander Pope (1638–1744), Jonathan Swift (1667–1745), John Gay (1685–1732), James Thomson (1700–1748), and George Lord Lyttelton (1709–1773) also wrote from a Tory perspective.

The literature of antiquity was also disseminated among and put at the service of eighteenth-century Americans principally through these civic humanist and republican writings. Both Italian Renaissance writers and their early modern English followers drew heavily upon the texts of many of the Greek and Roman authors, including especially such political treatises as the *Politics* of Aristotle (384–322 B.C.) and the *De legibus, De officiis,* and *De oratione* of Cicero (106–43 B.C.); the histories of Polybius (ca. 200–ca. 118 B.C.), Sallust (ca. 86–ca. 34 B.C.), Titus Livius (Livy) (ca. 59 B.C.–A.D. 17), and Tacitus (ca. 55–ca. 120); and the *Roman Lives* of Plutarch (ca. 46–after 119).

What interested early modern theorists most about these particular classical authors, all of whom, except for Aristotle, wrote about the Roman republic from the first century B.C. through the second century A.D., were the insights they provided into the nature and history of that remarkable political entity and the lessons those perceptions furnished about the character and fate of republics in general. Specifically, these works provided vast quantities of evidence to show that a strict separation of powers among the various components of government and high levels of personal independence and civic virtue among political leaders were absolutely essential for the maintenance of a stable republican polity against the efforts of corrupt men to monopolize the power and resources of the state. In vivid detail they chronicled the decline of the Roman republic into an arbitrary dictatorship after its senators had become dependent upon the emperor and its constitution had thereby been rendered incapable of maintaining the absolute separation of powers that for so long had made Rome the citadel of liberty. In Plutarch's *Lives,* the classical work most frequently cited by Americans of the revolutionary generation, men could find models in the biographies of the heroic figures—Brutus, Cassius, Cato the Younger—who, by opposing tyrants and warning against the encroachments of arbitrary power and corruption, defied and sought to stem these developments.

Along with the contemporary example of the successful mixed polity in the modern republic of Venice, the history of the Roman republic provided civic humanist and republican writers with the materials for the construction of an elaborate theory that analyzed the world in terms of two discrete and opposing patterns of political and social relations, which they referred to as virtue and corruption. In the virtuous state, the only sort of state in which men could attain genuine liberty, citizenship was the highest form of active life. Civic virtue—defined as public-spirited and patriotic participation in a self-governing political community in pursuit of the common good—was the primary goal of citizenship and the only legitimate mode of self-fulfillment for citizens. Absolute individual independence was another essential qualification for the achievement of civic virtue. For, the civic humanists believed, virtue was attainable only by men of independent property, preferably in land, whose independent holdings would permit them

to cultivate the intensely autonomous behavior that alone could preserve the polity in a stable and uncorrupted state.

The institutional device through which these independent citizens exercised their autonomous wills in pursuit of civic virtue and the common good was the balanced constitution, or mixed government. The necessary characteristic of such a government was that the constituent elements of the polity—usually defined as the one, the few, and the many (in early modern England, king, lords, and commons)—shared power in such a way that each was at once independent of the others and incapable of governing without their consent. Only by maintaining a strict balance, the primary obligation of all independent and virtuous citizens, could the polity be preserved in a state of perpetual stasis that would provide its citizens with full liberty, which was defined as the right of citizens to participate—to pursue virtue—in the public realm.

By contrast, in a corrupt state the three constituent components of the polity—usually the one, or, as it was commonly denoted in English politics, the court—sought through the calculated distribution of places and pensions among the members of the other two branches to extend its influence over them and thereby both to destroy their political independence and to make its own power absolute. Whereas a virtuous polity was presided over by proud independent citizens who gloried in their capacity to defend the state with a citizen militia, a corrupt polity was dominated by dependent clients, professional men of government and commerce—pensioners, placemen, officeholders, army and navy officers, rentiers, stockjobbers, and speculators in public funds—who were too addicted to the pursuit of private interests, too effete, and too lacking in moral fiber to defend themselves and so had to rely on a standing army.

Whereas a virtuous state was distinguished by its rulers' patriotism and concern with the public welfare, unfettered self-government, and a balanced constitution, a corrupt state was characterized by the selfish pursuit of private interest and power by the dominant group, arbitrary and tyrannical rule, and an unbalanced constitution. To prevent the degeneration of a virtuous government into a corrupt one, civic humanist writers stressed the utility of institutional devices such as rotation in office and frequent elections. They also emphasized the need both for a periodic return to the first principles on which the polity had been founded and for virtuous independent men to maintain a constant vigil against all efforts to aggrandize power on the part of the court.

For nearly a century after the Restoration of Charles II in 1660, this pattern of thought, with its obsessive emphasis upon virtue, independence, and corruption, its skepticism about change, and its suspicion of commercial activity exerted a powerful appeal among English political leaders who were out of power. In the 1670s and 1680s, Whig opponents used it to warn the polity of the Crown's efforts to employ patronage to render its power absolute and destroy the balance of the ancient constitution; they justified the Glorious Revolution of 1688 on the grounds that it had put a permanent stop to the Crown's anticonstitutional efforts and restored the ancient constitution to its pristine form.

But opponents and critics of the new Whig order that emerged in the wake of the Glorious Revolution and reached its fruition under the ministry of Sir Robert Walpole during the 1720s and 1730s found increasing evidence that the forces of corruption were yet powerful. While the spread of commerce and luxury threatened to undermine the independence and destroy the potential for virtue of the British citizenry, the growth of the standing army and the developments associated with the new financial order provided the court with vast new resources and opportunities with which to corrupt the constitution that only recently had been restored by the Glorious Revolution.

Especially during the 1760s and 1770s, the colonial opposition to Britain was deeply tinctured with the ideas of civic humanism, the traditional language of the excluded and the powerless in Britain for the previous century. In their attempts to explain why Parliament had suddenly thrown its support behind efforts, thitherto always associated with prerogative, to subvert colonial liberty, Americans turned instinctively to the opposition concept of corruption. Throughout the years from 1764 to 1776, they fretted about the corrosive effects of power and patronage upon the British constitution. The colonists saw themselves as the victims of a malign conspiracy of power on the part of the ministry to destroy liberty in both the colonies and Britain. The language of conspiracy, corruption, power, and virtue also infused the internal political struggles within the United States after 1776.

The Liberal Tradition

Complementing the jurisprudential tradition, the liberal tradition of social and political thought in which John Locke (1632–1704) was the pivotal figure was symbiotically related to the spectacular advances in science and natural philosophy during the seventeenth century. These included the development of an empirical approach to both science and philosophy by men like Francis Bacon (1561–1626) in England and René Descartes (1596–1650) in France, the brilliant work of Sir Isaac Newton (1642–1727) in mathematics and the mechanical and physical sciences, and Locke's own application of the principles of rational observation to the analysis of the human mind in *An Essay Concerning Human Understanding* (1690), an effort to provide a foundation for the science of man that would be comparable to that developed by Newton for the science of nature. Stressing the impossibility of any person's knowing anything through the medium of others, Locke made individuals autonomous in and responsible for their judgments in both religion and politics. The theory of knowledge that lay at the core of the *Essay* and to which Locke gave practical application in his shorter essays on religious toleration (1689) and education (1693) was radically antiauthoritarian and individualistic in its implications.

For the political realm, Locke developed these implications in his *Two Treatises on Government*. This work was written in the early 1680s during the crisis over efforts by some Whig politicians to exclude Charles II's Catholic brother James from the English throne. But it was not published until 1690, in the wake of the Glorious Revolution. Along with the *Leviathan* (1651) of Thomas Hobbes (1588–1679), the *Two Treatises* is one of the two main classics of early modern English political thought. Locke's immediate purpose in the *Two Treatises* was to refute the patriarchal doctrines of Sir Robert Filmer (ca. 1587–1653), whose *Patriarcha, Or the Natural Power of Kings* remained in manuscript during his lifetime and was published in 1680 but never elicited much resonance in the colonies.

Like Bossuet in France, Filmer worked within the providentialist stream of absolutist political philosophy that regarded political authority as having been divinely conferred by God upon a specific ruler and his descendants. He both traced the origins of that authority to the household and used the family as the symbolic representation of the state. The authority of kings within states, according to Filmer, was equivalent to that of fathers within families. Like the patriarchal authority of fathers, the political authority of kings was thus natural, divinely sanctioned, and, in the final analysis, absolute and unlimited.

In contrast to Filmer, Locke traced the origins of political society to the free consent of the individuals who composed it. In doing so he placed himself firmly within the classical tradition of the natural law theory of the state, the most prominent modern exponents of which were, in addition to Suaréz and Grotius, who were discussed earlier, the English ecclesiastic Richard Hooker (ca. 1554–1660), whose *Laws of Ecclesiastical Polity* appeared in 1594–1597; the German philosopher Samuel, Baron von Pufendorf (1632–1694), whose *De jure naturae et gentium* was published in 1672; and Thomas Hobbes, against whose doctrines Filmer had initially taken up his pen. All of these writers postulated the existence of an original state of nature in which men, living outside and free from the restraints of organized civil society, had, as individuals, total control over their own lives. They also employed the concept of consent, usually exercised through the medium of a social contract, to explain how free individuals came together to form a legitimate political society. For them, as for Locke, secular political authority derived not from God, the family, and force but from the consent of the parties to the initial social contract.

To some extent Hobbes had already departed from earlier natural law writers by emphasizing the egalitarian character of the state of nature and the excessively self-interested character of human nature. This self-interestedness, according to Hobbes, first drove men into the brutish patterns of behavior that produced a war of all against all in the state of nature and then made them decide, in a supremely self-interested act, to seek self-preservation by submitting their wills to an all-powerful sovereign. No less than for Suaréz and Grotius, however, Hobbes saw the social contract through which men consented to subject themselves to the sovereign as not merely a transfer but also, and much more importantly, as an abrogation of the sovereign authority that had, in the state of nature, resided in free individuals. Like Hobbes, Locke also used the imaginary construct of a state of nature and the ideas of consent and contract to explain the origins of civil society. As well, he emphasized the free, rational, and individualistic character of man in the state of nature. As long as men remained within the bounds of the laws of nature, according to Locke, each man in his natural state was equally beyond the jurisdiction of every other man.

Where Locke broke dramatically with Hobbes as well as with most earlier natural law writers was in his rejection of an absolutist theory of the social contract. For Locke men entered into society not from the terror generated by their brutish behavior in the state of nature, but out of a mutual recognition that the protection of individual natural rights to life, liberty, and property could best be secured against the vicious behavior of the degenerate men among them through mutual submission to civil authority. The sole function of government, in Locke's view, was thus to guarantee individual rights to life, liberty, and property to those who voluntarily put themselves under the jurisdiction of political society. In sharp contrast to Hobbes, Locke thus stressed the limited character of the grant of authority to the state. Indeed, he went on to emphasize the continuing rights of individual members both to withdraw from political society through the act of emigration and to resist—even to the point of revolution—any government whose exertions of authority went beyond or acted in violation of the limited ends for which it had been instituted.

For more than a half century following its initial publication, the *Two Treatises* seems to have had relatively little direct influence upon the development of either British or American political thought. But the doctrines espoused in the *Two Treatises* were popularized after the Glorious Revolution by more accessible writers, such as

James Tyrrell (1642–1718) and Bishop Benjamin Hoadly (1676–1761), as well as by the numerous defenders of the Whig order of Sir Robert Walpole during the 1720s and 1730s. Though apparently itself rarely read, the *Two Treatises* had come by the time of Walpole to be widely celebrated for having provided the theoretical justification for the Glorious Revolution.

Similarly, the *Two Treatises* figured prominently in all the important eighteenth-century contributions to natural law theory. These included *The Principles of Natural Law* (1748) by the Genevan professor Jean-Jacques Burlamaqui (1694–1748); *Institutes of Natural Law* (1754–1756) by Cambridge professor Thomas Rutherforth (1712–1771); and *The Law of Nations* (1760) by Burlamaqui's pupil, Emmerich de Vattel (d. 1767). The works of Burlamaqui and Vattel were particularly well-known in America. Each went through two American editions and was frequently cited in colonial polemical literature.

But the *Two Treatises,* which had no American edition until 1773, did not assume a prominent role in colonial political discussion until the last four decades of the eighteenth century, when the theory of politics it contained turned out to be very useful for Americans. Locke's theories became one of the key ideological foundations for opposing British intervention in colonial affairs before 1776 and providing a rationale for independence and for the process of constitution making thereafter. Crucial sections of the language of the Declaration of Independence in 1776 came directly from the *Two Treatises.* For members of the highly individualistic society that had grown up in colonial British America between 1607 and 1776, Locke's liberal individualism struck deep social resonances.

The Literature of Political Economy and Improvement

The doctrines associated with Lockean liberalism, with its emphasis upon the autonomous individual as the primary unit of social organization and the voluntaristic character of the social order, were ultimately subversive of traditional models of political society as they were espoused by civic humanists. Even more subversive were the economic changes associated with the spread of a market society in early modern England. Those changes, which to some extent had been a stimulus to the formulations of Locke, had also fostered the development of two additional and closely interrelated streams of thought, one in political economy and the other in a proliferating literature of socioeconomic improvement. By the early decades of the eighteenth century, these two streams were together providing a direct challenge to the old organic conception of the social order.

The literature of political economy was a direct product of the efforts of a number of writers, themselves mostly engaged in trade or other ventures associated with the emerging commercial society, to understand the workings of the market forces that governed the new social order in which they lived. Among the more prominent people who wrote in this tradition were Sir William Petty (1623–1687), Sir Josiah Child (1630–1699), Sir Dudley North (1641–1691), and Charles Davenant (1656–1714). To a man, these writers were optimists who unreservedly endorsed the effects of increased commercial activity upon English society and celebrated the workings of the market forces they sought to describe.

Whereas earlier writers of almost all hues and persuasions had conventionally decried self-interest as the bane of political society, these authors located the foundations of the new economic order in the undirected material aspirations of the individuals who composed it. In their view the self-interested behavior of individuals—the universal human tendency to seek one's own good—was the mainspring that kept the entire market edifice in motion and made its operation both comprehensible and rational. The individual desire for gain and the competition and instrumental behavior it engendered in a free market seemed to these writers at once a cure for idleness, an incitement to industry, a spur to achievement, and a stimulus to productivity. They recognized, moreover, that individual desires were the source of the rising demand for consumer goods that led to the enhanced productivity that in turn resulted in the augmentation of national greatness and the material enhancement of society as a whole as well as the betterment of the individuals who composed it. In a society based upon and animated by the pursuit of profit, egocentric behavior, they discovered, was thus both legitimate and benign. Unregulated, the natural operation of individual self-interest, they were convinced, would render the productive powers of society virtually limitless.

Their implicit plea for a free market unhampered by political interference during the eighteenth century never won the allegiance of people in power in Britain, where governments persisted in traditional policies of mercantile regulation. Nevertheless, their fundamental insights into the operation of commercial society were taken up, popularized, extended, and refined in later studies of political economy such as *Britain's Commercial Interest Explained and Improved* (1757) by Malachy Postlethwayt (1707–1767) and *Inquiry into the Nature and Causes of the Wealth of Nations* (1776) by Adam Smith (1723–1790).

In these forms, the new ideas of political economy helped to provide colonial British Americans with an understanding of the operation of the commercial world in which they had been so deeply enmeshed ever since the first settlement of the colonies. They also legitimized the individualistic and self-interested behavior that had been so manifest a feature of American life throughout the colonial era. By helping to foster an appreciation of the great extent to which the socioeconomic world in which they lived was the product of the unrestrained operation of self-interest in thousands of individuals, the literature of political economy also contributed further to enhance the liberal conception of political authority as a product of the consent of free individuals and to demystify those traditional conceptions that saw political society as deriving from the will of a sovereign and residing in authoritative governmental institutions.

Perhaps even more important in shaping the perceptual world of colonial British Americans was the related literature of improvement. Primarily concerned with enhancing productivity and bettering social and economic conditions, this literature was also intimately connected with the commercial revolution that had engaged the attention of the economic writers mentioned above. Throughout the seventeenth century, an increasing number of writers offered the public a wide range of proposals for improving agricultural yields, livestock, transportation, manufacturing, marketing techniques, housing, health, urban amenities, and general conditions of life.

The settlements in the New World were themselves seen as a means to improve the wealth and national greatness of England. Through the systematic application of human intellect, these writers assumed, nature could be made more tractable and man more productive. Poverty and idleness would be reduced, industry encouraged, standards of living enhanced, and society would be made ever more civil and refined as these improvements spread outward from its center to the peripheries. Improvement was thus a developmental concept that contained powerful implications for the possibility of social progress. For that reason it held a special appeal for people in the colonies, where the inhabitants saw themselves as engaged in an extraordinary effort to create societies in the image of the Old World through a constant process of improving the unimproved lands and "wilderness" they had wrested from the Indians.

Although the volume of improvement literature generated during the seventeenth century was substantial, its principal spokesman was the political writer and novelist Daniel Defoe (1660–1731). Defoe's literary output during the four decades beginning in 1690 seems to have been unrivaled by any other writer in early modern England. *An Essay upon Projects* (1697), which strongly influenced the young Benjamin Franklin, was perhaps the one work that most fully captured the optimism of the improvement writers and celebrated what Defoe called the "projecting spirit." Among Defoe's contemporaries the literary figures Joseph Addison (1672–1719) and Richard Steele (1672–1729) also contributed to this literature, explicitly linking the development of commerce and the passion for individual and social improvement to the rise of culture and politeness. By promoting exchange and contact among nations, regions, and classes, commerce, they suggested in a formula that would become a commonplace of social and political discourse by the middle of the eighteenth century, served as an active civilizing agent that made societies more polite, more urbane, and less barbarous. By providing society's ruder segments with higher standards and models of behavior, commercial exchange, they contended, at once eroded the rough edges of provincial behavior and improved manners, conversation, sociability, morals, and culture.

In this view enchanced refinement and civility came to be seen as the direct products of the individual striving and material achievements associated with the projecting spirit and the commercial age. The individualistic ethos implicit in this literature that continued to be published in quantity throughout the eighteenth century was highly influential among upwardly mobile colonial British Americans.

The Scottish Moral and Historical Tradition

The remarkable display of intellectual virtuosity known as the Scottish Enlightenment is usually said to have begun with the work of Francis Hutcheson (1694–1746), professor of moral philosophy at the University of Glasgow. Hutcheson challenged both Locke's epistemology and his concept of the state of nature, arguing that man's perceptions of good and evil, of right and wrong conduct, were the products not of reason but of what he called the moral sense, an innate extra sense implanted in every man by God. Contending that man, animated by his moral sense, was not a solitary but a sociable creature, Hutcheson argued that the moral sense gave rise to natural bonds of affection. These bonds made men sociable and benevolent, not autonomous and self-interested. From these premises, it followed both that society, being natural to man, preceded the formal establishment of civil government and that benevolence was its basic organizing principle. Whereas individual autonomy was the starting point for Locke's political thought, social interdependence provided the foundation for Hutcheson's moral philosophy.

Hutcheson's conception of the moral sense, of the supremacy of sentiment over reason in moral decisions, provided the point of departure for the considerable output of moral thought produced by Scots during the latter half of the eighteenth century. This was true for *An Enquiry Concerning the Principles of Morals* (1751) by David Hume; *Essays on the Principles of Morality and Natural Religion* (1751) by Henry Home, Lord Kames (1696–1782); *Theory of the Moral Sentiments* (1759) by Adam Smith; *An Inquiry into the Human Mind* (1764) by Thomas Reid (1710–1796); and many other works by writers such as Hugh Blair (1718–1800) and James Beattie (1735–1803). Gradually these moral sense proponents developed the idea

that the moral judgments of ordinary men were equivalent to those of the learned, with Reid even insisting that the common sense of plowmen, uncorrupted by the sophisticated musings of philosophers, might even render the moral perceptions of the lowly superior to those of philosophers. This egalitarian epistemology appealed to the anti-authoritarian instincts implicit in patterns of American social and political relations.

Because of his religious skepticism, David Hume, certainly the most sophisticated and impressive thinker to emerge from any part of the eighteenth-century British world, stood somewhat outside the main traditions of Scottish moral philosophy. His *Essays and Treatises on Several Subjects* (1753–1754) and his six-volume *History of England* (1754–1761) provided a systematic analysis of the operation of the new commercial society. In these works Hume employed a historical approach to contend that the modern age of commerce and refinement was the happiest and most virtuous period in the history of man. No believer in the alleged superiority of the ancient constitution so much celebrated by the civic humanists and contemptuous of Whig historians like Rapin, he showed in his *History of England* how English liberty had only slowly emerged out of changing social conditions between the Magna Charta and the Glorious Revolution. He insisted that authority had never been better regulated, liberty and law more secure, or commerce and the arts more thriving than they were in contemporary Britain.

The doctrine of social and economic progress articulated by Hume subsequently became the organizing principle of Scottish philosophical history as it was developed after 1750 by an impressive group of historians and social analysts, including Adam Smith, William Robertson (1721–1793), Adam Ferguson (1723–1816), and John Millar (1735–1801). In a variety of works, these writers elaborated a theory of the progress of societies from rudeness to refinement. This theory described the development of man not, as had Locke and other natural law theorists, as a movement from a state of nature to a state of society, but as a progress through time and space in four sequential stages—respectively the ages of hunters, shepherds, agriculture, and commerce. It sought to uncover the laws that governed this process and the range of possible variations.

At each of these stages, according to the conjectural historians, the mode of production was the primary determinant of the character of social institutions, manners, styles of life, and personality. The direction of movement was toward the division and specialization of labor, an intensification of exchange in goods and services, and an indefinite multiplication of goods. The desire for material improvement—the propensity of individuals, in emulation of those above them in society, to want to better themselves and to accumulate property and the social esteem and prestige conferred by that property—was the driving force in this process. For the philosophical historians, social progress was thus an unintended consequence of millions of individual acts of self-interest. They believed that the most rapid rate of material improvement occurred in situations in which there was minimal government regulation of the economy.

In place of the classical conception of man as a civic being and in amplification of the liberal image of man as a self-centered individualist, the philosophical historians substituted a modern conception of man as a transactional being ensconced in an ongoing and largely progressive cultural process characterized by increasing specialization, division of labor, and diversification and refinement of institutions and personality. Precisely because it provided a framework that seemed to situate their societies within a broader process of social and cultural development, a process they had all passed through at an accelerated rate in their own progress from rudeness to refinement, the work of Smith, Millar, Kames, and the other Scottish philosophical historians exerted a profound appeal for American leaders of the late colonial and revolutionary generations.

The Literature of the Continental Enlightenment

Generally connoting the era of rational scientific discovery, philosophical inquiry, and social criticism that stretched roughly from the closing decades of the seventeenth century through the first decades of the nineteenth century, the Enlightenment has always been a term without any very precise meaning. When contemporaries used it,

they certainly meant to include the great discoveries and writings of the Englishmen Newton and Locke and their eighteenth-century philosophical heirs and revisers, ranging from the idealist George Berkeley (1685–1753) to the materialist David Hartley (1705–1757). For most modern historians, however, the Enlightenment found its fullest and most prolific expression not in Britain but on the Continent, especially in France. Among the many important continental works to come out of the continental Enlightenment were the *Encyclopedia* (1751–1765) by Jean Le Rond d'Alembert (1717–1783) and Denis Diderot (1713–1784); the substantial tracts by the Swiss natural law theorists Burlamaqui and Vattel, mentioned above; the sympathetic discussion of the workings of the English political system by the Swiss political analyst Jean Louis De Lolme (1740–1805) in *The Constitution of England* (1771); and the poignant advocacy of the reform of criminal law by the Milanese Cesare Beccaria (1735–1794) in *An Essay on Crimes and Punishments* (1764). Except for the writings of Burlamaqui, Vattell, and Beccaria, however, these works, though present in a few American libraries, were neither widely known, readily accessible, nor especially influential in America during the colonial period.

This was less true of the work of three other eighteenth-century French philosophes. Almost all educated Americans were well acquainted with at least some of the voluminous writings of the philosophical skeptic François-Marie Arouet Voltaire (1694–1778) and the searching tracts of the iconoclastic Genevan Jean-Jacques Rousseau (1712–1778). But the philosophe who spoke most directly to American problems was the cautious Charles-Louis de Secondat, baron Montesquieu (1689–1755), whose massive analysis of ancient and modern political systems, *The Spirit of the Laws* (1748), was perhaps the single most important work of political analysis for Americans of the revolutionary generation.

Montesquieu's concept of the separation of powers—in his view the essential element underlying the comparative success of the British constitution in preserving liberty among British citizens—was both his most important contribution to modern political theory and the idea that most interested American political leaders of that era. Practically all earlier writers had conceived of a balanced constitution or mixed government in terms of a division of authority among the several constituent estates within the realm—the one, the few, and the many. By contrast Montesquieu modified this tradition by defining the concept of the separation of powers in modern functional terms, according to the ostensibly discrete and separable roles of the executive, legislative, and judicial branches of government. A strict separation of powers among these three branches, he believed, was necessary for any well-regulated polity that hoped to preserve intact the public liberty of its citizens. He argued that only if each branch of government was wholly independent of each of the others was it possible to maintain a government of laws and to prevent the degeneration of the government into a despotic regime. Although the authors of the early state constitutions between 1776 and 1780 had little success in applying Montesquieu's doctrine, it continued throughout the revolutionary era to be a goal for most American political leaders, especially for the framers of the federal Constitution of 1787, which represented the most ambitious effort up to that time to put his concept into practice.

AMERICAN VOICES

The emphasis in this essay has been upon the European intellectual heritage of colonial political thought. But the politically expansive societies of colonial British America were not merely passive vehicles uncritically dependent upon the Old World for their conceptions of society and the polity. Not only did they make highly discriminating use of those ideas, but they also made important contributions of their own to the particular intellectual worlds in which they lived, combining and refining the stock of political ideas available to them to meet the conditions they confronted in their own social polities.

Writers such as Thomas Hooker (1586–1647) of Connecticut and Roger Williams (ca. 1603–1683) of Rhode Island in the seventeenth century; David Lloyd (ca. 1656–1731) of Pennsylvania, Daniel Dulany, Sr. (1685–1753), of Maryland, Elisha Cooke, Jr. (1678–1737), of Massachusetts, and Sir John Randolph (ca. 1693–1737) of Virginia in the early eighteenth

century; and Benjamin Franklin (1706–1790) of Pennsylvania, Richard Bland (1710–1776) of Virginia, and William Livingston (1723–1790) of New York in the late colonial era produced tracts and speeches that revealed both an intimate familiarity with contemporary Old World political thought and enormous ingenuity in applying that thought to their own situations. After 1760 that learning and ingenuity would prove to be a major resource in their efforts to achieve independence and establish a new national state.

BIBLIOGRAPHY

Appleby, Joyce Oldham. *Economic Thought and Ideology in Seventeenth-Century England.* Princeton, N.J., 1978.

Bailyn, Bernard. *The Ideological Origins of the American Revolution.* Cambridge, Mass., 1967.

Breen, T. H. *The Character of the Good Ruler: A Study of Puritan Political Ideas in New England, 1630–1730.* New Haven, Conn., 1970.

Dickinson, H. T. *Liberty and Property: Political Ideology in Eighteenth-Century Britain.* London, 1977.

Dunn, John M. *The Political Thought of John Locke: An Historical Account of the Argument 'Two Treatises of Government.'* Cambridge, England, 1969.

Earle, Peter. *The World of Defoe.* London, 1976.

Fink, Zera S. *The Classical Republicans: An Essay in the Recovery of a Pattern of Thought in Seventeenth-Century England.* Evanston, Ill., 1945.

Forbes, Duncan. *Hume's Philosophical Politics.* Cambridge, England, 1975.

Gay, Peter. *The Enlightenment: An Interpretation.* 2 vols. New York, 1967–1969.

Gilbert, Felix. *Machiavelli and Guicciardini: Politics and History in Sixteenth-Century Florence.* Princeton, N.J., 1965.

Greene, Jack P. *The Intellectual Heritage of the Constitutional Era: The Delegates' Library.* Philadelphia, 1986.

———. *Peripheries and Center: Constitutional Development in the Extended Polities of the British Empire and the United States, 1607–1788.* Athens, Ga., 1986.

Greenleaf, W. H. *Order, Empiricism, and Politics.* London, 1964.

Gunn, John A. W. *Beyond Liberty and Property: The Process of Self-Recognition in Eighteenth-Century Political Thought.* Kingston, Ontario, 1983.

Hirschman, Albert O. *The Passions and the Interests: Political Arguments for Capitalism Before Its Triumph.* Princeton, N.J., 1976.

Hont, Istvan, and Michael Ignatieff, eds. *Wealth and*

Virtue: The Shaping of Political Economy in the Scottish Enlightenment. Cambridge, England, 1983.

Keohane, Nannerl O. Philosophy and the State in France: The Renaissance to the Enlightenment. Princeton, N.J., 1980.

Kramnick, Isaac. Bolingbroke and His Circle: The Politics of Nostalgia in the Age of Walpole. Cambridge, Mass., 1968.

Leder, Lawrence H. Liberty and Authority: Early American Political Ideology, 1689–1763. Chicago, Ill., 1968.

Lutz, Donald S. "The Relative Influence of European Writers on Late Eighteenth-Century American Political Thought." American Political Science Review 78, no. 1 (1984):189–197.

McDonald, Forrest. Novus Ordo Seclorum: The Intellectual Origins of the Constitution. Lawrence, Kans., 1985.

MacPherson, Crawford B. The Political Theory of Possessive Individualism: Hobbes to Locke. Oxford, 1962.

Meek, Ronald L. Social Science and the Ignoble Savage. Cambridge, England, 1976.

Morgan, Edmund S., ed. Puritan Political Ideas. Indianapolis, Ind., 1965.

Pagden, Anthony. The Fall of Natural Man: The American Indian and the Origins of Comparative Ethnology. Cambridge, England, 1982.

———, ed. The Languages of Political Theory in Early-Modern Europe. Cambridge, England, 1987.

Pocock, John G. A. The Ancient Constitution and the Feudal Law. Cambridge, England, 1957.

———. The Machiavellian Moment: Florentine Political Thought and the Atlantic Republican Tradition. Princeton, N.J., 1975.

Richter, Melvin, ed. The Political Theory of Montesquieu. Cambridge, England, 1977.

Robbins, Caroline. The Eighteenth-Century Commonwealthman: Studies in the Transmission, Development, and Circumstance of English Liberal Thought from the Restoration of Charles II until the War with the Thirteen Colonies. Cambridge, Mass., 1959.

Rossiter, Clinton. Seedtime of the Republic: The Origin of the American Tradition of Political Liberty. New York, 1953.

Schochet, Gordon J. Patriarchalism in Political Thought. Oxford, England, 1975.

Skinner, Quentin. The Foundations of Modern Political Thought. 2 vols. Cambridge, England, 1978.

Tuck, Richard. Natural Rights Theories: Their Origin and Development. Cambridge, England, 1979.

White, Morton. The Philosophy of the American Revolution. New York, 1978.

Wood, Gordon S. The Creation of the American Republic, 1776–1787. Chapel Hill, N.C., 1969.

*Jack P. Greene**

SEE ALSO **Colonial Political Culture** and **The Colonial Press.**

---

* The author wishes to thank Amy Turner Bushnell for her help with the section on Anglo-America Colonial Political Thought. The section on Anglo-America Colonial Political Thought is adapted from the author's study in *The Intellectual Heritage of the Constitutional Era.*

COLONIAL POLITICAL CULTURE

INTRODUCTION

THE CONCEPT "political culture," developed and widely employed by social scientists during the 1950s and 1960s, has never acquired any precise or generally accepted meaning. Scholars have often used it in a narrow sense to apply merely to political norms, concepts, and theories as they are articulated, expressed, and modified in political discourse.

This article uses the ideas in a far more expansive sense. Political culture includes not only the underlying intellectual propensities, orientations, imperatives, values, and expertise of a given political society but also the overt patterns of political and social behavior exhibited by the members of that society, the social processes through which those members acquire and exhibit those characteristic ways of thinking and behaving, and the institutional structures through which they act politically. The criteria for and extent of political empowerment and the forms of political association and mobilization are noted in this interpretation. This essay will not treat at length any of those aspects of the political cultures of colonial North America that have been covered in detail by other essays in this volume, including the ones on political thought and on frameworks and institutions and government.

Students of political cultures conventionally divide them into sets of broad categories. One such set distinguishes between subject and participatory political cultures according to the degree of public participation in the political process. Another school classifies political cultures in terms of forms of government: monarchical, aristocratic, republican, or democratic. Still a third group of scholars discriminates among primitive, traditional, and modern political cultures on the basis of the extent of their political resources and complexity.

All four of the early modern states to which the North American colonies were attached, Spain, England, France, and the Netherlands, had subject political cultures. Those of both England and the Netherlands involved significant amounts of participation. All were aristocratic in the sense that a titled and privileged segment of society wielded considerable formal power. All except the Netherlands were also monarchical. Those of both England and the Netherlands were in some respects even republican. During the sixteenth and seventeenth centuries, all four evolved from feudal to bureaucratic political cultures that in Spain, France, and England were also, to one degree or another, patrimonial. With political resources that were far too complex and developed for them to be considered primitive but not sufficiently differentiated to be thought of as modern, all four had political cultures that were traditional. This was not the case with their overseas colonies, several of which remained too small and too undeveloped—too primitive—to generate more than the rudiments of a traditional political culture. However, a few of the colonies were, by the end of the colonial era, displaying some of the characteristics of modern political cultures.

POLITICAL CULTURES OF THE NON-ENGLISH COLONIES

All non-English colonies in North America had subject political cultures that involved a minimum of participation on the part of the settlers. Those of the Spanish and French colonies represented a projection of the patrimonial and bureaucratic political cultures of Spain and France.

The Spanish Borderlands

Usually, the Spanish-American colonies began as private ventures by individual *adelantados* (enlargers of the king's domains) acting with authorization from the Crown or in its name. The more successful of these people initially managed, in places like Peru, to establish relatively autonomous centers of European power effectively under local control. But the discovery of precious metals and other riches provided the Spanish monarchy with the resources to slowly reduce these several enclaves of private power to some semblance of central control. Thenceforth, they established a system of imperial governance in which authority, at least in theory, flowed downward from the king through the Council of the Indies in Spain to the viceroys. From the viceroys, authority proceeded from the high courts (*audiencias*) and other royal officials and institutions of the colonies down to the larger community of settlers. In every Spanish colony, public life and the political culture growing up around it were dominated by a small cadre of administrative officials and their adherents.

This political system had been designed to secure and maintain royal hegemony. To this end the Crown took pains to try to prevent the large landowning or resource-owning elite class that developed in the larger colonies from acquiring heritable legal privileges. It sought to appoint nonlocals to religious benefices and civil offices and to treat those places as rewards for service. The Crown limited the tenure of royal appointees, subjected their performance in office to offi-

cial scrutiny, and dispensed law through royal decrees (*cédulas*). In any disputes over rights—for instance, to office, land, status, or exemption from certain types of taxes and punishments—recourse was to the head of the patrimonial state or to his representatives who were charged with handling adjudication. In practice local notables enjoyed considerable power through their domination of the governing *cabildos*, or town councils, the naturalization by marriage of officials sent from Spain, and the gradual creolization of the royal bureaucracy through the purchase of offices. At least before the implementation of the Bourbon reforms late in the eighteenth century, such people were able, through their domination of local institutions, to modify or resist the implementation of royal decrees they regarded as inimical to their best interests.

In peripheral colonies where the Spanish population was never very large and the office-holding and resource-owning classes were correspondingly small—including Florida and New Mexico, the two Spanish colonies that fall within the scope of this work—the number who participated in public life was confined to a very few people who were not part of the Republic of Indians. This republic was a system of governance for thousands of Indians in Florida whereby they lived under Spanish jurisdiction but possessed the rights to self-governance and the appointment of their own Native leaders. Those who participated in public life included governors and their staffs, treasury officials, regular army officers, priests, missionaries, merchants, prominent resource owners, ranchers in Florida, and *encomenderos* (those entitled to tribute from Indians) in New Mexico. Not counting wives and children, this population probably never numbered as many as a hundred in either Florida or New Mexico at any point before 1800. As a result the ostensibly traditional political cultures of those colonies were small in scope and resources. The cultures mostly revolved around the administrative application of royal decrees from Spain, relations between clerics and secular officials, and interactions with leaders, hereditary and elective, of the large Indian populations within their jurisdictions. Because both colonies were heavily subsidized by the Crown and by either Indian labor (Florida) or Indian tribute (New Mexico), local taxes were limited to customs duties, fees for administrative or religious services, and special Crown-imposed levies on elites during war. Neither colony had a printing press to serve as a vehicle for the expression of public opinion and debate.

New France

When the French Crown took the scattered trading posts and agricultural settlements in Acadia (Nova Scotia) and New France under its jurisdiction in 1663, it provided a similar system of governance. The Crown subsequently extended this structure to Louisiana following its establishment early in the eighteenth century. In contrast to the situation in Spanish Florida and New Mexico as well as in Acadia and Louisiana, however, New France slowly acquired a substantial white population that had increased to more than fifty-five thousand by 1763 and provided the basis for the emergence of a sophisticated traditional political culture in that colony.

Contrived during the last half of the seventeenth century, at the very moment when the absolutist state of old regime France was at its zenith, the political society of New France represented a conscious effort by Louis XIV's ministers to extend the absolutist principles of political centralization, royal paternalism, religious orthodoxy, and state control over economic life and the social order to the New World. In theory all authority flowed outward from the Crown through the Ministry of the Marine in France to the Crown's appointed officials in the colonies. These officials included the governor general and intendant at Quebec and extended to local governors at Montreal and Trois-Rivières, to parish militia captains (capitaines de milice), the chief agents of the provincial government in the localities, and to the wider population of traders and settlers. All colonial officials were appointed, those at the provincial level by the Crown and the capitaines de milice by the governors general. The judiciary was also dependent on the Crown. The members of both the highest court, called the Superior Council, and local courts were appointed by the Crown from the ranks of the local elite on the recommendation of the governor general and the intendant.

The authoritarian character of this system was mitigated by several factors. First, heavy subsidies from the metropolitan government meant that the inhabitants were not subjected to any taxes by the colonial government. Second, various forms of consultation at every level ensured that few political actions would be undertaken without the colonists' support. The Ministry of the Marine rarely issued decrees without first seeking the advice of the governor general and intendant. Before issuing ordinances and edicts, those officials in turn consulted with local notables through either the Superior Council or an annual advisory assembly held each summer at Quebec. Third, the fact that all offices were open to colonists and that many were actually filled by them also helped to make the colonial regime sensitive to local opinion. Indeed, as in the Spanish colonies, even when they were not themselves Creoles, royal officials, army officers, and merchants were all closely allied, sometimes through marriage, with prosperous colonials.

Throughout the era of French control to 1763, the paternalistic and bureaucratic political culture that emerged out of this system of governance was the preserve of the relatively small group in charge of the colony's administrative machinery. Yet through their willing cooperation with that system, the broader body of French inhabitants regularly both acknowledged that it was meeting their political needs and signified their satisfaction with it. Like the other non-English colonies in North America, New France had no printing press.

New Netherland

The government and political culture of the United Provinces of the Netherlands did not resemble the patrimonial bureaucratic polities of contemporary Spain and France in many ways. Authority was far more diffused and active citizen participation far more extensive. Nevertheless, the system of governance established in New Netherland, like those implemented by both Spain and France in North America, fostered a narrow subject, rather than a broader participatory, political culture.

Throughout its brief history until the English conquest in 1664, New Netherland had a company form of government. With its headquarters in Amsterdam, the Dutch West India Company had jurisdiction over the colony and placed authority in the hands of a small group of appointed officials. A director-general, a storekeeper (*kommis*), a sheriff or prosecuting attorney (*schout*), and a secretary (*fiscal*) who made ordinances and adjudicated disputes among inhabitants and traders constituted this set. More concerned with pursuing the interests of shareholders than with constructing a polity, these company officials tried to keep a monopoly of power in their own hands. Thus, although the director-general, acting on orders of company directors in Amsterdam, appointed a small advisory council composed of some of the leading men in the colony, he never permitted that body any significant exercise of authority. Similarly, company officials resisted demands from burghers and farmers for the establishment of a more participatory form of government and the extension of traditional Dutch municipal government to the colony, although they were unable to avoid granting New Amsterdam the privileges of a municipal government in 1653. With these sorts of provisional governing arrangements, the political culture of New Netherland never matured beyond a relatively primitive level.

POLITICAL CULTURES OF THE ENGLISH COLONIES

During the century and a half between the founding of Virginia, the first permanent English colony in America, in 1607 and the conclusion of the Seven Years' War in 1763, the Anglophone colonies in America underwent an astonishing political transformation. The tentative, cumbersome, and only marginally effective political arrangements by which the Virginia Company had sought to govern its first settlements at Jamestown gradually evolved into a series of remarkably sophisticated polities stretching from Barbados at the southeastern corner of the Caribbean to Newfoundland at the northeastern edge of North America. As the events of the American Revolution would demonstrate over the quarter century between 1763 and 1789, most of these participatory polities had by the mid eighteenth century developed extraordinary political resources.

Most of the seventeen colonies that constituted the organized Anglophone North American empire in 1776 had initially been founded as private colonies under the aegis of trading companies or proprietors. Only Georgia, originally administered by government-appointed trustees, and East and West Florida, both founded as royal colonies, did not have private origins. Reflecting the idiosyncrasies of the founders, the welter of institutions devised by their private sponsors to govern the rest of the colonies varied so enormously from one colony to the next as to defy simple categorization and description. By the late seventeenth century, however, the political systems of most colonies at the provincial level had assumed a roughly similar shape. In part this process was the result of the gradual conversion of the vast majority of the colonies into royal provinces directly under the control of the Crown. But it also occurred in the five remaining private colonies: the three proprietaries of Maryland, Delaware, Pennsylvania, and the two corporate colonies of Connecticut and Rhode Island.

Basic Properties

The political systems of all of the colonies exhibited, to one degree or another, certain basic features or properties that underlay and characterized their political cultures throughout the colonial period. The first and certainly among the most significant was their colonial status. The fact that they were colonial rather than independent meant that they were socially and economically truncated, that the highest echelons of the economic and social systems to which they were tied lay in the parent state. It also signified that the apex of authority—political, legal, moral, and cultural—rested there as well. They were subject to laws passed by the king-in-parliament, albeit before the 1760s this body limited its concern with the colonies almost entirely to trade and economic regulations. The laws of all royal colonies and Pennsylvania and the judicial decisions of all colonies were subject to review and approval by the Crown and its privy council in London.

The relationship between colonies and metropolis was thus of crucial significance. It bound the colonies within a system in which the ultimate determination of policy lay in large measure beyond their control. But it also gave them access to resources—to markets, credit, manufactures, staples, shipping, technical skills, military and naval protection, political rewards, preferment, and status. Perhaps most important of all, the bond gave the colonies normative standards and models of behavior and an intimate connection with a "great" metropolitan tradition that none of them could have commanded on their own. Finally, the connection guaranteed that the colonies would all be subcultures within a single Anglophone world and that, to an important degree, they would all be incorporated into the monarchical political culture of the parent state.

For colonial political life, this meant that institutions of government, systems of law and justice, and patterns of behavior and perception would all be to some extent clearly derivative of those of the metropolis. Thus, the three most important political institutions in the colonies were roughly analogous to those of Britain. The governorship was the provincial equivalent of the Crown. The governors' councils took on the multiple functions performed in Britain by both the privy council and the House of Lords. Finally, the lower houses of assembly were the colonial equivalents of the House of Commons; their lawmaking powers, though limited in the royal colonies and Pennsylvania by the requirement that all statutes be transmitted to Britain for review by the king-in-council and by the governor's veto power, were as extensive in their respective spheres as was that of the Commons in Britain. Their consent was required for all taxes.

A second and equally important feature of colonial political life was that each colony constituted an almost wholly separate political environment. Many colonies were to some extent offshoots of older colonies: Maryland and North Carolina of Virginia; Rhode Island, Connecticut, New Hampshire, and Nova Scotia of Massachusetts; South Carolina of Barbados; and Georgia of South Carolina. As such they exhibited important similarities in governmental and political structure and in political culture to the colonies that had spawned them. Yet because each colony had its own distinctive patterns of economic activity, social and ethnic composition, religious organization, and urban development as well as its own peculiar body of traditions, custom, and experience, it manifested its own characteristic configurations of political activity.

This individuality was reinforced by the fact that at least until the Seven Years' War, and really until the pre-revolutionary crises beginning in 1764, there was virtually no common political life among the colonies. Political contact among them was largely transitory and tangential to the central concerns of politics. The political involvement of each colony with the metropolis was considerably greater than that with its neighboring colonies. Not even the metropolis had sufficient power to eradicate the peculiarities of the political systems of individual colonies. Metropolitan influences were received, modified, ignored, or discarded according to their relevance to local circumstances and their correspondence with local conditions.

A third basic characteristic was that colonial political systems themselves were almost everywhere highly circumscribed in their operations. They performed all of the normal functions of government. The symbolic function entailed affirming—and embodying—social values through actions and laws. Another function, the regulative, involved formulating the ground rules directing the allocation of land and the process of settlement, setting forth prescriptions for individual conduct, and enforcing the law. The protective functions necessitated guaranteeing security of liberty and property, maintaining public order, and contributing to defense against alien attacks.

Because of the exigencies common to such new communities, however, provincial governments also engaged in a considerably wider range of activities than did the central government in Britain. First, they assumed responsibility for the initiation of a large assortment of both political and social institutions including counties, towns, parishes, courts, churches, and hospitals and social services such as roads, ferries, lighthouses, fortifications, canals, and public buildings. Second, they conferred a variety of privileges, benefits, and exemptions upon individuals charged with the creation of those institutions and the provision of those services. Finally, they sought to foster the economic well-being of the citizenry through regulations to produce new staples, improve the quality of old ones, or enhance the competitive advantage of the inhabitants in trade or at markets.

However broad the range of government activities in the colonies in comparison with that in Britain, by any modern standards colonists expected remarkably little from government.

Even in the late colonial period, government was a minuscule operation. Budgets—and taxes—were low; paid full-time public officials were few; civil, judicial, and police establishments were small, part-time, and usually volunteer; and before the Seven Years' War, military establishments were usually temporary and never large.

Because most of the responsibility for maintaining order, enforcing laws, mediating conflicts, handling routine litigation, and performing public services devolved upon agencies of local government in counties, towns, and parishes, colonists had considerably more contact with formal components of the political system at the local level than with the small establishments of the provincial government. But at most times and places, government weighed lightly upon the vast majority of colonists, whose usual involvement with the political system was limited largely to the payment of normally light taxes, the occasional performance of public-service obligations such as road maintenance or militia musters, and no more than annual participation in province elections and, in New England, town meetings. The results were that the political systems of the colonies provided a rather small scope for the active participation of citizens in the formal agencies of government. They placed few constraints on free individuals, the public sphere was relatively small, and the private sector was exceptionally large.

A fourth important feature of the political systems of the colonies was that they were all basically exclusivist in their assumptions and operation; that is, they denied full rights of participation in political society to most of the inhabitants. Virtually all offices were appointive. Outside New England a variety of town offices and, in Connecticut and Rhode Island, where even some provincial offices, were elective, only representatives to the general assembly were not appointive, and the voting franchise was limited. After the first few decades of settlement, all colonies followed traditional English practice by establishing property requirements for the suffrage to elective offices. A majority of colonies required voters to own landed property.

But the lack of sufficient property was not the only criterion for exclusion from the franchise. In both Britain and its colonies, whole categories of people were denied the franchise whether or not they met prevailing property stipulations. Women, minors, aliens, Catholics, Jews, and nonwhites were all categories of people who could not be excluded on the grounds of property requirements alone or by the stake-in-society argument. Like slaves, servants, short-term tenants, the indigent, and even sons over twenty-one still living with their parents, most married women and most minors could be refused citizenship on these grounds. For unmarried women and any other members of these groups who may have met the property requirements, the reasons for denial had to lie elsewhere.

Sir William Blackstone elaborated fully and precisely what these bases were in his *Commentaries on the Laws of England* in the 1760s: "The *true* reason of requiring any qualification, with regard to property, in voters, is to exclude such persons as are in so mean a situation that they are esteemed to have no will of their own." Property, then, was an essential precondition for the suffrage, not only or even primarily because it demonstrated a permanent attachment to the community, but because it alone conveyed personal—as well as economic and political—independence. Those without property and those who, because of religious, legal, or family obligations, were subject to the wills of others simply did not have the degree of autonomy necessary for full rights of civic participation. A corollary of this assumption, one that required the exclusion of women, minors, nonwhites, and Jews who could meet the property requirements and therefore presumably had the requisite personal independence, was that groups with believed emotional, physical, or "natural" disabilities were incapable of controlling themselves and, for that reason, also lacked the competence to be accorded full civil status in society.

If, however, the political systems of the Anglo-American colonies were just as exclusivist as that of the metropolis in their assumptions about who was entitled to the full rights of political participation, a considerably larger portion of colonial populations actually enjoyed those rights. As a consequence of the relatively easy availability of land, a very large proportion of the free adult male inhabitants in the colonies (up to 80 percent to 90 percent in some colonies) acquired land, built estates, achieved individual independence, and thereby empowered themselves.

This widespread empowering process gave rise to strong demands on the part of the large settler populations for the extension to the colonies of the same rights to security of property and civic participation that appertained to independent property holders in England. In their view English colonial government, like English government, should guarantee that men of their standing would be neither governed by laws nor subjected to taxes enacted or imposed without their consent.

Although the breadth of the franchise gave the political cultures of the colonies a distinctly popular tinge, it did not lead to the predominance of those medium and small property holders who everywhere made up the great majority of voters. Rather, people from these groups usually exercised their franchise to return their social and economic betters to office; in every colony, members of the emerging colonial elites dominated elective, as well as appointive, offices.

This domination cannot be explained by the coercive models favored by historians during the first half of the twentieth century. There were simply too many instances of tenants voting against landlords, of clients rejecting patrons. Since the late 1950s historians have tended to attribute elite dominance to the fact that the political systems of the colonies, like that of Britain, operated within a deferential, rather than a democratic, political culture. Prescriptively at least, they functioned within an integrated structure of ideas that was fundamentally elitist in nature and assumed that government should be entrusted to men of merit. Merit was very often associated with wealth and social position, and men of merit were obligated to employ their superior talents and greater learning and expertise for the benefit of the public; deference to these men was therefore the implicit duty of the rest of society.

But the extent of deferential behavior in the colonies seems to have been limited. Voters often rejected representatives who acted against their wishes and otherwise treated unpopular elite figures in ways that reflected neither awe nor respect. Elite dominance may well have been more a function of lack of political interest than of either deference or elite control. In ordinary times in a society that provided such broad scope for engagement in the private realm, interest in public affairs seems to have been low.

Central Variables

None of these basic properties of the colonial political systems—not their colonial status, their separation into largely discrete political environments, the circumscribed nature of their operations, nor their exclusivist character—remained wholly constant over time. Of the four, however, only the first varied in sufficiently important ways to produce major repercussions in colonial political life before the 1760s. Indeed, the changing intensity in the degree of colonial involvement with the parent society was one of three crucial variables affecting the character of colonial political cultures.

In two sectors—the economic and the cultural—the direction of change in metropolitan-colonial relations was virtually linear. The rate of modification was obviously not constant over time and the extent of alteration was not uniform throughout the colonies. But between the 1660s and the 1770s, there was a powerful movement in both the economic and cultural realms toward an ever more intense involvement. From the initial implementation of the navigation system in the 1650s and 1660s, the tendency everywhere was toward a closer involvement with the economy of the home islands. By the middle of the eighteenth century, the economies even of the nonstaple-producing New England colonies had become tightly integrated with that of the metropolis. This growing participation, together with an increasing volume of contacts among individuals and the improved communications that accompanied it, drew the colonists ever closer into the ambit of British life during the eighteenth century. The exposure provided them with easier and more direct access to English and, increasingly, Scottish ideas and models of behavior, and tied them ever more closely to metropolitan culture.

By contrast, in the political and military sectors, there was no linear movement from lesser to greater involvement between colonies and metropolis. To be sure the metropolitan political presence as represented by the number of royal officials in the colonies increased steadily after 1650, when Virginia was the only royal colony and there was not yet an organized customs service in the colonies. By the early eighteenth century, the metropolitan civil establishment in the colonies, excluding customs and admiralty officials, consisted of about 40 officers scattered throughout North America and the West Indies. This number increased to 57 in 1730, 87 in 1747, and 98 in 1761. At the same time, the customs establishment slowly expanded from about 90 in 1710 to 107 in 1744 and about 115 in 1760. Though never very numerous, admiralty officials perhaps reached as many as 20 by 1760.

But the rise in the number of metropolitan-appointed officials in the colonies did not represent a steady increase in levels of metropolitan political involvement with the colonies. Indeed, the amount of metropolitan energy and attention applied to colonial supervision ebbed and flowed over time according to a wide assortment of international and domestic, as well as colonial, considerations. Two long periods of more systematic and intensive efforts by the metropolitan government to impose stricter controls over the political systems of the colonies—one lasting from the mid seventeenth century to about 1710 and the other from 1748 to 1783—were separated by a period characterized by a much more casual posture towards the colonies.

Militarily the metropolitan presence was insubstantial on the continent before the Seven Years' War, which brought at its high point over thirty thousand British regulars to the colonies, most of them to the continent. Up until that time, the metropolis had kept few troops in North America, even during the earlier intercolonial wars of 1689 to 1713 and 1739 to 1748. In 1754 fewer than eight hundred regulars were in the continental colonies, and they were about equally divided between New York and South Carolina.

Even during periods of the most intense metropolitan political involvement, however, the extent to which the metropolitan political system imposed upon those of the colonies varied enormously from place to place according to the political vulnerability of each colony. The degree of a colony's vulnerability was in turn a function of several different local factors. The concerns included how dependent the colony was upon the metropolis for external and internal defense; the longevity, strength, and character of local charters, traditions, customs, and institutions;

and the autonomy and self-consciousness of local leaders. The integration of the social with the political system and the degree to which it was incorporated into the metropolitan patronage system were additional components. Together these many local considerations, as they changed over time, were thus themselves a second crucial variable in determining the character of political development and patterns of political activity in individual colonies.

The third and, in many respects, the most important of these crucial variables was the changing social and economic circumstances of each colony. With the Anglophone colonies, as with all societies, the ethnic, cultural, and religious composition of the population, the demographic and social structure, the organization of the system of production, the strength of community attachment, and the degree of social integration as they changed over time inevitably affected in profound ways the nature and direction of political development. Moreover, transformations in many of these areas in most colonies came particularly rapidly as the colonists had to adapt themselves and their societies initially to the conditions of the New World. After about 1710 the colonists' exposure to the new problems and opportunities created by the extraordinary and sustained growth in population, agricultural production, overseas exports, buying power, and the extent of settled territory prompted further modifications.

This tremendous expansion obviously was not uniform throughout the colonies. It proceeded at differential rates and produced varying effects. But it was everywhere one of the most salient features of colonial life between 1710 and 1760 and left rapid and extensive developments in its wake. By enlarging the size of the polity and the pool of potential leaders and politically relevant members of the population; by stretching institutional structures; by increasing social stratification and occupational differentiation and thereby either undermining or reinforcing the degree of social integration or strength of community; and by significantly enlarging the range and level of colonial aspirations, the remarkable expansion of the colonies affected the character of their political cultures.

Contrary to the assertions of post–World War II scholarship, these changes were by no means always disruptive or destabilizing. Perhaps because this process of growth seems, at least through its early and middle stages, to have been characterized by a major expansion in mobility opportunities, the increase in social aspirations that accompanied it did not lead to deep or widespread social frustration and political and social mobilization. In a few cases, as will be indicated later, it did create either social contenders for power who resorted to open political conflict to achieve their ambitions or an acute sense of political deprivation or discrimination among some aspiring segments of the population.

Patterns of Political Interaction

Within the context established by the basic properties discussed above, these three crucial variables—the degree of colonial involvement with the metropolis, the specifically local circumstances of politics, and the changing conditions of social and economic life—interacted to shape colonial political cultures. Because there were considerable differences in the nature and operation of these variables from one political environment to another, there were significant variations in the form and character of those cultures among the several colonies. Despite these many important variations, the political systems of the Anglophone colonies in America seem to have been moving, at different rates of speed, through a general developmental cycle. With some important exceptions, this cycle was roughly sequential in character and had three distinct, if also sometimes overlapping, stages.

Initially, the political systems of all of the colonies operated on a relatively primitive level. Political resources were sparse; virtually everywhere, leadership and institutional structures were weak and undefined, levels of political expertise and socialization were low, and political consciousness was inchoate and undeveloped. Under such conditions political life was usually brittle, often even explosive, as would-be leaders jockeyed with each other in a ruthless competition for power, wealth, and prestige.

This primitive politics of competition first appeared in Virginia during the earliest decades of settlement. For thirty-five years following the dissolution of the Virginia Company in the mid 1620s, a group of self-made tobacco magnates vied with each other and with royal officials for control over the economic spoils of the colony.

This ruthless struggle, occupying the very center of political life, was repeated up and down the seaboard and in the islands of Anglophone America. Maryland until 1689, Pennsylvania, South Carolina, New Hampshire, Rhode Island, and New Jersey until the 1730s and 1740s, and North Carolina until the eve of the American Revolution seem to have followed Virginia's early pattern. As long as social status and claims to leadership were unclear, political life remained chronically troubled.

But the vigorous competition that characterized the politics of most colonies during the first two or three generations of settlement was only one of two predominant patterns that marked the primitive stage in the development of politics in Anglophone America. A second was the politics of oligarchy, a situation in which public life was dominated by a single, unified group. Bound together by common religious beliefs, economic interests, patronage and kinship ties, or some combination of these factors, these dominant groups monopolized all avenues to political power and most of the primary sources of wealth. Massachusetts before 1684 and New York between its conquest by England in 1664 and Leisler's Rebellion in 1689 furnish clear examples of this type of politics.

Well into the eighteenth century, one or the other of these two types of primitive politics—the politics of competition or the politics of oligarchy—characterized the political life of every colony in Anglophone America, and some colonies actually shifted from one to the other and back again. Both types persisted in politically underdeveloped colonies until 1763, but the politics of oligarchy was possible only in very special circumstances in which small groups could monopolize political and economic power. Thus during the eighteenth century, it existed, on the continent, only in the relatively small and undeveloped colonies of Nova Scotia and New Hampshire during the 1740s, 1750s, and 1760s.

Beginning in the 1720s and 1730s, these primitive forms of politics began to give way to more traditional modes that more closely approximated the politics of the metropolitan state. The result was an era that, in comparison to earlier periods, was one of considerable political coherence and effectiveness that continued in most colonies at least into the 1750s and 1760s.

273

The history of Virginia provides a graphic example of one form this transition to traditional politics could take. At the end of the second decade of the eighteenth century, Lieutenant Governor Alexander Spotswood reached an accommodation with local leaders that finally broke the pattern of conflict that with the single exception of the brief period from 1660 to 1676 had characterized the public life of the colony from its very foundation. By carefully cultivating local leaders as well as imitating Sir Robert Walpole, Britain's own highly successful first minister, in his emphasis upon harmony and cooperation among all branches of government, Spotswood's successors, Hugh Drysdale and, especially, Sir William Gooch, who administered the colony from 1727 to 1749, managed both to extirpate faction and to achieve a new political cooperation that lasted for the remainder of the colonial period.

Both pragmatic politicians, Drysdale and Gooch studiously avoided transgressing local interests and cherished customs and traditions. In the process they managed, largely through the force of their own moral and political leadership and with almost no utilitarian resources at their disposal, to achieve a situation in which the vast majority of legislators routinely supported the administration. The legislators, thereby, in one of the very few such instances in the whole of the Anglophone colonial experience, actually exhibited habits of obedience to the Crown similar to those displayed by the independent members of Parliament in Britain, whose normal posture was one of support for the administration. With the exception of Robert Dinwiddie during the first years of his tenure in the early 1750s, subsequent governors obtained similar results by following the successful examples of Drysdale and Gooch.

In forging this system of politics, Drysdale and Gooch were, of course, aided by the new concern of metropolitan authorities after 1720 to achieve peace and order in the colonies, even at relatively high costs, and by the fact that, in contrast to the situation in earlier years, Virginia was no longer tied so closely into the British patronage system. They were helped as well by a fortunate set of circumstances within Virginia, where sharp political divisions were discouraged by a generally favorable economic situation, a

homogeneity of economic and social interests among all regions and all social classes among the free population, a high degree of social and religious integration, and a community of political leaders so large as to make it impossible for a single group to monopolize political power.

Virginia politics between 1720 and 1770 provides a classic example of what Samuel Huntington, a political scientist, has described as a situation of traditional stability. In the absence of large or important urban centers, the countryside was dominant in this situation. The rural elite governed unchallenged by endogenous groups, with the tenantry and yeomanry assuming a passive or only marginally active political role and the weak intermediate class of lawyers and merchants tending to ally itself with the dominant elite.

During the same period, South Carolina, Pennsylvania, and Massachusetts developed their own systems of traditional politics, each with its own underlying coherence and order. A slightly different configuration of forces produced a very similar pattern of development in South Carolina, after 1746, probably the Crown's wealthiest and most thriving (in terms of per capita wealth of free inhabitants) continental possession. Settled over six decades after Virginia, South Carolina, like most colonies, was the scene of violent political strife for much of its first fifty years, during which merchants were arrayed against planters, immigrants from the West Indies against those who came directly from Britain, Britons against French Huguenots, Churchmen against Dissenters, town against countryside, and local leaders against the proprietors. This discord culminated in the overthrow of the proprietors in 1719, but royal government did not immediately put an end to the political turmoil. A demand for an increase in paper money, stimulated by a severe depression during the late 1720s, brought renewed chaos, the provincial government broke down completely, and the colony came dangerously close to civil war. Only after the permanent implementation of royal government in 1730 was this tumultuous pattern of politics broken.

In contrast to the situation in Virginia, however, the moral leadership of the royal governors was not an important ingredient in the new era of public peace that began to take shape during the 1730s and continued to characterize the political life of the colony until the regulator troubles of the late 1760s. Although the prospects for this stability were enhanced by the absence of pressure emanating from the metropolitan government during the 1730s and 1740s, it was built primarily upon the gradual integration of hitherto competing and disparate interests and groups during the ever-increasing prosperity enjoyed by the colony through the middle decades of the eighteenth century.

With prosperity came not only the moving aside of earlier religious and ethnic differences but also a homogenization of economic interests. The common pursuit of profit in this bustling staple economy drew merchants and planters, town and country, into a symbiotic relationship and led to the development of close ties of consanguinity, a consciousness of shared economic interests, and a consensus about social and political priorities among the colony's emergent elite, which included a rising professional class of lawyers as well as merchants and planters. This new unanimity inhibited factionalism. There was a growing sense of need among the colony's small white population, composed of a relatively large elite and a comparatively small yeoman and artisanal class, to present a solid front against a burgeoning African slave majority (which had actually erupted in rebellion in 1739). Moreover, a series of minor crises during the late 1730s and 1740s underlined the necessity for internal political unity.

After 1750 the multiplication of the number of British placemen in executive offices and on the royal council and the renewal of pressure from the metropolitan government created tensions between the local elite and metropolitan representatives in the colony's administration. But these tensions, and the few open conflicts they generated, did not again divide the colony's leaders into factions. What South Carolina politics represented after 1730 was thus a stable town-country alliance in which a tightly interlocked urban-rural elite with a common vision of socioeconomic and political goals governed without challenge from inside the society and with remarkable social and political harmony.

A variation on the South Carolina pattern can be found in the experience of Pennsylvania,

one of the last settled of the major Anglophone colonies in America and, by the 1720s, already one of the most dynamic centers of demographic and economic growth in the whole of the Americas. Like South Carolina and Virginia, Pennsylvania was fraught with social and political turmoil for most of its early history. Disagreements between Proprietor William Penn and Quaker leaders in the colony over a variety of issues, the vigorous antiauthoritarianism of the predominant Quaker majority, and the attenuation of a sense of community among Quakers early split the colony into warring factions and established a pattern of political turmoil that persisted for nearly a half century. No sooner did an antiproprietary clique composed largely of leading Philadelphia Quaker merchants and their country allies wrest power from Penn's supporters than it found itself challenged by a coalition of lesser men organized into a loose country party under the leadership of David Lloyd. Two unfortunate choices as governor—Charles Gookin and Sir William Keith—and bitter disagreements over proprietary power, conditions of land tenure, and paper currency kept the fires of faction alive for another fifteen years.

Only after 1725 did this pattern finally begin to recede. The tactful administration of Patrick Gordon for a decade beginning in 1726, the disappearance of the old political issues, the death of Lloyd, and the emergence of Andrew Hamilton, a proponent of cooperation with the proprietor, as the colony's leading political figure, all worked to set the stage for a new era of harmony in public life and the virtual extinction of factional politics. During the 1730s the failure of the proprietor to exploit favorable conditions for the development of a strong proprietary political interest left the "Quaker party," a tight coalition of city and country leaders which controlled the powerful assembly, in a dominant position in Pennsylvania politics. This position was strengthened by the failure in 1740 to 1742 of a strong proprietary challenge led by Governor George Thomas over the issue of the Quakers' refusal to support the war effort against Spain, and for the next twelve years conditions of cooperation prevailed as Quaker control of the assembly went unchallenged.

During the early 1750s the growth of a powerful proprietary interest—composed mainly of an increasing body of wealthy Anglican merchants and proprietary officeholders in the city and some of the leaders of the Presbyterian and German settlers in the back country—along with the proprietor's attempt to shore up executive authority, secure exemption from taxation of proprietary lands, and gain financial support for the British war effort against France again brought factional politics to Pennsylvania, and the contention lasted for a decade. Significantly, however, the new factional competition did not yield the same sort of bitter and endemic conflict, civil disorder, and political breakdown that had marked the first decades of Pennsylvania politics.

In Massachusetts, the oldest and largest of the New England colonies, a similar pattern of development is observable. After a full half-century of conflict, the quarter century beginning in 1730 was one of basic political peace. A long-standing contest over the royal prerogative quickly abated during the late 1720s following a de facto constitutional compromise between the governor and the Assembly. In addition, the rural-urban antagonism that had underlain much of the factional strife of previous decades became much less pronounced as representatives from the rural towns increasingly deferred to the leadership of a small, socially prominent elite from the maritime east—at least as long as it served the interests of the rural, agricultural majority.

By working within and respecting this delicate balance of political forces, a governor could count on cooperation from the legislature and, from the point of view of local leaders, a successful administration. That he did not proved the eventual undoing of Jonathan Belcher. Despite a taste for compromise, he was unable during the land bank controversy in 1740 to 1741 to walk the narrow line between the inflationary forces in the colony and their opponents in Massachusetts and London.

His successor, William Shirley, who governed the colony for sixteen years from 1741 to 1757, operated in this new political milieu far more successfully. With strong connections in Britain and a talent for conciliation, he made skillful use of the limited local patronage at his command as well as the many contracts and offices at his disposal as a result of the military operations in the northern colonies during King George's War to attach many of the colony's leading men to the administration and to gain their support for his legislative programs. This administrative machine evoked fears among Shirley's opponents of a "Robinarchical" corruption of the kind charged against Walpole in Britain that by the 1760s, after his departure, had become sufficiently narrow and restrictive as to call forth widespread charges of "oligarchy" from those who were not a part of it. These charges took on additional resonance from the perspective of the revolutionary controversy.

But Shirley's machine was never so strong as to be able to ignore the wishes of the rural majority. The urban-rural alliance in Massachusetts—which, like those in South Carolina and Pennsylvania, was crucial to the achievement of a more settled political life between 1730 and 1760—was thus based less upon mutuality of interests, as in South Carolina, or the workings of an interlocking elite that brought town and country together in pursuit of shared, economic, political, and religious goals, as in Pennsylvania. Rather, Shirley's machine was an alliance born out of the necessity for compromise, in which, notwithstanding an occasional lack of congruity of interests or social goals, rural votes joined with eastern expertise to fashion a stable political environment.

In special circumstances a few colonies—those in which levels of conflict or the potential for conflict remained high—began to move beyond the boundaries of traditional politics and to develop informal structures for the routinization of conflict that gave their political cultures a distinctly modern cast. New York provides the most familiar model of this development. Marked by ethnic, religious, economic, and sectional diversity, New York society was never able to achieve the same levels of socioeconomic and cultural integration that characterized Virginia and South Carolina. Despite ties of consanguinity, the split between the mercantile elite in the towns and the Hudson River landlords—between the commercial and the landed interests—was too deep to permit the development of the kind of close-knit elite that bound town and country so tightly together in Pennsylvania and South Carolina. Never a large colony, New York, unlike Massachusetts, was not forced by the sheer complexity of social and economic circumstances to develop a differentiated political system that, by consent of all segments of the politically relevant, placed power in the hands of an identifiable and responsive elite in the capital. More closely tied into the British patronage system than any of the other four colonies, including even Massachusetts, the political life of New York was always less self-contained and always more sensitive to shocks from the vagaries of British politics than those of other colonies on the continent. In New York, moreover, politics seems to have continued to be looked upon as a source of economic gain by a much wider segment of the political leadership and for a much longer time than was the case in the other four colonies.

Except perhaps for a brief period in the early 1740s, New York never experienced the diminution of factional strife that characterized the experiences of so many other colonies for much of the period between 1730 and 1760. Instead it developed other ways to come to turns with the blatant factionalism of its politics. By the mid 1730s, the multiplicity of interests in the colony seems to have become too great. Too many interests had become too powerful and too assertive to permit a governor ever again to purchase political calm by systematically cultivating one interest at the expense of all others, as governors Robert Hunter and William Burnet had done between 1715 and 1729.

What seems to have evolved beginning in the late 1730s was a new mode of politics, the central feature of which was a vigorous, functional, and strikingly modern rivalry among the colony's multiplicity of interests within clearly defined—and agreed upon—political boundaries. Through the eventual creation of loose and semipermanent parties, this rivalry routinized and institutionalized competition at the same time that it discouraged or diminished the possibilities for explosive open conflict, civil disorder, and political disruption. Moreover, the rivalry gave expression to occasional apologies for parties as legitimate agencies for the expression of interests in society, a development that in the Anglophone American world would be highly uncommon for at least another half century. In a complex political society such as that of New York, parties thus seem to have been a necessary precondition for the achievement of political coherence.

Characteristics

Whatever form it took, the increasing political coherence exhibited by most colonies after 1730 was both a product and a reflection of a major development of political resources. This development can best be discussed as it was manifest in five principal areas: elite articulation; institutional development; configurations of political consciousness; patterns of relations between the elite and other politically relevant segments of society; and the expansion of the public realm.

Stable, coherent, and acknowledged political and social elites were slow to emerge in most of the Anglophone American colonies. Only Virginia, Massachusetts, and Connecticut had what might with some semblance of credibility be described as reasonably thoroughly articulated elites by the beginning of the eighteenth century. Elsewhere elites were unstable and inchoate and contained few men of substance and learning. In this situation political leadership fell to men who were at best only partially equipped for their tasks and who had a parochial and basically utilitarian orientation towards government. Men went into public life in large part because it provided them with concrete economic and social benefits in the form of easier access to land, special business or professional advantages, lucrative public office, or higher social status.

But the character, quality, and orientation of political leadership changed radically during the first half of the eighteenth century. By the 1730s and 1740s in all but a few of the colonies, the nascent elites had achieved considerable success in their efforts to establish themselves at the center of colonial life. By European standards they were, in many respects, peculiar elites. At their core was to be found, in every case, a group of first families or descendants of first families. Having successfully established themselves during the first or second generations after settlement, these families managed to retain their wealth and social standing in the discordant years of the late seventeenth and early eighteenth century. But especially in colonies like South Carolina, which experienced extraordinary economic booms after 1740, and like Pennsylvania and New York, where rapid commercial expansion opened up widespread new opportunities in commerce and the professions, the elites were, in some significant part, nouveau riche in compo-

277

sition. Even in older colonies like Virginia and Massachusetts, there was always room for the talented newcomer or upstart who managed to pull himself up the economic ladder. Membership in the elite thus depended at least as much upon achievement and merit as upon traditional ascriptive criteria such as family or inherited status.

With such origins and with no legally sanctioned sphere of influence, colonial elites, unlike their metropolitan model, developed neither an exclusive function nor that well-developed and secure sense of identity that derives from longevity and the illusion of permanence it creates. To a very large extent, the colonial elites remained loose categories and never developed into sharply defined corporate groups. For that reason none of the colonies ever elaborated an aristocratic political culture of the kind that existed throughout western Europe.

But these emergent colonial elites did acquire a high degree of coherence and visibility within their respective societies. Through intermarriage and personal and social ties, they early formulated those informal, inter-elite relationships and communications patterns that characterize elites in every society and, like their great estates and closer connections to metropolitan culture, helped to set them apart from people in other social categories. The imposing—by American standards—houses they built in increasing numbers through the middle decades of the eighteenth century in the country and in towns, like those of the English gentry, expressed in monumental form their accomplishments and standing.

These cohering elites, spreading, as one contemporary remarked, in size and influence as the colonies became more wealthy, provided a growing reservoir of political leaders. The progenitors of these elites—the men who between 1640 and 1720 had established and consolidated the positions of the elites in colonial life—had fulfilled themselves by acquiring estates, obtaining status in the community, and enhancing the family name. But their extraordinary success meant that their heirs, who were just coming into manhood during the 1720s and 1730s—members of the second generation in newer colonies like South Carolina, New Jersey, and Pennsylvania and of the third generation in older

provinces like Virginia, Massachusetts, Maryland, and New York—had to look elsewhere to find a suitable outlet for their energies and talents.

For men whose wealth and security of position provided them with the necessary leisure to direct at least part of their attention into noneconomic channels, politics provided the most exciting, challenging, and rewarding opportunities in mid-eighteenth-century Anglophone America. Many men—for the most part first-generation arrivistes like the Massachusetts merchant Thomas Hancock—still entered public life primarily to advance their economic or material interests. For a significant proportion of the established elite, however, and even many of the more thoroughly socialized among the new men, politics was becoming an important and time-consuming activity. Within a decade on either side of 1730 in most colonies, these elites had transformed themselves into communities of experienced and expert politicians who enjoyed the challenges and responsibilities they found in the political arena.

The majority of men in government at both the local and provincial levels continued to be men of narrow experience and vision. But the influence of the experts was far out of proportion to their numbers. Exhibiting attitudes and values that derived from the special inside roles they played within the political arena, they acquired the knowledge and the connections to give them authority in public life. The emergence of the colonial elites with a solid nucleus of men having a powerful commitment to politics thus led to a significant differentiation and specialization of roles within the colonial political systems.

The materialization of these communities of experienced politicians also produced important changes in the character of existing institutions. The royal and proprietary councils, and even the judiciary, were in most places through the first half of the eighteenth century local institutions in the sense that a large number of their members were drawn out of the colonial elites; but the largest and most dynamic of the institutions at the provincial level were the elected lower houses of assembly. By the 1730s some of these bodies were a century old. From the beginning they had been aggressive institutions, and by the last decades of the seventeenth century, most of them were displaying a marked tendency to claim privileges of the English House of Commons.

Although their role in the colonial political systems was enhanced by the demands of the first two intercolonial wars between 1689 and 1713, some of the lower houses still lacked independence and guarantees of regular meetings and frequent elections. The intense self-consciousness that characterized the English House of Commons after, if not to a great extent also before, the Glorious Revolution was also absent. Under the guidance of the new political experts through the early and middle decades of the eighteenth century, the lower houses consolidated their position in the colonial governments and acquired greater autonomy as the growing complexities of the political process made them indispensable to the functioning of the colonial political systems. They articulated a much more precise sense of their corporate rights and defined their procedures more clearly. They otherwise sought to give substance to the ideal that the lower houses, as the sole givers of internal public law and as the presumed equivalents of the British House of Commons, were endowed with charismatic authority and held in trusteeship all of the sacred rights and privileges of the public.

Other political institutions at both the provincial and local levels presumably underwent a similar process of corporate definition and consolidation of authority. This occurred especially in the localities, which with the rapid growth of the colonies during the eighteenth century seem to have assumed an ever higher burden of responsibility for maintaining social order.

In the area of specialized political infrastructure, the colonial political cultures were relatively undeveloped. To some extent the embryonic political parties in New York and Rhode Island and, to a much lesser degree, in Maryland and Connecticut during the late colonial period had developed rudimentary organizations and systematically cultivated bases of support. Elsewhere, however, political groups, as in the case of Massachusetts, were small, close-knit, and ephemeral. Even in New York and Rhode Island, where an interest group theory of representation was more thoroughly developed, there were no well-defined or reasonably permanent pressure groups, public associations, or other organizations to process demands and proposals from the citizenry. The absence or rudimentary character of such an infrastructure meant, of course, that the political institutions of the colonies were not highly developed in modern terms.

Within the context of the new political stability and under the influence of the newly formed community of expert politicians, traditional configurations of political consciousness also underwent important changes. These were a result of a shift in those agreed upon and unquestioned premises that shape patterns of political perception, provide guidelines for acceptable political behavior and a moral basis for political action, and determine the underlying propensities of the political system. Although political consciousness was not the preserve of the elite, it was concentrated in and most fully developed among that group. In the colonies, as in most societies, it was the elite that best understood and most consistently based its evaluations upon the generally accepted beliefs and values of the political systems.

Increasingly under the early Stuarts, politics in England began to display a new appreciation of political and constitutional issues. This appreciation—which revolved around a conception of political life as a perpetual struggle between prerogative and privilege, between a grasping and arbitrary monarch and a beleaguered House of Commons fighting valiantly to preserve the rights of the people—was transferred to the colonies in the seventeenth century; there it was given additional power and a continuing hold on the minds of colonial legislators because of the Crown's exaggerated claims for prerogative in the colonies. In Britain under the later Stuarts and increasingly during the first half of the eighteenth century, fears of prerogative were supplanted by fears of corruption. Court influence or ministerial corruption, which was associated with the standing army, placemen, pensioners, and a mounting national debt, came to be set in opposition against the ideal of the virtuous, uncorrupted, and independent (preferably landed) proprietor; the latter's economic independence, active patriotism, and sense of civic responsibility were regarded as both the primary bulwarks against the subversion of liberty by the minions of corruption and, ideally, the prerequisites for the exercise of a voice in the political system since it was believed that people who did not hold them should vote.

For aspiring political elites whose major claim to social position rested upon the amount of property at their command and for many of whom propertied independence was an undeniable reality, the appeal of this conception of politics was irresistible. But the ideal of the vigilant, independent, and patriotic landholder struck far greater resonances—and had a deeper and more lasting impact upon colonial political consciousness—than did the fears of corruption. Without a standing army, a large civil establishment, sinecures, pensions, secret service funds, or, indeed, much patronage, colonial administrations simply lacked the means for effective corruption in the style of Sir Robert Walpole. Colonial political leaders did indeed worry about corruption. However, it was the more primitive form of corruption arising from the evil and avarice of individual governors and other officials that concerned them and not corruption deriving out of court or administrative influence. Only in those places like Governor William Shirley's Massachusetts or proprietary Maryland, where the governors did have some patronage at their disposal, did the fears of ministerial corruption seem to have achieved much appeal or frequency of expression.

But there was an additional reason why this newer conception of politics as an adversary relationship between virtue and corruption did not achieve still wider acceptance and why the older notion of politics as conflict between privilege and prerogative lost some of its appeal through the middle decades of the eighteenth century. With the gradual relaxation of pressure from London beginning in the 1720s, colonial politics, under the accommodative ministrations of men like Gooch, came to be seen more as a cooperative and less as an antagonistic process. No longer faced with claims for excessive prerogative powers from the governors, many of whom were becoming increasingly domesticated, a rising community of expert politicians could feel free to cultivate a pragmatic concern for compromise and for accommodation with the executive in the pursuit of the public weal. In Virginia and Massachusetts where, for somewhat different reasons, political stability lasted for several decades. There even developed a vital tradition of such cooperation, along with a habit of following executive leadership that was not too dissimilar from the tradition among the British parliamentary elite of routine obedience to the Crown. The revival of prerogative claims by authorities in the metropolis beginning in the late 1740s seriously undermined this tradition.

These changes in the character of leadership, institutions, and consciousness were accompanied by an alteration in the relationship between leaders and constituents. This alteration was manifest in a transition from an essentially aggressive and participatory stance toward the political process on the part of constituents to one that was much more passive and deferential. Before 1725 popular involvement in the political process had often been extensive. Mostly characterized by open voting in the English tradition, elections could be rowdy affairs. Candidates appeared personally and solicited votes through promises and treating. Voter turnout was relatively high, contested elections normal, and turnover among representatives very high. With such extensive popular involvement in the electoral process, voters often expressed their preferences aggressively, and legislative leaders frequently found that they had to accede to the articulated wishes of the large political communities they served.

One of the most conspicuous features of the new era of political settledness after 1725 was the contraction of the role of the electorate. Suffrage remained high. Within the limits imposed by the exclusivist assumptions on which they were based, colonial political systems were extraordinarily inclusive. The contraction in political participation did not result from the systematic exclusion by the leadership of any segment of the traditional electorate. Rather, a larger proportion of voters seems merely to have withdrawn from active involvement in the political process and neglected to participate in elections. Unless a vital public issue was involved, voters simply did not vote in large numbers. As long as government did not threaten burdensome taxes or act in ways that seemed inimical to its interests, most of the electorate found no need to engage actively in politics, albeit it always retained the latent authority to thwart any political action it opposed.

This phenomenon can be seen in the relative turnover rates (the percentage of new people returned) in elections to the colonial legislatures during the eighteenth century. These rates were everywhere high at the beginning of the century, frequently reaching as much as from 70 percent to 80 percent, but they declined over the following seventy-five years as the political systems of the colonies became more settled. One group of colonies—Massachusetts, South Carolina, and Virginia—was characterized by a relatively steady long-term decline. Thus, turnover in Massachusetts, where elections were annual, fell from an average of 55 percent in the 1720s to 45 percent in the period 1730 to 1759, 32 percent in the 1760s, and 28 percent in the 1770s. In Virginia, where elections were irregular but never at intervals of more than seven years, turnover dropped from an average of around 50 percent in the 1710s and 1730s to 45 percent in the 1750s, 33 percent in the 1760s, and 26 percent in the 1770s.

In a second major pattern, found in Maryland, New Hampshire, New Jersey, New York, North Carolina, and Pennsylvania, turnover rates fell considerably earlier and more abruptly than elsewhere. After mid century, they began to rise more or less steadily, though not to the levels at the beginning of the century. Thus in New York, to take one example, the turnover rate declined precipitously to an average of just 29 percent in the 1710s and 27 percent in the 1720s. Though they increased to slightly over 40 percent during the turbulent 1730s, they fell again to 22 percent in the 1740s and 1750s before beginning to rise in 1759 to an average of over 40 percent for the remainder of the colonial period.

A similar development occurred with reference to officeholding. The steady spread of settlement, growth of population, and creation of new political units meant that in absolute numbers more people had access to and actually held office. But it was a declining proportion of the total population. Moreover, the extension of political jurisdictions meant that of the people in peripheral areas, only those with connections to the provincial capital did not live in a geographical isolation that effectively excluded them from access to office at the provincial level. In addition, growing social differentiation created a great social and technical gap between the elite and the rest of the members of society, who lacked the expertise and the social prerequisites for high office. The result was that a smaller and smaller percentage of the whole society could expect to hold important offices at either the provincial or local levels. Because this development was gradual, however, few seem to have felt any serious sense of relative deprivation.

The changing ratio of representatives in the legislature to potential voters (adult white males) between 1700 and 1770 provides a clear indication of the growing distance between constituents and leaders. During the first seven decades of the eighteenth century, those ratios rose relatively slowly in North Carolina, Rhode Island, Massachusetts, Connecticut, and Virginia and much more rapidly in New Hampshire, New York, Maryland, Delaware, South Carolina, Pennsylvania, and New Jersey. Especially in these last four colonies, the distance between voters and representatives was growing so rapidly that by 1770 their legislatures were less representative than those of other colonies and probably also less in touch with the constituents' needs or capacity to absorb new people with political ambitions.

The demobilization of the broad body politic represented by the low level of participation in elections, declining turnover rates, and the acceptance of the legitimacy of a more and more elitist leadership structure must be seen in part as the result of a broad satisfaction with the government provided by the new expert politicians. This approval was also revealed in the scope of support that the constituency regularly extended to the political system through paying taxes, obeying laws, and otherwise manifesting respect for and attachment to the political community and its symbols, institutions, and leaders. This widespread demobilization must also be seen as an indication of a growing degree of political socialization on the part of all segments of the free community, as they each found their places within and became increasingly more integrated into the political systems of the colonies.

Demobilization and political socialization, along with the increasingly deferential behavior that accompanied them, suggest, of course, that the political systems of the Anglophone American colonies were, under the guidance of the new professionals, performing the tasks assigned to them relatively well. As several scholars have argued for different colonies, they were both effective and responsive to the needs and wishes of their respective societies. They had also developed a capacity to avoid or resolve conflicts. As in Britain the localities were the primary conflict arenas, and a variety of potentially explosive issues were raised and resolved on that level. At the provincial level, rivalry among leaders and the push and pull of politics were perpetual, but civil disorder became extremely rare.

After 1715 civil discord tended to be confined to certain specific and well-defined situations. Discord erupted where the political system failed to perform its expected functions, as in the South Carolina revolt against the proprietors in 1719. Disagreements among strong contending parties over land titles, as in the land riots in New Jersey during the late 1740s and early 1750s and in New York in the 1750s, also provoked unrest. A loss of public confidence in the controlling leaders because of their failure to act on an issue of great moment to some significant segment of the population, as in Pennsylvania during the exclusion crisis of 1756 or the Paxton uprising in 1764, caused unease. A fourth instance happened when the political machinery had been stretched too far to provide adequate government, as in the case of the North Carolina Regulators. A deadlock between more or less equal contending forces resulted in a serious breakdown of government. The representation controversies in North Carolina and New Hampshire during the late 1740s illustrate this case. Finally, discord broke out when the traditional rights and privileges of the community were thought to be threatened by an external power. The impressment riots in Boston in the 1740s exemplify this point.

The colonial political systems had difficulty in dealing with such irregular occurrences, but neither the volume nor the range of such phenomena was very great. The susceptibility of the political systems to demands, the general level of political trust of leaders by constituents, and a new level of civility in the political arena all helped to avoid or routinize conflict. They also worked to promote a conception of politics as an accommodative, rather than a discordant, process in which the broad body of the people normally deferred to the leadership and decisions of a highly professional and competent political elite with confidence in its capacity to govern.

A final area in which there were significant developments during the middle decades of the eighteenth century was in the improvement of the modes of communication and the emergence of nongovernmental institutions that provided political training and dispersed political knowledge. These included a relatively vigorous, if not always entirely autonomous, press; a growing and increasingly sophisticated and competent legal profession; schools, including additional institutions of higher learning; voluntary associations such as coffeehouse groups, clubs, chambers of commerce, agricultural improvement associations, and professional societies; and expanding networks of trade. Along with an increase in travel, literacy, and books and other printed materials, these progressions contributed to the erosion of much of the traditional localism of rural America and provided easier access to metropolitan knowledge and technical skills. Moreover, they encouraged the rapid development of human capital—in sum to expand the cognitive map and augment the political potential of the colonists.

More directly, despite the low level of participation in elections and the declining proportion of the population that could expect to hold public office, men at all levels of society routinely engaged in an extraordinary number of public and private transactions. These dealings included property transfers, public obligations, and litigation that involved contact with government. Through these transactions British colonists obtained a range and a depth of political competence that was rare among contemporary political societies in either colonial America or Europe, and this capacity helped to create a relatively broad and informed citizenry.

But the political implications of the enormous expansion of the public realm represented by these developments remained largely latent before the 1760s. The emergence of an increased public participation in public affairs, a remobilization of the constituency, became much more manifest beginning with the Stamp Act crisis. Thereafter, the politicization of the colonists increased in response to the engrossing controversies that occurred during the last decade before independence. The potential for such broad and deep politicization had been growing rapidly over the previous generation. But in the more settled political world that obtained in most of the colonies for much of the period between the 1720s and the early 1760s, nothing happened to bring it to full development.

During the years from 1720 to 1760, the conflicted political systems of the seventeenth- and early-eighteenth-century Anglophone American colonies gradually gave way to a more settled, traditional, and, in a few cases, even somewhat modern political order. This new order depended upon and was characterized by the muting of longstanding issues that had earlier polarized the political community, the reduction of factional strife to levels at which it became either unimportant or routinized and functional, the acceptance by political society of existing institutional and leadership arrangements, and the regularization of relations among the several branches and levels of government. Lower rates of turnover among elected officials, the orderly transfer of authority or leadership through normal constitutional channels without serious disruption of the polity, and ordinarily low levels of collective violence and civil disorder completed the picture.

The extensive political development that both defined and contributed to the further elaboration of these new political cultures—in leadership, institutions, political consciousness, the socialization of the electorate to their political systems, and instruments of communication and nongovernmental political training institutions—was irreversible. And it provided the political systems of the Anglo-American colonies with vastly increased capabilities and resources that would prove indispensable in coping with the challenges that lay beyond 1763.

BIBLIOGRAPHY

Almond, Gabriel A., and G. Bingham Powell, Jr. *Comparative Politics: A Developmental Approach.* Boston, 1966.

Almond, Gabriel A., and Sidney Verba. *The Civic Culture: Political Attitudes and Democracy in Five Nations.* Princeton, N.J., 1963.

Archdeacon, Thomas J. *New York City, 1664–1710: Conquest and Change.* Ithaca, N.Y., 1976.

Bailey, Raymond C. *Popular Influence upon Public Policy: Petitioning in Eighteenth-Century Virginia.* Westport, Conn., 1979.

Bailyn, Bernard. *The New England Merchants in the Seventeenth Century.* Cambridge, Mass., 1955.

———. *The Origins of American Politics.* New York, 1968.

———. "Politics and Social Structure in Virginia." In *Seventeenth-Century America: Essays on Colonial History*, edited by James Morton Smith. Chapel Hill, N.C., 1959.

Baker, Keith M., ed. *The French Revolution and the Creation of Modern Political Culture.* Volume 1, *The Political Culture of the Old Regime.* Oxford, 1987.

Barker, Charles A. *The Background of the Revolution in Maryland.* New Haven, Conn., 1940.

Bonomi, Patricia U. *A Factious People: Politics and Society in Colonial New York.* New York, 1971.

Borah, Woodrow. "Representative Institutions in the Spanish Empire in the Sixteenth Century: III. The New World." *The Americas* 12, no. 3 (1956):246–257.

Brebner, John Bartlett. *The Neutral Yankees of Nova Scotia.* New York, 1937.

Breen, Timothy H. *The Character of the Good Ruler: A Study of Puritan Political Ideas in New England, 1630–1730.* New Haven, Conn., 1970.

Brown, Robert E., and B. Katherine Brown. *Virginia, 1705–1786: Democracy or Aristocracy?* East Lansing, Mich., 1964.

Buel, Richard, Jr. "Democracy and the American Revolution: A Frame of Reference." *William and Mary Quarterly*, 3rd ser., 21, no. 2 (1964):165–190.

Bushman, Richard L. "Corruption and Power in Provincial America." In *The Development of a Revolutionary Mentality*, by Library of Congress Symposia on the American Revolution. Washington, D.C., 1972.

———. *From Puritan to Yankee: Character and the Social Order in Connecticut, 1690–1765.* Cambridge, Mass., 1967.

———. *King and People in Provincial Massachusetts.* Chapel Hill, N.C., 1985.

Bushnell, Amy. *The King's Coffer: Proprietors of the Spanish Florida Treasury, 1565–1702.* Gainesville, Fla., 1981.

Cook, Edward Marks, Jr. *The Fathers of the Towns: Leadership and Community Structure in Eighteenth-Century New England.* Baltimore, Md., 1976.

Cremin, Lawrence A. *American Education: The Colonial Experience, 1607–1783.* New York, 1970.

Daniell, Jere R. *Experiment in Republicanism: New Hampshire Politics and the American Revolution, 1741–1794.* Cambridge, Mass., 1970.

Daniels, Bruce C., ed. *Power and Status: Officeholding in Colonial America.* Middletown, Conn., 1986.

——, ed. *Town and County: Essays on the Structure of Local Government in the American Colonies.* Middletown, Conn., 1978.

Dunn, Richard S. *Puritans and Yankees: The Winthrop Dynasty of New England, 1630–1717.* Princeton, N.J., 1962.

Ekirch, A. Roger. *"Poor Carolina": Politics and Society in Colonial North Carolina, 1729–1776.* Chapel Hill, N.C., 1981.

Gilsdorf, Joy B., and Robert B. Gilsdorf. "Elites and Electorates: Some Plain Truths for Historians of Colonial America." In *Saints and Revolutionaries: Essays on Early American History,* edited by David D. Hall, John M. Murrin, and Thad W. Tate. New York, 1984.

Greene, Jack P. *All Men Are Created Equal: Some Reflections on the Character of the American Revolution.* Oxford, 1976.

——. "Changing Interpretations of Early American Politics." In *The Reinterpretation of Early American History,* edited by Ray Allen Billington. San Marino, Calif., 1966.

——. "Foundations of Political Power in the Virginia House of Burgesses, 1720–1776." *William and Mary Quarterly,* 3rd ser., 16, no. 4 (1959):485–506.

——. "The Growth of Political Stability: An Interpretation of Political Development in the Anglo-American Colonies, 1660–1760." In *The American Revolution: A Heritage of Change,* edited by John Parker and Carol Urness. Minneapolis, Minn., 1975.

——. "Legislative Turnover in British America, 1696 to 1775: A Quantitative Analysis," *William and Mary Quarterly,* 3rd ser., 38, no. 3 (1981):442–463.

——. *Peripheries and Center: Constitutional Development in the Extended Polities of the British Empire and the United States, 1607–1788.* Athens, Ga., 1986.

——. "Political Mimesis: A Consideration of the Historical and Cultural Roots of Legislative Behavior in the British Colonies in the Eighteenth Century." *American Historical Review* 75, no. 2 (1969):337–360.

——. *The Quest for Power: The Lower Houses of Assembly in the Southern Royal Colonies, 1689–1776.* Chapel Hill, N.C., 1963.

——. "Society, Ideology, and Politics: An Analysis of the Political Culture of Mid–Eighteenth-Century Virginia." In *Society, Freedom, and Conscience: The American Revolution in Virginia, Massachusetts, and New York,* edited by Richard M. Jellison. New York, 1976.

Gutiérrez, Ramón A. *When Jesus Came, the Corn Mothers Went Away: Marriage, Sexuality, and Power in New Mexico, 1500–1846.* Stanford, Calif., 1991.

Hartz, Louis, ed. *The Founding of New Societies: Studies in the History of the United States, Latin America, South Africa, Canada, and Australia.* New York, 1964.

Hellmuth, Eckhart. *The Transformation of Political Culture: England and Germany in the Late Eighteenth Century.* Oxford, 1990.

Henretta, James A. *"Salutary Neglect": Colonial Administration Under the Duke of Newcastle.* Princeton, N.J., 1972.

Huntington, Samuel P. *Political Order in Changing Societies.* New Haven, Conn., 1968.

Kammen, Michael. *Deputyes and Libertyes: The Origins of Representative Government in Colonial America.* New York, 1969.

Katz, Stanley N. *Newcastle's New York: Anglo-American Politics, 1732–1753.* Cambridge, Mass., 1968.

Kim, Sung Bok. *Landlord and Tenant in Colonial New York: Manorial Society, 1664–1775.* Chapel Hill, N.C., 1978.

Klein, Milton M. *The Politics of Diversity: Essays in the History of Colonial New York.* Port Washington, N.Y., 1974.

Labaree, Leonard Woods. *Royal Government in America: A Study of the British Colonial System Before 1783.* New Haven, Conn., 1930.

Lax, John, and William Pencak. "The Knowles Riot and the Crisis of the 1740s in Massachusetts." *Perspectives in American History* 10 (1976):163–214.

Lovejoy, David S. *Rhode Island Politics and the American Revolution, 1760–1776.* Providence, R.I., 1958.

Lucas, Paul. "A Note on the Comparative Study of the Structure of Politics in Mid–Eighteenth-Century Britain and Its American Colonies." *William and Mary Quarterly,* 3rd ser., 28, no. 2 (1971):301–309.

Morgan, Edmund S. *Inventing the People: The Rise of Popular Sovereignty in England and America.* New York, 1988.

Murrin, John M. "Political Development." In *Colonial British America: Essays in the New History of the Early Modern Era,* edited by Jack P. Greene and J. R. Pole. Baltimore, Md., 1984.

Nash, Gary B. *Quakers and Politics: Pennsylvania, 1681–1726.* Princeton, N.J., 1968.

Pencak, William. *War, Politics and Revolution in Provincial Massachusetts.* Boston, 1981.

Phelan, John Leddy. "Authority and Flexibility in the Spanish Imperial Bureaucracy." *Administrative Science Quarterly* 5, no. 1 (1960):47–65.

Plumb, John H. *The Origins of Political Stability: England, 1675–1725.* Boston, 1967.

Pole, J. R. *The Gift of Government: Political Responsibility from the English Restoration to American Independence.* Athens, Ga., 1983.

———. "Historians and the Problem of Early American Democracy." *American Historical Review* 67, no. 3 (1962):626–646.

———. *Political Representation in England and the Origins of the American Republic.* London, 1966.

Purvis, Thomas L. *Proprietors, Patronage, and Paper Money: Legislative Politics in New Jersey, 1703–1776.* New Brunswick, N.J., 1986.

Rainbolt, John C. "The Alteration in the Relationship Between Leadership and Constituents in Virginia, 1620 to 1720." *William and Mary Quarterly,* 3rd ser., 27, no. 3 (1970):411–434.

Reid, Allana G. "Representative Assemblies in New France." *Canadian Historical Review* 27, no. 1 (1946):19–26.

Rink, Oliver A. *Holland on the Hudson: An Economic and Social History of Dutch New York.* Ithaca, N.Y., 1986.

Ritchie, Robert C. *The Duke's Province: A Study of New York Politics and Society, 1664–1691.* Chapel Hill, N.C., 1977.

Rothermund, Dietmar. *The Layman's Progress: Religious and Political Experience in Colonial Pennsylvania, 1740–1770.* Philadelphia, 1961.

Schutz, John A. "Succession Politics in Massachusetts, 1730–1741." *William and Mary Quarterly,* 3rd ser., 15, no. 4 (1958):508–520.

Sirmans, M. Eugene. *Colonial South Carolina: A Political History, 1663–1763.* Chapel Hill, N.C., 1966.

Steele, Ian K. *Politics of Colonial Policy: The Board of Trade in Colonial Administration, 1696–1720.* Oxford, 1968.

Sydnor, Charles S. *Gentlemen Freeholders: Political Practices in Washington's Virginia.* Chapel Hill, N.C., 1952.

Tully, Alan. *William Penn's Legacy: Politics and Social Structure in Provincial Pennsylvania, 1726–1755.* The Johns Hopkins University Studies in Historical and Political Science, 95th series, no. 2. Baltimore, Md., 1977.

Washburn, Wilcomb E. *The Governor and the Rebel: A History of Bacon's Rebellion in Virginia.* Chapel Hill, N.C., 1957.

Waterhouse, Richard. *A New World Gentry: The Making of a Merchant and Planter Class in South Carolina, 1670–1770.* New York, 1989.

Weir, Robert M. " 'The Harmony We Were Famous For': An Interpretation of Pre-Revolutionary South Carolina Politics." *William and Mary Quarterly,* 3rd series, 26, no. 4 (1969):473–501.

Williamson, Chilton. *American Suffrage: From Property to Democracy, 1760–1860.* Princeton, N.J., 1960.

Zeichner, Oscar. *Connecticut's Years of Controversy, 1750–1776.* Chapel Hill, N.C., 1949.

Zemsky, Robert. *Merchants, Farmers, and River Gods: An Essay on Eighteenth-Century American Politics.* Boston, 1971.

Zuckerman, Michael. *Peaceable Kingdoms: New England Towns in the Eighteenth Century.* New York, 1970.

Jack P. Greene

SEE ALSO **Colonial Political Thought; The Colonial Press; The Framework of Government;** and **Local Government.**

THE FRAMEWORK OF GOVERNMENT

SPAIN AND ITS COLONIES

IN THE AFTERMATH of the discovery of the New World, Ferdinand and Isabella laid the foundations for a system of government that was destined to exercise royal control, through a series of authoritarian institutions, during the more than three centuries of Spanish colonial rule. Based largely on medieval antecedents, these governmental institutions reflected the Hispanic imperial ideal.

Ferdinand and Isabella are credited with centralizing the Spanish monarchy. In the last quarter of the fifteenth century, they curbed the feudal rights of the nobility and created a national bureaucracy, treasury, army, and legal code. Further, they acquired royal patronage, or power, over the Roman Catholic church in Spain and imposed religious unity by forcing Muslims and Jews to convert or leave the country. The consolidation of all such authority and prestige under the Crown characterized the growth of nation-states in Western Europe at this time.

The rise of absolutism, buttressed by an all-powerful bureaucratic organization, proved to be the key determinant in the formulation and evolution of the Spanish colonial system. No-

where in Spain's overseas empire, for example, does one find the representative assemblies that later took root in English America. Neither Isabella of Castile nor her successors seem to have entertained any doubts about their sovereign rights in the New World.

At Spain's request, Pope Alexander VI in proclamations of 1493 and in the Treaty of Tordesillas of 1494, drew a line of demarcation west of the Cape Verde Islands that conceded possession of most of the New World to Spain and left Portugal in control of lands east of the line—the bulge of Brazil. The granting of pagan lands to Christian princes had long been considered a papal prerogative and was recognized by international law. The Spanish monarchy eagerly sought this concession as much to establish a basis for colonial rule as to legitimize its territorial claims. Subsequently, other European colonizing nations ignored the papal action and treaty when they occupied marginal sections of America left unsettled by Spain or seized Spanish territory by force of arms.

Since Isabella of Castile had underwritten the costs of the initial discovery and conquest, the New World possessions belonged exclusively to the Crown of Castile, and not to Spain as a whole. That theoretical position, which did not fade until the eighteenth century, allowed the Castilian monarchs free rein to exercise royal jurisdiction and impose unhindered their imperial policies abroad.

BEGINNINGS OF GOVERNMENT IN THE INDIES

Private entrepreneurs, of whom Christopher Columbus was merely the first, led the way in exploration and expansion of Spain's colonial realm. They operated under terms of contracts, called *capitulaciones,* with the Crown. These agreements specified the rights, economic privileges, and titles conceded to the entrepreneur and fixed the percentage of the venture's profits reserved for the royal government. Essentially they represented Crown grants of political power and furnished the legal basis for the creation of government in the new dominions. In that respect, these formal documents resembled the charters that Great Britain and France later issued to individual proprietors or corporations who wished to plant colonies in North America. The experiment with private enterprise, based on business contracts offered by the Crown, failed to last long. As soon as an area was settled, contractors found themselves shunted aside to make way for officials sent out by Spain.

This fate befell even Columbus, whose privileges were retracted so that by 1500 his career as a colonial administrator in the Caribbean was at an end. Ever fearful that powerful overseas subjects might assert their autonomy, the Spanish monarchy sought a solution by replacing them with a ponderous Castilian bureaucracy. The assertion of royal controls, initiated in the reign of Queen Isabella, was continued and expanded by her grandson, Charles I of Spain (r. 1516–1556), the first king of the Hapsburg dynasty, who also became Charles V of the Holy Roman Empire. Both he and his son and successor, Philip II (r. 1556–1598), contributed to the growth of a cautious and suspicious state: one whose chief aims in the Indies focused upon fortifying royal power, curbing the independent tendencies of conquistadors and colonizers, and forging some semblance of political unity among the scattered colonial kingdoms.

In the sixteenth century Spain created a series of kingdoms as settlers (*pobladores*) advanced the boundaries of the empire. Unofficially these entities varied in prestige and rank, according to their wealth and population. But legally, under the Crown, all kingdoms, whether of the Indies or of the Iberian Peninsula, were equal within a sort of commonwealth of nations. Union was achieved through the person of the sovereign. In recognition of that, Philip II titled himself "King of Spain and the Indies."

From the outset, the kingdoms of the Indies experienced tighter regulation than those in Spain. A flood of royal laws and edicts controlled colonial life down to the smallest detail. These paternalistic measures were designed to assure profit to the Crown, to promote the interests of the colonists, and to provide protection for Indian vassals. Representative of such laws were the celebrated Ordinances of Pacification of 1573, imposing systematic rules to be observed in the making of new discoveries and settlements. By 1681 more than one hundred thousand royal pronouncements were in force. In that year appeared, after a long period of labor, *Recopilación de leyes de los reynos de las Indias* (Recompilation of the Laws of the Kingdoms of the Indies), which through condensation reduced the laws to a mere sixty-four hundred. This became the guide and basic code on procedural law for all New World officials.

As much as the Crown wished to maintain firm centralist control over its Indies by means of absolutist policies and strict laws, distance and poor communication dictated that considerable discretionary powers be delegated to colonial administrators. Particularly in the early years, these administrators often made important rulings on their own, then waited months or even years to receive approval from Madrid. The efficiency of government was further impaired by the huge quantity of paperwork, centered on endless reports, that Madrid required of the colonial bureaucracy.

ORGANS OF IMPERIAL CONTROL

In 1503, the year before her death, Queen Isabella created the *Casa de Contratación* (Board of Trade) to oversee commerce and regulate the movement of people and ships between Spain and the Indies. Deriving from Italian antecedents and comparable with the *Casa da India* in Lisbon, the Board of Trade was headquartered in Seville. Its first challenge was to control the sudden trade based on gold from the Caribbean island of Hispaniola. It soon received sweeping powers and assumed a multitude of duties associated with colonial economic development. It was the first instrument of royal government specifically devoted to New World affairs.

Under the Crown, the functions of Spanish political administration came to be handled by a conciliar form of government. Some councils, such as the Council of State (*Consejo de Estado*) and the Council of Finance (*Consejo de Hacienda*), had responsibilities that extended generally throughout the empire. Other councils possessed a more specific jurisdiction, limited to advising on policy in a particular territory. Among these the most influential was the Council of Castile, which by 1500 had emerged as the linchpin in the administrative machinery of the peninsula. In addition to giving political advice to the monarch, it acted as a supreme court within Castile, supervised local government, and recommended appointments for office.

For the three decades following Columbus's discovery, a standing committee of the Council of Castile handled matters related to government in the Indies. But after the conquest of Mexico and the addition of extensive lands and millions of new subjects to the empire, the situation required something else in the way of colonial administration. Thus Charles V in 1524 founded by royal edict a new body called the Council of the Indies (*Consejo de Indias*) and gave it authority over all administrative, judicial, economic, and ecclesiastical matters pertaining to his overseas possessions. The members of this body, all Spaniards of lofty rank, both counseled the monarch and acted in his behalf. During the sixteenth and seventeenth centuries, the Council of the Indies remained the governing institution that most directly and significantly affected life in the American colonies.

FORMS OF NEW WORLD ADMINISTRATION

The vanguards of royal control over the Indies, in the conquest period, were men who held the title of governor. Columbus was granted a governorship, as was Hernando Cortés upon his conquest of the Aztecs and his founding of the Kingdom of New Spain in central Mexico. This office, which carried important political and military powers, was conceded to early conquistadors because of Crown belief that it served as an ideal vehicle for extending Spanish rule throughout the Indies. Explorer Hernando de Soto, before his death on the banks of the Mississippi in 1542, acted as joint governor of Cuba and Florida, as did Pedro Menéndez de Avilés from 1565 to 1574. Juan de Oñate, colonizer of the Kingdom of New Mexico in 1598, simultaneously held the title of governor and the supreme military rank of captain-general, as did many leading figures of that century.

The watchful Spanish sovereign, however, took pains to see that the first governors did not evolve into a line of feudal lords. Their terms of appointment were kept relatively short, and powers and privileges were progressively circumscribed. Upon completion of the conquest, in fact, governorships were reduced in status as they were gradually bureaucratized. The governor thereby became a colorless civil servant, unlike the early holders of the office, the conquistadors, who were men of action and of some independence.

At an early date the governorships were superseded in authority by the viceroyalty. The viceroy exercised power in the king's name, and with royal trappings presided at his own court. Only men close to the Crown and of proven loyalty were chosen to fill this delicate and influential position. Serving strictly at the pleasure of the king, the viceroys usually held the post for three to six years.

Within his vast domain, the viceroy functioned as the executive head of government. But in truth his duties intruded upon practically every other category of colonial affairs. He presided over the high court (*audiencia*) of his capital. Police and military powers were delegated to him. As vice-patron of the Spanish church, he played a role in ecclesiastical administration. The superintendency of finances was assigned to him. He also guarded the health and morals of colonial subjects, giving special attention to protecting the Indians from exploitation. Through the viceregal office, royal legislation emanating from the Council of the Indies was translated into political reality.

While the viceroy enjoyed considerable latitude in the interpretation and implementation of the laws, he was also under substantial restraint by the Council of the Indies not to undertake major enterprises without express authorization; that is, his decisions had to be referred to Madrid for approval. In regular metings the Council of the Indies reviewed viceregal dispatches and prepared summary documents (*consultas*), containing their views and recommendations, which were submitted to the king for his guidance in reaching a final decision. Once the Council received the sovereign's reply, it was sent to the viceroy for his action. Such a complicated chain of communications meant that government moved slowly and inefficiently, but it aided the Crown in keeping a close check on its viceroys.

The first viceroy to reign on the North American mainland was a Spanish nobleman, Antonio de Mendoza. In 1535 he arrived at his capital of Mexico City to assume direction of the far-flung Viceroyalty of New Spain. During his unusually long term in office—he remained until 1550—Mendoza set standards and established precedents that would guide all future viceroys. It fell to him to consolidate the conquest and improve upon the rough structure of colonial government devised in Spain. Mendoza proved a true statesman, an excellent administrator, and, above all, obedient to the king.

The territorial boundaries and governmental divisions of the viceroyalty shifted repeatedly during the nearly three centuries of colonial rule. The Kingdom of New Spain, as initially carved out and named by Cortés, embraced much of central and southern Mexico. When Mendoza became viceroy, he also acquired the titles of captain-general and governor over this area, giving him direct management of its political affairs. But the Viceroyalty of New Spain was much larger, including an assortment of kingdoms, provinces, and other administrative units.

Among these were the Kingdom of Nueva Galicia, west of Mexico City; the Captaincy-General of Guatemala (encompassing much of Central America); the Captaincy-General of Santo Domingo (later headquartered in Havana), which took in the West Indies and Florida; and the Captaincy-General of the Philippines, after their occupation in 1564. As the frontier advanced northward from Mexico City, the Spanish Borderlands were absorbed into the Kingdom of New Spain as each section in turn underwent political organization: the Kingdom of New Mexico (afterward downgraded to a province) in 1598, the province of Texas in 1718, and the province of Alta California in 1767.

The royal *audiencias* existed as another level of administrative jurisdiction within the viceroyalty. Not only were they the highest courts of appeal in the New World (subject judicially only to the Council of the Indies) but they also exercised executive and legislative functions over their districts. In the latter instance, they passed local ordinances, which were subject to royal approval. Each court with its justices (*oidores*) was headed by a president who might also hold the titles of governor and captain-general. Three of the *audiencias* of the Viceroyalty of New Spain were elevated to the status of a captaincy-general, which meant that each, for political matters, was answerable directly to the king and the Council of the Indies; the viceroy retained only nominal supervisory authority over them, mainly in fiscal affairs.

The three captaincies-general were Santo Domingo, Guatemala, and the Philippines, all granted nearly autonomous status because of their great distance from the viceregal capital. The *audiencia* in each, with its president and captain-general presiding, functioned in effect as a council of state, administering regional affairs. Owing to its proximity to Mexico City, the *audiencia* of Guadalajara (in Nueva Galicia) remained under its president a dependency subject to the viceroy. Special circumstances governed the *audiencia* of Mexico in the Kingdom of New Spain. Its executive head was the viceroy himself, giving the body exceptional prestige and power in fulfilling the duties assigned it by royal law. Further, in the event of the absence or death of the viceroy, the *audiencia* of Mexico assumed complete viceregal authority.

As part of the imperial system of checks and balances, the king decreed that all officials in positions of authority must undergo a judicial review (*residencia*) at the conclusion of their terms of office. An appointed judge (*juez de residencia*) conducted an investigation, called witnesses who might wish to testify against a retiring officer, and allowed the subject of the review to defend himself. Should an official be found guilty of misconduct, the judge imposed fines or other punishment and required him to pay the expenses of the proceeding. Although the procedure was occasionally subverted by an offender's bribing the judge to clear him, on the whole it had the effect of discouraging misgovernment.

A second device used by the royal government to acquire information on the conduct of colonial officials was the *visita*. From time to time, the king and council sent inspectors (*visitadores*) to America to hold secret and unannounced examinations of the workings of the imperial system. Their findings often resulted in administrative reforms and the removal of corrupt or incompetent civil servants. A celebrated and lengthy *visita* carried out in New Spain by José de Gálvez (1765–1771), for example, produced significant economic reform, reorganization of the Spanish Borderlands, and improvements in imperial defenses.

PROVINCIAL GOVERNMENT

In the hierarchy of colonial administration, provincial governorships occupied an intermediate but significant level. As was the case with the office of viceroy, that of governor was not constricted by the principle of separation of powers. In addition to executive duties, the governor's powers extended into the legislative, judicial, military, and religious spheres. He was nominally subject to the supervision of the viceroy, but officeholders remote from Mexico City, such as those on the far northern frontier, by necessity exercised greater independence. When viceregal oversight was lessened by distance, self-seeking or unscrupulous governors could become local tyrants.

Appointments to governorships were made directly by the king, usually from a slate of three candidates, listed in order of preference, drawn up by the Council of the Indies. Occasionally he ignored these nominations and chose a candidate recommended by the viceroy. As a rule, new governors were native-born Spaniards, a circumstance thought to guarantee loyalty to the royal government. If they were in Spain at the time of appointment, they took the oath of office before the Council of the Indies and received a document of title that outlined obligations to the Crown, fixed a salary, and set the term of office. Terms tended to range from three to five years but in fact varied widely.

In the sixteenth century, provincial governors, particularly those in frontier zones, generally held the military rank of captain-general. Later the lesser rank of colonel became standard, and with it went command of all local army troops and militia. In the northern provinces constituting the Spanish Borderlands, problems of defense remained a chief concern for the governors until the end of the colonial period. Hostile Indians posed the gravest threat, but in Florida, where new governors were regularly ordered "to guard and defend the province against all enemies," foreign invaders and pirates presented added dangers.

As chief executives of their provinces, the governors wielded administrative authority and limited appointive power. They issued local ordinances and decrees, supervised the founding of new settlements and the taking of a periodic census, assigned land and water rights to citizens, regulated public travel, appointed civil officials, and nominated persons for military positions. As part of the executive function, they also had fiscal duties associated with the royal treasury, such as the promotion of Crown revenues and collection of taxes.

The governor acted as chief judicial officer in his district although, being a soldier, he usually had no formal training in law. He was supposed to have a legal adviser (*asesor*) on staff to guide him in such matters, but in the poorer provinces on the northern rim of the viceroyalty, the crown, for budgetary reasons, seldom provided one. The New Mexico governor in 1802 complained that neither he nor his immediate predecessors had access to advisers, lawyers, or notaries who could prepare and direct a legal case in the proper manner. A California governor once instructed a subordinate magistrate, who was ignorant of formal court procedure, to administer the law in accordance with the principles of natural right and justice. That, together with occasional reference to printed codes such as the *Recopilación*, seems to have been all that was normally available to guide the frontier judiciary.

In his judicial capacity, the governor sat as a court of first instance, hearing both civil and criminal cases. If he was the only judge in the province, a condition that regularly prevailed in Florida, he presided over all cases, of both high and low degree. Elsewhere, as in Texas and New Mexico, petty magistrates (*alcaldes*) handled minor cases in the first instance, the governor sitting as a court of appeal from their decisions. Appeals from the governor's judgments were carried to the *audiencia*, which had jurisdiction over the province.

Boundaries of *audiencias* within the Viceroyalty of New Spain shifted during the centuries of colonial rule. Florida officially was attached to the *audiencia* of Santo Domingo, on the island of Hispaniola, but that tribunal was usually bypassed and appeals from the governor in Saint Augustine were carried directly to the Council of the Indies in Spain. Texas, initially subordinate to the *audiencia* of Mexico in the Kingdom of New Spain, was transferred to the *audiencia* of Guadalajara in the last quarter of the eighteenth century. New Mexico, except for a brief interval, was also subject to the court in Guadalajara, as were Sonora (whose upper reaches included today's southern Arizona) and California.

Governors, like all executive officers in Spain's New World realms, had special obligations to defend the legal rights of Indians, shielding them from mistreatment and economic exploitation. In judicial cases involving Indians, the governor held exclusive jurisdiction. Appeals were carried to a specialized tribunal established at Mexico City in 1573, the General Indian Court (*Juzgado General de Indios*), which facilitated access of natives to the legal system. At the provincial level, they had recourse to a government-appointed protector of Indians (*protector de indios*), who acted as their legal representative in court, notably in defense of land titles. Some of the northern districts of New Spain never had a protector, and even in a province such as New Mexico, where the office existed, it was occupied in the seventeenth and eighteenth centuries only sporadically.

Within the religious sphere, the governor held the title of royal vice-patron of the church. Under the doctrine of the Real Patronato, a body of rights and functions associated with ecclesiastical administration that had been conceded by the papacy to the Spanish Crown, provincial executives exercised authority in the name of the king. Numbered among the vice-patron's obligations were responsibility for maintenance and fiscal direction of the missionary program, support of the secular (or diocesan) clergy, and resolution of nondoctrinal religious controversies.

In carrying out their multifaceted tasks, Spanish governors in theory headed a battery of lesser officials who assisted in the conduct of provincial business. These might include a lieutenant governor, a secretary of government, a fiscal officer, and clerks. Often, however, these functionaries were wholly or partially lacking in the borderland provinces because the Crown was loath to fund them. Florida, prior to its cession to Great Britain in 1763, never had a lieutenant governor, while New Mexico during the seventeenth and eighteenth centuries had one only intermittently. Since the provinces returned virtually no revenue to the royal treasury and required constant subsidies (*situados*), the king kept the number of paid civil servants to a minimum, even though that worked a severe hardship upon beleaguered governors.

One practice available to governors, which afforded some relief, was the convening of a *junta*, an unofficial advisory council that met on a temporary basis to furnish support for a governor's policies and programs. It met when called by the governor and dissolved upon completion of its deliberations. Members included civic, religious, and military leaders of the colony, thereby providing one means for at least limited community participation in management of the local political system. In Florida, where the framework of government was particularly weak, the *junta* was convoked with some regularity and emerged as a significant political institution. By contrast, in the Spanish Borderlands to the west of Florida, *juntas* assembled infrequently and generally for the sole purposes of considering economic reforms or confronting an economic or military crisis.

LOCAL GOVERNMENT

At the lowest stratum of the Spanish colonial system were the district and municipal governments. Some uniformity existed in local institutions, but wide variance in form and names could be encountered, especially in the Kingdom of New Spain. The term *alcalde mayor*, for example, was used in the viceroyalty as the title for the chief executive and judicial officer who headed a province, in effect a petty governor. By contrast, in New Mexico the term *alcalde mayor* referred to unsalaried district officials, appointed by the governor, who administered their jurisdictions with the aid of a deputy (*teniente alcalde*). Such inconsistencies in nomenclature sometimes caused confusion among royal officials newly arrived from Spain, who were forced to seek clarification from knowledgeable civil servants.

Among Hispanic political institutions introduced in the New World, the municipal council, or *cabildo*, was virtually the only one with any tradition of popular participation. Spain since Roman times had placed strong emphasis on urban life and municipal government, with the result that during the later Middle Ages towns acquired a great deal of autonomy. Upon the occupation of the Indies, Spaniards quickly founded municipalities to serve as both anchors and agencies for colonization. Rural areas, therefore, were developed specifically to support the towns, the exact reverse of the pattern in the English colonies.

Initially the colonial *cabildos* drawing on the Castilian prototype had shown assertiveness and wielded considerable authority. But beginning with Charles I, the Crown moved to curb the independent spirit of the municipal corporations and bring them firmly under control of the authoritarian political system. Nevertheless, the *cabildo* enjoyed prestige among the citizenry and remained a viable unit of local government.

The jurisdiction of a *cabildo* was twofold. First, it had direct governing authority over the municipality itself. Secondarily, it exercised a kind of general authority over a large area outside its urban boundaries extending to the territorial limits of neighboring *cabildos*. This ensured rural populations at least tenuous access to local government. On the frontier, where *cabildos* were few, they tended to gain in influence, becoming spokesmen for large blocs of provincial citizens and on occasion challenging the wishes and policies of the governor.

In the organizational structure of the *cabildo*, power was vested in two classes of officials, councilmen (*regidores*) and municipal magistrates (*alcaldes ordinarios*). Provincial towns had four to six councilmen, while Mexico City had twelve. The usual number of magistrates was two, although small communities might have only one.

Originally the conquistadors and founding colonizers appointed the members of the first *cabildos*. Thereafter, following the custom in Spain, the councilmen were supposed to be elected by the male householders in the community, and they in turn elected the magistrates. That democratic practice failed to survive long, however, for Philip II, in order to raise revenue for his treasury, began the sale of the office of *regidor*. In outlying areas, such as the Spanish Borderlands, where positions in the *cabildo* were not in great demand, the councilmen were frequently appointed for a one-year term by the governor. Even so, they retained the privilege of annually electing the magistrates.

The council convened in closed sessions to conduct the everyday business of the municipality. It parcelled out lands to citizens, imposed local taxes, issued licenses, regulated public events, supervised market prices, and maintained roads and jails. The *regidores* were prohibited from engaging in any business that might create a conflict of interest.

The primary duty of the *alcaldes ordinarios* was to sit as judges of first instance in civil and criminal cases. Appeals from their courts went to the governor and thence to the appropriate *audiencia*. But the *alcaldes* also had an executive role as full participants in council meetings, where they enjoyed a vote equal to the *regidores*. The senior *alcalde* presided over the deliberations of the *cabildo*. In addition, the magistrates made weekly inspections of the jail and administered the municipal archives.

In much of New Spain, the *cabildo* had a fairly stable existence, but within the provinces on the northern frontier it had a checkered history. The town council, which first appeared in Florida during the 1560s, had become dormant by the 1750s, when colonists and clergy unsuccessfully attempted to reestablish it as a check on the arbitrary use of power by the governor. When Louisiana came under Spanish rule, its chief municipality, New Orleans, was given a *cabildo* with direct appeal to the Council of the Indies. The first and only *cabildo* in Texas was formed at the *villa* of San Antonio de Béxar (San Antonio) in 1731. It made an attempt to rule the province ad interim when the governor died in office (1799). In New Mexico, the first *cabildo* at the *villa* of San Gabriel was dissolved after the founding of a new capital at Santa Fe (1610) with its own municipal corporation. The Santa Fe *cabildo* lasted until the 1720s, after which it was abolished by the governor, who preferred to see local government in the hands of pliant *alcaldes mayores*. Spanish California, founded late in the colonial period, had elected *cabildos* with a single *alcalde* in its pueblos (corporate towns). Here the council's customary powers were severely limited by the governor's representative, the *comisionado*, who held real authority within the municipality.

ADMINISTRATIVE REFORM

In the seventeenth century, Spain and its empire experienced political decline and economic stagnation under the increasingly weak and ineffective Hapsburg dynasty. But with the advent of the Bourbons in 1700 a new spirit of reform was introduced, which reached its zenith during the reign of the progressive Charles III (1759–1788). A notable achievement was the movement away from Crown reliance on councils toward a new system of ministries more responsive to the need to rehabilitate Spain's ossified institutional structure.

José de Gálvez's prolonged inspection (*visita*) of New Spain, beginning in 1765, represented one step in the drive to overcome weaknesses in the imperial bureaucracy. From his survey Gálvez gained insights that allowed him to implement basic political and economic reforms when he was promoted to minister of the Indies (1775). One of these reforms involved the separation of the Internal Provinces (exclusive of Louisiana and Florida) from northern New Spain and their creation as a military department headed by a commandant-general. Another reform, in 1786, saw New Spain reorganized into twelve *intendencias* (administrative districts) under *intendentes* who were clothed with broad powers. Unfortunately the spirit of renewal was allowed to languish when Charles III's son, Charles IV (r. 1788–1808), failed to rise to the challenge of reformation.

The imperial crises growing out of the Napoleonic invasion of Spain in 1808 produced an upheaval in the colonial system and eventually contributed to the success of Spanish American movements for independence. While King Ferdinand VII of Spain was a captive of the French, a rump parliament or *cortes* that included representatives from the New World attempted to rule. In 1812 it promulgated a liberal constitu-

tion limiting the powers of the monarchy and, among other administrative reforms, reorganizing local government. Effects of the political change were felt as far away as the Spanish Borderlands. In New Mexico, for example, in outlying settlements there was a sudden rush to elect municipal councils, now termed *ayuntamientos* (following the language of the constitution) rather than *cabildos*. Ferdinand VII regained his throne in 1814, abolished the *cortes*, and restored royal absolutism. The return to autocratic rule was doomed to failure, for in 1821 the colonial Viceroyalty of New Spain was replaced by the independent nation of Mexico.

BIBLIOGRAPHY

Aiton, Arthur S. *Antonio de Mendoza, First Viceroy of New Spain*. Durham, N.C., 1927; repr. New York, 1967.

Benson, Nettie Lee, ed. *Mexico and the Spanish Cortes, 1810–1822: Eight Essays*. Austin, Tex., 1966.

Blackmar, Frank W. *Spanish Institutions of the Southwest*. Baltimore, Md., 1891; repr. Glorieta, N.Mex., 1976.

Burkholder, Mark A., and D. S. Chandler. *From Impotence to Authority: The Spanish Crown and the American Audiencias, 1687–1808*. Columbia, Mo., 1977.

Bushnell, Amy. *The King's Coffer: Proprietors of the Spanish Florida Treasury*. Gainesville, Fla., 1981.

Crouch, Dora P., Daniel J. Garr, and Axel I. Mundigo. *Spanish City Planning in North America*. Cambridge, Mass., 1982.

Cruz, Gilberto R. *Let There Be Towns: Spanish Municipal Orgins in the American Southwest, 1610–1810*. College Station, Tex., 1988.

Cutter, Charles R. *The Protector de Indios in Colonial New Mexico, 1659–1821*. Albuquerque, N.Mex., 1986.

Elliott, John H. *Imperial Spain, 1469–1716*. New York, 1966.

Floyd, Troy S. *The Columbus Dynasty in the Caribbean, 1492–1526*. Albuquerque, N.Mex., 1973.

Gibson, Charles. *Spain in America*. New York, 1966.

Haring, Clarence H. *The Spanish Empire of America*. New York, 1947: repr. 1963.

Parry, John H. *The Spanish Theory of Empire in the Sixteenth Century*. New York, 1974.

Priestley, Herbert Ingram. *José de Gálvez, Visitor-General of New Spain, 1765–1771*. Berkeley, Calif., 1916.

Simmons, Marc. *Spanish Government in New Mexico*. 2nd ed. Albuquerque, N.Mex., 1990.

TePaske, John Jay. *The Governorship of Spanish Florida, 1700–1763*. Durham, N.C., 1964.

Marc Simmons

SEE ALSO **Local Government; Relations with the Parent Country;** and **The Reorganization of Empires.**

FRANCE AND ITS COLONIES

FRENCH COLONIAL EXPANSION coincided with an era of metropolitan turmoil marked by religious wars, peasant revolts, and the two Frondes. The parliamentary Fronde (1648) sought to limit the power of the Crown and heighten the legislative responsibilities of the *parlements*. The aristocratic Fronde (1649–1652) sought to reassert the old aristocracy's privileges and role in government that had been undermined during the ministries of cardinals Richelieu (1624–1642) and Mazarin (1642–1661). During the first half of the seventeenth century, the French state continued to undergo a long process of modernization with the development of a centralized bureaucracy and the affirmation of the primacy of royal legislation over local customs. The crushing defeat of the feudal and parliamentary aristocracies during the Fronde left the Crown secure and allowed it to enact a series of administrative reforms during the personal reign of Louis XIV. Municipal government and provincial assemblies were brought under the tutelage of royal officials. Representative or democratic ideals had no place in this system. Unlike England, which succeeded in curbing the power of the Crown, France reinforced royal authority after 1661.

MONOPOLIES AND THE STATE

From Louis XI (1461–1483) to the beginning of Louis XIV's personal reign (1661), the Crown was more concerned with securing its frontiers in Europe, ending civil strife, and entrenching the power of royal officials over the resistance of provincial institutions than with administering colonial outposts. Private enterprise would bear the burden of colonization, the conversion of Native peoples, and the administration of new lands. Between 1541 and 1627, a succession of individuals and trading companies were given monopolies to exploit North America's resources generally on the condition that they attempt to Christianize the natives and form settlements in the region. Some, like the marquis de la Roche (a favorite of the Queen Mother, Catherine de Medici), were awarded the lofty title of viceroy with ownership of all the land they could conquer. Most were appointed lieutenant generals of the king with the power to grant seigneuries: substantial tracts of land in exchange for oaths of hommage.

Monopolies drew opposition from other traders who were excluded and few lasted their full term. Jacques Noël's twelve-year monopoly, granted in 1588, was revoked the following year while Pierre du Gua de Monts's ten-year monopoly, granted in 1603 for the area from the fortieth parallel to Newfoundland, was revoked in 1607 and then renewed for a single year. The failure of the Crown to respect its grants encouraged merchants to make a quick profit rather than to invest in providing missionaries and settling colonists. Most attempts at settlement ended after scurvy had demoralized prospective settlers during the first winter. Only at Port Royal after 1604 and at Quebec after 1608 were there any permanent residents, and their small numbers did not require elaborate administrative structures.

The principle of monopolistic control of French colonies was reaffirmed with the establishment of the Company of One Hundred Associates by Cardinal Richelieu in 1627. Modeled in part on the great Dutch and English trading companies, the One Hundred Associates was granted all of North America north of Spanish Florida in seigneurial tenure. The company received a monopoly over all trade to North America (except for the fisheries) along with an exemption from customs duties for fifteen years and a perpetual monopoly over the fur trade. In return it was to bear the costs of defense and administration, settle four thousand Roman Catholics by 1643, and provide for the upkeep of clergy to serve the needs of the French population and evangelize the Native peoples.

The administrative structure established by the Company of One Hundred Associates was simple. The governor general, named by the company and approved by the king, had supreme authority over military affairs, civil administration, and the law; he was the sole judge of both civil and criminal cases. He was assisted by one law officer, a clerk, who was usually his secretary. Only the financial management of the colony, entrusted to the company's agent in Canada, was outside his jurisdiction. With the founding of Montreal in 1642, Paul de Chomedey de Maisonneuve filled the role of governor in that isolated outpost.

Unable to meet its commitments, the company turned over the financial administration of the colony to the Communauté des Habitants ("community of [Canadian] habitants") in 1645. This company was directed by a half dozen of the leading colonial families. In 1647 the Crown established a council made up of the governor general, the Jesuit superior, and the governor of Montreal. Councillors could consult syndics, elected by permanent residents, for Quebec, Trois-Rivières, and Montreal along with the commander of the company's fleet on matters concerning the company. The company enlarged the council the following year to include any former governor-general living in Canada, the governor of Trois-Rivières, and two members elected by the other members of the council after consultation with the syndics. The council had important financial powers, but its existence in no way diminished the authority of the governor general, who could veto any council decision.

The closing years of company rule (1659–1663) were marked by administrative turmoil. Frustrated by the lack of troops to ward off Iroquois attacks, embroiled in quarrels with the clergy over the brandy trade with Native peoples, and embittered by petty disputes over precedence, governors resigned in rapid succession. The council, whose main responsibility now was to regulate the fur trade, was reorganized by the Crown in 1657 to include the governor general, a director named by the Company of One Hundred Associates, and four councillors elected for two-year terms by the inhabitants of Quebec

(two members), Trois-Rivières, and Montreal (one each). Bishop François de Montmorency de Laval and the Jesuit superior joined the council in 1661 just before it was dissolved by Governor Pierre du Bois d'Avaugour.

Syndics and councillors had little importance as democratic institutions. Syndics acted only in an advisory capacity. Although syndics continued to be elected into the period of royal government after 1663, little is known of their activities, and it is impossible to draw up a complete list of the officeholders. Nor does extant documentation permit understanding of the councillors' role. Public meetings were prohibited in the colony, but officials sometimes convened assemblies of notables to seek advice on policy. After 1717 merchant syndics were elected by the principal traders of Quebec and Montreal to discuss commercial policy. Initiative, however, always rested with the officials and never with the people.

The seigneurial system is sometimes seen as an administrative structure, although it was in fact the most common form of property found in ancien-régime France. It was therefore natural that this form of land tenure be imposed on the colony. Seigneurial grants could, however, entail some administrative responsibilities—notably the administration of justice and of local laws. Most seigneurial grants from this period conferred the right to establish a seigneurial court with jurisdiction over virtually all civil and criminal cases. The first known seigneurial jurisdiction was established at Beaupré in 1646 and a second at Montreal in 1648. The most important of these early seigneurial courts was the *sénéchaussée* of Quebec established by Governor Jean de Lauson in 1651. Composed of a judge, a deputy judge, a seigneurial attorney (responsible for prosecuting criminals and acting on the company's behalf in civil suits), a clerk and a process server, this court heard cases of first instance and appeals from other seigneurial courts such as Beaupré. Decisions of the *sénéchaussée* could be appealed to the governor general.

Supreme judicial authority was withdrawn from the governor general in 1659. A royal edict declared that all cases would henceforth be heard by the *sénéchaussée*, with appeals going to the *parlement* of Paris. This enactment added to the disillusionment of the last governors under company rule and contributed to sapping their authority.

ROYAL GOVERNMENT

By 1663 Iroquois depredations had wrought havoc with French Indian allies and almost completely disrupted the fur trade—the colony's economic lifeline. Unable to defend the colony and virtually bankrupt, the Company of One Hundred Associates resigned, returning New France to the king in March. Over the following decade the colony was integrated into the French royal administration on basically the same footing as a metropolitan province.

At the same time, French Caribbean colonies were given the same administrative structures. A governor general and intendant were sent to Martinique to administer the French Windward Islands while another government was established at Saint Domingue (present-day Haiti). Since all French colonies were structurally similar, the example of New France will be used.

The first royal governor general, Augustin de Saffray de Mésy, arrived in New France in September 1663, in the company of Bishop Laval. They were to appoint a sovereign council made up of five councillors, an attorney general, a clerk, and a process server. The new council was given broad legislative, executive, financial, and judicial powers. Although it initially passed some useful legislation and continued to function adequately as a law court, conflict between the governor and bishop disrupted its other roles. The situation was made more complex in 1664 when Louis XIV ceded the colony to the Compagnie des Indes Occidentales. With the arrival of the first intendant, Jean Talon, in 1665, conflict between royal officials and company agents intensified. The intendant's commission gave him control over justice, civil administration, and finance, leaving little room for the company's agent. By 1670 royal officials had asserted their preeminence, and the Crown resumed undisputed control of the colony in 1674. The royal government subsequently underwent only a few minor modifications.

In theory, the governor general commanded all of New France, which by 1700 stretched from Newfoundland to Louisiana. But, given the distances involved and the problems of communication, the lieutenant governors appointed to peripheral administrative centers such as Port Royal (later replaced by Louisbourg) or New Orleans were virtually independent, receiving their instructions directly from Versailles. In these areas the intendant was replaced by a *commissaire ordonnateur* in charge of justice, civil administration, and finance. The central colony of Canada was divided into three governmental districts: Quebec, Trois-Rivières, and Montreal. The area west of the Ottawa River, the *pays d'en haut,* was also under the direct responsibility of authorities in Quebec.

All French colonies were under the direct authority of the Minister of Marine (except for a short interlude during the regency, 1715–1723, when the Council of Marine was formed). Versailles made all major decisions regarding policy, appointments, and even pensions and issued precise instructions to colonial officials. With little ability to formulate policy, the latter could only make the best of poor communications between colony and the mother country and, by temporizing, hope to persuade the minister to change his mind.

The Governor General

Under royal government the governor general, as the king's direct representative, remained the foremost official in New France, although he had far less power than governors in the earlier period of proprietary rule. Appointed and dismissed at the king's pleasure, he was responsible for maintaining obedience to the king and respect for the monarchy. As the Crown's representative, he shared with the intendant the power to grant seigneuries and could interfere in matters of civil administration only if he felt the Crown's interests were threatened. In cases of conflict with the intendant, however, he had to justify his actions to the minister.

In two spheres the governor general had exclusive jurisdiction: military affairs and diplomatic relations. He was in charge of fortifications and was commander-in-chief of all military forces in the colony: both regular troops (the twenty-eight companies of *troupes de la marine* and, in time of conflict, any regular army reinforcements) and the militia. He directed the colony's Indian diplomacy and administered the *pays d'en haut,* the vast fur-trading hinterland to the west of Montreal studded with forts and trading posts. This involved him in commercial policy through the granting of trading licenses (*congés*) and in religious affairs, since missionaries in the West often acted as royal agents.

Only the minister's orders limited his actions in these spheres. Versailles had to approve all policy initiatives, but distance worked in the governor's favor since his correspondence was one of the two main sources of information for the ministry. The intendant could restrict the governor's authority through his control of the colony's finances, by virtue of which he could withhold budgetary approval for initiatives involving additional expenditures.

The governor general was represented in the governments of Trois-Rivières and Montreal by lieutenant governors. In each parish, a militia captain commanded units comprised of all able-bodied men from sixteen to sixty. These officers mustered the men periodically and ensured that they received some military training. In addition to his purely military role, the militia captain assisted the intendant by ensuring that regulations were observed and he could be called upon to perform police work in apprehending criminals. In the West, military post commandants who received their orders from the governor exercised administrative authority. These men were the main agents of the governor's Indian policy, informing Quebec of developments in their region and maintaining peace among the different tribes and the French traders. Post commandants were commissioned to render justice in their jurisdiction and their sentences could only be reviewed by the intendant and governor.

The Intendant

Though second in the royal administrative hierarchy, the intendant wielded the most important power. In France, the intendants were a fairly recent administrative innovation whose role was to reinforce central authority in the provinces. They oversaw the collection of taxes and the administration of justice, supervised major public-works projects, and coordinated economic policy. When the Crown assumed control of New France, the intendant became the main local architect of French colonial policy. With a title that described him as "responsible for justice, public order and finance," the intendant controlled all aspects of colonial government not specifically under the jurisdiction of the governor general or bishop. Through his control of the purse strings, he also exercised influence in many military and religious affairs.

The intendant had wide-ranging judicial powers. Although the governor general was the honorary president of the Sovereign Council, the intendant effectively presided. He supervised the lower courts, judges, and law officers and was charged with ensuring that all laws were enforced. He had the power to judge any case that was submitted to him and even call before himself cases pending in regular courts. He could revoke decisions of the Sovereign Council if he deemed them contrary to the interests of justice or of the state. He specifically had jurisdiction over crimes against the security of the state, smuggling, cases involving the king's domain, and questions regarding the seigneurial system. Despite holding these broad powers, most intendants referred even these specified cases to the regular courts. Intendants Claude de Bouteroue (1668–1670), Jacques de Meulles (1682–1686), and Jacques Raudot (1705–1711) were the exceptions who actively intervened in justice. Since appeals of an intendant's decision could only be made to the king's council in France, the expense involved effectively rendered an intendant's judgment final. Appointments to superior judicial posts in the colony were made by the king, but normally on the intendant's recommendation. The intendant granted commissions to all minor judicial officials: process servers, notaries, and surveyors.

Being responsible for public order meant not only ensuring law and order but adherence to the Crown's economic and social policies. Demographic growth was one of the ministry's main preoccupations, and one of Jean Talon's first tasks after his arrival in 1665 was to draw up a nominative census. Down to the end of the French regime in 1760, no fewer than forty-one censuses were sent to Versailles, making the demographic development of Canada one of the most closely monitored in the world. The intendant also supervised settlement of colonists and, in conjunction with the governor, distributed seigneurial grants. Theoretically, he was responsible for making sure that seigneurs recruited colonists and that pioneers cleared their land. The intendant applied economic policies set out by the minister in France, sending men to search for mineral deposits and for oak forests suitable for shipbuilding, subsidizing local industries such as the naval yards at Quebec City and the Saint Maurice ironworks near Trois-Rivières, and promoting the production of naval stores such as pitch, tar, and hemp. Intendants also encouraged trade between Canada and other parts of the French empire. But in years of crop failure, the intendant could prohibit the export of grain and flour to ensure that the local population was properly fed. He also fixed the prices of basic commodities such as beef and bread at urban markets to protect consumers from speculators.

The colonial budget was drawn up by the Minister of Marine, and the funds were forwarded to the intendant, who had absolute control over the financial administration in the colony. He approved all state expenditures, supervised the collection of duties that were levied by the Crown and of seigneurial dues on Crown lands, and regulated currency. Taxation, broadly defined, was a major preoccupation of French provincial intendants. However, it posed less difficulty in New France since Canadians were not subject to the most onerous taxes that impoverished the French peasantry: the *taille* (a tax paid by commoners roughly based on means) and the *gabelle* (salt tax). Taxation in the colony took the form of a 25 percent export duty on beaver pelts (until 1717) and a 10 percent duty on moose hides, while imports of wine, spirits, and tobacco were subject to a 10 percent duty. After 1749, a 3 percent duty was added on all other imports.

Because of a chronic deficit in its trade balance with the mother country, New France had trouble keeping hard currency in the colony. The problem was made more acute by delays in the arrival of specie to pay for state expenditures. In the summer of 1684, intendant Jacques de Meulles—in desperate need of cash to pay expenses—made credit notes out of playing cards reimbursable in specie when the fleet arrived. This temporary measure filled a genuine need and, in time, developed into a system of colonial paper currency, the *monnaie de cartes*.

The intendant was in charge of the colonial bureaucracy, which was divided into two main sections: the Bureaux de la Marine and the Domaine d'Occident. Another official, the *grand voyer*, supervised roads and urban planning.

The Bureaux de la Marine administered the king's storehouse, which was a supply depot for military provisions and ammunition. With the growing financial crisis that threatened the state with bankruptcy at the turn of the eighteenth century, the storehouse also sold trade goods to local merchants in the hope that profits would diminish the deficit. A comptroller of the Marine supervised this division, and there were stores in Quebec City and Montreal with staffs made up of a storekeeper, an accountant, and several clerks.

The Domaine d'Occident was responsible for the collection of customs duties and for administering crown lands—collecting seigneurial rents and dues and farming out fur-trading posts of the northeast, such as Tadoussac, which controlled trade along much of the North Shore and in the Saguenay region. Besides its director, this office was composed of a comptroller, three or four inspectors, and a half-dozen clerks.

Urban planning and road construction were supervised by the *grand voyer*, or road officer. He ensured that the alignment of houses did not encroach on roadways and saw to the upkeep of paved streets in Quebec City. His responsibilities included the planning, construction, and maintenance of roads and bridges throughout the colony. Militia captains in each parish organized statute labor for all road work.

The Judicial System

Civil law in the colony was derived from the Custom of Paris, one of the most widespread bodies of law used in northern France. Although the Company of One Hundred Associates did not impose a specific custom, most of their seigneurial grants stipulated that land was granted under the Custom of Paris. The edict creating the Compagnie des Indes Occidentales in 1664 specified that only the Custom of Paris was to be used in the future. Litigation followed the procedure established by the Civil Ordinance of 1667, which brought together in one code practices followed in most of the country's courts. Criminal procedure was defined by the Criminal Ordinance of 1670.

The Sovereign Council (the name was changed to Superior Council in 1702) was the highest court in the colony. Composed of the governor general, the bishop (or the vicar general in his absence), the intendant, five councillors (seven after 1675 and twelve after 1703), an attorney general, a clerk, and a half-dozen process servers, the council progressively lost its legislative power. By the beginning of the eighteenth century, it only heard appeals from lower jurisdictions.

Royal courts were established at Quebec, Trois-Rivières, and Montreal. These tribunals had both civil and criminal jurisdiction and were presided over by a *lieutenant-général* who was assisted by a *lieutenant-particulier,* a king's attorney, a clerk, and up to a dozen process servers. They also had an important role in ensuring that police regulations were obeyed, especially those concerning urban markets, fire prevention, and public sanitation. They also judged appeals from seigneurial courts within their government.

In a reform aimed at reducing court costs, expediting justice, and preventing the re-creation in the New World of one of the worst areas of abuse in the Old, lawyers were not allowed to practice in the colony. (There were nevertheless practicing attorneys in French North America.) Since the accused in criminal cases would have had no counsel in any event, the prohibition had little influence on criminal trials. This reform undoubtedly helped speed up procedure in civil suits and reduced costs. Some of the functions of lawyers were filled by notaries, process servers, or others familiar with the law who could represent litigants in court, but they could not plead.

Analysis of the Quebec court's records reveals that the vast majority of cases submitted to the courts were civil suits, with over half concerning debt collection. Those concerning property lines and leases or the settling of estates accounted for most of the others. Over three-quarters of the litigants came from Quebec City, suggesting that the royal judicial machinery had little influence in the countryside.

The structure of royal courts was modified by the creation of an admiralty court in 1719. Located in Quebec City, it dealt with all matters concerning shipping, including responsibility for registering ships entering or leaving the port of Quebec, inspecting cargos, and ensuring that all vessels had a full complement of men (including a surgeon). It judged cases concerning damaged cargo or equipment, prizes captured in wartime, and mutinies or other shipboard crimes. Apart from the court officials (a judge, king's attorney, clerk), a harbormaster was responsible for seeing that the port was clear of obstacles and that ships were loaded and unloaded in an orderly fashion.

The final royal judicial post was the *prévôt de la maréchaussée,* created in 1677. In France these officials had important functions in repressing banditism and vagrancy. They judged summarily and without appeal crimes committed by vagrants and by the military. In New France, their role was reduced and their principal function was to search out and arrest criminals and deserters.

The seigneurial courts established in several of the most populous seigneuries—such as Notre Dame des Anges, Beauport, Beaupré, and the island of Orleans—occupied the lowest rung of the judicial hierarchy. These private courts had full jurisdiction in almost all civil and criminal cases and were useful instruments of seigneurial administration, enabling seigneurs to collect quit rents and other dues. They also enforced royal ordinances and police regulations within their jurisdiction. Since costs in these courts were lower than those in royal courts and no time or money was lost in travel, they served the rural population well. In the Montreal district the seigneurial court of Montreal heard all cases until the establishment of a royal court in 1693.

The final judicial institution was the *officialité,* an ecclesiastical court created by Bishop Laval in 1660 but not officially recognized by the state until 1684. This court had jurisdiction in cases involving the clergy and sentences could be appealed to the Sovereign Council.

RELIGIOUS ADMINISTRATION

In the theory of French absolute monarchy, the king received his authority directly from God, and church and state were closely linked. Throughout the French regime royal authorities were ordered to promote Roman Catholicism. Although state authorities did not prosecute religious crimes such as blasphemy and witchcraft with the same vigor as their New England counterparts, they strove to uphold the dignity of the clergy and to suppress unorthodox religious views. The charter of the Company of One Hundred Associates had prohibited the settlement of Protestants in New France; those who did manage to arrive in the colony could not publicly practice their religion and were pressured to convert by both state and Catholic authorities. The ban on Protestants, although never rescinded, was relaxed in the eighteenth century when trade to the Canadian colony became dominated by Huguenot traders from Rouen and La Rochelle. Protestant agents of these companies, including François Havy and Jean Lefebvre of Quebec City, lived in the colony for long periods without harassment.

Religious administration was under the direct control of the bishop but closely supervised by the state. Until the establishment of the Bishopric of Quebec in 1674, Laval was vicar apostolic. During this period the church was organized as a mission, with all secular clergy being members of the Seminary of Quebec. Since Bishop Laval considered funds generated by the tithe (a tax on grain production) insufficient to support a parish clergy, priests were sent as missionaries to serve the needs of the colonial population. The Crown, however, insisted on having resident curates and, in 1679, established parishes and fixed the tithe at one twenty-sixth of grain production. Annual subsidies were paid to the church to ensure the clergy a decent standard of living. Parish clergy served the state by publicizing ordinances, helping with the census, and, in areas where there were no resident notaries, by drafting legal deeds. Subsidies were also paid to regular orders such as the Jesuits and Hospital sisters for their mission and diplomatic work with the Native peoples and for provision of social services such as hospitals and schools to the general population.

STATE AND SOCIETY

Bostonian Francis Parkman's vision of an ignorant and obedient peasantry mindlessly following the dictates of a paternalistic absolute monarchy has dominated the perception of New France's government by English-speaking North Americans for over a hundred years. In this overly simplistic, Whig interpretation, the Crown

helped stunt development of a viable community by restricting the local population's freedom of action and incentive.

Official correspondence between the ministry and colonial officials does indeed give the impression of an interventionist state meddling in the trivia of daily life. Instructions dictated how officials should behave in public, who was to receive holy communion first, and how pensions and contracts should be awarded. Measures such as the 1711 Edicts of Marly, which provided for the cancellation of seigneurial grants if seigneurs did not develop their lands and allowed seigneurs to reintegrate uncleared peasant lands into their domain, had a more significant impact. Most of the intendants' ordinances sought to protect consumers by putting the common good above individual interest. But they could, at times, be vexatious. Michel Bégon's prohibition against hiring stonemasons in 1715 while he rebuilt the intendant's palace is a good example.

Despite the apparent rigor of state intervention, enforcement was never mechanical and one of the distinguishing characteristics of this paternal system was the pronounced tendency of officials to deal with individual cases on a personal level and the taking into account of mitigating circumstances. The Edicts of Marly, for example, were not enforced until 1741, and even then most dispossessed seigneurs received new grants.

In ancien-régime France, family and social status were fundamental determinants of political influence. Royal absolutism relied heavily on personal and family linkages. A few families, usually related to the Pontchartrains—among them the Bégons and the Beauharnois, who provided several governors and intendants for New France—dominated the Marine bureaucracy in the eighteenth century. In France's highly structured society, one's place in the hierarchy defined social and political relations. The highest officials in New France developed their own networks of clients, recruiting army officers and civil administrators within their ranks, awarding fur-trade monopolies and contracts to their partisans. Thus, although New France had no representative institutions, its leading families did exercise some political influence within these networks. In the ancien régime, it was normal and acceptable to use position to better the condition of family and clients and, so long as officials were careful to make private interest coincide with state policy, this system permitted considerable individual initiative by the elite.

Apart from junior officials and militia officers, client networks rarely reached the majority of the population. New France was basically a peasant society in which family and local community came first. The state was relatively unobtrusive in the daily lives of most people, especially given the near absence of taxation. Militia service and the occasional billeting of troops were the most direct manifestations of state authority.

Royal institutions were urban and had little impact on most rural inhabitants. Although laws could be proclaimed, there was no effective means of enforcing unpopular measures since the captains of militia were more closely linked to the local community than to distant authorities. Popular protest was not unknown in New France. In 1704 residents of Montreal Island protested the high price of salt and, although the gathering was condemned by authorities, no arrests were made and the price of salt was regulated to meet their demands. In 1717 the *habitants* of Longueuil took up arms to protest statute labour on the Montreal fortifications. When armed resistance persisted, ten men were jailed but were released before winter by the governor who feared that they might freeze to death in their cells. Individualism and independence rather than blind subservience flourished as the predominant characteristics of the Canadian peasantry.

BIBLIOGRAPHY

Bosher, John F. "Government and Private Interests in New France." *Canadian Public Administration* (1967):244–257.

Crowley, Terence. " 'Thunder Gusts': Popular Disturbances in Early French Canada." Canadian Historical Association. *Historical Papers* (1979):11–32.

Dickinson, John A. *Justice et justiciables: La procédure civile à la Prèvöté de Québec, 1667–1759.* Quebec, 1982.

Dictionary of Canadian Biography. Vols. 1–3. Toronto, Ontario, 1966–1974. The first three volumes cover people who died before 1770; that is, the vast majority of those who held office during the French regime. Volume 4 covers those who died before 1801.

Dubé, Jean-Claude. *Les intendants de la Nouvelle-France.* Montreal, 1984.

Eccles, W. J. *Canada Under Louis XIV, 1663–1701.* Toronto, Ontario, 1964.

_____. *France in America.* New York, 1972.

_____. *Frontenac: The Courtier Governor.* Toronto, Ontario, 1959.

Lachance, André. *La justice criminelle du roi au Canada au XVIIIe siècle: Tribunaux et officiers.* Quebec, 1978.

Lanctôt, Gustave. *L'administration de la Nouvelle-France.* Montreal, 1971.

Lunn, Alice Jean Elizabeth. *Dévelopement économique de la Nouvelle-France, 1713–1760.* Montreal, 1986.

Miquelon, Dale. *New France, 1701–1744: "A Supplement to Europe."* Toronto, Ontario, 1987.

Standen, S. Dale. "Politics, Patronage, and the Imperial Interest: Charles de Beauharnais's Disputes with Gilles Hocquart." *Canadian Historical Review* 60, no. 1 (March 1979) 19–40.

Trudel, Marcel. *The Beginnings of New France, 1524–1663.* Toronto, Ontario, 1973.

Zoltvany, Yves. *Philippe de Rigaud de Vaudreuil: Governor of New France, 1703–1725.* Toronto, Ontario, 1974.

John A. Dickinson

SEE ALSO **Local Government; Relations with the Parent Country;** and **The Reorganization of Empires.**

ENGLAND AND ITS COLONIES

THE FRAMEWORK OF GOVERNMENT in England's North American colonies fluctuated over time. Ideas for a plan of government hardly existed at the dawn of settlement in 1600, and not until the end of the seventeenth century did a structure of imperial government and authority begin to take shape. But as imperial requirements changed, as the North American colonies grew in population and expanded in territory, and as the English monarchy itself shifted from absolutism to constitutionalism, the framework of

England's imperial government was remodeled. With the passage of time, as imperial needs, aims, institutions, and practices changed, even the idea of empire itself was transformed.

There were several elements built into the fabric of English imperial government that established the unique tensions which made the history of English rule in America exceptionally dynamic. While English imperialists aspired to establish a highly centralized, colonial administration patterned after the earlier successes of the Portuguese, the Spanish, the French, and even the Dutch who had preceded them, in practice England only managed to produce a "federal empire," an empire characterized by ongoing conflicts and tensions between "peripheries and center." Moreover, the empire of theory differed from the empire of practice. London's vision of what colonies ought to be was markedly distinct from what Americans thought the colonies had become. This was true from the earliest period of English settlement and became even more of an established fact as time went on. The inability of the English government to accommodate these tensions and to reconcile the division between perception and reality ultimately produced the War of Independence and the separation of the English mainland colonies from the mother country.

The continuing debate between the colonists and the English administration over what fundamental body of law lay at the foundation of legal authority in the colonies provides a good example of this. The Americans believed that English law was established in America. As subjects of the English Crown, they enjoyed all of "the rights, privileges and liberties" of Englishmen under the Common Law. As the first Maryland General Assembly declared in the Act for the Liberties of the People (1638):

All the inhabitants of this Province being Christians, slaves excepted, shall have and enjoy all such rights, liberties, immunities, privileges, and free customs within this Province as any natural born subject of England has or ought to have or enjoy in the Realm of England by force or virtue of the common law or Statute Law of England. (W. K. Kavenagh, ed. *Foundations of Colonial America*. Vol. 2, p. 1182)

Over a century later, however, on the very eve of the American Revolution, the author of the eighteenth century's leading compilation of English laws and the principal advocate of Parliamentary authority, Sir William Blackstone, would write in his influential *Commentaries on the Laws of England* (4 vols., 1765–1769):

If an uninhabited country be discovered and planted by English subjects all the English laws are immediately there in force. For as the law is the birthright of every subject, so wherever they go they carry their laws with them. But in conquered or ceded countries, that have already laws of their own, the king may indeed alter and change those laws. . . . Our American plantations are principally of this latter sort, being obtained in the last century either by right of conquest and driving out the natives . . . or by treaties. And therefore the common law of England as such has no allowances or authority there; they being no part of the mother country but distinct (though dependent) dominions. (*Commentaries*. Vol. 1, p. 104–105)

In short the Americans believed that they carried the common law with them when they settled across the sea. But the English resisted this notion, preferring to view the colonists as completely subjugated to the will of the sovereign. This unresolved difference in viewpoint on vital issues—the rights of English settlers, the fundamental laws in force in America, the authority under whom those laws remained in force, and the mechanisms by which they could be altered—typified the unfinished character of the English imperial framework of government even as the colonial period came to a close.

FOUNDING DOCUMENTS

British settlers on the American mainland often resorted to self-help in establishing the foundations of government and authority. The most striking example of this was the famous Mayflower Compact (1620). The compact was an agreement, or "covenant," entered into by the leaders of the newly founded Pilgrim community to enact "just and equal Laws, Ordinances, Acts, Constitutions, and Offices . . . for the general Good of the Colony." The Mayflower Compact was needed because the land patent from the Virginia Company to the Council for New England failed to provide for the establishment of proper legal authority or for a form of government. Consequently, the compact became the basis for the government the Pilgrims would soon put into place. While the Mayflower Compact was not a true constitution in the modern sense in that it did not establish a framework of government, it did provide a precedent for settlers covenanting together to set up a regime of law.

Other, less well-known examples of such documents of political and legal foundation abound in the early colonial experience. For example, in 1637 the people who first settled Providence, Rhode Island, entered into an "Agreement" in which they promised

to subject ourselves in active and passive obedience to all such orders and agreements as shall be made for the public good of the body in an orderly way, by the major consent of present inhabitants, masters of families, incorporated together in a Towne fellowship, and others whom they shall admit unto them only in civil things. (Donald S. Lutz. *Origins of American Constitutionalism*, p. 28)

Similarly, in 1641 inhabitants along the Piscataqua River in southern Maine entered into a "Combination" which, though short in length, had all the elements of a true secular compact for the establishment of "a body politick":

Whereas sundry Mischiefs and Inconveniences have befallen us, and more and greater may, in regard of want of Civill Government, his gracious Majesty haveing settled no order for us, to our knowledge, we whose names are underwritten, being Inhabitants upon the River of Pascataqua have voluntarily agreed to combine ourselves into a body Politick, that wee may the more comfortably enjoy the Benefit of his Majesties Laws, and doe hereby actually engage ourselves to submit to his Royall Majesties Laws, together with all such Laws as shall be concluded by a major part of the Freemen of our Society, in Case they be not repugnant to the laws of England, and administered in behalf of his Majestie. And this wee have mutually promised, and engaged to doe, and so to continue till his excellent Majestie shall give other orders concerning us. (Donald S. Lutz, ed. *Documents of Political Foundation*, p. 187)

Throughout the seventeenth century, settlers up and down the North American coastline, from Maine to the Carolinas, wrote solemn agreements in order to establish the basis of law and government. They were called different things in different places ("covenants," "compacts," "combinations," "agreements," "fundamentals," and "orders"), but collectively they show a strong and deep commitment to rudimentary forms of constitutionalism. The resort to written agreements of mutual understanding provide early evidence of what would later ripen into the formal written constitutions adopted by most of the new American states during the revolutionary period.

Within such rudimentary frameworks of authority, mainland settlers wrote, copied, invented, and transcribed the laws that would govern their lives. Given that law was a scarce commodity, it is not surprising that mainland colonists drafted legal codes and compilations of law to fill the vacuum. Dale's Code, adopted in the Jamestown settlement in 1611, was a draconian system of law designed to impose quasimilitary discipline because of the harsh conditions that early Virginians faced. In contrast, the Body of Liberties of 1641 and the Laws and Liberties of 1648, enacted by the Massachusetts Bay colony, contained significant elements of Mosaic as well as English law. The Laws and Liberties of Massachusetts were influential in other "Puritan" colonies where codes of law were adopted. Other examples of early colonial legal codes were Ludlow's code of Connecticut (1650), the Duke of York's laws for New York (1664), Cutt's code for New Hampshire (1680), and Trott's adaptation of English statutory law in Carolina (1712).

English law was not transmitted wholesale to the colonies. Each colony developed its own legal culture, often using original nomenclature for courts, judges, and forms of legal process. However, as new needs arose, as colonial societies and economies became more complex, and as legal professionals with training and experience came to America in the eighteenth century, the law of the mainland colonies grew closer to, rather than more distant from, English models. Still, the legacy of the colonial legal experience was that of originality, difference, greater informality, and simplification in law and legal practice in comparison to the laws and procedures of England.

THE IMPERIAL CONTEXT

As for the framework of government itself, certain assumptions were firmly established and generally acknowledged by all parties. It was well understood, for example, that the American colonies were political dependencies, which meant that the ultimate power of political decision resided in England. Moreover, Americans accepted the fact that the king rather than Parliament had responsibility for colonial rule. Even though the history of England during the seventeenth and eighteenth centuries was marked by the rise of Parliament as the cornerstone of England's modern constitutional system, the authority of the Crown over colonial administration was, if anything, greater at the end of the period than it had been at the beginning. Indeed, one explanation for the crisis of empire that commenced in the aftermath of the Seven Years' War (1754–1763) was the fact that the new Parliament coming to power with the accession of George III in 1760 attempted to usurp the traditional role of the Crown and the imperial bureaucracy in colonial affairs. This role was evidenced by an array of royal institutions that were directly implicated in the routine, day-to-day management of England's overseas dominions. But the competition between the Crown and Parliament for control of colonial policy, and the infighting that often took place within the agencies of the colonial bureaucracy, created a poorly coordinated system of colonial government.

Within this fragmented and decentralized framework of imperial government, the American mainland colonies developed political and legal institutions, as well as a body of law, that established unique but working systems of local government. These local governments were responsive to the particular needs of the colonists and counterbalanced British rule.

THREE COLONIAL MODELS

There were three types of government established by the British to govern the colonies: charter colonies, proprietary colonies, and royal colonies. They existed side by side from the early seventeenth century, but by the end of the colonial period, the royal colony had clearly emerged as the preferred model, at least from the British point of view, and certainly as the most common type.

Charter Colonies

The oldest form of government in this threefold typology was the charter colony. These were colonies established by trading companies, groups of enterprising merchants—or "merchant adventurers," as they were called at first—who received a grant of land, legal power to govern, and a written charter of incorporation directly from the king. The model for the charter colony was the joint stock company, popular in the sixteenth century as a method for developing trade with the New World as well as with Russia (Muscovy Company, 1555) and the Far East (East India Company, 1600). The first permanent English settlement in America, Jamestown (1607), was organized under the auspices of the London Company, a branch of a larger group of investors known as the Virginia Company. While the London Company lasted for less than two decades, it presided over the establishment of the first representative assembly in America, the Virginia House of Burgesses. In addition to employing the governor and his council, the House of Burgesses consisted of two representatives from every Virginia town, plantation, and "hundred." Representative institutions like the House of Burgesses came naturally to charter colonies. As companies they were structured to give authority to a wide group of people—first to stockholders and then to actual settlers, "freemen" or "freeholders."

Plymouth and Massachusetts Bay were two other examples of charter colonies. Plymouth was established by a group of investors called the Council for New England, an offshoot from the original Virginia Company. This enterprise was funded by a group of London merchants, but the principals were Puritan dissenters who wanted to separate themselves physically as well as theologically from the Anglican church. These "Separatists" or "Brownists" (after the radical Puritan theologian Robert Browne) were considered subversive by the English authorities. Fearing persecution, the "Pilgrims" (as they were later called) sailed aboard the *Mayflower* in September 1620. Even though most of the people on board the *Mayflower* were not themselves Separatists, the journey of the Pilgrims has long been celebrated as the single most dramatic immigrant voyage in American history. The signing of the Mayflower Compact by forty-one of the adult male passengers took place while still en route. Plymouth was to prosper but never to grow very large in population. It was to be absorbed by Massachusetts after the Glorious Revolution (1688).

If Plymouth was the forerunner of the charter colony in New England, the region where that form of government predominated, then Massachusetts, became the most significant charter colony. The Massachusetts Bay Company received its charter from Charles I in 1629. Prominent Puritan members of the company were willing to settle in New England when the company, in the Cambridge Agreement (1629), consented to the transfer of the government and the company charter to America. Under this agreement a contingent of about one thousand Puritan settlers set sail in eleven ships in 1630 in what came to be called the Great Migration. Settlements were established to the north of Plymouth. In the next ten years about fifteen thousand settlers, most of them Puritans, migrated to New England. The reason for this outpouring of people was that England was entering troubled times. The king had dissolved the Parliament, and a wave of Anglican conformity was sweeping the land under the direction of William Laud, the Anglican archbishop of Canterbury. The Puritans faced persecution plus an economic crisis in the cloth industry resulting from disruptions caused by the Thirty Years' War (1618–1648) in Europe. With the transfer of the charter and the company government to New England, the Puritan leaders were able to admit freemen as voting members of the company even though they were not investors in the enterprise. Freemenship was then made to depend upon orthodox Puritan church membership. As a consequence, in the first generation after 1630, Massachusetts was governed more as a theocracy than as a commercial enterprise or a normal polity.

The structure of government in Massachusetts Bay was typical of the charter form of government—a governor, a deputy governor, a group called the Court of Assistants (a governor's council), and deputies to the General Court elected on a township basis by the adult males who had been admitted to freemanship. The governor, the deputy governor, the assistants, and the deputies together comprised the General Court. The General Court elected the governor and the deputy governor. After some initial controversy, the freemen were allowed to elect the assistants. In 1644 the deputies and the assistants were divided and sat in two separate chambers, thereby establishing the precedent for the bicameral legislature.

Even though proprietary and royal colonies would also establish representative assemblies paralleling those of the charter colonies, the latter were always noted for their "democratical" tendencies and their heightened spirit of independence. This is well documented in the history of Rhode Island (charters, 1644 and 1663) and Connecticut (charter, 1662), where habits of independence and self-rule were strong and enduring. The English wanted a form of government that was less liberal and more in line with the centralizing themes of mercantilism then in the ascendancy in Britain's ruling circles. By the middle of the seventeenth century the charter colony form was supplanted by the proprietary grant and the royal colony.

Proprietary Colonies

As a method for settling colonies, the proprietorship became popular after 1630. Over the next half century, the monarchy established Maryland, New York, New Jersey, the Carolinas, and Pennsylvania using the proprietary grant as the primary model of colonial government. Most of these colonies were eventually converted into royal colonies as the process of imperial consolidation accelerated (none became charter colonies). Because of the political power of its proprietors, Maryland and Pennsylvania (with the Delaware counties) remained in the hands of proprietary grantees (the Calvert family and the Penn family) until the American Revolution.

As with charter grants, the proprietorship was based upon historical precedent. The specific model was the Palatinate of Durham, a feudal land grant that gave sweeping powers to the lord bishops of Durham, in the northeast corner of England, in order to defend the frontier of the realm (the "march") against Scottish marauders. While the Palatinate itself lay to the south of the Scottish border, a small triangle of land was detached from the county of Northumberland and placed under the authority of Durham. Dating from the time of the Norman conquest, this special land grant enabled the marcher lords to exercise absolute authority.

Similar thinking was now applied to America. "Palatine" dignities included broad military and political powers as well as control over land

306

distributions. This was the model used when Lord George Calvert, the first baron of Baltimore, received a grant of land north of the Potomac River from Charles I in 1632. This "Maryland Palatinate" was, in every respect, a feudal grant from the king of England to one of his great lords. As the charter itself stated:

We do by these Presents . . . Make, Create, and Constitute Him, the now Baron of Baltimore, and his Heirs, the True and Absolute Lords and Proprietaries of [Maryland] . . . To Hold of Us . . . in free and common Soccage, by Fealty only for all Services, and not in capite, nor by Knight's Service, yielding therefore unto Us . . . two Indian Arrows of these Parts, to be delivered at the . . . Castle of Windsor, every Year, on Tuesday in Easter-Week. (Henry Steele Commager, ed. *Documents of American History.* Vol. 1, p. 21)

Along with the exceptional rights and immunities of the lords of Durham, the proprietor was also given the power to establish manors with "courts baron" (baronial courts) in accordance with the ancient customs and traditions of English feudalism.

But while the proprietary grant of Maryland to Lord Calvert was retrospective in form, the grant also required that laws be made with the "Advice, Assent, and Approbation of the Freemen . . . or their Delegates or Deputies, whom We will shall be called together for the framing of laws." Indeed, the freemen of Maryland were quick to assert their role as participants in lawmaking. The Maryland assembly of freemen, called into being by the terms of the charter itself, demanded the power to initiate legislation and to affirm a body of liberties. The assembly also enacted an Act of Toleration (1649), a landmark in the history of American religious freedom. The Toleration Act declared that, as enforced belief in matters of conscience had produced dangerous consequences in other colonies, no person would be "Molested or discountenanced . . . in respect of his *or her* religion nor in the free exercise thereof . . . nor any way compelled to the beleife or exercise of any other Religion against his *or her* consent" (emphasis added). In addition to its prescient recognition of the equal rights of women in matters of conscience, the Toleration Act also created a private cause of legal action as a method of enforcing its provisions. Thus, in addition to the payment of a fine of twenty shillings to the government, violators of the statute could be sued by an injured party for treble damages. Although it was conditioned on belief in Jesus Christ, the Toleration Act nevertheless established Maryland as one of the most liberal settlements.

The same pattern is observable in Pennsylvania, a colony that was established on feudal models and forms but developed a reputation for a progressive political and social outlook. The proprietary grant from Charles II to the Quaker William Penn (1681) was made with similar purposes to those of the Calvert grant fifty years before: to shore up England's position along the Delaware River. But just as Maryland was to become a haven for religious dissidents (in its case, Catholics), so Pennsylvania would become a home not just for dissident Quakers but for an assortment of religious and ethnic groups: Scotch-Irish from Northern Ireland, Rhineland Germans, French Huguenots, and religious groups of almost every description and persuasion from the Continent as well as from Britain.

By 1750 no colony except New York had a wider diversity of population than Pennsylvania. This was due, in part, to the great productivity of the Pennsylvania economy: its rich agricultural, mineral, fur, and forest resources; its commercial development; its shipbuilding; and the highly developed cosmopolitan life of Philadelphia, the "Athens of America." By the middle of the eighteenth century, Philadelphia was the largest city in British North America and second only to London in all of the British Empire. But a rich economy was not the only reason for Pennsylvania's unusual liberal spirit. The other source was the vision of its founder who, despite the nearly absolute powers granted to him as proprietor, immediately established institutions of freedom through his Concessions (1681), a Frame of Government (1682), and the Charter of Privileges (1701). These acts established powerful traditions of limited government, constitutional rule, and individual liberties in Pennsylvania.

The Prevalence of Royal Colonies

By the time of the American Revolution, there were only two proprietary colonies in existence, Maryland and Pennsylvania. The dominant form of colonial government had become the royal colony. Eight of the original thirteen colonies (New Hampshire, Massachusetts, New York, New Jersey, Virginia, the Carolinas, and Georgia) had come under this form of direct Crown rule. By the eve of the revolution, royal government was in the ascendancy in America and appeared to be the wave of the future. Unlike the charter and proprietary colonies, where legal authority flowed directly from, and was bounded by, a written document (the company charter or the proprietary grant), in royal colonies there was no charter document. With the exception of Massachusetts, which did have a charter (1691), all of the royal colonies were ruled directly by royal prerogative through the king's representative, the royal governor.

First employed in Virginia in 1624, the royal colony model was used as a method for salvaging company colonies (such as Virginia) and proprietorships (such as the Carolinas) from financial ruin and political instability. By the end of the seventeenth century, the royal colony was preferred over charter or proprietary alternatives because the Crown was in a stronger position to project its power abroad and less dependent upon intermediaries. Moreover, with constitutional relations between king and Parliament stabilized after 1689, the king could turn his attention to the American dominions, where his political and constitutional authority did not threaten Parliament. The royal colony also provided the Crown with a great opportunity to bring about the centralization that had so eluded the privy council, the Lords of Trade, the Board of Trade, and the other agencies of colonial administration. Through the instrumentality of the office of royal governor, the imperial apparatus hoped to succeed in coordinating and rationalizing colonial affairs more effectively than it had in the past.

The formal legal powers of royal governors were considerable. As set forth in the typical royal commission—the public document governors received from the privy council at the time of their appointment—governors were charged with wide-ranging authority: to execute the laws; to call together legislative assemblies of freeholders (or deputies); "to make, constitute and ordain laws, statutes and ordinances"; to veto legislation that was contrary to the interest or policy of the Crown; to dissolve rebellious assemblies; to

establish civil and criminal courts; to appoint judges; to pardon offenders; and to command military and naval forces in time of war. The governors were also charged with the responsibility of seeing to the enforcement of the Acts of Trade and Navigation and the collection of customs duties. In addition to these executive powers, governors could act by proclamation, and proclamations had the force of law. They served in a judicial capacity as a court of equity, as a court of probate, and as the highest court of appeals in the colony's judicial hierarchy. Royal governors received detailed (and secret) instructions from the privy council as to how policy was to be implemented. Thus through its royal appointees in the colonies, the Crown had the ability to exercise great political leverage. Indeed, as the custodian of the royal prerogative in the colonies, royal governors enjoyed the formal legal power that English monarchs of the seventeenth century had aspired to but failed to achieve at home.

The royal governor's office, then, was one with significant legislative and judicial as well as purely executive functions. There is debate among historians, however, about whether or not the royal governors' authority translated into real political power. Bernard Bailyn, the distinguished historian of early America, has written that royal governors enjoyed what he calls "swollen claims and shrunken powers" because of certain inherent weaknesses in their real political position. Even so, when Parliament adopted a Revenue Act (1767) to increase colonial revenues to an anticipated sum of £40,000 sterling a year in order to provide "a more certain and adequate provision for . . . the support of civil government," a storm of protest erupted because of the fear that this would release the royal governors from their dependence on local assemblies for appropriations and salaries. While colonial assemblies would lose "the power of the purse," the governors would be able to rule as petty tyrants bent upon the establishment of absolute rule.

COMPONENTS OF GOVERNMENT

The formal differences between charter, proprietary, and royal colonies can easily be exaggerated. In fact, despite structural and legal distinctions, governmental institutions in most of the colonies developed along similar lines. For example, all of the colonial governors had a governor's council, something akin to an executive cabinet. Councillors were appointed by the governor in royal colonies and by the proprietor in proprietary colonies; in charter colonies councillors were elected by the people or the people's deputies. Massachusetts showed its true "hybrid" status as a cross between a charter colony and a royal colony because, from 1691, councillors were elected by the House of Representatives even though Massachusetts had a royal governor who normally would have had the power of appointment. Councillors served as advisers to the governor on such matters as expenditures, calling the assembly into session, legislation, Indian policy, and appointments. But the council was more than just an advisory committee. In royal colonies councillors served with the governor as a court of judicature and even as the highest court of appeals. The governors' councils also served as an upper house of the colonial legislature except in Pennsylvania, where the legislature was a unicameral body. By law governors were eventually excluded from the deliberations of the council when it was sitting in its legislative capacity.

Potentially a source of influence and power, this legislative role proved, in the long run, to be the undoing of the councils. Caught between ambitious governors and powerful lower houses of assembly, the councils failed to develop an independent political base. Usually much smaller in membership than the popular assemblies, the councils did not have a regular standing committee system that would have given them more institutional focus. In addition, councils sometimes gave legislative approval to particular measures only to advise the governor to disapprove of them afterwards, an action which undermined their credibility as legislative bodies. Moreover, council members often occupied a number of high positions in colonial government, and they simply could not discharge all of their responsibilities simultaneously. As a result councils frequently failed to muster the necessary quorum to do legislative business, and this further weakened their legislative role.

By the end of the colonial period, the governors' councils were already in decline. They virtually disappeared amidst the turmoil of the American Revolution. The very fact that they enjoyed executive and judicial as well as legislative powers made them unpopular because the councils conflicted with the principle of separation of powers. Vestiges of the councils did remain, however. In Massachusetts the governor's council survived into the modern era with mostly ceremonial functions, its only real power today being that of reviewing candidates for judicial appointment. However, the councils did provide an important precedent for bicameralism. Almost all of the early state constitutions (with the exceptions of Pennsylvania and Vermont) provided for an upper house, usually called the senate, which had its origins in the old colonial councils sitting as an upper legislative chamber.

The Courts

The colonial court system was very different from modern state court structures. In colonial times local courts performed many routine governmental functions. In the southern and middle colonies, county courts sat as courts of judicature in important civil and criminal cases, but they also performed other roles: they determined rules for the transfer of land and the terms of labor contracts; regulated the buying and selling of bonded servants and slaves; supervised the construction and maintenance of roads, bridges, and wharves; and controlled the surveyors and engineers who planned those public works. County courts also functioned as licensing authorities that regulated the professions, and they set fee schedules and prices for the goods and services of tradesmen. County courts served as tax collectors, established standards of weights and measures, and regulated the hunting of game and the destruction of insect and animal pests. The county courts were responsible for public health, the administration of poor relief, and the care of orphans. In time of hostilities, they saw to the levy of troops and made provision for their supply, housing, and defenses.

County courts had similar functions in New England, but there the town meeting was the principal organ of local government. The New England town meeting was the first truly democratic institution in American life. Based upon principles of direct democracy, all residents of the town, regardless of their wealth and ability to meet property qualifications, could participate. However, while property qualifications were relaxed, gender qualifications were not, since only male adults could vote in the town meeting. Most of the functions performed by the county court in the southern colonies were performed by the town meeting. In addition, the town meeting chose town officers and a board of selectmen, a small executive body that administered town affairs day by day. The town meeting itself convened only when it was called by "warrant" or "warning" to town voters, which generally was issued only once or twice a year. The English viewed the town meeting as a hotbed of resistance to royal government.

In 1774 Parliament enacted a series of laws to punish Massachusetts after the Boston Tea Party. In one of those measures, the Massachusetts Government Act, Parliament virtually suspended the charter of 1691 and declared that town meetings could gather only if their warrants were approved in advance by the royal governor. By this measure the English hoped to curb the town meetings because, in the words of the statute, "such meetings . . . have . . . been misled to treat upon matters of the most general concern, and to pass many dangerous and unwarrantable resolves." The Massachusetts Government Act, however, only served to intensify the spirit of independence.

The colonial court structure above the local level had characteristics that set it apart from the English judiciary. For example, colonial justices of the peace were called "magistrates" or "commissioners" in some localities. After centuries of growth, English courts had become highly differentiated into an array of courts performing specialized functions. In contrast, colonial courts were more unified; the same court would decide several types of matters that in England would be divided among different courts. For example, the colonists preferred to have equity law decided by regular courts rather than by equity courts as was the English practice. American courts were also more hierarchical; inferior courts dealt with minor criminal offenses or petty civil disputes and superior or "supreme" courts handled serious crimes and more substantial civil cases. In addition, because of the paucity of trained lawyers in America, judges in the colonies were often lay people with no significant legal training or experience. Consequently, appellate review was customary; the higher courts served as forums for the correction of errors committed by the lower courts. But the distinction between trial courts and appellate courts was often blurred.

Finally, there was at least the possibility of review by the privy council in England. The privy council considered about fifteen hundred cases coming from the colonies in the century preceding independence with most originating in Virginia, Massachusetts, and Rhode Island. Privy council review was not a common event, for it entailed great costs in money, time, and effort. In addition, there was no system for reporting decisions by the privy council, so that no body of case law developed to guide colonial courts and judges. The absence of a body of reported cases probably increased the number of appeals that were brought to the council. Privy council review was more administrative than judicial. The possibility of such appeals limited the freedom of colonial courts to develop new law or test English precedents as the council tried to bring colonial legal processes into conformity with English practice. But there were also cases in which the council deferred to colonial pressures to relax the stricter requirements of English law, particularly on issues like the divisibility of landed estates.

By the middle of the eighteenth century, the most important unresolved issue concerning the colonial judiciary was the nature of judicial tenure in the higher courts. Under the Act of Settlement (1701), English judges had achieved independence from the Crown and served during good behavior and not at the pleasure of the king. Judges could only be removed "upon address" by both houses of Parliament, thereby relieving judges from direct political control.

In the American colonies, however, the status of judges remained cloudy and uncertain. In New Jersey, for example, Robert Hunter Morris was appointed in 1739 by his father, Governor Lewis Morris, to the chief justiceship with a good behavior provision in his commission. In New York the judges of the Supreme Court sat for a brief time on terms of good behavior tenure until the Crown ended the practice in 1761. But

310

in some of the other colonies, judges served only at pleasure. The issue was finally joined upon the death of George II.

The death of the king meant that all royal commissions would have to be renewed in the name of the new king, George III. This provided an opportunity for the Board of Trade and the privy council to try to bring the colonial judiciary under greater royal control by requiring that all judicial commissions provide for tenure at the pleasure of the Crown. But the colonial assemblies refused to appropriate funds for judicial salaries unless the judges served during good behavior. The Board of Trade and the privy council remained adamant on the question and attempted to pay judicial salaries by other means. The Revenue Act of 1767, with its provisions for financing the colonial civil list through new colonial revenues, brought the issue into sharp relief. As Jefferson was to put it in the Declaration of Independence (1776) in his indictment of George III: "He has made Judges dependent on his Will alone, for the tenure of their offices, and the amount and payment of their salaries." The unwillingness of the English authorities to provide the colonies with an independent judiciary or to compromise on this sensitive question was a major source of division further polarizing England from its mainland colonies.

The People's Representatives

Of all the institutions of colonial government, the most dynamic and significant were the lower houses of assembly, which formed the cornerstone of representative government in America. Called into being by charter in the charter colonies, by grant in the proprietary colonies, and by the governors commission in the royal colonies, the assemblies of the peoples deputies became the principal forum for the expression of colonial interests and for resistance to British policies and rule.

The position of the assemblies in colonial political life was not static. Colonial historians have documented a "rise of the assembly" not unlike the rise of Parliament itself. By the time of the revolution, the reins of political leadership had passed to these institutions in most of the colonies, regardless of their formal structure. As James Glen, royal governor of South Carolina said of the South Carolina Assembly in 1748,

"The People have got the whole administration into their Hands, and the Crown is by various Laws despoiled of its principal flowers and brightest Jewels." Beginning in 1776 the popular assemblies led the fight in the War of Independence as well as in the struggle for written constitutions in the newly independent American states. The rise of the assembly did not necessarily mean that there was a commensurate decline of royal authority since the tendency of imperial and parliamentary policy was to strengthen the hands of the royal governors and to stiffen British rule. Thus, assembly "privilege" and royal "prerogative" were on the rise simultaneously, a trend that inevitably led to conflict. There is no doubt, however, that time and experience strengthened the position of the assemblies in the structure of colonial government.

At first a distinctly subordinate branch of government, by the middle of the eighteenth century the assemblies had established their right to meet separately from the governor's council, to elect their own speaker, to establish a regular committee system, and to hold regular sessions. Assemblies decided which deputies to seat in disputed elections; they defended the principle of legislative immunity and the right of legislators to speak freely in debate. Assemblies also claimed the privilege to investigate, to summon persons to appear before the bar of the legislature, and to exercise all of the powers of Parliament even though the English would not acknowledge such claims. As time went on, assemblies increased their output of statutes, a sure sign of growing maturity and institutional confidence. Assemblies even acted as judicial bodies deciding an assortment of civil and criminal matters. In fact the division of the Massachusetts legislature (the General Court) into two chambers was a direct result of a dispute between the deputies and the assistants over a lawsuit, the famous case of the stray sow (*Sherman v. Keayne*, 1642) that the legislature was hearing on appeal.

With the development of regular courts, however, the colonial assemblies gradually surrendered most of their judicial functions. But even as they abandoned their judicial powers, the lower houses of assembly asserted executive authority in areas of policy and administration traditionally within the purview of the governors. Assemblies not only exerted control over money bills (the power of the purse) but even insisted on the right to determine how revenues were to be spent as well as the right to audit the colony's financial accounts. Some assemblies tried to manage intercolonial relations and colony policy toward Native Americans. Assemblies even considered the appointment of officials such as the public printer, military officers, the colony treasurer, and the colony's representative in England (the colonial agent) as within the scope of their authority.

THE STRUGGLE FOR POWER

The "quest for power" by the colonial assemblies continued until the American Revolution. The intensity of the conflicts between assemblies and governors varied from colony to colony, but the rise of the assemblies typified the dynamic nature of the structure of British imperial government on both sides of the Atlantic. The failure to resolve the tensions and conflicts generated by assembly claims to power contributed mightily to the War of Independence.

BIBLIOGRAPHY

Commager, Henry Steele, ed. *Documents of American History.* 2 vols. New York, 1934; 9th ed., New York and Englewood Cliffs, N.J., 1973.

Dargo, George. *Roots of the Republic: A New Perspective on Early American Constitutionalism.* New York, 1974.

Greene, Jack P. *Peripheries and Center: Constitutional Development in the Extended Polities of the British Empire and the United States, 1607–1788.* Athens, Ga., 1986.

_____. *The Quest for Power: The Lower Houses of Assembly in the Southern Royal Colonies, 1689–1776.* Chapel Hill, N.C., 1963.

Katz, Stanley M. *Newcastle's New York: Anglo-American Politics, 1732–1753.* Cambridge, Mass., 1968.

Kavenagh, W. K., ed. *Foundations of Colonial America.* 3 vols. New York, 1983.

Labaree, Leonard Woods. *Royal Government in America: A Study of the British Colonial System Before 1783.* New York, 1958.

Lutz, Donald S. *Documents of Political Foundation, Written by Colonial Americans: From Covenant to Constitution.* Philadelphia, 1986.

_____. *The Origins of American Constitutionalism.* Baton Rouge, La., 1988.

Sosin, Jack. *English America and Imperial Inconstancy: the Rise of Provincial Autonomy, 1696–1715.* Lincoln, Nebr., 1985.

_____. *English America and the Revolution of 1688: Royal Administration and the Structure of Provincial Government.* Lincoln, Nebr., 1982.

Ubbelohde, Carl. *The American Colonies and the British Empire, 1607–1763.* Arlington Heights, Ill., 1975.

George Dargo

SEE ALSO **Local Government; Mercantilism; Relations with the Parent Country; The Reorganization of Empires; Social Tensions;** and **The Structure of Society.**

THE NETHERLANDS AND ITS COLONIES

THE GOVERNMENT OF the United Provinces of the Netherlands was shaped by war and held together by culture and history. The centralized government was embodied in the States General, a national assembly composed of delegations of representatives from the seven provinces that had formed themselves into a nation by written agreement. The agreement, known as the Union of Utrecht, was signed in 1579 in the midst of what would become the Eighty Years' War against the Spanish Hapsburgs.

The States General was a relatively weak institution. The seven provincial States (assemblies) were sovereign. Most delegates arrived in The Hague with detailed instructions from home, and few acted independently of their region or province. Decisions of importance regarding the union as a whole required a unanimous vote. The system worked by consensus, but it did not always work well.

Political leadership could come from at least two other quarters: the province of Holland, which carried 58 percent of the government's financial burden, and the stadholder (prince of Orange). When the chief advocate (*raadpensionaris*) and the stadholder cooperated, the government could act decisively. At other times the jealousies among the provinces paralyzed the government.

The government was a coalition forged in the context of the revolt against the Hapsburgs. The success of the coalition was dependent upon the maintenance of political consensus and the avoidance of issues that were particularly divisive. Consequently, the chartering of the two great joint-stock companies, the East and West India companies, with their complex chamber systems and decentralized administrations, suited the coalition well. By abdicating authority to privatized cartels, the government of the United Provinces could embark upon a policy of imperialism without having to debate the issue of sovereignty. This led to the assumption of government responsibilities by joint-stock companies.

THE WEST INDIA COMPANY AND NEW NETHERLAND

The West India Company (WIC) first sought to govern New Netherland as a military garrison. The instructions for Willem Verhulst (the commander of the expedition that in 1624 settled some thirty families of French-speaking Walloons in the colony) left no doubt as to the locus of authority. As commander he was authorized to administer corporal punishment and to deport wrongdoers to the fatherland "in order that they may be punished . . . according to their deserts." Most importantly he was to see to it that the colonists worked.

From the company viewpoint, the Walloons were employees, and the commander was both military leader and boss. It was a system designed to exploit the fur trade by creating a self-sufficient agricultural community to support a permanent company presence in the area. It was also a system easily abused.

Garrison government in the company's chartered territory tended to be brutal. Scandal seemed to surround all of the early commanders of New Netherland. In 1626 Willem Verhulst was literally overthrown by his own officers when he refused their demand for his resignation. When his successor, Peter Minuit, arrived in the colony, he found Verhulst under house arrest and the colonists scattered in unprotected hamlets from the Delaware to the Connecticut rivers. Company secretary Isaac de Rasiere reported that the settlers had been "very harshly ruled by Verhulst," and as a consequence he recommended that they be treated more humanely in the future, even if it meant that "owing to bad government hitherto prevailing, it is necessary to administer some punishment with kindness."

Minuit's term ended in controversy when he absconded with secret maps and information that enabled him to help found the Swedish West India Company. Minuit's successor, Wouter van Twiller, was recalled from office amidst charges of alcoholism and fraud. Willem Kieft, van Twiller's successor, foolishly triggered a series of Indian wars that nearly drove the European population into the sea. When he was replaced by Peter Stuyvesant in 1647, Kieft had so antagonized the council that the first item of business facing the new director-general was the cooling of tempers and the reestablishment of respect for the office.

A council had been created in 1626 to assist the director-general in his dealings with the colonists. The council, drawn from the officers of the company, proposed laws and assisted the director-general in enforcing them. The director-general took part in council meetings. In the case of a tie, the director-general could cast two votes.

The council's most important function was as a judicial bench. From its beginning in the 1620s until 1653 (when most of its judicial responsibilities were taken over by the municipal court of burgomasters and *schepens*), the council heard cases ranging from minor suits for debt collection to cases involving capital crimes. In later years, after the proliferation of municipal government had created regional lower courts, the council at New Amsterdam became an appeals court.

More change would come to government in New Netherland as the once-mighty company relinquished its hold on trade, opened the colony to free burghers, and conceded the development of local government. Stuyvesant's administration would span the last seventeen years of New Netherland's existence as a Dutch colony, and although his regime would be seen as autocratic by historians schooled in late-eighteenth-century Whig philosophy, it was in fact a period of great expansion of local government.

LOCAL GOVERNMENT COMES TO NEW NETHERLAND

One of Stuyvesant's first tasks after arriving in the colony was to calm the waters that had been stirred up by a conflict raging for months between Willem Kieft and the council. Kieft, in an effort to gain support for his unpopular Indian policy, had expanded the old council to a Board of Twelve Men. By expanding the older institution to include the leading citizens from New Amsterdam, Kieft had laid the groundwork for representative government.

The Board of Eight Men initially supported Kieft in his effort to crush the Indian uprising, but by the autumn of 1643 the director-general's autocratic rule prompted the board to write letters to the WIC and the States General describing Kieft's misgovernment and demanding his recall. When Stuyvesant arrived in 1647, the government had ceased to function.

Stuyvesant reorganized the council by adding nine men drawn from the leading citizens and company employees. In following Kieft's example, he was more cautious in allocating power. The council could not meet independently of the director-general, and even the three arbitrators who were to serve by rotation as a sitting court of justice were expressly limited to deciding only cases of small consequence.

One of the most persistent problems facing Stuyvesant as he settled into his new job was the lack of government institutions to communicate and enforce company policy. The West India Company had been ill-prepared to assume the mantle of government. The directors of the company's Amsterdam chamber, which was responsible for the colony, demonstrated little inclination to permit widespread public participation in an enterprise still considered a business venture by the stockholders. Furthermore, the people of New Netherland were a heterogeneous lot, sharing few common political traditions.

The English settlers who poured into eastern Long Island from New England chafed under the tyranny they perceived in company directives. They wanted town charters on the New England model, and they proved relentless in their pursuit of local rights. On the other hand, the predominantly Dutch villages around Manhattan and at Fort Orange on the Hudson River were generally less vocal in their demands for local autonomy. The situation changed, however, when the English villages on Long Island began to acquire burgher rights in the 1640s.

The success of the English towns in obtaining self-government was in part the result of their homogeneity. In stark contrast to the rest of New Netherland's population, the English settlers were culturally, religiously, and linguistically connected. Moreover as "foreigners" in a Dutch colony, they sought to maintain the familiar forms of English local government. The Dutch authorities, desperate for colonists after 1645 and unable to stop the tide of immigrants pouring in from New England, conceded to their demands. Beginning with Newtown in 1642, charters were issued to several English towns—Hempstead (1644), Gravesend (1645), and Flushing (1645). As the English villages succeeded in the quest for local government, the other Europeans in New Netherland came to take the English system of town governance as the model for their aspirations. Somewhat later Dutch towns received charters—Breuckelen (1646), Beverswyck (Albany, 1652), Midwout (Flatbush, 1653), and New Amsterdam (1653).

The establishment of municipal government in the two principal Dutch population centers of Beverswyck and New Amsterdam marked a significant change in the framework of government for the citizens of New Netherland. In both municipalities new courts of inferior justice were established to adjudicate cases that before had always been heard by the council.

At New Amsterdam the new Court of Burgomasters and Schepens began meeting in February 1653 in the old City Tavern, which was immediately rechristened the City Hall. Most of the time the two burgomasters and five *schepens* met to hear criminal and civil cases. Cases were tried in accordance with the laws of the city of

314

Amsterdam, and appeal was to the director-general and council. Dutch civil law governed the proceedings. Based on Roman law, it did not recognize the right to jury trial.

The Court of Burgomasters and Schepens sat also as an advisory board to the director-general. In this capacity it proposed laws for the city and made recommendations to the director-general and council. The court and council officially communicated through the *schout* (a combination sheriff, prosecuting attorney, and sergeant-at-arms). Laws were provisional until approved by the directors of the West India Company.

The beginnings of local government at Beverswyck were even more modest. Burgher rights for the people of Fort Orange and Beverswyck had come about as a result of a struggle between Peter Stuyvesant and Brant van Slichtenhorst, director of the patroonship of Rensselaerswyck.

The issue concerned the right to grant land in the area north of Fort Orange. Without seeking permission and in defiance of several company directives, Slichtenhorst granted building lots to Rensselaerswyck tenants and commenced construction in 1648 of a *Bijeenwonigh*, or community. When Stuyvesant heard of this, he ordered all building within a cannon shot of the fort (reckoned at approximately three thousand feet [900 meters]) stopped immediately. Slichtenhorst defied the company and Stuyvesant for nearly four years while other matters occupied the attention of the provincial government.

Finally, in 1652 Stuyvesant was in a position to deal with the situation on the upper Hudson. The Treaty of Hartford had recently been concluded with the New England colonies, securing the eastern borders of New Netherland. Fort Casimir had also been built at company expense on the Delaware to block further land grabs by the Swedes. With his southern and eastern flanks secure, Stuyvesant had an ordinance passed in council proclaiming the company's right to the land north of Fort Orange. When Slichtenhorst refused to recognize the ordinance, Johannes Dyckman, soon to be first chief magistrate of the Court of Fort Orange and Beverswyck, acting on orders from the council, arrested him and transported him to Manhattan. Slichtenhorst spent over a year under house arrest until his term of office as director of Rensselaerswyck had expired. In the meantime Dyckman proclaimed the founding of the Court of Fort Orange and Beverswyck.

The Court of Fort Orange and Beverswyck was established as a *Kleine Banck van Justitie* (inferior bench) to hear civil and minor criminal cases. The court was composed of the commissary of the fort and varying numbers of *commissarissen*, or local magistrates. The commissary served as the prosecuting officer for the company and was appointed by the director-general for an indefinite term. The magistrates represented the people of the town and were appointed by the director-general annually from a double number chosen by the townspeople. Like the burgomasters and *schepens* of New Amsterdam, the magistrates of the Court of Fort Orange and Beverswyck not only determined guilt or culpability but also determined the penalty, subject always to appeal to the director-general and council. The court's jurisdiction initially extended over the whole of the upper Hudson Valley, including the villages of Beverswyck, Schenectady, Kinderhook, Claverack, Coxsackie, Catskill, and the Esopus. On 16 May 1661 a court was set up at the Esopus to adjudicate cases in the central reaches of the valley. The director-general and council continued to function as the provincial government until the time of the English conquest in 1664, but the people of New Netherland had acquired a surprising amount of local autonomy in the last years of Dutch rule.

BIBLIOGRAPHY

Fernow, Berthold, ed. *The Records of New Amsterdam from 1653 to 1674*. 7 vols. New York, 1897.

Gehring, Charles T., ed. and trans. *Fort Orange Court Minutes, 1652–1660*. Syracuse, N.Y., 1990.

Laer, Arnold J. F. van, ed. and trans. *Documents Relating to New Netherland, 1624–1626, in the Henry E. Huntington Library*. San Marino, Calif., 1924.

Nissenson, Samuel G. *The Patroon's Domain*. New York State Historical Association Series, no. 5. New York, 1937.

Rink, Oliver A. *Holland on the Hudson: An Economic and Social History of Dutch New York*. Ithaca, N.Y., 1986.

White, Philip L. "Municipal Government Comes to Manhattan." *New-York Historical Society Quarterly* 37, no. 2 (1953):146–157.

Wright, Langdon G. "Local Government and Central Authority in New Netherland." *New-York Historical Society Quarterly* 57, no. 1 (1973):7–29.

Oliver A. Rink

SEE ALSO **Dutch and Swedish Settlements; Local Government; Relations with the Parent Country; and Social Tensions.**

RELATIONS WITH THE PARENT COUNTRY

THE SPANISH BORDERLANDS

COLUMBUS'S 1492 ENCOUNTER with and subsequent colonization of Hispaniola posed new challenges for the Crown of Castile. Early ad hoc forms of government created in Castile to govern the Indies, based on existing Castilian institutions, were transformed into a formal system of government. The Casa de Contratación (House of Trade, 1503), which organized flotillas and regulated trade between Spain and the Indies, evolved from an office set up in Seville to oversee the direct investments of the monarch in the Indies. Responsibility for the Indies originally was assigned to the Council of Castile, but in 1524 Charles V created a separate body, the Council of the Indies, to govern the New World territories. In the 1520s and 1530s, the king experimented with different forms of government for the individual colonies to replace the governments set up by the conquistadores. In New Spain, for example, the king appointed two separate *audiencias* (courts that combined judicial, legislative, and administrative functions) and then named a viceroy. The system developed in New Spain was later applied to the other New World kingdoms.

The government of New Spain drew upon many Castilian traditions. Towns established *cabildos* (town councils) and were governed by *alcaldes mayores* and *corregidores*. The viceroy was the chief executive, but his powers were limited by the *audiencia* in a system that at times created vague and overlapping jurisdictions which served as a form of checks and balances. Conquistadores rewarded themselves with feudal-like *encomienda* grants that gave them rights to the labor and tribute of subject Indians. The Crown recognized but at the same time attempted to limit *encomienda* rights. The New Laws of 1542 attempted to abolish the *encomienda* but failed when a revolt broke out in Peru and the viceroy in New Spain suspended the law in the face of a threatened revolt by *encomenderos* (holders of encomienda grants).

On paper the Spanish government in the Indies was a centralized regime. However, in reality there was considerable local autonomy. Communication between Spain and the Indies was slow, and local royal officials generally mediated between the desires of the Crown expressed in *cedulas* (decrees) and the interests of local elites. The formula *obedezco pero no cumplo*, "I obey but I don't comply," was frequently used to suspend laws issued in Spain pending an appeal to Madrid. Many royal officials became *radicados,* so called because they were "rooted" in the Indies by familial and economic ties. Often in violation of law, officials married into elite American families or established business interests in the jurisdictions they governed. In the late seventeenth and early eighteenth centuries, the sale of offices in the colonial bureaucracy gave local elites even more influence.

The northern borderlands was the northernmost extension of Spanish control in North America, but for a variety of reasons frontier communities enjoyed considerable autonomy. The northern frontier regions were sparsely populated areas that were in many ways different from the core of Spanish America. Government officials faced unique problems such as defense, and the institutions of the core areas either did not evolve in the frontier or developed in modified form. The most important frontier institutions were *presidios* (military garrisons) and missions where Franciscan, Jesuit, and Dominican missionaries attempted to convert Indians to Catholicism and integrate converts into colonial society.

Frontier policy was formulated both in Spain and in Mexico City, but royal officials in Mexico City or Havana and Santo Domingo had more say in the settlement of the frontier and made most decisions. The highest-ranking civil and military officials stationed on the frontier generally came from Spain, but most personnel were natives of New Spain or, in the case of Florida, Cuba and Hispaniola. The cost of the military, missionaries, and officials serving on the frontier was covered from American revenues. In real terms the colonization of the frontier was primarily an American enterprise.

The following sections discuss the institutions that evolved in the borderlands and the role that policy formulated in Madrid played in the evolution of frontier institutions. Florida, colonized after 1565, is considered separately because it was colonized directly from Spain but administered from the Caribbean. The other borderland regions—New Mexico (1598), Sonora–southern Arizona (1687), Texas (1690 and 1716), and Alta California (1769)—were colonized from New Spain, and the institutions in these four regions were similar. The discussion

of New Spain's northern frontier is topical, focusing on institutions that evolved throughout the region.

FLORIDA: A DEFENSIVE SETTLEMENT

Florida was the first region within the present boundaries of the United States to be colonized by Spain. The impetus for colonization was concern for imperial defense and the threat posed by French colonization in the area. Florida borders the Bahama channel, the principal route used by the annual *flotas* (treasure fleets) to return to Spain from the Caribbean. Several colonization schemes during the early sixteenth century failed, but the occupation of the peninsula gained urgency after Admiral Gaspar de Coligny planted a French Huguenot settlement in northern Florida in 1564.

The Spanish colonization of Florida occurred during a period when private exploration and colonization in the Americas was still common. Philip II appointed a high-ranking Spanish noble, Pedro Menéndez de Avilés, to finance and organize the expulsion of the French and the colonization of Florida. Menéndez de Avilés received extensive powers within Florida as *adelantado* (governor) and captain-general. In 1565 the *adelantado* destroyed Fort Caroline, the French colony. Between 1565 and 1571, Menéndez de Avilés established forts at Santa Elena (South Carolina) and Saint Augustine and brought Franciscan missionaries to evangelize the natives.

When Menéndez de Avilés died in 1574, the Crown took direct control over Florida. Throughout the first period of Spanish occupation (1565–1763), Florida was a defensive bastion and mission frontier. The major concern of the Spanish government was to ensure the defense of the peninsula against its European rivals and find the means to fund the garrisons and the missions in northern Florida and along the Georgia coast. The solution was to subsidize the Florida colony from other colonial revenues. In a royal decree of 15 November 1570, Philip II ordered the Panama–Nombre de Dios treasury to make an annual payment of 32,312 pesos of eight reales to help defray the costs of a garrison of 150 soldiers in Florida. His decree of 3 July

1573 directed the Veracruz (New Spain) treasury to pay the Florida subsidy, which was increased to 38,862 pesos for at least one year. In a 24 January 1580 decree, the subsidy rose to 65,859 to pay for a 300-man garrison in Florida.

Efforts to fund the *situado* (subsidy for outlying areas) constituted the most direct attempt of the colonial administration in Spain to oversee directly the administration of Florida. However, Crown desires often conflicted with fiscal realities in the Americas. The Veracruz treasury covered the costs of the subsidy until the English war in the late 1680s, which curtailed the *flota* sailings to New Spain and substantially reduced revenues at that port. The breakdown of subsidy payments from Veracruz led to the shifting of the responsibility to the Mexico City treasury. A 29 April 1592 decree directed the Mexico City treasury to make up shortfalls in subsidy payments from the Veracruz treasury; a second decree of 8 June 1595 permanently shifted the subsidy to Mexico City.

The subsidy became the lifeblood of the colony in Florida. Soldiers stationed in the garrisons and the small settler population benefited from what constituted the only reliable source of income for the province. The subsidy also supported the missionary effort. In 1616, for example, thirty-seven Franciscan missionaries received the same pay and rations as a common soldier, which amounted to 158 pesos per year. Throughout the seventeenth century, the Mexico City treasury encountered difficulties in paying the subsidy in a timely fashion, particularly during periods of prolonged warfare. In a sense American realities limited the effectiveness of initiatives from Spain, and local officials in Mexico City, Cuba, or Florida itself had more of an impact on the governing of Florida and the implementation of policy than did policymakers in Madrid.

Spanish policy in Florida changed in the late seventeenth and eighteenth centuries largely as a result of growing competition with the English. In the 1680s traders from South Carolina established commercial relations with interior tribes that previously had been loosely allied to the Spanish. Because of budget constraints, Spanish officials in Florida could not effectively compete with the better-supplied English traders, and Spanish influence in the region declined.

In the 1680s the Spanish abandoned Guale, a coastal province north of Saint Augustine. After 1700 foreign policy formulated in Madrid had more of an immediate impact on Florida as Spain's involvement in a series of international wars in alliance with France intensified Anglo-Spanish rivalry in the Southeast. In the years 1703 and 1704, during the War of the Spanish Succession, British colonial forces from Carolina destroyed most of the mission communities in Florida. The Spanish presence in Florida was now reduced to forts at Pensacola and Saint Augustine.

Spain lost Florida to Britain in 1763 at the end of the Seven Years' War. Florida was returned to Spain twenty years later in 1783 at the end of the American Revolution. Spanish policy in Florida during the second period of Spanish occupation was more limited in scope. Military garrisons occupied Pensacola and Saint Augustine, but little effort was made to revive efforts at evangelization. The major concern was growing pressure from an aggressive United States as Protestant settlers moved into Florida and challenged Spanish dominion; tensions grew over conflicting boundary claims, access to the Mississippi River, and the raiding of United States territory by hostile Indians who found refuge in Florida. In order to avoid war, Spain sold Florida to the United States in 1821 but also secured a settlement of boundaries further to the west.

SPANISH POLICY IN THE WESTERN BORDERLANDS

Frontier Defense

Spaniards expanding into northern New Spain from the sixteenth to eighteenth centuries encountered hostile Indian groups. From 1550 to 1600 Spaniards in what is now the southwestern United States battled nomadic groups collectively known as *chichimeca* in a conflict that typified Spanish-Indian hostilities along the frontier of northern New Spain. Spanish military garrisons and fortified towns attempted to protect trade routes and farming and mining towns in north-central New Spain from raids by small bands of warriors. The war with the *chichimeca* forced the viceregal government in New Spain to create a permanent military force. Up to that time, colonial defense relied upon a feudal levy from *encomenderos*, militias, and Indian allies.

As Spanish missionaries, miners, farmers, and ranchers advanced northward, raids by hostile Indians continued to be a problem. The government in Mexico City authorized the establishment of *presidios* for local or regional defense. In 1701, 1,006 officers and soldiers were stationed at twenty-three *presidios* at an annual cost of 251,883 pesos to the treasury in Mexico City. The actual cost of the military garrisons was reduced by requiring soldiers to buy their own horses and equipment at inflated prices. Moreover, cost-conscious officials conducted inspections with an eye to reducing the amount spent on defense. Nevertheless, the size of the frontier army and the defense budget continued to increase during the eighteenth century. In 1787, 3,087 officers and men were stationed at twenty-two *presidios* at an annual cost of 810,240 pesos.

The system of frontier defense evolved in a haphazard fashion, primarily at the initiative of officials in Mexico City. The establishment of new *presidios* was frequently prompted by the creation of new missions or chronic local defense problems, such as raiding by different Apache tribes. The defense of Texas was typical. At different times in the eighteenth century, six *presidios* existed in Texas. The occupation of Texas in 1716 led to the foundation of a short-lived *presidio* named Nuestra Señora de los Dolores facing the French in Louisiana, which was followed by the placement of a garrison at San Antonio in 1718. Other *presidios* were Los Adaes, founded in 1721 in east Texas; Nuestra Señora de Loreto de la Bahía de Espíritu Santo, established in 1722 to protect a mission on the Gulf Coast; a *presidio* located at different sites between 1751 and 1772 to protect several short-lived Apache missions; and San Agustín de Ahumada, established in 1756 near the Trinity River in east Texas (just east of modern Houston) to safeguard short-lived missions among the Orcoquisa.

Coordination of defense might be achieved at the local or provincial level, but rarely at the interprovincial level. The high cost and, as it appeared to officials in Spain and Mexico City,

inefficiency of frontier defense prompted a scheme for reorganization in the 1760s at the beginning of the military and bureaucratic reform known in Spanish-American historiography as the Bourbon reforms. Disastrous military defeat at the hands of the British during the Seven Years' War (1756–1763) prompted Madrid to expend resources on colonial defense. In 1765 the Spanish government sent regular troops from Europe to New Spain along with a cadre of officers to organize professional units and militias. In the same year, Madrid commissioned field marshal Marqués de Rubí to inspect the northern frontier garrisons in order to improve defense. Rubí's inspection led to a *reglamento* (regulation) for the *presidios* put into force in 1772.

The 1772 *reglamento* called for the suppression of garrisons that no longer fulfilled the purpose for which they had been established. It also provided for the relocation of other *presidios* to a single defensive cordon, roughly paralleling the modern international frontier between the United States and Mexico, that was designed to reduce the ability of hostile tribes to raid frontier communities. Only San Antonio and Santa Fe were to be beyond the new defensive line. Additionally, efforts were made to coordinate defense across the frontier. Madrid appointed Lieutenant Colonel Hugo O'Conor, a distinguished career officer with considerable European experience, to oversee the relocation of *presidios* and coordinate campaigns against Apache tribes. In 1772/1773 and 1776 O'Conor organized campaigns against Apache bands using troops from different *presidios* and provinces.

The need for coordinated frontier defense led to a major administrative reorganization in 1776. Madrid created a new super jurisdiction made up of the northern frontier provinces, which it called the Provincias Internas del Norte. The new jurisdiction was subordinate to the older viceroyalty of New Spain but was granted autonomy. Experienced soldiers, given the title *comandante-general*, were appointed to govern the Provincias Internas. The increased attention given to frontier defense led to gains against hostile tribes, including the creation of reservations for Apache bands, which in turn contributed to economic growth in the region. However, periodic realignments of the northern provinces, including the division of the Provincias Internas into two autonomous jurisdictions, limited the effectiveness of frontierwide coordinated defense.

Encomienda and Labor Drafts

From the very beginning of the colonial period in New Spain, tribute paid by free Indian vassals, particularly in the form of labor, became a bone of contention between conquistadores, Spanish settlers, and the Crown. The Crown had to find ways to promote the economic development of the region, which meant taking surplus agricultural production and, more importantly, labor from the Native population. At the same time, the Crown had at least one reason to try to limit the exploitation of the Indian population: a concern over the emergence of an overly powerful elite with pretensions to becoming a feudal aristocracy along the lines of the Castilian nobility.

Following the conquest of the Caribbean, Spaniards received grants of *encomienda* that entitled them to tribute and labor from the Indians. Abuses of the *encomienda* contributed to the rapid depopulation of the Caribbean Islands and led to efforts by the Crown to regulate the institution. The Laws of Burgos (issued in 1512, implemented in 1513) came too late to improve conditions for Caribbean Indians. Equally important was King Charles V's attempt to prevent the granting of *encomiendas* following the conquest of New Spain, albeit with little success. In 1522 Hernan Cortés, the conqueror of the Aztec state, wrote back to Charles V claiming that his comrades in arms had forced him to grant *encomiendas*, although Cortés gave himself the largest number of tributaries.

The New Laws of 1542–1543 attempted to extinguish the *encomienda* by not allowing the inheritance of grants, but with little success. A threatened revolt by *encomenderos* prompted the viceroy to suspend the application of the law in New Spain, and the Crown tried instead to modify and regulate *encomienda* grants. For example, royal decrees eliminated *servicio personal* (labor services) from *encomienda* grants, stipulated that royal officials set tribute levels and periodically revise the tribute rolls that were to be used to calculate the amount of tribute to be paid by individual communities, and have royal officials (*corregidores*) collect tribute. The Crown attempted to distance *encomenderos* from the Indian communities that constituted their grants and convert what was evolving as a feudal institution into a type of annuity paid to a class of pensioners. The *encomienda* declined in importance as a colonial institution during the sixteenth century, but mostly as a result of Indian population decline that reduced the number of tributaries and thus the tribute income of the *encomenderos*.

The royal government organized a labor draft in central New Spain in the 1550s known as *repartimiento,* which replaced the *encomienda* as the primary source of Indian labor. Created after a severe epidemic in the late 1540s and several decades of rapid Indian population decline, the *repartimiento* can best be understood as an effort to ration a declining Indian labor force. Indians periodically worked for Spanish entrepreneurs in enterprises deemed necessary for the well-being of the colonial economy, such as mining and, in the Valley of Mexico, wheat production for Mexico City. As was the case with the *encomienda,* Spaniards abused the *repartimiento* labor draft, and the Crown made efforts to eliminate the draft in the early 1600s. However, labor drafts, whether organized by civil officials or the clergy (especially the regular clergy), continued to exist in contravention of the law until Mexican independence in 1821.

Both *encomiendas* and *repartimiento* labor drafts existed in the Spanish Borderlands. Throughout the seventeenth century, New Mexico Indians paid a small group of *encomenderos* tribute in the form of corn and cotton cloth or deerskins. Formal labor drafts also existed in New Mexico and Sonora, including southern Arizona. However, the dynamic of the politics of Indian labor was different in the Spanish Borderlands. In New Mexico resentment over both the *encomienda* and *repartimiento* contributed to the 1680 Pueblo Revolt that expelled the Spaniards from the province for twelve years. In Sonora control of Indian labor caused friction between Jesuit missionaries and local civil officials and settlers who wanted greater access to labor through *repartimiento.* In the 1720s civil officials in Sonora, seconded by prominent settlers and miners, attempted to have the Jesuit missions secularized to secure land and labor and claimed that the Jesuits were personally benefiting from their control of Indian labor. Officials in Mexico City resolved the dispute in favor of the Jesuits.

Formal labor drafts providing Indian workers to settlers did not exist in either Texas or the Californias, but Indian labor was crucial in the development of both regions. The missionaries, acting as legal guardians for the converts living in the missions, controlled what was called mission temporalities: the lands assigned to the mission communities; the fruits of agriculture, ranching, and craft production; and, most significantly, Indian labor. The missionaries used Indian labor to build the complex of buildings at each mission, to develop agriculture and ranching, and at times, to help the military and settlers. In the Alta California missions, for example, Franciscan missionaries provided labor to the military garrisons for construction projects at the *presidios*. Moreover, the Franciscans rented Indian workers to individual settlers, with the proceeds going to the mission fund administered by the missionaries. The decision to grant the missionaries control over the temporalities was made in Mexico City, as were most decisions relating to the missions. For example, in 1773 Franciscan Junípero Serra, architect of the Alta California mission system, successfully petitioned royal officials in Mexico City to have the temporalities returned to the control of the missionaries after several years of lay administration.

Missions and Evangelization

From the beginning of the Spanish conquest and colonization of America, the Crown of Castile assumed responsibility for the evangelization of the Indian population. Papal bulls issued in 1493 confirmed Castilian claims to the lands discovered by Columbus, and to other non-Christian lands yet to be discovered, specifically for the propagation of the faith. Subsequent bulls gave the Crown virtual control over the New World church. Papal concessions in 1501 and 1508 granted rights known as the Real Patronato: the right to collect ecclesiastical taxes such as *diezmos* (tithes); the right to nominate high ecclesiastical officials such as archbishops and bishops; and the right to nominate lower clergy. The Crown directly sent nominations for higher church officials to the papacy but left most decisions regarding the clergy to officials in the New World. The Real Patronato made the Catholic church a branch of the government. The church legitimized the colonial government, and the Crown protected and promoted the church and its mission of evangelization in the Americas.

Franciscan, Augustinian, Dominican, and Mercederian missionaries spearheaded the evangelization of the Indian population of central New Spain in the decades following the conquest. The missionaries brought several traditions with them to New Spain. Iberian Catholicism was militant and exclusive as a result of seven hundred years of the Reconquest of Iberia from Muslims who had seized control of the peninsula in 711. The regular clergy in Castile had already been reformed on the eve of the evangelization of New Spain, and many members of the orders were influenced by humanism and utopianism and saw their conversion campaigns as an opportunity to create utopian communities where Indian converts would not be corrupted by secular Spanish society. There were problems associated with the evangelization of the Indian population of New Spain. The missionary orders carved up the *altepetl* (Native city-states) into territories that they disputed among themselves, and they often recruited their Indian parishioners into militias to battle for control of disputed parishes. After the first wave of conversions, which merely superimposed a veneer of Christianity over an inclusive Mesoamerican religious tradition, missionaries harnessed Indian labor to build impressive churches and convents and, in general, became more concerned with the profane. There were also disputes between the regular and secular clergy over control of parishes.

In the Ordenanza de Patronazgo, issued in 1574, King Philip II sided with the secular clergy in its dispute with the regular clergy. Once the regular clergy had outwardly converted the bulk of the Indian population of central New Spain, the time had come for it to step aside to allow the creation of an ordered episcopal system in the colony. Northward expansion also created new opportunities for evangelization as missions became an important element of the colonization of the semiarid and arid north populated by semi-sedentary agriculturalists and nomadic hunter-gatherers.

The mission system was an ideal adaptation to the challenges of the colonization of northern New Spain. The Spaniards easily exploited the sedentary populations of central New Spain which lived in nucleated communities that facilitated collecting tribute and rounding up Indians for labor drafts. Therefore, at the end of the sixteenth century, following considerable Indian depopulation, civil and religious officials attempted to recreate large nucleated communities through the *congregación* policy: the resettlement of the populations of small dispersed communities into larger nucleated villages. In the case of the borderlands, the Crown and viceregal government in New Spain assigned the regular clergy mission fields and empowered it to congregate the Indian populations into nucleated communities to re-create in the north the patterns of exploitation already developed in the center.

The establishment of a mission was a complex process that involved both the clergy and viceregal government. Officials in Mexico City approved the establishment of each mission and ensured that there was money for an endowment to buy supplies and provide a stipend to the missionaries. The government established each mission community as a separate corporate entity with grants of land and water rights theoretically protected by the government. In addition to being the spiritual heads of the community being established, the missionaries were also the guardians and legal protectors of the Indians. The objective of royal policy was to convert missions into autonomous municipal corporations, but until the time when the mission was secularized or converted into a town served by a secular priest, the missionaries retained control over the property, agricultural production, and even the labor of the Indians. Moreover, the government authorized most missionaries to use corporal punishment to maintain discipline among the converts. The viceregal government established *presidios* to protect the missionaries, and in some cases the missionaries used their control over mission temporalities to help subsidize the expense of maintaining military garrisons by selling food and clothing at low cost to the *presidios*, as was done in Alta California.

A symbiotic relationship existed between missionary, soldier, and civil official, but frictions also existed. Seventeenth-century New Mexico experienced the greatest dissension between civil and religious officials. On several occasions in the seventeenth century, the Franciscan missionaries challenged the authority of the civil governors appointed in Mexico City or Spain, a conflict that originated, in part, over conflicting economic interests. The Franciscans used their spiritual authority as pastors to New Mexico and as local representatives of the Inquisition to undermine the legitimacy of the governors and sent one governor to Mexico City in chains. Other serious frontier civil-religious disputes centered on the economic power of missionaries. As discussed above, in the 1720s settlers and local officials challenged the Jesuit control of mission lands and Indian labor in Sonora and petitioned for the secularization of most of the Sonora missions. One motive for this challenge was the fact that the Black Robes competed with influential ranchers in the supply of beef to the *presidios* and mining camps and enjoyed a significant advantage since they controlled an unpaid labor force. Settler usurpation of Indian lands in the Pimería Alta contributed to a major uprising in 1751.

A second source of civil-religious discord was related to the influence of enlightened humanistic ideas on Spanish officials and the officials' perception that the missions were anachronistic survivals from the past. This ideological rift was particularly evident in the colonization, beginning in 1769, of Alta California, the last mission frontier opened in northern New Spain. In the 1780s California governor Pedro Fages (1782–1791), who was considered mentally unbalanced by the Franciscans because of his views, challenged measures used by the Franciscans to maintain social control in the missions. In a 1798 report, Governor Diego de Borica (1794–1800) blamed high Indian mortality in Alta California on living conditions in the missions and measures taken to maintain social control, such as the practice of locking Indian women and girls up at night in unhealthy dormitories. However, not all officials assigned to the frontier in the late eighteenth or early nineteenth century criticized the Franciscans. In 1816 Alta California governor Pablo Vicente de Solá (1815–1822) exonerated Franciscan Andrés Quintana, assassinated at Santa Cruz mission in 1812, of charges of excessive brutality toward the Indians. Santa Cruz neophytes charged that Quintana planned to use a wire-tipped whip. Solá maintained that punishment of Indians with twenty-five lashes was not excessive.

More common were disputes that involved what the missionaries perceived as the immorality of soldiers who corrupted Indian women and challenged the authority of the missionaries. Missionaries, who frequently were puritanical in outlook, frowned upon soldiers having sexual liaisons with Indian women living at the missions. From the point of view of the missionaries, such liaisons exposed the Indian converts to ideas and attitudes that undermined the missionaries' authority. There was a second pragmatic motivation. The excesses of soldiers, who in some cases raped Indian women and killed men who defended them, caused resentment that led to active resistance to the new order being created by the missionaries. For example, Indians in the Los Angeles Basin in Alta California resisted the Spaniards after soldiers raped Indian women and killed and beheaded one chief.

According to law, missions were to operate for only ten years and then were to be secularized. In reality the missions in the Spanish Borderlands operated for more than the stipulated period. The rigid paternalism practiced in the missions delayed the acculturation of the Indians. Moreover, missionaries in Texas, Pimería Alta–northern Sonora, and Alta California continued to bring new converts to the mission communities. They argued that secularization should be postponed, since they were still engaged in active evangelization of non-Christian Indians. Nevertheless, pressure was building at the end of the eighteenth century to close missions, especially those establishments with small and continuously declining Indian populations. In 1794 one mission in the vicinity of San Antonio, Texas (San Antonio de Valero), was secularized, and the other four missions in the area were partially secularized. In the same year, two Baja California missions were suppressed. At the same time, Franciscan missionaries established new missions in both Texas and Alta California. In 1791 the Refugio mission was established among the Karankawa along the Texas Gulf Coast. Between 1790 and 1821 the Franciscans established nine new missions in Alta California.

The closing of missions in Texas and Alta California in the 1790s was a locally formulated policy. The government in Spain did not challenge the mission system until 1813, at the height of the Napoleonic Wars. In the absence of King Charles IV and his son, Ferdinand VII, who were both forced to abdicate their rights to the Spanish throne in 1808 by Napoleon, liberal-minded politicians drafted a constitution in 1812 that gave extensive powers to a revitalized Cortes (Parliament). In 1813 the Spanish Cortes passed a law calling for the secularization of frontier missions in the New World, especially the Alta California establishments. Officials in New Spain did not implement the law, and in 1814 the absolutist King Ferdinand VII returned to Spain. The king suspended the constitution and invalidated all laws passed by the Cortes.

In 1821 Mexico became independent from Spain. Anticlerical Mexican liberals argued that the missions were colonial anachronisms that prevented the full integration of Indians into society. Attempts by liberal politicians to reform Mexican society were resisted by the Catholic church and conservatives who wanted to maintain as much of the colonial world as possible, and especially their social control over the non-white population. The lack of consensus among Mexican politicians led to periodic civil war and frequent changes in government. During the periods that liberals governed Mexico in the 1820s and 1830s, they passed laws that led to the collapse of the frontier mission system. Moreover, anti-Spanish xenophobia became an important element in Mexican politics. In 1824 the government secularized the remaining Texas missions. In 1828 it ordered the expulsion of *peninsulares* (Spanish-born Spaniards) from the missions. Officials in Alta California refused to expel Spanish-born Franciscans staffing the missions. Franciscans in the Pimería Alta elected to leave. In 1833 the government sent Mexican-born Franciscans from the Apostolic College of Guadalupe de Zacatecas to staff half of the Alta California missions, but in the same year a short-lived liberal Congress passed a law secularizing the last missions. Although the liberal Congress was suspended and the laws it passed invalidated, local politicians in Alta California began the process of closing down the missions.

CONCLUSIONS

Several general conclusions can be made about the relationship between the Spanish Borderlands and Spain, and especially regarding the governance of the borderlands and the formulation of policy. Officials in Madrid directed while officials in Mexico City implemented the mandates of the king. But it was in Mexico City that the specific details of royal decrees were generally worked out, and the officials there had a more immediate impact on the governance of the northern borderland region than did those in Spain. Revenues generated in New Spain paid the salaries of all officials, from governors down to common soldiers stationed in frontier garrisons. Moreover, most decisions, including the establishment of *presidios* or missions, the organization of military campaigns against hostile Indians, labor policy, and the extent of missionaries' authority over Indian converts, were decided in Mexico City. Mexico settled the northern borderlands with guidance from Spain.

High-ranking civil, military, and religious officials generally were *peninsulares,* or at any rate in the case of the Jesuit frontier missionaries, natives of Europe. The Crown selected favored *peninsulares* in appointments to important New World positions, and patronage frequently played a role in nominations to posts in the colonial civil and religious bureaucracy and the military. In 1765 King Charles II sent José de Gálvez to make any changes he thought necessary in the administration of the colony. The King rewarded him with the position of colonial minister. In the new position, Gálvez practiced nepotism, giving jobs to a clique of friends and relatives from Malaga in southern Castile. His brother became viceroy of New Spain; his nephew, Bernardo de Gálvez, who also eventually became viceroy of New Spain, rose rapidly through the ranks through a combination of distinguished military service in the western borderlands, Louisiana, and Florida and the influence of his uncle. However, most of the people involved in the settlement of the borderlands were New World natives.

The administration of the borderlands underwent considerable change from the sixteenth to the early nineteenth century. The greatest change occurred in the years after the Seven Years' War as policymakers in Madrid directed military and fiscal reorganization in the New World, including Florida and the western borderlands. In many ways Spanish authority on the northern frontier region was strengthened in the last decades of the eighteenth century. New Indian policies, including trade and subsidies for previously hostile tribes, backed by military force brought a semblance of peace to northern New Spain, which in turn contributed to rapid economic growth. For example, New Mexico's economy grew in the last half of the eighteenth century as measured by increased trade with Chihuahua and the growth of tithes. The strengthening of frontier defenses also enabled Spain to fend off rival British and later American territorial claims. One incident in northeastern Texas exemplified Spain's enhanced military strength towards the end of the colonial period. In 1806 a force of one thousand soldiers was mobilized in a short period of time to turn back the Custus-Freeman expedition, sent by the U.S. government to survey portions of Texas claimed as a part of the Louisiana Purchase. A century earlier a total of only one thousand troops had staffed all *presidios* in northern New Spain, and even in the 1780s there had been only some three thousand troops stationed in the frontier region.

The French invasion of Spain in 1808 and the outbreak of Mexico's independence war in 1810 undermined Spanish frontier policy. Money previously spent on Indian trade and subsidies went to finance war in Europe and Mexico, and troops were diverted to the growing civil war in Mexico. The breakdown of the so-called Apache peace led to increased Indian raiding of frontier communities, which slowed or stopped economic growth. In Florida, Spain's weakness led to American encroachments. The United States absorbed much of West Florida in 1810 and 1814 and on two occasions invaded the parts of Florida still under nominal Spanish rule to suppress raids on U.S. territory by hostile

Indians. In 1821 Spain sold Florida to the United States because the former could no longer control the territory. In the same year, Mexico became independent.

BIBLIOGRAPHY

Bannon, John Francis. *The Spanish Borderlands Frontier, 1513–1821.* Albuquerque, N.Mex., 1974. Provides an overview to the settlement of the northern frontier region, although it is dated and contains a Eurocentric bias.

Burkholder, Mark A., and D. S. Chandler. *From Impotence to Authority: The Spanish Crown and the American Audiencias, 1687–1808.* Columbia, Mo., 1977. Discusses the composition of *audiencias* and the late-eighteenth-century reform of them.

Gibson, Charles. *The Aztecs Under Spanish Rule: A History of the Indians of the Valley of Mexico, 1519–1810.* Stanford, Calif., 1964. Offers a detailed analysis of the evolution of Spanish colonial institutions in central Mexico as they affected the Indian population.

———. *Spain in America.* New York, 1966. Examines Spanish colonization of the Americas, with an emphasis on institutions.

Gutiérrez, Ramón A. *When Jesus Came, the Corn Mothers Went Away: Marriage, Sexuality, and Power in New Mexico, 1500–1846.* Stanford, Calif., 1991. An interesting but very uneven study of the society of colonial New Mexico. It is useful for the discussion of relations between Franciscan missionaries and the governors of New Mexico.

Haring, Clarence H. *The Spanish Empire in America.* New York, 1947. A detailed institutional study of Spain in America.

Jackson, Robert H. "Population and the Economic Dimension of Colonization in Alta California: Four Mission Communities." *Journal of the Southwest* 33, no. 3 (1991):387–439. Discusses the political economy of the California missions as related to changes in the Indian population.

Lynch, John. *Spain under the Habsburgs.* 2 vols. London, 1969. Provides in-depth discussion of Spain and its relations with America, especially trade relations, from the sixteenth century to 1700. Lynch furnishes a useful overview to Spanish Catholicism.

Moorhead, Max L. *The Apache Frontier: Jacobo Ugarte and Spanish-Indian Relations in Northern New Spain, 1769–1791.* Norman, Okla., 1968. Outlines reform of the frontier military in the late eighteenth century as well as changing Indian policy.

———. *The Presidio: Bastion of the Spanish Borderlands.* Norman, Okla., 1975. A detailed study of the evolution and reform of the frontier military of New Spain.

Sluiter, Engel. *The Florida Situado: Quantifying The First Eighty Years, 1571–1651.* Gainesville, Fla., 1985. A study of the evolution of the Florida *situado* and the amount of the subsidy.

Robert H. Jackson

SEE ALSO **Church and State; Crises of Empire; The Framework of Government: Independence; Mercantilism; Roman Catholicism; and Settlements in the Spanish Borderlands.**

THE FRENCH COLONIES

APART FROM THE EARLY seventeenth century, when private companies controlled the destiny of French colonial expansion, France's American colonies were integrated into an empire whose administration was dominated by a centralized bureaucracy which operated under the principles of mercantilism. Government policy had a strong impact on colonial development but even the state was unable to overcome the influences of economy and demography that shaped each colony.

RELATIONS UNDER COMPANY RULE

From the first French attempts at settlement in the 1540s until the Crown took control in 1663, the French colonies were controlled by a series of monopoly companies. Embroiled in civil war and European conflicts, the state left government of its overseas possessions to private enterprise. This had important implications for New France where the main economic resource was the fur trade, an activity that relied heavily on Native labor and scarcely had need of European colonists. Merchants had little incentive to colonize and the state had few resources to devote to its American empire. As a result, few settlers arrived in North America before 1632.

The Company of One Hundred Associates differed from other monopoly companies in that the founding shareholders were picked by Cardinal Richelieu who insisted that settlement be given priority. Although the company was hampered by a precarious financial situation after the loss of its first two fleets to English privateers and by the fact that Canada was never perceived to be a very desirable destination, it managed to recruit colonists for the Saint Lawrence Valley. With the growth of population, a more elaborate civil administration was set up under the control of the company. While private companies could attend to the civil and commercial interests of colonists, they lacked the military strength to ensure their security. The Iroquois Wars (1641–1667) endangered the very existence of the Canadian colony and made more active state intervention imperative.

In the Caribbean, the Compagnie des îles d'Amérique (created in 1635) and the Compagnie de la France equinoxiale (founded in 1652) had more success in attracting colonists to the sugar islands. But, as in Canada, private enterprise was inadequate for the military challenge of wars with the local Carib population and the threat of attack by other Europeans. The southern colonies came under royal control at the same time as Canada and all French American colonies were included in the Compagnie des Indes Occidentale's monopoly in 1664.

FRENCH MERCANTILISM

Under royal control after 1663, colonial development was dominated by the mercantilist policies elaborated by Louis XIV's principal minister, Jean-Baptiste Colbert. Colbertism placed great importance on international trade as a means of acquiring bullion that would then circulate within France increasing investment and commercial transactions. To increase France's presence on international markets and ensure a positive balance of trade, domestic industry was encouraged by tariffs on foreign manufactures and by promoting imports of raw materials. Colonies were useful if they could supply materi-

als not found in France and could offer captive markets for the mother country's agricultural and industrial production. Finally, increased trade would augment the state's revenues through duties, inspection fees, and a more prosperous population able to pay higher taxes.

Colonies played a small but important role in this economic and fiscal program, and, because they were considered a component of international trade, they were placed under the responsibility of the Ministry of the Marine, or Navy and Colonies. The state support they received depended in part on their ability to meet mercantilist goals. The slave colonies of the Caribbean produced exotic raw materials that were transformed by French industry before being re-exported to other European countries. Their affluent white planters and rapidly expanding slave populations were ideal markets for French agricultural produce and manufactured goods. As a result they were highly valued. Canada produced essentially the same products as France except for furs which were not always easy to market, and its small population base consumed relatively few French imports. While it had strategic importance in the contest between the French and British empires, the ministry generally believed that it cost too much.

RELATIONS BETWEEN CANADA AND THE MINISTRY OF MARINE

Since the empire was seen as an organic whole, policy decisions were made at Versailles to ensure coordination. Theoretically, the governor general and intendant at Quebec were in charge of all of New France from the Atlantic to the Gulf of Mexico, but communications difficulties made it more efficient for the ministry to deal separately with the peripheral colonies of Acadia (later Île Royale) and Louisiana. Quebec was icebound seven months a year making it virtually impossible to exchange more than one letter per shipping season.

Officials at Quebec, Louisbourg, and New Orleans received an annual set of instructions and reported back to the ministry once a year. Ships normally arrived at Quebec with news from France in July or early August. After unloading their cargos, they awaited the fur brigades from the Great Lakes and sailed in October or, at the latest, early November. This left colonial officials just a couple of months to digest their instructions and to reply to the ministry. Dispatches were received by Versailles towards the beginning of December. Upon reception, a clerk made a resumé, which was submitted to the minister who annotated his copy so that a reply could be drawn up. Any new policy was also sent to the clerk to be included in the next set of instructions. Letters left the ministry in March or April for Rochefort to be put on the king's ship bound for Quebec.

Throughout the French Régime, financial considerations dominated the decision making of ministers and colonial officials. After the decade 1663–1672 when the Crown invested heavily in New France, war in Europe strained royal finances. Cuts resulted in the Ministry of Marine's spending.

Financial administration was complex. The governor and intendant annually drew up a proposed budget, which was invariably pared down at Versailles. Each year, money to pay for government expenses was shipped to cover the previous year's budget but expenditures always exceeded estimates and deficit financing was the rule. When the king's vessel was late, or worse yet when it sank, colonial officials found expedients such as creating credit by producing card money redeemable when the funds arrived. Since this money was needed for local transactions, many cards remained in circulation and the deficit increased. Bookkeeping practices carried the deficit from one year onto the next with the result that no one knew the exact state of the colony's finances.

The chaotic state of Crown finances had important repercussions in a colony where the state was a major economic player. The annual budget of over four hundred thousand livres covering military and civilian pay, fortifications, pensions, provisioning, Indian presents, and the like was a fundamental component of the Canadian economy providing essential specie and credit.

Although ministers complained continually about the cost of maintaining the colony and scolded colonial officials for exceeding the budget, they also urged the intendant to diversify the economy so that New France could better serve the mercantilist goals of the mother country. However, colonial merchants had little capital to finance new enterprises. As a result, the Crown had to subsidize the two large-scale industries created in the eighteenth century: the Saint Maurice iron works and the royal shipyards at Quebec. Both were expensive but did stimulate the local economy.

Because of delays in correspondence, colonial officials enjoyed greater freedom of action than their metropolitan counterparts. If the governor and intendant felt that a policy was ill-suited to the colony, they could temporize by protesting to the minister. Despite orders to close the western posts in 1696, for example, successive governors and intendants maintained a French presence in the West until official policy was reversed after 1717. Since they were the ministry's principal sources of information on colonial affairs, they also influenced policy by presenting only the facts that would support their viewpoint. This required close cooperation between the governor and intendant and the absence of strong opposition in the colony since private individuals could write directly to the minister. The minister, however, always had the final word and officials were bound to obey. For example, in 1701 Jérôme de Pontchartrain ordered the establishment of Detroit despite the protests of governor Louis-Hector de Callières and intendant Jean Bochart de Champigny. The latter's fears were justified in questioning Antoine Laumet de Lamothe Cadillac's scheme to settle Native allies so close to one another and to Iroquois territory.

This centralized administrative structure gave the French one decisive advantage over the English colonies: the coordination of military activities. Strategy was decided in Versailles and the united front of the French colonies contrasted sharply with the continuous divisions among the British American colonies. Massachusetts and New York rarely had the same priorities, not to speak of the more southern colonies, and they rarely managed to mount concerted action against New France.

PERSONAL RELATIONS AND ASPIRATIONS

Despite their relative freedom of action, colonial officials were servants of empire and their careers depended on the minister's patronage. New

France was rarely perceived as a senior posting. Appointment to Canada afforded governors the means of restoring lagging fortunes through participation in the fur trade, but most colonial executives aspired to postings in France, where life was easier. Intendants formed part of the marine bureaucracy and colonial postings were deemed mere steps on the ladder leading to the more prestigious posts such as the intendancy of important arsenals like Rochefort or Le Havre. Military officers were recruited from among a relatively small group of leading Canadian families. Military careers were linked to the empire and, when available commissions were too few to satisfy the numerous scions of the local gentry, they were sent to serve in Louisiana or the West Indies where disease quickly decimated their ranks.

Military officers and administrators were not the only ones whose personal interests coincided with those of the empire. Trade linked colonial merchants and the French Atlantic ports. Colonial merchants emerged elsewhere in the empire as a distinct group in the second half of the seventeenth century but, dependent on the credit of their metropolitan suppliers, they never freed themselves from their control. With the fur trade facing bankruptcy in 1702, colonial merchants formed the Colony Company and obtained a monopoly over beaver exportation. They felt exploited by metropolitan monopolists whom they blamed for the sorry state of the beaver market. With insufficient capital, this company sank into debt ruining some of the foremost Quebec traders. In 1706 metropolitan interests assumed the company's debts and the beaver monopoly, and colonial merchants were forced to accept their inferior status.

As in government, family was a crucial cement in merchant activity. Most merchants in New France came out as young men using the colonial trade as training for greater mercantile responsibilities in family businesses in France. Successful merchants usually returned to France leaving the colony with a disproportionate number of indebted merchants. During the eighteenth century, the most lucrative trade, the import-export business, was dominated by agents of Rouen, La Rochelle, or Bordeaux firms, such as François Havy and Jean Lefebvre who represented Dugard and Company of Rouen. Although these traders lived for long periods in the colony, they never considered themselves colonials. Many were Protestants, who were officially forbidden to establish families in the colonies.

In the same period, prosperity increased the colonial domestic market, leading some merchants to set up thriving businesses in rural parishes. The most successful maintained links with France. François Bailly de Messein, for example, sent his first two sons to the prestigious Louis Le Grand college in Paris. The eldest became coadjutor bishop of Quebec while the second sought his fortune in the Caribbean. A third son remained in the countryside living "nobly" off his father's estate.

Merchants were not the only social group that maintained close relations with France. The secular clergy, apart from the bishops who were all sent out from France, was recruited in Canada and trained at the Jesuit College and the Seminary of Quebec. But the important male regular orders—the Jesuits and the Sulpicians—were all metropolitans and usually members of the French elite. The Sulpicians were governed by the Paris Seminary, which set policy, controlled expenditures, and sent instructions on how to administer estates. The Jesuits followed an even more complex chain of command. The superior of the Canadian mission reported to the provincial of the order in Paris where he was represented by a *procureur* who published the annual *Relations* until 1672. An active correspondence was also maintained with the general of the order in Rome. However, as with civil government, distance permitted the colonial clergy significant independence in administering their own affairs. Religious orders were also tied to the Crown, acting as agents for government diplomatic initiatives toward Native peoples. Since they benefited from royal subsidies, they were effectively servants of the state.

Female orders, on the other hand, recruited their members in Canada and, after the first immigrant nuns died, had fewer contacts with their French mother houses. Yet they too were dependent upon state aid, especially the nursing orders, which relied heavily on royal funds since many of the hospitalized were soldiers and sailors.

The mass of the population had few contacts with the mother country. Most immigrants arrived in the seventeenth century and relations with friends and relatives broke off after the first generation. Many eighteenth-century immigrants were soldiers, often younger sons excluded from any family inheritance. Once they had married and settled, there was little to draw them back to France. The danger and expense of a trans-Atlantic crossing was also a powerful deterrent to continued links with the mother country.

With the colonial elite heavily dependent upon imperial ties for career advancement and prosperity, it is hardly surprising that few settlers thought of severing ties with France. For the common people, government was an abstraction in which they had no say. Their priorities were centered on family and personal economic well-being. In light of these social realities, there was no movement for independence in New France.

BIBLIOGRAPHY

Bosher, John F. "Government and Private Interests in New France." *Canadian Public Administration* (1967):244–257.

Dictionary of Canadian Biography. Vols. 1–3. Toronto, Ontario, 1966–1974. Although the *DCB* consists of twelve volumes published from 1966 to 1990, the first three volumes contain the most relevant material. Volume 4 has a few additional pertinent entries.

Dubé, Jean-Claude. *Les intendants de la Nouvelle-France*. Montreal, 1984.

Eccles, W. J. *Canada Under Louis XIV, 1663–1701*. Toronto, Ontario, 1964.

———. *The Canadian Frontier*, 1534–1760. New York, 1969.

———. *France in America*. New York, 1972.

———. *Frontenac, the Courtier Governor*. Toronto, Ontario, 1959.

Miquelon, Dale. *New France, 1701–1744. "A Supplement to Europe."* Toronto, Ontario, 1987.

Standen, S. Dale. "Politics, Patronage, and the Imperial Interest: Charles de Beauharnais's Disputes with Gilles Hocquart." *Canadian Historical Review* (1979):19–40.

Trudel, Marcel. *The Beginnings of New France, 1524–1663*. Toronto, Ontario, 1973.

Zoltvany, Yves. *Philippe de Rigaud de Vaudreuil. Governor of New France, 1703–1725*. Toronto, Ontario, 1974.

John A. Dickinson

SEE ALSO **Church and State; The Conquest of Acadia; The Framework of Government; Independence; Mercantilism; The Reorganization of Empires;** and **Roman Catholicism.**

THE BRITISH COLONIES

FOR OVER A CENTURY and a half, from 1607 to 1776, a minuscule British colonial administration managed to hold together the first British Empire. During that time imperial administration was constantly reflecting changes in British domestic politics, imperial attitudes, and the mother country's expectations of its colonies. It was never well staffed; never guided by a clear, comprehensive policy; never possessed of extensive authority. Nevertheless, for most of the time it worked.

COLONIAL ADMINISTRATION TO 1696

The machinery of administration developed slowly, very much by trial and error. Between 1607 and 1630 the first colonies were established by English mercantile companies (the Virginia Company, the Massachusetts Bay Company, and the Plymouth Company) chartered to run their own affairs in return for financial contributions to the Crown. When the companies failed or were bought out by the colonists, the governments they had created were replaced by a jumble of administrative arrangements. One mainland colony, Virginia, was taken over directly by the Crown in 1624. Massachusetts became a corporate colony largely running its own affairs, as did neighboring Plymouth, founded in 1620, and the colonies springing up alongside it in the 1630s—Connecticut, Rhode Island, and the briefly incorporated New Haven. One other colony, Maryland, was established in 1632 by a proprietor who paid nominal obeisance to the king but ran the province as his own domain.

Under the first two Stuart monarchs, such colonial administration as there was fell first to

King James I himself (1603–1625), then to the privy council in King Charles I's early years, and then in 1634 to a Commission of Plantations headed by William Laud, archbishop of Canterbury. Laud occasionally attempted to limit immigration to New England or Maryland, or to send over a ship to bring the colonists to heel, but he did not have the time or resources to carry out his plans. In 1640 Charles I, having ruled on his own for a decade, was forced by financial needs to summon Parliament to vote taxes. Parliament proceeded to appoint its own Committee of Plantations under the earl of Warwick. Although Warwick had connections with a number of Puritan leaders in the colonies, his committee was little more effective than Laud's because Parliament soon engaged in a civil war with the king (1642–1649) that consumed all its energies. The king was defeated and executed in 1649; the republican Council of State that took over the government after his death appointed the Committee for Trade and Plantations in 1650.

However, after a brief period of activity during which it passed the first Navigation Act (1651)—requiring colonial goods to be transported in English ships—and sent commissioners to subdue the Chesapeake colonies, it too lapsed into infighting and inactivity. When Oliver Cromwell became head of state in 1653, he hoped to use his personal friendship with Puritan leaders in both New England and the Chesapeake to establish closer cooperation between the colonies and the mother country. But he also found that distractions at home were too great to allow systematic consideration of colonial measures. The colonists, for their part, wanted almost as little to do with Cromwell as with his royal predecessors. They failed to support his recruitment of men for an expedition against Spanish Jamaica, refused to comply with the Navigation Act, and met regularly in the Confederation of New England, set up in 1643 ostensibly for mutual protection from Indians and foreign powers but actually to defend themselves against attempts by the home government to limit their autonomy.

Administrative Institutions in the Restoration Era

In 1660 the monarchy was restored, but colonial administration continued to be handled by trial and error for another fifteen years. In the first year after his return, King Charles II appointed a Council for Foreign Plantations, separate but overlapping in membership with a Council of Trade. Both committees lapsed in 1664–1665 but were briefly revived later as the Council of Trade in 1668 and the Council of Plantations in 1670. They were unwieldy (with from nineteen to sixty-seven members), were composed of a mixed lot of privy councillors, planters, merchants, and other "experts," lacked focus and information, and degenerated at times into debating societies. The councils were replaced by a single committee handling both trade and plantations in 1672, but the new panel, composed as it was entirely of paid advisers, proved expensive and was similarly short-lived. Finally, in 1675 a privy council committee composed of twenty-one councillors called the Lords of Trade was appointed. The Lords were to last twenty-one years, surviving a series of crises in English politics between 1675 and the Glorious Revolution (1688) and bringing some measure of continuity, if not stability, into colonial administration.

The establishment of the Lords of Trade coincided in time with a surge of English interest in the rapidly growing colonies. European-American population in the colonies increased from an estimated 70,000 in 1660 to about 250,000 at the end of the century. As the population expanded into new areas, English settlements ran up against those of the French, Dutch, and Spanish, and the colonies became potential theaters of international conflict. New York twice (1664 and 1673) became a scene of Anglo-Dutch warfare. In the same period, colonial trade with the mother country expanded rapidly: in 1663–1669 the colonies (including African trade stations) accounted for 12 percent of English imports and 8 percent of English exports. In 1699–1700 the percentages were 19 percent and 12 percent respectively. Such trade enriched the coffers of the government as well as the merchants. A steadily growing volume of American trade made customs duties on colonial products (an estimated £200,000 a year by the 1680s) crucially important to government finance at a time when the basis of government revenue was shifting from gifts and loans made by established institutions to indirect taxes levied on commerce.

The growth of North American population, trade, and settlement area continued to make Restoration monarchs, parliaments, and councils increasingly aggressive in their attempts to administer the colonies effectively. All sections of the government, but particularly the various committees of trade, began cultivating the acquisition of information from the colonies. Early committees were confined to such sources as merchants passing on news from their correspondents, colonists appealing against local authorities, and governors sending occasional reports. The committees soon turned to sending their own investigators to the colonies, beginning with Richard Nicolls in 1664. Later they began demanding that colonies have agents in London to provide information from home and that they also send provincial laws to England for review. By the 1680s Edward Randolph had become a professional troubleshooter reporting to the Lords of Trade on a variety of colonial transgressions, and Sir Edmund Andros and Francis Nicholson were on their way to becoming career governors. All this provided increasing amounts of information to the colonial committees; the Lords of Trade sought, and got, a secretary (William Blathwayt and Sir Robert Southwell were the best known holders of the office), a clerical staff, and an office (formally known as the Plantation Office) in which to store its records.

Shortcomings of Restoration Administration

Despite their growing awareness of the importance of the colonies and their growing access to information about them, however, Restoration governments were never able to bring either consistency or stability to colonial administration. Monarchs, parliaments, and committees never cooperated fully with each other, and those efforts they did launch, either jointly or separately, were resisted in the colonies.

Most important, the Restoration settlement had failed to resolve fundamental differences over claims to authority by kings and Parliament, so there was prolonged instability in domestic politics. During the tenure of the Lords of Trade, the government faced a plot against the king's life (the Rye House Plot of 1683), a full rebellion (Monmouth's Rebellion of 1685), and the Glorious Revolution that replaced one monarch with another. Throughout the period neither the monarch nor the legislature was willing to trust the creation of colonial policy to a committee that might fall under the control of the other. Parliament made some decisions, the monarchs made others, and both overlooked, or overrode, the decisions of the Lords of Trade.

From 1660 to 1673, Parliament passed a series of navigation acts restricting colonial trade to ships with English owners and English crews. The acts stipulated that certain enumerated commodities produced in the colonies be sent from them only to other English colonies or to England itself. European goods had to be imported into the colonies only by way of English ports and any duties on enumerated goods were to be paid at the place of export. Parliament also determined the level of duties. The monarch created proprietorships for friends and negotiated the terms of the proprietary charters, and secured removal of the Massachusetts charter in 1684 when the colony failed to comply with the navigation acts. The king also created the ill-fated Dominion of New England (1685–1688), which combined all the colonies from New York northward in one government. Monarchs closeted with close advisors decided a wide and random range of questions, leaving committees only the work of drawing up plans for their implementation.

Any exertion of English authority was likely to be opposed by colonists who resented any encroachments on the virtual autonomy they had hitherto enjoyed. Not having significant influence on decisions affecting them, colonists could do little but balk at cooperating. They flouted the navigation acts, and the royal colonies resisted demands that they vote long-term salaries for governors. (New Hampshire was successful in its resistance; Virginia was not.) Despite government demands, the colonists delayed sending agents to London. They smuggled extensively, passed laws for periods of time so short that the imperial government could not review them before expiration, and made life as miserable as possible for customs collectors appointed under the Plantation Duties Act of 1673. The colonists also rebelled successfully against the loyal governor of Virginia in 1676 and against governors identified with James II, the monarch overthrown in 1688.

In the aftermath of the Glorious Revolution, which replaced James II with William III, there was continued confusion over where the authority to administer the colonies actually lay. The privy council as a whole resumed consideration of some colonial matters, Parliament considered setting up a new committee of trade, the king handled various colonial problems himself, while the Lords of Trade began to lose heart as well as staff when fewer issues were referred to them. Increase Mather, seeking to restore the Massachusetts charter, went to the Lords of Trade, Parliament, and the king before William III himself finally made the decision not to restore it. Finally, in 1696 colonial administration was overhauled by a combination of royal action and parliamentary statutes.

A parliamentary navigation act of 1696 tightened imperial control over American trade by requiring bonds to be posted to ensure that enumerated products would be sent only to imperial ports. It also required that all colonial laws be sent to London for review and that all governors obtain royal approval before assuming office. The act established vice-admiralty courts to enforce trade laws in America, and provided a full-scale customs organization for the colonies. The Commissioners of Customs constituted a bureau within the Treasury Board to enforce the navigation acts and collect customs duties. The Admiralty in America was supposed to help the customs officers prevent smuggling. By the early eighteenth century, every colony had a naval officer, who was appointed in practice by the Crown and kept a record of ships entering and leaving ports, their cargoes, and their destinations. Customs officials also held posts in fifty ports along the American coasts.

ESTABLISHING THE BOARD OF TRADE

The royal contribution to revamping colonial administration was William's replacement of the Lords of Trade with a new committee, the Board of Trade. The new board rapidly became an effective committee and remained so for nearly seventy years until its powers were whittled away in the 1760s. It lasted formally until 1782. The Board of Trade's creation represented considerably more than the substitution of one committee for another, of new blood for old. The very fact of its appointment by the king reflected the

emerging resolution of the conflict between the kings and Parliament, with colonial affairs being left largely in royal hands; it showed also the rapid expansion of all English administration after 1689 and the ever-increasing value of the colonies to England. The new board, unlike the old, was an efficient instrument for bringing the colonies under tighter control, with access to more extensive and more reliable information than its predecessors, and the colonists complied far more willingly with its decisions than they had with those of Restoration agencies of government.

As William III created the board, he also aborted the efforts of parliamentary leaders to establish a committee responsible to themselves. The board had eight salaried and eight ex officio members, one of whom was the bishop of London. William III thwarted demands by the mercantile community that merchants trading to the colonies be represented, appointing instead men of gentry background. Though the board was not a committee within the privy council, it was responsible for reporting to the council as well as to the secretary of state for the Southern Department, the cabinet minister assigned to colonial matters (as well as relations with southern Europe). Many of the reports of the board were rubber stamped by the council or the secretary, though some were occasionally overruled because the minister thought the report's recommendations inexpedient or a colonial group with better connections on the council than at the board appealed against the latter and won. The board's specific assignments were four: it was to review colonial legislation, making sure that a law passed by a colonial legislature was not repugnant to those of England; to appoint colonial councillors; to assist non-English settlers in reaching the colonies; and to draft the instructions to governors of royal colonies.

Though the board and the council handled the bulk of colonial administration, they shared some authority with Parliament and with other royal officials. To Parliament belonged questions of policy, particularly questions of trade, manufacturing, or naturalization—questions involving all or a great number of colonies. To the king's ministers went responsibility for setting the parliamentary agenda and negotiating parliamentary majorities; to them also fell foreign policy decisions directly affecting the colonies and, in practice, the nomination of colonial governors.

Over the years the board slowly lost some of its power to both ministers and Parliament. Increasingly ministers, secretaries of state in particular, interfered in appointments below the gubernatorial level, leaving colonial appointees sent by the board to be undercut in the colonies by appointees owing their positions to other patrons. Increasingly the board also found itself referring to Parliament administrative questions it could not handle on its own. When proprietary and charter colonies resisted parts of the navigation acts, the board recommended to Parliament that their governments be resumed to the Crown. When colonies issued what the board considered to be excessive amounts of paper money, the board, after unsuccessfully instructing the governors not to agree to such emissions, turned over to Parliament first the question of regulating colonial currency and then the responsibility of making governors' instructions legally binding. The board threatened in the 1740s and again in 1755 to propose legislation disqualifying Quakers from serving in the colonial assemblies because they would not vote military support in colonial wars. On all these issues the initiative for the referrals to Parliament came from the board itself, but the referrals of the first half of the eighteenth century anticipated the rapid increase of Parliament's power at the board's expense in the 1760s.

TIGHTENING UP COLONIAL CONTROLS

Under William III and his successors, the American colonies were more closely tied to Britain than they had been during the Restoration, reflecting the rapidly growing importance of the colonies to the British political economy. The immediate occasion for tighter rule was the need for colonial cooperation in two French wars, which began with the king's accession in 1689 and continued, with only a short break, to 1713. Conflicts erupted up and down the east coast of North America from the Carolinas to eastern Canada, in contrast with the Restoration era, when fighting had centered on New York. Colonists were expected to contribute men and money to the wars and to vote supplies to the army and navy. The wars temporarily slowed the growth of American trade with the mother country; but commerce picked up quickly after the wartime disruption, and the growth of American trade and population enhanced both the value of the colonies to Britain and the need for colonial regulation. Over the first half of the eighteenth century, British imports from America increased by 235 percent and British exports to the colonies grew by 380 percent; population expanded from an estimated 250,000 in 1700 to nearly a million in 1740 and two million twenty years later.

The rapid growth of the colonial population, area of settlement, and economy meant that, from the mother country's standpoint, the colonies could no longer continue to enjoy the autonomy they had had in the seventeenth century. Between 1679 and 1729, seven of the mainland colonies—New York, Massachusetts, the Carolinas, New Jersey, and New Hampshire joined Virginia as permanent royal colonies and Pennsylvania and Maryland were temporarily brought under royal administration after the Glorious Revolution. Only two mainland colonies, Connecticut and Rhode Island, retained their corporate charters, which gave them the right to choose their own governors and councillors; but even they were expected to obey parliamentary legislation and submit their laws to the privy council (which meant the board) for review. All the royal and proprietary colonies had governors appointed in England, and all the colonies except Connecticut, Rhode Island, and Massachusetts had councils appointed there, too. The governors were sent to the royal colonies with a commission and instructions drawn up by the Board of Trade. Once in the colonies, a governor was to follow (though not to publish) his instructions and to obtain favorable legislation, including provision for his own salary. The provincial legislation was then sent back to the king in council, which referred it to the Board of Trade for review. The board sent all the laws to its attorney to measure their compatibility with existing parliamentary law and gave some laws additional consideration if they were likely to be controversial, unworkable, or prejudicial to groups within the colonies. In the end in the period from 1696 to 1776, 5.5 percent of all colonial laws reviewed were disallowed. (In addition, 30 percent of the judicial decisions of colonial courts were reversed.)

By and large colonial compliance with the new regulations was reasonably good, though it is impossible to measure precisely. Colonists certainly did continue smuggling, but on the whole they directed their trade in accordance with the navigation acts. They delayed sending some laws to Whitehall for review, but they occupied substantial parts of legislative sessions rewriting others to comply with the board's directives. They evaded some gubernatorial instructions on the grounds that the governors did not make them public, but compromised with others they did not like and welcomed new governors with more than ceremonial enthusiasm.

INFORMATION AND LOBBYING BIND THE EMPIRE

Such compliance was not the result of coercion. The British had no effective peacetime army in the American colonies and averaged fewer than a dozen royal officials in each; the compliance, therefore, was largely voluntary. It was motivated in part by loyalty to common conventions of the English world. Stability in the mother country also helped: English crises no longer spilled over into imperial relations as they had in the seventeenth century. Prosperity within the empire and wartime military protection also inspired American loyalty. More important than these, however, were two other factors, two sides of the same coin: the British government in the early eighteenth century had better information about colonial politics than its predecessors and could therefore make decisions more acceptable to the Americans; conversely, the colonists were able to influence decisions affecting them at both the imperial and the local levels.

More effective supervision required more accurate information about colonial conditions, and here the Board of Trade was much stronger than the old Lords of Trade, with the ability to call upon far more resources. By 1700 virtually all the colonies had standing agents to handle their business before the board. Governors appointed to the new royal colonies, judges in the Admiralty courts, and customs officials were all expected to send regular information. Perhaps most important, a number of London interest groups, particularly churches, foreign communities, and mercantile associations, developed connections with corresponding interest groups in the colonies and undertook to lobby with the British government, and especially the Board of Trade, on their behalf. (It should be noted that the bishop of London, in charge of all Anglican churches in the colonies since 1685 and himself an ex officio member of the Board of Trade, served as the church's chief lobbyist.) The lobbyists provided information about American conditions in return for favors for their American correspondents. The colonists' most effective influence at the board came through these lobbyists and through the agents of the provincial assemblies.

From these sources the board aggressively solicited information—requiring regular correspondence from the governors, summoning agents to appear with proper papers on relevant measures, and sending them off to obtain further information from the colonial legislatures. Representatives of the interest groups were notified to attend when matters concerning tthem were considered. Additionally, the board obtained information by asking leading members of interest groups to poll their members on particular questions and publishing the times of their meetings in coffeehouses where interested people would see them.

Such solicitude did not always produce reliable information. Royal officials in the colonies were spread too thinly; their numbers did not increase nearly as quickly as the colonial population upon whom they were to report. Even the few officials in the colonies and colonial spokesmen in London often disagreed with one another: governors and customs officials, agents representing the governors and those representing the assemblies, the governors and the lieutenant governors who hoped to dislodge and then succeed them, and spokesmen for competitive interest groups provided conflicting reports of colonial conditions. Nevertheless such sources, used with care, produced for the board significantly more information than Restoration councils had enjoyed and helped steer it away from decisions unpalatable to the colonists.

THE MATURATION OF THE COLONIAL ASSEMBLIES

In addition to shaping decisions at Whitehall, the colonists developed more effective control of their provincial institutions as the colonial assemblies, popularly elected by property owners, increased their local authority over the eighteenth century. They did so in two ways.

The first way was by cutting into the governors' powers. There was much variety in the structure of colonial governments and the governors appointed to them. Proprietary, royal, and charter forms of government all continued to exist in the eighteenth century, and the governors were a mixture of military and nonmilitary men, courtiers and lesser politicians, from America and from England. Yet for all the colonies but Connecticut and Rhode Island, where governors were locally elected, their pattern of service was similar. They arrived in the colonies needing to get the assemblies to vote both their salaries and the legislation suggested in their instructions. To do this they had to use patronage and favors to create alliances with factions, interests, or coalitions in their assembly. This in itself was difficult because what little patronage the governors possessed at the beginning of the century was eroded as English politicians increasingly used colonial jobs to reward their followers at home. Without a secure political base, the governors were forced to trade off some of their executive authority to the assemblies in return for their salaries.

Once a governor's colonial alliances were determined, angry provincial opponents appealed home in an effort to put pressure on the executive and remove him if he continued to be uncooperative. In London the discontented colonists had a variety of natural allies: other imperial officials whose priorities differed from the governor's, colonial agents representing the assemblies but often responsible to one or another faction within them, interest groups that disapproved gubernatorial policies, office seekers who wanted the governor's job, and the political patrons of those office seekers. With such constraints the governors could hold on to their positions for an average of from four to five years; only a few, like Governors Robert Hunter of New York, William Gooch and Alexander Spotswood of Virginia, and Joseph Dudley and Jonathan Belcher of Massachusetts, survived more than a decade. All the governors, however, were forced to compromise away some executive powers in an effort to gain local support and to keep colonial issues quiet enough so that they did not carry over to London, where they could threaten the governors' standing.

Far more important for the growth of colonial influence over provincial affairs, colonial legislatures learned to handle increasing numbers of constituent demands for legislation. Over the century the assemblies took up a growing number of issues that their constituents would earlier have taken to local or imperial authorities, and they handled such questions with increasing efficiency. The new issues, many but not all of them emerging from King George's War (1740–1748) and the Seven Years' War (1754–1761) concerned defense, transportation, and currency. To handle larger amounts of legislation the assemblies greatly improved their efficiency, expanding their committee systems, increasingly relying on elected speakers to focus debate, and systematizing their record keeping. They encouraged constituents to express their views through petitions, sent committees to consult constituents when drawing up particular measures, and sometimes even adjourned temporarily to let representatives go home and consult the voters on legislation. Legislative output increased unevenly from colony to colony, but overall the increase averaged over 60 percent. Through the improved handling of legislation by the assemblies as well as their growing control of the governors, colonial politicians could influence politics in the empire.

THE SHIFT OF AUTHORITY WITHIN THE EMPIRE

In the aftermath of King George's War and the Seven Years' War, the structure of imperial government did not change, but the locus of authority and influence within it shifted significantly, threatening the stability of the old empire. Britain ended the wars victorious over France but with a £147 million debt, with concerns about the colonists' lukewarm support during a good part of the wars, and with expectations that the colonists would be moving into even larger areas of settlement now that the French threat had been removed from most of North America. With a combination of motives, the British set about tapping the growing American wealth to help reduce the debt and make the Americans better imperial citizens; each measure moved the governance of the colonies more clearly toward Parliament and away from the royal councils.

As a first step in augmenting colonial administration after the Seven Years' War, Parliament passed an act permitting the British navy to aid the customs service in regulating American trade. From there it moved to the Sugar Act of 1764, which imposed new customs duties but also added regulations on American shipping and the erection of a vice-admiralty court at Halifax, Nova Scotia, with jurisdiction over all the mainland colonies. The next step was the Stamp Act (1765), imposing duties on colonial newspapers, diplomas, licenses, wills, playing cards, and a host of other items sold within the provinces. This legislation was shortly repealed in response to American opposition, but its revocation was coupled with an act declaring Parliament's right to legislate for the colonies in any circumstance. In 1767 Parliament passed the Townshend Duties Act, placing customs duties on a number of items the colonists imported from England, and though parts of this act, too, were repealed in response to American resistance, other provisions were left to stand.

In one sense the parliamentary legislation represented simply an extension of the administrative work the board had sent it earlier in the century. But it also represented a growing reluctance to leave the colonies under royal direction; if reforms were to be made, so went the thinking, it was safer for English liberties to have them made by Parliament. Correspondingly, the 1760s saw the powers of the Board of Trade so reduced that it was no longer capable of undertaking reform. Ministerial turnovers occurred almost annually in the turbulent decade, and each new group of ministers usurped some of the board's powers. In 1768 a secretary of state for American affairs was appointed. The board itself had a complete turnover of membership, so that the members during the 1760s were both inexperienced and lacking in personal contacts with colonial agents or members of interest groups who could provide information about the colonies. The board met less and less frequently; it ceased to seek out information from appropriate agents and interest groups, and relied entirely on the reports of its attorney when reviewing colonial legislation. Though George III was hesitant about particular legislative measures, he did not oppose Parliament's increasing intervention in colonial administration.

Some Americans, however, resisted losing their direct relationship to the king, not only because they did not want their assemblies to become subordinate legislatures, but also because they would not be able to inform or influence Parliament as much as they had the smaller, more specialized, more accessible Board of Trade. As late as 1767, however, the colonists hoped that Parliament might somewhat be responsive to their pressure. When governors prorogued assemblies about to condemn the Stamp Act or Townshend Duties Act, the colonial legislators met informally, hoping their protests would lead the British government to retract unpalatable legislation, as it had done before. The provincial protesters did succeed in getting the Stamp Act and most of the Townshend duties repealed. But they failed to secure repeal or change of the Tea Act of 1773, which reduced the cost of tea (still taxed by the Townshend duties) in the colonies by allowing the East India Company to ship it directly from India to America. Parliament responded not with concession but with punitive legislation, the so-called Intolerable Acts of 1774.

Later that year, when colonial representatives met in the Continental Congress to formulate their response to the Intolerable Acts, the colonists had seen the center of colonial authority in London shift from the kings' servants, whom they had learned to influence, to a Parliament they could not. Over the course of the eighteenth century colonial assemblies had gained experience in handling executive responsibilities and meeting constituent demands. Nevertheless it was with sadness as well as bitterness, surprise as well as resignation, that the colonists declared their independence from the mother country in 1776.

Until its very last decades, then, British colonial administration had worked rather well. Administrative staffs were always small, but they made the most of informal sources of information and on the whole proved responsive to colonial needs. By the time the colonists rebelled, the administration was no longer functioning responsively; it was no wonder that on the eve of the War for Independence, some of the colonists lamented that they could not turn back the administrative clock.

BIBLIOGRAPHY

Andrews, Charles M. *The Colonial Background of the American Revolution: Four Essays in Colonial American History.* New Haven, Conn., 1924; rev. ed. 1931.

Barrow, Thomas C. *Trade and Empire: The British Customs Service in Colonial America, 1660–1775.* Cambridge, Mass., 1967.

Basye, Arthur H. *The Lords Commissioners of Trade and Plantations, Commonly Known as the Board of Trade, 1748–1782.* New Haven, Conn., 1925.

Beer, George Louis. *British Colonial Policy, 1754–1765.* New York, 1907; repr. 1958.

———. *The Old Colonial System, 1660–1754: Part 1: The Establishment of the System, 1660–1688.* New York, 1912; repr. 1959.

———. *The Origins of the British Colonial System, 1578–1660.* New York, 1908; repr. 1959.

Clark, Dora Mae. *The Rise of the British Treasury: Colonial Administration in the Eighteenth Century.* New Haven, Conn., 1960.

Dickerson, Oliver M. *The Navigation Acts and the American Revolution.* Philadelphia, 1951.

Johnson, Richard R. *Adjustment to Empire: The New England Colonies, 1675–1715.* New Brunswick, N.J., 1981.

Kammen, Michael. *Empire and Interest: The American Colonies and the Politics of Mercantilism.* New York, 1970.

Labaree, Leonard Woods. *Royal Government in America: A Study of the British Colonial System Before 1783.* New Haven, Conn., 1930; repr. 1958.

Olson, Alison Gilbert. *Anglo-American Politics, 1660–1775: The Relationship Between Parties in England and Colonial America.* New York, 1973.

———. *Making the Empire Work: The Development and Cooperation of London and American Interest Groups in the Seventeenth and Eighteenth Centuries.* Cambridge, Mass., 1992.

Olson, Alison Gilbert, and Richard Maxwell Brown, eds. *Anglo-American Political Relations, 1675–1775.* New Brunswick, N.J., 1970.

Russell, Elmer B. *The Review of American Colonial Legislation by the King in Council.* New York, 1915.

Smith, Joseph H. *Appeals to the Privy Council from the American Plantations.* New York, 1950.

Sosin, Jack M. *English America and the Restoration Monarchy of Charles II: Transatlantic Politics, Commerce, and Kinship.* Lincoln, Nebr., 1980.

Steele, I. K. *The English Atlantic, 1675–1740: An Exploration of Communication and Community.* New York, 1986.

———. *Politics of Colonial Policy: The Board of Trade in Colonial Administration, 1696–1720.* New York, 1968.

Webb, Stephen Saunders. *The Governors-General: The English Army and the Definition of the Empire, 1659–1681.* Chapel Hill, N.C., 1979.

Alison Gilbert Olson

SEE ALSO **Framework of Government; Mercantilism; Trade and Commerce;** and various essays in TOWARD INDEPENDENCE.

THE DUTCH COLONY

FOR ALL OF ITS HISTORY, the Dutch colony of New Netherland was ruled by the chartered West India Company (WIC). Although explored as early as 1609 by Henry Hudson and exploited for its furs by private companies thereafter, it was not until 1624 that New Netherland received its first European colonists.

COLONIZATION AND RULE UNDER THE WEST INDIA COMPANY

New Netherland was the responsibility of the directors of the Amsterdam chamber of the WIC. The chamber system was unique to Dutch corporate capitalism and was designed to concentrate capital and control in the hands of local merchant investors. The company capital was divided among five chambers: Amsterdam, Middleburg (for Zeeland), Rotterdam, Enkhuizen, and Groningen. The central administration was in the hands of the Heeren XIX (College of Nineteen), a board of directors elected by the chambers, with representation based on the percentage of subscribed capital. The Amsterdam chamber provided eight delegates, Zeeland four, and each of the remaining chambers two. The nineteenth delegate represented the States General. The individual chambers conducted most of the company's operations. Chambers were authorized to keep their own books, outfit their own fleets and trading expeditions, establish their own colonies (with approval of the Heeren XIX), and compete with every other chamber. When the responsibility for developing New Netherland was assigned to the Amsterdam chamber, the colony at once became a principal focus of this, the most powerful chamber in the company.

The WIC's charter gave it far-reaching powers and responsibilities while separating most of its activities from the government of the United Netherlands. Some scholars have argued that a national joint-stock company with powers of sovereignty was an inevitable outcome of the inability of the government to assign sovereignty among the competing interests of the provincial legislatures, the merchant-oligarchs, and the House of Orange. By abdicating sovereignty to the company, the precarious balance of interests could be maintained without addressing the fundamental question of the locus of political authority.

In 1624 the Amsterdam chamber undertook an ambitious plan to settle thirty families of Walloons in the colony. The directors drew up a document known as the Provisional Orders specifying the colonists' responsibilities to the company and the fatherland. The colonists were to observe "the respective articles and instructions, during the voyage and their residence, and in changing their location, be bound to obey and to carry out without any contradiction the orders of the company." This severe and uncompromising language was softenened, however, by the articles that followed. In addition to specifying that all matters of a criminal nature would be dealt with in accordance with the laws of the United Provinces, the succeeding paragraphs weakened the authority of the post commander by requiring him to rule with a council drawn from among the settlers.

The Walloons dealt with the company as government and employer simultaneously. The company encouraged the colonists to engage in the fur trade as either trappers or traders. As the sole purchaser of furs, the company promised to pay "reasonable" prices. In other trades the colonists were given a freer hand, being encouraged to search for "mines of gold, silver, copper or any other metals." In return the colonists received free passage to New Netherland, as much free land as they could work, and livestock at "reasonable prices" or on credit without interest.

In 1629 the Amsterdam chamber tried a new approach to colonization in New Netherland. Led by Kiliaen van Rensselaer, the directors proposed to establish a string of feudal estates throughout the colony to be worked by a rural peasantry. On these patroonships the patroon or his designee would exercise legal jurisdiction through a manor court. The "Freedoms and Exemptions for the Patroons and Masters or Private Persons who would plant a colony and cattle in New Netherland" granted the patroons enormous privileges, including the unlimited right to all "fruits, flora, minerals, rivers, and springs." Moreover, the patroon could appoint officers and agents, levy taxes and fees, appoint all magistrates, and confer titles. In the patroon's court all cases could be tried, including capital offenses, which in effect gave the patroon the power of life and death over his tenants. In return for these privileges, the patroon had only to agree to settle fifty persons in a "colony" within the space of four years. For this he would receive an estate "four leages along the coast or one side of a navigable river, or two leagues along both sides of a river." From the coast or bank of a river the size of the patroonship was theoretically unlimited, being "as far inland as the situation of the residents shall permit." This vague terminology would permit Kiliaenn van Rensselaer and his heirs to claim an estimated one million acres in the vicinity of present day Albany, New York. This experiment with feudalism may be explained with reference to the peculiar circumstances of Dutch imperialism.

The resort to a medieval manorial system was less an anachronism than a matter of pragmatism. In the Amsterdam chamber, wealthy directors and perhaps the majority of the *hoofd-participanten* (principal shareholders) favored some method to shift the cost of colonization from the chamber to private merchants. When Kiliaen van Rensselaer and his backers offered to foot the bill for colonizing New Netherland, the reaction was one of relief. Only later did the stockholders come to regret this decision. When the first plan was abandoned in the late 1630s, only the patroonship of Rensselaerswyck remained. The experiment never really caught on among the Dutch, although the English were to have limited success with a manorial society in the same area.

In 1640 the company abandoned most of its monopolistic privileges and offered two hundred acres (80 hectares) of free land to any colonist who brought with him five family members or servants. The new Freedoms and Exemptions also opened the fur trade to all citizens of the United Provinces. The only vestige of the company monopoly that remained was the right to tax certain imports and exports. The abandonment of the trade monopoly left the once mighty and now nearly bankrupt company with all the responsibilities of government but little loyalty from the colonists.

DEMISE OF WEST INDIA COMPANY AND DUTCH NEW NETHERLAND

After the Indian wars of the 1640s, hundreds of English families migrated from New England and set up towns on the eastern end of Long Island. At the same time, thousands of Europeans arrived from Holland, Scandinavia, the German states, and France. This flood of new immigrants accelerated the process of town formation among the non-English and pressed company officials hard for recognition of town governance. The company granted charters to the English towns of Newtown (1642), Hempstead (1644), Gravesend (1645), and Flushing (1645), and to the Dutch towns of Breuckelen (1646), Beverswyck (Albany, 1652), and Midwout (Flatbush, 1653).

These years also witnessed direct outside intervention in the colony's affairs when the city of Amsterdam helped fund a 1655 company raid on New Sweden, led by New Netherland Director-General Peter Stuyvesant, that resulted in the ouster of the Swedes. As reimbursement to the city for its help in the conquest of the Swedish settlements on the Delaware, the company granted it a plot of land on the river from Christina Kill to Boompeties Hoeck. Christened New Amstel, it was to serve the city of Amsterdam as a colony to settle and exploit as it saw fit. This intervention, so out of keeping with the previous history of the colony, speaks both to the bankrupt state of the West India Company and to the continuing role of the Amsterdam merchant-oligarchs in the affairs of the colony.

The financial and political assistance of the city of Amsterdam came too late to save the colony. Ethnic and political divisions had already rendered the colony vulnerable to conquest. The generous land policies after 1640 and the end of the disastrous Indian wars resulted in a surge of European immigration in the 1650s and early 1660s. Only a fraction of the new immigrants, however, were ethnically Dutch. On Long Island two thousand or more English settlers, mostly from New England, served as a fifth column when the Anglo-Dutch wars of the late seventeenth century threatened New Netherland. Elsewhere in the colony European ethnic groups chafed under the restrictions of the WIC and resisted the attempts of the Stuyvesant administration to impose company rule. When the English war fleet appeared in the roadstead before New Amsterdam in 1664, the company had long since lost the political allegiance of most of the colony's citizens. As the later history of New York would prove, political alligiance tended to follow local ethnic divisions. The non-Dutch of New Netherland, comprising 50 percent or more of the total European population, refused Stuyvesant's call to defend the colony for the company, and few Dutch wished to defend it for the fatherland.

BIBLIOGRAPHY

Bachman, Van Cleaf. *Peltries or Plantations: The Economic Policies of the Dutch West India Company in New Netherland, 1623–1639.* Baltimore, Md., 1969.

Boxer, Charles R. *The Dutch Seaborne Empire: 1600–1800.* London, 1965.

O'Callaghan, Edmund B. *History of New Netherland; or, New York Under the Dutch.* 2 vols. New York, 1848.

Rink, Oliver A. *Holland on the Hudson: An Economic and Social History of Dutch New York.* Ithaca, N.Y., 1986.

Oliver A. Rink

SEE ALSO **Framework of Government; Mercantilism;** and **Trade and Commerce.**

LOCAL GOVERNMENT

THE SPANISH BORDERLANDS

THE SPANISH BORDERLANDS HAD a much longer life—from the 1520s to 1848—than did the English, French, or Dutch colonies, although, of course, after 1821 they were the Mexican borderlands. Theoretically, the Spanish possessions stretched from Florida and Georgia across the southern portion of the continent, up the West Coast of California and into much of the West past the Mississippi River. Reality was somewhat less grand. At the end of the eighteenth century, Spanish settlement was primarily grouped around a few urban nodules located in four clusters: San Antonio, La Bahia, and Nacogdoches, Texas; Santa Fe, Albuquerque, El Paso, Tucson, and Tubac in modern-day Arizona, New Mexico, and West Texas; San Diego, Los Angeles, San Jose, and San Francisco, California; and Saint Augustine, Florida.

Spanish civilization north of Mexico began in the early seventeenth century with the creation of a few tenuous settlements in New Mexico. Technically, Florida was the oldest of the borderland areas, having had an independent governor appointed in 1574, which confirmed its status as a separate province. Florida consisted, however, primarily of beleaguered military outposts and was the only one of the four North American provinces not to develop a functioning system of civilian local government. New Mexico, which became a province in 1598, developed the first

and most elaborate set of local institutions. Texas, which on paper became a province in 1690, did not have any significant Spanish settlement until 1718. And California remained unpopulated by Europeans until 1769, when the Spanish planted a mission at San Diego. In 1773 California became a province, and over two dozen Spanish settlements were begun in the 1770s and 1780s. Thus, local government in the borderlands originated in New Mexico in the seventeenth century and spread to Texas and California in the middle and latter years of the eighteenth century.

Throughout their history, the Spanish Borderlands faced two questions that also troubled the English colonies: Where should the boundary be drawn between church and state?; and what was the appropriate relationship between central and local power? The borderlands additionally confronted some problems the English colonies did not face when creating local institutions. Spanish settlement was geographically far-flung and relatively sparsely populated by Spaniards. In parts of the borderlands, Spain assumed much responsibility for the governance of natives within the boundaries of its possessions. And the military played a greater role in the Spanish colonies than in the English. Most English male colonists served in the militia, but few were professional military men. Spanish colonists tended to be male and often were professional soldiers. The Crown ennobled many of these military men in return for valiant service, and a formal Spanish nobility played a key role in local government.

Thus a distinct set of demographic, social, and geographical circumstances conditioned Spanish local institutions in North America. Spain governed local life in the borderlands through three sets of institutions that it developed for its three main types of settlement: the *presidio,* the town, and the mission. The power of the *presidios,* military fortresses garrisoned with professional soldiers, symbolized and guaranteed Spanish rule. Ranging from a handful to several hundred soldiers, *presidios* grew in number from the first ones at Saint Augustine and Santa Fe to a string of twenty forts that stretched from Florida through Texas and New Mexico and up the west coast to San Francisco at the end of the eighteenth century. Governed by a military commander and operating under martial law, they were part of a hierarchical imperial bureaucracy that allowed for virtually no participatory involvement of the citizenry.

Towns and missions, on the other hand, existed largely outside of the imperial hierarchy. Towns, urbane communities with diverse civilian populations, transplanted to the borderlands many of the municipal institutions that had evolved in late medieval Spain. The missions, sometimes called the pueblos or the pueblo missions, were Indian villages under the tutelage of representatives of the church. Usually these representatives were Franciscan friars, but occasionally they were Dominicans or Jesuits. Missions combined elements of Native and Spanish institutions and wove Spanish rule and custom into the local political fabric. Their purpose was to convert, civilize (by Spanish standards), and control the Native population.

The first northern province, New Mexico, was divided into a system of judicial districts, *jurisdicciones,* created by the Spanish royal officials. Each district was presided over by an *alcalde mayore* (chief constable and judge) appointed by the governor. *Alcaldes mayores* combined executive, legislative, and judicial authority in their persons and exercised strong local powers over rural settlers and missions. They conducted trials, supervised commerce and trade with the natives, administered land grants, regulated public travel, proclaimed royal law and decrees, kept records such as cattle brands, passed information

to superiors, and even served as a *capitán a guerra,* or war leader, for local defense if no *presidio* was nearby. Almost everything except towns lay within their competence.

Jurisdicciones were in turn subdivided into *partidos* presided over by a *teniente alcalde,* who also possessed authority in all spheres but had a limited competence and could act only in relatively minor matters. In much of New Spain, *alcaldes mayores* and *tenientes alcaldes* served for three-year terms at a provincial governor's pleasure. In the borderlands, however, they usually served for life due to a shortage of acceptable Spanish candidates to fill the jobs. Collectively *alcaldes mayores* and *tenientes alcaldes* were sometimes called *justicias* or simply *alcaldes.* Derived from a Moorish term for village judge, the word *alcalde* was used ubiquitously for a wide variety of magistrates, constables, and sheriffs and other administrative figures. Systems similar to that of New Mexico were later created for the new provinces of Texas and California but not for Florida, where the governor directly administered all matters of justice.

Two systems of courts existed throughout the *jurisdicciones* and the *partides:* the ordinary and the privileged. *Alcaldes mayores* and *tenientes alcaldes* presided over courts of *justicia ordinario,* which were for secular and civilian matters. Courts of *justicia privilegiado,* which were for the special interests of the church and military, were presided over respectively by clergy and military leaders. Both systems, of course, like that of the *presidio,* were part of a hierarchical structure that ran upward from the *partides* through many levels to the Council for the Indies and the king.

The town was more truly an agency of local governance that expressed local power and aspirations. During the latter years of the Reconquest by the Christians of the Iberian Peninsula, towns developed a tradition of self-government. The *ayuntamiento,* or *cabildo secular* as it was more commonly called, was the crucial governing instrument of Spanish towns. Similar to an English town council, the *cabildo* usually numbered from six to eight *regidores* (members), of whom one was designated the *alcalde ordinario* (mayor). The *cabildos* were elected by the substantial citizens of the town and were responsible to the Crown, not the local nobility. They enjoyed independent powers to tax, create and license markets, provide police protection, pass bylaws, and so forth, much like an English incorporated town or a modern municipality.

Although towns and *cabildos* developed early in many parts of Spanish America, in the first two centuries of the Spanish Borderlands only one town, Santa Fe, was granted the privilege of a *cabildo*. The 1680 Pueblo Revolt against Spanish rule in New Mexico ended Santa Fe's *cabildo*, and it was not reinstituted when the Spanish repossessed the area in the 1690s. In the 1730s and 1740s, the Bourbon rulers weakened town government in Spain as part of their attempt to strengthen the monarchy; they also tried to whittle down town autonomy in Spanish America. In the second half of the eighteenth century, however, town government revived in Spain and especially in the Spanish Borderlands. By the outbreak of the American Revolution strong, successful *cabildos* governed Santa Fe and El Paso in New Mexico, Laredo, and San Antonio in Texas, and San Jose and Los Angeles in California. Movement toward municipal government had begun in other communities such as La Bahia, Nacogdoches, Albuquerque, and Santa Cruz. Even in Florida, which existed as a series of *presidios* with virtually no institutions of local government, a *cabildo* was created in 1761 for Saint Augustine. However, its political life ended less than two years later with the transfer of Florida to England at the end of the Seven Years' War.

Peninsulares (Spanish citizens born in Spain) dominated *presidios* and usually the higher-level courts, but Creoles (Spanish citizens born in the western hemisphere) dominated the *cabildos*. This had the effect of tying the *cabildos* to the local interests. For example, when Spain established a *cabildo* for New Orleans in 1769 after assuming control of Louisiana, it allowed the first one to be staffed entirely by French colonists. Theoretically, the *cabildos* had the privilege of communicating directly with the king, although no evidence exists to show that any of those in the borderlands did. Structurally, they were under the authority of provincial governors, but were not required to report directly to the governor. In practice they were the most independent institution of Spanish local government. In the nineteenth century, *cabildos* became the training ground for secular political activity and provided the leadership of the revolutionary movements throughout Spanish America. The first *regidores*

were often appointed by a province's governor, but subsequent ones were elected either by the free citizens or by the remaining incumbents. Besides the *alcalde ordinario*, whom the *regidores* selected from among themselves, the *cabildos* also appointed lesser officers such as a sheriff, a variety of clerks, and inspectors of weights and measures. No regularly constituted town meetings were held, but towns occasionally held an emergency meeting of the citizenry, a *cabildo abierto*, which was an open assembly that offered advice to the town's leaders. Since most of the *cabildos* existed for towns that either had or were adjacent to *presidios*, they had a moderating effect on some aspects of royal military power by providing a parallel set of secular institutions for the same community.

Most towns were former pueblo missions grown big. The most numerous and basic institution of Spanish local government, missions were Native villages incorporated into the Spanish Empire through the agency of the church in the form initially of one or a few clergymen. Prior to the eighteenth century, the natives related to the Spanish government primarily through Franciscan missionaries. After a series of political reforms initiated by the Spanish government in 1693, the missions became more integrated into the Spanish secular institutions and less dependent on the friars. Both church and secular officials, however, agreed that the missions needed a participatory system of local government based on Native leadership.

The friars founded the first mission in New Mexico in 1621; from that date onwards they organized dozens of them, first in New Mexico and then in Texas and California. In Florida endemic military tensions and hostilities hindered the establishment of a large number of functioning missions. Typically, each mission elected a *gobernadorcello* (petty governor), an *alguacil* (local sheriff), and several lesser functionaries such as *mayordomos* (road supervisors) or *fiscales* (church wardens). In the seventeenth century, these Native leaders tended to be allies of the friars, often in opposition to royal officials. Partly to weaken the power of the church in local affairs, Spanish governors in the eighteenth century gave the missions more autonomy. After 1693 governors appointed a secular Spanish official, the *alcaldia*, to live in each mission and replace the church officials as the liaison to Spanish imperial government. Local elections of natives to the various positions in the missions were held annually in the first week of January. Suffrage requirements varied, but in general most respectable adult males could vote.

In summary, by the end of the eighteenth century the Spanish Borderlands had created a reasonably uniform system of local government for the three provinces of the Southwest. The military and church played important roles in this system; they functioned in a standard hierarchical manner as part of a chain of command. Judicial and administrative secular districts brought government to rural areas and unorganized settlements; the *justicias* of these districts were part of a royal system, but they enjoyed more independence than the military and clergy did within their spheres. Many of the *justicias* were *creoles* or *peninsulares* of long residence; they derived power and authority as much from their social position as from their office. And town *cabildos* and pueblo missions were urban agents of local government with a substantial degree of independence that was increasing throughout the second half of the eighteenth century. The province of Florida stood outside of this system and had virtually no local institutions save for those of the military. Santa Fe and El Paso, with populations of approximately five thousand residents each at the end of the eighteenth century, were the two largest towns, powerful political entities that had well-developed elites and bureaucracies guarding their local prerogatives. The extensive system of pueblo missions, which integrated European and indigenous institutions into a system of government, was unique in colonial North America. French missions founded by Jesuits and a few villages of "praying Indians" founded by Puritans brought Europeans and natives together in small numbers; but neither created a political system that blended French or English institutions with American ones.

NEW FRANCE

Governed in their early years by a series of private trading companies, the French possessions were placed under the control of the Crown by Louis XIV in 1663. With royal direction New France developed a rationalized, centralized, efficient, and primarily military governmental structure. The French outposts scattered around North America were governed directly by military commanders. At Île Royal the military governor of the fort administered all matters through a *commissaire*, attorney general, and six appointed councillors. The Crown entrusted local government in Louisiana to the commanders of the forts at Natchez, Natchitoches, and Le Chartre; this was also true in the case of the French fort at Detroit. In Acadia the military governor at Port Royal controlled local government in theory, although in practice he allowed the small settlement of farmers to manage many of its own affairs and to settle its disputes informally. No organized institutions of local governance, however, existed either in Acadia or in any of the other military settlements.

Canada, with a larger population that reached seventy thousand in 1763, developed a sophisticated system of local government. Its framework, too, was essentially military, but despite this the citizenry had numerous opportunities for involvement. Two figures stood at the head of New France's government in Canada: the governor-general, who commanded the military, conducted diplomacy, and served as the ceremonial head of state; and the intendant, who had lesser status than the governor-general but more power in the daily governing of the colony. The intendant had responsibility for maintaining law and order, administering justice, managing the colony's finances, and promoting economic development. He also marshaled all of the support needed—pay, food, shelter, medical treatment, fortifications—for the regular army troops stationed in Canada.

Most importantly, the intendant provided the liaison between royal officials in France and Canada's settlers. The intendant resided in Quebec and had deputies in three other major centers—Trois-Rivières, Montreal, and Detroit—to carry out his orders and report to him. In the capital of Quebec, the intendant chaired a body consisting of the governor, the bishop, five appointed councillors, an attorney general, and a recording clerk. In 1703 the king changed the council's name to Supreme Council and increased the number of councillors to twelve. It continued to possess the highest executive, legislative, and judicial authority in the colony. The governor-general had the title of president of the council; the attorney general made recommendation to it; and the councillors and bishop offered opinions. But the intendant presided over the council and made the final decisions after listening to all of the deliberations. Matters great and small came before the Supreme Council, which held weekly meetings on Mondays. Local business was referred up the hierarchical ladder to it for decisions. The Council enacted much legislation in the seventeenth century but in the eighteenth this function diminished as strong intendants governed more through executive actions. The Council became more occupied with civil and criminal legal cases.

Despite the authoritarian nature of the Supreme Council and the theory of royal government under which the council operated, the intendant and other members of the central government attempted to stay in touch with the concerns of the settlers remote from the capital. In the towns and rural areas, merchant councils and parish meetings developed in the early eighteenth century; both had essentially advisory functions. Councils existed for Quebec, Montreal, and Trois-Rivières, and parish meetings were held in the hundred or so rural parishes. Council meetings began in 1708, when the merchants of Quebec asked for and received the right to meet annually and elect two or three of their number to make representations to the intendant about local matters. In 1717 the merchants of Montreal and Trois-Rivières received similar privileges. Not formal assemblies, these merchant councils had no authority to do anything beyond their charge, which was to convey their concerns and wishes to royal authority. Similarly, parish meetings were called occasionally to solicit advice from the local men. And the majority of legislation initiated at all levels originated in requests that the people expressed at these meetings. If parishioners wanted an intendant's *ordonnance* enacted to force people to mend their fences or to maintain roads, they sent word up the chain of command, and the intendant usually responded favorably. Thus, parish meetings and merchant councils made important contributions to local government, but their powers were strictly advisory, falling short of those of town, city, and parish government in the English colonies.

In the rural areas, an officer called the *capitaine de malice* served as the linchpin of the administration and the liaison between the intendant and the parishioners. Each parish had one *capitaine*, a uniquely Canadian institution originally devised for military purposes. Appointed by the governor-general, the *capitaines* were chosen from among the habitants and quickly assumed important civil responsibilities in addition to militia duties. They communicated the orders of the intendant to the local residents and supervised public works such as bridges and roads. In turn the *capitaines* acted as the intendant's eyes and ears and reported anything untoward occurring in the parishes. When parishioners had complaints or requests, the militia captains passed them up the line. All *ordonnances* passed by the intendant were sent to the *capitaine* to be carried out.

Joining the *capitaines* in exercising local power was an elite group of landowners called seigneurs. After taking control of New France in 1663, the Crown created a landholding system of large tracts of land (seigneuries) in order to populate the colonies. The seigneuries received these grants in exchange for promising to promote immigration to their tracts. Seigneurs technically had the right to administer justice through seigneurial courts, but virtually none of them exercised the opportunity. Most emphatically, the seigneurial system was not feudal; seigneurs had no structural independence; approximately half of them were ennobled, and a majority of them held military commissions. By the fall of New France in 1760, almost 250 seigneuries existed in the regions along the Saint Lawrence River. Seigneurs did not assume formal civil responsibilities as the *capitaines* did. In general the seigneurs' importance lay in their role as land settlement agents and in their capacity as the elite of the local social structure.

Local government in New France had a paradoxical quality. In theory it was the most absolutist of any of the systems in colonial North America, and it existed in a society known for its insistence on Catholic religious orthodoxy and piety. Yet despite the hierarchical royal structure and unitary church, in practice local government allowed for a great deal of involvement by the governed. And local government was essentially secular. It proved to be a wise course of action for royal officials to minimize the roles of the church and the seigneurs, both of which could have been rivals to the Crown for power, and to maximize the importance of consulting with the merchants in the towns and the habitants in the rural parishes. No evidence exists to indicate serious dissatisfaction with local government or with government at any level in New France. This was due partly to the fact that until the last few years of the French regime, government at all levels functioned with efficiency and honesty. Order was maintained, justice was administered fairly, commerce and agriculture were nurtured, and military defense was provided successfully. And finally taxation, one of the greatest sources of political alienation, was virtually absent from political discussions at the local level. Import duties and excise taxes paid for the administration of New France; only a small amount of local tax was imposed, and it was always for immediate, visible needs such as defense or poor relief.

NEW NETHERLAND

New Netherland did not develop a mature system of government in its short forty-year history as a colony under the Dutch West India Company. From its founding in 1624 to its conquest by the duke of York in 1664, New Netherland's settlers waged a continuous political struggle to force the West India Company's director-general and council to make concessions to local initiative. The aggrieved citizenry was making gains, but the English conquest aborted this process.

In late medieval Holland, a similar drive for a measure of local self-government presaged the struggle in New Netherland. The two crucial local Dutch offices, that of the *schout* and the *schepen*—roughly equivalent to the English sheriff and justice of the peace, respectively—had traditionally been appointed by local lords and had functioned as part of a manorial court. By the end of the sixteenth century, both rural districts and towns had won the right to elect their *schout* and *schepens*. And these local officers, particularly the *schepens,* gained considerable power in the late sixteenth and early seventeenth centuries. They assumed executive and legislative functions in addition to their judicial one. Within

Holland, a small and relatively urban society, towns and cities developed a heightened sense of independence relative to rural areas.

Intended by the West India Company to be a settlement of traders and soldiers and not a recreation of European society, New Netherland functioned entirely without local institutions from 1624 until 1639. The Dutch colony existed as a combination of a business company and fort, governed by a corporate-military chain of command. The only exceptions to central rule were the patroonships created in the Hudson River valley. The company intended these quasi-feudal manors to attract and control settlers. Any wealthy man who transported and equipped fifty adults to the province was given title to a large tract of land and authority to govern it much in the manner of a medieval lord dispensing justice and order. Five of these patroonships were established on paper; had they become realities, the five would have represented a very real devolution of power from the company to a local elite. Only one, however, Rensselaerswyck, lasted throughout the Dutch period, and even it limped along with no established governmental structure. The other four collapsed for want of settlers, and so the patroonships had little effect on the political life of New Netherland.

In its first fifteen years, the company neither prospered nor attracted settlers. Hence in 1639 it embarked on a series of reforms to stimulate the fur trade and promote immigration. As part of these reforms, in 1640 the director and council promised to allow persons living in villages remote from the main settlement at New Amsterdam some involvement in their own local affairs. Under a directive called the Freedoms and Exemptions of 1640, persons who organized villages or towns could nominate nine men from whom the director and council would appoint one to be a *schout* for the community and two to be *schepens*. The *schout* and *schepens* were authorized only to hear petty civil and minor criminal cases, and all of which remained subject to appeal to the director and council.

From this small beginning, local government grew in New Netherland. New England Puritans organized the first towns under the terms of the Freedoms and Exemptions. In 1641 they settled Newtown, which was followed quickly by Hempstead in 1644 and Flushing and

Gravesend in 1645. Dutch settlers organized their first town, Breukelen, in 1646, and then six more at Harlem, Bushwyck, Wiltwyck, Bergen, New Utrecht, and Staten Island in the next few years. By 1664, the year of the English conquest, fourteen towns had obtained acts of incorporation and were operating under town courts composed of a *schout* and at least two *schepens*.

From the first grant to Newtown onwards, the central and local authorities disputed the limits and scope of each town court's power and jurisdiction. No town willingly accepted the extreme restrictions the director tried to impose on its capacity to act. English towns negotiated more successfully with the company government, probably because their future settlers had the wherewithal to do so in advance. They remained in Connecticut during negotiations and let it be known that they would not move to the proposed new town unless the director made some concessions to their demands. Among other powers, the English towns asked for and received final jurisdiction in civil cases involving less than one hundred guilders and in criminal cases with less than a £2 sterling fine. Several of the English town courts also notified the company that they wanted to assume some legislative power to enact bylaws. The company grudgingly acquiesced, although it maintained the right to disallow any local bylaws. Dutch towns followed the English lead and also secured limited local legislative power for their courts. And all of the towns succeeded in reducing the number of their nominees from which the director and council selected local officers from triple to double the number to be appointed. Finally, from their inception onwards the English towns regularly convened town meetings of the citizens to advise the town court, much as the New England towns met to shape the general policies of their communities. Within a few years of their creation, each Dutch town emulated the English ones and held regular meetings also.

Although the terms *schout* and *schepen* remained in use throughout the Dutch years, and although the formal grants of power to the communities remained restrictive, the towns of New Netherland had the towns of New England in mind as their model of institutional development. Year after year they sought to enlarge their legal and jurisdictional competence at the

expense of the central government. In 1647 Director-General Peter Stuyvesant bowed to pressure from a delegation of town leaders to create a committee of local residents—the Board of Nine, it was called—to advise the company government on local matters. Emphatically not a legislative council but a mere advisory group, according to Stuyvesant, the Board of Nine immediately acted as an independent body to press for more local autonomy. In 1649 the board sent three representatives to Holland to complain of the company's leadership; the petition cited, among other things, the "hairbrained people, such as the company flings thither." The delegation extolled the virtues of New England's town government, where neither "patroons, lords, or princes are known. Only the people." This remonstrance, like most, failed to prompt immediate action; yet over the ensuing decade, New Netherland's towns did slowly begin to evolve toward the New England ones to the north. Stuyvesant and the company talked tough; for example, they threatened Flushing with revocation of its town charter. But they invariably backed down and, as they did, town government became emboldened and strengthened. The structure of the town court, however, remained remarkably simple all during the Dutch years.

Only in New Amsterdam did a more elaborate form of government emerge to replace the town court of *schout* and *schepens*. In response to complaints by wealthy and socially prominent merchants to the States-General in Holland, Stuyvesant granted municipal status to New Amsterdam in 1652 and a Court of Burgomeisters and Schepens was established in 1653. In Holland incorporated cities had a great deal of freedom from interference from the central government; hence New Amsterdam, with its new municipal status, had a rich tradition of independence upon which to draw. And draw upon it the burgomeisters did. Director-General Stuyvesant continued to resist New Amsterdam's attempts to implement its charter to the full extent, and the city had to continue fighting for power point by point and issue by issue.

In sum, aside from the city of New Amsterdam, the emerging institutions of local government in New Netherland bore a similarity to those developing in New England. Upon reflection this should occasion little surprise. Protestant, small, maritime Holland, with a growing tradition of political rights and liberties, resembled England politically and economically more than did any other European country. Nestled alongside the English Puritan colonies to the north, and with a sizable number of English Puritans resident in Long Island's towns, the citizens of New Netherland saw at close hand institutions of local government that were attractive and appropriate to their historical experience. Thus, the embryonic local institutions of New Netherland could easily be integrated into the colony's English future as New York.

THE ENGLISH COLONIES

Historians customarily group the mainland English colonies into four regions: New England, the middle colonies, the Chesapeake, and the lower South. For the purpose of describing local government, these regional categories work well. In their founding years in the seventeenth century, each of the four areas developed a pattern of physical settlement and a social structure that created distinct identities, which in turn led to four distinct systems of local government. New Englanders based their local institutions on the town; southerners in the Chesapeake and lower South based theirs on the parish and county; and middle colonists based theirs on a diverse blend of town, parish, county, and several other institutions.

The most famous form of colonial local government, the New England town meeting, bore but a slight resemblance to English town government. Crucial to its early development was the inescapable fact that the New England town, unlike its counterpart in name, was not a corporation. New England towns were created by the governments of their colonies, which were corporations, and one corporation cannot legally create another. Hence in the first generation of settlement, New England towns did not draw upon the semiautonomous traditions of their English counterparts. Moreover, by an English definition, most New England towns would not be considered towns. In England the term town meant a nucleated settlement—an urban form of residential geography. In New England the term came to mean a combination of village residents and those living on outlying farms, who

sometimes were as much as fifteen or twenty miles (from 24 to 32 kilometers) from the village.

New England's towns, therefore, created a unique type of town-meeting government that drew on three English antecedents: the institutions of the manor and parish, of the borough and town, and of the Puritan Congregational church. Like manors and parishes, the New England towns regulated the lands and economic practices of an agricultural countryside, handled petty criminal matters, and administered poor relief. In the second half of the seventeenth century, however, the towns began to disregard their legally ambiguous status by assuming the semiautonomous outlines of English towns. Although unincorporated, they began to see themselves, in reality, as independent from most of the powers of external agencies. And they grafted onto the traditions of parish, manor, and town the Puritan conception of themselves as a commune. New England Puritans maintained their belief in hierarchy, but they also had a chance to put into institutional form the Puritan ideals of participatory involvement. The New England town meeting should be regarded as a secular version of a congregational meeting. Thus a system of local government developed that was thoroughly English in its origins but found nowhere in England. Called town government, it seemed to confound the very definition of town used by Englishmen.

New England's definition of a town confounded the definition used by Englishmen in the southern colonies of the Chesapeake and lower South as well. Southerners also shaped local government to their own needs, but they hung on to their mother country's definition of a town as a substantial economic and social center. Geography, tobacco cultivation, and religious values combined to make Virginia a rural society. The meandering river systems gave settlers access to the ocean without requiring them to live in villages, and tobacco required too many acres of land to allow a farmer to live in a village and walk out to his holdings each day. Besides, the Anglicans who went to Virginia did not share the communalism of the New England Puritans.

At first Virginia's governor and assembly tried to handle all matters of local governance, but the growth and dispersal of the population across the countryside made this impossible. In 1634 Virginia passed an act creating eight counties to assist the central government in dispensing local justice. Each county was to be governed in local matters by justices of the peace, who were to sit collectively as the county court to carry out major administrative functions and to sit individually as magistrates to hear petty civil and criminal cases. Virginia's county courts and justices were given powers similar to those enjoyed by their counterparts in England. The counties shared local power with the Anglican parish vestry, which traced its Virginia beginnings back to the code of "Laws Divine, Morall and Martial" proclaimed in 1611 by Sir Thomas Dale. Vestries levied taxes for religious support, made presentments to the county courts for petty crimes, and also performed secular functions such as the administration of poor relief and the binding out of apprentices.

The county-parish system became the norm for the southern colonies. Maryland, founded in the 1630s, South and North Carolina in the 1660s, and Georgia in the 1730s had different origins than Virginia's. Yet they shared with Virginia several common circumstances: a dispersed population, an absence of villages and of a communal religious impulse, and an economy based on the export of staples. These similarities inclined them to create institutions of local government more closely approximating the Virginia model rather than that of the New England.

The middle colonies blended the town system of New England with the county-parish system of the South and adapted both to local circumstances. In addition some vestiges of Dutch rule in New York, the influence of the Quakers in Pennsylvania, the power of their proprietors, the presence of genuine urban centers, and the force of geography combined to give the principal middle colonies of New York and Pennsylvania unique systems of local institutions differing both from each other's and from those of the regions to the north and south. The two smaller middle colonies, New Jersey and Delaware, had more diverse but less dramatic origins. Neither New Jersey, cobbled together out of disparate groups of migrants from New England, New York, Pennsylvania, England, and New Sweden, nor Delaware, settled as a division of Pennsylvania, developed a clear identity as a separate colony until the early eighteenth century.

By the end of the seventeenth century, the basic institutions characterizing each region's and most of the colonies' local governments were in place. With but a few exceptions, little basic change in institutional arrangements took place after 1700; rather, the eighteenth century witnessed an elaboration and development of seventeenth-century models. The institutions that had emerged by 1700 were more modern than medieval and reflected both the opportunity to experiment and the necessity to adapt to new conditions. The offices, terminology, and practices of local government in 1700 would not seem strange—in fact most would sound familiar—to today's local politicians, because most of the same institutions exist in parts of the present United States.

New England

The town meeting lay at the heart of New England local government. Every town in the region—with no exception and including urban centers such as Boston, Newport, and New Haven—had town-meeting government throughout the colonial period. Not until after independence did any town successfully seek incorporation as a city and abandon the town meeting in favor of municipal government. Thus, towns with populations ranging from over fifteen thousand in Boston to forty persons in the northern White Mountains of New Hampshire assembled regularly in meetings of the whole to order their local affairs.

How often towns met, who could attend and vote at these meetings, and who did attend and vote are matters of debate among historians, but many secure generalizations may be made. Massachusetts, Connecticut, New Hampshire, and Rhode Island had elaborate suffrage laws that were frequently amended, but all were based on the same principle; white, respectable, adult, male property owners could vote and serve in office; all others could not. Although this restrictive definition of a freeman seems shocking to twentieth-century sensibilities, the New England town meetings had one of the highest rates of participatory political involvement anywhere in the eighteenth-century Western world. Most adult white males could attend, vote, and be officers if they wished.

Every town held at least one meeting per year—the annual election meeting to vote for officers, each of whom served a one-year term. Held in the late winter or early spring before planting time, election meetings usually drew a large percentage of the freemen. New towns and small towns tended to hold many meetings, often as many as twelve a year, or one per month, but as towns grew older and more populous, they tended to hold fewer meetings between the annual election gatherings and instead turned the ongoing decision making over to the elected officers. All town meetings, however, retained the latent power to assert themselves on any matter; often a contentious issue would suddenly produce a flurry of meetings in a town that had previously been meeting only once or twice a year.

Towns held meetings in the most convenient places available, often a centrally located church meetinghouse but occasionally in taverns, private homes, or outdoors. Law required that they be well advertised in advance, and by custom meetings ended an hour before dusk in order to allow rural freemen time to get home before dark. The conduct of the meeting varied from colony to colony and from town to town, but some general principles characterized most of them. An elected chairman, called a moderator, presided over each meeting; open discussion was permitted on any issue being addressed; and voting usually took place orally but occasionally, upon request, was by written ballot. Meetings relied heavily upon reports from elected officers and usually elected an ad hoc committee to deal with emergencies or special problems. Most meetings strived to avoid settling controversial issues by a majority vote that left a sizable minority opposed to the decision; instead they preferred to work for a compromise that would produce consensus. The ideal meeting unified the community as well as governed the town.

In their early years, most towns elected a relatively small slate of officers: three or five selectmen (sometimes called townsmen) who functioned as the chief executives and took on many of the trappings of village elders; from one to five constables, who maintained the local peace, served legal writs, and arrested lawbreakers; a town clerk who kept minutes of meetings, recorded deeds, and registered vital statistics; two or three taxing officials; from two to four surveyors of highways, who supervised the building and maintenance of roads; and from four to six fence viewers, who ensured that fences be-

tween properties were accurately placed and effective. Aside from the selectmen, who enjoyed some discretionary authority, the officers functioned more like modern bureaucrats than political leaders. All of them, including the selectmen, were subject to the watchful eye and authority of the town meeting, and all of them faced yearly elections. Many of the jobs were onerous, and men accepted them as much or more from a sense of community duty than from personal ambition.

As a town matured, the number of offices and officers increased in proportion to its population and physical size. Most New England towns were at least fifty square miles (about 130 square kilometers), many were more than one hundred square miles (260 square kilometers) and a few approached or exceeded two hundred square miles (520 square kilometers). As population dispersed from the village center, new officers had to be elected to provide government services in distant areas. Most towns with more than two thousand people elected seven selectmen and correspondingly increased the number of the other officers. Not unusually, towns elected as many as thirty surveyors of highways, twenty fenceviewers, and ten constables. Also, new offices were being created, sometimes by mandate of provincial law or by local bylaw. The financial functions of local officers often were separated into several specialized offices such as assessors to list assets, ratemakers to calculate the need levies, and treasurers to pay bills on the towns' behalf. Constables were assisted in the maintenance of morality by lesser officers called tithingmen in Massachusetts and grand jurymen in Connecticut. New economic needs might be met by the creation of market officers. The crucial point to note in all of this elaboration is that virtually all of the local bureaucracy was elected by the town meeting. No matter how menial or trivial the job, the meeting wanted the holder to be accountable to it every year. Thus, towns often elected men "to sweep the meetinghouse," "keep the keys to the door," or "dig the graves." As New England local government grew, it continued and even enhanced its participatory nature.

Among Massachusetts, Connecticut, and New Hampshire, the three mainstream Puritan colonies, and even among the towns of maverick

Rhode Island, remarkably few basic differences existed in town-meeting government in the eighteenth century. Many of the distinctions that can be drawn derived from town size, age, and location. Connecticut's towns tended to be larger and more populous than those of the rest of the region; New Hampshire had a large number of small, lightly populated new towns; Massachusetts had a diverse blend of old, large, established centers, seafaring entrepôts, and frontier rural communities; and almost all of Rhode Island's towns were located on salt water and needed governments responsive to the needs of trade. Yet these variables produced but wrinkles on a standard form. Rhode Island called its executives councilmen instead of selectmen; allowed its towns more freedom from provincial interference than did its neighboring colonies; and had more difficulty collecting taxes. But in the main, the differences among town meetings in the four colonies were minimal.

New England's colonies had other institutions of local governance in addition to the town meetings. Justices of the peace, appointed by the colony government, served as local magistrates in all four colonies. In Connecticut and Rhode Island, the appointments were made by the governor, council, and assembly acting in concert; in Massachusetts and New Hampshire, they were appointed by the governor sitting with his council. In Massachusetts, Connecticut, and Rhode Island, the justices met collectively as a county court but performed primarily judicial duties, not administrative ones. New Hampshire was not divided into counties until 1769, on the eve of the revolution, and its county court system was in its infancy at independence.

Probably the greatest distinction among the four colonies derived from the fact that Massachusetts, Connecticut, and New Hampshire had established churches and Rhode Island did not. Both Massachusetts and Connecticut used the Congregational parish as a form of neighborhood government to help administer poor relief and education and, at times, to apportion town offices. Thus, the parish functioned as a subdivision of the town. In New Hampshire this was true in the early years of the eighteenth century, when each town was allowed to choose a church to support with tax money; but as royal officials increased their support of the Anglican church,

the parish became much less important as a form of government. In Rhode Island, which had no publicly supported churches, the parish had a purely private, religious function. But even in Connecticut, the most staunchly Puritan colony, time weakened the parish as a unit of government. By the revolution, Connecticut had been forced to concede legitimacy to Baptists, Anglicans, Separatists, and Quakers; with their incorporation as legal religious societies, the parish diminished as an organ of government. Thus time, growth, and economic forces all worked to lessen those small differences in local institutions that did exist among the New England colonies.

The South

Local government in the southern colonies was neither as elective nor as uniform as New England's. Appointed officials played more of a role than they did in New England, and the eclectic origins of the southern colonies led to a more diverse system of governance. Nevertheless, several common institutions and practices bound the region together, and they afforded most prosperous and some average residents opportunity for involvement.

Virginia and Maryland. The upper South —Virginia and Maryland—had the most well-defined system of local government and the one most familiar to historians. At its heart lay the concept of the magistracy. Maryland's governor appointed at least six justices of the peace per county; Virginia's appointed at least eight per county. Individually the justices sat as local magistrates in their neighborhoods and collectively as the county court. In Virginia the governor filled vacancies from a list of men nominated by the sitting justices. In Maryland the governor selected justices without formal nominations but usually consulted members of the provincial council and relied heavily on their knowledge of local personnel. Justices sitting as individual magistrates had a restricted jurisdiction that allowed them to decide only minor criminal and civil matters. Nevertheless, they were the first and most familiar agents of government to be encountered by the citizenry. The homes of justices invariably assumed the role of neighborhood courthouse.

When sitting collectively as the county court, the justices had the dominant share of local executive and judicial power. They also took on a quasi-legislative role by issuing regulatory orders that had the force of bylaws. Among its most important functions, the county court served as an appeals court for decisions made by individual justices; expressed original jurisdiction over cases involving serious punishments or large fines; administered all cases of probate and guardianship for minor orphans; licensed taverns; registered deeds; supervised elections; adjudicated conflicts between masters and servants; prepared grand lists of property and of tithables for the local poll tax; and oversaw the laying out of highways. In short, not much lay outside the county court's purview.

To aid them in performing all of these functions, the justices had a staff of subordinate officers who were also appointed by the governor but almost always upon nomination from the justices themselves. The most important of these, the sheriff, bore the brunt of the responsibility for carrying out the court's orders and making certain that the court's processes worked smoothly. The sheriff took bail, served writs, impaneled juries, conducted elections, and acted at the court's behest in dozens of matters. Most counties had but one sheriff, who occasionally had a deputy or two. The county court, however, directly appointed another local law enforcement officer, the constable; most counties had several of them, sometimes as many as ten, to assist the sheriff or to carry out the orders of individual justices. The governor also appointed a coroner for each county to conduct investigations into all cases of untimely death; a clerk to maintain records; and from five to twenty-five highway overseers to supervise road construction and maintenance.

Not surprisingly, given all of the functions of the court and the number of personnel involved, court days were hubbubs of activity that took on the flavor of a rural fair. Several hundred people usually attended the court over the course of a long day—the justices in their wigs and waistcoats, gentlemen in their finery discussing politics, small planters registering new deeds or serving on juries, vendors hawking food and drink, slaves attending the needs of their owners, and criminals and litigants awaiting judgment—and each group formed its own social circle. Despite a surface gaiety, much was at stake on court days: a hanging might take place, a great planter might be declared bankrupt, or a political battle might be fought over taxes. Positioned at a governmental stratum between the rarified deliberation of the colonial legislature and the simplicity of the justice of the peace's parlor, the county courthouse was the prism that brought law, government, and people together amidst much noise and dust to make the countryside run smoothly, honestly, and safely.

Located structurally below the county court another local governing body, the Anglican church parish vestry, exercised important power in some limited areas. Created in Virginia in 1611 but in Maryland not until 1692, after the Anglican church had been established, the parish vestry administered its affairs through twelve vestrymen in Virginia and eight in Maryland. Each vestry designated two of its members to serve as churchwardens, who acted as the parish executives. In Virginia vestrymen served at pleasure for undefined terms, and when one retired or died, the remaining members chose his successor. Thus, Virginia's vestries were self-perpetuating local oligarchies, as were the county courts. In Maryland the freeholders of the parish elected two of the eight members at an annual election. Thus, Maryland's vestries were the most open and the only directly elected institutions of local government in the Chesapeake.

Many of the functions of the vestry were clearly religious in nature, but because no Anglican bishop resided in the colonies, the vestries had much more opportunity to direct parish affairs than their English counterparts had. Nominally subject to the bishop of London, in reality the Anglican parishes in the South were nearly as autonomous as those of the Congregational church in New England. And because the Anglican church was legally established, no clear lines separated church and state; hence, the parish performed secular duties and functioned as a civil organ of local government. In Virginia the parish vestry was older and the Anglican church was rooted more deeply in the social bedrock than it was in Maryland. This created a political milieu that allowed Virginia's vestries to be much more active and powerful than Maryland's. In both colonies, however, the vestries had taxing power to raise money for a variety of church-state purposes. Among the most important of these was poor relief and welfare, most of which was also administered by the parish vestry, although it often worked in close cooperation with the county court. Invariably, several of the vestrymen were also justices of the peace. Most counties had two or three parishes, and vestrymen regularly attended the county court to keep the justices aware of the pulse of each neighborhood.

South Carolina. In the third major southern colony, South Carolina, parish government played a greater role than it did in the Chesapeake due to the fact that, except for a brief and unsuccessful attempt in the 1720s, the colony did not create a system of counties. As in the Chesapeake, the colony's governor appointed justices of the peace who sat as local magistrates; but the powers of individual justices in South Carolina were even more limited than those of their counterparts in Virginia and Maryland. In the early eighteenth century, they were given the power to act in cases of debt involving up to £20 of South Carolina currency, a relatively slight sum. South Carolina's justices also imposed small fines for petty criminal acts such as trespass or marketplace violations; they issued licenses to tavern keepers and peddlers; and they "warned" vagrants out of a parish. Aside from these minor functions, they had little authority over white colonists. But they exercised great power over blacks; two justices had the authority to sit with any three freemen and try blacks in all crimes whatsoever, including capital ones. In sum, the local magistrates could not fine a white person more than a sum equal to approximately a week's wages for a laborer, but they literally had powers of life and death over blacks.

In the absence of county courts and a magistracy strong in all areas, power devolved upon South Carolina's parish vestries that, by colony law, each had seven members. The freemen of each parish elected vestrymen to one-year terms. A provincial law of 1706 established the vestries and outlined their functions; laws in 1712 expanded the vestry's powers. Anglican parishes grew in number from the first ten created in 1706 to twenty-three in 1770. The vestries administered all poor relief, exercised a police and judicial power nearly equal to that of the county courts of the Chesapeake, built and maintained parish schools, and were the primary local agency charged with enforcing morality. Thus, South Carolina's parishes combined many of the functions of parish and county in Virginia and Maryland.

In addition South Carolina had another instrument of local governance that was unique in the South: the commission. The assembly appointed several for each parish. The road commission was the most important of these; others included those to regulate markets, to run workhouses, to organize military defense, to provide fire protection. The commissions gave the central authorities a direct role in the administration of many aspects of local government. Undoubtedly, this happened because Charleston played such a dominant role in the colony's political life. As a result South Carolina in general vested less autonomy in its local institutions than did the Chesapeake colonies in theirs.

North Carolina and Georgia. North Carolina and Georgia developed even weaker systems of local government. In some ways these two colonies had histories of striking contrast. North Carolina, settled in the 1660s as part of the Carolina proprietary, was an isolated outpost of unruly stragglers and dissenters wedged between Virginia and South Carolina. It existed for nearly thirty years with a minimum of government—a no-man's-land nearly out of touch with the regular channels of duly constituted authority. Georgia, founded in 1732 as part of a philanthropic impulse to uplift the poor, suffered from the opposite—too much control and too much government imposed by outside authorities. Yet both colonies had in common a weak system of local institutions with virtually no elective component.

Called Albermarle County for its first twenty-six years under the Carolina proprietors, North Carolina became formally detached from the Charleston settlement in 1689, had its first governor as a separate colony appointed in 1712, and became a royal colony in 1729 when the Crown purchased the proprietors' interests. At first Albermarle was technically one large county divided into precincts, but after 1739, the precincts each became counties. Their local governments, originally called precinct courts, then became known as county courts. Presided over by justices of the peace appointed by the proprietors or their designated governors, these courts had civil and criminal jurisdiction over small cases and administrative duties in areas such as roads, bridges, and local taxes in much the same manner as the county courts of the Chesapeake. The justices, in turn, appointed the other county court officers, the leading one of which was called the provost marshall until 1739, when the assembly changed the title to sheriff. The North Carolina sheriff became the most powerful one in the southern colonies and increasingly by mid eighteenth century functioned as a county executive.

Over two-thirds of the members of colonial North Carolina's assembly were justices of the peace; this overlap resulted in an extraordinary amount of centralization. To a lesser degree a similar situation existed in the Chesapeake, but unlike the upper South, North Carolina had weak parish vestries and no elected vestrymen for most of its colonial history. Parish vestries were created in 1703 and given civil functions in welfare, poor relief, and education in 1715. But the Anglican church was established in name only, and the Anglican parish vestries had little legitimacy in the eyes of the religious dissenters who constituted the majority of the population. Moreover, until 1751 all vestrymen were appointed by the assembly. After that they were elected, but only by the Anglican church communicants of the parish. The western half of North Carolina, which had very few Anglicans, treated local officials with contempt. The "sheriff and his bums," one disgruntled westerner called the county court and vestry officials who made up the local elite. A series of popular uprisings in pre-revolutionary North Carolina, known as the Regulator movement, nearly plunged the colony into civil war. Demands for reform in local government lay at the center of this rebellion.

Georgia, too, had a system of appointed local government. In 1733, the year Georgia was settled, its trustees in London created a town court for Savannah; between then and 1752, when the Crown took over the colony, the trustees created four more for Frederica, Augusta, Darien, and Medway River. Town courts had consta-

bles, tithingmen, and conservators of the peace, all appointed by the trustees. Constables and tithingmen impaneled juries, issued indictments for crimes, and acted as moral watchdogs. The conservators of the peace sat as magistrates. All of the officials reported directly to the trustees in London. From the first the colonists objected to what they regarded as arbitrary treatment. In response the trustees created two counties in 1741, each of which had a president and four assistants sitting as a court to hear appeals from the town courts. All of the county officials, however, were also appointed by the trustees.

In 1752 Georgia became a royal colony, but local institutions gained little legitimacy in the eyes of the settlers. Royal officials established the Anglican church and created eight parishes in 1758 and four more in 1765. Each parish elected two churchwardens and from five to ten vestrymen annually. On the surface this gave Georgians a greater level of participation than before. But the majority of Georgians who were not members of the Anglican church resented lodging any civil authority in its vestries; and so the vestries had little power and few duties. Thus on the eve of the revolution, Georgia, like North Carolina, had a system of local government with names and institutions resembling those of the upper South. Beneath the surface similarities, however, both colonies had a weaker system of local institutions, more dependent on provincial authorities and less rooted in the local social structure than were those of Virginia and Maryland.

The Middle Colonies
By the time of the English conquest in 1664, New Netherland's inhabitants had wrested significant concessions to local rule from the reluctant Dutch West India Company. A patchwork of several different forms of local government greeted the duke of York's representations. Added to these Dutch institutions was a system of town-meeting government on Long Island that had been created by settlers from Connecticut.

New York. The English proprietor tried, as the Dutch had, to minimize the powers of local authorities. The duke was no more successful, but the changes he attempted to impose further increased the colony's institutional heterogeneity.

In 1683 New York's newly appointed governor, Thomas Dongan, convened a provincial assembly that worked with him to reform all levels of government. Several of the acts passed by this assembly proved crucial for the development of local government. Working harmoniously together—a rarity in colonial government and especially rare in New York—the governor and assembly created ten counties, giving New York a territorial structure similar to England's; erased several vestiges of Dutch local institutions in Albany and Ulster County; created a municipal government for New York City staffed by both locally elected and provincially appointed officers; and created courts of oyer and terminer for each county to act on indictments above those for petty crimes.

With the Glorious Revolution of 1688, the assembly was dissolved and the Dongan years came to an end, to be replaced by three years of turmoil known as Leisler's Rebellion. After 1691 New York enjoyed a period of relative tranquillity, and the process of government reform was renewed. The provincial assembly established in 1691 by William and Mary laid the basis for the local institutions that were to endure throughout the colonial period. The county became the key unit of local government, but manor, town, and municipal institutions that already existed continued to function anomalously within county government. At the end of the colonial period, nearly half of the population of New York lived under either town or municipal governments. Manors eventually metamorphosed into towns, and new municipal institutions were created for several small but nucleated settlements.

New York's county government differed from that of the South. The sheriff emerged as the county's most formidable officer and enjoyed much more power than did southern sheriffs with the exception of North Carolina's, who was a similarly powerful figure. New York's sheriffs supervised all elections, carried out all the decisions of the county courts, exercised the police power, and collected all the revenues due royal government. Boards of supervisors handled administrative matters in New York's counties; all lesser officers reported to these supervisors rather than to the judges of the county court. County courts in New York, as in New England, functioned primarily as courts of trial, and their judges mainly exercised judicial duties. The governors appointed sheriffs and judges of the county courts; the freemen elected the boards of supervisors annually in a manner and place determined by the sheriff. The governor also appointed justices of the peace to act at a level beneath that of the county court to hear cases of debt, trespass, and civil disputes involving small sums or fines.

Additionally, the governor appointed some functionaries for each county: a clerk, a coroner, and occasional officers to answer specific local needs. All of these reported to the elected board of supervisors. A variety of other county officers were named by other bodies. The assembly appointed highway commissioners to build and maintain roads and selected excise tax collectors from among individuals who bid for the job; boards of supervisors, in consultation with the county court judges, appointed "loan officers" to enforce credit and market regulations. The county also served as an election district for the provincial government. Usually, provincial assemblymen also served as judges of the county court or justices of the peace.

The board of supervisors had no counterparts in English local government. The assembly subdivided each county into precincts based on the county's physical size and population; each precinct elected one supervisor. Thus, the number of supervisors, the crucial elective component of county government, varied by county. At the end of the colonial period, some counties had as many as ten precincts and hence had ten supervisors. All had a minimum of three.

Town and municipal institutions, which existed in an organizational layer beneath county government, underwent fewer changes in the post-1691 era. Towns, most of which were located on Long Island or in Westchester County, combined a few elements of town-meeting government from Massachusetts and Connecticut with some of the more traditional institutions of the English towns. The governor appointed magistrates for the towns, but the local freemen annually elected eight overseers and one constable who were collectively called the town court. It, in turn, appointed lesser officers to carry out local duties. Occasionally, by warrant of the town court the freemen gathered in a town meeting to advise the town officers on contentious issues.

Municipal government in New York City, Albany, Schenectady, and Westchester was patterned after city government in England. New York City and Albany in particular took on the structural outlines of English provincial cities. Divided into wards, each of which elected two aldermen, two assistants, and a constable, New York City and Albany became open corporations in 1731, which meant that rights of freemanship were extended to most respectable residents with a minimum amount of property. The governor appointed the mayor of each of the cities but usually did so upon the aldermen's suggestion. Together the mayor and elected aldermen functioned as the city court or council, which combined the executive functions of the county board of supervisors with the judicial functions of the county court.

Pennsylvania. By way of contrast, Pennsylvania had a much more rationalized system of local government that blended town and county. Founded by Quakers under the leadership of William Penn, Pennsylvania was one of the better-planned colonies and was settled amidst relatively orderly circumstances. Local institutions of government reflected this stability; they, too, along with the colony government, were prescribed in the colony's constitution, authored by Penn.

Pennsylvania had four units of local government: the county, township, borough, and city. The county was by far the most important of these; both the township and the borough were subdivisions of it. Only the city of Philadelphia had any claim to local autonomy outside the bounds of county government. At the end of the colonial period, eleven counties existed in Pennsylvania; their government was based upon the Charter of Privileges of 1701, which superseded Penn's Frame of Government of 1682, and upon various amendments to the charter adopted by the provincial government between 1701 and 1776.

In 1711 the provincial assembly created the county's key executive positions, those of county commissioner, and appointed commissioners at irregular intervals until 1722, when it made the office elective and set the number at three per county. Elected for three-year terms, commissioners could not stand for reelection. Terms were staggered so that each year one new commissioner joined the two incumbents. The freemen of each county also elected six assessors annually for one-year terms. Assessors were free to run for reelection. Commissioners had the overall executive power for the county; assessors were limited to estimating county expenses and levying and collecting the taxes to defray them.

As were their counterparts in Virginia, Maryland, and New York, Pennsylvania's counties were served by a sheriff and coroner. In Pennsylvania, however, they were selected by a relatively democratic combination of election and appointment. The freemen annually elected two men as nominees to each position, and the governor appointed one of the two to office. From 1730 sheriffs could only serve three one-year terms consecutively; coroners had no limit. The sheriff's job included both executive and judicial matters. He selected jurors for panels, made arrests, served summonses, executed the decisions of the commissioners and justices of the county court, and organized all elections. The coroner investigated and reported upon all unnatural deaths and served as the understudy for the sheriff, performing his duties in the sheriff's absence or incapacity.

Pennsylvania had the most orderly and rationalized county judicial system of any of the colonies. The assembly created three courts for each county in 1707: the Court of Common Pleas, the Orphan's Court, and the Court of Quarter Sessions. The same justices of the peace sat on all three. Appointed by the governor, the justices served as long as the governor stayed in office. New governors issued new appointments, although customarily they reappointed most justices.

A collection of other appointees rounded out county government. For each county the governor appointed a recorder of deeds, a register of wills, and a sealer of weights and measures. None of these were nominated; the governor had the freedom to select whom he wished. County surveyors were chosen by the provincial surveyor-general. The commissioners of each county appointed a county treasurer and a clerk for their own meetings. The assembly appointed one county officer, the collector of excise taxes, who served a one-year term.

Pennsylvania's counties were divided into townships, each of which had its own set of officers. These, too, were a combination of elected and appointed officials. The most important officer, the constable, corresponded at the township level to the sheriff at the county level. Each spring, the freemen of a township nominated two men, one of whom would be named the constable by the county's Court of Quarter Sessions. Townships directly elected an assessor, who joined the constable in gathering lists of assets for county and township tax purposes. Local freemen also chose election inspectors, a supervisor of the highways, and a poundkeeper. The County Court of Quarter Sessions appointed overseers of the poor, usually two or three in number, for each township. Townships did not hold meetings—local officials answered to the freemen only at the polls.

The three boroughs—Chester, Bristol, and Lancaster—had a system similar to, but more independent than, that of the townships. The boroughs had larger and more urbane village centers than did the townships and existed in limbo somewhere between townships, which were creatures of county government, and the city of Philadelphia, which had the autonomy of an English municipal corporation. In addition to a constable, assessors, and the entire range of elected and appointed township officials, boroughs elected from two to four burgesses, who acted as city executives. The boroughs had much greater powers of taxation than did the townships and could levy rates for many functions that in the townships would have had to be referred to the Court of Quarter Sessions.

Philadelphia had the most unique political structure of any city in the English colonies. From the first days of Pennsylvania's settlement, Philadelphia had the wealth, physical attributes, complex social groupings, and economic power of a major urban center. Philadelphians did not want to exist at the mercy of either the proprietor or their fellow Pennsylvanians in the colonial assembly. The city sought and obtained a special charter that gave it self-government in a manner reminiscent of a few closed and nearly autonomous medieval city-states. The special act of incorporation issued by William Penn in 1701

created the "Mayor and Commonality of Philadelphia." Penn named a common council for Philadelphia; the council chose aldermen from among its own ranks. The common council constituted the corporate body, with vacancies to be filled by the remaining members. Thus, Philadelphia was a closed corporation, a self-perpetuating elite political body limited only by a need to adhere to provincial statutes and English common law.

At first this extraordinary power did not offend Philadelphia's residents, most of whom were deprived of any significant role in local affairs. Some resentment among excluded groups developed, however, and the eighteenth century witnessed an erosion of Philadelphia's autonomy. Gradually, the common council lost power to various administrative agencies and voluntary efforts and metamorphosed into a venerable chamber of commerce. At the end of the colonial period in 1776, the Philadelphia corporation, a vestige of its original powerful self, was voided by the new state. Befitting the political culture of a republican society, a modern, open city corporation replaced the medieval, closed one.

Delaware. Probably no part of English America evolved under more unusual circumstances than did Delaware, which was consecutively part of New Sweden, New Netherland, and New York before being incorporated into William Penn's grant in 1682, although it was also claimed by Maryland's proprietors. Incorporated into the short-lived Dominion of New England, Delaware was returned to the Penn proprietary in 1691 and known afterwards as the lower three counties. For most of the eighteenth century, the lower counties occupied an ambiguous political position, set aside from the rest of Pennsylvania by geography, custom, and institutional arrangements but legally part of the Penn proprietary. The status of having some but not all of the attributes of a separate colony had an unusual and seemingly paradoxical effect on Delaware's mature colonial history. It had more autonomy than any of the other proprietary or royal colonies, rivaling the two charter colonies of Connecticut and Rhode Island in political freedom. This situation profoundly affected its system of local government.

New Sweden existed primarily as a military society with little room for citizen involvement in decision making. The Dutch appointed *schepens* (magistrates), and after briefly reconquering the area in 1673 they created three local courts, each with *schepens* and a *schout* (sheriff). After the English retook the area, New York's governor Edmund Andros created three counties—New Castle, Kent, and Sussex—based on the 1673 Dutch divisions. The Penn family maintained these county divisions, which became the backbone of Delaware's local government.

As in most colonies, the governor (the Penn family appointee for Pennsylvania) appointed the justices of the peace for the counties. Probably in no other colony, however, did the justices have as much power, both sitting as individual magistrates and as the collective county court, as they did in Delaware. The Penn family and Pennsylvania's governors tended to leave the lower counties alone in day-to-day matters. A unicameral assembly existed for the area, but in reality almost all authority devolved upon the county and its justices. The justices met as Levy Court to raise taxes, as Court of Common Pleas to hear civil cases, as Court of General Sessions to hear criminal cases, and as Orphan's Court to administer guardianships. A sheriff, coroner, assessor, and lesser officers were appointed for each county by Pennsylvania's governor from among a list of nominees elected by the freemen. In practice the governors invariably appointed the top vote getters. With little interference from above and with virtually no rivals from below, the justices exercised most of the power in eighteenth-century Delaware. Only in the city Wilmington, incorporated as a borough in 1739, were there other well-developed local institutions. The second smallest of the colonies at independence with about thirty-seven thousand residents, Delaware was a small-scale society governed by responsive local institutions throughout all of its English colonial history.

New Jersey. New Jersey's origins and early history were as diverse and complex as Delaware's. And its local institutions in the eighteenth century grew to be nearly as independent as those of Pennsylvania's three lower counties. Populated by Dutch from New Netherland; Swedes and Finns who moved north after New Sweden failed; Congregational Puritans from the New Haven colony and Long Island; Presbyterian Puritans from Scotland; and English and German Quakers, the area went through a bewildering series of political configurations before East and West Jersey were pulled together into one royal colony in 1701.

The first local government was Dutch in origin and consisted of a *schout* and *schepens* (sheriff and magistrates) for the town of Bergen. Town meeting government developed in the period 1667 to 1675 in the nine Puritan towns of East Jersey, and in the 1690s township government developed in West Jersey's Quaker communities. Both Puritan and Quaker towns and townships elected their magistrates and other officers. West Jersey created a county court system in 1686, and East Jersey did the same with the creation of four counties in 1693. During the second half of the seventeenth century, as diverse ethnicities, religions, and politicians scraped against each other in a struggle for place and power, the residents of the future colony of New Jersey developed a strong identity with and loyalty to local institutions. Royalization did not diminish this identity and loyalty.

In the eighteenth century, the county-township system that had developed in New Jersey's private years remained in place and was extended to all areas of the colony. New Jersey's assembly smoothed off some of the rough edges of local institutions, and the system that emerged by the second quarter of the century was remarkably consistent and simple considering the colony's history, social structure, and location. Justices of the peace appointed by the governor sat both individually as local magistrates and collectively as a county court. Administratively, counties were governed by a board of supervisors consisting of two supervisors elected from each township and the justices of the peace. Usually the boards had more elected supervisors than appointed justices. The freemen of each township annually chose two selectmen, who in turn appointed the community's other three major officers: a clerk, assessor, and tax collector. The selectmen also appointed an array of local bureaucrats: overseers of the poor, highway supervisors, and fence viewers. The county board of supervisors was not served by a large number of lesser officers. It had a clerk and frequently appointed special committees to deal with emergent problems, but in general the county supervisors worked through the township officers. In many ways New Jersey resembled New England as much as it did New York or Pennsylvania: its local government was indeed local, and much of it was elected.

OVERALL PATTERNS, PROCESSES, AND PERSPECTIVES

The English Colonies

Both professional and amateur historians often write about colonial America on a colony-by-colony basis. Each colony's unique origins and independent development encourage historians to treat it as a nation-state. The resultant historical literature emphasizes the differences among the various parts of colonial America, and indeed diversity was the historical reality. But amidst this heterogeneity some similar institutions and common practices are discernible in the local government of the thirteen colonies.

Institutional Structure. As they were in England, the justices of the peace were ubiquitous figures from northern New Hampshire to southern Georgia. All of them were appointed by provincial authorities and had a legal competence restricted to relatively minor matters. Yet the solitary magistrate assumed much of the responsibility for maintaining peace, order, civility, and morality at the local level. Invariably local justices were tied to many other agencies of local and provincial government, either directly through institutional connections or indirectly through multiple officeholding. In some regions the justices had lesser roles than in others—New England's magistrates had less administrative authority than the South's, for example—but in all colonies their authority went beyond a narrow reading of their commissions. The local men of most consequence, the justices carried with them the authority of patriarch, village elder, or rural squire.

Nearly as ubiquitous as the magistrate's court, church parishes and county government were a part of all but a few systems of local government. Both the parish and the county

played important roles in the English countryside. Colonial parishes and county government, however, diverged substantially from their English institutional ancestors. The two parishes of most consequence were the Congregational in New England and the Anglican elsewhere; both had more autonomy than Anglican parishes in England, as did the Quaker meeting, which functioned in Pennsylvania as an unofficial form of parish government. That was because the English parishes were more integrated into an organized hierarchy. County government, on the other hand, did not have more autonomy in the colonies than in England. Early modern Englishmen strongly identified with their home counties, and attempts by the Tudor and Stuart monarchs to reduce the power of counties were generally unsuccessful. Colonial county government developed unevenly and with various eccentricities. New England reduced the county's power relative to that of England's counties, while the South increased it. Several county officers, such as the sheriff in North Carolina, enjoyed unusual power and prominence and others, such as the county supervisors in New York or commissioners in Pennsylvania, were unique to the New World.

The American colonies departed most from English antecedents and differed most among themselves in their institutions of town government. In the six colonies north of Pennsylvania—New Jersey, New York, Connecticut, Rhode Island, Massachusetts, and New Hampshire—town (or township) institutions were far more important than they were in England and bore little resemblance to English town government. In the six colonies south of Pennsylvania—Delaware, Maryland, Virginia, North Carolina, South Carolina, and Georgia—towns were less important than in England and in fact were virtually nonexistent. Pennsylvania's boroughs were probably the only type of town government that would be readily recognizable to an eighteenth-century Englishman. A few municipal governments scattered across the middle colonies, such as those of Albany, New York City, Philadelphia, and Wilmington, also resembled English institutions; but by and large, local government in the English New World was most original in the way half of the colonies expanded village institutions and the other half eliminated them.

Functions, Philosophy, and Personnel. In the main, local government functioned to promote peace, order, and good will; to prevent crime; to provide and maintain what would today be called an economic infrastructure of roads, bridges, ferries, fences, and harbors; to monitor and regulate necessary economic institutions such as taverns, markets, and fairs; to punish minor crimes and adjudicate petty civil disputes; to provide poor relief for widows, orphans, the elderly, and the infirm; and to enforce codes of conduct and morality. These functions, of course, encompassed most areas of life, and colonial local government was, indeed, encompassing. Over three-fourths of all tax revenues went to governmental units at or beneath the county level.

Specialization by function obviously existed at the local level—men were elected or appointed to prescribed positions—but in general, the idea of separating powers into executive, legislative, and judicial branches was not a well-developed concept. In particular, the executive and judicial functions intertwined. County courts furnished the best examples of this, but individual justices, selectmen, vestrymen, and even lesser officers such as fence viewers issued orders in an executive capacity and adjudicated disputes in a judicial capacity. And almost all local boards of officers legislated orders in the manner of ordinances or bylaws. A practical rather than a theoretical matter, local government existed to bring order to communities of people who knew each other.

This philosophy of practicality and unity of power helped integrate the tangle of local institutions into a coherent whole. So, too, did patterns of leadership and officeholding. All of the colonies had a local elite that in most cases personally knew the nearby citizenry. This elite was based on values embedded in the immediate community: it was open and relatively accessible compared to local elites in England, and the gap between local leaders and the generality of the population was not wide. Most New England selectmen were prosperous farmers and pious Congregational church communicants. Most southern justices of the peace were large planters and respectable Anglicans. They made decisions for a white population that had access to land and opportunity. Boston had John Hancocks and

Virginia had Landon Carters, but men of their stripe did not typify the local elite. Local leaders were a cut above the rest of the citizenry, but they were seldom cut from a different bolt of cloth. Also, many leaders held several jobs simultaneously; this multiple officeholding oiled the parts of the political machinery, making them mesh with less friction.

Average citizens had ready access—often more than they wanted—to the vast array of lesser offices that were part of local government. Opportunity and obligation coexisted to entice and require average freemen to be involved in the elaborate network of decision making. Without doubt, officeholding opportunities were most widespread in New England, where more than 50 percent of adult men served in an elective office at least once in their lifetimes. But in most parts of the middle colonies and even in the South, where fewer offices existed and the majority of these were filled by appointment, not election, local government was not mysterious, remote, or intimidating but a familiar fact that fit comfortably into people's everyday lives. In colonies or anomalous communities where this was not true, such as North Carolina, Georgia, and Philadelphia, citizens complained bitterly about their lack of involvement. Awareness of opportunity elsewhere sparked and fueled the protests in these exceptional cases.

Institutions That Worked. By and large English Americans at the end of the colonial period felt happy with and well served by their local governments. The occasional protests in a few places such as North Carolina and the Hudson River valley were the exception. The American Revolution engendered a great amount of theory and questioning about the meaning and nature of government. It produced anger against elitism. As do most violent upheavals, the revolution unleashed forces that could be neither contained nor predicted. But little discussion or anger was directed at local government and local officials. Newly independent Americans agitated questions about the nature of the executive and legislative branches of the state governments, and they directed anger against some merchants and colonial leaders enmeshed in the imperial system. But local government went on during and after the revolution much as it had before.

The revolution did signal the end of the parish as a formal unit of local government. But this was merely an acceleration of a trend already occurring in late colonial America. The religious ferment of the Great Awakening, which questioned the religious establishment in every colony, had already quickened the pace of movements everywhere to end state-supported religion.

The citizenry of the new nation did not want to change its basic institutions or practices of local government because those institutions and practices worked. The distinctive historical circumstances surrounding each colony's founding created the differing needs and aspirations upon which local institutions were founded. England's past was sufficiently rich and diverse to be able to accommodate these needs and aspirations. From an ample stock of possibilities, colonists selectively borrowed the institutions that they found most conducive to their reality and vision. Religion, geography, and the composition of population shaped the outcome of the process. And of course the colonies had the freedom in their formative years to select, adapt, and discard as they wished from the constitutional smorgasbord laid out before them in the form of English local political and religious institutions. From their choices of English ingredients, the colonists produced a local political fare that was distinctively American.

BIBLIOGRAPHY

English Background

Barnes, Thomas. *Somerset, 1625–1640: A County's Government During the "Personal Rule."* Cambridge, Mass., 1961.
Clark, Peter, and Paul Slack, eds. *Crisis and Order in English Towns, 1500–1700: Essays in Urban History.* London, 1972.
Corfield, P. J. *The Impact of English Towns, 1700–1800.* Oxford, 1982.
Gleason, J. H. *The Justices of the Peace in England, 1588–1640: A Later Eirenarcha.* Oxford, 1969.
Homans, George C. *English Villagers of the Thirteenth Century.* Cambridge, Mass., 1941.
Stone, Lawrence. *The Causes of the English Revolution, 1529–1642.* London, 1972.
Webb, Sidney, and Beatrice Webb. *English Local Government.* 9 vols. London, 1906–1929.

Transatlantic Studies

Allen, David Grayson. *In English Ways: The Movement of Societies and the Transferal of English Local Law and Custom to Massachusetts Bay in the Seventeenth Century.* Chapel Hill, N.C., 1981.
Breen, T. H. "Persistent Localism: English Social Change and the Shaping of New England Institutions." *William and Mary Quarterly*, 3rd ser., 32, no. 1 (1975):3–28.
Cressy, David. *Coming Over: Migration and Communication Between England and New England in the Seventeenth Century.* New York, 1987.
Haskins, George. *Law and Authority in Early Massachusetts: A Study in Tradition and Design.* New York, 1960.
Karraker, Cyrus H. *The Seventeenth-Century Sheriff in England and the Chesapeake Colonies, 1607–1689.* Chapel Hill, N.C., 1930.
Powell, Sumner Chilton. *Puritan Village: The Formation of a New England Town.* Middletown, Conn., 1963.
Thistlethwaite, Frank. *Dorset Pilgrims: The Story of West Country Pilgrims Who Went to New England in the 17th Century.* London, 1989.

Intercolonial Works

Bridenbaugh, Carl. *Cities in Revolt: Urban Life in America, 1743–1776.* New York, 1955.
———. *Cities in the Wilderness: The First Century of Urban Life in America, 1625–1742.* New York, 1938; 2nd ed. 1958.
Daniels, Bruce C., ed. *Power and Status: Officeholding in Colonial America.* Middletown, Conn., 1986.
———. *Town and County: Essays on the Structure of Local Government in the American Colonies.* Middletown, Conn., 1978.
Nash, Gary B. *The Urban Crucible: Social Change, Political Consciousness, and the Origins of the American Revolution.* Cambridge, Mass., 1979.

New England

Akagi, Roy Hidemichi. *The Town Proprietors of the New England Colonies: A Study of Their Development, Organization, Activities and Controversies, 1620–1770.* Philadelphia, 1924.
Clark, Charles E. *The Eastern Frontier: The Settlement of Northern New England, 1610–1763.* New York, 1970.
Cook, Edward, Jr. *The Fathers of the Towns: Leadership and Community Structure in Eighteenth-Century New England.* Baltimore, Md., 1976.
Daniels, Bruce C. *The Connecticut Town: Growth and Development, 1635–1790.* Middletown, Conn., 1979.
———. *Dissent and Conformity on Narragansett Bay: The Colonial Rhode Island Town.* Middletown, Conn., 1983.

Gross, Robert A. *The Minutemen and Their World.* New York, 1976.

Lockridge, Kenneth A. *A New England Town: The First Hundred Years, 1636–1736.* New York, 1970.

Withey, Lynne. *Urban Growth in Colonial Rhode Island: Newport and Providence in the Eighteenth Century.* Albany, N.Y., 1983.

Zuckerman, Michael. *Peaceable Kingdoms: New England Towns in the Eighteenth Century.* New York, 1970.

Southern Colonies

Billings, Warren M. "The Growth of Political Institutions in Virginia, 1634 to 1676." *William and Mary Quarterly,* 3rd ser., 31, no. 2 (1974):225–242.

Carr, Lois Green. "County Government in Maryland, 1689–1709." Ph.D. diss., Harvard University, 1968.

Carr, Lois Green, and David William Jordan. *Maryland's Revolution of Government, 1689–1692.* Ithaca N.Y., 1974.

Hartdagen, Gerald E. "The Vestry As a Unit of Local Government in Colonial Maryland." *Maryland Historical Magazine* 67, no. 4 (1972):363–388.

Isaac, Rhys. *The Transformation of Virginia, 1740–1790.* Chapel Hill, N.C., 1982.

Kay, Marvin L. Michael. "The Institutional Background to the Regulation in Colonial North Carolina." Ph.D. diss., University of Minnesota, 1962.

McCain, Paul M. *The County Court in North Carolina Before 1750.* Historical Papers of the Trinity College Historical Society, series 31. Durham, N.C., 1954.

Porter, Albert O. *County Government in Virginia: A Legislative History, 1607–1904.* New York, 1947.

Rainbolt, John C. "The Alteration in the Relationship Between Leadership and Constituents in Virginia, 1660 to 1720." *William and Mary Quarterly,* 3rd ser., 27, no. 3 (1970):411–434.

Roeber, A. G. "Authority, Law, and Custom: The Rituals of Court Day in Tidewater Virginia, 1720 to 1750." *William and Mary Quarterly,* 3rd ser., 37, no. 1 (1980):29–52.

Waterhouse, Richard. "South Carolina's Colonial Elite: A Study in the Social Structure and Political Culture of a Southern Colony, 1670–1760." Ph.D. diss., Johns Hopkins University, 1973.

Middle Colonies

Bonomi, Patricia. *A Factious People: Politics and Society in Colonial New York.* New York, 1971.

Keller, Clair Wayne. "Pennsylvania Government, 1701–1740." Ph.D. diss., University of Washington, 1967.

Kim, Sung Bok. *Landlord and Tenant in Colonial New York: Manorial Society, 1664–1775.* Chapel Hill, N.C., 1978.

Klein, Milton M. *The Politics of Diversity: Essays in the History of Colonial New York.* Port Washington, N.Y., 1974.

Kross, Jessica. *The Evolution of an American Town: Newtown, N.Y., 1642–1775.* Philadelphia, 1983.

Tully, Alan. *William Penn's Legacy: Politics and Social Structure in Provincial Pennsylvania, 1726–1755.* Baltimore, Md., 1977.

Wolf, Stephanie Grauman. *Urban Village: Population, Community, and Family Structure in Germantown, Pennsylvania, 1683–1800.* Princeton, N.J., 1976.

New Netherland

Burke, Gerald L. *The Making of Dutch Towns: A Study in Urban Development from the Tenth to the Seventeenth Centuries.* London, 1956.

De Jong, Gerald F. *The Dutch in America, 1609–1974.* Boston, 1974.

Kenney, Alice. *The Gansevoorts of Albany: Dutch Patricians in the Upper Hudson Valley.* Syracuse, N.Y., 1969.

Wright, Langdon G. "Local Government and Central Authority in New Netherland." *New-York Historical Society Quarterly* 57, no. 1 (1973):7–29.

New France

Eccles, William J. *Canada Under Louis XIV, 1663–1701.* Toronto, Ontario, 1964.

———. *Canadian Society During the French Regime.* Montreal, 1968.

———. *The Government of New France.* Ottawa, 1965.

Trudel, Marcel. *Histoire de la Nouvelle-France.* 3 vols. Montreal, 1963–1975.

Spanish Borderlands

Crouch, Dora P., Daniel J. Garr, and Axel I. Mundigo. *Spanish City Planning in North America.* Cambridge, Mass., 1982.

Cruz, Gilbert R. *Let There Be Towns: Spanish Municipal Origins in the American Southwest, 1610–1810.* College Station, Tex., 1988.

Gutiérrez, Ramón A. *When Jesus Came, the Corn Mothers Went Away: Marriage, Sexuality, and Power in New Mexico, 1500–1846.* Stanford, Calif., 1991.

TePaske, John Jay. *The Governorship of Spanish Florida, 1700–1763.* Durham, N.C., 1963.

Simmons, Marc. *Spanish Government in New Mexico.* Albuquerque, N.Mex., 1968.

Bruce C. Daniels

SEE ALSO **Colonial Political Culture; Framework of Government;** and **The Suffrage.**

THE SUFFRAGE

Among the European settlements on the North American mainland, only the British colonies permitted any considerable degree of popular participation in government, so this essay on the suffrage and electoral system must of necessity focus on the thirteen British colonies. Studying the suffrage is important for understanding the gradual development of democratic institutions in the New World. To be sure, the British colonists did not settle in North America with the intention of creating a democratic political system, nor did they establish anything resembling a full-fledged democracy in the colonial period (1607–1776). Yet in creating a fairly broad electorate and a pattern of relatively free and frequent elections, the colonists were laying the foundations for such a system in the future.

To discuss the suffrage in the British North American colonies is no simple task. There were, after all, thirteen different mainland colonies, and each one had its own set of suffrage laws. In addition these laws changed over the course of time, and it is not clear whether they were uniformly obeyed. Nevertheless we can make a number of generalizations concerning how many people were qualified to vote, how frequently and in what manner they exercised their franchise rights, and what effect the suffrage had on society and government in that era.

VOTER ELIGIBILITY

Most of the suffrage laws framed in the North American colonies followed English precedent. In fact certain enactments in some provinces were reproduced exactly as they had existed in the mother country. However, the settlers did not simply copy all the British suffrage regulations. Often they introduced new measures prompted by the different conditions in the New World. While the British government would have preferred conformity to the system at home, it did not generally interfere with this new legislation. Except in its insistence on property qualifications for voters, the Crown more or less acquiesced in the colonial standards established.

In formulating their system, the colonists operated on the principle, originating in fifteenth-century England, that potential voters should have a positive stake in the welfare of society. Conversely, they believed that irresponsible elements—"people of small substance and no value" who could not be counted upon or might endanger the community's well-being—should be barred from the polls. These views were implied, for instance, in the preamble of the South Carolina election law of 1716, which declared, "It is necessary and reasonable, that none but such persons who have an interest in this Province should be capable to elect . . . members of the Commons House of Assembly."

In line with this position, leaders in the colonies sought to bar those people—women; racial and religious minorities; indentured servants and other men without property—who seemed to lack the qualities needed in an independent voter. As a result the size of the electorate was much smaller than today's, with several important segments of the community excluded.

Women

Interestingly, the exclusion of some groups stemmed more from custom than from any set of laws. Women, the largest group denied the vote, were directly excluded by statute in only four colonies. Elsewhere it was mainly a matter of tradition that the voters be male. To be sure, scattered evidence from New England and New York shows at least a few property-owning widows casting ballots at times, but this was not a widespread phenomenon. The arguments against a woman's voting were clearly expressed by John Adams, the famous patriot and future president who, like most men of the time, saw women as unsuited both by temperament and background for such a worldly pursuit as politics. "Their delicacy," Adams insisted,

renders them unfit for practice and experience in the great businesses of life, and the hardy enterprises of war, as well as the arduous cares of state. Besides, their attention is so much engaged with the necessary nurture of their children, that nature has made them fittest for domestic cares.

Religious Minorities

Different reasons underlay the exclusion of religious minorities. Persons not belonging to the established church in a particular colony allegedly posed a threat to the state as well as to religious harmony. Therefore, non-Puritans were denied the vote in early Massachusetts, and certain dissenting Protestant groups, such as the Quakers, Baptists, and Presbyterians, were frequently ruled ineligible in the Anglican colonies. The accession of William and Mary to the English throne in 1689 brought increasing toleration of Protestant dissenters both at home and in America, causing many of the earlier religious bans to be removed.

Nonetheless, soon afterward, perhaps in response to the start of the French and Indian wars, several colonies introduced voting restrictions against Catholics. These included Virginia (1699), New York (1701), Maryland (1718), Rhode Island (1719), and South Carolina (1759). Maryland, founded originally as a haven for Catholics by the first Lord Baltimore, eventually attracted a Protestant majority that took away the Catholics' vote "lest they make a Party, which would tend to the Discouragement of his Lordship's Protestant government." Jews, though far less numerous, found themselves disenfranchised for similar reasons. But it is not clear that enforcement against either group was very thorough, since members of both faiths appeared on the poll lists for some of these colonies from time to time.

Racial Minorities

Voting restrictions against racial minorities never became universal and tended to be based primarily upon custom. In the northern colonies, no statute banning nonwhites was ever enacted, while in the southern colonies, where the majority of the black, Indian, and mulatto population resided, legal disenfranchisement took place rather late. That Indians voted in Massachusetts can be seen in the report of a disputed election in the town of Stockbridge in 1763. It stated that thirty-seven Indian males were qualified electors, of whom twenty-nine actually cast ballots. That free blacks managed to vote occasionally in the Carolinas and Virginia in the early eighteenth century can be seen in various official documents.

However, the idea of extending the franchise to black men apparently bothered some whites, causing laws to be passed in South Carolina (1716) and Virginia (1723) completely barring them from the polls. The governor of the latter colony told his superiors in England that it was necessary to disenfranchise blacks in order to preserve a "decent Distinction between them and their Betters" until they were educated and reformed. Although efforts elsewhere to bar them did not usually go as far, there is little evidence of nonwhites' voting in the half century before the American Revolution.

Indentured Servants

Either by custom or statute, white indentured servants were also kept from voting in most colonies. Legislation in mid-eighteenth-century Virginia stated specifically that no servant could be enfranchised solely on the basis of being an inhabitant or resident of a town. To be acceptable such a man had to be duly apprenticed within the town for five years and certified as a householder. Servants in South Carolina were said to have cast ballots early in the eighteenth century but were definitely excluded under the election law of 1717.

The middle colonies of New York and Pennsylvania also passed laws denying the suffrage to those in any condition of servitude. An apprenticed tradesman in New York, however, could obtain the franchise after completing his apprenticeship. Connecticut was the sole colony where "hired servants" could be admitted as "inhabitants of a town" and allowed to vote in local affairs, provided that they met all other requirements, which included being a person of "honest conversation."

Age, Citizenship, and Residence

Restrictions based on age, citizenship, and residence were also part of the electoral system. Twenty-one was the standard age limit for voting virtually everywhere. If in their election laws all of the colonies did not invariably establish a minimum age, it was still customary to bar youths under twenty-one. Massachusetts and New Hampshire even briefly raised the level to twenty-four in the late seventeenth century, but none of the others ever deviated from the norm.

Citizenship was an important qualification, especially in places like Pennsylvania, where many non-English immigrants settled. Supposedly only natural-born subjects of England and its colonies or those naturalized in England or America could vote. Yet spokesmen for the proprietary interest in Pennsylvania often complained of "unnaturalized Moravians and other Germans" being permitted at the polls not long after their arrival. The most outspoken critic, the Anglican minister William Smith of Philadelphia (1727–1803), demanded that their suffrage rights be suspended for twenty years "till they have a sufficient knowledge of our Language and Constitution." "What can be more absurd and impolite," he asked, "than to see a Body of ignorant, proud, stubborn Clowns (who are unacquainted with our Language, our Man-

ners, our Laws, and our Interest) indulged with the Privilege of Returning almost every Member of Assembly?" Such nativist outbursts, however, did not succeed in causing stricter citizenship requirements to be instituted.

Residence requirements, although unknown in England, were established in several American colonies. Many of those in authority believed that only bona fide residents could have a proper concern for a colony's or community's welfare and so sought to restrict eligibility to persons who had lived there for a considerable length of time. The residence requirement generally ranged from six months, as in Georgia and North Carolina, to two years, as in Pennsylvania and Delaware.

In colonies such as New York and Virginia, which had no definite residential qualification, landholders with property in more than one county could theoretically engage in plural voting. A few of them may have done so on occasion, especially since elections in different counties were often held on different days. Nevertheless, it is doubtful whether more than a handful of men exercised this privilege on a regular basis.

Property Qualifications

Among adult white males, the most significant factor separating voters from nonvoters was the property qualification. Property ownership had been the chief requirement for English electors since the year 1430 and was supported by the most advanced political thinkers from that time onward. John Locke, for example, argued that only property holders had enough of a stake in society to be allowed a say in its governance. Other writers emphasized that possession of some wealth was necessary for a man to make a free and independent choice. Otherwise he could not withstand the pressure that might be placed upon him for his vote. Also, as John Adams stated in May 1776: "Very few men who have no property have any judgment of their own. They talk and vote as they are directed by some man of property, who has attached their minds to his interest." To be sure, not everyone agreed with these views. Yet few seem to have publicly challenged the idea of property qualifications for voting before the revolutionary era.

While property requirements became universal in the colonies by the end of the seventeenth century, their forms varied from place to place. In Rhode Island before 1724 the suffrage law was indefinite, stating merely that electors be persons of "competent estates." At least half the colonies, however, eventually insisted that voters must be freeholders. This move was encouraged by the Crown, which starting in the late seventeenth century, instructed the royal governors to exclude nonlandowners from the ballot. "You shall take care," said the order, "that the members of the assembly be elected only by freeholders, as being most agreeable to the customs of this kingdom."

Although the British government sought adherence to the freehold regulation, it did not stipulate any minimum amount; thus, it tended to vary. Massachusetts and Connecticut required a forty-shilling freehold, that is, land producing forty shillings in rent annually. In practical terms this meant real estate with a yearly rent equivalent to twenty-seven days' wages for a common laborer. Rhode Island allowed men to meet the requirement in the same manner or through the possession of a freehold rated at forty pounds. New York had the same forty-pound standard but also permitted those with a lifetime lease on a forty-shilling freehold to vote. New Hampshire, on the other hand, had only one criterion: an estate worth fifty pounds.

In the colonies farther south, freehold qualifications were expressed in terms of acres rather than in value of land or its income. Land there cost much less—in some places only a few shillings per acre. Since there were twenty shillings in a pound, it would have taken an inordinately large estate to satisfy a forty- or fifty-pound requirement. In Pennsylvania, Delaware, Maryland, Georgia, and the Carolinas, possession of fifty acres was a minimum for voting. Virginia ultimately decided on one hundred acres (40 hectare) of unsettled land or twenty-five acres (10 hectare) of improved land with a house upon it. What constituted a house was originally undefined and often depended upon the whims of local election officials. In 1762 one man in Elizabeth City County moved a structure measuring ten feet by eight feet onto his land and was allowed to participate, while another man with a "house" standing less than five feet by five feet (1.5 by 1.5 meters) was not. Finally, the legislature decided that the dwelling must be at least twelve feet square to qualify.

Six of the colonies had alternatives to the real estate qualification in the form of personal property or the payment of taxes. In addition to forty-shilling freeholders, Connecticut, Massachusetts, and Maryland permitted any owner of a forty-pound "personal estate" to vote. Pennsylvania established a fifty-pound estate as a substitute, and this proved to be the only way citizens of urban areas like Philadelphia could qualify. Some colonies established special alternatives for urban dwellers similar to the English borough franchise. Williamsburg and Norfolk, Virginia, Burlington and Perth Amboy, New Jersey, and Annapolis, Maryland, all permitted householders to vote. A number of towns in North Carolina even accepted tenancy of a house as sufficient to qualify. Residents of Albany and New York City could secure the franchise by becoming freemen of the corporation, another practice common to English boroughs. Freemanship was available at a nominal cost and allowed a man to practice his trade as well as vote.

Number of Eligible Voters
The number of colonists eligible to vote under this intricate web of restrictions is difficult to determine. The absence of complete census data, tax lists, and records of land ownership make any definitive statement impossible. Moreover, most of the contemporary estimates by government officials are of questionable accuracy. Nevertheless the existing evidence can give a reasonably reliable picture of the size of the electorate. Considering eligibility in terms of the total adult colonial population (including women, religious and racial minorities, etc.), the number qualifying was less than a majority. But if we count only adult white males, it would appear that from 50 to 80 percent satisfied the requirements, a fairly substantial figure and at least twice as high as in England or anywhere else in the world at that time. It should be added that accumulating enough property to vote was to a degree correlated with age, and that a greater percentage reached the required level as they matured into their thirties and forties. On the other side of the ledger, certain parts of New England and Maryland saw the number of landholders, and hence prospective voters, declining toward the last decades of the colonial period.

Regarding eligibility, some modern historians have argued that the qualifications for voting were not too meaningful, claiming they were rarely enforced. As evidence they cite the words of the Tory-leaning governor of Massachusetts, Thomas Hutchinson, who said in 1772 that in Boston "anything with the appearance of a man" was admitted to vote without scrutiny. To be sure, officials in certain locales did ignore the statutes at times and allowed persons of questionable status to participate when it suited their needs. Yet records of contested elections throughout the colonial period show that voter eligibility was carefully scrutinized on numerous occasions. Since a heated contest and strict enforcement were clearly possibilities on any election day, it seems doubtful that many among the unqualified would have risked spending their time traveling to the polls if there was a chance that their votes might be rejected. Also, the very fact that the revolutionary generation heard frequent calls for suffrage reform would indicate that not every man could vote before 1776.

Given the less than universal level of suffrage among adult white males, one question must be immediately addressed: Did the voting requirements of the time significantly limit the number of those who would have gone to the polls? Conceivably in some locales the restrictions may have reduced the total vote on a few occasions but never by more than from 10 to 20 percent. Perhaps equally important in excluding individuals from taking part in the voting process were factors regarding representation. People living in yet-to-be incorporated New England towns or along the unorganized southern frontier did not have an opportunity to vote, even if they could meet the legal qualifications. Such places did not hold regular provincial elections. Even many already-incorporated New England towns were too poor or too unconcerned with colonywide matters to send a representative to the legislature. (At that time, New England legislators received no stipend and had to be supported by the community that sent them.)

One can argue that even had there been no restrictions on voter eligibility beyond those of our own times no different candidates would have been elected nor different laws or policies made. Additional white males in the electorate would probably have voted along existing lines, if they would have voted at all. Surely the government and the society as a whole would not have changed.

Voter Turnout

How many men actually voted during the colonial era is not much easier to ascertain than the number of potential voters. Many of the returns have been lost or destroyed, and in quite a few cases when one candidate seemed the obvious winner, no precise count was made. The records merely report that the person won by a "substantial majority." Looking at the fragmentary statistical results, it would appear that approximately 20 to 40 percent of the adult white males voted. The highest single-race totals occurred in Pennsylvania and New York, where factional divisions, based partly on ethnic and religious differences and partly on conflicting political principles, brought heavy turnouts from time to time. (The city of Philadelphia surpassed 60 percent in 1765.) Overall, the highest average (over 43 percent) was in Virginia, where more than anywhere else people went to the polling place for reasons beyond just casting a ballot. Other than faction-free South Carolina, the lowest figures —often less than 20 percent—show up in New England where, except for Rhode Island, few open contests took place. On most occasions arrangements regarding which candidates should be supported were worked out by colony and local leaders in advance. Furthermore the atmosphere at the polling place was usually serious and somber, offering little incentive for people to attend other than the call of duty.

VOTER PARTICIPATION AND ELECTIONS

To understand why men did or did not exercise the vote in this era, we must turn our attention to the nature of colonial elections. Interest in elections or politics in general was not very high, particularly in the first century of colonization, when survival was often the main concern in life. Given the limited forms of communication back then, the majority had little knowledge of political events anyway. Even among the politically aware, few saw much reason to take part in the electoral process, since most major offices were appointive. In almost every colony, the governor and members of the upper house of the legislature received their appointments from the Crown or from a proprietor in England. Administrative and judicial posts also were not subject to public choice. Rhode Island and Connecticut stood alone in having all branches of their governments popularly elected throughout the colonial period. Elsewhere only the lower house of the legislature and certain local offices were elective for the entire era.

In fact, actual contests for elective office were extremely rare during the first several decades. Not until the eighteenth century did elections become competitive to any significant degree. By that time the homogeneity and close-knit leadership that characterized some of the early New England settlements had begun to break down. There and elsewhere many challenges began to be raised against traditional authority. New York and Pennsylvania, containing a mixture of ethnic and religious groups— English (Anglican, Presbyterian, and Quaker), Dutch, German, French, and Scottish—grew into hotbeds of factionalism. Even in some of the more homogeneous southern colonies, clashing interests frequently caused heated rivalries. Moreover, increasing numbers of individuals now had the affluence and leisure time to participate in politics and covet a seat in the legislature. All these factors led to a considerable upsurge in vote-getting activity.

Contested Elections

The reasons for contested elections varied. In some places competition stemmed from divisions over local problems—perhaps involving differences over land allocations, the apportionment of taxes, and religious regulations. In others colonywide matters dominated, for example, whether to print paper money to reduce economic strain or to build forts to defend against Indian attacks. Sometimes legislators who disliked the governor's policies would form a "country party" and oppose the election of the chief executive's supporters, known as the "court party."

In about as many cases, however, neither local nor provincial issues were of much consequence, so outcomes hinged mainly upon each candidate's rank and personal qualities. As one historian has written about contests in mid-eighteenth-century Virginia: "It seems not to have been so much a question of *what* as *who*." Robert Munford's play *The Candidates* (1770)

clearly illustrates this theme, for when the lead character, Worthy, at first declines to stand for reelection with his colleague Wou'dbe, a number of questionable figures enter the race. Among them we find Sir John Toddy, "an honest blockhead" with little ability except in consuming liquor; and also Smallhopes and Strutabout, two fellows of doubtful virtue. Eventually Worthy reconsiders, joins the fray, and easily triumphs over the undesirables.

THE SUFFRAGE, SOCIETY, AND GOVERNMENT

In general most of the successful candidates for office, like the fictional Worthy, were men of substance from the upper layers of society. The majority of colonies had high property qualifications for officeholding (ranging from one hundred [40 hectare] to one thousand [400 hectare] acres). But even where such requirements did not exist, it was usually individuals of affluence and learning who sought and won high positions in government. Most Americans, like the Europeans of the time, took for granted a stratified society in which deference to one's betters was the accepted norm. They believed that to preserve order in the community, each man should remain in the station to which God had called him and should respect those in higher stations. In regard to governing, this meant people in the lower strata should defer to the "rich and wellborn." Much of the election literature throughout the colonial period echoed the idea that only those "high and eminent" were fit to rule.

Of course it is necessary to point out that deference did not mean that the common people automatically elected the wealthiest and most prominent gentleman in every case. Other factors came into play, particularly when members of the gentry competed among themselves. Scholars investigating the matter of who got elected to high posts in colonial Connecticut have demonstrated that a candidate's ability and political achievement were typically more important than his wealth and family connections. Moreover, in order to remain in office, members of the elite had to fulfill certain minimum obligations to the populace. Both in personal behavior and in stands on issues, there were clearly bounds beyond which they could not go. Those who defied the public and, when challenged, ignored the need to campaign, often suffered quick defeat on election day.

Electioneering

The main method of campaigning during the colonial period was canvasing and handshaking. Probably more so than today, people felt it important to be personally acquainted with the men for whom they voted. Having less populated election districts gave representation a greater personal meaning back then. Thus, persons running for office sought to meet members of the electorate individually—at church, at court, at a tavern, or at a militia training. Candidates in urban areas often went from door-to-door or buttonholed potential voters in the streets. Sometimes the pursuit of votes was undertaken by surrogates who traveled around the district in the candidate's behalf. In addition to canvasing, one of the most accepted campaign activities was treating the voters to food and drink. Contemporaries frequently referred to this practice as "swilling the planters with bumbo." In the southern and middle colonies—especially Virginia, Maryland, and New York—it was customary to provide refreshments for the voters either before or after the balloting. George Washington was not unusual in spending a considerable sum of money (£39) for "treats" on the occasion of his first election to the House of Burgesses in 1758.

Despite the rise of active campaigning, many elections remained uncontested or minimally contested. Even competitive races tended to be conducted on a more modest scale than those in post-colonial times. The period given to soliciting votes was usually quite brief. Rarely did it extend beyond one week, and sometimes it lasted no longer than the morning of election day itself. The large majority of campaigns remained local in nature, with candidates relying on their own resources and the support of a few trusted friends. Even in colonies where highly partisan activity occurred during legislative sessions, members from each constituency normally managed their own reelection bids without seeking outside help.

There were times, though, when campaigning went much further. In New York, Pennsylvania, Maryland, and Rhode Island, during periods of extreme factional conflict, partisans engaged in more elaborate electioneering schemes, sometimes covering the entire colony. Faction leaders sent emissaries to the different counties to meet with local officials to better coordinate the vote-getting effort. As part of their strategy, they arranged tickets well in advance of the balloting, provided money to get voters to the polls, and sent letters to important persons requesting their assistance. In urban areas such as Boston, New York, and Philadelphia, they had their lieutenants out distributing handbills on election day and making sure that everyone on their side voted. If the scope of their activities did not quite equal that of later party bosses, certain aspects of their approach surely pointed in a modern direction.

Time and Place of Polling

There was no standard date for balloting in early America. Some colonies (Rhode Island, Connecticut, Delaware, and Pennsylvania) held annual elections on a particular date, while others followed the British system whereby elections occurred at the discretion of the royal governor. In the latter mode, the governor called an election within a certain span of years—two, three, or seven. The first step in the calling of a new election was the governor's issuance of a writ directing the sheriff to summon the voters to the polls by a particular date. Except in the colonies with standard annual contests, the actual time and place was left for the local officials to decide. Notices containing the details were posted in public places and, where possible, inserted in newspapers. In most colonies the election unit was the county and the voting site was the courthouse, while in New England the unit was the town and the site the town meetinghouse. Normally only one voting site existed in each election district, so voters often had to travel great distances to cast their ballots. A journey of five, ten, twenty miles (1.5, 3, 6 kilometers) or more was sometimes necessary. Bad weather was not usually an inhibiting factor, since most elections took place in the early fall or late spring.

Voting Procedures

At the polling place, the act of voting was accomplished either by voice or by paper ballot. Six of the provinces—New York, New Jersey, Maryland, Virginia, North Carolina, and Georgia—followed the English parliamentary tradition of oral voting. When a poll was taken, the electors would come up one at a time to a long table situated inside or in front of the courthouse. Standing there within the hearing of the election officials and all interested spectators, each man would state his name and, in a loud voice, announce his preferences for the offices to be filled. In Virginia and possibly elsewhere, the candidates themselves were often present and would thank those who had just voted for them. One of the clerks would then record the voter's name on the appropriate list. Voting in some locales might continue for more than one day, but just before the end of the proceedings, the sheriff would call out, "Gentlemen Freeholders, come into court, and give your votes, or the poll will be closed."

To a modern observer, oral voting may appear to place the elector in a pressure-filled situation and present an open invitation to undue influence or corruption. Yet the colonials, like the Europeans of the time, thought that secret, paper balloting was the method more likely to produce irregularities. Open voting, they believed, kept everything aboveboard. Nevertheless many of the northern colonies, including all four in New England, chose secrecy as the way of casting votes. For New Englanders in particular, consensus in political affairs was a highly desired goal and secret voting was seen as a better way of achieving it than an open form. In Massachusetts, Connecticut, New Hampshire, and Rhode Island, prospective electors went to the town meetinghouse, where a hat or other type of ballot box had been set down at the front of the building. Under the observation of a constable and the town selectmen, the voters came forward and deposited their filled-out ballots. Although some fraud did occur at times with both secret and open voting methods, colonial elections probably involved fewer charges of illegality than contests in later centuries.

Election Day

Outside of New England, election day provided a time of great excitement, often taking on a holiday atmosphere. It not only offered people a chance to see the candidates and deliver a vote but gave them several alternatives to the daily routine of town and farm life. In some colonies election day coincided with a session of the county court or a local militia training. Going to the polling place frequently included visiting with friends, enjoying some convivial drinking, or engaging in sports and games. Sometimes the festivities led to instances of violence, with many of the men participating in a major brawl.

One historian, Edmund S. Morgan, has seen in these proceedings many parallels to the yearly carnivals in Latin countries, where the lower classes fraternized with the upper classes and reigned for a day, taking part in rituals giving them temporary ascendancy before they returned power to the elite. Elections for many inhabitants, he says in *Inventing the People* (1988), became not so much a matter of choosing candidates as a way of exercising authority, albeit on a symbolic basis.

However, if colonial elections did contain some ritualistic aspects, only a few contests in pre-revolutionary Maryland and Virginia seem to fit his overall description to any extent. Elsewhere the excessive behavior that went on at the polls did not seem to follow any well-defined pattern. In the colonies farther north, elections generally had a more serious tone, and if violence did happen on occasion in the middle colonies, it was usually more purposeful and involved well-organized factions such as the Livingstons and DeLanceys in New York or the Proprietary party in Pennsylvania seeking to control the outcome.

CONCLUSION

In the final analysis, how do we characterize the electoral system in the colonial times? On the one hand, the suffrage requirements were many, and they somewhat restricted the size of the electorate. The number of those eligible who actually did vote was usually less than a majority. Even the highest offices, those of the governor and the upper house, were not usually subject to popular choice. Indeed even the positions that were elective tended to fall into the hands of representatives from the upper classes. Most colonists seem to have taken little interest in politics most of the time. Elections generally did not involve major issues and in quite a few cases appear to have possessed the qualities of modern-day sporting events.

On the other hand, the franchise among adult white males can be described as fairly broad, and the politically important lower house of the legislature was elective. Although only a minority of men regularly voted, the potential existed for the majority to turn out if it felt that its interests were at stake. Members of the elite normally dominated politics, but they could not fully control the electorate and had trouble getting it to support unpopular measures. Candidates who sought to defy the popular will often found themselves defeated at the polls on election day. While this system did not make for truly democratic politics, it surely set the stage for changes in that direction during the American Revolution and its aftermath.

BIBLIOGRAPHY

Brown, Robert E. *Middle-Class Democracy and the Revolution in Massachusetts, 1691–1780.* Ithaca, N.Y., 1955.

Dinkin, Robert J. *Voting in Provincial America: A Study of Elections in the Thirteen Colonies, 1689–1776.* Westport, Conn., 1977.

Gilsdorf, Joy B., and Robert B. Gilsdorf. "Elites and Electorates: Some Plain Truths for Historians of Colonial America." In *Saints and Revolutionaries: Essays in Early American History,* edited by David D. Hall, John M. Murrin, and Thad W. Tate. New York, 1984.

Morgan, Edmund S. *Inventing the People: The Rise of Popular Sovereignty in England and America.* New York, 1988.

Murrin, John M. "Political Development." In *Colonial British America: Essays in the New History of the Early Modern Era,* edited by Jack P. Greene and J. R. Pole. Baltimore, Md., 1984.

Nash, Gary B. *The Urban Crucible: Social Change, Political Consciousness, and the Origins of the American Revolution.* Cambridge, Mass., 1979.

Pole, J. R. *Political Representation in England and the Origins of the American Republic.* New York, 1966.

Snydor, Charles S. *Gentlemen Freeholders: Political Practices in Washington's Virginia.* Chapel Hill, N.C., 1952.

Williamson, Chilton. *American Suffrage: From Property to Democracy, 1760–1860.* Princeton, N.J., 1960.

Robert J. Dinkin

SEE ALSO **The Structure of Society.**

TAXATION

THE BRITISH COLONIES

LOCAL EXPENDITURES

TAXES IN THE BRITISH COLONIES were levied by the local, provincial, and imperial governments. This essay will not consider taxes levied by Parliament, which were unimportant until 1764 when they formed part of the background of the revolution and so fall beyond the scope of the present discussion. Almost everything historians have written about colonial taxation pertains to imperial policies, so that a survey of the subject at the local and provincial levels must be stitched together insecurely.

The towns and counties collected revenues for a number of purposes that varied little year after year. At both levels there were numerous officials, though most were not paid and received money only for expenses such as travel. Those who were paid included clerks, men to enforce the laws, assessors to determine the value of taxpayers' property, and tax collectors, though the last paid themselves by keeping a part of the revenue. The people paid a per diem for their delegates to the colonial legislature. Deputies living near the capital spent little time or money in traveling, but those farther away cost their constituents a good deal of money just getting to and from the sessions, renting rooms, and paying for meals. Because of the expense, poorer or more distant communities sometimes decided not to send anybody at all. As a rule the men who would best represent their constituents generally cost the most; a town that sent a local farmer instead of a well-known justice of the peace might save money but could not expect much of a return.

There were often other costs. In New England the provincial governments required the towns to support schools, and there were publicly supported schools in some other places, especially in the cities. In the matter of churches, New England (along with New York) again stood out in that a special town tax was levied upon every head of family to pay the minister's salary and other costs, particularly the building and repair of the church itself. Elsewhere everyone was expected to contribute in proportion to their ability, a kind of moral tax.

Another cost was poor relief. In Europe and elsewhere the problem of the destitute was often substantial. The failure of harvests, a virulent epidemic, destruction by invading armies or local nobles fighting for power left thousands crippled, starving, and homeless. Even in normal times, things were bad enough; there were always poor people. The burden of poor relief was carried not by the monarch but by the community, especially the churches and the lesser nobility—the gentry. For historic reasons members of the nobility did not pay taxes but were supposed to support the church and perform a variety of other public services, including care of the poor.

For several reasons this obligation did not carry over to the colonies to a significant degree. First, very few nobles—even gentry—immigrated to the colonies, and those who did were seldom wealthy enough to act the part of universal benefactor. Second, in colonies where such men did settle, or where a colonial equivalent developed, they became owners of servants and then of slaves. As masters of servants they perhaps performed according to expectations, but as slaveowners they generally did not. Third, neither they nor other men of wealth consistently and reliably acted the part of philanthropist, since most lacked the extensive, fertile landed estates to generate enough money, and because unlike the European nobility, they had to pay taxes. Accordingly much of the cost devolved upon the churches and local governments. In general, towns or counties took care of the rest, such as nonchurch members and all the poor when churches did not act.

Road building was also a local matter, except when the British government constructed a few roads for military purposes during the Seven Years' War. People used the old Indian trails on foot or by horse and created new ones in villages, connecting the church, the store, the blacksmith's shop, the mill, and the wharf. Middlesex County, Virginia, in 1669 had a road running the whole length of the county for thirty-five miles (56 kilometers), with four branches leading to two churches, a ferry, and a bridge. Fifty or more years later another branch curved off to link up a mill, a public landing on the Rappahannock River, the village of Urbanna, and another bridge. These roads were usually built by men and boys when they were not busy with farm chores and was a way of working out part of their taxes. This method also financed the labor cost of building or repairing the church, the courthouse, the town hall, and the school.

Finally, every town and county had at least one militia company. In theory every able-bodied male from sixteen to sixty, except for the minister, was called out for training periodically, supposedly with gun in hand. No public expenditure was involved, but in case of war local governments in practice bore some of the cost.

LOCAL TAXES

To finance these expenditures, local governments collected money (or articles such as farm products) by taxing the people's production; that is, whatever earned an income, primarily their money-making labor, land, livestock, polls (on individuals), and faculties (on earning ability), the last two of which will be discussed shortly. They could not tax incomes because so much of the annual farm production was consumed at home, and the services of families to one another did not involve exchanges of cash. Even businessmen did not add up their incomes at the end of the year. People simply recorded mentally or in an account book what they owed or were owed at a particular time. A sales tax also was impossible, since no records of sales existed. Only in the case of imports and exports did records exist, but taxes on these were not assessed locally.

On the other hand, a tax on land was relatively simple: an assessor could see land and estimate its value, and nobody could conceal land from a tax collector. Furthermore it was the major source of income and wealth. People were used to such a levy; in the Old World custom, landowners other than the nobles and clergy paid a tax on land. The colonials did have some trouble collecting taxes from the first group to receive large royal land grants. They often claimed exemption, especially if the land remained unoccupied, in which case they could claim that it was not making any money and so not taxable.

However, the land that most people owned clearly did earn income. The value of the land rose as people improved it, changing forest into field, and so there was heated debate about the appropriate level of taxation, especially because politically powerful men had a vested interest in the outcome. Everybody agreed that before the land had been taken from the Indians with an arguably legal title and properly surveyed, it lacked taxable value. Afterward, however, the land could be sold or rented and so bring a profit, which would normally increase over time; therefore it then possessed value that an assessor could reasonably determine. As the value increased, the amount of money raised by the land tax rose steadily and formed a substantial part of local budgets.

Almost as important were the receipts from livestock, primarily cattle and horses and far less often sheep, goats, and hogs. The tax was on income-producing items, not food; the colonists did not assess beef, pork, and so forth. Farm families might eat oxen, but their primary value was for plowing and hauling. Cows produced milk, cheese, calves, and hides for shoes and tallow. The horse was a draft animal in the less rocky soil of the South. Other productive articles, such as mills, the tools and shops of skilled craftsmen, and ships, were less often assessed.

The Poll Tax

Also producing substantial revenue was the poll tax. It was a flat tax on labor in the form of a levy on adult males and, sometimes, female slaves sixteen and up. It was their labor that produced the crops and manufactures which constituted the country's annual product. A boy of sixteen, a hired worker, a servant, or a slave as well as a farmer, craftsman, or shopkeeper all earned money, and those earning, it was believed, should be taxed. The labor of a tithable man in Connecticut was considered equal in value to six cows, or about two acres of meadow land. A farmer who had two grown boys at home raised three times as much surplus as one who had none; a slaveowner's yearly profit rose in proportion to the number of hands in the tobacco or rice fields. The tax for those not laboring on their own behalf was paid by the beneficiary—the father, employer, master, or owner—until such persons became independent, after which they paid for themselves.

Perhaps the greatest advantage of the tax, from the point of view of the collector, was its high visibility. Another was that no one considered the poll unfair at the time. It was normal in Europe, and the notion that every able-bodied man should contribute something to the community seemed obvious. Actually it fell mostly on employers and fathers, and in early America country villages adopted it at once. Moreover the truly poor were exempted, and so were ministers and men "past their labor."

The tax on polls did not begin to allow for the earnings of full-time artisans and professionals, who might employ no one, yet equal in wealth farmers who were aided by sons and hired workers for whom the tax had to be paid. To equalize the burden, communities began to levy a faculty tax on their earning capacity, "faculty" meaning ability plus training. The larger towns contained many such men, but even a country village had a few doctors and lawyers, especially in the eighteenth century, along with skilled workers such as tanners and millers. The tax also applied to shopkeepers and merchants for their ships and stock-in-trade—the goods they offered for sale. Those items, plus money—cash in hand—and debts owing to them were not taxed until near the end of the colonial period, and then only over strenuous objections. Most local governments relied almost entirely upon the revenue from land, livestock, and polls.

The local tax system seems to have been reasonably fair. It probably fell a little too heavily on farmers, who sometimes objected. However, some inequality is inherent in any system, and the only large-scale protests occurred where corrupt county officials clearly broke the law, as they did (among other sins) in backcountry North Carolina during the 1760s and 1770s. The poll tax taken by itself was unfair in that the poor paid as much as the rich; but considered in combination with the other taxes, it was only mildly regressive, since it was the only one a poor man did pay. The poll was commonly valued at eighteen pounds currency, assumed to be the profit of a year's labor. So with the tax at from one to three pence per pound, if a man was employed two-thirds of the time and spent eight pounds to support himself, he would pay on the average between 2 percent and 4 percent of his net earnings. Owners of slaves and servants had to list all of those capable of fieldwork, generally including female slaves in the South, despite the fact that many of them were household servants and so consumers rather than producers. Large landowners and ordinary farmers combined to constitute a political majority for these taxes on forms of property other than land; this practice encountered strong objections from everyone else. Historians like Robert Becker and Lawrence Gipson have sometimes taken sides but the fairness is not at all apparent.

PROVINCIAL EXPENDITURES

Major protest arose not with respect to local taxes but regarding those levied by the provincial legislatures or the royal and proprietary governments. By modern standards these bodies spent remarkably little, except during wars, because their functions were limited and their officials few; furthermore costs of living were much less than in the Old World. Public buildings were unassuming and few in number. In Williamsburg, Virginia, the capitol, governor's palace, jail, and guardhouse sufficed and were more modest than today's replicas. Yet Virginia was the oldest, most populous, and richest colony. The governor himself always received a relatively large salary, and so did other major officials such as a lieutenant governor, a treasurer, a receiver of taxes, a naval officer, the members of the governor's council, an attorney-general, and a secretary. These were chosen by the governor or by officials in England and were supposedly paid by the colonists. Only the governor's salary exceeded $100,000 in today's money.

In a few colonies the governors succeeded in obtaining permanent salaries from the legislatures but in most the colonists refused, and the issue became a perennial controversy. The British government then appropriated funds from other sources such as quitrents and export taxes, which royal officials collected and paid directly to the executive. In addition a variety of officers of the militia received their salaries either from the governors or more often from the representatives. The legislature had a clerk, and beginning with Massachusetts in the 1670s, many legislatures appointed agents to influence important decisions in London. All of these had to be paid. Other expenses were few and occasional. Colleges received some help, but of these there were only four until the 1750s. The colonial governments did not ordinarily concern themselves with the poor, for whom the local churches, parishes, or towns were responsible, nor about roads, bridges, ferries, or wharves. Moreover some functions and their costs were paid for by user fees or by allowing officials to keep a share of the revenue involved, a right readily subject to abuse. The collection of fees became a major burden toward the end of the colonial period.

The major expenditures stemmed from wars, threatening and fought at frequent intervals with the Spanish, French, Dutch, and assorted Indian peoples. The colonists themselves were responsible for many of these wars, especially the last variety, the cost of which they bore with little help from Britain. In addition some of the colonies spent money on gifts to Native Americans or on land purchases from them. The wars with European powers were fought primarily by England's army and navy, and with her money; however the colonies too contributed ships, men, and treasuries. King William's War (1689–1697) was fought in America entirely by New York and New England, and in Queen Anne's War (1702–1713), a force primarily from Massachusetts sailed in 1711 from Boston for Quebec and failed, at great cost in both men and money. To be sure many privateers captured enemy vessels, creating fortunes for their owners, but this did not help the budget.

In general the legislatures did not take in enough revenue to pay the cost and were obliged to borrow. They therefore issued promissory notes, IOUs, to be paid when sufficient taxes were collected. This enabled governments to spread the payment over a period of years, moderating the bite and adding to the supply of money in circulation. Too much money led to inflation, however, especially when the legislatures failed to impose the necessary taxes to maintain confidence that the debt would indeed be paid. As a rule the currency's value declined slowly enough to avoid trouble—at about the same rate as ours from World War II to the 1990s—and for most colonists the benefits outweighed the disadvantages. As a direct consequence of frequent wars, taxes and paper money proved a problem and would plague the new nation during the revolution as well.

PROVINCIAL TAXATION

The governments of each colony collected taxes for a variety of purposes and in many ways. Like the towns and counties, they relied quite heavily on the poll tax, in a few cases deriving from it more than half of the provincial income. The legislatures also raised money with a tax on land, adding to that imposed by the local governments and incorporating, in the case of the larger cities, assessments on urban real estate, including houses. There were two varieties of revenue from this source: the quitrent imposed and collected by the governor and the ordinary tax already discussed.

Land Taxes

Quitrents go back to 1618 in Virginia, when the Virginia Company of London promised gifts of land at no charge except a payment of two shillings per hundred acres, which exempted (or quitted) the owner from any of the customary obligations common in England and elsewhere. Later the proprietors who became the owners of the Carolinas advertised land for a quitrent of a halfpenny per acre, about twice the Virginia price. These early land grants were small, but in 1669 parts of Carolina were formed into twelve-thousand-acre squares (480 hectares) and granted in even larger tracts to proprietors who subdivided and sold them for a penny an acre annual rent. This principle was extended to all of the other southern colonies, to Pennsylvania by the Penns, and to some lands farther north by the king. The grantees expected the quitrents to pay the cost of governing the colony, with plenty left over for themselves. It was not, then, entirely a private matter, since it affected the colonial governments.

As an extension of this system, individuals could buy great landed estates or obtain them by influence almost anywhere and apply the same principle, simply dropping the obsolete word *quit* and becoming landlords with tenants. The objective was to create a colonial society similar to that of the Old World. The quitrents, therefore, became not only an economic but a political and social issue. The landowners, large and small alike, were not sufficiently "grateful"; they did not want to pay taxes, especially if the revenue did not benefit their community, and they did not want to strengthen the royal or proprietary executives and officials. Because of such opposition, quitrents raised far less money than anticipated, forming in South Carolina less than 12 percent of the provincial revenue.

The other species of land tax duplicated the local tax already described. The towns at the outset might set their own method of evaluation, but usually the legislatures made the decision, which varied depending on such factors as the desire for simplicity and the balance of political power. The simplest approach was to lump all real estate together and levy a flat tax per acre—the quitrent system. This benefited those who held the most valuable land—highly fertile and located on navigable water, the sort that the most wealthy farmers owned—because the alternative was an assessment varying with the quality of the soil.

However, wealthy landowners opposed a flat tax on all land regardless of value, because they often held extensive unoccupied tracts bought for future use—meaning these would be taxed even though they produced no income. They preferred, first, to evade the quitrent, second, to exempt unimproved land, and third, having done that, to have a flat tax levied on the remainder. Ordinary farmers favored assessing all improved land relative to its value. The result was that unimproved land was universally exempted (except for quitrents) and the rest was taxed either according to its value, as was the case in New England, or at a flat rate, as happened eventually in the southern colonies when money was desperately needed during the Seven Years' War and the great planters could no longer avoid a land tax. To them, exempting unimproved tracts and assessing all the rest at the lowest possible rate was the preferable evil.

Other Taxes

The legislatures, like the local governments, also raised money by assessments on livestock and on slaves or free negroes when white polls were not being taxed and by various imposts, export taxes, and excises. The impost, like a tariff, was levied on imported goods. By far the most imports came from England, but the British government did not permit an impost on those. The colonies did tax goods from Europe and the West Indies, usually unnecessary or luxury articles of doubtful moral value such as liquor or slaves, when a colony seemed to have imported more than the farmers needed in view of the price of their crops and their debts. Virginia, Delaware, and Maryland levied export taxes on their tobacco; South Carolina levied them on rice and New York on furs. The most common excise was on the sale of liquor; it was collected from the tavernkeepers, who also had to pay annual license fees.

Loan Offices and Paper Currency

The problem of taxation was profoundly affected in some colonies by the legislature's creation of loan offices that loaned money to landowners for the improvement of their land. That at least was the ostensible purpose, and these loans did enable farmers to obtain money at relatively low rates of interest and with relatively little danger of foreclosure. More importantly, though, when a colony was not burdened with a war debt, the money received from interest on the loans paid most or even the entire cost of government, as was the pleasant situation during various periods in New Jersey, Delaware, New York, Pennsylvania, and South Carolina. In fact Pennsylvania made so much money that by 1755 the colony had a substantial surplus. Rhode Island's loan office, on the other hand, aroused controversy among people at the time and among historians since. However, most of the colony's residents benefited, and it is arguable that Rhode Island bank notes furnished a currency for her neighbors at a time when they needed one. Massachusetts created a public land bank in 1714, issuing bills of credit that were divided among counties and towns. They apparently did not last long and so constituted an unusual failure.

An alternative way of paying the cost of government was by issuing IOUs made of paper. At first the legislatures simultaneously passed a tax law to bring into the treasury, over a fixed period, enough money to pay off the debt. (Without such a law, fear of the governments not accepting the bills at par would result in their decline in value.) The failure to attach a tax clause to a paper money bill usually began in wartime when a colony could not raise the necessary taxes to meet increased expenditures. Thus New York issued paper money beginning in 1709, appropriating enough revenue to retire (take in and destroy) the paper, which accordingly maintained its value. This practice, everything considered, enabled the colonies to balance their budgets except in times of war or depression and to pay wartime debts when peace or prosperity returned.

NEW ENGLAND

We can review the history of taxation by dividing the colonies into three groups, each of which had different experiences. The four New England colonies were peculiar, first, in having exceptionally strong local governments with their own tax systems, collectors, and expenditures. All of them assessed land and livestock according to value and taxed polls and (later) faculties. They kept expenditures low partly because almost none of the town officials were paid and because they required a good deal of labor on public works from the people. They provided so many of the essential services that the provincial legislatures had few expenses in normal times. Thus the total tax burden in Connecticut was usually about a shilling per person, one-twentieth that of England, and an ordinary laborer would pay no more than 5 percent of his net income in taxes.

The second peculiarity of the New England colonies was their heavy involvement in numerous wars. Geographically those colonies were, except for New York, closest to the French and their Indian allies, and they fulfilled their obligation to the empire while enthusiastically indulging their own desire for expansion. Military costs extended into the intervals of peace and the tax rate increased accordingly, doubling after the Seven Years' War just as a postwar depression hit. Luckily the British government agreed to pay a quarter of the wartime cost.

Only one of the four colonies—Rhode Island—established a land bank of long duration. New Hampshire, Massachusetts, and Connecticut all issued paper money that declined in value, resulting in a generally mild inflation, but the process was gradual enough, and the colonies' tax revenue sufficiently reliable, to prevent a crisis. Meanwhile they increased the supply of badly needed money, providing cheap capital for the region's expansion.

Even Rhode Island managed to pay all its debts by 1772. That colony's land bank was made possible by the exceptional political strength of the population's rural element, who started it, and the ability of the merchants, who brought order out of initial chaos. Once the banks were operated on a businesslike basis the interest they collected added to the colonial revenue and kept taxes low—a good thing because the farmers were not enthusiastic about paying taxes. New England emerged from the 1760s in excellent financial condition.

THE MIDDLE COLONIES

The group of colonies southwest of New England—New York, New Jersey, Pennsylvania,

Delaware, and Maryland—all began under the aegis of proprietors, and the last three continued as such throughout the colonial period. For the most part, they were well governed and had low taxes. New York's situation was unusual in that it suffered from the wars with France as did New England; New Jersey, Delaware, and Maryland escaped because they were some distance from the combat, while Pennsylvania was not involved because it was controlled by pacifist Quakers.

All established land banks to excellent effect. New Jersey's began in 1723 and enabled the colony to tax at a very low rate for twenty-eight years. Pennsylvania's supported the government entirely for twenty-five, and Delaware may have matched New Jersey. New York's bank paid half of the colony's expenses and was so clearly beneficial that Parliament passed a special act to continue it, while Maryland's, started in 1723, enabled the government to invest a substantial sum in the Bank of England.

Before that date and during the Seven Years' War, land taxes, and specifically the quitrent and assessments on undeveloped land, were debated in these colonies. In New England these were not major issues except in New Hampshire, where quitrents resulting from early royal grants were a concern. In New York, first the Dutch West India Company and then the English government gave away large areas along the Hudson Valley during the seventeenth century and then distributed additional land to the north and west. The English required quitrents, which the great landowners opposed because they had difficulty placing settlers on the more distant tracts. Attempts by the governors to collect the money sometimes cost more than the proceeds, which did not even pay the governor's salary. Arrears by 1767 amounted to nearly twenty thousand pounds, which would have supported Connecticut's government for five years. Collections in New Jersey were no more successful. Pennsylvania's quitrents belonged to the Penn family. They were not heavy, only from a halfpenny to a penny per acre in rural areas (though much higher for town lots), the equivalent of a dollar or two per acre in current United States money, yet everyone complained, nonetheless. The collectors were negligent or worse, and the Penns only received about a third of the amount due, which barely paid their own costs. The situation was

even worse in Delaware, also owned by the Penns, who appointed insufficient collectors and no supervisors. The Calverts in Maryland charged half as much but were efficient and fair and so received twice the profit of any other government in the colonies.

The proprietors in Pennsylvania, Delaware, and Maryland owned the unoccupied land, disposing of it little by little in return for quitrents, so the question of taxing it arose only when the legislatures tried unsuccessfully to collect money from the proprietors. Besides, the counties were able to take care of local costs and the land banks paid for the rest. In New Jersey the proprietors understandably exempted their own land entirely and at first taxed only improved, or settled, tracts. Eventually they did assess unimproved land but kept all such taxes reasonably low. Under the subsequent royal government, the legislature assessed unimproved land at only four pounds per hundred acres (40 hectares), far less than its value, but then New Jersey taxes were less than a shilling per capita including slaves, about five dollars in current money, plus the equally low county rates. From 1724 to 1752, the legislature avoided debate by passing no revenue bill at all. It added no new taxes during the Seven Years' War, even though between 1754 and 1764 it spent £347,000 by issuing paper money. When Parliament paid a third of its wartime expenses the assembly, instead of reducing the debt, lowered the tax rate.

New York contained many towns similar to those in New England in that, along with the county governments, they paid for community services. The province obtained a good deal of revenue from its flourishing commerce through imposts on imports and excises, levying taxes on property only in emergencies. Its extensive unoccupied estates might have furnished a substantial revenue, but the large landowners, dominating the government, saw to it that only improved real estate was taxed, except in a few of the southern counties. The small farmers and tenants benefited from the reliance on import and excise taxes, since they bought few of the goods involved, but any assessment on land hurt them; even many tenants had to pay taxes on their farms and sometimes a quitrent as well. Luckily for them loan banks and paper money relieved the financial pressure during most of the eighteenth century. Thus these five middle colonies experienced little difficulty with the costs of government, though they wrangled bitterly with each other over costs and taxes.

THE SOUTHERN COLONIES

The remaining colonies of Virginia, the Carolinas, and Georgia were royal provinces for most of their existence. They had the relatively expensive officialdom which went along with that form of government; lacked effective local governments except when they were provided by vestries; relied heavily on staple crops and had little in the way of a commercial class outside of Charleston; had most of the slaves; and were dominated by a self-conscious, aristocratic upper class without parallel to the north, except in New York and Maryland. All relied for revenue primarily upon the poll tax, a land tax in the form of quitrents, an export tax on tobacco, and a duty on imported slaves after 1700. They had more prolonged tax disputes than other colonies and had no land banks, except in South Carolina.

The earliest taxes in Virginia were levied in 1619 on all male tithables above sixteen so as "better to tax the products of labor." A levy of two shillings per hogshead of tobacco was added in 1658. Along with a poll tax on slaves, these remained the major and uncontroversial sources of income for local governments and the province. The British government did little to extract quitrents until 1684, after which it became important for the establishment of the College of William and Mary, support of the Anglican clergy, and military expenses. On the whole the planters managed their finances successfully; trouble arose only toward the end of the colonial period, when declining tobacco prices, the cost of war, and overspending by the planters created financial problems. They then had to impose a land tax in 1755—the first in more than a hundred years—which was assessed equally on all acres, so that the owners of the most valuable lands, presumably themselves, would not be overburdened. It was repealed as soon as possible in 1769.

North Carolina was relatively poor, with few exports and an inefficient government that cost more than it should have. The colonists resisted the collection of quitrents, and the collectors retained most of what they extracted. Otherwise the colony depended upon a poll tax on white males over sixteen and on blacks, both female and male, over twelve—an exceptionally low age. As with land these human assets could not easily be concealed.

South Carolina differed from the other southernmost colonies in its reliance on deficit financing. It began with paper IOUs in 1703 for military reasons. In 1712 the legislature, encouraged by that experiment, established the colonies' first public loan bank; it was backed by land, slaves, and, later, taxes on the export of rice. The bank notes declined in value, apparently for lack of sufficient support (the British government vetoed an impost on slaves), but eventually assessments and payments of interest brought in enough to balance the budget in normal times. According to one estimate, the colony's taxes amounted to between 2.5 percent and 5 percent of annual income. The colony's landowners also paid a quitrent that went to the royal government. It seems not to have been very popular, and the proportion of the colony's supposedly taxable acreage reported to the collectors declined from 37 percent in 1734 to 19 percent in 1772.

That was much better than the situation in Georgia, where the administration under the proprietors, after the first ten years of settlement, attempted to collect four shillings per hundred acres (a rate later increased fivefold) with no luck. The Crown then offered to forgive the delinquents if they would commence payments, but the inability to draw up an adequate rent roll prevented any collections, and the government apparently dropped the matter. A subsidy from Parliament kept the colony afloat.

During the period after the Seven Years' War, and sometimes earlier, many colonists complained of their taxes. In truth they paid less than 5 percent of their income, averaging about a shilling per capita. Large costs during periods of war for some colonies were partially balanced by the complete absence of taxes in others and by money received from London. The English people were paying twenty times as much around 1750. True, the Seven Years' War was costly and was followed by a depression, so the taxes proposed by Parliament after 1763 came at a bad time. But that is a later story: for the colonial period as a whole, despite the existence of real grievances, taxation had been exceptionally light.

BIBLIOGRAPHY

Becker, Robert A. *Revolution, Reform, and the Politics of American Taxation, 1763–1783*. Baton Rouge, La., 1980. Covers only the final decade of the colonial period, is political in orientation rather than economic, and has its biases but is generally sound.

Bond, Beverley W., Jr. *The Quit-Rent System in the American Colonies*. New Haven, Conn., 1919. First-rate.

Bonomi, Patricia U. *A Factious People: Politics and Society in Colonial New York*. New York, 1971.

Gipson, Lawrence Henry. *Connecticut Taxation, 1750–1775*. New Haven, Conn., 1933.

Greene, Jack P. *The Quest for Power: The Lower Houses of Assembly in the Southern Royal Colonies, 1689–1776*. Chapel Hill, N.C., 1963.

James, Sidney V. *Colonial Rhode Island: A History*. New York, 1975. Original in defending the colony's monetary policy.

Kammen, Michael G. *Colonial New York: A History*. New York, 1975.

Munroe, John A. *Colonial Delaware: A History*. Millwood, N.Y., 1978.

Pomfret, John E. *Colonial New Jersey: A History*. New York, 1973. Condenses his two earlier books.

Ritchie, Robert C. *The Duke's Province: A Study of New York Politics and Society, 1664–1691*. Chapel Hill, N.C., 1977. Combined with Bonomi and Kammen, furnishes exceptional coverage of New York.

Selesky, Harold E. *War and Society in Colonial Connecticut*. New Haven, Conn., 1990.

Sirmans, Marion. *Colonial South Carolina: A Political History, 1663–1763*. Chapel Hill, N.C., 1966.

Watson, Alan D. "The Quitrent System in Royal South Carolina." *William and Mary Quarterly*, 3rd ser., 33, no. 2 (1976):183–211. Unfairly criticizes Bond but is a valuable, full discussion of the subject.

Jackson Turner Main
Jerome Reich

SEE ALSO **Crises of Empire; The European Contest for North America;** and **Reorganization of Empires;** and various essays in ECONOMIC LIFE.

THE DUTCH COLONY

DESPITE THE DUTCH WEST India Company's purported commitment to pursue free trade, its efforts to colonize New Netherland resulted in extensive regulation of the commerce and productive activities of settlers in the Hudson River vicinity. Most taxation was initiated on behalf of New Netherland for one of three purposes: to raise the revenues necessary for supporting local defense and salaries; to establish fees that would encourage higher quality and better regularity in economic exchange among colonists; or to eliminate the commercial competition of neighboring New England and New Jersey settlers. Import and export duties were collected in earnest by the governments of William Kieft (1638–1646) and Peter Stuyvesant (1647–1664). They became a greater source of revenue—and elicited a far greater amount of contention—than the land or excise taxes first passed during this period.

LEVYING EXCISE TAXES

Excise taxes—those on goods exchanged within the colony—covered primarily two commodities. The tax on beer, three guilders[1] per tun, was levied beginning in 1644; it was paid by the tapsters at the time they acquired beer from brewers or by brewers who sold beer directly to customers with a tavern license. The taxes on various wines, from one stiver to four guilders per "pot," began in 1647 and were normally paid by the importing merchant. In both cases, if we can believe the weight of contemporary evidence, the burdens of these taxes were passed on to consumers in the form of higher prices. Only in 1656 was an additional excise levied, that of about 5 percent ad valorem on slaughtered cattle.

---

[1] A guilder comprised twenty stuivers (or stivers). Over most of the Dutch period, beaver and wampum passed as local currency with silver guilder equivalencies; one beaver was equivalent to eight guilders (or florins), or one "piece of eight." In 1664 English Governor Richard Nicolls decreed that residents would continue to follow this equivalency and added that one beaver, or eight guilders silver, were also equivalent to thirteen shillings and four pence English sterling. However, devaluation of colonial currency in relation to both Dutch and English currencies makes generalizations difficult; before 1664 Stuyvesant periodically tampered with the value of Dutch guilders in relation to local currencies, and under the English in 1672, a "piece of eight" went for six shillings sterling; in 1692 a "piece of eight" went for six pence. Hence, I have compared the level of taxation in the colony with its home country rather than judge its burden, sui generis, on colonists.

ESTABLISHING LAND TAXES

Land taxes were passed, but largely uncollected, for two reasons. In the first place, Dutch colonial ideology and economic efforts in the colony were more commercial than agricultural, more centered on extracting goods for international commerce than settled productive efforts. In the second place, settlement was concentrated in New Amsterdam and Beverswyck and remained quite sparse over large areas; Rensselaerswyck and a few tobacco and mixed farming plantations comprised only minor efforts at improved real estate. Nevertheless, the governor and council first established land taxes in 1638. The first ordinance stipulated the payment of "Tenths," or one-tenth of the annual crop of each free patent in the colony after the first ten years of its settlement. It also established a quitrent of "one couple of Capons for a house and lot." An ordinance of 1652 attempted to raise a small quitrent from outlying settlements after one year of improvements and a minimal real estate tax from city properties; although it was approved by the States General in Amsterdam, it failed to produce significant revenues. A 1654 ordinance eliminated the exemptions for unimproved land and new settlers and set the tax at 20 stivers for every morgen (roughly 2.1 acres [.84 hectares]) of land, twenty stivers for each one- and two-year-old cattle, and "the hundreth penny of the real value" for every city house or vacant house lot. However, at no time was it feasible to collect these land taxes.

Moreover, down to the English conquest in 1664, there is evidence of only one levy on New Amsterdam's real estate. This 1655 levy was based upon "voluntary subscription and contribution, each according to his condition," to repay loans made by city merchants in previous years. Should such contributions not be forthcoming, the burgomasters were authorized to levy a tax on New Amsterdam real estate to raise the necessary monies. The authority for this particular assessment came from the 1638 grant by the West India Company of limited political and commercial freedoms to the colonists; Article Eight of the company's grant stipulated that "each householder and inhabitant shall bear such tax and public charge as shall hereafter be considered proper for the maintenance of Clergymen, comforters of the sick, schoolmasters and such like necessary officers. . . ." Other than the Tenths and the 1655 assessment, most outlying towns were permitted to raise small revenues from land taxes to pay the salaries and expenses of clergymen and schoolmasters. Attempts to assess unimproved lots in New Amsterdam proved wholly impossible during the Dutch period.

IMPOSING PORT DUTIES

Commercial port duties were the most lucrative assessments, and most regular form of income available to the colony for its maintenance and defense. From 1621 to 1638, the Dutch West India Company reserved the fur trade to itself and imposed an export duty of one guilder per beaver and otter skin. Over the same years, colonists paid eighteen guilders per last (four thousand weight) in duties on particular goods sent from Amsterdam plus a 5 percent import duty at New Amsterdam and eighteen guilders per one hundredweight of salt. The 1638 articles of the company, granting colonists free trade to all allies of the home country, set a 15 percent duty on all foreign imports and 30 percent—the highest rate recorded for any imperial colony at that time—on all exports from the colony made in foreign ships. In 1642 the company required the colony to impose a duty of 10 percent on all of its own importation as a means of dissuading merchants from shipping through non-Dutch ports at lower costs than the Amsterdam merchants faced by exporting from the home country. In 1651 the company decreed that all Virginia and New England imports should be charged 16 percent while all exports to those places were henceforth to be free of export duties—changes that appeased importers who needed the encouragement of import discrimination as well as peltry exporters who wished to seek the highest prices possible among all trading nations. In the next year the company set a tax on each imported slave from western Africa.

The governor and council of the colony also eschewed the principles of free trade in order to regulate the colony's commerce and generate necessary revenues. In 1638, the year the West India Company relinquished its monopoly of peltry exportation, the council set an 8 percent duty on beaver peltry exported from the colony, to be paid at the point of export by merchants; the provisions of the act were renewed periodically until 1647, when the duty was set at fifteen stivers per good peltry. In 1652 the duty was revised; in addition to renewing the 8 percent ad valorem duty on beaver, four stivers per otter, bear, and elk was added. The duty was disallowed by the company from 1654 until the end of the Dutch colonial period, except for the brief reoccupation in 1673 when peltry exports were taxed at 2.5 percent ad valorem. However, even the minimal export duty on peltry consistently evoked protests from New Amsterdam merchants, whether employees of the company or independent residents trading on their own accounts.

Export duties were also levied on codfish and tobacco soon after 1638; by 1656 exports and reexports of wine, brandy, and beer were also taxed. Over most years the level of taxation on the latter three commodities was approximately the same as the internal excise taxes.

Export duties were easier to evade than import duties, given the ease with which exporters could conceal and transport peltry overland to New England and New Jersey settlers. In fact, export smuggling was a regular subject of Council denunciation and regulation. However, after 1638 provincial authorities began making import duties more specific, hoping to stem illicit trade by tightening inspection and port procedures. To the extent that these duties were successfully collected, there grew widespread protests from consumers and producers, for merchants were passing on their higher costs with markups of from 100 percent to 400 percent.

Provincial import duties, over and above the duty imposed by the company at Amsterdam, were only 1 percent ad valorem during the early years. In 1654 the governor and council, responding to popular petitions and protests against the high price of necessary consumer items, reset the 1 percent general import duties so that particular items bore the weight of the colony's revenue collection with specific duties, including Indian goods reexported up the Hudson River, wine, brandy, and salt. The law was renewed in 1656. In 1658 the council further amended the company's 10 percent ad valorem duty on Virginia, New England, and New Jersey imports; although the council ratified the duty in principle, it exempted malt, tobacco, indigo, oil, vinegar, provisions, and sugar from duties in order to encourage trade with the West Indies. In 1673, the year of reoccupation, import duties were set at 2 percent for Indian goods and 5 percent for wine, brandy, spirits, muskets, and ammunition.

CHANGING RATIONALE FOR HIGH TAXES

Paeans to "free trade" notwithstanding, the Dutch West India Company, the independent traders, and the colonial government all supported high levels of taxation to raise revenues for defense and development, to control the quality of colonial commerce and impose regularity in trade, and to defeat English competitors along the northeast coastline. Although colonists' need for revenue and orderly, standardized economic development did not diminish, the stronger motivation for high taxes by the end of the Dutch period was discrimination against rival colonists along the coastline and in the West Indies. By 1664 New Netherland's system of taxation was focused on international commerce with an intricate web of differential rates for the commodities central to its exporting and importing. In this the colony was distinct from the Dutch mother country, which was beginning a long period of rising internal taxation on personal property.

BIBLIOGRAPHY

There is no single secondary source that summarizes the taxation of either the Dutch West India Company in America; or the colony's taxation of its own, and neighboring, settlers. See the following printed collections of primary documents for the political discussion and legislative enactments about taxation.

Fernow, Berthold, ed. *Records of the City of New Amsterdam from 1653 to 1674.* 7 vols. New York, 1897; repr. 1976.
Gehring, Charles T., ed. *The Curacao Papers.* Syracuse, N.Y., 1986.
———. *New-York Historical Manuscripts, Dutch.* Vol. 5, *Council Minutes, 1652–1654.* Syracuse, N.Y., 1983. Vols. 28–29, *Delaware Papers.* Syracuse, N.Y., 1981.
O'Callaghan, Edmund B., ed. and trans. *Laws and Ordinances of New Netherland, 1638–1674.* Albany, N.Y., 1868.

O'Callaghan, Edmund B., and Berthold Fernow, eds. and trans. *Documents Relative to the Colonial History of the State of New York.* 15 vols. Albany, N.Y., 1853–1887; repr. 1969.

Cathy D. Matson

SEE ALSO various essays in ECONOMIC LIFE.

THE FRENCH COLONY

THE EARLIEST SETTLERS in New France paid no taxes, and even in the eighteenth century most people were taxed very little. So conclude the historians of New France. What they mean is that the principal French taxes on real estate, merchandise, and the king's subjects were not imposed on the colonists in North America. People in New France did not pay the *taille,* the *gabelle,* the *tabac,* the *aides,* the *capitation,* or most of the customs duties. Colonial trade was not heavily taxed; seigneurial dues were moderate; the royal government was hoping to encourage colonists. In 1663 Louis XIV (r. 1661–1715) imposed a modest tithe (*dîme*) of one-thirteenth of the harvest. In 1667 Louis XIV reduced it to one-twenty-sixth (3.8 percent). The clergy in New France never succeeded in having this low rate increased, and at least one-third of church revenues had to come from France as subsidies.

FISCAL POLICIES
IN NEW FRANCE

Other burdens appear if we look at New France as part of the French colonial empire and reflect on the fiscal methods of that age. The monarchy had neither central treasury nor budget of the modern kind, and it customarily sold its taxing rights to financiers or financial companies. Among the advantages to the throne of this system was that the financiers, not the government, drew the popular hostility that taxes aroused. With the purchaser's right to tax came a list of government services to be paid out of the sums collected. Thus the financial system consisted of many private enterprises, each collecting specified taxes and paying a list of specified services. One example was a company contracted in 1725 to build a wall around Montreal for thirty-five thousand livres that were to be raised by a tax on the townspeople. Another example were the army purveyors (*munitionnaires*) who supplied the colonial soldiers stationed but in turn levied 2.5 percent of the soldiers' pay to meet the cost of clothing.

Hidden charges lurked in the system of naval payments for goods and services in the colonies. The two naval treasurers-general in Paris, one for even-numbered years, the other for odd-numbered years, maintained an agent in each colonial capital. The treasurers-general, having bought their offices, essentially ran a private profit-making financial system. Their agent at a colonial capital usually paid for goods and services with promissory notes or, at certain periods, with playing cards bearing an official mark. Then, in autumn, the agent would redeem these with bills of exchange drawn on his employers, the treasurers-general in Paris. But these bills were sometimes cashed at a discount in France; payments were often much delayed; and when the government was bankrupt, as in 1705 and 1759, payments stopped altogether and the government found pretexts for repudiating large sums in bills. Many of the Canadians who became British subjects in the conquest of 1759–1760 were never able to cash the bills with which the French government had paid them in previous years; Acadian exiles were also unable to collect.

Other taxes may be seen in the processes of the monopoly companies to which the Crown committed its colonies: the Compagnie des Cent-Associés (Company of One Hundred Associates) (1627–1663), the Indies Company (1664–1674), the Compagnie de l'Occident (1674–1718), and their eighteenth-century successors, beginning with Antoine Crozat's Compagnie de la Louisiane (1712–1717) and the short-lived companies established by John Law. Their monopolies included the right to collect duties on beaver pelts, moose hides, and a few other commodities. Until

1717 the sale of moose hides was taxed at 10 percent and until 1702 beaver pelts at 25 percent. In the 1690s, the records show, a new tax on hats was purchased and collected by a certain Bailly, but about 1700 it was added to the taxes collected by the domaine.

The monopolistic companies customarily sublet collection of certain duties to other financiers. An exceptional partner in several companies was Charles Aubert de la Chesnaye, an Amiens merchant who grew rich in transatlantic trade and settled at Quebec. In 1663 and for many years thereafter he leased the Tadoussac fur monopoly, which gave him the right to control and tax the beaver skins, moose hides, and seal skins throughout a huge region centered on the mouth of the Saguenay River but reaching north along the Labrador Coast. In July 1675 Chesnaye was one of ten businessmen who leased the entire Canadian fur monopoly.

Meanwhile, waiting at La Rochelle, Bordeaux, and other French ports were the financiers who had bought the right to collect various duties on imported goods, and those costs were of course passed on to the public on both sides of the Atlantic. Duties on ships and their cargoes were imposed at colonial ports as well as in France. In wartime, the local admiralty office could charge 10 percent of the profits on enemy ships captured and sold as prizes. In most years of the eighteenth century, the bureau of the domaine at Quebec usually collected from one thousand to two thousand livres per cargo imported, about half of this for rum from the West Indian colonies or for wine and brandy from France. Whatever the cargo, a ship entering or leaving a harbor was charged various duties: at Louisbourg, for instance, seven duties totaling about thirty-five livres were charged each departing vessel. These were for the admiralty office's inspections, registrations, licenses, and passports, which entailed delays and paperwork as well as fees. Some of the bureaucratic controls were characteristic of authoritarian states like Bourbon France, which had repressive policies of trying to prevent ships from visiting foreign ports without official permission and of trying to prevent people suspected of Protestant heresies from escaping abroad. Legal charges were high enough to discourage even merchants from seeking redress in the courts.

The taxes on trade and shipping weighed only indirectly upon country folk; seigneurial dues were the principal taxes in the countryside. These varied so much that the amounts paid cannot be usefully summarized, but they were not heavy by French standards. The *cens* was a small levy assessed on land for the privilege of holding it *en censive*, under which it could not be sublet. *Cens* marked a paying tenant as a *censitaire*, a name used to describe a French seigneurial tenant until the French Revolution of 1789, but it was not as large as the *rente* paid annually to the seigneur in money, wheat, or other produce, according to contract. Added to the *rente* here and there was a *corvée* of one or two days compulsory labor. When a tenancy was sold the seigneur could claim payment of the *lods et ventes*, a sales tax which might be as high as one-twelfth of the sale price. In New France no seigneur could claim hunting rights, but he could collect payments for fishing, grazing livestock on common land, and the use of his flour mill. On the island of Montreal by 1731 there were fifteen mills for which the seigneurial religious order that held the island charged a *banalité* of one-fourteenth of the flour milled. Like other compulsory payments, these may be classified as service charges, but they looked very much like taxes to the people who paid them.

BIBLIOGRAPHY

Bosher, J. F. *French Finances, 1770–1795: From Business to Bureaucracy.* Cambridge, England, 1970.

Clark, John Garretson. *New Orleans, 1718–1812: An Economic History.* Baton Rouge, La., 1970.

Harris, Richard Colebrook. *The Seigneurial System in Early Canada: A Geographical Study.* Madison, Wis., 1966.

Lunn, Alice Jean. *Dévelopement économique de la Nouvelle-France, 1713–1760.* Montreal, 1986.

Mathieu, Jacques. *Le commerce entre la Nouvelle-France et les Antilles au XVIIIe siècle.* Montreal, 1981.

J. F. Bosher

See also The Framework of Government; Local Government; Relations with the Parent Country; and various essays under ECONOMIC LIFE.

THE SPANISH BORDERLANDS

INITIAL TREASURY ARRANGEMENTS

WHEN SPAIN BEGAN its colonization of the New World, the Crown believed that the combination of income generated from trade and tribute payments from its new subjects would greatly contribute to its wealth. With the discovery of rich silver mines in both Mexico and Peru, however, the main focus of taxation shifted to the payment of the *quinta real* (royal fifth), soon cut to a tenth, of total production. Spain used this immense treasure to pay for wars throughout Europe for the preservation of Catholicism and its greater glory.

The northern frontier, however, proved a significant exception to this pattern. Despite Fray Marcos de Niza's tall tales in the 1540s of Seven Cities of Gold, there proved to be no major mines in what are now Florida, Louisiana, Texas, New Mexico, Arizona, and Colorado, nor in California until 1849. The lack of mines influenced much of the nature of the colonization and taxation in these areas on the outskirts of empire. Without precious metals and so far from the major centers of Spanish life, these colonies suffered from lack of civilian population until almost the end of the eighteenth century.

That lack of population is reflected in the treasury arrangements designed in Mexico City for administering the far north. From 1598 until 1769, only one *caja real* (royal treasury) in Durango served the entire region, including five of the six Mexican states—Sonora, Chihuahua, Coahuila, Nuevo León, and Tamaulipas—which today lie along the border with the United States. Since that branch of the treasury received the vast majority of its funds from taxes on silver mining, historians cannot yet determine what proportion was contributed by the far northern areas.

THE BOURBON REFORMS AND THE PROVINCIAS INTERNAS

In 1772 the Crown altered its relations with the North by redesigning its system of frontier defenses, and four years later by creating a new administrative unit, the Provincias Internas. These changes were part of the Bourbon reforms, a series of measures designed to stimulate the colonial economy and, by so doing, to increase revenue collections. Part of the new policy was a concerted effort to maintain peace with Indian tribes by subduing them on the battlefield and by providing food, clothing, and other goods in exchange for continued tranquillity along the frontier. The campaigns against the Indians were spearheaded by soldiers stationed in New Mexico and financed by the royal treasuries of Mexico City, Durango, and later Chihuahua; their success led to significant economic gains throughout the region.

Royal officials had other instruments in mind for raising revenues as well. In November 1765 José de Gálvez, the viceroy of New Spain, directed the governor of New Mexico to organize the tobacco monopoly there, as had been done in other areas throughout the viceroyalty. The Crown hoped that monopolies would make the northern areas as self-supporting as possible. Governor Tomás Velez Cachupín replied that the monopoly would hurt the provincial economy because the region, like all other parts of the Spanish Empire, lacked circulating coin and would require the suppression of native tobacco (*punche*), grown both by *vecinos* (colonists) and by nearby Pueblo Indians. Although the Crown apparently never succeeded in outlawing *punche,* the monopoly became one of the major sources of revenue in the entire area and throughout the viceroyalty. The gunpowder, stamped paper, and playing card monopolies also did well in the far north, although most payments were made in kind or through barter.

Because the Crown was so concerned with foreign threats to its empire, it decided to opt for greater economic development of the North, which would ultimately stimulate population growth and, thus, greater protection, rather than short-term increases in treasury collections. This perspective is demonstrated in the case of *alcabala* (sales tax) collections in New Mexico and elsewhere. When Juan de Oñate agreed to establish a colony in New Mexico in 1598, the Crown exempted the new area from the payment of the 2 percent sales tax for the following decade. Extant records indicate that with the establishment of the Bourbon reforms, beginning in 1764, the Crown initially sought to raise revenues by insisting on *alcabala* collections on all merchandise purchased in Chihuahua. Those collections finally began in 1780 in the province of New Mexico including El Paso del Norte, but the taxes themselves were mainly invisible because they remained uncollected or were added to the prices in Chihuahua or in the *presidio* company store. In 1796 the Crown permitted a new exemption for a decade in order to protect the growing trade between New Mexico and Chihuahua, a decision that bore ample fruit in increased revenues. The *alcabala* was not collected in Texas or in California because the *situado* (subsidy for the maintenance of outlying areas) from San Blas was specifically exempted, since the territory was still being settled. Spanish Florida, too, was exempted from payments for the entire period from 1702 to 1763.

Frontier residents were hardly exempted from the payments of church tithe, however. The tithe was collected in kind and often farmed out to a local *rico* (rich man) for a fixed sum, although it was often difficult to find anyone sufficiently creditworthy to fulfill his part of the bargain.

As part of the Bourbon reforms and the creation of the Provincias Internas, the Crown opened four new *cajas reales* in the North (Los Álamos, Rosario, and Cosalá [1770], Arispe [1781], Chihuahua [1785], and Saltillo [1794]); none of these were located in the borderlands. Between 1773 and 1798 some 100,000 to 440,000 pesos annually left Durango and these *cajas* for the farther north. Arispe, the capital of the Provincias Internas, shipped moneys to support *presidios* in Tucson and Tubac; Chihuahua financed Santa Fe and El Paso del Norte; and Saltillo supplied Monclova and San Antonio. The system of payments facilitated the growth of a fiscal and commercial network throughout the North whereby communities on the frontier like Santa Fe were connected to better-established communities farther inland like Chihuahua; the latter supplied them with goods and were themselves much more closely linked to Mexico City. The ties that developed maintained crucial linkages with the rest of the viceroyalty and helped keep the area loyal to Spain.

CREATION OF NEW NATIONAL GOVERNMENTS

Crown concerns notwithstanding, it was the *vecinos* who had the most to fear from instability along the frontier. They recognized the danger and were not hesitant to supply voluntary loans to maintain necessary defenses, particularly during the 1790s and later. For that reason, the borderlands seemed hardly conscious of the wars to free Mexico from Spain.

After 1820 New Mexico in particular found itself threatened by hostile Indians due to the migration of the peaceful Comanche tribes who had protected them from the more aggressive Indian groups. In general residents of the area were forced to fend for themselves. In exchange for exemption from having to pay taxes, New Mexicans organized a citizen militia whose members defended the populace at their own considerable expense; the volunteers had to buy their own weapons and leave their fields for long periods to join the campaigns against the Indians.

Now freed from colonial rule, *vecinos* and settlers in other northern areas had to face two new and quite different enemies: the growth of the United States and the financial insolvency of the Mexican treasury. The Mexican Constitution of 1824 declared that Texas and its southern neighbor Coahuila would be considered one state, and that New Mexico and the Californias would be recognized as territories. In the beginning, national fiscal records lumped expenses for all frontier areas with that of San Luis Potosí, and they were rarely consistent.

The new treasury system relied on taxes on foreign trade rather than those on silver mining, which had dried up after independence. In 1829 the government abolished the profitable tobacco monopoly. The shift greatly benefited frontier areas with newly opened ports, such as Monterrey in California, and internal customs stations like that in Santa Fe. However, the newly opened ports and territories attracted merchants from the United States who brought large supplies of needed goods at prices more attractive than those from customary Mexican sources.

The new traders also encouraged contraband. Despite its good intentions, the republican government in Mexico City lacked the means to enforce tariff collections and trade restrictions.

Unpaid and underpaid customs officials often accepted bribes simply to survive, and the navy had only five vessels to defend ten thousand miles (160,000 kilometers) of coastline. Reliance on trade taxes also made the treasury more vulnerable as when in 1825 a financial crisis in Britain provoked a serious economic collapse in Europe and threw trade with Mexico into sharp decline. As a result, Mexico defaulted on its foreign loans in August 1827. In the following year, national expenditures earmarked specifically for the northern frontier dropped by 1.5 million pesos. The loss of revenue led to substantial internal borrowing for short periods at high interest rates (*agiotaje*) and added to the treasury's growing problems.

Whenever the government tried to increase revenues by raising tariff rates, smuggling increased, with traders employing the time-honored techniques of fake manifests, false bottoms, paying on only part of a shipment, or transacting business in the name of a willing Mexican citizen or a complaisant Mexican wife. Since foreign merchants were often the only source of needed items at reasonable prices, and because local governments found themselves dependent on revenues from trade, officials and settlers on the frontier resented laws from Mexico City that threatened their well-being and consistently turned a blind eye whenever the national government passed laws detrimental to such activity in their areas. Often these officials set their own tariff rates to stimulate trade, for, as California Governor Mariano Chico noted, "the Californias would disappear" without smuggling.

The result on the northern frontier was devastating. Unlike their Spanish predecessors, the new national governments were unable to fund troops to protect outlying areas against the constant threat from increasing Indian attacks. In addition, growing trade with merchants from the United States was gradually unraveling the ties that had been so carefully woven between the far north and merchants in Chihuahua and Sonora, as did the influx of Americans who flooded Texas as colonizers. Some officials suggested that the Mexican government take steps to link these areas more firmly to the national economy, but their advice was ignored, prompting even greater alienation from Mexico and greater dependence on the rapidly growing United States economy.

The Mexican government, however, was preoccupied with its own difficulties. In response to its fiscal distress and anticlerical sentiment, in 1833 Mexican Vice-President Valentín Gómez Farías tried to fill the national treasury with the tax moneys garnered when the government ordered the church to sell its nonessential property. That measure sparked revolts throughout Mexico, and Santa Fe "pronounced" in favor of a centralist government under Antonio López de Santa Anna in the hopes that such government could provide troops for protection against Indian raids. Once the centralist system was in place, Texas quickly took advantage of the opportunity and successfully rebelled against Santa Anna's troops, a fact Mexico refused to recognize.

Following the debacle in Texas, the Mexican government, now under Anastasio Bustamante, reorganized the national treasury and decentralized collections on 17 April 1838. Each state (department) was to use half of its revenues to support army units stationed there or elsewhere. As a result, Sonora subsidized presidial troops at Altar, Babispe, Bacoachí, Buenavista, Pitic, Santa Cruz, Tubac, and Tucson; Sinaloa supported those at Monterrey, Rosario, and San Diego. But as a result of the new constitution, the Mexican government declared that all departments had to pay taxes, which New Mexicans had never done before.

They learned of the new tax law in July 1837. Although the governor made no attempt to collect such taxes, rumors circulated that Mexico City wanted exorbitant amounts, perhaps totaling one-third to one-half of a family's property. By the end of the month the people of Santa Cruz de la Cañada had organized a revolt in Río Arriba against the new taxes. On 8 August 1837 the rebels killed Governor Pérez and defeated his forces at La Mesilla (Black Mesa). According to legend, they decapitated Albino Perez's body and carried the head on a pole, shouting to it, "Ah, you robber! You will no longer extort taxes; you will no longer drink chocolate or coffee!"

Alarmed by the excesses of the rebellion, the rest of the populace quickly banded together to support the status quo, much as a similar group had done in Guanajuato when faced with similar behavior at the start of the Mexican independence movement in 1810. Manuel Armijo, a former governor, trained volunteers and collected loans from both foreign merchants and wealthy local citizens. The threat of violence was enough to convince the rebels to sign a treaty in Santa Fe on 21 September 1837 that agreed to recognize Armijo as the political and military head of the area, disband their forces, and turn over the four leaders of the initial rebellion. Once they had quelled the uprising, government troops threatened rebellion unless they were paid. In that, too, Armijo was successful; by the end of the year he had collected nearly five thousand pesos to pay the troops. By 9 January 1838 the first centralist government troops arrived, as did the official pronouncement of Armijo's appointment as constitutional governor and head of the militia. Armijo kept the peace by fostering low (illegal) tariffs and by not collecting the taxes owed to the central government. In exchange New Mexico remained loyal to Mexico City until 1846, when American troops arrived.

CONCLUSION

Residents of the northern borderlands under Spain or Mexico never suffered the burdens of heavy or unreasonable taxation that British colonists under King George III bore. Whenever a government issued an unpalatable regulation, distance allowed officials to ignore its provisions. Yet ultimately they felt the effects of weakened administrations that could not protect their coasts from contraband or their territory from stronger neighbors.

BIBLIOGRAPHY

Frank, Ross H. "From Settler to Citizen: Economic Development and Cultural Change in Late Colonial New Mexico, 1750–1820." Ph.D. diss., University of California at Berkeley, 1992.

Lecompte, Janet. *Rebellion in Río Arriba, 1837.* Albuquerque, N.Mex., 1985.

Navarro García, Luis. *Las Provincias Internas en el siglo XIX.* Seville, 1965.

Tenenbaum, Barbara A. "The Making of a Fait Accompli: Mexico and the Provincias Internas, 1776–1846." In *The Development of the Mexican Political System,* edited by Jaime E. Rodríguez O. Wilmington, Del., 1993.

———. *The Politics of Penury: Debts and Taxes in Mexico, 1821–1856.* Albuquerque, N.Mex., 1986.

Weber, David J. *The Mexican Frontier, 1821–1846: The American Southwest Under Mexico.* Albuquerque, N.Mex., 1982.

Barbara A. Tenenbaum

SEE ALSO various essays in ECONOMIC LIFE.

CRIME AND LAW ENFORCEMENT

THE BRITISH COLONIES

A FUNDAMENTAL MAXIM of Anglo-American law, *nulla poena sine lege* (the state may not punish those who have not broken the law), would appear to reduce an examination of crime and law enforcement in British colonial America to a study of the formalities of law. Working English and colonial magistrates knew better. The language of the lawbooks might define offenses and frame procedure, but law enforcement rested then, as it does today, upon shared communal values. If, as was true for much of the colonial era, a tightly knit elite of trained lawyers and judges, serving and representing a landed gentry, drafted the law of crime and instructed the magistrates, authorities could only catch and prosecute criminals through the active participation of a broad segment of the community. If English and colonial criminal law favored those with wealth and power over those with neither, the weakest members of the community nonetheless had a stake in effective law enforcement, for they were most often the victims of crime.

CRIMINAL COURTS AND LAW

Colonial criminal courts and law followed the contours but diverged in significant details from English models. In both the mother country and the colonies the structure of courts was hierarchical. Local courts handled less serious crimes, assize (circuit) or central courts heard and determined cases that were more serious. In England, some jurisdictions like the Duchy of Lancaster and the Bishopric of Durham operated semi-autonomously; elsewhere, serious crimes were Pleas of the Crown and heard in the royal courts. The various colonies derived the right to try criminals from their individual charters and exhibited a variety of laws and courts, some closely modeled upon the mother country, others quite different.

Criminal Courts in England

The criminal courts in England evolved over the course of seven hundred years from the Norman invasion of Saxon England in 1066 until the American Revolution. The king impressed his law upon the countryside by commissioning trustworthy members of his council and leading lawyers to hold court throughout the realm. Under the Tudor kings, beginning late in the fifteenth century, the periodic but irregular tours of royal commissioners were replaced by the biennial "assize," or circuit, courts held in the major towns of the counties. The king also commissioned powerful and respected men in each county as justices of the peace. The justices kept order, inquired into accusations of crime, and convened "quarter-sessions courts" four times a year to enforce royal statutes, oversee the licensing of businesses, punish the immoral and corrupt, and keep the roads in good order. Serious crimes (called "felonies") were reserved to the courts of assize.

Criminal-law enforcement was a public affair in England. Local courts met in taverns, castles, and other familiar places, and commoners came to these courts to pay fines, give evidence, pray for the aid of the justices, or file legal papers. Some sat as jurors. When the assize judges arrived to "deliver" the jails of suspected felons and preside over their trials, many people came into the county town to view the spectacle. Trials might last a week, rarely longer, and punishment followed swiftly for those convicted of crime.

Criminal Courts in the Colonies

Colonial criminal courts were less formal and perhaps less awesome than those in England, but they were closer to the people and just as effective. Pleadings were in English, not Latin, and a larger proportion of the adult male population participated in the courts' operation. The lowest officer of colonial criminal jurisdiction was the justice of the peace, who dealt with petty offenses. Although he was not required to keep a record of his actions, and few such records survive, the personal diaries of some of these justices suggest that they relied on a system of fines and bonds that bound neighbors to keep the peace with each other and obey the laws. This semiprivate network of order-keeping drew its strength from the relative homogeneity of the community and the influence of leading figures in the village or parish. Often these men posted sureties that would be forfeited if the offender repeated the offense, indebting the offender to them as they indebted themselves to the court. This "watch and warn" system of law enforcement was cheap to administer.

The justices of the peace also met at county courts much like the English quarter sessions to hear grand juries present men and women for violations of law. Presentments for drunkenness, sexual misconduct, failure to attend church, assault, and battery dominated the dockets. The accused might ask for a trial jury, but juries were paid for by the party seeking them, and most suspects "put themselves upon the court." Any

free white male could be called by the sheriff for jury duty. Those who failed to appear were fined.

In all the colonies, serious crimes fell to the jurisdiction of the central courts. These might move about the colony, as did the Massachusetts Superior Court, or sit at the capitol, as did the General Court of Virginia, the council with which the governor presided over all capital offenses. To these courts came all felonies. In these cases defendants were much more likely to ask for a jury trial than in the county court, unless they had already bargained their admission of guilt for conviction on a lesser offense. Plea bargaining was common in the colonies.

At all levels of the system, colonial lawgivers and judges shared two of the ruling assumptions of their English counterparts. The first was that there was no clear line of demarcation between crime and sin. The pious person was law-abiding; the dissolute of spirit would commit or had committed crimes. The association was natural in a society whose lawmakers prosecuted Protestant religious dissent and threatened Roman Catholics with death. Sinful activities like drunkenness, failure to attend church, and fornication made up the vast majority of criminal prosecutions in both England and her North American colonies. The second assumption of authorities in both locales was that such "sinful misconduct" led to more serious crime: the profligate youth became the adult thief; the disorderly youth became the mature murderer.

In British colonial America, criminal courts had a dual function: to keep order and to determine guilt or innocence. These functions overlapped but did not coincide perfectly. In times of civil disorder, both England and her colonies used the criminal-justice system to suppress dissent. On these occasions, the determination of guilt or innocence was sacrificed to the goal of defending the interests of the existing government. In addition, seventeenth-century colonial courts operated under different demographic conditions than those in England. English authorities wished to rid the realm of its surplus of "sturdy beggars"—the wandering poor. In the first colonies, labor was always scarce and correspondingly valued. No colony ever duplicated the severity of punishment for petty crime on the English statute books.

Colonial courts differed from English courts in one even more important respect. English judges, particularly those sitting in the central courts, were well trained in the law. Many had practiced law themselves; some sought appointment as clerks in the central courts; others had been serjeants-at-law or king's counsel and represented the Crown in important matters of law. Colonial high-court judges, by contrast, were men of affairs and authority in their communities who were acquainted with law but rarely trained in it. Moreover, they were never full-time jurists. The highest courts of Massachusetts and Virginia, for example, rarely included more than one well-educated lawyer. The legal skills of the judges in Pennsylvania were no stronger. Only the duke of York's province could boast a legally literate bench. This pattern continued well into the eighteenth century in most of the colonies.

The result of laymen on the high-court benches might have been swift and sensible justice. Massachusetts Superior Court justices such as Samuel Sewall were deeply moral men, concerned about the quality of their performance, but other colonial judges were neither as ethical nor as able. Governors such as William Cosby of New York, doubling as judges, disgraced themselves by venality and partisanship.

Types of Crime

English and colonial criminal law defined two general types of crime: felony and misdemeanor. Felonies were serious crimes, including murder, treason, rape, burglary, robbery, counterfeiting, arson, forgery, and grand larceny. After 1650 in England, felonies comprised a mixed group of offenses against property that included acts of social protest such as breaking the factory machinery that was replacing handworkers.

The penalty for felony was death, but benefit of clergy, transportation, pardon, and jury mitigation could avert capital punishment for a host of offenses. Introduced in the fourteenth century, benefit of clergy could be pled by clerics and monks, exempting them from trial in the king's courts. By the eighteenth century, the plea could be made by anyone. Murder, treason, and a few other capital offenses were never "clergy-able." When benefit of clergy was permitted, a defendant was branded and allowed to go free.

In eighteenth-century England, capital punishment was also mitigated by "transportation" for a term of seven or fourteen years. Transportees were sent to the colonies under guard and placed with masters who paid for the convict's labor; they were more likely to end up in Maryland or Virginia than in any other colony. Transportees could not return before their term expired, upon penalty of death. Some of the convicts were political dissidents, others were poor farm laborers who had engaged in some form of protest against their working conditions—for example, by wrecking agricultural machinery or setting crops on fire. The majority of the transportees appear to have been professional criminals.

Many convicted felons were pardoned by the Crown. Upon the request of the home secretary and with the approval of the trial judge, the king issued pardons to more than 50 percent of those convicted of capital offenses. Such pardon was purely discretionary, a free gift of the king's grace. The use of pardon reaffirmed the king's authority and his mercy. The promise of pardon could turn offenders into informers; the threat of refusal of pardon hung over every unrepentant defendant. Succor from above reminded the convict and the potential wrongdoer that criminal law and courts were the agencies of the state.

The community also interposed itself between the severity of felony law and defendants. Victims, jurors, and judges wanted order and public safety, but they understood that some crimes were the direct result of poverty and want. Juries regularly alleviated punishment for children and first offenders in theft cases by altering the value of the object taken and reducing the offense from a felony to a misdemeanor. Judges often permitted and sometimes encouraged this common subterfuge.

Benefit of clergy, pardon, and jury mitigation were all exercised in those colonies where the list of capital offenses was similar to England's. Other colonies chose from the outset not to duplicate the severity of England's penal code. In New England, crimes against property, notably burglary and robbery, were not capital unless the convict was a repeat offender. The Puritans had protested against criminal prosecution of their co-religionists in England, but were not tolerant of dissent against their own colonial government. In New England, Puritans may have mitigated punishment for serious crimes against property because labor was so scarce and therefore so valuable, although New England was not a major producer of staple goods for the Atlantic market and did not need agricultural laborers as desperately as did the tobacco colonies to the south. The Quaker colonies of Pennsylvania and the Jerseys mitigated punishment for crimes against property with the express motive of reforming the severity of English penal law. Murderers were hanged, but those convicted of other offenses were shamed (for example, by having to stand in the stocks or wear a letter denoting their offense), fined, sold into forced labor, whipped, or incarcerated for short terms.

Misdemeanors were by far the crimes most frequently committed in the colonies. The most common misdemeanors were assault and battery, rioting, sexual misconduct, abusing the constables or the magistrates, vagrancy, and violating any of the multitude of economic and moral regulatory statutes—for example, by selling alcoholic beverages without a license, overcharging for bread, or failing to attend church. Punishment for misdemeanor was usually a fine, corporal punishment, or some form of shaming. Alternatively, or in addition, the offender might be required to post a bond ensuring future good behavior. Sureties were required as well from neighbors who would forfeit their bonds if the offender repeated the offense.

Transmission and Reception of Criminal Law

Information about English criminal law reached the earliest colonies in three ways. Some elements of the law were dictated to the colonies or were based on knowledge of precedent. For example, formal royal charters enabling merchant companies and individual proprietors in the North American colonies to hold and govern land contained strictures on criminal law. Acts of Parliament, rulings of the king's attorney general, and central court and privy council opinions later also became sources of criminal law for the colonies, as did special instructions given to the colonial governors by the king's secretary of state for the Southern Department. In later years, decisions by Crown courts on criminal cases that

had been appealed from colonial courts supplemented the former sources of official transmission of criminal law.

Lawbooks were a second means by which law was conveyed. Alphabetical abridgments of English law, such as Francis Bacon's and later Charles Viner's, were purchased by colonial assemblies or were carried to the colonies as the private possessions of individuals. English manuals for justices of the peace such as Michael Dalton's *The Countrey Justice* (1618) were very common, and expanded local editions including Virginia justice George Webb's *The Office and Authority of a Justice of Peace* (1736) were widely read. These manuals were also alphabetical, but they detailed the statutory bases for criminal jurisdiction as well as the managerial functions of justices of the peace. Treatises on criminal law such as Matthew Hale's *Pleas of the Crown: A Methodical Summary* (which went through many editions between 1678 and 1773) and William Hawkins's *A Treatise of the Pleas of the Crown* (also in many editions, beginning in 1716) circulated widely.

Finally, knowledge of English criminal law sometimes arrived in the colonies with the emigrants themselves. While few among the early settlers had practiced law or acted as magistrates in England, over time the number of trained English lawyers and judges who went to the colonies grew. Many colonists had prosecuted or given testimony in English courts. Sometimes these men and women were unhappy with the criminal justice system they had left behind and so brought to the New World a determination to reform criminal law and courts. These reforms manifested themselves in the first criminal codes of the Puritan colonies and the Quaker colonies. Never did transmission of English criminal law to the colonies result in mere duplication of that law, for in each of the colonies local needs and goals transformed English precedent and rules.

Virginia. When the first settlers of Jamestown, Virginia, weakened and died at a frightening pace, Captain John Smith, a lively and well-traveled mercenary soldier, seized control of the dispirited, rebellious settlement and refashioned it along military lines. Although Smith returned to England in 1609 to answer complaints from his disgruntled comrades, his approach to criminal law continued under his successors. Governor Sir Thomas Gates drew up the *Articles, Lawes, and Orders, Divine, Politique and Martiall,* modeling them upon the law which the English conquerors imposed upon Northern Ireland. Governor Sir Thomas Dale enforced them so energetically, they came to be called Dale's Laws.

With time and dispersion of settlement the colonists raised objections in Virginia and in London to the rigor of Dale's Laws. The introduction of some of the key features of English criminal law, particularly the trial jury, was well under way by 1624, when the Crown reclaimed the charter of the colony from the Virginia Company of London and made the tiny settlement on the James River into North America's first royal province. The leading planters had assembled in a House of Burgesses in 1619 and had already begun passing statutes on crime. These statutes, not English law per se, formed the criminal law of Virginia. Later, despite efforts by English authorities to control lawmaking from the center of empire, the North Carolina, South Carolina, and Georgia colonies followed the Virginia example.

The greatest initial variation between the criminal law of England and that of the southern colonies was in the area of game laws. In England, poaching in the king's royal forest preserves or upon the lands of noblemen, or even carrying firearms when not training with the militia, was a serious offense for commoners; repeaters could expect a death sentence. Colonial men and women could carry weapons, and freemen in almost all the colonies were expected to take part in militia exercises. Game was freely stalked, taken, and eaten from the forests, fields, and streams. In the South, where open fields and hunting for sport framed a way of life, game laws would have been unthinkable.

New England. While still in England, the Puritans, harassed by church courts and threatened by civil courts to cease their complaints, called for wholesale reformation of criminal law. Part of their justification for rebelling against Charles I, who succeeded his father James I in 1625, was his persecution of Puritans in the courts. Puritans called for simplification of the law in codes that were clear and fair. Crimes of immorality—for example adultery and blasphemy—were to be treated with greater severity;

Puritan dissent was to be tolerated; all penalties were to be rationalized; and procedure was to be made consistent and direct.

The leading Puritans who made up the board of the Virginia Company of Plymouth, after secretly transporting themselves and the charter of the company from London to Boston, Massachusetts, exercised supreme judicial authority within the new, self-governing colony. Led by the Massachusetts Bay Company's first governor, John Winthrop (elected in 1629), the company officers, known as the "assistants," heard and determined criminal cases without a code of laws. Pressure from the deputies elected by the towns eventually induced the assistants in 1641 to commission Nathaniel Ward, who had legal training, to draft a model code for Massachusetts, the Body of Liberties. The code was revised and adopted as the *Lawes and Libertyes* in 1648.

The Liberties combined a frame of government, the prototype of a bill of rights, and a penal code. Much of its language was based upon earlier English declarations of rights, including the Great Charter of 1215 and the parliamentary Petition of Right of 1628. Unlike the latter, which left the prerogative of the Crown intact, the Liberties limited the discretion of Massachusetts to prosecute crimes.

No mans life shall be taken away, no mans honour or good name shall be stayned, no mans person shall be arested, restrayned, . . . no mans goods or estaite shall be taken away from him, . . . unless it be by vertue or equitie of some expresse law of the Country waranting the same, established by a general Court and sufficiently published. . . . Every person within this jurisdiction, whether Inhabitant or forreiner, shall enjoy the same justice and law, that is general for the plantation.

Although the Liberties declared certain rights, the inhabitants of Massachusetts Bay understood that these rights were not abstract principles but were woven into the fabric of Puritan community life. Equal protection of the laws did not forbid special privileges—quite the contrary: gender, wealth, family, political position, and above all religious persuasion made a difference in how one actually would be treated under the criminal laws. Woe to the Quaker or other sectarian who persistently flouted the will or questioned the privileges of Puritan institutions.

A list of crimes and punishments followed the civil provisions. Some of this "penal code" was taken from English criminal law, but other parts were taken from the Old Testament—enough to be more than window dressing, but less than an attempt to rebuild Jersualem. In fact, although adultery, apostasy, and blasphemy were made capital crimes in Massachusetts, as was disrespect to parents, men and women were almost never prosecuted for these offenses, and even those few prosecuted rarely suffered the prescribed penalty. The borrowing of Old Testament injunctions was primarily a solemn public warning to those at the edges of the community against violation of the deeper social mores that held the Puritan towns in the wilderness together.

Connecticut criminal law was modeled upon that of Massachusetts, but prosecution of crime in the distinct colony of New Haven was closer to Old Testament precedent. Rhode Island's first criminal code was far more lenient than that of Massachusetts, reflecting the influence of the minister Roger Williams. Williams was not an absolute advocate of toleration, but at the same time he did not believe that people's consciences should be coerced by magistrates.

The Middle Colonies. The colonies of New York, Pennsylvania, and the Jerseys established their own distinct criminal-justice systems. When the Dutch colony of New Netherland fell to the forces of the Duke of York in 1664, the English generously allowed the Dutch to retain their property and practice their religion. The Duke of York's laws allowed the Dutch mayors' courts to function in New York City and Albany and made concessions to Dutch customary law as well. After a series of political upheavals ending with Jacob Leisler's revolt in 1689, the criminal-justice system attained the form it was to have for the rest of the colonial period. The law conformed closely to English practice: a central supreme court was established, local courts in each county heard minor offenses, and specially commissioned courts (courts of oyer and terminer) heard and determined serious crimes.

In the Quaker colonies of East and West Jersey (unified as the royal colony of New Jersey in 1702) and Pennsylvania, the criminal law was far more lenient than anywhere else in the colonies. William Penn, the first governor and pro-prietor of Pennsylvania, guaranteed leniency in the colony's 1682 Frame of Government and subsequently renewed his promise, a liberality based upon humane Quaker principles. The only capital offense was murder. Quaker local courts were busy with minor criminal offenses, but Quaker authorities encouraged parties to take their quarrels to church courts, and persuasion often sufficed to keep the peace. Although Quakers did assault, slander, and even steal from each other, they were never as contentious or criminally inclined as their neighbors.

Criminal Law for Native Americans. Like the stranger in biblical Jewish kingdoms, everyone in the Puritan commonwealths was to be judged by the same law. The price of such formal equality was that Native Americans, despite their different ways, values, and cultures, were not allowed to claim the protection of their own customs or laws. Indians accused of attacking English settlers were tried by the Puritans under the Liberties, in disregard of Native American customs concerning honor and retribution. Although the Puritans assured the Indians that Englishmen who victimized Indians would be similarly treated, in fact little protection was given to the Native Americans. When any Indians went to war, the Puritans' response was swift and thorough: Native American villages were burned to the ground; often women and children perished with the warriors. Indians at peace with the Puritans, even tribes of "praying Indians," were attacked by whites, forced to leave their villages, and confined in "safe" compounds.

Not all the New England governments were unscrupulous in their dealings with the Indians. Rhode Island's policy was far more enlightened and grew out of a mixture of genuine concern for the Indians and fear of the colony's own weakness. The middle colonies of New York, Pennsylvania, and the Jerseys also treated the Indians fairly, but could not prevent individual settlers from committing atrocities against Indians nor save colonial settlements from Indian retaliation. To the South, colonial lawmakers experimented with a reservation system, convinced that Native American and settler could not intermingle safely. When Indians were no longer needed to serve as troops against other Indians, the reservations were reabsorbed into the colonies.

Elaboration of the Criminal Law After 1660

Criminal law in England changed markedly after the Restoration. Although a final civil uprising ultimately drove the Stuarts from the throne, over the long course of time from 1660 to 1776 criminal law focused less upon religious dissent and political disorder and more upon protection of new forms of commercial and later industrial wealth. Strictures against vagrancy and wantonness gave way to statutes against breaking machinery, as organized acts of violence directed at an emerging "monied" class increased. Parliament doubled and then redoubled the number of criminal statutes, redefining all manner of offenses against property as felonies. At the same time, the actual rates of indictment and prosecution declined, proving not that the criminal law had become more effective in deterring crime but that the crimes of violence that had once dominated the dockets of English courts were in decline. A criminal bar emerged and began to take an active role in defending those accused of major crimes, a practice not fully sanctioned until an 1836 statute of Parliament.

Anglicization of Colonial Criminal Law.

The transformation of colonial criminal law followed changes in England, but distantly and with an American twist. Massachusetts, under a new charter, began after 1692 to adopt more English criminal law. The biblical cast of the old Body of Liberties was not entirely abandoned, but crimes against property became much more important and the significance attached to crimes against religious and sexual rules declined. A Supreme Court of Judicature, the members of which were named by the Crown, replaced the assistants. Parliament authorized courts of vice-admiralty, similar to those in England, to sit in the colonial ports and hear cases of smuggling and evasion of customs duties. These courts did not have juries.

Throughout the colonies the level of judicial expertise began to rise, but political abuses undercut this development, as did the adoption of laws that were sometimes less appropriate than the colonial statutes they replaced. For example, English-trained lawyer Nicholas Trott brought much-needed order to South Carolina law, but soon after his accession to the chief justiceship in 1703 he began to use the position to line his own pockets. For this, and for his avid partisan-ship, the colonial assembly impeached Trott in 1719. With increasing participation by non-Quaker immigrants, Pennsylvania adopted a criminal code much resembling English law in 1718. Harsher penalties against crimes like robbery and burglary were introduced, along with a stricter system of penal bonds.

Yet even as criminal law in the colonies began to resemble English law more closely, distinctly colonial elements of criminal law continued to emerge. Lawyers for the accused were by the early 1700s a feature of many colonial criminal courts, prefiguring a change in English practice by two decades. Prototype bills of rights—protecting the right to jury trial, legal counsel, public and speedy hearings of cases, and other procedural guarantees—appeared in over half of the colonies. At the same time, a unique law of slave crime representing the worst features of racial animus and unrestrained acquisitiveness was adopted in almost all of the colonies.

Colonial law stipulated that criminal defendants had a right to be represented by lawyers, a signal advantage to the accused. The Massachusetts Body of Liberties in 1641 and the Fundamental Orders of Connecticut in 1639 had each suggested that there was a right to counsel; the Concessions of the West Jersey Proprietors in 1677 and the 1682 Frame of Government of Pennsylvania gave the same assurances. After the dissolution of the first charter, the Massachusetts General Court tried to reenact a guarantee of counsel in 1692, but for other reasons the statute was disallowed by the privy council. In 1701, the General Court repassed the criminal counsel provisions, and the courts, on occasion, appointed counsel for needy suspects in felony trials. The Connecticut General Court followed this practice. Pennsylvania in 1718, Delaware in 1719, and South Carolina in 1731 each wrote an explicit provision for counsel in criminal cases into their laws. Some colonies resisted this reform—most notably New York—but by the 1760s, counsel was permitted felony suspects in more than half the colonies.

Slaves and Criminal Law.

Crimes by slaves had long posed a problem for colonies with growing concentrations of African slave laborers. The Virginia House of Burgesses, later followed by the assemblies of the Carolinas and Georgia, early on had borrowed the slave law of the British West Indies. Gradually but inexorably the colonies elaborated "black codes" that had no precedent in English law. These codes made color into the badge of slavery and slaves into chattels to be bought and sold, given away and inherited.

Slave law was not criminal law per se, for in law slaves were property. At the same time, slaves were men and women capable of committing acts dangerous to their masters or to each other. The progressive debasement of Africans and the elaboration of a separate and harsh code for criminalization of acts by these bondsmen and women went hand in hand. In 1669, the Virginia assembly prospectively exculpated any master who killed a slave in the course of "due correction" (punishment). In 1680, the legislature made it a felony for slaves to carry a weapon, leave the plantation without a pass, offer resistance to any free person, or lurk about, the last an open-ended offense subject to infinite extension. For any one of these transgressions punishment might include thirty lashes on the back "well laid on." In all the southern colonies, slaves were tried by "freeholders" courts, effectually denying Africans and African Americans the basic rights of any white inhabitant of the English colonies: the right to jury trial when accused of a serious crime, compulsory process against accusers, access to counsel, and permission to address the court in their own behalf under oath.

CRIMINAL PROCEDURE

Jurists and scholars conventionally separate criminal law from criminal procedure, although it may be argued that the two are so interconnected that one cannot tell where procedure ends and substance begins. Criminal procedure is supposedly neutral, but the process of determining innocence and guilt was and remains much influenced by the same elements that influenced the framing of the criminal law itself.

Criminologists liken the system of criminal justice to a funnel through which flow the suspects of crime. Criminal procedure shapes that funnel and historical forces—the values of a people and the aims of its governors—inevitably shape criminal procedure. Under colonial criminal justice in which suspects had fewer rights,

determinations of cases were much swifter, on the whole, than they are within modern criminal procedure, ruled by concern for the rights of the accused.

Distributions of Crimes and Perpetrators

At the mouth of the funnel are those offenses reported to the authorities. The percentage of crimes committed that were actually reported increased dramatically with the severity of the offense. Much petty theft, malicious mischief, and many assaults went unreported. Homicides, burglaries (breaking and entering with intent to commit a crime), and robbery (taking property using force) were very commonly reported.

Grand-jury presentments of misdemeanors and indictments of suspected felons constituted the first stage of criminal procedure in the colonies for which historians have some quantifiable evidence on the incidence of crimes. The grand jury was an assemblage of free, white men from the neighborhood selected by the sheriff who presented information on petty offenses to the court "on their own knowledge." The grand jurors also met to hear indictments against felons. When the grand jury found a true bill against a suspected felon, the suspect might try to bargain with the court for a lesser charge or demand bench or jury trial.

At any time before a verdict was brought in by a trial jury, the defendant could confess and seek the mercy of the court. Convicted, the offender was sentenced. The last stage of criminal procedure, punishment itself, ordinarily was swift, unless a point of law was in doubt or the defendant could give some other reason why punishment should be delayed. A pregnant woman, for example, could "plead the belly" and gain a reprieve from punishment until her child was born.

In seventeenth- and eighteenth-century England and in her North American colonies, there were no police forces. Towns had watchmen, and rural areas were patrolled by the sheriffs' constables, but these men were neither eager to discover crime nor trained to ferret it out. Reportage depended upon the victims or alert neighbors. Often suspects were tracked and caught after a "hue and cry" was raised by the community. The "dark figure" of unreported crime associated with this gap between precept and performance in criminal law varied over time and place in England and the colonies.

Reported crime can be categorized according to its object. Offenses against the person in the colonies—assault, battery, wounding, and homicide—were rooted in quarrels. Overwhelmingly, the perpetrator of these crimes was seeking not material gain but emotional satisfaction. Assault, battery, and fornication were common modes of crime. Rates of these offenses were highest in the southern colonies, but by all accounts colonial America in general was a rough and violent place to live and work.

Homicide—including murder, manslaughter, and killing by accident or in self-defense—never accounted for more than a small fraction of the violent encounters among colonists. Before 1660, only thirty-one cases of homicide went to trial in colonial courts. Although the actual number of homicides and manslaughter cases increased significantly in the years 1670 through 1776, the per capita rates of homicide in fact dropped over the course of the eighteenth century. A different pattern for a few urban areas including New York City and Philadelphia—higher initial levels and persistence of violent crimes—testifies to the heightened potential for violence in urban settings and to the growing frustration of the poorer people of colonial cities in the second half of the eighteenth century.

Offenses against property were crimes of opportunity: their commission was directly related to the deprivation of the perpetrator and the availability of movable wealth. Theft, called larceny in English law, was endemic throughout the colonies and increased dramatically with the growing density of population. Theft was four times more common in New York City than in the surrounding countryside, for example, and serious crimes against property—including grand larceny, burglary, robbery, counterfeiting, and forgery—occurred more frequently in the city of Boston than in the rest of Massachusetts.

Rates of theft also responded to external forces. When war took away numbers of young men, rates of crimes against property declined sharply. In times of economic depression, theft, robbery, and burglary skyrocketed. Women, less free to move about the colonies on their own than men, were more likely to be receivers of stolen goods than they were to be burglars, rob-

bers, or pickpockets. Women in the cities of Boston, New York, and Philadelphia, played a more active role in crimes against property than did women in the countryside.

In the colonies, as in modern criminal-justice systems, there were certain individuals and certain classes of individuals who were the first to be suspected of certain types of crimes. The "usual suspects" were outsiders: the servant or slave, the unwed woman, the foreign-language speaker—economically marginal men and women. The women and men accused of witchcraft in seventeenth-century Connecticut and Massachusetts were people considered threatening to the values of the majority culture; neighbors ultimately took accusations of sorcery to the magistrates in reaction to this perceived threat. Likewise, although the offense of fornication required two transgressors, one male and one female, unmarried servant women suffered prosecution far more often than men. This double standard became more pronounced as the interest of New England authorities in prosecuting sexual misconduct declined.

Closely watched for signs of disobedience or insubordination, slaves, Indians, and servant women were all indicted for crimes far less often than their presence in the population of the colonies would have predicted. Overall, women were never more than 10 percent to 20 percent of those indicted for crime. The Dutch in New York, slaves in the southern colonies, and Indians in Massachusetts were similarly underrepresented in the dock. Once a minority or a relatively powerless group was identified as a likely source of criminal activity, minority status directly affected treatment in the courts. Invariably, disenfranchised groups believed to be at the center of a crime wave—as with women in the surge of bastardy prosecutions of the 1720s or slaves in the New York City arson scare of 1741—were convicted in far greater numbers than they would have been had there been no perception of group-centered conspiracy.

"Deviance" theory argues that communities use public prosecution of such minorities—for example, the Quakers in Massachusetts in the 1650s or the "witches" of Salem in 1692 and 1693—to restate the values that hold the community together. Persecution of Quakers and witches in seventeenth-century New England publicly restated the values of that community. Persecution of slaves for arson, poisoning their masters, and petty treason (against masters) in the southern colonies served a similar purpose for the dominant culture.

Trial

In Elizabethan and Stuart England, criminal trial was short and straightforward. The defendant's life depended upon persuading a judge and jury that he or she was not guilty. The jury returned its verdict, often without retiring and always without "meat nor drinke nor fire"—one panel hearing case after case. Procedural rights were minimal. The defendant could challenge up to twelve jurors for cause, examine witnesses, and introduce evidence to support his other case. The community—represented by the jurors— played a vital, sometimes a controlling, role in particular cases, as did judges, whose instructions to juries were on occasion tantamount to directed verdicts. By the eighteenth century, first in the colonies and later in England, new players strode upon the trial stage—counsel for the prosecution and the defense. The lawyers never appeared in more than a small portion of the total number of cases, but in their cuts and thrusts with each other, their colloquies with the judges, and their caustic, sometimes brutal, examination of witnesses, they began to build a recognizably modern adversarial procedure within the trial system.

The colonists' earliest laws guaranteed jury trials in criminal cases, and colonial juries may have taken advantage of the relative amateurishness of colonial judges to carve out a larger role for juries in criminal trials than was the custom in England. The criminal jury was a redoubt that the colonists hotly defended against their own magistrates and English authorities, although few accused took advantage of their right to jury trial for petty offenses—these were heard "summarily" by the bench. Even in more serious crimes, defendants did not always insist on a jury trial, and in Virginia, for example, less than half of all prosecutions that might have been heard by juries were in fact brought before the jury. Defendants often plea bargained or tried to avoid undertaking the expense of a trial jury. In New England, defendants commonly but by no means universally asked for jury trial. In New York, upper-class defendants sought jury trials, while lower-class defendants only sometimes did the same.

Outcomes

Verdicts of trial juries and findings of judges in bench trials varied according to the nature of the offense and the jurisdiction in which it occurred. The more serious the offense, the more likely the accused was to be found not guilty. Over the long course of colonial rule, defendants in capital cases in Massachusetts, New York, and Virginia were convicted at trial as often as they were acquitted, but regional and temporal variations were also apparent in conviction rates at every level of criminal activity. In New England, where magistrates were diligent pursuers of immoral men and women, conviction rates for violations of laws forbidding fornication, drunkenness, and other moral offenses exceeded 90 percent. For serious crimes, conviction rates in Massachusetts varied from lows of 30 percent to highs of nearly 80 percent depending upon the offense and the period of time in which it occurred; in the first half of the eighteenth century, conviction rates were lower than they were in the years leading up to the revolution. Women had higher conviction rates than men in the seventeenth century, but these differences disappeared in the eighteenth century. Rhode Island's courts were more lenient than those in Massachusetts, and Connecticut courts were slightly more likely to convict than those of Massachusetts.

Conviction rates in the colony of New York varied around a mean of nearly 50 percent, with Dutch, Jews, and free blacks convicted least often and slaves most often. Conviction rates increased after 1750, as authorities began to perceive that the entire criminal-justice system was failing to keep order or protect property. Violation of public order was the offense most likely to result in conviction. To a lesser extent, Pennsylvania and New Jersey courts were also preoccupied with growing public disorder.

North Carolina courts, more concerned with assault than with other offenses, predictably had a higher conviction rate for this crime than for all others—nearly 50 percent. Overall, North Carolina courts convicted only 40 percent of all suspects. Richmond County, Virginia, courts convicted nearly 60 percent of defendants accused of serious crime, but this statistic is significantly inflated by the frequency with which the courts of oyer and terminer found slaves guilty of crimes and by the number of men and women sent to Williamsburg for trial on serious offenses.

One must bear in mind that these figures for conviction and acquittal do not include the many suspects who had already been discharged because grand juries found no bill or because judges dismissed the case for technical reasons. Even so, the conviction rates were two to three times higher than rates of conviction in modern felony trials, a disparity that reflects the general aim of colonial law courts to keep order at the sacrifice of reasonable doubt.

Punishment

The eighteenth-century procession of felons to the Middlesex Gallows near the Tyburn stream in London (now the Speakers' Corner of Hyde Park) was a spectacle of punishment meant to impress the majesty of the law on potential felons that instead brought out the worst in English conduct. The frenzy of the crowds, many of whom came to heckle the authorities as much as to see convicts "turned off" by the hangman, matched the viciousness of the penal code. Brawls were frequent among poor people swirling around the carriages of the affluent who had come to enjoy themselves, only to become the targets of pickpockets undeterred by the very lesson meant for them. The mob would occasionally riot when royal surgeons attempted to retrieve the hanged men and women for dissection. Public executions, in sum, did not check criminals or encourage social order at all.

Colonial punishment had a similar message for potential felons, but it never duplicated the riotous atmosphere at Tyburn. For those convicted at trial, punishment was swift and highly visible, but much more solemn than in England. In New England, ministers' "gallows sermons" seem to have had more impact than in England, and many a convict would warn the crowd against duplicating his or her sins. N. E. H. Hull depicts the setting in her work on serious crime in colonial Massachusetts:

Punishment is the most visible proof of the efficacy of the justice system. . . . Only a few men and women could crowd into the courts to hear the sentence spoken, but many could and did attend the punishments. . . . At this last stage of the criminal process the court no longer focused solely upon the individual defendant but upon the offense—and all offenses like it. Punishment became an expression of community censure, and the defendant a symbol of disorder, violence, and sin. (*Female Felons: Women and Serious Crime in America*, pp. 122–123)

To the pillory or the gallows went the convict and a throng of people—officials, ministers, and bystanders. The pain and shame of punishment could be and was meant to be seen by all.

At the end of the criminal procedure as at its outset, status mattered. In Massachusetts, servants, Indians, and slaves received far more lashes than others convicted of the same crime. In North Carolina, the master class was fined and the servant class whipped for similar offenses. Sometimes this variation in punishment was built into the law; sometimes it was left to the discretion of judges and magistrates.

These officers were always men and though there is little evidence that they conspired to mistreat women, the poorest women—servant girls and older widows—fared even worse than free men under the penal laws. Overwhelmingly, women bore the pain and shame of punishment for bearing the bastard children of their "betters." Proved to have concealed the deaths of their bastard infants, some were punished for murder. No man faced that risk. Proved to have "the devil's mark" on their bodies, they faced punishment for witchcraft. No man was examined for such marks. Convicted by all-male juries and sentenced by male judges for crimes that men defined and prosecuted, women were defamed as symbols of the inherent immorality of a weaker sex.

Reform of Punishment

Prison sentences in colonial North America were not usual forms of punishment, but every county and town had a place where lawbreakers could be confined; these jails were often rickety and dirty. Persons incarcerated as debtors or for minor offenses, or those who had not yet paid court costs, had liberty to move about the yard; others might be more closely confined, even chained. A term of months or even years in prison was rare but not unheard of.

By the end of the colonial era, a powerful current of reform was beginning to change ideas of sentencing and punishment. In England, under the influence of Enlightenment rationalism and direct experience of the bestial conditions of English prisons and public punishments, penal reformers such as Henry Fielding, David Coquohon, Samuel Romilly, and Jeremy Bentham demanded rational schemes of punishment linked to the severity of the crime. They also began to argue for punishment designed to rehabilitate criminals. In revolutionary America, the English reformers' ideas coincided with republican reformism, and England's "penitentiary" movement was welcomed in the new American states. Plans for prisons, in which incarceration was to replace whipping and branding, were adopted. These penitentiaries were to be asylums for socially maladjusted men and women, where the ways of crime would be replaced by habits of hard work and obedience to rules. Meanwhile, in the new state legislatures, reformers such as Thomas Jefferson pushed for revision of criminal codes. These revisions would reserve capital punishment for murder, treason, rape, and arson.

Colonial lawmarkers had encouraged genuine reform in criminal law and procedure, reform that modern Americans may take for granted. Bills of rights, legal counsel in criminal cases, and speedy and public trial were colonial innovations that have become fixtures in our criminal justice system. Not all of these revolutionary-era reforms attained their goals; crime and law enforcement remain high priorities in our own day. Acts that were not criminal in the eighteenth century—for example the use or sale of narcotic drugs—have become so, entailing major allocations of official time and money. Conditions in prisons have improved since the eighteenth century, but prisons are just as overcrowded and incarceration in them seems no more rehabilitative now than a term in the Old Bailey in Moll Flanders's day.

BIBLIOGRAPHY

Crime in England

Beattie, John M. *Crime and the Courts in England, 1660–1800.* Princeton, N.J., 1986.

Brewer, John, and John A. Styles, eds. *An Ungovernable People: The English and Their Law in the Seventeenth and Eighteenth Centuries.* New Brunswick, N.J., 1980.

Cockburn, James, ed. *Crime in England, 1550–1800.* Princeton, N.J., 1977.

Green, Thomas. *Verdict According to Conscience: Perspectives on the English Criminal Trial Jury, 1200–1800.* Chicago, Ill., 1985.

Hay, Douglas, Peter Linebaugh, John G. Rule, E. P. Thompson, and Cal Winslow, eds. *Albion's Fatal Tree: Crime and Society in Eighteenth-Century England.* New York, 1975.

Langbein, John. "The Criminal Trial Before the Lawyers." *University of Chicago Law Review* 45 (1978–1979): 263–316.

Sharpe, James A. *Crime in Early Modern England, 1550–1750.* London, England, 1984.

Thompson, Edward P. *Whigs and Hunters: The Origin of the Black Act.* New York, 1975.

Court and Crime in Anglo-America

Boyer, Paul, and Stephen Nissenbaum. *Salem Possessed: The Social Origins of Witchcraft.* Cambridge, Mass., 1974.

Chapin, Bradley. *Criminal Justice in Colonial America. 1606–1660.* Athens, Ga. 1983.

Demos, John P. *Entertaining Satan: Witchcraft and the Culture of Early New England.* New York, 1982.

Erikson, Kai T. *Wayward Puritans: A Study in the Sociology of Deviance.* New York, 1966.

Faber, Eli. "Puritan Criminals: The Economic, Social, and Intellectual Background to Crime in Seventeenth-Century Massachusetts." *Perspectives in American History* 11 (1978):81–144.

Flaherty, David H. "Law and the Enforcement of Morals in Early America." *Perspectives in American History* 5 (1971):203–256.

Goebel, Julius, Jr., and T. Raymond Naughton. *Law Enforcement in Colonial New York: A Study in Criminal Procedure, 1664–1776.* New York, 1944.

Greenberg, Douglas. *Crime and Law Enforcement in the Colony of New York, 1691–1776.* Ithaca, N.Y., 1976.

Haskins, George Lee. *Law and Authority in Early Massachusetts, A Study in Tradition and Design.* New York, 1960.

Hoffer, Peter Charles. *Law and People in Colonial America.* Baltimore, Md., 1992.

Hoffer, Peter Charles, and William B. Scott, eds. *Criminal Proceedings in Colonial Virginia: Richmond County, 1710/11–1754.* American Legal Records Series, vol. 10. Washington, D.C., and Athens, Ga., 1984.

Hull, N. E. H. *Female Felons: Women and Serious Crime in Colonial Massachusetts.* Urbana, Ill., 1987.

Karlsen, Carol F. *The Devil in the Shape of a Woman: Witchcraft in Colonial New England.* New York, 1987.

Koehler, Lyle. *A Search for Power: The "Weaker Sex" in Seventeenth-Century New England.* Urbana, Ill., 1980.

Murrin, John M. "Magistrates, Sinners, and a Precarious Liberty: Trial by Jury in Seventeenth-Century New England." In *Saints and Revolutionaries: Essays on Early American History,* edited by David D. Hall, John M. Murrin, and Thad W. Tate. New York, 1984.

Oberholzer, Emil, Jr. *Delinquent Saints: Disciplinary Action in the Early Congregational Churches of Massachusetts.* New York, 1956.

Powers, Edwin. *Crime and Punishment in Early Massachusetts, 1620–1692: A Documentary History.* Boston, Mass., 1966.

Schwarz, Philip J. *Twice Condemned: Slaves and the Criminal Laws of Virginia, 1705–1865.* Baton Rouge, La., 1988.

Scott, Arthur P. *Criminal Law in Colonial Virginia.* Chicago, Ill., 1930.

Spindel, Donna. *Crime and Society in North Carolina, 1663–1776.* Baton Rouge, La., 1989.

Reform of the Legal System

Foucault, Michel. *Discipline and Punish: The Birth of the Prison.* Translated by Alan Sheridan. New York, 1977.

Ignatieff, Michael. *A Just Measure of Pain: The Penitentiary in the Industrial Revolution, 1750–1850.* New York, 1978.

Newman, Graeme. *The Punishment Response.* Philadelphia, Pa., 1978.

Rothman, David J. *The Discovery of the Asylum: Social Order and Disorder in the New Republic.* Boston, Mass., 1971.

Peter Charles Hoffer

SEE ALSO **Civil Law; The Legal Profession;** and **Local Government.**

THE DUTCH COLONY

CRIME IN NEW NETHERLAND was defined according to the laws of the Netherlands, specifically the Roman-Dutch law of the province of Holland, where the Dutch West India Company (WIC) was located. *Introduction to the Jurisprudence of Holland,* written in the Dutch language by famed legal scholar Hugo Grotius in 1631, served as the standard reference for law enforcement officials in New Netherland. When company administrators confronted novel situations not covered by existing legislation, they improvised laws and ordinances for colony residents that were then submitted to the company directors in Amsterdam for approval.

ABSENCE OF SERIOUS OUTBREAKS OF CRIME

In New Netherland, criminal cases were adjudicated by the director-general of the colony and a council composed of the commissary, secretary, and *schout,* an official who performed the duties of both a prosecuting attorney and a sheriff. As the colony's population expanded, inferior courts were established in the towns. After New Amsterdam received a city charter in 1653, a municipal court composed of *schout,* burgomasters, and *schepens* decided criminal cases. Jury trials were not a part of Dutch practice.

Although a quantitative analysis of the data on crimes and criminals in colony records has not yet been produced, some generalizations can be made about the characteristics of those who perpetrated crimes and the nature of their offenses. The vast majority of criminals in New Netherland were men. One researcher has found that women appeared in only twenty-four criminal cases in New Amsterdam between 1653 and 1663. A disproportionate number of male miscreants appear to have been soldiers of the WIC or sailors at large in the port of New Amsterdam. Relatively few of the people tried in court as criminals were Africans or Indians.

Serious crimes such as murder and burglary were rare in New Netherland. Far more common were petty theft, slander, sexual misbehavior, and drunkenness. The most prevalent crimes among women were theft, assault, and violations of the liquor laws. Selling alcohol or firearms to the Indians ranked high on the list of major offenses, especially in the frontier area of Beverswyck.

Justice was swift in New Netherland, with no more than a few days elapsing between conviction and punishment. Though death sentences occasionally were pronounced for crimes such as murder and sodomy, they were rarely carried out. At the last minute, and usually as a sign of mercy, offenders were pardoned or banished from the colony. The symbolism involved in the ritual of execution, however, operated as a deterrent to prospective criminals, just as public executions in the seventeenth-century Netherlands were orchestrated to impress witnesses with the grave consequences that awaited transgressors of the law.

Public punishment rather than incarceration was the norm in a society in which the only jail outside Fort Amsterdam was a room in New Amsterdam's city hall. Colonists who broke the law were sentenced to be whipped, branded, or placed in the pillory. The punishments imposed by New Netherland courts were geared to the social position of the criminal. Corporal punishment was reserved primarily for men, while women were punished with banishment, fines, or an order to return stolen goods. Errant soldiers were forced to ride the wooden horse, which involved sitting in a saddle with weights attached to the feet for several hours. Men of lower social status whose misdeeds were not considered serious were assigned to work "at the wheelbarrow" with the WIC's slaves, a punishment designed to degrade white workers by forcing them to labor alongside a people defined as inferior to Europeans.

The punishments meted out to slaves varied according to the offense. In a few instances, slaves convicted of heinous crimes were sentenced to death by hanging or burning but reprieved at the last moment. One notorious case involved Manuel Gerritsen ("the Giant"), a slave belonging to the WIC who was chosen by lot to be executed for the murder of another slave after the person who committed the crime failed to confess. Gerritsen was saved from death after the rope on the gallows broke from his weight and the crowd, interpreting this as a sign, clamored for mercy.

A young slave girl convicted of arson and sentenced to be strangled and then burned at the stake was pardoned at the site of the execution on the pretext that she had learned her lesson. Her master's financial investment in her, however, may have influenced the decision not to impose the court's penalty. When a ten-year-old black girl was accused of stealing from her mistress, her mother was ordered to chastise her. Assisted by another black woman, she whipped her daughter with rods under the watchful eyes of the magistrates.

Stiff fines awaited those who violated laws concerning the sale of liquor to the Indians. But even these heavy penalties seem not to have reduced the practice to any significant degree. Neither were officials successful in curbing drunkenness among the population, despite strenuous efforts to enforce controls on those serving alcoholic beverages. Officials also struggled to uphold the sanctity of the Sabbath in the face of unruly townspeople who preferred drinking, gaming, and hunting to spiritual reflection.

New Netherlanders were a spirited people who rushed headlong into the pursuit of profit and pleasure. Predictably, they came into conflict with the law at times. Nevertheless, the colony never experienced any serious outbreaks of crime. While crime could not be eradicated, attempts could be made to preserve order. Toward this end, authorities in New Amsterdam and Beverswyck established a "Rattle Watch" that patrolled the streets at night carrying noisemakers to alert the populace of impending danger.

BIBLIOGRAPHY

Biemer, Linda. "Criminal Law and Women in New Amsterdam and Early New York." In *A Beautiful and Fruitful Place: Selected Rensselaerswijck Seminar Papers,* edited by Nancy Anne McClure Zeller. Albany, N.Y., 1991.

Christianson, Scott. "Criminal Punishment in New Netherland." In *A Beautiful and Fruitful Place: Selected Rensselaerswijck Seminar Papers,* edited by Nancy Anne McClure Zeller. Albany, N.Y., 1991.

Raesly, Ellis Lawrence. *Portrait of New Netherland.* New York, 1945.

van Rensselaer, Mariana Griswold. *History of the City of New York in the Seventeenth Century.* 2 vols. New York, 1909.

Joyce D. Goodfriend

SEE ALSO Civil Law; The Legal Profession; and Local Government.

THE FRENCH COLONIES

FRENCH CRIMINAL JUSTICE was deeply influenced by Roman law and by the thirteenth century had completely abandoned the Germanic adversarial system in favor of the more scientific inquisitorial system. Frenchmen considered administration of justice the foremost responsibility of kingship, and the development of a centralized state increasingly concentrated law enforcement in the hands of royal officials. Although manorial courts theoretically retained jurisdiction in criminal affairs, they rarely exercised their powers after the end of the seventeenth century.

France's American colonies followed the metropolitan pattern. Soon after the Crown took control of New France in 1663, royal jurisdictions were established in the colony's main towns, and these institutions processed the vast majority of criminal cases during the French Régime. Appeals were made to the Sovereign Council (Superior Council after 1703) and, occasionally, to the *Conseil des dépêches* or the *Conseil d'état,* the two sections of the king's council in Paris dealing with judicial affairs.

FRENCH CRIMINAL LAW

Trials in New France utilized the inquisitorial system, which emphasized secrecy and enabled royal judges to control the process at every stage. The ordinance of 1670 established criminal procedure. To dissuade criminality, punishment was exemplary, meted out in an elaborate public ritual that was itself a political statement destined to reinforce the state's power. Only the king, by virtue of divine right, could exact vengeance for a wrong.

In French law, individuals could sue for civil damages, but only the king's attorney could initiate criminal proceedings. The judge was obliged to determine the exact nature of alleged crimes and the identity of alleged criminals. Although judges had great latitude in gathering evidence, they had to follow strict guidelines in evaluating it. Evidence was divided into three categories: "complete proofs," "proximate indications," and "remote indications." Eyewitness testimony was considered the best evidence, but it had to meet certain criteria. Two eyewitnesses who agreed on all the particulars were required, and both of them had to make three distinct but identical and unimpeachable statements. Testimony from a single eyewitness was insufficient for a capital sentence. Written proof alone was adequate in cases such as forgery if the accused admitted the document to be considered "proximate indications," which could not lead directly to a conviction. They could, however, justify torture to extract a confession, which would then constitute a complete proof. The attitude of the accused when questioned was not given much weight.

Only when the judges were convinced of the defendant's guilt did they dispense justice. Judges could choose from over twenty different types of punishment authorized by the royal ordinances, but the ordinances failed to specify punishments for specific crimes. Judges thus enjoyed considerable latitude when dispensing justice, permitting them to weigh the unique circumstances of the crime and the defendant's social position. Three judges were required to sentence an accused to corporal punishment, and the most lenient opinion of the three always prevailed.

France had moved away from the medieval adversarial system still employed in England and her North American colonies, ostensibly because it gave too great an advantage to the rich and powerful. In the inquisitorial system, all stages of the trial were conducted secretly so that witnesses could testify without fear of retaliation. Even the king's attorney who acted as prosecutor was absent from the courtroom during testimony lest he influence the witnesses. Since the accused did not know the exact nature of the charges or the evidence against him, a defendant could fabricate an alibi only with great difficulty. Because of popular distrust of glib lawyers who specialized in freeing guilty people, this system prohibited any legal counsel for the accused. With no legal guidance and unable to cross-examine their accusers, suspects faced an uneven battle with the magistrate. Unlike the adversarial system, in which the judge was limited to the evidence presented by the accuser, colonial magistrates had to discover and validate all pertinent facts by conducting a complete investigation. The effectiveness and fairness of this system depended on the conscientiousness and impartiality of the judges. Yet, while not free of error, New France's judicial record was good.

Since judges controlled the proceedings and were responsible for gathering proof and weighing evidence according to well-defined rules, the professional training of judges was crucial to the system's effectiveness. In France, all judges had to be university law graduates, but there was no law faculty in the colony. Although several judges were recruited among French immigrants with law degrees, not all magistrates had formal legal training. Some, such as René-Louis Chartier de Lotbinière, who succeeded his father as chief judge of the Quebec royal court, received legal training from their fathers. The only colonial official who had to be a member of the Paris bar was the attorney general of the Sovereign Council. In the eighteenth century Attorney General Louis-Guillaume Verrier lectured on the ordinances, contemporary jurisprudence, and the Custom of Paris to the sons of officials who aspired to careers in the judicial administration. Despite the lack of formal legal training, most judges followed the ordinances scrupulously and read the most important contemporary criminal law commentaries. Their competence was rarely questioned.

CRIMINAL JUSTICE

Criminal trials went through different stages defined by the criminal ordinance of 1670. In a case where the guilt of the accused was clearly evident after the interrogation, there were only eight possible stages. If any doubt remained in the judge's mind, four or six additional steps were required.

Accusation

An accusation (*la plainte*) could be filed either by private citizens seeking redress for such crimes as theft or assault or by the king's attorney when a crime became public knowledge, most often in the case of murder, dueling, or arson. A *plainte*, addressed to the local judge, had to include all the circumstances of the crime: date, time, place, people present, and a brief description of what had transpired. Individuals took an active role only if they sued for civil damages, primarily in cases of assault, since the *partie civile* as they were called, was liable for many of the expenses incurred. Normally the king's attorney or public prosecutor brought forward charges following a denunciation, and the state paid all court costs. To avoid frivolous denunciations, informers were prosecuted for libel if the accused was acquitted.

Inquiry

Once the judge was convinced that a crime had been committed, he scheduled an *information*, the equivalent of a preliminary hearing. In cases involving physical violence, he awaited a doctor's report on the extent and nature of the injuries or the cause of death. Any witnesses mentioned in the accusation were summoned to court. People of all classes could testify, even children and servants, and only drunkenness invalidated testimony. In 1724, for example, Montreal process server André Dorien testified in an assault case while drunk, and he was ordered to return sober at a later date. Testimony was given under oath to the judge in the presence of a clerk. After identifying themselves, witnesses were read the *plainte* and asked to tell everything they knew about the crime. After they had finished, the clerk read them their statement; they were then asked if they wanted to change any part of it before signing or apposing their mark.

Witnesses were paid for testifying in court. The judge determined the remuneration based on the social position of the witness, and sums awarded usually equaled a day's labor for tradespeople and five to ten times that amount for merchants, officers, and nobles. The court clerk paid the witness, and the principals were barred from augmenting the officially specified amount.

If the preliminary hearing had not enabled the judge to determine the criminal's identity, he could ask for monitories to be published by the religious authorities. These documents, read at Sunday Mass for three consecutive weeks, described a crime and ordered all persons with any knowledge of it to testify under pain of excommunication.

Summons and Arrest

When the judge had sufficient evidence to identify a suspect he could choose from three kinds of writ. A summons ordered the suspect to appear in court for interrogation, while a personal citation prohibited the suspect from exercising any functions until sentencing or acquittal. An arrest warrant was issued only if the crime deserved "corporal or ignominious punishment." Judges were ordered to give highest priority to criminal trials, and they had to notify the attorney general of the incarceration of all prisoners. If the case did not proceed quickly enough, detainees could be freed. Jails in New France were not the gloomy dungeons of Europe but, rather, rooms in a minor judicial official's house. Given the difficulty of guarding prisoners, judges in New France tried to finish the trials as quickly as possible.

Once an arrest warrant had been issued, a process server, accompanied by soldiers, went to arrest the suspect. If he could not be found, the suspect was prosecuted in absentia and the sentence was executed on an effigy. In the case of suicides (which were considered murder) the dead person was represented in court by a relative, and then invariably the corpse was symbolically hanged at the public gallows.

Interrogation

Once arrested, the accused had to be interrogated under oath within twenty-four hours of incarceration in the presence of the judge and a clerk. The judge drafted questions, sometimes with the help of the prosecutor. The clerk recorded all replies, and the complete transcript was read to the accused before he was asked to sign and confirm his statements.

The transcript was immediately sent to the king's attorney, who then addressed his "conclusions" to the judge. In the case of a minor felony he could ask for a final judgment and suggest the penalty, recommend that the case be sent to civil jurisdiction since only civil damages were warranted, or suggest acquittal. In the case of a more serious crime, the prosecutor automatically called for an "extraordinary procedure," which involved hearing all testimony anew and then confronting the witnesses and the accused. The latter could then be tortured to extract a confession.

Confirmation of Testimony

Once the judge was convinced of a defendant's guilt in a felony trial, he summoned the witnesses to appear again. The clerk read their testimony, asked the witnesses to affirm their statements, and then asked the deponents if they wished to add any new information. In New France, no witnesses recanted their testimony, though many added a few details. Witnesses who subsequently changed their story could be charged with perjury. Witnesses could also demand remuneration for the court appearance.

Confrontation

After all the witnesses had verified their testimony, they were confronted with the accused. Only at this juncture did the defendant learn the exact nature of the charges and the identity of the witnesses. The confrontation also afforded the accused the only real opportunity to defend himself. At this time the accused could attempt to disqualify witnesses or try to point out contradictions in the damaging testimony. Once this step was completed, the trial was said to have been completed and all documentation was passed on to the king's attorney and the magistrates for judgment.

The king's attorney then motioned for a final sentence. In capital crimes, the attorney requested that the prisoner be tortured to extract a complete confession (preliminary torture) or, after a capital sentence had been handed down, to identify accomplices (preparatory torture).

Torture

When torture was necessary, the accused was brought to the court and seated on a stool. Theoretically, a doctor and two surgeons had to be present to establish how much punishment the prisoner could endure, but this rule was not always followed in Canada. In France, torture normally consisted of tying the prisoner in a prone position with limbs extended and then pouring several gallons of water into his mouth. In Canada, the courts resorted to the more dangerous method of using torture boots made of four two-foot-long (6 meters) oak planks fastened around each calf from the knee to the ankle. Four (ordinary torture) or eight (extraordinary torture) wedges were then driven between the planks on the inside of the legs, tightening the planks and increasing the pain. After each wedge was driven home, the accused was asked to confess. When the torture was finished the prisoner was laid out on a mattress to recover. The judges then asked the defendant to confirm any confession he had made. No confession extorted under torture was valid unless the prisoner repeated it after having had sufficient time to recover.

The results of the inquiry were then communicated to the king's attorney. His conclusions were submitted to the bench, and the three magistrates then sentenced the prisoner.

To prevent judges from abusing this method of interrogation, confession under torture was not deemed sufficient proof to warrant the death penalty. When it was used, the case against the accused was normally very strong, lacking only the defendant's admission of guilt. All orders for torture had to be confirmed by the Sovereign Council before a lower court could proceed. For these reasons torture was not widely used, and only eight criminals were tortured in New France.

Final Interrogation

Before sentencing, the accused went through a final interrogation before the three presiding magistrates. If doubt persisted regarding the guilt of the accused, the judges could decide on a sentence of *plus ample informé,* which meant that the prisoner was released, but could be recalled and retried if proof were later forthcoming.

Sentencing

If the evidence for guilt was overwhelming, the accused was again brought to court and seated on a stool before the bench. The criminal ordinance fixed a range of punishments but did not prescribe specific penalties for crimes. Penalties included capital punishment, torture, perpetual service in the king's galleys, permanent banishment, service aboard the galleys, flogging, the *amende honorable* (publicly asking forgiveness), banishment, and fines. Judges were obliged to fit the punishment to the crime. The sentence

did not have to cite all the facts but did have to state the basis for condemnation or acquittal. The convicted felon never had to pay the cost of the trial, but he often had to pay a fine that partially offset the costs. The government could also confiscate the defendant's estate in some capital cases.

Appeal

All convictions could be appealed to the Sovereign Council, where they were judged by seven magistrates. An appeal was automatic for sentences more severe than the *amende honorable.* Appellate judges merely examined the written documents produced by the lower court to ensure conformity with the ordinance and questioned the prisoner one last time. Beyond the Sovereign Council, convicted persons could appeal to the king's council in Paris and request letters of remission, which would clear them even of very serious crimes. Seven Canadians asked for and obtained letters of remission, among them army captain Pierre Le Gardeur de Repentigny, who was granted remission in April 1749, for having murdered Nicholas Jacquin.

Punishment

As soon as all avenues of appeal were exhausted, the judge and the clerk went to the jail, met privately with the appellant, and then formally pronounced sentence. The public executioner then meted out the prescribed punishment. (The execution was delayed only for a woman who claimed to be pregnant. In this case, she was examined by a midwife and if she was indeed expecting, punishment was deferred until after the birth of the child.) Executions were supposed to take place in the same venue as the crime, but because there was only one hangman in Quebec City, criminals from Montreal and elsewhere were executed in the colonial capital. This was done in part to save money, but also because it was sometimes difficult to find boatmen or carters willing to transport the hangman.

The official function of public executioner was the most despised job in Canada, and it was often difficult to find a willing recruit. Ten of the fourteen public executioners in New France were convicted criminals who accepted the post to avoid execution. In 1665, for example, Jacques

Daigre was condemned to death for theft along with an accomplice but avoided the noose by executing his associate. Public executioners were abhorred by the general population and had to be housed in a redoubt of the fortifications. A couple of executioners relapsed into crime, and one, the renegade Irishman Denis Quavillon, was executed for theft a few months after having accepted the position in 1755.

The type and severity of punishments generally fit their respective crimes. Killers, for example, were punished by hanging, while persons convicted of breaking and entering or of counterfeiting government notes were often punished by banishment, service on the king's galleys, and/or branding. Although the practice of branding individuals with a *fleur de lys* might appear cruel by modern standards, it was one of the most effective ways for early modern society to identify habitual criminals. Individuals found guilty of simple theft in daylight were punished by the lash. Common assault, disturbing the peace, and minor sexual misdemeanors were punished by fines, which were by far the most widespread punishment. The stocks were considered a serious punishment but were rarely used; only two men were chained to a post with a sign indicating their crime in the eighteenth century. This contrasts sharply with prevailing practice in the British American colonies. Imprisonment was considered not a suitable punishment but only a preventive measure. Occasionally officials ordered the confinement of prostitutes in the general hospital. Canadian judges could also impose less rigorous punishments. A severe reprimand (*blâme*) was addressed to people who, although guilty, were not aware of the severity of their offense. For minor breaches of the peace, people received a simple reprimand that was not considered dishonoring.

CRIMINAL ACTIVITY

The first French colony in Canada was made up largely of people conscripted in French prisons. The leader of the expedition, Jean-François de La Rocque de Roberval, ruled with an iron hand and had six people executed for theft during the winter of 1542–1543. One of Samuel de Champlain's first official acts, as commandant of the post at Quebec in 1608, was to execute Jean Duval, who had led a conspiracy against him on the outward voyage. Fortunately for the colony, this pattern of violent repression was not necessary for long.

It is impossible to know the exact extent of criminal activity in New France. Extant documentation reveals what types of crime were prosecuted and the fate of the accused; but, as with all early modern data, this picture is necessarily incomplete. Repression was most severe in towns where the state could exercise its authority; and 60 percent of reported crime had an urban setting, although towns represented only about 20 percent of the total colonial population. In the countryside, community solidarity often prevented cases from coming before official tribunals. Priests and other local notables such as notaries, militia captains, and rural merchants were undoubtedly called upon to mediate conflict, thereby avoiding costly recourse to the royal judicial machinery. Only when mediation failed or antisocial behavior persisted was an accusation brought before the courts. Most rural crime brought before tribunals was assault and battery, and in several instances the problem had clearly been festering before being prosecuted.

Apart from the urban-rural dichotomy, crime was not evenly distributed across the colony. The Quebec City region, which always had more than half of the colony's total population, generated only about 30 percent of the prosecutions. The far more unruly Montreal area witnessed almost 64 percent of the recorded criminal activity. Montreal in the French Régime was a frontier outpost with not only a large military garrison but also the disruptive presence of *coureurs de bois* and voyageurs returning from the West each autumn. It also underwent the most rapid demographic expansion of any region in the eighteenth century, and community and family solidarity networks were the weakest there.

Criminal behavior was overwhelmingly a male trait. Only 20 percent of all accused people in the eighteenth century were women; prostitution, simple assault, and theft were their main crimes. Most of the men were relatively young (between twenty and thirty-four); bachelors and the military contributed a quarter of all criminals. This is hardly surprising, since soldiers had considerable spare time to spend in taverns and rarely had family ties in the colony. They were also inured to a violent life that valued physical prowess. Although Christianized Indians were theoretically French subjects and liable for prosecution, Native peoples were not tried in the courts lest criminal proceedings jeopardize alliances necessary for New France's security.

As in the British American colonies, there was a sharp evolution in the types of crime that were prosecuted, illustrating changing levels of tolerance for various offenses.

Crimes Against God and the State

Despite its missionary origins, New France was never as zealous as the New England colonies in prosecuting religious and moral failings. Heresy was not considered a crime, and the courts left the conversion of Protestants to the Catholic church. Blasphemy and witchcraft together accounted for less than 4 percent of all seventeenth-century prosecutions (blasphemy cases virtually disappeared), with only one case each in the eighteenth century. Sexual misdemeanors, of which rape, seduction (gaining sexual favors by promising marriage), prostitution, adultery, and concubinage were the most important, constituted just over 20 percent of accusations in the seventeenth century, when the sexual imbalance condemned many men to long periods of celibacy. Once an equilibrium between the sexes was reached by about 1700, this type of case decreased dramatically, constituting just over 5 percent in the eighteenth century; almost all cases were for seduction or prostitution. Apart from rape, punishment for this type of crime was normally light, with most defendants receiving either an acquittal or a reprimand.

Crimes against the state (forgery, prison escapes, and resistance to property seizures) were relatively rare in the seventeenth century, accounting for only 6.4 percent of all prosecutions. This type of infraction increased significantly to 15 percent in the eighteenth century, mainly in two areas: forgery and resistance to property seizures. With the generalized use of card money, many literate soldiers tried to increase their pay by forging the intendant's signature on the back of a playing card or increasing the card's face value. Resisting judicial officials attempting to seize property or deliver a court summons was

a traditional means for the lower classes in France to protest authority. Sometimes process servers were chased away with brooms, but occasionally axes and knives were used to threaten the state's representatives.

Crimes Against the Person

New France, like New York, Virginia, and the Carolinas, was a violent society. Simple assault was undoubtedly one of the most common but least reported crimes, since Crown attorneys were hesitant to prosecute unless serious injury was involved. Many of these incidents were taken before the civil courts because punitive damages were the key issue. In a status-oriented society, people were very conscious of their good name, and insults often led to litigation even when they did not degenerate into physical confrontations. Peter Moogk has captured the essence of insults in New France in the title of his article " 'Thieving Buggers' and 'Stupid Sluts' "; men were accused of dishonesty, while the chastity of women was attacked. Insults accounted for about 10 percent of cases brought before the courts throughout the period.

Socialization in urban New France, as in France itself, often centered on the tavern; and when wine and brandy were added to fiery words, fists were wont to fly. Assault and battery was the single most important crime in the colony, accounting for 28 percent of accusations in the seventeenth century and 36 percent thereafter. Reported brawls were mainly confined to the lower classes. Royal justice was relatively tolerant of this behavior, refusing to impose severe criminal penalties and preferring instead to refer the disputants to civil courts, where damages could be assessed.

Army officers were more likely to be involved in duels to settle their differences, and the consequences were far more serious, resulting in injury or death. Despite very strict ordinances against dueling, the military ethos prevalent among many members of the colonial elite made recourse to swords the definitive method of settling a dispute. Twenty-two people were accused of dueling, but few were convicted since duelists were careful to fight in secluded places, where there would be few witnesses. Of those condemned to death, three army officers were pardoned.

410

Homicide was difficult to conceal, and the courts acted quickly as soon as a corpse was discovered. Killings accounted for about 5 percent of all cases, the same percentage as colonial Virginia, Britain, and France during this period. Most homicides were accidental and resulted from brawls. Occasionally, a servant accused of theft struck out at an employer—as was the case of Catherine Charland, who beat her mistress over the head with a pewter plate and was hanged 20 September 1721. Only six people were tried for murder in the eighteenth century; theft was the main motive in four cases, whereas the two other murderers killed their spouses to run away with their lovers. Again, suicide was treated as homicide and was punished by hanging the corpse in effigy; only six people were tried for this crime. The final category of murder is infanticide, a crime that the state considered abominable. All unmarried girls had to report their pregnancy as soon as they became aware of it, on pain of death. Six women were tried for infanticide in New France.

Crimes Against Property

Crimes against property, mainly thefts, made up almost one quarter of all cases. In French jurisprudence, theft was divided into simple and qualified theft. In the first case the crime was committed in daylight without breaking and entering and without threat of physical harm to the property owner; in the second the circumstances aggravated the crime. Some people, for example, stole food in the market or a shirt hanging out to dry out of need, whereas others stole while under the influence of alcohol; these crimes were rarely punished severely, unlike the English colonies. Nocturnal theft, involving breaking and entering, and thefts by servants or slaves were considered much more serious. Flogging, branding, banishment, and service aboard the king's galleys were the punishments most commonly prescribed for these crimes. The overall increase in prosecution for theft from the seventeenth to the eighteenth century was particularly marked in Quebec City, reflecting a greater concern for bourgeois values and private property.

The resale of stolen goods, fraud, and arson constituted the other major crimes against property. All were rare and considered very serious.

When black slave Marie-Joseph-Angélique protested her sale in 1734 by setting ablaze her mistress's house in Montreal, the fire ultimately destroyed forty-six homes. The local judge sentenced her to be burned alive; but the Superior Council amended the sentence, and she was hanged before her body was set on fire.

Criminal activity in New France was comparable to that of contemporary France and the Anglo-American colonies. Criminal justice was moderately effective as a means of social control in the towns, but lack of an efficient police force and the relative ease with which criminals could leave for the West or the English colonies limited its overall effectiveness. Despite the fearful array of punishments available to Canadian judges, only a quarter of all accused people were actually punished. The Superior Council usually imposed judgments less severe than the lower royal jurisdictions. As a result, only forty-one of the seventy-eight people convicted of capital offenses in the eighteenth century were executed.

BIBLIOGRAPHY

Boyer, Raymond. *Les crimes et les châtiments au Canada français du XVIIe au XXe siècle*, Montreal, 1966.
Cahn, Mark D. "Punishment, Discretion, and the Codification of Prescribed Penalties in Colonial Massachusetts." *American Journal of Legal History* 33, no. 2 (1989):107–136.
Dickinson, John A. "La justice seigneuriale en Nouvelle-France: Le cas de Notre-Dame-des-Anges." *Revue d'histoire de l'Amérique française* 28, no. 3 (1974):323–346.
Esmein, Adhémar, et al. *A History of Continental Criminal Procedure, with Special Reference to France*, Boston, 1913.
Foucault, Michel. *Surveiller et punir: Naissance de la prison*, Paris, 1975.
Greenberg, Douglas. "Crime, Law Enforcement, and Social Control in Colonial America." *American Journal of Legal History* 26, no. 4 (1982):293–325.
Isambert, François André, et al. *Recueil général des anciennes lois françaises, depuis l'an 420 jusqu'à la revolution de 1789*, 29 vols. Paris, 1821–1833.
Kealey, Linda. "Patterns of Punishment: Massachusetts in the Eighteenth Century." *American Journal of Legal History* 30, no. 2 (1986):163–186.
Lachance, André. *Le bourreau au Canada sous le régime français*, Quebec, 1966.

_____. *Crimes et criminels en Nouvelle-France*, Montreal, 1984.

_____. *La justice criminelle du roi au Canada au XVIIIe siècle. Tribunaux et officiers*, Quebec, 1978.

Moogk, Peter N. "'Thieving Buggers' and 'Stupid Sluts': Insults and Popular Culture in New France." *William and Mary Quarterly*, 3rd ser., 36, no. 4 (1979):524–547.

Morel, André. "Réflexions sur la justice criminelle canadienne, au 18e siècle." *Revue d'histoire de l'Amérique française* 29, no. 2 (1975):241–253.

Powers, Edwin. *Crime and Punishment in Early Massachusetts, 1620–1692*, Boston, 1966.

Séguin, Robert-Lionel, *La vie libertine en Nouvelle-France au dix-septième siècle*. 2 vols. Montreal, 1972.

Spindel, Donna J. "The Administration of Criminal Justice in North Carolina, 1720–1740." *American Journal of Legal History* 25, no. 2 (1981):141–162.

John A. Dickinson

SEE ALSO **Civil Law; The Legal Profession;** and **Local Government.**

THE SPANISH BORDERLANDS

THE JUDICIARY FIGURED prominently in the Spanish colonial regime as an instrument of political and social control. Indeed, it was through a virtual "government of judges" that Spain sought to maintain harmonious relations within society. Wielding considerable discretionary powers, colonial magistrates displayed both loyalty to the Crown and sensitivity to the community in fulfilling their duty to maintain public tranquility. As the Crown's primary agents of law enforcement, magistrates in the Spanish Borderlands sought to deter criminal activity.

Somewhat predictably, criminal behavior in the Spanish Borderlands covered a wide range—from petty thievery to brutal and treacherous murders. A variety of obstacles, however, hinders our understanding of the full extent of criminal activity. First, we have incomplete documentary records for most of the provinces. In the worst case, almost all local judicial records for Spanish

Alta California perished in the earthquake and fire of 1906. Second, magistrates apparently settled many petty disputes verbally, and the historical record consists only of those criminal cases that generated documentation. Finally, it seems likely that neighbors would try first to settle accounts privately before resorting to the courts. Thus, as today, some crimes undoubtedly went unreported.

CRIMINAL BEHAVIOR

Because of their seriousness, violent crimes loom large in the legal record of the Spanish Borderlands. Unlike other crimes, homicide required a judicial investigation by the state, which may explain the rather high proportion of murder cases found in the documentary record. In a sampling of court cases from 1700 to 1780 in New Mexico, for example, murders account for 17.14 percent of the total criminal cases. Spanish colonial law did not differentiate precisely among degrees of murder, but magistrates recognized in their sentences mitigating circumstances and punished unpremeditated murder rather leniently. Closely related to murder, assault represents an even higher proportion of reported criminal activity—28.6 percent. Combined, assault and homicide constitute 45.7 percent of the total criminal cases in this sample group.

Sexual crimes, some of them violent, also came under the scrutiny of the local magistrate. Reported incidence of violent rape is low, perhaps because of the prevalence of informal sexual unions among the lower strata and the easy access to females that the extended family afforded to men from the upper classes. "Deflowering" or breaking a promise of marriage after enjoying the sexual favors of a female, however, was a different matter. This breach of honor could result in a forced marriage or, if required, in monetary support for the child. Sexual crimes between consenting adults were more common. Authorities prosecuted both male and female in roughly the same proportions for the crimes of fornication, adultery, and cohabitation, but they seem to have done so only after the offending parties ignored repeated warnings to correct their behavior.

Homosexual behavior also was considered to be criminal, although evidence of its prosecution is rare. The documentary record indicates that magistrates proceeded rather cautiously in this matter. In a case of sodomy involving two Indian men, for example, the judge noted that only one witness verified the deed; he therefore terminated the case with an admonition to the accused to cease their illicit behavior. Bestiality, a crime in which written laws specifically called for the death penalty, was dealt with rather mildly by borderland magistrates. While all agreed on its seriousness, civil magistrates usually sought to reform rather than punish the behavior of the accused. The appearance of these crimes, in which males were nearly always the defendants, is infrequent and statistically insignificant.

Other crimes that upset the moral order of colonial society were those of witchcraft and sorcery. Jurisdiction in these cases was hazy (at times the Inquisition prosecuted them), but civil officials had legal sanction to investigate reports of magical rites and hexes, which usually terminated for various reasons before the sentence. The accused included both women and men, almost invariably from the lower strata of society. As in other crimes that involved morality, magistrates were inclined to treat the accused in a moderate fashion.

In contrast to late-eighteenth-century trends in other parts of the colonial world, crimes against property were somewhat less evident in the Spanish Borderlands. In the New Mexico sample, trespass and theft account for only 11.4 percent of the total criminal cases. The incidence of such crime, particularly trade in contraband, had increased considerably in early-nineteenth-century Texas, probably because of the heightened possibilities for economic intercourse with non-Spaniards. No precise figures exist for Louisiana or Florida, but those provinces provided easy opportunities for illegal trade.

THE BORDERLAND MAGISTRATE

To maintain social order and to enforce the law, the Crown relied principally on the judiciary. A wide variety of jurisdictions and specialized courts existed in the empire. Fewer specialized courts could be found in the borderlands and only three dealt with crime—civil, ecclesiastical, and military courts. This discussion derives mainly from archival records of civil courts of ordinary royal jurisdiction, which heard the vast majority of criminal cases in the Spanish Borderlands.

A striking feature of the colonial judicial system was the prominent role of the magistrate in every step of the criminal judicial proceedings. Courtroom procedure in criminal cases lay rooted in the inquisitorial system of the Roman-canon law tradition. Under this system, the magistrate played an active role in prosecuting crime and in shaping the nature of judicial proceedings, rather than serving merely as the impartial referee found in the common-law tradition. Furthermore, because of the combined executive, legislative, and judicial attributes of provincial authorities, these men often served as the equivalent of sheriff, court investigator, prosecuting attorney, and judge (the jury system was not a feature of Spanish law). Magistrates received their appointments from either the Crown (in the case of provincial governors and *alcaldes mayores*), or from the municipal corporation (as in the case of the *alcaldes ordinarios*). Provincial governors in the borderlands tended to be military men—outsiders whose career advancement depended on the effective discharge of their duties, including maintenance of public order. The various *alcaldes* normally came from the ranks of the local population. The most important duties of all these officials were to maintain community harmony and to correct antisocial behavior.

While they often displayed diligence and shrewdness in carrying out their duties, no magistrate on the northern frontier of New Spain or in Florida ever had any formal instruction in law. Nor, in contrast to their counterparts in the centers of empire, did they enjoy the benefit of trained legal advisers. This lack of expertise, however, characterized judicial administration throughout the empire, save in the large urban centers. In this regard, the borderlands were not exceptional. The Crown recognized the legitimacy of simplified or summary procedure, especially in cases of lesser importance. Criminal procedure in the borderlands thus conformed generally to contemporary Spanish legal practice.

PROSECUTING CRIMINALS

The preliminary phase of a criminal case, the *sumaria,* similar to the Anglo-American indictment, began in one of three ways—by a direct complaint of the aggrieved to the magistrate (*querella*), by notification by a third party (*denuncia*), or, because of the Crown's obligation to maintain public order, by initiative of the magistrate himself (*de oficio*). Next in the *sumaria* came an investigation of the alleged crime, including verification of the corpus delicti and preliminary testimony from witnesses. Satisfied that a crime had been committed, the magistrate issued either a summons to appear in court or an order to apprehend and arrest the accused, sometimes sending a subordinate to do so. Once in custody, the suspect gave a signed declaration, known as the *confesión,* in which he generally denied any wrongdoing.

Somewhat surprisingly, suspected criminals showed little tendency to resist arrest or to flee. Some provinces, such as California, lay virtually isolated from others; unfriendly Indian groups encircled New Mexico. Easier communications between Texas and other provinces perhaps facilitated criminal flight from this province. In rare instances a militia group might be organized to pursue a criminal.

Unlike the apprehension of criminals, which posed few problems, their physical custody proved to be more vexing. Under Spanish legal rules, jailing was not a punishment in itself but simply a phase in the judicial process. Magistrates often released suspected criminals on their own recognizance or, less frequently, placed them under house arrest. The non-punitive nature of prison, the strength of community social controls, and generalized poverty combined to make jails almost nonexistent in the borderlands. (In a celebrated mid-eighteenth-century incident, local citizens in San Antonio, Texas, simply refused the governor's orders that they build a community jail, citing more pressing business at hand.) Typically, from California to Florida, such structures as military garrisons and storerooms in the *casas reales* (government buildings) served as makeshift jails when the necessity arose. In outlying districts that had no such facilities, officials normally sent dangerous suspects to larger settlements for incarceration.

The next phase of the trial, the *plenario,* was subject to stricter procedural rules than the preceding phase. Lacking juridical training, however, borderland magistrates acted in rather haphazard fashion to ratify previous testimony, admit new testimony and evidence, and hear arguments from both plaintiff and defendant. Conventional views to the contrary, these magistrates do not seem to have unduly discredited the testimony of women and of Indians, who often served as key witnesses in criminal cases.

During the *plenario,* legal representation for the accused was inconsistent. Only in Spanish Louisiana did trained lawyers ply their trade in the borderlands, mostly in civil cases. In other areas, local citizens gained judicial expertise in an informal manner and thereby satisfied the needs of a relatively simple judicial system. Especially in the late eighteenth and early nineteenth centuries, provincial governors often drew on military personnel to serve as court-appointed legal counsel for defendants. In criminal cases, minors almost invariably had the legal representation of a *curador;* adult defendants had the sporadic aid of a *defensor.* Although in theory considered as legal minors, adult Indians often had the services of a *defensor* and, if not fluent in Castilian, an interpreter. The arguments of these representatives were relatively unsophisticated, but they nevertheless reflected a familiarity with the rudiments of Spanish law.

DISPENSING JUSTICE

The *sentencia,* the final phase in a criminal proceeding, exemplifies well the flexibility of the Spanish legal system and its respect for local prerogative in defining and controlling illegal behavior. Although the Crown legislated extensively, the lack of prescriptive punishments afforded magistrates a wide range of possibilities in dealing with—and, thus, giving definition to—criminal activity. Exercising "judicial will" (*arbitrio judicial*), colonial magistrates judged each case on its own merits and assigned a punishment that often reflected local community values as much as it did the royal will.

In meting out justice, magistrates throughout the Spanish Empire drew from a diverse normative system that embraced written legislation, *doctrina* (the legal opinions of national and Roman law jurists), custom, and *equidad* (not Anglo-American "equity," but a communally defined sense of fairness). The mechanism of "judicial will" allowed magistrates to choose from these constitutive elements as each case dictated. Evidence reveals that judges in the borderlands utilized all of these sources, but that they resorted more to custom and *equidad* in their decisions than did their highly trained counterparts in the centers of empire.

Contemporary Hispanic jurists agreed that punishments had a dual purpose—to discipline the offender and to serve as an example to others. To effect both objectives, the community as well as the culprit was made aware of the sentence. Public proclamation, often in the "most public place" of the settlement—at the church portal after mass on a feast day—functioned as a forceful reminder that antisocial behavior was a community affair. In the Hispanic world, public shame and humiliation figured prominently in the punishment of crime.

For example, in San Antonio *alcalde ordinario* Vicente Amador in 1792 sentenced a cattle thief, Francisco Hernández, to be "walked through the customary streets with the [animal's] entrails hanging from his neck," no doubt a humiliating and rather fitting punishment. In a case from mid-eighteenth-century New Mexico, a well-to-do citizen, Eusebio Chaves, had physically assaulted his father-in-law. Not only did Chaves have to pay the man's medical expenses and court costs but he also was made to beg forgiveness of his father-in-law in full view of the community. Humiliation and shame are most effective, no doubt, in close-knit communities, where public opinion carries considerable weight. Their use as a means of social control reflects the values of the traditionalist, largely pre-modern society that existed in the borderlands.

Those who continually overstepped the bounds of acceptable behavior—defined both communally and institutionally—often found themselves exiled from the immediate community or, at times, from the province. In the New Mexico sample, 20.8 percent of all criminal cases in which some form of punishment was applied resulted in banishment. While authorities banished both men and women, especially for repeated instances of fornication and adultery,

they applied this punishment usually to the lower strata of this racially tinged social hierarchy.

Another frequent form of punishment was to impose fines (18 percent in the New Mexico sample), many of which were assigned to cover court costs. Ranging from a few to several hundred pesos, fines were often paid in kind because of the lack of specie in the borderlands. Evidence indicates that magistrates in the borderlands normally charged less for court costs than the fixed rates (*aranceles*) set by the Crown, perhaps because of the generalized poverty of the inhabitants in their jurisdictions. Often some portion of the fine went to the plaintiffs to cover costs of property damage or physical injury.

Forced labor was another popular punishment throughout the borderlands, as it was in the rest of the Spanish colonies. For petty crimes, convicts might find themselves assigned to some public works project, such as the construction or repair of a government building. Crimes of greater severity brought harsher work punishments. Particularly violent criminals or habitual offenders might be sent to one of the dreaded *obrajes* ("workshops") in the mining districts of Nueva Vizcaya (the modern Mexican states of Chihuahua and Durango) or Coahuila (the modern Mexican state of the same name). Such a severe punishment from a borderland magistrate was quite exceptional.

In 1775, for example, four Indians from the mission of San Bernardo, on the Rio Grande, confessed to the murder of a Spanish settler whom they did not know. Tried by Texas governor Barón de Ripperdá, the defendants admitted that they had all robbed and assaulted the victim—one beat him with a rifle barrel, another speared him with a lance, the third shot him with a bow, and the fourth beat him with a stick. Despite the brutality of their crime, the men each received initial sentences of six years at the *obrajes* of either Patos or Bonanza (both in Coahuila). But when their mission father interceded, Governor Ripperdá reduced the sentences to only three years.

While public humiliation, banishment, forced labor, and fines were common, corporal punishment figured less prominently. Magistrates assigned lashings almost always to the lower classes, but normally only as punishment for serious offenses such as murder or aggravated assault. As in other parts of New Spain, capital punishment was rare in the borderlands. Magistrates there meted out capital punishment only for a particularly brutal, cruel, or treacherous crime, or for treason, and then only after review of the case by a trained legal adviser (*asesor*) or, from 1765 on, the appropriate *audiencia*.

Authorities in Texas, for example, after lengthy consideration, executed a notorious character known as *Quemaculos* (literally, "Butt Burner"). An accused rustler, adulterer, murderer, thief, and jailbreaker, Rafael Gutiérrez had earned his unsavory sobriquet by allegedly having burned his wife's genitals with lighted corn husks. Local authorities convicted Gutiérrez of murder and theft, and sentenced him to two hundred lashes and six years of hard labor. Yet the cruel and "scandalous" treatment of his wife, for which he was not technically being tried, sealed his fate. Upon reviewing the case, the Audiencia of Guadalajara (the highest Court of appeals for much of the borderlands) ordered the execution of Rafael Gutiérrez.

Crimes less heinous sometimes ended in a pardon from the Crown (*indulto*). Milestones in the personal lives of the royal family—marriages, births, accessions to the throne, and so forth—were the usual occasions for these empire-wide general pardons. Surely, a convict sweating in an *obraje* or working on a local construction crew derived hope from hearing of some such felicitous event. By dint of these pardons, authorities freed petty criminals, such as José Guadalupe Urrutia at San Antonio in 1808, with a warning to change their ways. Dangerous criminals, such as the infamous *Quemaculos*, were specifically exempted from these pardons and remained in custody.

The moderation in punishing criminals in the borderlands paralleled general practice in the Spanish Empire. By way of comparison, among the 265 criminal trials heard in 1798, the Audiencia de Guadalajara did not pronounce a single death sentence (though seven defendants were so condemned *in absentia*); in fact, 53.6 percent of the defendants received no punishment whatsoever. The percentage of unpunished defendants from the New Mexico sample (52 percent) is remarkably similar. In a sense, moderate punishments helped maintain social order by displaying the magnanimity of the Crown. For many ordinarily productive citizens, the public ordeal of being brought before the local magistrate was sufficient to curb inappropriate behavior.

THE JUDICIARY: AN INSTRUMENT OF SOCIAL CONTROL

An overview of the sentences pronounced by magistrates in the borderlands reveals some important characteristics of the judiciary as an instrument of social control. First, the system itself proved to be quite adaptable to diverse conditions found throughout the Spanish colonial world. Local prerogative, as embodied in locally selected magistrates and in the mechanism of *arbitrio judicial*, allowed considerable discretion at the time of sentencing. Rather than applying laws in mechanical fashion, magistrates might modify punishments to suit each particular case. While the potential for corruption and abuse in such a system is apparent, evidence has failed to corroborate the conventional view that Spanish colonial legal administration was capricious and corrupt. Indeed, magistrates in the borderlands fulfilled reasonably well their duty to control crime and maintain community harmony.

The sentencing process also reflects the relationship that local citizens had with the law. Entering into criminal proceedings, a plaintiff often requested that a judge impose a specific punishment on the defendant. This phase of the judicial process exemplifies well how the community and the state each played a role in shaping the everyday legal practice found in the borderlands. Despite the authoritarian nature of the state, magistrates showed moderation in dispensing justice. Law enforcement in the borderlands depended not on rigid, heavy-handed, and authoritarian administrators. Instead, the judiciary served as a nexus between state and community in shaping a common vision of proper social order in the Spanish colonial world.

BIBLIOGRAPHY

General Works

Castañeda, Carlos E. *Our Catholic Heritage in Texas 1519–1536*. 7 vols. Austin, Tex., 1936–1958.

Gutiérrez, Ramón A. *When Jesus Came, the Corn Mothers Went Away: Marriage, Sexuality, and Power in New Mexico, 1500–1846.* Stanford, Calif., 1991.

TePaske, John Jay. *The Governorship of Spanish Florida, 1700–1763.* Durham, N.C., 1964.

Works on Hispanic Law

Alonso Romero, María Paz. *El Proceso Penal en Castilla (Siglos XIII–XVIII).* Salamanca, Spain, 1982.

Cutter, Charles R. "Judicial Practice in Northern New Spain, 1700–1810." Ph.D. diss., University of New Mexico, 1989.

Langum, David J. *Law and Community on the Mexican California Frontier: Anglo-American Expatriates and the Clash of Legal Traditions, 1821–1846.* Norman, Okla., 1987.

Tomás y Valiente, Francisco. *El Derecho Penal de la Monarquía Absoluta (Siglos XVI–XVII–XVIII).* Madrid, 1969.

Charles R. Cutter

SEE ALSO **Civil Law; The Legal Profession;** and **Local Government.**

THE LEGAL PROFESSION

THE BRITISH COLONIES

ALTHOUGH THE BRITISH colonies had law-trained individuals in their populations throughout the colonial period, the rise of the legal profession was an eighteenth-century development. Indeed it was only after 1750 that the colonial bar began to flourish and to provide lawyers and judges competent to sustain a full-scale importation of English law into the British colonies.

The legal profession in the colonies developed in proportion to the economic and political development of each colony and mirrored the colony's commitment to the reception of English law. Four stages of evolution can be identified: (1) the earliest years of settlement (1607–ca. 1685), which were characterized by informal systems of law and procedure administered by untrained law practitioners; (2) a time of transition (ca. 1685–1700), during which some English barristers and solicitors settled in the colony, along with judges and attorneys general who were placemen from England; (3) the establishment and growth of the bar (1700–1750), based upon the founding of colonial colleges, the development of legal clerkships, and the beginning of systematic efforts to impose educational requirements for bar admission as well as the formation of generally accepted practice rules; and (4) the

maturation of the legal profession (1750–1776), marked by anglicization of the bar, including some differentiation between barristers and those of lesser rank and experience, the growth of extensive law libraries, and the creation of bar associations and societies for mooting points of law. During the last period, lawyers and some judges took a principal role in articulating Patriot and Loyalist constitutional positions and in leading the colonies into revolution against Great Britain.

Although colonial courts were patterned after the English court system, there was wide variation in the names and functions of these courts. All colonies, except South Carolina, had a system of local courts and a group of central courts that exercised both original jurisdiction and appellate authority over the local courts. Local courts exercised limited jurisdiction in civil litigation and criminal jurisdiction concerning misdemeanors. In New England and Virginia, these courts were unified into county courts, but in the other colonies common pleas courts handled the civil business while general sessions courts dealt with the criminal cases.

At the provincial level the jurisdiction of the Westminster Courts (Common Pleas, King's Bench, and Exchequer) were usually combined into one court (Superior Court in Massachusetts; Supreme Court of Judicature in New York; General Court in Maryland, Virginia, and North Carolina) that handled major civil and criminal cases.

Colonies that had a separate system of equity utilized a High Court of Chancery (called the Equity Court in Pennsylvania). Since the colonial governor held ecclesiastical jurisdiction, the probate of wills and grant of administration over intestate estates were also administered centrally (Probate Court in Massachusetts, Prerogative Court in New York and New Jersey, Court of the Commissary in Maryland, General Court in Virginia and North Carolina, Court of the Ordinary in South Carolina).

Jurisdiction in admiralty and maritime cases was granted to the colonial governor. After 1696 it was regularly delegated to a vice-admiralty court that met at the colonial capital or at the largest seaport if the capital was inland. With the exception of lawyers who served as attorneys general or advocates general in admiralty, few colonial attorneys practiced criminal law since legal counsel was available in relatively few criminal cases.

THE EARLY SETTLEMENTS

There were few trained lawyers in the earliest settlements, and some of these were in nonlegal occupations. While the absence of legal practitioners reflected formal policy in some colonies, it more frequently signified that the low level of economic development, coupled with pressures toward arbitral settlement of lawsuits, provided little opportunity to make a living from law practice alone.

Some colonies had well-established prohibitions against the practice of law, either with or without remuneration. Most significant were the New England colonies with their Bible codes and criminal sanctions against those who represented another for compensation. Throughout the seventeenth century, the all-encompassing scope of the Puritan church diminished the need to litigate. As strangers not subject to congregation discipline began to intrude into the economic activities of towns hitherto subject to the authority of a single congregation, church control decreased toward the end of the seventeenth century. Even among inhabitants of the same town, a diversity of religious belief and church membership rendered less pervasive the biblical injunction that disputes be settled in the church. With economic development Bible codes became less relevant to the needs of society in the latter part of the seventeenth century, and more frequent recourse to English common law resulted in a growing need for specialists in that area.

Much later in the seventeenth century, Quaker Pennsylvania also attempted to eliminate practicing lawyers from its court system. Many of the same religious considerations were behind Pennsylvania's reluctance to sanction law practice, but the Quakers did not attempt to institute a Bible-oriented code in their commonwealth. Within a short time after settlement the proprietor, William Penn, began to utilize English-trained lawyers to administer the colonial government. One of these attorneys, David Lloyd, deserted the proprietor's service and gained leadership of the anti-proprietorial political party, merging political power with the establishment of a law practice based upon defense of the artisans and laborers of Philadelphia. In colonies with large German immigrant populations—Pennsylvania, New York, and colonies to the south—another basis for excluding professional lawyers lay in traditional Lutheran attitudes toward the bench and bar. Based upon his experience with the delays and exorbitant fees of imperial and local German courts, Martin Luther was strongly opposed to lawyers. Luther's distinction between Jewish and canon law—covenants of works and the Christian Gospel, which he considered a covenant of grace—led his followers to generalize that all resort to law was a repudiation of salvation "by faith alone." This kept virtually all Germans away from law practice and solidified their opposition to a paid legal profession.

In the middle colonies (New York, New Jersey, and Pennsylvania), arbitration and mediation served as substitutes for courts and a legal profession in the early decades of settlement. Preference for the negotiated settlement of disputes derived from biblical injunctions directing first resort to church authorities and, perhaps, from a utopian outlook that preferred consensual resolution of civil disputes.

Religious persecution in the English prerogative courts of High Commission and Star Chamber triggered Puritan and Quaker opposition to the establishment of any noncommon law courts in the American colonies. This included the Court of Chancery, which administered a vast body of law for the prevention of fraud, unfair dealing, and breach of fiduciary relationships.

These equitable powers traditionally exercised by the English High Court of Chancery were, in New England and Pennsylvania, assigned to the regular courts, where colonial magistrates and judges applied all of the English law they felt appropriate to the case at hand.

South of the Chesapeake there was less opposition to an organized legal profession since colonists there had little resentment against the operation of English common or ecclesiastical law. Most of the early practitioners were primarily planters, whose well-being did not depend upon their part-time profession. However, as the South's economy matured, full-time lawyers became common. Lacking the social status and part-time status of their planter colleagues, these legal professionals sought wealth and social rank through their profession, generating jealousy among established gentry and at times displacing them from local and provincial political office. At no time, however, did opposition to the legal profession gain the strength evidenced in early New England and Pennsylvania.

With few if any lawyers available, litigation before seventeenth-century colonial courts tended to be simple in content and procedure. The parties themselves appeared before the court, usually making oral statements of their position. Witnesses provided testimony that, along with the parties' statements, were written into the court record book. When a jury was utilized, it then deliberated and returned its verdict. When the case did not require a jury, the judge or panel of judges gave its decision, which also was duly recorded in the court record book. It was permissible for a party to use the assistance of a more eloquent friend or neighbor to present or argue the case, but in no instance was the representative to be compensated. There were also attorneys-in-fact who appeared for litigants unable to be present on court day. Frequently wives represented husbands or a father, mother, brother, or sister represented a party absent from the hearing. On the rare occasion when trained legal professionals appeared in these informal courts, they raised technical objections to the proceedings that halted the wheels of justice and raised public opposition to those who would complicate fairly simple techniques of dispute resolution.

Although it has been said that the lack of trained professionals generated a vast army of unethical and incompetent practitioners in seventeenth-century America, qualified English lawyers generated opposition because of their behavior. Thomas Morton, a member of one of the English Inns of Chancery, arrived among the early settlers at Plymouth. By 1627 he had moved to Merrymount (Wollaston), where he erected a Maypole for bacchanalian orgies with Indian squaws and also sold guns and ammunition to their menfolk. It is not clear whether the Pilgrim fathers took less kindly to his sexual immorality than to his giving firearms to the Indians; at any rate Morton soon found himself denounced to the Crown and shipped home to England in chains. The second trained lawyer, Thomas Lechford, achieved little more for himself than did Morton, despite his more conventional social behavior. Received in the Massachusetts Bay colony with hostility because of his profession, Lechford at first was content to act as a scrivener of wills and deeds. However he soon began to try cases for others. His enthusiasm for one client's cause induced him to tamper with the jury in a civil case, and he was sharply disciplined. By 1641, having given up hope of reestablishing a practice, he returned to England, leaving behind his legacy to the Bay colony—a colonial law that required all courts to record their judgments and the evidence supporting them.

In the seventeenth century, the legal system was administered by judges without formal legal training, and an organized legal profession did not exist. As a consequence the elaborate and time-consuming procedures of English common law and chancery were not adopted. While the lack of sophistication in law and procedure might have been troublesome in areas more heavily involved in trade and commerce, the relative isolation of North America permitted the continuance of this primitive state of legal practice.

THE PERIOD OF TRANSITION TO ENGLISH LAW

The last two decades of the seventeenth century were a time of rapid change and shifting political loyalties in the English colonies. Each province experienced some of the disruptive influence that shook seventeenth-century England to the core. Whether the colonies remained loyal to the Stuarts deposed in the civil war or rejoiced in hopes for a Bible commonwealth on English shores, they were doomed to disappointment. The 1660 Restoration brought with it political uncertainty and left untouched the Cromwellian mercantilist system imposed on the empire through the Acts of Trade.

When King James II decided to unite all colonies from New England to Pennsylvania into his short-lived Dominion of New England (1685–1689), he inadvertently fostered the development of the colonial legal profession. Maladroit administration of the Dominion by the imperious governor, Sir Edmund Andros, triggered numerous protests. American political tracts proliferated expressing concern for the survival of rights conveyed by the colonial charters and fears that freedoms and prosperity would be curtailed by the reinvigorated imperial administration. To counter these threats, men with legal training and experience were needed, and wealth gained from commercial activity made it possible for New England and the middle colonies to recruit a small but well-trained legal profession. Although crops like tobacco and indigo in theory provided colonists in the South with the needed capital to fund a legal education, the high standard of living in practice kept colonists at an economic disadvantage.

Meanwhile, British political chaos produced more emigrant lawyers than colonial America would need. Jacobite supporters of the Stuarts, both north and south of the Tweed River, saw little opportunity in England after the Glorious Revolution (1688–1689). The Inns of Court were training skilled and well-educated barristers, including two giants of the English judiciary, Lords Mansfield and Hardwicke. William Brown's treatises on chancery law and practice, Michael Dalton's study of the office of sheriff, Henry Curson's text on estates tail, and countless other volumes were products of men trained at the Inns of Court at the end of the seventeenth century. The bar was exceptionally well-qualified and overcrowded; many competent practitioners were available and eager to seek their fortunes in the New World.

Initially many of these law professionals arrived in America as officials of the Crown or the proprietors. Included in this group were Nicholas Trott of South Carolina, David Lloyd of Pennsylvania, and Dr. John Bridges and Roger Mompesson of New York. These immigrant lawyers joined a group of practitioners that had grown in numbers and competence on American soil, including Daniel Dulany of Maryland and William Pinhorne, David Jamison, and John Tuder of New York.

Through its effort to consolidate all provinces into one large administrative unit, the Dominion had another impact upon the legal profession. While the attempt was frustrated by the Glorious Revolution and the deposition of James II, the preliminary steps disrupted traditional court systems within each colony. With the restoration of colonial independence under governors dispatched by William and Mary, the way was clear for the creation of new court systems. For the most part, these new judicial arrangements established one superior court that incorporated the common law jurisdiction of the English courts of Common Pleas, King's Bench, and Exchequer. In New York, New Jersey, and South Carolina, courts of chancery were erected early in the eighteenth century. Since both the law and equity courts held their principal sessions in the colonial capital, a geographic focus for law practice existed for the first time. Each provincial capital became a center for legal education as well as for trial and appellate practice. Among the southern colonies, Virginia maintained her traditional county courts, where local practitioners dominated. However appellate litigation centered in the General Court at Williamsburg, which had broad general common law jurisdiction and original jurisdiction of all felonies committed by free inhabitants. South Carolina never developed strong local institutions in the colonial period, and all litigation, original or appellate, took place before the Courts of General Sessions, Quarter Sessions, and Chancery held at Charleston.

Admiralty jurisdiction grew with prize litigation during King William's War (1689–1697), Queen Anne's War (1702–1713), and as a consequence of imperial efforts to suppress piracy. Earlier governors had exercised admiralty jurisdiction powers through specially commissioned courts. Beginning in 1697 distinct admiralty courts were established with permanently appointed judges and an appropriate array of staff and marshals. Probate jurisdiction, previously vested in the governor or delegated to the provincial secretary, devolved into distinct courts to supervise the administration of wills and intestate estates. Increased wealth, coupled with expanded commercial activity, guaranteed practitioners substantial fees from practice in these courts.

THE RISE OF THE COLONIAL BAR, 1700–1750

After 1700 the legal profession experienced steady growth, both in numbers and in qualifications. Many of the native-born American practitioners received their formal training at the Inns of Court and were admitted as barristers before they returned home to petition for colonial admission. Some colonies automatically admitted English barristers to practice, but others, conscious of variances between English and colonial law, insisted that the gentlemen of the gown pass examinations in the colonial courts before they were admitted. A growing number of American lawyers were trained in colonial colleges and then served a law clerkship that might extend to five years duration. This was the preferred mode of education in the northern and middle colonies, but Virginia and South Carolina persisted in sending most of their law students to London for training at the Inns.

Within each colony admission to practice was subject to licensing by the governor, usually upon the recommendation of the courts and of a committee of lawyers appointed to examine the candidate. The courts also exercised light-handed discipline over members of the bar, evidenced most strikingly in the case of Paroculus Parmyter of New York, who was disbarred five times before he finally abandoned practice. Maximum fees, established either by act of the assembly or by an ordinance issued by the governor's council, were a source of professional discontent. They were responsible for the establishment of bar associations in New York (1709), Pennsylvania (1722), and Maryland (1730) and for intermittent organizational efforts elsewhere.

Professional organizations were not limited to programs for raising legal fees. The Rhode Island bar association, established in 1745, united its members into agreements not to accept unsecured credit in place of fees. County bar associations in Massachusetts, begun about 1750, exerted their influence to increase the requirements for admission to practice and to eliminate unauthorized practice of law. The New York bar association, reestablished in 1744 after a period of inactivity, engaged in a struggle with the governor over admission standards and the constitutional foundation for colonial courts. A Rhode Island bar committee in 1749 helped draft a statute that received a number of English statutes into provincial law. Many of these associations also exerted pressure to limit the number of attorneys licensed within the colony.

During the first half of the eighteenth century, there was a substantial increase in litigation. The dockets of the New York Supreme Court of Judicature increased from 51 cases in the summer of 1724 to 144 by the summer of 1751, while the Mayor's Court of New York increased its caseload from 46 cases in June 1720 to 268 cases in June 1751. Caseloads in the Massachusetts Superior Court from 1760 to 1765 increased from 104 cases to 587 cases per annum, declining to 498 cases in 1766 as a result of the Stamp Act protests.

Substantial fortunes might be amassed from law practice, and the legal profession on the whole earned ten times as much as medical doctors and teachers. A number of prerevolutionary attorneys in South Carolina made more than three thousand pounds sterling per annum; Josiah Quincy of Massachusetts made about two thousand pounds sterling per annum in the 1770s, and as early as 1745 James Otis, Jr.'s annual income was about one thousand two hundred pounds per year. Earnings for medical practitioners averaged about eight hundred pounds per annum.

The prosperity of the bar enhanced the social and political reputation of its members. By mid century lawyers were a powerful leadership group within the lower houses of the colonial legislatures. From 1720 to 1776 three of the four Virginia House of Burgess speakers were lawyers. In the New Jersey Assembly, there was a marked increase in the number of lawyers elected after 1738, and in that year the first lawyer was elected to the Massachusetts General Court (legislature). By 1770 nearly 9 percent of the Massachusetts General Court was composed of lawyers.

In New Jersey and Massachusetts members of the judiciary, either superior court judges or county justices, dominated the legislative assemblies from 1740 until the revolution.

Some lawyers, like Andrew Hamilton of Pennsylvania, who defended John Peter Zenger in 1735, practiced in several colonies by virtue of their wide reputations for competence and advocacy skills. This group of intercolonial lawyers included James Alexander of New York and New Jersey, William Smith, Sr., of New York, and John Read of Massachusetts.

Although many lawyers gained success through their individual efforts and competence, most drew upon family wealth and connections to sustain their practices. Virtually all colonial lawyers, either by birth or intermarriage, were related to the landed or mercantile gentry of their province. In Maryland, Virginia, and the Carolinas, some planters practiced law in addition to their agricultural endeavors, but these part-time lawyers decreased in number with the approach of mid century. By 1750 law practice in Massachusetts was a road to fortune and social position, even for men of modest means. Although most lawyers were sole practitioners, it became common for older Massachusetts attorneys to take junior members of the bar as partners.

In the seventeenth century, American public life was dominated by clergymen in the New England colonies, by merchants in the middle colonies, and by planters south of Pennsylvania. By 1750 the leadership balance had begun to shift toward the legal profession throughout the English colonies of North America.

THE MATURATION OF THE LEGAL PROFESSION, 1750–1776

The third quarter of the eighteenth century witnessed a continued increase in legal sophistication and political and social status for attorneys. The Seven Years' War (1756–1763), designated the French and Indian War in America, reopened the flood of admiralty cases dealing with illegal trade and prize condemnation. That war generated a need for additional revenue and a consequent British effort to tax the colonies to pay for the conflict, a situation that ultimately led to constitutional debate and then to the War for Independence. It also provided proof, to both Whitehall and the colonial political leadership, that there were substantial differences of opinion concerning imperial relationships. Those disagreements were, for the most part, either constitutional in nature or economic with constitutional overtones. Public attention, despite occasional adverse editorial and electoral reaction to the activities of lawyers, turned to the legal profession and found there the leadership for the American Revolution.

Paradoxically, as the colonists were forced into articulating their view of the imperial constitution, American private law became more English, both in its content and in formalities of practice. The bar experienced marked anglicization. Some colonies instituted a system whereby only veteran attorneys could practice in the central courts, and virtually all courts insisted that lawyers wear gowns in the courtroom. On the eve of the revolution, the Massachusetts Superior Court and the New York Supreme Court of Judicature adopted the English practice of attiring judges in immense wigs as well as in the traditional gowns of office.

Although each major city and colonial capital had a supply of conveyancers, scriveners, and notaries public not admitted to the bar, these practitioners were narrowly restricted in their activities and subordinated to a growing professional monopoly of legal business. English barristers were no longer freely admitted to practice in many colonies, and many were harassed when they attempted to support themselves by drawing wills and deeds. Since licensing attorneys was a gubernatorial function, the practicing bar had no means of limiting its size except through refusing to accept law clerks. This was done through agreements among the practitioners either not to accept any clerks at all, to employ only a limited number of clerks in each office, or to increase the educational requirements necessary for a young man to begin clerkship. By 1776 the legal profession's increased standards for admission to clerkship resulted in most attorneys having completed their college degrees as a preliminary to their legal education. Undoubtedly the founding of a large number of colonial colleges in the third quarter of the eighteenth century facilitated this development.

On the other hand, the attempt to limit the number of practicing attorneys failed, and competition for business remained brisk. Family and marital connections continued to serve as sources of legal employment, and young lawyers began to associate together in partnerships, thereby pooling their resources and sharing the burdens of riding circuit or attending local courts away from the capital.

To supplement incomes artificially depressed by maximum fee regulation, lawyers resorted to land speculation as well as commercial and industrial investments. They actively sought public office, both as an additional source of income and as a means of serving their communities. Among those lawyers with diverse sources of income was John Tabor Kempe, the last royal attorney general of New York, who was an active speculator in colonial land grants, obtained revenues from several Crown offices, and maintained a lucrative private practice, in addition to drawing his salary as attorney general. In South Carolina, Sir Egerton Leigh followed a similar strategy until political hostility and moral outrage against him for seducing his sister-in-law caused his career to languish. Kempe and Leigh, both sons of English placemen sent to occupy Crown offices in the colonies, were barely tolerated by their fellow attorneys, who were drawn from the landed and mercantile aristocracy of their respective colonies. John Jay, a very junior member of the New York bar in 1770, did not hesitate to berate the well-established Kempe for failing to consult him in a case where they were co-counsel.

The quest for public office became more earnest. As the revolution approached, the Crown used patronage and honors to secure continued loyalty from members of the legal profession. It is estimated that in some colonies as much as 50 percent of the bar remained loyal to the Crown.

Increased reliance upon English law and practice caused a large importation of case reports, abridgments, digests, English statutes, and treatises. Many treatises appeared in American editions, including Sir William Blackstone's *Commentaries*, published in Philadelphia in 1771–

1772, just six years after the appearance of the first English edition. However most law books were imported either from England or from Ireland, which seems to have been a source of slightly cheaper imprints.

Modest libraries of less than one hundred volumes were the rule in the English colonies before 1725, but William Byrd of Virginia, a member of Middle Temple and Lincoln's Inn, possessed a library of about 3,625 books, of which 350 were legal titles. In the quarter century before the American Revolution, substantial libraries were not uncommon among the legal profession. Sir Egerton Leigh of South Carolina had an 800-volume collection, and James Grindley, a junior member of the South Carolina bar, died with 530 volumes in his possession. The preeminent colonial libraries were those of Thomas Jefferson (over 6,000 titles; among the 606 books and manuscripts classified as law, about 400 were acquired before 1776) and John Adams (2,756, including what Adams considered "the best Library of Law in the State"), both exceptional for their content and variety. James Alexander, Joseph Murray, and William Smith, Sr., of New York had large collections of law books, as did Ralph Assheton and John Guest of Pennsylvania and Robert "King" Carter of Virginia. The sophistication of Virginia law practice can be seen in the 1730 reports of Sir John Randolph of Virginia, which contain several cases dealing with the rule against perpetuities. Similar resort to complex principles of English law have been identified in Maryland, Pennsylvania, and New York.

The American colonial bar took considerable interest in its own statutes and precedents. The acts of each session of the assemblies were printed in pamphlet form, and periodically the statutes in force were published in a carefully edited version, prepared by one or more lawyers appointed to the task by the legislature. While no court opinions appeared in book form during the colonial period, a number of manuscript collections might have been printed except for the coming of the revolution. These included opinions collected by Sir John Randolph and Edward Barradale (General Court of Virginia, 1728–1741), Thomas Jefferson (General Court of Virginia, 1730–1740, 1768–1772), Josiah Quincy

(Superior Court of Massachusetts, 1761–1772), and Alexander J. Dallas (Supreme Court of Pennsylvania, 1754–1776). In addition a volume of colonial precedents from the Maryland Provincial Court and Court of Appeals (1658–1776) appeared after the revolution as the first volume of *Harris and McHenry's Reports*. We know that some legal organizations within the colonies were interested in regularly reporting court opinions, and in some instances lawyers and their clerks attended sessions of the court on motion days in the hope of reducing oral decisions to writing. This extensive concern for establishing a system of case reporting reflects the growing maturity of the bar and its wish to preserve local law as a supplement to the substantial amount of English and foreign materials available in the libraries of American lawyers.

Colonial lawyers in the period immediately prior to the revolution were in a unique position to enhance the cultural level in their respective colonies. William Byrd of Virginia gained admission to the Royal Society in 1696 based upon his botanical observations, and other lawyers followed his example. James Alexander of New York and New Jersey was a prominent surveyor who corresponded with Benjamin Franklin and others on scientific subjects. Thomas Jefferson and Sir Egerton Leigh of South Carolina were amateur musicians; Leigh wrote poetry and prose, and St. George Tucker of Virginia added playwrighting to his poetic activities. Leigh may have been one of the first art connoisseurs in North America, boasting paintings by Veronese and Corregio in his collection.

Members of the colonial bar also established and edited influential literary magazines published in the English colonies. Philadelphia attorney John Webbe began publishing the *American Magazine* in 1741, which was followed by Boston lawyer Jeremiah Gridley's *American Magazine and Historical Chronicle* (1743) and *The Independent Reflector* (1752), edited by William Smith, Jr., and William Livingston of the New York bar.

Beginning with the *Sodalitas* of Massachusetts (1765), lawyers began to form debating societies that argued issues of law, political theory, philosophy, and ethics. In 1770 New York City lawyers formed The Moot, and their neighbors in the bar of Newark in New Jersey established the Institutio Legalis. These groups survived the political animosity between Loyalists and Patriots that by 1772 had resulted in the collapse of other unifying associations of the bar.

The years following 1763 witnessed increased tension between colonial authorities and the legal profession. When George III succeeded to the throne in 1760, the tenure of colonial judicial appointments was changed to "at pleasure" rather than the English tenure of "good behavior." Even while judges enjoyed the greater protection of "good behavior" tenure, New York Governor William Cosby had summarily dismissed Chief Justice Lewis Morris, Jr., in 1734 for independently ruling against the governor in a case concerning Cosby's salary. Because of the Crown's insistence upon "at pleasure" judicial tenure, one of the associate justices of the New York Supreme Court of Judicature refused his new commission. The bar defended his position, and a year later its members were unified in their opposition to Lieutenant Governor Cadwallader Colden's attempt to have his council review the verdict of a common law jury.

These inroads into the prosperity and tranquillity of colonial law practice were minor compared to the impact of the Stamp Act of 1765, which imposed a tax upon all papers filed in civil litigation. Throughout the colonies the legal profession opposed the stamp tax. In cases where the courts would not permit pleading on unstamped paper, the lawyers refused to bring or defend actions, and litigation ground to a halt because of the "lawyers' strikes." Rents went uncollected, wills went without probate, and chaos resulted when tenants refused to pay back rents once the tax was lifted.

While the bar was united in its opposition to the Stamp Act, reactions to the 1766 Declaratory Act were varied. Because of the political and constitutional ramifications of acknowledging the supremacy of Parliament, the American bar at this time began dividing into Tory and Whig camps. In 1761 James Otis, Jr., had taken the Whig position while unsuccessfully arguing against the Massachusetts Superior Court's right to issue a writ of assistance. While opposing the writ because of its general nature and the lack of safeguards for individual rights, Otis asserted that any statute of Parliament that was contrary to custom and right reason was null and void. His introduction of the reasoning of Dr. Bonham's Case (1610) into American jurisprudence is considered a foundation for the concept of judicial review in the United States. Witnessing the argument as a law student, John Adams later claimed that the American Revolution began with Otis's argument of this case.

Growing disorder marked the decade before American independence, and the bar played an important role in the criminal litigation that resulted. When tenants in Dutchess County, New York, rioted because of rent collection efforts in 1766, New York lawyer Benjamin Kissam mounted a strong attack upon the British concept of constructive treason. His tenant clients were convicted but later pardoned by the Crown before their execution for treason. In 1770 John Adams accepted assignment to defend the officer and eight soldiers accused of perpetrating the Boston Massacre, in which a number of young men and boys were wounded or killed. His skill in defending the men and avoiding the impact of local prejudice resulted in the acquittal of all but two, who were convicted of manslaughter. Those two successfully pleaded benefit of clergy. Derived from the medieval privilege of clergy to stand trial in church courts, benefit of clergy permitted any literate person to escape capital punishment for his first capital offense. For his efforts Adams earned the scorn of his fellow townspeople, but he upheld the traditional obligation of the bar to provide criminal defense.

The maturation of the legal profession provided the American colonies and states with a rich reservoir of talent. The revolution produced a division in the legal profession and a significant number of colonial lawyers remained loyal to Great Britain. Some migrated to England where they lived out their days on Crown pensions, while others moved to Nova Scotia, New Brunswick, or the British Caribbean colonies. Many rose to professional prominence or judicial office in their new locations. Those who chose American allegiance found themselves involved in the demanding task of preparing constitutions for the newly independent states. They served as administrators, lawmakers, and judges in the new nation and brought with them the wealth of knowledge and experience they had ac-

quired in the course of their prerevolutionary practice.

BIBLIOGRAPHY

Botein, Stephen. "The Legal Profession in Colonial North America." In *Lawyers in Early Modern Europe,* edited by Wilfred Prest. New York, 1981.

Calhoon, Robert M., and Robert M. Weir. " 'The Scandalous History of Sir Egerton Leigh.' " *William and Mary Quarterly,* 3rd ser., 26, no. 1 (1969):47–74.

Canady, Hoyt P. *Gentlemen of the Bar: Lawyers in Colonial South Carolina.* New York, 1987.

Chafee, Zechariah, Jr. "Colonial Courts and the Common Law." *Proceedings of the Massachusetts Historical Society* 68 (1952):132–159.

Chroust, Anton-Hermann. *The Rise of the Legal Profession in America.* Vol. 1, *The Colonial Experience.* Norman, Okla., 1965.

Coquilette, Daniel J., ed. *Law in Colonial Massachusetts 1630–1800.* Boston, 1984.

Crary, Catherine S. "The American Dream: John Tabor Kempe's Rise from Poverty to Riches." *William and Mary Quarterly,* 3rd ser., 14, no. 2 (1957):176–195.

Day, Alan F. *A Social Study of Lawyers in Maryland, 1660–1775.* New York, 1989.

Dewey, Frank L. *Thomas Jefferson, Lawyer.* Charlottesville, Va., 1986.

Eaton, Clement F. "A Mirror of the Southern Colonial Lawyer." *William and Mary Quarterly,* 3rd ser., 8, no. 4 (1951):520–534.

Gawalt, Gerard W. *The Promise of Power: The Emergence of the Legal Profession in Massachusetts, 1760–1840.* Westport, Conn., 1979.

Goebel, Julius, Jr., and T. Raymond Naughton. *Law Enforcement in Colonial New York, 1664–1776: A Study in Criminal Procedure.* New York, 1944.

Hamlin, Paul M. *Legal Education in Colonial New York.* New York, 1939.

Johnson, Herbert A. "John Jay: Lawyer in a Time of Transition, 1764–1775." *University of Pennsylvania Law Review* 124, no. 5 (1976):1260–1292.

Klein, Milton M. "From Community to Status: The Rise of the Legal Profession in Colonial New York." *New York History* 60, no. 2 (1979):133–156.

———. "The Rise of the New York Bar: The Legal Career of William Livingston." *William and Mary Quarterly,* 3rd ser., 15, no. 3 (1958):334–358.

McKirdy, Charles R. "Before the Storm: The Working Lawyer in Pre-Revolutionary Massachusetts." *Suffolk University Law Review* 11, no. 1 (1976):46–60.

Main, Jackson Turner. *The Social Structure of Revolutionary America.* Princeton, N.J., 1965.

Morris, Richard B. "Legalism *versus* Revolutionary Doctrine in New England." *New England Quarterly* 4, no. 2 (1931):195–215.

———. "The Legal Profession in America on the Eve of the Revolution." In *Political Separation and Legal Continuity,* edited by Harry W. Jones. Chicago, 1976.

Murrin, John M. "The Legal Transformation: The Bench and Bar of Eighteenth Century Massachusetts." In *Colonial America,* edited by Stanley N. Katz and John M. Murrin. 3rd ed. New York, 1983.

Roeber, A. G. *Faithful Magistrates and Republican Lawyers: Creators of Virginia Legal Culture, 1686–1810.* Chapel Hill, N.C., 1981.

Rosen, Deborah. "Civil Practice in Colonial New York: The Supreme Court of Judicature in Transition, 1691–1760." *Law and History Review* 5, no. 1 (1987):213–247.

Rowe, G. S. "The Legal Career of Thomas McKean, 1750–1775." *Delaware History* 16, no. 1 (1974):22–46.

Warren, Charles. *History of the American Bar.* Boston, 1911.

Whittenburg, James P. "Planters, Merchants, and Lawyers: Social Change and the Origins of the North Carolina Regulation." *William and Mary Quarterly,* 3rd ser., 34, no. 2 (1977):215–238.

Herbert A. Johnson

SEE ALSO **Civil Law; Crime and Law Enforcement;** and **Higher Education.**

THE DUTCH COLONY

THERE WAS NO formally constituted legal profession in New Netherland (New York) that represented private individuals before courts of law. The administration of justice did depend, however, on the services of public officials who were knowledgeable about Dutch law and who had the authority to execute certain responsibilities, such as initiation of criminal prosecutions or the drafting of legal instruments. The exercise of these specific functions was often subject to dispute given the problems of political instability, institutional weakness, and conflicting jurisdictions within the colony.

THE ROLE OF PUBLIC OFFICIALS

Beginning in 1624 the Dutch West India Company (WIC) committed the government of New Netherland to a director-general and council that had supreme executive and legislative authority and that also served as the highest colonial tribunal. The chief legal officer responsible to this body was the *schout-fiscaal,* a magistrate combining the roles of sheriff and attorney general. As in the Netherlands, the *schout* was empowered to file criminal charges, arrest malefactors, oversee prosecutions and suits, and execute the sentences of the court. In his capacity as *fiscaal,* he acted as a financial agent to ensure compliance with the company's commercial regulations and to prosecute suits (at the council's express order) that protected these business interests. The *schout-fiscaal* might sit in the council, but he had no vote in governmental matters. Paid out of fines and penalties pertaining to his office, he was forbidden to accept presents or gifts from any person.

In addition to this provincial officer, the government also allowed over time for the appointment of *schouts* in local jurisdictions. In some cases local magistrates obtained permission to select the *schout,* while in other instances he was chosen by the director-general and council. (English towns within New Netherland usually obtained greater autonomy than Dutch villages in the matter of appointment.) In the *colonie* (colony) of Rensselaerswyck, the patroon appointed the *schout,* authorizing him not only to prosecute criminal offenses, but also to cite and fine tenant farmers who failed to pay their rent and to punish unlicensed traders who intruded upon the Indian trade. Brant Aertsz van Slichtenhorst, *schout* from 1648 to 1652, was so aggressive in defending the patroon's domain against the WIC that Director-General Peter Stuyvesant finally had him arrested and removed from office. The director-general thereafter appointed the *schout*

THE LEGAL PROFESSION: DUTCH

of Rensselaerswyck, while the patroon chose a director to manage his business affairs.

Adriaen van der Donck, *schout* of Rensselaerswyck from 1641 to 1643, was one of the few public officials in New Netherland who had formal legal training, having studied law at the University of Leyden. He subsequently used his legal skills as a member of both the provincial council and the board of nine men, an advisory group of prominent burghers who consulted with the government on public issues. As a leading critic of government corruption and inefficiency, van der Donck was responsible in 1649 for preparing a complaint against Stuyvesant's rule to the authorities in Holland. Once the director-general learned of these plans, he had van der Donck's papers seized, arrested him under accusation of libel, and expelled him from the board and later from the council. Van der Donck soon departed for Holland, presented his *Remonstrance (Vertoogh)* before the States General of the Netherlands, and after much delay obtained some satisfaction when the WIC consented in 1652 to allow a limited form of self-government for New Amsterdam (Manhattan).

Once New Amsterdam gained its own municipal government the following year, the burgomasters and *schepens* (city magistrates) demanded their own local *schout* and also sought to curtail the powers of the provinical *schout-fiscaal*. Their petition to the Amsterdam Chamber of the WIC attacked Cornelis van Tienhoven, the then–*schout-fiscaal*, as one who "imprisons and releases citizens without the [municipal] court's knowledge, and executes the court's judgments with contempt." This suit had partial success, as the Company's directors agreed in 1654 to separate the offices of *schout* and *fiscaal*. They did not, however, accede to the burghers' demand that the city magistrates have some role in the *schout's* appointment, instead leaving this solely to the discretion of the director-general and council.

A LITIGIOUS SOCIETY

Though New Netherland had almost no lawyers, it was a litigious society with a high number of suits between private parties, especially for the payment of debts. Recognizing the problems caused by these disputes, the director-general and council ruled in 1647 that a system of mandatory arbitration be instituted to help deal with the civil case load. On each Thursday three representatives from the advisory board of nine men were to sit at court and to familiarize themselves with current business. These men—one from the board's merchants, one from the farmers, and one from the burghers—were then to decide cases whenever the council called upon their judgment. All parties had to abide by their decisions or pay a fine before making an appeal to the council.

In a new colony, the government's authority necessarily depended upon establishing an orderly system of law. During the 1640s the director-general and council enacted three ordinances regulating the drafting of legal documents. Citing abuses in the writing of promissory notes, the government declared invalid any obligations or legal papers that were not drafted by the provincial secretary or a designated official. This decree acquired a political dimension as discontented colonists began to prepare written complaints as the basis of their remonstrances to authorities in the Netherlands. In response, ordinances of 1646 and 1649 declared invalid "all Affadavits, Interrogatories, or other Instruments serving as evidence, which are written by private Individuals and not confirmed by oath before the Court here or other Magistrates." This rule indicated the government's concern with the issue of dissent, but it did not prevent dissatisfied burghers, including some public officials, from forwarding their grievances to Holland.

The demand for legal services in New Netherland increased with the growth of the population and economy. In addition to court secretaries and clerks, notaries came to assume a major role in meeting this demand. Dirck van Schelluyne, the first notary public appointed for New Netherland, arrived in the colony in 1650. At least four others also served in this capacity before the English conquest. Notaries' fees were closely regulated by a provincial ordinance of 1658. Dirck van Schelluyne himself faced Stuyvesant's wrath, since the notary had attested to a copy of Adriaen van der Donck's *Remonstrance of New Netherland* in 1649 while still executing his office at the Hague. The director-general forbade him to practice his profession, though he later rescinded this prohibition upon orders from the States General.

Notaries in Dutch civil law were highly responsible court officers who were generally better educated and who possessed greater authority than those men who assumed that title in English law. In English common law, the notary served primarily to administer oaths and to take acknowledgments of deeds and other instruments. In the Dutch system, the notary was the principal public official responsible for drafting formal legal contracts. He was authorized, moreover, to keep an official register of those documents and to issue copies only to the interested parties themselves. Contracts and testaments were regarded as authentic once they were sworn before a notary and signed by the parties, the official himself, and at least two witnesses (the latter being males over twenty-four years of age).

The role of Dutch legal officials did not end suddenly with the English conquest of New Netherland in 1664. The *schout*, for example, continued to execute the functions of sheriff and public prosecutor before New York City's municipal court for at least a decade thereafter. (This period included the brief restoration of Dutch rule in 1673–1674). The English provincial government licensed notaries and other court secretaries during the late 1600s who served the Dutch community in much the same manner as they had formerly done. Willem Bogardus, the most active notary in Manhattan, began his career in 1656 as a clerk to the provincial secretary in New Amsterdam. He drafted or witnessed many last wills and testaments for city residents between 1664 and 1691, thereby helping to preserve Dutch social customs under English rule. Some of these documents were in the form of a mutual will executed by husband and wife— a practice common to Dutch law but contrary to English common law. Notaries continued to draft some wills in eighteenth-century New York, especially in Albany County, though their role diminished significantly once English legal procedures were instituted during the 1690s. The compliance with English law proceeded even as Dutch colonists maintained certain social traditions from the New Netherland era.

BIBLIOGRAPHY

Bielinski, Stefan. "The *Schout* in Rensselaerswijck." In *A Beautiful and Fruitful Place,* edited by Nancy A. Zeller. Albany, N.Y., 1991.

Houghtaling, Earle H., Jr. "Administration of Justice in New Amsterdam." *De Halve Maen* 43, no. 3 (1968):9–10, 15–16; no. 4 (1969):17–19.

Johnson, Herbert Alan. "The Advent of Common Law in Colonial New York." In *Law and Authority in Colonial America,* edited by George Athan Billias. Barre, Mass., 1965.

Kammen, Michael. *Colonial New York: A History.* New York, 1975.

Narrett, David E. *Inheritance and Family Life in Colonial New York City.* Ithaca, N.Y., 1992.

Nissenson, Samuel G. *The Patroon's Domain.* New York, 1937.

O'Callaghan, Edmund B. *History of New Netherland; or New York Under the Dutch.* 2 vols. New York, 1846–1848.

———, ed. *Laws and Ordinances of New Netherland, 1638–1674.* Albany, N.Y., 1868.

Pearson, Jonathan, and Arnold J. F. Van Laer, trans. and eds. *Early Records of the City and County of Albany, and Colony of Rensselaerswyck.* 4 vols. Albany, N.Y., 1869–1919.

Rink, Oliver A. *Holland on the Hudson: An Economic and Social History of Dutch New York.* Ithaca, N.Y., 1986.

Van Alstyne, W. Scott, Jr. "The *Schout:* Precursor of Our District Attorney." *De Halve Maen* 42, no. 1 (1967):5–6, 15; no. 2 (1967):7–8.

Wright, Langdon G. "Local Government and Central Authority in New Netherland." *New-York Historical Society Quarterly* 57, no. 1 (1973):7–29.

David E. Narrett

SEE ALSO **Civil Law; Crime and Law Enforcement;** and **Higher Education.**

THE FRENCH COLONIES

THE MODERN UNDERSTANDING of "the professions" has been heavily influenced by the nineteenth century's culture of professionalism and by the twentieth century's sociological models for studying professionalization. As a result, a profession has come to be regarded as a discrete occupational group with specialized knowledge or expertise, a monopoly (usually statutory) over the application of that knowledge, and powers of self-governance enabling each group to control admission, discipline, expulsion, and fees for services. That modern conception of a profession does not fit North America's colonial experience comfortably. Few of the modern criteria of a profession existed in any occupational group in the colonial period. Nonetheless, a variety of lawyers' roles were performed during the colonial period, and the people who filled those roles can be regarded as legal professionals if a functional rather than a cultural or sociological conception of the legal professions is adopted.

Louisiana and Canada, which became Quebec in 1760, Lower Canada in 1791, and Canada East in 1840, are the North American colonies where continental French influences on the structure and responsibility of the legal professions were most strongly felt. But there are also similarities between lawyering in those two jurisdictions and the Roman-Dutch-oriented legal profession of New Amsterdam and colonial New York, about which much more has been written. There is virtually no secondary literature on Louisiana's colonial bar, and scholarship dealing with the legal professions of New France and colonial Quebec is largely anecdotal.

CITIZENS' ROLE IN LEGAL TRANSACTIONS

That gap in scholarship is partly because there were few qualified or certified lawyers in either of North America's French colonies in the early period and partly because modern conceptions of professionalism often do not describe colonial occupational groups. Although a series of royal ordinances prohibited lawyers from operating in Canada and Louisiana, numerous inhabitants performed a variety of lawyers' roles. The imperially appointed intendant of New France had supervisory responsibility for the colonial judiciary: notaries sometimes appeared before the courts as *procureurs;* the clergy often acted as notaries, recording and publicizing commercial transactions; and seigneurs were typically empowered in their Crown grants of property to establish and operate seigneurial courts although they were not required to do so. The cost of maintaining courts significantly outweighed any fees received. Juristic roles were thus being filled in New France even if their personnel were not a full-fledged, self-governing profession.

Although lawyers could not practice in the colonies, in Canada many litigants hired court bailiffs or notaries to plead for them. These *procureurs* served for a fee and were lawyers in all but name. Occasionally the required quorum of up to five judges could not be mustered; thus eminent citizens were brought in to serve as *assesseurs* (acting judges). In 1733 Louis-Guillaume Verrier, attorney general, began offering courses in law to young Canadians who aspired to become judges on the Superior Council, and they were given the preference.

Following the English conquest, governors James Murray, Guy Carleton, and Henry Hamilton granted a substantial number of royal commissions to practice law to untrained, newly arrived British merchants. Recurring disputes between members of that group and Verrier's certified assessors led to the enactment of an ordinance in 1785 that stipulated five years' apprenticeship and a formal bar examination for aspiring lawyers. That regime was, in turn, modified in 1849 when the provincial bar was incorporated as a self-governing agency with three regional sections. Under the new Bar Act, law students were entitled to a two-year reduction in their apprenticeships if they completed, consecutively or concurrently, a structured program of law lectures. McGill College and the Montreal branch of Laval University immediately established such programs, which survive today as the faculties of law at McGill University and the University of Montreal.

By the close of Quebec's colonial period and Canadian confederation of the remaining British North American provinces in 1867, most of the modern benchmarks of a self-governing profession had therefore been achieved by Quebec's lawyers. The separation of those lawyers into a bar that performed attorneys' roles and advocacy before the courts and a branch of notaries public that drafted and recorded deeds persisted on a European model. But both branches of the profession had been incorporated by statute, a monopoly over the provision of legal services had been conceded by the provincial legislature, and official and unofficial legal literature suitable to the management of specialized knowledge had begun to be produced locally. Law training had been formalized in university settings. The professions themselves had achieved firm control over the admission, discipline, and expulsion of lawyers.

BIBLIOGRAPHY

Buchanan, Arthur William Patrick. *The Bench and Bar of Lower Canada Down to 1850*. Montreal, 1925. One of the leading works on the bar of New France and colonial Quebec.

Dickinson, John Alexander. *Justice et justiciables la procédure civile à la prévôté de Québec, 1667–1759*.

Cahall, Raymond Du Bois. *The Sovereign Council of New France: A Study in Canadian Constitutional History*, New York, 1915.

Isambert, F.-A. *Recueil général des anciennes lois française,* 29 vols. Paris, 1822–1833.

Prest, W. R. "Why the History of the Professions Is Not Written." In *Law, Economy, and Society, 1750–1914*, edited by G. R. Rubin and David Sugarman. Oxford, 1984. A good overview of the theoretical difficulties associated with studying the early modern professions.

Roy, J.-Edmond. *L'ancien barreau au Canada*. Montreal, 1897. One of the leading works on the bar of New France and colonial Quebec.

Vachon, André. *Histoire du notariat canadien, 1621–1960*. Quebec, 1962. The standard source on notaries public.

G. Blaine Baker

See also **Civil Law; Crime and Law Enforcement;** and **Higher Education.**

THE SPANISH BORDERLANDS

IN STARK CONTRAST to the more developed centers of empire, the Spanish Borderlands suffered from a paucity of legal professionals. This situation arose, in large measure, from the precarious geographic setting and the economic malaise of the borderland provinces. As highly vulnerable frontier areas, the borderlands were governed almost exclusively by military personnel who also served as chief magistrates of their jurisdictions. Although generally quite capable, they lacked formal legal training and, except in Louisiana, had only limited access, usually from a great distance, to expert legal advice.

THE SCARCITY OF LEGAL PROFESSIONALS

The poverty of the region also contributed to a lack of legal professionals. Instruction in law had been available at Spanish-American universities since the mid sixteenth century, but opportunities for formal study in the borderlands were scant. Spanish-American *letrados* (lawyers) had first to complete requisite university courses and then pass an examination before the regional *audiencia*. Those who became *letrados* tended to concentrate in the administrative and commercial centers of the colonies, where a ready clientele might be found. Few gravitated to smaller cities, and none, apparently, to the borderlands.

Another source of judicial expertise in the Hispanic world was the *escribano* (notary), who lacked a university degree but whose services in drafting and recording legal instruments were crucial. He was familiar with proper legal form, especially in drawing up wills, testaments, contracts, bills of sale, and similar legal documents. In theory, only notarized documents were legally binding, but authorities recognized the validity of non-notarized documents if there were no notaries in a given area.

Escribanos were most conspicuous in Spanish Louisiana, undoubtedly because of the commercial importance of the region and because a cadre of legal professionals had developed prior to the Spanish occupation. More typical of the borderlands was Texas, which enjoyed the services of Francisco de Arocha, an *escribano de cabildo* (town council or municipal official) who served from 1731 until he renounced his office in 1757. The position lay vacant for the remainder of the colonial period. New Mexico also had an *escribano de cabildo* during the early eighteenth century until some time in the 1710s, when the *cabildo*, and the position, disappeared. The ecclesiastical judge of that province, however, often employed a *notario eclesiástico,* who was more likely to be a civilian involved in affairs of civil government. Other scattered borderland municipalities, among them Pensacola, Saint Augustine, and El Paso (present-day Ciudad Juárez), also had *escribanos.* California seems to have lacked these legal functionaries.

Despite the lack of legal professionals, Hispanic settlers in the borderlands shared with their compatriots a strong legalistic sense. They maintained the formulas and values of the Hispanic legal culture, and they passed along their judicial knowledge in informal ways from generation to generation. In some provinces a local elite served as a second tier of government functionaries and was instrumental in preserving rudimentary legal precepts among frontier settlers. In New Mexico and Texas, for example, these individuals helped others draft legal petitions and frequently appeared as courtroom representatives. These men evidently received remuneration of some sort, but they were not full-time legal professionals.

Some have suggested that the absence of a true lawyer class, combined with Anglo-American chauvinism, explains why the Hispanic civil law tradition of the borderlands succumbed to the Anglo-American common law system.

BIBLIOGRAPHY

Baade, Hans. "Número de Abogados y Escribanos en la Nueva España, La Provincia de Téxas y La Luisiana." In *Memoria del III Congreso de Historia del Derecho Mexicano (1983)*, edited by José Luis Soberanes Fernández. Mexico City, 1984.

Cutter, Charles R. "La Magistratura en el Norte de la Nueva España: El Caso de Nuevo México." In *Memoria del V Congreso de Historia del Derecho Mexicano*, edited by Guillermo F. Margadant S. Mexico City, 1993.

McKnight, Joseph W. "Law Without Lawyers on the Hispano-Mexican Frontier." *The West Texas Historical Association Year Book* 66 (1990):51–65.

Charles R. Cutter

See also **Civil Law; Crime and Law Enforcement;** and **Higher Education.**

CIVIL LAW

THE BRITISH COLONIES

IN THE UNCERTAIN WORLD of colonial enterprise and domesticity, law offered the hope and the semblance of stability. Men and women went to court to assert old values and test new ways. Law interceded between disputants and intruded into the everyday lives of towns and parishes.

For much of the seventeenth century and into the first decades of the eighteenth century, law was handed down in writing by an authoritative governing body but was spoken in a tongue ordinary people could understand. In the course of the eighteenth century, that informality was joined by more and more sophisticated technical pleading. At the same time, American law inched toward English law. Local elites still functioned as officers of the courts, but by the middle of the eighteenth century, law practice had become the preserve of trained lawyers.

THE RISE OF THE COLONIAL BAR

The crucial element in the formalization of civil law was the increasing prominence of professional lawyers. There were "attorneys" in the first colonies simply representing others in court, but they did not earn fees for pleading others'

cases. In colonies like Virginia that permitted "lawyers" to charge their clients for services rendered, few men made a living solely on the practice of law. The rise of the legal profession to an elite position in America commenced in the early eighteenth century. Increased litigation in the 1720s and 1730s made lawyering lucrative and attracted able young men. Women were not accepted as apprentices in lawyers' offices, nor were they licensed to practice law by the superior courts. By the 1730s most of the statutory barriers to law practice enacted by colonial legislatures in the seventeenth century had fallen in the rush of plaintiffs and defendants demanding trained assistance in litigation.

American lawyers most often trained by "reading" law as clerks and juniors in established lawyers' chambers or offices. A few had learned their craft in England's Inns of Court. Bar associations created by the leading lawyers soon gained the approval of the colonial legislatures, themselves increasingly penetrated by members of the legal profession. Bar examinations went hand in hand with licensing examinations by judges, the result of which was a more influential profession as well as a more English one.

PLEADING A LAWSUIT

Like the colonial courts in which the lawyers practiced, legal procedure varied from colony

435

to colony. In general, pleading in the colonies during the eighteenth century followed the English model sufficiently to be recognizable to a lawyer from the mother country. The suit at common law, called an "action," began with the filing in court of a "writ." Originally these writs were in Latin. Writs were quite specific, so that filing the wrong writ led to dismissal of the action. The purpose of common-law writ pleading in England and the colonies was to reduce the legal issue to a single "cause of action" and confine juries to deciding a narrowly defined factual question.

Once the "original" writ was filed, the colonial court informed the defendant that litigation had begun and summoned the defendant to appear. In court, plaintiff's declaration laid out one version of the facts. Defendants had to answer the declaration. They might confess judgment; there the action ended and payment of damages and costs was arranged. They might deny all the facts, assert facts excusing them, or challenge the technical correctness of the writ on which the action was brought. The defendant might even admit some or all of the factual allegations in the declaration to be true but insist that they were not sufficient to sustain the particular action brought by the plaintiff.

The defendant's reply was not confined to the version of the facts presented in the writ but was limited to the underlying transaction or event that brought the plaintiff to court. If the defendant wanted to respond that he was owed money by the plaintiff in some other matter or that a third party was responsible for the damage done, the defendant had to bring a separate action into the courts as a plaintiff or go into the courts of equity and seek relief there.

Back and forth the pleas went. If the plaintiff failed to appear in a colonial trial court, he was "nonsuited" and the case ended. If the defendant failed to answer or appear, he was held in "default" and had to pay the judgment plus the court costs. In order to insure that defendants did not disappear or squirrel away their property, plaintiff could obtain a variety of intermediate writs to "attach" the defendant's property or "arrest" his flight. Defendants jailed by the sheriff were ordinarily freed on bail or given the right to move freely about the jail and its environs.

Most suits did not go to trial. They were settled in the shadow of the courthouse by negotiation, confession and payment, or by arbitration of some sort. If a trial began, the evidence offered was primarily documentary. Witnesses could be called and examined on oath, but the testimony of persons who had any monetary interest in the suit was barred. Emphasis rested upon a very narrow base of evidence, and there was little cross-examination of witnesses. The jury was expected to reach its verdict upon its independent assessment of evidence, not upon its judgment about who was telling the truth and who was lying.

After the trial verdict, judicial order, or default was entered, a final series of writs, paid for by the parties, began the "execution" of judgment. Sometimes a successful plaintiff had to pay for many rounds of writs before the sheriff found the defendant and obtained the damage award or took possession of the defendant's land and chattels and sold these at auction to pay off the plaintiff.

SUBSTANTIVE LAW

As procedure varied from colony to colony, so did "substantive" law, the law that determined the outcome of disputes, although no sharp boundary separated procedure from substance—a writ, for example, was both a procedural device and a substantive claim. In its overall contours, colonial substantive law was English common law, but there were differences that were almost as important as the similarities.

Real Estate

The common-law lawyers had liberated much of English real estate and inheritance practice from the dead hand of feudalism by 1607, but the first magnates to be granted proprietorships in the colonies wanted to reestablish feudalism. The seven noble proprietors of the Carolinas, for example, believed that they could send their estate managers and servants to America and rule in the style of medieval barons. In New York leading Dutch and English families pried great swaths of land from the government to set themselves up as the lords of vast manors.

The feudal dreams of these men vanished when they came face-to-face with the labor shortage in the colonies. Even when the proprietors could find men and women to till the soil, there was so much land that people had no need to bind themselves to serve others. In Virginia indentured servants, whose labor contracts required that they work for their masters for a term of years, knew that the end of service would bring them ownership of a small farmstead. New York's great landowners were in reality landlords, not feudal barons. Their tenants had leases whose terms were based upon contractual agreements. In Pennsylvania the many tenants on the proprietors' manors gained customary rights based upon multiyear leases.

Early in the course of settlement, the colonists opted for a clean, straightforward approach to the transfer of title to lands. Almost all the colonies adopted the "deed" and "record" system. In "deed and record," title passed with the exchange of a deed, a memorandum of sale. The deed was then recorded in a county or colonial record book. The title was fully secure only on the basis of the record. (A prior deed lost out to a later deed which had been recorded first.) The deed described the property, giving its boundaries and extent. Subsequent sellers merely endorsed the deed to new buyers; the latter bore the burden of recording the transaction.

Despite the availability of land and the ease with which it could be bought and sold, possession of it was not evenly distributed among the settlers. Most land grants by the colonial and imperial governments were patronage. Hundreds of thousands of acres in the colonies were tied up in this way, and courts in all the colonies became political arenas when political factions sought to test each others' control of land.

Inheritance

In the colonies as in England, inheritance law was partly statutory and partly based upon common law (judicial precedent). Many created probate courts or devoted separate portions of the superior courts' sessions to hearing and approving the provisions of wills. Commissioners were appointed to take inventories of estates if one was not included in the will.

Wills reflected family strategies for building funds of capital or distributing accumulated wealth. Sometimes they concentrated the wealth in a few hands; more often they distributed it among the surviving spouse and children. In Bucks County, Pennsylvania, for example, testators tended to give equal shares to all their sons and favored sons over daughters, though early in the county's settlement daughters were also given some land. In the tidewater South, testators generally treated their sons equally and left nearly equal portions of their estates to their daughters, albeit tying these up in life estates or irrevocable trusts rather than allowing the daughter to take the property without strings.

When there was no will, widows of intestates retained a life estate (an estate that could not itself be devised, or disposed of by will) in one-third of the land and one-third of the personal estate. In New England, statutes provided for partible inheritance, with a double share—the biblical portion—going to the oldest son. In the middle and southern colonies, the English rule of primogeniture was retained, the oldest son getting all of the land, though he had to settle for an equal share of the personal property with his brothers and sisters.

GENDER AND PROPERTY

Colonial law discriminated against women. American courts retained the common-law view of a married woman as a "feme couvert" whose legal rights and property were totally merged with her husband's. The wife could not sell off property without her husband's consent, nor could she bind herself by contract. Her husband had the right to sell off any or all of the couple's property without the consent of his wife, even if the property was brought into the marriage by her, though there were qualifications upon this sort of sale. Husbands could not sell property the wife inherited, and if she appeared to consent to such a sale, she would be privately examined about her true feelings by a magistrate.

Some colonial courts enforced premarital agreements under which women could protect their own property against their husbands. These agreements often involved the creation of a "trust" into which brides-to-be put their property. Southern courts tended to be more solicitous of these agreements than northern courts, and southern chancellors protected the trust funds from the husbands' creditors. So,

437

too, southern chancellors insisted that the widow keep her dower (the one-third lifetime interest in the marriage's real estate) against all claims. Indeed southern courts assured widows a one-third portion of the personal property as well, enabling women to retain household goods and personal articles of value.

Marriage and Divorce

In the colonies as in England before the Marriage Act of 1753, a man and a woman could enter into marriage by mutual consent and open cohabitation. No formal steps were necessary, though many couples did choose to have religious ceremonies.

Ending the marriage was much more difficult. In England the church courts could annul marriages for cause (impotence, affinity, consanguinity) or allow separation on condition that the partners lived celibate until one or the other died. In 1670 Lord de Roos was able to obtain permission from the House of Lords to remarry after he proved his wife guilty of adultery. In effect the Lords had granted him a legislative divorce. After de Roos's successful plea, legislative bills of divorce were theoretically available, but there were still very few legislative divorces in England—only ninety between 1692 and 1785, and they cost more than a poor person could afford.

Divorce was easier and more frequent in many of the colonies. New England Puritans regarded marriage as not a sacrament but a contract that misconduct by either partner might breach. The Massachusetts General Court, and later the governor and his council, took upon themselves the power to grant a divorce on grounds of adultery of either partner as well as cruelty or desertion. At first couples did not rush to the General Court to get divorces. In Rhode Island and Connecticut, whose divorce practices were even more liberal than Massachusetts, there was rarely one petition per year in the seventeenth century. During the next century, however, the number of petitions steadily increased. The assemblies of Rhode Island and New Hampshire also severed marriages upon petition of one of the spouses and a finding of adultery or, more commonly, desertion.

New York and Pennsylvania allowed divorces, but only for adultery. Southern courts and legislatures refused to liberalize divorce, allowing only annulments and celibate separations. Legislative bills of divorce could be obtained when one partner had disappeared, although these were sometimes disallowed by the privy council in England.

CHURCH AND STATE

English divorce law rested upon the authority of the "established" church. Established churches, like the Church of England in the southern colonies and the Puritan churches in much of New England, enforced a broad range of religious regulations running from sexual conduct to conformity in worship. Although the ministers did not prosecute misfeasors, under colonial statutes the magistrates or justices of the peace insured that public authority reinforced religious precepts.

Over time the nature of settlement in the colonies undercut the relationship between civil and religious authority. The Puritans had no sooner fled the persecution of the high church in England than they attempted to reinstate the ideal of religious uniformity in their new home. Rhode Island, a safe haven for Puritans driven out of Massachusetts, adopted a policy of official toleration—of Protestants only. This concession led not to harmony but to campaigns by Baptists for full religious freedom. Connecticut attempted to achieve harmony by instituting synods of elders—in effect switching from the Massachusetts plan of Congregationalism to a form of Presbyterianism. The result was not uniformity but conflict over the proper form of church governance. Pennsylvania was more tolerant of religious dissent than New England, which ironically fostered splits among the Quakers. Throughout the northern colonies, civil authorities, hard put to protect the settlers against Indian and European raiders, weakened by disputes over colonial autonomy with English authorities, and underfunded and understaffed from top to bottom, simply could not insist on strict conformity to any church regime.

In the southern churches, where Anglican worship was theoretically established, the very mixed state of the ministry—some ministers were able and well born, others were not so respectable or competent—did nothing to amend the colonies' unofficial but pervasive religious pluralism. In Virginia and South Carolina, Anglican ministers were often ill paid. Vestrymen, chosen for their status in the community rather than their piety, were supposed to ensure that the churches and the churchmen were well kept. Instead, they often quarreled with their ministers over salaries. Some of these quarrels ended in the civil courts, where the juries joined with the vestrymen against the ministers.

A CRISIS OF LAW AND ORDER

Colonial law at mid century was riven with paradoxes. With Anglicization of the law came needed sophistication and unwanted formality. Lawyers were everywhere abused for stirring contention and everywhere employed to bring suits. The openness and fluidity of the law gave rise to a litigiousness that flooded court dockets and delayed legal redress. The iniquities of private law became the inequities of public law in what seemed to contemporaries to be a spiral of private avarice and official corruption. The law promoted greater equality for some and progressively debased the status of others to chattel slaves.

These tensions in the American law could not be wholly contained within the colonial legal system. Popular dissent took many forms. Farmers and tenants in New York and the Carolinas demanded legal reform. In Virginia grand jurors refused to serve. In a voluntaristic, face-to-face society, such indifference to public duties was calamitous. Parliament would shortly add to these local disorders the burden of almost unenforceable customs regulations and taxes. A crisis of law and order fast approached the colonies.

BIBLIOGRAPHY

Baker, John H. *An Introduction to English Legal History.* 3rd ed. London, 1990. Provides a general overview of English law.
Hoffer, Peter Charles. *Law and People in Colonial America.* Baltimore, Md., 1992. Gives a good summation of American law in the colonial period.

The Lawyers

Day, Alan F. *A Social Study of Lawyers in Maryland, 1660–1775.* New York, 1989.
Gawalt, Gerald. *The Promise of Power: The Emergence of the Legal Profession in Massachusetts, 1760–1840.* Westport, Conn., 1979.
Murrin, John M. "The Legal Transformation: The Bench and Bar of Eighteenth-Century Massachusetts." In *Colonial America: Essays in Politics and Social Development,* edited by Stanley N. Katz. Boston, 1971.
Roeber, A. G. *Faithful Magistrates and Republican Lawyers: Creators of Virginia Legal Culture, 1680–1810.* Chapel Hill, N.C., 1981.

Pleading and Substance

Bridenbaugh, Carl. *Mitre and Sceptre: Transatlantic Faiths, Ideas, Personalities, and Politics, 1689–1775.* New York, 1962.
Klein, Milton M. "From Community to Status: The Development of the Legal Profession in Colonial New York." *New York History* 60 (1979):133–156.
Mann, Bruce. *Neighbors and Strangers: Law and Community in Early Connecticut.* Chapel Hill, N.C., 1987.
Morris, Richard B. *Studies in the History of American Law.* New York, 1958.
Nelson, William E. *Americanization of the Common Law: The Impact of Legal Change on Massachusetts Society, 1760–1830.* Cambridge, Mass., 1975.
Phillips, Roderick. *Putting Asunder: A History of Divorce in Western Society.* Cambridge, England, 1988.
Salmon, Marylynn. *Women and the Law of Property in Early America.* Chapel Hill, N.C., 1986.
Shammas, Carole, Marylynn Salmon, and Michel Dahlin. *Inheritance in America, from Colonial Times to the Present.* New Brunswick, N.J., 1987.

Peter Charles Hoffer

SEE ALSO **Crime and Law Enforcement** and **The Legal Profession**.

THE DUTCH COLONY

EVERY CITIZEN IN NEW NETHERLAND was subject to Roman-Dutch law, a jurisprudence that by the late sixteenth century combined the laws and ordinances of the Netherlands, the privileges of established custom and usage, canon law, and Roman civil law. This civil system had evolved from the Middle Ages, when the Netherlands was a group of individual states, each governed by a count or duke who received his land from the emperor to whom he owed his fealty. The power of the towns had increased during the Crusades, however, as the counts borrowed money from them in order to go on crusade. In return the towns received certain privileges, such as the right to elect their own magistrates or to levy taxes.

Each town had its own particular customary laws, charters, freedoms, and privileges, as well as the right to make its own regulations. These rights accrued over time through contractual arrangements with the lord of the town and were jealously guarded by the people. By the fourteenth century, the rights and laws were entered into local *stadboeken* (law books), to ensure their protection and continuity. The extensive laws dealt with everything from regulating weights and setting fines and penalties to determining the law of intestate succession and marriage.

However much these rights and laws increased the strength and freedom of the towns, their local nature was of little help in a growing urban society whose commerce extended across provinces and throughout Europe. Frequently, therefore, when Dutch jurists could find no remedy for complex cases in customary law they would turn to Roman law for instruction.

Through a series of centralizing ordinances, the house of Burgundy, followed by the Hapsburgs, regularized the laws and in the process promoted Roman law as the common law of the several provinces of the Netherlands. The culmination of the ordinances of the fifteenth and sixteenth centuries was the Political Ordinance of 1 April 1580, issued by the states of Holland and West Friesland. Noting the abuses and confusions that had arisen concerning the laws of marriage, succession, sales, leases, mortgages, registration, and fees, the ordinance enacted thirty-seven articles dealing with those subjects. The ordinance also repealed all the laws that were in conflict with those in the ordinance. An ordinance regulating the civil procedure of the courts was enacted the same day.

ROMAN-DUTCH LAW TRANSPLANTED

These laws, with their subsequent revisions and ordinances, governed the Netherlands in 1621 when the States General, the supreme governing body of the Netherlands, chartered the West India Company (WIC) as a joint-stock trading company. They were therefore the laws of the company and thus the laws regulating New Netherland. The thirty Walloon families who comprised the first colonists were instructed in the Provisional Regulations to observe the articles and instructions and "be bound to obey . . . the orders of the Company already given them or still to be given."

The first set of instructions issued, probably in January 1625, for the second director of the colony, Willem Verhulst, were specific guidelines for maintaining discipline during the voyage. A second set of directives was issued in April 1625 to Verhulst; these concerned the colony's management and supplemented the first set of instructions. The new decree required, among other things, that the customs and common written law of Holland and Zeeland be followed and that no new laws or ordinances were to be passed or any new customs sanctioned unless they were sent to the company for approval with an argument as to why they should be adopted.

Moreover in the Freedoms and Exemptions of 1629, which established patroonships in New Netherland, the States General of the Netherlands mandated that the Political Ordinance of 1580 be followed. To these laws the Amsterdam chamber of the WIC added that city's municipal ordinances. Ordinances that dealt with such specifics of daily life as the regulations for oath taking or penalties for contempt of court or the drawing of a weapon thus became law in the colony. The chamber provided the colonial council with copies of the ordinances for distribution to the courts.

ADAPTING ROMAN-DUTCH LAW TO NEW WORLD REALITIES

Obviously Roman-Dutch law, or even the customary law, would not cover all situations encountered in a frontier society in the New World, such as the complex relationships with the Indians or the mundane but vexing problem of roaming hogs. The new laws and ordinances necessary for these problems were the responsibility of the director-general and his council, who were charged with administering civil and criminal justice. As closely as possible, and always with the concurrence of the Amsterdam chamber's directors, these laws were to conform to those of the Netherlands.

The extant collection of laws and ordinances for New Netherland begin in 1638 with the term of the fifth director, Willem Kieft. Ordinances promulgated under the previous directors, Peter Minuit and Wouter van Twiller, are lost. In the nine years of his administration (1638–1647), Kieft enacted thirty-four colonial ordinances that dealt with a range of problems from trespassing and the drawing of legal instruments to prohibiting liquor sales to the Indians to setting the price of duffel, the coarse cloth used in the Indian trade. It was under Peter Stuyvesant's administration (1647–1664) that the majority of the colonial ordinances were promulgated.

A staunch Calvinist and devoted company man who served with distinction in the West Indies, Stuyvesant was charged by the directors to promote "the interests of the Company and the welfare of the Commonalty" and to establish good relations with the Indians. Faced with a colony angry over Kieft's autocratic administration and reeling from four years of Indian wars, which were the result of Kieft's misguided management, Stuyvesant let loose a barrage of regulatory ordinances aimed at bringing order to the society. His first of twenty-two ordinances came a little more than two weeks after he assumed command. Like many of the ordinances, it dealt with more than one situation—drinking on the Sabbath and the drawing of knives. In his first three and a half years in office, Stuyvesant issued thirty-six ordinances, two more than Kieft's administration produced. The people did not respond with the total fidelity to which the former general was accustomed, and Stuyvesant frequently reissued ordinances as if by reiteration he would gain compliance.

While the directors of the Amsterdam chamber required that the ordinances be sent to them for approval before they were enacted, in actual practice they were enacted and then sent, no doubt because Stuyvesant believed that immediate problems needed prompt action. For purely local situations, this practice did not disturb the chamber. Regulations concerning fencing, controlling livestock, trespass, taverns, galloping fast with wagons, carts, or sleighs inside the city walls, and the like brought little or no comment. But when a law was made contrary to the chamber's interpretation of the customary or general law, the directors sternly rebuked Stuyvesant and either disallowed the ordinance or rewrote it. Aware that the colony was low on people and needed trade, the chamber also censured Stuyvesant and his council on numerous occasions for laws that might negatively affect settlement and commerce, even though Stuyvesant and the council may have justifiably believed they were acting within the sense of the law.

The reins of New Netherland's legal institutions were held firmly in the hands of the fatherland. Nothing was left to chance or went unnoticed as the Amsterdam chamber maintained a constant correspondence with the director-general on every aspect of the colony's government. To implement management, the chamber established a New Netherland bureau to deal specifically with colonial matters. Since the directors required the director-general to keep the bureau informed on a regular basis of everything that was done, contemplated, or needed in the colony, there was little room for colonial innovation. With the exception of Indian relations, there was probably little need for such innovation. The jurisprudence of Holland had evolved to meet the needs of a commercial society, and it was therefore eminently suitable for the needs of New Netherland—a colony bred for commerce.

FORM AND FUNCTION

Both government and justice were dispensed by the courts of New Netherland, making them central to many aspects of the inhabitants' daily lives. As the court met weekly in most villages, it could be called into extraordinary sessions by the people at any time. Requests, suits, and petitions received immediate attention. Regardless of their place in society—rich or poor, servant or slave, male or female—everyone had access to the court. From requests for land and petitions requesting a change in an ordinance to suits for debt and defamation, the court was the forum for the community's economic, political, and social concerns.

The first court in New Netherland was established in 1625 with Verhulst's administration. The director-general and the council, who were appointed by the WIC, comprised the colonial government. They acted in executive, legislative, and judicial capacity, and as surrogate court and a court of admiralty. Cases could be appealed from the lower courts to the council, but there was no appeal from the council's decisions.

Until the establishment of the first inferior court in 1644, the only other court in the colony was the patroon's court of Rensselaerswyck, 150 miles (256 kilometers) north of the colonial government in New Amsterdam. Rensselaerswyck was the only surviving colony of the five patroonships started under the WIC patroonship plan for colonizing New Netherland. Under the Freedoms and Exemptions of 1629, it was allowed its own court with high, middle, and low jurisdiction over its colonists. The colonists could appeal judgments above fifty guilders to the director-general and council. While the patroon appointed his own officers and magistrates, the government was to conform to the law of the Netherlands.

The Freedoms and Exemptions of 1640 contained the provisions for local courts. It also eliminated the West India Company's monopoly on the fur trade, in the hope of increasing the population of New Netherland. With that hope in mind, the company said that when "the dwelling places of private Colonists become so numerous as to be accounted towns, villages or cities" they should be accorded their own courts. Just how many people qualified for a town or village was unspecified and was left to the judgment of the director-general and council. Until a settlement received its own court, its administrative and judicial affairs were either handled by the council or were placed under the jurisdiction of a neighboring village.

At the time of the English conquest of New Netherland in 1664, there were seventeen inferior courts in the colony. Patterned after the inferior courts of the Netherlands, called the court of *schout* and *schepenen,* they consisted of a *schout,* who was appointed by the director-general and council with company approval, and a set number of *schepenen,* or magistrates, which varied throughout the colony from three to six. Initially the burghers submitted a group of names, from which the council chose the magistrates, who served a two-year term. Thereafter the council chose the magistrates from a double number of nominees submitted by the incumbent magistrates and sent yearly to the director-general and council for selection. The eighteenth town, New Amsterdam, received a municipal government in 1653, comprising a *schout,* two burgomasters (mayors), and four magistrates.

In the inferior courts, the *schout,* who acted as sheriff and prosecuting attorney, sat as president of the court, sharing an equal vote with the magistrates. When acting as prosecutor, however, the *schout* could make recommendations to the court but could not vote. During those times, or when the *schout* was away, one of the magistrates served as president of the court. Unlike the English jury system, which decided cases based on fact alone, Dutch magistrates made their judgments based on both fact and law. The vote of the majority bound the court's decisions.

The inferior courts were civil courts. Criminal matters, such as smuggling or murder, were referred to the colonial council for adjudication after the local courts had amassed the evidence and examined the suspects and witnesses.

While legal expertise was not a requirement to serve as *schepenen* or *schout,* the courts did use authoritative legal references to help in their decisions. Director-general Peter Stuyvesant and the notaries quoted frequently from sixteenth-century sources that dealt with criminal, civil, and notarial procedures. Hugo Grotius's famed *Introduction to the Jurisprudence of Holland* (1631) was an important source on Roman-Dutch law; it clearly and concisely systematized the existing collections of laws and had the advantage of being written in Dutch. All the courts had as well copies of the laws of Amsterdam, which informed many of their rulings.

The way in which the court went about its business was governed by detailed procedural laws and customs of the Netherlands. For instance, there were sixteen articles regulating duties and fees in the ordinance for the court messengers, which painstakingly described such things as how to handle summons both with the defendants and before the court. This was not only a firmly regulated society, it was also one whose legal system was based on written instruments that provided evidence for matters in dispute or made legal certain acts. All the regulations, certificates, licensing, bonds, and procedures conformed "to the customs of the fatherland."

CONCLUSION

The Roman-Dutch law of Holland was the unalterable general law of New Netherland. Developed to a large extent to support a commercial economy, it served well the needs of the trading society of New Netherland. Furthermore, the court system of government and justice provided a uniform structure for the civil society of New Netherland, as the inhabitants were accustomed to turning to the court for the ordering of their lives and the protection of their rights. While the colonial council added ordinances to serve the needs of the New World, the language of the law, the form of the proceedings, and the constitution of the court were rooted firmly in the legal institutions and customs of the Netherlands.

BIBLIOGRAPHY

Grotius, Hugo. *The Jurisprudence of Holland.* Translated by R. W. Lee. Oxford, England, 1926.
Shattuck, Martha Dickinson. "A Civil Society: Court and Community in Beverwijck, New Netherland, 1652–1664." Ph.D. diss., Boston University, 1993.
Wessels, J. W. *History of the Roman-Dutch Law.* Grahamstown, South Africa, 1908.

Martha Dickinson Shattuck

SEE ALSO **Crime and Law Enforcement** and **The Legal Profession**.

THE FRENCH COLONIES

CIVIL LAW IS A TERM generally used to describe a system of private law inspired by landmark Prussian, Swiss, or French legal codifications of the late eighteenth and nineteenth centuries. Those European codes were themselves derivative of Justinian's ancient Roman legal digests. Civil law, therefore, connotes a particular historical tradition, distinctive legal doctrines, and a systematic way of presenting legal knowledge. It is often contrasted with England's uncodified, customary, and precedent-based common law system.

New France, Louisiana, and New Amsterdam were the three North American colonies in which imported law and custom most closely resembled continental European models. Significant continental influences were also felt in such other colonies as Pennsylvania, Texas, and Florida. Yet it is difficult to speak of discrete, national systems of imperial law during most of North America's colonial period, which ended in the late eighteenth century, since those European systems developed later as an important part of the nineteenth-century ascendance of cultural nationalism, territorial sovereignty, and political unity. The key point is that at the time ideas like European law were first being transferred to North America's emerging civil law colonies, those colonies could only have received a mélange of precodification local customs not yet thoroughly structured by Roman norms or unified by statutory fiat in imperial jurisdictions. Therefore to refer to civil law regimes in North America's colonial period is to impose the reality of a later period onto an earlier one. That problem is not unique to the French colonial tradition, since similar difficulties present themselves in searches for uniform, identifiably common law regimes in North America's early English colonies. National European legal systems of a civil or common law variety are a post-colonial phenomenon.

Louisiana reformed and codified its private law in 1808, and Quebec did so in 1866. In both jurisdictions, therefore, the predominant civil law influence was felt at the close of a colonial period. The extent to which Quebec and Louisiana's codifications followed the French Code of 1804 or merely restated regional European law transplanted to those colonies at a much earlier date remains a disputed issue among legal scholars. It is, however, undeniable that Quebec and Louisiana's civil law heritage had become an important part of nationalistic rhetoric in those jurisdictions by the last third of the nineteenth century. That rhetoric is a fascinating post-colonial development, and it often achieved a modern life of its own without much grounding in Quebec or Louisiana's colonial history. Quebec provides a good case in point of that tendency to impose the reality of a later period onto an earlier one.

CUSTOM OF PARIS IN NEW FRANCE

New France was quickly established as a proprietary colony by the Compagnie des Cent-Associés (Company of One Hundred Associates) in the early seventeenth century. Responsibility for the administration of law was delegated by the French Crown to the associates by charter as part of the quid pro quo for their trading monopoly. Further delegations of legal authority began in the 1640s with seigneurial land grants that required seigneurs to establish local courts on a seigneury-by-seigneury basis with first-instance jurisdiction over most civil and criminal matters. Supreme judicial authority remained in the colony's governor general, who acted as an appellate bench and general coordinator of private seigneurial courts.

Officially, the substance of private law applied in New France was the Custom of Paris, reduced to written form in 1580 and publicized by continental commentators like Robert-Joseph Pothier and Jean Domat. That custom was one among hundreds of regional bodies of customary law in precodification France. Medieval in origin, three-quarters of the Custom of Paris's sixteen titles dealt with property relations and inheritance, while half of the remainder treated commercial matters such as debt. Thus it emphasized landed property and the social rights or duties that followed from status-based legal identities. Putting aside the law that was

in books, little is known about the daily operations of New France's local seigneurial courts. Lawyers and legal literature were virtually absent from the early colony, and notaries (who recorded public accounts of transactions) did not achieve a significant presence until the eighteenth century. Seigneurial courts were probably used primarily by seigneurs themselves to collect feudal dues owed to them by their *censitaires*, who were like English yeomen farmers.

Centralization and standardization of justice began in earnest in New France during the last third of the seventeenth century. High points in that process included the establishment of a Conseil Souverain (Sovereign Council) with sweeping legislative and judicial powers in 1663, the creation of an intendant's office to superintend the colonial judiciary in 1665, the establishment of royal courts at Quebec City, Montreal, and Trois-Rivières to implement municipal regulations and hear intermediate appeals from seigneurial courts, the founding of a Court of Admiralty in 1717, and the formalization of an Ecclesiastical Court with jurisdiction over the clergy in 1684. That institutional regime was modified following the British military conquest of New France in 1759 by the introduction of English public, criminal, and judicial law. But substantive private law remained more or less intact throughout the colonial period until the eve of Canadian confederation, in 1867.

The cornerstone of the Custom of Paris's persistence in colonial Quebec was Britain's Quebec Act of 1774, which preserved French Canadian systems of property and civil rights, despite the change in imperial rule. Property and civil rights essentially meant the seigneurial kind of land tenure and a colonial settlement scheme derived from continental models and modified by royal ordinances applicable to New France, from colonial practice, and from local legal commentary that began to appear in the late eighteenth century. It had close analogues in the patroon system of New Amsterdam and Central America's latifundium systems. The key features of the seigneurial regime were seigneurs' monopolies over mill sites, annual ground rents paid by *censitaires* to their seigneurs, land sales taxes payable by purchasers to their seigneurs on sales out of the family, priorities of rights in land based on social statuses, and a structured system of inheritance that placed significant limits on freedom of willing. The essence of seigneurialism was thus the merely nominal role that it allowed for liberal ideas like freedom of contract, alienation, or succession.

Quebec's seigneurial system was abolished in stages between 1840 and 1856 in favor of a regime of freehold interests in landed property. That statutory substitution was the major law reform event of Quebec's colonial period. It also complemented and made possible a comprehensive reform and codification of private law on a Napoleonic model undertaken between 1857 and 1866. As one of the Civil Code Commission's members said of those two companion reforms: "It is one of the characteristics of the olden legislation that it appears to have had in view things before persons . . . [but] the tendency of this age is to make things subservient to persons, and to bring immovables as well as all other things under complete subjection to the will of man."

Quebec's colonial period thus ended with its 1867 participation in the political confederation of five British colonies that created the basis for modern Canada. (With its ascension to American statehood, Louisiana ended its colonial period in much the same way.) Land law reform and comprehensive private law codification on nineteenth-century European civil law models significantly buttressed those jurisdictions' claims to membership in the international community of civil law at precisely the moment they abandoned their colonial political status.

BIBLIOGRAPHY

Allen, David Grayson. *In English Ways: The Movement of Societies and the Transferral of English Local Law and Custom to Massachusetts Bay in the Seventeenth Century.* Chapel Hill, N.C., 1981. Provides an outstanding framework for a general consideration of colonial legal transplants.

Brisson, Jean-Maurice. *La formation d'un droit mixte: L'évolution de la procédure civile de 1774 à 1867.* Montreal, 1986. A microstudy of specific aspects of the administration of justice.

Cook, Charles M. *The American Codification Movement: A Study of Antebellum Legal Reform.* Westport, Conn., 1981. One of the best introductions to North Amer-

ica's nineteenth-century rediscovery of the civil law tradition.

Dargo, George. *Jefferson's Louisiana: Politics and the Clash of Legal Traditions.* Cambridge, Mass., 1981. The classic work for Louisiana.

David, René, and John E. C. Brierley. *Major Legal Systems in the World Today: An Introduction to the Comparative Study of Law.* Birmingham, Ala., 1988. Another outstanding introduction to the rediscovery of the civil law tradition in North America.

Dickinson, John A. *Justice et justiciables: La procédure civile à la Prévoté de Québec, 1667–1759.* Montreal, 1982. Examines a particular area of the administration of justice.

Kim, Sung Bok. *Landlord and Tenant in Colonial New York Manorial Society, 1664–1775.* Chapel Hill, N.C., 1978. The classic work on the subject for colonial New York.

Lareau, Edmond. *Histoire du droit canadien depuis les origines de la colonie jusqu'à nos jours.* 2 vols. Montreal, 1888–1889. Remains the best overview of the legal system of New France and colonial Quebec.

G. Blaine Baker

THE SPANISH BORDERLANDS

SPAIN BROUGHT TO the New World a strong and well-developed legal tradition. While circumstances in the new environment forced some modification of laws and judicial practice, the legal culture of the colonies retained the unmistakable imprint of the Castilian legal system. Thus, judicial activity throughout the Hispanic world fell under the rubric of civil, or Roman/canon, law. Key features of the Spanish colonial legal system included the absence of a jury and the prominence of the magistrate in all phases of legal proceedings—investigation, prosecution, and sentencing.

THE CIVIL LAW TRADITION

The civil law system of Spain was rooted in the intellectual and political currents of the High

Middle Ages. The *Siete partidas* (1265?), attributed to Alfonso X of Castile, represented a major step in both the reception and the Hispanicization of Roman/canon law. Attuned to intellectual currents emanating from northern Italy, Iberian monarchs encouraged this juridical trend largely because of the preeminent position of the monarch under this system. Adherents of Roman/canon law soon found positions in government and at Spanish universities, and the popularity of legal studies by the sixteenth century reflected the juristic bent of the early modern Spanish state. *Ius commune* and canon law were staples in the curriculum, and not until well into the eighteenth century did Spanish universities offer courses in *derecho patrio* ("national" law).

Despite the intellectual prominence of the Roman/canon law tradition, Iberian countries never adopted it wholesale (as happened, for example, in Germany). In Castile and, by extension, in the Americas, royal legislation and corporative privileges (*fueros*) always took precedence. Roman/canon law served only in a supplementary capacity, to be used as a guide when no specific royal law applied. Its practical importance, though, transcended its subordinate position in the normative system of the Indies because the rules of procedure in Hispanic law—both civil and criminal—stemmed directly from the Roman/canon law tradition. In this respect, almost every special jurisdiction—royal, ecclesiastical, military, guilds, and corporations—felt the influence of the Roman/canon law tradition.

CIVIL LAW IN PRACTICE

Colonial Spanish American courts located in the administrative centers tended to follow rules of procedure rather closely. University-trained judges, prosecutors, and advocates of the regional *audiencias* or other important tribunals carried on a legal discourse steeped in Roman method and peppered with erudite citations of the doctors of law known as *doctores*. But Hispanic law allowed for procedural simplification, and in most parts of the colonial world officials with little or no legal training attended to judicial affairs as best they could.

In the Spanish Borderlands, strict adherence to procedural rules in both civil and criminal cases tended to be lax, though not illegal. Distinctions between civil and criminal law differed from modern ones, but in what we would refer to as civil cases, provincial magistrates tended to pay closer attention to legal prescriptions, especially in matters of succession and transfer of property. Furthermore, wills, testaments, and petitions drawn by provincials replicate the standard contemporary legal idioms of the Hispanic world. Evidence suggests that borderland settlers learned proper style from formularies and by copying documents. The few who had substantial property recognized the importance of adhering to legal convention.

Spanish Louisiana, the most active commercial region of the borderlands, was unique in having a cadre of legal professionals who maintained a level of expertise and consistency unknown in other peripheral areas. In addition to wills, testaments, and dowries, noncriminal matters also centered on questions of contractual obligations and property transfers of various kinds, often involving considerable sums.

In contrast, civil cases in poorer regions such as Florida, New Mexico, and Texas usually dealt with small claims. The Crown allowed and encouraged their summary dispatch. A squabble over nonpayment for *una vaca parida* (one milk cow), a hunting knife, or meager back wages could not generate the fees necessary to sustain a lengthy trial. When large sums were involved, however, litigants sometimes pursued their justice beyond the local magistrate, appealing to the provincial governor or, rarely, to the regional *audiencia*. Clearly, the lack or presence of wealth shaped the nature of legal administration in the borderlands. Most cases involved trifling amounts and were dealt with in simplified, summary fashion. Nevertheless, summary justice appears not to have deterred litigation, and colonial subjects in the borderlands evidently viewed litigation as a normal way to resolve both criminal and noncriminal conflicts.

In many parts of Spanish America, Indians appeared frequently as litigants in civil cases. With one notable exception, however, they rarely did so in the borderlands. Under the close scrutiny of Franciscans and Jesuits, who drastically altered traditional political, social, and economic arrangements, mission Indians took little active part in the colonial legal system. The Pueblo Indians of New Mexico loom as the exceptions to this general tendency. Like their counterparts throughout much of the Spanish colonial world, the Pueblo people pursued their rights as Indians under Spanish law and became adept courtroom participants. Their litigation often centered on questions of communal land ownership, usually against Hispanic neighbors though sometimes against other Indian villages. The use of colonial courts proved to be an important and often effective strategy by which the Pueblo people maintained their village lands—a key part of their communally centered identity.

THE LEGACY OF SPANISH CIVIL LAW

Because of their modern importance, certain aspects of the Spanish colonial legal system merit special attention. Regions in the United States that once fell under Spanish jurisdiction have incorporated into their common law systems some elements of Spanish civil law. Community property laws (by which husband and wife share in the assets of a marriage) and some elements of laws of succession, for example, stem from Hispanic practice and are found mostly in regions once held by Spain.

Scholars continue to debate the Spanish influence on water law of the arid western United States. While Spanish colonial practice often coincides with modern legal precepts, the direct connection is harder to pin down. Texas and New Mexico seem to have retained the most features of Spanish water law, especially with respect to community regulation and allocation of water. Because of the Treaty of Guadalupe Hidalgo (1848)—by which the United States rec-ognized property rights of former Mexican citizens—American courts continue to consider the nature of ownership, control, and use of water under Spanish and Mexican sovereignty (to 1821 and 1848, respectively), and to interpret how these precepts might apply to current regional legal practice.

An important event in the unique legal history of Louisiana was the introduction of "O'Reilly's Code" in 1769, based largely on the *Nueva recopilación de Castilla* and the *Recopilación de leyes de los reynos de las Indias*. Well received by the French-speaking population, this collection of written statutes served to consolidate and make understandable the Spanish civil law tradition and, thus, contributed noticeably to Louisiana's legal tradition.

Aside from these legacies, little of the Hispanic legal tradition survived the United States acquisition of the borderlands. Unfamiliar with the civil law system, and convinced of the superiority of the common law system, Anglo-American settlers almost completely supplanted Hispanic legal practice with their own.

BIBLIOGRAPHY

Baade, Hans. "Marriage Contracts in French and Spanish Louisiana: A Study in 'Notarial' Jurisprudence." *Tulane Law Review* 53, no. 1 (1978):1–92.

Cutter, Charles R. *The Protector de Indios in Colonial New Mexico, 1659–1821.* Albuquerque, N.Mex., 1986.

Meyer, Michael C. *Water in the Hispanic Southwest: A Social and Legal History, 1550–1850.* Tucson, Ariz., 1984.

Yiannopoulos, A. N. "The Early Sources of Louisiana Law: Critical Appraisal of a Controversy." In *Louisiana's Legal Heritage,* edited by Edward F. Haas. Pensacola, Fla., 1983.

Charles R. Cutter

INDIAN GOVERNANCE

ANY DISCUSSION OF Indian governance at the time of contact and for the early years of colonial involvement must be prefaced by several important caveats. The continent north of Mexico, a vast area in excess of 7.4 million square miles (19.2 million square kilometers) and containing every gradation of climate from subtropical to arctic, does not yield easily to analysis. Within this area approximately seven million Native people lived in thousands of villages and tens of thousands of family units. Their social and political organizations mirrored the diversity of the land.

The problems of determining the political systems of these social units deserve consideration. First is the nature of the data. The cultures of Native peoples were rich in folklore, epics that described their origins, tales of migrations assisted or directed by mythological culture-heroes, and complex, intriguing cosmologies that defined and explained the universe. But none had a written language. While many of the great epics explained the origins of political systems, none detailed their contemporary functioning. We are therefore dependent to a large degree on archaeological research and the journals, letters, reports, and commentaries of non-Native observers.

As to archaeology, while it can provide many insights into social life, it offers precious little direct evidence of political organization. What archaeology does show is that there existed be-fore known European contact extensive trade networks covering tens of thousands of square miles. This has important ramifications, as will be shown later in this essay.

The second primary source for an understanding of precontact governance is the written material of early explorers, settlers, adventurers, colonial officials, traders, and slavers. These sources, although useful, must be read with care. Almost without exception, they present a negative picture of Native peoples or, conversely, an idyllic one. In most cases the commentators did not speak the languages of the natives they met, and so they imposed their own sense of political organization on the Native communities they observed. Often, the commentators were hardly more literate than the observed; their interests were in trade, conquest, and enslavement—the latter two, at least, hardly representing the basis for unbiased observation. Because of the limitations resulting from the absence of Native records and little available from the archaeological record, we remain dependent on the reports of early explorers for our understanding of Indian governance at the time of contact and during the colonial period.

One additional caveat deserves mention: the idea of contact as a fixed point is illusory. Contact was not a single event, but rather a series of invasions and intrusions spanning more than two hundred years, whose objectives were to plunder the land for gold, slaves, and furs and to prosely-

449

tize the survivors. It is nearly universally true that the earliest contacts, particularly those of the Spaniards, were marked by violence.

Thus, contact and colonization occurred at different times throughout North America, and the colonial periods varied in lengths of time and the intensity of their impacts on Native peoples. For example, along the East Coast the colonial period did not end until the close of the Revolutionary War; in the Ohio Valley it took another decade for the process to complete itself. And so it went elsewhere on the continent. The process did not end until the early 1800s on the Plains, 1803 in Louisiana, 1820 in Florida, until the 1830s in the Southwest, 1848 in California, and 1867 in Alaska. Canada, like the United States, had various dates, depending on the region and the settlement patterns of Europeans, but it certainly was completed by the time of Canadian independence from England; that is, by 1867. Regardless of the time or the colonizer, there was an inexorable quality to the process. Native polity changed or disappeared under the pressures from imperialism.

By the beginning of the nineteenth century most of the Native groups north of Mexico had had contact with Europeans. More important, even the groups that had avoided direct contact had been significantly and irreversibly changed by that contact. The records of these contacts, imperfect as they are, form the bases for an analysis of Indian governance. Because of the incomplete, biased, and serendipitous nature of the documentation, many of the details of Indian governance are unknowable. Therefore, to understand aboriginal polity, anthropologists must use comparative and other inadequate evidence derived from data collected in North America as well as elsewhere in the world. This being the case, they have developed three ideal types: bands, tribes, and chiefdoms. (A fourth type, states, is omitted from this essay because it is not applicable to the area north of Mexico.)

Bands consist of a small number of nuclear and extended families, generally related to each other, who tend to forage together. Bands have no formal political structure or codification of law, and leadership commonly accrues to the individual who demonstrates particular talents. These leadership positions carry with them no institutionalized power or authority. This is not

to say that bands are anarchic; rather, they maintain order by customary law and by the social pressures placed on individuals by other members of the band.

Tribes tend to be more sedentary, with larger populations than bands and with more complex kinship systems. Like bands, tribes tend to be egalitarian, with leadership vested in those who are respected and who, in some cases, have accumulated wealth. In many cases, tribes are led by a headman and an informal council made up of the elder members of the tribe. Often tribe and village are synonymous. The larger the village, the greater is the tendency to vest authority in the hands of one or a few leaders. The presence of clans, moieties, and sodalities adds to the complexity of the sociopolitical organization of the tribe.

The chiefdom is significantly different from the band and tribe in that it represents a ranked rather than egalitarian society. It is similar to the tribe in that it is kinship-based and village-centered. It is characterized by the institutionalization of political authority in the office of chief, who with a council controls the activities of the general population. Chiefs control the production, distribution, and consumption of resources. Individuals achieve the status of chief through descent and seniority, although ability certainly has an impact on the determination.

Having mentioned the serial, serendipitous nature of early contact and colonization, the remainder of this essay concentrates on what can be said about Indian governance based on the extant sixteenth- and seventeenth-century documentation.

Band societies were common throughout Canada (north of the Great Lakes and the Saint Lawrence Valley), the Great Basin, California, and interior and northern Alaska. Bands, which relied wholly or primarily on hunting and gathering, were generally small social units that acted autonomously. They consisted of a few related families, with leadership vested in the heads of the households. Decisions were based on consensus, most of the social order was determined by custom, and disputes were settled by divination, contests, and, as a last resort, violence. There were, of course, variations among the many bands that lived in North America at the times of contact.

The political system of North American Indian bands was informal and without much structure. Individuals who did not agree with the actions of the leader were free to leave the local group and join another. Political decision making was tied to and was a function of the kin network. There was no higher political organization than the band, and that was functional only in the most minimal way. The local group was the effective political unit.

The Micmac Indians, an Algonquian-speaking people who occupied an area from the Gulf of Saint Lawrence south to the eastern shore of Nova Scotia, including Prince Edward and Cape Breton islands, provide one example of this type of organization. For most of the year, the Micmac lived in small kin-based households, which joined together to form local groups of related families. Each group had a local leader, or sagamore, who possessed limited authority. The position of sagamore could be inherited, assigned by an elder sagamore, or acquired by skill and charisma. The sagamore's power was limited to assigning hunting territories, greeting and questioning visitors, leading the seasonal movement of the local group, counseling on peace, and directing the group's men in times of war. Sagamores were advised and assisted by shamans and by the local group's elders. Since shamans were thought to possess the power to divine the future, their advice weighed heavily on all deliberations.

During the summer the local groups came together for feasting, at which time the local-group sagamores had the opportunity to discuss matters of common interest. The Micmac divided themselves into seven bands or districts, each with a relatively well-defined territory. Although there was no higher organization, the seven bands recognized Onamag (Cape Breton Island) as the head district and its sagamore as the chief sagamore. Disputes between individuals were settled by wrestling matches or fights when the sagamore and his advisers were unable to work out a compromise. In such instances, the sagamore or neutral elders in the community acted as judges. More serious crimes, such as murder,

were settled by revenge killing or the acceptance of compensation by the aggrieved.

TRIBES

Tribes were common throughout North America, particularly in areas where horticulture was possible or where there was an ample, relatively stable food supply. This includes most of the eastern seaboard, the Ohio-Missouri-Mississippi River system, parts of the southwest, the Great Lakes area, the Plains (particularly after the introduction of guns and horses), and along the Northwest coast from Oregon north to the panhandle of Alaska.

Tribes were more sedentary than bands and, with few exceptions, relied on horticulture for a significant part of their diet. Their political organizations were characterized by leaders chosen on the basis of achievement and personality. Generally speaking, these leaders (generally referred to as sachems, sagamores, chiefs) did not possess coercive power but instead relied upon their personal prestige to achieve consensus. In addition to a civil chief, many tribes had a war chief who took over when the tribe was threatened or threatening. Decisions were made by a council consisting of the elders from the various extended families; on the more serious matters the council might include all the adult members of the tribe, although not all tribes permitted women to speak in council. As with bands, customs and beliefs provided the basis for individual behavior, but there were no institutionalized means of enforcing conformity. Both types of political organization were essentially egalitarian.

The Western Abenaki, who lived west of the Micmac, represent one example of a tribal type of political organization; other tribes, although displaying similar political structures, vary in detail. They occupied most of what is now New Hampshire and Vermont, and they extended into Canada as far as the headwaters of the Saint Lawrence River, an area they used primarily for hunting and trapping. The tribe followed a seasonal cycle similar to that of the Micmac. The Western Abenaki exhibited several important differences from their neighbors to the east. The society was patrilineal; the basic social unit was the household. Several related households lived together in a longhouse, and the total of the extended families made up the tribe.

The tribe consisted of a number of villages, each of which had a civil chief and a war chief. Chiefs were chosen for their abilities, and because of their personal prestige they exerted considerable influence over the affairs of the village. They lacked coercive power, however, and instead relied upon persuasion to accomplish any objective. Issues of general concern to the village were discussed at a council that included the civil chief, war chief, and elders representing the various extended families. Decisions were based on consensus, as witnessed by this excerpt from the Dutch observer Isaack de Rasieres, circa 1628 who attended a meeting of a similar tribe in southern New England:

When any stranger comes, they bring him to the Sackima. On first meeting they do not speak—they smoke a pipe of tobacco; that being done, the Sackima asks: "Whence do you come?" the stranger then states that, and further what he has to say, before all who are present or choose to come. That being done, the Sackima announces his opinion to the people, and if they agree thereto, they give all together a sigh—"He!"—and if they do not approve, they keep silence, and all come close to the Sackima, and each sets forth his opinion till they agree; that being done, they come all together again to the stranger, to whom the Sackima then announces what they have determined, with reasons moving them thereto. (J. Franklin Jameson, ed. *Narratives of New Netherland* [New York, 1909], p. 109)

More serious concerns, such as war, were discussed at a general meeting of all the adult tribal members; both women and men were able to address the council and participate in the decision making. If war was chosen, the war chief called for the formation of war parties. Each war party consisted of up to ten men with a leader; ten or more war parties required an overall leader, but each party was relatively free to act on its own.

CHIEFDOM

Chiefdoms were far less common than bands and tribes. They developed where there were unusually rich resources; in particular, the Southeast and Northwest.

Along the southwestern portion of the Chesapeake Bay, in what is now Virginia, lived a collection of tribes bound together in what has been described as a "chiefdom." These tribes lived principally along two major river systems—the York and the James—and depended largely on horticulture, supplemented by hunting and fishing for subsistence. Perhaps as many as twenty-five tribes were so linked together, to a greater or lesser degree, by the beginning of the seventeenth century.

The formation of the chiefdom coincided with, but was independent of, European exploration and was the work of Powhatan, who in the latter half of the sixteenth century conquered or coerced the tribes into submission. He created a political structure that provided for a chief over each tribe and subchiefs controlling the smaller settlements. Chiefs could be male (*weroance*) or female (*weroansqua*). Their duties included welcoming guests with feasts and oratory, collecting tribute in the form of tanned hides, peak, maize, and so forth from the commoners and subchiefs, and consulting with and carrying out mandates of the supreme ruler, the *mamanatowick*. Chiefs possessed the power of life and death and could summarily execute individuals who were disobedient by having them clubbed to death.

The position of chief was most commonly inherited through the matriline and went from the sons in order of birth to the daughters in order of birth, although it was possible to become chief through acts of bravery and loyal, exemplary service. Chiefs commanded the services of the commoners who tended their fields, hunted game for them, and provided tribute, some of which was passed on to the *mamanatowick*.

Above the tribal chiefs was Powhatan, the supreme ruler, the *mamanatowick*. While Powhatan did not control every aspect of the affairs of the tribes in his domain, on the major issues of war, peace, alliances, and the payment of tribute, his word was law, and he was not averse to the use of force to punish a recalcitrant tribe. For example, in 1608 he wiped out the Chesapeake for refusing to join his "empire." As supreme leader Powhatan had a monopoly over all copper, which he used as rewards and payments to the chiefs for their participation in wars against tribes that opposed his will. The copper came to Powhatan from the Ohio Valley through the extensive trade networks that existed in the precontact period.

While Powhatan's empire consisted of tribes united by force and intimidation, to the west and south, along the Mississippi, in the vicinity of the present-day city that bears their name, lived the Natchez Indians, a tribe that had developed the most elaborate hierarchal social and political structure north of Mexico. The tribe was first contacted by the Hernando de Soto expedition in 1542, as it passed through the Natchez territory on its return to the coast. The meeting was far from amiable, and the expedition was attacked repeatedly by the Natchez. The next contact came in 1682 when the French explorer René-Robert Cavelier de La Salle was received with hospitality and was smart enough to act accordingly. By 1700 the French had established cordial enough relations so as to allow traders and priests to operate out of the territory, although the latter were not very successful in converting the Natchez. The tribe's religious system was far too well integrated into the political and social life of the tribe to permit the easy establishment of a rival belief system.

The social and political life of the Natchez centered around the leader called the Great Sun, the incarnation of the Supreme Being, who possessed absolute power over the tribal members. Assisting the Great Sun was a council of advisers made up of two war chiefs, two priests, two men who dealt with external relations, one man in charge of public works, and four who arranged for public feasts. These individuals acted as the administrative branch of the tribal government. In addition, there was a council of elders, representing the various villages, who met with the Great Sun. By and large, their responsibility was to see that the will of the Great Sun was carried out at the local level and to provide information as requested. So elevated was the Great Sun that individuals bowed in his presence, stayed four paces from him when conversing, assented to all he said, and walked backward, bowing, as they left him. Failure to follow the etiquette meant death. The Great Sun was the personification of the highest supernatural authority on earth, a god-king, and he was treated accordingly.

Natchez society was divided into two classes of people; nobility and commoners, or Stinkards. The nobility consisted of three subclasses: Suns, Nobles, and Honored People. The tribe followed a matrilineal descent pattern, with the nobility practicing exogamy; that is, members of the nobility were required to marry commoners. When a woman of the nobility married a commoner, the offspring remained in the same subclass as the mother. When a man from the nobility married a commoner, the offspring dropped down one class; Suns became Nobles, Nobles became Honored People, Honored People became Stinkards. Since polygyny was permitted, and since men of the nobility had access to more resources, they could marry more women, thus creating a shortage of common women for common men. This was at least in part alleviated by bringing in captured women from other tribes. The Natchez also practiced slavery, although it is not clear whether slaves could marry tribal members and whether they could be manumitted.

Another area where chiefdoms developed was the Northwest Coast from approximately Puget Sound north to the United States–Canada boundary. Here the Haida, Tsimshian, Bellacoola, Kwakiutl, Makah, Quileute, and Nootka, among others, developed complex social, ceremonial, and political systems. For example, the Nootka on Vancouver Island had three hereditary classes: chiefs and their families, commoners, and slaves. Within the first class were a number of subclasses determined by the relationship of the individual to the chiefly line. Kinship and rank were inextricably tied together, and inheritance moved through the kin lines with the eldest son succeeding the father.

A chief received tribute from those under his control, and he redistributed the largesse through potlatches and gift giving. In return, he gained prestige and acknowledgment of his status. For those reluctant to contribute, the chief had slaves to enforce his will, but his power was limited to those in his aggregate. Raids against other clans were conducted for revenge and to capture slaves. The chief's political power did not extend beyond his clan, and struggles between clans were not uncommon. Feasts and potlatches were two means to maintain political ties with other clans. Thus, there was no single leader for all the members of the chiefdom. Instead, a series of alliances kept the political situation in a dynamic, if at times delicate, balance.

As one might expect, not all cases fit neatly within the schema of ideal types. Such is the case, for example, with the Pueblo of the Southwest. Although all have villages based upon horticulture, they show a wide variation of governance, not quite fitting either the criteria for tribes or chiefdoms.

The Pueblo are divided into two groups, Western and Eastern. The Hopi, Zuni, Acoma, and Laguna are Western Pueblo, while the Eastern Pueblo consist of eighteen villages including Taos, San Juan, Santa Clara, Isleta, and San Ildefonso. While the two groups differ in social and political organization, they share a core of beliefs. (There are also differences within the groups such that the differences from east to west are more of a continuum than a polarity.) In general, the Western Pueblo were organized around matrilineal, matrilocal, exogamous clans, while the Eastern Pueblo villages were divided into two patrilineal moieties with descent reckoned bilaterally.

The political system of the Western Pueblo was essentially theocratic, with the kachina cults providing the means to enforce public opinion. The Eastern Pueblo developed a more centralized political system with a chief or cacique and a council responsible for village order and the allocation of village land. Among some Pueblo there are hierarchically arranged classes of people. San Juan Pueblo and Santa Clara are examples. Thus it is not altogether clear just where the Pueblo fit in the typology.

IMPACT OF COLONIZATION

European exploration and colonization quickly and radically altered Indian polity. Even before large-scale settlement, European-introduced pathogens ravaged many of the tribes along the coast. Smallpox, measles, and influenza, among a host of others, wiped out entire settlements; in other instances, diseases killed so many that for the survivors, the fabric of social life was effectively destroyed. It is estimated that between 50 percent and 90 percent of Native populations died in the early days of contact. Tribes and bands were affected long before they had direct contact. Europeans did not just move along the coast; explorers penetrated the river systems, moving the pathogens deep into the continent. What Europeans did not carry directly, tribes in contact with them transmitted to others. The continent was laced with trade routes over which Native traders moved with ease. And so did the diseases.

Contact increased trade and in the process altered the Native societies. European products—among them beads, tools, metal utensils, axes, knives, and guns—were in high demand. In exchange, Europeans desired furs, deerskins, precious metals, slaves, and wampum. The competition set tribe against tribe, European against European. Tribes and bands lined up with European colonists to raid each other, quickly adopting the total-war motif of Europe. With the establishment of colonies, Europeans, particularly the English and Dutch, sought title to land. The result was the extermination of some tribes and, within the span of a few decades, the alteration of the political systems of most remaining tribes.

Tribes that opposed Europeans faced annihilation at the hands of the colonial officials or their paid surrogates, other tribes. The Beothuk of Newfoundland, for example, earned the enmity of the French for what amounted to petty theft. The French offered a bounty for every Beothuk head, and their neighbors waged incessant raids that resulted in the near-total destruction of the tribe by the end of the seventeenth century. The Pequot are an even more striking example. A large and powerful tribe governing the area between the Mystic and Connecticut rivers, they also controlled a major fur-producing area and the center of wampum production. The English coveted the tribe's lands and feared its power. Joined by the Mohegan and Narraganset, the English launched a surprise attack on the main Pequot village, which they set afire, and then slaughtered the fleeing inhabitants, mostly women and children. The tribe's sachem, Sassacus, fled to the Mohawk to seek their assistance; they responded by cutting off his head and sending it to Hartford as proof of their fealty. A similar fate awaited the Narraganset in 1675 and the Wampanoag under their sachem, King Philip, a year later.

Nor was this warfare limited to New England. Tribes along the eastern seaboard were set against each other; old injuries revived and new ones developed. Many tribes just disappeared or merged with other tribes. The chiefdom of Powhatan was destroyed after an extended war of attrition, its constituent members becoming subject tribes of the colony of Virginia. The Natchez were also destroyed by the combined forces of the French and their Indian allies; the survivors either joined other tribes or were captured and sold into slavery—the fate of many unfortunate Indians in the seventeenth and eighteenth centuries.

Throughout North America, the colonial governments combined their efforts at conquest with equally severe efforts at conversion. In most cases, conversion meant first and foremost the suppression of Native social, religious, and political institutions. In New England, Praying Towns were established to facilitate conversion. Missionaries from all religions and sects fanned out across the continent to proselytize. Where possible, force was combined with prayer to persuade the recalcitrant. Among the Pueblo the combination of brutal Spanish practices and overly zealous priests led to a revolt in 1680 that resulted in the elimination of Spanish control. By the end of the century the Spanish had regained control of the Pueblo, but they were unable to suppress the religio-political system. Instead, they superimposed their system of civil governance, which the Pueblo co-opted by appointing the representatives. Their religious practices continued in secret.

Although the pressure from colonial governments often resulted in tribes being pitted against each other, in some instances it had an opposite effect. It led to the formation of confederacies. A number of such confederacies appear in the records: Abenaki and Wabenaki in New England; Huron in the Great Lakes region; Illinois in the Ohio Valley; and the Creek in the lower Mississippi Valley. By far the most famous of the confederacies was the one formed by the Iroquois (also known as the Five Nations confederacy and Six Nations confederacy). Initially, it was made up of the Mohawk, Oneida, Onondaga, Cayuga, and Seneca tribes; later the Tuscarora tribe from North Carolina was added. It is by no means clear that a confederation existed prior to European colonization, although there was certainly a shared ceremonial cycle.

Within the Iroquois confederacy each tribe maintained its autonomy, and common action required unanimous agreement. While the rhetoric of the confederacy suggests a relatively tightly organized group led by fifty hereditary sachems unevenly representing the five tribes, the historical records indicate little unanimity. Whatever coherence that existed ended with the American Revolution, when the confederacy covered its council fire and its members divided over whom to support in the war. The Oneida and Tuscarora joined the colonial cause while the other three remained loyal to the British.

Other, more ephemeral, confederacies formed to meet the pressures from the colonizing powers. They generally formed around a charismatic leader advocating nativistic themes. These organizations brought together a number of tribes in a region and were often supported by one of the colonial powers. Their demise came with military defeats. Such was the case of the Ottawa chief Pontiac in the 1760s, of the Indians in the Ohio Valley tribes in 1794, and of the movement led by the Shawnee chief Tecumseh and his brother, the Prophet, in the first decade of the nineteenth century.

Tribes that survived the European onslaught changed their political organizations to fit the new political realities. Europeans tended to reward leaders who could command the loyalties of the fighting men. The result was that in many of the surviving tribes, the traditional political organization atrophied, although the terminology of leadership may have remained the same. Often tribes split into two groups, with one maintaining the traditional ways and the other, commonly those who had converted to Christianity, accepting the European precepts. This was particularly true of the tribes under the control of the English. Colonial governments pressured the tribes by passing laws dictating the forms of tribal government and the limitations of tribal power and authority over tribal members and land.

This is not to say that all aspects of Indian polity disappeared in the face of European pressure. Many tribes continued to rely on consensus for decision making. Leaders often were chosen by families, and councils were formed that represented the constituent families. In some cases, such as the Mashpee Wampanoag on Cape Cod and Gay Head Wampanoag on Martha's Vineyard, the conversion to Christianity did little to alter the underlying political processes, although it brought superficial changes to the political structures.

Thus, the stability of Native political systems depended upon a number of conditions over which the tribes and bands had little or no control. Epidemics, disputes among European sovereigns, competition for trade, exploitation of resources, the desire to proselytize, and the insatiable appetite for land affected the Native entities in differing ways and at different rates. Those who could modify their political organizations to adjust to the pressures or who could avoid the worst effects survived the longest, but in the end, all Native groups were altered by the processes of exploration and colonization.

BIBLIOGRAPHY

Campisi, Jack. *The Mashpee Indians: Tribe on Trial.* Syracuse, N.Y., 1991.

Denig, Edwin Thompson. *Five Indian Tribes of the Upper Missouri: Sioux, Arickarqs, Assiniboines, Crees, Crows.* Edited by John C. Ewers. Norman, Okla., 1961.

Handbook of North American Indians, edited by William C. Sturtevant. Vols. 4–10, 15. Washington, D.C., 1978–1990.

Hudson, Charles. *The Southeastern Indians.* Knoxville, Tenn., 1976.

Jameson, J. Franklin, ed. *Narratives of New Netherland, 1609–1664.* New York, 1909; repr., 1967.

Jennings, Francis, et al., eds. *The History and Culture of Iroquois Diplomacy: An Interdisciplinary Guide to the Treaties of the Six Nations and Their League.* Syracuse, N.Y., 1985.

Rountree, Helen C. *The Powhatan Indians of Virginia: Their Traditional Culture.* Norman, Okla., 1989.

Swanton, John R. *The Indian Tribes of North America.* Bureau of American Ethnology Bulletin no. 145. Washington, D.C., 1952.

Jack Campisi

SEE ALSO **The First Americans; Interracial Societies; Mission Communities; Native American Economics;** and **Native American Families and Life Cycles.**

V

ECONOMIC LIFE

MERCANTILISM

OVER THE SECOND HALF of the second millennium of the Christian Era, the Western world has experienced the impact of three successive, interrelated, overlapping economic doctrines: mercantilism, capitalism, and socialism. Mercantilism called upon government to develop the economy in the best interests of the state. Capitalism called upon government to develop the economy in the best interests of business. Socialism called upon government to develop the economy in the best interests of the workers. None of these three doctrines necessarily denied the need for attention to the concerns of the other partners in the enterprise. All three recognized the symbiotic relationship of the state, business, and workers. The focus of each was simply a matter of emphasis, of subordination. Historical imperatives and historical opportunities dictated the form and gait of these doctrines. Cognizant always of the continuum, this essay dwells on the first in this sequence of three: mercantilism.

GOAL OF MERCANTILISM

The goal of mercantilism was to fortify the central governments of Europe. The pivotal proposition of mercantilism was that the entire economy could be, and should be, harnessed to power the engine of the state. From the fifteenth century on, nationalism was the prime political force in northern and western Europe. Strong central governments were formed from and replaced the feudal patchwork that had characterized the previous thousand years. The creation of the nation Spain at the end of the fifteenth century provided a model for others to follow. France and England were quick to enter the competition. The Portuguese and the Dutch initially surpassed them only later to be surpassed by them.

Every ingredient in the establishment of the nation-state cost money, especially the suppression of internal and external rivals. Grants and bribes, armies and navies, all required secure and expandable sources of revenue. To increase local taxes seemed unwise, given domestic opponents who might exploit consequent discontent. The rising nation-states of Atlantic Europe turned, instead, to the foreign sector of their economies as a source of money with which to buttress their central governments.

Foreign trade gathered treasure for the coffers of kings in two ways. In normal times, customs duties collected from imports and exports were an immediate and regular source of revenue for the central government. Any increase in the nation's foreign trade translated directly into more money for the government's use. In times of national emergency, it became necessary to borrow. Loans from subjects of the Crown were easier and cheaper to obtain than loans from others, but required that the nation have individuals able and willing to lend money to the monarch. Any increase in the number and wealth of such people, especially if they felt that they owed their initial and continuing success to the bounty of the monarch, translated into easier funding of the debts of government. Merchants engaged in foreign trade were a likely group.

The power of the nation-state could be used to protect and promote the kinds of enterprises that would enhance foreign trade and enrich the merchants who organized and conducted it. The expansion of a nation's foreign trade brought quick and continuing benefits to the central government. The stronger the central government, the stronger the support for foreign trade; the stronger the support for foreign trade, the stronger the central government. Or so sounded the mercantilist mantra. Mercantilist doctrine, based on these realizations, suggested a way to accomplish—and to justify—policies in pursuit of these ends.

Given the essentially predatory nature of a mercantilist world, contests between governments followed almost as a matter of course. The sixteenth century saw Spain and its empire decline as it failed to defeat challenges from rivals near and far. Chief among them was the Netherlands, which, in its own triumph, crafted a "Golden Age" and became a target for others. In the seventeenth century, the Netherlands lost a succession of wars fought first with England and then with France. The two victors then turned upon each other and fought seriatim their own Second Hundred Years' War (1689–1815) to decide which of the two would rule the world. The outcome of that mercantilist struggle, the Pax Britannica, ushered in—indeed, encouraged—the enunciation of the next economic doctrine, capitalism.

The enthronement of the supremely powerful nation-state, Great Britain, as controller of the world permitted devising a doctrine that called for government now to foster the economy in the best interests of business. It was hardly coincidental that Adam Smith wrote *The Wealth of Nations*, his tract denouncing the worst features of mercantilism and setting out the guidelines of classical capitalism, on the heels of the stupendous British victory over France in the fourth phase of that series of Anglo-French wars, the Seven Years' War. Nor was he alone, in Great Britain or on the Continent, where French

Physiocrats like the marquis de Mirabeau argued much as Smith did. The era of "free trade" that Smith and Mirabeau called for, and that the Pax Britannica ultimately enshrined, was the obvious successor to successful mercantilism.

NATURE OF MERCANTILISM

Just what constituted mercantilism has so bedeviled historians that a few commentators have even tried to deny that it ever existed. (One almost has the feeling that they do not like it and, in not liking it, have dismissed it.) Some fail to find either coherence or consistency in theory or in practice and conclude that, without them, there was no such thing as mercantilism. In the words of Arthur V. Judges, "Mercantilism never had a creed; nor was there a priesthood dedicated to its service." Yet to argue from the lack of a cogent creed, dedicated votaries, or even a coherent congregation to the nonexistence of a doctrine is to disregard the likes of Christianity or Judaism because of their diversity and discordancy.

Mercantilism existed—just as capitalism and socialism still exist—despite the difficulty we may have in defining its ideas and detecting its agents. Governments and peoples acted on its doctrines, organized themselves to put its principles into practice, and fought to attain mercantilist goals that promised them benefits. People and governments also questioned and ignored the tenets of mercantilism. More frequently, they bent them. By the last third of the eighteenth century, many had begun to reject outright the doctrines of mercantilism, arguing, with Adam Smith, for change. That capitalism and socialism, the successors of mercantilism, are neither more or less clearly defined nor consistently practiced than mercantilism establishes them merely as similar in that all three are doctrines.

By "doctrine" we mean something far less than dogma. Indeed, we mean to connote just the opposite of dogma: not all of the tenets of mercantilism were observed by all the adherents, everywhere, all of the time. There was mercantilist theory; there was mercantilist policy. That such theory as there was contributed little to the advancement of economic science matters little in any assessment of its impact upon its own time. Sometimes policy and proposal were at war with each other. Frequently other considerations overrode what a mercantilist would have preferred. Such is the fundamental conflict between theory and practice.

The relationship between theory and policy was never one-directional and sometimes not even clear. Policy decisions did flow from the dictates of the doctrine, but not all policies were mercantilist. And not all the economic ideas current at the time in the Atlantic world were mercantilist. Sometimes mercantilist actions were justified with reference to propositions that seem not very mercantilistic at all. Doctrines are like that. Mercantilism was a set of beliefs, a pattern of practices—in the words of Jacob Viner, "a folk doctrine." It was hardly a "system," despite Adam Smith's self-serving opinion to the contrary.

By "mercantilism" we mean simply the shared perception, among those who controlled the rising nation-states of northern and western Europe from the sixteenth to the eighteenth centuries, that the economy should be made to support the interests of government—and vice versa. By "mercantilism" we also mean the body of policies, regulations, and laws developed over the period to implement that perception. We are left to infer much of the former from an exegesis of the latter. There was no formulary for mercantilism.

The leadership of those nation-states, originally just the political rulers of the countries and their supporters, came over time to include the more powerful representatives of the landed and commercial interests. A fiercely belligerent world environment induced disparate political and economic groups increasingly to cooperate, once they realized not only that they would survive better working together but also that they could prosper, politically and economically. (The rise to power of country and countinghouse interests over these centuries laid the foundation of the changes that were to characterize the next era.) Of primary concern, given a dangerous world, was the maintenance of a strong central government that could protect and promote the nation's economy. In turn, that economy could provide the central government with the monetary and financial support it needed to survive and grow stronger. Everyone would benefit—everyone

who counted, that is. In the words of one English writer, the self-styled "Philopatris," "Foreign Trade produceth Riches, Riches power, Power preserves our Trade and Religion." Mercantilist doctrine pointed the way to a most fruitful collaboration.

TENETS OF MERCANTILISM

All of this can be made somewhat clearer by outlining the basic tenets of mercantilist doctrine. There were three elements common to the thinking of mercantilists. It will be useful to appreciate that they were accredited and articulated in most of the nation-states of Atlantic Europe. These ideas constitute what Jacob Viner called "the solid core of mercantilist doctrine, from which there was little dissent before the 1750s."

First, as has already been suggested, mercantilists accepted that the economy should be structured by the state to serve the interests of the state. This perception is a direct outgrowth of the transition during this period from weak, local, feudal governments to strong, central, national governments. The need for and the value of individual and corporate participation in the economy were recognized, but mercantilism insisted that prime consideration be given not to individual or corporate aspirations but to the usefulness to the nation of any particular enterprise. Thus, for instance, both the British and the French governments were content to ban the domestic production of tobacco in order to promote the overseas trade in tobacco, despite the adverse effects such a ban had on their own farmers. The tobacco trade yielded customs revenues; tobacco farming did not.

Central government structuring of the economy took many different forms. Nevertheless, all can be seen to have the kind of point suggested already: the more a plan or a program had a direct bearing on increasing the power of the central government, the more the central government pushed it. Thus mercantilist policies rarely addressed domestic agriculture unless there were implications for the nation's foreign trade. Nor were mercantilists much concerned with the internal commerce of the country. Manufacturing, too, did not loom large in the mercantilist mind unless its decrease meant more foreign imports or its increase meant increased domestic exports. The financial sector of the economy rarely attracted the attention of mercantilists except for the part that facilitated the organization and capitalization of trading companies or the buying and selling of government securities. By contrast, the central government was heavily involved in granting lucrative monopolies in the trade from the nation's ports to various parts of the globe. It did so because that trade enriched the investors, who could then be counted on to support government, and it enriched the monarch, who collected the customs duties.

Second, mercantilists believed that the intermediate goal of mercantilism was to build up the nation's wealth, which they measured by its stock of money. Wealth meant gold and silver, coin and bullion. Preserving or enhancing human capital or capital goods was not part of mercantilist thinking. In the bullionist corollary to mercantilism, the world's supply of gold and silver was fixed and limited. Thus it was possible to improve one's own position and weaken one's competitors at the same time. The more gold and silver a nation had, the better it was. The more *we* have, the less *they* have, by definition. All means were to be employed to acquire and keep as much gold and silver as possible.

The money stock of the nation was, of course, not an end in itself but a means to an end. The goal was political strength; gold and silver helped a nation attain and retain that strength. Money allowed the nation to protect itself and to expand by funding all of the things necessary to be a true nation-state.

France under Louis XIV (ruled 1661–1715) exemplified this perfectly. The Sun King required the accoutrements necessary to display his majesty; the fortifications necessary to protect his Crown; the diplomatic corps necessary to enhance his kingdom; and the armed forces necessary to expand his territory. Thus his need for Versailles and its splendors; his need for Sébastien de Prestre, marquis de Vauban, and his fortresses; for Hughes de Lionne and his diplomats; and for François Michel Le Tellier, marquis de Louvois, and his generals. Thus, too, the necessity for Jean-Baptiste Colbert, the controller general of finances whom the Sun King charged with securing the requisite resources. Colbert accomplished his task brilliantly—at least for a while—and he did so by blatantly copying the mercantilistic modes of his king's rivals across the English Channel. Expanded French foreign trade, he expected, would yield more money for the central government, immediately by way of increased customs revenues and eventually by creating a class of French businessmen who could be relied upon to make loans to the government. The first part of his plan worked better than the second part.

Third, mercantilists believed that if a nation was to gain full benefit from its expanded trade then that trade had to be structured in precise ways. While they did not set out their ideas using the terms of modern balance-of-payments accounting, their arguments can best be understood in such language. Essentially the balance must always tip in favor of one's own nation, and government must do all that it can to tip that balance. The premise was clear and obvious. A balance in one's own favor meant that the flow of gold and silver in the bullion account necessary to offset a trading partner's excess of debits in the current and capital accounts would always be inward. How to ensure more credits than debits in the current account became one of the consuming passions of mercantilists.

The theory was fairly simple. To keep the carrying trade in ships that were built, owned, and operated by your own nationals guaranteed that the earnings from these voyages came home when the ships came home. To export more goods by value than one imported meant that the balance of trade was always in your favor. Thus both elements in the current account worked to the country's benefit. And, reciprocally, they worked to the detriment of any trading partners whose goods were carried in your ships, not their ships, and who imported more from you than you imported from them. They had to make up for the debits in the carrying and the commodity trades in any way they could. The only way available, in theory, was by sending you gold and silver. An excess of debits in the current account was to be offset by an excess of credits in the bullion account. They lost; you gained. It was, to the mercantilistic mind, a zero-sum game.

COLONIES AND MERCANTILISM

Colonies fit into this picture just at this juncture. In mercantilist thinking they were mere extensions of the metropolis. To the degree that they produced something that previously the kingdom had had to import, they helped reduce debits in the current account. To the extent that any of their produce could be reexported from the metropolis, they helped earn credits in the current account. Their use of metropolitan shipping services profited the nation's businessmen. The duties collected on their produce when it entered or exited metropolitan ports replenished the monarch's treasury. Clearly colonies were a worthy addition to the kingdom—again, in theory.

Much effort was expended to realize these theories and, especially, to establish colonies exclusively for imperial benefit. Left to their own devices, however, individual colonists naturally pursued their own comparative advantage. Their actions, where they contravened the mercantilist canon, frequently caused much distress in the halls of metropolitan government. Laws and regulations sharing considerable common content strove to bind the trade of the colonists to the interests of the mother country. The famous English "Acts of Trade" of the early 1660s, reinforced by the Plantation Duty Act of 1673, the Navigation Act of 1696, and a plethora of eighteenth-century rules and regulations, found parallels promulgated by every continental regime. The Spanish (with the ordinance creating the Casa de Contratación in 1503) and the Portuguese, the Dutch and the Danes, and the French (witness the *Lettres Patentes du Roi* of April 1717 and October 1727)—just like the English—all strove to keep foreign merchants and foreign merchant ships away from their colonial ports and out of their colonial trade. They all expected to be the sole purveyor of imports into their colonies and the exclusive market for colonial exports, at least the most important commodities. They all insisted that their businessmen be the only ones to carry on such commerce.

The Spanish imperial system, the English navigation system, and *le système exclusif* of France codified in a cacophony of statutes and edicts the commercial designs of the mercantilist mind, for the colonies and beyond. Without fail, all such regulations hearkened to doctrines we can identify as mercantilistic. That colonists balked at first and kicked against the goad; that central government brooked little nonsense and soon organized the means—economic, political, military—to enforce its will; that by the end of the seventeenth century the English colonists at least found it more to their advantage to conform than to fight; and that some colonists eventually discovered opportunities within their empire to turn a "system" to their own best advantage, to prosper thereby, even to the undoing of that empire, however unintentionally: none of this should surprise us. And, certainly, the existence of mercantilism is neither proven nor disproven by the success or the failure of this empire or that one.

MERCANTILISM IN SUM

To sum up, then, it is fairly easy to grasp the thrust of mercantilism. The rising nation-states of early modern Europe needed money to consolidate and enhance their power. Everyone understood that the Crown had the right to control the economy—and everything else—in the best interests of the state. The proposition was generally accepted if only because the alternative to a strong central government was a reversion to feudal anarchy. All lost if that happened, or so all believed. The money governments sought was most efficiently acquired through a controlled expansion of the nation's foreign trade. Increased trade produced more money immediately through increased customs duties and ultimately through the growth of that class of wealthy individuals who would lend the government money when it needed more. This arrangement required government protection and promotion of the economy to ensure that trade proceeded in ways that yielded the greatest amount of national and corporate gain. One hand washed the other. Neither hand was invisible.

Later writers looked at all of this and called it mercantilism. No single contemporary author set it all out in anything like the formulation presented here. British philosopher David Hume came closest in his 1752 essay on the balance of trade. In 1776 Adam Smith erected it all in a somewhat more finished form the better to attack it as both inappropriate and irrelevant. Most other authors who wrote in a mercantilist vein addressed only part of the picture. They argued the need for the state to structure the economy, or the need for the state to acquire bullion, or the need for the state to organize foreign trade. They argued numerous related matters. But they were largely men of affairs who had a personal ax to sharpen, a particular row to hoe. We can see in their arguments the tacit acceptance of the other premises—attitudes—we call mercantilism. So we can fit their arguments, like pieces of a jigsaw puzzle, into the larger picture even if they themselves did not. Sometimes, of course, the rest of what they said makes such a fit difficult. There were no general theoreticians of mercantilism. But there were enough writers and practitioners, from several centuries and many countries, that it is possible to see, in theory and in practice, that something called mercantilism existed.

Indeed, as a practical program set down by practical people, we can best assess its results by seeing how it worked out in practice. This is particularly germane in the case of the European colonies in North America, where, at least until the middle of the eighteenth century, most of the policies adopted by metropolitan governments were based on the tenets of mercantilism. The consequences of such policies and programs, immediate and prolonged, are the subtext of many of the other essays in these volumes to which the reader is warmly invited to turn.

BIBLIOGRAPHY

Modern Essays

Allen, William R. "Mercantilism." In *The New Palgrave: A Dictionary of Economics,* vol. 3, edited by John Eatwell, Murray Milgate, and Peter Newman. London, 1987.
De Roover, Raymond. "Ancient and Medieval [Economic] Thought." In *International Encyclopedia of the Social Sciences,* vol. 4, edited by David L. Sills. New York, 1968.
Viner, Jacob. "Mercantilist [Economic] Thought." In *International Encyclopedia of the Social Sciences,* vol. 4, edited by David L. Sills. New York, 1968.

All three of these essays have important bibliographies that include all the major works on the subject.

Contemporary Writers

Hume, David. "Of the Balance of Trade." In *Political Discourses.* Edinburgh, 1752. The most accessible modern edition of this work is in *Essays, Moral, Political, and Literary,* edited by Eugene F. Miller. Rev. ed. Indianapolis, Ind., 1985.
Philopatris. *A Treatise Wherein Is Demonstrated That the East-India Trade Is the Most National of All Foreign Trades.* London, 1681. The author was *not* Sir Josiah Child.
Smith, Adam. *An Inquiry into the Nature and Causes of the Wealth of Nations.* London, 1776. The definitive edition of this work, part of the modern Glasgow Edition of all of Smith's writings, was edited by Roy H. Campbell, Andrew S. Skinner, and William B. Todd and was published in two volumes in Oxford in 1976.

The Theory of Mercantilism

Hutchison, Terence. *Before Adam Smith: The Emergence of Political Economy, 1662–1776.* Oxford, 1988. Immensely valuable for putting mercantilist theory into the context of developing European political and economic thought.
Schumpeter, Joseph A. *History of Economic Analysis.* Edited by Romaine Elizabeth Boody Schumpeter. New York, 1954. The magisterial treatment of the subject, especially chapter 7. Objections to the usefulness of the construct have been voiced by several authors, to which Schumpeter and Hutchison are important correctives.

Objections to "Mercantilism"

Coleman, Donald C., ed. *Revisions in Mercantilism.* London, 1969. A summary of the arguments that mercantilism did not exist, in selections from several authors.
Judges, Arthur V. "The Idea of a Mercantile State." *Transactions of the Royal Historical Society,* 4th ser., 21 (1939):41–69. One very particular set of objections, by way of example.

The Practice of Mercantilism: General

Kellenbenz, Hermann. "Probleme der Merkantilismusforschung." In Twelfth International Congress of Historical Sciences. *Rapports,* vol. 4, pp. 171–190. 5 vols. Horn and Vienna, Austria, 1965–1968.
———. "Wirtschaft und Gesellschaft Europas, 1350–1650." In *Europäische Wirtschafts- und Sozialgeschichte*

vom ausgehenden Mittelalter bis zur Mitte 17. Jahrhunderts, edited by Hermann Kellenbenz. Vol. 3 of *Handbuch der europäischen Wirtschafts- und Sozialgeschichte,* edited by Wolfram Fischer et al. Stuttgart, Germany, 1986.

Included in these broader discussions is mercantilism in such places as Sweden, the German states, and the Austrian Empire, which are omitted elsewhere in the present exposition because they did not found colonies in the Western Hemisphere.

The Practice of Mercantilism: Spain

Hamilton, Earl J. "Spanish Mercantilism Before 1700." In *Facts and Factors in Economic History: Articles by Former Students of Edwin Francis Gay,* edited by Arthur H. Cole et al. Cambridge, Mass., 1932.
Larraz López, José. *La epoca del mercantilismo en Castila, 1500–1700.* 2nd ed. Madrid, 1943.

The Practice of Mercantilism: Portugal

Gonnard, René. *Les doctrines mercantilistes au XVIIe siècle en Portugal.* Paris, 1935.
Hanson, Carl A. *Economy and Society in Baroque Portugal, 1668–1703.* Minneapolis, Minn., 1981. See especially chapters 5 and 7.

The Practice of Mercantilism: The Netherlands

Van Dillen, Johannes G. "Betekenis van het Begrip Mercantilisme in de Economische en Politieke Geschiedschriving." In *Tijdschrift voor Geschiedenis,* 72 (1959):177–205.
Voorthuijsen, Willem D. *De Republiek der Verenig de Nederlanden en het mercantilisme.* The Hague, 1964.

The Practice of Mercantilism: France

Cole, Charles W. *Colbert and a Century of French Mercantilism.* 2 vols. New York, 1939.
Deyon, Pierre. *Le mercantilisme.* Paris, 1969.

The Practice of Mercantilism: Denmark

Nielsen, Axel E. *Dänische Wirtschaftsgeschichte.* Jena, 1933. See especially pp. 112ff.

The Practice of Mercantilism: Great Britain

Harper, Lawrence A. *The English Navigation Laws: A Seventeenth-Century Experiment in Social Engineering.* New York, 1939. The classic text on the workings of English mercantilism.
McCusker, John J., and Russell R. Menard. *The Economy of British America, 1607–1789.* Rev. ed. Chapel Hill, N.C., 1991. See especially pp. 35–50 and the works cited there, a list not repeated here.
Rees, James F. "Mercantilism and the Colonies." In *The Old Empire: From the Beginnings to 1783.* Vol. 1 of *The Cambridge History of the British Empire,* edited by John Holland Rose, Arthur P. Newton, and Ernest A. Benians. Cambridge, England, 1929.
Speck, William A. "The International and Imperial Context." In *Colonial British America: Essays in the New History of the Early Modern Era,* edited by Jack P. Greene and J. R. Pole. Baltimore, Md., 1984.

John J. McCusker

SEE ALSO **Emergence of Empires; The European Contest for North America; Relations with the Parent Country;** and **The Reorganization of Empires.**

GROWTH AND WELFARE

"THE COLONY OF A CIVILIZED nation," Adam Smith noted in 1776, "which takes possession, either of a waste country, or of one so thinly inhabited, that the natives easily give place to new settlers, advances more rapidly to wealth and greatness than any other human society." Several things about Smith's assertion now seem wrongheaded, particularly his use of the passive "easily give place to" as a way of disguising the harsh reality of the European invasion of the Americas, the suggestion that America was "a waste country" before that invasion bent its resources to the European project, and his implied contrast between civilized Europeans and savage natives. *From a European perspective,* however, Smith hit on the central theme in the economic history of North America during the colonial era.

This essay explores that rise to "wealth and greatness" in the several European empires of North America through a focus on the growth of their economies and on the welfare it produced—that is, on the way the benefits of growth were distributed among the empire's inhabitants. It begins with a brief discussion of how social scientists now determine economic performance and of the problems encountered when modern methods of analysis are used to assess the economy of a premodern population. The first substantive section focuses on the British colonies that became the United States. Since we know much more about that region than about the

other parts of North America, the bulk of the essay concentrates on the thirteen colonies. Economic performance in French and Spanish North America are explored, in an attempt to compare developments there to those in the British colonies. Having described growth and welfare in North America from a European perspective, this chapter then examines how the economies of Indian peoples were affected by the process of colonization. The essay concludes with a continental overview, offering some comments on the growth of the North American economy taken as a whole.

ON MEASURING ECONOMIC PERFORMANCE

Modern efforts to measure economic performance focus on estimating total output (or income), either for a national or regional economy as a whole (gross national product, or GNP) or on a per capita basis. Gross national product is computed by summing the value of all goods and services produced by an economy; a per capita figure is derived simply by dividing GNP by the total population. To facilitate comparisons over time, GNP is usually expressed in constant dollars to produce a "real" figure with the impact of any monetary inflation or deflation removed.

Ideally, one would like to measure economic performance in the colonial era after the modern style, by constructing estimates of real GNP per capita that would chart the growth of the North American economy before the nineteenth century and permit precise comparisons with our own time. Unfortunately that is impossible, owing to some central differences between the North American economy of the late twentieth century and that of the colonial period.

The major difficulty is a lack of evidence: no one tried to keep track of all the goods and services produced in the colonial economy. Government looms much larger today than it did in the eighteenth century. Although rulers were held responsible for the general welfare, no one expected the great range of services, the purposeful economic interventions, or the vast array of information that we routinely expect of our political institutions. Colonial governments did collect some valuable economic information, primarily for tax purposes or in the course of regulating foreign trade, but it falls far short of the requirements for reliable estimates of GNP.

Even with the equivalent of modern data we would have difficulty constructing comparable performance measures for colonial and twentieth-century America because the economies are so different. How does one compare, in quantitative terms, well-being in a society that has (for instance) a vast telecommunications network, a biomedical-engineering industry, a major public university system, and modern transport facilities to well-being in a society in which such assets are not even conceivable? Even if we made the needed leap of faith (as economists routinely do) and accepted that the dollar value of such services can be calculated, other problems would remain. For instance, typically, household production—goods and services provided and consumed within the family—has not entered into calculation of GNP. That poses only minor problems today since household production is now only a small part of total economic activity, but in the colonial era such goods and services accounted for perhaps one-half or more of the whole. Finally, we can note a conceptual difficulty of another order. Modern measures of economic performance imply some element of choice and assume that the purpose of economic activity is to promote the well-being of the entire population. What sense does it make to apply such in-

dices to a society where a large part of the population was enslaved—forcefully denied the right to choose—and where slavery for some was so critical to prosperity for others?

Such difficulties cannot be entirely overcome. We cannot measure performance in the colonial economy in ways that are fully comparable to the twentieth century. Nonetheless, there do exist ways to chart growth during the colonial era and to make some rough comparisons to the present. Fairly reliable data on population are available that will permit some preliminary calculations, while other demographic measures—of life expectancy, for example, or of how tall our colonial forebears were—provide important insights. There is a variety of material on living standards—on the houses colonials lived in, the clothes they wore, the food they ate. And there are several classes of documents that can be made to yield fairly precise quantitative measures of wealth and welfare. Probate records, particularly estate inventories that list and evaluate the property of decedents in extraordinary detail, are especially valuable. Tax lists, although hardly comprehensive, furnish useful guides to shifting distributions. And trade statistics, although confined largely to exports and imports, chart the growth of a foreign sector crucial to colonial incomes. Taken individually, any of these data sets or approaches would be a weak reed, but woven together they form a rich tapestry that describes the growth of the North American economy and the distribution of its benefits with surprising precision.

THE BRITISH CONTINENTAL COLONIES

The British continental colonies that became the United States have received more attention from economic historians than have the settlements of the regions of the other European invaders of North America. It is thus useful to start with their history—in the light, as it were—before venturing into the relative darkness of the other colonial enterprises. We can chart the growth and distribution of wealth in the British colonies with some precision, and that information becomes a guide to the economic performance of other regions and a standard against which that performance can be judged.

A variety of evidence points to a remarkable and broadly based prosperity among British North Americans on the eve of the revolution. Colonists in 1774 enjoyed a standard of living that Alice Hanson Jones describes as "probably the highest achieved for the great bulk of the population in any country up to that time." Colonists, it seems, were well-fed by the standards of the time, even though free families spent a smaller share of their household budget on food than did their European counterparts. This is hardly surprising given the abundance of land and the overwhelmingly agricultural focus of an economy in which 80 percent of the labor force worked on farms or plantations. The quality of the colonial diet is revealed in the stature of the population: by the time of the revolution American-born men of European ancestry were, on average, just over 5′8″ tall. They were about three inches taller than their English counterparts and only a fraction of an inch shorter than Americans who served in the military during World War II.

Colonists in the eighteenth century were also well-clothed, in part because membership in the British Empire during the early stages of the industrial revolution gave them easy access to English textiles. And even families with modest incomes were able to acquire various amenities that made life easier and more comfortable: good bedding, tableware and ceramics, sugar, tea, spices, and the like. Such high levels of comfort were not always the case. Food was ample in the colonies from the beginning, at least after the terrible "starving times" that afflicted a few of the first settlements were overcome, but the standard of life remained crude for decades after the initial English invasion. By the end of the colonial era, however, there is substantial evidence of considerable improvement.

Apparently those advances were less marked in housing, and by this measure colonists did not live as well as their peers in the parent country. The early modern era witnessed a "great rebuilding" in England, where an increasing proportion of the population put houses on foundations; installed floors, ceilings, chimneys, and window glass; switched from clay, timber, and thatch to more durable brick and stone building materials; and increased the size of their dwellings by building a second story with stairs (replacing ladders) and adding rooms that permitted the spatial separation of functions.

Colonists lagged behind. Their houses were generally smaller and had fewer rooms, more often without foundations or wood floors, and were more frequently of wood construction. As late as 1798, only about 15 percent of the housing stock in the United States consisted of substantial two-story brick and stone structures with stairways, differentiated rooms, brick chimneys, and glass windows. On the frontier at that time, two-thirds of the houses were less than four hundred square feet (thirty-six square meters) in area— a size that could be achieved with a one-room house of twenty feet by twenty feet, while fully 90 percent were built of logs.

The inferiority of colonial dwellings compared to those owned by persons of similar means in England in large part reflects the rapid growth of population in America, which put great pressure on the housing stock. It also reflects the low price of wood in a region still heavily forested, the scarcity of skilled building craftsmen, and the high price of labor generally, all of which made substantial brick dwellings relatively expensive in British America. Despite their prosperity, colonists put up with houses that were cramped, poorly insulated, dark, unsafe, impermanent, and inelegant by the highest standards of the contemporary English-speaking world.

Evidence on diet, clothing, housing, and the like is important to understanding the growth of the British American economy and the distribution of its benefits, but such material is unwieldy: it is too detailed and too varied to permit easy yet precise comparisons between different groups in a population or across space and time. Demography provides some of the needed precision, and strong confirmation for the argument that colonists shared an impressive prosperity. Contemporaries were fascinated with the population of British America, especially its "rapidity of increase . . . without parallel in history" as Thomas Robert Malthus expressed in *An Essay on the Principle of Population* (London, 1798). Estimates of total population for the thirteen continental colonies (see table 1) suggest why the issue was so interesting: the number of inhabitants grew from 40,000 in 1650 to 250,000 in 1700, past 1 million by 1750, and to more than 2 million by 1770. The contrast with Europe was striking. From 1700 to 1750, when colonial population quadrupled, England's population increased by 14 percent, from 5.1 million to 5.8 million, while that of Europe as a whole grew by 17 percent, from 125 million to 146 million.

or northwestern Europe. In the early modern era women in England usually married in their mid to late twenties and some 15 to 20 percent or more were unmarried at age forty-five; in the colonies, by contrast, women usually married in their late teens or early twenties and perhaps 5 percent were unmarried at forty-five. These distinct marriage patterns led to much larger numbers of children and played the main role in accounting for the high American growth rate.

Table 1   Estimated Population of the Thirteen Continental Colonies, 1610–1780 (in thousands)

Date	European Americans	African Americans	Total
1610	0.3	—	0.3
1620	1.0	—	1.0
1630	4.6	0.1	4.7
1640	23.2	0.5	23.7
1650	38.7	1.2	39.9
1660	62.4	2.1	64.5
1670	100.5	6.0	106.5
1680	143.2	6.7	149.9
1690	200.2	12.6	212.8
1700	239.4	21.2	260.6
1710	296.0	37.8	333.8
1720	412.0	60.2	472.2
1730	551.9	97.0	648.9
1740	755.6	159.2	914.8
1750	934.3	242.1	1176.4
1760	1267.8	325.8	1593.6
1770	1674.3	456.9	2131.2
1780	2158.7	569.2	2727.9

Source: John J. McCusker and Russell R. Menard. *The Economy of British America, 1607–1789,* pp. 103, 136, 172, 203.

Thinking about the sources of population growth clarifies the relationship between demographic performance and prosperity. Immigration made an important contribution, as several hundred thousand Europeans crossed the Atlantic in search of the better life that colonial opportunities promised. Most of the high American growth rate, however, was a product of natural increase. That was not a result of mortality: death rates in New England were lower than in old England, but those in the South were higher. Rather, the rapid increase reflected colonial marriage patterns. Americans, especially female Americans, white or black, rich or poor, from the North or South, married earlier and in higher proportions than was the case in England

Benjamin Franklin noted in his "Observations Concerning the Increase of Mankind" (1751), these "more general, and more generally early" marriages were rooted in colonial prosperity, especially the abundance of land and the consequent "Ease and Convenience of supporting a Family."

Demographic evidence makes a compelling case for a broadly shared prosperity in the colonies of British North America, but it is indirect and it remains unwieldy for purposes of comparison. What is needed is a simple quantitative index that will provide an exact summary assessment of colonial well-being. Fortunately, we have such an appraisal in the work of Alice Hanson Jones, who used probate inventories—evaluations of property by owners made shortly after their death—to construct an estimate of income per capita for the thirteen continental colonies in 1774. Jones's work provides a benchmark figure from which we can elaborate a focused yet comprehensive account of the growth of the American economy.

Jones's concern was to estimate private wealth in the thirteen colonies on the eve of the revolution and to describe its components and distribution. She drew a small, unbiased sample of probate inventories for the three major regions—New England, the middle colonies, and the South. The inventories were supplemented with other sources and adjusted to comprehend otherwise omitted assets and wealth owners in order to describe fully the property of the population. Since probated decedents were older on average than living property owners and since wealth rose with age, the figures were weighted to reflect the age distribution of all wealth holders and then "blown up" to represent the private wealth of the living circa 1774. The results are reasonably accurate estimates of the distribution and components of wealth for several categories of inhabitants at the end of the colonial period. Per capita wealth figures were then multiplied by a range of likely income-to-wealth ratios to estimate income per head. The procedure indicates that—in 1990 dollars—real annual income per capita for the thirteen colonies ranged between $1,172 and $1,369 on the eve of the revolution.

Jones's figures are very rough—indeed, they are best considered educated guesses—but they are reliable enough to place the British American economy in a broad historical context. In 1985, for example, gross national product per capita equaled $20,020 in the United States, $4,069 in Greece, $974 in Nigeria, and $333 in India (1990 dollars). Such figures should not be read literally: it is not clear that Americans in 1774 had one-fifteenth the wealth of Americans, one-third that of Greeks, or one-third more than Nigerians in 1985. The economies of those places differed too widely and the index is too imperfect to support so exact a comparison. Such figures nonetheless do suggest both how well off British Americans were in the late 1700s and how far we have come in the two centuries since the revolution.

Combining Jones's benchmark figures with evidence of population size and assumptions about rates of productivity gain makes it possible to chart the growth of the British North American economy from the middle seventeenth century to the end of the colonial era. The calculations in table 2 assume that per capita incomes rose at 0.5 percent annually over the 125 years following 1650. The 0.5 percent rate is near the midpoint of the range of estimates suggested by scholarship in the late twentieth century, slightly ahead of the English and French achievements of the eighteenth century but well behind the growth registered by the U.S. economy during modern times. Under that assumption, per capita income in the colonies was roughly $677 (in 1990 dollars) in 1650 and $964 in 1720. In the aggregate, the economy expanded at a rate of 3.9 percent annually over the entire period. That is an impressive performance by any standard. For the early modern era, when stagnation and decline were more common than growth and when even the highly successful English economy increased at only 0.5 percent per year, it is truly remarkable.

Table 2   Estimated Income in the Thirteen Continental Colonies, 1650–1774 (1990 dollars)

Year	Per Capita GNP	Aggregate GNP (Millions)
1650	$ 677	$ 27
1720	$ 964	$ 455
1774	$1264	$3070

Sources: The calculation begins with the midpoint of Alice Hanson Jones's estimate of per capita GNP in 1774, in her *Wealth of a Nation To Be: The American Colonies on the Eve of the Revolution* (New York, 1980), 63. Figures for 1650 and 1720 were then derived assuming an annual growth rate of 0.5 percent. Aggregate GNP was derived by multiplying the per capita figure by the population estimate in table 1. Figures were converted to 1990 dollars by the price index in John J. McCusker, "How Much Is That in Real Money? A Historical Price Index for Use As a Deflator of Money Values in the Economy of the United States," American Antiquarian Society *Proceedings* 101, no. 2 (1991):323–332. Compare with John J. McCusker, and Russell R. Menard, *The Economy of British America, 1607–1789*, p. 57.

Some scholars find the emphasis on growth and improvement in living standards in the colonial economy misleading. For them, the colonies existed in an economic "steady state" characterized by rapid expansion as population grew and new land was brought into cultivation and by the absence of major structural changes or big gains in efficiency. They point out that the early American economy remained overwhelmingly agricultural, that there was no shift of the work force out of farming and into commerce or industry, no shift of population out of rural areas and into cities. Growth was largely "extensive" rather than "intensive." These scholars add that the distribution of wealth and income in the colonies remained stable at low levels of inequality.

While such an interpretation implies no increases in incomes per capita, it is not entirely incompatible with the growth rate of 0.5 percent yearly posited here. True, in an era when population increase usually meant economic decline, that rate was a remarkable achievement given the rapid growth of the American people and it was sufficient to double incomes over the colonial era. If the growth rate were constant, however, annual improvements in per capita incomes at one-half of one percent would have been barely perceptible to contemporaries who might well have found the notion that they lived in an economic steady state persuasive. Contemporaries such as Benjamin Franklin were not so persuaded. They extolled the accomplishments of the colonial economy, the progress it had made since the early days of the invasion, the wealth it generated, the high living standards it supported, and the opportunities it provided free settlers who were industrious and frugal.

In part contemporaries celebrated the impressive "extensive" performance of the American economy—the growth of population and the spread of settlement—but they also responded to the actual pattern of change in incomes per head. Improvements were not constant but rather occurred in two growth spurts sandwiching a longer period of little change. The first spurt followed the initial settlement of each colonial region and lasted for roughly a generation. It was largely a product of farm making, as families cleared land and fenced fields; raised barns and other outbuildings; planted orchards and gardens; built up livestock herds for meat, hides, and dairy products; erected bigger and more comfortable houses, and the like. Other gains during the early years of settlement followed

from higher population densities that supported the growth of local markets in foods, household crafts, and services. The second spurt began in the 1740s and lasted to the revolution, although it seems to have slowed toward the end of the period. It was rooted in a revitalized export sector, as renewed population growth in Europe led to growing demand for American agricultural products and as England's industrial revolution lowered prices for the manufactured goods colonists purchased from abroad. These growth spurts bracketed a period of stagnation or perhaps slight decline, its length varying by date of settlement. During the growth spurts, increases in income per head served as a major engine of change in the colonial economy.

Economists divide the sources of growth into changes in the supply of resources and changes in their productivity. As emphasized by those who insist that early American economic growth was largely an extensive process without major structural change, the major part of the rise in aggregate GNP is explained by increases in the supply of resources. Calculating from GNP in 1650 estimated at $27 million, annual productivity gains of 0.5 percent, and no increases in population, colonial GNP would have been just over $50 million in 1774, less than 2 percent of its actual size. Productivity increases cannot be dismissed as inconsequential, however if we extract increases in income per capita from the calculation in table 2, colonial GNP would have been slightly more than half its estimated size in 1774. The interaction of even modest improvements in efficiency with rapid increases in the supply of resources made for explosive economic growth.

Economists attribute productivity gains to three sources: better technology; improvements in the skills of the work force, in what is sometimes called "human capital"; and gains in economic organization. All three contributed to the advance of the colonial economy, although not in equal proportions. Technological change played the smallest role, although there were some notable gains in shipping and in the rice industry of the Carolina Low Country. Colonists also benefited from technical gains in England, as the industrial revolution lowered prices for manufactures and helped shift the terms of trade in favor of agriculture. Improvements in human capital were also of minor importance, although "learning by doing" as colonists gained familiarity with the environment and with crops such as tobacco, rice, and indigo not previously grown in England led to some gains in efficiency. Most of the productivity gains achieved in the colonial economy stemmed from better economic organization, especially shifts away from self-sufficiency and toward production for markets, which fostered specialization and the more efficient use of available resources.

The British American economy registered impressive gains over the colonial period. How were the benefits of growth distributed? As the analysis of productivity gains suggests, incomes varied with the extent of engagement with markets. This led to two regional patterns, one on an east-west axis, the other north-south. Given that major markets for colonial produce were abroad, those who lived near the coast and thus had easy access to those markets earned higher incomes than those living farther inland, where high transport costs imposed a greater degree of self-sufficiency. If incomes fell as one moved west, they rose as one moved south, where plantations that specialized in the production of tobacco, rice, and indigo generated greater returns than the more generalized farms that dominated northern agriculture.

Historians are divided on the issue of changes in the distribution of wealth and income over time. There is general agreement that abundant resources and scarce labor kept the degree of inequality among free colonists low by European standards, but many historians argue that the poor were on the increase and that a growing share of the benefits of growth were concentrated in the hands of a privileged few. Evidence for that position comes largely from studies of long-settled communities near the coast, where overcrowding led to higher rents, lower wages, diminished opportunities, and rising inequality. Further evidence comes from the cities, where growing numbers of urban workers were trapped in low-paying, seasonal jobs that kept them poor while a handful of merchants grew rich from a burgeoning trade in colonial products.

Scholars who view the growth of the American economy as an extensive process marked by little structural change find the case for the progress of inequality wanting. What happened in cities, they argue, is hardly relevant to the aggregate level of colonial inequality; city dwellers amounted to only 5 percent of the population in 1775. Further, rising inequality in older settlements on the coast led to high rates of migration to the interior, where wealth and income were more evenly distributed. The evidence on changes in distribution is thus mixed: inequality rose in cities and in older settlements but this was matched by migration to the frontier. Whether movement to regions of low inequality fully offset trends along the coast is uncertain. What is clear is that the level of inequality was low by comparison to later periods in U.S. history: in 1774 the richest 10 percent of wealth owners controlled slightly more than half the wealth in the colonies, a figure that approached 75 percent for the United States in 1860. It is also clear that colonial inequality remained low by eighteenth-century European standards and that the benefits of early American economic growth were widely shared among free colonists.

The issue has a different look if we think of the population as a whole and consider slaves and slavery. The African-American population—nearly all of them slaves—of the thirteen continental colonies grew rapidly over the period (see table 1). Roughly twelve hundred blacks (3 percent of the total population) in 1650 had become twenty-one thousand (8 percent) by 1700 and nearly half a million (21 percent) by 1770. Slaves played a critical role in the development of the early American economy, especially in the southern plantation districts, and they made a major contribution to the living standards of the free population. Their presence must temper romantic notions of early America as an economy marked by equality, opportunity, and a widely shared prosperity. This is not to say that slaves had no income or even that those incomes did not rise over the colonial period. Slaves had to be fed, housed, and clothed, and there is reason to believe that their material conditions improved during the eighteenth century. The best evidence for such improvement (as is often the case with early modern economies) is demographic. Beginning in the 1720s in the Chesapeake region and in the 1750s in the Carolina Low Country, the African-American population grew rapidly through reproduction, a rare achievement among New World slave societies. But slaves paid a frightful price for those modest gains.

The economy of the thirteen continental colonies grew impressively in the 125 years following 1650, and it distributed the benefits of that growth widely among Americans of European ancestry. Given the evident material benefits of membership in the British Empire, why did colonists mount a resistance to that empire after 1760 and then fight a long, costly war for independence? The puzzle deepens when it is recalled that the economy grew at an especially rapid pace in the years just prior to the revolution; it deepens further when the costs of independence are assessed. Per capita incomes plummeted in the aftermath of the war and were slow to recover: as late as 1805 there is evidence that incomes in the young United States lagged behind those achieved in the colonies in 1774 by as much as 15 percent. Colonists, one might argue, committed "econocide." Why?

One answer is that economic concerns were unimportant to the revolutionary leadership, which focused instead on politics, especially issues of liberty, representation, and self-government. That is a narrow view of the movement, however, for economic developments provided the means for independence and shaped the aspirations that gave colonists the nerve to take the risks of revolution. Independence was thinkable by the 1770s because the rapid growth of the colonial period had created an economy that seemed capable of standing alone and supporting a government able to hold its own against the great powers of the day.

Perhaps more important, economic progress filled colonists with pride in their accomplishments and nurtured visions of a bountiful future. Americans were surrounded by evidence of their rise to "wealth and greatness" in the form of prosperous farms and big plantations, bustling port cities dispatching ships throughout the Atlantic world, impressive fortunes accumulated by the elite, great crops of tobacco, wheat, and rice, and, especially, the substantial growth of population and settled area. That evidence was projected into the future by revolutionary leaders whose aspirations were defined by visions of a New World empire that would extend the accomplishments of the colonial economy into the next century and across the vast North American continent.

NEW FRANCE AND ATLANTIC CANADA

While historians agree on the prosperity of the thirteen continental colonies, there is no such consensus on the economy of New France. The dominant view is that the economy was weak and stagnant throughout the era of French control. The region was dominated by a fur trade that enriched a handful of merchants but provided few jobs and generated little linked activity in supply, processing, or transport. Agricultural development, the main source of growth in the English colonies, was hampered by poor soil, a short growing season, small markets, and a regressive seigneurial system that blunted incentives for farm-building. A dissenting voice, growing in volume in recent years, contends that the economy became stronger and more diverse in the eighteenth century, and that shipbuilding, the lumber industry, and especially an increasingly productive agriculture led to impressive gains in income and a rising standard of life.

Anecdotal evidence supports the dissenting view. Visitors to New France from Europe and the English colonies were astonished by the affluence of ordinary Canadian farmers and their families, who are repeatedly described as well dressed, well housed, well fed, and able to afford some of life's comforts. There were no very rich in the colony, none who lived on a grand scale by the standards of the French nobility. But the bulk of the population of small farmers and artisans, benefiting from low taxes, cheap rents, and high wages, enjoyed a standard of living much higher than that of the French peasantry and not noticeably below that of people of similar status in the British colonies.

The demographic record is mixed. Few immigrants came to the region—perhaps ten thousand during the entire period of French control—in part because little was done to encourage settlement but also because prospects were not sufficiently attractive. On the other hand, those who did immigrate reproduced at an extraordinary rate. Quebec's population grew at about

2.6 percent per year, from a few hundred in 1650, to fourteen thousand in 1700, and to sixty-three thousand in 1760, the eve of the end of French domination (see table 3). In part this reflected low mortality rates by European standards, but as was the case in British America the main source was marriage patterns. Women in New France married young—in their late teens during the seventeenth century, their early twenties in the eighteenth—and in high proportions—only about 5 percent remained unmarried at age forty-five. At the very least the colonial economy was sufficiently prosperous to provide men and women the opportunity to marry early and often.

as prosperous as the free colonists of British America, but the distance between them was smaller than is often admitted. Given the stagnation of incomes per head in the thirteen colonies before the 1740s, that gap narrowed considerably during the first four decades of the eighteenth century.

As was the case in Anglo-America, most of the expansion of the economy in Quebec reflected a growth in the supply of resources, especially in population and settled area. Nonetheless, there were also some clear gains in agricultural productivity stemming from farm-building and an increased engagement with markets in the French West Indies and Quebec

Table 3   Estimated Population of Quebec and Atlantic Canada, 1650–1780 (in thousands)

Year	Quebec	Nova Scotia	Newfoundland
1650	0.7	0.2	1.7
1660	4.0	0.3	1.8
1670	6.6	0.4	2.0
1680	9.7	0.6	2.2
1690	10.8	0.9	2.3
1700	14.1	2.0	3.8
1710	18.3	3.4	3.3
1720	24.5	5.5	3.7
1730	34.1	8.0	4.8
1740	44.2	10.5	5.9
1750	51.9	17.1	6.9
1760	63.1	22.0	13.1
1770	82.2	26.4	11.4
1780	106.9	38.1	10.7

Source: John J. McCusker and Russell R. Menard. *The Economy of British America, 1607–1789,* p. 112.

More direct evidence on economic performance is provided by Morris Altman, who has used census records to estimate real domestic product for Quebec over the years 1695 to 1739. These estimates provide powerful support for the dissenting view that the economy registered impressive gains during the eighteenth century. The economy as a whole grew at about 3.2 percent per annum from circa 1700 to the late 1730s, a bit slower than the pace achieved by the thirteen continental colonies but very fast by early modern standards. On a per capita basis, growth averaged about 0.4 percent per year over the period, roughly the same as in the English colonies. The habitants of Quebec may not have been

City. What is perhaps most remarkable about this growth is that it occurred despite the sluggish performance of the fur trade, still the colony's dominant export in 1740, where earnings failed to keep pace with the growth of population.

Unfortunately, no evidence currently available permits extension of this description of growth to the years before 1700 or after 1740. There is a consensus that the seventeenth-century economy was too dependent on the fur trade for successful development, although the material just presented suggests a need for a closer look. For the later eighteenth century, concern has focused on how the transfer from

French to British control shaped economic prospects.

Some historians are persuaded that the British conquest was a critical turning point in the development of the economy and that it played a key role in shaping the subsequent distribution of incomes and opportunities between Anglophone and Francophone Canadians. In particular, they argue, the conquest led to a "decapitation" of Quebec society. Some two thousand colonials left for France in the 1760s, a migration that deprived the Quebecois of entrepreneurial leadership, created a vacuum quickly filled by English-speaking merchants, and placed direction of the economy in British hands.

While the issue is far from settled, it is difficult to demonstrate that the great majority of Francophone Canadians suffered as a result of the change in metropolitan control, at least for the short term. Many of the emigrants were in fact military men and administrators dependent on the French government for salaries, privileges, and patronage, while there is clear evidence of a lively French-speaking merchant community in the decades after 1763. Population continued to grow at preconquest rates, and the improvements in agricultural productivity evident before 1760 were extended into the 1770s as farmers gained access to new markets for grain in the British West Indies. Finally, with the Quebec Act of 1774, the British guaranteed some of the central pillars of Francophone culture: the seigneurial system, a tax-supported Catholic church, French civil law, and the French language. During the War for American Independence, the Quebecois could have seized the opportunity to protest British rule. Their determined neutrality argues that there was as yet no significant decline in their welfare nor widespread dissatisfaction with the new institutional arrangements.

There were also colonial settlements elsewhere in the northeast, at Nova Scotia and Newfoundland, in what can be called Atlantic Canada. As the demographic record indicates, both were slow to get started but showed signs of more rapid development late in the colonial period (see table 3). Newfoundland was a fishing outpost with only a few thousand permanent residents; the population swelled by a factor of three when the fleet arrived each spring, but fell again when the ships departed in the fall. In 1700 Nova Scotia—then the French colony of Acadia—had a population of about two thousand. It became a British possession in 1713, and the Acadians were expelled from the settlement in 1755. By 1775 both Nova Scotia and Newfoundland had been integrated into a greater New England economy, in part by the steady migration of New Englanders "down east," in part by the aggressive entrepreneurship of Boston merchants. It is not possible to offer reliable estimates of living standards in these regions at the eve of the revolution. It is unlikely, however, that incomes there lagged far behind those elsewhere on New England's northeastern frontier, where settlers built an economy on forest products, fishing, and an agriculture hampered by rocky soil and a harsh climate.

THE FRENCH AND SPANISH IN THE SOUTHEAST

The economies of British North America and Quebec were the great success stories of the colonial era—from a European perspective. Elsewhere, the invaders accomplished much less. In 1565 the Spanish founded Saint Augustine, the earliest continuous European settlement within what would become the United States. It served as a military post and mission as well as a base from which other missions were established elsewhere in Florida and in Georgia. Expansion northward was eventually blocked by the British and the Spanish presence concentrated in and around Saint Augustine. By demographic and economic measures, Saint Augustine was a failure. In 1715, a century and a half after its founding, the European-American population amounted to only fifteen hundred (see table 4). The next fifty years saw some upturn, as new migrants from Cuba brought African slavery to the colony, apparently in hope of introducing plantation agriculture. In 1760, however, on the eve of the end of the first era of Spanish control, the colony was home to only twenty-seven hundred Europeans and about five hundred Africans.

The economy was also a failure. Throughout the first Spanish era, Saint Augustine remained an impoverished military outpost and

Table 4 Estimated Population of Florida and Greater Louisiana, 1685–1775 (in thousands)

Year	Florida		Louisiana	
	European American	African American	European American	African American
1685	1.5	0.0	0.0	0.0
1700	1.5	0.0	0.1	0.0
1715	1.5	0.0	0.3	0.1
1730	1.7	0.1	1.7	3.6
1745	2.1	0.3	3.9	4.1
1760	2.7	0.5	4.0	5.3
1775	1.8	1.0	10.9	9.6
1790	1.4	0.5	19.4	23.2

Source: Peter H. Wood. "The Changing Population of the Colonial South: An Overview by Race and Region, 1685–1790," in *Powhatan's Mantle: Indians in the Colonial Southeast.* Edited by Peter H. Wood et al., pp. 38–39.

mission, unable to raise enough food to feed itself or to produce a valuable export, dependent on irregular subsidies from Crown and church for its continued existence. Nor was it able to protect the Native population to which it ministered from the ravages of disease or from slaving raids by the South Carolina English and their Indian allies. A sharp decline in Native American numbers began early in the history of the invasion, but we cannot now estimate its magnitude with any confidence. By the mid 1680s, however, there were roughly sixteen thousand Indians in Florida. By 1760 that number had fallen to about seven hundred, stark testimony to the danger that even a minimal European presence posed to Native peoples.

Things did not improve when the Spanish ceded the Saint Augustine colony to the British in 1763. The British reorganized the region as East Florida (a territory including all the modern state except the panhandle) and approached the colony's development with a burst of enthusiasm. Indeed, the English went "Florida mad," their visions immortalized in Samuel Taylor Coleridge's "Xanadu," but they accomplished little of substance. By 1775 the colony could claim fewer than twenty-eight hundred non-Indian inhabitants and a floundering economy based on a small indigo industry and a trade in deerskins. In 1790, after British Loyalists and their slaves left following the return of the region to Spain, only about fourteen hundred whites and five hundred blacks remained. The Native popula-

tion rebounded, however, largely because of the growth of the Seminole, Lower Creek Indians who moved into the region and assimilated both the remnants of Florida tribes and runaway slaves into their group. The Indian population of East Florida, after falling to as little as seven hundred in 1760, reached fifteen hundred in 1775 and surpassed two thousand in 1790. By then Indians again outnumbered the population of European ancestry, indicating that success and failure are sometimes matters of perspective.

The European settlements along the Gulf coast and in the lower Mississippi Valley, usefully thought of as a "greater Louisiana," did better than the Spanish or English ones around Saint Augustine, although their achievements are hardly impressive by the standard of the thirteen colonies that became the United States. It took time for colonists to establish a firm foothold: as late as 1715 there were perhaps four hundred non-Indians (most of them soldiers, officials, or clerics) scattered among the more than half a dozen administrative outposts (see table 4). The region experienced a minor population boom around 1720, however, shortly after the French government turned responsibility for the development of Louisiana over to John Law's Compagnie des Indes in 1717. Over the next fifteen years, the company shipped about seven thousand Europeans and an equal number of Africans to the Gulf coast, most arriving before 1721. Conditions there were terrible. "Numbers died of misery or disease," Pierre de Charlevoix explained in his *History and General Description of New France* (1866–1872), "and the country was emptied as rapidly as it had filled." By 1730 the colonial population of Greater Louisiana amounted to only fifty-three hundred inhabitants, a majority of them African slaves.

While the efforts of the Compagnie des Indes produced only an unimpressive increase in population, they did lead to a substantial deterioration in relations with neighboring Indians, which culminated in the destructive Natchez uprising of 1729. In the aftermath, the company relinquished control of the region to the French government, which showed little interest in developing the colony. Immigration was reduced to a trickle and population grew slowly. In 1760, on the eve of French surrender of the territory, the inhabitants of European and African ancestry in Greater Louisiana numbered fewer than ten thousand.

Colonial development in the region quickened when Greater Louisiana was partitioned in the aftermath of the Seven Years' War. France ceded its territory east of the Mississippi above Lake Pontchartrain to Great Britain, which reorganized the region as West Florida. New Orleans, the lower delta, and the west bank became Spanish Louisiana. Both colonial powers worked to promote trade and plantation agriculture, to attract immigrants, and to encourage investment. As a result, population boomed, more than doubling between 1760 and 1775, doubling again by 1790. By that time the entire territory was under Spanish control, albeit temporarily, as a result of Spain's conquest of West Florida in 1783.

The performance of the economy mirrored that of the population. Until the very end of the French period Native peoples outnumbered Europeans in the region and the economy was dominated by the trade in deerskins. The French were at a competitive disadvantage in the deerskin trade to British traders working out of Charlestown, South Carolina, who offered the Indians higher-quality, lower-priced English manufactured goods. That made them the partners of choice in the vast southeastern interior, a region that remained "Indian country" until late in the eighteenth century where neither European power could dominate militarily. Thus the French were never able to make as much

of the Indian trade in the lower Mississippi Valley as their advantageous geographic position and experience in the Great Lakes region led them to expect.

A small plantation sector began to emerge in Greater Louisiana during the 1720s as a result of the development efforts of the Compagnie des Indes. Concentrated around New Orleans and upriver at Pointe Coupee, planters used slaves to produce modest quantities of tobacco, indigo, and timber products for export as well as foodstuffs for the local market. Plantation agriculture expanded slowly during the next forty years, but it remained subordinate to the more lucrative Indian trade throughout the French period.

Greater Louisiana was transformed into a plantation colony during the era of partition. By the early 1780s annual exports of indigo and tobacco from Spanish Louisiana were worth more than six times the value of peltry exports. Plantation development was less rapid in British West Florida, and peltries remained the dominant export there for a longer time. However, that colony also shipped substantial quantities of indigo and forest products by 1775.

There is not now sufficient information available to support exact comparisons between the standard of living or the degree of inequality among colonials in Greater Louisiana, the thirteen continental colonies, and Quebec. Certainly the Louisiana economy was much smaller than either of the other two if only because there were so many fewer people. There is evidence of a rising standard of living in the region—although much of it remained raw frontier—and of an impressive prosperity for a handful of successful planters and big New Orleans merchants as the American Revolution approached. On the other hand, the importance of slavery to Louisiana's economic success—blacks were 47 percent of the population in 1775, 54 percent in 1790—suggests a high level of inequality rivalled elsewhere in North America only in the Carolina-Georgia Low Country.

The French also established a small but by some standards quite successful cluster of settlements on the Mississippi below present-day Saint Louis. By the middle of the eighteenth century these villages contained roughly three thousand inhabitants, about one-third of them African or

Native American slaves. The economy of French Illinois turned on the fur trade, lead mining, and, especially, the production of food for the settlements of the lower Mississippi, as yet unable to feed themselves. This activity brought an impressive prosperity and a standard of living which approached that achieved in New England. The proportion of slaves in the population, however, indicates a much higher level of inequality than in the small towns of the British American northeast. The prosperity achieved at mid century failed to last, in part because Spanish control of New Orleans closed off some commercial opportunities after 1763 but also because the growth of the plantation sector in the lower valley ended the need to import food. When Anglo-Americans poured into the region after 1800 they encountered a subsistence economy and a people that struck them as poor, backward, and lazy.

THE SPANISH IN THE SOUTHWEST

It is difficult to compare the economic performance of the Spanish settlements in the Southwest with that of European colonies to the east of the Mississippi. The region remained a borderlands throughout the colonial period, the Spanish occupation largely limited to military posts and missions aimed at trading with, extracting tribute and slaves from, and converting the Native American population. The Spanish effort was also a preemptive colonization designed to deny the region to other European invaders and to form a buffer around the more important and productive core regions of New Spain. It was only in the last decades of the eighteenth century that economies comparable to those of the English along the Atlantic or the French in the Saint Lawrence Valley began to appear.

The Spanish invasion of what is now the southwestern United States began in the late sixteenth century but was not fully successful until after 1700. By the 1670s there were roughly twenty-nine hundred Spanish speakers in New Mexico, most at Santa Fe and El Paso. The Spanish were expelled in the Pueblo Revolt of 1680, a violent Native rising against Spanish demands for tribute, the enslavement of Indians, and reli-

gious oppression. New Mexico was reconquered by the late 1690s, but nearly endemic warfare with nomadic groups, particularly Apache and Comanche, inhibited development: the Spanish-speaking population numbered only about five thousand in 1750.

Things began to change after 1760 as the Spanish government launched a series of measures, known collectively as the Bourbon reforms, designed to restore Spain's international stature and reinvigorate its American empire. In New Mexico this led to a determined government effort to pacify the province, to end the slave trade in Indian captives, and to integrate the area into a regional economy centered on Durango and Chihuahua. The reforms brought prosperity and more rapid growth in the closing decades of the eighteenth century. By 1790 the Spanish-speaking population of New Mexico had passed twenty thousand, and a small ranching industry producing cattle and sheep had been established. There is not now sufficient information available to compare living standards in New Mexico with those in other North American regions. In 1800, however, per capita income in Mexico as a whole was a bit less than half that in the United States. That ratio suggests that the standard of living in the Spanish southwest lagged far behind that of the thoroughly Europeanized regions along the Atlantic and in the Saint Lawrence Valley.

The Spanish also established outposts in both East Texas and California during the eighteenth century, but in neither region was their presence impressive. In 1790 the Spanish-speaking population of East Texas was about eighteen hundred, mostly soldiers and missionaries. The colony was also home to several hundred slaves who worked on small frontier plantations along the Red River. Alta California had a Spanish population of roughly one thousand in 1790, most of them attached to the handful of missions that had been established in the region during the previous twenty years.

THE WELFARE OF INDIANS DURING THE INVASION

From a European perspective, the record of economic performance in North America before

1800 is mixed. Some regions achieved spectacular increases in population, settled area, and total production while supporting an impressive, broadly shared prosperity. In other regions results were less impressive, with the invaders holding only tenuous control and living under raw frontier conditions despite decades of effort. Thinking about the economy from a perspective that considers its impact on Native Americans introduces further ambiguity. Again, it is useful to start with the demographic record.

We do not know how many people lived in North America on the eve of the European invasion, nor is it likely that we ever will. Estimates show wild variation, from one million and less suggested by some anthropologists during the 1930s to eighteen million advanced in the 1980s by at least one scholar. It would be a mistake to imply that a consensus is emerging around a particular figure, but an estimate of four and a half million, cautiously offered with a range of 33 percent (three million to six million), could be said to reflect the opinion of many historians now at work on the question. That range is large, but it is nevertheless a robust result, sufficient to establish that the European invasion of America initiated one of the great demographic catastrophes of human history. At the end of the eighteenth century there were only about one-half to three-quarters of a million Native people remaining in North America.

Continent-wide estimates of the extent of the Native population's decline across several centuries following the Columbian encounter will always be controversial because the evidence is so thin. It is possible to be more precise by a focus on particular groups for more restricted periods. The population of the New Mexico pueblos was at least 130,000 at the time of Francisco Vásquez de Coronado's expedition in the 1540s; in the late eighteenth century it barely exceeded ten thousand. The Indian population of the Southeast was about two hundred thousand in the mid 1680s; by 1760 it was slightly more than fifty thousand. In New England, the Native population fell from more than seventy thousand in 1600 to fewer than twelve thousand by 1675.

At one level, the economic consequences of such a demographic collapse are clear: the economies of Native America experienced staggering declines in the course of the European invasion. Beyond that simple statement, however, it is difficult to generalize. Population declines of such magnitude meant more than a simple shrinkage in the size of the various Indian economies. Demographic collapse forced economic reorganization as the ratio of population to resources changed, as trade and production were disrupted during epidemics, and as groups became too small to support particular technologies or specializations.

Europeans brought other pressures—and opportunities—not all of them detrimental, at least in the short run. For those who survived the epidemics and who were able to produce something Europeans wanted—food, peltries, slaves—or to act as trade brokers between Europeans and other Indians, the invasion brought a higher standard of living in the form of access to horses and to manufactured goods, especially textiles, tools, and weapons. Such gains were often bought at a high price in terms of endemic warfare to control peltry supplies or acquire captives to sell as slaves. And they were usually short-lived, disappearing once Europeans began to produce their own food or when the supplies of peltry or slaves in a region were exhausted. For most Native peoples the long-term consequence of trade with Europeans was dependence and poverty. In the eighteenth century, however, the continued presence of several European powers on the North American continent enabled some Native groups to play one against the others and thus delay the result. Whatever the benefits accruing to a particular group and however long obtained, access to better textiles, to horses, and to more efficient tools hardly seems compensation for such a massive loss of life.

BROADENING THE PERSPECTIVE ON COLONIAL ECONOMIES

What then do we make of Adam Smith's characterization of colonial economic history as a rapid "advance . . . to wealth and greatness" if all of North America provides the context? Certainly from a European perspective Smith's phrase is a fair description of developments in Britain's thirteen continental colonies. There, population approached two and a half million in 1775, the aggregate economy grew at a rate of nearly 4 percent per year, and the free inhabitants shared widely in a general prosperity. But where else? Perhaps in New France, although with a total population in 1775 of less than one hundred thousand, with most of the settlers spread thinly in a long narrow strip along the banks of the Saint Lawrence, it is difficult to celebrate that enterprise as a similar success. Certainly Smith's description does not hold in Spanish Florida, in Greater Louisiana, or in the Spanish Southwest, despite some signs of progress in the latter two regions late in the eighteenth century.

Even from a European perspective, then, the performance of colonial economies was mixed. Thought of more broadly, from the perspective of North America as a whole, Smith's representation of colonial economic history as a simple progression to wealth and greatness becomes a major ethnocentric distortion. Indeed, it is not clear that the North American economy was as large in 1775, on the eve of the revolution, as it had been in 1500, on the eve of the invasion. Given a population of European and African ancestry in 1775 of about 2.7 million and less than a million Native peoples, it is possible that the total product of North America in 1775 remained well below that of 1500, even allowing a substantial increase in output per head in recognition of the record of England's Atlantic colonies. Advances to wealth and greatness, it would seem, in this case depend on the breadth of the beholder's vision.

BIBLIOGRAPHY

Altman, Morris. "Economic Growth in Canada, 1695–1739: Estimates and Analysis." *William and Mary Quarterly*, 3rd ser., 45, no. 4 (1988):684–711. Provides estimates of income per capita based on early census materials.

Armstrong, Robert. *Structure and Change: An Economic History of Quebec.* Toronto, Ontario, 1984. A good short survey and guide to the literature.

Carr, Lois Green, Russell R. Menard, and Lorena S. Walsh. *Robert Cole's World: Agriculture and Society in Early Maryland.* Chapel Hill, N.C., 1991. A detailed analysis of farm-building and its contribution to economic growth.

Eccles, W. J. *France in America.* Rev. ed. Toronto, Ontario, 1990. Offers a broad overview and guide to the literature.

Hall, Thomas D. *Social Change in the Southwest, 1350–1880.* Lawrence, Kans., 1989. A survey of the Spanish colonization in the region.

Hoffman, Ronald, John J. McCusker, Russell R. Menard, and Peter J. Albert, eds. *The Economy of Early America: The Revolutionary Period, 1763–1790.* Charlottesville, Va., 1988. Essays on aspects of economic change in the British colonies.

Jones, Alice Hanson. *Wealth of a Nation To Be: The American Colonies on the Eve of the Revolution.* New York, 1980. Provides benchmark estimates for wealth and income per capita and useful material on distribution drawn from an innovative use of probate records.

McCusker, John J., and Russell R. Menard. *The Economy of British America, 1607–1789.* Rev. ed. Chapel Hill, N.C., 1991. Furnishes a summary of the field and a comprehensive bibliography.

Meinig, D. W. *Atlantic America, 1492–1800.* New Haven, Conn., 1986. An expansive overview from the perspective of cultural geography.

Perkins, Edwin J. *The Economy of Colonial America.* New York, 1980. A brief study of the thirteen continental colonies.

Price, Jacob M. "The Transatlantic Economy." In *Colonial British America: Essays in the New History of the Early Modern Era,* edited by Jack P. Greene and J. R. Pole. Baltimore, Md., 1984. An overview of the external trade in the British colonies by the leading historian in the field.

Shammas, Carole. *The Pre-Industrial Consumer in England and America.* New York, 1990. A useful discussion of living standards in the thirteen continental colonies.

Sheridan, Richard B. "The Domestic Economy." In *Colonial British America: Essays in the New History of the Early Modern Era,* edited by Jack P. Greene and J. R. Pole. Baltimore, Md., 1984. An assessment of the internal economy of the colonies.

Thornton, Russell. *American Indian Holocaust and Survival: A Population History Since 1492.* Norman, Okla., 1987. An introduction to Native American demography.

Usner, Daniel H., Jr. *Indians, Settlers, and Slaves in a Frontier Exchange Economy: The Lower Mississippi Valley Before 1783.* Chapel Hill, N.C., 1992. Describes the economy of Greater Louisiana. Footnotes provide a guide to the literature.

Walton, Gary M., and James F. Shepherd. *The Economic Rise of Early America.* Cambridge, England, 1979. A short survey of the thirteen continental colonies. Especially good on foreign trade.

White, Richard. *The Roots of Dependency: Subsistence,*

Environment, and Social Change Among the Choc-taws, Pawnees, and Navajos. Lincoln, Nebr., 1983. A view of economic developments from a Native perspective.

Russell R. Menard

SEE ALSO **The Structure of Society** and various essays in THE SOCIAL FABRIC.

POVERTY

THE NATURE OF POVERTY and the way in which a society treats its indigent reveals a great deal about the social and political character of the society itself. America's mythology of equality, for example, does not rest in easy accord with the present-day existence of widespread poverty. Given the rich natural resources and the general scarcity of labor in the North American colonies, many historians have concluded that, although the poor may always be with every society, their numbers in early America were few; that most unfortunates, especially able-bodied young men, were able to improve their economic situation; and that the colonies, therefore, were predominantly middle-class and the destitute received relatively good care. Other analysts disagree; they detect growing poverty during the eighteenth century, especially in the cities. This phenomenon may have been an important factor in the American Revolution if the economic difficulties encountered by many lower-class people weakened their allegiance both to the British Empire and to their own domestic political systems.

Some scholars link the peculiar "solution" of the poverty problem in the southern colonies to the development of a general commitment among wealthy landowners to a republican form of government. Political philosophers and the elites in both England and America often feared that the "lower sort," if accorded power, naturally would attack the lives and the property of the wealthier classes. Racial bondage, however, meant that many of the poorest and potentially most menacing people were controlled by slavery. The resulting feeling of security engendered in many planters and slaveowners enabled them more easily to embrace the revolutionary ideal of representative government, which would automatically exclude the poorest people—the slaves.

As the distribution of wealth has grown even more unequal and the existence of an "underclass" even more permanent in the United States during the late twentieth century, considerable study has been devoted to the contemporary and the historical dimensions of poverty. In general, the colonies suffered considerably less than did Great Britain or Europe from the problem of poverty. Yet America did not escape poverty in the seventeenth century, and the number of indigents increased during the eighteenth century, both in urban areas and among bound black workers. In addition, the causes of poverty and the characteristics of the indigents changed during the colonial era as more able-bodied white laboring people sought assistance and as slaves began to comprise the majority of the American poor.

Before exploring the nature and extent of poverty in the North American colonies and the policies and practices of colonial governments and private citizens in dealing with the destitute, it is necessary to offer a working definition of "poverty." Early Americans generally agreed that anyone dependent on aid (excepting wives and children) was poor. Yet poverty encompassed people other than merely those who relied on outside assistance. "The poor," according to John Andrew, an eighteenth-century Bostonian, "always liv'd from hand to mouth, i.e. depended on one day's labour to supply the wants of another." The *Pennsylvania Packet* reported in 1772 that a poor person earned "a living by the work of his hands" and "must either work or starve." Indeed, the precariousness of life for many laboring people meant that no clear line separated the working poor from the dependent poor. In this essay, "poverty" and its synonyms will be used to describe both types of individuals: aid recipients, on the one hand, and, on the other, ordinary laboring people who worked each day for their survival, frequently experienced material standards similar to those who received assistance, and continually risked falling dependent on public or private charity.

THE BACKGROUND IN GREAT BRITAIN

Poverty was much more deeply entrenched in the seventeenth- and eighteenth-century British Isles than in the American colonies. While Great Britain's population increased rapidly from the early sixteenth century until the middle of the seventeenth century, its economy did not expand quickly enough to provide employment for many of its inhabitants. By 1700 perhaps 25 percent of the population of England and Wales required regular assistance, and an equal number occasionally sought help to obtain the basic necessities of life. Even worse, as many as 60 percent of the Irish lived close to subsistence during these years. As the population stabilized and economic growth increased, conditions for the poor generally improved in the British Isles during the eighteenth century, although in years of bad harvests nearly 20 percent of British citizens still relied on relief.

Fearful of the multitudes of migrants who wandered the country searching for employment and begging for money and food, English officials passed legislation designed to aid and to control the destitute. The Elizabethan Poor Law of 1601, which continued in effect with but minor revisions for several centuries, established four major principles that served as a model for much subsequent colonial welfare policy. First, the state assumed partial responsibility for relieving suffering among and ensuring the maintenance of life for its down-and-out citizens. Second, this responsibility was to be exercised at the local level with each parish authorized to organize its own relief system and to raise taxes for its support. Third, individuals were held accountable for the care of their kin; only unfortunates lacking such support could qualify for public assistance. Fourth, overseers of the poor were afforded broad power to apprentice needy children, to force the able-bodied or "unworthy" poor either to work or to suffer punishment, and to provide aid to the helpless or "worthy" poor either in their homes ("outdoor relief") or in institutions ("indoor relief") like almshouses.

Many British officials viewed the colonization of America as an additional component of the solution to their poverty problem. Not only would the destitute of the British Isles move to the New World and enjoy the opportunities available there, but the demand by both colonists and Indians for English goods, especially cloth, would create jobs to enable the poor at home to earn a decent competency.

THE SEVENTEENTH CENTURY

The myths of American abundance began with European explorers, many of whom envisioned the New World as a paradise containing unlimited land and incredible bounties of nature. Settlers surely could prosper in such an environment and might even be able to eradicate destitution from their new communities. And, indeed, the colonists suffered relatively little from poverty during the seventeenth century and small sums of money sufficed to assist most unfortunates. The "traditional poor"—the elderly, infirm, widowed, and orphaned—constituted most of the needy in seventeenth-century America.

Despite the real opportunities for success, however, early colonists did not escape the scourge of poverty. The general scarcity charac-

POVERTY

teristic of all preindustrial societies kept many people close to the edge of subsistence. Material suffering was further intensified by such common features of daily life as seasonal and irregular employment, high rates of mortality and morbidity, periodic epidemics, poor harvests, regular economic fluctuations, and the special difficulties always encountered by the young, the sick, and the aged.

During the initial decades of settlement, Europeans often were unable, for a variety of reasons, to produce sufficient food to sustain their lives, and a great many of them died during the "starving times" in Virginia and Massachusetts. American diets during the remainder of the colonial era usually were adequate, and the colonists suffered little from the food shortages familiar in Europe. In material terms, the first several generations of colonists led a primitive existence often associated with poverty in Europe, living in crude dwellings containing few amenities. During the seventeenth century, for instance, a majority of the poorest householders in rural Massachusetts and a large minority in rural Maryland owned the "essentials" of a Bible and bed linens, while only one in three possessed coarse earthenware from which to eat. But few poor families enjoyed such "luxuries" as knives, forks, spices, secular books, timepieces, mirrors, or pictures. If these regions are representative, the poorest segment of the American population did not significantly increase their stock of either the essentials or the luxuries during the eighteenth century.

Both social and religious theory encouraged early European settlers to assume responsibility to aid their neighbors in need. Most colonists clung to the traditional ideal of a well-ordered, hierarchical society where people of all ranks enjoyed certain rights, privileges, and duties. If the lower sort should work hard and show deference to their betters, the well-to-do were obliged to help the less fortunate. Such conduct would maintain stable social relations and, especially important to the Puritans, also would please God. The demands of life on a frontier during the initial decades of colonization reinforced the sense of communal responsibility for the destitute since farmers were required routinely to help one another clear fields, construct homes, care for animals, and reap the harvest.

Yet attitudes toward the poor were by no means universally benevolent in the British colonies. In New England, where Puritans deeply believed in the virtue of hard work and the sin of idleness, officials complained continuously about lazy persons who refused to labor and accused them of creating their own financial difficulties. In the Chesapeake Bay area, wealthy landowners often were contemptuous of indentured servants and slaves, envisioning them as mere pieces of property to be bought and sold. That many British communities adopted the English precedent of forcing people who received public assistance to wear some form of identifying badge illustrates the stigma attached to being poor.

Still, colonial legislators rather quickly assumed the task of providing relief to the indigent, and most copied the four major principles of England's poor laws in part or in whole. In its very first meeting in 1647, for instance, Rhode Island's assembly implemented the concept of local responsibility for the care of the needy and specified that overseers of the poor were to be appointed to levy and collect a tax for the indigent. Virginia and Plymouth colony passed similar legislation in the 1640s, Connecticut in 1673, and Massachusetts in 1692. In general, the smallest unit of government—town meetings in New England, county governments in the middle colonies, and parishes in the Chesapeake Bay region—was assigned the administration of the poor laws.

American communities adopted mixed approaches combining four types of relief: contracting with local families to assist the needy, aiding dependents in their homes, selling the care of paupers to the lowest bidders, and institutionalizing the indigent in almshouses. In the seventeenth century, the colonies relied primarily on the first two types of familial assistance. But during the eighteenth century, when the cost of public aid grew, officials increasingly turned to auctioning off the poor or to building workhouses in an effort, usually futile, to minimize costs.

In New England, town meetings made decisions regarding most individual relief cases and then directed overseers of the poor to make the arrangements. Typically, the meeting authorized paying local householders to maintain unfortunates as a part of their families. Healthy adult paupers and underaged indigents often were indentured, sometimes against their own or their parents's desires. The meetings also enjoined overseers to dispense food, firewood, clothing, and other provisions directly to the needy in their own homes. Early New Englanders experienced relatively little poverty and the traditional poor comprised most of the destitute.

Considerably more people in distress lived in the seventeenth-century Chesapeake Bay region. Extremely high mortality rates destroyed families and left numerous orphans and widows in need. Thousands of indentured servants who flocked to the area discovered that opportunities to acquire land after their servitude began to narrow after the middle of the century. A good many of them, some of whom joined in Bacon's Rebellion (1676), languished in poverty. The shift from indentured servants to slave labor at the end of the seventeenth century meant that fewer servants achieved their freedom each year, thus adding fewer able-bodied whites to the potential poverty rolls. But large numbers of slaves, most of whom lived at the subsistence level, began to replace white workers at the bottom of the economic ladder.

Poor relief was administered somewhat differently in the South than in New England. Virginia, for example, was divided into parishes in 1641, and each parish was governed by the vestry, a group of twelve men. In that same year, a petition to the House of Burgesses complained that "Divers poore men have longe inhabited heere and nowe are growne decrepped and impotent." The following year a general law empowered the vestries to set tithes to support public assistance for people who could not work due to illness or old age. Vestries also were to administer the poor laws, apprentice orphans, bastards, and children of the bereft, and allot aid according to the needs of each case. The church wardens, the executive arm of the vestry, brought to the vestry's attention the individual cases of the poor and distributed the allocated funds. Early Virginia, like New England, most commonly depended on a familial system of relief, paying families for housing the indigent.

The Dutch colony of New Netherland (New York), first settled in 1624, was a notable exception to the wholesale adoption by the British colonies of the major features of the Elizabethan Poor Law. The Dutch settlers adopted their mother country's approach to poor relief, establishing poorhouses in Beverswyck (Albany) in 1652 and in New Amsterdam (New York City) in 1655. The also instituted an ecclesiastical system of assistance to the poor, instituting voluntary contributions rather than mandatory tax collections to raise funds for the bereft. Officers of the Dutch Reformed church dispensed aid and decided who was qualified to receive it. When England conquered the colony in 1664, its policies were restructured to more closely match the English model.

Like the early English colonies, New France (1663–1760) experienced relatively little poverty since its flourishing fur trade, plentiful lands, and labor shortages provided abundant opportunities and a relatively high living standard for its inhabitants. As it did in France, the Catholic church played a pivotal role in assisting destitute settlers, constructing almshouses beginning in the late seventeenth century to care for the aged, the sick, and others incapable of working. When beggars multiplied during the economically difficult decades of the late seventeenth and early eighteenth centuries, royal officials established a new institution unique to New France, the Bureau des Pauvres (Offices of the Poor), to help indigents in the major towns. The local authorities who staffed these offices were authorized to collect voluntary alms from the citizens, examine the cases of the needy, find jobs for the unemployed, and apprentice the children of the poor. Apparently the agency was short-lived since poverty was not very acute.

Unlike the British colonies, the ethos of paternalism permeated every aspect of Canadian society and government. The family—the basic unit of society—was responsible for taking care of its own members. If families failed to carry out these duties or if indigents had no family, then royal officials took charge. The Intendant at Quebec in New France and the Commissaires-Ordonnateurs in the other French colonies thus saw to it that colonists did not live in complete deprivation.

Historians have paid scant attention to the nature of official policies toward poverty in the American Southwestern regions controlled by New Spain. The Penitentes, a lay religious society of the Roman Catholic church, ostensibly were committed to aiding Hispanic and Native Americans in the Rio Grande Valley during the seventeenth and eighteenth centuries, although their success in that venture is unclear.

The English colonies departed from the paradigm of the Elizabethan Poor Law by excluding specific racial groups—Indians and blacks—from public assistance. On first settling in the New World, Europeans were puzzled by the paradox of the poverty of coastal Native Americans in a land filled with nature's blessings. By the standards of the invaders, Indians eked out a spartan existence without proper clothing or housing or many other personal belongings. Indians commonly exploited the seasonal diversity of their environment by moving their villages to areas with the greatest natural food supplies. One part of this strategy meant that some coastal Indians, especially the hunters and gatherers in northern New England, went without much food during the winter shortages, a tactic that startled the colonists who equated hunger with destitution. The early settlers remained confident that the desire for material commodities among the natives would increase rapidly as they came to appreciate the value of European civilization. In later decades, as Indians were exterminated, forced westward, or confined in a state of perpetual poverty on small tracts of land, the colonists made little attempt to ameliorate the plight of the natives, viewing it as extraneous to their responsibility to aid the needy.

White colonists rarely thought of African Americans as proper beneficiaries of the welfare system. Because masters were supposed to furnish the basic needs of their slaves, bondspeople did not qualify for poor relief. Officials usually denied aid to free blacks as well, even though one popular argument offered against the emancipation of slaves was that, because of their supposed natural laziness, free African Americans would be a drain on public assistance.

THE EIGHTEENTH CENTURY

Although scholars disagree on this assessment, the proportion of the colonial rural population that lived below or near subsistence probably increased during the eighteenth century. It is difficult to make more than educated guesses as to their numbers, but the poor may have comprised nearly one-third of the white residents of the northern colonies on the eve of the revolution, and another 10 percent fared little better. Perhaps 20 percent of whites and, when slaves are included, nearly 40 percent of the total population in revolutionary British America could not afford to purchase all of the daily necessities of life. While these figures are tentative, the response to poverty and the growth of both landlessness and tenancy during the eighteenth century suggest that poverty and economic marginality may have been common in many agricultural regions.

Many agrarian areas, responding to escalating poor relief expenditures, experimented with new methods to rationalize the economics of public assistance. One solution was to auction the care of paupers on the open market to the person who made the *lowest* bid. Towns in New York boasted of the savings realized by placing paupers on the auction block since, as one supervisor noted, "none except those that are objects of charity, will apply to the town for assistance, and be exposed for sale, and liable to labor." In 1771 John Ryder received a lump sum of twenty-three pounds to care for two three-year-old orphans until their eighteenth birthday. As many contemporaries recognized, this method of relief often was deleterious for the poor since the bidders were tempted to supply minimal provisions in order to increase their profit.

Other rural locales began to build or rent structures to cope with what they perceived was a growing poverty problem. After mid century, unions of small Virginia parishes, New York counties, and Massachusetts towns constructed almshouse-workhouse combinations designed to sustain those unable to work and to force others to labor for their keep. But, as in England and larger American cities, this system ultimately saved few pounds. Virginians consequently sold or abandoned most of their institutions during the revolutionary era, although almshouses remained the wave of the future and did not reach their full flowering until the nineteenth century.

One intent of much poor-relief activity in both the seventeenth and the eighteenth century was to prevent nonresident prospective indigents from gaining legal settlement in the community and, thus, from claiming public assistance. Shipmasters and others who brought people into town, even if they were only visitors, were required to notify local officials and to provide security for those likely to become destitute. Overseers often warned out newcomers, enforcing their decision with fines and whippings, or bodily transporting the offender out of the area. Authorities in Virginia even sent some poor immigrants back to England. The growing concern with poverty among rural inhabitants and the continued vigilance of officials to minimize the cost of relief may have reflected merely the increase in the number of bereft individuals that naturally accompanied demographic growth. Nevertheless, considering that a town like Braintree, Massachusetts, came to spend more than a third of its budget on poor relief, that southern parishes paid thousands of pounds of tobacco to doctors for attending the needy, and that overseers in New England warned out ever-growing numbers of itinerants, it appears more likely that the level of indigence in proportion to the population was indeed expanding during the eighteenth century.

The extent of tenant farming and landlessness provides another barometer of the material difficulties in rural areas. Obviously, not all people without property suffered privation, but agricultural laborers and farmers who rented land were more susceptible than landowners to experience serious financial distress, and the number of propertyless men and tenants increased throughout much of British America during the eighteenth century.

Many historians, like Kenneth Lockridge and Douglas Jones, have forwarded a Malthusian interpretation of eighteenth-century New England, arguing that as a rapidly expanding population pressed on a limited supply of land, poverty necessarily increased. By the late eighteenth century, for example, poor transients accounted for one out of every three adult males in Kent, Connecticut. In many communities the poor became both more numerous and relatively poorer, creating conditions that more closely resembled some European areas.

A considerable number of people tramped through the northeast during the late eighteenth century, many of them destitute. The characteristics of Massachusetts itinerants indicate that few may have established a beachhead of stable employment in their personal war against deprivation. Most came from the bottom of the social order, toiling as lesser-skilled laborers, artisans, washerwomen, and domestics. More than half were single, a good portion probably the younger sons and daughters of farmers who could not provide all their children with land. Families accounted for the second-largest category of migrants, and their seasonal pattern of movement suggests they searched primarily for temporary employment. Women, especially widows, deserted wives, and single females also numbered heavily among the vagabonds. Some paupers walked the roads of New England for years in a futile search for economic security.

Residents of the Middle Atlantic region suffered less economic difficulty than New Englanders, although there are signs of growing hardship. For example, conditions in southeastern Pennsylvania—often considered the "best poor man's country" and one of the most prosperous agricultural areas in the region—appear to have deteriorated for a portion of the population. Throughout the century, the distribution of wealth gradually became more unequal and the proportion of non-landowners, tenant farmers, and cottagers correspondingly increased. By 1750 the assessor of one Pennsylvania township described nearly a third of the inhabitants as "poor." Indeed, the majority of males were propertyless by mid century, a startling statistic in an area where freeholders supposedly dominated. Cottagers probably enjoyed adequate living standards throughout most of the period, but the material conditions of freemen likely deteriorated during the final decades of the colonial era.

The South, especially the Chesapeake Bay region, contained a sizable group of white tenants who expanded in both absolute and relative terms during the eighteenth century. In some older settled areas of Maryland and Virginia, propertyless white males constituted more than half of the household heads at the end of the colonial period. In All Hallow's Parish, Maryland, for instance, the proportion of households that were tenants grew from one-fifth in 1675 to one-third in 1707 to one-half by the revolution. Many of these farmers barely scraped by, since rent for their land was not far below their total production of cash crops. Their poverty prevented most of them from ever becoming freeholders in their own right.

In Middlesex County, Virginia, the number of relief recipients and the cost of welfare rose precipitously during the early eighteenth century. Between 1668 and 1724 the proportion of inhabitants who received aid tripled while the percentage of public funds spent on welfare multiplied by ten. The nature of welfare recipients also changed, with illegitimate children in the seventeenth century giving way to adult women by the mid 1720s as the primary benefactors.

The most salient feature of the southern colonies was the massive number of slaves who resided there. Like white tenants, their proportion of the population increased during the eighteenth century; blacks accounted for about 40 percent of the inhabitants by the eve of the revolution. Nearly all of these bound laborers lived in continuing poverty. Slaves did enjoy one important advantage over free poor whites—the vested interest of their masters in keeping them alive and in a condition capable of working. African Americans rarely went without the absolute necessities of life, but owners minimized the outlay on their labor force by providing food, shelter, and clothing of the cheapest possible sort.

Yet the material lives of slaves were not uniform over time or place. For example, physical standards may have followed a cyclical pattern in the low-country regions of South Carolina and Georgia. As the Low Country changed from a frontier area to one of vast plantations during the early eighteenth century, blacks lost important individual freedoms. But the increasing popularity of the "task system" of labor in the latter part of the century enabled some slaves to regain some authority over their work lives, to improve their living standards, and even to accrue their own property. In strict material terms, these African Americans may have been better off than some whites who lived in poverty. Still, when slaves are counted with the most economically marginal white tenants, as many as 60 or 70 percent of Southerners lived near subsistence.

Slaves who lived in Louisiana, a colony alternately controlled by the French and the Spanish during the eighteenth century, suffered under the brutal conditions common to New World areas that produced sugarcane. In general, life expectancies were short and work routines arduous. Yet here, as in much of the rest of North America, many African Americans were able to improve their living conditions by tending their own gardens, raising poultry and hogs, and selling their produce in local markets.

URBAN CENTERS

Poverty cast its shadow over relatively few residents of the major colonial seaports during the late seventeenth century. Life for the urban lower classes compared quite favorably with conditions for their counterparts in the British Isles. Breeches in the family structure accounted for most penury, and remedies generally assumed a familial form as well, with the traditional poor receiving the bulk of outrelief in their homes or in the households of others.

The consensus among scholars is that the nature of poverty in metropolitan areas changed significantly during the eighteenth century. The level of indigence increased, particularly during the final decades of the colonial era. The flow of tax money to the materially unfortunate outpaced population growth in most cities even though officials continually adopted new strategies to minimize the cost of assisting those in distress. The causes of impoverishment likewise changed. As the century progressed, able-bodied men and women who could not find jobs or, even though employed, did not earn enough to support themselves and their families, joined the traditional paupers on the relief rolls.

Bostonians encountered poverty earlier, more continuously, and with the most severity of any seaport dwellers during the eighteenth century. Increasing competition from other coastal towns and a series of costly and debilitating wars compounded the difficulties created by the city's economy, which remained weak throughout much of the century. After constructing an almshouse in 1685, Boston's officials spent relatively small amounts subsidizing indigents during the next twenty years.

When the city's economy stagnated during the 1720s and 1730s, poverty increased, driving more people to seek refuge in the almshouse than could be accommodated. In 1735 the overseers of the poor, perceiving greater employment problems and rising poor taxes, began construction of a workhouse designed specifically for individuals who could not or would not find jobs, thus distinguishing them from the deserving almshouse inmates who were physically incapable of labor. Attempting to shorten relief rolls, the overseers successfully petitioned for a law that broadened their power to eject newly arriving immigrants who potentially might require aid. The efforts of municipal authorities to curb the cost of maintaining the needy were ineffective, since public expenditures rose by 50 percent and taxes for support of the poor by 138 percent (after adjusting for inflation and population growth) between 1727 and 1742.

The wars of the 1740s benefited some Bostonians but devastated others, especially disabled war veterans and the widows and children of men killed in the struggle. Almost 2 percent of the inhabitants took refuge in the almshouse or workhouse; one of every three adult women was widowed, and many of those women led a hand-to-mouth existence; and nearly one of every four taxpayers could not pay their taxes. By 1753 the overseers claimed that the cost of public relief was twice as high in Boston as in any other city in the world. Four years later 6 percent of the city's residents received some form of public assistance.

During the 1760s and 1770s, the almshouse contained as many as 4 percent of the city's residents, outrelief was dispensed to an additional 15 percent of householders, and religious benevolent societies and private philanthropic organizations nurtured numerous other families. As town officials funded more people in need, they also warned out an ever-greater number of new arrivals. By the end of the colonial era, the specter of poverty haunted many Bostonians who previously had felt its presence only at a distance. Even if they managed to avoid the public dole, many ordinary working people struggled hard to cover the cost of daily necessities. As many as 30 or 40 percent of the city's residents lived at or below subsistence and were continuously liable to fall into a state of dependency.

New Yorkers felt the impact of poverty later and less severely than Bostonians. In 1683 the colonial assembly directed the city to make provisions to assist its poor. Five years later, officials expended a mere twenty pounds for that purpose. During the next half century, church wardens—the equivalent of the overseers of the poor—dispensed public aid primarily as outrelief. The first surviving list of the "permanent" poor in 1700 numbered only thirty-five people, nearly all of them orphaned, disabled, or aged. But two years later, 10 percent of the populace expired from yellow fever, leaving one in five families headed by a woman, many of whom fell onto hard times. Particularly harsh winters during the early years of the century caused a great many others to seek help. The city's per capita expenditures on the poor increased by 62 percent between 1698 and 1714.

During the depression of the late 1720s and 1730s, poor relief became the most costly item in the municipal budget, as the city government maintained almost 1 percent of the population permanently and provided periodic subsidies to others who could not find work. The Common Council proposed constructing a combined almshouse and workhouse, completed in 1736, to contend with the worthy and the unworthy poor. This institution not only housed the "deserving" poor but the building's keeper also tried to correct the "undeserving" needy who did not display the correct values of hard work, discipline, and thrift. The living and working quarters of both categories of people were separated. But all inmates were subject to a highly structured environment: bedtimes were strictly enforced, people could not leave the facility without permission, and those who did not attend regular prayer sessions forfeited meals. The institution, however, helped the city to stabilize the cost of poor relief until mid century.

The material difficulties of many residents intensified during and after the Seven Years' War. When the conflict disrupted trade, municipal relief expenditures skyrocketed and beggars wandered the streets. The postwar economic dislocation idled many workers, provoking the church wardens to appeal for additional funds to keep the destitute from perishing for want of necessities. Private citizens responded to the crisis by establishing a linen factory employing three hundred jobless people, loaning spinning wheels to impoverished women, and founding a trade school for poor children. Meanwhile, mutual-aid societies mushroomed among various occupational and ethnic groups, and some wealthy individuals contributed money directly to indigent families. Imitating Benjamin Franklin's efforts in Philadelphia, Dr. Samuel Bard founded the New York Hospital for the sick poor in 1771. Religious groups supplemented these activities with various aid programs and "charity sermons" preached to raise funds for those in need.

Even with the private sector's assistance, the municipal government struggled with growing poverty. Adopting a fiscally conservative approach, town leaders attempted to force people off public relief by apprenticing more children of the poor, transporting greater numbers of questionable characters out of the city, and tightening the residency requirements for aid. They also financed the construction of a house of correction to punish idle vagabonds and separate them from almshouse inmates. Despite these efforts, officials still spent three times more per capita subsidizing the destitute during the early 1770s than they had two decades earlier. On the eve of the revolution, 2 percent of New York's inhabitants occupied the almshouse and at least 3 percent more received outrelief.

Like its urban neighbors to the north, Philadelphia developed a significant poverty problem during the eighteenth century. But the level of indigence increased more slowly in the Quaker City; rarely did more than 1 percent of its residents depend on public relief during the first six decades of the century. The financial problems of less-fortunate Philadelphians grew substantially during the Seven Years' War, and, by the late 1760s and 1770s, 5 percent of the inhabitants received public aid. In 1772 nearly 25 percent of the city's adult free males qualified as being poor or near poor by contemporary standards. In addition, 16 percent of adult females were institutionalized, and another 10 percent of men and women either fled their debts or were escorted out of town by the overseers.

Philadelphians responded to poverty in ways similar to their counterparts both in other American metropolitan areas and in England. When poor rates escalated, officials devised more stringent residency requirements for aid recipients and increasingly ushered nonresidents out of the city. In the 1760s they financed a "Bettering House" with tax money and placed it in the hands of a private corporation. This almshouse-workhouse combination served a dual purpose, minimizing the cost of care for indigents and forcing able-bodied paupers to labor for their livelihood. As they reduced support for people receiving outrelief, city leaders began to abandon the familial system of aid in favor of institutional solutions. Private citizens established a host of organizations, associated primarily along ethnic, occupational, or religious lines, to supplement public relief.

Conditions in Philadelphia demonstrate that it was not only economic stagnation, as in Boston, that gave rise to greater poverty, but that a growing economy could produce more distress as well. The Pennsylvania capital enjoyed the brightest economic record of any major Atlantic port during the eighteenth century, and its overall wealth increased markedly. But the processes of economic change enriched some classes of citizens while harming others, simultaneously generating greater wealth, greater poverty, and greater inequality.

By the estimates of various historians, most notably Gary Nash and Raymond Mohl, public-welfare dependents may have constituted roughly 5 percent of the urban populace during the third quarter of the eighteenth century. This figure, however, does not include those who received aid from public or private agencies for which records no longer exist, men and women who did not qualify or apply for public assistance, slaves and servants who were prevented from receiving help, or working people who daily lived at or just above subsistence. Although precise statistics are impossible to compute, these people may have constituted as many as one-third or, during hard times, one-half of the residents of America's largest metropolitan centers during the pre-revolutionary decades.

THE POOR

Poverty declined in New France during the eighteenth century. But in British North America, poverty not only increased during that century, but it also affected new groups, afflicting "respectable" working people more frequently than ever before. While designed primarily to serve the needs of the elderly, widows, orphans, and the infirm, colonial relief systems began to assume the additional burden of assisting ordinary laboring people who for various reasons could not make ends meet.

Growing poverty did not mean that scenes of massive misery characterized the colonies. The vast majority of the poor were able to maintain their lives. Still, some indigents experienced appalling conditions by any standards, lacking adequate food, clothing, and shelter to prevent their physical deterioration and premature demise. In 1776, for example, the Philadelphia almshouse managers disclosed that "most" of the unfortunates admitted during the previous year were "naked, helpless and emaciated with Poverty and Disease to such a Degree, that some have died in a few Days after their Admission" (*Pennsylvania Gazette*, 29 May 1776). And even though it was illegal, beggars routinely appeared at country and urban markets to solicit food, money, and firewood.

Officials continued to dispense aid for the traditional reasons throughout the eighteenth century. Old age caused many people to seek help, although it did not automatically qualify a person for relief. Illness and disease were widespread, especially in the cities, and when heads of households grew ill, their family's financial situation often became desperate. Employment-related injuries likewise impaired the ability of many workers to earn a living.

Irregularity of employment exacerbated the problems of the poor as the availability of jobs varied with the seasons, especially in farming areas. Equally serious were employment problems created by business slumps. People who lived near subsistence possessed a very thin cushion and a difficult task of surviving and recovering from these periodic crises. Moreover, during the decades preceding the revolution, wages for many workers, especially those in urban centers, did not keep pace with inflation. Consequently, many men and women did not earn enough to maintain themselves and their families even when fully employed.

Women endured poverty more often than men. Women's employment opportunities were circumscribed, their marketable skills few, and their wages low, generally only about half that earned by less-skilled men. If their spouses died, left, or grew ill, married women and widows usually carried enormous economic burdens, especially if they had young children. Single women often fared little better.

CONCLUSION

Increasing poverty in much of British North America during the eighteenth century helped stimulate the political mobilization that resulted in the American Revolution. The specter of poverty that haunted many middle- and lower-class residents of northern cities encouraged their radical demands for American independence and the establishment of republican governments to solve their own problems. Detecting growing economic difficulties among their neighbors and kinfolk, New England farmers felt personally threatened by English imperial measures which might lead to their own impoverishment. And many southern whites, relying on slavery to control their society's poorest members, were free to develop and to pursue an ideology of equality, albeit one which included only white propertied males and left an indelible mark on the new nation.

BIBLIOGRAPHY

Alexander, John K. *Render Them Submissive: Responses to Poverty in Philadelphia, 1760–1800*. Amherst, Mass., 1980. Examines the struggle over the type of funding to be extended to the "deserving" and the "undeserving" poor in Philadelphia.

Cray, Robert E., Jr. *Paupers and Poor Relief in New York City and Its Rural Environs, 1700–1830*. Philadelphia, 1988. Traces the evolution of public aid to the needy.

Daniels, Bruce C. "Poor Relief, Local Finance, and Town Government in Eighteenth-Century Rhode Island." *Rhode Island History* 40, no. 3 (1981):75–87.

Eccles, William J. "Social Welfare Measures and Policies in New France." In his *Essays on New France*. Toronto, Ontario, 1987. Argues that French officials dealt with poverty relatively effectively, and that it was not a significant problem during the eighteenth century.

Jernegan, Marcus W. *Laboring and Dependent Classes in Colonial America, 1607–1783*. Chicago, 1931.

Jones, Douglas Lamar. "The Strolling Poor: Transiency in Eighteenth-Century Massachusetts." *Jour-*

nal of Social History 8, no. 2 (Spring 1975):28–54. Detects growing poverty in eighteenth-century New England.

Katz, Michael B. *In the Shadow of the Poorhouse: A Social History of Welfare in America.* New York, 1986.

Lee, Charles R. "The Poor People: Seventeenth-Century Massachusetts and the Poor." *Historical Journal of Massachusetts* 9, no. 1 (January 1981):41–50. Discovers that poverty declined in seventeenth-century Massachusetts.

Lockridge, Kenneth A. "Land, Population and the Evolution of New England Society, 1630–1790; and an Afterthought." In *Colonial America: Essays in Politics and Social Development,* edited by Stanley N. Katz. Boston, 1971. Argues that overcrowding created a significant poverty problem in eighteenth-century New England.

Main, Jackson Turner. *The Social Structure of Revolutionary America.* Princeton, N.J., 1965. This classic study detects significant levels of poverty in the midst of a middle-class society, although Main's subsequent scholarship argues that many needy people were young adults who eventually prospered.

Mohl, Raymond A. *Poverty in New York, 1783–1825.* New York, 1971.

Morgan, Edmund S. *American Slavery American Freedom.* New York, 1975. Links slavery and the evolution of republican ideology among white elites in Virginia.

Nash, Gary B. *The Urban Crucible: Social Change, Political Consciousness, and the Origins of the American Revolution.* Cambridge, Mass., 1979. Identifies the connection between growing poverty and the American Revolution.

———. "Urban Wealth and Poverty in Pre-Revolutionary America." *Journal of Interdisciplinary History* 6, no. 4 (Spring 1976):545–584. Measures increasing levels of both poverty and economic inequality in early American cities.

Smith, Billy G. "Poverty and Economic Marginality in Eighteenth-Century America." *Proceedings of the American Philosophical Society* 132, no. 1 (March 1988):85–118. Reviews the historical literature on poverty in early America.

Stiverson, Gregory A. *Poverty in a Land of Plenty: Tenancy in Eighteenth-Century Maryland.* Baltimore, Md., 1977.

Trattner, Walter I. *From Poor Law to Welfare State: A History of Social Welfare in America.* New York, 1989.

Virgadamo, Peter R. "Charity for a City in Crisis: Boston, 1740–1775." *Historical Journal of Western Massachusetts* 10, no. 1 (January 1982):22–33.

Walsh, Lorena S., Gloria L. Main, Lois Green Carr, and Jackson Turner Main. "Toward a History of the Standard of Living in British North America." *William and Mary Quarterly,* 3rd ser., 45, no. 1 (January 1988):116–170. Concludes that most whites in early America enjoyed relatively high living standards.

Billy G. Smith

SEE ALSO **Growth and Welfare; Hired Labor;** and various essays in THE SOCIAL FABRIC.

TRANSPORTATION AND COMMUNICATION

THROUGHOUT THE NORTH AMERICAN colonies, settlers sought to facilitate trade, travel, and the dissemination of information and ideas. The most significant changes in transportation and communication were brought about for economic reasons, as those in commerce and trade demanded both a greater circulation of market information and swifter, cheaper delivery of commodities. Technological and financial obstacles slowed development of road networks, reliable shipping, and a dependable means of communication. Further complicating the situation was a lack of centralized administrative direction, as the responsibility for the construction and maintenance of transportation facilities resided at various levels of government. Nonetheless, by the last quarter of the eighteenth century, most of the North American colonies had achieved integration in economic empires, and most settlers enjoyed a reliable, though not necessarily swift, means of communication.

TRANSPORTATION BY SEA

The vessels plying the Atlantic in the seventeenth and eighteenth centuries were of various sizes and types. The Portuguese sailed massive carracks with up to two-thousand-ton (1,800-metric ton) displacements. The English, too, employed several large ships. In 1610 the East India Company (VOC) launched the *Trade's Increase,* a ship of almost one thousand tons (900 metric tons), and in 1683, construction was completed on the eight-hundred-ton (720-metric ton) *Charles II.* There were small coastal packets and ships involved in the trade between the West Indies and North America that were no larger than forty to fifty tons (36 to 45 metric tons). Most Spanish, English, French, and Dutch ships entering the Atlantic in the seventeenth century, however, had displacements of two hundred to two hundred fifty tons (225 metric tons) and averaged about one hundred feet (30 meters) in length.

By the time of the American Revolution, vessels of three hundred to four hundred tons (270 to 360 metric tons) were becoming more common in the transatlantic crossing. Constructed with multiple decks to accommodate cargo, crew, passengers, and ordnance, ships of this era featured ever more streamlined hulls for greater speed. Still, these largely three-masted ships with square sails could average only two to five knots per hour, depending upon the currents, prevailing winds, and the skill of the shipmaster.

The preferred course from Europe to the Americas was southward past the Madeira and Canary islands, down to the Cape Verde Islands, and then westward to the islands of the Caribbean. While this route remained the favorite with those pursuing the valuable Caribbean sugar trade, several variations had developed by the early eighteenth century. English shipmasters involved in the tobacco trade, for example, experimented with several routes to the Chesapeake Bay region both to shorten travel time and to evade interception by hostile vessels that circulated throughout the Caribbean. Some preferred sailing to the Madeiras, then to Bermuda, and on to the Chesapeake. Others sailed to the Azores and on to the Chesapeake. Still others preferred sailing directly from England. A few even took the northern route, sailing to Newfoundland and down the coast. By the late seventeenth century English shipmasters were sailing directly to all the key northern colonial British ports—Boston, New York, and Philadelphia.

After the English conquest of New Netherland (New York) in 1664, Dutch shippers developed a number of alternative routes to evade English mercantilist restrictions. Eager to maintain trade ties with merchants in New York, they developed several illicit, indirect routes. Their shipmasters obtained safe-conduct passes in southern Europe, the West Indies, and the Orkney Islands off Scotland before proceeding on to New York.

In the sixteenth century the Spanish developed a lucrative Pacific route between New Spain and their Philippine possessions. Merchants exchanged Mexican silver and gold for a variety of valuable East Asian goods—silks, spices, and china. In 1593 merchants in Spain, fearful of losing their New World markets, persuaded the king to limit this trade to two seven-hundred-ton (630-metric ton) vessels per year. Subsequently, two Manila galleons annually made the eastward voyage to Mexico. Shipmasters sailed north from the Philippines to catch the prevailing westerlies and rode them to the North American coast. From near Monterey, the Manila galleons skirted the coast to Baja California and on to Acapulco.

The voyage from Manila was a long one, often taking from four to eight months. The average time required for the westward voyages from Europe, though shorter, varied dramatically. From London to Boston took just over fifty days. From Plymouth, England, to Barbados in the West Indies took at least sixty days, and

from England to Virginia almost eighty days. The voyage from La Rochelle, France, to Quebec usually required more than sixty days. Shipping was seasonal.

Shipmasters learned to avoid the North Atlantic winter gales and iced-in ports. Once the last ship departed in November, Canadian settlers knew they would not see another for the next six months. Similarly, shipmasters avoided being in West Indian ports in the late summer and early autumn because of seasonal hurricanes. Shipmasters also faced a variety of conditions at port facilities in the North American colonies. The English had several excellent harbors along the east coast, but ships heading for the French possession of Louisiana faced a myriad of problems. Nowhere along the Gulf coast was there safe anchorage. The threat of ravenous worms destroying their hulls kept shipmasters from remaining long at their moorings. Most significant, oceangoing vessels could not sail up the Mississippi to New Orleans because of shifting sandbars and floating debris. Sailing through the Gulf of Saint Lawrence and up the Saint Lawrence River to Quebec was also a journey fraught with danger. Icebergs off Newfoundland, treacherous reefs, rapidly developing fogs, and sudden gusts of wind sweeping down the steep shoreline mountains combined to challenge the best of shipmasters.

The traveling conditions aboard these vessels, for the freeman as well as the indentured and the enslaved, were almost universally deplorable. Except for the ships' officers and the few passengers who could afford private quarters, those sailing the Atlantic did so in steerage, that is, between the decks. Seldom was there more than five feet of headroom. At best, passengers and crew slept on cots, hammocks, or wooden bunks. At worst, they were consigned to the deck. Besides being cramped and unsanitary, these accommodations were unbearably hot in summer and bitterly cold in winter. Dietary allotments were often unsavory as well as insufficient. Normal fare was hard-baked biscuits, salt pork, peas, and oatmeal. Drinking water was scarce or contaminated or both by journey's end. Because only one Manila galleon could trade between the Philippines and Mexico, shipmasters loaded cargo into space usually allotted to food and water. Consequently, crews on those lengthy voyages frequently suffered from scurvy, malnutrition, and thirst.

Gottlieb Mittelberger's 1750 voyage revealed the conditions passengers from Europe sometimes faced. This organist from the German duchy of Württemberg wrote a vivid account of his miserable trip to Pennsylvania. He described the food as oversalted, filthy, or spoiled; the bread as crawling with red worms and covered with spiders. The water supply had turned a sickening black by the voyage's end and, like the bread, was fouled by worms.

The cramped conditions and inadequate diet contributed to numerous illnesses. Dysentery, malnutrition, smallpox, measles, and influenza were always a threat, and seasickness was an almost universal complaint. Knowing the potentially dangerous conditions associated with transatlantic voyages, many boarded ships fearing they would not survive the trip. Rarely, however, did the voyages result in the loss of the ship. In the 1630s, for example, of almost two hundred voyages from England to New England, only one ship went down, and most of its passengers survived.

TRANSPORTATION ON RIVERS

Travelers on the rivers of North America utilized a variety of vessels. Canoes, dugouts, barges, and rafts of many sizes could be found on the Hudson, Savannah, Delaware, Mississippi, Saint Lawrence, and hundreds of other rivers. Most often, settlers turned to one or the other of three types of boats. The variously spelled pirogue ("perriauge," "pirogu," and "perriauger" were three common variations) was the favorite in South Carolina, Georgia, North Carolina, and all along the Mississippi. Little more than a long hollowed-out log, the pirogue was simple to construct and maintain and was particularly suitable for small cargoes. For larger ones, settlers turned to a flat-bottomed boat most often called a bateau. Up to forty feet long and ten feet wide (12 by 3 meters), the bateau usually had an enclosed area and could carry cargoes of up to twenty-five tons (about 22 metric tons). This shallow-draft boat usually had a sail and a crew of four to eight men to pole it upstream. Though they could be seen throughout North America, bateaux were particularly popular on the Mississippi.

In Canada, the birchbark canoe remained the favored craft through the eighteenth century. As long as thirty-five feet (about 11 meters), these vessels could accommodate up to eight men and a three-ton (about 3-metric ton) cargo. French colonists relied upon the birchbark in their pursuit of the fur trade of the vast North American interior. Using these light vessels, the famed voyageurs traveled up the Saint Lawrence and Ottawa rivers to the Great Lakes, and via the Saskatchewan, Mississippi, and Missouri rivers as far as the Rocky Mountains and the Gulf of Mexico.

Whether in a canoe, bateau, or pirogue, transportation on the rivers was slow. The two hundred and fifty miles (400 kilometers) from Augusta to Savannah, Georgia, took four to five days to travel. The trip from Sainte Genevieve in upper Louisiana (Missouri) to New Orleans required almost three weeks, and the return trip often took four months.

Aside from the languid pace, there were a host of other problems associated with river transportation. Disruptions caused by ice floes, low water, floating debris, and floods were common. Some rivers posed particular challenges. Rapids made the Susquehanna in Pennsylvania difficult to navigate. Likewise, numerous sandbars and mudbars tested the skills of boatmen on the Savannah River. The Saint Lawrence was navigable for only a short season due to ice, and thick fogs, treacherous reefs, and strong currents made even seasonal passage troublesome. The French voyageurs faced particularly arduous travel conditions. Leaving Montreal in spring, they traveled to the western fur-trading posts, not to return until late August. The voyageurs needed strength and stamina, not only for the daily paddling of their canoes, but also for carrying two to three hundred pounds (90 to 135 kilograms) of gear over often grueling portages.

Despite these conditions, the best, and sometimes the only transportation option available to colonists was by river. In the early Chesapeake settlements, planters took advantage of the many slow-moving, navigable rivers such as the James to deliver their tobacco to market. In eighteenth-century Georgia, farmers who raised rice, corn, tobacco, and other heavy produce, settled near streams because they provided the only affordable means to transport their crops to market.

Because they lacked a good road system, early North Carolina settlers had to travel by water. In New York, the most important seventeenth-century trade and communication links to Manhattan were by streams and rivers. The Mississippi River provided eighteenth-century French and Spanish settlers the only effective contact with the outside world. The same was true of French settlers along the Saint Lawrence. Since virtually every farm fronted on a river, there was little need for roads. Farmers could take their products to market by boat at a relatively low cost. Once the Saint Lawrence froze, settlers moved about on horse-drawn sleighs; the government even required each habitant with river frontage to use small spruce trees to indicate safe passage on the ice.

LAND TRANSPORTATION

Still, it would be wrong to conclude that most settlers in North America traveled by boat. Even in the Chesapeake Bay settlements, fewer than a quarter of the planters by the late seventeenth century owned a boat of any kind. Oceangoing vessels often could sail up the Chesapeake to a planter's dock, where tobacco bound for European markets was loaded. While they continued to rely largely upon the waterways to transport their tobacco to European markets, Chesapeake planters developed and maintained personal contact by travel over land. As early as 1680, 80 percent of Maryland's planters owned at least one horse. There were sound economic reasons for most in tidewater Maryland, at least, to opt for land over water transport. Watercraft required more skill to maneuver and were costlier to maintain than wagons and horses, which could graze in the woods and were less expensive to purchase by the 1690s.

The most notable aspect of land travel was the uneven pace of road building in the colonies. Maryland, Connecticut, eastern Massachusetts, and Delaware River towns had established extensive road networks by 1700. New York, particularly under the Dutch regime, had paid little attention to road building by that date. Neither had North or South Carolina. There were few roads beyond thirty miles (48 kilometers) from Charleston in 1720. Georgia had almost none as late as 1750. Likewise, roads in upper and lower Louisiana were virtually nonexistent until after the American Revolution. In eighteenth-century Canada, French settlers belatedly built a road connecting Quebec and Montreal on the north shore of the Saint Lawrence, an arduous task because of the numerous bridges required between the two towns.

The types and quality of roads also varied dramatically. By the late eighteenth century, there were several primary roads in the colonies. Settlers could travel the great eastern road between New York City and Portsmouth, New Hampshire, passing through Boston, Salem, and Newbury, Massachusetts, along the way.

The Great Wagon Road, a more significant route, extended from Philadelphia to backcountry Georgia, a distance of about eight hundred miles (about 2,900 kilometers), essentially following old Indian trails. Begun in the 1730s, the route was improved over the next two decades to permit wagon traffic as far south as Staunton, Virginia, and by the American Revolution, travelers could reach Augusta, Georgia. By the 1770s thousands were using this road, the most traveled route in all English America.

The third and longest road was the *Camino Real*, or Royal Highway, established by Juan de Oñate in 1598. Extending about eighteen hundred miles (about 2,900 kilometers), this road served as the crucial link for the mining towns, missions, garrisons, and ranches between Mexico City and Santa Fe in New Mexico. Wagon-train caravans required about six months to complete the journey from the capital of New Spain to its northern frontier. The caravans usually consisted of thirty-two wagons, an escort of about a dozen soldiers, occasionally some settlers, and a herd of cattle and reserve draft animals. In its first century of existence, the *Camino Real* served essentially as a supply line for the Franciscan missions in Pueblo country. By the eighteenth century commercial traffic dominated the route.

A fourth route, which became more important in the early national period, followed the trails widened by British general Edward Braddock during the Seven Years' War. Built to accommodate the supply wagons for his army dispatched to seize Fort Duquesne, built and held by the French, Braddock created a route of expansion from the Potomac to the Monongahela.

In addition to these major roads, settlers in some colonies built a network of secondary roads. Beginning in the 1730s, for example, settlers living along the Great Wagon Road in the Shenandoah Valley began the construction of west-to-east roads. Winchester in the north and Staunton in the south became the main focal points of land connections to eastern Virginia. Similarly, the Spanish constructed several roads that branched off the *Camino Real* to serve the settlements that emerged in Texas and Arizona in the eighteenth century. In the mid 1770s Juan Bautista de Anza opened an important route between Sonora in northwest Mexico and San Francisco.

Besides the networks of roads radiating from the primary routes, the major colonial towns developed links to their hinterlands. Boston, by the late seventeenth century, became the "hub" of an extensive network of roads linking over seventy inland and coastal towns. In 1742 farmers from as far away as one hundred miles (160 kilometers) could reach Philadelphia by road. By the 1770s a road connected Savannah, Georgia, with Saint Augustine, Florida. Smaller networks developed around county courthouses, churches, and mills in several colonies.

Some roads barely deserved the name. Those on the margins of settlement were no more than inadequately marked trails for two-wheeled carts, such as the route connecting Sainte Genevieve to local lead mines in upper Louisiana. Even in the more established locales, the earliest roads were often little more than paths that followed Indian trails. Once individuals and governments began to construct roads, few used anything other than sand or dirt for the surface. In particularly marshy areas, local governments sometimes commissioned the construction of corduroy roads made from ten-to-twelve-foot (about 3 to 4 meters) logs laid side by side. There was little effort to impose standards on the roads built. Between New York and Philadelphia, the eighteenth-century road varied in width from ten to twenty feet. In early-eighteenth-century Maryland, the Assembly ordered that public roads be twenty feet (6 meters) wide. The first roads in Georgia were twenty-four feet (about 7 meters) wide and, in 1770, the provincial government ordered that future construction include a thirty-three-foot-wide

(approximately 10-meter) roadbed. Not only did road widths vary from region to region, but few road builders attempted to create straight ones. Since cost was the critical concern, most roads meandered, avoiding ravines, gullies, and streams.

Not all rivers could be avoided, however. When possible, travelers searched for a convenient place to ford. In all regions there were ferries on the most traveled routes. Whether private or publicly subsidized, ferries were expensive. They were also slow, and often the operators were unreliable, causing extended delays. Bridges were rare because of the cost to build and maintain them. The few built in the colonial period were generally located over narrow creeks and usually were unstable makeshift wooden structures.

As the road network expanded, printers began offering road maps, and in the 1730s and 1740s, New York officials ordered the placement of stone markers along roads to inform travelers of the distance to key locations in the province. The best aid came from Daniel Henchman and Thomas Hancock in 1732. That year the two published *The Vade Mecum for America; or, A Companion for Traders and Travellers*. In addition to a street map of Boston, they included information on the roads and taverns between New England and the Chesapeake.

MODES OF LAND TRANSPORT

Most colonists traveling overland went on horseback or walked. By the eighteenth century, horses were so numerous in New France that virtually every male colonist had one. This development worried authorities, who claimed that the Canadians had become lazy and were unfit for military campaigns. A few, however, did adopt the natives' pedestrian mode of travel, particularly in winter. The French in Canada soon recognized the virtues of snowshoes and toboggans. The demands of agriculture and commerce and the desire for greater comfort, however, prompted the adoption of a variety of vehicles.

From Georgia to Massachusetts and from Maryland to the Spanish Borderlands, farmers from the early years of settlement used carts to haul stones or hay or to transport corn or wheat.

Most carts were crudely constructed. Farmers usually fashioned these two-wheeled vehicles, including wheels and axle, from wood. Found throughout the North American colonies, these simply designed rigs were called oxcarts by the English settlers, *charettes* by the French in upper Louisiana, and *carretas* by the Spanish. For long-distance hauling, early settlers relied upon pack-horses. Traveling in caravans, they were particularly important in the transport of goods over the Allegheny Mountains. The pack trade also remained the crucial commercial link between settlers in the Shenandoah Valley and eastern Virginia until the mid eighteenth century. Into the nineteenth century, pack mules remained the favored method of transporting goods in New Mexico. They could carry up to four hundred pounds (180 kilograms) each and could go where neither wagon nor horse could.

Heavier loads required a more substantial means of conveyance. Wagons of all descriptions came into use by the early eighteenth century. The Conestoga easily became the favorite of colonists in Pennsylvania and the backcountry of Virginia and the Carolinas. Brought into use by German settlers, this covered, high-wheeled, boat-shaped wagon with a curved bottom could haul more than any other land vehicle in the colonies. Depending upon what was being transported, the Conestoga could carry between four and six tons (about 4 to 5 metric tons), about four times the capacity of the carts used by most farmers. Fully loaded, the Conestoga required a team of four to seven horses. In the 1760s there were over ten thousand Conestoga and other types of wagons in use in Pennsylvania. By the next decade farmers were using perhaps three thousand wagons to haul produce from the Carolina backcountry to Charleston. Colonists in the Spanish Borderlands adopted a similar vehicle. Their four-wheeled, iron-tired wagons could carry up to two tons (about 2 metric tons) and required an eight-mule team when fully loaded.

As ever more wagons came into use, colonists became interested in alternatives to riding on horseback when making trips. By the mid eighteenth century, a wide variety of two- and four-wheeled passenger vehicles could be found in newly settled regions like Spanish Illinois as well as in communities over a century old. The ownership of chaises, buggies, chariots, carriages, or coaches not only afforded more comfortable travel but also served as a symbol of economic standing in the community. The prosperous in New York, Philadelphia, Boston, and Montreal, for example, often utilized sedan chairs in inclement weather. Although often carried by servants, some sedans were wheeled vehicles pulled by horses. There were over one thousand private carriages in Massachusetts by 1750, and in Philadelphia alone, over eighty citizens had private coaches. For those without their own vehicles, there were several stagecoach lines in operation by 1750: from Philadelphia to New York, Boston to New York, Boston to Rhode Island, and Amboy to Trenton, Burlington, and Philadelphia.

Regardless of the means of transportation, travel on land, like that on the seas and by river, was slow in the colonial period. Under the best of conditions, a rider on horseback could average no better than seven miles (11 kilometers) an hour. A teamster on a fully loaded Conestoga wagon was fortunate to make thirty miles (48 kilometers) in a day. A coach ride from Philadelphia to Portsmouth, New Hampshire, in 1750 took eighteen days. In 1775 a group of Quakers moving from Savannah to Wrightsborough, Georgia, needed eight days to travel only one hundred sixty miles (256 kilometers).

Travelers had many other complaints about the roads. Regardless of the region, colonists grumbled about roads that were crooked, ungraded, filled with ruts or holes, rocky, obstructed by overhanging branches, or blocked by fallen trees. Stephanie Grauman Wolf tells of settlers of Germantown, Pennsylvania, for example, who said of the soil on the road connecting them to Philadelphia that "in summer it was ground to fine choking dust, while in winter and spring it was almost impassable for wheeled vehicles on account of the mud." Harold E. Davis notes that early colonists in Georgia complained not only about the poor quality of roads, but also the lack of them. "Several People are obliged to go to their Lotts thró Swamps up to the middle in Water," one official noted, "which not only prevents their bringing any crop home, but is the cause that men get violent illnesses in winter time."

Amid the chorus of complaints, however, there were some who praised the ease of getting about. In 1699 a tidewater Maryland clergyman wrote that because of the sandy soil in the region, roads there were free of stones. This permitted the ambitious traveler to ride fifty or more miles (80 kilometers) in a day. Some foreign travelers in the English colonies even argued that the roads in America were superior to those in Europe.

ROLE OF GOVERNMENT

Governments played an important role in the development of the colonial transportation systems. The planning of roads, wharves, and bridges was largely a public function, although some individuals planned and then sought government permission to construct a road. Officials at all levels might be involved. Edward Hyde, who was Lord Cornbury and royal governor of New York and New Jersey, granted a monopoly in 1706 for a stage line between Amboy and Burlington, New Jersey, and for a ferry from Burlington to Philadelphia. The viceroy of New Spain, Antonio Bucareli y Ursúa, ordered the opening of a route between Sonora and San Francisco in 1773. In New France, orders for maintenance of roads and bridges came from the "Grand Voyer," the appointed surveyor of roads.

In the English colonies, most provincial assemblies got involved by passing legislation providing for publicly supported roads, ferries, and bridges. For example, according to Michael Kammen, in 1703 the New York Assembly approved a law for "Laying out, Regulateing, Clearing and preserving Publick Comon highways thro' out this Colony." Usually, the responsibility for the construction of roads fell to the county governments. Whether in New England, the Middle Atlantic colonies, or in the South, county officials usually responded to the petitions of inhabitants in deciding the location of roads.

The administrative and maintenance responsibilities for the roads, ferries, and bridges also fell to local officials. They fulfilled their obligation in a variety of ways. Officials in Georgia required all males between sixteen and sixty to serve six days on road maintenance. The county courts in Maryland appointed road overseers who "warned" taxpayers to complete road re-

pairs. In New York, users paid for their construction through taxes and fines and also had to help with their repair.

IMPACT OF IMPERIAL WARS ON TRANSPORTATION

Imperial wars significantly disrupted colonial shipping routes. During the second Anglo-Dutch war (1665–1667), Dutch warships virtually severed commercial contact between New England and the West Indies. Similarly, during the War of the League of Augsburg (1689–1697), there was a dramatic decrease in the number of ships conducting trade between the two regions. French transport between the homeland and Louisiana was normally perilous because of the risk of pirates in the Caribbean. The additional threat of privateers and the English Royal Navy in wartime almost eliminated travel between the two areas. The imperial wars also inhibited land transport. Fierce fighting in the northern end of the Shenandoah Valley during the early years of the Seven Years' War (1756–1763) not only slowed improvements being made along the Great Wagon Road, but also kept many from traveling that route.

Yet warfare also served as a catalyst for transportation improvements. When English officials saw how difficult it was to move troops to meet the recurring French threat, they often acted to improve the quality of roads in their colonies. A noteworthy example occurred in 1755. When General Edward Braddock attempted to move his troops, packhorses, and wagons from Fort Cumberland on the Potomac to Fort Duquesne at the juncture of the Allegheny and Monongahela rivers, his column could only make about two miles (about 3 kilometers) each day. Improvements on this and other roads following Braddock's defeat made the Virginia town of Winchester a major center in the transportation network of the Shenandoah Valley.

TRANSPORTATION AND ECONOMIC GROWTH

The expansion of the transportation system in the colonies led to new opportunities in ancillary business. In the major port towns, demand increased for workers in shipbuilding, ship repair, and the provisioning of ships. From shipwrights and caulkers to rope workers and blacksmiths, good-paying jobs emerged. Similarly, the increased use of wagons and coaches provided employment for wheelwrights as well as wagon, carriage, and harness makers. Wherever wagons rolled, there were men to repair them and shoe the horses. The escalating use of wheeled vehicles also had a dramatic impact on agriculture in some colonies. To maintain a team of three horses, a farmer had to devote three acres (about 1 hectare) to pasture, three (about 1 hectare) to hay, and about six acres (about 2 hectare) to grain, usually oats. In Pennsylvania, where there were thousands of wagons by 1760, such demands played a critical role in farmers' allocation of resources and time as well as their crop decisions. Finally, since the vehicles and vessels used by colonists were built in America, the expanded use of them proved a boon to those involved in lumbering.

The growth of urban areas was closely linked to access to an adequate transportation system. Ideally, that meant location on a good harbor with a dependable water or land route to the hinterlands. Most sizable towns in the colonies—Boston, Philadelphia, New York, Norfolk, Charleston, Savannah, and Quebec—had at least the former if not both advantages. Many smaller towns developed along navigable streams and rivers and roads. By the mid eighteenth century a string of towns had sprung up along the Great Wagon Road: Martinsburg, Winchester, Strasburg, Woodstock, and Staunton in Virginia; Hillsboro, Salisbury, and Charlotte in North Carolina; Camden and Orangeburg in South Carolina; and Augusta in Georgia. Travelers utilizing that major route had many needs ranging from repairs and supply to refreshment and accommodations that created employment opportunities particularly at these locations.

As transportation facilities improved, more colonists gained access to external markets. North Carolinians, through most of the colonial period, experienced slow economic growth because of a shortage of labor and currency, but more important because they lacked good roads and a good port. A. Roger Ekirch, in his study of the colony, documents the prevailing frustration: "Within the whole province," he quotes, "there is not one good harbour, being all ob-

structed with bars, and fluctuating sand-banks." This complaint was an overstatement, since the port at Wilmington could accommodate ocean-going vessels, but the consequences of inadequate river traffic were difficult to exaggerate. "The badness of our Navigation makes our Land and Slaves of very little profit to us," wrote one wealthy planter. "And as our Navigation is bad so we have very few Vessells except those that are very small, which makes freight excessive."

Complicating their difficulties was a lack of a good west-to-east road from the interior to the coast. Without ease of access from the backcountry to the Atlantic through their own province, many planters had to rely upon merchants in South Carolina and Virginia, a move that cost them in high freight charges and markups on imports. As a result, many in the colony were unable to participate fully in external markets until the provincial government acted in the mid eighteenth century to begin the construction of a road from the backcountry to Wilmington. In 1703 the New York Assembly likewise noted the important connection between better roads and increased commercial activity. They promoted the building of roads to each town to facilitate the shipment of goods.

The expansion of the road network and the growth of port towns created an opportunity for those willing to offer food, shelter, and drink to weary travelers. In his study of urban life in the first hundred years in the British colonies, Carl Bridenbaugh reports the observation by town officials that the dramatic increase in the number of taverns and ordinaries in late-seventeenth-century Philadelphia occurred because their community had "become the road where sailors and others doe frequentlie pass and repass between Virginia and New England." The port towns had dozens of taverns by the late eighteenth century, but so did small communities located on well-traveled river and land routes. On long trips to markets, farmers, merchants, and teamsters sought refreshment and a place to sleep.

CONTEMPORARY ASSESSMENTS OF TRAVEL CONDITIONS

The conditions of travel clearly improved over the course of the eighteenth century. A comparison of the assessments of colonial roads, bridges, and ferries by two particularly observant travelers, Sarah Kemble Knight and Alexander Hamilton, illustrates the positive changes that were made. In October 1704 Sarah Kemble Knight set out on horseback on a journey that took her from Boston to New York City and back. Almost without exception, she found the roads to be in deplorable shape. At best they were rocky, with uneven grades. She faced an unending series of obstructions and hazards. Mrs. Knight rode through fog-shrouded swamps, streams, and thickets of shrubs and trees. Although she employed a number of escorts and guides along the way, she occasionally got lost.

She describes several treacherous crossings of rivers on ferries, in canoes, and over poorly constructed bridges, particularly in Connecticut. Mrs. Knight tells of her crossing on the New London ferry, when fierce winds tossed the boat about wildly, frightening all on board, including her horse, which reared in panic, making the ride even more hazardous. On her return trip, she describes how, on approaching Norwalk, she had to creep over a tottering wooden bridge suspended fifty feet above the water. Between Stratford and Milford she had to make a dangerous, late-night ferry crossing over an ice-choked river. The most perilous incident occurred when she was just a few miles from her home. As she neared Dedham, Massachusetts, Knight's horse stumbled in a muddy roadway and fell and could not continue the journey. After obtaining another horse, she came upon a bridge in such disrepair that the river flowed over the walkway. Knight claimed it was a virtual miracle that she and her horse were able to cross the bridge unharmed.

Forty years after Sarah Kemble Knight made her harrowing journey, Alexander Hamilton, a physician from Maryland, traveled over sixteen hundred miles (2,560 kilometers) from his home in Annapolis to York, Maine, and back. Unlike Mrs. Knight, Hamilton found most of the roads to be smooth, affording a pleasant ride on horseback. He had praise for the roads in Maryland, New Jersey, Long Island, Rhode Island, and Massachusetts. To be sure, there were exceptions. Some stretches of road in Pennsylvania were quite rough, and officials in Connecticut apparently had made little effort at improvement in the four decades since Mrs. Knight's excur-

sion. Hamilton's most vivid recollection of his sojourn through Connecticut was the extraordinarily rough roads. He also noted, as Mrs. Knight had learned, how easy it was to get lost in that colony of winding trails and divided paths. Hamilton encountered a few dilapidated bridges, one at Brandywine, Pennsylvania, and one over the Connecticut River, but most were in good repair. Likewise, he had little complaint about the fifty ferries that he used.

Hamilton's experience illustrates how people of means could enjoy the leisurely pace of eighteenth-century travel. He encountered an intriguing variety of people along the roads between Maryland and Maine and delighted in chatting with most, whether it was the captain of a tobacco ship, an iron works proprietor, a lawyer, a physician, a Quaker, or any number of "inquisitive rusticks."

Improvements in the transportation system in the English colonies enhanced the ability of colonists to communicate with one another. They communicated in a variety of ways, but the most simple was by means of conversations, such as those which Hamilton enjoyed as he traveled up and down the East Coast.

ORAL COMMUNICATION

Although a significant proportion of the colonial population was literate, most people preferred face-to-face communication to the written word. The many taverns in the towns and countryside were a favorite place for such exchanges. By the mid eighteenth century, Boston, New York, and Philadelphia, offered dozens of licensed and illegal taverns. Newport, Rhode Island, and Charleston, South Carolina, could boast many fewer, but their numbers were growing. Most villages and hamlets, especially in the northern English colonies, had at least one tavern. Besides food and drink of varying quality, some of these establishments afforded travelers lodging. Colonists used a variety of terms to describe these establishments. References to inns, dramshops, grogshops, ordinaries, alehouses, tippling houses, coffeehouses, and taprooms, as well as taverns can be found in the legal documents and advertisements from the seventeenth and eighteenth centuries. Before the development of a reliable mail service and the printing of newspapers, besides serving as places to eat, drink, gossip, and be entertained, taverns functioned as key centers for the exchange of information. They were generally convivial places to debate political and religious questions, post broadsides and notices, be informed of the latest shipping news, arrange cargoes, make purchases, and discuss future business.

Churches were even more important as centers of oral communication. In Catholic and Protestant settlements alike, the Sabbath provided opportunity for more than religious observance. After the worship services in French colonies, parishioners visited, discussed politics, conducted business, and held auctions. In Puritan New England, churchgoers often heard government proclamations read from the pulpit, and in the churchyard before and after the sermon they debated political issues and negotiated deals.

Philip Fithian, a Presbyterian tutor, lamented the emphasis upon the secular side of Sabbath observances in late-eighteenth-century Virginia. For the gentry, the time before services was spent "giving & receiving letters of business, reading Advertisements, consulting about the price of Tobacco, Grain &c. & settling either the lineage, Age, or qualities of favourite Horses." Following a service of brief prayers and a short sermon, the local elite spent nearly an hour "strolling round the Church among the Crowd" waiting to be invited to some gentleman's home for dinner.

Colonists exploited many other opportunities to share news and renew acquaintances. Market days, annual fairs, muster days, elections, and meetings of the county court provided occasions for those living in isolated areas to learn of the latest political and economic developments.

For those living on the margins of settlement, who were too far from the church or county court to attend regularly, peddlers brought news of the outside world. Throughout the backcountry of the English colonies, settlers eagerly looked forward to the irregular appearance of these itinerant hawkers. Peddlers initially carried their goods in tin boxes or trunks, but many switched to packs slung over their backs that often held up to 120 pounds (54 kilograms). Eventually, they began using packhorses, carts,

and light wagons to transport their wares over land, and rafts on rivers. They carried cloth, thread, needles, pots, bowls, patent medicines, knives, nails, glass, guns, books, almanacs, jewelry, and sundry other items to settlers far from country stores. The number and impact of peddlers is best measured by the reaction of merchants to them. Angered by the peddlers' encroachment on their retail trade, merchants often persuaded officials in their town or county to compel peddlers to obtain a license or to forbid them from selling their wares. For backcountry settlers, however, the legitimacy of the peddlers' trade was often a secondary issue. The news the peddler shared, whether it be political or personal, was as important as any other commodity, because it briefly broke a family's isolation.

POSTAL SERVICE

Colonists communicated with one another and with those across the Atlantic by letter. Those unable to read or write called upon a schoolmaster or clergyman to draft their messages for them. In the seventeenth century, getting a letter written was less of a problem than getting it delivered. Individuals could usually make arrangements for overseas delivery with a shipmaster. Port-town taverns frequented by mariners were good places to find mailbags headed to or arriving from Europe. Once dispatched, letters faced a number of hazards at sea, such as water damage or loss, and their delivery was dependent on the safe passage of the vessels that carried them, which were threatened by storms and piracy. Some letters were censored or confiscated by imperial officials. In New France, three copies of official correspondence to the minister of marine were sent from Quebec on three different ships to ensure delivery.

The biggest problem, however, was the time required to complete the communication. Transatlantic delivery took at least a month and usually much longer in the seventeenth century. Since ships could not make it up the Saint Lawrence six months of the year, settlers in Canada faced extraordinary delays in receiving responses to their letters. The spring arrival of ships from France was a momentous occasion. Settlers eagerly awaited news of family as well as the latest information about the international scene. Within the colonies, letter writers had to depend upon the willingness and trustworthiness of travelers to get their letters conveyed. As late as the mid eighteenth century, settlers from the Georgia coast to the rivers in upper Louisiana had to rely upon the irregular arrival of ships and boats for the dispatch of their mail.

Initial efforts to establish a regular postal service in the colonies achieved mixed results. In 1639 the General Court of Massachusetts permitted Boston tavern owner Richard Fairbanks to charge a small fee for delivering and receiving letters. Thirteen years later in New Amsterdam (New York City) a small office opened to handle that community's mail. In 1673 the first attempt to operate regular postal service between these two towns proved abortive, lasting only a few weeks. In the colony of Pennsylvania, William Penn initiated mail service to Maryland in 1683. In Canada, the postal system remained simple under French rule. Postal couriers from France arrived in the spring and delivered mail to a designated merchant's shop. From there a court clerk was responsible for the distribution of the post, and the recipients paid the charges. Not until the eighteenth century was a courier service established between Montreal and Quebec. Once set up, however, normal delivery time between the two towns was only four days.

In 1691 the British government finally attempted to bring order out of the early sporadic efforts at mail service by granting a royal patent to Thomas Neale, a favorite at court, to operate a postal service in the British colonies. Neale selected Andrew Hamilton, soon to be appointed governor of New Jersey, as his deputy. Because of Hamilton's efforts, the northern colonies enjoyed improved service. A "General Letter Office" opened in Boston and New York, regular service began between Philadelphia and New York, and by 1698, weekly service connected the towns between Portsmouth, New Hampshire, and Newcastle, Delaware. Moreover, Hamilton encouraged colonial assemblies to implement uniform postal rates.

Hamilton's efforts to extend regular service to the southern colonies, however, met with little success. Service from the northern colonies to the Chesapeake was halted when Hamilton discovered that fewer than one hundred letters a year had been exchanged between the two regions. The settlers of Maryland and Virginia wrote and received many letters, but they chose not to use the royal postal system. They preferred entrusting their mail delivery to ship captains who came to their wharves on the navigable tidewater rivers. This circumstance frustrated government officials in the northern colonies, who needed to communicate with counterparts in the Chesapeake. They had to dispatch their messages with express riders. Seldom could these riders make a trip from New York to Maryland or Virginia in less than three weeks. Although Charleston, South Carolina, had a post office as early as 1698, initial attempts to link it with the northern port towns failed because of insufficient demand for the service.

When Neale's patent expired in 1707, Parliament established a more centralized system. The postmaster in England appointed deputies for each of the colonies. Under this new regime, postal service between Philadelphia and colonies to the south slowly improved. In 1722 there was regular service to Annapolis, Maryland, and in 1732 to Williamsburg, Virginia. By 1740 Edenton, North Carolina, and Charleston, South Carolina, were finally brought into the system. By then, private mail service had begun to connect the Carolinas with Georgia.

BENJAMIN FRANKLIN AND POSTAL REFORM

This intercolonial system of mail delivery, although ever more extensive, remained undependable. Furthermore, it always operated with a deficit. The situation changed dramatically when Benjamin Franklin was appointed postmaster general of the colonies. After two years of lobbying for the job, Franklin received a joint appointment with William Hunter of Virginia in 1753. Following the latter's death eight years later, Franklin shared the position with John Foxcroft until 1774.

With Hunter, Franklin, who had served as Philadelphia's deputy postmaster for sixteen years, quickly set about reforming the much maligned intercolonial postal system. The Franklin years featured inspections of branch offices in 1754, 1755, 1756, and 1763 and carefully drafted instructions to the local postmasters to improve the speed and frequency of delivery. The effort resulted in a more careful monitoring of branch post-office accounts and in increased accountability of post riders, who were required to travel by night as well as by day. A rigorous adherence to the rate schedule, local delivery of letters in larger towns, the development of shorter routes, and the advertising of undelivered letters in the local press encouraged confidence in the system. These changes permitted one-day delivery of mail between Philadelphia and New York and reduced from twenty-one to six days the time required for a letter and response between Philadelphia and Boston.

The reforms, nonetheless, had little impact on mail service in the southern colonies. After England's substantial acquisition of territory with the 1763 Treaty of Paris following the Seven Years' War, Parliament established a northern postal district that extended from the North Carolina–Virginia border to Quebec, and a southern postal district that included North and South Carolina, Georgia, Florida, and the Bahamas. Haphazard delivery and chronic deficits plagued the southern district through the end of the colonial period.

Initially, the reforms implemented in the northern colonies cost a good deal of money; in Franklin's first four years, the postal service remained a deficit operation. After 1757, however, it made a profit each year until Franklin was removed from the post because of his sympathy to the patriot cause.

Besides an improved, profitable postal system, Franklin also left a less desirable legacy. Establishing a tradition that would be honored for many generations, Franklin regularly appointed relatives and friends, including his son William, brother John, and New York publishing partner, James Parker, to positions in the colonial postal system.

MAIL DELIVERY

For most of the colonial period in the English territories, post riders, working in relays, carried the mail overland, although mail coaches had begun to be used in some areas by the 1730s. Some post riders supplemented their small wages by carrying merchandise, and a few even acted as commission agents in the purchase of livestock and drove cattle along their routes, slowing mail delivery considerably. Still, the arrival of a post rider was a significant event in the life of most communities. Crowds would gather in hopes of receiving news from family or friends, or to acquire the latest issue of a newspaper or hear the news the rider himself brought. In the Spanish Borderlands, mail, as well as commerce, was delivered by pack animals or by wagon-train caravans. Between New Amsterdam and Fort Orange (Albany) in the early years of those settlements and during the whole of the colonial period in Louisiana, there was virtually no delivery overland; mail arrived like other goods, in boats.

Transatlantic news and mail for the English colonists usually came aboard commercial vessels. For most of the seventeenth century, colonists on Barbados were the first to receive mail because most shipmasters still preferred to sail to the Madeira and Canary islands before heading westward, a route that brought them to the Leeward Islands. After brief stops there, they proceeded on to the continental colonies. To shorten the delivery time, the English established a packet service to the West Indies in 1702. Set up in response to the War of the Spanish Succession, this service's armed vessels carried only mail. The government-funded operation provided a dependable service with regular schedules and routes.

In the aftermath of Braddock's defeat in 1755, the English government decided to initiate a packet service to North America as well. From Falmouth, England, to New York City, monthly packets made their way directly across the Atlantic. By the end of the Seven Years' War, the packet service had been extended to Boston and Charleston. Besides transatlantic service, there were intercolonial packet routes. At the end of the colonial period, Charleston had a packet service to East Florida and Pensacola.

HUGH FINLAY'S SURVEY

The most thorough evaluation of the English colonial postal service on the eve of the American Revolution came from Hugh Finlay, designated by the British postmaster general to survey the post offices and the post roads from Falmouth, Maine, to Savannah, Georgia. Finlay began his nine-month inspection in the fall and during his survey kept a journal from 13 September 1773 to 26 June 1774. In the northern colonies, he found most of the local postmasters to be trustworthy, with up-to-date accounts. Generally, the roads were in good shape; some Finlay deemed in excellent condition. As a consequence, service to the communities along the post roads was reliable. Still, there were problems. Some of the post riders were lazy, too many others carried on private enterprises on their routes, and a few pocketed the postage. Finlay also believed service could be speeded up by developing alternative routes to avoid ferries, which often delayed mail delivery. He advocated that action be taken to diminish the competition from private stage drivers and that more communities be added to the post road network.

While he found an improving postal system in the northern colonies, Finlay found that conditions in much of the South were deplorable. There was mismanagement, and post riders were even less punctual than in the North. The condition of the roads and accommodations, however, were the greatest encumbrance to a more efficient system. Finlay described most of the taverns and inns on the post roads as miserable huts. The roads, often of heavy sand, quickly tired out the horses. He characterized the road between Charleston, South Carolina, and Wilmington, North Carolina, as "certainly the most tedious and disagreeable of any on the continent of North America."

NEWSPAPERS, MAGAZINES, AND LIBRARIES

The mail pouches carried on packet ships or conveyed by post riders in the eighteenth century usually contained newspapers. The intimate link between an expanding postal system and the development of newspapers in the English colonies is unmistakable. John Campbell, the publisher of the first successful newspaper, the *Boston News-Letter,* had served as that town's postmaster for four years before he began his paper in 1704. Likewise, William Bradford, publisher of Philadelphia's first newspaper, the *American Weekly*

Mercury, was the town postmaster for nine years. During Benjamin Franklin's years as joint postmaster general of the colonies, nine printers received appointments as postmasters.

These men had clear advantages in the increasingly competitive business of journalism. Printers who were also postmasters could prevent post riders from distributing rival papers, they sometimes received direct government subsidies, assemblies and governors often awarded them the contract for printing laws and proclamations, they could circulate their papers postage free, and like William Bradford, coordinate the printing of their paper with the schedule of post riders or packet ships. Benjamin Franklin, always with an eye to the main chance, saw other advantages to accepting the position of postmaster of Philadelphia in 1737. In his biography of Franklin, Ronald Clark quotes him as explaining, "Tho' the Salary was small it facilitated the Correspondence that improv'd my Newspaper, encreas'd the Number demanded, as well as the Advertisements to be inserted, so that it came to afford me a very considerable Income." Not all early printers had government support. Those without it, however, had difficulty attracting advertising and focused upon literary rather than political and economic news.

Printed with or without public support, newspapers played a key role in the expansion of intercolonial communication. By 1739 there were thirteen newspapers in the British colonies including ones in Barbados and Jamaica, and twenty-one years later there were twenty active papers in the continental colonies alone. Circulation averaged between two hundred and three hundred per issue. Only a few attracted as many as five hundred subscribers. At the end of the colonial period, *The Pennsylvania Journal* had the highest circulation figure, about twenty-three hundred. The low circulation figures do not reflect a lack of interest, but rather the cost of subscribing. A one-year subscription to most newspapers was roughly equal to a week's income for most colonists. While only about 5 percent of all white families could afford to subscribe, those who did often shared their copies. Also, the ubiquitous taverns and coffeehouses usually had issues of one or more newspapers, and many patrons took advantage of their availability.

Most colonial newspapers conveyed the same kinds of information. They relied upon reprints from the English press focusing upon domestic politics. There were also some accounts of events from other areas of the empire and in Europe. Local news received little attention. What there was of it usually dealt with commerce. In port towns, for example, shipping schedules were an important item. Such an approach is not surprising for printers dependent upon the government for their continued success. Criticism of the royal government or satirical pieces on local affairs typically came from printers with no affiliation with the government. James Franklin's *New England Courant* and John Peter Zenger's *New York Weekly Journal* were independent papers that dared criticize public officials.

In contrast to the proliferation of newspapers in the English colonies, neither newspapers nor printing presses were established in New France. Although not opposed to a private enterprise, the Crown twice rejected requests from governors-general for government-subsidized print shops.

Magazines contributed only slightly to wider communication in the colonies. There were none until the early 1740s, when printers in Boston and Philadelphia each issued one. Most came out monthly and featured essays, poetry, and fiction. Even the most popular magazines had difficulty attracting more than five hundred subscribers, and as a consequence, all failed, usually within eighteen months. Jeremiah Gridley's *The American Magazine and Historical Chronicle* lasted the longest, from 1743 to 1746.

Another means of communication, subscription libraries, also had short lifespans. There may have been as many as sixty before the American Revolution, but few survived. Most were dependent upon the payment of dues or fees, which were seldom paid on a regular basis, forcing directors to close them.

CONCLUSION

While the pace of change varied considerably from colony to colony, significant progress in transportation and communication in North America had been made by the 1770s. The impact of this change was clear, most notably to entrepreneurs, who saw an increasingly favorable climate for enterprise. Indeed, imperial officials most often cited commercial opportunity as the rationale behind funding improvements in communication and travel networks. Reform of the postal system, the introduction of packet ships, and the increased number of newspapers all helped reduce the risks and uncertainties colonists faced. Through much of the colonial period, merchants and planters had had to rely on badly out-of-date market information. With improved communication, they had access to more reliable information on prevailing prices in distant as well as regional markets that enabled them to make sounder business decisions. Moreover, the development of more direct, more reliable shipping routes and better roads reduced transportation costs and permitted greater specialization. By the mid eighteenth century, the easier circulation of commodities and news permitted merchants in each of the great Western European powers to forge more integrated imperial markets.

At the same time, the growth of newspapers and the improvement of mail service contributed to the development of an American political community in the English colonies. The process advanced slowly, but by the 1770s, the colonists' sense of national affiliation had begun to assume as strong a role as their feelings of local and regional identity. This was a particularly fortuitous development for the patriot cause during the pre-revolutionary crisis. The press provided an impetus to debates over imperial authority in the 1760s and 1770s, and helped galvanize opposition to British actions. An extended road network speeded the exchange of information among the many committees of correspondence. By 1774 virtually all the English colonies had an intercolonial committee that contributed to a growing conviction of common cause.

In religion as in politics, there was greater intercolonial contact. Improved communication clearly aided expansion of the interdenominational religious "awakening" of the mid eighteenth century. Contacts across the Atlantic as well as among colonists increased in other ways. Europeans in significant numbers traveled through the colonies; over eight hundred in the eighteenth century kept accounts of their journeys in the English provinces. A growing number of students in the English colonies went to Europe for their advanced education. There was a continued exchange of letters across the Atlantic, and the increase in merchant ships docking in colonial ports meant an ever greater flow of books, newspapers, and magazines from Europe. This permitted colonists in North America to keep abreast of the major intellectual and cultural trends of the eighteenth century. Private libraries from Quebec and Saint Louis to Philadelphia and tidewater Virginia contained works on the new scientific worldview and political philosophy as well as the classics and books of theology and sermons.

Continued emigration from Europe produced extensive business, political, and kin networks, and most colonies experienced an increase in internal migration in the eighteenth century as road networks expanded and improved. This ever larger movement of people into and within the North American colonies contributed to greater ethnic diversity and diminishing local attachments.

There were also some negative repercussions for colonists brought about by the improvements in communication and transportation. Officials in Spain, France, and England, with sufficient energy, occasionally emerged to exploit the improvements in communication to centralize their empires. Whether imposing or enforcing mercantile regulations, issuing instructions to royal governors, or disallowing provincial legislation, more effective means of communication between mother country and colony gave vigorous imperial officials the opportunity to create a more unified empire. Regular shipping routes also facilitated the spread of devastating epidemics to the Atlantic empires. Smallpox and yellow fever, for example, reached the major English colonial ports on several occasions in the eighteenth century from both Europe and the West Indies.

On balance, however, colonists benefited from the improvements in transportation and communication. Because of them, the colonies were more prosperous, cosmopolitan places in the 1770s than they had been a century earlier.

BIBLIOGRAPHY

General Studies

Bridenbaugh, Carl. *Cities in the Wilderness: The First Century of Urban Life in America, 1625–1742.* New York, 1938.

Clark, Ronald W. *Benjamin Franklin: A Biography.* New York, 1983.

Cressy, David. *Coming Over: Migration and Communication between England and New England in the Seventeenth Century.* New York, 1987.

Dunbar, Seymour. *A History of Travel in America.* New York, 1937.

Earle, Alice Morse. *Stage-Coach and Tavern Days.* New York, 1900.

Kielbowicz, Richard B. *News in the Mail: The Press, Post Office, and Public Information, 1700–1860s.* New York, 1989.

Parry, J. H. *The Age of Reconnaissance.* Cleveland, Ohio, 1963.

Quinn, David B. *North America from Earliest Discovery to First Settlements: The Norse Voyages to 1612.* New York, 1977.

Steele, Ian K. *The English Atlantic, 1675–1740: An Exploration of Communication and Community.* New York, 1986.

Wright, Louis B. *The Cultural Life of the American Colonies, 1607–1763.* New York, 1957.

Regional Studies

Davis, Harold E. *The Fledgling Province: Social and Cultural Life in Colonial Georgia, 1733–1776,* Chapel Hill, N.C., 1976.

Earle, Carville V. *The Evolution of a Tidewater Settlement System: All Hallow's Parish, Maryland, 1650–1783.* Chicago, 1975.

Ekirch, A. Roger. *"Poor Carolina": Politics and Society in Colonial North Carolina, 1729–1776.* Chapel Hill, N.C., 1981.

Kammen, Michael. *Colonial New York: A History.* New York, 1975.

Lemon, James T. *The Best Poor Man's Country: A Geographical Study of Early Southeastern Pennsylvania.* Baltimore, Md., 1972.

Merrens, Harry Roy. *Colonial North Carolina in the Eighteenth Century: A Study in Historical Geography.* Chapel Hill, N.C., 1964.

Mitchell, Robert D. *Commercialism and Frontier: Perspectives on the Early Shenandoah Valley.* Charlottesville, Va., 1977.

Moorhead, Max L. *New Mexico's Royal Road: Trade and Travel on the Chihuahua Trail.* Norman, Okla., 1958.

Morse, Eric W. *Fur Trade Canoe Routes of Canada: Then and Now.* Toronto, Ontario, 1979.

Rink, Oliver A. *Holland on the Hudson: An Economic and Social History of Dutch New York.* Ithaca, N.Y., 1986.

Trudel, Marcel. *Introduction to the History of New France.* Toronto, Ontario, 1968.

Wolf, Stephanie Grauman. *Urban Village: Population, Community, and Family Structure in Germantown, Pennsylvania, 1683–1800.* Princeton, N.J., 1976.

Contemporary Accounts

Bridenbaugh, Carl, ed. *Gentleman's Progress: The Itinerarium of Dr. Alexander Hamilton, 1744.* Chapel Hill, N.C., 1948.

Farish, Hunter Dickinson, ed. *Journal and Letters of Philip Vickers Fithian, 1773–1774: A Plantation Tutor of the Old Dominion.* Williamsburg, Va., 1957.

Knight, Sarah. *The Journal of Madam Knight.* Edited by Malcolm Freiberg. Boston, 1972.

Journal Kept by Hugh Finlay, Surveyor of the Post Roads on the Continent of North America, during his Survey of the Post Offices between Falmouth and Casco Bay in the Province of Massachusetts, and Savannah in Georgia; begun the 13th Septr. 1773 and ended 26th June 1774. Brooklyn, N.Y., 1867.

Kalm, Peter. *The America of 1750: Peter Kalm's Travels in North America.* New York, 1937.

Larry D. Gragg

SEE ALSO **Internal Migration; Rural Life;** and **Travel and Lodging.**

TRADE AND COMMERCE

THE BRITISH COLONIES

INTRODUCTION

IT IS A COMMONPLACE of economic geography that some areas are better endowed than others for specific productions or economic activities. The relevant endowments include climate, soil, minerals, and access on advantageous terms to markets, capital, labor, and other inputs not always available locally. The total significance of such present or missing endowments constitutes what economists call the "comparative advantage" of a particular region or district in a specific activity. In the long run, capital and labor are normally mobile, but natural endowments are not; hence, the frequently observable tendency of both capital and labor to move toward natural endowments under favoring market conditions.

For example, when the movement of market prices makes the production of a specific commodity noticeably profitable, market considerations should, within the scope allowed by political impediments, encourage the movement of capital and labor toward areas where they can be more advantageously employed in the now-attractive production. Market considerations should also encourage the similar reallocation of capital and labor *within* such favored areas.

If the comparative advantages are sufficiently substantial, such movements will normally lead to the expansion of production and exports in the favored areas and, under ideal circumstances, should also result in "export-led growth"; that is, an increase in their income per capita. Historians commonly refer to the linked phenomena of "export-led growth" as the "staple thesis," particularly when used as an explanation of the economic dynamism of newly settled areas concentrating upon an export production.

The British colonies in North America contained a quite wide range of natural endowments, from the semitropical marshes of Georgia and South Carolina to the frigid wastes about Hudson's Bay. For development all these areas needed the importation of capital and labor. That some were settled and developed much sooner than others can in part be explained by the relative significance of their comparative advantages in the markets of the day. However, whether rapid or slow, development in colonial areas usually required a significant volume of exports and imports and, from the first, settlers were conscious of the necessity of basing their local decisions about making, getting, and spending upon the realities of wider and often very distant markets.

If an export commodity appeared to play a governing role in the economic progress of a colony, the market-oriented inhabitants came to think of it as their "staple." From their earliest days, the settlers in some colonies expected to devote much of their market activity to the procurement or production of goods for export markets. In this category would fall the fur traders around Hudson's Bay and in the Dutch trading stations along the Hudson and Delaware, the fishermen of all nations who first set foot on Newfoundland, and those Englishmen who established the first fishing stations on the coasts of northern New England. Similarly, within the first generation of settlement the planters of Virginia and Maryland knew that their labor and capital could most advantageously be devoted to the production of tobacco for the ever-expanding European market. It took longer for the settlers in South Carolina to reach an equivalent state of concentration, but by the second quarter of the eighteenth century it was clear that the future of their colony, and later of Georgia, was to lie in the production of the newer export staples of rice and indigo rather than in the earlier combination of Indian trade and subsistence agriculture. Other areas had to wait similarly long times before they found the staples for which they had a natural or man-made advantage. The subsidies adopted by the British government in 1705 to encourage the importation of masts and naval stores from the colonies helped concentrate the attention of North Carolina on pitch and tar and New Hampshire on masts.

The alertness with which colonists responded to outside market opportunities for their potential staples in good part reflected their need for the wherewithal to purchase European, Asian, and other goods that they could not produce locally either at all or in acceptable qualities at acceptable prices. Some colonists found that they really could produce very little that could be sold in the mother country. Except for furs and skins obtained through Indian trade, there was for a long time little available in New England and the middle colonies for which there was a good market "at home." Britain was well supplied with fish by its own fishermen and with cereals—during most years—by its own farmers (protected by the late-seventeenth-century Corn Laws). Thus to obtain the European and Asian and tropical produce they desired, the New Englanders at an early stage in their settlement found it necessary to export their provisions and forest products to the West Indies and their fish to both the Antilles and southern Europe. Part of the proceeds of such sales was brought back in their own vessels in the form of sugar, molasses, coffee, salt, and wine. Part, however, was sold for bills of exchange that created credits in England which could be used to purchase both European and Asian goods.

At a very early stage, then, the colonists had developed not only bilateral exchanges with Britain and the West Indies but triangular trading (not necessarily shipping) patterns by which credits earned in the West Indies or southern Europe could be used to pay for imports from Britain. There were other multilateral trading patterns observable. New Englanders in the seventeenth century imported from England more European goods than they needed and soon were peddling the surplus to the colonies to their south. New York and Pennsylvania traders brought back more West Indian produce than they needed and tried to sell the surplus in Europe.

The Impact of British Trade Regulations

Not all multilateral trading opportunities could be exploited. Throughout the colonial period, the home government spent increasing sums of money on the defense of the colonies, particularly during the long cycle of wars with France that started in 1689. At the very least, the English and later British Parliament expected the colonists in return to order their trade in ways that would add to the strength and security of the whole metropolitan-colonial complex or imperium. The specific rules that governed trade within the complex were embodied in the Acts of Trade and Navigation. These were enacted and codified in ever more rigorous form between 1651 and 1696, though subsequently—particularly under Robert Walpole in the 1730s—Parliament allowed a number of significant exceptions that diminished the rigor of regulation for some products.

The main features of the legislation are well known: first, certain colonial products desired in England—the "enumerated commodities"— could be exported to Europe only by way of England or, after 1707, Scotland. The original listing of 1661 had included sugar, tobacco, cotton, indigo, and some dyewoods, but the list was expanded to include rice and molasses in 1704– 1705; tar, pitch, turpentine, hemp, masts, yards, and bowsprits in 1705–1706; beaver skins and other furs in 1721–1722; copper in 1721–1722; and coffee, pimento, coconuts, whale fins, raw silk, hides and skins, potash and pearl ash, and European-bound iron and lumber in 1764. However, the liberalization of the 1730s permitted the export of sugar and rice to places in Europe south of Cape Finisterre (in the northwest corner of Spain). Second, other colonial commodities (the "nonenumerated" goods) could be sent anywhere in Europe, and after 1731 to Ireland as well. Third, European and Asian goods could be sent to the colonies only from England, though exceptions were made for servants, horses and provisions from Ireland and Scotland, salt needed by the fisheries from Newfoundland down to Pennsylvania, and later, Irish linen. Fourth, all commerce between the colonies and the mother country had to be carried in empire-built and -owned vessels whose masters and three-fourths of whose crew were native-born English, or later, British subjects. Fifth and finally, for trade and customs Scotland ceased being a foreign country and was treated the same as England after the union of their two parliaments in 1707.

The burden of these regulations has been a subject of great controversy, and any assessment must be tentative and imprecise. The need to use only empire-built, -owned, and -manned vessels was an advantage rather than a burden for the colonies by the eighteenth century, creating employment for colonial crews, shipyards, and vessels. In addition, colonial shipbuilders had by mid century developed a substantial market in Britain for their output. The obligation to import European and Asian goods only from Britain undoubtedly added something to the cost of some of those goods in the colonies, even though the customs duties were generally refunded in whole or in part when continental goods were reexported to the colonies. The total package of such regulation was unlikely to have been too much of a burden, since by 1789–1791 the former colonies were importing considerably more from Britain than they had before independence.

The burden of the acts of trade on colonial exports varied considerably among regions and commodities. They had relatively little significance for the northern colonies' exports of fish, cereals, and flour to southern Europe or the shipment of these commodities plus other provisions, forest products, and livestock to the West Indies. In the Antilles, aside from the expected demand in the British colonies, there was also a market for some of these items in both the French and Spanish colonies, despite prohibitory legislation on every side. In the British market, imports of most colonial products, if taxed at all, were charged a significantly lower duty than competing foreign productions. Moreover, as already noted, colonial exports to the mother country of hemp, flax, masts, and naval stores received a bounty from the British government from 1705; other subsidies were subsequently added for indigo in 1749, raw silk in 1770, and timber in 1766, while the liberalization of Ireland's colonial trade in 1731 made it the only important market for the flaxseed of the middle colonies.

However, when the operation of the acts of trade directed much greater quantities of a product to Britain than the British market could absorb—most noticeably tobacco and rice—the surplus had to be reexported. For tobacco, reexports were 65 percent of English imports around 1700 but about 85 percent of English and Scottish imports on the eve of the revolution. Rice reexports ranged from 87 percent of English imports in 1718–1723 to 89 percent in 1753–1762 and 95 percent for Scotland in 1756–1762. Even though the retained duties on reexported rice were low and all duties on reexported tobacco were refunded after 1723, the costs of unloading and reloading plus customs house fees and freight charges on the final shipments to the Continental market should have reduced the net yield to the owner-consigner of the tobacco or rice and thus would have had a depressing effect on prices in the colonies. For rice this outcome was partly mitigated by the freedom to ship from North America to the West Indies and southern Europe. There were no such mitigating concessions for tobacco, but it must be remembered that in most European countries there was a tobacco monopoly and thus no free market for that product. After independence colonial merchants found it very unattractive to ship tobacco to countries where the local monopoly was the sole buyer. Thus, had there been no navigation acts, the only realistic regular alternative destination for colonial tobacco would have been in the open markets of Amsterdam, Rotterdam, the free port of Dunkirk, and the

EXPORTS OF THE THIRTEEN COLONIES, CIRCA 1770

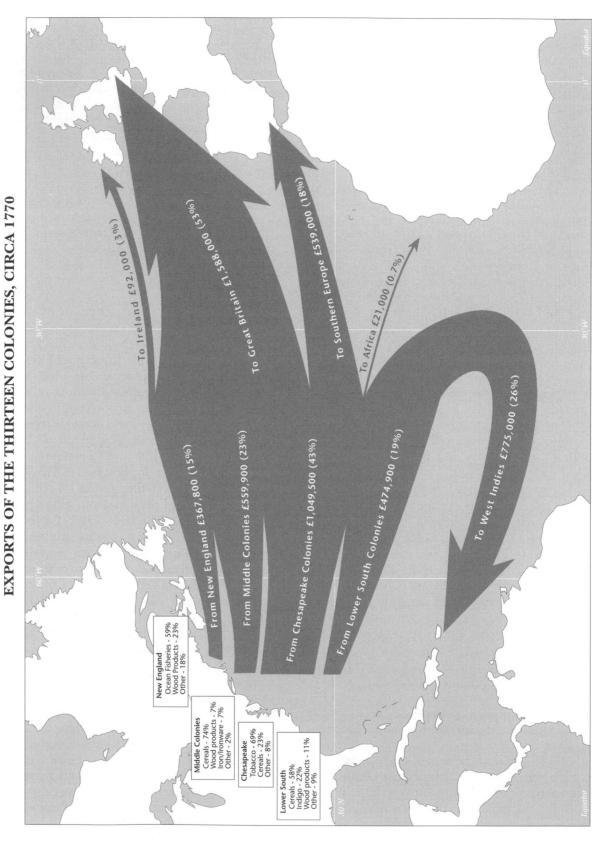

To Ireland £92,000 (3%)

To Great Britain £1,588,000 (53%)

To Southern Europe £539,000 (18%)

To Africa £21,000 (0.7%)

To West Indies £775,000 (26%)

From New England £367,800 (15%)

From Middle Colonies £559,900 (23%)

From Chesapeake Colonies £1,049,500 (43%)

From Lower South Colonies £474,900 (19%)

New England
Ocean Fisheries - 59%
Wood Products - 23%
Other - 18%

Middle Colonies
Cereals - 74%
Wood products - 7%
Iron/Ironware - 7%
Other - 2%

Chesapeake
Tobacco - 69%
Cereals - 23%
Other - 8%

Lower South
Cereals - 58%
Indigo - 22%
Wood products - 11%
Other - 9%

Hanse port towns. Since most of the tobacco shipped to such entrepôts would ultimately have had to be reshipped to a further destination, handling and transit charges would have been incurred comparable to those paid in Britain. In short the navigation system taken as a whole provided benefits as well as imposing burdens on the colonial exporter; the burdens, if irksome, were never heavy enough to check the growth of productions for which there was a real outside market.

EXPORTS

In 1768–1772 the British North American colonies exported goods worth about three million pounds sterling per annum. For the thirteen colonies, exports in 1770 came to about £1.32 per head of population. Considering that their income per capita at that time has been estimated at £10.70–£12.50, exports at this level are im-

pressive, but perhaps not as high as the emphasis on staples may have led some historians and economists to expect. There was, however, a significant difference between regions in the per capita value of exports, a difference reflecting the varying weights of staple exports in the economies of different colonies. Thus, the exports of the tobacco colonies of Virginia and Maryland averaged £1.80 (sterling) per head and those of the lower South—the source of naval stores, rice, and indigo—came to £1.55 per head, while the middle colonies' exports were worth but £1.10 per head and those of New England only £0.85. However, if estimated "invisible earnings"—mostly from shipping services—are added to the value of commodity exports, the external earnings of the two northern regions rise to £1.56, much closer to the £1.85 of the Chesapeake and southern colonies.

The importance of the major staple commodities is self-evident. Table 1 lists the nine

Table 1. Exports of British North American Colonies

	1770 (official values) Sterling ('000s)	1768–1772 (annual averages) (estimated current prices) Sterling ('000s)
Cereals and Cereal Products	1,021 (29.7%)	936
flour and bread	*505*	*412*
rice	*341*	*312*
wheat, maize, etc.	*176*	*212*
Tobacco	907 (26.4%)	766
Ocean Fishery Products	502 (14.6%)	?
dried fish	*375*	*287*
pickled fish	*23*	*?*
whale products	*104*	*80*
Wood Products and Derivatives	265 (7.7%)	?
boards, masts, staves, &c.	*165*	*144*
potash and pearl ash	*65*	*?*
pitch, tar, turpentine	*36*	*47*
Peltry	149 (4.3%)	?
furs	*91*	*?*
deerskins	*58*	*83*
Indigo	132 (3.8%)	117
Livestock	80 (2.3%)	82*
Iron and Ironware	67 (2.0%)	59
Beef and Pork	66 (1.9%)	53
SUBTOTAL	3,189 (92.8%)	
Other	248 (7.2%)	?
TOTAL TRADE GOODS	3,438 (100%)	3,015

* = cattle and horses only

515

principal commodity groups that, together, accounted for almost 93 percent of the exports of the British North American colonies in 1770, with the first four alone accounting for over 78 percent: cereals and cereal products, tobacco, ocean fishery products, and wood products and derivatives. The distribution of the geographical destinations of all colonial exports in 1768–1772 is equally clear:

to Great Britain	£1,588,000 (52.67%)
to Ireland	£ 92,000 (3.05%)
to Southern Europe and Wine Islands	£ 539,000 (17.88%)
to the West Indies	£ 775,000 (25.7%)
to Africa	£ 21,000 (0.7%)

We do not have long time series of export-import data that would enable us to follow the history of each branch of the colonies' trade through the years before 1768. However, we do have useful data on British imports from and exports to the colonies. For England we have a detailed series starting in 1696; for Scotland the detailed series starts only in 1755, though we do have summary data from 1740 (table 2). To understand these time series, we must remember that the population of the colonies increased over ninefold between 1700 and 1773. The growth in population meant both an increased market in the thirteen colonies for European and Asian goods and an enlarged colonial work force, slave and free, to produce the export goods that paid for those imports. However, English imports from the colonies did not grow *pari passu* with the increase in colonial population: we see only a fourfold increase from £319,851 per annum

in 1699–1701 to £1,333,863 in 1772–1774, representing a decline in shipments per head of colonial population from £1.27 in the earlier period to £.57 in the later. Part of this is to be explained by the diversion of a significant section of British-colonial trade to Scotland after 1707, particularly after 1740. While it is true that when we add shipments to Scotland to those for England in 1772–1774, we get the more impressive total of £1,844,837 per annum, this is still only £.80 per head of colonial population and represents only a sixfold increase since the beginning of the century. It is clear that, as the colonial export economy developed in the eighteenth century, non-British destinations, particularly those in the West Indies and southern Europe, became relatively more important, as did the internal market within the colonies.

Table 2 also casts some light upon the effect of the mid-century wars between the two great colonial and maritime powers, Britain and France, wars in which the Atlantic commerce of both suffered from the depredations of enemy privateers. The trade data for the war of 1744–1748 show a not-unexpected decline both in British exports to and imports from the North American colonies. However, in the Seven Years' War (1756–1762 in the table), while imports from the colonies declined again for Britain as a whole (even if not for Scotland), exports to the colonies rose by over 40 percent. This is explained by the British government's heavy expenditures on pay and subsistence for the military forces maintained in North America in the war, at least until the fall of Montreal in 1760. The military agents obtained most of the cash they needed for pay and subsistence by selling bills of exchange on

Table 2. British Data on Trade with the Thirteen Colonies
(annual averages; official values; Sterling ['000s])

	English Imports	English Exports	Scottish Imports	Scottish Exports	British Imports	British Exports
1699–1701	320	364	—	—	—	—
1740–1743	793	832	90	100	883	932
1744–1748w	632	698	121	149	753	847
1749–1755	891	1,238	185	136	1,076	1,374
1756–1762w	705	1,811	275	147	980	1,959
1763–1769	1,117	1,861	392	230	1,510	2,090
1770–1774	1,271	2,762	524	298	1,796	3,061

w = years of war with France

London. The bills passed into the hands of local merchants who used the windfall to order and pay for more goods from Britain. In peacetime years the gap between British exports to the colonies and the smaller British imports thence should have been made up by colonial earnings in the West Indian and south European trades.

Fishery Products

Looking more closely at the colonial export trade to Britain (more than half of the whole), one notes that the fortunes of the five key commodities or staples differed considerably. The first enterprise that drew English vessels to the waters and shores of North America was the cod fishery on the Grand Banks of Newfoundland, visited in the late sixteenth century by the fishermen of the southwest counties (particularly Cornwall, Devon, and Dorset) as well as by their competitors from France and Portugal. The cod fishery could be most efficiently carried on when the cod could be dried on shore, leading in the seventeenth century to the establishment of temporary settlements in Newfoundland and points to the south. Though permanent British settlements in Newfoundland did not come till the eighteenth century, there were some semipermanent fishing settlements on the northerly coast of Massachusetts Bay before the first Puritan settlers arrived in Boston in 1630. Since the British home market was more than adequately supplied by the fishermen of England and Scotland (exploiting both home waters and the Grand Banks), the New England fisheries from their first day had to look further afield for their markets. The fish merchants of Boston and Salem found these markets first in the West Indies and then in southern Europe: 62 percent to the former and 38 percent to the latter for New England's fish exports in 1768–1772. By contrast the fisheries of Nova Scotia, Quebec, and Newfoundland, financed and controlled in good part by English merchants, sent over 86 percent of their fish to southern Europe in the same years.

Peltry

Another natural resource contributing to the colonists' export earnings from the earliest days was the peltry of the large and small mammals of the forest. From their first arrival, Dutch, French, and English colonists attempted to enter into peaceful trade with the indigenous population around them. In this trade the settlers customarily bartered European manufactures (and sometimes rum) for furs and deerskins. As the volume of trade increased, there was a tendency for the principal fur-bearing animals to be over-trapped, diminishing the potential of the trade except in the remoter areas of the north. However, the deerskin trade appears to have left the deer population less depleted, so that it continued at a fairly high level down to the revolution. Since beaver was needed for the felt hat trade, fur was an enumerated commodity. In 1770–1775 close to 95 percent of the fur imported into England came from North America, and almost 80 percent of the North American imports came from Canada and Hudson's Bay—not yet depleted—with smaller but significant amounts coming from New York and Pennsylvania. Nearly half the furs imported then were beaver, followed far behind by otter, bear, musquash, mink, marten, wolf, raccoon, fox, and many others. By contrast around 80 percent of the deerskins exported from British North America in 1769–1772 came from the southern colonies between the Chesapeake and the Floridas. This trade went back to the last quarter of the seventeenth century both at Charleston, where it was the preeminent trade, and in Virginia, where the first William Byrd carried on an extensive Indian trade based on the James River but ranging hundreds of miles to the south. In the 1690s most of the larger Chesapeake merchants of London received some skins with their tobacco each year. In the thirteen colonies proper (excluding Canada and Hudson's Bay), deerskin exports were much more important than fur exports in the generation or more before the revolution.

Wood Products and Derivatives

The third great natural resource available to the earliest settlers was the forest itself. From its wood they built houses and furniture as well as barns, bridges, and vessels of every size and description. Wood was burned to provide heat for homes, places of business, and many industrial processes. If anything there was too much wood, and new settlers clearing the land burned much of it promiscuously. At first there was not much of an export market for wood products because of transport costs, though some was sent to the West Indies in vessels carrying other products. The colonies there particularly needed barrel staves for their sugar products; such staves could be fitted into any spare space in the hold of a vessel.

The objective situation of colonial forest products was changed, however, by the mother country's strategic needs during the British-French wars of 1689–1713. England had only limited forests and imported much timber. In 1699–1701 about 70 percent of it came from northern Europe, primarily Norway, and only 14 percent from the American colonies. As already noted, the costs of transport made such imports from North America uneconomic, except for special products like barrel staves. The needs of the shipbuilding industry were often embarrassingly precise and particularly pressing in wartime. It was estimated in 1686 that five-sixths of the timber used in English shipbuilding was imported. The remaining sixth was largely English oak, insisted upon for ships built for the Royal Navy and preferred by many private owners for the frames of merchant ships. A particular problem was created by the great conifers used for masts, particularly the tallest masts required by the Royal Navy. Masts were available from Norway, but the most preferred were those from Riga, whither they came down the River Dvina from the interior of the Polish-Lithuanian commonwealth. With the start in 1700 of the Great Northern War between Peter the Great of Russia and Charles XII of Sweden (and their respective allies), Swedish Riga was cut off from its hinterland by Russian armies, and masts no longer got through. The English navy was greatly perturbed, but all the efforts of the most adroit English diplomats could not correct the military situation. As the Great Northern War dragged on (1700–1721), the London government's relations with Sweden deteriorated, threatening in addition both the Royal Navy's and the mercantile navy's supplies of pitch and tar, most of which came from Sweden and Swedish Finland. The northern countries so deeply involved in their war were also the principal sources of hemp and flax needed to make cables and cordage for ships' rigging and sails of every description.

The English government and the new Board of Trade tried very hard in the 1690s to encour-age greater shipments of masts and naval stores from the American colonies. These efforts proving not too successful, the government procured from Parliament an act in 1705 providing subsidies for the importation from the American colonies of certain products of strategic importance to the navy: bounties of £4 per ton for pitch and tar; £3 per ton for rosin and turpentine; £6 per ton for hemp; and £1 per ton for masts, yards, and bowsprits. This act and previous measures also attempted to prevent the unlicensed cutting down of mast trees and "Pitch, Pine or Tar Trees." The tree protection measures had only a limited effect. More successful if controversial were the subsidies, even though their level was reduced in 1722. By 1772–1774, 29 percent of England's much-increased timber imports were coming from America instead of the 14 percent at the beginning of the century. While only 45 "great masts" had been imported annually from New England during 1701–1704, 603 were imported thence in 1759–1760, though the Baltic was still the principal supplier of masts of every size. No pitch or tar was imported from New England or the Carolinas during 1701–1705, but once the bounty was adopted, some started to trickle in and then indeed to pour in when British relations with Sweden became quite strained around 1718. The Navy Board, though, was highly critical of the quality of colonial pitch and tar in the 1720s, when more was coming from the plantations than from Europe; thus, in the long run—1705–1775—the board bought twice as much European pitch and tar (almost all from Sweden and Russia) as North American. Private buyers in Britain, however, were not so demanding and, as table 1 suggests, colonial exports of pitch and tar were quite substantial around 1770.

Among the wood products not covered by the subsidy policy of 1705 were potash and pearl ash. They were alkaline salts prepared from the ash of many varieties of burnt wood, particularly birch and alder. They were used in a wide range of industrial processes, including the manufacture of soap and glass and in fulling and bleaching textiles. The forests of North America were well suited for such production, provided that the necessary technology could be procured from Europe and the necessary encouragement was given by the home government. Down to 1750

British potash imports came largely from Norway and the countries around the Baltic, while pearl ashes came mostly from Germany. However, to encourage their production in the colonies, Parliament in 1751 removed all import duties on such ashes imported from British America. It was thus only in the last decades before the revolution that these products became significant colonial exports.

Tobacco
The exploitation of the seas and forests of North America was but the first stage in the development of an export economy. Of much greater potential was agriculture, once the forests had been cleared and the necessary labor obtained. Tobacco was the first colonial agricultural export of importance and the first English colonial product to establish itself as a real staple influencing world markets. As early as the 1630s, when the tobacco-using habit was only beginning to become established, Virginia was a major supplier of tobacco. By the 1680s the Chesapeake Bay region was by far the major supplier of American tobacco to Europe. However, the great expansion of Chesapeake production between the 1630s and 1680s would appear to have exceeded the growth of demand in Europe, with a resulting sharp drop in prices that was most discouraging to planters in the bay region. When the procurement of labor, both free and slave, became increasingly difficult during the wars of 1689–1713, and some former servants drifted out of the tobacco colonies towards the north or the south, tobacco production stagnated and continued to stagnate during the first peace years. Thus British tobacco imports (virtually the entire Chesapeake production) were no higher in the period 1721–1725 than at the beginning of the century. However, the higher prices of the postwar years of 1713 to 1725, reflecting this stagnation in production, gave planters the wherewithal to buy more slaves so that a growth in Chesapeake production and British imports could resume after 1725. This was also encouraged by rising demand for tobacco on the Continent, particularly after John Law banned its cultivation in France in 1719–1720 and the succeeding French tobacco monopolists found it in their interest to buy their tobacco in Britain. With this resumed growth, British tobacco imports in 1771–1775

were three times the volume of 1721–1725, almost all from the Chesapeake in both periods. This growth is all the more noteworthy because tobacco prices started falling in the late 1720s and remained discouraging until the early 1750s and unstable thereafter. The chief short-term influence on prices in America was the state of each year's crops, while alternations between war and peace could keep prices quite unsettled in Europe.

More than any other export trade, that in tobacco was strongly influenced by the union of England and Scotland in 1707. Some Scots had settled in the colonies in the seventeenth century, and by the 1690s complaints were being made of illicit trade between Scotland and the tobacco colonies. After the union the Scots were to play a conspicuous role in the trade from about 1720 and a major role from the 1740s. As late as 1738, Scottish ports accounted for only 10 percent of British tobacco imports. By 1744 this had become 20 percent, and the figure advanced to 30 percent in 1758 and 40 percent in 1765. The Scottish share of such imports peaked at about 50 percent in 1768–1770 but dropped to 45 percent in the larger trade of 1771–1775. The 85 percent of British tobacco imports that were reexported around the 1771–1775 period went primarily to Holland (36.1 percent of exports), France (26.2 percent), Germany (14.5 percent), Flanders (7.7 percent), Ireland (6.2 percent), and Scandinavia and the "East Country" (5.1 percent).

During 1768–1772 tobacco, still in first place, accounted for 25.4 percent of the exports of British North America (at current prices). In 1699–1701, when exports to Scotland were not permitted, it had accounted for 77.8 percent of English imports from the North American colonies (official values based on valuations by customs agents). In between there had been a considerable development of other agricultural productions and exports, particularly cereals and cereal products.

Cereals and Cereal Products
The thirteen colonies were not all equally suited to cereal production. The figures for 1768–1772 show Massachusetts (with Maine), New Hampshire, and Rhode Island as regular importers of wheat, maize, and flour from the middle colo-

nies and the upper South. This dependence was of long standing. In the far South, South Carolina and Georgia regularly imported flour from the north in those years, even while exporting maize and rice. The middle and Chesapeake colonies, which supplied their northern and southern neighbors with cereals and flour, were also the center of the export trade in such commodities. Most important was the flour and bread group (13.7 percent of all colonial exports in 1768–1772). Quite early in the history of Pennsylvania, the settlers along the Delaware had developed a significant milling industry. By the 1720s flour was already a more valuable export there than cereals. In 1768–1772 this flour and bread from all the colonies went principally to the West Indies (46.5 percent), southern Europe (34.9 percent), and elsewhere in North America (11.4 percent). Maize went to these same areas in roughly the same proportions, but wheat went overwhelmingly (79.6 percent) to southern Europe.

Very little of these cereal products went to Great Britain, except for some wheat in years of bad harvests. In the late seventeenth century, England had adopted a series of Corn Laws which placed very high import duties on foreign wheat, rye, and oats and subsidized English exports in years of glut. However, the growth of population in Britain in the second half of the eighteenth century proceeded more rapidly than the increase in the productivity of the soil, making the country increasingly dependent on cereal imports in ever more frequent years of inadequate harvests. Between 1697 and 1766, there were only three years in which Britain was a net importer of wheat and wheat flour: 1728, 1729, and 1757. By contrast Britain was overall a net importer during the next nine years, 1767–1775, with substantial deficits in 1767, 1768, and 1772–1775. As soon as prices reached alarming proportions (usually over fifty shillings per quarter, or eight bushels), the government obtained emergency legislation from Parliament suspending the export subsidies and removing the protective import duties. In 1757 Parliament went as far as temporarily prohibiting exports of cereals or flour from the American colonies to places in Europe south of Cape Finisterre in the hope that this would direct more American foodstuffs

to the British Isles. There was also an intermittent market for colonial wheat and flour in Ireland, with which the middle colonies were developing closer trade relations from the 1740s, encouraged by the Irish market for North American flaxseed. After 1764 about 58 percent of Ireland's flour imports came from the colonies.

However, taken together Britain and Ireland provided not a regular but an intermittent market for colonial wheat and flour. There could be moderate shipments in a year like 1768 and then nothing in 1770 or 1771. The grain and flour export merchants of Philadelphia, Baltimore, and New York depended on the erratic mails (improved by the packet service to New York established in the 1740s) to keep them informed of prices in both Britain and southern Europe so that they could send their products to the most promising markets. (The 1757 prohibition was not repeated.) Sometimes European speculators intervened and sent orders to commission merchants in Philadelphia and New York to ship wheat or flour on European account, even to France. Though the markets were very unstable, the export earnings of the wheat-exporting areas clearly improved between 1767 and 1774. This improvement was to become more marked after the revolution.

Rice and Indigo

Even more important in the cereal category were the exports of rice from South Carolina and Georgia. The real beginning of this cultivation and trade came with the introduction into South Carolina in the 1690s of a superior larger-grained variety of rice from Madagascar. Starting on a rather modest scale at the beginning of the eighteenth century, rice exports from South Carolina and, later, Georgia increased very rapidly down to the start of the French war in 1744, going from 5.8 million pounds (2.6 million kilograms) per annum in 1715–1724 to 29.5 million pounds (13.3 million kilograms) in the period 1735–1744. After a pause in the next decade growth resumed, reaching 46.6 million pounds (20.8 million kilograms) per annum in 1755–1764 and 72 million pounds (32.4 million kilograms) in 1765–1774. During 1768–1772 about 65 percent of colonial rice exports went to Great Britain, 18.3 percent to the West Indies, and

16.7 percent to southern Europe. However, as already noted, most (sometimes over 90 percent) of what was shipped to Britain was reexported to the Continent, primarily to Holland and Germany.

A much newer production in South Carolina was indigo. Since woolens and other textiles were Britain's leading industry, the supply of dyestuffs was particularly strategic. Dyestuffs imported by England alone rose in value from £226,000 in 1699–1701 to £506,000 in 1772–1774. Since those that could be grown in Britain itself did not usually produce colors of the first quality, the British textile industries required substantial imports of dyestuffs originating in warmer climates. Some of these (for example, logwood, brazilwood, and cochineal) could not be produced in the British colonies; but others, including braziletto and indigo, could be so grown, and it was in the national interest to encourage their cultivation. Indigo, as its name suggests, had first been obtained by Europeans from India, but its cultivation had in the late sixteenth century been taken up by Spanish settlers in Guatemala and Mexico and diffused from there to the Antilles in the next century. However, in the second quarter of the eighteenth century the cultivation of this product in the British West Indies declined as planters found sugar more profitable. (The share of England's dyestuff imports that it was able to get directly from the Americas declined from 48 percent in 1722–1724 to 25 percent in 1752–1754.) Of necessity British drysalters had to buy the needed supplies of indigo from France, whose West Indian colonies had continued production. This dependence became dangerous when Britain and France found themselves once more at war in 1744.

Planters in South Carolina had learned by experiment that indigo might thrive on the higher, dryer lands not suitable for rice. Parliament helped out in 1748 with a bounty of sixpence per pound. With such encouragement the planters' efforts were sufficiently successful so that during the next war, from 1756 to 1763, substantial quantities of Carolina indigo began to reach Britain. Production spread to the Floridas, Georgia, North Carolina, and even Virginia, where Landon Carter was an interested experi-menter. There were, of course, problems: most of the colonies mentioned were a bit far north for indigo, and so their cultivators did not get as many crops per year from their plants as those in the West Indies; and the textile interests in Britain were not fully satisfied with the quality of the North American product. Even so, indigo was the second most important export from the lower South on the eve of the revolution.

Other Exports

The few remaining commodities mentioned in table 1 can be dealt with briefly. Both livestock (horses and cattle) and beef and pork (in barrels) were exported primarily to the West Indies; the livestock came principally from New England, the beef and pork mainly from the lower South.

The trade in iron was more complicated. There had been experiments with iron smelting in New England in the previous century, but at the beginning of the 1700s there was no significant iron making in the colonies. In England during the sixteenth and seventeenth centuries, the iron-using trades had grown much more rapidly than iron production, largely because of the high cost of labor and of charcoal then essential both for the furnace and the forge. Even in the 1580s England was importing iron equivalent to 13 percent of its domestic production; by the end of the seventeenth century, the country was importing as much iron as was produced domestically. At that time, about four-fifths of the imports were from Sweden. The trend of increased import dependence continued in the eighteenth century, with Russia also becoming an important source. This dangerous reliance on foreign supplies led to a crisis in 1718, when deteriorating political relations caused a suspension of imports from Sweden. At this juncture a serious division of interest appeared between the iron-making trades (furnaces and forges) and the iron-fabricating trades. The iron users, allied with the Virginia merchants, tried in 1718–1720 to persuade Parliament to encourage iron production in the American colonies by removing import duties on iron produced there. In this effort they were defeated by the greater political weight of the ironmasters and their landlord allies. Nevertheless, in the years following the Swedish crisis of 1718, serious beginnings were made toward iron production in the colonies, particularly Pennsylvania and Virginia.

In the long run, *raison d'état* proved stronger than special-interest politics. A new deterioration in British-Swedish relations in the 1740s led to an act of 1750 finally removing the import duties on American colonial pig iron entered at all ports and on bar iron imported at London. (London was far from the iron-producing areas in the west and north and imported most of its iron from Sweden.) In 1757 this customs exemption for colonial bar iron was extended to the other ports. Since the old duty was not very high, its removal did not have very striking results. Even so, British iron imports from the colonies in the early 1770s were roughly double what they had been in the 1730s. A rather varied trading pattern emerged in iron. Virginia and Maryland continued their practice, substantial since the 1730s, of producing pig iron to be sent to Britain as ballast—with low freight—on tobacco vessels. At the beginning of the century, both English and Swedish bar iron had been sent to the colonies, particularly New England, for the use of local smiths and fabricators. With the development of local production, such shipments had ceased by mid century, and after the customs concessions of 1750, bar iron as well as pig iron was exported from the colonies, particularly New York and Maryland, to Britain. There was also a significant intercolonial trade in bar iron, much of it originating in Pennsylvania.

Finally, there was one further colonial export that completely escaped the attention of the government clerks who prepared the data that appears in table 1. With their abundant and inexpensive supplies of every sort of timber, the colonies were well situated to develop a shipbuilding industry. In fact, almost all the colonies between New Hampshire and Georgia had developed at least the beginnings of such an industry by the middle decades of the eighteenth century. It would appear that in 1763–1775, shipbuilding in the thirteen colonies totaled about 40,000 measured tons (36,000 metric tons) annually and was worth about £300,000 sterling, of which at least 18,600 tons (16,740 metric tons) worth £140,000 were sold abroad. If anything, this estimate is too cautious, particularly in its omission of possible sales in the West Indies that would not have come to the attention of *Lloyd's Register*

(the publication of the marine insurance exchange), the source of much of our hard information.

IMPORTS

So much for the export earnings of the thirteen colonies. All of the effort to create exports was, of course, for obtaining cash or credits that could be used to pay for imports, including a wide range of consumer goods, capital goods, industrial raw materials, and labor.

Servants and Slaves

For development, the most essential import was labor, slave or free. Throughout the seventeenth and eighteenth centuries, a good number of immigrants came to the colonies on their own. Such, however, were not enough to satisfy the labor needs of the new and, from a military perspective, dangerously exposed colonies. The growth of population in seventeenth-century England had contributed to a rise in the cost of living, greater competition for farm rentals, and noticeable pools of unemployment, all associated by contemporaries with increased poverty. Such experiences, exacerbated perhaps by the serious political disturbances of the mid century, helped persuade many poor young men and some women to sign contracts providing for their immigration to the colonies as indentured servants. In the seventeenth century, the shipping of indentured servants to any particular colony was largely in the hands of merchants sending ships to that colony for general commerce. Outbound vessels usually had spare capacity that could be used for the servant trade, particularly when those in the vicinity of London and Bristol who wished to go under indentures were numerous and the market for servants was lively in the colonies. In the Chesapeake, for example, the services of indentured servants were sold for tobacco, providing a convenient return commodity and usually eliminating the problem of credit. Conditions changed in the first half of the eighteenth century, when England's population stagnated and it became much more difficult to recruit indentured servants there. Regular merchants in the English ports still recruited a few skilled workers for their correspondents—rarely indentured—but the main indentured emigrant business moved to more remote and backward areas, such as the west coast of Scotland and northern Ireland. In such regions the indentured trade became less that of the ordinary merchant house trading to America and more that of a smaller group of firms prepared to make a particular effort to find servants. The same held true for the German redemptioner trade from Rotterdam and for English convict contracts.

In the eighteenth century, the slave trade was much more important than the servant trade. Slave imports into the thirteen colonies are estimated to have risen from an annual average of 1,100 (with a market value of £28,000) in the decade 1701–1710 to 4,400 (worth around £155,000) in the decade 1761–1770. The slave trade tended to be a specialized business from the beginning. In the late seventeenth century, the English African slave trade was in the hands of monopoly companies: first the Company of Royal Adventurers of England (1660–1672), then the Royal African Company from 1672. Both these concerns concentrated on the West Indian market and tended to neglect North America, though on several occasions the Royal African Company agreed to deliver whole shiploads of slaves to Virginia for the account of syndicates of London merchants trading there. The representatives of the London merchants paid on delivery (in bills of exchange on London) and then sold the slaves in the colony at their employers' risk, thus freeing the African company from the worry of collecting the sale price from the planter-buyers.

Such arrangements did not satisfy the demand in the West Indian or continental colonies, and so both the Royal Adventurers and the African Company had to contend with the competition of outside slave traders, or "interlopers." Between 1698 and 1712, Parliament legalized the activities of the interlopers, or "separate traders," provided that they paid a toll to the Royal African Company. During this period a major part of the trade passed into the hands of the interlopers, who completely dominated the trade from the 1720s. At London only a very few of the regular traders to North America ventured into the slave trade. And of those who did, most tried only a few "adventures" and then dropped out, leaving the interloping trade also in the

hands of specialized firms. By contrast at Liverpool, where the slave trade became a major activity after 1740, many of the merchant houses trading to the American colonies also ventured in the slave trade. The colonies' own slave trade, particularly the well-known "triangle trade" of the Rhode Islanders, was also understandably in the hands of more specialized firms. Of course, many men who were not conspicuously active in the slave trade may have had small shares in slave-trading firms or "adventures" that have left little trace on the record.

Compared with the dangers and horrors of the slave trade, the other colonial import trades seem prosaic indeed. Such importations can be divided into two main groups: in the first, products of the West and East Indies that could not be raised in the North American colonies themselves, and in the second, European merchandise that conceivably could have been produced in the colonies but whose importation was preferred for reasons either of price or of quality.

The West Indies and the Wine Islands

The trade with the West Indian islands can be considered analogous to and basically a geographical extension of the intercolonial traffic on the North American continent in which some colonies supplied others with products for which they were better situated. The West Indies were of course by the second half of the seventeenth century the "sugar islands," and sugar products led the six most important of their commodities imported by the North American colonies in 1768–1772:

rum	£285,000 p.a. sterling (current
molasses	£201,000 prices)
sugar	£132,000
salt	£ 31,000
cotton	£ 19,000
coffee	£ 16,000

Sugar was, of course, the major production of the British West Indies, but about 94 percent of their output was exported to Great Britain and only 5 percent to North America. Molasses, a by-product of the first stages of sugar refining, was sold as a drug on the markets in the British, French, and other sugar islands but either there or on the mainland could be distilled into rum for which there was a ready American market. (American rum was heavily taxed in Britain and totally banned in France.) While the West Indies' shipments of sugar and rum went to all the continental colonies, molasses went disproportionately to New England, where there was a major distilling industry. Much of New England's molasses came, of course, from the foreign West Indies and provoked the political hostility of the British West Indian sugar interests. But from the Molasses Act of 1733 onwards, parliamentary efforts to discourage the continental colonies' importation of foreign molasses were not very successful. Most of the North American colonies' resulting supply of rum, whether imported or distilled locally, was consumed by the thirsty colonists themselves, whose annual consumption in 1770 was 4.2 gallons per head. Much attention has been paid to the fraction exported for the slave trade, but though Africa took almost 30 percent of the colonies' rum exports, that represented only 3.7 percent of the total available colonial supply.

Both cotton and coffee were originally Asian products that had been introduced into the British West Indies relatively recently. Their great importance in the agriculture and commerce of the Americas was to come only after the American Revolution. Salt, however, was absolutely necessary for the New England fisheries, and from 1664 its importation there directly from southern Europe had been permitted, adding to the supply from the West Indies. (The desired freedom to import European salt was later extended to New York and Pennsylvania.) Some also came from England.

The only other product whose direct importation from Europe had been legal since 1664 was wine of the Portuguese islands of Madeira and the Azores. Portugal had been an important ally of England from the time of its separation from the Spanish Crown in 1640. There was a large community of English and later Scottish merchants in Lisbon and Oporto, some of whom took advantage of their influence to insinuate their way into Portugal's trade with Brazil. Madeira, where there was also a significant British mercantile element, was an important way station on the English sailing route to America. For most of the seventeenth century, the most

frequented course westward took English vessels bound for America first southward from the Channel to Madeira, then westward on the trade winds to the West Indies, and then northward to the Chesapeake and other continental colonies. For their return or eastward voyage, the same vessels normally took advantage of the westerly winds on the shorter North Atlantic route but did not attempt the northerly route for the outward-bound voyage until the end of the seventeenth and beginning of the eighteenth century. To sail westward by the northerly route usually meant taking advantage of the easterly winds prevalent in British waters in January, February, and March, a season earlier navigators had considered too dangerous. However, in the years when ships for America normally followed the southerly route and stopped at Madeira, their owners found it quite convenient for them to take on a consignment of the local wine traditionally supposed to be improved by an ocean voyage and quite acceptable to the colonists, who had difficulty getting any other.

Irish Provisions

A comparably specialized role in supplying the colonies was played by Ireland. Because the importation of Irish cattle was prohibited in England from 1666, the Irish were forced to develop a significant industry of slaughtering and packing salted beef. In peacetime a good part of the beef was sold in the French western ports, whence it was shipped to the French Antilles. Because all provisions were cheaper in Ireland, English ships outward bound for the plantations were often instructed to stop at Cork or another Irish port for ship's provisions, particularly butter and barrels of salted beef and pork. Substantial quantities of these products were also shipped from Ireland to the British West Indies and to some of the more northerly continental colonies, particularly those now part of Canada. When the new cycle of wars between Britain and France started in 1744, the growing colonial market helped cushion the blow to the Irish of the loss of the French market for their beef and butter. Since 1705 the direct exportation of Irish linens to the colonies had been permitted, and this in time became a significant addition to the supply of Irish linens sent to the colonies from Britain.

Imports from Britain

It has already been noted that, though colonial exports to England grew rapidly in the eighteenth century, they did not grow as rapidly as the population of the thirteen colonies, so that such exports per capita were less in 1772–1774 than they had been around 1700. This lack of dynamism was ascribed in good part to the diversion of colonial production to the growing internal market and of colonial exports to destinations other than England. A similar pattern can be detected in the serial history of colonial imports from Britain. Although English exports to the thirteen colonies increased from £364,000 sterling per annum in 1699–1701 (official values) to £2,561,000 in 1772–1774, they did not increase as rapidly as population, which went from an estimated 251,000 in 1700 to 2,320,000 in 1773. Thus shipments per head of colonial population declined from £1.45 in 1699–1701 to £1.10 in 1772–1774. If we add Scottish exports to the figures for the latter period, the annual average rises to only £1.22. (Substituting current for official values does not change the picture significantly.) A small part of this lack of dynamism may be ascribed to newly permitted imports from non-British areas prohibited in 1700 (e.g., linen from Ireland and salt from southern Europe) or increased imports from other areas, particularly the West Indies. A weightier cause may be increased competition from local manufactures within the thirteen colonies. For, as shall soon be quite apparent, the principal British exports to the colonies were goods that the colonists could at least in part manufacture for themselves. The choice between "homemade" and imported was for consumers of most goods—at least in peacetime—an ordinary market decision based on price and quality. The preferences of the consumer were converted into trade statistics by orders sent to Britain by merchants and planters.

It should be remembered that English emigrants to America came from a society in which industrial skills were widely diffused, even among the rural population. The degree to which such skills were utilized and thereby affected the volume of colonial imports obviously reflected myriad decisions about both demand and supply. On the demand side, the colonial consumer had to decide whether he or she preferred goods made "in the country" to those that were imported. Labor was comparatively expensive in the colonies, and some imported utilitarian commodities were cheaper than the local product. At the other end of the price spectrum were luxury products (including coaches, watches, fashionable clothing, and house furnishings) that were superior to almost anything that could be found in the colonies. On the supply side, would-be entrepreneurs in the colonies had to decide whether it was sensible to transfer capital and labor from agriculture and commerce to manufacturing. By the eighteenth century, the decision rarely involved complete manufacture within the household for household use. (Surviving inventories show that very few households had looms or other major manufacturing equipment.) Colonial manufacturing was more often the activity of small firms with limited but adequate capital. Millwrights who built gristmills for the flour trade could also make rolling mills and slitting mills for the iron trade (even when illegal) and fulling mills for the textile trade. Other enterprises that manufactured consumer goods in the late colonial period included saltworks, sugar refineries, distilleries, potteries, glassworks, paper mills, and the shops of silversmiths and furniture makers well known to antique collectors today.

Despite such competition the volume of imports from Britain was substantial in 1772–1774, even if not as much per head of population as at the beginning of the century. There were interesting variations between regions. Whether one consults official values or (estimated) current values New England, which probably had the most highly developed manufacturing sector at the time, imported less per capita from Britain than did the other regions. Such imports in the lower South, while above those of New England, were behind those of the Chesapeake and middle colonies. However, it is likely that a significant fraction of the goods imported into Virginia and Pennsylvania found their way southward to North Carolina.

The available printed sources on British exports to the colonies are not as complete as might be desired. Table 3, however, can give some idea of the range of commodities exported in 1772–1774 from England to the American colonies generally and to the thirteen colonies in particular.

Table 3.   Values of English Exports to America, c. 1772–1774 (annual averages; official values; Sterling ['000s])

	To 13 Colonies 1772	To America 1772–1774
Woolens and woolen products	926 (30.7%)	1148 (22.3%)
Linens (Brit. and Foreign)	462 (15.4%)	966 (18.8%)
Metalware	—	755 (14.4%)
Wrought Iron	218 (7.2%)	—
Silk Fabrics	—	343 (6.7%)
Silk Yarns etc.	—	102 (2.0%)
Cottons and Calicoes	—	261 (5.1%)
Hats	—	93 (1.8%)
Tea	53 (1.8%)	82 (1.6%)
TOTAL	3013	5148

Woolens and Linens. About 80 percent of the merchandise exported from England to the colonies consisted of British manufactures. The most important English manufacture and export was woolen (and worsted) cloth. In 1699–1701 it accounted for 85 percent of England's domestic manufactures exported to all countries and 48 percent of England's total exports and reexports; by 1772–1774, in a considerably expanded trade, the woolen-worsted share of exports was 49 percent of domestic manufactures and 27 percent overall. However, the role of the American market had changed over this time: in 1699–1701 North America and the West Indies together took only 6 percent of England's woolen exports, but by 1772–1774 the figure had grown to 27 percent. From a North American perspective, British woolens in 1768–1772 accounted for from 30 percent to 35 percent of colonial imports from England at official value.

The next most important item shipped from Britain to the colonies was linen, a commodity whose strategic importance was much greater in the eighteenth century than today. With no synthetics then and cotton still a relatively exotic fabric, linen had to satisfy a wide range of needs, from sacking and sailcloth to tableware and bedware to diapers and work clothes to the fanciest men's shirting and ladies' chemises. Because the work of harvesting flax and extracting the fibers from the stalks was rather labor intensive, England was at a disadvantage in this manufacture compared with countries enjoying lower labor costs. For the first three-quarters of the seven-

teenth century, England got much of its linen from France, including both the Vitry canvas and coarse dowlas of Britanny and the fine cambrics of French Flanders. When, however, political relations between England and France deteriorated and all imports from France were prohibited between 1678 and 1685 and again during the cycle of wars that started in 1689, alternative varieties had to be found. The first, and for a time the most important, were the inexpensive linens of Westphalia (including the oft-cited "ozenbrigs"), sometimes shipped from Bremen but often finished in Holland, particularly at the bleacheries in Haarlem. Later, additional supplies were tapped farther east from Saxony and Bohemia (obtained via Hamburg) or within the Baltic from Silesia, Poland, and Russia. However, closer to home the British Crown also ruled over underdeveloped territories with labor costs lower than those in England, areas whose questionable political loyalties made some economic nurturing seem prudent. First in Ireland and later in Scotland, legislative encouragement was given to the linen industries, making linen cloth the most important industrial export in both countries by the mid eighteenth century.

Complaints were often made by the friends of the new Irish and Scottish linen manufacturers that they could not compete with the cheap continental linens in the colonial markets because the relevant British import duties were in great part refunded when foreign linens were reexported to the colonies or elsewhere. The Irish and Scottish linen industries wanted the British Parliament to end the "drawback" or refund of these duties on the reexport of continental linens to the colonies. For this they had to wait until 1764, because of the considerable economic and political weight of the London merchants trading to the Low Countries, Germany, and the Baltic; together they were probably the weightiest sector of the London business world and included a good number of aldermen of London, members of Parliament, and directors of the Bank of England. The London merchants also had much support from the great woolen interest in England, because the continental areas from which linen was imported were great markets for English woolen exports. As a compromise Parliament in 1743 raised the import duty on the more expensive foreign cambrics and used the proceeds to pay a subsidy or bounty on export to the plantations of lower-priced British and Irish linens. As amended in 1745, the bounty reduced the effective export price (to the colonies) of British and Irish linens by 8.3 percent to 25 percent. Thus after 1743 colonial importers had three choices: they could order German and Baltic linens shipped from Britain with most of the import duty refunded (until 1764), Irish linens shipped from Ireland with no duties on them, or British and Irish linens shipped from Britain with a subsidy on the less expensive grades.

The Irish linen industry benefited from these policies. After sugar, linen was England's principal import. The proportion of England's linen imports coming from Ireland rose from around 11 percent in 1722–1724 (by value) to 28 percent in 1752–1754—after the adoption of the export bounties to the colonies—and then to 52 percent in 1772–1774 after the removal of the drawbacks on continental linens reexported to the colonies. By contrast continental linens, which had accounted for 89 percent of England's imports in 1722–1724, had by 1772–1774 (i.e., after the legislation of 1743, 1745, and 1764) fallen to 48 percent (including 28 percent from Germany and 11 percent from Russia). More Irish linen was exported to the colonies with bounty from Britain than without bounty from Ireland. The Scottish export linen industry, in effect starting later than the Irish, was working hard to catch up. In the decade following the adoption of the bounty, more Irish linen than

British linen was exported with bounty from Britain to the American colonies. But in the decade preceding the American Revolution, the British product passed the Irish in the booming bounty trade. (From 63 percent to 74 percent of Scotland's linen exports were then going to the thirteen colonies.) However, since Irish linen was also going directly to the plantations without bounty, it appears that over 50 percent of the linen imports of the thirteen colonies came directly or indirectly from Ireland in that period. Although declining in relative importance, at least 20 percent of the linens exported from England to the colonies in 1772 were "German" or continental. The only other significant product reexported from England to the colonies was tea, though it was of greater political than commercial importance.

Iron and Other Imports. Wrought iron was also a significant colonial importation from Britain in 1768–1772, even if its value was much less than woolens or linen. In a land rich in uncleared forests, there was always a strong demand for axes to fell trees and for nails with which to build wooden structures. Farmers needed sturdy scythes and mariners always needed anchors. There was also a regular intercolonial trade in wrought and cast iron products, but it did not equal in weight imports from Britain.

Even if bar iron was no longer needed, there were other noteworthy industrial raw materials imported into the colonies on the eve of the revolution. Cotton has already been cited among the imports from the West Indies. There were other products which, though not of great value, hinted at considerable manufacturing activity. Textile makers usually need dyes to enhance the appearance of their products (particularly woolens) and chemicals to bleach white linens. Even in the late seventeenth century, we can find among the goods sent out from London to Virginia wool cards (for carding or combing wool before spinning), smalts (a dye), alum (a mordant for dyeing), and brimstone (a bleach). In the eighteenth century, those venturing into cloth manufacturing could get indigo from South Carolina and a wide variety of other dyestuffs from the West Indies (including logwood, indigo, and braziletto), but they would still need alum as a mordant or fixing agent. A list of British products imported into the colonies in 1769 included over 30 long tons (67,200 pounds) of alum plus the dyes copperas and madder as well as wool cards; among the foreign goods sent to the colonies that same year were quite substantial amounts of brimstone and saltpetre (useful, inter alia, for gunpowder and glassmaking) plus almost five hundred tons of hemp for the ropeworks of Boston and Salem. The values of these items are not necessarily impressive, but their inclusion suggests a wide variety of manufacturing activity requiring foreign imports. Alum, for example, may not be too valuable in itself, but it does make possible the dyeing that could double the value of a piece of cloth.

SHIPPING

These substantial volumes of commodity movements into and out of the thirteen colonies required the service of a significant quantity of shipping. In addition, much of the carriage between the colonies or within some of the colonies went by oceangoing vessels. In 1760–1762, for example, an annual average of some 3,940 vessels (214,381 tons; 192,943 metric tons) entered the ports of the thirteen colonies plus Nova Scotia and Canada, while some 4,080 vessels (235,081 tons; 211,573 metric tons) cleared outwards. The missing 20,700 tons (18,630 metric tons) would cover ships taken by the enemy or lost at sea, as well as vessels sold abroad. In 1768–1772 the average cleared outward was 262,034 tons (235,831 metric tons) compared with 245,198 (220,678 metric tons) inward—a loss of almost 17,000 tons (15,300 metric tons). While nearly all vessels in the shuttle trades between the southern colonies and Britain were owned in Britain, most of the vessels serving the intracolonial trade and the scattered foreign trade of the New England and middle colonies were owned in the colonies. It has been estimated that earnings from the carriage of freight added some £600,000 per annum to the income of the colonies during 1768–1772. In addition, as already noted, sales abroad of vessels built in the colonies brought in at least £140,000 per annum at the end of the colonial period.

COMMERCIAL ORGANIZATION AND CREDIT

The differences just observed between the northern and southern colonies in the pattern of shipowning suggests other contrasts in commercial organization and the need for town services. Precisely because the New England and middle colonies in their early decades produced very little that metropolitan merchants found commercially attractive, the country traders of those areas were forced to become their own export merchants and shipowners. They had to build or acquire oceangoing vessels and send them to the West Indies and southern Europe in search of markets for the fish, forest products, cereals, flour, and other commodities that they could produce at competitive prices. Thus at an early stage in the history of these colonies, we find clusters of shipbuilders, shipowners, and export-import merchants harkening to the call of distant markets. Because physical proximity facilitated linkages between buyers and sellers of commodities and services, the needs of the emerging export economies encouraged the growth of significant port towns such as Boston, Newport, New York, and Philadelphia, towns characterized by large mercantile and marine service sectors. (Marine services would include ship and insurance brokers as well as ship repair yards and vendors of sails, cordage, and naval stores.)

By contrast the more southerly colonies produced goods that were wanted in England at an early date: tobacco, naval stores, indigo, rice, and deerskins in particular. English and later Scots merchants found it in their interest to send vessels to such areas to vend European and even Asian goods and buy the desired American produce. In the Chesapeake colonies the first commercial forays were usually the joint speculations of ad hoc syndicates of small merchants entrusted to a supercargo who would return on the same vessel with the produce of the "adventure." Experience soon taught that this method involved the unwelcome expense of keeping the supercargo's vessel too long "in the country." To reduce such shipping expenses, the English adventurers came to prefer establishing a factor in the colony who could adjust his trading activities to the agricultural calendar and the needs of his planter customers, develop a circle of friends there, and accumulate return cargo before the arrival of his principal's next vessel. Although many such factors, whether on salary or commission, started without capital of their own as dependents of the metropolitan merchants for whom they acted, a fortunate few managed to accumulate some capital and became local independent merchants dealing with English merchants as "correspondents," with each side performing commercial services for the other—buying, selling, arranging shipping—for a commission. Some of the larger planters followed the local merchants' lead and experimented in dealing with English merchants on a commission basis. More were encouraged to consign their tobacco to London or Bristol rather than sell it in the colonies when war conditions created a widening gap between American and European prices for tobacco. However, the planter consignment system, probably of the greatest relative importance between 1713 and 1740, never accounted for as much as half the trade. It became relatively less important after 1740, when the increasingly successful Scottish firms pushed their chains of "stores" into the newly settled, more inland regions that were often far from waters navigable by oceangoing vessels. However, a numerous class of indigenous merchants persisted in the tobacco colonies, even at the height of the Scots' success.

For the Chesapeake tobacco trade, neither the seventeenth-century English factors, the eighteenth-century Scottish storekeepers, nor the indigenous merchants found it necessary or useful to congregate in major port towns. Deliberately dispersed through tidewater and Piedmont, they preferred locations near their customers but with ready access to navigable rivers, the maritime highways on which ships from Britain brought their imports and took delivery of their tobacco from public riverside warehouses. The significant port towns in the Chesapeake were not centers of the tobacco trade; rather, they specialized, like equivalent northern towns, in the wheat and flour trade (Baltimore) or the West India trade (Norfolk). The colonies farther south also had their indigenous merchants, but only at Charleston did a major port develop, trading in every direction.

Because undeveloped land was so abundant and inexpensive in the colonies while capital and labor were so scarce, credit was particularly valued by all who had or hoped to have something to sell. The growth of population, even more than of export earnings, greatly increased the value of land—roughly 70 percent of nonhuman wealth in the colonies on the eve of the revolution—and thereby provided a solid underpinning for mortgage and every other kind of credit. (By terms of the British Colonial Debts Act of 1732, land, slaves, and every other type of property could be attached for debts on mortage, bond, note, or open account.) Credit could be used for current consumption, but the larger advances were usually associated with development: credit to acquire land, buildings, slaves, slave clothing, and agricultural tools. Behind the credit that a farmer or small planter might obtain from a local trader was the credit the trader got from a port merchant; behind that the credit the colonial port merchant got from a metropolitan merchant; and behind that the credit such a metropolitan merchant got from a wholesale ironmonger or draper or from monied people who lent him cash on bond. This chain of credit was formalized in the decades preceding the revolution in the "cargo trade." In this the colonial merchant sent an order for goods to a metropolitan merchant to be purchased from wholesalers on one-year's credit with the understanding that the colonial merchant would remit bills of exchange or staples to the metropolitan merchant in time to clear the debt. Because the colonial merchant had purchased his imports on credit, he could reasonably offer credit to his customers.

Even longer terms had become usual in the slave trade, with wholesalers and manufacturers furnishing trading goods to English slave traders on up to eighteen-months' credit. In the colony of destination, the slaves were usually entrusted for sale on commission to a local substantial factor who, to get this valuable business, had to find some affluent person in Britain or the colony to act as his surety or "guarantee." The slaves were then sold to planters, usually on long credit secured by bond, but long before the planter was expected to complete payment, the factor had to remit to the English slave traders his own twelve to eighteen month bills of exchange drawn on his "guarantee." The slave trader could get cash immediately for these bills by selling them at a discount to a banker or other monied person, but the arrangement put great pressure on the factor to get enough from the planter purchasers to remit to his surety the appropriate amount before each bill became due.

Thus both the slave trade and the general import trade were characterized by complex networks of debt that could lead to litigation and much trouble for all concerned when commodity prices fell. On the eve of the revolution, this transatlantic debt was thought to total around £6 million sterling. Contemporaries tended to condemn credit most when it was used for luxurious consumption; they were more tolerant when it was used for productive investment, particularly for slave purchases. For the slaves, however, the association of their condition with planter debt only compounded their misery. In the event of death or bankruptcy, the executors or assignees might have to sell at auction all property of the deceased or bankrupt, breaking up the slave community and family.

CONCLUSION

The introduction to this article referred to the historian's "staple thesis" and the economist's related "export-led growth" model. The discussion above of colonial exports has emphasized the importance of the well-known staples: tobacco, rice, wheat, flour, fish, forest products, indigo, and the like. Insofar as usable data survive, the record shows that the export history of these staples was one of buoyant growth, even if that growth was not as exuberant as that of the colonial population, and even if some colonies, particularly Virginia and Maryland, appear to have been diversifying or moving away from monoculture between 1700 and 1775. However, given aggregate growth, the historian must wonder whether there was also any observable "real growth"—that is, growth in income per head of population—that can be linked to the major export staple commodities.

The concept of export-led growth presupposes the power of a favorable market for a commodity to attract to areas suitable for that commodity's production both capital and labor. The impressive growth of the thirteen colonies' population suggests that the labor needs of their expanding staple productions were in good part

being met. Most of the population growth in the eighteenth century was through natural increase. However, over the whole colonial period, immigration was significant, and most immigrants being poor and often unfree, someone other than the immigrants had to pay for their passage. Most often the ultimate payer was the staple producer who bought the slave or the services of the indentured servant. Thus a staple production in effect imported its own labor.

At first settlement, unimproved land had almost no market value. However, with the passage of time, the growth of population and the resultant improvements to the land combined with healthy markets for colonial staples to create the substantial land values that made land and buildings add up to about 70 percent of the colonists' nonhuman wealth on the eve of the revolution. If one includes the value of slave property in wealth totals, then the colonists, most of whose families had started with hardly anything, held per capita wealth comparable to that of their fellow subjects in England. The fact that land values, so large a portion of the colonists' wealth, varied not just with the degree of improvement but also with proximity to ports and navigable rivers and the roads that served them, is but another suggestion of the degree to which the export staples had created colonial wealth as well as colonial population. Landed wealth in turn was the explicit or implicit underpinning of most colonial credit, the credit that helped provide producers with the labor, tools, vehicles, crafts, buildings, and so forth needed to expand staple production more and more.

BIBLIOGRAPHY

General Accounts

Gray, Lewis Cecil. *History of Agriculture in the Southern United States to 1860.* 2 vols. Washington, D.C., 1933.
Greene, Jack P., and J. R. Pole, eds. *Colonial British America: Essays in the New History of the Early Modern Era.* Baltimore, Md., 1984. Note articles by R. S. Dunn, J. M. Price, and R. B. Sheridan.
Jones, Alice Hanson. *Wealth of a Nation to Be: The American Colonies on the Eve of Revolution.* New York, 1980.

McCusker, John J., and Russell R. Menard. *The Economy of British America, 1607–1789.* Chapel Hill, N.C., 1985. Indispensable bibliography; valuable text.

Price, Jacob M. *Capital and Credit in British Overseas Trade: The View from the Chesapeake, 1700–1776.* Cambridge, Mass., 1980.

———. "New Time Series for Scotland's and Britain's Trade with the Thirteen Colonies and States, 1740 to 1791." *William and Mary Quarterly,* 3rd ser., 32, no. 2 (1975):307–325.

Shammas, Carole. *The Pre-Industrial Consumer in England and America.* Oxford, England, 1990.

Shepherd, James F., and Gary M. Walton. *Shipping, Maritime Trade, and the Economic Development of North America.* Cambridge, England, 1972. Indispensable.

Tracy, James D., ed. *The Political Economy of Merchant Empires.* Cambridge, England, 1991. Note articles by R. R. Menard, A. Perotin-Dumon, and J. M. Price.

Special Topics

Barnes, Donald Grove. *A History of the English Corn Laws from 1660–1846.* New York, 1930.

Bischoff, James. *A Comprehensive History of Woollen and Worsted Manufactures.* 2 vols. London, 1842.

Carr, Lois Green, et al., eds. *Colonial Chesapeake Society.* Chapel Hill, N.C., 1988. N. B. articles by L. G. Carr, R. R. Menard, and J. B. Russo.

Clemens, Paul G. E. *The Atlantic Economy and Colonial Maryland's Eastern Shore.* Ithaca, N.Y., 1980.

Clowse, Converse. *Economic Beginnings in Colonial South Carolina, 1670–1730.* Columbia, S.C., 1971.

Condon, Thomas J. *New York Beginnings: The Commercial Origins of the New Netherlands.* New York, 1968.

Davies, K. G. *The Royal African Company.* London, 1957.

Davis, Ralph. "English Foreign Trade, 1700–1774," *Economic History Review,* 2nd ser., 15 (1962):285–303.

Devine, Thomas M. *The Tobacco Lords: A Study of the Tobacco Merchants of Glasgow and their Trading Activities.* Edinburgh, 1975.

Dickerson, Oliver M. *The Navigation Acts and the American Revolution.* Philadelphia, 1951.

Doerflinger, Thomas M. *A Vigorous Spirit of Enterprise: Merchants and Economic Development in Revolutionary Philadelphia.* Chapel Hill, N.C., 1986.

Durie, Alastair J. *The Scottish Linen Industry in the Eighteenth Century.* Edinburgh, 1979.

Earle, Carville V., and Ronald Hoffman. "Urban Development in the Eighteenth Century South." *Perspectives in American History* 10 (1976):7–78.

Ernst, Joseph A. *Money and Politics in America, 1755–1775: A Study of the Currency Act of 1764 and the Political Economy of Revolution.* Chapel Hill, N.C., 1973.

Galenson, David W. *White Servitude in Colonial America: An Economic Analysis.* Cambridge, England, 1981.

Goldenberg, Joseph A. "An Analysis of Shipbuilding Sites in *Lloyd's Register* of 1776." *Mariner's Mirror* 59, no. 4 (1973):419–435.

———. *Shipbuilding in Colonial America.* Charlottesville, Va., 1976.

Harper, Lawrence A. *The English Navigation Laws.* New York, 1939.

Harrington, Virginia D. *The New York Merchant on the Eve of the Revolution.* New York, 1935.

Land, Aubrey C., et al., eds. *Law, Society, and Politics in Early Maryland.* Baltimore, Md. 1977. Valuable articles by R. R. Menard and others.

Lawson, Murray G. *Fur: A Study in English Mercantilism.* University of Toronto Studies, History and Economic Series, no. 9. Toronto, Ontario, 1943.

McCusker, John J. *Rum and the American Revolution: The Rum Trade and the Balance of Payments of the Thirteen Continental Colonies.* 2 vols. New York, 1989.

Malone, Joseph J. *Pine Trees and Politics: The Naval Stores and Forest Policy in Colonial New England, 1691–1775.* London, 1964.

Menard, Russell R. "The Tobacco Industry in the Chesapeake Colonies, 1663–1730: An Interpretation." *Research in Economic History* 5 (1980):109–177.

Ommer, Rosemary E., ed. *Merchant Credit and Labour Strategies in Historical Perspectives.* Fredericton, New Brunswick, 1990. Note articles by J. A. Ernst, M. L. Nicholls, and D. Vickers.

Price, Jacob M. "Economic Function and the Growth of American Port Towns in the Eighteenth Century." *Perspectives in American History* 8 (1974):123–186.

———. "The Economic Growth of the Chesapeake and the European Market, 1697–1771." *Journal of Economic History* 24, no. 4 (1964):496–511.

———. "The Last Phase of the Virginia-London Consignment Trade: James Buchanan & Co., 1758–1768." *William and Mary Quarterly,* 3rd ser., 43, no. 1 (1986):64–98.

———. "A Note on the Value of Colonial Exports of Shipping." *Journal of Economic History* 36 (1976):704–724.

———. "The Rise of Glasgow in the Chesapeake Tobacco Trade, 1707–1775." *William and Mary Quarterly,* 3rd ser., 11, no. 2 (1954):179–199.

Price, Jacob, and Paul G. E. Clemens. "A Revolution of Scale in Overseas Trade, 1675–1775." *The Journal of Economic History* 47, no. 1 (1987):1–43.

Solow, Barbara, ed. *Slavery and the Rise of the Atlantic System.* Cambridge, England, 1991. A valuable collection of articles.

Steele, Ian K. *The English Atlantic, 1675–1740: An Exploration of Communication and Community.* New York, 1986.

Truxes, Thomas M. *Irish-American Trade, 1660–1783.* Cambridge, England, 1988.

Jacob M. Price

SEE ALSO **Relations with the Parent Country** and **The West Indies and North America;** and the map accompanying this article and **The West Indies and North America.**

THE DUTCH COLONY

THE GLOBAL SCOPE OF DUTCH TRADE

THE TRADE OF THE United Provinces spanned the globe by 1650. Although the Netherlands was initially an intra-European trading nation with a dominant position in the Baltic trade, by the middle of the seventeenth century its merchants had journeyed to the farthest reaches of the earth in search of markets and profits. The two great Dutch trading companies aggressively pursued trade and conquest from southeast Asia to Brazil. The trading companies were the *Vereenigde Oostindische Compagnie* (United East India Company, VOC), established in 1602 and given a national monopoly of all trade from the Cape of Good Hope east to the Strait of Magellan, and the *Westindische Compagnie* (West India Company, WIC), chartered in 1621 and given as its monopoly all trade west of the Cape of Good Hope to the Strait of Magellan.

By 1650 the VOC was the most successful joint-stock company in Europe. Its success in southeast Asia had already relegated the once powerful Portuguese to second place in the lucrative spice trade. From the Cape of Good Hope to Japan, the company's great sailing ships, called "Indiamen," sailed the "roaring forties," the parallels of latitude so named for their hard and steady easterly winds, to the straits of Sunda and back again, a voyage that on the average took nearly three years to complete. The voyage took them due east and south from the Cape of Good Hope to the thirties and forties of south latitude. Ships then ran east before turning north to catch the trade winds for the Sunda Strait. Sailing the roaring forties required superb seamanship and fast and seaworthy ships. The Dutch were the first to employ this route regularly in trade. This route would remain the preferred and fastest east-west crossing of the Indian Ocean until the last days of sail.

The huge ships, sometimes exceeding one thousand tons, returned loaded with nutmeg from the Banda Islands, cloves from the Moluccas, pepper from the Coromandel coast of southeast India, and cinnamon from Ceylon. In a little over a quarter century the VOC made Amsterdam the spice capital of Europe and enriched the merchants who had wisely purchased its stock. The company remained a bankable investment for over two centuries, and its activities would establish the Dutch presence in South Africa at Capetown, in Indonesia at Jakarta, and for a while on the island of Taiwan.

The WIC, by contrast, had much less success. From the moment of its founding in 1621, its directors squandered millions of florin on war fleets to attack Spanish silver fleets returning from America. On one occasion in 1628, the efforts paid off spectacularly, but most of the time the ships returned empty, to the anger of stockholders and investors. The most serious financial hemorrhaging took place in South America, where the company's Brazilian colony of New Holland fell to a Portuguese rebellion in 1654.

Financially, the loss of the sugar plantations in Pernambuco (the Luso-Brazilian capital of New Holland) was a heavy blow to the company. The decline in sugar imports signaled economic difficulties for the company both at home and in the chartered territory. The loss of its trade facilities on the South American mainland also created difficulties in the slave trade, which by the mid 1650s was already a major profit-making enterprise for the company. In the years following the retreat from Brazil, the WIC would reorganize its trade with South America through the island of Curaçao and devote more attention to the management of its colony in North America.

NEW NETHERLAND AND THE ATLANTIC TRADE

The responsibility for developing New Netherland's trade fell to the directors of the Amsterdam chamber of the WIC. After experimenting with a factory system in the 1620s, a feudalistic manorial system in the 1630s, and a land incentive system based upon something akin to the Virginia headright system in the 1640s, the company abandoned all but a few of its trade prerogatives while maintaining its political authority.

New Netherland was part of an Atlantic trading community that included the English colonies to the north and south. Of critical importance was the special relationship with Curaçao, which provided access to African slaves and salt. Slaves were in demand throughout the Caribbean and in English Virginia, and salt was an important commodity in the trade with New England.

New Netherland became an important slave entrepôt in the last years before the English conquest. Shipping records reveal that regular voyages from the West African slave coast were being made to New Netherland in the 1650s. So common were such voyages that Director-General Peter Stuyvesant had special forms printed that left blanks for the name of the ship, her captain, and the locations on the West African coast where the slaves were purchased. Although exact figures are hard to obtain, it appears that the number of Africans in New Netherland was larger than in New England and probably second only to Virginia and Maryland in the seventeenth century. Nonetheless, most slaves brought to New Netherland probably did not remain long in the Dutch colony. In the 1650s the WIC regularly exported Africans to English Virginia and charged a 10 percent export tax on slaves destined for the Chesapeake. The size of this trade remains something of a mystery, but a conservative estimate would put the number at about three hundred souls per year for the period from 1657 to 1664.

Within the Atlantic trading community, New Netherland's products were in high demand. Furs, the most lucrative of colonial commodities, were highly valued in Europe for hats and clothing. At the height of the company's fur trade as many as forty-six thousand pelts per year were shipped to Amsterdam from Fort Orange, the company's fur trading outpost near the confluence of the Hudson and Mohawk rivers. By the late 1650s, however, the fur trade appears to have begun its decline. A number of factors may have accounted for this, not the least of which was overhunting. Moreover, other colonial products were beginning to crowd out furs. The colony's timber and grain were needed in the West Indies; in turn, New Netherland could provide the salt of Curaçao and Bonaire to New England fishermen to preserve their catch. New Netherland thus became a vital port in the North American coastal trade and the West Indian regional trade. With the passage of the first English Navigation Act in 1651, New Amsterdam also became a smuggling enclave for citizens of both empires.

The hemispheric scale of Dutch trade drew the merchants of New Netherland into the web of the Atlantic trading community. Although orchestrated by powerful Amsterdam cartels and sustained with bills of exchange guaranteed by the Exchange Bank of Amsterdam, the trade of New Netherland was part of a much larger movement of goods around the perimeter of the Atlantic. The notarial archives of the city of Amsterdam contain thousands of charter contracts, bottomry bonds, and partnership agreements that sketch the outlines of this trade.

Goods sent to New Netherland directly included the two primary commodities of the Indian trade: cloth goods and liquor. Firearms were also an important part of this trade as were iron goods, copper pots, knives, and the traditional gifts used in exchange: beads and small trinkets. In addition, the company developed a lively trade in seawan, or wampum, that enabled the Dutch to take advantage of various exchange rates among Native Americans in New Netherland. Eventually the company came to control the sources of the most highly valued seawan. By rapidly increasing the "money supply" and transporting the highest quality shells and wampum belts to seawan-poor areas, Dutch merchants increased their profit margins while simultaneously setting off inflationary trends in the local economy.

As the European population grew, so too did the demand for the accoutrements of European civilization. Cargo lists from the late 1650s, for example, often contained references to French soap, fine porcelain ware, spices from the East Indies, books, oil lanterns, and furniture. Some Amsterdam merchants specialized in the European provisioning trade, and the profit margin may have exceeded that obtainable in the fur trade.

Charter contracts for the late 1650s and early 1660s preserved in the Amsterdam notarial records suggest that direct annual shipping to New Netherland probably exceeded two thousand tons. The coastal trade with the English colonies and the regional trade with the West Indies probably added another one thousand tons to the annual figures, making New Amsterdam the most important seaport in North America in the first half of the seventeenth century.

A good example of a charter contract was one signed by Cornelis Coij, Cornelis Leenaertsz, and Jacob Jansz Staets in 1652. These merchants hired the ship, the *Vergulden Kreef*, out of Amsterdam under the command of Dirck Ariensz of Texel. The charter stipulated that the captain was to make a voyage from Amsterdam with a cargo of trade goods "to the English Virginias, Manhattan in New Netherland, and the South River [Delaware River]." The voyage turned out to be successful, the result in no small part of the effective control maintained by Staets as supercargo. The charter, with its clear delegation of responsibilities, had made it possible for Staets to order a longer stay in Virginia than the captain thought proper, thus ensuring a full cargo for the homeward journey. When the *Vergulden Kreef* unloaded its cargo in Amsterdam, the manifest showed half Virginia tobacco and half New Netherland pelts.

The use of multiple ports of call became a characteristic of the New Netherland trade after 1640. Amsterdam merchants and their American agents watched closely the market conditions for the different colonial products. They were well aware that a glutted market in tobacco, for example, could render an expensive Virginia voyage unprofitable. Dutch merchants kept their eyes open to profit. When the fur trade declined, they turned to the slave trade or the European provisioning trade. When the demand for food grew in the West Indies, they were quick to exploit the grain and fish trade between North America and the Caribbean. The result was a trade system that followed the markets and often ignored the arbitrary boundaries between empires.

DECLINE OF THE AMSTERDAM–NEW YORK TRADE

The English conquest of New Netherland in 1664 ended abruptly the reign of Dutch authority in North America. Although a Dutch naval squadron recaptured New Amsterdam (New York) during the Third Anglo-Dutch War (1672–1674) and held it for fifteen months, the government of the United Provinces formally abandoned claim to New Netherland in the Treaty of Westminster (1674). The States-General gave up New Netherland in return for the South American colony of Surinam.

Amsterdam merchants would continue to trade with New York, but the increasing burdens of the English Navigation Laws cut deeply into profit margins. By the late 1670s the direct Amsterdam–New York trade was in irretrievable decline.

The loss of New Netherland redirected Dutch commercial interests south to the Caribbean and east to Africa where they would dominate the sugar and slave trade for half a century. New York would be rapidly integrated into the emerging British navigation system. The colony's strategic location allowed colonial entrepreneurs to exploit the trade patterns established during the period of Dutch occupation. New York's fur exports dropped significantly as the eighteenth century opened, but the colony's farm products, as well as its ability to offer maritime financial services (notarials, insurance, financing), soon reestablished it as the North American entrepôt for the Atlantic trade.

BIBLIOGRAPHY

Boxer, Charles R. *The Dutch in Brazil, 1624–1654.* Oxford, 1957.
———. *The Dutch Seaborne Empire, 1600–1800.* London, 1965.
Davies, David W. *A Primer of Dutch Seventeenth-Century Overseas Trade.* The Hague, The Netherlands, 1961.

Gehring, Charles T., and J. A. Schiltkamp, eds. *New Netherland Documents*. Vol. 17, *Curaçao Papers, 1640–1665*. Interlaken, N.Y., 1987.

Rink, Oliver A. *Holland on the Hudson: An Economic and Social History of Dutch New York*. Ithaca, N.Y., 1986.

Oliver A. Rink

SEE ALSO **Relations with the Parent Country** and **The West Indies and North America;** and the map accompanying this article and **The West Indies and North America.**

THE FRENCH COLONIES

ANY HISTORY OF TRADE and commerce in New France must acknowledge the key roles played by politics and culture in its development. Society in France and colonial society in North America acquired a distinctive character in which military and aristocratic strains predominated but interacted with rapidly changing economic and political structures. These structures mingled with commercial ambition and were equally important in determining Canada's economic life. Even religion was not without its effect, shaping features of commercial behavior in French North America. In brief, no evaluation of trade and commerce in French America can be obtained by a simple appeal to economic man. Everywhere culture and politics wove a delicate structure in which commercial life was merely part of the larger pattern.

BEGINNINGS: PRIVATEERING AND FISHING

Early French commercial interest in the New World centered on plunder and fish, but neither encouraged settlement or fostered trade. During the early sixteenth century, French privateers attacked Portuguese shipping north of the equator near the Atlantic islands off the coast of North Africa and fishermen flocked to the vast fishing grounds of the North Atlantic. Early voyages of reconnaissance and exploration of North America between 1524 and 1542 were examples of sporadic royal interest in investigating the potential for pursuing anti-Spanish policies overseas. These voyages were soon abandoned because merchants in the Atlantic and Channel ports of France began to explore growing opportunities for plunder and illicit trade in the Caribbean, where Spanish shipping more than doubled during the 1540s owing to the discovery of rich silver mines in present-day Mexico and Bolivia.

The year 1549 marked the beginning of renewed French corsair activity in the Caribbean and within five years Spanish shipping had declined to its lowest point in thirty years. During the period 1555 to 1565, French royal, religious, and commercial interests briefly combined to establish settlements in Brazil and Florida, on the shoulders of the Spanish trade routes. But Spanish reaction proved to be fierce, ruthless, and overwhelming and these attempts to establish France in America failed. Privateering continued for another half century, but colonial commerce and plunder never united with religion and patriotism as they did later in England and the United Provinces to produce a national effort to expand overseas.

During the sixteenth century, French merchants revealed a hesitancy to invest in colonization and overseas ventures proposed by the court and the nobility. This behavior was rooted in the priorities shaping their lives. Initial unprofitability, for example, led to the diversion of further investment at La Rochelle and Rouen to licit and illicit trade with Spanish and Portuguese colonial markets rather than to more risky French ones in the northern part of America. Like other merchants, those of Rouen sought swift commercial profits to invest in land, annuities, offices, and other forms of noncapitalist wealth. The object was to obtain stable incomes that in effect drained away investment from colonial and commercial enterprise.

Understanding the development of French fishing on the Grand Banks and off the northeast coast of Canada has always been problematic for colonial historians. This shift in France's priorities may have been closely related to the growth of Europe's population and its search

535

for new protein sources—thus it may better be viewed as a part of the expansion of agriculture rather than as overseas trade. Little more than a decade after Columbus's first voyage, "new land" fish were being sold in the Rouen marketplace and Indian captives were being displayed. But while a close connection existed between fishing and overseas activity, the former never encouraged exploration or settlement, nor did it require or seek state intervention for its success.

Fishing was, and continued to be, carried on primarily from France, and while its importance to the French economy is undeniable only merchants and seamen in several selected seaports appeared interested. Fishing was a highly structured business, labor intensive, and with heavy overhead costs and low profitability. It did not encourage other commercial activities. Although by 1578 more than half of all the fishing vessels on the Grand Banks were French, they had little effect on the development of colonial trade. As with privateering and merchant priorities, fishing heightened preexisting urban rivalries, religious animosity, and intense regional competition and conflict. It did not promote commercial consolidation, economic unity, or national identity.

THE FUR TRADE

The fur trade appeared to be the only activity that might encourage increased French activity overseas. But the fur trade was not a natural outgrowth of the fishery as some historians have claimed. Interest in the fur trade grew slowly and sporadically among fishermen, and it is significant that the first ventures in the fur trade were initiated not by fishermen but by merchants of Saint-Malo, Rouen, and Dieppe who sought to collect old unpaid debts of the Crown owed to Jacques Cartier's family. As early as 1534, natives had shown a desire to trade furs for European goods, but it is not at all clear that Europeans were similarly inclined. The fur trade only appeared during the early 1580s in the Gulf of Saint Lawrence. As was the case with other French commercial activity in the New World, however, exploration of America's natural re-

sources led to urban rivalry and fierce unfettered competition.

Merchants sought to eliminate this competition by obtaining exclusive trading monopolies from the French Crown. They did not seek to promote colonization but to consolidate commercial gains. Not surprisingly, the monarchy sporadically sought to promote its own overseas aspirations on the backs of petitions for exclusive jurisdiction to trade. For the next forty years, from the first grant of monopoly to Jacques Cartier's nephew in 1588 to the establishment of a state-supported monopoly in 1627, the pattern remained consistent. One group of merchants would obtain a grant of a royal monopoly only to be met by other rival groups who ignored its terms or sought, usually with the help of noble patrons, to have the monopoly revoked on the grounds of nonperformance and regranted to superior claimants. With the Crown preoccupied by civil war and internal ruction, and with no end of merchants anxious to apply for monopoly trading rights, it seems clear why the procedure was repeated again and again. An outstanding matter of debate, however, remains the degree to which trade in America was shaped by these conditions or by the nature of the fur trade and the cultural attitudes and behavior of the Indians.

Fur was a most unusual colonial staple and stands in sharp contrast to others produced in the New World. Unlike tobacco, sugar, indigo, rice, timber, or other New World commodities, gathering fur for export depended upon a free, indigenous labor force. Native Americans harvested the animals, processed the pelts and, until late in the seventeenth century, transported them to places of trade to exchange for a limited range of manufactures—chiefly muskets, powder and shot, woolen and linen cloth, copper and brass kettles, wire, steel hatchets, knives, scissors and needles, brandy, and tobacco. An important consequence of this fundamental characteristic of the fur trade was that very few Frenchmen were required to carry it on. Secondly, no other colonial staple gave rise to anything resembling the partnership that was established between French and Indians. It also gave rise to a unique paradox. As characterized by historian W. J. Eccles, the trade brought most of the continent

536

under nominal French control, and led to its destruction.

While the staple itself gave shape to much of the fur trade, the attitude of the Indians contributed to the trade, and the meaning they gave to exchange also molded the institution. All witnesses emphasize Indian shrewdness and self-interest, but many historians disagree about a common Indian attitude toward trade, especially since a type of division of labor existed between different Indian tribes. While some Indians hunted and trapped animals, others acted as middlemen between the Indians and the French. Nevertheless, it would be wrong to view Indian traders as having the same view of commercial transactions as Europeans even though they understood the nature of prices and competition.

Many Indians and their French counterparts understood that trade encompassed much more than markets and economic gain. Ceremonial exchange, gift giving, political stability, and ritual expressions of diplomatic and strategic alliance were all involved in trade and did not operate independently of it. Moreover, it does not appear that European goods were distributed within Indian societies among their members by trading mechanisms. Individual rights and property consciousness appeared not to exist. In addition, crude economic determinism ran into the nearly incomprehensible spiritual matrix that made up the Indian world.

While Indians and their culture shaped the conditions by which trade was conducted, trade itself ultimately drew them into the market and transformed their world, reorienting it toward capitalist notions of land and labor. Although Indians and French remained partners for nearly two centuries, trade ultimately aided in destroying Indian subsistence economies and reducing Native people to dependency.

The evolving fur trade also forced important changes in French trade practice for it soon became apparent that the chief institution for its prosecution, the monopoly company, could not carry on successfully. Solutions to the two major problems facing traders, limiting competition and ensuring a regular, adequate supply of furs, often proved mutually contradictory. In 1627 government officials established a royally backed joint-stock company, the Compagnie des Cent-Associés (the Company of One Hundred Associates), in an effort to suppress internal competition among French merchants and to respond to growing external pressure from English and Dutch competitors for furs. But war between the French and Indians—chiefly the Iroquois—and between the French and English revealed the monopoly company to be a clumsy form of trading organization. The company proved unable to respond to rapidly changing conditions in North America and Europe. Successor companies, the Community of Habitants and the West India Company (WIC), proved to be no better.

Individuals in increasing numbers began to penetrate the interior. Beginning in the 1650s Frenchmen traveled beyond the lower Saint Lawrence Valley into the continent until by the mid 1680s they had reached as far as ninety-five degrees west longitude (approximately present-day Minnesota), pushed north to Hudson Bay, and traveled southward along the entire length of the Mississippi River. This energetic activity, while increasing the supply of furs, had thoroughly subverted all attempts by monopoly trading companies to limit competition and control exchange. Indeed, by the final quarter of the seventeenth century anarchy and glut characterized the fur trade.

REGULATING THE FUR TRADE

Reliance upon the fur trade to maintain a French presence in America and advance royal interests there had long been abandoned by French officials but alternatives proved difficult to identify and initiate. Noncommercial, religiously motivated colonization brought French missionaries to New France and implanted an apostolic church in Canada but the only long-term solution lay in finding commercial alternatives to the fur trade. In 1663 Louis XIV revoked existing monopolies and made New France a royal colony, and while the following year he approved the creation of yet another monopoly company, the WIC, its primary focus lay in the Caribbean and its chief raison d'être was political rather than economic.

French state intervention in the economy went well beyond the provisions of protective

537

legislation observed elsewhere in Europe. Under Louis XIV's minister Jean-Baptiste Colbert the state achieved unprecedented heights in participation and direction of commercial and manufacturing activity. But French government policy during most of the seventeenth and early eighteenth centuries was formed chiefly in response to short-term fiscal demands for revenues to pay for the ever-increasing military designs of the absolute monarchy. Like other states, France sought to impose a series of regulations designed to drive European, chiefly Dutch, competitors out of French overseas trade by restricting the transport of French goods to French ships. Extension of these navigation laws and tariffs to include the French colonies followed naturally.

Colbert also intended to reduce Canada's dependence on the fur trade. He promoted immigration, agriculture, and a crude industrial strategy that aimed to make the colony more self-sufficient than before on the one hand, and well-integrated into a nascent French colonial trading system on the other. In terms of trade, he sought to promote increased domestic consumption and more diversified export production. From the time of Jacques Cartier's discovery of the Saint Lawrence River until the present, Europeans have believed that the northern half of America contains untold riches. Canadian historian Michael Bliss points out that throughout history extracting wealth from Canada has been handicapped by the harshness of the land, its small population, and the great expectations of its people and their government. These factors forced development beyond real resource bases and added to costs. Colbert's attempts to stimulate France's and New France's social and economic development proved to be just such an example of state-forced development that exceeded expectations.

Much that Colbert promoted proved ambiguous or downright contradictory. Colbert relied heavily, but with little effect, on legislation to regulate production of beaver hats at home but ignored the effect that a fixed-price system for the purchase of beaver skins in New France had on the growing anarchy and glut in the colonial trade. Increasingly, during the half century following the outbreak of the Franco-Dutch War in 1672, the exigencies of war finance drove government policies and legislation affecting colonial trade and development.

In 1675, the year after the abolition of the WIC, Colbert leased its monopolistic rights, including the beaver trade, to a syndicate of tax farmers, a type of financier. In return for an annual fee paid to the Crown, these men gained the exclusive privilege of purchasing at fixed prices all beaver and moose hides offered for sale at Quebec. Monopoly had been exchanged for monopsony, but the effect was the same. Furs poured into the colony from the frontier, but by the final quarter of the seventeenth century the trade was more strongly tied to Indian alliances of growing complexity than ever before and any attempt to reduce production appeared to threaten the very existence of New France.

By 1696 French authorities and colonial merchants were desperate, and the fur trade was drastically curtailed. All but one western post were to be closed and their garrisons recalled. No permits were to be issued for trade. Colonists were forbidden to travel west of Montreal. Such drastic orders, creating a power vacuum in the west, could not be allowed and the resultant compromise that permitted a partial withdrawal from the west and a partial reduction in the trade proved no solution at all. The exigencies of French war finance did not permit abandonment of the tax farm on the beaver trade.

LOUISIANA AND THE WEST INDIES

During the first decade of the eighteenth century this continuing chaos led to the virtual abandonment of New France by metropolitan merchants and a new focus by the French government on Louisiana. Changes in French foreign policy directed new attention to the mouth of the Mississippi and initiated a sudden decision to strengthen French interests there. For reasons that had nothing to do with economic exploitation and everything to do with geopolitical realities in Europe, the French government decided to found the colony of Louisiana. Not surprisingly efforts to place the new French establishment on a self-supporting basis proved impossible. The founding of Louisiana in 1700 illustrates a most important feature of French colonial trade and commerce in North America. It was ancillary to France's strategic, noneconomic reasons for a continuing presence in America.

Despite all that has been written about Colbert and his successors' encouragement of colonial self-sufficiency and economic diversification, little occurred during the half century between 1665 and 1715. Attempts to encourage shipbuilding and timber exports and to initiate trade between Canada and the West Indies suffered from overstimulation, on the one hand, and irregularity, poor quality, and the high price of colonial production on the other. Colonial initiatives replaced government encouragement during the first decade of the eighteenth century, but these efforts were weak and proved no match for the tyranny of distance and the harsh climate that prohibited navigation between Quebec and the islands for nearly half of each year. The attempts also could not rival the growing competition from New England and New York merchants who enjoyed a vigorous, illicit trade with Martinique. The glut of furs in New France also promoted a similar illicit trade in beaver pelts between Montreal and Albany, New York. Officials in France and in America might have hoped that New France would develop more than a fur trade and cease to be a drain on government, and they did much to stimulate new ventures, but few examined policies with a view to determining their consistency or profitability.

During the decades after the Treaty of Utrecht (1713), France experienced great success in developing her West Indian possessions. The Atlantic port cities of Bordeaux and Nantes grew rapidly along with the slave and sugar trades. Sugar exports from Saint Domingue increased twice as rapidly as those from Jamaica while secondary staples of coffee, indigo, cacao, and cotton enhanced a diversified economy. French foreign and colonial trade grew between 1716 and 1748 at an astonishing annual rate of slightly more than 4 percent and nearly quintupled by the mid 1780s. But New World markets did not grow in similar fashion, and the French Atlantic trades never developed beyond a series of temporary commodity booms in the port cities. The fur trade was too small to be of much economic significance to this spectacular growth, and New France was both too specialized and too minuscule a market for French manufactured goods.

AGRICULTURE AND FISHING

Business opportunities that did arise were closely tied to privilege because prior to 1720 New France could not produce anything other than fur cheaply. Because they were separated from trade, colonists, indentured laborers, discharged colonial soldiers, and women were slowly transformed from a disparate collection of individuals into a relatively homogeneous, noncapitalist, preindustrial European peasant society based on subsistence agriculture. The degree to which commercial agriculture was practiced in New France occupies much space in current debates over the nature of trade. According to some historians, habitant producers had little of their surplus appropriated through tithes and seigneurial burdens; other scholars maintain that nearly half of the colonial surpluses were lost to them. There can be no doubt, however, that a lack of markets for colonial surplus production left settlers with few or no incentives to produce beyond the household unit. Between 1717 and 1793 the population increased eight times while the volume of exports only tripled. The countryside was virtually cashless and resistant to capitalist pressures; these conditions discouraged accumulation of large holdings and did not promote the appearance of even a nascent agrarian bourgeoisie.

Most historians claim that little or no connection existed between the fur trade and agriculture, the two main areas of economic activity in the colony, before the second half of the eighteenth century. As a consequence the colony was oversupplied with a growing abundance of cheap, unemployed rural labor. During the first quarter of the century, however, a French government decision to construct a great fortified town on Île Royale (Cape Breton) led to new conditions that stimulated agricultural production and permitted, in some small degree, the diversification long sought but never achieved by government economic policies. During the 1720s and 1730s the garrison town of Louisbourg developed a vigorous maritime trade based on the production and export of dried codfish. Indeed, the value of cod exports grew to three times the value of the Canadian fur trade. The trade involved significant colonial participation and Louisbourg became an entrepôt for Canadian produce from farm and forest—West Indian sugar, the tafia rum, and molasses— and illicit trade and fish from New England. During these years farm produce, chiefly flour and peas, sawn lumber, and barrel staves were also shipped directly between Canada and Martinique and other French West Indian islands. Whether Louisbourg became a major market for Canadian agricultural surpluses and forest products, as some have claimed, is open to speculation.

Regularity of Canadian production was never established as the growing market outstripped supply. Moreover, a growing illicit trade in cheaper lumber and foodstuffs from New England left Canadians in an increasingly uncompetitive position that was worsened by the imperatives of climate and geography. During the 1740s overfishing also appeared to threaten Louisbourg's own commercial well being, and major crop failures in Canada during the late 1730s and early 1740s led to a decline in intercolonial trade. The outbreak of King George's War in 1744 brought it to an end. Attempts to revive the trade at the war's conclusion in 1748 foundered on growing demands in Canada for foodstuffs as the colony increasingly assumed the characteristics of a military fortress with a large garrison of unproductive soldiers to feed.

GOVERNMENT INTERVENTION AND INFLUENCE

Although it has been argued with good reason that fish and not fur was the focus of French imperial activity in North America, as late as the eighteenth century, after two centuries of involvement, the government still knew very little about the cod fishery. Statistics sent to Versailles were imprecise and incomplete, and they were never analyzed to obtain a picture of the fishery. Though conscious of the fishery's importance as a source of manpower for the navy, the government's attitude, as in the case of the beaver trade, was primarily fiscal. Its interest in the fishery focused on its potential as a source of revenue. The duties on codfish were heavy. The system of duties and exemptions was more irrational than burdensome. Indeed, as prices

rose the burden declined, for most duties were levied on quantities not prices. Merchants sought and obtained protective tariffs against English and Dutch cod and exemptions from French duties.

Two developments occurred in the eighteenth century that reflected changing conditions. First was a tendency to equalize merchant privileges rather than to rationalize them in order to increase production; and second, later in the century, the government shifted from attempting uniformity of revenue collection to a system of bounties in support of the fishery. This move from milking to supporting, from fiscal to strategic imperialism, was brought on by the loss of Île Royale and the Canadian inshore fishery during the Seven Years' War and consequent penetration of English dried cod into once-secure Iberian and Italian markets.

The government had never stopped trying to stimulate the colonial economies, but precisely because official focus was as much on fiscal as on geopolitical realities its policies remained inconsistent, ambiguous, and irrational. In Canada, the government stepped in with a number of overly ambitious, pump-priming schemes for iron-founding and shipbuilding during the 1730s. But the end result endowed the colony with costly, unprofitable industries that damaged local initiatives and required large subsidies to remain in existence.

Colonial initiatives in trade often illustrate the important role of privilege that characterized business success in Canada as well as the continual search for exploitable products to send to France. Successful efforts to establish porpoise and sealing stations along the north shore of the Saint Lawrence River and Gulf depended upon the use of influence and interest to obtain monopolistic concessions from colonial authorities in order to cover the high capital outlays in ships, buildings, and men needed to exploit the resources of the region. Successful entrepreneurs were almost always established merchants or well-connected colonial officials. The profitability of these enterprises always remained in doubt and the chief end in establishing these ventures seems to have been to find additional returns to pay for French imports in the continuous, unrelenting struggle to overcome the always unfavorable terms of trade.

THE MARGIN OF EMPIRE

Two broad general explanations have been offered for the deplorable state of Louisiana's export economy during the French regime. The first, used by all who have written the colony's history in political terms, blames "the system"—the restrictive, so-called mercantilist policies of the Crown. The second is a more vague, less coherent claim that France lacked the resources necessary to exploit such distant frontiers, namely capital, a navy, and an emigrating population. Both explanations, however, fail to address the issue of what immigrants and capital would have done had they been present in greater number and amount. A third explanation that we may term fiscalist could provide a better answer.

Although the original reasons for establishing Louisiana were geopolitical, government officials quickly sought relief from the economic burden of the new colony. The chief problem that emerged, however, was that the revenue needs of the French Crown proved stronger than its colonial ambitions.

One obvious possible colonial staple was tobacco, but during the late seventeenth century wartime demands for additional state revenues had led to the creation of a state monopoly on the purchase of all tobacco for sale in France. Owing to the high value of the sums paid by tax farmers and their ability to purchase much cheaper, better quality tobacco abroad (such as, in Virginia and Maryland), the French government thereafter discouraged the cultivation of domestic and colonial tobacco. Indeed, so strong was the influence of tax farmers that Colbert, the supposed promoter of colonial staples production and trade, allowed the monopolists to destroy tobacco cultivation in the French colonies, and also manufacturing in France and trade with European markets.

Although John Law obtained a tobacco monopoly for his Compagnie de l'Occident (Western Company) in 1718, on condition that it undertake to develop production in Louisiana so as to free France from dependence on British supplies, the ambitious scheme failed. Financial manipulations; a failure to observe the terms of the agreement; mismanagement by successive holders of the monopoly; and lack of capital, labor, and technical skills were to prevent delivery of sufficient quantities of good quality leaf at low enough prices to compete with foreign tobacco.

The Louisiana fur trade could not successfully rival that of Canada. The government's solution, already failed half a century before, was to place Louisiana's export trade in the hands of various monopolists between 1712 and 1731. Other factors also constrained trade in Louisiana. Capital and labor were both lacking, and the few settlers, traders, and soldiers were left to their own devices. They raised a little indigo and tobacco together with agricultural produce, but the chief means to pay for imports was found in trading with the Indians for deerskins.

As a consequence, while Canadian settlers became even further removed from market exchange, Louisiana settlers continued to trade directly with the Indians. Accordingly, prior to 1780 little emphasis on commercial agriculture existed in the colony and trade in the lower Mississippi generated economic roles and ethnic relations between Indians, whites, and blacks that were unique and possessed considerable flexibility. A small trade in foodstuffs and forest products developed between Louisiana and the French West Indies but was carried on chiefly by French rather than local merchants. Metropolitan merchants, however, sought chiefly to carry away bills of exchange from the colony rather than local commodities, and this inhibited growth and profitability. Similarly local exchange with Spanish American ports, such as Veracruz and Pensacola, served largely as cover for illicit trade practiced by metropolitan merchants. Indeed, there was very little export trade. Commerce between France and Louisiana remained quite insignificant under these conditions. Bordeaux merchants were indifferent, and those from La Rochelle remained hesitant even after receiving subsidies from the government. Fewer than sixty ships cleared the latter port for the colony between 1731 and 1744, and about half belonged to a single company. The problem always was lack of returns and scarce money that hindered trade.

The loss of Canada and transfer of Louisiana to Spain during the 1760s coincided with new ideas about colonies in France. The rise of physiocratic theory, which claimed that society

541

should be governed according to a natural order by which the soil is the only source of wealth and the only proper object of taxation, embraced free trade and included strong hostility toward colonies. But territorial losses and new ideology did not signify an end to French interest in America. The wealth of the West Indies and in the waters of the North Atlantic remained; the same decade was also marked by a large, new initiative to establish a French colony in Guyana in South America, but unfortunately the venture failed after the expenditure of millions of livres and the loss of thousands of lives.

As exclusive privileges became restricted in favor of reduced internal tariffs and trade barriers, trade in the French West Indies became virtually free by 1774. This development, however, was as much an acknowledgement of the already existing commercial relations between American traders and French planters as a reflection of new thinking among ministers and senior government officers.

APOGEE AND AFTERMATH

Following the loss of Canada, the French government attempted several times to stimulate the trade in dried codfish to the West Indies, but failed for reasons that were as much technical, demographic, and political as economic. With its fishing fleet based in France and only a tiny colony of fishermen remaining at Saint Pierre and Miquelon, off the south coast of Newfoundland, no amount of subsidies could overcome the greater manpower, shorter distances, and available time enjoyed by New England fishermen to supply the ever-growing demand for food to feed the rapidly increasing number of slaves in the French islands, whose economies were growing more rapidly than before.

Although there were some hopes that France would obtain most favored nation status from the United States such aspirations played a minor role in drawing the government into the new nation's War for Independence. French motives were almost entirely geopolitical and for the first and only time in history France could concentrate its resources on an overseas, colonial war. From the French point of view, the result was a sensible restoration of the strategic balance

of power so seriously overthrown in 1763, but the cost of success had been more than the kingdom could bear. In 1783 the minister of the marine, the marquis de Castries, restored partial limits on foreign trade in the West Indies, but four years later Controller General Charles de Calonne proposed to the Assembly of Notables that these restrictions be abolished, an idea enacted by the National Assembly in 1789–1790. During this final decade, however, the French saw not only that they had failed to gain commercial preference from the United States, in whose interest they had invested so much treasure, but also that American traders had gained virtual command over the trade of the French Antilles.

The history of the French in America is, to a large degree, a history of trade. The exploration and exploitation of the northern half of the continent always depended upon an ever-expanding search for more and more furs. Fashion dictated the shape of New France. The development of the cod fishery governed the foundation and nature of French establishments on Canada's east coast, and Louisiana's history was shaped by the unsuccessful search for commercially exploitable commodities. At the same time, however, the history of French colonial trade and commerce forces one to eschew any crude economic or demographic determinism. All things considered politics and culture played fundamental roles in shaping the nature of trade and commerce and the history of colonial development.

BIBLIOGRAPHY

Balcom, B. A. *The Cod Fishery of Isle Royale, 1713–58.* Hull, Quebec, 1984.

Bliss, Michael. *Northern Enterprise: Five Centuries of Canadian Business.* Toronto, Ontario, 1987.

Brière, Jean François. *La Pêche française en Amérique du Nord au XVIIIe siècle.* Montreal, 1991.

Clark, John G. *New Orleans, 1718–1812: An Economic History.* Baton Rouge, La., 1970.

Dechêne, Louise. *Habitants et marchands de Montreal au XVIIe siècle.* Paris, 1974.

Eccles, W. J. *Essays on New France.* Toronto, Ontario, 1987.

Miquelon, Dale. *New France, 1701–1744: "A Supplement to Europe."* Toronto, Ontario, 1987.

Moore, Christopher. "The Other Louisbourg: Trade and Merchant Enterprise in Ile Royale, 1713–58." *Histoire Sociale–Social History* 12, no. 23 (1979):79–96.

Ouellet, Fernand. *Economy, Class, and Nation in Quebec: Interpretive Essays.* Edited and translated by Jacques A. Barbier. Toronto, Ontario, 1991.

Phillips, Paul C. *The Fur Trade.* Norman, Okla., 1961.

Price, Jacob M. *France and the Chesapeake: A History of the French Tobacco Monopoly, 1674–1791, and of Its Relationship to the British and American Tobacco Trades.* 2 vols. Ann Arbor, Mich., 1973.

Pritchard, James. "The Pattern of French Colonial Shipping to Canada Before 1760." *Revue française d'histoire d'outre-mer* 63, no. 231 (1976):189–210.

Quinn, David B., ed. *New American World: A Documentary History of North America to 1612.* 5 vols. New York, 1979–.

Surrey, N. M. Miller. *The Commerce of Louisiana During the French Regime, 1699–1763.* New York, 1916.

Tarrade, Jean. *Le Commerce coloniale de la France à la fin de l'ancien régime: L'évolution du régime de 'l'exclusif' de 1763 à 1789.* 2 vols. Paris, 1972.

Trudel, Marcel. *The Beginnings of New France, 1524–1663.* Translated by Patricia Claxton. Toronto, Ontario, 1973.

Usner, Daniel H., Jr. "The Frontier Exchange Economy of the Lower Mississippi Valley in the Eighteenth Century." *William and Mary Quarterly,* 3rd ser., 44, no. 2 (1987):165–192.

———. *Indians, Settlers, and Slaves in a Frontier Exchange Economy: The Lower Mississippi Valley Before 1783.* Chapel Hill, N.C., 1992.

James Pritchard

SEE ALSO **Relations with the Parent Country** and **The West Indies and North America;** and the map accompanying this article and **The West Indies and North America.**

THE SPANISH BORDERLANDS

OCCUPATION OF FAR NORTHERN New Spain was an essentially defensive enterprise requiring the cooperation of frontiersmen, who made up the presidial companies and supporting populations, and the church, mostly in the form of Franciscan and Jesuit missionaries. With the possible exception of New Mexico, the Spanish outpost provinces of what is now the southern United States never developed strong and diverse economies. Until the end of the colonial period, the northern rim of Spanish America relied on intercolonial trade and foreign commerce to obtain all but the most basic subsistence items. Moreover, in the course of the eighteenth century, pacification of potentially hostile Indians along a large portion of the frontier depended on the distribution of gifts, often in competition with French and British traders. Distances, imperial security considerations, and limited demographic growth also help account for the fact that the region experienced only marginal economic development.

THE IMPERIAL COMMERCIAL STRUCTURE

As the first of the European powers in the New World, the Spanish had to invent a colonial structure that could be managed from across an ocean. The Spanish were interested not in mere trade with the newly discovered lands but in their incorporation; therefore the commercial system devised had to be closely linked to a governmental structure geared to that end. Because Spanish Crown policy at the turn of the sixteenth century focused on consolidating power to itself, it is not surprising that the commercial apparatus designed at the time should be highly centralized.

In 1503 Ferdinand and Isabella established the Casa de Contratación (House of Trade) in the city of Seville to manage the transatlantic empire. The Casa served as customs and emigration agency, admiralty court, and clearinghouse for nautical information. In these roles it issued licenses for sailing and passports to emigrants, collected customs duties, made sure the Crown got its royal fifth of precious metals produced, and trained the pilots who guided Spanish shipping across the Atlantic. In 1717 the Crown transferred the Casa to Cádiz, where most of the American traffic had moved in the latter part of the seventeenth century because of Seville's inadequate facilities for handling large ships. Changes in Spanish commercial policy toward the end of the eighteenth century, including the opening of a number of Spanish ports to American trade, led the Crown to close the Casa in 1790.

To further regulate, as well as to protect, its American trade, the Crown organized its commercial shipping into a dual convoy system around the mid sixteenth century. New Spain was serviced by the flota, a fleet of armed merchantmen and warships that sailed from Spain in May for Veracruz. South America was serviced by the *galeones*, which sailed in August for Cartagena and then went to Portobelo. After collecting American products brought from colonial centers to these ports, the fleets rendezvoused in Havana for the return voyage the following spring. The highly profitable transpacific trade was regulated through the Manila galleon, which sailed to and from Acapulco. Changes in naval technology and inroads by British and Dutch merchants into American markets contributed to the decline of the fleet system in favor of licensed independent merchantmen during the eighteenth century.

While the Casa de Contratación regulated American trade, transatlantic commercial activity was monopolized by the *consulado* (wholesale merchants' guild) of Seville from 1543 to 1594. The commercial houses represented in the *consulado* maintained agents in American ports who set the prices for goods traveling in both directions. As the prices and quality of Spanish commodities became uncompetitive toward the end of the sixteenth century, Seville *consulado* merchants became the agents of French and Italian merchants who controlled the vast majority of goods going to America. In 1594 the Crown granted the wholesalers of Mexico City a monopoly of trade in that viceroyalty, and in 1613 Lima's *consulado* received the same privilege for Peru. With the transatlantic trade in the hands of tightly run guilds that were able to set the prices for commodities being exported to Europe and Asia, wholesale commerce became the single most profitable business activity in the Indies from an early period.

In the course of three centuries, the commercial hierarchy that developed in Spanish America came to include not only dedicated import-export merchants, local retailers, and traders but a variety of individuals who made trade an ancillary activity to their main profession. At the top of the commercial world were the *comerciantes*, members of the appropriate *consulado*, most of whose business was in long-distance trade but who might operate a retail establishment in the colonial capital through an employee. Unlike modern corporate trading companies, these merchants most often operated in partnerships on contracts lasting no more than a few years. Many also acted as bankers to miners, *hacendados* or large landholders, and manufacturers. Investment by these men extended to the ownership of merchant ships, mule trains, and in later times, haciendas where the export products they dealt in were produced.

Beneath the *comerciantes* there operated a broad range of specialized commercial agents, retailers, and vendors. Factors or commission merchants represented the interests of *consulado* merchants in port cities. *Aviadores* or *habilitadores* specialized in supplying miners as well as frontier garrisons and missions. The *mercaderes* were shopkeepers, either independent retailers or agents of *comerciantes*. Tying the countryside into the imperial commercial network were the *tratantes*, dealers or traders who operated on credit extended by import-export houses. At the bottom of the ladder were the retail clerks, bookkeepers, and stock clerks hoping for advancement.

In competition with merchants, and sometimes acting in partnership with or as agents of *comerciantes*, were a number of officials, clergymen, viceregal court favorites, landowners, and entrepreneurs. *Encomenderos*, Spaniards granted a certain number of Indian tributaries in return for service to the Crown, soon found that their Indians constituted a captive market. Gathering locally produced goods, the *encomenderos* exchanged them or sold them to the Indians at inflated prices, a practice that became known as the *reparto de mercancías* (distribution of merchandise). With the waning of the *encomienda* system, *alcaldes mayores* and *corregidores*, royal officials equivalent to governors, took up this practice. Priests, too, looked to augmenting their earnings by participating in local trade, and it was common for bishops to take part in wholesale enterprises.

The empire's increasing size, the inflated price structure for imports caused by monopolies, and the undervaluation of American products in the Spanish trade all contributed to contraband. By the seventeenth century, most European goods being purchased by Spanish Americans came from elsewhere than Spain. Americans stood to gain by bypassing *consulado* merchandise, which was marked up to give Spanish *comerciantes* their profits, and dealing directly with French, Dutch, and English merchants. European merchants stood to gain by cutting out the Spanish middlemen in Seville-Cádiz and the additional costs of transshipment. Although contraband was a sizable problem in some areas, lack of documentation makes it almost impossible to study effectively.

Expanding economic activity in Spain and Spanish America and efforts to restore the empire's fortunes in the eighteenth century contributed to a series of changes in imperial policy commonly referred to as the Bourbon reforms. The process of administrative reforms begun in Spain under Philip V, following the War of the Spanish Succession, was extended to Spanish America in the 1760s. Under the intendant system, the most ambitious administrative reform undertaken between the 1760s and 1790s, the Crown made an effort to create a new class of royal officials responsible for public administration, finances, defense, and justice. The intendants oversaw large districts and operated through subdelegates, the replacements for the *corregidores* and *alcaldes mayores* who had previously controlled regional government and wielded substantial economic power. The reform ultimately proved a disappointment, as underpaid subdelegates resorted to the same economic practices, particularly the *reparto de mercancías,* as the officials they replaced.

The Bourbon reforms also included a series of trade reforms designed to expand business and commercial opportunities on both sides of the Atlantic. The Portobelo fleet, which carried the Peruvian trade, was abandoned during the first half of the century as newer and bigger independent merchantmen capable of rounding Cape Horn serviced that market directly. Trade with the new viceroyalties of Nueva Granada and La Plata was not organized in fleets. Finally, the Veracruz fleet was abandoned in 1789 in favor of independent Spanish merchant ships and those of friendly or neutral powers in times of war.

No longer tied to well-organized convoys sailing from central locations, the Crown slowly opened transatlantic trade to a number of peninsular and American cities between 1765 and 1789. Consequently, local commercial interests lobbied for the removal of the wholesale monopolies held by the *consulados* of Mexico City and Lima. In the mid 1790s other major colonial cities were granted their own *consulados,* including Veracruz and Guadalajara in New Spain. The Crown also experimented with chartered companies based on Dutch and British models and made efforts to curtail the illicit commercial activities of government officials and the clergy.

GENERAL CHARACTERISTICS OF BORDERLAND TRADE

The borderlands were linked to this imperial commercial network both through the military and missionary supply systems as well as through an irregular and limited civilian trade. Inefficiency and expense were hallmarks of the frontier trade network. The vast distances through uninhabited country, hostile Indian territories, and perilous coastal waters added to the cost of goods forced to travel to Veracruz and Havana before distribution. The small frontier populations and consequent limitations on profits resulted in a lack of interest in investment by large commercial houses. Specie scarcity and an absence of valuable export commodities hindered the growth of trade much beyond subsistence needs. French and English efficiency in trading with the Indians denied the Spanish much of the lucrative fur trade.

The strong military character of the Spanish Borderlands forms a good starting place for discussion of both long-distance and local trade from Florida to California. The *situado* (military payroll) formed a vital financial resource for most provinces. Although the system worked slightly differently for Florida, the *situado* formed the backbone of all the borderland economies except that of New Mexico. Paid in Mexico City until the latter part of the eighteenth century, most of the money never reached the hands of the soldiers. Instead, the garrisons had agents in the capital who purchased needed supplies as well as luxury items and arranged for their transportation to the frontier. Foodstuffs and locally produced goods were often bought by these officers for resale to the soldiery. The soldiers, each of whom had an account book, were credited with their salary and debited each time they took something from the company store. The local population could also buy at the garrison stores, which were staffed by civilian employees of the officer who controlled the *avío* (supplies). Although price schedules were occasionally issued to prevent gouging, inspections often revealed overcharging and the distribution of inferior quality goods.

Until the 1770s, when the presidial ordinances forbade *presidio* commanders from participating in the commercial exploitation of the soldiery, it was common for governors and captains to join forces with Mexico City merchants to extract a profit from the payroll and run the stores. In an effort to see that more of the salary made it into the hands of the soldiery, either in cash or merchandise, the reform regulations of 1772 required that each company elect an officer to act as *habilitado* (paymaster). It was his responsibility to personally purchase the supplies and maintain the appropriate accounts. The process was also made more efficient by allowing the *habilitados* to collect the *situado* at subtreasuries closer to the frontier, where they could then buy the needed supplies.

Like the *presidios,* the frontier missions were part of the imperial governmental structure. The missionaries received an annual *sínodo* (stipend) of from 350 to 450 pesos, payable in Mexico City and used to purchase the *avío,* which was then shipped directly to the missions. As a result this governmental payroll and provisioning system acted to inhibit the development of commercial activity on the frontier by limiting independent merchants' access to a large portion of the frontier population. On the other hand, in areas where *presidios* and missions constituted the only Hispanic markets, the *avíos* constituted the only available sources of supply of manufactured goods.

As frontier colonies matured and their populations and economies grew, the doors opened

to a small number of merchants who usually dealt in a variety of commodities rather than specializing in any one kind of merchandise. These men can be broadly categorized as either local producers turned part-time merchants or full-time immigrant petty merchants. In either case they were individuals willing to sink social as well as economic roots into the communities in which they operated and accept the limited profits inherent in operating in small markets. Of course in the specie scarce environment of the borderlands that fostered an essentially barter economy, almost anyone who produced more than he could consume became a trader of some sort.

Successful local producers often found their first market with a neighboring *presidio* by meeting its agricultural and livestock needs from the closest inexpensive source. Livestock and livestock by-product exports constituted the next step up in the commercialization of the frontier economies. Ranchers often purchased or took payment for their produce in merchandise, which they brought back to their provinces for sale. In some instances these individuals became traveling merchants, picking up and disposing of commodities along the routes they followed to and from their final destinations. Among these items were Indian trade goods, including buffalo hides and other skins, pottery, pine nuts, and blankets, as well as Hispanic products such as sheep, raw wool, soap, candles, and dried beef.

Full-time merchants were scarce on the far northern frontier. Everywhere they existed they operated on credit supplied by merchants of the interior, either in Mexico City or one of the northern regional centers in New Spain, and Havana or Veracruz in the case of Florida. The limitations of the frontier markets required these retailers to avoid specialization. Their establishments were often little more than poorly stocked general stores carrying a variety of hardware, kitchenware, dry goods, and comforts such as chocolate, liquors, coffee, and sugar. Most often working on the fringes of military communities, they found themselves forced to extend credit to soldiers whose pay was often in arrears. Barter for commodities that might find a market somewhere along the route of their next resupply trip to a commercial center was another mode of operation for frontier retailers.

Aside from the limitations on borderland commerce imposed by military and religious regulations, local producers and merchants faced competition from the missions. As livestock, grain, and textile producers, missions continually competed with civilian producer-marketers. Sometimes the competition extended into the realm of manufactures, which missionaries were accused of importing for sale rather than mission consumption. Often, however, the missions became involved in commercial transactions with local merchants, buying or selling on credit on behalf of the mission Indians.

Contraband was also a part of life on the Spanish Borderlands. Not only frontier merchants but governors, priests, military officers, and civilians participated in an active trade with Spain's European rivals. Guns, textiles, tools, and a wide variety of English and French notions were exchanged for pelts, grain, livestock, and sometimes even silver. British, and later American, traders dealt with Florida settlements both before and after British rule from 1763 to 1783. In California, too, English, American, and even Russian ships became common visitors. French traders found their way into New Mexico, Texas, and West Florida, both directly and through the agency of Indian intermediaries, but were replaced by Anglo-Americans even before the Louisiana Purchase.

REGIONAL VARIATIONS

Florida, the oldest of the Spanish Borderland colonies, remained the least developed at the end of the Spanish colonial period in 1821. During the seventeenth century, when Spanish control was effectively limited to Saint Augustine, the *situado* supplied almost all of the colony's needs. The absence of any meaningful development of commercially viable economic activities relegated the colony to dependence on New Spain, Cuba, and the British North American colonies for almost all its needs.

Not surprisingly, the British presence in North America enabled English merchants to become important players in Florida trade during the eighteenth century. Among the eighteenth-century reforms aimed at correcting the inadequacies of paying the Florida *situado* in New

Spain and organizing the *avíos* there was the transfer of commercial responsibility to the Royal Havana Company. By 1740 the company had come to the same conclusion Florida residents had reached in the late 1600s: that the British colonies made the most logical source of trade goods for Saint Augustine. Pensacola, which until its transfer to the British in 1763 had relied on French trade for survival, became a center of British-Indian trading, a situation which was allowed to continue during the second Spanish period after 1783.

One distinctive feature of Florida commerce was that it could, during times of war, supplement its normally lean pickings through disposal of ships and cargoes taken by privateers. Despite the fact that the Royal Havana Company used British colonial merchants to supply the province, most prizes brought into Saint Augustine during the eighteenth century were English. These cargoes found eager buyers among the few Spanish merchants of Saint Augustine, who were otherwise dependent on the irregular arrival of *avíos* and *situados*.

California, the last of the Spanish Borderland provinces, had a commercial history similar to Florida's. Settled by overland expeditions from Sonora and Arizona, California's overland link to the rest of New Spain was cut off during the 1780s, making the province totally dependent on supply ships from the Pacific port of San Blas in Nueva Galicia, northwest of Guadalajara. Although the Spanish managed to keep their English, Russian, and American rivals out of California until 1790, interest in seal and otter skins and provisions from the missions resulted in regular contacts thereafter. The eagerness of missionaries and a few successful *rancheros* to find markets for their grain, hides, and skins combined with the inadequate military resources of the province to prevent governors from effectively impeding foreign trade.

The missions soon proved to be the most effective commercial actors in Spanish California. It was through the missions that Spanish authorities hoped to establish an active trade of otter furs with China in exchange for mercury to be employed in refining silver in present-day Mexico. Competition with English and Russian traders soon led to an opening of the Spanish otter trade to nonmission suppliers. This was followed up by other liberalizing laws that allowed Spanish traders to deal with the coastal Indians as far north as Nootka. Disruption of the supply system at the outbreak of the Mexican War of Independence created a demand for goods that the foreigners, Americans in particular, were eager to fill. The missions, with access to Indian labor, produced large surpluses of grain and livestock for which they were eager to find markets, even on illicit terms.

The search for markets by frontier producers was complicated by the absence, in most regions, of commodities of sufficient value to attract substantial investments. Texas faced this dilemma throughout the colonial period. Because Indian hostilities and remoteness discouraged settlement and the missions enjoyed access to neophyte communal labor, the small Hispanic population found it difficult to expand agriculture beyond a subsistence level. Only San Antonio regularly had surpluses of maize to sell to other communities in Coahuila and Nuevo Santander, as well as to the downriver *presidio* of La Bahía. This was a sporadic commerce, however, one often carried on by the farmers themselves, individually or in a group.

The most important trade item Texas had to offer was cattle. As early as the 1740s, the same mule trains that brought merchandise for the *presidios* and missions in the San Antonio region returned to Coahuila with dried beef, tallow, soap, and candles. The rapid, and feral, propagation of the cattle that came to be called longhorns in the nineteenth century allowed long drives to take place starting around 1770, about one hundred years before the Chisholm Trail was opened. The destination of cattle drives from San Antonio and La Bahía were neighboring *presidios* in Coahuila, towns in that province and Nuevo Santander, and the annual trade fair in Saltillo. A number of legal drives from the San Antonio region were also made into Louisiana, particularly to supply Spanish forces fighting the English during the American War of Independence. And toward the end of the eighteenth century, the East Texas settlement of Nacogdoches developed a considerable trade in horses with Louisiana.

Throughout the frontier the availability of communal mission labor to the Franciscans gave them an often unfair advantage over civilian producers in commercializing their products. In New Mexico this was the case up to the time of the Pueblo Revolt of 1680. In fact that province's reliance on the mission convoys for imports made the missionaries powerful commercial actors throughout the seventeenth century. Matters changed after the reconquest, however, as the missionaries were relegated to the margins of the Pueblo communities and lost access to most of the Indian labor.

It was in New Mexico that the Spanish formed the most meaningful trade relations with unincorporated Indians. Gaining access to pre-Hispanic trade fairs at which Plains Indians traded buffalo products for cotton goods, pottery, and maize, the seventeenth-century Spanish settlers introduced ironwares and firearms into the equation. Later, horses and mules were added to the list of Spanish goods; this trend reversed itself toward the end of the eighteenth century, when the Comanche brought horses and mules to trade for other goods.

One item of trade that proved very lucrative beyond the colonial period was Indian captives. In the seventeenth century, Indian slaves taken in "just wars" were often destined for agricultural or other commercial work. Captives obtained in trade with Plains Indians often became domestics in Spanish households. Slave raiding for purposes of obtaining children to be raised as servants was also common in Texas until dying out in the late 1740s, but in New Mexico the practice continued well into the Mexican period.

The constant raiding, by both Spanish and Plains Indians, created a very volatile climate for trade. The solution proved to be an annual mule convoy in the late fall, which brought in those manufactured and luxury goods in demand in the province and left with the local produce—buffalo and cattle hides, woolens, cotton blankets, piñon nuts, wine from the El Paso area, and sheep. The large size of the convoys provided safety but also put New Mexicans at the mercy of the Chihuahua merchants, who had the funds or credit to organize the expeditions. Because these merchants made sure that the value of the merchandise brought into the province exceeded the value of goods leaving New Mexico, the province existed in a continual state of debt.

548

BIBLIOGRAPHY

Archibald, Robert. "The Economy of the Alta California Mission, 1803–1821." *Southern California Quarterly* 58, no. 2 (1976):227–240.

Bethel, Leslie, ed. *Colonial Spanish America.* Cambridge, England, 1987.

Deagan, Kathleen. *Spanish St. Augustine: The Archeology of a Colonial Creole Community.* New York, 1983.

Gillespie, William R. "Survival of a Frontier Presidio: St. Augustine and the Subsidy and Private Contract Systems, 1680–1702." *Florida Historical Quarterly* 62, no. 3 (1984):273–295.

Gutiérrez, Ramón A. *When Jesus Came, the Corn Mothers Went Away: Marriage, Sexuality, and Power in New Mexico, 1500–1846.* Stanford, Calif., 1991.

Hinojosa, Gilberto Miguel. *A Borderlands Town in Transition: Laredo, 1755–1870.* College Station, Tex., 1983.

Jones, Oakah L., Jr. *Nueva Vizcaya: Heartland of the Spanish Frontier.* Albuquerque, N.Mex., 1988.

Lockhart, James, and Stuart B. Schwartz. *Early Latin America: A History of Colonial Spanish America and Brazil.* Cambridge, England, 1983.

Moorhead, Max L. *New Mexico's Royal Road: Trade and Travel on the Chihuahua Trail.* Norman, Okla., 1958.

———. *The Presidio: Bastion of the Spanish Borderlands.* Norman, Okla., 1975.

Officer, James E. *Hispanic Arizona, 1536–1856.* Tucson, Ariz., 1987.

Ogden, Adele. *The California Sea Otter Trade, 1784–1848.* Berkeley, Calif., 1941.

Simmons, Marc. *Spanish Government in New Mexico.* Albuquerque, N.Mex., 1968.

Teja, Jesús F. de la. "Land and Society in 18th Century San Antonio de Béxar: A Community on New Spain's Northern Frontier." Ph.D. diss., University of Texas at Austin, 1988.

Thomas, David Hurst, ed. *Columbian Consequences.* Vol. 1, *Archeological and Historical Perspectives on the Spanish Borderlands West.* Washington, D.C., 1989.

Jesús F. de la Teja

SEE ALSO **Relations with the Parent Country** and **The West Indies and North America;** and the map accompanying this article and **The West Indies and North America.**

CURRENCY AND FINANCE

THE BRITISH COLONIES

DURING THE EIGHTEENTH CENTURY, the thirteen colonies made substantial progress in the development of their monetary and financial systems. Their use of inconvertible fiat currency (paper money not backed by specie) was particularly innovative compared with practices in other countries. Contrary to the interpretative framework found in many older historical accounts, subsequent scholarly research has revealed that the colonies enjoyed more successes than failures in their monetary experiments. Fiat currency differed from bank notes, another contemporary form of paper money, because it was not legally convertible into specie at a fixed rate of exchange; instead it was backed by colonial governments and redeemed by the payment of taxes and the payment of debts to public loan offices.

In Britain on the other hand, private bank notes were the only form of paper money in circulation. These monetary units were readily convertible into coinage at the holder's option. They circulated in Great Britain, particularly Scotland, but were notably absent in the colonies, since no private firms were organized to issue convertible monies on a sustained basis. While they recognized the legitimacy of specie-backed paper monies, British political leaders univer-

sally condemned inconvertible fiat money as inherently unsound and economically destabilizing because of its potential for uncontrollable depreciation. Nonetheless nine colonies continued to issue fiat money and give it legal status in their financial systems right up until independence. Indeed, confrontations between several colonial legislatures and the Board of Trade over fiat paper were the second most identifiable source of political friction with the mother country during the 1760s, trailing only imperial taxes in public debates.

Most colonies showed progress in strengthening their embryonic capital markets. Everywhere except Virginia persons with equity in real estate periodically had the opportunity to borrow funds for long-term investment from public loan offices at low interest rates. Private markets for mortgage debt likewise thickened and broadened over the course of the eighteenth century in many regions. Public borrowing from private sources emerged as well; after mid century the four New England legislatures periodically drew on indigenous capital markets to finance modest deficit budgets. These colonies sold treasury notes with maturities ranging from two to five years to local investors, and their repayment record was unblemished. Overall, holding personal wealth in interest-bearing financial instruments—as a supplement to more traditional investments in land and other tangible assets—became more common in British North America as the decades passed.

Another innovative feature of the colonial financial services sector was the formation of the first successful insurance company in North America. Organized by Benjamin Franklin in 1752, the Philadelphia Contributorship for the Insurance of Houses from Loss by Fire was a nonprofit mutual company. The policyholders were the owners; in addition to the payment of annual premiums, they were subject to joint assessments in the event of extraordinary fire losses. The company recruited brigades of fire fighters which fought blazes that threatened insured properties. After independence numerous companies, both profit oriented and nonprofit, were formed to provide fire insurance, and others were organized to cover the risk of loss of ships at sea.

COLONIAL MONEY: COIN AND PAPER SUBSTITUTES

Money in the colonial era had two fundamental economic functions. First, it served as a store of value for persons who sought to preserve accumulated wealth. High-value specie coins were especially useful for this purpose. Since money was a sterile asset generating no income stream, few persons, including the very rich, actually held large money balances relative to their overall wealth. In similar fashion credit balances with merchants and bankers usually paid no interest. Few households held more than 5 percent of their net assets in monetary units.

The second useful purpose of money was to act as a medium of exchange in all forms of trading activity, thereby providing a convenient alternative to crude barter arrangements. Since money had universal properties, it facilitated mutual exchanges of goods and services by allowing the population to settle promptly differences in valuation whether large or small. Merchants frequently used gold coins to negotiate wholesale transactions. The typical farm or artisan household kept a pouch of intermediate- and low-value coins to pay for routine purchases of everyday goods and services.

For most of the seventeenth century, monetary policies in the colonies conformed with British precedents. Before 1690 most of the monetary units in general circulation were metallic.

Because Parliament refused to allow the private export of English coin or the establishment of a mint overseas, the colonies relied mostly on foreign coinage. The Crown could export coin to buy military supplies and pay soldiers wages, but private parties were required to send overseas bills of exchange, foreign monies, or bullion. While French, Portuguese, and Dutch monies were fairly common, Spanish coins minted in Mexico and other parts of Latin America constituted the core money supply for the thirteen colonies. The colonies exported much of their surplus output of goods to Caribbean islands, and inflows of hard monies from that region added regularly to the money stock. Some English coins entered the colonies as the result of routine British military expenditures—the purchase of local supplies and the payment of wages to hired troops—and even larger quantities arrived in bulk when Parliament reimbursed certain colonies for expenses incurred in raising armies to battle native tribes and French outposts.

High-value coins were universally gold. Silver coins represented intermediate values. Copper, tin, lead, and compounds of these less valuable metals were the main components of so-called token coins (counterparts of modern quarters, dimes, nickels, and pennies). The Spanish silver dollar, along with its fractional divisions, called *reales,* were popular with the general population and became the model for the United States coinage system after independence.

To discourage the shipment of foreign coins overseas and simultaneously promote their retention in the home market, several colonial legislatures, beginning in the mid seventeenth century, began assigning foreign coins somewhat higher legal tender values than was fully justified by their measurable metallic content. In an effort to create greater monetary uniformity within the empire, Queen Anne proclaimed in 1704 that foreign coins circulating in the colonies could be officially overvalued by one-third. Sometimes ignoring the exact terms of the royal decree, the thirteen colonial governments adopted diverse overvaluation schedules, and several went beyond the one-third increase authorized by the Crown.

The sole uniform monetary standard throughout the British Empire was the designated value of coins struck at the royal mint in England. Commonly known as sterling, the money was denominated pounds, shillings, and pence at the rate of 12 pence to 1 shilling and 20 shillings to 1 pound. To distinguish these official values from their overseas counterparts, contemporaries usually cited the colonial units as "proclamation" monies. Since the colonial legislatures had no means of enforcing a rigid exchange ratio between sterling and proclamation monies, their market rates fluctuated from month to month and year to year in response to trade flows and capital movements. The rating systems used by the colonies for foreign coins as well as for fiat paper were varied and complex. Unless otherwise specified, monetary units will be given at their proclamation values.

The Money Supply in the Colonies

The colonies maintained, on balance, a sufficiently large money supply, consisting of coins supplemented by paper currency, to finance a comparatively high level of per capita economic output throughout the colonial era. Prices rose gradually during the eighteenth century, which suggests that money supplies in the Western Hemisphere were growing faster than the production of goods and services. The persistent complaints of contemporaries about shortages of monies must be taken with a grain of salt; these statements were not the unbiased accounts of disinterested observers. Periodic shortages of monies in certain colonies, which sometimes lasted for months or even several years, did occur. Yet, the problem was never chronic, since the free flow of specie in international financial markets kept the distribution of the stock of money in general equilibrium. If more monies had been desired to support economic activity, the colonists had other tangible goods in abundance that could have been exchanged overseas to build up the supply of domestic coinage. Based on their increasing understanding of money flows in this era, economic historians have concluded that the population held about as much of its wealth in monetary assets as most households normally required during the seventeenth and eighteenth centuries.

To supplement the supply of coins, the colonies injected various paper substitutes into the monetary system. Commodity monies were the

first addition. In some regions farmers received transferable certificates in return for depositing tobacco and grains in governmentally regulated warehouses, and these warehouse certificates circulated widely as a medium of exchange. In Virginia, for example, tobacco certificates were the only form of paper money in circulation until the 1750s.

Fiat currency, unsupported by either specie or a marketable commodity, entered the economy beginning in the 1690s. The colonial legislatures invariably designated fiat currency as legal tender in the payment of taxes and public debts and sometimes in the settlement of private debts. Currency was issued in a range of denominations—from large bills such as £20 to amounts as small as 1 shilling. Over half the bills had a face value of less than 10 shillings, which made them widely accessible and convenient for negotiating everyday transactions. The fiat paper issued in one colony often spilled over colonial borders into contiguous provinces, where recipients accepted it on a voluntary basis at prevailing exchange rates. Merchants in Philadelphia often held—in addition to quantities of Spanish, Portuguese, Dutch, and English coins—the fiat currencies of Pennsylvania, New York, New Jersey, Delaware, and Maryland.

COLONIAL FIAT CURRENCIES AND MONETARY POLICIES

Tax Anticipation Bills

There were two broad categories of fiat currency, which were distinguishable by the backing mechanisms devised to support their values. In the first category were tax anticipation bills, defined as temporary monies issued in advance of the collection of taxes. The first emission occurred in Massachusetts in 1690. The treasury was short of coinage to cover the salaries of soldiers returning from a campaign against the French, and the legislature voted to issue a modest volume of "bills of exchange" (the contemporary terminology for fiat currency) as an expedient. Over the next few years the legislature collected the necessary taxes, and the outstanding paper was retired on schedule. The success of this monetary experiment led Massachusetts to repeat the procedure in future decades, and other colonies soon became imitators. The necessity of financing military adventures, usually against Native tribes on the frontier or against the French in Canada, was the main justification for new issues of fiat currency.

On other occasions fresh monies were emitted in an effort to stimulate lethargic local economies. Some economic historians have cited this policy as a forerunner of modern Keynesian pump priming—deficit spending to boost aggregate demand. When Virginia joined the ranks in 1755, all thirteen colonies had emitted some form of tax anticipation notes. The terms of issuance varied greatly, not only from colony to colony but also within a single province. Some issues carried a compound interest component, while others were redeemable merely at face value. Colonial legislatures routinely authorized overlapping currency issues, with maturity dates ranging from two to twenty years after emission.

When legislatures acted responsibly by limiting the volume of fiat currency outstanding, collecting the necessary taxes, and diligently meeting redemption schedules, their currencies resisted long-term depreciation and maintained purchasing power for decades. Colonies in this grouping included Maryland, Pennsylvania, New Jersey, New York, and Virginia—plus South Carolina after 1731. The exchange rates for their respective currencies vis à vis British sterling fluctuated at times in response to changing market conditions, but these emissions never suffered spiraling depreciation. These adventuresome colonies were successful innovators in the maintenance of financial systems with fiat currency as a substantial component. Other colonies were less successful.

During the first half of the eighteenth century, the currencies of certain colonies lost purchasing power, depreciating steadily and irreversibly. Their legislatures became lax about applying the taxes required to retire old issues; meanwhile, new emissions were authorized to finance budget deficits. Gresham's law went into effect: bad money (depreciating paper) drove good money (coin) out of circulation. Gold and silver coins were subject to hoarding or export. The main offenders were the four New England colonies from 1730 to 1750 plus South Carolina

from 1710 to 1725. Their performance affirmed the views of European critics of fiat currency, who had predicted that fiat issues would ultimately result in a heavily depreciated currency. South Carolina allowed the situation to get out of control in the 1720s, and Parliament responded by freezing the size of its outstanding fiat currency at the level prevailing in 1731.

In New England heavy depreciation of fiat paper in the second quarter of the century led Parliament to enact the Currency Act of 1751. Previously emitted currency issues were allowed to remain in circulation until their assigned maturity dates, but no new emissions were permitted in the four northernmost colonies. The goal was to return the region over a period of years to a monetary system based strictly on specie. To ease the transition from paper to hard money, Parliament paid a substantial subsidy—mainly in Spanish coin—to reimburse the colonies for expenses incurred in recent military campaigns against French forces in Canada. The four colonies used the proceeds of this shipment to retire much of the fiat currency in circulation. From mid century until the outbreak of the War for Independence, the monetary system in New England generally paralleled its counterpart in the mother country.

During the Seven Years' War, the middle and southern colonies issued large volumes of fiat currency to finance the military effort, while the New England colonies sold an increased number of treasury bills to local investors. Parliament ultimately reimbursed the colonies for about 40 percent of their aggregate wartime expenditures. During the late 1750s and early 1760s, taxes rose everywhere to retire the excessive volume of fiat currency and treasury bills outstanding. The three colonies that bore the largest share of the financial burden—Massachusetts, Virginia, and Pennsylvania—made remarkable progress in terms of sinking the debt associated with war. The goal of most legislatures was to retire their war debts within a decade, and the majority met that challenge according to schedule. The successful management of their finances during the Seven Years' War gave Americans a great deal of reassurance about their capacity to support military operations over vast territories and for lengthy periods of time.

Asset-Backed Fiat Currency

The second type of fiat currency placed in circulation arose from transactions initiated by public loan offices—or land banks, as these institutions were called by contemporaries. Every colony except Virginia created a loan office. These institutions performed too few financial services to qualify as banks by modern standards; for example, they accepted no deposits and made only mortgage loans. These public agencies provided support for their currency based on the security of real estate pledged as collateral. All citizens with equity in real estate were eligible to borrow up to one-half of the market value of land or one-third of the market value of residences. The eligibility of residences permitted landless artisans to obtain funds, although the vast majority of borrowers were yeoman farmers or the owners of large tracts. Most borrowers used the funds to enhance their productive assets—land, agricultural improvements, bonded workers, and the like—but they were free to use the money for the repayment of pressing private debts or the purchase of luxury goods.

To guarantee wide access to public credit facilities, the legislatures placed modest limits on how much money an individual could obtain from the loan office. The rules were designed to prevent a few very wealthy people from gaining access to a disproportionate share of the loan pool. For example, the minimum loan in New York was £25 and the maximum £100, the latter a fairly modest figure. The repayment period ran from eight to twelve years for original borrowers, with amortization schedules stipulating annual payments of interest and principal. The inflowing currency was either retired from circulation or reloaned to other eligible borrowers.

This mechanism of issuance was highly conducive to preventing monetary depreciation, since in the absence of a collapse in real estate values, which never happened in the colonies on a grand scale, the currency was amply secured by mortgages. These monies were in steady demand because borrowers regularly needed funds to make their annual amortization payments. Unlike tax anticipation bills, the responsibility for retiring these issues lay with private parties; retirement was not dependent on the willingness of legislators to vote the requisite taxes. If a borrower failed to repay an outstanding mortgage, the loan office could foreclose, sell the property at auction, and use the proceeds to sink that portion of the paper money outstanding. As a result defaults were low and losses rare in most colonies. The major exceptions to this generalization were the loan offices in South Carolina and Rhode Island prior to mid century, where hundreds of irresponsible debtors conspired to evade repayment. Elsewhere this type of asset-backed fiat currency had an outstanding record in terms of maintaining its value relative to specie and financial instruments denominated in sterling.

In addition to injecting a reliable currency into the money stock, mortgage loans generated a stream of interest income for provincial governments. The interest rates on loans varied from colony to colony, but the general range was from 5 to 8 percent. The low rates reflected, in part, religious concerns about usury, but they also revealed a general consensus about the validity of public subsidies for programs designed to promote economic development. The legislatures also welcomed these interest revenues as a supplement to regular taxes. In the middle colonies—New York, Pennsylvania, and New Jersey—interest income was sufficiently large to cover all, or nearly all, expenditures in annual budgets for a series of years. Taxpayers benefited, since their assessments were correspondingly lower; in some years the tax burden fell to zero.

TRADE AND THE ANGLO-AMERICAN CREDIT NETWORK

The absence of commercial banks and other financial institutions tends to obscure the critical role of the credit system in supporting the flow of goods and services through the colonial economy. Nonetheless the existence of facilities to permit merchants and their customers to acquire goods before making final payment was no less important in this period than after independence. Besides accommodating transactions in the mercantile sector, financial services were also available to fund investments in land, bonded workers, and other capital improvements. Persons seeking small cash loans usually turned to local elites who sometimes accommodated prospective borrowers in order to preserve access to local labor supplies in critical times—for example, during the harvest season—or simply out of a sense of noblesse oblige.

Because of the seasonal nature of this largely agricultural economy, reliable financing between harvests was critical in stimulating output and facilitating trade. The use of book credit was common in financing direct exchanges of goods between households as well as indirect exchanges through merchant intermediaries. Farm households typically purchased supplies on credit in the winter and spring months and then paid off their debts in summer and fall when their crops went to market. The sums needed to finance working capital—which consisted mainly of inventories plus accounts receivable from customers—typically accounted for the bulk of the investment in a mercantile firm. The suppliers of goods, whether foreign or domestic, routinely offered credit services in conjunction with merchandising functions, since granting a customer sufficient time to make payment was a vital factor in promoting sales. Given slow communication and transportation networks, payment terms often stretched out over long periods of time—from twelve to eighteen months was not unusual for overseas debts and up to nine months was common in the domestic market.

A substantial amount of the credit extended to merchants originated in London and other locales of England. The volume of credit outstanding climbed steadily over the course of the eighteenth century in response to population growth and the expanding size of markets in North America. By the early 1770s, British mercantile capital provided sufficient funding to support approximately one-quarter of colonial aggregate debt. The extension of overseas credit was skewed, however, for up to 80 percent went to residents of the southern colonies. British merchants loaned up to £7 per capita to the free population in the southern colonies compared with only £1.5 to persons in the middle colonies and New England.

The regional differential in the level of foreign credit was a reflection of prevailing trading patterns. The southern colonies regularly shipped huge quantities of tobacco, rice, and indigo to British merchants and received finished goods on return voyages, whereas exports from the northern colonies directly to Great Britain were limited. British merchants sometimes played a dual financial role in the Chesapeake colonies. They not only financed retail customers—namely, those planters whose purchases of finished goods exceeded the value of tobacco shipped overseas for sale—but after 1750 they were also actively engaged in financing an increasing number of indigenous wholesale accounts with credit lines running as high as £5,000 or even more.

The entire mercantile community was tied together through long chains of credit that extended from domestic and foreign wholesalers and manufacturers, who rested at the top of the ladder, down to part-time storekeepers in remote areas. Individual merchants invariably granted each other credit facilities to promote the flow of goods and generate sales; however, remittances were often slow. In frontier regions, for example, the process of remitting funds back to the original source of credit did not begin until a storekeeper had sold the goods in question to a local farmer or artisan, also probably on credit. Six months later the buyer paid the debt in cash, or perhaps in kind, and the frontier storekeeper remitted the proceeds to a mercantile firm in a nearby town, who was likewise in debt to counterparts in more populous towns nearer the coastline. Several more remittances between merchants in progressively larger trading centers might be necessary before the original seller of merchandise, who had also provided the initial credit, finally received payment. From start to finish, the whole process of selling goods wholesale and collecting payments from retail customers through a chain of intermediaries could easily take from twelve to twenty-four months.

Mercantile operations were risky in general because of the slow movement of goods, the possibility of losses in transit due to bad weather, and periodic financial crises. A minor disturbance in financial markets in one part of the world could quickly escalate into a full-blown panic affecting economic activity in distant lands. A credit crunch in London in 1772, largely unrelated to events in the Western Hemisphere, had unfortunate consequences for debtors in the colonies. British creditors as a group sought to bolster their liquidity in an effort to survive the panic, and a substantial number demanded immediate settlement of the debts of their long-standing North American customers. British mercantile firms refused to honor the bills of exchange (documents similar to checks) drawn on them by American exporters and returned these financial instruments back across the ocean to their endorsers.

These efforts at self-preservation in London put unanticipated financial pressure on colonial accounts with outstanding debit balances, some of which had not been paid down to zero for years. The net result was hardship for many indebted Americans and in some cases bankruptcies. The main impact was in the Chesapeake region, where numerous customers were angered by the unfortunate turn of events. Some planters felt betrayed by their creditor "friends" in London, who had generously offered financing for extended periods of time and had then suddenly insisted on a complete settlement of accounts. Coming on the eve of the outbreak of hostilities, the fallout of this credit crisis served to undermine the attachment of many influential colonial planters to their business connections in London, and this episode may have contributed to the momentous decision to declare independence in 1776.

In the domestic market, credit was often available to finance purchases of real property—land and structures. As discussed earlier, prospective borrowers with equity in real estate periodically had the opportunity to obtain monies from public loan offices. But most mortgages were routinely financed by private parties rather than through governmental agencies. The goal of most colonial households was to acquire their own farmland, and arrangements to finance land transfers were fairly common. Buyers seeking mortgage money turned almost exclusively to local sources. Households with accumulated wealth were sometimes willing to diversify their holdings by adding financial instruments to their portfolio of assets. Indeed the inclusion of mortgages in the estates of deceased persons increased over the course of the eighteenth century. Many real estate transactions were financed by the seller who accepted a down payment and took back a mortgage maturing in from two to five years. (Americans in the 1980s called similar transactions "creative financing," not realizing that before the rise of organized financial institutions, such arrangements were the norm in rural areas for generations.)

The credit system that served the colonial economy was peculiar in regard to its extremely decentralized structure. The system was institutionally immature, yet it functioned sufficiently well to support high rates of economic growth for a premodern economy—higher than anywhere else around the globe in that era. Since no banks existed to act as intermediaries, loans were negotiated directly between savers and borrowers. Communities were still small enough and personal networks broad enough that lenders seeking safe havens for their accumulated wealth were typically able to find and come to terms with borrowers seeking funding for worthwhile projects. Most investments that merited funding eventually received the financial support to make them a reality. The informality and personal character of the colonial financial system belied its unusual degree of responsiveness to the requirements of the free population. Much of this heritage of communal interdependence and personal contact was preserved after independence; in the nineteenth century, Americans chose a financial system characterized by an atomized structure with thousands of independent commercial banks in thousands of small towns across the nation.

CONFRONTATION WITH PARLIAMENT

When Parliament had debated the currency legislation passed in 1751, some members advocated banning fiat currency everywhere in North America, not just in New England. The leadership demurred because the agents of the other nine colonies argued persuasively that depreciation was not a serious problem within their borders. After Virginia issued its first volume of fiat currency in 1755, however, those London merchants heavily involved in the Chesapeake trade became increasingly agitated about the risks associated with the settlement of long-standing debts in fiat monies. Rumors circulated in London during the early 1760s that judgments in colonial courts often discriminated against British creditors, who ostensibly were forced to accept, under prevailing legal tender laws, fiat currencies that sometimes passed at substantial discounts relative to sterling. In truth the claims of inequities in colonial courts were exaggerated, but the pressure mounted for legislative action to calm the fears of influential London merchants.

In response to intense lobbying, Parliament passed the Currency Act of 1764. It outlawed all future emissions of fiat currency with any legal tender provisions whatsoever—public or private—in the nine colonies not covered by the earlier act. The colonial legislatures deeply resented this unprecedented interference in their domestic affairs, and they behaved defiantly. They objected because, in most instances, their monetary systems had been managed responsibly for decades, and none had experienced irreversible depreciation. Colonial political leaders saw no logical reason for denying legal tender status to fiat monies in public transactions—tax payments and loan office payments—since private creditors were not threatened by such provisions. Many citizens viewed the punitive act as another aspect of a conspiratorial British plot to exert increasingly greater control over political and economic affairs in North America.

For most of the next decade, the colonial legislatures continued to pass laws authorizing fresh issues of fiat currency irrespective of the parliamentary prohibition. By threatening to refuse payment of executive salaries, they coerced their royal governors into submitting these currency acts to the Board of Trade for approval in direct violation of explicit governance instructions. The board predictably disallowed some currency acts, but after listening to the pleadings of colonial agents stationed in London, it reluctantly assented to others.

The controversy died down after 1773, when Parliament consented to amend the law to allow the continued issuance of fiat currency with legal tender status in public but not in private transactions. British merchants raised no objections to this change in the statute, since they and other creditors remained fully protected from the risks of fluctuating exchange rates for colonial currencies. In retrospect Parliament's application of the 1764 law to public-sector payments had served no useful purpose; its net effect had been to stir up colonial senti-

ments against the impact of British rule. The Crown's attempt to root out the alleged heresy of fiat paper and to purify thereby the monetary system in all of North America was perhaps a well-intentioned effort at reform, but it was extremely unpopular in the colonies and ultimately proved counterproductive. When Thomas Jefferson drafted the Declaration of Independence, many signers from the middle colonies vividly remembered the clashes with imperial officials over the legitimacy of fiat currency and the controversy surrounding the colonists' rights to determine their internal monetary affairs.

With the benefit of two centuries of hindsight and a clearer understanding of how monetary events unfolded in the colonies, it seems fair to conclude that the Board of Trade's reservations about the propriety of fiat currency were unfounded. Contrary to British expectations and to the exaggerated reports circulating within the London mercantile community, all nine colonies exempted by the Currency Act of 1751 had managed their currency issues exceedingly well in the third quarter of the eighteenth century. Uncontrollable depreciation was never a problem anywhere in North America after mid century. Colonial fiat currency was not only useful as a medium of exchange, but it also served as a reliable store of value over the long run as well. In truth colonial legislatures were genuine innovators in the use of inconvertible public monies; since the abandonment of the gold standard in the twentieth century, a similar form of paper money has been in universal use.

On the eve of independence, fiat currency remained popular in the nine colonies south of New England, and in most areas inconvertible paper had been a component of the money stock for decades. Under the circumstances it is not surprising that the Continental Congress and the states relied primarily on tax anticipation bills to finance over half the war effort. In the late 1770s, however, the sums issued were too massive and the taxes imposed too low. The public lost faith in the backing mechanism, and the wartime issues succumbed to persistent depreciation from 1777 to 1780. By 1781 fiat currencies, issued by both the Congress and the several states, had fallen to near zero in terms of purchasing power. Seven states later reinstituted systems of currency finance in the 1780s, but the Constitution drafted in 1787 outlawed fiat paper as a future option for state government. Once independent the United States reverted to the money system that had prevailed in Great Britain during the eighteenth century. The money stock after 1790 was composed of coinage and the bank notes issued by private financial institutions chartered by the federal and state legislatures.

BIBLIOGRAPHY

Brock, Leslie V. *The Currency of the American Colonies, 1700–1764: A Study in Colonial Finance and Imperial Relations.* New York, 1975. A reprint of a 1941 dissertation and probably the best single source on the topic.

Ernest, Joseph Albert. *Money and Politics in America, 1755–1775: A Study in the Currency Act of 1764 and the Political Economy of Revolution.* Chapel Hill, N.C., 1973.

Ferguson, E. James, "Currency Finance: An Interpretation of Colonial Monetary Practices." *William and Mary Quarterly,* 3rd ser., 10 (1953):153–180.

Hanson, John R. II. "Money in the Colonial American Economy: An Extension." *Economic Inquiry* 17 (1979):281–286.

Jones: Alice Hanson. *Wealth of a Nation To Be: The American Colonies on the Eve of the Revolution.* New York, 1980. A valuable source on the per capita holdings of monetary assets.

Lester, Richard A. "Currency Issues to Overcome Depressions in Pennsylvania, 1723 and 1729." *Journal of Political Economy* 46 (1938):324–375. Argues for the stimulative effect of currency issuance on local economy.

McCusker, John J. *Money and Exchange in Europe and America, 1600–1775: A Handbook.* Chapel Hill, N.C., 1978.

Michener, Ron. "Fixed Exchange Rates and the Quantity Theory in Colonial America." In *Empirical Studies in Velocity, Real Exchange Rates, Unemployment and Productivity,* edited by K. Brunner and A. H. Meltzer. Amsterdam, The Netherlands, 1987. Argues that the quantity theory of money is applicable to the colonial era.

Nettels, Curtis. *The Money Supply of the American Colonies Before 1720.* Madison, Wis., 1934.

Perkins, Edwin J. *The Economy of Colonial America.* New York, 1980; 2nd rev. ed., 1988. See the chapters on money and taxes.

Price, Jacob. *Capital and Credit in British Overseas Trade: The View from the Chesapeake, 1700–1776.* Cambridge, Mass., 1980.

Rothenberg, Winifred B. "The Emergence of a Capital Market in Rural Massachusetts, 1730–1838." *Journal of Economic History* 45 (1985):781–808. Reveals how much wealth was held in financial instruments.

Sheridan, Richard. "The British Credit Crisis of 1772 and the American Colonies." *Journal of Economic History* 20 (1960):61–186.

Smith, Bruce O. "Some Colonial Evidence on Two Theories of Money: Maryland and the Carolinas." *Journal of Political Economy* 93 (1985):1178–1211. Argues the importance of reliable backing in supporting the value of monies.

Weiss, Roger W. "The Issue of Paper Money in the American Colonies, 1720–1774." *Journal of Economic History* 30 (1970):770–784.

West, Robert Craig. "Money in the Colonial American Economy." *Economic Inquiry* 16 (1978):1–15. Asserts the importance of book credit.

Wicker, Elmus. "Colonial Monetary Standards Contrasted: Evidence from the Seven Years' War." *Journal of Economic History* 45 (1985):869–884.

Edwin J. Perkins

SEE ALSO **Local Government** and **Relations with the Parent Country.**

THE DUTCH COLONY

THROUGHOUT ITS BRIEF HISTORY, the economy of New Netherland struggled with a perennial shortage of specie. The mercantilistic relationship with the Amsterdam merchant cartels, which operated under license from the West India Company, prevented the accumulation of hard currency in the colony. The exchange of low-cost manufactured goods for colonial products meant most hard currency stayed in Amsterdam as profit on the account books of merchants. Cheap textiles, metal goods, and liquor were exchanged in New Netherland for furs, tobacco (mostly from English Virginia), and timber. By extending credit through their book accounts to colonial clients, the Amsterdam merchants came to enjoy a dominant position in New Netherland's trade. The activities of the Amsterdam merchants and the restrictions imposed by the

West India Company combined to create an unfavorable balance of trade between the colony and the fatherland. The deficit in colonial accounts drained New Netherland's economy of hard money.

DUTCH AND EUROPEAN COINS IN NEW NETHERLAND

The guilder or florin (expressed as fl.) was one of the least volatile and most highly prized of all currencies in the seventeenth century. The standardization of its metallic content, which remained unchanged for nearly two centuries, made it, along with sterling, the currency of choice among merchants. The florin contained 20 stuivers and a stuiver contained 16 *penningen*. A seventeenth-century florin would be worth about $9.90 in 1991 United States dollars.

There were various issues of florin circulating in the colony. The following types of florin are mentioned in New Netherland colonial documents: guilder or florin, goud guilder (2 fl., 8 stuivers), and Carolus guilder (1 fl., 10 stuivers). The Carolus guilder was equal to a *daelder,* and the *rijksdaelder* was the equivalent of 2 fl., 10 stuivers. A *rijksdaelder* of 50 stuivers traded for £0.23 in 1651.

The Spanish "piece of eight" was the most common and trusted of the foreign coins circulating in New Netherland. The piece of eight, or *pathienje* (expressed as P in colonial account books), was worth about 2 fl., 8 stuivers. In addition documents mention the Amsterdam ducat (3 fl., 3 stuivers), the *pond Vlaamsche,* or "Flemish pound" (6 fl.), and English shillings and pound sterling.

The exchange rates among the various coins fluctuated with the quality of the coin and the balance of payments. The quality of the coins was always a problem. So many shaved and clipped coins were in circulation that merchants had to set prices by weight rather than face value.

WAMPUM AND FURS

In the 1620s the directors of the Amsterdam chamber of the West India Company received reports from the company secretary in New Netherland suggesting that the specie problem might be solved by manipulating the money supply of the Indians. Dutch traders had observed a lively exchange between the coastal Indian tribes and those of the interior in what appeared to be black and white shells. They discovered that wampum (*sewant* in Dutch) was used as a currency of exchange by the Indians. The woodland Indians of the interior placed a high value on the tiny marine shells harvested by the coastal tribes along the beaches and inlets of Long Island Sound and elsewhere. The Dutch devised a system that exchanged cheap textiles, liquor, and firearms with the coastal tribes for wampum. They then traded wampum for furs with the interior woodland tribes. As the coastal tribes increased their harvests to purchase European goods, the supply of wampum grew, setting off an inflationary trend that persisted until the end of the Dutch period. In the meantime wampum, along with beaver pelts, had become the currency of the colony. In the last decades before the English conquest, New Netherland magistrates struggled to control the inflation in wampum by a series of laws.

In the spring of 1650, the director-general and council at New Amsterdam issued an ordinance to stop "the decline and depreciation of the loose wampum, among which is found much unpierced and only half finished [beads], made of stone, bone, glass, shells, horn, nay even of wood." The decline in the value and quality of wampum had caused "many inhabitants to complain, that with it they cannot go to market and buy any commodities, not even a little white bread or a mug of beer, from the traders, bakers and tapsters." In an effort to stem the tide of inflation, the council established an official exchange rate of one stuiver for six white beads or one stuiver for three black beads. Two categories of wampum were recognized as legal tender: good wampum that traded at the above rate and bad wampum that traded at the rate of eight white or four black beads for one stuiver. The effort was apparently unsuccessful, because eight years later the council officially devaluated wampum and set a new exchange rate of eight white or four black beads per stuiver.

Furs, also used as currency in New Netherland, traded at a rate of from 6 to 8 fl. per whole beaver pelt. As with coins and wampum, the quality determined value. Numerous cases in the colonial courts testify to the differences of opinion that often arose in such matters, and complaints about moldy and bare pelts are found throughout the notarial records of Amsterdam merchants.

Other colonial products, including tobacco and timber, occasionally served as legal tender for debts. But wampum and furs were the most common currencies for intra and intercolonial trade.

OTHER REMEDIES FOR THE SPECIE SHORTAGE

Bills of exchange circulated around the Atlantic trading community and served as currency for transactions involving exchange at great distance. Most bills of exchange in New Netherland were drawn on the Exchange Bank of Amsterdam, which issued the bills in florin accounts.

The growth of the European population in the colony stimulated the rise of merchant activity and encouraged the use of instruments of account to facilitate exchange. Bills of exchange served as a partial solution for the shortage of specie.

The specie shortage exacerbated the credit situation in the colony. Since many colonial trade transactions required months and sometimes years to complete, the availability of credit became a critical problem for the colonial merchant. Several remedies were tried.

The West India Company served as a source of credit for colonists, especially in the early years when the company store maintained a monopoly on European imports in the colony. As the company declined in financial strength in the late 1640s, it came to play a smaller economic role in the colony, although its expenditures for military expeditions, fortifications, and construction remained an important source of hard currency for New Netherland.

Merchants with sufficient capital simply carried their customers on their account books for specified monthly interest rates. By the late 1650s, the magistrates of New Amsterdam were willing to accept book accounts as proof of debt obligations. Merchants or their heirs were highly successful collecting on these obligations, which in turn made such arrangements less risky.

Another source of credit was the Dutch Reformed church, which became a lending institution of some importance, especially in New Amsterdam. Notarized promissory notes between debtors and the deacons of the church of New Netherland have survived in several documentary collections. One example from the Register of the Provincial Secretary for 1638 obligated Wolphert Gerritsen to "honestly and truly . . . pay into the hands of the . . . deacons" the sum of 216 fl. "arising from the receipt of such sum from the hands of the deaconry, and that at five per cent interest per annum." During the crises brought on by the first and second Anglo-Dutch wars, the deacons sometimes earned over 10 percent interest on their loans.

The overall effect of forty years of chronic specie shortage was a credit economy financed by merchants and regulated by company officials. When New Netherland became New York in 1664, its merchant community was already tied into the Atlantic trading community.

BIBLIOGRAPHY

Boxer, C. R. *The Dutch Seaborne Empire, 1600–1800.* New York, 1965.

Fernow, Berthold, ed. *The Records of New Amsterdam.* 7 vols. New York, 1897.

Gehring, Charles T., and J. A. Schiltkamp, eds. and trans. *New Netherlands Documents: Curaçao Papers, 1640–1665.* Interlaken, N.Y., 1987.

McCusker, John J. *Money and Exchange in Europe and America, 1600–1775: A Handbook.* Chapel Hill, N.C., 1978.

Rink, Oliver A, *Holland on the Hudson: An Economic and Social History of Dutch New York.* Ithaca, N.Y., 1986.

van Laer, Arnold J. F., trans. *New York Historical Manuscripts: Dutch.* 4 vols. Baltimore, Md., 1974.

Oliver A. Rink

SEE ALSO **Local Government** and **Relations with the Parent Country.**

THE FRENCH COLONIES

THE STORY OF currency and finance in French America is a variant of Gresham's Law: bad money replaced good, which was bound to leave the colonies in any case. The story had public and private aspects. Money and public finances came within the jurisdiction of the intendant and, on Île Royale and in Louisiana, the commissaire-ordonnateur. Practical supervision of finances in New France fell to the local comptroller from the Department of Maritime Affairs, which administered the colonies. The officials' work is substantially recorded in government correspondence. The private realm of currency and finance is not well-documented because some activities were illegal. Archaeology, however, has revealed the fruit of clandestine trade, and it provides evidence of foreign and copper coins whose presence was sometimes denied by administrators.

French coins seldom stated their worth, and it was customary for the Crown to manipulate currency values for revenue. By legislative *réformations* old bullion coinage was discounted, then purchased by royal mints, overstruck, and reissued at inflated values. Specie in silver and in a copper-silver alloy called billon was most frequently revalued. Since domestic coins had no fixed value, calculation was done with counters on counting boards or in partitioned drawers whose compartments represented livres, sols, and deniers of the Tours city standard (twelve deniers equal one sol; twenty sols equal one livre). Financial records were kept in stable and reliable livres tournois, whatever the current value of specific coins. Canadiens sometimes expressed values in so many beaver pelts or bushels of wheat to obtain a fixed standard, just as West Indian Creoles set values in quantities of raw sugar. There was usually a delay between legislation of new currency values in France and proclamation of the new scale in the colonies. This encouraged merchants and peddlers to bring discounted coins to North America to profit from the difference in values. This activity, although condemned by civil authorities, helped satisfy the need for metallic currency.

A HOUSE OF CARDS

Like other North American colonies, New France did not export enough to equal the value of manufactured goods brought from the mother country. In 1734 Canada dispatched produce worth 809,933 livres to France and other French territories in return for 2,100,271 livres in imports. Île Royale and Louisiana had a smaller deficit. Some of the difference between exports and imports was made up by sending bullion back to France. This outflow created a shortage of gold and silver coins in Canada. The situation was made worse by colonials who converted specie into silver plate and gold jewelry—coins were used in the absence of native minerals. Refounding coins satisfied a practical need for dinnerware and church ornaments, and it also secured the owner's assets from government currency revaluations and laws against hoarding old coins. Quantities of French gold and silver coins were shipped to the colonies to pay administrators' salaries and for military expenditures, and these coins quickly returned to the kingdom in payment for imports. They were partially replaced by Spanish colonial silver obtained through illicit trade with British and Spanish possessions. For example, the Spanish garrison at Pensacola supplied much of Louisiana's silver. Plaisance and Louisbourg, because they sheltered vessels from southwestern France, also received milled silver coins from adjacent Spain. Louisiana received Spanish specie through illicit trade with Spanish Florida, Texas, and Mexico.

In the early 1680s Quebec's Conseil Souverain decreed that Spanish cobs and other foreign coins be appraised by weight, and it employed a silversmith to stamp cobs with a valuation mark. Silver currency from the Spanish Empire was more familiar than French silver in France's American colonies. As a consequence the Spanish eight reales dollar, or piastre, was used as an accounting unit, especially in the West Indies. "Piastre" is still the colloquial term for a dollar in French Canada.

Traders from France who insisted on payment in metropolitan gold and silver made purchases in the colonies with devalued copper, bronze, and billon coins. From 1672 onward French specie in Canada commanded a one-third premium over the original value. Debased silver four-sol coins of the 1670s and 1690s, subsequently demonetized in France, were also brought out to New France for an additional profit because of their higher value there. Archaeological excavations in Quebec City's Place Royale identified these low-value coins, including one of the disliked four-sol pieces of the 1670s. The commonest types were copper doubles tournois (worth two deniers) from Louis XIII's reign and sixteenth-century billon douzains bearing the 1640 countermark, which raised their value from twelve to fifteen deniers. In seventeenth-century Canada, douzains were worth from sixteen to twenty-four deniers. Ineffective attempts were made in the 1660s by Quebec's Conseil Souverain to stop the influx of copper doubles and liards (worth three deniers) by lowering their official value. Price inflation eventually drove the doubles tournois from circulation, just as tiny copper deniers had been purged, but liards from the 1650s remained the commonest copper coins in eighteenth-century New France. They were supplemented, but not superseded, by bronze Dardennes, worth six deniers, minted in 1710–1712.

Countermarked douzains were called sols marqués by colonials, and this description was later applied to all billon pieces circulating in French North America. Fifteen-denier sols minted in the 1690s—some struck over countermarked douzains—received this name, which passed on to other billon coins minted at the end of Louis XIV's reign. Despite being called sols (worth twelve deniers), they were rated at eighteen or twenty-four deniers in the colonies during the early 1700s. Old sols accounted for two-thirds of the billon coins found on the fortress of Louisbourg site. Copper coins were twice as numerous. Canada's intendant and Île Royale's commissaire-ordonnateur were unable to prevent merchants from trafficking in old, base coins, and so they too ordered quantities of billon sols in the 1730s and 1740s to share in the profits. The appearance of a new, good quality, 25 percent silver double sol (worth twenty-four deniers) in 1738 brought about an official devaluation of the older billon coins, but only after colonial officials had disposed of their own stocks. There never was a shortage of billon sols. In 1749 Peter Kalm observed: "I hardly ever saw any coin [in New France], except French sols, consisting of copper, with a very small mixture of silver. They were quite thin, [worn] by constant circulation, and were valued at a sol and a half."

The abundance of old metropolitan coins of copper, bronze, and billon in French North America also showed the failure of experiments with a distinctive colonial coinage. Administrators hoped that a highly rated colonial currency would keep specie in the Americas. In 1670 the Gloriam regni series of silver five- and fifteen-sol coins was struck for the American colonies. The coins were of good quality—too good to remain in the Americas. Despite the 1672 augmentation in value for the colonies, they disappeared within a decade. In 1717 an issue of clearly marked six- and twelve-denier copper pieces for the colonies was begun and then suspended. Their weight matched metropolitan coins of the same value, and it may be that the metal's brassy tone made them unacceptable.

Using good-quality copper in the form of blanks or Swedish flans, the Colonies françoises series was produced in 1721–1722 at the La Rochelle and Rouen mints. No value was marked on the coins. The Compagnie des Indes, holding the fur trade concession, wanted to pay them out at eighteen deniers apiece, even though their weight was the same as the bronze Dardennes and copper half sols valued at six deniers in France. Eighteen deniers was three times the coin's intrinsic value. Naturally, colonials balked at surrendering furs for such overvalued coins. The company reduced the coppers to twelve and then nine deniers, but the coins' reputation had been destroyed. Even at six deniers value in 1724, the colonists' disdain for this coin was unconquerable. The offensive coppers were shipped back to France and subsequently dispatched to Louisiana, where the initial rating was twelve deniers. The 1731 to 1732 issue of six- and twelve-sol coins for the Windward Islands was struck in silver, which was not a base metal, and this might have been a tacit admission that earlier coppers were grossly overvalued.

Although card and paper colonial currency were more likely to remain in New France than gold and silver coinage, the former first appeared only by accident. When the annual shipment of coins failed to arrive in 1685, Intendant Jacques de Meulles paid the troops with playing

563

cards that he signed after giving each card a monetary value. The Crown disapproved of this innovation, yet subsequent intendants resorted to de Meulles' precedent in financial emergencies, and in 1704 Acadia's naval commissaire issued card money to take the place of high-value coins. Card money was almost as acceptable as cash to colonials, and only a fraction was surrendered for redemption. France's nearly bankrupt government reduced its liability and the cards' value by half in 1717. Twelve years later the intendant, governor general, and naval commissaire-comptroller jointly issued a new series on plain cards with embossed seals and their signatures. Twenty-four livres was the highest value in this issue, which continued until 1757.

Fiscal restraint was abandoned during the Seven Years' War in the 1750s: Intendant François Bigot supplemented card money with his own printed treasury notes, called ordonnances. They were assigned values from one to ninety-six livres. The uncontrolled flood of paper currency exacerbated wartime inflation and note holders only recovered a small fraction of the face value after the war. So painful was the Canadiens' memory of paper money that they absolutely refused the printed Continental currency offered by invading American revolutionaries in 1775 to 1776.

Paper credits had a much more respectable career in private transactions. Individuals wrote out notes entitling a creditor to draw goods to a certain value from the author's own debtors. These were known as *bons* because the text included the phrase "bon pour ——— livres." Colonial merchants made purchases in France with letters of credit drawn against their metropolitan partners. Because of the risk of shipping coins across the Atlantic Ocean, merchants also bought letters of exchange from the Department of Maritime Affairs or the Compagnie des Indes, which could be tendered to naval or company treasurers in France. Paper remittances accompanied the gold and silver coins shipped to France to offset the trade deficit.

CONCLUSION

Public finances in Canada were indeed a "house of cards" (later papered over demonstrating their nature as a stopgap measure); the house, however, only suffered an official declamation of face value for redemption in 1717 and did not collapse until the late 1750s. Île Royale and Louisiana had more durable economies. And despite the plenitude of debased currency and paper credits, commerce throughout French North America operated quite happily for a long period.

BIBLIOGRAPHY

Cunningham, Ann. *Coins from Fort Beauséjour, N.B.* Ottawa, 1971.

Moogk, Peter N. "A Pocketful of Change at Louisbourg." *Canadian Numismatic Journal* 21, no. 3 (1976):96–104.

———. "When Money Talks: Coinage in New France." In *Proceedings of the Twelfth Meeting of the French Colonial Historical Society*, edited by P. P. Boucher and S. Courville. Lanham, Md., 1988.

Niellon, Françoise, and Marcel Moussette. *Le site de l'Habitation de Champlain à Québec: étude de la collection archéologique (1976–1980)*. Quebec City, Quebec, 1981.

Shortt, Adam, ed. *Documents Relating to Canadian Currency, Exchange and Finance During the French Period*. 2 vols. Ottawa, 1925.

Surrey, Nancy M. *The Commerce of Louisiana During the French Regime, 1699–1763*. Columbia University Studies in History, Economics, and Public Law. New York, 1916.

Peter N. Moogk

SEE ALSO **Local Government** and **Relations with the Parent Country**.

THE SPANISH BORDERLANDS

WITHIN THE SPANISH BORDERLANDS, the government of New Spain and individual settlers responded to special problems in matters of currency and finance posed by their changing position in the larger Spanish economy. Fiscal adaptations, often innovative ones, determined the level of economic activity and the pace of growth in the provinces on the northern border of New Spain. In the face of serious obstacles to the foundation and operation of commercial markets on the frontier, settlers and officials during the last decades of the colonial period fashioned a financial system that began to establish local and provincial markets and attempted to connect them to a coalescing interregional economy. By 1821, at the end of the colonial period, this movement had only begun to yield appreciable results in many parts of the Spanish Borderlands. The financial patterns forged during the late colonial era, and the mechanisms established for adapting to rapid and profound economic changes, conditioned the response of the northern provinces to the changing economic picture of the Mexican period and to their eventual political incorporation into the United States.

GENERAL CONSIDERATIONS

New Spain

Silver mining constituted the basis for the monetization of the colonial economy in New Spain and elsewhere in Spanish America. In addition to providing the coin for circulation, mining activity generated regional economies to feed and clothe those engaged in the industry. Long-distance trade evolved to transport the silver elsewhere and provide the mines with supplies that the local economy could not produce. By design, both the 10 percent royal tax on silver and the imperial commercial structure moved silver from the American colonies to Spain. The flow of resources allowed Spain to finance its own imports from other European nations, as well as to finance political ventures in Europe, but it also served to drain the colonies of specie and to limit the accumulation of capital in the colonies. Goods entering the colonies outside of the official commercial system were carried largely by English merchants, who in receiving payment for their contraband in colonial silver exacerbated the situation.

Areas of New Spain—such as Mexico City and its environs, Puebla, the mining districts of Guanajuato and Zacatecas in the north, and the ports of European and Asian trade, Veracruz and Acapulco, respectively—felt the financial effects of the extraction of capital less severely. These central markets and areas of production functioned as conduits through which commercial goods and products from both sides of the Atlantic traveled to their ultimate destinations. The flow of money out of New Spain established credit as the preeminent medium of exchange in many parts of the viceroyalty. Capital and credit emanated from the major commercial houses of Cadiz in Spain, and from the members of the guild of merchants (*consulado*) in Mexico City, who controlled commerce in both directions. Through a complex network of distribution, powerful merchant establishments in Mexico City extended credit to agents, officials with local economic interests, and merchants, who in turn serviced individuals throughout New Spain. The continuous pressure of the overarching imperial financial needs enhanced the economic power of those who could obtain capital and extend credit as a normal part of commercial activity.

Today banks perform a number of financial functions that other institutions handled in colonial New Spain. Besides the commercial credit extended by the large merchant houses, commercial agents, and individuals involved in buying, selling, or trading in any degree, the church and monastic organizations—with income-producing lands and money from tithes and religious bequests—served as bank and banker to the commercial and landowning elite. Religious organizations provided capital, normally at 5 percent interest, for meeting other debts, purchases of or capital improvements to haciendas, investments in mining, and all sorts of commercial ventures. Lending money at a fixed rate of interest represented a conservative compromise to managing church wealth, a compromise between squandering the economic potential of religious property through inaction and making a direct investment in commercial undertakings that bore greater risk and offered financial gains bordering on the usurious.

The other important service that banks manage in today's economy, the safekeeping of capital and the resolution of financial transactions, formed another part of the daily function of commercial houses, merchants, haciendas, the church, and the financial departments of the

Spanish colonial government. Before the advent of paper money as a medium of exchange among European nations, letters of credit and bills of exchange became the preferred manner of avoiding the risk and expense of transporting large quantities of specie in order to settle debts and execute commercial transactions. Known as *libranzas*, these instruments of exchange functioned in New Spain as a form of payment in lieu of hard currency. A merchant in Chihuahua, for example, could purchase his wares in Mexico City, Puebla, or another commercial center using an agent who would present a bill of exchange in payment drawn on a commercial house in Mexico. That *libranza* could represent hard currency that the merchant in Chihuahua had previously deposited in Mexico, or it could entail a new extension of credit, depending upon the arrangement between the Chihuahuan merchant and the commercial house in the capital. The recipient of the bill of exchange could either present it for payment to the establishment in Mexico City or could give it to yet another party as part of a separate transaction. At each point of transaction, the value of the *libranza* depended on both the reputation of the party on whom the bill of exchange was drawn and the personal knowledge of the party receiving the *libranza* in payment. This mechanism limited the range within which bills of exchange held value and further enhanced the financial power of the largest commercial houses and the church.

Areas outside of the major arteries of trade and commerce, by no means limited to the northern border provinces, remained only imperfectly connected to the more formal colonial commercial system. Regions that produced valuable commodities within a non-Spanish, indigenous Indian economy, like cochineal dye, a scarlet dye extracted from the cochineal insect, in the valley of Oaxaca, experienced the intrusion of a monetized, commercial economy by means of financial adaptations that mediated between the two different economies. In Oaxaca, merchants and colonial officials adopted a practice called *reparto de mercancias*, or *repartimiento de comercios* (literally "distribution of merchandise"), which involved the involuntary allocation of imported and local goods on credit by officials or their agents among the population. The Indians repaid these loans in cochineal dye, which the great Mexican mer-chant houses imported to Europe for use in the production of textiles.

Spanish Borderlands

As in the valley of Oaxaca, the provinces of the northern borderlands developed their own regional financial adaptations to chronic shortages of currency and the lack of easy access to the network of credit dominated by Mexico City. Until the growth of the colonial population during the eighteenth century in the northern provinces of Nueva Vizcaya, Coahuila, Nuevo León, and Nuevo Santander, frontier outposts in Texas and settlers in New Mexico contended with only the most rudimentary components of the colonial financial system. The salaries of soldiers and the stipends (*sínodos*) of the missionaries represented the two possible sources of currency in the northern provinces until the last quarter of the eighteenth century. In New Mexico, in the seventeenth century and after the reconquest in 1692, the Franciscan friars contracted for an annual caravan to make the four-month journey from Mexico City, bringing with them supplies for the missions unavailable locally. Since the friars satisfied the bill for their imports out of their stipends payable in Mexico City, little if any of the money due them entered the province.

In the mid eighteenth century the salaries of the soldiers of the northern frontier garrisons, or *presidios*, fared little better. In the 1740s the commander of the *presidio* at San Antonio de Béxar in Texas supplied his soldiers by securing their power of attorney and instructing his agent in Mexico City to withdraw their salaries. The agent would then purchase the goods ordered by the soldiers and arrange for their shipment to Texas. Not only did both the commander and agent often profit by this arrangement, but the cost of transportation of goods charged at generally inflated prices also made sure that little specie entered the provincial economy. The governor of New Mexico handled the purchase of supplies for the *presidio* of Santa Fe in the same manner. One missionary in the 1760s charged that the soldiers paid a third of their salary for clothing of the worst quality, and then they paid double the going rate to the governor for maize and wheat collected from local Pueblo Indian farmers.

The lack of hard currency noted in the colonial records of New Mexico and Texas during the same period led to local systems of barter that dominated the internal economies in these regions, supplemented by the extension of private credit between individuals. The exchange of goods depended upon private or communal understandings as to the relative value of goods, particularly those produced or manufactured locally. In New Mexico, organized trade fairs allowed the Spanish settlers and Pueblo Indians to exchange goods with groups of Apache, Ute, Navajo, and Comanche that visited the Rio Grande Valley. In order to manage these exchanges, and to avoid misunderstandings that often led to violence between New Mexicans and the bands of nomadic Indians, in 1754 Governor Tomás Vélez Cachupín established a list of prices and regulations governing the trade fairs. Cachupín expressed the price of common trade goods in pesos or reals to establish their equivalence for the purpose of barter, even though no money actually changed hands. The schedule of "prices" set by Cachupín in the mid 1750s still functioned almost unchanged thirty years later. Further, the Spanish settlers and Pueblo Indians followed the schedule to calibrate barter of goods within the province.

A local system of understanding of the relative value of trade goods probably functioned in Texas as well, although perhaps in a less formalized fashion than in New Mexico. In general, provincial economies based largely on barter reflected a lack of interregional trade and a constant shortage of currency. This in turn limited the growth of internal markets, restricted economic opportunities, and hampered any meaningful connection between these regions and the larger colonial economic system.

Over the course of the eighteenth century, new settlements brought the frontier outposts in Texas and New Mexico into somewhat closer contact with communities and markets in neighboring regions. After the settlement of the mission of Nombre de Dios in 1697, miners and settlers moved into the valley in 1705 to found the town that became La Villa de San Felipe el Real de Chihuahua. Significant silver strikes stimulated a rapid influx of settlers and encouraged the population of the vast distance between New Mexico and the older mining settlements farther south. Instead of the four-month journey to Mexico City, the annual caravan from Santa Fe reached Chihuahua in about forty days. Unlike the already-established settlements in New Mexico and in some sense Florida, which at the end of the sixteenth century had jumped far ahead of the northward extension of the Spanish colonial frontier, the settlement and resettlement of communities in Texas throughout the eighteenth century proceeded from the gradual population of the frontier provinces of Coahuila and Nuevo León and from immigration from the Canary Islands. Similarly, the establishment of the missions in Alta California during the 1770s represented the fruits of a century of settlement and expansion in Sonora, Sinaloa, and northwestern Nueva Vizcaya.

The decade of the 1770s saw important changes that affected the situation of finance in the borderland provinces. Significant new discoveries of rich veins of silver ore in the north propelled a new cycle of economic development over a wide area from Guanajuato to Chihuahua. The boom in silver production in the 1770s received additional impetus from Spanish government policies that halved the price of mercury (one of the royal monopolies used to extract silver from ore), exempted silver from the sales tax known as the *alcabala,* and reduced other taxes on mining equipment. The changes in fiscal policy that aided the increase in silver production during the 1770s formed a part of the fiscal and economic changes collectively known as the Bourbon reforms. Part of this campaign to revive the economies and revenues of the Spanish American colonies included significant investments in northern Mexico to bolster the defense of the silver-producing regions against the raids of Apache and Comanche bands and to prevent any possible foreign encroachment. In 1772 the Crown began to establish and regularize a line of *presidios* extending across the northern frontier of Mexico. In order to establish the financial infrastructure necessary to collect revenues and disburse moneys for the new system of defense, the Bourbon government gradually extended the system of regional treasuries (*cajas reales*) to the north, mirroring that region's growth in economic importance.

Like the fiscal adjustments that the Bourbon government made in order to stimulate the Mexican mining industry, administrators concerned with the economic development of the far north realized that the money expended on building and maintaining the *presidios,* purchasing military supplies, and paying salaries represented an opportunity to influence the supply of currency and stimulate markets in the north. The commitment to the defense of the northern perimeter of New Spain also represented an enormous infusion of money that had potential economic benefits throughout the region. During the period 1773 to 1798, between 100,000 and 440,000 pesos per year left the Durango treasury alone for the *presidios internos,* the garrisons built in Sonora, Nueva Vizcaya, and New Mexico. Combined, the officials of the treasuries of Mexico and Durango earmarked almost 18,500,000 pesos for the northern frontier between 1770 and 1810; more than 12,500,000 pesos of this amount was allocated before 1786. Durango, and through Durango the Real Caja of Chihuahua, acted as a funnel for money provided by the richer regions farther south, especially Guanajuato and Mexico. Officials at all levels understood the important role that royal expenditures for the line of *presidios* could play in the creation of a strong regional economy.

A series of reforms in the regulations governing the supply of the *presidios* exemplifies the concern of Bourbon officials that some of the money invested in defense in the north enter and remain in circulation in the borderland provinces. The government instituted new regulations in 1773 that provided for an elected paymaster (*habilitado*) from each *presidio* to take charge of purchasing and arranging for the transportation of the goods ordered by the soldiers. The paymaster picked up one-half of each soldier's pay every six months at the nearest provincial treasury; this provided the officer with the finances necessary to negotiate with merchants for the best prices when making the presidial purchases. In this manner the soldiers could avoid some of the middlemen who tended to keep prices high and force the soldiers into debt. The soldiers received another portion of their salary in cash in the form of a daily allowance.

This procedure seemed to work relatively well in Texas in the 1770s, but in New Mexico and much of Nueva Vizcaya the new system soon showed its flaws. The paymaster did not secure the *presidio* funds in a locked box. He seldom kept the soldiers' accounts in order, and he rarely performed audits or kept track of the distribution of provisions. Some paymasters, arriving at a large market town with one half the annual wages of the presidial company, fell to the temptation of gambling or other misuse of the money entrusted to them. Further, few *habilitados* used their purchasing power to negotiate the lowest price for goods bought for the company, preferring to give their business to a single merchant. As a result, an inspection of 1777 revealed that five of the *presidios* had amassed a combined debt of fifteen thousand pesos, and some of the paymasters from companies in Nueva Viscaya had declared bankruptcy, leaving the soldiers in debt and without adequate provisions.

During the early 1780s, officials experimented with a system of contracts with private merchants to provide the annual supplies for the *presidios* in Nueva Viscaya and New Mexico. Behind the new system lay the idea that, although the private merchant who won the contract in a given year charged higher prices for the goods delivered to the *presidios,* the commercial connections and financial arrangements of merchants in Chihuahua had developed sufficiently to ensure a more efficient and dependable supply operation. Although ultimately not successful, in part due to a cumbersome bureaucracy that delayed critical payments to the first contractor, the episode illustrates the effort that Bourbon administrators took to try to bring a larger part of the presidial salaries into the northern provinces in the hopes that access to currency would stimulate the formation of vigorous internal markets.

REGIONAL ADAPTATIONS

Texas

Despite the attention and concern of Spanish officials, the general development of the northern provinces of Nuevo Santander, Coahuila, Nueva Vizcaya, and Sonora during the height of the Bourbon reforms had vastly different effects on each of the borderland provinces. In Texas, the 1770s saw the beginning of the export of live cattle to meet the demand for meat and hides in the settlements on the Rio Grande and Coahuila. Texas settlers—*tejanos*—added cattle to the goods that they traded at the annual fair in Saltillo, and the American War of Independence opened a market in cattle to Louisiana. The cattle sold internally to provision the *presidio* at San Antonio brought cash, but most of the *tejano* goods—mostly dried meat, tallow, pecans, and livestock traded in the Saltillo fair—returned to the province in the form of products that Texas settlers could not grow or manufacture at home. As the hostilities with the Plains Indians made normal ranching and animal husbandry difficult, the herds exported consisted of wild cattle rounded up and branded. The sudden opening of new markets prompted exports that threatened to reduce the breeding stock to the point of killing the industry at its inception, and Governor Domingo Cabello in 1780 responded by limiting export to bulls and steers. A system of licensing and tax payment developed, adding to the restrictions on the market already created by distance and problems of supply.

Increased economic activity in Coahuila and Nuevo Leon in the 1770s seemed to offer new markets that could connect the province more firmly to a regional money economy, alleviating the problems of lack of currency and capital. At the same time, the Bourbon government began to enforce regulations against trade in contraband from outside of the province, taking advantage of the relative high prices and paucity of imported goods. After a decade of tolerance, Spanish officials began to crack down on the trade in cattle with Louisiana because the settlers brought back in return illicit trade goods, again due to lack of specie. Continued efforts to enforce the ban on trade, first in cattle, and then in horses toward the turn of the nineteenth century, deprived *tejanos* of a source of economic activity that could have provided capital for expanded commerce with Coahuila and Saltillo.

The financial affairs of the few merchants who operated in Texas at the end of the eighteenth century show the effect of distant markets, lack of capital, and the high cost of credit. Many ended their careers in commerce after tying up their affairs inextricably in a web of debt. In the 1770s, when informed that the province had to pay tax on salt as a part of the new royal monopoly, Governor Juan María Ripperdá responded that the lack of money in circulation made payment impossible. Two decades later, Governor Manuel Muñoz could not recommend anyone to take over administration of the tobacco monopoly in Texas because no one in the province had the means to guarantee the proceeds to the Crown. When the administrator at Monclova, Coahuila, appointed Juan Timoteo Barrera, he quickly fell behind in his payments, owing more than five thousand pesos in 1800.

The commercial problems faced by the *tejanos* at the end of Spanish colonial rule suggest that the province had been left out of economic changes that had taken place elsewhere in the north and within some of the other borderland provinces. Having failed to develop a viable system of commerce outside of Texas that could sustain at least a portion of the provincial economy, financial affairs became immediately an issue after Mexican independence. Dependent on the states of Coahuila administratively and Saltillo judicially, communities in Texas found themselves with autonomous responsibilities under the Federalist Constitution of 1824, but with very few powers to pursue their own policies.

The municipal council (*ayuntamiento*) of San Antonio Béxar provides a good example of the fiscal problems faced by Texas under Mexican rule. Revenue to meet obligations that now fell on the town came from rents on common lands owned by Béxar, judicial fines, and taxes paid to slaughter unbranded cattle within the municipality. After its formation, the council attempted to raise revenue by taxing all forms of economic activity within its purview. They assessed the import and export of horses, wagon and mule cargoes, shops and market stalls, and irrigation water used on secularized mission lands. Activities of the populace such as dances, serenades, and food and gambling stalls also owed fees to the municipal council, but these measures could not raise the revenues needed by the town and served to place additional burdens on economic activity. Béxar's financial bind stemmed from an undeveloped provincial economy and continued federal (and now state) control over other sources of revenue. In order to spur trade, the national government exempted the province from *alcabala* for goods shipped into the province for consumption, and for most agricultural products produced within the province, through most of the Mexican period. Unlike New Mexico or Alta California, Texas had little trade with foreign countries that could bring in customs revenue. In an economy already strapped for currency and credit, provincial towns now had to bear the burden of supporting their own local government.

The situation also made Texas especially vulnerable to interruptions in the supply of specie to pay the soldiers of the *presidio*. After the difficulties of the central government in Mexico City delayed payment for the troops in 1821 and 1822, Governor José Félix Trespalacios established the National Bank of Texas at the end of 1822 and issued scrip instead of silver to the men. Soldiers could cash in the paper money when the silver arrived, or they could use it to pay taxes and buy land. Silver to pay the garrison came soon after from Mexico City, but the specie to redeem the scrip did not appear until 1830.

For the average *tejano*, the first decade as a part of an independent Mexico proved a frustrating experience financially. At every point it appeared that government policy prevented actions that might alleviate some of the obstacles that men and women faced daily in their struggle for subsistence. Pressure for expanded and streamlined economic contact with neighboring provinces, Spanish or American, increased due to the heightened internal demand fueled in part by the American colonists in Texas. Unlike New Mexico or Alta California, the Texan access to the Gulf coast made neighboring Mexican provinces unwilling to allow less-regulated trade for fear of undermining their own markets.

In 1830, when a seven-year exemption on tariffs for goods imported into the province expired, the government's attempt to collect customs duties led to the first act of overt resistance to Mexican authority. A group of American colonists expelled the customs officers at Anáhuac, on Galveston Bay, in protest of the collection of customs that to them seemed arbitrary. These actions, and others that followed, attested to the failure of the Spanish colonial system to begin the integration of the Texas economy into a larger regional system during the last decades of Spanish rule. During the 1820s and early 1830s the obvious effects of a financial system inadequate to sustain economic development

made *tejanos* more vocal in their grievances before state and national assemblies. By that time Mexico no longer had the resources or bureaucratic muscle to implement solutions that could fundamentally reorganize the economic system of the province.

Alta California

The plans of visitor-general José de Gálvez for the occupation of Alta California came to fruition beginning in 1769 with the expedition led by Gaspar de Portolá and Fray Junípero Serra that resulted in the foundation of the settlement at San Diego. By 1800 the Spanish presence in Alta California comprised eighteen missions for converting and "civilizing" the Californian Native Americans; *presidios* at Monterey, San Diego, Santa Barbara, and San Francisco; three civil settlements; and individual ranchos. Communities of Spanish settlers also grew up alongside the *presidios*. The Franciscans designed missions as self-sufficient communities that could sell surplus foodstuffs, livestock, and other products to the soldiers of the *presidios*. The dependence of the colony on goods shipped by sea from San Blas in Nueva Galicia added tremendous cost and unpredictability to the lives of the settlers. In 1777 and 1781 respectively, Governor Felipe de Neve established the civil settlements of San José and Los Angeles to provide grain to the settlers throughout the province.

As the Crown invested directly in the settlement and building of Alta California, a money economy predominated from the beginning of the province. *Presidio* salaries, along with the missionary funds used to found new missions and the stipends of the friars, provided the financial backbone of a commercial agrarian society. After the expedition of the governor of Sonora, Juan Bautista de Anza, opened a trail to Alta California at the end of 1775, new colonists came to settle in California. Emigrants from Sonora and Sinaloa could claim weapons, livestock, and tools for farming, as well as 120 pesos for each of the first two years, and they could draw upon supplemental provisions for the next three years. Those who moved to the Río de Porciúncula to found the new town of Los Angeles in 1781 received ten pesos per month, livestock, clothing, seed for starting crops, and farming tools. The settlers repaid the money over the next ten years;

they received an exemption from paying the tithe for five years.

Despite the success of the settlements in growing enough grain in the 1780s to supply the province, the real industry developed by the settlers lay in ranching and livestock. As in Texas, tallow and hides formed the principal products from cattle, and horse raising prospered as well. At times the settlers had to slaughter surplus animals in order to control damage to agriculture. Nonetheless, visits from foreign vessels to California ports began to tap some of the agricultural and animal products of the land. Besides the celebrated interest shown by the English navigator George Vancouver in the early 1790s, and the mission in 1805 of the Russian-American Company representative Nikolai Petrovich Rezanov to collect supplies in San Francisco, beginning in the late 1780s ships bound for the Far East via the United States made regular stops at California ports. California lay conveniently along the emerging sea-trade route between New England merchants and China. English, Russian, and American vessels all showed interest in harvesting sea otters for pelts off the northern California coast. All of this economic activity introduced a modicum of specie into the local economy and provided a direction that influenced internal markets for livestock and agricultural produce.

The trade in sea-otter pelts, and the secondary trade in tallow and cattle hides, blossomed in the 1820s after Mexican independence changed Spanish commercial regulations. English and American traders now openly and legally traded with individuals and missions that they had already dealt with on an occasional basis during colonial times. This accounts for the speed with which most of the Alta California missions signed multi-year contracts with British agents for their surplus production of hides and tallow in exchange for supplies that the mission needed. After 1822 California producers could rely on British or American companies to market their goods in South America, England, and the United States.

The particular circumstances of California's access to sea trade, too distant from ports in Mexico to become integrated into the Spanish or Mexican regional economies, created a narrow commercial export economy dominated by foreign merchants. Within the territory, letters of credit played a far lesser role in financial matters, although debt still tied the lower classes of settlers to the emerging landed elite who could benefit most easily from the export trade. The connection with the commercial system in Mexico through agents, *libranzas*, and credit accounts that formed economic bonds with Texas and New Mexico did not function in California. Despite its creation as an expression of the economic expansion of northern New Spain during the 1770s, Alta California's financial system proved a largely autonomous creation of a niche export economy carried by foreign vessels.

As the contracts with the missions suggest, American and British traders often received tallow, hides, and pelts in exchange for imported merchandise. Rancheros and missionaries paid a handsome premium on goods purchased in this fashion and could commit their future production a few years in advance. Duties on imports collected at the customs house in Monterey prompted widespread smuggling and more direct forms of evasion, none of which contributed toward financing a stronger local government. This system did not encourage the circulation of money or aid significant capital accumulation even in the hands of the major California beneficiaries of trade. On the other hand, neither the province under Spain nor the Mexican territory afforded much opportunity to invest large amounts of cash. Unlike New Mexico or Texas, where more currency in circulation might have significantly increased the level of overland trade, imported goods presented the only obvious place to put wealth to use in California.

Under the circumstances, the issuing of a large number of land grants to Americans in the 1840s represented little change in the financial direction of the territory. During the previous two decades, the small number of foreigners who had settled in California resided in or near Californio (the original Spanish) communities and generally married into Spanish society. In the 1840s, responding to the overland land rush of Americans to the West and the limited resources in the departmental treasury, California governors approved some 370 grants for individual ranchos, many for Americans or other foreigners. Many Americans took up their grants and established their ranchos in the Central Valley, apart from the older California regions of settlement. The economic and financial pattern of life in California established in the preceding decades did not change dramatically as a result, until the discovery of gold in 1848, and by then the United States had taken the territory by force of arms.

Florida

Of the northern borderlands, the Spanish settlement in Florida proved the most purely defensive. From its establishment in 1565 as a military outpost, the population of the colony of Saint Augustine did not surpass one thousand during the seventeenth century. Until worries over English expansion from Charleston began in the 1670s, the colony figured as a minor military post in the Spanish colonial scheme. Unlike Alta California, neither the mission system nor the military garrison established adequate farming or ranching economies. With very little output of its own, the colony survived almost entirely on the annual royal subsidy.

As in the northwestern frontier areas, the payment of the annual *situado* (garrison salary) and the shipment of supplies over great distances created a major financial problem for the settlers in Florida throughout the first period of Spanish government (c. 1602–1763). Every year, the governor of Florida and the viceroy of New Spain negotiated the value of the salaries on the basis of the number of men serving in the garrison. The viceroy then instructed the treasury to make available the funds, and an appointed agent of the Florida garrison would purchase supplies in Mexico and arrange their transportation overland to Veracruz, along with the portion of the salaries remaining in specie. The *situado* then embarked by sea to Havana, for transshipment to Florida, where the governor distributed it to his men and their families. The royal subsidy frequently did not arrive in Florida on time, often because the viceroy claimed either that he had no ships available to transport the supplies to Cuba or that he did not have the necessary information from Florida used to calculate the *situado*.

In this situation, the governor had to take measures to see the colony through the period. Normally this entailed borrowing money from moneylenders and purchasing supplies for ra-

tions and other necessities from Cuba at higher prices. From 1638 until 1654 the soldiers received certificates for back wages that became a virtual currency in the region. For necessary supplies, however, the soldiers had to take loans from moneylenders against their overdue salaries. In addition to the loss of purchasing power due to the interest on the loans, the goods that the soldiers received from the company store came from suppliers in league with the moneylenders at whatever price the monopolized market would bear. In 1654 payments from Mexico City caught up with the shortfall and the paymaster found a brief period of respite from the current monopoly, but the difficulty of organizing the annual *situado* and shipping it to far-flung Florida remained a serious threat to the viability of the garrison. To make matters worse, the cost of provisions in Florida underwent a general increase until at the turn of the eighteenth century food purchases alone consumed about 70 percent of a soldier's pay. With such a system, the colony retained little money from the *presidio* that could stimulate a local economy.

The financial system that had served to discourage much economic activity in Florida outside of the *situado* itself received a major reorganization as a result of Queen Anne's War. The siege of Saint Augustine by the English in 1702 prompted Philip V to authorize the recruitment of 150 additional men for the *presidio* of Saint Augustine; at the same time, he significantly increased funds for supplies and for rebuilding important buildings damaged in the siege. The new official interest in the defensive integrity of Saint Augustine resulted in a reordering of the Florida *situado* in an attempt to end the inefficiency of the previous system. Beginning in 1707 the Florida *situado* came from the 2 percent *alcabala* levied on commerce that traveled to and from Puebla de Los Angeles. The bishop of Puebla administered the collection of the tax and held responsibility for releasing the annual funds to the agent from the Florida *presidio*. As Puebla lay astride the road from Mexico City to Veracruz, the *alcabala* brought enough revenue to make an annual payment in specie toward reducing the sizable debt still owed by the governor of Florida, and it decreased the distance that goods and specie had to travel to reach the port of embarkation.

572

Within the next decade, some of the old abuses and inefficiencies had reappeared in the system. Governors complained of high prices in Puebla made higher still by the process of transporting money and goods to Florida. The occasional capture of the vessels carrying the *situado* did not help matters, leaving the governor in 1712, 1723, and 1747 without the specie and supplies with which to pay the garrison. The bishop did not always arrange the purchase of provisions of the highest quality in Puebla, and this problem compounded by the length of their passage to Saint Augustine often led to spoilage. Despite several proposals to reform the system, a more direct way of solving the problem of supplies arose through opening Saint Augustine to English traders who sold their goods illicitly to the Spanish soldiers and their dependents. From the mid 1730s, cheaper, higher quality goods came in large quantities from the Carolinas. One contemporary Florida resident remarked that the English merchants walked the streets of Saint Augustine as if in London.

Although this illicit trade did not continue—the English again attacked Saint Augustine in 1740—it did presage the pull of English trade as a solution to an inefficient system that left individuals, the governor, and the colony in constant debt and poorly supplied in the bargain. In 1746 Governor Manuel de Montiano even proposed the institution of free trade with the English colonies as a way out of the predicament of the *situado*. Montiano's superiors ignored the proposal, but the practice of applying to English merchants to relieve distress on an occasional basis grew into constant commercial contact by the 1750s. In 1740 Philip V allowed the incorporation of the Havana Company, a joint-stock company patterned after the English East India Company and the already-established Spanish Caracas Company involved in the cacao trade. The Crown gave the new company the responsibility for carrying the *situado* in specie from Puebla to Havana, from where the paymaster from Florida could purchase better supplies at lower prices. Difficulties between Governor Montiano of Florida and the Havana Company directors led to a difficult decade, but by the early 1750s the company began to contract with English merchants in New York and Charleston to sell goods in Florida. In addition, Spanish privateers operating from Saint Augustine also improved the supply of necessities in the colony. Even the subsidy appeared to reach Florida with more regularity, allowing the governor to pay for the supplies.

Ironically, Florida showed the first signs of real economic development in the 1750s with the production of naval stores for the shipbuilding operations of the Havana Company. Beginning in 1756, Floridians sent tar and pitch to Havana, and the next year began shipments to Veracruz. In addition to tar and pitch, the governor and Spanish officials in Cuba and Mexico envisioned shipping resin, masts, and spars from the colony. In 1760 Charles III exempted products exported from Florida from paying port taxes for ten years in order to encourage the fledgling industry. The establishment of the new industry in Spanish Florida ended abruptly three years later when Spain agreed to give Florida to the English as a part of the Treaty of Paris, ending the Seven Years' War.

The difficulties that pursued the *situado* during the first Spanish period in Florida complicated already-difficult conditions and severely limited the development of a viable local economy. Unlike circumstances in the other borderland provinces, currency circulated in Florida, at least when the *situado* arrived from New Spain. That a glimpse of commercial enterprise took hold at just the moment when the most glaring inefficiencies of the subsidy system had been solved by contracting supplies from the English is probably not a coincidence. The savings realized by the Florida treasury and the improvement in the lot of the common soldier seems to have stimulated the initial steps taken toward economic self-sufficiency. The case of the *situado* in Florida serves as an example writ large of the problem that Spanish colonial officials faced in the supply of the *presidios* on the northern frontier, especially those in New Mexico and Texas.

New Mexico

New Mexico responded to the general economic conditions of late-colonial northern New Spain and the particular interest of Spanish officials in stimulating development with more vigor than any of the borderland provinces. With a far larger population than Texas, Alta California, or Florida, New Mexicans found themselves in a favorable position to expand trade to Nueva Viscaya and Sonora in the mid 1780s, spurred by increased demand and the conclusion in 1786 of an alliance with the Comanche. Exports of sheep and wool grew at a rapid rate, and a range of finished woolen and cotton textiles and pottery made by the Pueblo Indians found new markets in the north, supplementing the old staples of livestock, hides, *punche* (a native tobacco plant), and pine nuts. The spurt of economic activity beginning in the mid 1780s began to incorporate New Mexico into a coalescing regional economy centered around Durango, Chihuahua, and the *presidios* of northern Sonora and Nueva Vizcaya.

Driven by a larger population at home, increased trade with Chihuahua and other settlements outside of the province, and influenced by regional policies toward trade and finance discussed earlier, New Mexico developed the rudimentary structure of a market system to complement its changing economy. This development proceeded in three stages. First came a period of simple barter, from the 1760s (for the purpose of this discussion) into the 1770s. An economy based largely on barter reflected the lack of connection between the province and the larger regional economy. Next occurred a transition period, extending from the 1770s into the 1790s, in which settlers tried to reconcile growing, yet uncertain, economic links with the south with the existing system of barter. Finally, a conversion began in the 1790s to a full-fledged commercial, money-based economy driven by a more intensive and extensive economic connection to the developing regional economy of northern New Spain.

As in the case of Texas, at mid century colonial officials and visitors to the province described an economy with very little circulating currency and carried out principally in barter. In order to regulate abuses in the exchange of goods to the Comanche and other Native groups, Governor Cachupín in 1754 promulgated a list of common trade items pegged to a set value in silver. *Vecinos* (Spanish citizen settlers) within New Mexico used these same "prices" to arrive at equivalent values in barter transactions.

During the 1770s, owing to the increased economic activity of a burgeoning *Vecino* population, continuing lack of specie, and changes in the monetary policy of the royal treasury, the barter system became more elaborate by evolving a number of "imaginary moneys," as Fray Juan Augustín de Morfí called them, that reflected different levels of participation in the regional, market-oriented, money-based economy. Discussions of the New Mexico economy during the late colonial period ordinarily rely heavily on the description of trade and the examples that Morfí provided in his two reports on New Mexico to explain the functioning of the colonial economy during the late 1770s. The complaints of Morfí about the practices of merchants in New Mexico have received an interpretation that has completely obscured their significance to the understanding of the system that he criticized. If one analyzes his examples closely, they demonstrate an attempt to integrate an internal economy based on barter with a commercial export market only imperfectly accessible owing to distance and Indian hostility.

The use of the imaginary moneys described by Morfí began to disappear in the 1790s as the use of circulating currency increased, at least among the wealthier classes of society, normally those involved most closely in the export trade to the south. Increasing integration of the New Mexico economy into the larger regional northern economy manifested itself in the form of long-term contracts for the delivery of New Mexican wool to the public *obraje* (textile workshop) in Chihuahua and for finished textiles in official and merchant account books in Chihuahua and Durango. Public donations to support Spain's foreign wars and to crush the Hidalgo and Morelos insurrections in New Spain in the early nineteenth century also attest to the availability of specie on the part of citizen-elites.

The emergence of an active internal commercial economy as well as a thriving export market in New Mexico during the last decades of colonial rule helps to explain the success of the overland trade route from Missouri that opened in 1821 and became known as the Santa Fe Trail. During the first years of the Mexican period, American merchants undertook the eight-hundred-mile (1,280-kilometer) journey to sell manufactured goods in Santa Fe and other New Mexico towns; they realized large profits both in local textiles and other goods and in silver. Excise taxes collected by the customs post at Santa Fe accounted for a large portion of the revenue collected in the Mexican territory of New Mexico. Repeated attempts to set up customs houses in Taos and San Miguel del Vado, to regulate imports at the principal ports of entry to the north and east, respectively, met with little success, demonstrating the susceptibility of the system to bribes and contraband.

By the early 1830s the primary destination of merchants using the Santa Fe Trail had become Chihuahua instead of Santa Fe, because New Mexicans could not absorb the volume of goods imported from the United States. Once again the region experienced a chronic shortage of currency and capital, leaving many local merchants and inhabitants alike in debt. The significant increase in the pace and size of land grants made during the Mexican period, particularly to foreigners, represents one manifestation of a process that began to tie the New Mexico elite to financial interests that emanated from the United States rather than from Mexico. This phenomenon may account in part for the reluctance of Governor Manuel Armijo and other prominent New Mexicans to oppose the inferior military force that occupied Santa Fe in August 1846, led by Colonel Stephen Watts Kearny of the United States Army.

BIBLIOGRAPHY

Brading, David A. *Miners and Merchants in Bourbon Mexico, 1763–1810.* Cambridge, England, 1971.

Bushnell, Amy. "The Expenses of Hidalguía in Seventeenth-Century Saint Augustine." In *America's Ancient City: Spanish Saint Augustine, 1565–1763,* edited by Kathleen A. Deagan. New York, 1991.

Chacón, Fernando de. "Report of Governor Chacón, 1803." In *Coronado's Land: Essays on Daily Life in Colonial New Mexico,* edited and translated by Marc Simmons. Albuquerque, N.Mex., 1991.

De la Teja, Jesus F. "Land and Society in Eighteenth-Century San Antonio de Béexar: A Community on New Spain's Northern Frontier." Ph.D. diss., University of Texas, 1990.

De la Teja, Jesus F., and John Wheat. "Béxar: Profile of a Tejano Community, 1820–1832." In *Tejano Origins in Eighteenth-Century San Antonio,* edited by Gerald E. Poyo and Gilberto M. Hinojosa. Austin, Tex., 1991.

Domínguez, Fray Francisco Atanasio. *The Missions of New Mexico, 1776: A Description with Other Contemporary Documents.* Translated and edited by Eleanor B. Adams and Fray Angelico Chavez. Albuquerque, N.Mex., 1956.

Gerhard, Peter. *The North Frontier of New Spain.* Princeton, N.J., 1982.

Gregg, Josiah. *Commerce of the Prairies.* Edited by Max L. Moorhead. Norman, Okla., 1954.

Gutiérrez, Ramón A. *When Jesus Came, the Corn Mothers Went Away: Marriage, Sexuality, and Power in New Mexico, 1500–1846.* Stanford, Calif., 1991.

Jackson, Jack. *Los Mesteños: Spanish Ranching in Texas, 1721–1821.* College Station, Tex., 1986.

Jones, Oakah L. *Los Paisanos: Spanish Settlers on the Northern Frontier of New Spain.* Norman, Okla., 1979.

MacLeod, Murdo. "Aspects of the Internal Economy of Colonial Spanish America: Labor, Taxation, Distribution, and Exchange." In *The Cambridge History of Latin America,* vol. 2, edited by Leslie Bethell. Cambridge, England, 1984.

Moorhead, Max L. *New Mexico's Royal Road: Trade and Travel on the Chihuahua Trail.* Norman, Okla., 1958.

———. *The Presidio: Bastion of the Spanish Borderlands.* Norman, Okla., 1975.

———. "The Private Contract System of Presidio Supply in Northern New Spain." *Hispanic American Historical Review* 41, no. 1 (1961):31–54.

Morfí, Juan Augustín. "Account of Disorders, 1778." In *Coronado's Land: Essays on Daily Life in Colonial New Mexico,* edited and translated by Marc Simmons. Albuquerque, N.Mex., 1991.

———. "Geographical Description of New Mexico." In *Forgotten Frontiers,* edited by Alfred Barnaby Thomas. Norman, Okla., 1932.

Poyo, Gerald E., and Gilberto M. Hinojosa, eds. *Tejano Origins in Eighteenth-Century San Antonio.* Austin, Tex., 1991.

Solana, Juan Joseph. "Juan Joseph Solana Report on the Condition Saint Augustine, 1760." In *America's Ancient City: Spanish Saint Augustine, 1565–1763,* edited by Kathleen A. Deagan. New York, 1991.

TePaske, John Jay. "Economic Problems of the Governor." In *America's Ancient City: Spanish Saint Augustine, 1565–1763,* edited by Kathleen A. Deagan. New York, 1991.

Weber, David J., ed. *The Mexican Frontier, 1821–1846: The American Southwest Under Mexico.* Albuquerque, N.Mex., 1982.

Ross H. Frank

SEE ALSO **Local Government** and **Relations with the Parent Country.**

THE COLONIAL MERCHANT

THE BRITISH COLONIES

TRADE, LIKE CAPITAL, DEPENDS on the production of a surplus, on goods and services in excess of short-term consumption needs. It also requires having wants that can be satisfied more economically through trade than by using relatively expensive resources in production. Both of these conditions obtained to some extent almost everywhere during most of the colonial period, certainly after the early experimental years.

Agriculture was the overwhelmingly dominant form of economic activity, so surpluses varied with soil quality, labor availability, technology, and distance from markets. Where soil was poor and settlement remote from markets, as in the New England uplands, the economy produced only a small surplus above subsistence needs. Largely self-sufficient farm villages, Jackson Turner Main has found, were "the most common type throughout New England and perhaps in the entire North." Yet even villages like these needed, but could not themselves produce, such articles as gunpowder, tools, iron wares, and salt. To obtain them, farmers relied upon retail stores where they could exchange their surpluses of pork and beef, corn, rye, wheat, flaxseed, or other produce for what they needed.

RETAIL STORES IN THE COLONIES

Although they were most abundant in the coastal cities, retail stores dotted the landscape of the backcountry. Except on the remote reaches of the frontier, where a wandering peddler might occasionally visit, stores appear to have accompanied the westward movement of the population in the eighteenth century. On a journey to the Ohio country in 1789, Colonel John May of Boston was surprised when he came upon "a settlement of five log huts, or cabins, & not more than fifty acres of land cleared," called Mingo Bottom. (The first white settlements had been established only a year earlier.) "Yet, small as the settlement is," the colonel confided to his journal, "here is a store, with a very good assortment of goods, to the value, as I suppose, of £1,000."

Such a store sometimes occupied one room in a house, but usually it was a separate structure. The storekeeper might obtain his merchandise from a store nearer the coast, or from one in a coastal city, if there were convenient roads or rivers. Representative of backcountry commerce was the store kept by Jonathan Trumbull in Lebanon, Connecticut, in the 1730s and 1740s. Trumbull sold an incredible variety of items, all of them purchased from merchants on the coast. His stock in trade ranged from pepper, lace, gloves, gunpowder, drugs, pots and pans, needles, and knives to molasses, rum, and copies of Watts's *Psalms*. He exchanged these items for hogs, oxen, sheep, pork, beef, deerskins, firewood, turkeys, potatoes, and numerous other forms of "country pay." Trumbull carted the latter to Norwich and Boston for sale and there obtained the merchandise for his shelves. Retail stores in the coastal cities generally carried a wide variety of goods, but in the later eighteenth century some began to specialize in particular kinds of merchandise.

BARTER, COIN, AND CREDIT

Purchasers of goods sometimes paid for them by tendering gold or silver coins, the most common being the Spanish silver coin known as the piece of eight. As a rule, however, the precious metals were too scarce to serve as lubricants of trade. Coins and bullion that found their way to the colonies as proceeds of sale of cargoes in the West Indies or South America (for example, Portuguese "joes" and "half-joes," Spanish pistoles, and English guineas) did not long remain in circulation. Instead, they were used to offset the persistent deficits in the balances of payments with the mother country.

For the most part, formal evidences of claims and obligations do not appear to have been necessary, although bills of exchange, IOUs, and tobacco warehouse receipts sometimes passed from hand to hand. Essentially, goods and services were bartered. However, it is only rarely possible to exchange goods or services that are exactly equal in value. Barter therefore requires the recording of the difference between the value (price) of what is bought and what is sold. It also requires trust that this difference will be paid at an agreed upon time in the future. In sum, barter depends upon bookkeeping and credit, both of which were available in the colonial period.

The merchant who wholesaled his imported merchandise to a retail storekeeper in the same coastal city charged the buyer's account for those goods and credited it for the country pay received in exchange. The respective values were, of course, unequal, but because the merchant had usually received a year's credit from his British supplier, he was able to give several months' credit to the buyer. The latter, in turn, passed on a similar credit to retailers in the backcountry.

Eventually, the lifeline of credit thrown out by British mercantile firms reached the farmers of America, who exchanged their surplus produce for merchandise at the country store.

Unsurprisingly, British colonials recorded debits and credits in their account books in pounds, shillings, and pence. But these did not signify sterling values, for English law forbade both the export of English coin and the establishment of mints in the colonies. Rather, they signified the value assigned by colonial law to the piece of eight. Intrinsically, during the colonial period, this coin, of 17½ pennyweight, was worth 4s. 6d. sterling. Because of the shortage of precious metal coins, however, almost all of the American colonies competed with each other in efforts to attract them. This they did by legalizing their acceptance for all public payments at values higher than sterling, say at 6s. instead of at 4s. 6d. The aim was to induce pirates to bring their coin to New York, for instance, where the highest ratio of colonial money to sterling was 155:100, rather than to Virginia, where the rate was only 111:100. It was hoped that traders with coin would also be attracted. In sum, the "lawful money" or "currency" of New York, say, differed from that of Virginia.

Currency, therefore, did not refer to coins in circulation but to the standard by which they were evaluated. Currency was not money but the measure of money. As so often in history, the two basic functions of money—to serve as a medium of exchange and to serve as a standard or measure of value—were separated. The pounds, shillings, and pence that served as the standard of value differed from the denomination of the money actually in circulation.

Debits and credits were recorded in account books in the lawful money (currency) of the colony in which the transaction occurred. In Maryland and Virginia, however, traders often devoted one column of an account in their ledgers to tobacco. This practice reflected the utility of the staple as a means of paying taxes and other obligations. Whether these traders differed in this respect from those in the lower South is unknown.

MARKETING METHODS

Certainly those engaged in trade differed in their marketing methods, and this was due to the geographic features of the region in which they lived. In both Maryland and Virginia the numerous streams navigable by seagoing vessels permitted English ship captains to call at planters' wharves. There they unloaded merchandise that had been ordered and put on board tobacco that was consigned to the same English merchant who had shipped the goods. Larger planters seem typically to have bought tobacco from smaller ones, or afforded them a means of getting it to market by having it shipped along with their own. Also typically, they kept a store or two from which they retailed imported merchandise to their neighbors. The store of John Rousby of Calvert County, Maryland, who died in 1686,

held the usual yardgoods, shoes, hats, and stockings, with a miscellany of hardware items for work and the house, plus 100 pounds of soap, 400 pounds of muscavado sugar, 80 gallons of rum, 20 gallons of brandy, 30,000 nails, and quantities of wheat, corn, oats, and even rye, a rarity in the Chesapeake. (Gloria Main. *Tobacco Colony,* p. 234)

Planters often owned small sloops or other craft suited to river and bay traffic. That they used such vessels to dispose of some of their imports is clear from the letters of Colonel William Fitzhugh of Virginia (1651–1701). The colonel not only kept two stores in which to sell his imports; he also traded some of them upriver. Certainly by the eighteenth century, if not before, strong tendencies toward diversification led to increased numbers of merchant-planters with investment interests not only in the sale of imported merchandise and ownership of shares in one or more ships, but also in sawmills, iron mines, mortgages, and other lending.

In the early eighteenth century private "rolling houses" began to be used as warehouses for imported goods. With the movement of tobacco growing into the interior, these houses had been built on tidewater as places to which tobacco hogsheads could be rolled so they would be readily accessible to ships. Movement into the interior brought change in the way tobacco was gathered for exportation. The older consignment system was increasingly displaced in the eighteenth century by sale of the tobacco to resident middlemen. Scottish mercantile houses established partners or resident agents (factors) in Virginia, Maryland, and North Carolina, and the latter opened stores in the backcountry as centers

for both the purchase of tobacco and the sale of imported merchandise. As a result, the Scots enjoyed an increasing share of the American trade after mid century. Imports of tobacco into Scotland began to mount in the 1750s in relation to those entering London and other English ports, increasing from roughly one-third to one-half of the total by the end of the decade, and continuing to rise thereafter.

Under both the consignment and the Scottish marketing systems trade was diffused throughout the provinces rather than concentrated in port cities. Lacking economic functions to perform, cities did not spring up, nor did native mercantile houses that could serve as intermediaries between foreign supply and native demand. Although the exports of Maryland and Virginia to Great Britain were worth nearly as much as those of all the other colonies combined, neither Baltimore nor Norfolk became important until after the revolution.

In contrast with the upper South, the shoal channels of the inland streams of the lower South were not navigable by oceangoing vessels. For this reason, seaports developed at the available harbors: Wilmington, North Carolina; Charles Town (Charleston), Georgetown, and Beaufort, South Carolina; and Savannah, Georgia. Charleston became the commercial capital of the entire region, the funnel through which its principal products—rice, indigo, naval stores, and deerskins—were exported to England. With an estimated population of eleven thousand in 1770, Charleston was the fourth most populous city in British America and its flourishing seaport created commercial opportunities for numerous natives. For although English merchants dominated the external trade of the Charleston District, they did so via native representatives known as Charleston factors. These factors or commission agents wholesaled imported British merchandise to local retailers and shipped cargoes of rice and other produce back to Britain. The 5-percent commission earned on both purchases and sales was standard throughout the colonies.

Those factors, who imported merchandise supplied them by British firms on one year's credit and sold it on their own account, also acted as independent merchants in their own right. Leading colonial merchants had correspondents not only in Great Britain but also in the West

Indies, the Wine Islands (Madeira and the Canary Islands), Portugal, Spain, and the cities of Flanders, Holland, and Germany. Correspondents exchanged information on current prices of commodities and bills of exchange and other market news. And they acted as agents for each other in filling orders for goods. Henry Laurens, one of the greatest of the Charleston factors, had correspondents in numerous European and West Indian ports, as well as in Boston, New York, and Philadelphia. As did other merchants, Laurens disposed of imported merchandise by selling it in wholesale quantities to both urban and rural retailers.

Rural retailers, known as country factors, acted as the commission agents of the Charleston factors and of the planters as well. Like the Charleston factors, they also did business on their own account. They frequently imported their stock-in-trade directly from the West Indies, from the northern colonies, and even from England. Sometimes they owned shares in the vessels that brought them their goods and, like the great merchants of Charleston and other coastal cities, sold in wholesale quantities and loaned money to backcountry farmers and planters on the security of land and slaves.

Despite this overlapping of functions, neither in the South nor elsewhere did retailers who succeeded in setting themselves up as small independent merchants account for more than a relatively small proportion of the overseas trade, finance, and shipping of the colonies. These businesses were dominated by merchants, who were distinguished from other traders, such as storekeepers and merchant-planters, by the fact that they were *primarily* engaged in foreign trade. Most of their investable assets or capital was employed in exporting and importing, and their purchases and sales were primarily at wholesale.

The businesses engaged in overseas trade were typically formed as partnerships, especially family partnerships, but such mercantile firms, both British and colonial, were by no means of equal size and worth. Some conducted numerous and far-flung enterprises and were relatively rich. They owned vessels or shares in them, engaged in the mercantile insurance business, made loans at interest, speculated in western land, invested in urban real estate and in such

manufacturing enterprises as iron bloomeries, sugar refineries, flour mills, and distilleries, and bought and sold bills of exchange. In a word, they possessed sufficient capital to be jacks-of-all-trades. In the later decades of the eighteenth century and increasingly in the nineteenth, the growth in demand for these various functions generated even more occupational specialization.

By necessity, less wealthy firms engaged in overseas trade operated on a smaller scale and tended to specialize in a geographic area, concentrating, for example, on the provisioning of West Indian ports. These smaller firms, it is safe to assume, predominated in number in all the coastal cities of colonial America. Yet it is also safe to say that their numbers exceeded their importance in relation to foreign trade. Of 503 merchants present in Philadelphia between 1756 and 1775, the top 50 alone bought about half of all the shipping tonnage purchased by merchants. Only 57 firms imported 54 percent of the goods entering Philadelphia during a three-year period in the 1780s. These were the great oaks of the city, and although comparably detailed analyses of other mercantile communities have not yet been made, the situation was undoubtedly similar in them.

MERCHANTS AND AGENTS

The beginnings of business administration are implicit in the kinds of decisions the colonial merchant made. Unlike his European predecessors, or even some of his colleagues in colonial America, he did not accompany his wares to market. Seated in his countinghouse (office) in one of the coastal cities, he necessarily depended upon others for market information in making investment decisions and for transacting his business at distant ports. His most important decisions were these: what commodities to ship and in what assortments; where to ship them; to whom to entrust their sale; what terms to sell on; what disposition to make of the proceeds of sale; and what to load for the homeward cargo. As a rule, the man to whom he entrusted their execution was either his ship captain or some resident merchant at the port of destination, who thus served as his commission agent. He himself typically served merchants of other ports, both foreign and domestic, in the same capacity, so that nearly every merchant acted now as principal, consigning goods on his own account, and now as commission agent, selling consignments received from distant ports and remitting the proceeds either in bills of exchange or in the form of a return shipment. Bills on London were normally preferred to those drawn on any other place, partly because bills on London formed a means of payment that Britain's extensive commerce made acceptable in almost any area of the trading world, and partly because the colonists needed to pay for their own imports of manufactured goods from Britain.

The resident merchant sometimes employed a supercargo, or traveling agent, especially when the trading area was distant and unfamiliar. He might also employ one if he wished to give a start to the mercantile career of the son of a fellow merchant or to a relative or friend. In the familiar West Indies he typically employed the services of a ship captain, not infrequently one who was part owner of the vessel or its cargo, or both. The consignment of an outgoing cargo to the captain gave him the authority to move from port to port in an effort to locate the most favorable market. This arrangement was especially desirable in the West Indies, for even in the eighteenth century only three ports—Bridgetown in Barbados, Kingston in Jamaica, and the Dutch island of Saint Eustatius—had markets of sufficient size or could provide price and other information concerning the insular and South American ports of the Caribbean. The capitals of the lesser islands were so small as to be glutted by a very few cargoes. Only a limited number of commodities (principally sugar, rum, molasses, and coffee) were imported from the West Indies, and they were far easier to select than an assortment of European goods. Finally, except for lumber, nearly every article of North American produce was perishable in the tropics. In general, it could not be stored by a resident merchant to await an upturn in the market.

Nevertheless, the services of resident agents even in the West Indies were often indispensable to the success of a voyage, and ship captains were commonly directed to consult with them. As residents they were far better informed than distant men could be of changes in the credit standing of local merchants and of price and market conditions. And they could sometimes assemble and have ready for loading at least part of a desired return cargo. Such arrangements, made beforehand, enabled a captain to give his business and vessel "dispatch"—a word that is common in the correspondence of the era—and beat some rival captain to the better prices enjoyed by the first man home. Where goods could be stored, the resident agent often performed the indispensable service of permitting the captain to "value" on him, that is, to draw a bill of exchange representing an advance of some part (a quarter, half, or more) of the estimated value of the cargo. The advance permitted the captain to proceed to whichever port looked most promising as the source of a return cargo.

A merchant's ability to select dependable ship captains and agents was critical to the success of his business. Not all captains were men of discretion. The late-eighteenth-century Baltimore mercantile firm of Robert Oliver & Brothers conceded that Frederick Folger was "a good master of a vessel," but because of the firm's attachment to him "we remained a long time blind to his incapacity to transact business, attributing to ill-fortune & other Circumstances, what was entirely owing to want of Capacity, indolence, and irregularity." Various captains were alleged by the same firm to be drunks or to be inattentive to business or to the cargo. One was blamed, along with the supercargo, for detaining a vessel an unwarranted length of time, another with suppressing a letter. "There are some Captains belonging to this Port that we would not trust with our Letters to you," the Olivers wrote to one of their correspondents in the West Indies. They thought one man honest and well-intentioned, "but he is not so smart as might be expected." More than once they referred to a lack of suitable captains or remarked that "good Captains are very scarce." On the other hand, they informed the employer of one master that they had found him a "very valuable Man," recommended one for his sobriety and capability, and wrote that their "great confidence" in another was an inducement for engaging in a voyage. They summed it up: "Our Captains are like the Captains of every other Country[,] some good and some bad."

So, too, were the resident merchants who served as the Olivers' commission agents in the various ports of their trading world. The Olivers sought constantly to place their business "in the hands of Men of Stability, good information & undoubted integrity." When they found a correspondent who was *Solid, Liberal* [in making advances on unsold cargoes] *& Active*[,] qualities which we consider absolutely necessary for an agent," they endeavored to hold on to him. They were highly reluctant to change correspondents, and almost always did so only after long and repeated efforts to accommodate differences. But when a Venetian merchant sent them "so particular" an order that they preferred not to fill it, the Olivers rather majestically wrote: "We have no desire to do commission business unless we can give perfect satisfaction and if you should hereafter think proper to give us any orders, we advise you to state your views and expectations and leave us to Judge of the propriety of carrying them into effect."

James Beekman of mid-eighteenth-century New York seems to have had a similar problem. He "frequently spelled out in his orders price specifications which bore little relation to the actual state of the British market into which his orders came." In other matters, states his biographer, Philip L. White, he displayed "a remarkable talent for vagueness and ambiguity." According to Elva Tooker, merchants like Nathan Trotter of early-nineteenth-century Philadelphia "often . . . left so little discretion to their agents that the latter were prevented from taking action when opportunities arose quite unforeseen."

In general, however, relationships between merchants and their foreign agents appear to have been characterized more by elasticity than by rigidity. The primary reason for this was their separation in distance and time, and thus their inability to foresee changes that might affect their interests. Under these circumstances, an informed judgment was usually preferable to meticulous obedience to instructions. When on one occasion a cargo did not do as well as expected, the Olivers blamed their agent for failing to comply with "our positive orders . . . to sell immediately." Yet they concluded that "your intentions were no doubt very good and we must rest satisfied." The Olivers undoubtedly agreed with Robert Gilmor, another leading Baltimore merchant,

who believed it was the "duty of an agent to do everything in his power to promote the Interest of his employer." And David Parish, a merchant of Hamburg and Antwerp, promised "to bestow our unremitting attention on the Concern & to study the interest of our principals as we would our own."

The Olivers of eighteenth-century Baltimore typified merchants earlier and later. The biographer of the Pepperells of Piscataqua concludes that an important element in the success of these late-seventeenth- and early-eighteenth-century New Hampshire merchants "was their ability to maintain satisfactory relations with their correspondents." Speaking generally of New England merchants during almost the same years, Bernard Bailyn remarks that the "heart of a merchant's business lay in his reputation and in the number and quality of his correspondents." These examples of the importance of the mutual dependability of widely separated commission agents have been taken from studies of mercantile firms from the late seventeenth to the early nineteenth centuries, and others might be cited both before and after those years. Dependability and trust were so important to merchant concerns because colonial and early national merchants lived in an age of slow communications dependent upon sailing ships. Price and other market information routinely included in letters between mercantile correspondents enabled them to make their investment decisions.

BOOKKEEPING AND BUSINESS DECISIONS

Did bookkeeping records of the success or failure of past investments influence investment decisions? The question is not easily answered because few account books have survived, especially from the earlier colonial years. In the only substantial study of colonial accounting practices yet made, W. T. Baxter concludes that the overwhelming majority of merchants kept their books by crude single-entry techniques. He finds accounting records to have been little more than lists of debtors and creditors, employed primarily to facilitate barter. Few accounts were for cash or merchandise, and there is little evidence that the profit and loss account served as anything more than a means of writing off bad debts. While merchants had a nodding acquaintance with the standard ledger, they seem generally to have been dilatory in their bookkeeping habits. Baxter explains this situation by the tiny scale of operations, the prevalence of barter, the snail-like pace of transport, and a preference for a relaxed tempo in business, together with a relish for negotiation on the part of the colonial businessman.

One may cite exceptions to these conclusions. There is, for example, Jonathan Trumbull, who periodically balanced his accounts in the 1730s and 1740s. But pending a thorough canvass of all surviving records, it is difficult to be sure of the significance of such examples. In view of the fact that even at the end of the eighteenth century in England it was mainly wholesale merchants who utilized double-entry bookkeeping—and by no means all of them—the hypothesis may be advanced that as trade increased in volume in the eighteenth century the larger merchants were the ones most likely to adopt the more efficient housekeeping technique that double-entry affords.

The same can be said of the larger merchant-planters. One of the most frequently read books in George Washington's library was *Book-Keeping Moderniz'd: Or, Merchant-Accounts by Double Entry, According to the Italian Form.* Even today the balance of international payments is calculated by the technique of double entry, which means that for every entry made in the journal, two must be made in the ledger. This duality reflects the nature of a business transaction wherein something is paid out (for example, cash) and something is received (for example, a suit, a car, or a day's labor). Double entry keeps track of both sides of the transaction.

Virginia Harrington reports that most wholesale houses in New York appear to have used the double-entry system on the eve of the revolution, and she cites the ledger and wastebook (daybook) of the Livingstons as "models of the double-entry books." Similarly, one may point to the Baltimore records of Oliver & Thompson in the 1780s, of Robert Oliver & Brothers in the 1790s, and of Alexander Brown & Sons after 1800 as excellent examples of full double entry. All these men, however, were post-revolutionary migrants to America who evidently brought their knowledge with them. The extent to which earlier residents responded to such newspaper advertisements as John Miller's offer in the *South Carolina Gazette* of May 1733 to teach "the Italian method of bookkeeping" is yet to be determined.

When a more complete understanding of colonial practices is possible, it most likely will be found that bookkeeping records of past profit or loss had very little weight in investment decisions compared with the influence of current market information. If so, external management will be seen to have been more important than internal. Advanced double-entry records such as those kept by the Olivers of Baltimore did not afford the kind of information on past profits or losses that could have influenced decisions. In the first place, a very large number of "adventure accounts," the type usually employed to record the costs and sales proceeds of shipments, did not show the net outcome of a voyage. Whenever the Olivers imported or exported in a vessel they owned wholly or in part—and such shipments were very numerous—some of the costs of the voyage were recorded in *other types* of accounts.

The value of the cargo, costs of loading it on board, and insurance on the goods were charged against the adventure account. But the cost of the vessel and its outfit, insurance, and expenditures for repairs were entered in an account set up in the name of the vessel. Also charged to a vessel expense account were the wages of captain and crew, costs of stores and supplies, and such miscellaneous expenses as consular fees and fees paid harbormasters to stow the cargo. These various costs were sometimes consolidated. In general, vessel expenses were transferred to the vessel account as soon as voyage costs were known. And sometimes the gain or loss from the adventure account was transferred to the vessel account. But as a rule, adventure and vessel accounts were independently closed to profit and loss, so that the net proceeds of the voyage emerged only after the vessel account was closed to the partners' capital accounts. Net proceeds almost never emerged as a single figure.

There are many instances in which even the *gross* profit or loss of what was essentially one venture is found partly in one account and partly in another. When the Olivers bought flour, for example, they charged the purchase price to a "flour account." But when they exported it, they sometimes valued it at a figure higher than cost. When they did so, part of the profit was in the flour account and another part in the adventure account. Sometimes the article sold for less than the value assigned at the time of export. In either case the actual gross gain or loss emerged only after both the commodity and adventure accounts had been closed to profit and loss, and the latter to the capital account(s).

The puzzle of determining the gross profit of a voyage becomes insoluble in many of the instances in which the firm imported a cargo and later reexported all or most of it. The Olivers preferred selling their imports in Baltimore, but it was often necessary to go into new ventures to dispose of them. In one instance they were obliged to sell a cargo by making eight reshipments to different ports. Examples of multiple reexports are numerous. The problem of ascertaining the outcome of such shipments derives from the fact that the cost of the reexported goods had previously been charged to the adventure-of-import account. The value of reshipped parcels, however, was entered separately in adventure accounts set up for the reexports. Two related problems emerge: it is frequently impossible to determine whether the reexports were valued at cost; and it is frequently impossible to determine the prices at which they were sold abroad. For they were often reexported along with other goods and no record was kept of the proceeds from the separate parcels.

In sum, many adventure accounts reveal the gross profit of a voyage, but frequently the gross profit is found partly in a commodity account and partly in an adventure account. Often the gross profit is in two or more adventure accounts; frequently it cannot be determined at all. These complexities are compounded by the Olivers' practice of using an adventure account to record the costs and sales proceeds of two or more voyages. Their adventure-to-Veracruz account ran for three and a half years before being closed to profit and loss, and the resulting gain came from a very large number of shipments. In view of the uncertainties generated by the interrelationships of accounts pertaining to a single investment, it is safer to speak of the gross result

of a particular account than of a particular venture. It is difficult to believe that records so maintained were of much help in making investment decisions. What mattered was not past results but fresh news, and that is why good correspondents were vital to the success of a firm.

CONSTRAINTS UPON TRADE

Luck also played a part, as it usually does. It was an age of sailing ships dependent upon wind and tide. It was also an era of mercantilist rivalry between great powers, each convinced that the benefits of colonial possessions ought to be confined to the nationals of the mother country. Frequent wars added to the uncertainties, and a merchant's best-laid plans might go awry.

Round trips between Baltimore and the West Indies were usually made in six or seven weeks, and westbound passages from Liverpool, London, or Le Havre to New York in five weeks. But individual voyages might take twice as long, or longer. Yet the degree of uncertainty and irregularity of communications is often exaggerated. For although the time required for a particular voyage depended on such variables as the direction and strength of the winds, the design, size, and rigging of the vessel, and the captain's judgment, merchants seem generally to have formed expectations based on normal or average runs. The merchant's ability to choose wisely and manage well were his main hedges against the power of luck.

Imperial Laws

How much room for discretion and judgment was there, in view of the compulsions of Britain's mercantile system? As British subjects, colonial merchants were governed by a number of imperial laws affecting shipping and trade. Acts of trade and navigation, first enacted in the mid seventeenth century, stipulated that no goods could be imported into the colonies or exported from them except in English or colonial ships, of which the master and three-fourths of the crew should be English or colonial. The purpose of the law was to exclude foreign vessels, especially those of the archrival Dutch, from trade with the plantations. Naturally, this law would increase the demand for English and colonial ships; the merchant marine would expand in size, freight rates would tend to fall, and auxiliary vessels as well as seamen would be available in case of war. Although foreigners were not permitted to trade with the colonies, English and colonial ships could trade freely with the foreign plantations, provided they did not export to them certain enumerated colonial commodities. The latter were required to be shipped only to England, Ireland, Wales, or Berwick-on-Tweed (on the Scottish frontier), or to other colonial plantations.

Tobacco and indigo (and other dyes) were the first commodities to be enumerated. Over the years the list swelled to include beaver and other skins, naval stores, and rice, the last being permitted to go directly to any European port south of Cape Finisterre, an exception that allowed direct colonial trade with the Iberian Peninsula and the Mediterranean. With enumeration, the officials sought to increase customs revenues; to supply the needs of the Royal Navy (naval stores), the textile industry (dyes), and the consuming public (tobacco); and to generate income for merchants and shippers handling reexports to continental markets. Finally, the Staple Act (1663) required that all European goods destined for the colonies be shipped from England, Wales, or Berwick-upon-Tweed in English or colonial vessels and not from the country of origin. Salt (obtained largely from southern Europe) and wines from the Portuguese islands were later excepted.

Whether this legislation inhibited the economic growth of the colonies has been much debated by scholars. It is no easier to assess its impact on colonial merchants and domestic marketers of such enumerated articles as tobacco. The shipping clauses of the Navigation Acts tended to confine the trade of the empire to ships built, owned, and navigated by Englishmen (including colonial Englishmen), but it is difficult to measure the effect of this restriction on freight rates. Did the exclusion of Dutch vessels, which were built and navigated more efficiently than those of the British, narrow the available supply and result in higher charges to shippers of tobacco and other products? Or did the laws, by encouraging the growth of the colonial shipbuilding industry, increase the available supply and hence tend to lower freight rates?

If both, which effect predominated, and by how much?

As for enumeration, many scholars argue that most colonial articles would have gone to the British market even in the absence of law. After the revolution most American tobacco continued to be exported to England, where it was graded, sorted, and packed before being reexported to its main continental markets. Although smuggling undoubtedly took place, these scholars suggest that most importing and exporting may have been conducted within the framework of law because the law conformed to the natural conditions of trade. Where it did not, the law was easily evaded. Of course, this situation changed when the old colonial system gave way after 1763 to a regime of strict enforcement culminating in the American Revolution.

Religion

It is likely that imperial law did not in any substantive or prolonged way impede the functioning of a market economy in the colonies. Can the same thing be said of religion? At first glance the question may seem a strange one. It becomes less so when one recalls that religious belief was one of the significant forces to which the colonial merchant was subject. Indeed, the two most important mercantile colonies, those founded by the Puritans at Massachusetts Bay and by the Quakers on the banks of the Delaware, were initially settled during an age of faith by people belonging to dynamic Nonconformist groups. Having only minority status in England, both groups had been made cohesive by harassment. And both were led by people of conscience determined to found communities in which the practice of life conformed with their vision of the right. Governor John Winthrop and William Penn looked upon their colonies in the New World as holy experiments.

While Calvinists of New England and Quakers of Philadelphia differed in some fundamental articles of religious faith (for example, the Quakers rejected the Calvinist belief in predestination), they had shared the Puritan environment of Commonwealth England, and the ideas girding their economic ethic were remarkably similar. Both emphasized that every person had been summoned by God to his life task, his calling, and both stressed the importance of pursuing that calling with diligence and industry. Both deprecated idleness and counseled frugality. Not surprisingly, such behavior often culminated in worldly success. Both Quaker and Calvinist, however, warned against the snares of success and cautioned the true believer to lay up his true treasure in heaven. The Puritan ethic thus contained both promotive and restrictive elements, and many people who sought faithfully to follow its injunctions found themselves in a dilemma, none more so than the merchants.

Bernard Bailyn has shown that the resulting conflict within the ruling body of religious doctrine was paralleled by conflict within the Puritan social body. Implicit from the beginning, it broke into the open before the end of the first decade of settlement in the Massachusetts Bay Colony. One social group, composed of men who, like Winthrop, traced their origins to the lesser English gentry, tended to regard middlemen with suspicion. Agrarian in outlook and deeply religious, they strongly supported the emphasis of the church on the restrictive elements within the Puritan heritage. In enacting wage, price, and profit controls, however, the Puritans were responding to the requirements of a primitive economic situation—one that threatened starvation—as well as to the compulsions of religion. The non-Puritan, southern colonies enacted similar legislation in an effort to safeguard the community from the shortages of food and other necessaries that they feared might arise from uncontrolled individualism. But while a southern merchant might violate the law of man, his counterpart in the North also risked the judgment of God if he followed the promotive strand within Puritanism too zealously.

It was the merchants who won. In New England their growing economic power was translated first into social prestige and, before the end of the century, into a measure of political leadership as well—a leadership used to protest the economic disadvantage to which they felt subjected by the Trade Acts. A shift in the balance of social values also took place as new immigrants arrived and as early threats of starvation yielded to increasing plenty. But to people of faith the advance of materialism, and to a lesser extent the advance of secularism in the eighteenth century, signaled degeneration. In Quaker Philadelphia as well as in Calvinist Boston, jeremiads lashed out at the rising generation, struggled to keep aloft a declining standard, and spoke darkly of the future.

THE RISE OF THE MERCHANT ELITE

Despite such misgivings, successful merchants continued to accumulate wealth and the social prestige that accompanied it. Possessing dominant economic power in late-seventeenth-century Boston, they show up in scholarly studies of probated estates and other sources as those on top of the economic order in eighteenth-century Connecticut, and as members of the economic elite (along with planters) in late-seventeenth- and early-eighteenth-century Maryland. In eighteenth-century Charleston, a city with a black majority most of whom were slaves, "a small number of planters, merchants, and lawyers controlled the town, largely determining its look, feel, and general milieu." By the eve of the revolution the white population of the Low Country, which included Charleston, was by far the richest single group in British North America. In New York City at the same time, the merchant represented society, wealth, and power: the city was an "aristocracy of wealth rather than of lineage." Analysis of the mercantile community of revolutionary Philadelphia has shown, however, how small this aristocracy might be: only about 15 percent of the city's mercantile community belonged to its "social elite, or upper class." In sum, there existed no simple congruence between a city's aristocracy and its mercantile community.

Whatever their number, there can be little doubt about the social aspirations of many of the leading merchants. Emulating the English gentry, the successful merchant sought the social distinction that attended ownership of a landed estate. Bernard Bailyn has perceptively analyzed the psyche of New England's seventeenth-century merchants.

For centuries the goal of the London businessmen had been to prosper in trade, marry into a family of higher social standing, provide themselves with landed estates, and begin the process of transferring their family from the status of tradesmen or merchants to that of gentlemen. The great social magnet was a secure place among the landed country families where alone might be enjoyed "the unbought grace of life."

THE COLONIAL MERCHANT: BRITISH

The New England merchants sought the same goal. (*The New England Merchants*, p. 102)

And so did their confreres in all the coastal cities of colonial America.

Merchants either could not or did not choose to purchase a large estate all at once. In late-seventeenth-century New England most "were engaged throughout their active lives in accumulating contiguous pieces of land which they eventually consolidated into large estates." Thomas Doerflinger asserts that in late-eighteenth-century Philadelphia, merchants usually built relatively simple structures on their country estates "in stages, as the money for construction became available. . . . Though dictated by financial constraints such simplicity had the positive effect of focusing attention on the splendid sites on which many of the buildings were constructed. Promontories overlooking the Schuylkill and Delaware rivers were favorite locations." The roads leading to the north of New York City "were lined with the estates of merchants whose orchards and formal English gardens often reached to the water on the east or west."

Successful merchants had mansions in the fashionable parts of town as well. The "square brick house, five windows wide, with stone trimmings" was the characteristic structure of the well-to-do in late-eighteenth-century New York City. Charleston's most imposing structure after 1740 was the double house. Thoroughly English in origin, it was a large symmetrical structure, generally of brick, with two floors of four rooms each. In revolutionary Philadelphia the great houses of the men at the pinnacle of the mercantile pyramid bespoke an emulation of the English gentry in an urban setting.

They generally lived in the heart of the city in three-story town houses that were graced by high ceilings, elaborate trim in the main parlors and dining room, and a fine garden in the back. In designing these residences the merchants favored elegance over size. Although they expected to accommodate many guests, sizable household staffs, large families, and sometimes business quarters as well, the town houses usually had only two or three medium-sized public rooms, with the balance of the floorspace given over to bedrooms, kitchen, and pantry. But the parlors and the dining rooms of the finest town houses were indeed magnificent. Lavish carving around the windows, doorways, mantelpieces, and cornices depicted all sorts of natural and unnatural objects. . . . A chandelier hanging from an ornate ceiling illuminated expensive mirrors and portraits of the master and his family, and the smooth mahogany and walnut furnishings set off porcelain figurines and locally crafted silver. Imported carpets and drapes completed the effect. (Thomas Doerflinger. *A Vigorous Spirit of Enterprise*, p. 21)

Whether in their town houses or at their country seats, wealthy merchants and their families enjoyed a wide variety of luxuries. They could set their tables with fine imported wines, rum, fruits, spices, and other gourmet foods. Many had their own cows and at least one horse, which could be hitched to a phaeton or chariot and used for summer touring or for city visiting. Many merchants had such larger vehicles as light, four-wheel carriages, while fewer owned a coach.

The possessions of the merchant-planters of the southern rural gentry bespoke their greater interest in agriculture. The inventory of the estate of Maryland's richest merchant-planter, Samuel Chew, who died in 1718, listed 88 slaves, 3 servants, nearly 350 cattle, over 500 hogs, almost 50 sheep, and a dozen horses, besides a variety of household and other goods, silver plate, and a share in a ship. Robert ("King") Carter, ruler of Corotoman, was not only the richest man in Virginia but the wealthiest of all Chesapeake planters. At his death in 1732 he possessed 300,000 acres, 1,000 slaves, and £10,000 in personal estate.

Most of the wealthier merchant-planters lived relatively simply in the earlier years of the eighteenth century. Ralph Wormeley II's Rosegill, widely viewed as the most beautiful home in Virginia at the beginning of the eighteenth century, was only a nine-room wooden structure. Even so, its attic was so large that it contained enough beds to accommodate thirty guests. Furniture and hangings were as fine as Wormeley's London factors could supply, and his sideboard was heavy with silver plate marked with the family crest. By the late eighteenth century the outward and visible signs of wealth among rich merchant-planters were even more conspicuous—indeed, hardly less so than those favored by comparably fortunate urban merchants.

There nevertheless existed a notable difference in the life-styles of the two groups. With slaves and servants to do the work of the field and house, or to build or repair fences, barns, and other structures, the rural merchant-planter enjoyed the leisure to emulate the tradition of public service long associated with the squire-archy of England. Colonel George Wells of Baltimore County, who died in 1696, was not only the chief militia officer of his county but also a justice of the peace and a member of the Assembly. "Judging from the composition of his assets as reported in the inventory of his estate, he acted as a doctor, merchant, and distiller as well as a planter." Ralph Wormeley II was a justice of the county court, commander of the militia in two counties, naval officer on the Rappahannock River, receiver of Virginia duties, member of the council, and secretary of state. By 1720 not only did a small number of relatively rich merchant-planters own most of the bound labor in Maryland, but their sons and grandsons "came to hold most of the major and lesser political offices of the province." In a sense, officeholding belongs to the pattern of economic diversification of the merchant-planters, for it provided a significant source of income. Ralph Wormeley II, for example, is said to have drawn a considerable revenue from his various public offices.

The relationships between urban merchants and government were as a rule more circumscribed. Unquestionably, some were eager to accept contracts to supply British or colonial troops in wartime. Henry White and John Watts of New York, for example, held British supply contracts during the Seven Years' War, as did Thomas Hancock of Boston. But they appear generally to have been disinclined to pursue or accept positions in government. Commercial rather than political concerns were matters of priority with them except when the two became linked in time of crisis. Such a time, certainly, were the years following the end of the Seven Years' War. But the story of the British enforcement of the Trade Acts and of the mercantile response in Boston and elsewhere belongs to the struggle for American independence.

BIBLIOGRAPHY

Bailyn, Bernard. *The New England Merchants in the Seventeenth Century.* Cambridge, Mass., 1955; repr. New York, 1964. A classic study of the merchant community of Boston, which elucidates the close relationships among trade, society, politics, and religion.

Baxter, William T. "Accounting in Colonial America." In Ananias C. Littleton and Basil S. Yamey, eds., *Studies in the History of Accounting.* Homewood, Ill., 1956; repr. New York, 1978.

———. *The House of Hancock: Business in Boston, 1724–1775.* Cambridge, Mass., 1945; repr. New York, 1965. A professor of accounting's able analysis of bookkeeping records of foreign trade. Explains bookkeeping barter.

Bruchey, Stuart. *Robert Oliver: Merchant of Baltimore, 1783–1819.* Baltimore, 1956. Uses bookkeeping and other business records to trace the career of a leading merchant.

———. "Success and Failure Factors: American Merchants in Foreign Trade in the Eighteenth and Early Nineteenth Centuries." *Business History Review* 32, no. 3 (1958): 272–292.

———, ed. *The Colonial Merchant: Sources and Readings.* New York, 1966. Describes mercantilism and the Navigation Acts, the Puritan economic ethic, the southern staple trade, and the merchants of the middle and northern colonies.

Coclanis, Peter A. *The Shadow of a Dream: Economic Life and Death in the South Carolina Low Country, 1670–1920.* New York, 1989. Examines in great depth the economic rise and fall of the South Carolina Low Country, which includes Charleston.

Doerflinger, Thomas M. *A Vigorous Spirit of Enterprise: Merchants and Economic Development in Revolutionary Philadelphia.* Chapel Hill, N.C., 1986. A splendid analysis of the economic and social structure of the merchant community.

Fairchild, Byron. *Messrs. William Pepperrell: Merchants at Piscataqua.* Ithaca, N.Y., 1954.

Harrington, Virginia D. *The New York Merchant on the Eve of the Revolution.* New York, 1935; repr. 1964. Describes the organization and conduct of business, minimizing the impact of the Navigation Acts, and places merchants in provincial life.

Hedges, James B. *The Browns of Providence Plantations: Colonial Years.* Vol. 1. Cambridge, Mass., 1952. Analyzes diversified investment interests of an important Rhode Island mercantile firm; especially good on slave trade and rum distilling.

Main, Gloria L. *Tobacco Colony: Life in Early Maryland, 1650–1720.* Princeton, N.J., 1982. Careful reconstruction of changing living standards of tobacco planters based on inventories of probated estates.

Main, Jackson Turner. *The Social Structure of Revolutionary America.* Princeton, N.J., 1965. A pathbreaking analysis.

———. *Society and Economy in Colonial Connecticut.* Princeton, N.J., 1985. Uses probate estate inventories to plot the distribution of property and associated social status of merchants, traders, and others.

Porter, Kenneth W. *The Jacksons and the Lees: Two Generations of Massachusetts Merchants, 1765–1844.* 2 vols. Cambridge, Mass., 1937; reiss. New York, 1969. Contains many letters illuminating mercantile and other relationships.

Sellers, Leila. *Charleston Business on the Eve of the American Revolution.* Chapel Hill, N.C., 1934; repr. New York, 1970. Useful descriptions of activities of factors, planters, and British merchants.

Weaver, Glenn. *Jonathan Trumbull: Connecticut's Merchant Magistrate, 1710–1785.* Hartford, Conn., 1956.

Wertenbaker, Thomas J. *The Planters of Colonial Virginia.* Princeton, N.J., 1922; repr. as part of *The Shaping of Colonial Virginia;* New York, 1958. Older but still useful, especially for tobacco trade.

White, Philip L. *The Beekmans of New York in Politics and Commerce, 1647–1877.* New York, 1956. Some Beekmans were politicians; others, merchants. For the latter, see especially chapters on Gerardus and James. Good on flax trade of former.

Stuart Bruchey

SEE ALSO **Relations with the Parent Country; The Slave Trade;** and **Urban Life.**

THE DUTCH COLONY

POLICIES OF THE WEST INDIA COMPANY

THE DEVELOPMENT OF AN indigenous merchant community in New Netherland was delayed for years by the policies of the West India Company (WIC). In the first decade of company administration, the directors of the Amsterdam chamber—the segment of the company responsible for North American development—debated various types of colonial arrangements. In 1624 the chamber, with the approval of the company's Heeren XIX (College of Nineteen), settled some thirty Walloon families in several locations in the colony in the hopes of establishing a core of employees and free burghers to support the fur trade. The restrictions placed upon the settlers in matters of trade and exchange precluded the development of a merchant community among this vanguard of Europeans.

In addition to the company monopoly on furs, the colonists were restricted to 10 percent of the return on gold, silver, pearls, or other treasures they might find. Furthermore, company fees were charged on virtually all exchanges. Many Walloons turned to livestock farming or tried their hand at smuggling furs in the private chests of those returning home after their contracts had expired. There was also a lively clandestine trade between the settlers and the seamen who came ashore at Manhattan. Several cases involving accusations of smuggling were settled in Amsterdam long after the sailors had arrived home, their sea chests stuffed with illegal pelts. Thus while it appears certain that smuggling received its impetus from company policy in the first five years of New Netherland's existence, there is no evidence of a viable merchant community in the colony at this time. The company monopoly was too great a barrier to merchant enterprise.

The Patroonship Plan

In 1629 the Amsterdam chamber adopted a new colonization plan for New Netherland. Its patroonship plan clearly favored the Amsterdam merchants by giving the wealthiest and most influential the right to exploit the colony as patroons. Although much has been written about the feudal rights of the patroons allowing them to hold a manor court and mete out justice, of greatest concern to those within the company who opposed the patroons were the trade provisions in the plan. Among other things, these provisions allowed patroons to outfit their own ships and conduct trade along the entire coast of North America, subject only to the presence of a company supercargo on board.

The effect of these provisions was to permit the development of trade between private agents of the patroons of New Netherland and the colonists of New England and Virginia. By legalizing the intercolonial trade for the patroons or their agents, the company opened the trade up to the Amsterdam merchants, who responded in the 1630s by building, chartering, and freighting dozens of ships for the North American trade.

The advantages to patroons were great: a reduction of the company assessment on freight from 10 percent to 5 percent of total value; the removal of the time limit on its payment; free passage for the patroons' livestock on company ships; and permission to ship goods directly to the fatherland, provided that "contrary currents and other things" prevented stopping off at Manhattan first. This last provision virtually guaranteed the development of the direct Amsterdam-Virginia and Amsterdam-New England trade. It also stimulated the growth of the coastal trade, financed largely from Amsterdam but managed by New Netherland merchants.

Kiliaen van Rensselaer was the only patroon to succeed under the provisions of the 1629 Freedoms and Exemptions. A large and critical part of his success was due to the rapidity with which he and his heirs took advantage of the trade provisions of the patroonship plan.

Articles and Conditions

The growth of New Netherland's merchant community accelerated after 1639, when the company finally gave up its efforts to monopolize the trade of the colony. In that year the States General, after a long and protracted struggle with the Heeren XIX, approved a plan that drastically altered the relationship between the colony and the company.

Under the so-called Articles and Conditions, colonists were free to trade in all colonial commodities, including furs. Private ships from the fatherland could sail freely to the colony and trade throughout the chartered territory, provided a company supercargo was on board. The company retained the right to tax certain imports and exports and to levy a 10 percent "farm tax" based upon a farm's production in its fifth year of operation. These changes marked a transition in the company's history, a transition from a trade monopoly to a government of free burghers.

Freedoms and Exemptions

It would take some years for the transition to be complete, but the seeds of change were planted permanently in 1640 when the company issued a new set of Freedoms and Exemptions that, among other things, provided two hundred acres (80 hectares) of free land to each colonist who brought with him five family members or servants. This Dutch version of the Virginia headright system spelled the end of the company's dominance in economic matters. Thereafter the merchants of Amsterdam would engross the transoceanic trade in their web of cartels, and the merchants of New Netherland would exploit intercolonial trade opportunities first as agents and partners of the Amsterdam merchants and eventually as competitors.

CREDIT AND EXCHANGE

The transoceanic trade in furs, timber, and tobacco remained firmly in the hands of the Amsterdam merchants until the English conquest in 1664. The trade itself was a credit trade, requiring the commitment of capital for at least two years and sometimes longer. A number of instruments were used to pool and leverage capital.

The regulated partnership was a common feature of the trade. It usually involved a notarized agreement among a number of freighters (*bevrachters*) who pledged a certain portion of the capital in return for a like percentage of the profit. Such agreements were negotiable instruments on the exchange and could be used as collateral for loans. Usually the agreement required the freighters to pay the company its "recognition fee" and to take out an insurance policy on the ship and its cargo. Insurance alone could add from 10 percent to 12 percent to the costs.

The owner of the vessel could borrow capital through a bottomry bond (*bodermerijbrief*). Bottomry bonds were loans secured, literally, by the "bottom" or keel of the ship. The owner, in effect, mortgaged his ship, and it was up to the creditor to assure that the ship was worth the loan. In the event of a poor voyage, the creditors could attach the ship and sell it to recover the loan. Bottomry bonds, like regulated partnership agreements, were bought and sold on the exchange, and their fluctuating values tell us much about the Amsterdam merchant community's assessment of the risks of the New Netherland trade.

By and large the trade was considered risky. Between 1651 and 1664 the interest rates for bottomry loans fluctuated between 20 percent and 23 percent. This was twice as high as the rates paid by shippers to the Baltic and about the same as that charged borrowers for the African slave trade.

The process of exchange involved both "real money" (gold, silver, and copper coin) and "moneys of account" (written instruments, such as bills of exchange). In New Netherland and elsewhere in the company's chartered territory, specie was short, and exchange was usually by barter. In New Netherland this meant furs (reckoned at about 8 florins per beaver pelt), wampum (reckoned at 1 stuiver for 6 white or 3 black beads), and tobacco (reckoned at 114 florins for a 240-pound hogshead of Virginia "leaves"). If a colonist owed money to a merchant in Amsterdam, he could assemble a cargo of goods for shipment to the fatherland, where it would be sold by an agent and the money paid to the creditor. This type of exchange was common for small sums, but it was exceedingly cumbersome for large amounts and ongoing accounts of the type developed by the Amsterdam merchants and their clients after 1640. For such transactions the bill of exchange was the preferred method of payment.

Bills of exchange were usually drawn on and guaranteed by the Wisselbank van Amsterdam (Exchange Bank of Amsterdam) founded in 1609. Colonial bills of exchange were calculated in the specie of the fatherland; that is, in gulden or florins. Since colonial bills were invariably discounted in Amsterdam to account for the inflation in colonial currency, the result amounted to an "exchange tax" on the colonial merchants and an "exchange dividend" for the home country merchant.

Access to the credit markets of Amsterdam and an exchange system that favored the merchants of the fatherland combined to strengthen the hold of the Amsterdam merchants on New Netherland's transoceanic trade. After 1640, however, a rising tide of European immigration and the expanded Freedoms and Exemptions provided new opportunities for the development of an indigeneous merchant community in the colony.

NEW NETHERLAND'S MERCHANT COMMUNITY

New Netherland's merchant community expanded rapidly in the late 1640s and 1650s to become an important economic and political force in the colony. Here again the role of the large Amsterdam merchants was crucial. After 1639 the merchant cartels in Amsterdam took advantage of the new opportunities to settle their agents in the colony. These agents channeled credit into the colony through the use of bills of exchange drawn on the Exchange Bank of Amsterdam. They relied on the West India Company to guarantee their credit agreements through formal written debt instruments and the adjudication of debt disputes before the director-general and council.

Written credit agreements in the form of notarized promissory notes were produced by New Amsterdam notaries as early as 1651. The establishment of professional notaries in New Netherland was an important step in transferring the credit system from the fatherland to the colony.

The system operated within the framework of Dutch civil law (which was based on Roman law) and derived its customs and practices from the city of Amsterdam, whence most of the notaries came. It involved several types of credit documents besides promissory notes drawn before notaries. The "mortgages" issued by the *schepens* (magistrates) may suffice as one unique example.

In New Netherland a mortgage seldom concerned real estate. Instead it was usually a written guarantee of debt certified as valid by the *schepens*. In actuality it was something akin to the deal struck between a pawnbroker and his customer. In the document the debtor swore to "specially hypothecate and mortgage" some designated piece of property as security for the loan. The mortgage constituted a legal lien on the property until the settlement of the debt. Should the debtor default, the creditor had first claim on the property as well as rights to all profit from its sale.

Historian Dennis J. Maika's survey of "mortgages" registered by the secretary of the city of New Amsterdam–New York from 1655 to 1674 suggests a high level of merchant activity over the twenty-year span. He notes that of the more than 250 separate entries, only about one-third involved the purchase of real estate. The other two-thirds were dominated by the extension of credit for the purchase of goods and the lending of money.

The adjudication of debt disputes brought the merchants into contact with the company as government. Indeed the dissatisfaction they felt in their dealings with the WIC's administration led directly to the establishment of municipal government in New Amsterdam. The number of cases involving questions of credit before the colony's council rose from twenty cases in 1638 to more than one hundred cases a year by 1652, leading to a call by Manhattan merchants for a "suitable municipal government" for New Amsterdam. As early as 1649, colonial merchants petitioned the States General to establish a municipal corporation for New Amsterdam. They were particularly angered by Director-General Peter Stuyvesant's harassment of merchants who appeared before him to collect debts. His reluctance to repay company debts owed Manhattan merchants was another factor in the merchants' drive for municipal government. After a three-year struggle and numerous petitions, the States General issued a charter for the city of New Amsterdam, which took effect in February 1653.

The city charter established the new court of *schout*, burgomasters, and *schepens*. From 1653 until at least 1674, long after the colony had become New York and the titles of municipal officials had been changed to sheriff, mayor, and aldermen, the court continued to adjudicate debts. The continuity of its procedures and the steady support it gave for debt collection enabled the merchants of New Netherland–New York to expand their operations, secure in the knowledge that contracts and notes were enforceable.

The expansion of colonial trade in the 1650s can be traced in a number of laws and ordinances approved by the director-general and council for New Amsterdam. The cumulative result of these was the institutionalization of business activity in the city and the formalization of the free marketplace.

To protect resident merchants from the competition of itinerant foreign traders, the director-general and council imposed a three-year residency requirement for all merchants in the colony in 1648. The purpose of the regulation was clearly stated:

Whereas the Honorable Director General and Council have seen and learned than many of the Scottish merchants and small traders, . . . do not nor intend to do anything else, but to injure trade with their underselling, by selling their goods quickly, . . . and having sold out returning in the ships, . . . to the injury of the inhabitants, having houses and lots and bearing all burdens. (Berthold Fernow, ed. *Records of New Amsterdam.* Vol. 1, p. 10)

In 1649 the director-general and council approved a law ordering "all wholesale and retail merchants, also bakers and others, who sell by the ell [about two feet English (60 centimeters) measurement], measure or weight, not to use in delivering or receiving any other ell, weight or measure, than that of Amsterdam." The law stipulated that "all inhabitants and traders" had to procure "genuine Amsterdam ells, measures and weights" within one year. In the meantime all ells, weights, and measures presently in use had to be brought to the company warehouse in the fort for certification. The law also charged the fiscal (the company officer in charge of accounting and bookkeeping) with inspecting all weights and measures used in the city "as often, as he thinks fit." Merchants discovered using nonstandard weights and measures were fined according to the customs of the fatherland. In 1658 the municipal government of New Amsterdam decreed that measures and weights had to be certified at the City Hall (Stadhuis) and a fee paid to the city treasury.

The director-general and council even attempted to control the money supply by issuing ordinances regulating the quality of and setting prices for wampum, the currency of the colony. In 1650, with an internal economy suffering from the depreciation of loose wampum, "among which is found much unpierced and only half finished [beads], made of stone, bone, glas, shells, horn, nay even of wood," the council declared that henceforth no loose wampum would be considered legal tender in New Netherland. The ordinance further stated that strung wampum "shall pass as good pay . . . at the rate of six white or three black beads for one stiver and bad, strung wampum at the rate of eight white or four black for one stiver."

Indirect evidence of increased merchant activity is found in an ordinance of 1656 establishing Saturday as market day in the New Amsterdam. The market was to be held "on the Strand near the house of Master Hans Kierstede," and all who wished to sell farm products or anything else were directed to conduct their business there. Numerous contemporary accounts and observations by foreign visitors in later years testify to the vibrant role the market played in the city's commercial history. Many of New Netherland's most prominent merchants spent their apprenticeship in New Amsterdam's free market.

Similar developments in Beverswyck (Albany) point to the growth of indigenous merchant activity in the upper Hudson Valley during this period. The minutes of the inferior court of justice (Kleine Banck van Justitie) for Fort Orange and Beverswyck reveal that many of the cases adjudicated before this body involved suits for the payment of debts and requests for enforcement of commercial contracts. Out of approximately 1,586 entries for the years 1652 to 1660, some 626 are easily identified as creditor requests for payment of debts. In most of these cases, a written debt obligation virtually assured judgment for the plantiff. It appears that the magistrates of Fort Orange and Beverswyck were as attentive to the needs of merchants as the magistrates of New Amsterdam.

By the end of the Dutch period, a merchant class had come to dominate the politics of the city of New Amsterdam and was vying with the landed interests of the Hudson Valley for control of local government. The Dutch merchant community, although less than a generation old at the time of the English conquest, would grow and prosper under English rule as it had in the last years of Dutch rule. Moreover it would remain ethnically Dutch for several generations, becoming at times a thorn in the side of English governors and a potential source of political unrest.

BIBLIOGRAPHY

Bachman, Van Cleaf. *Peltries or Plantations: The Economic Policies of the Dutch West India Company in New Netherland, 1623–1639.* Baltimore, Md., 1969.

Barbour, Violet. *Capitalism in Amsterdam in the Seventeenth Century.* The Johns Hopkins University Studies in Historical and Political Science, ser. 67, no. 1. Baltimore, Md., 1950.

Fernow, Berthold, ed. *The Records of New Amsterdam from 1653 to 1754.* 7 vols. New York, 1897.

Gehring, Charles T., ed. and trans. *Fort Orange Court Minutes, 1652–1660.* Syracuse, N.Y., 1990.

McCusker, John J. *Money and Exchange in Europe and America, 1600–1775: A Handbook.* Chapel Hill, N.C., 1978.

Maika, Dennis J. "The Credit System of the Manhattan Merchants in the Seventeenth Century." *De Halve Maen* 63, no. 2 (1990):1–3 and no. 3 (1990):5–7.

Rink, Oliver A. *Holland on the Hudson: An Economic and Social History of Dutch New York.* Ithaca, N.Y., 1986.

Oliver A. Rink

THE FRENCH COLONIES

A SOCIAL ANALYSIS

THREE PRINCIPAL KINDS of people carried on the ocean going commerce of the French Empire. Roman Catholic and Huguenot merchants were, in the final analysis, different social groups. The most powerful, however, was the third group: royal officials, financiers, magistrates, and military officers who dominated the monopoly trading companies and who traded on the side whenever they could. Such persons numbered about two-thirds of the 108 partners in the famous Compagnie des Cent-Associés, also known as Compagnie de la Nouvelle-France or Company of One Hundred Associates, founded in 1627. Merchants, so called, were no more than one-third of the partners. After that company disbanded in 1663, groups of officials and financiers managed the importing and selling of Canadian beaver pelts throughout almost the next hundred years. They also provided nearly half of the capital invested in the Indies Company (Compagnie des Indes) that monopolized the Canada trade from 1663 to 1674 and controlled the later Indies Company that monopolized trade with Louisiana until 1731. Some of these businessmen were merely investors, but many were part-time traders—*marchands* or *négociants*—in all but name.

Officials, officers, and financiers commonly traded on the side, especially when their careers took them out to a colony. At New Orleans in the middle of the eighteenth century, Governor Rigaud de Vaudreuil's officials—and even his wife—were busily trading. At Quebec nearly all of the intendants, government storekeepers, naval treasurers, and senior military officers imported cargoes of food, supplies, and trading goods, sometimes on a grand scale. The famous governor Louis de Buade de Frontenac owned a one-third share of a ship, *Le Saint Louis,* in the 1690s. Much of the fur trade, too, was in the hands of officers and officials. The fifty-one from Quebec who were arrested and tried on various charges of corruption in the notorious *affaire du Canada* (1761–1763) had only been trading as usual, but they were made scapegoats for the French naval defeats by which Canada was lost in the Seven Years' War.

Businessmen of this type were nearly all Roman Catholic, at least publicly, as the monarchy required them to be. Huguenots remained Huguenots, under the surface in many cases. For the age of the Roman Catholic Counter-Reformation, this is not surprising. The authoritarian governments of Louis XIII (r. 1617–1643) and Louis XIV (r. 1661–1715) had a decisive social effect upon the French merchant class by persecuting Protestants and by holding up purchasable offices, titles of nobility, and life at the royal court as the goals of a successful career. Two different social groups formed in consequence: on one hand, Roman Catholic families that aspired to venal offices leading to noble rank and a place in the approved society of the kingdom, and on the other hand, Protestant families (Huguenots) that were barred from royal offices by law but had a place in the cosmopolitan society of the Protestant Atlantic.

The differences between these two, reinforced by the policy of preventing Huguenots (identified by law as "new converts" to Catholicism) from establishing their families in French colonies, were more profound than the differences between French and colonial merchants. Catholic and Protestant merchants traded with one another, but their families, which were what they cared about most, remained largely separate. Even more separate were the families of those few Jewish merchants who were allowed to live at Bordeaux and Bayonne in the eighteenth century. Thus merchants in the French Empire were socially divided along religious lines. In studies of trade, it has been easy for historians to ignore religious and social factors, but the study of the merchants themselves brings religious identity into focus and shows it to have been as powerful an influence in merchants' lives as their pursuit of profits.

Two examples may illustrate the case. Pierre Garrisson (d. 1774), from a Huguenot family of Montauban, settled as a merchant at Bordeaux in partnership with other Protestants. Like so many others in the business classes, Garrisson's family and social affinities were entirely Protestant and included a wife from the Lafon family, relatives in most of the Protestant communities in southwestern France, uncles and cousins in Amsterdam, and family memories of his uncle Jacob Garrisson, arrested at Bordeaux in May 1705 for trying to escape to England with his family on a Dutch ship. In 1747 Garrisson and his partners were about to dispatch a ship to Canada, *Le Dragon,* which they had bought as *Le Saint-Esprit de Québec* and renamed.

Meanwhile several other ships were being fitted out at Bordeaux by another new arrival, Pierre Trottier Desauniers (1700–1757), born to a prominent Catholic family at Quebec. Having made a fortune as a businessman in Canada, Desauniers retired in 1747 to a country estate near Bordeaux, bought an office of *secrétaire du roi* for sixty-three thousand livres, married his daughters to noblemen, and settled his sons in the army, the church, or in trade. Unlike Garrisson and his circle, Trottier Desauniers was part of the social fabric of the French Empire.

Desauniers and Garrisson had one thing in common, however: they were outsiders newly arrived at Bordeaux. In this they were typical of the merchants in the French North American colonial trades. Established, prosperous families preferred to invest in the West Indian trade or the Newfoundland fisheries, both more profitable, and few sent their ships to New France, except in wartime under pressure from the royal government. Most ships were sent to New France by smaller or less-established traders, often patronized by church and state. Two types of information lead to this general conclusion: the relatively small number of sailings to the northern colonies—far fewer than to the West Indies or to the Newfoundland banks—and the humble origins of many merchants in these branches of trade.

To cite a few prominent late-seventeenth-to mid-eighteenth-century colonial traders at La Rochelle as examples, Antoine Grignon (c. 1612–1675) was illiterate and used to sign "AG" in a shaky hand. Jean Gitton (1633–1690) began as a baker in the dockside parish of Saint Nicolas supplying hardtack, *pain biscuit* (twice-cooked bread), to the ships at La Rochelle. Hilaire Bourgine (1650–1725) began as a shopkeeper's son from Poitiers who married a poor glazier's daughter. Paul Berry (1665–1709), Pierre Plassan (1670–1716), and Antoine Pascaud (1665–1717) all began their careers as indentured servants (*engagés*) contracting to work for two or three years in Canada at a fixed wage. Michel Rodrigue was born into a family of mariners at Louisbourg. All worked for years in Canada or were born there, but all returned to France and settled at La Rochelle. All of them were Roman Catholic. Life in the colonies offered them opportunities but reduced their prospects for social advancement, venal offices, titles of nobility, and the civilized country life they longed for. The few who settled in Canada or Acadia were usually either poor or else anchored by well-rooted families.

Some merchants did become true colonists. Among the earliest was Nicolas Denys (c. 1599–1688), who migrated to Acadia about 1647 from La Rochelle, where he had been in the colonial trades since the early 1630s. At Quebec, Charles Aubert de la Chesnaye (1632–1702) emerged in the 1660s as the leader in a trading partnership that drew together men from several ports of France. Later he was a founder and director of the French Compagnie du Nord ou de la Baie d'Hudson (1682–1700). No less prominent and prosperous was Jacques Le Ber (c. 1633–1706), who emigrated in the mid seventeenth century from Normandy as a young man. He sold imported goods at stores in Quebec and Montreal and exported cod, timber, barrel staves, and furs, all in partnership with other merchants and with a son who worked as his agent at La Rochelle. Le Ber eventually bought seigneurial properties

in Canada and in 1696 paid the Crown six thousand livres for royal *letters de noblesse*. He and Chesnaye chose to live at a colonial port, as did more and more merchants in the eighteenth century. But few of them traded on a large scale. Most transatlantic traffic was owned and managed by men at ports in France.

Even Chesnaye's success was due in some measure to his nephew, François-Louis Aubert (c. 1663–1711), who spent years selling beaver pelts in Amsterdam as a director of the official French beaver monopoly. There Aubert lived discreetly as an international Protestant merchant. Amsterdam and London, the shipping capitals of the world, welcomed Huguenot refugees from France, including many merchants. Large communities of them had been gathering at Dutch and English ports since early in the sixteenth century. As a result the Huguenot merchants in France maintained close but more or less secret connections in Holland, England, and their colonies. These connections served them well in their sales of furs abroad and in the sugar, tobacco, and indigo trades of the Caribbean that flourished from the 1650s. Thus Huguenot merchants worked within a worldwide network that included not only the "new converts" at French ports but also refugees in New England trading illegally with New France in the late seventeenth and early eighteenth centuries, men such as Henri Brunet (d. 1686), David Basset (d. 1724), Philippe Langlois (1651–1736), Gabriel Bernon (1644–1736), and the famous Faneuil brothers of Boston. Theirs was a relatively open society, the liberal world of the future that was to take over New France in 1759–1763 and France itself after 1789.

ORGANIZATION AND METHODS

Most merchants traded alone or in brief partnership with one or two others. Large, stable companies such as Robert Dugard's Compagnie du Canada were rare, and joint-stock companies were almost unknown. A partner in one of the big royal monopolies signed for a specified sum in a notarized agreement with the official company figurehead. The typical private partnership in an Atlantic port was formed for three years by a renewable notarized contract. More often than not, partners were relatives, for the family was the basic social unit in that age and dominated the lives of merchants, as of other classes. In any case, partners were usually of the same religion; partnerships of Catholics and Protestants were rare.

Trade in colonial towns was in the hands of four principal kinds of merchants. The most numerous were the established *marchands domiciliés*, Roman Catholics with the rights of permanent residents and relatives among the clergy, accustomed to dealing in many different commodities as there were no guilds in the colonies. Nicolas Pinaud (c. 1665–1722) and his partners in the Perthuis family are good examples, active in every branch of trade open in the colony. Such established men were sometimes at odds with the *marchands forains,* who typically came and went with the ships or who could not establish themselves as permanent residents because they were Huguenots. During the last quarter century of the French regime, Huguenot families such as the Dumas and Rauly families from Montauban, specializing in woolens, conducted more and more of the colonial trade in New France.

A third type of merchant, including men from both the *forains* and *domiciliés,* was the factors serving metropolitan firms either for salaries or on a commission of 5 percent of the profits on imports and 2.5 percent of the value on exports. For instance, François Havy and Jean Lefebvre, two Huguenots from Normandy, represented Dugard and Company of Rouen at Quebec in the 1730s and 1740s. Joseph Lustre was sent out from Bordeaux to Louisbourg as the factor of the Baron d'Huart fishing company. Much trade was managed by a fourth type of businessman, the magistrate, government official, or military officer whose commercial activities are all too often left out of account because they would not have wanted to be described as merchants. Good examples are Guillaume Estèbe, a government storekeeper, eventually a member of the colonial council, and the post commander, Pierre-Joseph de Céloron, sieur de Blainville, who married a merchant's daughter at Montreal and traded in furs and supplies at the various western posts he commanded in the 1730s and 1740s.

As soon as they could, French merchants invested in land and houses, though they also kept large sums of cash in chests at home to meet unexpected claims, to pay dowries for daughters' marriages, to advance the wages of departing ships' crews, and to sustain the family's credit in general. Cash was scarce in that age. Most merchants depended upon credit. Payments were made by book balances, by promissory notes, or by bills of exchange redeemable in a specified number of months. In such circumstances, a merchant's reputation was one of his principal assets, and in this respect French merchants were no different from others.

Merchants in the colonial trades usually lived within a few minutes' walk of one another near the docks: in Lower Town Quebec; near the Mississippi in New Orleans; in the parish of Saint-Michel at Bordeaux; near the Seine flowing through Rouen; on the tiny island where Saint-Malo perched; or within the walls of such small ports as La Rochelle, Bayonne, and Louisbourg. In New Orleans, small-time traders and merchants, called *caboteurs* and *gaboteurs,* lived in the interior. Much of their business life was collective. Shipping insurance was underwritten by subscription, bottomry loans were locally obtained, and creditors normally assembled to deal with a bankrupt debtor. Bankruptcies were frequent, and their causes seldom clear.

Except for the West Indies, colonies furnished little that could fill the ships returning to France, and the trade with New France was mainly in outward-bound supplies of textiles, hardware, and foodstuffs. All the furs from New France scarcely filled four ships in a year. Return cargoes of fish, timber, and coal were sometimes profitable, but merchants hoped for more from triangular voyages that included a stop in Martinique, Saint-Domingue (later Haiti), or Guadeloupe. Without the missionary efforts of the Counter-Reformation and the imperial ambitions of the Bourbon kings, there might have been no French colonies in North America.

Poorer than merchants in the West India or East India trades, those in New France depended fundamentally on the activities of church and state for their business. The Company of New France was mainly a missionary enterprise. With its demise Louis XIV created employment for merchants by making New France a Crown colony to which a governor, an intendant, a bishop, regiments of soldiers, and new colonists

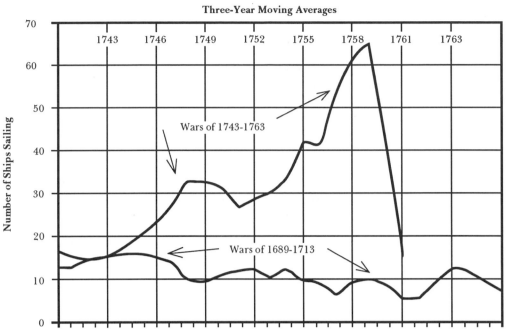

Shipping to Canada in Wartime
The Trends in 1686-1713 and 1740-1763
Three-Year Moving Averages

The rising trend during the wars of 1743-1763 reflects French imperial efforts and immense spending.

were to be sent. Shipping and trading increased in the 1660s and 1670s, and La Rochelle, the principal port in the Canada trade, drew Bordeaux merchants into that trade from 1671. Thereafter four wars resulting from imperial policies affected the rise and fall of merchant fortunes more than any other factors. These were the wars that filled most of the years from 1689 to 1713 and from 1744 to 1763. Annual totals of shipping to Canada rose at the beginning of each war—in 1684–1689, 1701–1704, 1743–1749, and 1755–1758. Government orders were the dynamic factor in this wartime trade, and it collapsed when government credit failed, notably in 1705 and 1759. Merchants' fortunes were severely taxed as a result, and bankruptcies followed.

In the eighteenth century, government initiatives brought into being the new colonies of Louisiana and Île Royale (Cape Breton Island). About 1730 Louisbourg and New Orleans began to draw more and more trade from Quebec as well as from France. But the wars that broke out in 1744 soon ruined the merchants in these trades, such as Charles-Polycarpe Bourgine

(1696–1756) and Jean Jung (1698–1753). Only the authority and credit of the royal government, based on a hope of victory, sustained French transatlantic trade between 1744 and 1759. Had this trade been left to market forces, it would have died out as did nearly every other branch of French seaborne traffic in those years. A general collapse did come in 1759, when the French government went bankrupt in October and November; most of the merchants who specialized in the colonial trades were ruined then. Yet some did not give up hope. In the spring of 1759, François Lavaud of Bordeaux was planning to establish a trading company at New Orleans in Louisiana, and on 11 February 1762 he sent off his youngest son, Bernard Lavaud, to take charge of it. The Crown later sued François Lavaud for embezzling the funds allocated for the purchase of goods for Louisiana.

THE FRENCH IMPERIAL ENVIRONMENT

Merchants had much less influence in the French Empire than their counterparts had in the Dutch and British empires. For one thing they ranked much lower on the social scale in France. For another they did not have the representation that the Dutch had in the Estates General and the English had in Parliament. The Bourbon monarchy, the Roman Catholic church, and the official financiers dominated French life in an authoritarian manner. This was especially so during the long rule of Louis XIV, who developed an aggressive imperial policy to impose his authority and his religion upon the Atlantic world. The Bourbon government saw to it that Quebec, Montreal, and later New Orleans and Louisbourg remained imperial bases with few of the institutions found at metropolitan ports. There were no mayors or town councils, no active chambers of commerce, no money markets (*bourses*), no commercial courts (*jurisdictions consulaires*), no guilds, no representative Deputies of Commerce, and no journals or printing presses. The merchant at a colonial port worked in circumstances different from those at French ports like Bordeaux, Bayonne, Rouen, or Saint-Malo, where a certain spirit of independence, local and provincial, survived.

Even more, the freedom enjoyed by merchants at Dutch and English ports, where gazettes and newspapers flourished, especially in the eighteenth century, made a striking contrast. Boston had its first news journal in 1704, New York and Philadelphia a short time later; but Quebec and Montreal had no public press at all until after the British conquest. Merchants depended upon news in order to make informed decisions about cargoes, prices, and other matters, but French merchants had to depend upon private letters or illegal foreign gazettes because church and state maintained an oppressive censorship. Beneath the surface of imperial policy, however, much colonial business was driven by the private commercial and social motives of the merchants.

BIBLIOGRAPHY

Biggar, Henry Percival. *The Early Trading Companies of New France: A Contribution to the History of Commerce and Discovery in North America.* Toronto, Ontario, 1901; repr. Clifton, N.J., 1972.

Bosher, J. F. *The Canada Merchants, 1713–1763.* Oxford, England, 1987.

———. *Men and Ships in the Canada Trade, 1660–1760: A Biographical Dictionary.* Ottawa, 1992.

Dechêne, Louise. *Habitants et marchands de Montréal au XVIIe siècle.* Montreal, 1974.

Francis, Daniel, and Toby Morantz. *Partners in Furs: A History of the Fur Trade in Eastern James Bay, 1600–1870.* Kingston, Ontario, and Montreal, 1983.

Giraud, Marcel. *Histoire de la Louisiane française.* 4 vols. Paris, 1953–1968.

Menkis, Richard. *The Gradis Family of Eighteenth-Century Bordeaux: A Social and Economic Study.* Ph.D. diss., Brandeis University, 1988.

Miquelon, Dale Bernard. *Dugard of Rouen: French Trade to Canada and the West Indies, 1729–1770.* Montreal and London, 1978.

Ray, Arthur J., and Donald Freeman. *"Give Us Good Measure": An Economic Analysis of Relations Between the Indians and the Hudson's Bay Company Before 1763.* Toronto, Ontario, 1978.

J. F. Bosher

SEE ALSO Mercantilism; Relations with the Parent Country; and Trade and Commerce.

THE SPANISH BORDERLANDS

MERCHANTS OF THE COLONIAL SPANISH Borderlands served a vast region that stretched from the Pacific to the Atlantic oceans and at times from the Canadian border of colonial Spanish Louisiana to the Gulf Coast. These diverse men and women of several nations and socioeconomic statuses operated within both an international commercial system and a cross-cultural frontier exchange network. Ideally, at least from the Spanish Crown's perspective, mercantilism governed the transactions of borderland merchants, but in reality, local officials and participants practiced flexibility in their commercial dealings, both formal and informal, as a matter of necessity. For such frontier, marginal, peripheral regions as Spain's North American Borderlands, merchants functioned not only within a formal sphere of trade-alliance relations but also among those informal, intimate forms of cross-cultural trade.

Several trading systems prevailed across Spain's diverse northern frontier, with variations based on geopolitical, economic, and demographic characteristics of the region, as well as temporal changes. Spain experimented with these systems as means to expand and defend its borderlands. The *presidio*-mission system functioned primarily in Florida and northern New Spain, the trading-post system along the Gulf Coast of Louisiana and West Florida and up the Mississippi River valley, and the urban market system in settled areas throughout the borderlands (of which there were very few until the eighteenth century).

THE MISSIONS AND THEIR DECLINE

Jesuit missionaries in California and Arizona and Franciscans in California, Arizona, New Mexico, Texas, and Florida initially supplied food and other necessities to the civilian and military establishments (*presidios* and pueblos) located near their missions. Jesuit and Franciscan friars also obtained farm implements and livestock for their converts. The missions acted as primary suppliers from the time of settlement in the second half of the sixteenth century through most of the seventeenth century. The period of decline begins in the late 1600s and continues into the 1700s, when lay merchants eclipsed the friars. Through their control of mission populations and economies, friars administered the disposal of mission surpluses, often demanding payment in coin for goods manufactured by Native American laborers and foodstuffs such as corn, wheat, vegetables, fruits, meat, and poultry. In turn, missionaries procured cloth, tobacco, tools, medicines, and ceremonial items from their agents in Mexico City and Havana or by means of the *situado* (annual subsidy from the Crown).

California and Arizona Jesuits controlled the mission, and for all practical purposes the regional economy from production to distribution. A source of bitter controversy, the Jesuits' dominance of material surpluses and their insistence on payment in hard currency stunted the growth of a mercantile sector, incurred the jealousy of non-Indian settlers, and eventually contributed to the Jesuits' rapid expulsion.

In Florida, Indians in the Franciscan missions that surrounded Apalachee Bay supplied the nearby military garrison of San Marcos de Apalachee (about twenty miles [32 kilometers] south of modern-day Tallahassee), marketed their products far to the east at Saint Augustine, and sold additional surpluses to ships departing from Apalachee Bay. Floridians often depended on mission products for their survival but also resented the friars' control of regional resources.

During the eighteenth century, laymen gained control of these mercantile activities and displaced the missionaries as major suppliers to the Spanish populations of northern New Spain and Florida. As long as Native Americans overwhelmingly outnumbered Hispanics, the missions could maintain their monopoly over indigenous land, labor, produce, and markets. The lure of silver discoveries, favorable prospects for commercial agriculture and husbandry, threats from hostile Native American nations, demographic decline among mission Indians, and competition for territory from the English and French brought growing numbers of Spaniards—military and civilian. They began to challenge the missions' monopoly. As prosperity came, albeit gradually and sporadically, to Spain's northern frontier, it generated more intense competition for resources. Those secular merchants attracted to the region resented mission control of trade. All across the Spanish Borderlands, the missions themselves and their mercantile pursuits experienced declining influence during the eighteenth century.

English and French encroachment in the southeast borderlands intensified in the 1700s. It contributed to replacement of the *presidio*-mission with the trading-post system in some parts of Florida and to the continuation of this system in areas along the Gulf Coast and Mississippi River (the province of Louisiana) that Spain acquired from France and England. These nations seemed to have greater success with the Native Americans of eastern North America, so Spanish officials began to imitate their methods. British raids on the Apalachee region decimated the Franciscan missions; what natives remained resettled near Saint Augustine. Spanish officials, in turn, established a string of trade centers along the Florida Gulf Coast and into the Florida interior. Like the French and English, they intended to win alliances with Native peoples through trade and goodwill.

AGENTS OF THE CROWN

Royal authorities granted monopolies and commissioned agents to conduct this trade. Because Spain had few traders skilled at dealing with Native Americans and lacked the supplies and funds necessary for such trade, authorities turned to Anglo (primarily Scot) agents. When Spain acquired Louisiana from France in 1763 and West Florida from England in 1783, the Crown elected to maintain already established Indian trade centers, the principal one being Mobile, as well as the French and Anglo agents who directed the centers' mercantile activities. One of the most influential, extensive, and active firms along the Spanish Gulf and Atlantic coasts was that of Panton, Leslie and Company (Established in late 1782 or early 1783, its name was officially changed to John Forbes and Company in 1784.) With primary trading centers at Saint Augustine, San Marcos de Apalachee, Pensacola, and Mobile, Panton, Leslie and Company acted on behalf of Spain to provide Native Americans in the southeast borderlands with the British cloth, arms and ammunition, and trinkets they desired. Spain hoped to exchange these goods for deerskins, alliances, and, if necessary, warriors to check United States aggression.

The five founding partners of Panton, Leslie and Company—William Panton, John Leslie, Thomas Forbes, Charles McLatchy, and William Alexander—were all born in Scotland, came to the Americas in the 1760s and 1770s, and entered into the southern Indian trade prior to the American Revolution. They made each other's acquaintance while acting as merchants in and between Charleston, Savannah, Saint Augustine, and Nassau; all remained loyal to England during the colonies' struggle for independence. With England's loss of the thirteen original colonies and acquisition of East and West Florida in 1783, these Scotsmen left Charleston and Savannah and established residences in the Floridas and the Bahamas. They also merged to form Panton, Leslie and Company, building trade networks throughout the southeastern borderlands and the British West Indies. In addition to their mercantile activities, the partners acted as attorneys, public officials, and prominent landholders in their communities.

Although Thomas Forbes's younger brother John did not become a partner until 1792, he emerged as leader of the firm following Panton's death in 1801. By the time the firm's name was officially changed to John Forbes and Company in 1804, only one of the original partners (Thomas Forbes) still lived. Other Scotsmen—William Simpson and James and John Innerarity—perpetuated the firm's involvement in the southeastern Indian trade until the mid nineteenth century.

One of the Scots' rivals was Gilbert Antoine de Saint Maxent, a wealthy, experienced French fur trader to whom Spain granted a monopoly for the Mississippi valley Indian trade when the Crown acquired Louisiana. Panton, Leslie and Company, however, eclipsed Saint Maxent as Indian traders when Saint Maxent ran into problems supplying the Crown with adequate trade goods in the 1780s. Many years of experience with a variety of Native nations and better, more reliable access to the English trade goods that southern tribes preferred gave the Scottish firm a decided advantage.

THE ROLE OF LOWER-LEVEL TRADERS

A host of smaller-scale agents and middlemen (and women), often financed by colonial wholesale and retail merchants, also scoured the Spanish Borderlands to trade cloth, arms and ammunition, and liquor for Native American deerskins and foodstuffs. They were especially active within eighteenth-century trading-post centers, providing goods not only to the natives but also to white and free black inhabitants and black slaves. Though the Spanish Crown tried to create a monopoly of exchange through its contracted agents (such as Panton, Leslie and Company and Saint Maxent), the borderland Indian trade actually involved many persons of all races, nationalities, and socioeconomic groups. Wholesalers and even large retailers forwarded goods on credit

600

to many small traders, who in turn advanced goods to Native Americans in anticipation of that season's hunt.

These peddlers and traders, many of them *castas* (of mixed race) and a few of them women, played a vital role in the frontier exchange economy of the Spanish Borderlands; they facilitated immediate distribution of goods, furnished and used a long-term credit network, and contributed to the commercialization of marketing throughout the region. Of course, when extended too far, credit transactions often resulted in long-term debts and even bankruptcies over a series of bad years. The myriad of colonial court cases involving "collection of a debt" attests to the grievances sparked by an overextended credit network.

Persons of many races also participated in the many levels of urban marketing. Merchants who served the cities and towns of Spain's northern borderlands ranged from wholesalers to brokers and agents, retailers and shopkeepers, and vendors and peddlers. In general, the higher-level merchants—wholesalers and brokers— were white (Spanish, French, or Anglo) male agents for large commercial houses in Philadelphia, New York, Mexico City, Havana, Cádiz, Seville, Bordeaux, and London. Familial relationships often connected these frontier agents with their metropolitan suppliers and distributors. Overall, colonial wholesale merchants imported manufactured products (especially cloth), alcohol, weapons, flour (wheat was scarce in southern climes), and African slaves. The wholesale merchants exported furs, skins, lumber, indigo, tobacco, rice, corn, sugar, cotton, and some precious metals.

Colonial retailers and shopkeepers obtained imported goods from wholesalers and regionally produced goods from vendors, peddlers, and the general populace. Although primarily white and male like the wholesalers, this next level of merchants—retailers and shopkeepers—also had some female and mixed-blood practitioners. They in turn competed with vendors and peddlers, many of whom were women, slaves, and/or *castas,* for local suppliers and customers. Traders of Spanish, Anglo, French, German, West Indian, African, and Native American descent contributed to the vitality of multiethnic markets at New Orleans, Mobile, Pensacola,

Saint Augustine, Natchitoches, El Paso, Taos, Santa Fe, Tucson, San Diego, and Los Angeles. The role of Native Americans in urban mercantile exchanges declined during the eighteenth century throughout the borderlands, due primarily to demographic factors. They were replaced—or displaced—by European immigrants, American migrants, and free and enslaved persons of African descent.

The African tradition of market activity persisted most strongly in urban areas along the Gulf Coast where slave and free black populations congregated. Free people of African descent hawked their own wares, produce, and baked goods, and slaves hawked those of their masters on city streets, from market stalls, and along levee banks. Slaves sold the produce of their subsistence plots and fresh wild game at urban markets; in New Orleans they joined Native American, free black, Acadian, Isleño (Canary Island), and German traders at *el mercado de la Conga* (Congo Square) and the riverside market established by the Spanish city council on the site of an ancient Indian trading ground (the French market).

ILLICIT TRADE

In addition to participating in a cross-cultural regional network of exchange, merchants at all levels engaged in smuggling and illegal trade. Both regional trade and smuggling constituted practical responses to the metropolis's failure to provide sufficient, reliable supplies according to the mercantilist model. Colonial merchants along Spain's northern frontier exchanged goods across national borders, ethnic and racial lines, and intercolonial boundaries (for example, between Louisiana and Texas or Florida and Cuba). Some of the most prized items that borderland merchants smuggled into the colonies included African slaves from the West Indies or directly from Africa, New Mexico and Texas livestock into French Louisiana, wheat and flour from Anglo America, and wine and luxury goods from France. Against their masters' wishes, African slaves secretively sold produce (cultivated on their subsistence plots) and game (hunted in the forests and swamps) to Mississippi River traders, called *caboteurs;* enterprising slaves used these funds to purchase tobacco, extra clothes, trinkets, and sometimes even their freedom.

CONCLUSION

Whether engaged in wholesale trade on a grand scale or in the small individual transactions that collectively amounted to a substantial proportion of subsistence trade, merchants in the colonial Spanish Borderlands contributed to the daily survival of colonial populations and cultures, and occasionally even to their prosperity. Jesuit and Franciscan friars, Native American producers and hunters, Anglo Indian traders, Spanish wholesale merchants, slave and free African-American vendors, European truck farmers—all participated in and shaped the cross-cultural exchange network that characterized Spain's North American frontier.

BIBLIOGRAPHY

Coker, William S., and Thomas D. Watson. *Indian Traders of the Southeastern Spanish Borderlands: Panton, Leslie & Company and John Forbes & Company, 1783–1847.* Pensacola, Fla., 1986. A comprehensive history of these Scottish traders. Based in Florida, the firm virtually monopolized Indian trade throughout the southeast Spanish Borderlands in this period.

Hu-DeHart, Evelyn. *Missionaries, Miners, and Indians: Spanish Contact with the Yaqui Nation of Northwestern New Spain, 1533–1820.* Tucson, Ariz., 1981. The author's thorough study of the struggle between Jesuit, military, and mining interests for dominance in the region provides a detailed assessment of mission mercantile and other economic activities, as well as laymen's usurpation of these pursuits.

Matter, Robert Allen. "Economic Basis of the Seventeenth-Century Florida Missions." *Florida Historical Quarterly* 52, no. 1 (1973):18–38. An examination of the Franciscan mission system that flourished among Florida Native Americans in the seventeenth century; concentrates on the economic basis of this system.

Moorhead, Max. *New Mexico's Royal Road: Trade and Travel on the Chihuahua Trail.* Norman, Okla., 1958. Looks at commerce between New Mexico and Mexico City, in particular how Chihuahua merchants gained control of supply caravans from the missions. Chihuahua merchants profited as middlemen in the Mexico City–Santa Fe trade.

Scholes, France V. "The Supply Service of the New Mexican Missions in the Seventeenth Century." *New Mexico Historical Review* 5, nos. 1, 2, 4 (1930):93–115, 186–209, 386–404. The author gives a detailed history of the missions' mercantile activities during their high point. He provides translations of supply contracts, including lists of goods, prices, and terms of exchange.

Usner, Daniel H., Jr. "The Frontier Exchange Economy of the Lower Mississippi Valley in the Eighteenth Century." *William and Mary Quarterly*, 3rd ser., 44, no. 2 (1987):165–192. Argues that a cross-cultural exchange network operated throughout the Gulf Coast and Mississippi valley region and played a significant role in the economy and society of the frontier (and can be applied to other frontier regions).

Kimberly S. Hanger

SEE ALSO **Mercantilism; Relations with the Parent Country;** and **Trade and Commerce.**

ARTISANS

IN THE NOT-YET-INDUSTRIALIZED economy of colonial America, the artisan was a ubiquitous and pivotal figure. Whether crafting such simple and commonplace items as shoes, coats, and nails or producing more complex colonial commodities such as homes, furniture, and transatlantic sailing vessels, early American society depended on the labor of the skilled craftsman. Together with commerce and agriculture, artisan production lay at the very heart of the North American colonial economy.

Artisans were among the earliest European settlers to come to America. Indeed, as the leaders of the craft-starved Virginia Company discovered soon after they landed in the Chesapeake in 1607, successful settlement depended on having ready access to the services of carpenters, blacksmiths, and leather workers of all kinds. The early successes of the better-planned Spanish, French, Dutch, and later English settlements of the sixteenth and early seventeenth centuries rested in large part on the fact that these ventures began with full complements of artisans drawn from the construction, metalworking, and leather working trades.

Within a generation of their initial founding, each of the major European settlements supported developed craft economies. In rural areas farmer-artisans supplied the local milling, blacksmithing, and construction needs of their communities, while in the seventeenth-century cities of Quebec, Boston, and New Amsterdam (present-day New York City), French, English, and Dutch artisans practiced trades ranging from bricklaying to barrelmaking. Blacksmiths and carpenters could be found in even the smallest communities of northern New Spain. By 1700 the English seaport cities of Boston, New York, and Philadelphia counted more than a hundred trades, and contemporaries pointed to the fact that American artisans produced virtually any article available from Britain. In fact before the American Revolution ended the transatlantic connection, British and Scottish merchants regularly purchased American-made ships, not only for their competitive prices but because of their superior quality and oceangoing durability.

Artisans fabricated a wide variety of products falling into a handful of categories in colonial North America. Ship carpenters, sail makers, caulkers, riggers, and rope makers made up the bulk of the maritime trades that formed the backbone of the urban seaboard economies. In the major English colonial seaport cities, artisans crafted large oceangoing merchant ships for local and British mercantile houses, while others produced a myriad of sloops and smaller boats for local merchants engaged in the coastal and inland water trade. In New France, skilled boatmakers built the canoes that enabled France to dominate the interior of North America for a century and a half.

The construction and furnishing trades were equally vital elements in the North American economy, providing shelter for growing numbers of American colonists as well as supplying the wharves, shops, and countinghouses that made the colonial economy hum. Artisans in the leather and clothing trades—shoemakers, harness makers, tanners, tailors, and stocking weavers, to name but a few—met the needs of a local clientele, as did those—including butchers, bakers, and brewers—who labored in the food and refreshment trades. Women dominated the female clothing trades and, in the Spanish Borderlands, tanned hides, fashioned pottery, and made moccasins. Coopers and stave makers produced containers for the agricultural export trade that was the mainstay of the export economy, while highly skilled craftsmen such as printers, silversmiths, and clock and instrument makers produced their goods for local and overseas consumers.

Like the colonial population itself, artisans came from diverse national backgrounds. Spanish artisans predominated in the borderlands of New Spain, although by the late sixteenth century increasing numbers of Spanish-trained Indians practiced trades alongside their Iberian counterparts. While French artisans dominated laboring-class life in New France, it was Native American craftsmen who prepared the furs and hides that were the foundation of the Indian-French trade. In New Netherland (present-day New York), Dutch artisans plied their trades in Holland's American colony and continued to constitute a major portion of the labor force after the colony came under English rule in 1664. And with the exception of New England, where the population remained almost entirely English throughout the colonial era, the Anglo-American colonies were ethnically heterogenous, with Middle Atlantic and southern artisans tracing their ancestries to England, Ireland, Scotland, and beginning in the 1730s, the Palatine region of Germany. Later, following the capture of Quebec by the English in 1759, small groups of expatriate French artisans drifted into the port cities of British America, where they joined the Huguenot craftsmen who had fled to America at the beginning of the eighteenth century to escape religious persecution in their homeland.

ARTISANS AND THEIR CRAFTS

There were many ways to define an artisan in the seventeenth and eighteenth centuries, and the early American lexicon reflected the fundamental ambiguities involved in any formal definition. In addition to the word "artisan" (or "artizan"), colonists frequently referred to producers as "handicraftsmen," "artificers," "mechanics," or simply "craftsmen." The uses of the terms were in practice so variable that they reflected less the level of skill or accomplishment of an individual producer than the regional dialect of the speaker. Yet despite this nominal ambiguity, colonists from Canada to the northern borders of New Spain had little difficulty in recognizing those men and women who worked up raw materials into the finished commodities that appeared in every local and regional market.

At any time during the colonial era, the surest way to define an artisan was by reference to his or her possession of a skill. It was the knowledge of materials, tools, techniques, production processes, and marketing strategies that set the artisan apart from those whose income depended on their brawn alone. In a world that was already divided into those who worked with their heads and others who worked with their hands, artisans occupied a middle ground, combining in their trade a degree of manual labor with the intellectual refinement of prior training, thought, and planning.

Artisans purchased this skill through a long term of apprenticeship to their craft. As potential artisans reached the age of thirteen or fourteen, their parents sought to secure their future by indenturing them to a master craftsman, in whose shop they would learn "the mysteries of the trade" that would make them full-fledged craftsmen. While Dutch parents usually relied upon informal family connections to secure apprenticeships, most apprenticeship indentures were written contracts negotiated between parents and masters which stipulated that the children live in the home of the master until adulthood, learn the skills of the craft as well as the fundamentals of reading, writing, and basic mathematics, and receive a gift of clothing and perhaps tools at the expiration of their term. Depending on the difficulty and lucrativeness of the trade, the parents might be required to pay the master an entry fee to take on the aspiring apprentices, although the relative lack of labor in colonial America made many trades accessible for only a token sum. In the English colonies small numbers of aspiring women artisans were apprenticed in the same way, although to master craftswomen in the seamstressing, mantuamaking, and hatmaking trades.

Apprenticeships lasted through the adolescent years and generally ended by the age of twenty-one. The average period of apprenticeship thus lasted about seven years. Trades requiring less skill often ended earlier while those that required highly refined skills, like instrument making and engraving, generally lasted a year or two longer. But whatever the term, the young apprentices typically spent the first year or so of their indenture performing the drudging tasks of hauling, lifting, cleaning, and errand running that formed the common introduction to all trades. After proving their allegiance to the craft and to the master by enduring hard physical labor and the taunts of senior apprentices and journeymen, the neophytes, now in their mid teens, were relieved of their most onerous tasks and taught the rudiments of their trade. By the time they approached the end of their service, the apprentices were well versed in the everyday operations of their craft and possessed most of the skills necessary for the practice of their trade. With their "freedom dues" in hand, the young craftsmen were now ready to embark on the next stage of their training, the journeymanship.

In France and in Europe generally, journeymanship was a formalized institution in which semi-trained craftsmen traveled from town to town learning new techniques in different shops while they saved money and honed their skills. In America this journeyman phase was never formalized. Instead, young American craftsmen who possessed skills but few funds spent the years immediately after their apprenticeship saving the money that would allow them to marry and enter their trade as full-fledged masters. In English America this meant working for a few years on a piecework basis for an established craftsman in one of the seaport cities or the larger country towns. In New France, on the other hand, most young craftsmen bypassed this stage of dependency entirely and typically earned their savings by joining fur trading expeditions or by entering into partnerships with merchant-investors, established craftsmen, or tradesmen's widows. Thus, while young American journeymen might move about in search of the most lucrative employment, in contrast to Europe the journeyman's "tramp" never became a widespread American practice.

So too with the guild. Although a few masters attempted to establish guilds in the seventeenth century, the guild system never took hold outside Spanish America. A major reason was that the relative scarcity of labor in America made guilds unnecessary as regulators of labor, and the widespread dominance of European guilds by a small coterie of wealthy and exploitative masters did little to recommend the institution to Americans. Thus, unlike their European counterparts, American journeymen were not required to apply to a guild for permission to practice their trade, nor were they required to produce a "masterpiece" to demonstrate their skills to a local guild examining committee. When American journeymen had accumulated the savings and credit necessary to rent a shop, buy tools and materials, and set up a home, they were ready to join the ranks of the community's master craftsmen.

Until the middle of the eighteenth century, entry into an independent mastership required only modest capital. While the less skilled and less lucrative trades, such as shoemaking and tailoring, might require an investment of as little as from £5 to £20 local currency, the majority of trades required something between £50 and £75. Only the most skilled and remunerative trades, such as jewelry and instrument making, or those few trades that required expensive machinery and equipment, like ropemaking, printing, tanning, and iron founding, required more than a £100 initial investment. This situation began to change after 1750, however, as increasing numbers of American journeymen found that disruptions caused by the colonial wars between England and France, the growing instability of the imperial economy, and mounting competition from English manufactured goods made entry into the ranks of master craftsmen increasingly difficult, especially in those trades requiring more than modest capitalization. But while the colonial era ended on a note of anxiety and heightened insecurity, the path to independent proprietorship remained open to many young craftsmen.

Before the end of the eighteenth century, most master craftsmen operated as independent producers; that is, as individuals who owned their own tools, purchased their own materials, and relied on the help of their families, apprentices, journeymen, and, less frequently, free or bound laborers to fashion their goods. Most worked in small shops (often attached to their homes) that in urban areas they rented and in rural areas they generally owned. The workday, which typically ran from ten to twelve hours in winter and from fourteen to sixteen hours in summer, was regulated by the available hours of sunlight, candles being too expensive to use for nighttime work. Most artisans worked five and a half days during the week, with Sunday reserved for rest, recreation, and worship. The craftsmen's tools were hand-held and machinery was primitive, usually nothing more than a foot-driven potter's wheel or a hand-cranked wood lathe. Power thus came from the exercise of human muscle, and the pace of work was governed as much by the strength and endurance of the producers as by the nature of the work itself.

While most colonial products came directly from the shops of small masters, some were too large, complex, or expensive to be produced by a single craftsman. In some of the more capital-intensive enterprises—shipyards are the most prominent examples—individual artisans worked as subcontractors to the owners of the concern, providing their own tools and hiring their own journeymen and apprentices to work beside them. In others, such as iron foundries, ropewalks, and tanneries, artisans simply hired their time for an agreed-upon amount. In both cases, however, artisans retained the personal and work autonomy that marked the life of skilled craftsmen everywhere in colonial America. Negotiating work, hours, and payment directly with the owner (who might also have an artisan background), the artisans worked on their own terms, limited only by the necessity to complete the task and by the customary rules of the trade.

Defined in this way, artisans were found throughout colonial America. Craftsmen were located in the countryside as well as the city, in the South as well as the North, and on the high seas as well as on terra firma. In short, artisans were present wherever more than a small handful of colonists congregated for trade or settlement.

Urban artisans made up between one-third and one-half of the adult male population (and less than 1 percent of the female population) in the port cities of Quebec, Louisbourg, Boston, New York, Philadelphia, Charleston, Mobile, and New Orleans. These seaport economies were directly tied to regional and overseas trade, and their commercial nature was reflected in the occupational structure of each community. The port cities supported a wide variety of crafts, but the shipbuilding and the maritime support trades dominated artisan production in the English ports of Boston, New York, and Philadelphia while the processing of furs by Native Americans, and of lumber and naval stores by local white artisans dominated production in the French cities of Canada and the Gulf region. The construction, tanning, leather working, and metalworking trades rounded out the list of the largest urban crafts in these cities, with the remainder ranging from a few dozen to more than a hundred other artisan occupations.

While urban artisans played a prominent role in North American life, most colonial artisans lived in rural rather than urban communities. It was the rare agricultural village that did not have its resident blacksmith or carpenter, and many rural towns supported at least a dozen trades. In the smallest villages, these local craftsmen were usually part-time farmers as well as practicing artisans, but in the larger agrarian trading centers like Concord, Massachusetts, artisans practiced their trades year-round. One important distinction between the rural and urban artisan was that rural craftsmen often served shorter apprenticeships (typically with a nearby craftsman) and practiced more than one trade. This was especially true in the agrarian villages, where the demand for skilled labor was seldom sufficient to attract the kind of specialized craftsmen found routinely in seaport centers. But whether they lived in town or village, the wealth and social standing of most rural artisans made them virtually indistinguishable from the farmers with whom they lived.

Before they were displaced by African-American slave craftsmen in the mid eighteenth century, white artisans practiced their trades in the Anglo-American South as well. Like many of their northern counterparts, the rural artisans of the South were concentrated in the woodworking, leather, clothing, and smithing trades. Most lived close to the plantations that dotted the tidewater and Piedmont settlements of the Chesapeake and Carolinas, and most were tied exclusively to the local plantation economy. After 1730, however, increasing numbers of plantation owners began to bind their slaves as apprentices to local artisans, and by the close of the colonial era, competition from slave artisans drove growing numbers of white craftsmen from the slaveholding regions of English America.

ARTISAN TRADITIONS

Colonial artisans shared with their European counterparts a body of moral precepts and a distinctive view of the world. The content of their small-producer tradition is especially clear in the case of Anglo-American urban craftsmen, but similar traditions existed among French, Spanish, and Dutch artisans in the early modern era.

The cornerstone of the artisan moral tradition was labor, and from this foundation flowed the related notions of democracy, competency, independence, and community. Given the critical services rendered by artisans to early American communities, it is easy to understand that craftsmen thought of their skilled labor as a central element in the smooth functioning of colonial society. As one Connecticut artisan put it, skilled labor was the accumulated "genius of the people," and a popular New York writer went so far as to claim that mechanics formed the very "axis of society." The time spent in apprenticeship, the skills laboriously learned and honed through years of practice, and the lifelong contribution to the well-being of the community gave to the artisan a deep-seated feeling of pride, purpose, and social respectability. Artisans viewed their labor as something more than work alone, and they thought of themselves as more important than a worker simply earning his or her living. In practicing their trade, the artisans saw themselves as performing a service, not only to family and customers, but to the larger community in which they lived. The artisans' view of their place in community life was forcefully captured in a declaration written by Philadelphia craftsmen during a debate with city merchants

in 1779. Arguing against the merchants' claim that the city's artisans were nothing more than hired workers and subcontractors, the artisans reminded the community of the indispensability of their skilled labor:

[After the British occupation of the city in 1777–1778,] there was not a vessel, scarcely a boat, to be seen in the river. It was therefore impossible that those who then professed themselves merchants . . . could exercise their professions without the accumulated assistance of the several trades and manufacturers concerned in the art of building and fitting out vessels for sea. Ship carpenters, joiners, blacksmiths, gunsmiths, blockmakers, tanners, curriers, painters, and labourers of numerous kinds, contributed their several portions of service to this purpose. When the vessel was on float and capable of sailing, another set of men were employed to victual her, and a third to man her; and without the previous assistance of all these, the merchant would have been only an unserviceable name applied to an occupation extinct and useless. (*Pennsylvania Packet* [Philadelphia], 10 September 1779)

For Philadelphia artisans, their labor was more than a simple commodity, and the skilled labor they imparted in practicing their craft gave them a special claim on their products, even after the work was performed.

We conceive that these men [the builders, victuallers, and mariners] and all others concerned had something more in view than their meer wages when employed in the constructing and fitting out vessels for mercantile purposes, and that they naturally considered themselves as furnishing such vessels, not so much for the particular emolument of the merchant who employed them, as for the more beneficial purposes of supplying themselves and their fellow citizens with foreign necessities; and therefore we hold, that though by the acceptance of wages they have not, and cannot have any claim in the *property* of the vessel, after it is built and paid for, we nevertheless hold, that they and the state in general have a right in the *service* of the vessel, because it constitutes a considerable part of the advantage they hoped to derive from their labours.

As this argument reveals, colonial artisans viewed skilled labor as at once a social, moral, and economic act, and in their minds it made little sense to divide it into its constituent parts. To work was to employ skills in equal service to self, family, and the community at large.

Artisan thought surveyed the world from the perspective of the utility of skilled labor, and this led colonial craftsmen to form their own distinctive views about other aspects of early American life. This was especially true in the world of politics. In the colonial era, the possession of property was the sole way to establish a stake in political life. Only by owning substantial property in land or stock-in-trade, according to contemporary political theory, could one claim to have an interest in the running of community affairs and also have the wherewithal to exercise independent political judgment. A person without independent control of property was thought to be open to the coercion of husband, employer, or master and was thus a dependent incapable of independent political action.

Against this bias, which threatened to limit political participation to the colonial elite and the more prosperous master craftsmen and farmers, artisans laid claim to their own property in the form of skill. That skill, gained through long years of apprenticeship and journeyman service, was for the artisan a form of property fully as legitimate as the land and inventory of the greatest colonial landholder or merchant. As Walter Brewster, a Connecticut craftsman, phrased it, skill was "that property which is . . . the product and natural profits of the quantity of industry and oeconomy bestowed [by] seven years strict application to a particular science." "Such property and such abilities," he argued, "are acquired and not natural, they are actually the purchase of industry in the strictest sense." For Brewster and other colonial craftsmen, the indispensable utility of the artisans' skill and labor not only made them central figures in community life; it also gave them a rightful claim to a voice in community affairs.

Given this view of political inclusion, it is not surprising that colonial artisans were, with independent farmers, among the first spokesmen for democracy in the early modern world. At a time when most educated observers equated democracy with anarchy, artisans drew their ideas of social and political equality from the day-to-day functioning of their shops. Beginning with their apprenticeship, artisans participated in a kind of rough democracy within shop walls. Hierarchy existed, to be sure, and the lines of authority ran down from master or employer to senior journeymen and beyond; yet the norm (if not always the practice) in the shop was mutuality, not authoritarianism. Not only did each trade have its set of ancient rituals that regulated shop activities and personal relations, but the most important decisions—the assignment of tasks, the pace of work, the ordering of production—were decided by shop leaders in informal meetings of shopmates. When artisans came to consider the wider government of provincial society, it was to the rough-hewn democracy of their shop that they most often turned for guidance and example.

The artisan's economic goals were those of a preindustrial society. Until the end of the colonial era, when the American economy showed the first signs of actual development, the domestic economy grew no faster than the rate of population growth, or about 0.5 percent each year. Faced with this slow but steady growth, most artisans expected their skills and labor to provide not great wealth (that was left to large landholders and overseas merchants) but a middling existence. For mature craftsmen this meant providing for their family's needs, owning or renting a modest house with respectable furnishings (including floor coverings and, perhaps, a mantel clock), and accumulating a small savings for use in times of illness, slack trade, or eventual retirement. Artisans expected to achieve this middling status, called a competency, through the exercise of their skills in everyday life. In fact craftsmen thought of the practice of their trade as an informal covenant between themselves and their community, an implied contract in which they offered their services to the community in return for a respectable competency. In short most colonial artisans expected to be neither rich nor poor but comfortable, an expectation captured in Thomas Dilworth's brief couplet, which, though written at the end of the eighteenth century, accurately reflected the thoughts of colonial craftsmen:

Let me, O God, my labours so employ,
That I a competency may enjoy;
I ask no more that my life's wants supply,
And leave their due to others when I die;
If this thou grant (which nothing doubt I can),
There never liv'd or di'd a richer man.

(*A New Guide to the English Tongue*, 1791, p. 120)

Artisans lived out their lives within the bounds of small and often tightly knit communities. This was especially true of rural artisans, but even urban artisans lived in communities of between just twenty-five hundred and twenty-five thousand people during the colonial era. Social relations in these communities were personal, and the craftsmen not only knew their customers on a face-to-face basis but relied on their reputation within the community for their livelihood and well-being. Equally important, the artisan worked within a tightly knit community of fellow craftsmen in which techniques, work, and credit were commonly shared. Even the shop itself was a kind of community, a family-like gathering of masters, journeymen, and apprentices who labored together ultimately for the well-being of one another. Dependent upon collective life, artisans developed a passionate commitment to community and its norms of mutuality and equity, both in their shops and in the world at large. Artisans thought of society as a community structured much like their trades. And like the best of communities, a well-run society was populated by people who subordinated their individual interests to the collective well-being of the whole.

If any one word captured the crux of artisan thought and defined the goals for which they strove, that word was independence. Whether they sought a competency, political representation, or community respect, colonial artisans employed their skills to attain a state of independence. It was independence that separated skilled craftsmen from the unskilled and increasingly poor population below them, and it was the economic independence secured by their labor that underwrote their claims for respectability and a voice in political affairs. This notion of independence was the foundation of artisan struggles for recognition during the eighteenth century, and it would form the core of artisan resistance to the new world of manufacturing capitalism that began to appear early in the next century.

NON-ENGLISH NORTH AMERICA

Historians know a great deal more about the artisans of English North America than their counterparts in the Dutch, French, or Spanish colonies. Yet rural and urban artisans plied their trades in the Dutch, Spanish, and French colonies much as they did in the English coastal settlements. Certainly the urban centers of Quebec and New Amsterdam required artisans to supply local residents, to process and package the raw materials of the timber and fur trades, and to provision and maintain the ships engaged in the transatlantic trade. And it is likely, given what we know about their European counterparts, that Dutch, French, and Spanish craftsmen valued their skills, competency, and independence as much as any English artisan.

Yet there were variations as well. In colonial New France, immigrant French artisans attempted to follow the traditions of their homeland by forming trade groups and religious confraternities. But as they quickly discovered, New France was not a simple reflection of French society. Fearing any challenge to its authority in this tightly administered colony, the imperial government actively discouraged all voluntary organizations, viewing them as potential threats to royal authority and the colonial social order. By the end of the seventeenth century, the royal government had successfully suppressed all trade groups in New France and placed the religious confraternities under the strict control of the Catholic church. Thus by the beginning of the eighteenth century, native-born Canadian artisans looked to individual and family strategies for survival and advancement, eschewing collective organization as a means to address their most pressing needs.

Historians of the Spanish Borderlands have focused most of their attention on the crafts rather than the craftsmen. Because of this lack of systematic study of artisans themselves, comparatively little is known about the social and economic history of borderland artisans as a whole. Nevertheless, enough is known about artisans in a few trades to allow some general comments to be made.

Throughout the Spanish colonial period, the settlements of northern New Spain were outposts in a barely colonized marchland populated by Apache, Comanche, Pueblo, and other Native American peoples. Artisan life along this Spanish-American frontier was, like frontier life itself, a loose replica of the social relations at the center of Spain's colonial empire in the valley of Mexico.

While central New Spain attracted artisans of various types, from humble shoemakers to the makers of luxury goods for the newly risen hidalgo class of wealthy landowners, the Spanish Borderlands drew a far more restricted range of practicing craftsmen than did the English colonies. From the limited information available, the most important artisans in frontier New Spain appear to have been those who directly supported the military, religious, and trading purposes of borderland society. Among them, iron workers, textile workers, cart makers, and religious-image makers called *santeros* predominated.

The first settled ironworkers in the western borderlands came with Juan de Oñate's expedition to New Mexico in 1598. From the inventory of the expedition, we know that blacksmiths made the trek from Chihuahua with at least one small forge, numerous anvils, and a variety of ironworking tools ranging from taps and dies to equipment for making nails and horseshoes. By 1600 the region's first permanent forge had been built of local rock and adobe and was used, among other things, to repair the expedition's harquebuses (an early form of rifle).

The records of these early expeditions and settlements into the borderlands of New Spain suggest that much of the smiths' work in the colonial era was taken up in the manufacture and repair of arms and armor and in the shoeing of local horses, donkeys, and mules. Beyond this ironworkers fashioned stirrups, bits, and spurs and built and maintained the iron rims that were attached to the wooden wheels of long-distance trading carts. As the frontier settlements grew, blacksmiths provided a myriad of commonplace but essential items such as hinges, door bolts, tortilla griddles, skillets, and knives. By the eighteenth century, many of these everyday items were also produced for an extensive Spanish–Native American trading network that reached from California to the western banks of the Mississippi River.

Because the borderlands failed to produce hoped-for mineral wealth, residents depended on imported bar iron from Spain. The needs of Spanish settlers for iron and steel products were soon subordinated to those of Franciscan missionaries, who established a near monopoly on the imported iron and trained local Indians in the art of metalworking. The Native American artisans learned their trades well, and even after the Spanish were driven from New Mexico by the Pueblo Revolt of 1680, these Indian craftsmen continued to practice their trades, making, among other things, the iron-tipped lances with which they fought Spanish attempts at reconquest.

Following the ultimate victory and return of the Spanish in 1692, Santa Fe became the center of borderland ironwork. There, from the early eighteenth century, the best work was associated with the Sena family of provincial ironworkers. The family's founder, Bernardino de Sena, came to New Mexico as a young blacksmith in 1693. By the time he drew up his will in 1758, Sena (now known locally as Don Bernardino, a term of status and deep respect) had substantial landholdings in the capital and lived in a substantial, two-story house. He bequeathed his blacksmith tools and shop to his son, Tomás, who maintained the family business until his death in 1781. Members of the Sena family continued to produce iron products well into the nineteenth century.

If New Mexico was the center of borderland ironworking, colonial Texas, Arizona, and California were never without blacksmiths to perform essential duties for local *presidios* and missions: repairing weapons, fashioning horseshoes, and fabricating small-scale iron products such as nails, hinges, and locks. As in New Mexico, Franciscan friars in these eighteenth-century outposts trained Native Americans as ironworkers in order to supply local mission and community needs.

Ironworkers were not the only craftsmen of importance in borderland society. Carpenters, like blacksmiths, were vital to the functioning of their local communities, building churches, homes, and making the cabinets, chairs, and tables that constituted the furnishings of most frontier houses. While the evidence is fragmentary, carpenters came to the borderlands with the earliest settlers and, along with Catholic missionaries, trained local Indians in the woodworking crafts.

Closely related and equally vital to the frontier economy were the cartwrights who fashioned the carts that transported goods between Mexico and the outlying provinces. These *carros* and *carretas* were small, two-wheeled carts made from local cottonwood trees and built by cartwrights who were likely trained as general carpenters before specializing in the production of these rough-hewn conveyances. Before the Pueblo Revolt of 1680, many of these cartwrights employed Indians as assistants and apprentices, especially since Spanish youths were reluctant to enter this relatively unskilled trade.

Artisans in what is today the southwestern United States included numerous blanket makers and textile weavers. Indigenous Pueblo weavers were already accomplished artisans when the Spanish first arrived in the region in the sixteenth century. Initially working in locally grown cotton, these weavers quickly adapted their techniques to take advantage of the wool from the merino sheep that the Spanish introduced as they settled the region. The Pueblo, and later the Hopi and Navajo, wove cotton and wool into rectangular blankets for their own use, and the Spanish readily assimilated these Native textiles into their trade and tribute system. Curiously, although Native-made goods and patterns were popular among the Spanish settlers, Spanish weavers appear never to have adopted Pueblo techniques or designs, preferring instead to retain Old World techniques and traditional patterns.

Perhaps the most artistically developed of the borderland crafts was the making of religious images and figures. These *santos* (flat, painted images) and *bultos* (three-dimensional figures) were an important part of the religious life of the settlements, where almost all homes had at least one image or figure. The *santeros* (image makers) worked on wood planks, making their own *gesso* (gypsum and glue) and colorings and using their knowledge of saints and the Catholic liturgy to create some of the most captivating folk-art figures of the colonial era. *Santeros,* who were generally farmers, millers, or herdsmen, produced these religious paintings and figures during the winter months or at other slack times. Most worked on direct commissions from local or nearby residents, although the increasing popularity of *santos* in the eighteenth and early nineteenth centuries led many *santeros* to move their family and tools to more distant villages during the winter season.

Little is known about the artisan community itself; however, it was probably organized like that of its counterparts in Spain and the Spanish-American heartland, but with a significant differ-ence. While Spanish artisans brought traditional guild organizations and religious confraternities from the Old World into the New, borderland artisans did not carry these traditions north of the Rio Grande. As a result, although craftsmen were recognized as essential members of every Spanish borderland community, this economic prominence would not translate into an effective artisan identity as it did in the more populous regions of New Spain.

BIBLIOGRAPHY

The European Background

Malcolmson, Robert W. *Life and Labour in England, 1700–1780.* London, 1981.

Montias, John Michael. *Artists and Artisans in Delft: A Socio-Economic Study of the Seventeenth Century.* Princeton, N.J., 1982.

Rule, John. *The Experience of Labour in Eighteenth-Century Industry.* London, 1981.

Sewell, William H., Jr. *Work and Revolution in France: The Language of Labor from the Old Regime to 1848.* New York, 1980.

Wrightson, Keith. *English Society, 1580–1680.* London, 1982.

Colonial English America

Bridenbaugh, Carl. *The Colonial Craftsman.* New York, 1950.

Foner, Eric. *Tom Paine and Revolutionary America.* New York, 1976.

Innes, Stephen, ed. *Work and Labor in Early America.* Chapel Hill, N.C., 1988.

Morris, Richard B. *Government and Labor in Early America.* New York, 1946.

Nash, Gary B. *The Urban Crucible: Social Change, Political Consciousness, and the Origins of the American Revolution.* Cambridge, Mass., 1979.

Quimby, Ian M. G., ed. *The Craftsman in Early America.* New York, 1984.

Rediker, Marcus. *Between the Devil and the Deep Blue Sea: Merchant Seamen, Pirates, and the Anglo-American Maritime World, 1700–1750.* New York, 1987.

Russo, Jean B. *Free Workers in a Plantation Economy: Talbot County, Maryland, 1690–1759.* New York, 1989.

Salinger, Sharon V. *"To Serve Well and Faithfully": Labor and Indentured Servants in Pennsylvania, 1682–1800.* New York, 1987.

Schultz, Ronald. *The Republic of Labor: Philadelphia Artisans and the Politics of Class, 1720–1830.* New York, 1993.

Smith, Billy G. *The "Lower Sort": Philadelphia's Laboring People, 1750–1800.* Ithaca, N.Y., 1990.

Walsh, Richard. *Charleston's Sons of Liberty: A Study of the Artisans, 1763–1789.* Columbia, S.C., 1959.

Non-English North America

Boyd, E. *Popular Arts of Colonial New Mexico.* Santa Fe, N.Mex., 1959.

Goodfriend, Joyce D. *Before the Melting Pot: Society and Culture in Colonial New York City, 1664–1730.* Princeton, N.J., 1992.

Johnson, Lyman. "Artisans." In *Cities and Society in Colonial Latin America,* edited by Louisa Schell Hoberman and Susan Midgen Socolow. Albuquerque, N.Mex., 1986. This article is useful for an understanding of artisans and their institutions in mainstream Spanish-American society.

Monthan, Guy, and Doris Monthan. *Nacimentos: Nativity Scenes by Southwestern Indian Artisans.* Flagstaff, Ariz., 1979.

Moogk, Peter N. *Building a House in New France: An Account of the Perplexities of Client and Craftsmen in Early Canada.* Toronto, Ontario, 1977.

———. "In the Darkness of a Basement: Craftsmen's Associations in Early French Canada." *Canadian Historical Review* 57, no. 4 (1976):399–439.

———. "Manual Education and Economic Life in New France." *Studies on Voltaire and the Eighteenth Century* 167 (1977):125–168.

———. "Reluctant Exiles: Emigrants from France in Canada Before 1760." *William and Mary Quarterly* 3rd ser., 46, no. 3 (1989):463–505.

Rink, Oliver A. *Holland on the Hudson: An Economic and Social History of Dutch New York.* Ithaca, N.Y., 1986.

Simmons, Marc, and Frank Turley. *Southwestern Colonial Ironwork: The Spanish Blacksmithing Tradition from Texas to California.* Santa Fe, N. Mex., 1980.

Weigle, Marta, ed. *Hispanic Arts and Ethnohistory in the Southwest.* Santa Fe, N.Mex., 1983.

Wroth, William. *Christian Images in Hispanic New Mexico: The Taylor Museum Collection of Santos.* Colorado Springs, Colo., 1982.

Ronald Schultz

SEE ALSO **Bound Labor; Crafts; Hired Labor; Manufacturing and Extractive Industries; Technology;** and **Trade and Commerce;** and various essays in THE SOCIAL FABRIC.

MANUFACTURING AND EXTRACTIVE INDUSTRIES

INTRODUCTION

THE NINETEENTH CENTURY CONSTITUTED a watershed for the economic development of nations. New capital-intensive machine technologies, often accompanied by abundant mineral resources, propelled a few nations to unprecedented wealth and power while leaving most to languish with low levels of productivity. The industrial revolution had scarcely begun by the end of the colonial era, but its impact has distorted our perception of colonial manufacturing. Focusing upon both method and material, post–World War II historians have dismissed the manufacturing industries in the colonies, arguing as John McCusker and Russell Menard have in *The Economy of British America* that "they were of little consequence at the time and of real importance only for what they portended for the future." If "manufacturing hardly counted," as Susan Lee and Peter Passell held, explanation was found in the fact that "the technology of manufacture—sources of power, tools—had been roughly the same for a century."

Both theory and empirical evidence can be marshaled to support these assertions. Throughout the colonial period, manufactures were much more likely to be found on the import side of the ledger than the export side. Simple comparative advantage can rationalize this pattern: regions specialize in the production of goods that maximize their relatively abundant factors and, through trade, exchange these goods for those which are intensive in scarce factors. All of the colonies suffered in varying degrees from relative labor and capital shortages while enjoying plentiful resources. When compared with the other major economic sectors, commerce and agriculture, manufacturing was particularly labor intensive. Moreover, many lines of manufacture enjoyed economies of scale, so that larger producers could reduce unit costs through specialization and the division of labor. But the small and scattered colonial markets rarely justified investment in firms large enough to reap economies of scale.

Transportation costs compounded European advantages. Bulky colonial staple exports demanded more shipping tonnage than did imports, resulting in competition for inbound colonial freight that drove down Europe-to-America rates. Finally, those possessing industrially relevant skills, much more important then than a century later, were not likely to migrate to America. These skilled workers could earn higher wages in their own countries with their larger markets, greater specialization, and better techniques. Whenever the nations of Europe had the raw materials required, the quality of their wares equaled or exceeded those of the colonies.

In spite of these obstacles, manufactures grew in both quantity and variety, particularly in eighteenth-century America. The abundant resources that lured settlers to the New World also gave them low-cost inputs for processing industries. And nearly ubiquitous rivers and streams enabled colonials to apply waterpower to a range of arduous tasks, thereby minimizing labor inputs. Fed by the expanding world of trade, resource-based, power-using industries such as milling, shipping, and iron smelting thrived. Growing local populations with rising incomes supported a host of lesser craft-based manufactures that clustered in towns and cities throughout the North. On the eve of the revolution, Benjamin Franklin could boast with only slight hyperbole, "I do not know of a single article imported into the northern colonies, but what they can either do without or make themselves."

If colonial manufacturing achieved greater sophistication and scale than most post–World War II historians have acknowledged, production beyond local needs remained concentrated along the coast from Maine to Maryland. The highly specialized fur and fishing communities to the north and tobacco and rice regions to the south remained heavily dependent upon manufactured imports. Since their highly profitable staples had eager customers within expanding European and West Indian markets, they used the foreign exchange generated by extensive specialization to buy foreign and, by the end of the colonial period, domestic wares.

THE COLONIAL RELATIONSHIP

The sixteenth to the eighteenth centuries have been labeled the age of mercantilism, as governments sought to increase their power and wealth through the promotion of trade and industry. The American colonies contributed to the growth of the European nation-states as suppliers of raw materials for home consumption, manufacture, or reexport and as markets for metropolitan industrial goods and commercial and mercantile services. All nations attempted to cement these economic relationships through a wide array of prohibitions, duties, bounties, grants, and exemptions. The effectiveness of this legislation varied not only with the ability and willingness to enforce the rules but, more importantly, with the fit of colonial resources and metropolitan needs. Although colonists did trade outside of their emerging empires, they remained heavily dependent upon their fellow countrymen in Europe and the West Indies for capital, labor, and markets.

Mercantilist programs reflected shifts within the economies of the emerging nation-states. Rapid population growth pressed against resources, inducing the English, French, and Dutch to expand their trade with the Baltic, Russia, and Germany for resource-rich products such as grain, lumber, naval stores, and furs. In exchange they offered commercial services, imports from their tropical colonies, and mounting quantities of home manufactures, particularly textiles. Growing markets at home and abroad encouraged the expansion of industry, with its increasingly capitalistic organization and greater dependence upon raw materials imported from abroad. By 1700 these nations were the industrial powers of the world, possessing large, diversified, and relatively efficient manufacturing sectors. But such specialization brought dependence; the colonies offered the potential for more assured supplies of temperate-zone resources and, with sufficient development, more certain markets. To realize this opportunity, the home countries would not only have to invest in development and defense but would have to subsidize—at least initially—the less efficient colonial producers and compensate them for their higher cost of transportation.

The experience of the Dutch, who had the shortest-lived of the four major North American empires, illuminates the difficulties of colonization. The seventeenth century was the golden age of the Dutch Republic as it became the most successful of the economic powers. Amsterdam emerged as the principal trading and financial center of Western Europe. With cheap credit and efficient shipping services, no nation could best the Dutch in trade. In 1621 the republic chartered the Dutch West India Company, giving it a twenty-four-year monopoly on trade with portions of North and South America, Africa, Asia, and Australia. From the start the North American enterprise suffered in the competition for funding, becoming the "have-not" of the Dutch seaborne empire. For most of its history,

New Netherland earned its profits by trading with Native Americans for furs, an activity that required only modest investment in men and materials. The company encouraged colonization by direct subsidy and by grant to patroons, calculating that such efforts would yield grain, timber, pitch, tar, and dried fish, all products that were prized in European markets. Colonists were prohibited from entering on their own account the fur trade, mining, and certain artisanal crafts such as weaving. This ensured that the profits from the exploitation of the most valuable resources would go to the company and also protected Dutch textile manufacturers from colonial competition.

Settlement proceeded sluggishly during the period of West India Company rule; even with virtually free land and subsidized transportation for settlers, the colony had only ten thousand inhabitants when the British conquered New Netherland in 1664. The failure of the enterprise could be attributed to the difficulties of developing colonial resources in the face of established, better-located European producers. Dutch capital and labor sought more profitable outlets, and even the Amsterdam traders who came to dominate the exchange with New Netherlands were unwilling to plough back earnings into the colony. Rather than sink money into longer-term, essentially developmental projects, the Dutch West India Company invested in trade with Native Americans for furs and with other North American colonies for staple exports.

The French experiment lasted a century longer than that of the Dutch, but it, too, suffered from the absence of employment-generating staples desired by the mother country. The French government did make a concerted effort to develop industry. From the era of Jean-Baptiste Colbert, Controller General of Finances (1662–1683), forward the French government entertained high hopes of obtaining supplies of ship masts, spars, and ship timbers, along with pitch, tar, turpentine, hemp for rope, and other naval stores, from Acadia (Nova Scotia) and Canada in order to end reliance on supplies from the Baltic merchants. However, skilled labor was in short supply and the cost of importing artisans from France was high—skilled laborers would go to the New World only on short-term contracts and at double the wages then current in

France; moreover too many of them proved to be incompetent and had to be shipped back to France. These proved to be almost insurmountable problems.

In the 1660s and 1670s and again in the eighteenth century, the Ministry of Marine sought to have ships built in Canada for the navy. The first attempts failed because the minister contracted for ships of up to a thousand tons to be built at Quebec, but vital ship timbers were not to be found in the surrounding area. Similar attempts several decades later yielded a few large warships but at alarming cost. Shipbuilding in New France was an economic success only in its construction of vessels of under two hundred tons to provide for the colony's needs. These craft included fishing vessels for the local market, birch bark canoes for trade and communication with the far west and military transport on the Great Lakes, and small boats for freighting goods from Quebec to Montreal. The most lucrative center for canoe manufacture was Trois-Rivières, with women doing most of the skilled work. Each canoe could carry some twenty-five hundred pounds of trade goods.

For the import of goods into Canada, the maritime fortress of Louisbourg (well established by the 1720s), obviated the need for ships to make the long and dangerous voyage up the Saint Lawrence to Quebec; they could unload at Louisbourg and then continue to the Antilles while local ships took the goods intended for New France up to Quebec.

New France, however, proved to be a disappointing market for its mother country. The colony needed only twenty ships worth of imports a year to supply the manufactured wares it could not provide for itself. These imports consisted of goods to be swapped for furs: ironware, muskets, brandy, coarse woolens, and goods to be sold to the affluent colonists, such as silks, taffetas, colored cottons, and felt hats. For the less well-off, every attempt was made to satisfy their needs locally, especially with regard to food, fuel, housing, and some of the clothing they required. This freed them to spend their scarce specie on hardware, powder, lead, clothing, and wine. Worried that the British would supply even these small markets with manufactures, the French colonial minister sought to encourage local production, saying, "Nothing is of greater importance than to accustom them [the colonists] to industry, and means must be adopted to establish manufactures suitable to the country." But the local needs of the French in Canada remained too modest to engender much industry. Meanwhile, the fur trade and fishing required little resident labor. So when Canada was ceded to the British, it had but eighty thousand inhabitants.

The Spanish experience in New Spain and in the borderlands stretching from Florida to California witnessed only minimal development of manufacturing industries, since everywhere either agriculture or mining emerged as the mainstay of the colonial economy. Indeed, Spain's royal government deliberately impeded overseas industries that might compete with goods produced in the mother country. The colonies were expected to absorb finished European products and to export raw materials such as precious metals, cattle hides, hardwoods, tobacco, sugar, and dyestuffs. The subsistence economies offered little other than livestock for export. Economic reforms introduced late in the colonial period simply reinforced earlier policies, so that manufacturing remained underdeveloped in both New Spain and the Spanish Borderlands.

Even in the English colonies, the most successful extractive and manufacturing industries took off only in the eighteenth century. The richest of its possessions in North America, the tobacco colonies of Virginia and Maryland, used their income from tobacco to purchase European wares and slaves. Secondary industry languished as capital, labor, and entrepreneurship were drawn to the tobacco crop. The New England colonies, the poorest of the lot, specialized in extractive and manufacturing industries simply because there was little else they could do to accumulate products for extraregional sale. Peopled by a great religious migration, New England thrived as established settlers provisioned newcomers. But with the English Civil War, migration ceased and Massachusetts Bay, the major colony in the region, sank into depression.

Recovery came with exploitation of the first major nonlocal market, the West Indies. Highly specialized sugar planters needed timber, lumber, staves, flour, cornmeal, salted provisions, iron, and the ships to convey them. Colonial

Americans entered England's markets only under conditions of unusual scarcity; for example, when war decimated the stock of shipping at the turn of the eighteenth century or when England endured a succession of poor grain harvests in the mid 1700s.

In the absence of firm data, the impact of English mercantilist legislation remains open to conjecture. Like the other great powers, England envisioned a self-sufficient empire in which it supplied manufactures and services while the colonies provided raw materials. Worried about the threat of colonial manufacturing in New England, the home country tried to promote extractive industries with bounties for naval stores. But these inducements yielded few exports. Prohibitions designed to protect English industry—applying to manufactured exports of wool and woolen cloth (1699), hats (1732), and the construction of slitting and rolling mills, tilt hammers, and steel furnaces (1750)—caused little harm. Americans remained high-cost producers, and in those periods when they could be competitive, they ignored the regulations. Most would agree with Victor Clark that colonial manufactures "seem not to have been retarded or furthered decidedly by subordination to the British government."

For most of the colonial era, the Dutch, French, and English settlers could not substitute their grains, timber, and iron for Baltic, German, and Russian equivalents. Unable to peddle these specialties in European markets, the northern colonies lacked the foreign exchange to purchase metropolitan wares. This forced them to fashion most of their own goods. When colonial populations and incomes multiplied in the eighteenth century, colonials discovered that they could meet most of their own needs for manufactures. They had not forsworn European textiles and hardware, but for most other goods they had a market large enough and skills sufficient to underwrite colonial production.

Mercantilism's often unacknowledged legacy was what has been called an "acquired habit of legislation." Particularly in the seventeenth century, when the colonies found manufactured imports cut off by war or depression, they passed a host of laws promoting industry by, for example, ordering households to spin textile fibers and plant flax, prohibiting the export of hides and supporting tanneries, and offering subsidies and monopolies to mills and forges. This legislation tended to be short-lived; when good times returned, it was allowed to expire, was repealed, or was simply evaded. Whether enacted at home or in the mother country, legislation did far less to shape the colonial economies than did resources and markets.

THE WOODEN AGE

When European settlers came to the continent, they invariably commented upon the expanse of forests, which made a stark contrast to the increasingly denuded lands they had left. Colonists used wood for fuel, shelter, transport, power generation, fencing, containers, and implements. Some was so valuable—for example, the tall pines of northern New England or the live oak of the lower South—that governments tried to monopolize it for ship construction. But most timber was used for more mundane projects. Pine and firs were employed in construction; cedar in the North and cypress in the South were used for shingles. The lighter hardwoods could be used for vessels, although careless use of oak gave early American-made ships a poor reputation. Cherry, walnut, and maple were favored for furniture; oak and hemlock bark were used for tanning. The yellow pines of the South were tapped for naval stores, while cheap woods everywhere were burned for heat. Whenever possible colonists substituted wood for other materials. The plentiful supply of wood in New France encouraged the design of a new architectural type, the "pièces-sur-pièces" farmhouse, where wood replaced the traditional stone in virtually every part of the dwelling.

Lumber

The forests gave rise to four major industries: lumbering, naval stores, potash, and shipbuilding. While farmers everywhere felled trees for local use, the lumber industry required more than an ax. It needed access to cheap, invariably waterborne transportation and to waterpower. The Swedish, Dutch, French, and English colonists all built water-powered sawmills. The waterwheel turned a crank that pushed the saw (or several parallel saws) up and down. A man would push the log into the teeth of the saw, but with a windlass the log could be fed mechanically. These sawmills saved an enormous amount of labor; in the more advanced, one man could operate all the machinery. Hailed by frontier communities, sawmills permitted settlers to build frame rather than log dwellings and to have plank rather than dirt floors.

But lumber was rarely exported to European markets. Using seventeenth-century records, Van Cleaf Bachman has estimated that while New Netherland occasionally sent timber back in ballast to Amsterdam, it cost two times as much to haul this timber from New Netherland than to carry an equivalent amount from the Baltic ports. Even when the value of a standing tree in the Baltic amounted to only 5 percent of its selling price in Amsterdam, most of the remaining 95 percent went to those who transported the tree from the place where it was cut to the metropolitan market. On the other hand, where the North American colonies had a transport advantage over the Baltic ports, they could dominate the market. The West Indies took appreciable quantities of North American timber in the form of lumber, planking, firewood, and staves. The last-named were particularly important; in an age of wooden containers, staves "knocked up" into casks held such staples as sugar, molasses, rum, rice, and tobacco.

Naval Stores

The constant threat of war and the growing size of navies fostered the demand for a secure supply of naval stores. In 1705 England offered bounties for colonial pitch, tar, hemp, masts, and bowsprits and placed these articles, as well as rosin and turpentine, on the list of enumerated goods. The pine from Acadia (Nova Scotia) to New Jersey could be cut down to yield tar or its boiled variant, pitch. When applied to rope, tar retarded rot, while pitch was used to seal caulking material in hulls. The British navy protested Board of Trade policy; not only were colonial prices higher, but the quality of the materials was inferior. With the reduction in the bounty in 1729, New England's production—never large to begin with—languished. North Carolina became the center for naval stores; its pines could be bled, often by slave labor, to yield a gum that when distilled became rosin or turpentine.

Again colonials found European markets hard to penetrate. Their greatest success came in the export of great masts over thirty inches (750 millimeters) in diameter. Royal Navy agents scoured the colonial forests, taking only the very largest trees and purchasing lesser sizes from the Baltic.

Potash and Pearl Ash

The third of the wood-based industries, potash and pearl ash, grew rapidly with improvements in technique after 1750. A chemical used in the manufacture of soap and glass, potash consumed great quantities of wood, requiring some three to five acres (about 1 to 2 hectares) of timber for each ton of output. Wood, primarily elm and maple, was stacked in piles and ignited; then the ashes were collected. They were leached in barrels to produce lye, which was boiled to obtain the alkali called potash. Pearl ash, made from potash by applying heat in an oven to burn off the carbon, was not widely made in the colonies. Potash, however, became an important by-product of northern farming. In the late colonial period, farmers devised new ways of manufacturing potash in old sugar kettles and captured some two-thirds of the British market.

Shipbuilding

One of the three great resource-dependent manufactures of the colonial area (along with iron and flour milling), shipbuilding was born of necessity. Colonials needed coasters and riverboats to carry on trade, but the often turbulent Atlantic Ocean made importation of small craft nearly impossible. All along the coast, small shipyards turned out small vessels for intraregional commerce and fishing. But larger ships demanded skills, capital, and intermediate inputs not easily assembled by local builders. With abundant supplies of maple, oak, and pine, New England quickly became the center for ship construction, building larger coasting vessels and West Indian traders. The eighteenth century brought another leap forward for the industry as wars decimated the stock of oceangoing shipping and the Navigation Acts mandated the use of British ships in British trade. By 1730 one-sixth of the English merchant fleet had been built in America; by the eve of the revolution, it was one-third. Low site costs and cheap raw materials drew skilled shipwrights to the colonies, where they could construct vessels some 40 percent more cheaply than in England. With frequent wars and burgeoning trade, shipbuilding was one of the growth industries of its day, earning colonials some £140,000 a year in export sales alone.

Shipbuilding required only modest capital and organization. Most shipwrights built only one or two ships a year, usually on contract, with progress payments made throughout the period of construction. Builders did not retain a permanent labor force but hired up to a dozen artisans at a time, depending upon the skills needed. American ships tended to be built in shorter periods of time than European ones; a full-sized merchant vessel could be turned out in as little as four months. With reduced sail and simple rigging, colonial ships required smaller crews. These designs and practices fit colonial factor proportions. Rapid construction conserved scarce capital, while simpler designs and more intensive work regimens saved labor. By the end of the colonial era, shipbuilding centered in New England, Pennsylvania, and the Chesapeake, and while the industry did not always enjoy a reputation for quality, American ships were widely employed in river, coastal, and ocean trade.

PRODUCTS OF THE EARTH

The industrial supremacy achieved by the United States at the turn of the twentieth century can be attributed in large measure to the mineral abundance of the North American continent. But these extraordinarily rich and varied resources went untapped until the nineteenth century; none of the mines being worked a century after the colonial era dated back to colonial times. Moreover, minerals did not matter much. Coal, which would become the vital fuel for steel and steam engines, had been identified early in the colonial period, but few uses could be found for it.

And as for Coals, it is not likely they should ever be used there in anything . . . for, in [Virginia's] Country Plantations, the Wood grows at every Man's Door so fast, that after it has been cut down, it will in seven Years time, grow up again from seed to substantial Fire Wood. (Robert Beverly. *The History of Virginia* [1720], p. 108)

Only the production of iron employed substantial numbers in the colony. On the eve of the revolution, the British colonies in America yielded one-seventh of the world's iron, ranking third behind only Sweden and Russia. Even here Americans faced withering competition in European markets. With the revolution in British metallurgy during the late eighteenth century, Americans fell further behind, becoming net iron importers for most of the nineteenth century.

Each of the colonial powers viewed its colonies as potential sources of the three great minerals of the age: copper, silver, and above all, gold. Mineral rights were reserved for the Crown, which encouraged expeditions into the newly discovered territory and often sent skilled miners to search for these relatively pure, easily worked metals. Early encounters with Native Americans fed colonial hopes as Indians frequently wore gold, silver, or copper ornaments. The early French, Dutch, and English settlements struggled at one time or another because workers needed for agriculture wandered off to prospect for gold or silver.

Exploration of the Western Hemisphere had been launched by early mineral discoveries. Native Americans worked mines of gold, silver, lead, tin, and copper. These metals were so abundant that the skilled Native craftsmen had no need to exploit the much harder to process iron ore reserves. Intrigued by Native success, the Spanish sought to develop their own supplies, canvassing the borderlands from Florida to California between 1513 and the end of the colonial era. The remains of mining apparatus—shafts, ore crushers, smelters, and tools—attest to searches in present-day Georgia, the Carolinas, southern Arizona, east and west Texas, and even California. The most extensive investments centered in New Mexico, probably before the Pueblo Revolt in 1680. But if Spaniards explored this vast area and dug mines, they recovered very modest quantities of gold, silver, and copper. The robust success of the Mexican silver mines drew off labor and capital; the discoveries in the borderlands tended to be far less valuable; explorers did not identify what later proved to be the richest deposits in the area.

Similar experiences characterized the Dutch settlements in the Middle Atlantic. In the 1620s and again in the 1640s, the directors of the West India Company advertised for mineralogists to search for gold, silver, copper, iron, lead, and sulphur. Two ships laden with ore samples sank before reaching the Netherlands, postponing what would have been bad news anyway. Some evidence indicates that the Dutch operated two copper mines in the 1650s, but they never developed the iron ore reserves of the region; iron worked by the Dutch in New Netherland was imported from Europe.

The French explored some of the most minerally rich areas of the North American continent. Hearing stories from the Indians, they diligently sought the Lake Superior copper lode. But two expeditions in 1668–1672 failed to locate more than small deposits of copper. They did mine lead in the Illinois region, relieving colonials from having to import the mineral. As late as 1774, however, an English trader and investor, Alexander Henry, claimed

It was never for the exportation of copper that the company was formed; but, always with a view to the silver it was hoped the ores, whether of copper or lead, might in sufficient quantity contain. The copper-ores of Lake Superior can never be profitably sought for but local consumption. The country must be cultivated and peopled, before they can deserve notice. (James A. Mulholland. *A History of Metals*, p. 52)

For all the effort expended, the colonies to the north of the Rio Grande yielded virtually no gold, silver, or tin. By the end of the colonial era, copper and lead mining had all but ceased. During the first third of the eighteenth century, copper mining occurred in present-day New Jersey, Connecticut, and Virginia. Most of the ore was shipped to England unrefined; since the ore contained some 50 percent copper, it could bear the costs of long-distance transportation.

If the colonists rarely produced their own supplies, they still developed crafts based upon nonferrous metals. From the seventeenth century forward, silversmiths worked imports or scrap to fashion items that not only advertised their owners' affluence but also served as a store of value. With the growth of population and wealth in the eighteenth century, metals craftsmen proliferated throughout the northern cities, often specializing in one or two precious metals. While silversmiths remained the most common, coppersmiths satisfied local demands for warming pans, kettles, stills, funnels, and ladles. Alloyed with other metals, copper was cast or forged into bells, buttons, buckles, and andirons. Pewter became the trendy metal of the eighteenth century; well-off colonials bought it largely in the form of utensils and dinnerware. Most of this tin-based alloy was fashioned abroad, although with increasing demand, intercontinental migration of skills, and the mounting stocks of scrap, pewtersmithing and tinsmithing joined the list of colonial crafts.

Iron Manufacture

Iron overshadowed all colonial metals. Much more difficult to smelt than the nonferrous ores, neither the Native Americans nor the Spanish exploited the continent's ore resources. As early as 1621, English investors poured money into a major iron facility at Falling Creek in Virginia. Wiped out by an Indian massacre, this experiment was not repeated for a century. It was typical of a style of iron production normally associated with the upper South, where English or American merchants invested in huge furnaces designed to produce crude iron, or pig, for refining in England. Most pig iron, however, was destined for local or regional consumption. The ill-fated furnaces at Braintree and Lynn, Massachusetts, were supposed to free the specie-starved colony from dependence upon British imports.

Sizeable iron facilities usually failed in the seventeenth century because they lacked capital, skills, and appreciable markets. Even when the industry grew to impressive size in the eighteenth century, it tended to serve regional demand. For example, high quality bog iron was mined near Trois-Rivières, where the Forges de Saint-Maurice were established. After a rocky start in 1731, the furnaces eventually produced iron of a quality reputed to be equal to that of Spain or Sweden. But they did not export to France or other European countries; instead the output was cast into pots, pans, stoves, cannon, and cannon balls, all for local use. It is reported that the newly arrived iron masters from France had been sent early on to the English colonies to learn about methods of operation there.

Abundant ores, forests, and moderate local demand, often protected by high transport costs, encouraged small-scale production. A bloomery was well within the reach of a colonial capitalist.

Ores, either bog or rock, were retrieved from the bottoms of ponds or from shallow mines. Local farmers, eager to clear their lands before planting, provided the timber, which was reduced to charcoal. The ore was heated in a shallow hearth, fanned by hand or by water-powered bellows. The resulting pasty ball contained ore, slag, and dirt. Repeated hammering at a forge while at red heat broke away the slag and yielded a tough yet malleable iron. These blooms would then be sold to local smiths to make implements, nails, and tools.

Larger-scale output depended upon blast furnaces to produce pig and forges to refine it into bar iron. These capital-intensive enterprises have often been dubbed iron plantations since they encompassed, on average, three thousand to four thousand acres (1,200 to 1,600 hectares) of forests and fields, the former to feed the furnace, the latter to feed the work force. The centerpiece of the business was the blast furnace, a stone structure some thirty-feet (9-meters) high. It was usually built alongside a hill. Workmen loaded charcoal, ore, and limestone at the top. After heating, usually with the assistance of water-powered bellows, a plug was removed from the bottom of the furnace and the iron flowed into sand. Harder than bloomery iron, this pig could be immediately cast into hollowware or stove backs. Most of it went to the forge, where the pig was reheated until soft and beaten with a water-powered trip-hammer, which reorganized its crystalline structure so that the iron was fibrous, tough, shock resistant, and easily weldable. From here the forged iron could be sold to smiths or worked in rolling or slitting mills.

Iron, the second of the great colonial resource-using industries, took off after 1715 with the construction of eighty furnaces, including twenty in Pennsylvania, seventeen in Maryland, and fourteen each in Virginia and Massachusetts. They fed at least 175 forges, most of which were concentrated in the northern colonies from Massachusetts to Pennsylvania. At the time of the revolution, colonial pig iron output exceeded that of England and Wales, averaging some twenty pounds (9 kilograms) per person. But England had hoped for more, as it had become heavily dependent upon Sweden and Russia for this increasingly important metal. During the early eighteenth century, wars cut off Swedish imports, spurring investment in major enterprises in Maryland and Virginia. It also occasioned considerable debate in England, since the home pig and bar producers opposed aid to colonial industry, while the iron-using firms lobbied in support of assistance. Only in 1750 did Britain take action, reducing the tariff on imported colonial iron (a minor gesture) and prohibiting the construction of new facilities for rolling or slitting iron or making steel. Exports from the colonies rose slightly, although trade data indicate that about 1770, iron constituted only 6 percent of colonial exports. While England remained uncomfortably reliant upon northern European supplies, colonial iron imports roughly matched exports, suggesting that the British colonies could satisfy their own needs.

Blacksmithing. Throughout the colonies the number of blacksmiths and naileries multiplied. In the early years, houses were constructed without nails, because imported nails cost so much. With growing domestic stocks of iron, builders used nails to attach shingles, planks, and boards—but only sparingly, since nails remained expensive. Many of these nails were hand forged by New England farmers, who spent their evenings during the winter at a small anvil, pounding iron rods into large nails and spikes. Located in almost every town and city, blacksmiths hammered out tools, hardware, kitchen utensils, critical parts for ships, wagons and waterwheels, and even their own smithing tools. The business required little in the way of capital: a hearth, a hand-operated bellows, an anvil, and some hammers. The smith would heat charcoal on a hearth, usually fanning it with bellows, place the iron into the coals, and—once it reached sufficient temperature—take it to an anvil to be hammered into shape. Physically demanding, blacksmithing required considerable skill, especially in urban areas where imports offered vigorous competition. Expanding markets encouraged specialization; some smiths concentrated solely on locks, cutlery, or ship fittings or branched into gunsmithing.

Blacksmiths assumed vital roles in New Netherland as well, serving both the Dutch and Indian populations. With a population of almost one thousand in the mid 1650s, the village of Beverswyck had six smiths. In addition to servicing the company's and patroonship's needs in repairing agricultural tools and the metalwork on sawmills and gristmills, these smiths were frequently called upon to repair the tools and firearms of the Native population. In 1659 the Mohawk requested that the blacksmiths be required to repair their possessions whether they could offer compensation or not; the request was denied on the ground that the smiths could not be "compelled to repair the guns of our brothers without receiving pay for it, as they must earn a living for their wives and children, who would otherwise perish from hunger."

With no local production of iron, smithing remained underdeveloped and unspecialized in the Spanish colonies. All hardware had to be carried into the borderlands, and when bar stocks were short, metal objects were forged from worn-out pieces with, for example, horseshoes being converted to nails and old files being forged into knives and other edged instruments. The few smiths also kept the weapons of royal frontier troops in good repair.

Pottery, Brick, and Glass

The earth also contained minerals essential for the pottery, brick, and glass industries. In New England the red glacial clay was dug up in the fall, washed and dried during the winter, and thrown and kiln fired in the summer. Virtually every town had a potter's shop, where a potter fashioned cheap mugs, porringers, jars, chamber pots, plates, pans, pitchers, bowls, and bottles. Stoneware, a higher-quality pottery, was made from the white clays of the Middle Atlantic. Probate inventories indicate that just about every household had at least four or five shillings worth of pottery, although those of greater social standing preferred imported dinnerware.

Bricks, among the least valuable items relative to weight, were imported on occasion, giving testimony to the existence of cheap backhaulage rates. At first the Dutch settlers imported their yellow brick so that they could recreate some of their distinctive architecture. Soon the New Netherlanders made their own bricks and tiles at New Amsterdam (New York), Fort Orange, and Albany. For most cities brick and stone construction was more than a matter of taste.

Wooden houses were a constant fire hazard; Montreal, Quebec, and Trois-Rivières all suffered from severe conflagrations that destroyed most of the towns' housing stock. The authorities decreed that houses there had to be of stone construction, with slate or metal roofs and end walls. In addition the fortifications at Quebec, the environs of Montreal, and at the upper end of Lake Champlain kept masons hard at work for decades. With such governmental prompting, stone quarries were at a premium and masons in great demand. Hispanic colonists in New Mexico and southern Arizona relied on sun-dried adobe blocks, while those in California produced these and fired clay bricks and roof tiles. Adobe blocks and quarried stone were the preferred building materials of missionaries and settlers in Texas. Whether undertaken in New France, New Netherland, or the English and Spanish colonies, all of the production was for local use. Except for a stray cargo or two to the West Indies, there were no colonial exports of stone, bricks, or slate.

From the earliest days colonials tried to make glass, but they were thwarted by a shortage of skills and impurities in the local resources. While low-quality bottle glass was manufactured throughout the northern colonies, most window glass had to be imported. A German baron, Henry William Steigel, built a huge flint glass facility in Pennsylvania, along with several iron furnaces and a castle or two for his personal residence. The colonial market may not have been sufficient to justify the extraordinary scale of his enterprise; it failed in five years, when the War for Independence cut off his supply of funds from Germany.

PRODUCTS OF AGRICULTURE

Most Americans labored in the agricultural sector, which had important ramifications for manufacturing. They raised a variety of crops and livestock that normally had to be processed before consumption. Farm families butchered their own animals, distilled their own beverages, churned butter, made cheese, and on occasion, ground grain. If they lived at points remote from markets, household manufactures also encompassed most of the family's clothing, shoes, furniture, illumination, farm tools, household imple-

ments, and vehicles. Much of this activity was undertaken because rural dwellers could not afford to buy these goods.

Virtually prohibitive overland freight costs discouraged agricultural production for distant markets; with modest money incomes, farm families had to be very selective in their purchases of capital and consumer goods. Moreover, the seasonal nature of farm tasks released labor to fabricate wares that most urban dwellers bought through markets. Nineteenth-century industrialization drew much of its impetus from the ability of American manufacturers to drive down the prices of industrial goods so that farmers would buy them rather than rely upon household production.

Textiles and Clothing

The most difficult market for American manufacturers to capture has been that of textiles; for virtually all of U.S. history, the nation has been a net importer of cloth. This dependence dates from initial settlement and was a cornerstone of colonial policy. In New Netherlands the West India Company ordered that "the colonists shall not be permitted to make any woolen, linen, or cotton cloth, nor weave there, on pain of being banished, and being arbitrarily punished as perjurers." From 1699 the British prohibited colonial wool exports and, with drawbacks and other trade preferences, encouraged colonial importation of linens, cottons, and woolens. In both the Netherlands and England, the home governments encountered demands from large, well-established textile producers facing increasingly vigorous competition in world markets. During the eighteenth century, English merchants frequently flooded the American market with dry goods, dumping their overstocked wares at bargain prices. Not surprisingly most Americans looked abroad for English broadcloths, serges, flannels, hosiery, and caps, for India cottons, and for Scotch, Irish, and Dutch linens. According to trade data for 1768–1772, some 40 percent of British exports to its colonies consisted of woolen goods and another 25 percent were linens.

While colonists drew most of their textiles and clothing from international trade, household production did rise over time. Local manufacture required spinning wheels to produce the yarn and looms to weave the yarn into cloth. Careful analysis of estate inventories reveals that only a small proportion of New Englanders owned spinning wheels before the mid seventeenth century, while southerners did not report appreciable numbers until the turn of the eighteenth century. Looms were even scarcer, suggesting that colonials either knit the yarn they spun into stockings or hats, "put out" the yarn to itinerant weavers, or used the homespun to settle storekeeper's accounts. During the eighteenth century, the proportion of inventories listing textile equipment rose sharply, although the figure varied by place. In the rural North, perhaps three-quarters of the farm households were forced into the frequently unpleasant and time-consuming tasks of preparing fibers and twisting them into yarn. Only one-quarter of Bostonian estates listed spinning wheels, permitting the inference that they could readily purchase imported textiles. Meanwhile, as slavery spread in the South, plantation owners purchased textile implements to employ their female slaves. Usually it was the wealthier people within each region who raised the sheep, flax, or cotton, and who invested in spinning wheels and looms. But such efforts normally resulted in low-quality, often mixed, fabrics to satisfy some of the demand for table linen, bedding, and inner garments. Textiles, produced in mills or workshops called *obrajes,* constituted one of the few examples of colonial-era manufacturing that experienced widespread growth. Domestic output was restricted to coarser fabrics, the demand for finer-grade textiles being supplied by French, Dutch, and Chinese imports. Spanish settlers in the borderlands had access to locally produced woolen or cotton cloths in those places where friars taught Indians to weave in mission workshops or where, as on the upper Rio Grande, a Native textile tradition already existed. In colonial New Mexico, weaving gradually emerged as a cottage industry, allowing residents to export quantities of rough cloth to Mexican mining centers.

Tanning and Leather Goods

The leather industry paralleled that of textiles. With plentiful game—deer, fox, beaver, wolf, elk, moose, and raccoon, supplemented by multiplying domestic stocks of cattle, sheep, hogs, and horses—the production of leather was a by-product of frontier and farming life. The more prosperous of farm operators dug a tanning pit, tossed in layers of hides and either hemlock or oak bark, and left the mixture for as long as a year. During the winter months they retrieved the hides, scraped off the fur, softened the hides with a lapstone, and then either made leather items themselves or turned over the hides to local or itinerant artisans for manufacture into shoes, breeches, vests, or jackets. Many Spaniards similarly engaged in home tanning, using pits and vats. Alternatively, they obtained leather from mission shops, whose surpluses found a ready market elsewhere in the empire.

As settlement increased, tanning in the British colonies became a specialized business and every town had a tannery or two. Larger markets encouraged the proprietor to construct a horse-powered or water-powered bark mill, several vats, lime pits, and storage sheds. In northern cities and towns, tanneries ranked among the largest enterprises of their day, absorbing considerable capital in inventories, land, and equipment. Growing markets and plentiful hides underwrote an increasingly sophisticated leather industry.

Tired of traversing the countryside, shoemakers opened their own shops, using leather they had purchased to sew shoes on order. To occupy journeymen and apprentices in slack times, master craftsmen worked up stock on hand, hoping to sell or exchange it at some future date. Soon in areas of eastern Massachusetts, in New York, and in Philadelphia, some shoemakers ceased doing custom work and simply manufactured shoes in bulk for sale in the colonies and the West Indies. Lynn became a center of ready-made shoe manufacture, reportedly turning out some eighty thousand pairs at the height of nonimportation in 1768. Most attribute its emergence to John Adam Dagyr, a Welshman, who trained local craftsmen in foreign styles and techniques. Women's and children's shoes, such as those made at Lynn, always faced rigorous competition from foreign manufacturers, while American producers dominated the colonial market for men's boots and brogans.

Meat By-products and Rum

A handful of other agricultural products were processed for nonlocal sale. Butchers salted pork and beef, provisioning West Indian slaves and sailors at sea. Since these meats often required as many as twenty pints (about 9 liters) of salt per barrel, most colonists avoided consuming these highly seasoned, low-quality products. Slaughter by-products underwrote a number of small industries, such as soap, glue, neats-foot oil (for leather), and candles.

Not all agricultural products came from the northern colonies. West Indies sugar planters found few markets for their molasses; only the poor would consume it. In the mid seventeenth century, New Englanders began to distill molasses into rum, and with it introduced most Americans to the pleasures of highly alcoholic beverages. A century later, 140 distilleries were to be found on the continent, processing up to 6.5 million gallons (24.7 million liters) of molasses and accounting for some 60 percent of American rum consumption. By then, however, whiskey had displaced rum as the beverage of choice in the backcountry. And as Americans came to prefer refined white sugar over cheaper imported muscovado, twenty-six American sugar refineries were built, mostly in the major cities of Massachusetts, Rhode Island, New York, and Pennsylvania. Processing of West Indian staples was an anomaly; rarely did the colonies import primary products for local manufacture.

Wine and grape brandy were the preferred beverages on the Spanish frontier. Vineyards appeared from Texas to California with the establishment of the first missions, which attempted to meet their own needs for sacramental wine and to obtain a surplus for local sale. The El Paso Valley emerged after 1700 as a center of commercial production, its fine wines and brandies being broadly distributed in northern New Spain.

Flour Milling

The third and arguably the greatest of the colonial resource-using industries was flour milling, an industry that stands as a reproof to the generalization that little if any technological change or sophisticated manufacturing took place in the colonial era. By the mid eighteenth century, Middle Atlantic millers had built and equipped the world's most modern facilities and supplied an Atlantic market with the finest grades of flour. Their success stemmed from the conjunction of

resources and markets. Again the West Indies provided the first major market, and those islands remained among the largest and most stable of American outlets. Beginning in the 1740s, wars and harvest failures opened up Europe to American producers. These international markets spurred both the growth in scale and the improvement in technique that made American milling the envy of the world. And farmers in the middle colonies and the upper South, who had languished for want of markets, responded to high wheat prices with mounting quantities of this dietary staple.

Grinding grain was one of the most laborious of processes. A day's supply for one family required from two to three hours of effort with mortar and pestle or hand mill. Eager to avoid this labor-intensive task, farmers from New France to New Spain quickly sought out mills to grind their wheat, corn, barley, and rye for a share of the final output. These custom mills often anticipated settlement; the first sites to be taken in new areas were those with waterpower potential, and once waterpower was harnessed it proved to be a magnet for further settlement. The small mills would grind only a couple of bushels a day, usually drawing upon the from one to five horsepower generated by a horizontal waterwheel, dubbed a tub wheel because it was encased in a wooden tub. Inexpensive to construct, these wheels were often idle, either awaiting sufficient flow of water or demand for services.

Merchant milling involved much greater technological sophistication, organization, and power. In the English colonies millwrights erected enormous, vertically positioned waterwheels. These required considerable investment in developing the waterpower sites, digging hundreds of feet of raceways, and constructing millponds and dams to store and channel the water to the wheel. With more consistent flow of water across the seasons of the year, millwrights designed larger wheels, ones that were driven not by the impact of water against the blades but by the weight of falling water. The breast or overshot wheels generated from ten to twenty horsepower, enough to turn several pairs of stones, fans, sifters, bolters, and hoists. Assisted by eight or ten machines, millers needed little if any hired labor. But the quantity of labor saved in these automated mills was small, since older-style mills often employed only one or two workers. The gains came from the application of capital; mechanization of every step enabled millers to process immense quantities of wheat into a much higher quality of flour. Foreign markets recognized excellence, and Philadelphia super-fine flour commanded premium prices.

These great merchant mills absorbed sizable amounts of capital. A Middle Atlantic mill incorporating integrated machinery cost upwards of £1,000, ranking it with the largest sawmills, tanyards, and paper mills. Only iron plantations cost more, and perhaps half of their expense was attributable to the need to buy thousands of acres of forest. This scale of milling operation could only be justified by consistently large overseas markets and by location in the heart of grain-producing America. Once launched, scale and mechanization became intertwined in a mutually reinforcing relationship. Oliver Evans's famous automated mill, built after the revolution, represented the culmination of a half-century of pervasive innovation.

CONCLUSION

In comparison with Europe, the American colonies had to adjust to markedly different factor costs. They overcame shortages of skilled labor either by purchasing goods intensive in skills from abroad, enticing skilled workers to migrate, or simply accepting lower-quality domestic wares. Unskilled labor presented greater challenges. So long as land was virtually free for the asking and the rewards from its use were high, raw labor would always be much more expensive in America than in Europe. Even the landless could find remunerative employment; in New France, for example, a six-month engagement in the fur trade paid as much as an artisan made in a year. In the English colonies, labor costs in manufacturing were double those of England. Expansion of manufacturing output beyond the household and handicraft stages turned upon developing specialties that used resources extensively and upon developing techniques that saved unskilled labor.

The substitution of resources for labor can be seen in the American propensity to utilize nonhuman sources of power. Colonials har-

nessed horse, wind, and water to grind grain, clay, bark, and snuff; to beat rags (for paper), iron, and textile fibers; and to press oil, saw timber, pump air, sift flour, and hoist heavy materials. What distinguished the American practice was not the application of power; it was employed in England, France, Spain, Sweden, and the Netherlands. But Europeans lacked the sheer abundance of high-quality, readily available, cheap mill seats equivalent to those found along the rivers emptying into the Atlantic from the Saint Lawrence to the Delaware. When describing the abundant natural resources of the North American continent, the swiftly flowing streams should be included along with the forests, minerals, and soils. Secondly, Europeans did not experience the pressures of labor scarcity as intensely. The differences between the home countries and their colonies can be summarized by noting that in the two greatest power-using industries, saw and flour milling, colonial output per worker exceeded that of any other manufactory in the world. Americans appropriated a technology that fit their factor endowments and improved upon it. By the end of the eighteenth century, colonials had become, according to George S. Gibb, "as advanced as any other country in the basic applications of water power to mechanical movement." They were "on the threshold of undisputed supremacy in the field of practical hydraulics."

The North American colonists did not liberate themselves from a taste for European manufactures and tropical foodstuffs. Estimates vary as to the extent of importation; it may have amounted to as much as one-fourth of disposable income. Even so the surge in imports only matched population increase across the first three-quarters of the eighteenth century. With rising incomes, Americans must have been buying more at home. The multiplication of colonial crafts and craftsmen in North American cities testified to an ability to meet burgeoning domestic demand. But the most dramatic and portentous stirrings were to be found just outside of the North American cities, where resource-using industries employed unprecedented amounts of power to fabricate goods that competed effectively in world markets. The best was yet to come, but even in 1776 British America had already ceased to have a colonial economy.

BIBLIOGRAPHY

The English Colonies

Bishop, John Leander. *A History of American Manufactures from 1608 to 1860.* 3 vols. Philadelphia, 1864; 3rd ed. 1868. Discusses manufacturing in the New Netherlands as well.

Clark, Victor S. *History of Manufactures in the United States.* Vol. 1, *1607–1860.* New York, 1929. Includes material on the Dutch.

Goldenberg, Joseph A. *Shipbuilding in Colonial America.* Charlottesville, Va., 1976.

Hazard, Blanche Evans. *The Organization of the Boot and Shoe Industry.* Cambridge, Mass., 1921.

Hindle, Brooke, ed. *Material Culture of the Wooden Age.* Tarrytown, N.Y., 1981.

Hunter, Louis C. *A History of Industrial Power in the United States, 1780–1930.* Vol. 1, *Waterpower in the Century of the Steam Engine.* Charlottesville, Va., 1979.

Lee, Susan Previant, and Peter Passell. *A New Economic View of American History.* New York, 1979.

McCusker, John J., and Russell R. Menard. *The Economy of British America, 1607–1789.* Chapel Hill, N.C., 1985. See particularly chapter 15.

Mulholland, James A. *A History of Metals in Colonial America.* University, Ala., 1981. Covers New France, the Spanish Borderlands, and the New Netherlands as well as the English Colonies.

Nettles, Curtis. "The Menace of Colonial Manufacturing, 1609–1720." *New England Quarterly* 4, no. 2 (1931):230–269.

Paskoff, Paul F. *Industrial Evolution: Organization, Structure, and Growth of the Pennsylvania Iron Industry, 1750–1860.* Baltimore, Md., 1983.

Tryon, Rolla Milton. *Household Manufactures in the United States, 1640–1860.* Chicago, 1917.

Watkins, Lura Woodside. *Early New England Potters and Their Wares.* Cambridge, Mass., 1950.

New France

Fauteux, Aegidius. *Essai sur l'industrie au Canada sous le regime francais.* 2 vols. Montreal, Quebec, 1927.

Lunn, Alice Jean E. *Developpement economique de la nouvelle-France, 1713–1740.* Montreal, Quebec, 1980.

Surrey, N. M. Miller. "The Development of Industries in Louisiana During the French Regime, 1673–1763." *Mississippi Valley Historical Review* 9, no. 3 (1922):227–235.

Trottier, Louise. *Les forges.* Montreal, Quebec, 1980.

Spanish Borderlands

Bowen, Dorothy Boyd, et al. *Spanish Textile Tradition of New Mexico and Colorado.* Santa Fe, N.Mex., 1979.

Hale, Duane Kendall. "Mineral Exploration in the Spanish Borderlands, 1513–1846." *Journal of the West* 20, no. 2 (1981):5–20.

Simmons, Marc, and Frank Turley. *Southwestern Colonial Ironwork: The Spanish Blacksmithing Tradition from Texas to California.* Santa Fe, N.Mex., 1980.

New Netherlands

Bachman, Van Cleaf. *Peltries or Plantations: The Economic Policies of the Dutch West India Company in New Netherland, 1623–1639.* Baltimore, Md., 1969.

Rink, Oliver. *Holland on the Hudson: An Economic History of Dutch New York.* Ithaca, N.Y., 1986.

Diane Lindstrom[*]

SEE ALSO **Technology**.

[*]The author is indebted to Professor W. J. Eccles for his assistance with the industries of New France, David Dauer for sharing his unpublished research on Middle Atlantic milling, Charles Gehring for his information on the New Netherlands, and to Marc Simmons for broadening the treatment of the Spanish Borderlands.

MARITIME ENTERPRISES

ONCE THE INITIAL PHASES of European discovery were complete, the task of exploiting the new discoveries fell to the mariners and merchants who created the empires that followed. At first this was the work of European cities, but as the colonies prospered, they created their own maritime centers. These towns were unique because they looked toward and participated in an Atlantic community of shipping and markets, whereas the vast majority of the colonists lived in small agricultural villages. In the port towns, where less than 5 percent of the population resided, the inhabitants created the necessary infrastructure that made it all possible. They built and sailed the ships that made once-unthinkable voyages commonplace. Their exploits in shipbuilding, navigation, and seamanship were hardly the stuff of the heroic age of expansion but were just as important to the long-term future of the new empires.

SHIPS AND SHIPBUILDING

European maritime enterprise was based upon the evolution of the craft of shipbuilding. Shipowners and captains could never escape from the calculus that ruled during the days of sailing ships. They had to maintain a balance among the size of the hull, which determined the amount of cargo, foodstuffs, water, and naval supplies the ship could carry; the sails and rig-

ging that controlled the speed and maneuverability of the ship; and the number of men in the crew, a factor that often determined the profitability of the voyage. Ships had to be designed so that they could accomplish the intended voyage and still make a profit. This did not stop small ships, not much bigger than a small yacht, from making dangerous voyages across vast oceans; such ships could never exploit a trade effectively, however, because of the size of the cargo (unless they carried a commodity of very great value). Such a cargo attracted attention from thieves, and in short order it required a very large vessel to protect it. So the cargoes of the time were carried by ordinary merchant ships built for the requirements of the trade.

The Iberians were the first to bring together the elements of ship design that made European ships unique in their maneuverability, carrying capacity, and firepower. The Spanish and Portuguese melded aspects of ship construction from the Mediterranean and northern Europe. During the Middle Ages, northern ships were stout and tublike, with a single mast and square sail. The Mediterranean had a more complex tradition of oared galleys and sailing ships with two or three masts that used lateen (triangular) sails. There were many other differences between the two shipbuilding traditions, but over a long period of experimentation the Spaniards, more particularly the Basques, melded them and created large cargo carriers called carracks. These

627

ships had three masts: the foremast and mainmast carried square sails for power when the wind was astern, and the mizzen or rearmost mast had a lateen sail that allowed the ship to sail closer into the wind. The carrack also had high castles fore and aft that made it easier to handle the sail and to defend the ship. Three-masted ships of this type, called full-rigged, were subject to considerable variation to suit the needs of their owners.

Some of these variations were national. The English, who faced enemies wherever they sailed, preferred ships that carried good-sized cargoes but could also sail fast and fight. Such vessels had another advantage in that they could be brought into the navy on short notice to supplement regular warships. The Dutch followed a different path, and the solution to their problems had great long-term significance. Their most important trade in the sixteenth century was in bulk commodities such as salt, herring, grain, and timber. Dutch shipowners wanted large cargo carriers that could be built and operated cheaply. Dutch shipbuilders slowly evolved the perfect craft. From the *boyer* to the *vlieboot* and finally the *fluyt*, they searched for the right combination.

The *fluyt* emerged after 1550 and came to dominate the carrying trades of Europe as the Netherlands became the great entrepôt. Basically an oblong box with masts, the *fluyt* was the perfect bulk carrier. The Dutch had traditionally built vessels with little or no keel that could operate in their shallow inland waterways. The *fluyt* continued that tradition but was built much wider than earlier ships. Broad and shallow with a rounded stern, it could accommodate bales and barrels in every corner. The hold was decked over to protect it; only the rear of the ship had a castle, and that was not very high. To save money, the upper works used pine rather than oak, which also made it lighter. The other great area of saving came from an advanced system of sails and rigging. The three masts were kept short and the sail area was relatively small, with an extensive use of blocks and pulleys, which meant the ships carried fewer men per ton than any other full-rigged vessel. Thus speed, hardly necessary when carrying most bulk cargoes, was sacrificed for efficiency; fewer crewmen meant lower wage bills, and thus lower costs for trans-

portation. Having arrived at this formula, Dutch shipbuilders built thousands of these cheap bulk carriers mostly in the range of three hundred to five hundred tons. Their competitors would learn to do the same, but not before the Dutch captured a large percentage of the carrying trade of Europe.

The nature of the *fluyt* as a bulk carrier made it unable to defend itself, a fact that shaped Dutch naval policy. To protect their trade vessels, they formed convoys for the great fleets that sailed to the Baltic or went out on the herring fishery. Because of their primacy in the carrying trade, the Dutch also pressed the rights of neutrals in wartime. During the repeated Anglo-French wars of the late seventeenth to early nineteenth centuries they were often victimized by both sides.

While the *fluyt* dominated European shipping, it was not the solution to all problems. Warships needed speed and strength in their hulls, so they were built long and narrow and made of oak in all the vital areas. The masts were tall, and there was a constant push for ever more elaborate sail design that could bring maneuverability and speed. All of this produced a platform on which to place larger numbers of ever bigger cannon. Needless to say, these ships were expensive to build and required large crews. Thus only governments could afford to build them, and when they were not needed, the largest warships were sent immediately to the dock, to await the next conflict.

In fishing there were different issues. Close inshore, fishermen used nearly any craft that fitted their needs. However, as the fishermen started to go further and further away to exploit new fishing grounds, ships changed to meet the new conditions. The Dutch developed the *buss*, designed to exploit the herring fishery by carrying bigger nets, more men, and large amounts of salt, allowing it to go further and catch larger hauls. These sturdy ships would evolve into generations of tough, flat-bottomed ships that could sail anywhere, haul out on shore while the crew salted or dried the catch, and get back to Europe in a season. Some even had boxes in the hold that were partially filled with seawater to keep fish fresh so that they would bring higher prices.

Commercial voyages that involved sailing great distances or to dangerous areas also required different solutions. Given the prevalence of piracy in the Caribbean, Spanish merchantmen needed to be tough fighting ships as well as cargo carriers. That meant more crewmen and cannons on board and less cargo. This drove up the price of the goods going to the colonies but made much sense when it came to shipping back to Spain the high-value goods that dominated the return commerce. The East Indies trade, the longest voyages of all—some lasted up to three years—required ships of eight hundred tons (720 metric tons) or larger because of the need to pack large volumes of goods in order to pay for such long voyages. Also, the ships had to be able to fight their own battles since they were far from home during most of their voyage, well beyond naval protection.

COLONIAL SHIPBUILDING

In the New World shipbuilding started in 1496 when Christopher Columbus's crew built the *India* out of the wreckage of three other ships. Numerous other craft followed, for if there was enough suitable wood close to shore, most ship's carpenters could build a small boat for use in local waters. The French in Florida built oceangoing ships in 1562, and in 1607 the English built their first ship in Maine. Once the colonies were founded, their markets were controlled by Europeans, as was their shipping. They had to rely on the ships and men that came from Europe to keep them supplied with goods and to take away their exports, but as soon as there were sufficient numbers of carpenters, ships were built everywhere in the colonies from Quebec to Cartagena. Only the Spanish government attempted to control shipbuilding in the colonies. For a while the government banned it entirely except in the Pacific where the great expense and danger of sailing ships around Cape Horn made it sensible to build ships locally to serve the needs of the Spanish Empire in the Southern Sea. In the other empires colonists constructed ships as they needed them. Most of their vessels were small ships, such as pinnaces, barks, and shallops. The shallop was the commonest vessel: small, thirty feet (9 meters) or less, and undecked, it was an all-purpose ship that was used for transatlantic voyages. Barks and ketches were larger and, because they had a deck, could be used

for fishing or coastal trade. From these small beginnings grew colonial shipbuilding.

The shipbuilding industry in the English colonies got under way during the seventeenth century. While all the colonies made ships, those in New England were by far the most successful. The abundant woodlands made for easy transportation of timber, resulting in significant savings. Gradually, in ports and large river estuaries, shipwrights constructed stages on which to assemble ships that entered colonial fishing or commerce. Because of the low timber costs the colonists were able to export their ships. This was usually done by sending the ships on one-way trading voyages whose profits were derived from the goods on board and from the sale of the vessel at its final destination. In this way colonial ships became a significant part of the British carrying fleet.

Most of the vessels constructed in the colonies were for short voyages from port to port and were often undecked ships of twenty to forty tons. For longer voyages ships of one hundred to two hundred tons were common. Sugar, tobacco, fish, timber, furs, and the other commodities of the American colonies sailed in the descendants of the *fluyt*. During the eighteenth century various new ship types such as the brigantine, the snow, the ketch, the sloop, and the schooner emerged. Although there were changes in the hull, these ships were mainly marked by significant variations in sail plan. In the English colonies the two favored ships were the sloop and the schooner. The schooner was perhaps the most elegant solution yet evolved for carrying cargo in a ship with a turn of speed. A two-masted ship, it carried a large amount of canvas in a variety of sails that were easily managed by a small crew. It became the most common cargo vessel by the end of the eighteenth century. Ingenious shipbuilders on both sides of the Atlantic constantly sought the perfect configuration of cargo space and speed to meet the needs of a particular trade.

THE FISHERMEN

The first European ships to sail regularly to the New World were fishing boats. Though gold and silver represented the sought-after prize to be

629

wrested from America, one of the most constant sources of wealth came from the salted and dried fish that were brought to Europe in ever-greater amounts from the early sixteenth century. The harsh conditions of the North Atlantic were no impediment to the fishermen of northern Europe. By medieval times they were already fishing off Iceland and Greenland, where their lines and hooks caught cod and ling. They also brought goods to trade with the Icelanders, a practice they continued in the American fisheries.

During the sixteenth century this northern fishery gave way to the richer fishing grounds to the south on the Grand Bank, relatively shallow shoals that are part of the continental shelf. The Gulf Stream and the Labrador Current collide in the area, creating rich feeding grounds for many fish. The most important of these was the cod. It was prized for its flesh whether it was green (fresh), dried, or salted; its liver produced a valuable oil. The precise time when European fishermen arrived at the banks is still in dispute. Like good fishermen everywhere they did not talk openly about their favorite new fishing ground. The likelihood is that by the late fifteenth century the first contacts were made, and by the early sixteenth century fishermen were not only on the Grand Bank, just off Newfoundland, but also fishing the banks to the south and west along the North American coast. The evidence for this lies in such episodes as Giovanni da Verrazano's discovery in 1524 of Maine Indians wearing copper earrings of European manufacture. The habit of fishing and trading while drying the fish had already arrived in the New World.

The banks were long-distance fisheries, requiring the fishermen to develop new methods in order to spend months at sea and return with an edible cargo. For the Spanish, Portuguese, and French fishermen who had large supplies of indigenous salt used to preserve the fish, old techniques were refined to put the fish under even more salt. The English did not have large supplies of salt and so had to buy it; thus they preferred the technique of "dry" fishing. They sailed to the fishing grounds, acquired a catch, landed and erected stages (simple sheds with long tables), off-loaded their catches, boned them, and then lightly salted them before drying

them for as long as three months. Other nations also used this technique, but the English used it almost exclusively.

Because they needed to land in order to prepare their catches, the English were the most aggressive of the Europeans in seizing the sites on the Avalon Peninsula, the land closest to the Grand Bank. Contests for these stages soon ensued with the French, Portuguese, Spanish, and Dutch fishermen, who also landed a portion of their catch to dry, but it was the English who thrust their way forward and took over the choicest areas of Newfoundland. To avoid them, the French, who were the first to exploit the new fishing grounds, were forced to move farther west to concentrate on the Saint Lawrence fishery; there they developed a headquarters at Placentia, Newfoundland, where they could protect themselves from the English. Newfoundland witnessed many aggressive acts as men-of-war, pirates, and privateers swept in to rob and pillage or to assert the rights of their particular nation. The French and the English managed to remain the dominant powers in the area, forcing everyone else to seek their permission to land, and if granted, seamen had to sail to inaccessible areas, or to fish and then head home. The fisheries around Newfoundland were a seemingly endless source of fish, whales, and seals for the men who made the voyage across the Atlantic. They fed substantial numbers of people with their catches and enriched the merchants and shipowners who financed the voyages. The fishermen profited in ratio to their luck, for they held shares in the voyages and a good catch meant that they and their families survived another year.

To policymakers and admiralties, fishing was an essential training ground for the men needed on fighting ships in wartime. The English, in fact, regarded them as the "nurseries" of the navy, for more men were trained to the sea in the harsh conditions involved in fishing than in any other way. Because of their importance as food suppliers and a source of manpower, the fishing ships were hunted by ships of war, privateers, and pirates. Men-of-war sought to deny the enemy valuable cargoes, and the privateers and pirates sought them as easy prizes. The pirates also liked to recruit the sailors onto their ships to replace missing colleagues.

630

Fishing played a role in the beginning of colonization. As fishermen sailed farther south and west to the coast of North America, they continued to need places to dry their catches; they found these places in the harbors and bays that dot the coast of New England and the Gulf of the Saint Lawrence. Once again this was an international movement, for by the time the English came to these shores, the Indians already knew "baccalaos," a generic Iberian term for cod. By the end of the sixteenth century the English dominated the shorelines of New England and started to trade with the natives during the summer months. From these contacts came the devastating epidemics that scourged the coastal Algonquian prior to the arrival of the English colonists. It was from the fishermen that Samoset, the Indian who aided the Pilgrims, learned the English that he used to greet the startled colonists.

Learning the best local fisheries from the Indians, the colonists soon took advantage of this knowledge to expand their own efforts. In the Chesapeake the English found that they were living on the verge of one of the most productive fishing grounds in the world. They quickly learned the seasonal rhythms of the bay that produced such a wide variety of marine life. The Chesapeake Bay fisheries remained mostly local and fed the ever-growing population around the bay. New England came to be the premier fishery in the colonies because of its proximity to the banks. At first English fishermen continued to make the long spring voyage out to New England, where they set up their stages and then went out to the banks (particularly Georges) to fish, then dried the fish before the long voyage home. Some fishing companies decided to create their own settlements in order to take better advantage of year-long occupation. Gloucester, for instance, was created in 1623 by a fishing company in need of a local base. Such communities matured into towns that built their own boats and fished in their own right.

WHALING

Whaling played a significant role in American culture beyond its function as an economic activity. The heroic nature of whaling called forth many songs, paintings, and, of course, *Moby-Dick*, published in 1851, all of which gave whaling greater status than mere fishing. When Europeans arrived in the New World to fish, they discovered whales and an indigenous whaling fishery. The most abundant whale along the coast was the right whale, found as drift whales on the beach, where the Indians cut them up for meat and the bone. Some of the coastal people hunted the whales from canoes, using wooden harpoons. They usually hunted in groups and, after striking the whale, attached a log to the harpoon and followed their catch until they could close in and kill it. They then had the arduous task of moving the whale back to the shore, where it could be cut up.

The Europeans started whaling around Newfoundland and Labrador where the Basques and later the French were particularly active. Whaling in the English colonies was concentrated in southern New England and Long Island. On the eastern end of Long Island there was a particularly active Indian whaling culture. Their expertise in the hunt caused the English to hire the Indians, and throughout the colonial period they were found on colonial whaling vessels. The Indians aided the English in developing a whaling industry just offshore, where their iron harpoons were more efficient, as were their flensing tools. Once the whale was brought ashore, the blubber was boiled down and the baleen, or whalebone, was stripped from the carcass. The oil was used for lighting in lamps or was made into candles. The whalebone was used for stays in ladies' clothing and anywhere else stiffening material was needed. By the end of the seventeenth century whaling had moved to the islands of southern New England, and Nantucket had started its cultivation of whaling.

On Nantucket, as elsewhere, whaling was still a coastal affair: small boats and a few men went out to hunt as the whales moved north in the spring. Early in the eighteenth century the nature of whaling changed when whalers started to catch sperm whales, which were prized because they yielded greater amounts of a finer oil. But the sperm whales were found away from the coast and nearer to the Gulf Stream, and were more abundant to the south. To catch them, larger ships of thirty to fifty tons (27 to 45 metric tons) set out on longer voyages and new techniques were required to cut up the whales at sea before returning the blubber to port, where it was reduced to oil. By 1774 American whaling employed 4,700 men sailing in 360 ships who hunted as far afield as Africa and Brazil. The revolution was a catastrophe for the whalers, however. Of the 150 vessels in the Nantucket fleet, 134 were captured by the English. The industry did not recover until after 1800. By then whaling was concentrated in the Pacific, where ships of 250 to 350 tons sailed on voyages extending thirty-five to fifty months. These were the epic years of whaling.

MEN AND THE SEA

The "romance" of the sea has a long tradition that celebrates life at sea, though much of it is a romantic fiction. Not that life at sea lacked adventure, thrills, beauty, and strong emotion; however, the day-to-day life of early modern mariners does not transcribe well into song and story. Theirs was a life so bound up in hardship that it compares with few experiences today. The sea still exacts a toll on all those who make their living from it, no matter how modern the technology or how great the engineering.

In the seventeenth and eighteenth centuries men went to sea with few navigational instruments and very few creature comforts. The men dressed in rough and ready fashion. Along with a shirt they wore a pair of short trousers or breeches that were tarred to keep out the cold water. Over this went a jacket of heavy wool. Shoes were worn infrequently because leather was hardly fit for clambering on rigging. The harsh environment in which they lived slowly destroyed clothing, and the longer the voyage, the greater the likelihood that it would slowly disintegrate; thus, when a man died, his clothing was quickly auctioned off "before the mast." The same environment gave the men deeply tanned skin and made them easy to spot when they came ashore. While on board they slept wherever they could; if the weather was truly awful, they slept among the bales and boxes of the cargo. An invention of the Caribbean Indians that mariners quickly adopted was the hammock. It could be hung nearly anywhere and gave the men, for the first time, a permanent berth. However, on small ships they still slept on deck or on top of the cargo for lack of space.

Disease and injury were the common lot of mariners. Voyages to distant or tropical areas brought the possibilities of scurvy, always present in the absence of fresh fruits and vegetables, and the all too numerous viruses and parasites that could incapacitate or kill a person. In the confined space of a ship, especially a slave ship, a new disease could sweep the crew and leave them unable to work, or even dead, in large enough numbers that the ship was endangered by the lack of hands needed to run it.

Sailors' lives were full of danger, and the possibility of accidents was very high. In port they had to store the cargo properly, since this could affect the sailing qualities of the ship. Too much heavy cargo in the stern meant a high bow and a ship that was difficult to steer. Once at sea the men had to clamber up and down in the rigging to match the sails to the wind conditions, and to do so in all weather, so that a sudden squall in the middle of the night could find the men clambering about in hammering rain and lightning. When not tending sail, they mended the sails and kept the rigging and hull in repair; and if the ship was leaky, they spent endless hours pumping out seawater. In all, they experienced a harsh regime of labor where broken bones and lacerations were common and the loss of life an ever-present fact.

Besides bearing the dangers of the sea, the men had to deal with unique conditions of labor. In medieval times most seamen worked for a share in the profits of the voyage, but by the early seventeenth century more and more of them were working for wages. Only the fishermen and whalers continued to have shares in the profits of the catch. At a time when most labor was in a relationship of apprenticeship or some form of servitude, sailors were the first major group of laborers to deal with contracts for wages. Their wages changed very little over time. They rose slowly from about twenty shillings per month at the beginning of the seventeenth century to about twenty-five shillings by 1700. Wages remained stable until the middle of the eighteenth century, when they slowly started to drift upward again. Wartime always pushed wages higher as the navy and privateers competed for scarce labor. Wages could then reach sixty to sixty-five shillings, as they did during the Seven Years' War. While this was a bonanza for the men, it also meant that the dangers of a voyage were that much greater due to enemy action. Not all men were paid the same. Newly recruited men or boys got lower wages while experienced topsmen, those who could handle sails while out on the highest spars, commanded the highest wages.

On the voyages they were fed by the shipowners, who were supposed to feed them well. But often the men were cheated and short-rationed. The food was salt pork or beef, hard biscuit (often filled with weevils), dried or salt fish, cheese, beans, and beer. The monotonous diet was supplemented with fresh food while in port or whatever the men could catch while at sea.

Disputes over wages and victuals were common. Some of these disputes came from changes in the voyage due to weather or more attractive cargoes elsewhere, but many related to penurious treatment by the owners or captains. Admiralty court records are full of these disputes, and though mariners could—and did—win many cases, their wages could be withheld while they waited to catch another ship and return to the sea, so they could lose even when they won. The one small area the men controlled and could profit from was their sea chests. These chests were unexamined by officers or officials, and the men could carry on small trades of their own if they could afford to. Most mariners tried, in this small way, to supplement their wages, but it would never make them rich.

The officers were given very great powers over the sailors. The captain, or master, had the responsibility for navigation and the general management of the ship. The mate exercised the captain's authority when the captain was off duty and was mostly responsible for managing the men. Each of them took a four-hour watch, four hours on and four hours off, and the crew was divided into two watches that tended the ship twenty-four hours per day. Full-rigged ships had a carpenter who watched over the fabric of the ship; and if it was a voyage to a dangerous area, there would be a gunner to care for the armaments and a surgeon to tend the men. Captains could make five or six pounds per month and as much as ten pounds on long, dangerous

voyages. Mates, carpenters, and surgeons made from three to four pounds; gunners, from two to three pounds. Their wages were remarkably stable over the eighteenth century. Like the men, the officers were allowed to have private cargoes, although theirs were much larger than those of the seamen. Captains were the chief beneficiary of this privilege, and a well-managed private trade could easily put them in the middle class, far above the workers.

While at sea the men were expected to obey the officers, whose personalities and experience had a direct bearing on the conditions for the men. If the captain was a good sailor who cared for his men, they were willing to obey and sign on with him again, but there were always brutes whom sailors would shun if they had a choice. These were the drunks, psychopaths, or strict disciplinarians, such as famed *Bounty* captain William Bligh, who could make a ship a living hell. Needless to say, such captains took a great toll in the navy, where law and armed marines were on their side and where refinements of cruelty were practiced. While mutiny in the navy was uncommon, it was much less so on merchant ships, where the men could use all sorts of go-slow techniques to annoy the captain and could also jump ship or take it over in extreme circumstances. Mutiny was always dangerous, and more often than not the mutineers would turn to piracy rather than return to normal life.

Regardless of these harsh conditions, men still sought a life at sea. It was, after all, the quickest escape from life in a hierarchical society in which there was little hope for change. At sea, adventure could come over the horizon and there was always contact with new people and places. There was also the camaraderie with fellow sailors. They shared life together inside wooden walls and acquired the skills necessary to maneuver and guide the ship in all conditions. To do so they developed a unique language that bound them together, particularly on land where their gait and behavior set them apart from landsmen. They created a set of ceremonies to mark the passage of dangerous places or navigational points, such as the equator, that initiated newcomers into life at sea. Their songs also added to a culture that bound them together and made the mariners' life palatable if not exciting on a daily basis.

PRIVATEERING AND PIRACY

The sea was always dangerous, but in the colonial period there were dangers other than those of the weather. Piracy and privateering were ever-present aspects of life at sea. In Europe pirates had a long history, and as the trade that accompanied European expansion grew, piracy grew along with it. Only when the new states became sufficiently well organized at sea did their navies gradually suppress old pirate communities such as Dunkirk. However, as piracy declined, privateering increased in importance and intensity. During wartime, states commissioned privately owned vessels to capture enemy shipping. Once the investors obtained a commission for the ship and had agreed to obey all the relevant laws and ordinances relating to privateering, they could prepare their vessel for sea. They signed on officers and a crew, and agreed with them on what share each would have of the prize money. Experienced captains tried to get out to sea as soon as war was declared, so as to catch enemy ships that might not know about the war. The most profitable voyages were made in this period prior to the organization of convoys and naval guardships. After a prize had been captured, it had to be brought back to port and condemned before a properly authorized admiralty court. Then the vessel and its cargo were evaluated and sold, and the profits distributed to the investors and the men.

The lure of prize money attracted colonial shipowners and merchants, who started investing as soon as they could. In the Caribbean the proximity of colonies of so many nations and the prevalence of war between the colonizing powers meant that an enterprising captain could get a commission at any time if he did not care which prince he served. During the eighteenth century, when France, Spain, and Britain frequently went to war, the colonists in all the American colonies enjoyed the benefits and suffered the consequences of privateering. For example, during the wars from 1739 to 1748, the colonists captured 829 enemy ships, but French and Spanish privateers seized 736 English ships. So while the merchants of New York and Newport piled up significant profits from privateering, large amounts of English sugar, tobacco, and rice enriched the enemy.

If the seventeenth century witnessed a significant increase of privateering, it also saw a new and far more potent form of piracy. In the New World the rising imperial powers—France, England, and the Netherlands—sought to undermine the Spanish Empire with attacks that were nothing short of piratical. Covetous of the treasure that Spain was extracting from its American colonies, they sought to steal it. In wartime this was done under cover of privateering, but the rest of the time individual entrepreneurs or great companies organized ships and even fleets to capture the annual Spanish treasure fleets. One of the more spectacular of these actions occurred in 1628 when Piet Heyn, commanding a fleet under orders of the Dutch West India Company, managed to seize the Spanish treasure fleet near Havana valued at roughly 11.5 million guilders. Year after year the Spanish suffered attacks in the Caribbean and the Atlantic as the emerging powers permitted, or at least overlooked, the activities of their mariners. In the end the Spanish retreated behind their defenses and the *flota* system (annual convoys to protect their ships) while their enemies colonized the islands and continued to seek booty where they could.

In the turmoil of the Caribbean a new form of piracy emerged. Thousands of men—mariners, former soldiers, escaped servants, and others—fled the rigidities of ship life, the army, or the plantation system to create a new life-style. Traditional pirates were usually identified with a community that served as their base. In the Caribbean the buccaneers were uprooted men who sailed from any port that suited them or simply camped on a convenient beach. They accepted commissions as privateers whenever they were available, or simply set out to steal without permission. At times they aided the expansion of the new powers, but they were unpredictable allies.

Many of them started as "cow killers" who made their living on the Greater Antilles by hunting cattle and raiding Spanish settlements for supplies. These men also took to the sea in search of supplies, joining those pirates who sought booty wherever they could find it. At first their victims were Spanish ships and towns. They were encouraged in their activities by Spain's rivals, who sought to cripple Spain and to prevent

Spanish attacks on their own new and weak colonies. The buccaneers provided a first line of defense at no cost to the French, English, and Dutch. In fact, they brought valuable Spanish commodities of all kinds (besides the fabled gold and silver) into port, thereby enriching colonial merchants. To tie them more closely to colonial regimes, the buccaneers were given commissions to sail as privateers; many preferred the slender legitimacy of these pieces of paper to sailing as pirates.

The life of a buccaneer was one of deprivation punctuated with great feasts. Buccaneers tended to pack as many men as possible into a ship in order to overawe their intended victims, an overmanning that produced a cruel calculus. More men meant a need for greater amounts of supplies of all kinds in a tightly packed ship. If they did not successfully capture a ship or town, the men went on short rations and even starved. In their weakened condition they were more susceptible to the wide variety of tropical diseases, so that they suffered from high mortality rates.

Why would men subject themselves to such conditions? They did so not just because of the hope of great fortune but also because of the life-style. On board a buccaneering ship the men enjoyed a democratic regime that allowed them to elect a captain and get rid of him when they were dissatisfied. They divided their spoils according to predetermined shares and even provided for a primitive form of workmen's compensation by granting designated amounts to men who lost a limb or suffered a disabling wound. As members of the "brethren of the coast," the men had a great deal of control over their lives, so that no matter what the risks, they preferred to live as buccaneers. And if they did strike it rich, there was the promise of a great debauch in Port Royal, Jamaica, or Tortuga before returning to sea. Some men who made it rich preferred to return to normal life, where their small fortunes could open new vistas for them.

The 1670s were the heyday of the Caribbean buccaneers. They raided in numbers never seen before and struck terror into Spanish hearts in every corner of the empire. Leaders such as Edward Mansfield took large numbers of men on raids against Spanish ports. The best of these leaders was Henry Morgan, a daring man who knew how to handle large numbers and was lucky enough to seize considerable amounts of treasure. The climax of his career was a raid on Panama City, the Pacific terminus for the silver shipments coming from Peru. The silver was transported across the rugged Isthmus of Panama before being loaded onto the treasure fleet. Most attempts to capture the annual silver shipments were made at the Caribbean terminus of Portobello. Morgan led two thousand men on the exhausting overland journey and then proceeded to sweep aside the Spanish defenders before entering the city. While most of the treasure had been removed from the city prior to the arrival of the buccaneers, they still made off with a fortune. Morgan took most of the bounty to Jamaica, where some of his men accused him of cheating them.

For this and other reasons Morgan settled down to life as a planter and politician where his wealth and political connections (wealthy and charming pirates usually have friends in high places) brought him a knighthood and a term as lieutenant-governor of Jamaica. While this appears strange, Morgan always sailed with a privateering commission and could claim his actions were legal. He made this claim stick even as his detractors attacked him, and as a legitimate privateer against an ancient enemy such as Spain he was a hero to many, thus easing his transition into politics. His raid was an impressive achievement that frightened many in the Spanish bureaucracy and caused them to tighten up their defenses.

With the knowledge gained from Morgan's crossing of the Isthmus of Panama, other buccaneers soon decided to try their luck in the Pacific; before long, the "Spanish lake" was no longer safe for Spanish ships. After these raids the men returned overland to the Caribbean or made the difficult passage around Cape Horn. Two ships decided to hunt for the Manila galleon by crossing the Pacific; though they missed the galleon, the men returned home after completing an incredible circumnavigation. This voyage revealed the oftentimes foolhardy nature of the buccaneers, but it also testified to their toughness and skill as mariners.

While some men raided in the Pacific, conditions in the Caribbean caused other buccaneers to seek their fortunes elsewhere. By the 1680s a number of conditions made the Caribbean less attractive. Spanish defenses, slow to develop, had improved, especially the tough *barcas longas* that sought out pirate ships and often defeated them. Conditions had also changed in the ports that had given hospitality to the pirates. Merchants made more money from trading with the Spanish directly than from waiting for the buccaneers to come to port. This trade, though illicit, was growing rapidly, and the merchants preferred it to the irregular profits derived from piracy. To get supplies and a warmer reception, the buccaneers turned to cruising along the coast of North America, where the port towns were happy to receive cheap goods and sell the pirates whatever supplies they needed. The buccaneers were also sailing with greater frequency to Africa and then around to the Indian Ocean, where they opened up a new pirate frontier. The men settled on Madagascar, particularly the island of Sainte-Marie. From this base they raided north into the Red Sea and the Arabian Sea, in search of treasure and merchant ships. Some of the ships that went to the Indian Ocean returned immediately to their home base, while others remained in the East.

The needs of these men created one of the most incredible examples of entrepreneurship in this period. Merchants in New York saw an opportunity in the needs of the men on Madagascar. They sent ships filled with food, munitions, clothing, liquor, and other supplies that were traded for spices, jewels, silk cloth, and drugs. Those men who wanted to return home could buy passage for one hundred pieces of eight. Once the ships had returned to New York City, most of the goods were put on vessels headed for ports such as Hamburg, Germany. The profits from this voyage were returned to New York.

By 1700 buccaneering had spilled out of the Caribbean, endangering vessels in many areas of the new empires. When the War of the Spanish Succession ended in 1714, attention turned to protecting peaceful commerce. The British government reformed its laws, making piracy cases easier to prosecute; more important, the Royal Navy was sent out to attack the pirates and destroy their bases. The pirates were hunted down in all their favorite haunts. As they came under attack, they raided shipping regardless of its origin, including that of the colonial ports which had formerly offered a safe haven. By 1730 large-scale buccaneering was crushed, leaving local pirates to cause occasional problems; if they were too successful, the navy was brought out to hunt them down.

The Caribbean remained a favored place for piracy and privateering. The late eighteenth century witnessed an upsurge in both. The Age of Revolution brought many changes to the region as new governments were created in response to war and revolution in Europe. These governments commissioned privateers whose papers were suspect, returning the Caribbean to the state it had been in during the seventeenth century. Such confusion opened the door to real pirates, who thrived on anarchy. But the numbers of men and ships involved never matched that of the era of buccaneering.

MARITIME COMMUNITIES AND THE NEW NATION

By 1800 mature maritime communities thrived throughout the Americas. Ships and men were available for any venture. The United States built warships equal to those of the Royal Navy. A 60-gun ship was built at Quebec in 1748 and a 104-gun ship was built by Spanish colonists at Havana in 1787, proving that such skill was widespread. Of all the new nations, the United States had the most extensive maritime culture. It had large port cities where mariners were readily available for voyages to any part of the world. After 1783 the Americans pushed beyond the constraints of the British Empire and sailed their own ships as far afield as China to open up new trade. Their shipbuilding industry could turn out large numbers of brigs, skows, and, in ever-increasing numbers, the most popular ship in the new nation: the schooner. The American whaling and fishing industries had suffered from the war and had a contentious time asserting their rights on fishing grounds claimed by European powers, but their aggressiveness soon allowed Americans to fish and whale as equals. Thus in the nineteenth century the Americans played a highly significant role in the maritime scene in the New World and controlled the trade of large areas, resembling the Old World empires of trade in the eyes of other new nations.

BIBLIOGRAPHY

Ackerman, Edward A. *The New England Fishing Industry*. Chicago, 1941.

Bélanger, R. *Les Basques dans l'estuaire du Saint-Laurent, 1535–1635*. Quebec, 1971.

Brière, Jean-François. *La Peche Francaise en Amerique du Nord au XVIIIe siecle*. Montreal, 1990.

Cell, Gillian T. *English Enterprise in Newfoundland, 1577–1660*. Toronto, Ontario, 1969.

Davis, Ralph. *The Rise of the English Shipping Industry in the Seventeenth and Eighteenth Centuries*. London, 1962.

Earle, Peter. *The Sack of Panama: Sir Henry Morgan's Adventures on the Spanish Main*. New York, 1982.

Goldenberg, Joseph A. *Shipbuilding in Colonial America*. Charlottesville, Va., 1976.

Goslinga, Cornelis C. *The Dutch in the Caribbean and on the Wild Coast, 1580–1680*. Gainesville, Fla., 1971.

Haring, Clarence H. *Trade and Navigation Between Spain and the Indies in the Time of the Hapsburgs*. Cambridge, Mass., 1918; repr. Gloucester, Mass., 1964.

Harris, R. Cole, and Geoffrey J. Matthews, editor and cartographer. *Historical Atlas of Canada*. Volume 1. Toronto, Ontario, 1987.

Innis, Harold A. *The Cod Fisheries: The History of an International Economy*. Toronto, Ontario, 1940; rev. ed. 1954.

Israel, Jonathan I. *The Dutch Primacy in World Trade, 1585–1740*. Oxford, 1989.

Marcus, Geoffrey J. *The Conquest of the North Atlantic*. New York, 1981.

Millar, John F. *American Ships of the Colonial and Revolutionary Periods*. New York, 1978.

Nash, Gary B. *The Urban Crucible: Social Change, Political Consciousness, and the Origins of the American Revolution*. Cambridge, Mass., 1979.

Rediker, Marcus. *Between the Devil and the Deep Blue Sea: Merchant Seamen, Pirates, and the Anglo-American Maritime World, 1700–1750*. New York, 1987.

Ritchie, Robert C. *Captain Kidd and the War Against the Pirates*. Cambridge, Mass., 1986.

Rodgers, N.A.M. *The Wooden World: An Anatomy of the Georgian Navy*. London, 1986.

Starbuck, Alexander. *History of the American Whale Fishery from Its Inception to the Year 1876*. New York, 1964.

Swanson, Carl E. *Predators and Prizes: American Privateering and Imperial Warfare, 1739–1748*. Columbia, S.C., 1991.

Unger, Richard W. *Dutch Shipbuilding Before 1800: Ships and Guilds*. Assen, The Netherlands, 1978.

Weddle, Robert S. *Spanish Sea: The Gulf of Mexico in North American Discovery, 1500–1685*. College Station, Tex., 1985.

Robert C. Ritchie

SEE ALSO Mercantilism; Relations with the Parent Country; Trade and Commerce; and The West Indies and North America.

637

THE FUR TRADE

INTRODUCTION

THE FUR TRADE ENTAILED AN exchange of goods that each side found necessary, useful, or desirable: European manufactured goods for Native North Americans, and North American furs and hides for Europeans. The earliest trade goods were those already made for European consumption; goods exported thereafter for the North American trade were made especially for it or were surplus to European requirements. Native North Americans wanted a range of items: firearms and ammunition; metal tools, implements, and utensils; clothing and ornaments; tobacco and alcohol. Europeans wanted deerskins and other hides for a rapidly expanding leather market that European sources could not satisfy. They wanted beaver pelts for a felt hat market that rode the crest of fashion for more than two hundred years. And the affluent among them wanted luxury furs for coats, collars, and trim at reasonable prices rather than the furs of common animals or increasingly expensive rare varieties from northern or eastern sources.

The European Market About 1500
Before the North American trade began, western European markets were in transition. The production of textiles, metal tools and implements, firearms, and alcoholic beverages was steadily growing. Craft specialization by country or city, still evident in the origin of goods exchanged at the great fairs, was breaking down. Rapidly growing national armies required not only up-to-date weapons but also great quantities of leather goods (such as harness, saddles, boots, and clothing).

The European fur market was much affected by change in the complex Baltic supply system. Several northern species much valued for their fur were rapidly diminishing in number, and more common species were now in demand by the affluent. Rabbit could be used in the making of felt hats, but beaver was much preferred. When Chaucer's fourteenth-century merchant flaunted his "Flemish beaver hat," the industrious animal still frequented western European rivers; now, virtually the only remaining European source was Muscovy. Under such conditions, European furriers, felters, and tanners were more likely to meet the requirements of their customers by exploiting new sources of material at reasonable cost than by paying and charging higher prices.

European Trade Goods
Metal objects that Amerindians found useful included axes, hatchets, awls, needles, knives, files, hoes, traps, kettles, and fire steels, as well as silver ornaments such as armlets, brooches, gorgets, rings, and earrings. Cloth included blankets of several types and various other woolens from France and England, coarse canvaslike hempen fabrics, and various items of clothing. Combs

639

and looking glasses, as well as beads for ornament and as a medium of exchange, were in demand. Cheap rum from the Caribbean and brandy from France (dearer, but more pleasant-tasting) competed for favor. Firearms for warfare and hunting required spare parts, powder, shot, flints, and instruments for cleaning.

Although manufactures before the industrial revolution were often small-scale enterprises, the export of trade goods to North America became large-scale business. Organization was intricate. Bankers, great merchants (*négociants*), and smaller merchants and agents advanced, possessed, or acquired the capital necessary to buy, assemble, ship, distribute, and sell goods of a quality and in quantities satisfactory to the customer. Everyone from the hardware and textile manufacturers, and the vintners and the distillers, to the colonial merchant or independent trader who exchanged goods for furs, could expect to profit. As the trade developed, the demand for goods tended to increase, which implied growth in the size or number of shops and in consignments to be shipped, from which the organizers and operators of the business were able to benefit. Most of the merchants involved in the French and British trade were of those two nationalities but others, such as Dutch, German, and Swiss with business associates in France and Great Britain, invested in aspects of it.

North American Furs and Hides

The most marketable furs were the luxuriant ones found in the northern climates, where winters were coldest and longest. They included (in addition to beaver) marten, muskrat, mink, otter, wolf, bear, and lynx. The sea otter of the North Pacific was much sought after late in the eighteenth century. The most marketable hides were those of deer, elk (wapiti), bison, and moose, of which deerskin was by far the most common and moose the one most valued in the north. Deerskins were collected in enormous quantities from the Ohio Valley to the Gulf of Mexico and from the Atlantic to the Rocky Mountains.

THE FRENCH AND ENGLISH FUR TRADE THROUGH 1700

The organization of the fur trade was complex, whether it involved individuals and small companies, large companies such as Hudson's Bay (founded 1670) and the Compagnie des Indes (founded 1719), or all of them. Sometimes a hunter or trapper sold furs directly to a company employee, as occurred at Hudson's Bay Company posts; more usually, he sold them to a middleman: a Native trader, an independent European trader, or a trader's employee.

Europeans were governed by the profit motive; natives were not. The exchange of gifts was essential to Amerindian belief systems. Game and agricultural produce were to be taken only as required, and the taking to be accompanied by a gesture of reciprocity toward the powers of nature that had supplied them. With difficulty, Amerindians attempted to adjust their beliefs to the fur trade. European goods were acquired for personal use, which often entailed very particular preferences for certain qualities of merchandise: size, appearance, feel, and so forth. Nations that tended to trade what others hunted also sought territorial hegemony— but certainly not the accumulation of capital. Attributing that to any of them is a farfetched notion, contrary to the evidence, that has been discredited.

European traders, judging values in European terms, considered the Indians dupes for accepting cheap goods in return for fine pelts and skins. The Indians, for their part, were happy to obtain goods that, in their eyes, greatly improved their economic and social existence, in exchange for common animal skins, some of them sweaty and well-worn beaver coats. Of course, the capitalistic notions of risk taking and usury were completely alien to them. Before the winter hunting season, Native hunters expected advances in the form of trade goods; if hunting conditions proved unfavorable, however, they postponed repayment of these debts and refused outright to pay interest on them.

The fur trade was large-scale capitalism: for the European traders, merchants, voyageurs, indentured canoemen and packhorse men, shippers, bankers, furriers, hatters, tanners, cobblers, and saddlers, there were handsome profits to be made and wages to earn. Although higher prices had to be paid for furs and skins once Native North Americans demanded larger quantities and a wider variety of trade goods, profit margins did not decline appreciably throughout the seventeenth and eighteenth centuries.

Trading was a partnership between Europeans and Native North Americans, but the French and English apparently had different notions of this relationship. The French dealt with Amerindians as equals in fact, and did not covet their land, even though their rhetoric was at times paternalistic. They wished to trade rather than to colonize in great numbers, and they needed trading partners—whom the church, incidentally, wished to Christianize. French missionaries were excellent ambassadors for their country, showing it in a good light, opposing debauchery of the natives, and dealing tactfully with those whom they hoped to convert. The English of the seaboard colonies were primarily interested in settlement and were merciless in driving away or exterminating Indian nations that stood in their way. Traders did not sympathize with an attitude that would destroy their livelihood, but were ambivalent in their own relations with Native associates. There were exceptions to these generalizations—for example, in the relations of the two powers with the Iroquois—but essentially the French went well beyond business relations with natives in their endeavor to keep them as customers and allies.

The Beginnings of the Trade in the Northeast

Throughout the sixteenth century, Europeans came to northeastern North America to fish commercially on an increasingly large scale for cod and other species. Competing for this bountiful resource, vessels ventured into bays and rivers in search of sheltered fishing grounds; those engaged in the "dry" fishery landed crewmen on the coast to dry their catch, a process that lasted several weeks. In such cases, Europeans encountered Amerindians ready to trade furs of excellent quality for European manufactures. The profitable bartering for furs supplemented a less spectacular return from the fishery—even though it included the value of the return voyage across the ocean. By the 1580s this adjunct to the fishery became commerce in its own right.

Seeking to forestall English and Dutch defiance of a prior claim by France to colonize and develop the Saint Lawrence River valley, the French Crown experimented there and in Acadia with fur-trading monopolies, in return for which colonists were to be settled and evangelizing missions were to be financed. These measures culminated in the establishment of Port Royal (Acadia) in 1605 and Quebec in 1608. Along the Atlantic coast, from Newfoundland to New Netherland, traders ventured inland in search of furs, establishing trading relationships that profoundly affected indigenous nations.

The Amerindian belief in a nature in harmony morally restricted the killing of game to what was needed for food; it was to be complemented by other sources. This contrasted sharply with the Judeo-Christian concept of human primacy, placing nature at the service of man. Self-sufficient producers of food, clothing, and shelter thus became specialists dependent upon an alien economic, social, and cultural system. The Micmac, for example, partners of the French in the Acadian fur trade, were forced to abandon their traditional subsistence economy and to rely on food inferior to their former diet. This exacerbated their vulnerability to European disease, which drastically reduced their numbers and, by undermining the authority of the shamans who had traditionally explained and treated illness, diminished their confidence in their own culture.

The first New Englanders in the 1620s exported furs to pay off the initial costs of colonization. Indeed, as the seventeenth century progressed, furs were by no means insignificant in New England, and for decades on the Connecticut River there was a thriving trade. In the long run, however, trade gave way to colonization of the fertile hinterland. Amerindians, decimated by European diseases, could not resist the often violent advance of settlement. What Europeans unwittingly transmitted through their Native trading partners entailed the disappearance of forests, fur-bearing animals, and the partners themselves. By the eighteenth century the trade, confined chiefly to Maine, was minor in comparison with that of New York, which had begun about 1614 at the beginning of Dutch colonization.

The Dutch trade, which came to overshadow agricultural settlement, became firmly established on the Hudson, spread from there in various directions, and for a time competed in the Connecticut Valley with the New England trade.

The Beaver Trade: Montreal, Albany, and Hudson Bay

Among the skins taken in Canada the best-known, that of the beaver, was obsessively pursued to satisfy the requirements of the hatters. Although it has been singled out for more scholarly attention than fine furs or moose hides, it was by no means alone in commercial significance; and the beaver market was subject to fluctuation. Prime winter pelts worn for months by natives with the fur inward ("coat beaver" or *castor gras d'hiver*) were preferred by hatters: the guard hairs were worn off and the underfur was greasy, matted, and cohesive, ready for felting. This product fetched higher prices than winter pelts that had not been worn (*castor sec d'hiver*), but the latter, particularly the pelts of the highest quality, had a market of their own. They were sent through Dutch merchants to Muscovy, where "combed pelts" bearing the guard hairs were removed by a secret technique from the velvety underfur, without diminishing the usefulness of either (as fur or as felt). The *castor sec* of a quality suited to this market was often classed in the Canadian trade as *muscovie*.

Three bases of operation developed in the seventeenth century: the French on the Saint Lawrence (Quebec 1608, Montreal 1642), the Dutch (1612, 1613, and 1614) and English (1624) on the Hudson River (Fort Orange, later Albany), and the English at various posts on James Bay and Hudson Bay (1670). During the first half of the century, the French traded with Algonquian and Iroquoian nations of the eastern Great Lakes, at first through Algonquian, and by the mid 1620s through Huron, intermediaries. Trade with the Neutral Nation and the Petun (Tobacco Nation), and Algonquian bands to the north of them, brought the French between twelve thousand and fifteen thousand pelts a year. Dutch plans to gain access to this rich area through Mahican connections were frustrated by the Mohawk of the Iroquois confederacy. By about 1628 the latter had eliminated the Mahican with a view to monopolizing the Dutch trade, regardless of the origin of the furs and the ultimate destination of the trade goods. Their interest was firearms and ammunition; their goal, to assimilate their traditional enemies, several of whom were direct or indirect trading partners of the French.

In New Netherland, what had begun as financial support for an agricultural community became a sustaining element. A monopoly of the fur trade was granted to the Netherlands West India Company (chartered 1621), which was expected in return to administer and develop the colony. Patroons (seigneurs) acquired, through negotiation with Indians, large tracts of land that they held in fief from the company for the purpose of settling colonists, developing agriculture, and conducting "limited" trade. By 1638 the colony had fewer than one thousand settlers, of whom more than half were in New Amsterdam (Manhattan), but the fur trade thrived—in spite of, not because of, the company's monopoly. One absentee patroon, Kiliaen van Rensselaer, who by 1630 had seven hundred thousand acres (280,000 hectares) in the Fort Orange (Albany) area, circumvented company rules in order to gain personal control of the trade of the upper Hudson Valley. He encouraged his settlers to sell furs to his agents at a mutually advantageous price, and he provided trade goods. His initiatives did much to establish Albany, where Dutch traders loomed large for decades after it ceased to be called Fort Orange, as the center of the New York fur trade until 1763.

The French showed greater resolve than the Dutch to control the fur trade. From 1628 until 1760 a succession of entities were leased the responsibility for the beaver trade. In return for the right to collect a 25 percent duty on beaver pelts exported from Canada and a 10 percent duty on moose hides, they were obliged to buy from Canadian merchants at a fixed price all the marketable pelts brought to their premises. The first of these entities was the Compagnie des Cent-Associés (Company of One Hundred Associates, 1628), which had undertaken in its agreement to settle colonists on the land and to administer the infant colony. Except for three years early in its mandate, during the military occupation of Quebec (1629–1632), when the trade was under Anglo-Scottish control, the company held the lease until 1664.

Between 1650 and 1665 the Iroquois made a concerted effort to displace the nations trading with the French, who, by 1645, were exporting thirty thousand pounds (13,500 kilos) of fur a year from Quebec. By 1648 the Mohawk had accumulated eight hundred muskets, and by 1653 the Iroquois had eliminated or dispersed the Algonquian, Huron, Neutral Nation, Nipissing, and Erie. In 1656 and 1657, when annual exports from Fort Orange were roughly forty-six thousand pelts, western natives were making comparable offers at Montreal, but after that they were intimidated. Not until 1665, when French troops devastated Mohawk villages and secured peace with the Iroquois confederacy, could trade be conducted without interference. Two years earlier, a royal administration had replaced the Compagnie des Cent-Associés, and the fur-trade lease had been transferred to the Crown-owned Compagnie des Indes Occidentales. In 1664 New Netherland became New York. The Iroquois retired to villages south and north of Lake Ontario, traded with the Ottawa and Ojibwa on Lake Huron, and sold the furs thus obtained at Albany.

With the establishment of the first Hudson's Bay Company (HBC) posts on James Bay, the Canadian trade seemed threatened from two directions. Iroquois were redirecting the former Huron trade to Albany, and Cree were trading at the HBC posts. The French wished to have an agriculturally self-sufficient colony with a diversified economy, but their policy of officially forbidding new fur-trade initiatives succeeded only in fostering illegal commerce. In a colony desperately short of women, few of the men brought to Canada at Crown expense to clear land and build farms found wives to share the work and raise families. Instead, they followed the lure of adventure and quick gain, sponsored by Canadian merchants who could sell all the marketable pelts they collected. By 1679 between two hundred and three hundred of these unlicensed traders (coureurs de bois) were trading in the West, often living there for years with Native women. Also conducting trade, under the cover of exploration and imperial defense, were the agents of silent partners in high places (such as Governor Louis de Buade de Frontenac). Fort Frontenac (1673) and Fort Niagara (1676), controlling the trade on the lower Great Lakes, and the posts that Robert Cavelier de la Salle established in the Illinois territory, were examples of this kind of enterprise.

In the same period, illicit trade between the fur merchants of Montreal and Albany was developing. It was mutually profitable because the English beaver market seems to have grown more rapidly than Albany and Hudson Bay could supply it, and Canadians could make up the shortfall at prices the Albany merchants could afford (and sell them French goods as well). In return, the Canadians purchased English goods that were popular with their Native customers, particularly certain woolen cloths made especially for the trade. The authorities at Quebec and New York could not prevent the "mission Iroquois" from transporting goods to and from their home near Montreal over the Lake Champlain route.

In 1681 the French inaugurated the congé system. Hoping to limit the number of independents, it authorized the issuance of congés (trading licenses) to twenty-five teams of three men, each with one canoeload of trade goods; no one was to receive a permit for two consecutive years. The expected profit, based on two canoeloads of furs for one of trade goods, ranged from 40 percent to 60 percent. Congés could be sold, and were even issued for the express purpose of resale, and the governor and intendant could issue private licenses of their own. Obviously these rules made the size of the birchbark canoe, the key transport vehicle of the trade, crucial to commercial success for both the holders of congés and the coureurs de bois. Light and portable, and fast in the hands of skillful paddlers, by the late 1680s the canoe had reached a length of some twenty-eight feet (almost 15 meters) and a capacity of twenty-two hundred pounds (one metric ton).

English competition did not prevent the spread of the Canadian trade southwest of Lake Michigan, and north and northwest of Lake Superior. The "factories" established by the HBC at the mouths of rivers flowing into Hudson Bay did not preclude Canadian trade with the natives of that drainage basin; the latter were put in a good bargaining position, weighing the advantages of cheaper goods at distant HBC posts against a smaller selection nearby that included better-quality merchandise. The French capture in 1686 of three HBC posts on James Bay, along with fifty-thousand prime beaver pelts, sharply narrowed the choice for the aboriginal nations.

In 1696 the glut of beaver in the warehouses finally decided the French to curtail the trade and terminate the congé system. There is no evidence that demand in Europe had declined, only that there was overproduction in Canada resulting from fixed prices paid to Canadian merchants for unlimited quantities of beaver. It was decided in 1706 to reduce the price of *castor gras* in effect since 1677 by 60 percent and to limit strictly the quantity that must be accepted, in contrast with an unlimited quantity of marketable *castor sec,* the price of which was reduced by 57 percent. Obviously merchants were to be discouraged from adding to the surplus of *castor gras,* but this was not all: beaver was being redirected to other markets (such as Muscovy), and hatters had developed a ratio of *gras* to *sec* quite different from the traditional two to one, yet suited to the requisite quality in pure beaver hats (by 1753 it was one to four).

The Beaver Trade: Virginia and Maryland

A relatively prosperous beaver trade that began in the Chesapeake region about 1607 developed concurrently with that of deerskins because the ruling oligarchy was dominated for a time by businessmen astute enough to form alliances with inland natives when it was too late to reverse a virtually genocidal policy against those of the coast. The quality of the beaver hardly matched that of skins taken in Canada, New England, and New Netherland, but trading networks of Londoners, Virginians, and people such as the Susquehannock harvested pelts that had a market among English hatters. The success of these enterprises encouraged the founders of Maryland to challenge them. Yet, over twenty-five years (1630–1655) of frequently violent competition that depleted the populations of natives and beaver alike, the Marylanders were never able to establish the lasting kind of Native alliances that characterized those of Virginia, nor were their metropolitan associates impressed by the quantity of fur exported to England. After 1655, once the beaver supply of the Chesapeake was almost exhausted, the power of the partisans of settlement and tobacco increased. There was, in their scheme of things, no useful role for the Amerindians of the Chesapeake. From 1675 to 1677 the two colonies together turned viciously on the natives who had been their allies, and all but exterminated them.

Marketing

The French beaver market was regulated by government and managed by private entities under government lease. Prices were fixed, and production quality, demand, and supply controlled, in response to the perceived needs of the hatters and their customers. Under the British system, even such trading monopolies as the Hudson's Bay Company could not demand of the hatters more than the "market price"; that is, what they could afford to pay relative to other costs and expected revenues. The French government could successfully manipulate the market (for instance, to overtake foreign competitors, as after 1748), but unless prices and other fixed elements were changed in time to respond to external influences, the results were harmful (as in 1696). In Great Britain trade was governed by legislation subordinating colonial to metropolitan interests, so that colonial attempts to regulate it were disallowed at Whitehall (Virginia monopoly; New York bans on trade with Montreal). The British mercantile class, well represented in Parliament, lobbied vigorously against measures that might reduce output (and hence profits). French lobbies were by no means ineffective, but they lacked the opportunity the British had of influencing shifts in political power. Yet the results demonstrate that the system's strength gave the advantage to France, though its built-in rigidity had obvious drawbacks.

THE TRADE IN HIDES

The deerskin trade of Virginia and the Carolinas began with Sir Walter Raleigh's Roanoke colony in the 1580s, was interrupted for a generation, and developed after the founding of Jamestown, Virginia, in 1607. It quickly became a lucrative supplement to tobacco as an earner of sterling.

Virginia

The deerskin trade was to move hundreds of miles to the west. The development of tobacco plantations was rapid: by 1660 Virginia had some twenty-five thousand settlers; by 1680, about sixty thousand. As early as 1643, the factors leading to the demise of the beaver trade were rapidly diminishing the number of tidewater deerskins. By the 1670s and 1680s, the packhorse trains of William Byrd and his partners, comprising as many as one hundred horses (each carrying up to two hundred pounds [90 kilos] of goods) and fifteen or sixteen persons, were traveling to distant Native villages, quickly trading, and returning. Under ideal conditions, the trains could cover twenty miles (32 kilometers) a day. An astute dealer like Byrd could realize much greater profits from skins than from tobacco, because he kept abreast of the knowledge required to make the right decisions: prices, quantity and quality, availability of transport, changes in customer preference. Others lost interest in the West, fearing that overland transport would devour too much of the profit.

Around 1700, London's disallowance of a colonial monopoly near the North Carolina boundary induced the governor to sponsor expeditions across the Appalachians.

Pennsylvania

Though Pennsylvania lay farther north, its chief product in the seventeenth-century fur and skin trade was also deerskins; and the destiny of its traders, like those of Virginia, was in the Ohio Valley. At first the proprietor, William Penn, thinking the northern limits of the colony would be promising, had his agents try to acquire tracts of land on the upper Susquehanna River. Before they were thwarted in this by New York, significant numbers of skins had been shipped down the Susquehanna, Schuylkill, and Delaware rivers to Philadelphia, where the friendly Delaware Indians came to trade. In spite of Quaker disapproval, trade advanced to the headwaters of the Ohio.

The Carolinas

In 1677 five of Carolina's eight proprietors set up a seven-year monopoly of the interior trade. Caravans of twenty to thirty packhorses, each bearing three fifty-pound (23 kilo) packs of skins, were usual among traders who owned six to seven horses each; larger groups sometimes sent a contingent of one-hundred or more. And it was not unusual for Native "burdeners," employed in place of packhorses, to be expected to carry fifty to sixty pounds (32 kilos) over three-hundred to five-hundred miles (almost 500 to 800 kilometers). By 1690, contact had been made with the Cherokee west of the Appalachians, in 1698 with the Chickasaw, and the same year with the Quapaw at the junction of the Arkansas and Mississippi rivers; another expedition to the Mississippi followed in 1700. Carolinians were

thus approaching overland the trading territory of the Creek, Alabama, and Choctaw, which Spaniards from Florida and French from Mobile reached by river.

FUR TRADE AND EMPIRE IN THE EIGHTEENTH CENTURY

After the founding of Lousiana in the late seventeenth century, French policy turned on a plan to link the Saint Lawrence and Mississippi colonies by a series of strategic posts that would serve both military and commercial purposes. Trade provided a timely opportunity for this strategy, for furs again had to be acquired from the interior for the French market. Two years after the discovery in 1714 that moths and vermin had destroyed the surplus in warehouses and French hatters were clamoring for *castor gras,* it was decided to restore the *congé* system.

A Change in French Policy

From having been tolerated as a business that might benefit the state, the fur trade now became its instrument. France had to prevent control of the vast area between the Appalachians and the Mississippi from passing completely to Anglo-American traders, who would be followed by settlers making territorial claims. On Hudson Bay, the British had to be confined to their coastal bases. Alliances had to be established with as many Indian nations as possible, even at the risk of conflict with their enemies. French respect for aboriginal rights to these territories, and the English threat to them, would be stressed and the posts portrayed as centers for friendly exchange and support in times of danger. A renewed legal fur trade was expected to pay for much of the French imperial presence.

The posts therefore had a dual purpose: commercial and military. Most were dependent on Montreal and the remainder on New Orleans, and they were of three types: the major entrepôt, the district post, and the small dependent post. The first were advance headquarters for the traders and transshipment points for trade goods and furs. Dependent on Montreal were Michilimackinac, at the junction of Lake Huron and Lake Michigan, and near the outlet of Lake Superior; and Detroit, a short distance from Lake Erie. Kaskaskia, on the upper Mississippi, was dependent on New Orleans. All of the district posts were fortified, and those on the southern frontier were garrisoned. The small posts were not necessarily permanent: they were opened and closed at the dictate of Native relations and the market.

Trade at all posts was authorized by the Crown but conducted by small companies of Montreal merchants, often in partnership with post commanders. At entrepôts, the right to trade was obtained by purchasing a *congé* to carry goods to the post. The number of *congés*, which was limited, varied from one post to another. At other posts, monopoly leases were awarded for specified periods to the highest bidder or to military commanders, who were expected in return to help bear the costs of building, operating, and defending posts and to maintain, at considerable expense by means of regular presents, the goodwill of Amerindian neighbors. Only the king's posts, maintained for strategic reasons around Lake Ontario (and in the 1750s in the Ohio Valley), were paid for entirely by the Crown, whose agents operated the trading monopoly.

Hides and Empires

In the territory bounded roughly by the Great Lakes, the Mississippi, the Gulf of Mexico, and the Appalachians, a potentially enormous quantity of deerskins was in contention among Amerindian nations dealing directly or indirectly with British and French traders from Virginia, Pennsylvania, South Carolina, Georgia, Louisiana, and Canada. Trade with particular nations depended on several factors. Local prices fluctuated in fact, but Indians insisted on an official fixed tariff as a political bond, for traditional friendships and enmities, together with the strict observance of Amerindian ceremonies such as the exchange of gifts and smoking the peace pipe, were indispensable to good trading relations. Between 1712 and 1718 traders from South Carolina accused French and Spanish competitors of inciting and arming the Creek and Yamassee against them and, in response, armed such enemies of the Creek as the Cherokee and Chickasaw.

In the 1720s the French set up a chain of district posts from Mobile to Fort Toulouse (Ala-

bama), west to Natchez, and up the Mississippi to the Illinois country, to bring the trade under French control and isolate the Choctaw from the British. Failure to supply enough trade goods, however, forced the French to devote an inordinate amount of energy to guerrilla warfare. The Chickasaw attacked allies of the French as far north as the Wabash and Illinois rivers; the French retaliated in kind. In 1746 a Choctaw civil war, in which the majority pro-French faction defended itself against a pro-British revolt, devastated that Indian nation.

Nevertheless, the exportation of deerskins, alongside that of tobacco and indigo, increased steadily in Louisiana and in the British colonies. Throughout the period 1730–1748, despite intermittent frontier conflict in the 1720s and full-scale war in the 1740s, South Carolina exported sixteen thousand deerskins with an estimated value of £36,000, and imported £10,000 in trade goods from Great Britain, a volume of business rivaled by that of Georgia (chartered 1732). In the Illinois country, trade eventually thrived, although not exclusively under Louisiana auspices. The authority of the government at New Orleans, which could not obtain trade goods in adequate quantities at competitive prices, was weak. The result was a de facto free-trade area in which pelts were sent not only to New Orleans merchants by their associates in the posts but also to Montreal through Detroit or Michilimackinac by Canadian traders, and by Anglo-Americans via the Ohio and overland to the eastern seaboard. West of Lake Michigan, the Fox nation repeatedly disrupted the Canadian trade, and it was not until after several French punitive expeditions against them between 1728 and 1735 that their raids ceased.

The Ohio Valley

Pennsylvanians and Virginians were already accustomed to brief trading sojourns in the Ohio Valley at prearranged meeting places, where they were in contact with Shawnee and Miami, as well as with resettled Indians near Detroit. In 1739 a French expedition from Canada against the Chickasaw, in support of Louisiana, entered the region. The war of 1744–1748, when trade goods to New France were reduced, provided British traders with an opportunity to pour into the region, selling goods to trading partners of the French at one-quarter to one-third the French price. Once peace was restored in 1749, 230 soldiers were sent for the purpose of confirming long-standing French claims, rejecting British pretensions, and driving out some 300 British traders. Disgruntled by this, the Miami in 1751 destroyed Fort Vincennes, to which the French (with Indian allies) responded the following year by destroying a British post in the Miami village of Pickawillany and coercing the Miami back to the French interest. The subsequent construction of French and British forts and the outbreak of hostilities between the two nations in 1754 demonstrated the strategic interest of the region, which had long overshadowed its potential commercial value.

The Montreal–Albany Trade

In addition to merchants of Montreal and Albany, English hatters and some English manufacturers of trade goods profited from the illicit trade. The hatters got more high-quality pelts at a good price than was possible through the Hudson's Bay Company and legal Albany trade, and were thereby able to increase their European sales. The manufacturers increased their sales through the Canadian trading system. The trade was, however, injurious to others: the Compagnie des Indes, French hatters and manufacturers, the French Crown and the government of New France, and the New York colonial authorities. The Compagnie des Indes could make no profit on those furs; the hatters and manufacturers lost business to their English rivals; the trade was seen as helping the imperial adversary; and French traders could make a profit selling English goods to natives. The French Ministry of Marine ordered the trade stopped again and again. New York enacted legislation against it in 1722, 1724, and 1725, but it was disallowed in 1729 by the British government. In 1725 Governor William Burnet had a fort built at Oswego on Lake Ontario, similar to Fort Frontenac and Fort Niagara, to facilitate direct New York trade with the Mississauga across the lake and to reduce illicit trade between Montreal and Albany. The French responded by permitting their posts to sell brandy to the Mississauga and to sell other goods at a loss if necessary.

By 1748 so much Canadian prime beaver was diverted to Albany that French hatters lost to the British the lucrative Portuguese, Spanish, and German markets for beaver hats. Yet before 1764 they had completely regained those markets. The French authorities had cut the price of trade goods in half, so that British hatters were supplied with only enough beaver for their domestic market. Spanish and Portuguese consumers now bought only French hats, which were much cheaper, according to English hatters, because the French paid low wages.

The Northwest

Between 1725 and 1755 the Canadian trade gradually advanced into the Hudson's Bay Company hinterland at least as far as the forks of the Saskatchewan River, less than thirty-five miles (56 kilometers) east of present-day Prince Albert. Pierre de la Vérendrye, searching for a great western sea reputed to bear the same relationship to the Pacific that Hudson Bay bears to the Atlantic, may have reached the foothills of the Rockies. The canoes of the Canadian voyageurs continued to grow in order to carry more goods over longer distances. Many were as long as thirty-five feet (almost eleven meters) with a cargo capacity of sixty-six hundred pounds (3 metric tons); a crew of eight, under good conditions, could cover sixty-eight to one-hundred miles (almost 110 to 160 kilometers) a day. The HBC was late in exploring the interior: Anthony Henday did not set out until 1754 on the voyage that was to take him to the foothills of the Rockies.

French and British sought to trade with the same people; the goal of the natives was European goods, particularly firearms, on which they became dependent for their own protection, and the introduction of which changed relations among them and affected patterns of settlement. After the posts on the coast of Hudson Bay were confirmed as British (1713), some Cree families settled nearby, content to supply provisions and to trade in locally obtained pelts. Most Cree, and the Assiniboine, better equipped with firearms than their neighbors, expanded their trapping into the territory of others, consolidating their trading position on the Nelson River and stirring up the enmity of Chipewyan and Blackfoot. Once the Chipewyan were better armed, they checked Cree expansion to the north. And once the Blackfoot and other Plains Indians had acquired horses, they spent more time hunting bison and relied on the Cree and Assiniboine as middlemen in the trade with York Factory. Some Cree and Assiniboine were diverted from being go-betweens for the Plains Indians and the Hudson's Bay Company by trade with the French, which embroiled the latter in warfare with the Ojibwa until 1736 and with the Dakota until 1750. Once peace had been attained, however, treaties with the eastern Dakota in 1752 opened up trade around the headwaters of the Mississippi.

Posts had been built on the Assiniboine River and on the northwest shore of Lake Winnipeg by 1739, and Canadian traders had entered the trading area of the key Hudson's Bay Company post, York Factory. In 1755 a Native band destroyed Henley House, the Hudson's Bay Company post on the Albany River. In spite of a loss of trade to the company during and immediately after the war of 1743–1748, the Canadian share of the trade of the Hudson Bay drainage basin was approximately 50 percent in 1755. The total Canadian fur production from all sources was then about five times that of the Hudson's Bay Company.

The British Trade After 1760

The French had subordinated the Canadian and Louisiana fur trade to strategy, but as a business it had a strong attraction for British traders, who moved in quickly to capture it for themselves. Under Spanish rule, foreign commerce in Louisiana was precarious, but British ships brought to New Orleans trade goods that the Spaniards could not supply. Immigration, by 1767 including a thousand Acadian refugees expelled from Nova Scotia twelve years earlier, reduced Amerindians in lower Louisiana to a minority by 1780 and steadily shifted trade to the upper part of the province. British merchants opened shops in New Orleans to receive skins sent down the Mississippi from the Illinois country by British traders, and from Saint Louis by former French subjects like Maxent, Laclède and Company. Between the end of the War for Independence (1783) and Jay's Treaty (1796), British traders continued to dominate the western American posts. After that Americans, of whom the most notable was John Jacob Astor, took their place.

In the Northwest, Scottish and Anglo-American merchants, using British capital, took over the Canadian trade. They employed Canadian voyageurs, canoes, posts, and techniques, and they competed as forcefully with the Hudson's Bay Company in its own hinterland as the French had done. Carrying the trade through the Canadian Rockies and into the far Northwest, these traders comprised a number of small firms that eventually were forced to amalgamate into the North West Company (1787). This was the only way of competing with the Hudson's Bay Company, which had now abandoned the sedentary trade of the coast and ventured inland. The clashes between the two companies were violent, but in the long run the Nor'westers could not prevail against the size, wealth, and organization of the older concern. They held out until 1821, when their company was absorbed by the competitor.

THE SPANISH TRADE, 1540–1820

New Mexico

The Spaniards from Mexico learned as early as 1540 that the agrarian Pueblo Indians of New Mexico customarily purchased from nomadic tribes of the Plains, in exchange for surplus corn and pottery, well-dressed deerskins and buffalo hides which they made into clothing and footwear. Commerce with the Spaniards took root when they returned in the 1580s with European goods. The first hides were used by the colonists themselves; in due course, others were purchased for export to Mexico.

In the seventeenth century, coarse furs and hides were among the few exportable resources left after a quest for silver had proved fruitless. Some skins, sent to Mexico three times a year in the supply caravan, were exacted from the Pueblos as a levy; some were purchased from Navajo and other Indians with the intention of bypassing Pueblo middlemen. Fragmentary statistics suggest that substantial, if not spectacular, quantities were exported, along with such finished products as leather jackets and breeches from workshops in Santa Fe. Governors profited personally to such an extent that they completely dominated the trade and controlled the colony's economy. Bernardo Lopez de Mendizabal (1659–1660) set up a store in his residence, stocked with European manufactures and delicacies, for which he accepted hides as payment.

The trade was interrupted between 1680 and 1694 by a fierce Pueblo revolt against Spanish authority. Afterward the colonists traded with Apache, Comanche, and Ute, making tentative ventures into Ute country as early as 1712. By 1724 commerce at Chihuahua, where New Mexico colonists sold skins, became an annual event. By 1750 the Comanche, who had migrated to New Mexico from Wyoming, regularly attended the autumn fair at the pueblo of Taos, bringing hundreds of hides. After 1749 the Ute, enemies of the Comanche, traded regularly and on a large scale in the mountains with colonists who traveled great distances. Hides were an important part of the freight of thousand of mules that traveled between Mexico and New Mexico late in the eighteenth century, emanating from trade with several nations: Comanche who had moved to the Canadian River in northern Texas, Kiowa in Colorado, Pawnee in Nebraska, and Arapaho in Wyoming.

Texas

When Louisiana was under French rule (1682–1762), the missions and garrisons of Texas served as a buffer against French access to New Spain's silver mines. French traders who nevertheless penetrated the region ignored Spanish claims to exclusivity and traded directly with local natives, frontier officers, and other Spanish subjects. They bought no furs nor hides, however, because little trapping or hunting was done in Texas. Indeed, Spanish ships visiting New Orleans were more interested in buying furs than in selling them. Even after the Spanish acquisition of Louisiana in 1762, attempts to promote trade in hides near the mission stations failed, largely because of the fierce antagonism of the Comanche and the Apache to Spanish rule. It was not until after 1776, when Texas was incorporated into the Interior Provinces of New Spain, peace with the natives had been gradually restored, and a new liberal policy welcomed foreigners tied to the raw-fur markets of Paris and London, that trade began to thrive.

California

Franciscan friars were among the chief agents of Spanish penetration into the northern part of Alta California between 1769 and 1776, the purpose of which was to forestall the movement of Russian traders and colonizers south from the Aleutian Islands and the Alaskan mainland. Primitive missions established in fertile valleys or on mountain plateaus were expanded into stations with a church, a Native village, an orchard, irrigated fields, pastures, shops, and living quarters for clergy and a garrison. Unlike their brethren in New Mexico, who had been intimidated by the trading monopoly of the governor, the Franciscans developed a thriving trade in hides. Part of this trade emanated from leatherwork shops manned by Native converts whom they had instructed in the art.

THE BEGINNINGS OF RUSSIAN TRADE IN ALASKA

Between 1747 (following Vitus Bering's voyage of discovery) and 1791, furs worth more than 6.3 million paper rubles (about £800,000 sterling) were exported from the Aleutian Islands to Russia. The most highly valued pelt was that of the sea otter, but beaver, fox, and other inland furs were also taken. The reception of Russian traders by various Native groups at different times was quite mixed: some were very pleased to trade under peaceful conditions; others suspected the Russians of wishing to take possession of their land and to dominate them, and violence ensued. The fur trade was virtually the sole economic base of the colony that followed, but colonial imperialism and proselytizing of the Aleut and other Native peoples by the Russian Orthodox church were secondary factors in its establishment.

THE EUROPEANS, INDIANS AND THE FUR TRADE

Unlike the Aztecs and Incas, Native North Americans had little to offer in trade that was of interest to Europeans except furs and hides. The Europeans had much to offer them that was useful or pleasant, but trade became obsessive because of European voracity. No longer did North American Indians hunt and trap to satisfy their own needs, or perhaps the modest requirements of agrarian neighbors. Trying to fit traditional aspirations into a world not of their making, they contributed unintentionally to ecological dam-

649

age and the decimation of their own numbers. Balanced diets gave way to unhealthy ones. Alien diseases contracted through the trade took a tremendous toll in lives. The excessive use of alcohol wrought much social damage. Firearms, a boon to hunters, destroyed more people more effectively than arrows and tomahawks: they represented a passing triumph for some Indian nations but the total demise of others. And European belief in human predominance, purporting to justify the destruction of native animals and forests, undermined a general Amerindian acceptance of equality with other beings in the world of nature.

Although the subjects of France and Great Britain were the principal players in the trade, in the national economies of those countries furs played an insignificant role. Compared with the tropical products of their Caribbean colonies and the African slave trade that provided a cheap labor force for the producers of sugar, coffee, chocolate, indigo, and tobacco, fur in both kingdoms was a minuscule segment of imperial commerce. For the economy of Canada fur exports were a mainstay, but not for France; when France surrendered Canada and the fur trade, it retained its share of the lucrative Newfoundland cod fishery, a metropolitan, not a Canadian, interest. In the Anglo-American colonies, furs were an initial cash crop that tided them over until they could put their economies on a firm basis, or a supplementary source of revenue that facilitated western expansion. Their traders in the West served British imperial ends until New France was defeated; afterward, they were suspect because they were usually the forerunners of land-hungry settlers.

It seems likely that those in France and Great Britain who profited from the fur trade had investments in several fields. In the colonies, where opportunities were more limited, individual fortunes were made: several families in Montreal were known as l'aristocracie du castor (beaver aristocracy); in colonial New York, Stephen De Lancey, Cornelius Cuyler, and Robert R. Livingston grew wealthy on the Albany (and Montreal) trade; in Virginia, the first William Byrd increased his wealth and stature through the large-scale commerce in deerskins.

And finally, the role of the fur traders in increasing geographical knowledge was crucial: it is extremely doubtful that the interior of the continent would have been explored and mapped as soon as it was without the enterprise of European traders and the cooperation of their Native North American partners.

BIBLIOGRAPHY

Braudel, Fernand, and Ernst Labrousse, eds. Histoire économique et sociale de la France. 4 vols. Paris, 1970–1982. Vol. 1, pts. 1 and 2 are valuable for the economy of France in the sixteenth century.

Clark, John Garretson. New Orleans, 1718–1812: An Economic History. Baton Rouge, La., 1970. Useful for the Louisiana fur trade.

Crosby, Alfred W. Ecological Imperialism: The Biological Expansion of Europe, 900–1900. Cambridge, England, 1986. Includes a geographer's explanation of an aspect of European-Amerindian relations.

Diderot, Denis, and Jean Le Rond d'Alembert. Encyclopédie, ou Dictionnaire raisonné des sciences, des arts et des métiers, par une société de gens de lettres. Compact ed., 5 vols. New York, 1969. The article "Chapeau" explains the composition of a beaver hat about 1753 and how it was made.

Eccles, W. J. The Canadian Frontier, 1534–1760. New York and Toronto, 1969; rev. ed. Albuquerque, N.Mex., 1983. Thorough, up-to-date scholarly treatment of the Canadian trade.

Fausz, J. Frederick. "Merging and Emerging Worlds: Anglo-Indian Interest Groups and the Development of the Seventeenth-Century Chesapeake." In Colonial Chesapeake Society, edited by Lois Green Carr, Philip D. Morgan, and Jean B. Russo. Chapel Hill, N.C., 1988. Explains the process by which European-Amerindian fur-trading and social partnerships developed in the Chesapeake and were later eliminated in favor of tobacco production directed by Europeans.

Harris, R. Cole, ed. Historical Atlas of Canada. Vol. 1, From the Beginning to 1800. Toronto, Ontario, 1987. Very detailed cartographic and narrative treatment of the fur trade of New France by historians, geographers, and anthropologists.

Miquelon, Dale Bernard. New France, 1701–1744: "A Supplement to Europe." Toronto, Ontario, 1987. Contains excellent analyses of fur-trade questions.

Norton, Thomas Elliot. The Fur Trade in Colonial New York, 1686–1776. Madison, Wis., 1974. Contains a brief summary of the Dutch period (based on Trelease) and a detailed analysis of the British period. Should be used with caution where the Canadian trade is concerned.

Robinson, Walter Stitt. *The Southern Colonial Frontier, 1607–1763*. Albuquerque, N.Mex., 1979. Useful summaries of the Virginia and South Carolina deerskin trade.

Salisbury, Neal. *Manitou and Providence: Indians, Europeans, and the Making of New England, 1500–1643*. New York, 1982. Valuable explanation of the process of change in European-Amerindian economic, cultural, social, and political relations during the heyday of the New England fur trade.

Simmons, R. C., and P. D. G. Thomas, eds. *Proceedings and Debates of the British Parliaments Respecting North America, 1754–1783*. Vol. 1, *1754–1764*. Millwood, N.Y., 1982. Contains representations to Parliament by English hatters concerning the loss of trade to the French (1764).

Stock, Leo Francis, ed. *Proceedings and Debates of the British Parliaments Respecting North America*. 5 vols. Washington, D.C., 1924–1941; repr. New York, 1966–1970. Covers the period 1542–1754.

Tikhmenev, Petr Aleksandrovich. *A History of the Russian-American Company*, translated and edited by Richard A. Pierce and Alton S. Donnelly. Seattle, Wash., 1978. A mid-nineteenth-century chronicle written for the future researcher. The first chapter deals with the company's eighteenth-century predecessors.

Trelease, Allen W. *Indian Affairs in Colonial New York: The Seventeenth Century*. Ithaca, N.Y., 1960. Contains material on the Dutch period.

Usner, Daniel H., Jr. "The Frontier Exchange Economy of the Lower Mississippi Valley in the Eighteenth Century." *William and Mary Quarterly*, 3rd ser., 44, no. 2 (April 1987):165–192. Useful elucidation of multiple European-Amerindian relations in the southern part of the colony of Louisiana.

Veale, Elspeth M. *The English Fur Trade in the Later Middle Ages*. Oxford, 1966. Carries the study into the sixteenth century, thereby setting the stage for the North American trade.

Weber, David J. *The Taos Trappers: The Fur Trade in the Far Southwest, 1540–1846*. Norman, Okla., 1971. A very useful chapter on the Spanish colonial period in New Mexico.

Frederick J. Thorpe

SEE ALSO **The Colonial Merchant; Relations with the Parent Country;** and **Trade and Commerce;** and various essays in COLONIAL SETTINGS.

LANDHOLDING

THE BRITISH COLONIES

IN BRITISH NORTH AMERICA landholding patterns reflected both the economic beliefs of particular groups of colonists and the transferal of English ideas about property rights. To gain land colonists knew they first had to negotiate with Indians and impose English notions of land ownership on what they believed was a wilderness. In the next stage, land speculators often acted quickly to gain title, and they made an indelible impression on the real estate market in the colonies, though small farmers no doubt comprised a far larger group than these would-be developers.

In spite of certain shared experiences, regional differences relating to the proper uses and distribution of land existed in eastern North America. In seventeenth-century New England, groups of Puritan settlers divided land according to an individual's status within the community. In the Chesapeake and the South, generally, colonists acquired land in the process of creating a staple economy; those who contributed the most to economic development, particularly those who helped to people the early settlements with migrants, received greater portions of land as a result of their efforts. In the middle colonies, the earliest settlers benefited from close political connections with the proprietors of the new provinces, though over time each colony developed its own land policies that limited the power of government officials to some extent.

However, though these regional differences emerged, many aspects of purchasing land, such as the availability of credit, crossed provincial boundaries; creditors, both domestic and foreign, demonstrated greater concern about creditworthiness than regional landholding patterns. Further, the chances of owning land tended to increase for individuals as they aged. This lifecycle opportunity was common in the British colonies and helped to create a society where small farmers constituted the majority of the colonial male population in an overwhelmingly rural world.

ENGLISH ATTITUDES

When colonists arrived in Anglo-America, they carried with them inherited ideals about landholding. They held to the notion that landownership conferred a sense of security not otherwise obtainable in an agricultural society and that America, unlike England, offered more than enough land to suit their purposes. The distribution of land within the colonies thus reflected an effort to reconcile traditional beliefs and practices with the availability of land (once Indian titles to it had been extinguished). Acting on long-standing principle, royal and proprietary governments—that is, the governments of all of the colonies outside of New England—assessed quitrents on the lands they granted to colonists. Fixed rents in commutation of services, quitrents were intended to free tenants from a series of obligations to their landlord. They were a legacy of manorialism, which had appeared in England after the Norman invasion of the eleventh century. Nowhere in the colonies were quitrents especially onerous, but colonists nonetheless developed a hostile attitude toward them.

Often ignored by colonists and at times manipulated by colonial proprietors for their own gain, quitrents came to symbolize the direct connections between the colonies and the Crown. Had they been effectively collected, quitrents could have generated perhaps over thirty-seven thousand pounds per year; these funds could then have been used by royal officials in the colonies to enhance their authority by expanding their limited patronage powers. But no uniform system for collection existed, and actual collections averaged only nineteen thousand pounds each year. Rather than becoming a source of revenue for the Crown's officeholders, quitrents became, by the time of the revolution, a widely detested symbol of attempted royal control of the colonies. When colonists protested against paying quitrents, they were demonstrating that they held a different set of ideas about landholding than those prevailing in England. In particular, when they purchased land from Indians, their actions revealed a more market-oriented attitude than that which existed in early modern England.

COLONISTS, INDIANS, AND LAND

In eastern North America, groups of settlers knew they had to treat with Indians in order to obtain land. The colonists' unwitting transportation of European pathogens to the Western Hemisphere, and the resulting demographic catastrophe experienced by all groups of Indians with whom the colonists came into contact, proved to be of great assistance for colonists seeking land. Groups of Indians decimated by epidemic diseases such as smallpox were often willing to sell land to colonists, and colonists proved eager to purchase whatever was available.

In the process of transferring ownership from Indians to colonists, however, deeply held cultural beliefs about landholding led to conflict between the peoples vying for control of what was becoming British America. The sale of land by Indians to colonists, which took place all along the East Coast, proved especially troublesome, since these transactions did not always appear as simple as colonists believed. When they purchased land, they did so with certain ideas about landownership firmly in mind. Derived from English law and customary practice, colonists believed that ownership was exclusive and permanent, so that no one else could use the land without the owner's permission; the land did not revert to anyone after a certain time if it was already paid for; and the owner could, within limits imposed by law, dispose of property as he or she saw fit.

However, many Indians did not share this conception of land alienation. In New England (as elsewhere), Indians sold not the land itself to colonists but the right to use the land equally with them; they sold what the land could produce, not the soil itself. Their usufruct notion of landownership allowed for multiple owners and had already been employed by Indians in precontact times, especially when different groups claimed overlapping hunting territories. To be sure Indians had notions about property; agricultural groups believed that the person who planted a field had the right to what grew there, and Indians who depended on annual hunts or shellfish expeditions felt a proprietary right to their catch. However, land was not yet a commodity for them. Colonists made it so when their conception of real estate became the law throughout the colonies, but not without first inciting hostility from Indians.

Further, colonists did not always respect Indians' claims to property. The colonists came from a far more densely settled portion of the Atlantic world, where most land had long been cleared in order to create the farms needed to feed a population seemingly (with the exception of plague times) growing at a substantial pace; therefore they generally believed that only land actually being farmed could be owned. With little understanding of the role of forested lands in the economies of many eastern woodlands Indians, colonists often felt that Indians had no rights to these substantial unfarmed reserves. To English colonists such tracts were *vacuum domicilium*, or empty land, that needed to be "improved" through cultivation in order to be owned. Patents issued in England to loosely defined expanses of North American land further encouraged colonists to gain actual possession as quickly as they could.

In addition not all colonists traded fairly with Indians for land. Some tried to get Indians drunk in order to seize their lands, though colonial officials, ever sensitive to the dangers they faced from Indians, generally were quick to prevent such transactions. Yet even where colonists had the best relations with Indians, disputes over the transfer of property arose over what local Indians perceived as the greed and trickery of colonists.

No better example of this exists than the infamous Walking Purchase in Pennsylvania in 1737. At the time Pennsylvania's most powerful officials were the heirs of the colony's founder, William Penn, who had in his time sought to treat fairly with Indians whenever possible. The new proprietors, however, did not strive for such a standard. In an attempt to clear up an earlier land agreement, they made a deal with a group of Delaware to purchase as much land as a man could walk in one and one-half days. Figuring that the distance involved would not be too great, the Delaware agreed, especially since the map they were shown seemingly indicated that they had already sold most of the territory. But the map misled the Indians, and the walkers turned out to be very fast, covering sixty-four miles (102 kilometers) in the allotted time; in the end Pennsylvania officials claimed the Lehigh Valley between the Lehigh and Delaware rivers, as well as other territory. Yet however unfair the business seemed to the Delaware, the deal nonetheless held, a legacy of conflicting notions about how land should pass from one party to another.

LAND SPECULATION

Land speculators were among the colonists who dealt most directly with Indians for lands, though some did so more successfully than others. In most of the colonies eager investors sought to gain control of the economic development of the hinterland by speculating in western lands. The sizes of these speculative efforts differed dramatically, and so did individual speculators' ideas about how to maximize their profits. From northern New England to Georgia, however, speculators managed to gain title to sometimes enormous tracts. Three seventeenth-century patents issued in England—the Pejepscot, the Plymouth, and the Waldo—together comprised most of mid Maine (a part of Massachusetts during the colonial period), though these patents alone did not confer clear legal title to the lands, and settlers would eventually battle over who would control development on them. Speculative efforts elsewhere at times led to the engrossment of tracts totaling over one million acres (400,000 hectares), but such grants did not always guarantee any success to putative developers in New York, Virginia, or elsewhere. Speculation in lands also took place on a far smaller scale and became a common feature of the economy of towns and rural settlements throughout the colonies.

Successful speculators in early America ultimately learned that they could not sit back and wait for their investments to bring profits. Instead they needed to become actively involved in the economic development of the hinterland. They learned how to deal with Indians for land and how to create the social and economic climate necessary to draw settlers to their particular tracts; some, such as Sir William Johnson, the superintendent of Indian affairs for the northern colonies, were high government officials. However diverse their origins or the location of their holdings, successful speculators worked to make their real estate profitable. They sold land to, and provided mortgages for, some prospective settlers; rented to others; set up stores to provide for migrants' needs; and joined with government officials to improve the prospects of particular inland regions. Yet speculating in western lands was not a certain way to fortune, as many failed speculators discovered when they could not pay their debts; their hopes for creating inland estates disappeared when their own ventures collapsed.

NEW ENGLAND

Whether they acquired land in small parcels from deals with Indians or through massive speculative ventures, colonists knew that they needed more than title to land to make their settlements work. They also had to figure out how the land, once acquired, would be distributed. In seventeenth-century New England, landholding policies reflected the specific influence of Puritan ideas, and the initial parceling out of land within towns demonstrated their far-reaching power. Yet even in New England, entrepreneurs, many of them government officials or colonists with close connections to established authorities, acquired substantial tracts, especially in inland regions. Absentee ownership prevailed among these speculators and greatly skewed the distribution of landholding in a region where colonists sought to use land as much as possible for agriculture, though their economy remained committed to mercantile and seafaring ventures as well.

During the first half of the seventeenth century, Crown officials granted charters to groups of migrants that included title to particular tracts of land and the power to divide it as they saw fit. Though the town fathers, the proprietors who received control of the land, at first held the tracts in common, they quickly set about to divide them. To do so they were guided not only by their understanding of the resources of the region, which prompted them to set aside land for specific purposes such as woodlots or pasture, but also by preexisting economic and status distinctions within the group; a man's initial share could depend as well on the size of his family or his contribution to the purchase of land from Indians.

Further, since town groups often shared a common regional background in England, the initial mode of dividing land followed prevailing British practices, particularly the adoption of open- and closed-field systems. In open-field areas, the proprietors of towns chose to release very little land to private hands at first, preferring to retain strong corporate control. In closed-field systems, proprietors of towns quickly moved to transfer title from the town to individuals. By about the end of the seventeenth century, the closed-field system had become the more common one, thereby allowing for individuals to gain permanent and exclusive control of parcels of

land. Some of these colonists proceeded to buy and sell land whenever they chose, and on a few occasions, enterprising land speculators, at times in partnership with powerful government officials, used their connections as well as their capital to amass enormous tracts.

The system of land division can best be understood by focusing on a particular example. In Andover, Massachusetts, the initial distribution of land followed the status and economic standing of the head of each household. Those with the highest status received, in the initial allotment of land, a 20-acre (8-hectare) house site, while those with lesser status or finances received smaller tracts, ranging down to house sites of 4 acres (about 2 hectares); the rest of the land, the majority of the initial grant, remained undivided and set aside for later use. The discrepancy in landholding grew over time when town proprietors decided to divide up some of the remaining land. All subsequent divisions derived from the initial allotments. This meant that those who received 20 acres in the beginning got five times as much land as those who received 4 acres in each of the successive divisions of land. Subsequent divisions of upland and meadow and woodlots, then, benefited those who received the most at the beginning or their heirs (who ended up with 610 acres [244 hectares] if their original house lot was 20 acres [8 hectares]) more than they benefited those who received less or their heirs (who finished with 122 acres [49 hectares] if their original house lot was 4 acres).

Over time the growth of the regional population, evident by the latter decades of the seventeenth century, altered landholding patterns. In New England parents rejected English notions of primogeniture and entail on principle and chose to divide their holdings among their children when they died; male children received land, with the eldest getting a double portion, while their sisters generally received movable goods. Rather than a single household commanding enormous estates as a result of subsequent divisions of common land and the maintenance of the land within a single household, few were able to maintain substantial tracts. The limited fertility of land in New England and the continued proliferation of large families into the third and fourth generations, as well as the availability of land to the west and north, led to substantial out-migration; it occurred as early as the third generation in many families and by the fourth generation in those possessing enough land to maintain farmable tracts into the early eighteenth century.

Rapid growth of the New England population over the course of the seventeenth century, a result of long life expectancy and large families, led to increased pressure on the available arable land in the region; over time many colonists who wanted to own farms found they could not do so easily, in part because of the decreasing availability of land, in part because of an inability to raise sufficient funds to purchase a tract sizable enough to support themselves and their families. Some chose to become tenants, such as those who went to Springfield, Massachusetts, then under the control of the Pynchon family. However, in New England such a status remained relatively rare, at least for married couples, thus suggesting that tenancy here was almost always correlated to a stage of life (youth) rather than a permanent condition.

Over time colonists arranged new ways for parceling out still-available land. In recompense for their efforts in boundary disputes, the governments of Massachusetts and New Hampshire offered land to colonists who took up arms on behalf of their province; this approach was often used in other colonies as well, at times to pay soldiers for fighting Indians.

Perhaps more significant was a change in the relation between landholding and membership in a community. During the seventeenth century, when towns were being created, obtaining land in a particular area meant becoming a member of a community in the most complete sense of the term. Owning land became, like church membership for those who passed the strict examination process, a sign of one's identity; gaining it depended on receiving the favor of those who had obtained the initial grant from the government and had accepted conditions for the prompt and regulated settlement of the parcel. But landholding practices soon changed. With land being bought and sold frequently, the process of acquiring it came to have a different meaning. By the eighteenth century, earlier sensibilities had faded. Rather than needing the approval of a community, would-be landowners had only to purchase their lots; the growing prevalence of such practices led to a growth in absen-

tee landholders. This shift in practice underscored a more profound shift in economic and social values. Landholding remained important, to be sure, but it no longer entailed the sort of commitment required of earlier colonists.

THE CHESAPEAKE AND THE SOUTH

In early Virginia, Maryland, and the Carolinas, the distribution of land differed substantially from the landholding system in New England, especially in the seventeenth century—though there were similarities as well, such as a predisposition to treat land as a commodity. The differences stemmed largely from the region's peculiar demography and the colonists' search, from the start, for profitable exports through staple-crop production. In the Chesapeake labor was often more important than land; owning land had, at first, little advantage if the colonists and their families did not have sufficient labor to work it. Still the rate at which locally produced crops, especially tobacco, exhausted land did place those who could gain control of large plantations in an advantageous position. In South Carolina, where settlement began from two to three generations after the founding of Jamestown, the earliest colonists were emigrants from Barbados, some of whom could no longer afford to own land because of the spread of sugar plantations. Here, too, the division of land followed economic needs and the rising power of the export-oriented elite. Those who gained control of good land, particularly the lowland areas best suited to rice production, soon dominated the economy of the colony. Their decision to bring their slaves with them from Barbados had a long-lasting impact on the region, and laid the basis for what would become South Carolina's peculiar (among mainland colonies) demographic profile, with its black majority. In North Carolina and Georgia, colonial officials had hoped to create societies dominated by small freeholders, but over time landholding patterns in each came to mirror those of other southern colonies.

Early colonists to the Chesapeake, like other migrants to British America, had fairly precise ideas about what sort of land offered the greatest possibilities for economic development. Their close attention to trade in particular shaped early settlement patterns. Like other colonists Chesapeake residents knew that settling along navigable waterways facilitated commerce; without access to a reliable stream or river, colonists would face higher costs in transporting their tobacco to market. Further, from the start colonists sought to patent contiguous lands. It made far better sense to live near to than far from one's neighbor; neighbors could provide necessary assistance in many circumstances and were especially important given the high morbidity and mortality rates experienced by early settlers.

The demographic history of the region shaped landholding patterns in specific ways. In an effort to attract migrants to the region and thus create the labor pool necessary for staple-crop production, stockholders in the Virginia Company, which was already proving to be a failure by the mid 1610s, devised what became known as the headright system. Beginning in 1616 any colonists who paid their way across the ocean or anyone who paid for the transportation of another person received a headright entitling them to fifty acres (20 hectares) of land.

Over time headrights joined other commodities in the developing market; colonists sold them back and forth repeatedly, in part because they remained relatively inexpensive well into the seventeenth century. Even when headrights rose in value by the end of the 1650s, these fifty-acre (20-hectare) parcels still changed hands for as little as from forty to fifty pounds (18–22.5 kilograms) of tobacco, an amount easily produced, given sufficient labor, on most plantations. The ease with which colonists conveyed headrights demonstrates that the demographic problems suffered by colonists in the Chesapeake—skewed sex ratio and high mortality rate—continued to make landholding a precarious investment for many settlers and thus not necessarily as desirable as landholding was for people in England or New England. Only colonists willing to hold onto tracts for a long period of time, perhaps as long as a generation, could actually profit through real estate, and few had the resources to tie up their limited disposable wealth in unproductive real estate ventures. Still, some colonists did manage to join large tracts. Before 1640, along the Eastern Shore of Virginia at least, the top 10 percent of all landholders owned 40 percent to 50 percent of the land claimed by colonists.

During the second half of the seventeenth century, however, the situation changed dramatically, again because of the region's demography. Mortality rates improved, and continued immigration as well as some natural population increase led to an expanding population. Knowing that a larger labor force could produce more tobacco, those with existing capital began to speculate in available lands, purchasing tracts farther upriver and thus expanding the boundaries of land actually owned by colonists. A land boom from 1650 to 1675 resulted in a dramatic expansion in the amount of lands patented in Virginia; the total rose by 2.35 million acres (940,000 hectares), which constituted over 50 percent of all land patented in the colony from the mid 1630s to the end of the century. Those who purchased land or headrights correctly sensed that they would be able to attract laborers to their holdings, particularly those who would be unable to purchase land at the end of their terms of servitude. Lacking the capital necessary to purchase the tools, livestock, seed, and food necessary to support their households for as long as eighteen months before they could begin to survive on what they produced, freed servants found tenancy their most realistic option.

In both Virginia and Maryland, tenancy rates rose after 1650, a direct result of the increasing difficulty freed servants faced in purchasing land, though tenancy often (but not always) tended to be, in the seventeenth century at least, a life-cycle phenomenon rather than a permanent status; over time many one-time tenants became landowners, though the chances for becoming an owner decreased toward the end of the seventeenth century. To be sure, land in the Chesapeake was never evenly distributed among colonists, especially in longer settled areas. The opening of new settlements to the West, however, probably made tenancy less common in the developing regions, where freed servants presumably had a better opportunity to purchase land since prices tended to be lower. Migrants seeking economic betterment continued to arrive in large numbers into the 1660s by signing up as indentured servants to work on tobacco plantations. These servants had presumably shared an economic dream common in England; they believed that ownership of land would confer a degree of economic security. That idea would continue to inform American political culture until well beyond the revolution. Thomas Jefferson articulated it especially well in his *Notes on the State of Virginia,* written in 1782, in which he argued that freeholders could sustain a republic because no individual could exert economic control over them and thereby influence their political behavior.

While tenancy became increasingly common in the region, the lives of tenants, contrary to American mythology, were not necessarily more miserable than those of freeholders. In the Chesapeake as elsewhere, particularly in the middle colonies, those who owned land desperately needed laborers to work it. Further, provincial legislation intended to prevent engrossment of valuable land by individuals not having the labor to work it meant that anyone willing to invest in land had to find people to live on it. Prospective landlords thus had to offer prospective tenants good terms lest the tenants choose to lease elsewhere. Early leases in particular were attractive for newly freed servants, since the landlord at times offered to advance the tenant the necessary tools, stock, and food to begin a farm.

Further, rents tended to be low, perhaps from one hundred to three hundred pounds (45–135 kilograms) of tobacco a year for a tract from fifty to one hundred acres (20–40 hectares) of land not yet exhausted from years of tobacco production. To be sure the landlord gained a great deal from the arrangement; namely, maintaining ownership of the tract (by keeping it "seated," or occupied, in the eyes of the law) and having it improved. Over time, with population continuing to grow, landlords were also able to raise rents, thereby gaining even further income and maintaining control of an increasingly valuable commodity. By the early 1780s, when perhaps a majority of householders in the longer-settled counties of Maryland had signed leases, landlords were drawing rents from a sizable proportion of the province's householders.

In the most desirable tracts throughout the Chesapeake, then, those with access to substantial amounts of capital or credit built their plantations with the labor of tenants and, increasingly, slaves. Initially worth little, land came to compete with labor as one of the most highly valued commodities in the region.

In South Carolina similar processes took place, though at a different pace and under markedly different conditions. Here, too, demography shaped landholding patterns. The development of the colony at the end of the seventeenth century took place amidst a profound change in racial sensibilities in British America, and this was evident in the colony's headright system, which rewarded immigrants who transported slaves into the province. Rather than English or other European servants dominating the labor force, African slaves, barred by law from owning land in most instances, became the majority of workers in the rice, and later indigo, plantations. In South Carolina those able to gain access to capital or credit amassed substantial tracts of the most desirable land, particularly in the rice-producing lowlands, and they began to gather the slaves needed to make their lands profitable in a regional economy committed to labor-intensive crops. The distribution of land in the coastal areas of these colonies thus became far more skewed than it ever became in the Chesapeake or elsewhere. Like the economic development of the West Indies in the seventeenth century, South Carolina's economy favored those who could gather large numbers of laborers to produce desired staple crops. The result was a social system featuring enormous stratification of wealth, evident most clearly in the differences in slave ownership and landholding.

Landholding patterns in North Carolina and Georgia differed somewhat from those in South Carolina. Under North Carolina's headright system, which prevailed until 1729, heads of households received one hundred acres (40 hectares), and an additional fifty acres (20 hectares) for every servant or slave they added to the colony; fifty-acre grants went to others. After 1729, though headrights continued to be granted, most colonists obtained land by buying it. But a desire to settle the colony had led Crown officials to grant large tracts of land, far larger than the headrights allowed by law. As elsewhere, colonists holding high office, such as governor or council member, received substantial tracts. These practices elicited protests and some colonists tried to use local statutes to prevent the engrossment of large parcels. But official acceptance of large landholders, combined with the relatively low price of land in the colony and prevailing practices of primogeniture and entail, enabled wealthier colonists to evade restrictions and to amass considerable estates. To be sure, small farmers still held most of the land in the colony; the upper 10 percent managed to gain ownership of only about 40 percent of the land, a figure lower than in either Virginia or South Carolina.

The trustees of Georgia, who received a charter for settling the colony in 1732 and who governed it from London until 1752, apparently shared the belief that small landholders would be the ideal settlers in their colony. They carefully controlled the distribution of tracts and attempted to impose a specific economic system on the colony, with a particular concern for developing the silk industry; their regulations thus demanded that landholders, whether they paid for their tracts or got them for free, plant white mulberry trees. For colonists who paid their own way, the trustees set a limit of five hundred acres (200 hectares) on the size of the tracts each could purchase, but they demanded that each parcel have at least one male present, thus indicating their sense that the colony was at risk of attack. This fear also influenced the trustees' policies toward charity colonists; these people received fifty-acre contiguous units. Charity settlers did not own the land in fee simple, at least not at first; farmers held land for the duration of their lives only, and could will it only to male heirs. This practice of limiting heirs, known as tail-male, fit well into the trustees' plans to keep men on each parcel and thus enhance the defense of the province. The land policies of the trustees fit their vision of a colony designed for poor people who would develop small plots of land; the initial ban on the importation of slaves further demonstrated their commitment to creating a society of small freeholders.

Over time the trustees' plans became increasingly inadequate for life in Georgia. Those granting land paid insufficient attention to local variations. Many settlers who received allotments in pine barrens, with their characteristic sandy soils, found farming difficult if not impossible. And tail-male discouraged settlers who wanted, like settlers elsewhere in the colonies, to alienate land in whatever manner they saw fit. Perhaps sensing the need for change, the trustees in 1741 transferred control over the granting of tracts to the president of the colony, and he and his assistants allowed for greater variation in landholding (including the issuance of larger tracts with fee simple titles). And in 1750, while still in control of the colony, the trustees decided to get out of the business of controlling land distribution in the colonies; thereafter land entered the market, and settlers could alienate it or pass it down in any manner they saw fit. Already by that time land practices had deviated substantially from the ideas of the trustees. Consolidation of lands into more sizable tracts had begun earlier, in part because widows, who successfully won dispensations allowing them to maintain control of their deceased husbands' lands, remarried and thus joined their lands to those of their new spouse. Further, especially in the latter years of the trustees' power, grants to colonists able to pay their own way, typically in parcels of 300 acres to 500 acres (120 to 200 hectares), became more common than smaller grants to charity settlers. After the trustees gave up power, royal officials began to award tracts up to 1,000 acres (400 hectares) including 31 grants of 500 to 999 acres (200 to 400 hectares) to women between 1755 and 1775.

THE MIDDLE COLONIES

In the middle colonies—New York, East and West Jersey, and Pennsylvania—landholding patterns again reflected prevailing demographic and economic developments. Since the demographic and economic history of these colonies differed substantially from that of the colonies to the south, and the regional economy differed from that of New England, landholding patterns reflected these dissimilarities. In these colonies some wealthy residents were able to amass vast tracts, yet they did not control the economy as plantation owners did in the South. A long history of settlement by migrants and their heirs led, in some places, to a much greater equality in landholdings. This rough equality of modest-scale farms was epitomized by cereal farmers in southeastern Pennsylvania who inhabited the softly rolling hills of Chester and Lancaster counties, which have come to symbolize freeholders in early America in the opinion of some historians. The image was not always correct—land speculators eagerly sought large tracts in the region and immediately to its west—yet its development suggests the importance of landholding patterns for the definition of regional identity in British America.

Perceptions of the land's potential here, as elsewhere, shaped landholding patterns. Would-be farmers in the middle colonies correctly believed that, in contrast to the poor soils and harsh weather of much of New England, their soil and climate were ideal for cereal farming and that large profits could be made through exporting grains, especially to the West Indies. Given the seasonal demands of that type of production, they avoided the importation of large numbers of slaves, preferring instead to find the labor for their farms within their own families or to hire help locally during times of peak need for labor.

By the mid eighteenth century, colonial legislators had passed laws to prevent speculation in lands. In New York these statutes were a response in part to the granting of vast patroonships during the Dutch occupation of the colony and to later English grants to political favorites. In Pennsylvania, legislative initiatives reflected the ideas of the colony's proprietary family. These laws set strict limits on the amount of land any individual could purchase (300 acres, [120 hectares] according to one 1768 Pennsylvania law), though speculators knew how to accrue land despite the limits.

Ties between land speculators and government officials were clearest in the Hudson Valley of New York. By the 1680s, some twenty years after the colony was seized from the Dutch, English officials believed that the colony's economy needed assistance, particularly in attracting settlers. Purportedly in an effort to encourage what Governor Thomas Dongan (1682–1688) once termed "the future Settlement" of land in New York, he and Governor Benjamin Fletcher (1692–1698) granted title to large tracts to a select group of would-be developers, who also received manorial rights to establish courts baron (for civil affairs) and courts leet (for criminal and administrative affairs). The grants confirmed two tracts granted by the Dutch totaling almost one million acres (400,000 hectares) to the Van Renssellaer family; the largest, encompassing approximately 850,000 acres (340,000 hectares) ran along twenty-three miles (36.8 ki-

lometers) of the Hudson River and extended twenty-four miles (38 kilometers) in each direction, though the town of Albany and other relatively small amounts of land were excluded. Dongan granted five other manorial patents (the largest being the 160,000-acre [4,000-hectare] Livingston Manor) and Fletcher five more. Together these two governors issued manorial patents for several million acres of New York. Dongan further supported the creation of the manors by charging only nominal quitrents, even though the Duke's Laws of the province specified set amounts of two shillings and six pence per 100 acres (40 hectares). At Rensselaerswyck, the rent fell to fifty bushels of wheat at a time when a bushel cost approximately four shillings. On their holdings of 850,000 acres, then, the Van Rensselaers were assessed an amount approximating that levied on a landholder who had 1,250 acres (500 hectares). Though tenants, at times acting with the support of Massachusetts colonists (who sought to expand their province's holdings), occasionally protested the engrossment of land and battled over titles, especially after the mid eighteenth century, the manorial system survived.

To be sure, the overwhelming majority of the people in the middle colonies were small farmers (as was the case throughout much of the southern backcountry and Piedmont), such as the Quaker population of the Delaware Valley and the German and Scotch-Irish migrants to the Pennsylvania and New York hinterland in the eighteenth century. For many in these groups community ideals served to define landholding patterns. These ideals originated in Europe and were given more concrete form in the Western Hemisphere when colonists gained land as they could not earlier. Like New England farmers, settlers in the middle colonies strove to keep their tracts within their families, though many parents also purchased land for their children rather than divide their own tracts into farms insufficient to support their childrens' families. The appearance of small farms, which in Chester County averaged 245 acres (98 hectares) in 1710 (though they dropped to 125 acres by the late colonial period) and only slightly higher in Lancaster County; the relative ease with which settlers in the region gained access to land; and some useful propaganda spread by colony promoters led Pennsylvania to gain its eighteenth-century nickname as "the best poor man's country."

The promise of gaining land lured thousands to the region, though when they arrived, many discovered that obtaining it proved more difficult than they had imagined. Throughout the middle colonies, from the vast estates of the Hudson Valley to the smaller holdings of southeastern Pennsylvania, many people, especially in the eighteenth century, found themselves either unable to purchase land or unwilling to do so. Further, enterprising land speculators found ways to avoid existing statutory limitations. Provincial officials, some of whom became land speculators themselves, seemingly encouraged widespread evasion of provincial statutes by the mid eighteenth century. When land speculators sought to gain substantial tracts in the wake of the Fort Stanwix Treaty of 1768, which opened hundreds of thousands of acres of western land to colonial settlement, they obtained title by organizing groups of alleged settlers to purchase land and then arranged for the rapid transfer of the title to them, usually for a modest fee.

Speculators often chose to work together in companies to facilitate their quest to become a landed elite. Their pursuit of lands reflected the belief that growth of the colonial population, which was particularly impressive beginning in the 1710s, would force colonists to move west to find new land. Prominent colonists, including Benjamin Franklin, became actively involved in efforts to establish new colonies. In the mid eighteenth century the Susquehannah Company, composed of Connecticut colonists who sought western land, relied on the sea-to-sea clause of the province's 1662 charter and proceeded to claim all the land west of New York (already settled at the time of the charter) between forty-one and forty-two degrees north latitude. The claim brought them into conflict, at times armed, with settlers from Pennsylvania who held land in territory patented to William Penn in 1681. The company failed in its efforts, though many of its settlers did remain in the area, often challenging the legitimacy of their neighbors' Pennsylvania titles in the Wyoming Valley.

Other companies sought the fertile lands of the Ohio country, including the Ohio Company, which hoped to gain 500,000 acres (200,000 hectares) and the Loyal and Greenbrier companies, which sought one million acres. But, taken together, their talents and capital did not match their ambitions; the companies eventually failed, occasionally heaping catastrophic economic burdens upon those involved who had to sell off lands they had purchased earlier in desperate efforts to satisfy their creditors.

While speculators often failed, colonists with less capital also frequently could not obtain the land they sought. Many with limited resources chose to become tenants, though some did take out mortgages to purchase lands from wealthier landholders. Those who signed leases did so because landlords in the region made tenancy desirable. In order to attract tenants to their holdings and thus prevent would-be settlers from moving west where lands were cheaper, landlords built roads for settlers, provided remarkably easy leasing terms (with rents as low as one peppercorn per year for the first seven years in some instances), and let settlers establish credit at their stores so they could purchase needed goods more easily. Though these efforts no doubt improved the economic standing of the landlords themselves, especially when settlers raised the value of land by clearing it and when their store purchases made them ever more indebted to the landlord, they also enabled poorer settlers to gain access to land. Tenancy rates were high in places, especially where land speculators had been able to amass tracts of over 100,000 acres (40,000 hectares). Yet even in areas dominated by freeholders, tenants appeared in substantial numbers; perhaps 20 percent to 30 percent of the farmers in southeastern Pennsylvania were tenants by the late colonial period, though it is possible that tenancy here, as elsewhere, represented a stage in any individual family's economic development and not a lifelong status.

With tenancy growing even in "the best poor man's country," it became evident to many colonists that the dream of owning land in fee simple (that is, an absolute type of ownership including a right to alienate the property) was not to become a reality for them in British America. Yet only on relatively rare occasion did anger about their economic status lead them to take up arms against their landlords, and when they did, no great redistribution of land resulted. By and large even those who rented lands in the middle colonies concentrated upon improving whatever economic prospects they enjoyed, perhaps always hoping to raise enough money so that they could purchase land later in their lives or if not for themselves, at least for their children.

CONCLUSION

Landownership was more widely distributed in the British colonies than in England or on the Continent, though it never became universal in the rural areas that comprised most of British America and contained the vast majority of its population. And though rates of tenancy seemingly increased in particular places at particular times (such as the Chesapeake after the mid seventeenth century or Pennsylvania a century later), the possibility of eventually obtaining a freehold remained far greater in America than in much of western Europe in the early modern period. In addition the proportion of colonists owning land was always higher in the colonies than in England, which meant that a greater percentage of the colonial population was able to meet the property qualifications necessary for voting and holding office. Everywhere, or so it seems, colonists tried to improve their economic standing by speculating in land. Some chose to stay in one place, purchasing nearby lands or sending their agents into less densely settled territory; others chose to try their luck by moving west, though their chances for economic improvement remained precarious.

Given the importance of economic development to British colonists and the emphasis within the empire on the production and distribution of desirable goods for both short- and long-distance trade, it was perhaps not surprising that landholding patterns reflected these realities. The idealized yeoman celebrated by Jefferson and Hector St. John de Crèvecoeur might have been an almost universal image of an American in the late eighteenth century, but as with almost any broadly drawn description, it needs clarification. American-born married men conformed to the image more closely than immigrants, younger men, or women, and it was always easier to obtain land in the less densely settled interior than near the coast. Yet even though the opportunity for owning land seemingly decreased for many in certain times and places, especially in longer-settled areas, the possibility of gaining a freehold remained one of the enduring characteristics of the colonial economy.

BIBLIOGRAPHY

Bailyn, Bernard. *Voyagers to the West: A Passage in the Peopling of America on the Eve of the Revolution.* New York, 1986.

Bond, Beverly W., Jr. *The Quit-Rent System in the American Colonies.* New Haven, Conn., 1919.

Bushman, Richard L. *From Puritan to Yankee: Character and the Social Order in Connecticut, 1690–1765.* Cambridge, Mass., 1967.

Caldwell, Lee Ann. "Women Landholders of Colonial Georgia." In *Forty Years of Diversity: Essays on Colonial Georgia,* edited by Harvey H. Jackson and Phinizy Spalding. Athens, Ga., 1984.

Carr, Lois Green, Russell R. Menard, and Lorena Walsh. *Robert Cole's World: Agriculture and Society in Early Maryland.* Chapel Hill, N.C., 1991.

Coleman, Kenneth. *Colonial Georgia: A History.* New York, 1976.

Cronon, William. *Changes in the Land: Indians, Colonists, and the Ecology of New England.* New York, 1983.

Daniels, Bruce C. *The Connecticut Town: Growth and Development, 1635–1790.* Middletown, Conn., 1979.

Davis, Harold E. *The Fledgling Province: Social and Cultural Life in Colonial Georgia, 1733–1776.* Chapel Hill, N.C., 1976.

Greven, Philip J., Jr. *Four Generations: Population, Land, and Family in Colonial Andover, Massachusetts.* Ithaca, N.Y., 1970.

Higgins, Ruth L. *Expansion in New York, with Especial Reference to the Eighteenth Century.* Columbus, Ohio, 1931.

Innes, Stephen. *Labor in a New Land: Economy and Society in Seventeenth-Century Springfield.* Princeton, N.J., 1983.

Jennings, Francis. *The Ambiguous Iroquois Empire: The Covenant Chain Confederation of Indian Tribes with English Colonies from Its Beginnings to the Lancaster Treaty of 1744.* New York, 1984.

Kim, Sung Bok. *Landlord and Tenant in Colonial New York: Manorial Society, 1664–1775.* Chapel Hill, N.C., 1978.

Lefler, Hugh T., and William S. Powell, *Colonial North Carolina: A History.* New York, 1973.

Lemon, James T. *The Best Poor Man's Country: A Geographical Study of Early Southeastern Pennsylvania.* Baltimore, Md., 1972.

Lockridge, Kenneth. "Land, Population, and the Evolution of New England Society, 1630–1790." *Past and Present* 39 (1968):62–80.

Main, Gloria L. *Tobacco Colony: Life in Early Maryland, 1650–1720.* Princeton, N.J., 1982.

Main, Jackson Turner. *Society and Economy in Colonial Connecticut.* Princeton, N.J., 1985.

Mancall, Peter C. *Valley of Opportunity: Economic Culture Along the Upper Susquehanna, 1700–1800.* Ithaca, N.Y., 1991.

Martin, John Frederick. *Profits in the Wilderness: Entrepreneurship and the Founding of New England Towns in the Seventeenth Century.* Chapel Hill, N.C., 1991.

Menard, Russell R. "From Servant to Freeholder: Status Mobility and Property Accumulation in Seventeenth-Century Maryland." *William and Mary Quarterly,* 3rd ser., 30, no. 1 (1973):37–64.

Mitchell, Robert D. *Commercialism and Frontier: Perspectives on the Early Shenandoah Valley.* Charlottesville, Va., 1977.

Morgan, Edmund S. *American Slavery, American Freedom: The Ordeal of Colonial Virginia.* New York, 1975.

Perry, James R. *The Formation of a Society on Virginia's Eastern Shore, 1615–1655.* Chapel Hill, N.C., 1990.

Rutman, Darrett B., and Anita H. Rutman. *A Place in Time: Middlesex County, Virginia, 1650–1750.* New York, 1984.

Simler, Lucy. "Tenancy in Colonial Pennsylvania: The Case of Chester County." *William and Mary Quarterly,* 3rd ser., 43, no. 3 (1986):542–569.

Stiverson, Gregory A. *Poverty in a Land of Plenty: Tenancy in Eighteenth-Century Maryland.* Baltimore, Md., 1977.

Taylor, Alan. *Liberty Men and Great Proprietors: The Revolutionary Settlement on the Maine Frontier, 1760–1820.* Chapel Hill, N.C., 1990.

Wood, Peter H. *Black Majority: Negroes in Colonial South Carolina from 1670 Through the Stono Rebellion.* New York, 1974.

Peter C. Mancall

SEE ALSO **British Settlements; Farming, Planting, and Ranching; Gender Relations; Marriage;** and **Rural Life.**

THE DUTCH COLONY

FOR ITS FIRST FIFTEEN YEARS, New Netherland was a Dutch colony without colonists. It was not the land that Henry Hudson discovered in 1609 which was considered valuable by his Amsterdam sponsors, but rather the pelts of the fur-bearing animals who inhabited the land.

The first attempt to people the territory was made by the Dutch West India Company, which was chartered in 1621 to exploit trade opportunities between the Netherlands, the west coast of Africa, and the eastern seaboard of North and South America. The company established Fort Orange (Albany) in 1624 and New Amsterdam (New York City) in 1626 with French-speaking Protestant families from the southern Netherlands. Considered employees of the company, the families were paid a salary for their work. Settlers were not allowed to own the land they cleared nor to profit from its production. For this reason—and also because political and economic conditions in the Netherlands were not unsatisfactory—Dutch farmers had little interest in settling the new colony.

To entice settlers the company in 1628 and 1629 offered plans of "Freedoms and Exemptions for the Patroons and Masters or Private Persons who would plant a colony and cattle in New Netherland." In the 1629 plan, patroons (or patrons), at their own expense and over a four-year period, would equip fifty persons to settle in New Netherland. In return for their capital investment, these entrepreneurs would receive a grant of riverfront land—a patroonship—that stretched eighteen miles (29 kilometers) along one side of the Hudson River, or nine miles (14 kilometers) on both sides, and as many miles into the hinterland as they wanted. They were also given wide-ranging judicial authority over their tenants that included jurisdiction over capital offenses as well as the right of taxation, full powers of administration, shipping space on company vessels, and permission to trade from Newfoundland to Florida. Most important, patroons were permitted some access in the 1629 Freedoms and Exemptions to the lucrative fur trade on which the Dutch West India Company had hitherto maintained a strict monopoly. The company itself retained ownership of the island of Manhattan.

Despite the generous terms, only one patroonship, Rensselaerswyck, ever flourished. Between 1630 and 1646, 216 settlers immigrated to the lands of Patroon Kiliaen van Rensselaer on the upper Hudson River. Dissatisfaction with the feudal character of their tenancy, however, prompted many of the settlers to leave Rensselaerswyck at the end of their contracts either to return to the fatherland or to acquire land of their own. In the cases of failed patroonships, the company purchased the land from the patroons.

CONCESSIONS TO ENCOURAGE SETTLEMENT

In the hope of enlarging the small trickle of settlers to New Netherland, the 1629 Freedoms and Exemptions provided opportunity for ordinary persons as well as those with capital to obtain land. Under a form of land tenure known as "free and common socage," settlers could have as much land as they could "sow or mow," for as long as they occupied it, in return for a payment after the first ten years of one-tenth of the produce of the soil and one-tenth of the "increase of all sorts of cattle." Again the Dutch West India Company's offer was taken up by only a few persons because the land would revert to the company when they no longer occupied it—a condition unpalatable to most potential settlers.

In 1638 and 1639 the Dutch West India Company presented revised conditions for the settlement of New Netherland. Land could now be held in perpetuity, and trading privileges were extended to all commodities, including fur. With these incentives more settlers took up the company's offer, and the population of New Netherland increased from three hundred in 1630 to five hundred in 1640.

In that year the company issued a revised set of Freedoms and Exemptions, further liberalizing the terms by which land in New Netherland could be acquired. It offered two hundred acres (80 hectares) to settlers who brought five adult family members and/or servants with them and also provided the opportunity for settlers to develop their own towns and govern themselves on a local level. Local officeholders were to be nominated by the settlers and chosen from a double slate by the director general and council. Now Long Island, Brooklyn, and the Hudson and Hackensack valleys began to be settled in earnest, and by 1643 the colony's population had reached nearly two thousand, about half of whom lived in New Amsterdam and half in the hinterland. Unfortunately a devastating war with the Indians in the early 1640s interrupted the progress of settlement for a time.

Between 1644 and 1664, at least seventeen municipalities were established in New Netherland on both the Dutch and the English town models—the latter being accorded somewhat more autonomy than the Dutch.

ACQUIRING LAND TITLE

Once relations with the Indians had returned to a better footing, the original and rather enlightened Dutch policy toward Native American land rights was followed. To avoid dissension with the Indians, whose concept of land ownership vastly differed from that of the Europeans, Director General Peter Stuyvesant in 1652 required prospective buyers to receive government permission before purchasing. If the buyer could prove that the Native Americans were willing to sell and had agreed to the terms, and if the director granted permission, a license was filed, the land was surveyed, and a deed was drawn up. Then the buyer petitioned the director for a formal grant, or patent. Finally the buyer was required to appear before the director for a third time to receive official confirmation of the patent. This process eventually extinguished Native American titles to the land.

On Manhattan Island, which continued to be owned by the Dutch West India Company, settlers' guarantees to their land were in the form of legal instruments recorded by the provincial secretary. Conveyances between private individuals were also duly recorded. Since land was not surveyed, land papers were curiously vague—failing to specify metes and bounds or even to designate clearly the location of a particular tract or lot.

The 1642 appointment of a surveyor-general obligated proprietors of new communities formed on the Dutch model during the 1650s and 1660s to survey the land, allocate home lots, and set aside common lands for grazing. Once the land was fenced and adequately defended, the settlers, with the approval of the director general, drew lots for their individual shares of the common lands. Woodland and swampland were also allocated in this way, with fairness being a prime consideration. Subsequently, the community was allowed to form a local court, overseen by a *schout* (sheriff) and three *schepens* (judges) appointed by the director general and his council from a slate of nominees furnished by the settlers.

ECONOMIC USES OF LAND

Trapping and trading peltry were the original uses to which land in New Netherland was dedicated. But as the territory became settled, agriculture grew in importance. In the absence of a developed market economy, land was used first to feed and clothe oneself and one's household. Cattle were raised for slaughter and for dairy, hogs for slaughter, sheep for wool, and oxen and horses for their labor. By the end of the Dutch period, markets had developed and surpluses of all of these commodities were finding their way to buyers.

The third use to which land was put was economic betterment through speculation. Activity in real estate was widespread in New Netherland. Following the example of the large landowners of the period, ordinary settlers also bought and sold land for speculative purposes, often banding together in joint ventures. On Manhattan Island most small farmers subdivided and sold the land they had received free and used the proceeds to purchase other lots and land. Even those having as little as an acre to spare entered the lively market in real estate.

Mortgages, or sworn agreements between two individuals, were officially recorded by the government in New Amsterdam. The government set conditions for their repayment. Mortgages were a preferred form of credit since, in case of default, the mortgage holder had first claim on the property. In this pre-banking era, however, private loans secured with notes were common within families and among friends.

DUTCH LANDHOLDING AFTER 1664

After the British took possession of New Netherland in 1664, they recognized all Dutch land titles, although all landowners—both towns and individuals—were required to have their grants and patents confirmed. Similarly the rights of the patroon of Rensselaerswyck were recognized. The seignorial system there continued, serving as a model for a manorial system introduced by the British.

BIBLIOGRAPHY

Kammen, Michael. *Colonial New York: A History.* New York, 1975.

Nissenson, S. G. *The Patroon's Domain.* New York, 1937.

Rife, Clarence White. "Land Tenure in New Netherland." In *Essays in Colonial History Presented to Charles McLean Andrews by His Students.* Freeport, N.Y., 1966.

Rink, Oliver A. *Holland on the Hudson: An Economic and Social History of Dutch New York.* Ithaca, N.Y., 1986.

Firth Haring Fabend

SEE ALSO **Dutch and Swedish Settlements; Farming, Planting, and Ranching; Gender Relations; Marriage; and Rural Life.**

THE FRENCH COLONIES

As EARLY AS THE sixteenth century, the titleholder of territory in New France had the right to concede fiefs in the form of seigneuries. Nevertheless, the mode and degree of the institution varied markedly from one colony to another. The seigneurial tenure system evolved considerably in Canada, while it remained rather ineffectual in Acadia and largely marginal in Louisiana.

CANADA

The seigneurial system had its most profound effect in Canada, where most of the land was divided into seigneuries by the Compagnie des

Cent-Associés (Company of One Hundred Associates) from 1627 to 1663 and by the Crown thereafter. These seigneuries were granted along both banks of the Saint Lawrence River from the urban centers of Quebec, Trois-Rivières, and Montreal. In the seventeenth century, the concessions spread into the Richelieu Valley and in the 1730s into the Chaudière. At the end of the French regime, 210 seigneuries had been granted. They usually extended from one to three leagues in width (the French league equaled five kilometers, or about 2.75 English miles) and, with several exceptions, they were about the same in length. That was the extent of settled land in the colony. In Canada, the axiom "No land without a lord" had a real significance.

Seigneuries were not conceded haphazardly. The seigneurs were, for the most part, nobles, military officers, senior officials, the religious orders, and a small number of individual bourgeois who had acquired merit in the eyes of the authorities. The Crown clearly intended to establish a landholding social order similar to that in France at the time. A seigneury was a privilege in the sense that the seigneur could demand that certain rather burdensome dues be paid him annually. Some, like the *cens,* were more honorific than a source of profit; they merely established the social difference between the seigneur and his *censitaires.*

Some seigneurs sought to extort a fee for the use of the common land where the *censitaires* grazed their livestock, but with scant success. Nor could the seigneur hope to charge his *censitaires* for the right to fish in the river that their concessions faced. The seigneur could require that his *censitaires* grind their grain in the seigneury's communal mill, and he then collected the *banalité,* which permitted him a share—usually a fourteenth—of the grain that the habitants ground. First, however, he had to build the mill, at considerable cost. Should he fail to provide a mill, then anyone who chose to build one on the seigneury could do so and charge the customary fee. Only when a seigneury had at least fifty *censitaires* using a mill was a profit to be made. The seigneur could also legally benefit when the property of one of his *censitaires* was sold to anyone not in the right of succession. All land in New France was entailed and had to pass, by right of succes-

sion, to the heir. Were it to be sold to someone other than the heir, the seigneur could levy *lods et ventes,* a fee of one-twelfth of the purchase price of the transferred property.

In the contracts for the *censives,* pieces of land granted by a seigneur and charged with the *cens,* the seigneur often inserted clauses that guaranteed him advantages such as days of statutory labor or the right to cut wood on any conceded land. Certain clauses were intended to facilitate the administration of land—for instance, by permitting the seigneur to appropriate uncultivated lands or to reclaim a *censive* sold by a *censitaire* by reimbursing the price agreed by the buyer. To these rights were added merely ceremonial ones, such as the right to bear a sword, to be first in processions and first in being presented with the *pain bénit,* or consecrated bread, to occupy a complimentary church pew, and to be buried within the church—ways of marking the primacy of the seigneur over his *censitaires.* In principle, the ownership of a seigneury guaranteed considerable rights, and such rights could be protected by the prerogative that allowed the seigneur to establish courts of justice in his fiefs.

These seigneurial rights were matched, however, by obligations. First, the seigneur had duties to the state, a fact that he acknowledged by the act of homage and by proffering an enumeration of his possessions. If he sold his property, he paid the state a fee equal to one-fifth of the price. Any oak trees and any mines on seigneurial property belonged to the state. The seigneur also had obligations toward the *censitaire,* such as building the flour mill and maintaining a "fire and place"—and to live on and cultivate the land, by himself or by a representative. Finally, the seigneur was required to grant land to anyone who asked, except the portion reserved for his own use.

The granting of *censives* was usually made on an egalitarian basis, one tract per individual or per family. The *censitaire* was given a rectangular tract, measured in arpents (one arpent equals 192 feet or 58 meters), that was usually about three arpents wide and twenty, thirty, or forty arpents deep. Along with paying fees and showing respect to the seigneur, the *censitaire* was himself required to maintain "fire and place." Moreover, he was obliged not only to allow the public passage through his land but also to assist in and maintain this public thoroughfare. Despite the conditions imposed by the seigneurial regime, the *censitaire* could be considered a landowner. He could sell the land or exchange it as he wished, as long as he paid the prescribed transaction fees to the seigneur, who remained the overall proprietor as confirmed by payment of the *cens*.

During the seventeenth century, and even during the first few decades of the eighteenth, seigneuries in sparsely populated Canada might have few or no *censitaires* for years, so that most seigneurs gained little profit from their land. Without sufficient population, the construction of a mill and the establishing of a court of justice were rarely profitable. Even the recovering of dues had irregular success during this period.

As the number of settlers grew, however, the seigneurial regime became stronger. The seigneurs no longer hesitated to demand the entirety of their dues; some tried to increase the fees and invent new ones. The *censitaires'* property deeds were more carefully checked when land rolls were drawn up. By the end of French rule, the system had become more and more restrictive for the *censitaire* and more and more advantageous for the seigneur.

ACADIA

The feudal system never took hold in Acadia as it did in Canada. Grants of seigneuries were in fact made until the cession of the colony to England in 1713, but the seigneurial system existed on paper more than in reality. Several factors explain this situation, particularly the vagueness of the land grants and the interminable disputes that resulted, the sparsity of Acadian population, and the continual military tensions in the region. Under these circumstances, seigneurial authority never asserted itself fully.

Nonetheless, the feudal concept of landholding persisted in Acadia in a simplified version. Thus, the tenants seem to have paid symbolic *cens et rentes*, probably more to establish their rights of ownership than to acknowledge their dependence. This system is found in the oldest settlements, where it seems commonplace. It was even an object of discussion between the

seigneurs and British authorities after 1713. Elsewhere, seigneurial landholding did not even maintain an appearance.

LOUISIANA

The landholding situation in Louisiana differed from that in other French North American colonies because of early confusion about land distribution and because of the peculiar seigneurial system that prevailed thereafter. Indeed, from the foundation of the colony at the end of the seventeenth century to the creation of the Compagnie de l'Occident (Company of the West) in 1717, land distribution in Louisiana took place without any formal framework. This practice came about because France, displeased by the slow progress of colonization in Canada and Acadia, refused to grant seigneuries in the Mississippi colony. This period is characterized, therefore, by profound incertitude because, although the land was granted without any fee at all, its possession was not guaranteed by any official deed. Only in 1717 did France grant Louisiana to the Compagnie de l'Occident "in ownership, seigneury, and justice." The extension of the feudal system in Louisiana was nonetheless limited, since the Compagnie de l'Occident and the Compagnie des Indes (Company of the Indies) could not themselves grant individual seigneuries. From then on, land was granted either in *censives*—that is, with payments of *cens et rentes* to the company as seigneur—or in *franc-alleu*, which was entirely without fee. The coexistence of these two forms characterized Louisiana but had little effect on development in a colony where survival was the principal occupation of the population.

BIBLIOGRAPHY

Clark, Andrew Hill. *Acadia: The Geography of Early Nova Scotia to 1760.* Madison, Wis., 1968.
Giraud, Marcel. *Histoire de la Louisiane française.* 5 vols. Paris, 1953–1992.
Harris, Richard Colebrook. *The Seigneurial System in Early Canada: A Geographical Study.* Madison, Wis., 1966.

Trudel, Marcel. *Les débuts du régime seigneurial au Canada*. Montreal, 1974.

Alain Laberge

SEE ALSO **Architecture; Crafts;** and **Urban Life;** and various essays in ECONOMIC LIFE and FOLKWAYS.

THE SPANISH BORDERLANDS

BACKGROUND

SPAIN CONQUERED FLORIDA AND WHAT IS NOW the American Southwest by arms, but it secured its newly acquired territories by land grants. Beginning as early as the sixteenth century in New Mexico and continuing there and in Florida, Texas, and California until 1821, Spain extended its control over the vast expanses of the borderlands by conceding land to deserving citizens. In 1821, Spain lost Florida for the last time. But between 1821 and 1848, when sovereignty over the borderlands's soil changed once again, the Mexican Republic honored, continued, and extended Spanish land policy by granting from Mexican public domain additional, often extensive, tracts of land.

By the time the United States officially acquired Florida from Spain in 1821 and the bulk of the southwestern United States from Mexico in 1848, some of the most valuable land had already become private property by virtue of the previous land grants of Spain and Mexico. In the treaties that formally transferred sovereignty, the United States guaranteed to respect property of every kind, including land grants. Thus the land grants that the United States inherited fundamentally affected the distribution of private and public lands in the old borderlands and established the settlement patterns in the region.

Land grants made by Spain and Mexico represented the transfer of national property belonging to the sovereign into the hands of private citizens. In the case of Spain, the Southwest initially belonged to the Crown by virtue of the international law of discovery and conquest. In the case of Mexico, the new republic in 1821 acquired all land except what Spain previously had granted or lost to the United States. Thus Spanish and Mexican land grants represented the ultimate exercise of sovereign control over land, the power to convey private title to it.

Spain and Mexico both recognized limitations on this power over the land they had won. As the first European nation in the Southwest, Spain acknowledged that some of the indigenous people who resided in the area before Spain's arrival had rights to land. This aboriginal title put this permanently occupied territory beyond sovereign ownership and thus outside the sovereign land-grant power. In addition, Spain recognized that other indigenous but nomadic peoples had a preferential right to a permanent, settled home base. Preexisting Indian pueblos of New Mexico represented the first kind of restraint imposed on Spain's land-grant power. The creation of the missions in Florida, in Texas, and most prominently in California represented the second kind.

On succeeding Spain as sovereign in that portion of the borderlands outside Florida, Mexico honored Spain's previous commitments of land to indigenous people. At the same time it altered the special protections given to those lands and allowed their institutional protectors, the Franciscans, to sink into obscurity. As a result, both Spain's and Mexico's recognition of the special land claims of indigenous settled and nomadic peoples significantly changed. Protected communal Indian lands fell into private hands; nomadic Native Americans lost a home base; and the United States, as succeeding sovereign, lost public domain.

Spanish and Mexican land grants came in a variety of forms. They created a range of private interests and presented the United States with a variety of problems when it succeeded as sovereign in 1848. Some land grants were made to individuals and thus resembled the classic form of private property. Other land grants, particularly in Texas, were made to contractors who were obliged to bring others to settle the land. Finally, still other grants, especially in New Mexico, were made directly to communities. It fell to the United States to sort out the various forms of ownership that these Spanish and Mexican land grants created. This aspect of land-grant confirmation turned out to be as controversial as the United States' decision on whether to honor the grant in any form.

In whatever form a new Spanish or Mexican land grant finally appeared, the process of creating it in the first place was fairly uniform across the borderlands. The persons desiring a grant began the process by filing a petition for land with the appropriate official, usually the governor. The petition identified the applicant as proper and worthy, and the land applied for as vacant and eligible. Previous government service made an individual "proper and worthy" in the eighteenth century; need for land became the basis for that perception in the nineteenth. A series of subsequent steps verified the petition. If the governor ultimately approved, he ordered the land grant made. In the final and most crucial step in the process, the governor returned the matter to the local investigating official. That official put the new owner in physical possession of the land grant, sometimes making a map of the land. Thereafter the land was private property.

However, the creation of land-grant ownership only began the process of settling and using the land. First, Spanish land-grant law imposed the condition that grantees actually settle on the land granted to them. Only after a period of residency did the granted title become perfect. Thereafter, owners might sell, and private purchasers could buy, granted land just like any other private property. There quickly developed, in New Mexico as early as the eighteenth century and in California and Texas by the nineteenth century, a lively market based on perfected land-grant titles.

In addition, both Spanish and Mexican law recognized title by simple possession. This powerful law of possession guaranteed the right to land no matter what the formal land-grant title might say. Both because of the merchantability of land-grant property and because of the possibility of title by adverse possession, by the time the United States acquired sovereignty over the area, borderland landholding had become more complex than the grant documents indicated.

Succeeding sovereigns adjudicated those private land-grant titles which had originated under Spain and Mexico. In the borderlands, different entities performed this adjudicatory function. In Florida, two federal boards of commissioners and the courts took on the task. In Texas, the job fell to the Republic of Texas in the period between 1836 and 1845 and thereafter to the state of Texas. In the rest of the territory acquired from Mexico in 1848, the federal government decided on the validity of previous Spanish and Mexican grants. But even these decisions were made under different procedures at different times and at different places. Not surprisingly, the determinations themselves varied. As a result, the often contradictory adjudications of land-grant titles by the succeeding sovereigns added another level of complexity to the already complicated landholding scheme that the United States inherited from Spain and Mexico.

FLORIDA

Spanish settlement of Florida began and ended earlier than it did in the Southwest. Spain had lost the Floridas to the United States by 1821, the year that Mexico achieved sovereignty over Texas, the New Mexico territory, and California, and began to form its own land legacy that the United States did not inherit until 1848. The period of exclusively Spanish control was interrupted from 1763 to 1783, when Great Britain controlled Florida and instituted its own sometimes contradictory, often different, land controls. As a result, British and Spanish land policies overlay and undercut each other through the eighteenth century. In addition, neither England nor Spain succeeded in permanently settling more than a fraction of Florida land. Finally, the Florida coastal and interior terrain differed substantially from the arid heartlands of south Texas and New Mexico. All of these factors tended to develop a distinct landholding system in Florida.

Still, the land law of Florida prior to its acquisition by the United States was basically Spanish. The Spanish Crown, usually through authorized delegates in Florida, granted town lots within the principal settlements of Saint Augustine in the east and Pensacola in the west. After 1800 and the restoration of Spanish sovereignty, many private grants were made outside the settled areas in the hope that permanent settlement would reduce the constant threat that Creek Indian resistance posed. Sometimes these grants were settled; often they were not. Many times Indian hostility made it impossible for a grantee to establish the ten years' possession that Spanish law was thought to require (in New Mexico, Spanish law was thought to require only four years of actual service) before grant ownership was final.

As a result, by 1818, when Spain lost its authority to make land grants in Florida, it had granted only approximately 130,000 acres (52,000 hectares) for the purpose of settlement and cultivation. (Other much larger grants rewarding military service and supposedly to establish logging mills covered many more acres.) Many of these acres in fact had not been settled. Those that had been were held tentatively by members of the Hispanic community. Farther west, where the very different terrain was equally inhospitable, Hispanic landholding had taken much deeper root and would survive for three decades longer than it had in Florida. But it was Florida that established the outline and New Mexico that supplied the detail.

NEW MEXICO, COLORADO, AND ARIZONA

By the time sovereignty passed to the United States in 1848, Spain and Mexico already had given title, in the form of recognized land grants, to more than twelve million acres (4,800,000 hectares) in what are now the states of New Mexico, Colorado, and Arizona but what was then a distinct administrative area, separate from Texas to the east and California to the west. These twelve million acres represented only 15 percent of the land, but they signified a much higher percentage of arable land in this area of vast expanses of desert interspersed only occasionally with easily watered areas suitable for intense human occupation. The central Rio Grande corridor from Socorro on the south to Taos on the north was the heartland of Pueblo and early His-

panic settlement in the borderlands. As a result, the area was the first center of land-grant activity in the Southwest.

The first surviving grants of land to Hispanics in this area date from the late 1690s, although Hispanic settlement began a century earlier. The number and size of grants grew through the eighteenth century. By 1800, if not before, the Spanish Crown, through its royal administrators in the New World, had granted almost all the usable land along the Rio Grande in north-central New Mexico. Ironically, the oldest of these New Mexico land grants, the ones that determined where subsequent grants had to fit in, were not land grants at all.

Spanish law recognized that land occupied and intensively used by indigenous peoples should be retained by them and could not be granted to other people. This recognition clearly extended to the Pueblos of New Mexico and to the nine or more Indian settlements spread along the Rio Grande. At some point around the turn of the nineteenth century, Spaniards and Pueblo Indians alike began to refer to these recognized aboriginal holdings as "land grants." By the time the United States acquired New Mexico in 1848, everyone understood—incorrectly, as it turned out—that the ancient Pueblo settlements held their lands by virtue of the oldest Spanish land grants.

Because subsequent land grants to Hispanics could neither replace nor displace these earliest Pueblo "land grants," they had to be patched and fitted in between. As a result, the land grants first made to Hispanic settlers along the northern Rio Grande and its tributaries come in many sizes, shapes, and forms of ownership.

Some of the early-eighteenth-century New Mexico land grants in the central Rio Grande corridor were made in order to settle and colonize the frontier area. Others, however, rewarded civil or military service and were never settled. Still others restricted use to grazing; others were made for mines. A rich pattern of prescribed and proscribed land uses overlay the different sizes, shapes, and ownerships of early New Mexico land grants.

In addition, the ownership of these early grants differed markedly. At one extreme, some very large, very early grants were made to individuals who never settled them. At the other extreme were the earliest "pueblo grants," made to the indigenous corporate community in recognition of continuous occupation that predated the Spanish arrival in the New World.

Between the extremes fell the community grants, a crucial form of Spanish and Mexican land concession apparently peculiar to New Mexico. The government made these grants for the purpose of creating new settlements. The original settlers received as private property only the small tracts where they built their homes and established their irrigated fields. The balance of these large grants was held in common for the use of existing settlers and for new settlers who might want to locate on the grant.

This arrangement guaranteed the existing community use of the grant's common lands while offering parts of those common lands to any person who might want to settle on them. It fit perfectly the intricate subsistence economies of land-grant communities in its balance between intensively used private irrigated lands and collectively used uplands for extensive grazing. But this mixed use raised a real issue about who owned the unallotted common lands, the existing community or the national government. Whatever the correct and formal legal answer, New Mexico community-grant residents believed that in some sense they owned the unallotted common portions of their grants.

In New Mexico the 1821 change in sovereignty from Spain to Mexico had little effect on the broad outlines of land-grant policy. Now land grants were made in the name of the new Mexican nation, not the Spanish Crown. Lands owned by Indian Pueblos lost some of their protected status and were acquired by non-Indians—sometimes honestly, sometimes not. By 1848 as many Hispanics as Pueblos lived on what had been exclusively Indian lands. Mexican officials continued to grant land from the remaining public domain both to private individuals and to communities.

Most of the Mexican grants lay on the periphery of the earlier Spanish grants. Some overlapped or even replaced earlier grants. Others lay beyond any existing settlements, on the very frontier of Mexican New Mexico. In particular, five huge private Mexican land grants, each larger than five hundred thousand acres (20,000 hectares), all made between 1832 and 1848 and together rimming existing Hispanic settlement in New Mexico, covered huge contiguous tracts of Mexican public land on New Mexico's north and east. Probably designed by the last Mexican officials in New Mexico as a buffer of private property against United States incursion from the east, these grants forever changed the balance of public and private land in the state without much altering its long-established landholding and settlement patterns.

In 1848, at the final change of sovereignty from Mexican to United States rule, New Mexico had enjoyed the longest and most intense history of land settlement and use of any of the Spanish Borderlands. Land grants had only partially confined and directed those settlement patterns. In at least two ways, the deeply entrenched living habits of established New Mexican families went against the grain that three centuries of existing land grants had created.

First, New Mexicans living on frontier community grants had refused to remain in the compact settlements that Spanish law had contemplated. Instead, they moved along the rivers and tributaries that ran through the grants and up into the hills surrounding them. By 1848 residency on community grants in New Mexico resembled the small private *ranchos* typical of California.

New Mexicans transformed private grants as well. Often made and either settled or sold early in the eighteenth century, grants to individuals had became by the mid nineteenth century, through intermarriage and less formal means, the residences of large extended families constituting communities. Thus, by 1848 the length and depth of landholding in New Mexico had blurred the fundamental distinctions on which colonial Spanish and Mexican land law was based, replacing them with the intricate webs of a deeply entrenched, long-standing Hispanic society.

CALIFORNIA

In contrast with New Mexico, Hispanic landholding in California prior to the 1848 change in sovereignty was relatively recent and not nearly so fully articulated or deeply entrenched. Non-Indian settlement in New Mexico began in 1598.

672

Alta California, as the state was known prior to 1848, was not settled by Hispanic immigrants until the mid eighteenth century, and then only lightly. As a result, the sudden tidal wave of land-hungry immigration brought to California by the gold rush completely overbore the much more tenuous landholdings established by early Hispanic settlers.

The *rancho* provided the means by which Spanish and Mexican officials created individually owned, private land grants prior to 1848. *Ranchos* did not begin in Baja California until about 1730. The first permanent *rancho* grant was not made in the area between present-day San Diego and San Francisco until 1784. Significantly, Spanish officials made that first grant to retiring Hispanic military officers attached to the San Diego *presidio,* not to voluntary immigrants and their descendants. Between 1784 and 1848 Hispanic officials granted hundreds of additional *ranchos.* Some were occupied by their grantees; many were not. In any case, these private *ranchos* never grew and changed in the way older and more deeply rooted New Mexico private grants had.

As in New Mexico, private California *ranchos* were interspersed between various types of older or preferred landholdings. The California version of the New Mexico community grant was the "pueblo grant." In Alta California these civilian pueblo grants were made to foster compact urban settlements. Unlike New Mexico, settlement patterns never came to contradict the form of the grant. But by 1848 only three civilian pueblos had been established in Alta California: at San Diego, at Los Angeles, and at San Jose. These civilian towns were preferred as settlements but never fully developed prior to 1848.

Instead, in California the critical, or most productive, lands were held by the Franciscan missions, a form of landholding also important in Texas but largely unknown in New Mexico. Technically, only the lands and buildings of the missions belonged to the Franciscan order, but the fathers exercised delegated administrative control over land use in a much wider area. They exercised this control for the benefit of nomadic Indians whom the Spanish Crown hoped to "civilize" by inducing them to settle on the land, as the Pueblo Indians of New Mexico had done. Thus the missions served a central function in the Spanish plan to pacify Alta California and make lands outside the missions safe and available for non-Indian settlement.

In 1784, when the first private *ranchos* were established in California, there were nine Franciscan missions between San Diego and San Francisco, and the population of Alta California was predominantly Indian. By 1821 and the end of Spanish rule, officials had added twelve more missions. Grants of *ranchos* to non-Indians initially fit into the available land between the extensive lands the missions controlled for the benefit of the Indians.

In New Mexico, the 1821 change from Spanish to Mexican sovereignty primarily effected landholding by relaxing the protections that Spanish law had extended to the recognized land rights of Pueblo Indians. In California, the arrival of Mexican sovereignty accomplished the same end by secularizing the holdings of the Franciscan missions. After 1821 mission lands were available for purchase by private non-Indian citizens or for new grants as *ranchos.*

Most *rancho* grants after 1821 reached within the borders of mission lands and converted the protected public property to alienable private property. The change in policy devastated the already moribund missions but enhanced the ranchos as the primary landholding mechanism. Land settlement in California had not reached the stage of deeply interwoven, tangled complication that it had in New Mexico by 1848.

TEXAS

The way Texas separated from Mexico and eventually joined the United States adds a layer of complexity to its land-grant history that makes the pattern of preexisting Hispanic landholding more difficult to discern than it is in New Mexico or California. Texas separated from Mexico and entered the United States in two stages: in 1836 it proclaimed itself an independent republic, and in 1845 it became a state in which the federal government retained no public domain. As an independent republic, Texas claimed the Nueces River as its southern boundary. Only upon entering the United States did it reach to the Rio Grande.

In addition, Texas is special because no federal adjudicatory body gathered together all land claims originating under the state's antecedent sovereigns and ruled on their validity, as the United States did in New Mexico and California. Instead, Texas itself ruled piecemeal on the Hispanic land claims that it had inherited. Still, in extent and nature Hispanic landholding in pre-independence Texas fell roughly between the situations in New Mexico and California.

The best estimates show that Texas recognized that Spain or Mexico had granted about 15 percent of its land, roughly twenty-six million acres (10,400,000 hectares), to private owners before it achieved independence in 1836. The bulk of these acres lay in south Texas. For the most part they comprised missions, private *ranchos,* and pueblo municipal grants, as in California.

Settlement patterns along the south-running San Antonio River and its tributaries in the area of present-day San Antonio show how Hispanic settlement in Texas developed and changed. The Hispanic presence began early in the eighteenth century with the establishment of a military *presidio.* Five California-style Franciscan missions followed. As in California, the Texas missions owned the lands on which the mission proper was situated and controlled settlement of the public land surrounding them for the benefit of Indian settlers. The San Antonio River missions dotted the river from south to north like beads on a string. At the north end of the string sat San Antonio de Béxar, a military *presidio* established in 1718 that started to grow into a non-Indian civil community beginning in 1731 with the arrival of the first immigrants from the Canary Islands. The non-Indian municipality grew through the eighteenth century, pressing against the church-administered lands to the south. With the secularization of mission lands beginning in 1794, San Antonio absorbed first administrative control over mission lands and water, and then actual control of the lands. By the time Texas declared independence in 1836, non-Indians owned the land and the water of the river.

Thus landholding patterns in south Texas developed along lines similar to those in California and New Mexico. However, Texas did develop a unique form of land grant, the empresario grant. These grants were authorized by Mexican national and state law after 1821, primarily for the purpose of securing national borders by populating them.

The often huge empresario grant was made to a principal contractor who was required to bring others to settle on the grant and was authorized to convey title to these settlers. As his reward, the contractor received a generous bounty of land. Thousands of Americans emigrated to south Texas between 1836 and 1848 and took up lands offered by empresario contractors like Stephen F. Austin. However, most empresario grants in Texas were not fully settled when sovereignty changed.

CONCLUSION

Across the borderlands, the forms of Hispanic landholding varied. Each region had its distinctive forms. The size, purpose, and ownership of land created by the Mexican and Spanish sovereigns differed in critical ways in Florida, Texas, New Mexico, and California. The rich tapestry of Hispanic land use that the United States inherited when it finally acquired sovereignty was born of differences in topography, in climate, in remoteness, and in tenacity of local settlers. But the tapestry shared a common heritage which came directly from the Spanish and Mexican goal of securing property by settling it.

BIBLIOGRAPHY

Bannon, John Francis. *Spanish Borderlands Frontier, 1513–1821.* New York, 1970; Albuquerque, N. Mex., 1974. Provides the best starting point for understanding the general background of the various land policies.

Barker, Eugene C. *Life of Stephen F. Austin, Founder of Texas, 1793–1836.* Dallas, Tex., and Nashville, Tenn., 1925; 2nd ed. Austin, Tex., 1969. This work remains so influential that writers use Austin's land dealings to understand Texas land policies.

Engstrand, Iris H. W. "An Enduring Legacy: California Ranchos in Historical Perspective." In *Spanish and Mexican Land Grants and the Law,* edited by Malcolm Ebright. Manhattan, Kans., 1989. A short, elegant essay on the development of private land grants in California.

Hall, G. Emlen. *Four Leagues of Pecos: A Legal History of the Pecos Grant, 1800–1933.* Albuquerque,

N. Mex., 1984. A detailed study whose first two chapters cover the relationship of Indian and non-Indian land policies in pre–United States New Mexico.

Hutchinson, Cecil Alan. *Frontier Settlement in Mexican California: The Hijar-Padres Colony and Its Origins, 1769–1835*. New Haven, Conn., 1969. A carefully researched, broadly focused case study of land settlement in Mexican California.

Miller, Thomas Lloyd. *The Public Lands of Texas, 1519–1970*. Norman, Okla., 1972. A useful but mechanical presentation of the special and basic role of land in Texas. The first two chapters deal with colonial landholding patterns.

Servín, Manuel P. "The Secularization of the California Missions: A Reappraisal." *Southern California Quarterly* 47 (June 1965):133–149. A clear statement of the role of California missions in land settlement policies.

Simmons, Marc. "Settlement Patterns and Village Plans in Colonial New Mexico." *Journal of the West* 8 (January 1969):7–21. An elegant essay by New Mexico's preeminent historian which shows how much actual settlement in New Mexico varied from the formal legal requirements of colonial law.

Tebeau, Charlton W. *A History of Florida*. Coral Gables, Fla., 1971. Still the best account of landholding in Florida prior to 1821, against the background of the area's general history.

Weber, David J. *The Mexican Frontier, 1821–1846: The American Southwest Under Mexico*. Albuquerque, N. Mex., 1982. A marvelous general study of California, New Mexico, and Texas during the critical last years of pre–United States rule. Much of the book necessarily focuses on land.

Westphall, Victor. *Mercedes Reales: Hispanic Land Grants of the Upper Rio Grande Region*. Albuquerque, N. Mex., 1983. The basic reference work on land grants in the heavily settled area between Socorro and Taos, New Mexico.

G. Emlen Hall

SEE ALSO **Farming, Planting, and Ranching; Gender Relations; Marriage; Rural Life;** and **Settlements in the Spanish Borderlands.**

FARMING, PLANTING, AND RANCHING

THE BRITISH COLONIES

PRODUCTION IN EARLY rural America was organized by households. Farming, planting, and ranching were undertaken by husband, wife, and older children, and those paid or forced to work for the family. There were exceptions, of course. In the early seventeenth century, many households, especially in the southern colonies, were headed by single men, and increasingly in the eighteenth century, single women managed rural households. Moreover, on the coastal rice plantations of the Carolinas and Georgia and on the largest tobacco plantations of the Chesapeake, the scale of operations and, in some cases, the physical separation of slave laborers from the owner's household, created a distinctive agricultural regime. These exceptions acknowledged, however, we begin by noting that most early American farming was undertaken by families and that the farm household was the basic unit of production in the rural economy.

Householders farmed with three goals in mind: to meet the food and clothing needs of the family; to provide an inheritance that would sustain the family over generations; and to earn profit. As a rule subsistence, family, and profit were not conflicting goals. Buying land, for example, provided arable land or pasture to meet immediate needs as well as creating an asset that could be "banked," improved, or rented, and then turned over to children. In fact only the largest farms and plantations, those most thoroughly involved in commercial agriculture, had the resources and labor to provide most things that a farm family needed. What these large farmers did by choice, others did of necessity; only by buying and selling could they clothe and feed their families fully.

Farming changed over the life cycle of a family. Young families often lacked the resources and labor to meet all their own needs. Men sold their crops and labor for food, clothing, and household goods, while young mothers, when they could, took on help to watch children, do washing, or prepare food. With time families accumulated capital—cattle, improved acreage, and farm implements—and young children grew, took on household responsibilities, and were hired out to add to family income. Laborers could be hired at harvest time to help with a commercial crop or to assist in craft work. In later years both production and labor needs diminished as land and livestock were turned over to children. Agriculture in the southern staple colonies modified this pattern, primarily by creating a greater reliance on dependent labor, but did not eliminate it.

While labor in the rural economy of early America was defined by sex and age, women and men often worked at separate tasks in the same process, and when challenged by necessity, sex roles became blurred. Men did field work and usually managed livestock, but women ground corn, worked with flax, made butter, and preserved meat. At harvest time wives might work in the fields with their husbands; other responsibilities, such as tending gardens, fell almost entirely to women. Servant and slave women were usually expected to do the same field work as their male counterparts and had less opportunity to escape such drudgery by acquiring craft skills.

The discussion that follows begins with Native American agriculture and then surveys farming, planting, and ranching by region. A regional approach emphasizes staple agriculture and production for the market, for it was the combination of crop specialization and labor systems that made regions distinctive. Within each section, however, analysis of the raising of crops and livestock focuses on the farm household, and while distinctions among households and changes over time are suggested, the overall picture tends to be static. Only by keeping in mind both aspects of early American agriculture—the dynamic development of staple economies and the repetitive process by which farm households sustained and reproduced themselves—will the picture seem complete. More generally, once a particular aspect of farming, planting, and ranching has been discussed in one region, that discussion is not repeated unless there is a particular need to do so; thus, for example, flax was grown everywhere, but the processing of the plant is only described for the middle colonies.

NATIVE AMERICAN AGRICULTURE

Native American agricultural practices were as diverse as the peoples themselves and the ecological systems of which they were a part. But viewed broadly there were at least four aspects of Indian agriculture that were fundamentally important to most Native peoples of the Atlantic Coastal Plain and that contrasted sharply with the practices of the European invaders of North America: the seasonal relationship of hunting to cultivation; the sexual division of labor; the reliance on corn, pumpkins, and beans as basic food crops; and the absence of domesticated farm animals (and, less critically, metal farm implements).

Native Americans lived both by hunting and gathering and by cultivating food crops. Hunting was men's work, gathering predominantly women's, and both activities carried Indian peoples through the winter months. Cultivation was a warm weather activity; it was women's work, though men helped clear fields. Men exerted themselves periodically: on the hunt; at warfare; and in constructing buildings. Women labored continuously: making pottery and baskets; cooking food; tending gardens; planting crops; gathering roots, nuts, berries, and oysters; and minding children. Hunting provided meat for food, fur for clothing, and bones for tools; deer, bear, and buffalo as well as smaller game animals were all hunted. In deer hunting men would often set large semicircular fires to force the deer toward the waiting hunters, who could then kill them more readily at close range. Similarly in fishing, weirs and creek dams were used to trap and collect large numbers of fish at one time. In short, efficiency was valued as much as skill.

Agriculture was a part of Native American life but hardly the dominant activity it was for Europeans. Men used slash-and-burn techniques to clear Indian fields: underbrush was burned away; trees were slashed with stone implements, then burned, and then slashed again. Hardwoods might resist the technique, but once their branches fell, there was ample sunlight to plant between dying trees. After being cropped several years, fields could be abandoned to "forest fallow," the village moved, and the process repeated, although many Indian peoples, especially in the Southeast, cultivated their crops in rich river-bottom lands that could be cropped almost continuously without serious loss of yields. Women cultivated with what Europeans called hoes, mattocks, and spades made of wood, stone, and bone. They had no metal tools and no domesticated animals to help with cultivation. The basic crops were corn, beans, and squash; corn was planted in hills, beans allowed to grow up the corn stalks, and squash put in between the rows. Women and children weeded, picked, husked, and ground the corn and prepared an enormous variety of different foods from this relatively simple crop mix.

Once the European invasion of North America began, Indians generally survived best by keeping Old World settlers at a distance, with purposeful contact limited to trade and warfare. Settlers, however, adopted Indian crops, slash-and-burn techniques, and hoe culture (for few brought plows and harrows with them); they appropriated Indian fields; and they forced Indians into slavery and servitude. In the eighteenth century, some Indian peoples (the Iroquois and Cherokee, among others) absorbed European agricultural ways: small grains; plow culture; domesticated livestock; and new work roles for women and men.

THE CHESAPEAKE

In 1606 the English Crown chartered two Virginia companies, one that would eventually undertake the Pilgrim settlement of Plymouth colony, the other, based in London, that almost immediately began the exploration and exploitation of the Chesapeake Bay region. The colony the company established in 1607 at Jamestown, on the James River in the lower Chesapeake Bay, barely survived—disease, malnutrition, lack of supplies from England, and terrible retribution in 1622 from the Powhatan Indians for years of mistreatment and misunderstanding each took their toll of the settler population. It seems fair to say that the Virginia colonists did a poorer job of establishing an agriculturally viable outpost in the New World than any subsequent settler population.

The introduction of tobacco (a Native American crop, the first commercially successful variety of which in the Chesapeake came from West Indian seeds) did not end these troubles, but it saved the settlement. In 1617 the company shipped the first crop to England; extraordinarily high prices relative to any other agricultural product caused a rapid extension of planting and lured growing numbers of colonists to the James River settlement. The subsequent agricultural history of the Chesapeake went through three stages. The first lasted until the late seventeenth century and was the era of the small planter. Field work was done primarily by householders and indentured servants. Settlement and tobacco culture spread up the bay, moving inland along its five great fingers—the James, York,

Rappahannock, Potomac, and Patuxent rivers—and, more gradually, along the Eastern Shore. Population, fueled mostly by immigration, and that predominantly male, grew from some eight thousand people in 1640 in Virginia and the new colony of Maryland (settled in 1634) to about sixty thousand in 1680.

The second stage of Chesapeake agricultural history, lasting from the late seventeenth to the mid eighteenth century, witnessed the transition from servant to slave labor, the rise of a gentry class, and the creation of large-scale agricultural units. By mid century the Chesapeake's white population had increased, primarily through natural population growth, to more than 200,000 and its black population to more than 150,000. This population surge pushed tobacco cultivation from the tidewater into the Virginia Piedmont. The diversification of commercial agriculture marked the third stage of Chesapeake development. Wheat became an important second crop along the upper Eastern Shore and in northern Maryland as well as in some of the older tidewater counties of Virginia. Perhaps even more critically, the flow of settlers south from the mid Atlantic into the Maryland Piedmont and down the Shenandoah Valley in Virginia created an economy of small farms, mixed grain-livestock husbandry, and thriving commercial towns. Overall in the thirty years after mid century, both white and black populations doubled in number.

Two institutions, found throughout the colonies but of crucial importance in the Chesapeake, shaped the initial development of Chesapeake agriculture: the headright system and indentured servitude. The first was the policy of granting to anyone who transported himself or someone else to a colony the right to patent a certain number of unclaimed acres. Headrights were thus an incentive not only to settle but also to pay the cost of bringing others, too poor to pay their own way, to Virginia or Maryland. Poor immigrants were primarily servants. Most signed contracts, or indentures, in England agreeing to work a specified number of years (usually four to five) in the colonies in return for free passage and "freedom dues" when their terms expired. Headrights and indentured servitude underwrote the development of small tobacco farms throughout the seventeenth-century Chesapeake.

On such farms (called plantations), the agricultural regime revolved around the planting of corn and tobacco. In mid winter planters, their servants, and slaves prepared tobacco seedbeds using mulch to protect the young plants once they sprouted. In March hoe work began in the fields; hills (but not yet seeds) for both corn and tobacco were spaced evenly along parallel rows; and time allowing, perhaps some English grains were sown. In early spring workers seeded corn. When the plants appeared, they were thinned and thoroughly weeded several times. The weeding gave way to tobacco work, however, as spring lengthened. In late May the arduous task (done, ideally, during rainy weather) of transplanting the tobacco seedlings to the prepared fields had to commence if the crop were to be picked before fall frost. Young tobacco also required several weedings, as well as "topping" and "priming"—removing top and bottom leaves to enrich the remaining ones—and repeated inspections ("worming") for insect infestation. Spring, then, was a period of almost continuous, strenuous field work in which the planter's own labor and the labor he could compel or cajole from servants and slaves set absolute limits on the size of his crop.

In late summer planters cut the tobacco stalks; cutting at the right time, when the leaves were fully ripe but before frost ruined them, was crucial to the quality of the crop. The leaves were then allowed to dry or cure, first on the ground and then hung by the stalk in a tobacco house—an airy barn that was one of the most distinctive signposts of the rural landscape that English settlers created in the Chesapeake. After drying, the leaves were packed in hogsheads, which by the eighteenth century were of fairly standard dimensions and which weighed, when "prized" (pressed and sealed with a lever), upwards of one thousand pounds (450 kilograms). Hogsheads were rolled or dragged to the riverside and loaded on waiting vessels destined for English or Scottish ports. While workers proceeded to bring in the tobacco crop and prepare it for shipment, laborers also picked corn and stored it in a barn or "corn house" and harvested any other grains that had been cultivated. They then turned their attention to clearing new land, cutting firewood for the winter, and repairing fencing before the cycle began anew.

In the seventeenth century, hoe cultivation and the corn-tobacco cycle dominated the agricultural routine on Chesapeake plantations. Unlike in England servant women might work in the fields and some farm wives, on farms without other workers, probably did as well. Other traditional tasks were abandoned or altered by the new routines: livestock were not fenced in; instead fields were fenced to keep livestock out, and cattle and swine were allowed to forage in the woods. Few households had spinning wheels, cider presses, or butter churns; virtually none had looms. Clothes were presumably washed occasionally, but there is little evidence in Chesapeake probate records of how it was done. Pounding corn with mortar and pestle for several hours a day, milking half-wild Chesapeake cows, cooking for husband and servants, and minding small children wore down housewives and left little time for household production.

In the century or so before the American Revolution, two major changes occurred in Chesapeake agriculture: crop and craft diversification and the transition from servitude to slavery. The first "domesticated" the Chesapeake and made farming more like that in England and the northern colonies; the second fundamentally altered the social context in which that farming occurred. Diversification had several causes. As a society of predominantly male immigrants was replaced by one of family farmers, the demand for food increased; simultaneously, falling tobacco prices, and more critically, the periodic disruption of the tobacco trade by the Atlantic wars endemic to the era, directed land and labor to other pursuits; finally, well before the wheat boom of the mid eighteenth century, a growing demand for corn, meat, and timber in the West Indies provided alternatives to exclusive reliance on tobacco as a cash crop. Diversification appeared in a number of ways: a wider diffusion of craft skills; the extension of more time and acreage to orchards; the acquisition of tools for spinning, churning, butchering, and the like; and the cultivation of a wider range of crops in the Chesapeake.

In the late seventeenth century, tidewater tobacco planters began to substitute slaves for indentured servants in their labor force. English women and men had long been race conscious, and they came from a culture that had overworked and brutalized dependent laborers; moreover the English had already built the West Indian sugar economy by literally working African slaves to death, and West Indian merchants had long shipped Afro-Barbadian slaves in small numbers to all the mainland colonies, including Maryland and Virginia. What distinguished the late seventeenth century was not the introduction of slavery, which was already present, but the creation of a new system of labor. As the supply of servants dwindled, planters turned to slaves and began receiving direct, large importations from Africa. First through importation, then through natural population growth, the number of blacks in Maryland and Virginia increased rapidly. By the time of the American Revolution, about half the population of both the tidewater and Piedmont was black, and because slave women worked alongside men in the fields, blacks made up far more than half of the agricultural labor force.

The contributions to early American agriculture made by Africans adapting their own agricultural experience to new crops, a changed environment, and the system of coerced labor imposed upon them are extremely difficult to document. Even as historians piece together a picture of how blacks lived and labored on tobacco and rice plantations, the question of how much this experience was African remains.

English and, in the early seventeenth century, Dutch traders brought slaves to North America from the Caribbean and from numerous trading regions on Africa's west coast: Senegambia, the Windward Coast, the Gold Coast, the Bight of Biafra, and Angola, among the most prominent. In each of these regions, Africans from numerous ethnic groups were sold into slavery. The agricultural practices (crops grown, methods of cultivation, sexual division of labor, and the like) of these groups might differ substantially. Rice, cotton, indigo, and millet were all grown in West Africa. Hoe culture, practiced in Africa, would prevail in rice and tobacco fields instead of English plow culture. Some of the tools slaves used they fashioned themselves from African designs, and some of the plants they cultivated in their own garden plots were of African origin. Working to the rhythms of the agricultural clock, celebrating the harvest, and using fires to clear new lands were all part of the Afri-

can (as well as the English and the Native American) experience. It would be well to keep these facts in mind without ignoring how new crops, a new environment, and coercive white power reshaped the black world of agricultural labor.

After the transition to slavery, Chesapeake agriculture was carried out on larger units than were common in the mid Atlantic and New England, but smaller than units on the Carolina rice coast. The typical plantation was about two hundred acres (80 hectares), and the typical slaveowner owned three or four adult slaves. About half of all householders did not own slaves, and an equal percentage did not own land. Tenancy, then, was common, and after mid century it was not uncommon for tenants to own slaves. Livestock holdings were, on average, large: several dozen swine; more than a dozen cattle; a half-dozen horses; and two dozen sheep.

The pattern of slave and land ownership in the 1730s in Talbot County, on Maryland's Eastern Shore, provides some sense of what these averages meant across an entire population in a long-settled, tidewater tobacco county. The county had over sixteen hundred free, taxable residents; approximately half were householders, and approximately half of them owned land. Two of every five landowners owned slaves. Half of the landowners owned less than two hundred acres (80 hectares), and one in nine owned over one thousand acres (400 hectares). One slaveowner in nine owned at least ten adult slaves, while more than four out of five held five or fewer adult slaves. Talbot County had its great planters, families that owed much of their wealth to mercantile activity, but most farming was done by tenants, landowners without slaves, and owners of a small number of slaves.

If the Chesapeake remained an agricultural regime of small farms and modest plantations, it did have a gentry class, and wealth, land, and slave ownership was concentrated in the hands of gentry families. More than the scale of their undertakings distinguished the way the gentry farmed: they negotiated with their overseers and, occasionally, with their slaves, but seldom did field labor themselves. They not only grew a greater variety of crops than their lesser neighbors, they experimented with new cropping systems and new techniques. Their holdings were generally scattered over several counties, each "quarter" with a resident slave population. To the dwelling house, kitchen, and tobacco barn found on most plantations, they added milk houses, smokehouses, and corn houses, and in building their homes they replaced wood with brick. While they bought European goods readily from English merchants, they could produce virtually everything they needed for self-sufficiency on their own plantations. And with the flexibility that control over land, labor, and credit gave them, they led the effort to diversify market production and find new outlets for their crops.

In the mid eighteenth century, the Chesapeake tobacco economy was modified in two ways, one directed by the gentry, the other by new settlers moving down through the Maryland Piedmont to the Shenandoah Valley. In many regions of the tidewater, wheat farming complemented tobacco production. Stimulated by demand in southern Europe, wheat prices rose significantly, and first large planters, then ordinary farmers, began growing grain commercially. If planters had enough land, they could grow wheat without seriously cutting back on tobacco production; commercial grain cultivation nonetheless brought change to Chesapeake agriculture: land had to be conserved more carefully and fertilized more thoroughly; crop rotation schemes had to be followed more systematically; hired labor was needed at harvest time; and plows, harrows, wagons, and the like were added to the stock of tools in a household. Wheat processing provided opportunities for rural craft workers to earn a living and stimulated the development of numerous trading towns.

The settlement of the Shenandoah Valley created a mixed grain-livestock economy. As in the tidewater, farmers looked to wheat for a profitable market crop, and as in the east, a network of towns sprang up to handle wheat processing and crafts linked to diversified farming. Unlike in the east, slavery had not gained too great a foothold by the time of the American Revolution. Hemp production also flourished in the Piedmont and the valley, albeit briefly, as an alternative to wool and flax, from which coarse but serviceable clothing could be made. (The processing of hemp was similar to that of flax, which is discussed in some detail below.) As war with Britain approached, the Chesapeake suggested two futures for American agriculture: one, in the tidewater, of slavery and staple crops; the other, in the valley, of mixed farming and family labor. Yet in both production was organized by households, and householders farmed for personal use, local exchange, and the export market.

NEW ENGLAND

The settlement of some hundred colonists, most of them English Separatists (the Pilgrims), at Plymouth in the winter of 1620 created the first permanent English agricultural society in what would eventually be known as New England. Ten years later the great Puritan migration established the Massachusetts Bay colony, and in the difficult and hectic years from 1630 to 1643, some twenty thousand English men and women would arrive. The steady pulse of immigration pushed the center of settlement from Cape Ann to Cambridge, and then Boston, and led to the establishment of secondary, inland towns, first around Boston, then in the rich Connecticut River valley. Eventually branches of the Puritan tree would stretch throughout Connecticut, south to eastern Long Island and East Jersey, and north to what would become Maine and New Hampshire; meanwhile religious dissension within the Puritan fold would lead to the settlement of Narragansett Bay and eventually to the establishment of Rhode Island. In the mid eighteenth century, after the British expulsion of French settlers from Acadia (Nova Scotia), New England "planters" would recolonize the Maritimes. Fed initially by immigration but sustained by high birth rates and long life expectancy, the population of New England rose to twenty-three thousand by mid century, to some ninety thousand by the end of the century, and to more than half a million by the time of the American Revolution.

Bay colony Puritans were as concerned about the economic viability of their undertaking as were the organizers of the initial English effort to settle the Chesapeake Bay region, and the early settlers quickly established with England and the West Indies commercial links that served the region well through the outbreak of war in the 1770s. Furs, timber, and fish could all be harvested bountifully in New England and brought good returns to those with the capital to exploit such resources. The day-to-day life of ordinary farm families in New England, however, was probably less oriented toward export agriculture than in any of the colonies to the south, and family and community food requirements probably took up more time. Puritans clearly placed salvation above profit, and Puritan towns regulated economic behavior in the name of community welfare, but neither religion nor regulation clearly constrained the desire to improve and develop farmland. Rather, in the long run a short growing season, rocky soil, and plant diseases restricted agricultural options and shaped a farm life which was different from that of other regions of British North America.

Much of New England was settled in townships. The colonial government or the English Crown made land grants of several square miles to a group of proprietors rather than to individual settlers. The proprietors were essentially entrepreneurs, men with the capital to underwrite settlement and a willingness to take economic risks for profit; some were speculators who never took up residence in towns they founded. The proprietors, in turn, parceled out home lots, tillage (arable) plots, and the meadowlands among themselves, with new allotments sometimes spaced over two or more generations. Pasture land was, in contrast, often held and fenced in common. In some cases, settlement was tightly nucleated; in others, settlers dispersed. Initial allotments were generally small, on the order of from ten to thirty acres (4 to 12 hectares), and individual holdings were often fragmented (especially in nucleated townships), with upland fields being some distance from home lots. Farmers, accordingly, left home for their fields in the morning and returned when their work was done. Town meetings (in which all the proprietors, but not necessarily all residents, participated) regulated critical aspects of agricultural life—the shape of fields, the crops that were to be planted, the dates on which sowing or harvesting began—and imposed on inhabitants collective responsibilities for such tasks as cleaning woods, fencing fields, killing predators, and building roads.

Over time the communal character of new towns was modified in two important ways. Small groups of settlers would break off from the original settlement and move away, often to a location promising more ample tidal or river marsh grass for their cattle or more fertile arable fields.

Towns became collections of neighborhoods, often with individual taverns (ordinaries) and churches. But this fragmentation was, in fact, part of a more general pattern of individualizing economic resources and decision making. Proprietary rights were bought and sold, holdings concentrated, common pasture divided, and communal responsibilities abandoned. New England towns long remained tightly knit social units, but in agricultural life most farmers made their own decisions about their own land.

The preeminent crop of the first New England townships was Indian corn, or maize. Maize was easy to cultivate, produced a higher food value per acre than the grains that settlers knew in Europe, and ripened early, which was particularly important after a long, cold winter had depleted food reserves. Not surprisingly, when immigrants acquired the crop from North America's Native inhabitants, they also adopted their method of planting. Corn was planted among the stumps of girdled trees on fields burned clear of underbrush; seeds were distributed in rows, from five to six feet (1.5 to 1.8 meters) apart in both directions, hoed in several inches deep, four or five seeds to one spot. When the plants were a hand's height, weeds were hoed out and a hill of dirt built up around the base of the stalk to secure the roots and support the growing plant. Fish were used to enrich the soil, beans planted alongside the corn so that the veins could climb the stalks, and pumpkins and squash set between the rows, their foliage helping control weeds. Until harvesting little more needed to be done.

As farmers built up a stock of traditional farm implements, methods of corn cultivation changed. In older settlements the practice was to plow perpendicular rows, harrow over, cross plow again, and then plant seeds at the hilly intersections. Subsequent light plowing through the rows killed the weeds and built up the hills as the young plants grew. Picking and husking were work for farm boys or the occasion for a neighborhood "frolic" that might extend well into the night until the last ears were shucked. Little was wasted; stalks and husks were set aside as cattle fodder. Over time, however, corn cultivation took a toll from New England's soil. A remarkably productive crop, corn also drew more nutrients from the land than other grains; the problem was compounded by allowing cattle to feed in corn fields on the residual vegetation that might otherwise have served to reinvigorate the soil.

While relying on corn, settlers, not surprisingly, tried to replicate the husbandry with which they were familiar in England. Along with corn they planted the basic English grains, wheat and rye, as well as some barley and oats. Based on English experience, wheat seemed to offer the best possibilities as a market crop, but neither the climate nor the soil in New England were particularly favorable to cultivation. Even more seriously, Europeans introduced the black stem-rust fungus, known as the wheat blast, along with the crop, and by the 1660s the fungus had begun its attack on the New England crop. Nonetheless many farmers grew some wheat up through the revolution, and in regions such as the Connecticut River valley merchants accumulated enough from small producers to do a sizable export business. Shifting cultivation north and west to lands previously unaffected by the blast (and, of course, where the soil was less worn), planting in late autumn when the fungus seemed to disappear, and eradicating bayberry bushes, which were thought by some to contribute to the blast, all probably helped a little. (Much later agriculturalists discovered that the bayberry hosted the fungus, whose spores were borne by the wind to wheat fields.) In the mid eighteenth century, wheat cultivation received a last and almost fatal blow from the Hessian fly, which was brought to Long Island and spread quickly to Connecticut.

In most places rye did better than wheat. With corn it was the chief source of bread in New England households, often mixed with wheat to create maslin. New England housewives baked muffins and biscuits directly on the hearth and baked loaves in small ovens built in the back of fireplaces. The ovens were heated by allowing a fire to burn down and raking out the coals. Dough made from flour, warm water, and yeast was set near the fire to rise, kneaded, shaped into loaves, and then baked in the heated oven; if the process sounds similar to bread making today it was, but it also required considerably more skill to stoke and regulate the fire and to time each step in the process. Grain was also the source of a family's beer; while some towns had brewers, more often housewives brewed beer

themselves from barley, drawing off enough foam from the fermenting mash to supply yeast for their bread making. What stands out in these processes is the way in which the work of husband, wife, and community were integrated: men sowed and (often with the aid of wife and children) harvested the crops; the miller turned grain into flour; and women baked and brewed.

To virtually every New England farm family, livestock mattered as much as grain. In an economy where labor was expensive, land cheap, and at least initially, natural grasses in coastal and river marshes abundant, raising livestock made sense. At first, of course, there were more English settlers than farm animals in New England, as ships carried more people than cattle, swine, or sheep to Plymouth and then to the Massachusetts Bay colony. But flocks and herds built up quickly, and after the great migration ended in the early 1640s, there was little reason to import more livestock. In established towns almost every farm had several cattle and most had a few swine. In coastal areas and on islands where meadow land had been cleared of undergrowth and where predators had been eliminated, flocks of ten to twenty sheep were not uncommon.

In some seventeenth-century New England villages, livestock management was a cooperative endeavor. The town hired a cowherd or shepherd to collect the village animals each morning, drive them to pasture, and return them in the evening to individual owners. To expedite the manuring of arable fields, the village flock might be left overnight on an individual holding and then, through the use of movable fencing, shifted to a different proprietor's tillage land when the shepherd returned the animals from the pasture the next evening. Fencing was crucial, not only for manuring but more generally, both to keep animals away from predators in the forests and to protect crops, and so maintaining fencing was a collective village responsibility. In regard to sheep, this collective concern could extend to the colony as a whole. Legislation encouraged sheep raising by providing tax rebates, by mandating the clearing of brush on pasture lands so sheep could graze more freely, and even by requiring sheep raising. Swine were the exception; in new settlements, they were allowed to roam freely to grub nuts from the forests and shellfish along the coast. Large, strong, and lean, a tusked boar was a match for New England's wolves.

Both contemporary observers and modern historians have taken early America's free-roaming swine as a symbol of a more general inattention among farm families to the care and improvement of livestock. They have stated that stock breeding was done with little concern for quality; animals were left outdoors during harsh winters; too much reliance was placed on natural grasses, and too little effort went into creating artificial meadows. The result, they have claimed, was the perpetuation of scrawny livestock: sheep with short, coarse fleece and cows that gave considerably less milk than they might have. If there is truth in this analysis, much of it can be explained in terms of the land and labor conditions in New England, but in fact historians have not done the research necessary to provide an adequate answer.

What can be established is that plowing grain fields, felling timber for homes and fencing, and cattle grazing seriously eroded New England's farmland, and that before the revolution efforts to reverse the process were not particularly successful. On the coast and along rivers, farmers fertilized with fish, and by the eighteenth century cow and sheep dung were used regularly, and ashes occasionally—but application was not systematic, nor was the supply adequate. Crude crop rotation schemes—alternating planting with fallow periods—remained the rule, and when in the mid eighteenth century nitrogen-rich English grasses were purposely introduced into the rotation, early spring grazing (because the land did not supply enough hay to see livestock through the winter) could negate much of the benefit. Still, sowing English grasses, such as clover, and Herd's grass (timothy) on tilled uplands, harvesting the hay, and using it to fatten cattle brought some farmers productivity gains that translated into more food and greater profits from careful livestock management.

In late fall or early winter, the family slaughtered the livestock it needed for food; hogs, steers, and lambs had to be killed (usually with a knife), soaked in hot water and skinned, cut in sections, and then preserved by soaking the meat in brine; once salted, pork was often hung and smoked. From the entrails to the skin, virtu-ally the entire animal was put to some use. At slaughtering time day laborers might be hired on to assist a family, but wives and husbands were as likely to do the work themselves.

How viable and how productive were New England farms? The literature on early New England abounds with depictions of what the "typical" farm family was like, but as necessary as such descriptions are, they can hide as much as they illuminate. One would like to know, for example, not only the average number of livestock on a typical farm, but how many families had insufficient cattle, swine, and sheep to supply their food and clothing needs, and how many had enough to market surplus meat and wool. Unfortunately such questions cannot be fully answered, but at least some suggestions can be made.

The town of Concord lay in an intensely farmed area of eastern Massachusetts where production was stimulated by the demand of coastal seaports for grain and livestock. In 1771 Concord had some 273 taxpayers, three-fourths of whom were landowning farmers. (Most of the rest, presumably, were agricultural laborers.) On average, landowners held fifty-seven acres (23 hectares), about one-fourth of which was devoted to tillage. Again on average, taxpayers held one horse, three oxen, four adult cows (three years of age or older), two pigs, and six sheep. But only one owner in twenty had ten or more cows; one in three farmers did not own oxen, one in four did not own a horse, and one in two did not own sheep. These deficiencies were undoubtedly handled by local exchange: at plowing time those without oxen hired plows and teams to work the soil, paying with their own labor and crops as often as with cash. Annual grain production was approximately ninety bushels per farmer, well above the minimum a family needed for subsistence (perhaps twenty bushels for a family of four), and thus many farms had a sizable surplus to market or exchange locally. But even in an agriculturally rich town like Concord, small farmers had to purchase some of the grain, meat, or wool that they needed.

Land in Massachusetts's Connecticut River valley towns was not as productive as the fields of Concord. Productivity, evaluated in the 1771 Massachusetts tax valuation, was only from six to nine bushels per acre, below the colonywide median of ten bushels per acre, but farmers compensated by devoting a significantly higher percentage of their land to grain crops. The result was large yields, marketable surpluses—on which the agricultural fame of the valley rested—and correspondingly smaller livestock holdings (two cows and one ox per farm). But here as elsewhere in Massachusetts, many farms were viable not in the sense of producing all that a farm family needed, but rather because farm members could work for others to pay for what they did not have the resources to produce themselves. In the colony as a whole, using the baseline of twenty acres (8 hectares) of improved land as the minimum needed to sustain a farm family, almost half of Massachusetts farmers in 1771 did not have adequate acreage. Half of this group had neither oxen nor horses for farm work; nearly half had no arable land, or no pasture, or no meadow (or lacked more than one); and about one-third had no sows, boars, or pigs.

Farming appears to have been more prosperous in Connecticut than in Massachusetts. The typical farm was over one hundred acres (40 hectares), and by the revolutionary era perhaps half that acreage was improved. Such a farm had thirteen cattle, three horses, seven pigs, and sixteen sheep, and the distribution of livestock suggests that a greater percentage of Connecticut than Massachusetts farmers were able both to meet subsistence requirements and to market surpluses. More than nine out of ten farmers had at least five cattle, and one in five had at least twenty; two out of five had twenty sheep or more (and one in five had none); and two out of three had at least five swine. Average yields per acre were seven bushels for wheat, ten for corn, and five for rye—figures similar to but a little lower than those in Massachusetts (remembering that Massachusetts figures were primarily for corn). What the Connecticut data, drawn from probate records, makes clear is that most farmers who lacked the land or farm animals to meet subsistence requirements were young, and that trading labor for food, wool, or the use of oxen was an expected stage in the life cycle of rural inhabitants. As significant as regional variations appear to historians—and they had their consequences, especially in the export trade—there was a fundamental texture to farming in early America that varied little as one moved from colony to colony.

THE MIDDLE COLONIES

At first glance the mid Atlantic seems to have had less regional identity than New England or the Chesapeake; its diversity was, in fact, its defining characteristic. A product of Dutch settlement in New York, Swedish settlement in the lower Delaware Valley, Quaker proprietary undertakings in Pennsylvania and West Jersey, and Puritan expansion into Long Island and East Jersey, the mid Atlantic continued to attract immigrants from throughout Europe, especially Germans and Scotch-Irish, until the outbreak of the American Revolution. The most urban and the most industrial region of early America, the mid Atlantic was a many-colored quilt in which each of its distinctive farming communities was only a part of a larger pattern. Yet there was another sense in which the separate parts were tightly stitched together: family farming and the mix of livestock raising and grain cultivation so familiar to the rural population of Western Europe flourished in this, "the best poor man's country." Market agriculture underwrote a gradual improvement of rural life and helped fuel the dynamic commercial growth of Baltimore, Wilmington, Philadelphia, and New York City.

A region of no more than six thousand European settlers as late as 1660, most of them in New York, the mid Atlantic had more than fifty thousand inhabitants by 1700 as the Quakers organized the settlement of West Jersey and Pennsylvania. Four decades later the population had grown to over two hundred thousand and had reached more than half a million when the revolution began. But such figures are somewhat deceptive; the boundaries of the mid Atlantic were not static but dynamic as its produce flowed down the Susquehanna and through northern Maryland to Baltimore's mills and wharves, and its people moved down the Shenandoah Valley, lured by generous land grants. On distant backcountry farms as well as on prosperous homesteads a day's wagon trip from Philadelphia and New York, mid-eighteenth-century farm families made the mid Atlantic the wheat belt of early America.

While the mixed livestock-grain husbandry of the mid Atlantic was similar to that in New England, several distinctive aspects of mid-Atlantic farm life require comment. Cultural geographers have noted that various settler groups shaped the rural landscape in particular ways; barns were built, cheeses flavored, and fences constructed following practices that originated in Holland, the Rhine Valley, and northern Ireland, as well as in England. It is much less clear whether cultural heritage shaped the way in which fields were cultivated or the choice of crops. The mid Atlantic was also the site of large manorial estates in the Hudson River valley; such estates were not entirely unique, for there were also manors of a sort in Maryland, and the families that occupied manor lands were more like independent householders than feudal tenants. Nevertheless the concentration of tenancy in the valley contradicts the notions that most northern farming was carried out by freeholders.

Perhaps a more critical distinction between New England and mid Atlantic farming was the greater reliance on dependent farm laborers in the latter region. Unlike in New England, where most agricultural laborers were boys or young men awaiting their inheritance of land or livestock, rural laborers in the middle colonies were more likely to be permanently dependent. Wealthy farmers owned slaves and bought indentured servants, and most middling householders regularly used wage laborers. After mid century cottagers (families who survived by negotiating yearly work arrangements that brought them a home, garden, perhaps a little pasture land for a sheep or cow, and occasionally other "privileges") were found on more and more farms, and tenancy became increasingly common. Slaves never constituted more than 10 percent of the work force, and ownership concentrated in certain areas (on Long Island, in the Dutch areas of northeastern New Jersey, in the Philadelphia hinterland); but dependent laborers generally did a substantial part of the fieldwork and contributed to the diversity of craft endeavors in the mid Atlantic.

From the probate records of Chester County, Pennsylvania, in 1764, the estate inventory of Thomas Baily, a middling landowner in Newlin township, provides an example of a fairly typical mid Atlantic farm household. Baily had lived with his wife and several children, and they had farmed 150 acres (60 hectares) of land of which, a few years earlier, 60 (24 hectares) had been improved and 10 (4 hectares) sown with grain. His estate inventory indicated a harvest of 171 bushels of wheat, 37 bushels of rye, and 13.5 bushels of barley. In addition he left several tons of hay, perhaps thirty pounds of wool, and some timber. The livestock included five cows, three calves, and five young cattle; twenty-four sheep; a mare and colt, a riding horse, and three plow horses; and several swine. As regards farm equipment, Baily had owned a market wagon; a plow, with irons and swingletrees; an iron-tooth harrow and clevis (harrows might still occasionally be found with wooden teeth); and a grindstone, 2 mattocks, 2 hoes (used for general weeding, as he had grown no corn), a shovel, 3 axes, a mall and wedges, a dung fork, horse gears, and some carpenter and cooper tools (enough to suggest he had done some craft work). He also had owned a pair of sheep shears, a hackle, and 2 spinning wheels. Such tools, in Pennsylvania and elsewhere in the colonies as well, were probably better than the heavy, poorly fashioned farm implements of the seventeenth century but were still far from the lighter and stronger specialized equipment that farmers would utilize and for which agricultural entrepreneurs would seek patents from the new government in the post-revolutionary era.

Baily's household goods, distributed in a three-room farmhouse, were unexceptional. The only book listed was the Bible; the only furniture wood, walnut; the only luxury item, a clock (appraised for the same amount as his wagon, eight pounds in Pennsylvania currency).

Wearing Apparel	Pewterware
2 Feather Beds	Earthenware
2 Chafe Beds	Woodenware
11 Chairs	Jugs & Glass Bottles
Arm Chair	Clothespress
3 Tables	Dressing Box
3 Iron Pots	Clock
2 Brass Kettles	Sugar Pot
2 Chests	Irons & Fire Shovel
Dough Trough	Bible
Frying Pan	

Completing the estate inventory were some thirty-two pounds in outstanding bills and book accounts, indications of credit transactions and exchanges of produce and labor common to rural life.

The layout of the Baily farmstead is not indicated in the probate records, but if he was typical of the period, he probably had a wood frame dwelling house, a barn, several other small, functional wood structures, and a small orchard. Such a homestead was typical, but again, the notion of typical obscures the range of experience in rural America. At one extreme were the small stand-alone dwellings occupied by cottagers and their families, usually with little more than a garden attached. At the other extreme were the large estates commonly worked with slave and servant labor. Such large farms were impressive and rivaled some of the estates found in the Chesapeake. Frequently mentioned in newspaper advertisements announcing farm sales were brick farmhouses with separate kitchens; a dairy house, smokehouse, and cider house for processing food; fruit orchards of several varieties containing several hundred trees; vegetable gardens; barns, stables, and a corn house; and artisan shops.

Baily's farm of 150 acres (60 hectares) was close to the average in Chester County in the 1760s. Holdings in Chester at the beginning of the century had averaged about 500 acres (200 hectares); by the 1760s this figure had dropped to about 140 acres (56 hectares); and when the revolution ended, the average was about ten acres less (52 hectares). The pre–Revolutionary War average for Chester County was substantially greater than the average in New England and less than half the figure for the northern Chesapeake. Scholarly work on New Jersey and New York suggests that the Chester County figures were typical of the long-settled coastal regions of the mid Atlantic; the average holding was 120–150 acres (48 to 60 hectares) with one farm in five less than 100 acres (40 hectares) and with one in four over 300 acres (120 hectares).

As in New England, mixed livestock and grain farming was the rule in the mid Atlantic; unlike in New England, wheat was the most important crop. At first both spring and winter wheat were cultivated, but by the mid eighteenth century most farmers cultivated only winter wheat which, as previously noted, better withstood black stem rust. Extremely high yields were occasionally mentioned by travelers recounting trips through New York and Pennsylvania, but on long-worked farms yields of perhaps eight bushels per acre were the average. Sustaining such yields probably required efforts to improve the soil beyond periodically allowing fields to run to weeds, but the nature, extent, and success of such efforts is still a matter of considerable disagreement among agricultural historians.

The importance of wheat to mid Atlantic farmers must be kept in perspective. Relative to corn, rye, and barley, wheat probably constituted in value more than half the harvest, and wheat and maslin (wheat and rye mixed) together composed more than three-fourths. But relative to the total produce of a farm—hay, meat, flax, cider, wool, and the like—the wheat harvest generally accounted for less than a third of the value. Only after the mid eighteenth century, when grain prices rose generally and wheat prices rose spectacularly, can it be argued that wheat farming dominated the rural economy of the mid Atlantic.

Many farm families not only sowed grains but also about an acre of flaxseed, enough to provide clothing for the family. Flax production, from sowing to finished linens, was labor-intensive work shared by most of the family. Men broadcast the seeds in spring; women and children helped pull up the plants by the roots in mid summer, tied them together in small bunches, and laid them out to dry for several days. The plants were then drawn through a comb that removed the seeds (for separate sale or replanting) and then soaked and left until the vegetable matter had rotted. The latter process, called retting, might involve sustained soaking in a creek or pond, or simply laying the fiber on the ground so that morning dew would rot it.

Once retted and dried the flax was "broken," the fibers separated, and the chaff discarded; this was heavy work, done by placing the flax between the two metal blades of a flax brake and crushing the fiber. When completely dry, the fibers could then be cleaned, or scutched, with a knife; "scutching frolics" often took their place alongside barn raisings and corn huskings as days of neighborly cooperation and communal drinking. Next, farm wives or their husbands hackled the flax by drawing it repeatedly through a set of metal teeth that separated fibers by length and quality. From this process came oakum for caulking, tow for coarse clothing, and fine linen for bed and table.

Processing wool was somewhat easier than working with flax. The wool had to be sheared and the oil and dirt washed out. The wool was carded to untangle it (in the late eighteenth century, mills did this) and then spun. Spinning woolens and linens was usually girls' work, learned at home or through apprenticeship; weaving was most often men's work and done not by the farm family but by a local weaver (who, to be sure, was most likely a farmer as well). Perhaps two out of every three farmers owned spinning equipment, but even in sheep-raising regions adjacent to urban markets, weaving was a specialized trade and was engaged in by no more than one household in ten. Early Americans wore homespun, but theirs was not a homespun economy. Store-bought European fabrics were more common than local linens and woolens, and weaving was generally done outside the home. The farm household was not so much a self-sufficient entity as part of a local network of exchange tied to Atlantic markets.

Spinning symbolically united the two branches of mixed farming: linens from cultivation and woolens from grazing. As in New England, livestock management probably improved somewhat over the long run as farmers built stables and barns and introduced English grasses. In addition, in Pennsylvania's York, Lancaster, and Chester counties, significant progress was made after mid century by diverting spring and stream water to irrigate meadows, which both improved hay quality and increased the number of times a field could be mowed annually. Cattle driving to serve urban markets was also common. Men could buy surplus animals, for example, from small farmers in southern Delaware, drive them north, stall feed them to fatten them for market, and then sell them in Wilmington. Drivers brought cattle to Philadelphia from as far away as the Carolinas and, somewhat later, the Ohio Valley.

Mid Atlantic herds and flocks were roughly equivalent in size to those to the north. A survey of the probate records in the 1760s provides the following averages: cattle per owner in Chester County, Pennsylvania, eight; in Fairfield County, Connecticut (northeast of New York City), nine; and in Kent County, Maryland (in the northeastern Chesapeake), sixteen; but as previously noted, New England farms were smaller than those in Chester, and Chesapeake farms were much larger. The averages for swine (about seven) and sheep (about fourteen) were also virtually the same for Chester and Fairfield, and in both counties about two of every five decedents had sheep. In Kent farmers had larger flocks of sheep (twenty-five animals) and much larger numbers of swine (thirty).

While cattle were raised primarily for their meat and for pulling farm equipment, dairying became an increasingly significant aspect of rural life over the course of the eighteenth century. If initially this work was done primarily to feed the family or for local exchange, producers around Newport, New York, and Philadelphia increasingly sold to an urban and export market. The work involved the entire family. Men cared for the cattle and raised the hay crop, perhaps with help from their wives at the harvest; women and their daughters milked the cows; and women made butter and cheese.

Having milked the cows, farm women placed the milk in pans in a cool place to allow the cream to separate, then skimmed the cream off the top with a paddle and stored it in a bucket. When enough was collected, the cream was churned. The wooden churns were fashioned by local coopers; the basic plunger design was copied from long-standing European practice. A churn was an irregularly shaped barrel, wider on the bottom than the top, with a plunger inserted through a hole in the top. The plunger had either a flat, circular piece of wood or two crisscrossed pieces of wood attached to its lower end. By raising and lowering the plunger, the cream was churned and butter separated from the skim milk. The butter then had to be worked by hand (or with a wooden implement) to remove additional moisture and then salted. By one common estimate, a cow could give two gallons of milk a day; that milk, once churned, produced a pound of butter.

Dairying also included cheese making. Adding soured milk or rennet (an enzyme obtained from the stomach linings of calves) to milk or cream separated the liquid into curds and whey; the curds were then cut, drained through a cheesecloth, and placed in a press to draw off the remaining whey. The whey went into livestock food; the cheese was aged, then consumed or sold. Just as a carpenter might identify his work with a specific design, the women who made cheeses individualized the process and added distinctive flavorings to their product.

As dairy farming became a significant rural industry, farm families adapted. Many built separate work spaces, spring houses, and milk houses where milk was cooled, butter preserved, and women did most of the work. They also acquired more efficient churns. The barrel churn, in particular, became especially popular in the pre-revolutionary era; it was essentially a barrel, laid on its side, set on a stand, and turned by a hand crank. Not every family, of course, had dairying equipment; in the immediate Philadelphia hinterland in the decade before the revolution, probate records suggest that perhaps one farm in three had a churn and one in five a cheese press.

LOWER SOUTH

Permanent English settlement of the lower South began when Virginia colonists moved south during the 1650s into the Albemarle region of what would become North Carolina; it accelerated with the establishment in 1670 of a settlement at the Ashley River in the future colony of South Carolina. From around four thousand settlers in the 1670s, the population of the Carolinas grew to over 16,000 at the turn of the century and then to perhaps 60,000 as the new colony of Georgia was laid out in 1732. On the eve of the American Revolution, the population of the entire lower South approached 350,000 blacks and whites.

The agricultural economy of the lower South would mirror patterns established to the north, in the Chesapeake, and to the south, in the West Indies. The first settlers to cross into the future colony of North Carolina from Virginia were looking for cheap land on which to extend tobacco and grain farming; to the south many of those in the initial Ashley River undertaking were West Indian planters. By the early eighteenth century, settlers had created three distinct, if overlapping, agricultural economies in the lower South: along the sparsely settled outer coastal plain (the low country), they grew tobacco and extracted wealth from the forests in the form of naval stores and timber products; in the southern section of the Low Country, from

the Cape Fear region of North Carolina through Georgia, rice culture and large-scale slavery had begun to create a plantation regime that would evolve unlike any other agricultural economy on the North American mainland; and along the inner coastal plain (the middle country) and extending west to the Piedmont (the up-country) as new settlers entered the region, farming had much the same look as in the Chesapeake, with an emphasis on corn and tobacco or corn and wheat husbandry and extensive cattle raising. In all areas corn and livestock products met the basic household subsistence requirements.

The English settlers who moved to the Low Country during the last quarter of the seventeenth century lived a crude and dangerous life; most, we can be reasonably sure, had come with the hope of profit, but few had yet the capital or labor at their disposal to do more than establish homesteads and grow the food they needed to survive. And survival itself was always a question. For those facing a "seasoning" period in a new disease environment, hot weather and stagnant swampy water created a lethal mix in which malaria, yellow fever, and dysentery all became frequent killers. But the environment, in particular cheap land and extensive forests, also offered rewards to those survivors favored by luck, entrepreneurial skill, and access to a little capital. Trial and error with a hodgepodge of potential staple crops—silk, ginger (representing a direct attempt to replicate West Indian experience), grapes, and even rice and indigo—came to naught; only tobacco offered any real promise of allowing settlers to cash in quickly on cheap land.

One enterprise, however, brought quick returns with little demand for capital or labor: cattle raising. The same conditions that drove English colonists from Barbados worked to the advantage of Carolina settlers. As Barbados sugar planters enlarged their estates, squeezing out small landholders, they also left themselves without adequate land on which to grow food. In the Carolinas colonists found that cattle and swine turned loose in the woods to forage multiplied rapidly; barreled beef and pork could then be shipped back to the West Indies on the same sloops that had just brought new settlers to the Carolinas. The extension of sugar planting also stripped Barbados of its woodland and again provided an opening for enterprising Carolina householders to turn a quick profit through lumbering (though with considerably more effort than went into cattle raising).

Money made from lumber and livestock could be plowed back into labor and farm development, which gradually paved the way for more profitable, and more labor intensive, undertakings. Settlement of the Carolinas opened up vast pine forests for exploitation at a time of crucial British demand for naval stores such as pitch, tar, and turpentine. Almost continuous war between Britain and France from 1689 to 1713 increased the British demand for naval stores. Traditionally Britain supplied that demand from the Baltic, but Swedish restrictions on the shipment of naval stores and the Great Northern War of 1700–1721 between Russia and Sweden made this traditional source of supply less dependable. In response the British government in 1705 offered generous bounties for the production of naval stores, and Carolina settlers responded.

Tar and pitch were relatively easy to manufacture. Householders and their slaves built tar kilns on knolls by digging circular pits that sloped slightly downward toward the center. The pits were lined with pine billets and covered with sod, except for small air holes around the base; then the billets were set on fire. The carefully regulated, smoldering fire produced tar, which ran out of a hole at the center of the pit and then through a trough to containers below; it was then barreled or boiled to produce pitch.

Turpentine took more time and labor to manufacture, but the process could be integrated with the production of tar and pitch. Turpentine was drained from pine trees. Farmers, and more often their slaves, made deep cuts in a tree, running down the trunk and converging at the bottom, where a trough collected the raw turpentine resin as it ran out; alternatively they made rectangular cuts in the trunk in which the resin was allowed to collect and was then ladled out. Often bark was stripped from the tree so that the warmth of the sun could speed the flow of resin; when the tree was drained, experienced foresters let the wind blow it over, then split it into billets (lightwood) for use in tar kilns. The raw turpentine could then be barreled and shipped or mixed with water, boiled, and separated into spirits and rosin.

Probably the same farmers whose skilled slaves felled trees, tended kilns, and boiled tar

and turpentine began efforts to grow rice commercially in the Carolinas. The early history of rice cultivation in the lower South is poorly documented. Native Americans harvested wild rice before the arrival of European settlers, but the rice seeds that Carolina colonists first experimented with successfully between the 1690s and the 1720s came from either Asia or Africa. The high average temperatures of the growing season, ample moisture, and existence of rich alluvial soils, continuously enriched by water deposits, made the low country ideal for rice cultivation.

Between the 1690s and the era of the American Revolution, rice cultivation went through three stages, each representing a distinctive way of supplying water to the rice crop: first, upland planting, similar to that used for small grains, dependent on rainfall; later the flooding of fields adjacent to inland swamps; and at the end of the colonial era, the tidal flooding of fields on coastal plantations.

After initial attempts to water rice with rainfall, planters found they could improve yields and control weeds more effectively by flooding fields with water drawn from nearby swamps. Their slaves built dams that regulated the flow of water from a swamp onto a rice field, then employed a second dam, at the opposite end of the field, to drain the field. The field itself had to be cleared of trees and leveled, and in some cases, laced with ditches to help control the water flow. Slaves seeded rice fields in early spring. Once the seeds germinated, the fields had to be weeded constantly, usually by slaves standing in ankle-deep water. In early fall slaves cut the rice crop with a sickle, laid it out to dry, threshed it with a flail, and winnowed it to separate grain from chaff. A mortar and pestle were then used to remove the coat from the kernel.

Inland swamp cultivation brought diminishing returns. Fields lost their fertility and swamps were gradually drained; extensive inland lumbering and grazing produced low-country flooding that washed over fields and destroyed crops. Tidewater culture developed around the time of the American Revolution and became the dominant production method in the antebellum era; despite its dominance it was restricted to the thin strip of land between the tidal salt flats along the coast and the freshwater swamps beyond the tides. In this zone planters located rice

691

fields along rivers whose level rose and fell with the tides and utilized dams to control the flooding and drainage of fields. Yields went up remarkably and kept the low country, from Cape Fear in North Carolina to southern Georgia, a rice coast into the twentieth century.

Profits from rice, naval stores, and livestock grazing were channeled back into slave labor, and, by the end of the first decade of the eighteenth century, South Carolina had become the only North American colony with a black majority. At that time and before rice had become *the* staple of the Carolina Low Country, there were approximately four thousand whites and four thousand black slaves in South Carolina (and perhaps another fourteen hundred Indian slaves). Thirty years later, by 1740, and with the rice boom in full swing, blacks outnumbered whites almost two-to-one in a population of about sixty thousand. More directly, then, than in any other region, black agricultural labor created white wealth, wealth unmatched anywhere else in British North America.

As already noted, many Low Country slaves had come from rice-growing regions of Africa, but the extent to which their African background shaped their experiences in the Carolinas and Georgia is a matter of considerable uncertainty. Relative to other colonies, South Carolina received a higher percentage of slaves from African regions (Gambia and the Windward Coast) in which rice growing predominated, and by the mid eighteenth century, it was not uncommon for slave traders to advertise that they were selling slaves skilled in rice cultivation. Their African background may have served them in another way as well: by making them more likely than whites to survive in the deadly disease environment of the hot, swampy Low Country. Africans were more resistant than whites to two Low Country killers: malaria, against which many had partial, inherited immunity (associated with the sickle-cell trait), and yellow fever, against which they had acquired resistance because of the prevalence of the disease in their homeland. Beyond this, however, the connection between rice cultivation and the African background of Low Country slaves is more tenuous. While the number of slaves brought to the Carolinas from rice growing regions of Africa was disproportionately high, almost half came from regions (Congo-Angola) in which rice was not as significant a crop.

More critically, African cultivation methods differed significantly from those employed in the Low Country, and the system of task labor under which slaves worked (individual slaves were assigned specific tasks for the day, and when completed, had their time to themselves) had no African counterpart and little parallel elsewhere in the southern colonies (where gang labor under direct white supervision was more common). From the perspective of African and African-American workers, what can be said is that many, working in the backcountry forests or the watery coastal rice fields, gained considerable autonomy in managing their own time and working conditions, and this autonomy, in turn, helped them maintain the connection with their African past.

By mid century the rice economy had created a unique plantation regime in the Low Country. A typical South Carolina Low Country district was 80 or 90 percent black, and most of the land and slaves were owned by planters who held over one thousand acres (400 hectares) and fifty slaves apiece.

Exact data are hard to come by, but scattered returns provide a general picture of concentrated economic wealth. In Saint George's Parish, South Carolina, in 1726, eight of every ten white householders owned slaves, and 7 percent of the householders owned fifty slaves or more; in Saint James's, Goose Creek, South Carolina, in 1745—at the height of its prosperity as a rice-growing area—virtually every householder owned slaves, and more than a quarter of the householders owned at least fifty slaves. By contrast in 1769, in Brunswick and New Hanover counties in North Carolina's Cape Fear rice-growing region, only half the white taxables owned slaves, and only one owned as many as fifty slaves.

Landholding data is even more difficult to come by, but again the general pattern of concentration is clear. In Saint James's in 1745, almost half the householders had more than 1,000 acres (400 hectares) of land (within and outside the parish) and almost two-thirds had at least 500 acres (200 hectares). The contrast with Brunswick and New Hanover counties, North Carolina, in 1769 is again instructive; land there was much more widely distributed and far more people were smallholders, but the average size of holdings was the highest in North Carolina (over 850 acres [340 hectares] per taxable), and 76 of the 425 landowners were taxed on a thousand acres or more. We can be reasonably sure that late-colonial Georgia, except in the rice growing districts, looked more like North than South Carolina.

The increase in slave labor also fueled the Carolina timber economy. Not only did slaves work at producing naval stores, but as skilled sawyers they fashioned lumber, shingles, and staves for the British market. Sawmills along Low-Country rivers turned pine trees into sawn lumber; shingles were cut from cedar and cypress; and red and white oak supplied staves. Though Carolina forests produced wealth for the farming population throughout the Low Country, activity centered on the coastal stretch from Port Roanoke to Cape Fear (south of the tobacco counties and north of the rice parishes).

As the coast was dominated by large landowners and was cleared, cultivated, and built upon by African and African-American slaves, white immigrants moved inland, settling the backcountry. Some of the settlement took place in ethnic enclaves—such as Wachovia, established in 1752 by Moravians in North Carolina, or the Welsh Tract, created along the Pee Dee River in South Carolina—but initially much of the migration was by individual farm families with a few slaves. Then in the third quarter of the eighteenth century, a great southward migration from the mid Atlantic down the Piedmont and Shenandoah Valley brought a flood of Irish, German, and Scotch-Irish settlers to the backcountry, most of them intent on grain and livestock farming. By the 1760s the South Carolina backcountry (that area at least sixty miles [96 kilometers] from the coast) had thirty-five thousand settlers (three-fourths of the white and one-tenth of the black population of the colony). At about the same time in North Carolina, where coastal land was not so densely occupied and farming remained on a smaller scale, perhaps half the colony's inhabitants lived in the backcountry.

While the Piedmont remained an area of small farms and limited market production, farmers in the middle country (or inner coastal plain) produced wheat and tobacco for sale, raised large herds of cattle, and extended cultivation of a new Low-Country crop, indigo, to their own region. In the pre-revolutionary era, the inner coastal plain was dotted with tobacco inspection sites and flour mills that served as shipping points to dispatch processed crops to the coast. Even more noticeable were the cattle and swine herds, most of moderate size (the average in North Carolina around the time of the revolution being eleven cattle per owner), but some of over one hundred animals. By the mid eighteenth century, herders were driving swine to Virginia as well as to the Carolina coast, and cattle to as far away as Pennsylvania and New Jersey.

In the mid eighteenth century, indigo also became an important cash crop in South Carolina and Georgia. While the crop had been tried much earlier, competition from the West Indies made commercial growth unprofitable. In 1739, however, war curtailed British supplies, and in 1748 Britain granted a bounty on North American indigo to stimulate Carolina production. In the Low Country, planters turned to indigo when rice cultivation left land and labor available; in the middle country, indigo was often the primary crop, and profits helped build up slave estates and may have paved the way for the post-revolutionary cotton boom.

Labor demands for the planting, harvesting, and processing of indigo were high, and (outside the middle country) slaves did most of the work. Seeds were sown in holes made with mattocks and then covered over; while the plant grew, laborers weeded repeatedly and then cut the crop with sickles before the stem had hardened and as the leaves were acquiring a bluish tint. Two or three harvests a season were possible (considerably fewer and of poorer quality than in the West Indies). Workers processed the plant using a series of vats: one in which to steep the leaves initially; a second to draw off the liquid and beat it before allowing the indigo to settle; and a third to remove the remaining liquid from the indigo in the second vat. The indigo was then placed in sacks, allowed to drip until almost dry, and finally cut into squares and shipped in barrels.

The future, of course, did not lie with indigo, the cultivation of which virtually ended with the revolution, but with cotton, which had long been planted (and exported) in small quantities, along with flax, to provide clothing for slaves. The nonimportation agreements of the early 1770s and the outbreak of war in 1775, however, cut off British supplies of cheap fabrics and shifted attention to domestic cloth and linen production.

In the post-revolutionary era, cotton would change the daily lives, work routines, and prospects of the lower South's black and white inhabitants.

REFLECTIONS

What themes unify the history of farming and planting in British North America, and what questions invite further inquiry? One valuable perspective is to consider Native American agriculture in relationship to that of the European and African settlers of North America. From such a perspective it is easier to see the commonalities shared by those settlers and the distinctiveness of Native American agricultural practices. The corn-livestock husbandry pursued on family farms attached both to local trading networks and international markets differed fundamentally from the Native American mix of cultivation, hunting, and gathering.

Some historians, however, have emphasized how the commercialization of agriculture set apart a group of prosperous farmers from much of the rural population. In turn, they have shown how small farmers, tenants, hired laborers, and servants long continued to share an early-modern world in which, as with Native Americans and Africans, nature was animate and time cyclical. When we turn from the specific problem of agricultural practices to the more general question of rural culture the sharp contrasts suggested above blur and leave us with a continuing inquiry into the relationship of behavior and values in early America.

Such concerns are related, as well, to the problem of change in early American agriculture, and again, perspective is critical. In the era before the European settlement of North America, agriculture was not static; this was as true in North America as in Africa and Western Europe. The interaction of human populations and the environment reshaped agricultural life continuously, sometimes in recurrent patterns, sometimes in fundamental and permanent ways. Nonetheless, the conscious altering of the environment in response to market incentives created a pattern of change, best measured in increases in per capita productivity, and, by extension, in per capita wealth, that distinguished

farming in the early American era (and its European counterpart) from agriculture in the past. The problem for historians, not all of whom agree on this characterization, is that such change occurred in small increments and very slowly, and measurement of such variances, given the extant documentation, is very difficult. Some transformations—the remaking of the landscape as settlements were established and farms were built and the shifts in crop selection and livestock concentration in response to Atlantic markets—are clear and have been emphasized here; others are far more difficult to discern and remain the focus of study.

Finally, the question of change brings us to the American Revolution, in particular, and, the post-colonial era, in general. What was new? The expansion of cotton production in the lower South, the spread of rural industry in the northern countryside, and the accelerating tempo with which improved agricultural implements were invented by and marketed to American farmers were all significant changes. The revolution itself may have worked some changes—providing incentives for home manufacturing, realigning traditional trade relations with Great Britain and France, and clearing the way for new encroachments on Indian lands in the Ohio and Mississippi valleys—but much still needs to be done to understand the revolution as an event in economic and agricultural history. Perhaps, however, we will find that the Enlightenment, with its emphasis on innovation, experimentation, and invention had even more far-reaching consequences on the ways farmers imagined and reshaped American agriculture.

BIBLIOGRAPHY

Secondary Accounts

Ball, Duane Eugene. "The Process of Settlement in Eighteenth-Century Chester County, Pennsylvania: A Social and Economic History." Ph.D. diss., University of Pennsylvania, 1973. Using probate records and tax lists, Ball finds more evidence of intensive agriculture and economic growth than does Lemon.

Bidwell, Percy Wells, and John I. Falconer. *History of Agriculture in the Northern United States, 1620–1860.* Carnegie Institution of Washington Publication no. 358. Washington, D.C., 1925. The companion to Gray's history of southern agriculture but not as thorough on the colonial era.

Carr, Lois Green. "Diversification in the Colonial Chesapeake: Somerset County, Maryland, in Comparative Perspective." In *Colonial Chesapeake Society*, edited by Lois Green Carr, Philip D. Morgan, and Jean B. Russo. Chapel Hill, N.C., 1988. Crop and craft diversification as they related to tobacco production.

Carr, Lois Green, Russell R. Menard, and Lorena S. Walsh. *Robert Cole's World: Agriculture and Society in Early Maryland*. Chapel Hill, N.C., 1991. By far the best account of the operation of a seventeenth-century Chesapeake tobacco plantation.

Chaplin, Joyce E. "Creating a Cotton South in Georgia and South Carolina, 1760–1815." *Journal of Southern History* 57, no. 2 (1991):171–200. Cotton production before the cotton gin.

———. "Tidal Rice Cultivation and the Problem of Slavery in South Carolina and Georgia, 1760–1815." *William and Mary Quarterly*, 3rd ser., 49, no. 1 (1992):29–61. Valuable analysis of causes and consequences of changes in rice cultivation.

Clark, Andrew Hill. *Acadia: The Geography of Early Nova Scotia to 1760*. Madison, Wis., 1968. Good for comparisons with British agriculture in the northern colonies.

Clemens, Paul G. E. *The Atlantic Economy and Colonial Maryland's Eastern Shore: From Tobacco to Grain*. Ithaca, N.Y., 1980. How wheat became a staple in a tobacco colony and the economic consequences of the shift; see also Earle.

Clemens, Paul G. E., and Lucy Simler. "Rural Labor and the Farm Household in Chester County, Pennsylvania, 1750–1820." In *Work and Labor in Early America*, edited by Stephen Innes. Chapel Hill, N.C., 1988. Cottagers, wage laborers, servants, and slaves in the mid-Atlantic farm economy.

Coclanis, Peter A. *The Shadow of a Dream: Economic Life and Death in the South Carolina Low Country, 1670–1920*. New York, 1989. More useful on economic growth than on planting and farming.

Cohen, David Steven. *The Dutch-American Farm*. New York, 1992. Focus is on the distinctive aspects of Dutch farms and folk life.

Cronon, William. *Changes in the Land: Indians, Colonists, and the Ecology of New England*. New York, 1983. Hunting, agriculture, and the continuous reshaping of landscape; an exceptionally important study.

Daniels, Christine Marie. "Alternative Workers in a Slave Economy: Kent County, Maryland, 1675–1810." Ph.D. diss., Johns Hopkins University, 1989. Wage laborers, apprentices, and debt servants; includes an excellent account of the workings of an eighteenth-century tobacco plantation.

Earle, Carville V. *The Evolution of a Tidewater Settlement System: All Hallow's Parish, Maryland, 1650–1783*. University of Chicago, Department of Geography, Research Paper No. 170. Chicago, 1975. Especially good on the extent and causes of diversified economic activity in the upper Chesapeake.

Fletcher, Stevenson Whitcomb. *Pennsylvania Agriculture and Country Life, 1640–1840*. 2nd ed. Harrisburg, Pa., 1950. Compendium of information on rural life.

Gray, Lewis Cecil. *History of Agriculture in the Southern United States to 1860*. Carnegie Institution of Washington, Publication no. 430. 2 vols. Washington, D.C., 1933. The unsurpassed introduction to early southern agriculture and economic history.

Gross, Robert A. "Culture and Cultivation: Agriculture and Society in Thoreau's Concord." *Journal of American History* 69, no. 1 (1982):42–61. Description and analysis of agricultural decline in an established New England farming community.

Gwyn, Julian. "Economic Fluctuations in Wartime Nova Scotia, 1755–1815." In *Making Adjustments: Change and Continuity in Planter Nova Scotia, 1759–1800*, edited by Margaret Conrad. Fredericton, New Brunswick, 1991. Extremely valuable overview of economic life in the British Maritimes.

Hudson, Charles. *The Southeastern Indians*. Knoxville, Tenn., 1976. Detailed discussion of hunting, gathering, and farming.

Innes, Stephen. *Labor in a New Land: Economy and Society in Seventeenth-Century Springfield*. Princeton, N.J., 1983. A different type of New England village, this one in the Connecticut River valley and with an economy largely dependent on John Pynchon.

Kim, Sung Bok. *Landlord and Tenant in Colonial New York: Manorial Society, 1664–1775*. Chapel Hill, N.C., 1978. Landlord-tenant relations on the great Hudson River manors were based more on market factors and less exploitive than previously thought; contains considerable information on agriculture and tenancy.

Klein, Rachel N. *Unification of a Slave State: The Rise of the Planter Class in the South Carolina Backcountry, 1760–1808*. Chapel Hill, N.C., 1990. The first chapter provides a detailed overview, based in part on the use of probate inventories, of the development of the backcountry economy in the late colonial period.

Kulikoff, Allan. *Tobacco and Slaves: The Development of Southern Cultures in the Chesapeake, 1680–1800*. Chapel Hill, N.C., 1986. A sweeping interpretation, bringing together much of the late-twentieth century literature on gentry, planter, and African-American life in the Chesapeake.

Lemon, James T. *The Best Poor Man's Country: A Geographical Study of Early Southeastern Pennsylvania.* Ithaca, N.Y., 1972. Detailed analysis of mixed farming and extensive agriculture; the most important study to date of rural life in the mid Atlantic.

McCusker, John J., and Russell R. Menard. *The Economy of British America, 1607–1789.* Chapel Hill, N.C., 1985. An excellent overview and synthesis as well as an exploration of needs and opportunities for further research, with a lengthy bibliography and statistical summaries of trade and population data. Population estimates in this essay were drawn from here.

McMahon, Sarah F. "A Comfortable Subsistence: The Changing Composition of Diet in Rural New England, 1620–1840." *William and Mary Quarterly,* 3rd ser., 42, no. 1 (1985):26–65. Based on the author's dissertation, "A Comfortable Subsistence: A History of Diet in New England, 1630–1850" (Brandeis University, 1982); both provide extremely valuable insights into everyday farm life and agricultural practices.

Main, Gloria L. *Tobacco Colony: Life in Early Maryland, 1650–1720.* Princeton, N.J., 1982. Detailed portrait of the material lives of tobacco planters drawn from probate estate inventories.

Main, Jackson Turner. *Society and Economy in Colonial Connecticut.* Princeton, N.J., 1985. Detailed portrait of material life and wealth holding based on probated estate inventories; includes chapters on farmers and farm laborers.

Merrens, Harry Roy. *Colonial North Carolina in the Eighteenth Century: A Study in Historical Geography.* Chapel Hill, N.C., 1964. Based primarily on tax lists and travel accounts, this is a valuable study and virtually the only one of North Carolina agriculture.

Mitchell, Robert D. *Commercialism and Frontier: Perspectives on the Early Shenandoah Valley.* Charlottesville, Va., 1977. The best study of backcountry agriculture.

Morgan, Philip D. "A Profile of a Mid-Eighteenth-Century South Carolina Parish: The Tax Return of Saint James's, Goose Creek." *South Carolina Historical Magazine* 81, no. 1 (1980):51–65. Brings together what little statistical data is available on slave and land ownership.

Morris, Francis Grave, and Phyllis Mary Morris. "Economic Conditions in North Carolina About 1780; Part I: Landholdings; Part II: Ownership of Town Lots, Slaves, and Cattle." *North Carolina Historical Review* 16, no. 2 (1939):107–133; no. 3, 296–327. Statistical study based on tax lists; supplements Merrens.

Pruitt, Bettye Hobbs. "Self-Sufficiency and the Agricultural Economy of Eighteenth-Century Massachusetts." *William and Mary Quarterly,* 3rd ser., 41, no. 3 (1984):333–364. Important corrective to earlier studies about rural self-sufficiency that should be read in conjunction with Bidwell and Falconer, Russell, and Lemon. The author's dissertation, "Agriculture and Society in the Towns of Massachusetts, 1771: A Statistical Analysis" (Boston University, 1981) contains additional statistical information.

Russell, Howard S. *Indian New England Before the Mayflower.* Hanover, N.H., 1980. Overview with an emphasis on agriculture.

———. *A Long, Deep Furrow: Three Centuries of Farming in New England.* Hanover, N.H., 1976. A compendium of useful information on northern farming, less systematic than Bidwell and Falconer but more reliable.

Rutman, Darrett B. *Husbandmen of Plymouth: Farms and Villages in the Old Colony, 1620–1692.* Boston, 1967. Extensive use of wills and inventories to describe farming in the first English agricultural villages in New England. Short and readable.

Silver, Timothy. *A New Face on the Countryside: Indians, Colonists, and Slaves in South Atlantic Forests, 1500–1800.* Cambridge, England, 1990. An environmental history of the ongoing reshaping of the landscape by Indians, free settlers, and slaves in the south Atlantic.

Smith, Julia Floyd. *Slavery and Rice Culture in Low Country Georgia, 1750–1860.* Knoxville, Tenn., 1985.

Taylor, Alan. *Liberty Men and Great Proprietors: The Revolutionary Settlement on the Maine Frontier, 1760–1820.* Chapel Hill, N.C., 1990. Some attention to early agriculture.

Ulrich, Laurel Thatcher. *Good Wives: Image and Reality in the Lives of Women in Northern New England, 1650–1750.* New York, 1980. Excellent chapter on work in rural households.

———. "Martha Ballard and Her Girls: Women's Work in Eighteenth-Century Maine." In *Work and Labor in Early America,* edited by Stephen Innes. Chapel Hill, N.C., 1988. How one woman organized and employed rural labor.

Usner, Daniel H., Jr. *Indians, Settlers, and Slaves in a Frontier Exchange Economy: The Lower Mississippi Valley Before 1783.* Chapel Hill, N.C., 1992. A finely crafted study that helps put British settlement in comparative perspective.

Wacker, Peter O. *Land and People: A Cultural Geography of Preindustrial New Jersey: Origins and Settlement Patterns.* New Brunswick, N.J., 1975. First of a projcctcd two-volumc study of carly Ncw Jcrscy and its people, paying particular attention to the geography of ethnic diversity.

Wood, Peter H. *Black Majority: Negroes in Colonial South Carolina from 1670 Through the Stono Rebellion.* New York, 1974. Illuminates not only slavery and slave life but much of the early social and agricultural history of the colony.

Contemporaneous Descriptions

American Husbandry. Edited by Harry J. Carman. Columbia University Studies in the History of American Agriculture, no. 6. New York, 1939. Originally published in 1775.

Betts, Edwin Morris, ed. *Thomas Jefferson's Farm Book with Commentary and Relevant Extracts from Other Writings.* Princeton, N.J., 1953; repr. Charlottesville, Va., 1987. Agricultural life on a large Virginia plantation.

Bordley, John Beale. *Essays and Notes on Husbandry and Rural Affairs.* Philadelphia, 1799; 2nd ed., 1801. The author was familiar with the northern Chesapeake in the last half of the eighteenth century.

Dwight, Timothy. *Travels in New England and New York.* Edited by Barbara Miller Soloman. 4 vols. Cambridge, Mass., 1969. Post-revolutionary, but one of the most important sources of information on agricultural practices in the region.

Eliot, Jared. *Essays upon Field Husbandry in New England, and Other Papers, 1748–1762.* Edited by Harry J. Carman and Rexford G. Tugwell. Columbia University Studies in the History of American Agriculture, no. 1. New York, 1934. Probably the most cited contemporary work on New England agriculture.

Greene, Jack P., ed. *Diary of Colonel Landon Carter of Sabine Hall, 1752–1778.* 2 vols. Charlottesville, Va., 1965. Excellent introduction; the diary itself contains a wealth of information on agriculture and plantation management.

Kalm, Peter. *Peter Kalm's Travels into North America: The English Version of 1770.* Revised and edited by Adolph B. Benson. New York, 1937.

Woodward, Carl Raymond. *Ploughs and Politics. Charles Reed of New Jersey and His Notes on Agriculture, 1715–1774.* New Brunswick, N.J., 1941. Analysis and the edited manuscript; extremely valuable reflections on agricultural practices in the mid Atlantic.

Paul G. E. Clemens

SEE ALSO **Landholding** and **Rural Life**.

THE DUTCH COLONY

THE INITIAL EMPHASIS of the Dutch West India Company in New Netherland was on the fur trade rather than on establishing an agricultural colony. However the existence of permanent British colonies in New England and Virginia soon prompted the company to encourage agricultural settlements as well. Market-oriented rather than subsistence from the early 1600s, Dutch-American farming remained regionally distinct for almost three centuries. During the Dutch period (1624–1664), three distinct agricultural settlement types emerged in New Netherland: the isolated farm, the patroonship, and the agricultural village. All three had prototypes in different regions of the Netherlands.

THE FORMS OF AGRICULTURAL SETTLEMENT

A tradition of small, isolated farms can be traced back to the scattered farms settled by individual reclaimers in the wastelands of the Netherlands. The Dutch drew upon this settlement pattern in the wilderness of America.

A provisional order of 1624 granted all colonists free land, but they had to settle at places assigned to them and were told what crops to plant. In January 1625 the company instructed Provisional Director Willem Verhulst to give families "as much land as they can properly cultivate," each person drawing his share by lot. The Charter of Freedoms and Exemptions of 1629 allowed freemen to "choose and take possession of as much land as they can properly cultivate for themselves." In addition the West India Company hired farmers to work for a set number of years on farms owned by the company.

A 1639 map of Manhattan shows both *bouweries* and plantations; a *bouwery* had both livestock and crops, whereas a plantation had only crops. *Bouweries* and plantations are shown on Manhattan Island, Nutten Island (Governor's Island), and Long Island. Six of the *bouweries* on Manhattan Island were owned by the West India Company.

In addition to the farms and plantations, the Dutch settled large patroonships or manors. The Charter of Freedoms and Exemptions of 1629, which established the patroonship system in New Netherland, stated that anyone who agreed to bring fifty people over the age of fifteen within four years would receive four leagues (about eighteen miles [29 kilometers]) along one side of a navigable river or two leagues on both sides and as far inland "as the situation of the occupants will permit." Patroonships were established by company directors Michiel Paauw at Pavonia (Jersey City), Kiliaen van Rensselaer at Rensselaerswyck (near Albany), and Samuel Godijn at Swanendael (in Delaware).

The only one of these early patroonships to survive for more than a few years was Rensselaerswyck. In 1635 van Rensselaer reported that his patroonship consisted of one farm on the west side of the Hudson River, one farm on the east side, three farms on an island in the river, and a dwelling house outside Fort Orange (Albany). A typical contract was that made between van Rensselaer and a farmer named Gerrit Theusz de Reux, dated June 1632. The patroon agreed to supply de Reux with livestock and farm equipment and to pay him and his servants wages until January and May 1634, respectively. In return de Reux would have to pay back the patroon with half the winter wheat planted in the fall of 1633 and one-half of the surplus milk, butter, cheese, and livestock as of January 1634. These patroonships were modeled after feudal estates along the Rhine River in the Netherlands dating back to the late eighth and ninth centuries.

The third type of agricultural settlement, agricultural towns, developed later than the dispersed farms and patroonships in the 1640s. The Charter of Freedoms and Exemptions of 1640 provided for a town form of government, but the Dutch colonists had to be ordered by the West India Company to settle in towns as a defensive measure during the Indian war in the 1640s. In 1645 the company sent an instruction to the director and council in New Amsterdam ordering the colonists to settle in villages, towns, and hamlets "as the English are in the habit of doing, who thereby live more securely."

Five agricultural towns were founded on Long Island: Breukelen (Brooklyn) in 1646, Mid-wout (Flatbush) in 1652, Amersfoort (Flatlands) in 1654, and New Utrecht and Boswyck (Bushwick) in 1661. The village of Bergen (Jersey City) was surveyed in 1660 on the New Jersey side of the Hudson, and Harlem on Manhattan Island was surveyed in 1658. The division of the lands in Harlem was typical of these agricultural towns. House lots in town were arranged along two parallel streets. Each farmer was assigned a garden plot and four morgens (about eight acres [3 hectares]) of farmland along the river flats, and a small parcel of marsh to provide salt hay for his cattle. It is not necessary to look to New England for models for these Dutch agricultural towns. There were similar towns on the Drenthe plateau in the eastern part of the Netherlands.

When the English conquered New Netherland in 1664 and divided it into New York and New Jersey, the Dutch settlers remained. The English replaced the Dutch patroonships with manors and patents. The patent was a grant of fee-simple ownership of land to a group of unrelated individuals, whereas the manor involved tenancy and a title of lord. Several of the manors granted by the English were regrants of the old patroonships such as Rensselaerswyck, which was regranted to the van Rensselaer family in 1685. Other English manors were new land grants to old Dutch families, such as the Philipsburgh manor in 1693 and the Van Cortland manor in 1697. The chartering of towns also continued under the English. Many of the Dutch towns in New Jersey were granted charters by the English, including Aquackanonk (Passaic) in 1679 and Hackensack in 1693. The transition from Dutch to English landholding patterns was relatively smooth because the Dutch and English had similar traditions of isolated farms, agricultural towns, and large estates.

Contrary to the stereotype of subsistence agriculture in colonial America, a market-oriented economy developed early in the seventeenth century. In 1632 Kiliaen van Rensselaer sent instructions to the *schout* (a combination sheriff, prosecuting attorney, and sergeant-in-arms) and council of his patroonship that they should try to sell "the milk, butter, cheese, and further all kinds of grain and root crops that everyone has in store" either to other colonists or the Indians or else send them to the Netherlands. In 1656 the director-general and council of New Netherland established Saturday as market day in New Amsterdam because "the people from the country bring various wares, such as meat, bacon, butter, cheese, turnips, roots, straw, and other products of the farm to this city for sale." By 1680 cash crops were being shipped by sloops traveling up and down the Hudson River to New York City. In that year Jasper Danckaerts wrote that, in the vicinity of Esopus (Kingston), there was a warehouse along the river "where the farmers bring their grain, in order that it may be conveniently shipped when the boats come up here."

THE PRODUCE OF THE LAND

In 1655 Adriaen van der Donck wrote a detailed description of Dutch crops. He noted that Dutch farmers in New Netherland grew large gray peas known as Old Wives; they also cultivated European grains such as wheat and rye. Barley grew well in New Netherland, but it was not cultivated as much as in Europe, where it was a staple. Van der Donck noted that the Dutch settlers were lovers of fruit, and they brought over various kinds of apple and pear trees. The English introduced the first quinces, but the Dutch had brought over their own stock and seeds. Their garden produce included cabbages, parsnips, carrots, beets, endives, succory (chicory), finckel, dill, sorrel, spinach, parsley, chervil, cresses, onions, leeks, and radishes. In their herb gardens they grew rosemary, lavender, hysop, thyme, sage, marjoram, balm, onions, wormwood, belury, chives, pimpernel, dragon's blood, fivefinger, tarragon, laurel, artichokes, and asparagus.

Among the crops borrowed from Native Americans were maize, which the Dutch called "turkey wheat," tobacco, squash, and pumpkins. In Europe, van der Donck noted, pumpkins were "generally despised as a mean and unsubstantial article of food," but in America they were "of so good a quality that our countrymen hold . . . [them] in high esteem." Melons thrived in New Netherland, and one variety that grew especially well was the *citrull* or water citron (watermelon). It was not grown in the Netherlands but was known there as an occasional Portuguese import.

In addition, the Dutch grew cucumbers and calabashes (gourds). They also raised turnips, peas, and various kinds of beans, including horse beans, Turkish beans, and large Windsor beans, called *tessen*.

THE VARIETIES OF LIVESTOCK

In addition to arable farming, livestock was an important element in New Netherland agriculture from the outset. In 1625 the Dutch West India Company dispatched to the new colony two ships containing "one hundred and three head of livestock—stallions, mares, bulls and cows—for breeding and multiplying, besides all the hogs and sheep that they thought expedient to send thither." Initially kept on Nutten Island (Governor's Island), the livestock was then transferred to Manhattan Island, where the animals were put out to pasture. In 1655 van der Donck noted that "the tame stock, which at the settlement of the country were brought over from the Netherlands . . . differs little from the original stock."

The horses brought from Utrecht were supplemented by the English breed, which were lighter and not as suited for agricultural work. There were also some Arabian horses that the Dutch had imported from the West Indian island of Curaçao. The horses were used as draft animals to pull plows and wagons. But in contrast with Pennsylvania, where horses were the main draft animal, and New England, where oxen were mainly used, the Dutch used both horses and oxen.

The cattle were mostly of the Holland and Utrecht breeds. At first, when they fed only on fresh hay, the cattle were subject to disease. But the problem was solved by feeding the cattle salt hay and giving them salt and brackish water to drink. The Dutch also purchased English cattle from New Englanders. While the English breed did as well as their Holland counterparts and did not require as much care, since they were able to survive unsheltered during the winter, the English cattle did not grow as large and did not give as much milk as did the Dutch cattle. But they were cheaper and provided an equal amount of fat and tallow. Van der Donck added that "they who desire to cross the breeds, and raise the best kind of stock, put a Holland bull to their English cows, by which they produce a good mixed breed of cattle without much cost."

Hogs were "numerous and plenty" in New Netherland. "Some of the citizens," wrote van der Donck, "prefer the English breed of hogs, because they are hardy, and subsist better in winter without shelter; but the Holland hogs grow much larger and heavier, and have thicker pork." The hogs were allowed to forage for acorns in the woods and lowlands. When acorns were scarce, the hogs were fattened on maize.

The Dutch in New Netherland did not keep as many sheep as did the English in New England, and the New Netherlanders raised the sheep primarily for wool, not mutton. However, the sheep had to be protected against wolves, and they lost much of their wool as a result of rubbing against trees, stumps, and brushwood. Thus more goats were kept than sheep. Unlike the sheep, the goats were in no danger when they became lean. They gave good milk and were prolific yet did not cost much.

Estate inventories provide insight into the relative numbers of each kind of livestock. The farm named Emmaus, owned by Jonas Bronck (after whom the Bronx is named), had at the time of his death in 1643 two five-year-old mares, one six-year-old stallion, one yearling stallion, two one-year-old mares, five milch cows, one two-year-old cow, two yoke of oxen, one bull, three yearling heifers, and hogs "number unknown, running in the woods." The meticulous listing of the livestock by age reflects its value.

Typically the patroon supplied the livestock for his tenants, and the increase in livestock was divided between landlord and tenant. A 1654 lease of a farm to Jean Labatie specified that "the lessee shall receive two mares, two stallions or geldings, one filly, three cows and one full-grown heifer, one half the increase of which shall belong to the lessee." The division of the increase was to occur every three or four years, but the initial number of livestock had to be returned before any division took place.

In the Dutch towns, cattle grazed on the commons from April until November, usually under the care of a herder. Young horses, cattle, and swine were branded or marked and were turned out in the common woods in the spring and summer. During the fall and winter, they were sheltered in barns.

FARM BUILDINGS, TOOLS, AND EQUIPMENT

Two agricultural structures became common features of the Dutch-American landscape: the hay barracks and the Dutch barn. The barracks was a covered stack for storing unthreshed grain or hay. In America it typically consisted of four or five poles and a movable roof. The hay barracks, common in Europe among Germanic people, can be traced back as far as the Middle Ages in Germany and the Netherlands. As early as 1631, there was mention of several hay barracks in Rensselaerswyck, and a 1638 inventory of a Flatlands farm lists "one hay rick, with five posts, forty feet tall."

The Dutch barn had a large door on the gable end and a characteristic framing consisting of a series of H-bents. It was derived from farm structures found in the eastern provinces of the Netherlands and the adjacent areas of Germany in which the animals lived at one end and the family at the other, sometimes without a wall between them. While there is evidence that such combination farmhouse-barns were constructed in New Netherland in the early seventeenth century, separate farmhouses and barns became the typical pattern. In 1748 the Swedish naturalist Peter Kalm described the interior of a Dutch barn in New Jersey:

In the middle was the threshing floor and above it, or in the loft or garret, they put the unthrashed grain, the straw, or anything else, according to the season. On one side were stables for the horses, and on the other for the cows. . . . Here under one roof therefore were the thrashing floor, the barn, the stables, the hay loft, the coach house, etc. (John Fitchen. *The New World Dutch Barn*, p. 82, n. 9.)

Most of the tools and equipment found on Dutch-American farms were similar to those on Anglo-American farms, but three implements were distinctly Dutch: the Dutch plow, the Flemish scythe or sith, and the Dutch wagon.

The Dutch plow, or hog plow as it was sometimes called, differed from the English or bull plow. The implement had a pyramidal-shaped plowshare, a wooden moldboard, and usually only one handle. It seldom had a coulter and sometimes was mounted on wooden wheels. Its origins can be traced to the province of Zeeland in the Netherlands and the northern and eastern regions of Belgium.

The English plow usually had two handles: a relatively flat, horizontal plowshare, which was either triangular or V-shaped; and a coulter. Like the Dutch plow, it originally had a wooden moldboard. Despite its name the English plow is thought to have originated in the Low Countries. Found in parts of the Netherlands, the flat, triangular plowshare was introduced into England in the sixteenth and seventeenth centuries.

The sith, also known as the Hainault or Flemish scythe, was indigenous to the Low Countries. It was a type of scythe with an L-shaped wooden handle, and was used with a mathook, which was a straight wooden handle with a small iron hook on the end. The user stood nearly upright, held the mathook in his left hand, and cut the crop with the sith in his right hand. While the sith and mathook were more efficient than the sickle, which required the user to stoop low and grasp the crop with his hand, the sith and mathook required greater skill. The Dutch in America continued to use the sith and mathook until the end of the eighteenth century.

The Dutch wagon had two pairs of narrow-tired, eight-spoke wheels, with the rear wheels usually larger than the front ones. The body had a deep front board, a somewhat less deep tailboard, and vertical spindles on the sides. Its top rail had a distinctive curve. It differed from the German or continental wagon, which normally had four small wheels of equal size, a V-shaped body, and unboarded sides consisting of long spindles. It is believed that wagons spread from central Europe to the northern European plain, replacing the two-wheeled cart that was subsequently restricted to the fringes of Europe, including most of France, the Mediterranean, and Scandinavia. It is believed that the wagon was introduced to southeastern Britain by way of the Netherlands, but the cart continued to be used throughout the northern and western parts of the British Isles.

While we have no detailed descriptions of the wagons used in seventeenth-century New Netherland, they were most likely Dutch wagons. Hector St. John de Crèvecoeur described a Dutch wagon in Orange County, New York, in the 1760s:

You have often admired our two-horse wagons. They are extremely well-contrived and executed with a great deal of skill; and they answer with ease and dispatch all the purposes of a farm. . . . On a Sunday it becomes the family coach. We then take off the common, plain sides and fix on it others which are handsomely painted. . . . If it rains, flat hoops made on purpose are placed in mortises, and painted cloth is spread and tied over the whole. (*Sketches of Eighteenth-Century America*, pp. 138–139)

The similarity of the Dutch wagon to the famed covered wagon of the American West is no accident. These large freight wagons originated in the Conestoga region of Pennsylvania and are more similar to the Dutch wagon than the modern European wagon.

CONCLUSION

From an early date, Dutch-American farming was a mixed agricultural tradition with a market orientation. Dutch breeds of livestock and strains of crops were mixed with English breeds and strains, and new crops were borrowed from the American Indians. Distinctively Dutch farm structures were built, and Dutch tools and equipment continued in use well after the English conquest. Dutch-American farming was regionally distinct, and it maintained its unique identity throughout the nineteenth century.

BIBLIOGRAPHY

Bachman, Van Cleaf. *Peltries or Plantations: The Economic Policies of the Dutch West India Company in New Netherland, 1623–1639.* Baltimore, Md., 1969. Makes the case that the Dutch West India Company was interested in agricultural settlement as well as in the fur trade.

Cohen, David Steven. *The Dutch-American Farm.* New York, 1992. A description of Dutch-American farmhouses, landscape, farming, family, and folk life in New York and New Jersey.

Cousins, Peter H. *Hog Plow and Sith: Cultural Aspects of Early Agricultural Technology.* Dearborn, Mich.,

1973. A history of distinctively Dutch agricultural implements: the Dutch plow, the sith, and mathook.

Donck, Adriaen van der. *A Description of the New Netherlands.* Edited by Thomas F. O'Donnell. Syracuse, N.Y., 1968; repr. of 1655 original. A seventeenth-century account of New Netherland that includes details of Dutch farming practices.

Fitchen, John. *The New World Dutch Barn: A Study of Its Characteristics, Its Structural System, and Its Probable Erectional Procedures.* Syracuse, N.Y., 1968. Fitchen surveys the construction and design of Dutch barns in America.

Jenkins, J. Geraint. *The English Farm Wagon: Origins and Structure.* Lingfield, England, 1961. A study of the prototypes of the English farm wagon, with descriptions of German and Dutch wagon types and the regions of Europe where ox carts were used instead of wagons.

David Steven Cohen

SEE ALSO **Landholding** and **Rural Life.**

THE FRENCH COLONIES

A UNIVERSAL CHARACTERISTIC of preindustrial European communities, in Europe and in America, is that the majority lived primarily by farming. In the early years of French settlement in Canada (the Saint Lawrence Valley), colonists were predominantly males who frequently farmed, or gardened, as a supplement to labor in a skilled trade or in the fur trade. After a few decades, when modest immigration and natural increase established a gender balance and a social infrastructure, farming became the vocation and expectation of most—75 to 80 percent of the inhabitants, or habitants as they preferred to call themselves. The process was achieved in Canada by the end of the seventeenth century. In Acadia (Nova Scotia and New Brunswick), there appears to have been demographic sexual balance somewhat earlier. In Louisiana and the

Illinois country, which were colonized later, the pattern emerged in the 1720s and 1730s respectively.

WHEAT FARMING IN CANADA

Methods of farming and farm products varied among the different colonies according to climate, soil, and markets. In the north where it could be grown, wheat was the dominant crop from the earliest years; it was the exclusive crop when a farm was first cleared, stabilizing between 50 percent and 75 percent in the eighteenth century. This reflected the bread staple of the French diet. Wheat was supplemented by lentils, root crops, and fodder crops, such as oats. These last sustained a small number of cows, pigs, the occasional pair of oxen, and possibly a horse or two. The ox was the usual draft animal, suitable for the heavy work of clearing fields from forest and for plowing. Horses, too, were draft animals, but were likely used more for transportation, especially in the winter, when snow and ice facilitated land transportation by sled and *carriole* (sleigh). From spring to fall cart tracks were often impassable because of mud or potholes. Then the river was the highway, supporting traffic in bateau, pirogue, and especially canoe, "the vehicle of Canada" according to Bacqueville de La Potherie. It was for access to the river and ease of communication that farms were surveyed perpendicular to the waterways in long rectangles, commonly in a ratio of about one to ten frontage to depth.

There has been debate over whether Canadian farming methods were primitive and backward compared with others at the time. Several practices have been noted: the use of oxen instead of horses as draft animals (also true in Louisiana), the use of heavy wheel plows instead of lighter versions, inattention to regular crop rotation and fallow, and small numbers of cattle. It has been argued that as a consequence of soil exhaustion yields of wheat were lower than in France and were kept barely tolerable by the incremental addition of newly cleared, high-yield virgin land. This notion of backwardness in farming methods has been challenged, because practices in extensive farming differed little from those in the northeastern English colonies at the time and into the nineteenth century. Documentation for calculating wheat yields on family farms is scarce or nonexistent and is difficult to interpret.

The limits of preindustrial agriculture provide an important context for understanding the local farm economy. Contemporary critics of colonial farming methods usually reflected the views of metropolitan elites. Upper clergymen and royal officials were predisposed to find laziness in social inferiors, and their ambitions for colonial development overlooked many realities faced by the habitant.

Dependent entirely upon manual labor and hand tools (mostly farm-made of wood), a family could work a maximum field area of 30 to 40 arpents (1 arpent equals 0.85 acres or 0.34 hectares) out of a usual farm size of 80 to 120 arpents. In Louisiana the field area workable by a family was less than 30 to 40 arpents because of the climate and much greater difficulty in removing hardwood forests. If a farmer started from virgin forest and cleared it at the rate of one arpent each year, it took a dozen years for a farm to support a family and most of a working life to improve a farm to its maximum level. Surpluses produced by most could not be large, and in any case the local market was limited. By the 1730s only modest amounts of flour, biscuits, and lentils found their way to wider markets through Louisbourg and in the Antilles. With a climate that excluded winter foraging, larger numbers of cattle and other animals would have required substantial fodder crops in competition with wheat and other produce. The slaughtering of animals in late fall was thus a seasonal ritual. In winter grain was threshed and wood was cut, especially cordwood both for consumption on the farm and for sale. Winter foraging was possible in Louisiana.

The choices made by habitants when investing their time and labor presumably made good sense to them. Fundamental in their calculations was a strategy for social reproduction—the survival of their families, including the provision of a livelihood for their children in adult life. Until the early nineteenth century at least, there was abundant, conveniently located arable land to provide new farms for each expanding generation. In Canada and Acadia the population doubled about every twenty-five years.

Although inheritance laws required the equal division of property among all children, in practice ways were found to keep farms a viable size. They were often passed on to one of the children, frequently a younger son, with other children's shares being a charge against the farm. Other strategies are evident, for example the purchase of an unimproved or partially improved farm nearby, or the taking out of a second concession on the same, or on a neighboring seigneury, for subsequent use by one of the children. When old enough, a son might start improving his own concession while still living at home and helping with the family farm, as a way of ensuring earlier returns when he married and began his own family.

Common to all strategies was the contribution of all family members to farm income: indeed, without a wife, farming was not viable. Her labor, more domestic and in the barnyard than in the fields (though important there as well), was indispensable. Similarly, children did chores and after puberty were expected to contribute adult labor. Success depended upon fortune as well: more than the average number of children (four to six) could overburden the farm's resources, and illness or death of a spouse early in the life course could impose an extra cost of hired labor.

Faced with such risks, security was paramount and found expression in strategies of diversification and self-sufficiency. The term subsistence farming is frequently used to describe the farm economy of New France. As a comparative description the term is useful, but it can be easily misapplied. From the perspective of agricultural specialization and market economies such as have developed since the nineteenth century, the preindustrial "subsistence" farm may look stagnant, isolated, and backward. It would be utterly false, however, to imagine a countryside of self-contained farms whose occupants themselves produced or manufactured everything they needed and had little or no intercourse with the world outside their immediate community. Certainly they tried to produce as much as they could for their own consumption, but the establishment and operation of a farm required capital as well as land and one's own labor.

Assuming that land was virtually free, tools, provisions, draft animals, livestock, and hired labor were nevertheless all required to start and operate a farm. The credit forwarded to pay for these was in the expectation of a future return. Farm indebtedness, a universal experience, was not necessarily due to the burden of seigneurial dues and tithes but reflected also some integration of the farm economy into the larger colonial economy. Skilled labor and a variety of goods (notably textiles, hardware, and distilled spirits) were purchased with or exchanged for products of the farm or for labor, likely through the agency of rural merchants. Hiring farm labor, though likely done as little as possible, was unavoidable at different times of the year or in the life cycle.

There were opportunities to supplement farm income by earnings off the farm. In the seventeenth century exchanges with Amerindians were common, but as the rural population expanded in the eighteenth century, its contact with the Amerindian economy became indirect and relatively less significant. It is estimated that as much as 30 percent of the male population of the Montreal region, and 18 percent of the entire colony, hired on as canoemen in the western fur trade for at least one season in their lives after the 1720s.

The standard of living of habitant farmers in Canada during the French regime can be described only comparatively. Those who possessed their own land sufficient to provide a living and their own draft animals, tools, and equipment enjoyed an independence of income comparable with the better-off 10 percent of French peasantry. This same standard prevailed in Acadia as well but to a lesser degree in Louisiana. However, farm inventories and assorted notarial documents suggest that there was considerable inequality in equipment and possessions among farmers. Some of this reflects different stages of establishment in the life cycle, but it also reflects different levels of prosperity. Family strategies brought varying success, and some failures. Even so, the fact that most habitants possessed enough land to farm distinguished them from most of their French cousins.

Their seigneurial dues and tithes—the only direct tax burdens—have been estimated at 10 percent to 15 percent of total farm income: if accurate, this is a light burden compared with that endured by their countrymen in France. There is evidence in the eighteenth century that seigneurs were pressing more systematically for payment of their dues, and that some habitants were resisting to the point of being taken to court. It is claimed by some historians that by the end of the French regime these burdens were increasing and weighed heaviest on the less prosperous farmers. After the cession of Canada to Britain some British and *Canadien* seigneurs began raising their seigneurial dues arbitrarily. The new environment weakened the force of customary law in this matter.

SALT-MARSH CULTIVATION IN ACADIA

Farming in Acadia, particularly at Minas and Port Royal (later Annapolis Royal), shared many significant features with that in the Saint Lawrence Valley. The preindustrial stamp was evident: modest-sized family holdings; a limited inventory of largely wooden hand tools and equipment; the primacy of the wheat crop supplemented by a variety of lentils and vegetables; a familiar variety of animals; an exchange within the local economy of food and nonfood products and labor; the purchase from outside of a number of goods, notably hardware, textiles, and distilled spirits; evident inequalities in wealth despite an overall modesty of household inventory. There were variants. The sea permitted more fish for consumption and sale. Orchards were more prevalent and diverse, supporting pears, plums, and cherries as well as apples. The sea also afforded more immediate contact with the Atlantic economy, not only with French fishing settlements but with New England as well. Settlement patterns and the shape of farm holdings did not follow the symmetrical rows of elongated rectangles fronting on the water as in Canada. Fields were more clustered around the farm, perhaps reflecting the influence of administration by New England in the still formative years 1654–1670. Even more likely, long stretches of English rule in the seventeenth century and after the British capture in 1710, lightened the weight of seigneurial obligations, which appear to have been irregularly enforced when not totally ignored.

The most distinctive feature of Acadian farming was the extensive salt-marsh cultivation undertaken on land reclaimed from the sea by dykes, particularly at Minas. Dyke building required specialized knowledge, skill, and cooperation among large numbers of laborers. Many Acadians were recruited from the Atlantic shores of France for their experience in this technique. There can be no doubt that dyke building contributed to a heightened sense of communal interest, but claims that this eclipsed the importance of the familial labor force in Acadian farming can be taken too far. Disputes over property rights indicate that concern for family property and its succession was not extinguished by a sense of higher communal purpose.

COMMERCIAL PLANTATION PRODUCTION IN LOUISIANA

Farming in Louisiana was quite different, largely because of climate, topography, and location. Officials and promoters conceived of commercial plantations in the lower Mississippi Valley similar to those in the Antilles and in the southern English colonies on the Atlantic Coast. For more than two decades after 1700 their dreams produced failures and financial disasters more than successful plantations, but from the 1720s a distinctive farm economy emerged. Most visible were the larger-sized plantations producing export crops of tobacco, indigo, some cotton, rice, and sugar, and wood products, whose labor-intensive production in a hot, enervating climate was achieved by numbers of black slaves.

Less visible but far more numerous, and significant because of the diversity they represented in the farm economy of the Gulf colony, were the family farms of small producers employing one or two slaves at most. Among the larger export crops, tobacco and cotton were apparently the ones that small producers could profit from most. Although labor-intensive (hoeing, planting, pruning, weeding, picking, drying tobacco, and ginning cotton), tasks could be done on a modest scale by hand, avoiding heavy capital investment in equipment.

As in the northern colonies, much farm produce was consumed on the farm. Even the larger commercial owners planted gardens for some provisions. Perhaps more than in the north, small producers found a local market for a wide range of produce. Except for wheat (which the climate prevented from being successfully grown in the lower Mississippi region), maize, lentils, vegetables, fruit, and meat were needed to provision New Orleans, Mobile, Biloxi, and also slave field workers. There was also a local market for cordwood and construction wood. In the early years when the colony had to import flour and other food from France, the deliberate location of settlements near Amerindian villages where provisions were purchased underscored the demand. These locations also provided opportunities for other exchanges with the Amerindians for pelts, notably deer skins. Natchitoches on the Red River was located for its trade potential with the Spanish, and the settlements at Biloxi and Mobile traded provisions with Pensacola. Farms in upper Louisiana at Kaskaskia, Cahokia, and Vincennes, though they employed some black slaves, produced wheat as their major crop, as in Canada, and sold it to the lower colony. Thus, there was a network of exchange between settlements that provided diverse sources of income for local farm households.

SIMILARITIES

Behind the distinctive features of small-scale wheat farming in Canada, salt-marsh farming in Acadia, and commercial plantation production with slaves in Louisiana, there existed common features of preindustrial farm economies in all three regions. Most farms were family ventures of a scale that could be managed largely by the family's labor with simple equipment. Part of the farm strategy was to achieve self-sufficiency in many things, but another part was evidently to diversify income, the result of which was to link the farm to the local economy at many points. Even during the period of French colonization, which was early in the settlement process when populations were relatively small, there is evidence of differentiation of farm wealth, as some producers managed better than others to take advantage of the opportunities that this diversity provided.

BIBLIOGRAPHY

Brown, Margaret Kimball. "La Colonisation française de l'Illinois: une réevaluation." *Revue d'histoire de l'Amérique française* 39, no. 4 (1986):583–591.

Clark, John G. *New Orleans, 1718–1812: An Economic History*. Baton Rouge, La., 1970.

Dechêne, Louise. *Habitants et marchands de Montréal au XVIIe siècle*. Paris, 1974.

Desbarats, Catherine. "Agriculture Within the Seigneurial Régime of Eighteenth-Century Canada: Some Thoughts on the Recent Literature." *Canadian Historical Review* 73, no. 1 (1992):1–29.

Dessureault, Christian. "L'Égalitarisme paysan dans l'ancienne société rurale de la vallée du Saint-Laurent: Éléments pour une ré-interprétation." *Revue d'histoire de l'Amérique française* 40, no. 3 (1987): 373–408.

Dunn, Brenda. *The Acadians of Minas*. Ottawa, 1985.

Eccles, W. J. *France in America*. Toronto, Ontario, 1972; rev. ed. Markham, Ontario, 1990.

Ekberg, Carl J. *Colonial Ste. Genevieve: An Adventure on the Mississippi Frontier*. Gerald, Mo., 1985.

Giraud, Marcel. *Histoire de la Louisiane française*. 4 vols. Paris, 1953–1974.

Goubert, Pierre. *The French Peasantry in the Seventeenth Century*. Cambridge, England, 1986.

Greer, Allan. *Peasant, Lord, and Merchant: Rural Society in Three Quebec Parishes, 1740–1840*. Toronto, Ontario, 1985.

Griffiths, Naomi E. S. *The Contexts of Acadian History, 1686–1784*. Montreal and Kingston, 1992.

Harris, Richard Colebrook. *The Seigneurial System in Early Canada: A Geographical Study*. Madison, Wisc., 1968.

Miquelon, Dale. *New France, 1701–1744: "A Supplement to Europe."* Toronto, Ontario, 1987.

Ouellet, Fernand. "Economic Dualism and Technological Change in Quebec, 1760–1790." In *Economy, Class, and Nation in Quebec: Interpretive Essays*, edited and translated by Jacques A. Barbier. Toronto, Ontario, 1991.

Reid, John G. *Acadia, Maine, and New Scotland: Marginal Colonies in the Seventeenth Century*. Toronto, Ontario, 1981.

Surrey, N. M. Miller. *The Commerce of Louisiana During the French Regime, 1699–1763*. New York, 1916; repr. 1968.

Usner, Daniel H., Jr. "The Deerskin Trade in French Louisiana." In *Proceedings of the Tenth Meeting of the French Colonial Historical Society, April 12–14, 1984*, edited by Philip P. Boucher. Lanham, Md., 1985.

Zitomersky, Joseph. "The Form and Function of French-Native American Relations in Early Eighteenth-Century French Colonial Louisiana." In *Proceedings of the Fifteenth Meeting of the French Colonial Historical Society, Martinique and Guadeloupe, May 1989*, edited by Patricia Galloway and Philip P. Boucher. Lanham, Md., 1992.

S. Dale Standen

SEE ALSO **Landholding** and **Rural Life**.

THE SPANISH BORDERLANDS

A VAST REGION of diverse climate and topography, the Spanish Borderlands spread west from Florida's Atlantic coast, continued along the Gulf of Mexico, sprawled untidily across the Mexican border, and finally ended in California at the Pacific Ocean. Although the borderlands included parts of other states on both sides of the international boundary, in this essay we will consider only the area within the present states of Florida, New Mexico, Texas, Arizona, Louisiana, and California.

When pioneers from New Spain (Mexico) first came to settle in the borderlands, they brought a varied assortment of plants and animals unknown to the area. To provide food and re-create a familiar way of life, Spaniards introduced Old World grains, particularly wheat, and many kinds of garden vegetables. They planted several types of fruit trees, as well as grapevines for winemaking. The newcomers also learned to value the staples that had sustained the indigenous peoples for centuries: corn, beans, and squash.

Introduction of European livestock proved to be especially significant for both the Spaniards and the Indians. The original herds of cattle, horses, and sheep thrived, creating a ranching industry that continued to be important long after the colonial era ended. The spread of Spanish horses by trade or raiding had a profound effect on Indian tribes throughout the West, as did the acquisition of sheep by the Navajo Indians of New Mexico and Arizona. Although farming and ranching evolved in similar ways throughout the borderlands, each colony developed some characteristics of its own and will be considered individually here.

FLORIDA

Spanish conquistadors entered Florida as early as 1513, but permanent settlement did not begin until 1565, when Pedro Menéndez de Avilés founded Saint Augustine on the Atlantic coast. A daring and resourceful sea captain, Menéndez had contracted with King Philip II to root out an intrusive French colony at Fort Caroline, fifty miles (80 kilometers) to the north, and to secure the region for Spain. Although he succeeded, Spain's plan to establish hegemony from Newfoundland to the Florida Keys remained an unrealized dream. For many years, the actual occupation was confined to a narrow strip on the sea coast, reaching north from Saint Augustine to the islands of southern Georgia.

Maintained by the Crown as a defensive outpost, Saint Augustine depended for its subsistence on food supplies imported from New Spain and Cuba. But since weather conditions and pirate raids made sea travel uncertain, the local population sought ways to feed itself between deliveries. Although Indian corn became the staple food grain, Spaniards much preferred wheat. For colonial officials, obtaining enough corn to provide for the needs of the town and garrison at Saint Augustine became a constant preoccupation.

In 1573 a contingent of Franciscan friars arrived in Florida to spread the Christian faith among the region's Indian tribes and win their allegiance to Spain. During the seventeenth century the friars gradually established a chain of missions extending west from Guale on the Georgia coast to the Apalachicola River in Florida. Neophytes absorbed the fundamentals of church doctrine and tended the missions' corn fields. As in other colonies, the friars planned to use proceeds from grain sales to purchase images, candles, wine, and other items needed to maintain their churches. Frequently, however, military authorities seized even their smallest surplus so that they might feed the troops. Such seizures, predictably, annoyed the friars. Transporting bulky grain supplies to Saint Augustine from distant missions also caused difficulties. Some corn came by boat; much of the rest arrived on packhorses or on the backs of native porters. At the capital, grain was raised on plots on the town commons, which were assigned to individual soldiers. Like the friars, the men-at-arms also depended on drafts of Indian labor to perform the tasks of cultivating and harvesting.

Although largely dependent on corn, the Spaniards also experimented with wheat farming. In 1645 Governor Benito Ruiz Salazar de Vallecilla planted a large tract in wheat to satisfy his countrymen's continual craving for white bread. During the next several years, the governor established an impressive hacienda, even arranging for millstones and a miller from the Canary Islands. Then, in 1649, Salazar died suddenly in an epidemic that spread rapidly from Cuba to Florida. After his death the Franciscans, who regarded his farm as an encroachment on Apalachee Indian lands, persuaded the next governor to abandon it lest it incite a rebellion. Subsequently, the friars themselves grew some wheat and other grains. By mid century, military needs had slackened enough to allow occasional sales of church surpluses in Havana.

In addition to grains, the colonists raised all kinds of European vegetables and several varieties of fruits. Florida's huge citrus industry, so important in the state's economy today, originated at Saint Augustine, where oranges, lemons, and limes all flourished in the colonial era.

During Florida's earliest years, Menéndez de Avilés, following the explorers who had preceded him, introduced cattle into the colony in the hope that livestock breeding could be made a viable enterprise. Conditions proved unfavorable at first, and it was not until the mid seventeenth century that ranching began to succeed. Because the king sometimes withheld the subsidies that usually sustained the colony, officials sought ways to bolster the local economy by developing exportable commodities, such as hides and dried beef. For that strategy to succeed, potential ranchers had to have access to grazing lands, which previously had been severely restricted by governmental policy. Although documentation is lacking, it is probable that Governor Luis de Horruytiner inaugurated a liberalized land policy during the 1630s, awarding a number of grants suitable for stock raising to his relatives and other prominent citizens.

One of the first important cattle ranches belonged to Florida's royal treasurer, Francisco Menéndez Marquez, who seems to have obtained his original capital by simply helping himself to funds deposited in the king's treasury. Known as "La Chua," the Menéndez hacienda was located in the Timucua region, near today's Gainesville. Ranching also became important along the Saint Johns River, west of Saint Augustine, and on the Saint Marks River, around present-day Tallahassee. At those locations, the Menéndez Marquez and Horruytiner families, along with their relatives and allies, developed a profitable industry, despite occasional setbacks caused by Indian revolts, epidemics, and pirate raids. Florida ranchers made regular trail drives of beef cattle to Saint Augustine, where they found a strong demand. By-products went from Gulf ports to Havana, where they were exchanged for trade goods to be sold at home.

By the 1690s the number of cattle had increased greatly, resulting in a general price decline. As reduced profits were making the business less attractive, stockmen soon faced even graver problems. Between 1702 and 1706 British forces from South Carolina, reinforced by Indian allies, overran Spanish Florida, destroying missions, ranches, and every settlement but Saint Augustine. Cattle that escaped being slaughtered or stolen became feral, running wild over Florida's savannahs in the eighteenth century.

NEW MEXICO

Spanish settlement in the American Southwest began in 1598, when Don Juan de Oñate led a large expedition north from a camp in the present state of Chihuahua. Heir to a fortune amassed from the Zacatecas silver mines, Oñate had contracted with the Spanish Crown to provide the military equipment, livestock, men, and supplies, which included seed grain, needed for a successful occupation of the remote province. When the colonists set forth in January, the party included 10 Franciscan friars and 129 citizen-soldiers, many accompanied by families. According to one scribe, the train of baggage carts, pack animals, and loose livestock spread over the countryside for more than a league (2.6 miles; 3.52 kilometers).

After an arduous journey up the Rio Grande del Norte, Oñate's advance guard reached the area above today's Española early in July. There, near the confluence of the Rio Grande and the Rio Chama, the Spaniards established headquarters at the Pueblo village of Ohke, which they renamed San Juan Bautista. Almost immediately, Oñate's followers took steps to secure a reliable water supply, recognizing that in New Mexico's dry climate successful agriculture would depend on irrigation. Assisted by fifteen hundred "barbarous Indians," they began construction of an *acequia* (irrigation ditch) to flood lands chosen for farming.

In his proposal to Viceroy Luis de Velasco, Oñate had included 150 mares with colts, 4,000 sheep, 1,000 goats, and 1,000 cattle. Making an interesting distinction, he also promised to bring one hundred head of "black cattle." Some historians have speculated that Oñate brought the blacks to start a herd of fighting bulls. It seems more likely that these one hundred head traced their ancestry to Avila and Andulusía in central and southern Spain. From ancient times, herdsmen in those provinces had bred black cattle that served as both meat and draft animals. Demonstrating admirable foresight, Oñate probably wanted to provide oxen for farming and transportation.

The sheep assembled by the Spaniards for the colonization of New Mexico also served a dual purpose. Known as *churro*, they were descended from the common sheep of southern Spain, whose long but humble heritage extended back to the Roman era. Although small of stature and shearing only a minimal quantity of coarse, long-staple wool, the *churro* adapted readily to the semi-arid grasslands of the New World. Its meager fleece proved well-suited to hand processing, and all agreed that meat from the *churro* was unsurpassed in flavor. By substituting morning dew and succulent plants for drinking water, these tough little sheep could withstand drought better than cattle, sometimes surviving for days on the trail without streams, springs, or ponds.

In planning for the long journey, Oñate's followers had assembled an enormous *caballada*, or horse herd, comprising over twelve hundred head. Unfortunately, detailed descriptions of the *caballada* are nonexistent. However, Pedro Saucedo Montemayor, a Mexican historian, has provided some information concerning the horses of New Spain during the post-Conquest period. Of Arab and Moorish breeding, the *caballo criollo* inherited such valuable traits as great stamina, good heads, and an intelligence rare in other strains. Among *caballo criollo,* bays, blacks, and sorrels predominated because dark colors were hard to see from long distances in times of war. But it seems that not all Oñate's mounts measured up to the high standards suggested by Saucedo. During the final review before Oñate's departure for New Mexico, the Inspector General complained that part of the herd failed to qualify as army horses and described them as "old nags."

Once settled, Oñate wrote enthusiastically about the wonders of his conquest to New Spain's viceroy, the Count of Monterrey. Impressed by the region's potential for agriculture, he extolled the crops produced by Pueblo Indians, declaring that "their corn and vegetables . . . are the best and largest . . . in the world." Some of the colonists also praised native farmers, observing that they grew bumper crops of corn, cotton, beans, squash, and melons. In fact, were it not for Indian surpluses, obtained by purchase or extortion, the colony probably would have collapsed during the first winter. Contrary to Oñate's glowing reports, life was hard at this new outpost of empire, and the inexperienced pioneers complained bitterly to authorities in Mexico City. These grievances, added to alleged irregularities in his administration, caused Oñate to fall from favor and face a lengthy investigation of his performance.

During the inquiry, officials collected depositions from Oñate's adherents and detractors, some of whom had fled New Mexico for the comforts of Mexico City. In describing the colony's agricultural production, the two sets of reports diverged widely. Witnesses supporting Oñate claimed that wheat harvests had risen significantly each year, from 188 fanegas (1 fanega equals 1.6 bushels) to 1,500 fanegas between 1599 and 1601, allowing the colony to subsist with only a small supplement of Indian corn. Similarly, livestock numbers had increased so

much that cattle alone provided meat for a year and a half, leaving the sheep for breeding and wool production. Speaking in opposition, one former settler summed up New Mexico's rigorous climate with the phrase, *"ocho meses de invierno y cuatro de inferno"* (eight months of winter and four months of hell). Others declared that chronic drought curtailed crop production and inhibited livestock breeding.

After weighing the evidence, the viceroy decided that the settlement's agricultural problems were not insurmountable. More significantly, he resolved to maintain New Mexico as a Crown colony supported by royal subsidies in order to continue the Franciscan missions. Oñate failed to redeem himself, however. On 24 August 1606 he resigned as New Mexico's governor and was replaced by Pedro de Peralta, who later founded a new capital city, *La Villa de Santa Fe* (City of the Holy Faith), in 1610.

With Peralta installed as governor, New Mexico's future seemed assured. During the 1600s the population slowly increased as more immigrants came from New Spain to establish small agricultural settlements along the Rio Grande from Socorro to Taos. Franciscan missions extended from the east side of the Manzano Mountains to as far west as the pueblos of Zuni. Irrigated farming and stock raising became the principal occupations. Far from commercial centers and without mineral wealth, the economy remained primitive, with barter the usual means of exchange. Despite modest growth, the colony faced difficult problems. For many years before the great Pueblo Revolt of 1680, relations between the Spaniards and the Pueblos deteriorated because of religious differences, mistreatment of the Indians, and encroachment on Pueblo farmlands. And among the Spaniards themselves, secular officials engaged in a long struggle with the Franciscan hierarchy for control of the province.

Although religious doctrine and political power became the principal issues in the church-state dispute, economic matters were also involved. During the 1620s, as the Franciscans established missions at various pueblos, disagreements arose concerning the use of adjoining fields and pastures. Besides absorbing the rudiments of Christian doctrine, Indian converts were expected to tend the crops and livestock of their teachers. Mission herds increased remarkably as colonists exchanged sheep and cattle for church ceremonies—baptisms, marriages, and burials. The friars also instructed their pupils in the manufacture of woolen cloth, producing New Mexico's first textiles. Although Franciscans portrayed mission agriculture as a source of food for the poor in times of scarcity, growing church wealth excited the envy of provincial governors and other laymen.

The two factions also vied for control of New Mexico's export trade, which then consisted of a few coarse textiles and an assortment of raw materials—salt, hides, piñón nuts, and livestock. Because buyers from other regions proved willing to pay much-needed cash for cattle, sheep, and horses, secular and religious officials alike sometimes made imprudent livestock sales that stripped the province of its feeding herds and food supply. For example, in 1634 a viceregal decree ordered an investigation into charges that Governor Francisco de la Mora Ceballos had "destroyed" the colony by sending four hundred mares, eight hundred cows, and a large number of sheep and goats down the Camino Real for sale at the mines near Santa Barbara. Later one of his successors, Governor Bernardo López de Mendizábal, attempted to monopolize the livestock trade by denying entry into the province by dealers from "other kingdoms." At the same time, the Franciscans defended their own animal sales, claiming that the proceeds allowed purchase of vestments, images, and other religious paraphernalia. In 1659 Governor López banned removal of stock from New Mexico, an embargo ignored by the friars.

Dismayed by the chronic disagreements that divided their oppressors and fearing obliteration of their own culture, the Pueblo Indians rose in revolt in August 1680. After the initial attack, the settlers retreated down the Rio Grande to a location near present-day El Paso, Texas, where they remained for twelve years. When Spanish forces under Captain General Diego de Vargas made a triumphant reentry in 1692–1693, they found that the Pueblo Indians had retained some cattle and sheep, although the herds had dwindled.

Once peace had been restored, after a series of bitter campaigns, Vargas realized that recolonization would fail without additional men and resources. With approval from Mexico City, agents assembled a relief expedition at the mining town of Parral, in present-day Chihuahua, which included stocks of textiles, munitions, and a large herd of cattle, sheep, and goats. Soon after the caravan arrived in Santa Fe in late April 1697, Vargas distributed everything among the settlers according to family size. During the apportionment, approximately 1,000 New Mexicans received more than 4,000 ewes, 170 goats, and 500 cows. They also accepted 150 bulls intended for breeding and draft purposes. When Vargas finished, the settlers took their animals and scattered to various communities along the Rio Grande and its tributaries. Herds increased slowly at first, but New Mexico's livestock industry had been revived.

Since the entire population depended on farming for subsistence, colonial officials established a system of land grants; portions of the royal domain were to be allocated to needy individuals or groups of household heads according to a well-defined procedure. Landless citizens first submitted a petition for a specific tract to the governor, who then commanded the nearest *alcalde* (chief local official) to investigate. If no adverse claim by an interested third party resulted, the governor gave his approval and ordered the grantees placed in possession. After designating external boundaries, the *alcalde* conducted a ceremony that had originated in medieval Spain, in which he led the grantees over the land as they pulled up tufts of grass, threw a few stones, and shouted, "Long live the king!" In community grants, each family received a house lot facing an enclosed plaza and a parcel of irrigated farmland. All the grantees enjoyed access to a large commons area for grazing livestock and cutting wood.

Once a grant had been confirmed, the proprietors made construction of an irrigation system their first priority. To assure crop production in New Mexico's dry climate, an advance guard sometimes would begin building the necessary works even before their grant received official approval. Although familiar with irrigation practices originating in Spain and Mexico, settlers in New Mexico were handicapped by their lack of engineering expertise, surveyors' equipment, and suitable tools. But since everyone depended on irrigation for subsistence, the entire community assembled to help construct major ditches and diversion dams. Community leaders usually began by laying out an *acequia madre* (mother ditch), which originated at a point far enough upstream to provide sufficient fall for water to reach the fields below. Workmen used crude shovels and crowbars made of fire-hardened oak or other native woods. Teams of oxen skidded away large amounts of loosened earth on cowhides. Without transits or other surveying instruments to guide them, work parties frequently turned water into the ditch to locate the proper grade.

After completing the mother ditch, irrigators extended the network by digging lateral canals branching from the new acequia and, then, a series of still smaller ditches, known as *sangrías* or *venas*, to carry water to individual plots. To protect the project from flash floods, they established a relief channel (*desagüe*) that carried excess flow back to the stream. Finally, the ditch builders completed the system by erecting a diversion dam. Usually made of logs and brush reinforced with earth and river rock, most dams on the northern frontier were simple structures that frequently washed out during times of high water. Overcoming many difficulties, irrigators in New Mexico designed and built some remarkable water projects during the colonial era. A few are still in use. These include the diversion of the North Fork of the Rio Quemado, near Las Truchas, and the Cuchilla Acequia, a large ditch that appears to run straight uphill from the Rio Hondo to water fields on the plain above at Desmontes, north of Taos.

After construction had been completed, management of the acequia system continued to be an important matter for every community. Sometime during the winter, water users (*parciantes*) from each acequia gathered for the election of an overseer (*mayordomo*). An officer with enormous prestige and responsibility, the *mayordomo* divided the available flow among his *parciantes* each day, levied fines for infractions of acequia regulations, and attempted to resolve disputes with users from other ditches. Every spring he took charge of a thorough cleaning procedure, in which all landowners contributed labor and equipment in proportion to the size of their holdings. Those unable to perform such work personally were required to hire substitutes. With a few modifications, irrigators in New Mexico follow the same administrative procedures today.

Of all the European plants introduced by the Spaniards, wheat became the most important. As in other regions of New Spain, newly arrived colonists in New Mexico yearned for white bread and disdained native corn. (However, recurrent food shortages soon made corn tortillas much more palatable to the settlers, and both grains became staples.) On the northern frontier, farmers made use of only the most primitive technology. To till the soil, they often used plows made from the crotch of a tree, sharpened on one end to approximate a plowshare, with a branch angling upward as its handle. Such crude devices usually lacked iron reinforcement of any kind and proved extremely fragile in rocky ground. At harvest time, farmers cut sheaves of wheat with a sickle or a long knife and gathered them into piles. To separate wheat from straw, they drove herds of goats or other livestock around the stacks again and again until the grain was threshed. After the harvest, trains of burros or mules carried sacks of grain to one of the many small, water-powered grist mills that abounded in New Mexico. Because cash was short, the miller customarily accepted flour or cornmeal as payment.

Although mules and their smaller cousins served well as pack and draft animals, most New Mexicans rode horseback when traveling. Wills and other documents from the colonial period indicate that horses suitable for long-distance travel (*caballos de camino*) commanded extremely high prices. Wealthy ranchers took great pride in their mounts; each presented a colorful picture when turned out in a silver mounted saddle, bridle, and spurs, topped off with a broad sombrero and brilliant sarape from Saltillo.

Once horse breeding had been established by Oñate's followers, neighboring Indians soon learned to value this large and somewhat frightening animal. As early as 1609 Fray Francisco de Velasco suggested that Pueblo converts to Christianity be rewarded with gifts of cows, ewes, and mares for breeding stock. Beginning with the Apaches, nearby nomadic tribes acquired increasing numbers of horses through trade or raiding. By 1700 most of the southern plains tribes up to the confluence of the Missouri and Mississippi rivers had obtained horses this way.

Once plentiful, horses became scarce because of continuing thefts. Frequently, troops headquartered at the presidio in Santa Fe had difficulty taking the field against hostile Indians because of a lack of mounts. In 1775 officials in New Spain sent fifteen hundred head to Governor Pedro Fermín de Mendinueta to replace those crippled, lost, or stolen, which incurred a heavy expense for the royal treasury.

As the eighteenth century progressed, sheep ranching gradually developed as New Mexico's most important agricultural enterprise. With peace restored after the Vargas reoccupation, citizens hoped to renew commerce with towns below the Rio Grande. Lacking the rich mines that brought wealth to Zacatecas, Durango, and Chihuahua, New Mexicans continued to depend on exports. In exchange for tanned skins, piñon, woolen textiles, and *churro* sheep, they obtained tools, weapons, hardware, dry goods, and other manufactured goods so necessary on the frontier.

In the early 1700s provincial governors banned exports of wool and livestock to prevent the depletion of these resources. As flocks slowly grew, officials relented somewhat, allowing outside sales of woolen products and wethers (*carneros*). Ewes remained under embargo to conserve breeding stock. Because of their value in distant markets, sheep became a medium of exchange locally, often replacing cash in retail transactions.

Toward the end of the eighteenth century, sheep numbers began to outstrip local requirements, allowing exports to increase dramatically. Entrepreneurs assembled enormous flocks of wethers, known as *carneradas,* at La Joya de Sevilleta, near Socorro. Taking advantage of summer rains, which filled water holes and improved grazing conditions, the caravans usually departed in August for the long, slow drive down the Camino Real to Chihuahua, then the leading trade center. Protected by a military escort, the expeditions were large enough to discourage Indian depredations.

Most of the commerce in sheep was controlled by a few wealthy families, often related through marriage, who also dominated economic and political affairs. By 1800 annual exports totaled twenty to twenty-five thousand head, worth from one to two pesos each, according to figures compiled by Governor Fernando Chacón. An important part of the provincial economy, the proceeds provided credits with wholesale merchants in Chihuahua and Durango for the purchase of goods to be retailed in New Mexico. After Mexican independence, in 1821, the number of wethers driven south each year increased even more. Throughout the colonial period, sheep sales far exceeded the value of any other agricultural commodity produced in New Mexico.

TEXAS

Approximately one-half the size of the present state, Spanish Texas extended in a broad arc from the Nueces River on the southwest to an area west of the Red River in what is today Louisiana. The lands between the Nueces and the Rio Grande, now the boundary between Texas and Mexico, were part of the province of Nuevo Santander (Tamaulipas) during the colonial era. Spanish settlement began as an attempt to block the French intrusions into Texas that had originated with the ill-starred expedition led by Robert Cavalier, Sieur de La Salle, to Matagorda Bay in 1685. As a countermeasure, Spaniards established a mission among the Indians of East Texas in 1690. Known as San Francisco de las Tejas, it was abandoned three years later when the French threat faded temporarily. After the turn of the century, however, renewed French expansionism in Louisiana convinced Spain to defend her interests once again. Between 1716 and 1721, Spanish officials organized three major colonizing efforts, resulting in the permanent occupation of Texas.

The first of these, a party of seventy-five persons commanded by Captain Domingo Ramón, left the mission of San Juan Bautista, on the Rio Grande, for East Texas on 27 April 1716. Ramón's followers included nine Franciscan friars and twenty-five soldiers, some accompanied by their wives and children. By the end of the year, the expedition had founded several missions and a small presidio near the Neches River, intending to introduce Christianity among the indigenous tribes and thereby secure their loyalty to Spain.

Far from any other Spanish settlement, the new arrivals found themselves perilously isolated. To help mitigate the danger, New Spain's viceroy, the Marqués de Valero, authorized Martin de Alarcón, governor of Coahuila, to establish a new community on the upper Rio San Antonio, midway between San Juan Bautista and the missions. After arriving, Alarcón's party selected a site west of the river for Mission San Antonio de Valero on 1 May 1718. Four days later military leaders laid the foundations for a presidio called San Antonio de Béxar. Later relocated, the mission became famous in Texas history as the Alamo, a landmark in the present-day city of San Antonio. To sustain the colony, as Oñate had done in New Mexico, Alarcón provided large numbers of livestock: some 548 horses, several droves of mules, and herds of cattle, sheep, and goats.

The third expedition, which came to Texas between 1720 and 1722, also brought many domestic animals and a large supply of corn. Led by the Marqués de San Miguel de Aguayo, that group located a presidio, which they named Nuestra Señora del Pilar de los Adaes, only eighteen miles (29 kilometers) west of the French outpost at Natchitoches, in East Texas. In 1722 the Marqués also founded an important mission and presidio close to the Gulf coast, at La Bahía del Espíritu Santo, completing the first phase of Spanish settlement in Texas.

As the eighteenth century progressed, the community founded in 1718 by Alarcón became the largest in Texas. By March 1731 the Franciscans had located four additional missions downstream from San Antonio de Valero and the presidio. At the missions, the friars endeavored to gather Indians from various semi-nomadic tribes, a process known as *reduccíon*, to facilitate their conversion to Christianity. Once congregated, the Indians received instruction in religious doctrine and European farming methods. Unlike New Mexico, where the missionaries established themselves on lands that the Pueblo Indians had used for many years, their counterparts in Texas received allotments of land from the Crown as payments for their roles as trustees for the neophytes until the conversion and acculturation process had been completed. According to official policy, title to mission lands would then pass to the Indians congregated on them, although the process seldom produced the desired results. At San Antonio each of the five missions received an allotment of irrigable farmland near the river and a larger tract for grazing farther away. When the missions were secularized—a process that began in 1793 and continued for three decades—church authorities divided their lands among those Indians still remaining, but they soon passed into the hands of land-hungry settlers.

To strengthen Spain's hold on the region, government officials recommended recruiting two hundred families from Spain, Cuba, and other places for settlement in Texas. Although well short of the goal, fifteen families from the Canary Islands arrived at San Antonio de Béxar on 9 March 1731 to supplement its small collection of settlers. A new community, the Villa de San Fernando de Béxar, was founded to accommodate this growing number of colonists. According to one estimate, the newcomers swelled the Spanish population in the Béxar district to two hundred, perhaps 40 percent of all Spaniards residing in Texas.

As the *isleños* (islanders) settled in, they received from the governor individual grants of irrigable land west of the Rio San Antonio and upstream from the mission fields. The expanding population soon caused competition for available natural resources, particularly irrigation water. Each community had its own diversion dam and *acequia madre,* but the problem of equitable allocation persisted. According to local custom, the five Franciscan missions had exclusive use of water from the Rio San Antonio, while the settlers and presidial personnel depended on a tributary that originated at San Pedro Springs. The arrangement proved unsatisfactory to the latter group and they coveted part of the flow from the main stream, causing disputes that lasted for generations.

As the community grew, residents developed an elaborate irrigation system on the Rio San Antonio—a system much more sophisticated than those in New Mexico. Mission records from the eighteenth century indicate that diversion dams were large structures made of stones joined together with lime mortar. The dam at Mission San Francisco de la Espada, for example, was forty-seven varas long, two wide, and three high (1 vara equals 33 inches; 825 millimeters). Flumes and intakes were also made of stone, which was used to reinforce the ditches as well.

Thanks to excellent craftsmanship, portions of the *acequia* network have remained in use until recent times. In his research, Thomas F. Glick, a scholar specializing in irrigation history, has found that the administrative procedures and terminology currently used at San Antonio to regulate water use can be traced directly to the Canary Islanders who arrived there in 1731. Many of these customs have persisted for more than two centuries. At Béxar, irrigation became much more important than in any other Texas settlement during the colonial period. Residents of La Bahía failed to build the necessary infrastructure, relying instead on Béxar for grain and other food supplies; in East Texas ample rainfall eliminated the need for irrigation.

Whether practicing irrigation or not, most farmers produced for home consumption, although the presidios provided occasional markets for grain. In colonial Texas corn was the staple food grain, far exceeding wheat in importance. Some of the mission farms were particularly large producers. At San Antonio de Valero in 1772, missionaries supervised the planting of three corn fields, each about one league long, enclosed by pole fences, and irrigated from the river. During the same year, neophytes at San Francisco de la Espada cultivated 123 acres (9 hectares) in one field and planted corn and beans. Another area was devoted to fruit trees that included two varieties of peaches, according to a mission inventory. The same document also listed a smaller field that produced up to one thousand fanegas (1,600 bushels) of corn annually and enough beans for the congregation to observe Lent and other days of abstinence during the year. Occasionally, calamities such as drought caused grain shortages, which induced provincial officials to impose price controls on corn. In 1789, for example, Governor Rafael Martínez Pacheco attempted to prevent both missions and settlers from profiteering by banning exports and setting a ceiling of two-and-one-half pesos per fanega. In addition to a variety of vegetables, Texans also raised sugarcane and cotton, but neither crop became significant economically during the colonial period.

Although Texans depended on farming for a necessary part of their subsistence, ranching rapidly became the most important branch of agriculture in the province. During the first ex-plorations of the late seventeenth century, the Spaniards lost a few animals that soon became feral and began to multiply on the verdant plains. Later, when Alarcón and Aguayo arrived, they found wild Castilian cattle already there, augmenting those brought by the colonists. In the next few decades, a thriving livestock population grew up at the missions and settlements. Unlike New Mexico, where sheep prevailed, cattle and horses became the dominant species in colonial Texas, although sheep gained importance later, after statehood. As it developed in Spanish Texas, ranching engendered a distinct culture that came to be identified with the cowboy. Highly romanticized, this cultural image has spread all over the United States and much of the world beyond.

By 1750 cattle numbers had increased dramatically, allowing ranchers to seek outside markets for their excess stock. Like settlers in New Mexico and California, Texans hoped to exchange livestock for badly needed manufactured goods. Spanish mercantilist policies hindered their efforts, however. Government regulations prohibited trade with foreign countries and severely limited commerce between Spain's own colonies. Undaunted by bureaucratic restrictions, Texans turned east toward the French settlements in Louisiana. Much in need of beef and breeding stock, residents there could provide high quality merchandise in return. At mid century, the illegal livestock trade had grown enormously, prompting a suggestion to the viceroy from Governor Jacinto de Barrios y Jáuregui that such activities be regulated and licensed. Mexico City ignored his advice, however, renewing the ban on intercolonial trade, which remained in effect even after Louisiana became a Spanish possession in 1763.

Following a wide-ranging inspection of the northern frontier, conducted between 1777 and 1778, Teodoro de Croix, Comandant General of New Spain's Interior Provinces, again recommended that trade with Louisiana be allowed so that Texas might be made self-supporting. Bureaucratic wheels turned slowly, but, at last, cattle exports became legal in 1780. The change of heart resulted largely from Spain's decision to declare war on England during the American Revolution. Both Spanish troops and American rebels needed Texas beef for campaigns in the

Mississippi Valley and West Florida. With barriers lowered, most livestock moved through legal channels, but imposition of an export tax of two reales (about twenty-five cents) per head caused some smuggling to continue. After 1780 Texas stockmen drove thousands of cattle into Louisiana, realizing handsome profits. Animals worth four pesos each at Béxar brought up to eleven pesos across the Sabine River in the Opelousas district, west of present Baton Rouge. Drovers also trailed herds south to Coahuila, but prices were much lower there.

When fortune smiled, trail drives paid well, but cattlemen faced serious difficulties as they struggled to start a viable industry. Taxes on unbranded cattle and Indian raids were particularly vexing. During his inspection tour, Comandant General Croix marveled at the enormous herds of wild horses and cattle that roamed the prairies. Needing revenues to finance a new Indian policy, he suddenly decreed that all unbranded stock on the public domain belonged to the king. After a four-month grace period, ranchers were required to pay a roundup fee known as *la mesteña*—four reales per head on cattle and six on horses—for animals gathered for branding or slaughter. Enraged by the preemption of property they had always regarded as their own, missionaries and settlers alike attempted to subvert the new regulations. Their efforts led to almost endless litigation. Officials occasionally forgave these fees through an amnesty, but the restrictions remained in place.

While Texans found Croix's taxes burdensome, the plundering of their herds by hostile tribes, particularly the Apache and Comanche, was a much greater problem. Although provincial military forces conducted frequent campaigns, Indian wars continued intermittently throughout the colonial era. Missions, ranchos, and presidios all suffered heavy losses. In 1777, for example, the Apache struck the Béxar missions, carrying off seven hundred cattle at San José y San Miguel de Aguayo and an equal number at San Francisco de la Espada. Several years later, one observer declared that some ranchers were losing as many as twenty head each day. Although usually well protected, trail herds bound for market offered particularly tempting targets. In June 1780 Comanche warriors fell on a herd of one thousand mission cattle headed for Louisiana, killed one *vaquero* (drover), wounded two, and destroyed some livestock. As the news spread, *vaqueros* refused to hire out for other drives, almost shutting off the hard-won marketing connection as soon as it opened. But such difficulties failed to discourage colonial stockmen for long.

By the end of the eighteenth century, cattle in Louisiana had increased sufficiently to provide most of the meat, tallow, and hides needed for local consumption. As a result, exports from Texas declined. But this decline was offset both by traders, who began marketing large numbers of horses and mules across the Sabine to supply Louisiana cavalry posts, and by the growing number of Anglo-American settlers moving into the Mississippi Valley. As early as 1791, adventurers such as the famed Philip Nolan crossed into Texas, with or without authorization, to catch wild horses worth fifty dollars apiece in New Orleans or Natchez. Occasionally Ohio River boatmen, eager to reinvest proceeds from a successful trading venture, returned overland driving bands of Texas mustangs. Delivered to Kentucky, the mustangs were in great demand, despite their unpleasant gaits and cantankerous dispositions. After the United States took over Louisiana in 1803, trade in horses and cattle continued, as high profits lured speculators from both sides of the border. Spanish officials tried hard to maintain control, but were unable to do so, a portent of the political turmoil to come.

ARIZONA

Endowed with an environment very different from that of Texas or Louisiana, Arizona originated as an extension of New Spain's northwestern province, Sonora. During the colonial era, Spanish settlement in Arizona was concentrated in a small area in the southern part of the state, below the Rio Gila and along the Santa Cruz and San Pedro river valleys. The Gila marked the northern boundary of a region called Pimería Alta (Land of the Upper Pima Indians), which extended south across the present international boundary to the Altar River in Sonora. Between 1687 and 1711 the famed Jesuit missionary, Eusebio Francisco Kino, explored widely in

Pimería Alta, visiting remote Indian villages and befriending the inhabitants. In 1700 Kino founded Mission San Francisco Xavier del Bac at a large Pima settlement on the Santa Cruz, situated near the current site of Tucson. Well versed in agriculture, Kino introduced cattle ranching and wheat culture to the Pima, but, despite his efforts, the Arizona missions failed to prosper and consequently fell into neglect. In 1732, however, new priests arrived and reinvigorated the missionary effort among the Pima and other nearby tribes. Hispano settlers came to the area after the discovery of silver at "Arizonac," a few miles southwest of today's Nogales, in Sonora.

Not surprisingly, increased settlement caused friction with the Indians, leading to the Pima Revolt in 1751. To protect the missions from further unrest, in 1752 the governor of Sonora, Diego Ortiz Parrilla, founded Tubac presidio on the Santa Cruz, which became the first permanent Spanish community in Arizona. Twenty-four years later, during a major realignment of military installations on the northern frontier, Colonel Hugo O'Connor, an Irish expatriate, moved the presidio to Tucson, which then became the region's largest town. After a period of decline, Tubac regained its garrison in 1787. Civilian communities grew up at both locations, but population growth languished. In 1821, at the time of Mexican independence, Hispanos in Arizona numbered around one thousand, far fewer than those living in New Mexico, Texas, or California.

Like the Pueblo Indians in New Mexico, the Pima had practiced irrigated farming for many years before the Spaniards arrived. In the 1690s Kino found them cultivating "splendid fields" in which they raised the usual food crops—corn, beans, squash, and melons. The Pima also grew cotton for the manufacture of blankets and other fabrics. At the missions, Jesuit priests depended on Indian labor to establish agriculture, persuading native farmers to work in church fields three days a week. Along with wheat, the fathers brought an assortment of European vegetables, including peas, lentils, lima beans, radishes, and mustard. They also set out fruit trees and grapevines, but failed to make good wine, probably because of the high mineral content in the soil and water.

Eventually, both wheat and corn became important food staples for Indians and Hispanos alike. Any surplus not consumed at the missions was sold to miners from Arizonac or, in later years, to the presidial garrisons. As the civilian population increased, settlers along the Santa Cruz succeeded in raising significant quantities of grain, although Apache raids and the region's remote location discouraged major development. To promote agriculture, military authorities set aside four square leagues of land around the two presidios for allocation in small parcels to individuals or families. Yet, despite such incentives to Hispanos, Indian farmers continued to be the largest agricultural producers during colonial times.

Both groups depended heavily on irrigation. Experts in water management, the Pima not only channeled part of the flow from the Gila and Santa Cruz to innundate fields in the valleys, but also built check dams and dikes in the arroyos to guide rainfall toward plantings away from the rivers. After establishment of the Tubac presidio, irrigators constructed a large *acequia* out of the Santa Cruz, which watered a patchwork of fields west of the river below post headquarters. As might be expected, need for water at the presidio caused controversy with the Pima mission at Tumacácori, a short distance upstream. To prevent discord, Tubac's commanding officer, the intrepid frontiersman Captain Juan Bautista de Anza, imposed a rotation system: the mission and the presidio were to use the river in alternate weeks. A similar situation existed at Tucson, where authorities allocated three-fourths of the flow from the Santa Cruz to the mission and one-fourth to the presidio. The arrangement broke down in 1796, after Father Juan Bautista Llorens of San Xavier had persuaded 134 Papago to join the Pima already congregated at the mission. Despite urgent pleas from the religious sector, civil functionaries refused to provide enough water for the Papago, causing them to flee back into the desert. Although Spanish officials usually managed to find an equitable solution to water disputes, in this instance they failed to do so.

While documentation is scanty, historians agree that ranching was the most important industry in Spanish Arizona, as in all the borderland colonies. As we have seen, Jesuit missionaries brought the first cattle into the region at the end of the seventeenth century. In the 1720s a scattering of ranchers drifted into the area south of Guevavi, a movement that accelerated after the discovery of silver at Arizonac. Few bothered to obtain title to the lands they used, preferring instead to graze their herds on the fringes of the missions or on the royal domain. Prospects for the industry seemed bright, but by mid century, merciless Apache attacks had decimated the region's livestock. Ranching proved difficult until the late 1780s, when an imaginative new Indian policy conceived by Viceroy Bernardo de Gálvez began to show results. By alternating vigorous military campaigns with offers of trade and presents, Spain managed to convince the Apache to sue for peace.

When hostilities ended, herds began to increase slowly. A military census conducted in 1804 indicated that Tucson's stockmen—including soldiers, settlers, missionaries, and Indians—tallied 3,500 cattle, 2,600 sheep, and 1,200 horses. Significantly, out of 300 cattle slaughtered annually, 130 were donated to nearby Apache bands for their continued goodwill. Up the Santa Cruz at Tubac, the inventory comprised one thousand cattle and five thousand sheep, which provided wool for a nascent weaving industry. Each year the weavers turned out six hundred blankets worth five pesos each; theirs was the only manufacturing enterprise in the region at that time. Although Arizona's livestock numbers were small compared with inventories in other borderland colonies, they represent a significant turnaround.

Just before independence, stockmen began to petition for land grants once again, a sure sign of renewed confidence. Located in the Santa Cruz, San Pedro, San Rafael, and Sonoita valleys, many of the grants were old ranchos that had been deserted for fifty years or more. The rancheros experienced a few decades of prosperity until the 1830s, when renewed Apache hostilities brought another period of desolation and despair.

LOUISIANA

Situated across the Sabine River from Texas, Louisiana, originally a French colony, came under Spanish rule through the fortunes of war.

On 3 November 1762 France ceded Louisiana to Spain, her ally, under the terms of the Treaty of Fontainbleau, as compensation for losses suffered in the Seven Years' War. During sixty years of French administration, the colony had never been successful and had been maintained only at great expense to the Crown. Concentrated in a triangle extending from Natchitoches to Mobile to New Orleans, the population totaled no more than seventy-five hundred persons, a figure that included a large number of black slaves.

After the change in administration, Louisiana's first Spanish governor, Don Antonio de Ulloa, arrived at New Orleans early in 1766. Once in office, Ulloa inaugurated a vigorous policy to promote immigration and increase agricultural output. As an incentive to outsiders, the governor and his successors made numerous small land grants, stipulating that each settler must occupy his tract, clear a portion for planting, and build fences to protect his crops. Immigrants, who often received government subsidies, were required to swear allegiance to Spain. A heterogeneous lot, the grantees included refugees escaping British jurisdiction in West Florida, Acadians from Nova Scotia, Germans who had been unhappy in Maryland, and a sprinkling of Anglo-Americans. In the 1780s and 1790s government officials made several much larger land concessions—ranging in size from two hundred thousand to one million acres (8,000 to 40,000 hectares)—to French, Spanish, German, and American entrepreneurs who promised to establish communities of settlers.

In contrast to the bounty that subsequently characterized Louisiana agriculture, the colony under France had never raised enough crops to support its population. Hoping to increase food supplies, Governor Ulloa encouraged production of wheat, corn, livestock, and other commodities. He also imported gristmills, both water-powered and horse-driven, to facilitate the processing of flour and cornmeal. Although Frenchmen and Spaniards alike scorned it at first, corn became an important staple. Wheat did not thrive in Louisiana because of an unfavorable climate. Many Louisianans, particularly farm families and soldiers serving at colonial garrisons, depended on rice for a significant part of their diets. Unlike wheat, rice flourished in the colony and still continues to be important in the regional economy. Under Spain, production increased sufficiently to allow significant rice exports to Cuba.

In addition to grains for local consumption, Spanish authorities also promoted cultivation of other crops for export, with varying degrees of success. Commodities such as tobacco, indigo, sugar, and cotton promised to provide the colony with credits in outside markets, to offset the high costs of imports. In 1777 Governor Bernardo de Gálvez heartened Louisiana's tobacco growers by purchasing their entire crop at guaranteed prices, both to supply the government monopoly in New Spain and for export to Europe. In the first year planters received more than fifty thousand pesos; by 1790 tobacco exports from Louisiana had climbed to two million pounds annually.

Indigo proved less successful as a cash crop. Used widely in Europe for the manufacture of dyes, indigo enjoyed a strong demand during the eighteenth century. After a short period of expansion, indigo harvests declined rapidly in Spanish Louisiana because of insect infestation, poor crop years, and competition from superior plants originating in Guatemala, Cuba, and East India. Furthermore, planters discovered that indigo cultivation caused sickness in their slaves, resulting in death after a few years of exposure. Although valued at one peso per pound in 1794, indigo production had fallen to a few thousand pounds by 1800.

According to legend, Jesuit priests brought the first sugarcane to Louisiana from Santo Domingo in 1751. In fact, the plant had arrived much earlier, during the first years of French occupation, but difficulties in refining the raw cane made extensive cultivation impractical. In 1790, however, growers introduced new varieties of seed from Tahiti and soon began experiments with a granulation process that made shipment in casks or barrels possible. The technology was further improved by Etienne de Boré, a planter from New Orleans who later served briefly as the city's mayor. Boré realized more than twelve thousand pesos from his sugar crop in 1795, earning the title "father of sugar making in Louisiana." By 1802 seventy-five plantations were growing cane, and sugar manufacture had become an important industry.

French colonists had raised small amounts of cotton. Labor shortages and unsuitable soils discouraged large-scale production in some localities, however, causing cotton production to languish until planters pushed north into the fertile lands near Baton Rouge, Opelousas, and Atakapas (now Saint Martinville). In those regions, farmers often grew four hundred pounds of cotton per *arpent* of land (about an acre), worth one hundred pesos. Slaves could pick sixty pounds a day, although cleaning reduced their output by two-thirds. In 1802, when Louisiana had legally reverted to France but was still governed by Spanish officials, cotton exports had risen to two million pounds.

In addition to increasing agricultural productivity, Spanish Louisiana also developed a vigorous livestock industry. At mid century, as we have seen, Texas cattle growers began to market their stock in Louisiana, despite efforts by Spanish officials to prevent them. After 1780, when regulations were relaxed, the trade increased, allowing settlers east of the Sabine to establish ranches of their own or expand existing operations. Grass conditions were particularly favorable in the regions near Atakapas, Natchitoches, and Opelousas. At Atakapas an innovative entrepreneur, Antoine Bernard d'Hauterive, encouraged stock growing among a group of Acadians who hoped to settle there. Beginning in 1765 d'Hauterive gave each family eight cows and a bull annually for six years, with the donor accepting responsibility for death losses. When the agreement terminated, the recipients returned the same number of animals to their patron and divided the increase with him.

Thanks to the availability of Texas breeding stock, cattle multiplied rapidly and soon became a nuisance in some places. In 1770 Governor Alejandro O'Reilly decreed that ranchers must keep their cattle fenced in for most of the year, allowing them free range only in winter. He also ordered that all animals be branded and that, after a grace period, those remaining could be slaughtered by anyone. Of course, rustlers made good use of his ruling, which was soon revoked, and wild cattle remained a problem.

The rapid increase in livestock numbers especially benefited residents of New Orleans, who, during the French era, had depended on salt beef from the West Indies, bison, and other wild game for much of their meat supply. To facilitate cattle deliveries, officials in 1782 approved construction of a new road from Atakapas to New Orleans. As slaughter increased, the New Orleans *cabildo* (municipal council) imposed a tax of three reales for each head killed. City fathers used these revenues for a system of street lighting and other municipal improvements. Louisiana cattle also found a ready market across the Mississippi at Natchez and, during the American Revolution, among troops fighting the British in West Florida.

Both the favorable environment and the seemingly insatiable demand for beef and breeding stock encouraged cattlemen to continue to expand their herds throughout the Spanish period. Comprehensive figures for the entire province are unavailable, but local censuses give an indication of prevailing trends. When sovereignty changed in 1762, the Opelousas and Atakapas districts tallied about one thousand head each. During the next eight years, the combined total climbed to ten thousand. At the time of the Louisiana Purchase in 1803, observers from the United States estimated the Opelousas herds alone at fifty thousand head, with another sixty to seventy-five thousand grazing at Atakapas.

CALIFORNIA

Although Spaniards had explored Alta (upper) California much earlier, they did not attempt to settle there until the latter part of the eighteenth century. Having decided that the region was vital to Spain's national interests, the king's advisers dispatched a series of colonizing expeditions into Alta California to achieve a variety of religious and political objectives. As in other borderland colonies, the Franciscan hierarchy yearned to introduce Christianity among the regional Indian tribes; secular officials hoped to block Russian intrusions along the Pacific Coast. Early in 1769 Governor Gaspar de Portolá and Father Junípero Serra, the famous Franciscan missionary, organized a four-pronged expedition that traveled north by both land and sea from Baja (lower) California to establish a base for further settlement. Although some of the seafarers experienced a harrowing voyage, the four parties reunited at San Diego, where they founded Alta California's first mission.

From San Diego the Spaniards continued north, locating a presidio and Mission Carlos Borromeo at Monterey early in June 1770. During the next three years, Father Serra organized additional missions at San Antonio de Padua, San Luis Obispo de Tolosa, and San Gabriel Arcángel, the last near present-day Los Angeles. To consolidate Spain's hold above Monterey, Viceroy Antonio María Bucareli ordered Captain Juan Bautista de Anza, commanding officer at Tubac presidio, to lead a larger party of settlers overland to California from Sonora. Extremely well organized, Anza's expedition founded the mission and presidio at San Francisco in 1776. By the turn of the century, the Franciscans maintained a chain of eighteen missions in Alta California, while military forces occupied four presidios.

When the colonizing expeditions came to San Diego in 1769, they brought the usual seed grain and livestock to begin planting and breeding. The founders believed that with Indian labor the missions would not only feed the neophytes but would produce a surplus for the presidios as well. The Spaniards discovered, however, that developing agriculture in a strange land was no easy task. At San Diego the first crops were either flooded out or withered by drought, causing the missionaries to rejoice if the harvest recovered their seed. Famine threatened frequently, while the newcomers remained dependent on long, unpredictable sea routes for the most basic food supplies. To eliminate the expense and uncertainty of ocean transport, Governor Felipe de Neve decided to establish two pueblos, which in California were unchartered Spanish towns. Civilian farmers would raise wheat, corn, and other commodities for the presidios, and the increased population would strengthen Spain's presence in California.

In 1777 Neve founded the first community, San José de Guadalupe (now the city of San Jose), about three miles (about 5 kilometers) from Mission Santa Clara and near the south end of San Francisco Bay. Each of fourteen households received a house lot, a plot of farmland, a yoke of oxen, a few other animals, and the necessary agricultural implements. Characteristically, the settlers joined together almost at once to build a dam across the Rio Guadalupe for irrigation. Four years later Neve's representative repeated the process at a site in the south near Mission San Gabriel; named "El Pueblo de Nuestra Señora la Reina de los Angeles de Porciúncula," it is now Los Angeles. The colonists consisted of eleven families who, having recently arrived from Sonora and Sinaloa, had agreed to stay ten years. As in the missions, agriculture at the two pueblos started slowly, but a measure of success came after a decade or so, particularly at Los Angeles. Between 1783 and 1790 total crop production at the two settlements increased from 3,750 bushels to 6,750 bushels. In 1790 Los Angeles harvested more grain than any of the missions except its neighbor, San Gabriel. Yields of grain, especially corn, continued to increase at Los Angeles in the next decade, ranging from a low of 2,700 bushels in 1796 to a high of 7,800 bushels the following year. Despite such progress, the presidios still found it necessary to buy large quantities of mission grain to fill their needs, although pueblo farmers enjoyed a priority over other sellers.

By the early 1780s mission agriculture had increased sufficiently so that it now provided adequately for the neophytes and allowed some sales to the presidios. The military did not lay out scarce cash for commodities purchased, but instead gave paymaster drafts redeemable in Mexico City. The Franciscans welcomed those exchanges because they furnished the credits needed to buy a wide variety of manufactured goods and religious articles unavailable in California. In 1781 Governor Neve imposed a code of price regulations that effectively prevented the missions from realizing excessive profits on agricultural products until the pueblos were able to offer some competition. Under Neve's schedule, grain prices were set unrealistically low: two pesos for a fanega of wheat, one-and-a-half pesos for the same amount of corn. Naturally the Franciscans, who had always opposed the civilian communities, complained bitterly. But the price ceilings remained in effect, although both missionaries and soldiers sometimes found pretexts to ignore them. The dispute became academic after 1810, when the Hidalgo Revolt brought economic chaos to New Spain. Subsequently, the presidios continued to requisition commodities from the missions, even though everyone knew that the royal treasury lacked funds to pay for them.

Government regulations may have bothered the friars, but even manipulated prices failed to impede the missions' rising prosperity at the end of the century. Between 1786 and 1798 Father-President Fermín Francisco de Lasuén added nine new missions to the nine previously established by Father Serra. Agricultural production continued to expand and church livestock multiplied at an amazing rate, bringing on a "golden age" for California's mission system. In the 1790s grain harvests varied between thirty and seventy-five thousand bushels annually; widespread famine ceased to be a threat, thanks to enlarged storage facilities. During that period, the missionaries initiated a number of industries, such as weaving and tanning, and introduced some new crops to diversify their agricultural base.

Recognizing a need for cordage and canvas to outfit Pacific naval vessels, officials in New Spain sent a technical expert, Sergeant Joaquín Sánchez, to San José in 1801 to promote the planting of hemp and flax. Although Sánchez decided that California lacked the capital needed for flax processing, he believed that hemp culture had real potential. Encouraged by a price guarantee well above the market, several missions began growing the crop, with considerable success. Between 1803 and 1810 production rose from less than 500 to 120,000 pounds. After the Hidalgo Revolt, however, regular shipping connections ended, the treasury could no longer pay subsidies, and the hemp enterprise collapsed.

Of course, Father Hidalgo's famous *grito* (shout) had far more important economic effects in California than did the decline in hemp raising. As contacts with the central government diminished, provincial residents believed themselves abandoned and began to cast about for ways to survive. Mounting agricultural surpluses offered a solution to their problems. Ironically, Californians received a commercial windfall from their old adversaries the Russians, who had remained active as fur buyers along the coast south from Alaska. Like the Texans before them, the populace simply ignored official regulations that interfered with desired trade.

A connection was established in 1806, when the charismatic Russian diplomat, Count Nikolai Petrovich Rezanov, brazenly sailed into San

Francisco Bay, hoping to obtain food supplies for his base at Sitka. Once officers at the presidio had recovered from shock, they allowed Rezanov to exchange his stock of Russian merchandise for a shipload of flour, corn, and beans, all sorely needed in Alaska. Trade with the czar's subjects became more frequent after Russian fur hunters founded a small settlement called Ross in 1812. Located about eighteen miles (29 kilometers) north of Bodega Bay, Ross soon became the center of an illicit exchange of Russian manufactured goods and California grain, which proved highly beneficial to both sides. Although officials in Madrid frequently demanded that the post be evacuated, the Russians politely ignored them, and the illegal commerce at Ross continued until after the end of Spanish rule in California.

As we have seen, ranching provided a distinctive element to the lifestyle in all the Spanish Borderland colonies. This was particularly true in California, where every social group—missions, pueblos, presidios, and ranchos—was deeply involved in raising livestock. From modest beginnings, animal numbers burgeoned remarkably on the ample grasslands, giving the province a pastoral character that entranced outside observers.

In 1769, when Serra, Portolá, and their followers arrived at San Diego, they brought several hundred horses and cattle and a handful of sheep. Additional stock came with Anza in 1776 and with the settlers who founded Los Angeles five years later. Livestock increased slowly at first, but by 1783 missions and pueblos together owned five thousand cattle and eight thousand sheep. Growth accelerated sharply during that decade, as others entered the ranching business. To provide remounts and beef for the troops, officers at the presidios established enterprises known as "Ranchos del Rey," where they grazed large herds of horses and cattle. By 1790 the presidio at Monterey was running five thousand cattle and two thousand horses on pastures along the Salinas River.

As an incentive for further production, the Spanish Crown authorized grants of land to disabled or retired presidial veterans who wanted to start ranchos suitable for grazing. Although the grants conferred only a usufructuary title, each recipient was expected to build up a herd of two thousand head. In 1784 Governor Pedro Fages made three large grants named "San Pedro," "San Rafael," and "Nietos" on the coastal plain near Los Angeles. During the next year, he made three similar concessions in the north, near Monterey and present-day Castroville. Other grants followed, but the number remained small until after 1821, which began the period of Mexican sovereignty.

In the ensuing years, livestock numbers continued to balloon. A count conducted in 1800 revealed that 74,000 cattle, 24,000 horses, 1,000 mules, and 88,000 sheep grazed ranges in Alta California. Of the total 187,000 head, more than 82 percent belonged to the missions: strong evidence that the church continued to hold most of the wealth within the province. By 1805 horses had become so numerous that huge numbers had to be killed to prevent damage to crops. In the north thousands of horses and cattle escaped to the Sacramento and San Joaquín valleys, where they ran wild.

Although there was some demand for exportable by-products, such as hides and tallow, a lack of markets caused prices for live animals to remain low. In 1786 Governor Fages requisitioned mission cattle for as little as three pesos per head. After their slaughter, the governor sold the meat for a like amount and pocketed a profit of three pesos for the hide and tallow. While the friars preferred to retain their cattle and process the hides into shoes, harnesses, and other leather products, they continued deliveries of cattle to the presidios. Despite the low prices, their large sales volume brought the missions sufficient wealth to arouse jealousy among other Californians. Those feelings led to demands for secularization of church property, which eventually took place after 1834 under Mexico. Prior to independence some commerce in hides and tallow grew with merchants from New Spain and Peru, but a lack of shipping prevented its full development until New Englanders became active in the trade, following independence.

BIBLIOGRAPHY

Almaráz, Félix D., Jr. *The San Antonio Missions and Their System of Land Tenure.* Austin, Tex., 1989.

Archibald, Robert A. "The Economy of the Alta California Missions, 1803–1821." *Southern California Quarterly* 58, no. 2 (Summer 1976):227–240.

———. "Price Regulation in Hispanic California." *The Americas* 33, no. 4 (April 1977):613–629.

Arnade, Charles W. "Cattle Raising in Spanish Florida, 1513–1763." *Agricultural History* 35, no. 3 (July 1961):116–124.

Bancroft, Hubert Howe. *History of California.* 7 vols. San Francisco, 1884–1890.

Baxter, John O. *Las Carneradas: Sheep Trade in New Mexico, 1700–1860.* Albuquerque, N.Mex., 1987.

Bushnell, Amy. *The King's Coffer: Proprietors of the Spanish Florida Treasury, 1565–1702.* Gainesville, Fla., 1981.

———. "The Menéndez Marquéz Cattle Barony at La Chua and the Determinants of Economic Expansion in Seventeenth-Century Florida." *Florida Historical Quarterly* 56, no. 4 (April 1978):407–431.

Davis, Edwin Adams. *Louisiana: A Narrative History.* Baton Rouge, La., 1971.

Glick, Thomas F. *The Old World Background of the Irrigation System of San Antonio, Texas.* El Paso, Tex., 1972.

Hammond, George P., and Agapito Rey. *Don Juan de Oñate, Colonizer of New Mexico.* 2 vols. Albuquerque, N.Mex., 1953.

Holmes, Jack D. L., ed. *Documentos Ineditos para la Historía de la Luisiana, 1792–1810.* Madrid, 1963.

Jackson, Jack. *Los Mesteños: Spanish Ranching in Texas, 1721–1821.* College Station, Tex., 1986.

Jones, Oakah L., Jr. *Los Paisanos: Spanish Settlers on the Northern Frontier of New Spain.* Norman, Okla., 1979.

Meyer, Michael C. *Water in the Hispanic Southwest: A Social and Legal History, 1550–1850.* Tucson, Ariz., 1984.

Morrisey, Richard J. "Early Agriculture in Pimería Alta." *Mid-America* 31, no. 2 (April 1949):101–108.

Myres, Sandra F. *The Ranch in Spanish Texas, 1691–1800.* El Paso, Tex., 1969.

Officer, James E. *Hispanic Arizona, 1536–1856.* Tucson, Ariz., 1987.

Saucedo Montemayor, Pedro. *Historia de la Ganadería en México.* Mexico City, 1984.

Simmons, Marc. "Spanish Irrigation Practices in New Mexico." *New Mexico Historical Review* 47, no. 2 (April 1972):135–150.

Worcester, Donald E. "The Spread of Spanish Horses in the Southwest, 1700–1800." *New Mexico Historical Review* 19, no. 3 (July 1944):225–232, and 20, no. 1 (January 1945):1–13.

John O. Baxter

SEE ALSO **Landholding; Mission Communities;** and **Rural Life.**

NATIVE AMERICAN ECONOMIES

When Europeans arrived to colonize North America, a complex and elaborate Native economy already existed on the continent. Although mostly based on farming, the Native economy also included hunting, gathering, manufacturing, and some mining, and it was executed across a network of roads, trails, and waterways that spanned the entire land mass. One might argue, then, that Europeans did not so much invent an American economy as they stimulated and modified an economy already in existence.

For example most of the crops that formed the basis of the colonial economy—corn, beans, squash, and tobacco—were not European in origin but rather were Native plants of the New World. For another example colonial roads were not carved from the wilderness but rather represented improvements of Indian trails taken over to form part of the infrastructure of the colonial system. Concerning habitation, in some cases New England colonists did not even clear land or build houses but instead bought or expropriated Native villages and fields and simply moved into them. They were able to do so both because of European military superiority and because the population of many Indian villages had been drastically reduced by diseases introduced by Europeans, with the few survivors being displaced to other villages. While the land of North America was not truly vacant in the early colonial period, it was at least "widowed," or as a modern geographer might say, it was underpopulated.

NATIVE AGRICULTURE

Agriculture in the Western Hemisphere is very ancient, having its origins about eight thousand years ago. The early Indian farmers experimented agriculturally with many local plants, some of which still grow wild in North America today, including marsh elder, knotweed, and pigweed. Only two of these early experiments in North America produced plants that are still farmed commercially—sunflowers and Jerusalem artichokes. The plants that came to dominate continental agriculture were borrowed from the tropical regions of Mesoamerica and South America. The most prominent of these was corn, which became a staple crop in North American agricultural systems about three thousand years ago. The advantages of these new crops from the south were that they were more productive than the North American crops, and easier to cultivate.

Corn, known to much of the world as maize, was the most productive and most important agricultural crop in Indian America. Over the centuries many different varieties of corn had been developed by such horticultural tribes as the Iroquois, Choctaw, Osage, and Pueblo, with most of the agricultural work being done by women (although both men and women worked in gardens). These varieties were suited to different climates and served different purposes. The most spectacular was popcorn that was prepared merely by toasting it until it exploded. Another specialized variety was sweet corn that was intended to be eaten when it was immature and which contained a high proportion of sugars as well as starches. A variety for grinding was flour corn that had soft hulls and thus required less labor for making cornmeal. Two harder and more substantial varieties for winter storage and transport were flint and dent, the latter so-called because an indentation developed on the kernel as it dried.

Hundreds of varieties of beans existed in the New World, many of which were domesticated in tropical areas and later spread to North America. These included lima beans, butter beans, pole beans, kidney beans, navy beans, snap beans, and string beans. Their particular contribution to the Native diet was protein, a definite advantage where there was a shortage of meat. A nutritionally lesser contribution was made by pumpkins and squashes—some native to North America—which were planted among the corn and beans in Indian gardens. These three crops—corn, beans, and squash—constituted the agricultural triumvirate that dominated Indian agriculture in North America.

The fields for growing these crops were organized differently in different parts of North America. Even within the same region, there was variability in the kinds of crops planted and the timing and techniques of cultivation. Like good farmers everywhere, Indian people varied their farming practices so that they did not risk all of their production in some singular manner that invited a catastrophe from weather or pests. Consequently some gardens were planted early and some late, some along the streams and others on high ground.

Two climatic conditions limited the extent of agriculture in North America—the length of the growing season and the amount of rainfall. Corn, the staple crop, required about 120 frost-free days to come to maturity, and so it could not be raised reliably north of the corn line, which roughly parallels the modern boundary between Canada and the United States. From the Atlantic Coast westward across the continent, the other limiting condition, rainfall during the growing season, was unreliable as one approached the Great Plains, from about three hundred to five hundred miles (480 to 800 kilo-meters) west of the Mississippi River. On the Plains and in the desert Southwest, special techniques had to be used to assure that the crops had adequate moisture.

East of the Mississippi, where rainfall was sufficient for farming, the major problem was finding a place to plant. The most desirable area was on the nearly bare floor of a mature forest, after the trees had been killed by burning or girdling. Here the Indian farmers planted their corn, beans, and squash together in hillocks consisting of from four to twenty seeds of corn and about the same number of beans, with squash and pumpkins planted both at the edges of and between the hillocks. Planting the different crops together in the same hillock allowed the nitrogen fixed in the soil by the beans to fertilize the corn and squash and permitted a thick root cluster, which conserved water, to build up among the plants.

In different places, depending on soil and rainfall, the hillocks were constructed higher or lower and closer or farther apart. The chosen soil was sandy loam, because it was more easily worked than soils containing clay. The preferred pattern of rainfall for these crops was in small increments all summer, with a total of from twelve to twenty inches (30 to 50 centimeters) for the growing season.

The implements used for cultivation were very simple, the most common being a pointed digging stick, from four to six feet (1 to 2 meters) long, which could be used for planting and some weeding. For serious weed problems a hoe was used, consisting of a handle made from a piece of wood carved from the side branch of a large tree and an integral blade carved simultaneously from the trunk of the tree, or the scapula of a large animal lashed to the wooden handle. Stones, clam shells, and antlers also were sometimes bound to wooden handles for tools, depending on the local availability of these materials and the kind of work to be accomplished. For farming, European tools were not notably superior to their Native counterparts. Only when steel hoes became relatively cheap in the late eighteenth century did Indian people begin to use them.

The same techniques used for farming in the Eastern Woodlands could also be used in the riverine forests along the major rivers of the

Great American Plains. Where the rainfall was scarce, crops could be planted near enough to streams and rivers to achieve subirrigation, which is the movement of water through the ground to the crops planted in the garden. To prevent sun damage, gardens were sometimes planted so that they were shaded by trees for part of the day.

In the more arid parts of the plains and desert, more sophisticated techniques had to be used. In the Southwest, tribes such as the Hopi and other Pueblo Indians selected garden plots where the natural features of the land channeled rainwater into a restricted area—at the base of cliffs, for example, or in low spots with no outlet. In these cases the hillocks were planted far apart, so as not to draw water from one another, and the corn was planted in thick bunches, so that the outside stalks could protect the inside stalks from the hot wind. Even so desert farmers did not expect success every year.

As the crowning achievement of Native American farming techniques, southwestern tribes such as the Papago, Zuni, Hopi, and other Pueblo Indians dug large irrigation systems, similar to those in Egypt and India, that channeled water from permanent streams into their fields. Some of these systems, known from archaeological evidence, covered thousands of acres. These agricultural systems were among the most productive in the world, and European travelers in the Southwest, from the first Spanish explorers of the sixteenth century to the forty-niners of the nineteenth century, were fed from these enormous resources.

HUNTING, FISHING, AND COLLECTING

North of the corn line and west of the Rocky Mountains, agriculture was not the foundation of Native American economies. In the interior of the sub-Arctic and Arctic regions and in the Great Plains as well, the hunting of large mammals was the most important activity. All along the Pacific Coast, along the Atlantic Coast north of Maine, and in southern Florida, the fishing and the hunting of sea mammals were the dominant economic activities. But everywhere in North America, Indian people hunted to some extent to obtain most of the proteins and fats in their diets. In general hunting was done by men, both men and women worked in gardens.

In the agricultural areas of the Eastern Woodlands, deer and small animals such as squirrels, rabbits, and raccoons were the most important game. Deer were stalked with bow and arrow, while small animals and migratory birds such as ducks, geese, and passenger pigeons were hunted with throwing sticks, nets, and blowguns. Because the peoples were sedentary, however, they could not wander very far to hunt, and because they maintained relatively large populations, game was usually not very plentiful near the agricultural villages. By comparison the Indian societies based on hunting, fishing, and collecting exercised great mobility to take them where game was abundant. Either they were nomadic, had a seasonal pattern of migration, or like the Nootka, Tsimshian, and other peoples of the Northwest Coast, practiced a seafaring way of life that gave them access to many kinds of tidal and ocean resources.

In the north the major game animals were moose and elk as well as deer. Their meat was either dried in summer for storage or allowed to freeze in the winter and chopped off as needed. Animals such as bears and beavers were hunted for their skins as much as for their meat, and traps and deadfalls were also employed. Along the coasts salmon were a main source of food, caught as they ascended the rivers to spawn. But the ocean was also fished with hooks and nets for halibut and cod. Smaller fish, such as candlefish and herring, were netted near the shore.

Sea mammals such as seals, porpoises, and whales were hunted all around the northern coast of North America and occasionally in the south. Most often sea mammals were speared, lanced, or harpooned with a point attached to a rope or stout line for hauling in or following the animal until it died. The harpooning of large whales, such as blue, sperm, and right whales, was practiced on the east coast by Algonquian Indians and became the foundation for a large colonial industry that was based between Massachusetts and Long Island Sound.

European tools, weapons, and implements had a larger influence on Indian hunting and fishing than on farming or collecting. Of immediate use to Indians were guns, which were superior to bows and arrows for stalking deer and other forest animals, since the shot could be fired from a longer distance. Firearms were of less value for sea mammals, however, since the animal was likely to be lost in the water after it was shot. Also it did not pay to hunt small animals with firearms, since powder and shot were expensive in the beginning and there was little meat to show for each shot fired.

Steel traps also had an impact on the Native economy; in fact they caused a considerable reorganization of Indian life, since Indian people began to emphasize trapping over other activities so that they could obtain furs to trade for the European goods on which they had come to rely. Although Indians had traps aboriginally, theirs were complicated and hard to set compared with a steel trap. Also of value to Indian hunters and trappers were the steel knives and axes obtained from white traders. Although they were not necessarily sharper than flint tools, they were less likely to break under hard use and could easily be resharpened.

Generally speaking Indian people used the same kinds of tools for collecting as for farming, with an emphasis on digging sticks, spades, crooks for reaching fruit and nuts, and baskets. For collecting as for farming, European tools did not offer significant advantages. Within most Indian societies, it was women who collected vegetable foods, working in groups and accompanied by children.

Women also managed the preparation of food, and here European trade goods contributed an important item—iron and brass kettles. As with knives or axes, the advantage was that the metal pots were hard to break, unlike Native clay pots, which often broke and spilled their contents into the fire. The European pots, by contrast, were not only sturdy but versatile, and women could use them for boiling, baking, or frying. Brass pots were light and, therefore, easily portable.

Only in California and the Great Basin could women's collecting activities be described as dominating the domestic economy. In these areas acorns, piñon nuts, and mesquite seeds were staple foods, supplemented by fish, shellfish, and game animals where available. Elsewhere across the continent the collection of wild plants was always important if not essential, especially the seasonal berry crops and prairie turnips on the Great Plains. Hundreds if not thousands of other fruits, roots, and vegetables were collected by Indian societies and are listed in various compendia and standard textbooks.

In every locality of North America, Indian people had to make choices among the seasonal foods that were available; that is, they needed to schedule their yearly round of activities to maximize the productivity of their labor. Wherever there were salmon runs, local people tended to include salmon netting in their activities, even such bison-hunting tribes as the Kutenai and Nez Perce. The annual migrations of caribou and bison were also usually incorporated into the schedule, since a large amount of meat could be obtained and dried in a short time to last the winter. The gathering of plant foods also required scheduling, since many of them, too, were only ripe or available at a certain time, like blackberries in the spring or cattail roots and Jerusalem artichokes in the fall.

Agricultural groups also included hunting and collecting in their schedule of subsistence events. After the gardens had been cultivated several times and were considered safe from weeds, hunting and collecting parties set out from the villages to obtain seasonal foods. After the fall harvest, Indian societies almost universally mobilized themselves for a large fall hunting expedition to put away meat for the winter. Those societies near the ocean also sent parties to obtain fish and shellfish in season. In general the horticultural and subsistence activities included in any society's schedule represented an intelligent selection from the many activities possible in the local area.

MINING, MANUFACTURING, AND TRADING PATTERNS

Native peoples in North America traded among themselves because certain natural resources were unevenly distributed and because certain peoples maintained levels of manufacturing skill that their neighbors did not have. The most dramatic trade was the transcontinental exchange of luxury goods that included eagle feathers, metallic copper mined in the Great Lakes area, mica from the Appalachians, hematite from New Mexico, catlinite for pipes mined in Minnesota, dentalium and abalone shells from California, conch shells from the Gulf of Mexico, obsidian cores from the Rocky Mountains, and orange-wood bowstaves from the Ozarks. This trade in luxury goods is very ancient, as attested from archaeological sites, and is continued even today among some Indian tribes.

Because of the concrete economic conditions of North America, the items selected for long-distance trade had to possess certain characteristics. First of all there were no large pack animals on the continent, although dogs were used for such purposes on the Plains. Consequently the Indian trader had to carry everything on his or her back, which meant that the items of the long-distance trade had to be very valuable by weight. When the trading destination was reached, these items were exchanged for other lightweight items that could be carried back home. Parrot feathers, for example, could be carried from the Rio Grande to the Ozarks and exchanged for bowstaves. Mica could be carried from Appalachia to the Gulf and exchanged for shells. This did not mean, however, that a single person had to make the whole trip. Just as often the items were traded from village to village over a period of months, changing hands many times but always increasing in value by moving away from the source.

In some areas of the continent, waterways were more important than trails for moving goods. Powered by paddle, the same boats that were used on the Northwest Coast for fishing and harpooning were also used for coastal trade from California to Alaska. In the Great Lakes and north across Canada, bark canoes were used among the many lakes and rivers. They were made of bark so that they could be portaged—that is, carried by hand across land barriers that separated one network of streams from another.

In the rest of the continent, dugout canoes and rafts were more common. On the slower and larger streams of the Missouri-Mississippi drainage system and in the Southeast, portages were not as necessary, and so large boats (dugouts measuring about fifteen meters and bark canoes eight) were made to stay permanently within one system of waterways. Consequently

trade routes in these areas were simply up and downstream along the same river. By contrast canoe traffic in Canada went for hundreds and thousands of miles in the same direction, portaging across several systems of waterways.

For local transportation cruder and less substantial boats were often used. These included bull boats, made from the skin of a single buffalo stretched across a hemispherical framework of branches, and brush boats, made of bound reeds or rushes. Simple rafts were also used, made of two or more logs bound together. These kinds of craft were used especially along the Missouri River and in California.

Large dugouts and plank boats, however, were very stable and were seaworthy in light weather. Aboriginal trade between Florida and the West Indies has been documented, and a Pacific Coast trade existed between the mainland and offshore islands, including even Santa Catalina, some twenty-six miles (42 kilometers) from the mainland.

Local trade in North America was different from long-distance trade and included many bulky, everyday items such as corn, dried meat, rope, baskets, pots, twine, deerskins, and fur—in fact any item that a society preferred to acquire by trade rather than produce for itself. Such trade implies a difference in manufacturing skill between groups, so that a particular village, for example, specialized in pottery and traded it to all the surrounding villages.

Certain localities in North America were famous as the sites of annual trade festivals. At some appointed time, many different tribes would arrive for several days of trading, feasting, and dancing. Famous among these locations are the Falls of Saint Anthony on the upper Mississippi, the Shoshone Rendezvous in southwestern Wyoming, the Dalles Rendezvous on the Columbia River, and the Taos Pueblo. In some regions of the continent, certain tribes specialized in trading, and their language became the regional language, the lingua franca, in which people negotiated for the exchange of goods. On the Northwest Coast, the Chinook language was the trade language, while in the Southeast the Mobilians took the role of traders, later replaced by the Chickasaw. In the Great Lakes region, the Potawatomi were noted as traders and travelers, while on the Missouri River, the Mandan were the focus of exchange. Among the Arctic groups, Cree became the language of trade and negotiation. A unique trade language by manual signs developed on the central plains in a situation where ten or more tribes did not understand each other's speech.

INDIANS IN THE COLONIAL ECONOMY

In the first stage of contact between British colonists and Native Americans, the colonists were learning how to survive in the New World, while Indians struggled with the effects of epidemic disease. After that a new and even more traumatic situation developed for the Indians, with colonists undertaking to exterminate or enslave them. One representative of this new political tendency was Governor William Berkeley of Virginia. To motivate soldiers to join a military campaign in 1644, Berkeley suggested that only Indian men would be killed and that, as compensation for their services, soldiers could take Indian women and children as slaves. Virginia saw little enslavement, but by the middle of the century thousands of Indian people had been enslaved in other colonies either to work on mainland colonial farms or to be sold as slaves to the West Indies. These slaves had either been captured in war by the colonists or bought by colonists from allied Indian tribes, who were encouraged to raid other tribes, especially those in Spanish and French territory, to obtain slaves.

In reaction to these events, a considerable pro-Indian, antislavery sentiment developed in the British colonies, led by such religious leaders as Roger Williams. Toward the end of the seventeenth century, many colonial governments had been persuaded to outlaw Indian slavery, in large part because the slavery of Africans had proven to be much more successful from the standpoint of the plantation owners; for example, while Indian slaves frequently escaped to join their relatives across the frontier, fugitive African slaves found it more difficult to find refuge. After Indian enslavement was abolished, Indian tribes were employed as slave catchers for plantation owners, particularly in Virginia, the Carolinas, and Georgia.

Other roles for Indians in the British colonial economy were as hunters both for meat and as participants in the developing deerskins trade. Also, local patterns of trade between Indian and colonial villages became established on the same pattern as aboriginal trade, with the Indians exchanging baskets, cordage, and meat for metal tools, beads, and other trade goods. More and more, Indian people on the frontier came to depend on these European trade goods, and they reorganized their domestic life around the availability of kettles, knives, axes, firearms, and cloth.

More than the British, the French mobilized Indian societies for manufacturing and trade with the homeland. Not only were French traders the leaders in penetrating the continent and stimulating trade in furs, they also trained Indian women in Canada to produce patterns of beadwork that were popular in France. The flowery Chippewa-style beadwork made even today is based on French patterns of the colonial period.

Wherever there were permanent French settlements, however, they tended to follow the British colonial pattern of enslaving Indians. Especially around New Orleans, slaves from the Natchez and nearby tribes were put to work on plantations and in the houses of slave owners. More often, however, Indians worked for wages in French colonies as trappers, voyageurs, teamsters, and boatmen.

The Spanish mobilization of Indian labor was different both from the British and the French. In California missions and rancherias were organized with Indians as a peasant class, recruited from tribes defeated and dispersed by the Spanish military. The military expeditions themselves were brutal, and thousands of Indian people were enslaved by Spanish soldiers and used as servants, porters, and prostitutes. After the military expeditions, Indian slaves were numerous in the Spanish colonial administrative centers and were sold into Mexico for work in the mines or to the West Indies for agricultural work.

The Dutch colony of New Netherland seems to have been little different from the British colonies in its treatment of Indians. The Dutch participated with the British in the 1643 Pavonia Massacre against the Algonquian in New Jersey. Afterward, Indian slaves were present in the colony despite the fact that the Dutch publicly eschewed slavery. The Dutch were also precocious traders along the Hudson River system, and, like the Europeans that followed, they mobilized many Indian people into the fur trade.

THE EFFECTS OF EUROPEAN CONTACT ON INDIAN ECONOMY

For many Indian societies, the contact with Europeans was beneficial, at least in the short run. At first tribes near the colonies, such as the Powhatan and the Iroquois, profited greatly as middlemen in the trade for European goods, and they extended their political influence to the interior. In these early days, Indian tribes jockeyed for position, both to be nearest the Europeans and to form political alliances with them. But when the European colonists became more numerous, these same tribes were the ones most often attacked by the Europeans, and they suffered the most. Many became extinct as political entities, such as the Yamassee and Wappinger, and still others—Mahican, Pequot, and Lumbee—melted into the rural areas as refugees.

In the Spanish colonial areas, only the Pueblo Indian tribes of New Mexico and Arizona managed to maintain themselves as semi-independent nations. In Florida the Spanish mission Indians ultimately were captured as slaves by the British and allied tribes, were sold into slavery in the West Indies by the Spanish, or took refuge with the Creek and Seminole. In southern California, Indian people maintained an Indian identity but were organized around the Spanish missions. In central and northern California, however, many Indian tribes retained an autonomous existence, trading first with the missions and later with the Russian traders coming down the coast from Alaska.

The Indians benefiting most from European contact, however, were the tribes around the Great Plains. Before the Europeans brought horses in the late sixteenth century, buffalo hunting was slow and difficult. Hunted on foot, the buffalo had to be driven or surrounded, with lines of stone cairns used to drive the animals off cliffs or into box canyons during the fall migrations. But with horses it became possible to chase the buffalo and kill large numbers in all seasons, and the Indians were quick to see this possibility.

An entire complex of economic activities was soon developed by the Plains peoples around horses. Since horses required frequent changes of pasture, the people became nomadic. Because horses could pack and pull travois with large loads, Indian peoples developed buffalo-skin tipis that could be quickly erected and torn down. All kinds of horse gear was invented by Indians or borrowed from Spanish practice—saddles, bridles, bits, and hobbles.

Firearms did not become important for buffalo hunting, however, because they were not suited for the style of chasing and killing developed by the Plains Indians in the seventeenth and eighteenth centuries. The guns of that period fired but one shot and were hard to load—in fact impossible to load while riding a horse. So Indian hunters used lances instead and short arrows fired by stiff bows at close range to penetrate the buffalo's skin. The usual technique was to ride as close to the buffalo as possible and then fire an arrow down through the ribs to the heart and lungs. A hunter might kill three or four animals during a single chase.

Their new efficiency in hunting buffalo enabled the Plains Indians to develop a trade in surplus buffalo hides and robes. Also the nomadic tribes were able to trade their dried or jerked buffalo meat to surrounding agricultural tribes such as the Arikara, Hidatsa, and Mandan for corn and vegetables. Those mostly horticultural tribes themselves kept horses, and sometimes they competed with the nomadic groups for access to the buffalo herds.

Some Plains tribes became specialized horse breeders and horse catchers and, ironically, made profits by selling horses to Europeans. On the southern Plains, the Comanche traded both with New Orleans and with the Spanish of New Mexico and had a reputation for eating horses when buffalo were scarce. On the northern Plains, the Blackfeet were the preeminent horse raisers, along with the Nez Perce and Shoshone, who both supplied horses to the Lewis and Clark expedition.

Among eastern Indians stock also quickly became important, because the only native domestic animals were dogs. For the Cherokee, hogs and corn quickly became mainstays of the economy in the colonial period, and both were traded across the frontier. Farther south the

Creek and Seminole ran herds of Spanish cattle in the savannahs of Georgia and Florida and traded cattle and beef to the British colonies and the Spanish missions of Florida.

Eastern Indians also had horses, although not nearly as many as the Plains tribes. In the east horses were used mostly for transportation and warfare. After eastern Indians adopted plow agriculture, some horses were used for that purpose, although oxen were the most common plow animals. Sheep were also adapted for Indian purposes, specifically in the Southwest and most notably by the Navajo.

Fruit trees of European origin were also quickly adopted by Indian peoples, from the Seminole of Florida to the Pueblo of the Southwest. For Indians the most popular fruits were oranges, apples, and peaches, all of which were widely distributed in North America, far in advance of the European frontier.

CONCLUSION

In general both Indians and Europeans had to adapt to each other's economic needs in the colonial period. For the Europeans to survive at all, they had to use New World domestic plants and incorporate hunting into their economy. For transportation they adopted canoes and bark dugouts. They even squared their villages in the Indian manner for defense and surrounded their forts with palisades and ditches. From the standpoint of Europeans still in Europe, being an American or a colonial meant that a person had been considerably Indianized in culture and habits.

For Indian peoples the two major effects of the European invasion were death, from disease and warfare, and displacement, as the frontier moved west. But many tribes adapted well, reorganizing their own domestic economies and taking a role in the colonial economy. Most often this role was to supply raw materials for colonial and European enterprises, but there were special situations in which the Indians supplied staples or worked for wages.

By the end of the colonial period, the tribes in the British colonies either had been demolished or dispersed or had been relegated by treaties to discrete reservation territories, within which they pursued a modified economy based on the European pattern. In Spanish Florida and California, there were no reservations, and the Indians occupied the place of a peasantry on the European and Mexican models. In French Canada the Indians around the permanent French communities lived in conditions similar to those in the British colonies, while those Indian people involved in the fur trade were more coequal with their French colleagues and intermarried with them to form the considerable Métis communities of later times. At the end of the colonial period, there were truly free societies of Native peoples only in the central part of the country, and there this remained true only for another hundred years.

BIBLIOGRAPHY

Crosby, Alfred W., Jr. *The Columbian Exchange: Biological and Cultural Consequences of 1492.* Westport, Conn., 1972.

Hodge, Frederick Webb, ed. *Handbook of American Indians North of Mexico.* Bureau of American Ethnology Bulletin 30. 2 vols. Washington, D.C., 1907–1910.

Hulbert, Archer Butler. *Red-Men's Roads.* Columbus, Ohio, 1900. In addition to this, there are many regional and statewide surveys of the aboriginal transportation system.

Murdock, George Peter, and Timothy J. O'Leary. *Ethnographic Bibliography of North America.* New Haven, Conn., 1941; 4th ed., 5 vols., 1975. This is the standard modern bibliographic reference, augmented by a three-volume supplement published by the same publisher in 1990 and edited by M. Marlene Martin and Timothy J. O'Leary.

Sturtevant, William C., editor. *Handbook of North American Indians.* 20 vols. projected. Washington, D.C., 1978– . The descendant of Hodge's handbook.

Weatherwax, Paul. *Indian Corn in Old America.* New York, 1954.

John H. Moore

SEE ALSO **Ecological Consequences of Economic Development; The First Americans; Native American Families and Life Cycles;** and **Technology;** the maps accompanying **The Natural Environment.**

ECOLOGICAL CONSEQUENCES OF ECONOMIC DEVELOPMENT

WHEN EUROPEANS FIRST contemplated North America, they believed that they had found an abundant supply of all of the natural resources they could want. From the towering straight pine trees they needed for ship masts to the beavers whose pelts they coveted for felt hats, the resources of the Western Hemisphere seemed inexhaustible. To succeed in America, many colonists believed, they need only harvest what God or nature had already provided; nature's bounty appeared unlimited to both those already in North America and to the European readers of promotional literature celebrating and cataloging the resources of the Western Hemisphere. For the duration of the colonial period, migrants from Europe and their descendants acted as if every natural resource had a price; great profit would be theirs if only they could bring what they saw as commodities to market.

But these migrants were wrong about the supply of desirable resources. Although Americans would continue to look to the West and believe that there existed a virtually endless supply of raw materials, already by the mid eighteenth century many colonists realized that their pursuit of economic gain had indeed altered, and perhaps seriously damaged, the environment. By the time of the American Revolution, anyone who traveled across the continent, especially the region between the Atlantic Ocean and

the Mississippi River, looked out upon a landscape vastly different from the one that existed before Europeans ventured westward in the wake of Columbus's voyages. Though ecological shifts in New France and the Spanish Borderlands were not as extensive, the environment of the entire continent changed because of the spread of Old World peoples, plants, and animals. From the perspective of colonists who feared the loss of the continent's precious resources, the changes in the appearance of the land suggested a potentially less bountiful future.

To be sure, the North American environment showed marks of economic development long before 1492. Indians across the continent, from the Atlantic to the Pacific, had for generations changed the landscape through their economic systems. Eastern Woodland Indians had earlier cleared thousands of acres of forest for their fields and for fuel. They had also altered the populations of certain game animals, though not nearly so drastically as colonists later would. The population of deer, for example, increased after the Indians had cleared parts of the forest; the resulting edge habitats proved ideal for deer, whose population swelled in response to the larger supply of food such habitats afforded. Birds and insects that consumed farm products similarly experienced growth in their numbers when Indians grew crops, though the agricultural practices of most Indians did not attract as many pests as colonial monoculture.

The landscape also actually looked different as a result of Indian use of the land. In the Northeast, for example, areas that resembled parks, at least to European eyes, dotted the environment; in the Southwest efforts to irrigate crops had altered riparian regions, shifting the population of animals and fish dependent on the most precious natural resource in the desert—water. And everywhere that Indians had used fires to clear fields, no matter how limited the extent of the burning, the forests showed the signs of human intervention in pursuit of economic gain. Even when Indians limited the extent of fires by burning only during certain seasons and in specific areas, fires no doubt often went out of control and cleared large portions of woodland, though such fires did not permanently threaten many species of animals or vegetation.

Still, while Indians consciously altered the ecosystem of North America, the changes they imposed on the landscape were far less severe than those effected by colonists in the seventeenth and eighteenth centuries. That the landscape actually looked different after two hundred years of European settlement came as no great surprise to colonists. After all, with the exception of the small minority who migrated to find religious freedom, Europeans went to America to enhance their material prospects. The pursuit of economic gain had already transformed the European landscape by thinning its forests and depleting its indigenous game populations.

Further, the search for profit through the attempted mastery of the natural world had ethical foundations for transported Europeans and their descendants. The well-known biblical injunctions of Gen. 1:28 had taught a specific lesson for those interested in economic development: nature existed to serve mankind. English terminology reinforced this ethical imperative. Those who sought to farm had to "improve" the landscape. That is, the environment was better when it served the economic interests of those who lived there. Early modern Europeans did not, in general, greatly respect nature in its most pristine forms. Though migrants had to modify their expectations to adjust to the climate of North America, with those who failed to do so

suffering for their intransigence, by the end of the seventeenth century, if not earlier, colonists and explorers acted in ways that might best be termed "imperialist." They sought to take control of the environment and make it yield its benefits for their profit.

Far-reaching ecological changes—alterations in the entire web of life, human and nonhuman—took place in North America in the aftermath of European expansion westward at the end of the fifteenth century. The most dramatic ecological effect of European colonization, though not directly related to economic development, was the spread of Old World pathogens among North American Indians, precipitating the most profound demographic catastrophe in recorded history. But most ecological changes on the continent followed directly from economic activity, especially the pursuit of profit through trade and agriculture. Among these changes the best-known at the time was the decline in the number of furbearing animals.

Yet change was also evident in other ways. The composition of forests shifted dramatically when colonists logged them extensively in pursuit of fuel, building supplies, masts, and charcoal for making iron. Fish populations altered as a result of extensive fishing and changes in streams and rivers due to the spread of logging and farming. Further, colonists' actions altered the environment in more subtle ways as well: the earth became less able to hold water, thus increasing the risk of floods; summers became hotter and winters colder in once-forested areas when the insulating effects of trees diminished; erosion shrank the amount of arable land in riparian regions. Everywhere, it appeared to some observers by the end of the eighteenth century, the apparent cornucopia that had greeted the earliest European explorers had diminished as a result of economic development.

THE FUR TRADE AND ITS AFTERMATH

Pelts brought profit, or so most European explorers and colonists believed, from the time of contact to the late eighteenth century. Therefore they quickly set about to acquire the skins they thought would find a market in Europe. From the Arctic reaches of Hudson Bay to the more temperate climate of the Southeast, English, Dutch, and French colonists killed animals, or enlisted Indian hunters to do so, for their hides. By the eighteenth century, the progress of the skin trades had taken an enormous toll on a variety of animals, particularly beavers and deer. Changes in various animals' habitats further added to the loss of wildlife in the colonies.

The Decimation of the Beaver

The fur trade developed early in the colonial period, carried out by British, Dutch, and French explorers, traders, and colonists. Migrants to New England no doubt sought to free themselves of the religious encumbrances of the Anglican establishment, but they could not so easily flee their economic obligations. As William Bradford made clear in his history of the settlement at Plymouth, colonists quickly latched onto the export of beaver pelts, mostly obtained from Indian hunters who wanted what the migrants offered in trade, as a way to retire their debts. When a group of French thieves robbed an English trading post at Penobscot in 1631, they took mostly beaver pelts, an assault so heinous that Bradford felt compelled to describe the assailants' methods in his history of Plymouth. He knew too well the threat such an action posed to the migrants who relied on those pelts to maintain their credit with their partners in England. Still, by 1636 colonists in Massachusetts had shipped 12,530 "Pounds of Beaver" to England, along with over 1,100 otter skins. Thus, Bradford wrote, "they conceived their debts had been paid, with advantage or interest." The fur trade in New Netherland, later New York, also became vital to the economic interests of colonists.

The Dutch and French, too, shipped furs in sizable quantities. Dutch traders gathered approximately 4,700 beaver and otter skins in 1624 and almost 7,700 skins in 1638, all presumably intended for shipment across the Atlantic; by the late 1650s the Dutch annually exported approximately 46,000 pelts from their post at Fort Orange, located on the Hudson south of its confluence with the Mohawk River. Later, English exports from New York underscored the importance of the trade for the colony. Pelts totaled one-fifth of all exports to England during the first half of the eighteenth century, and in some

peak years, such as the late 1710s, they totaled almost two-fifths of the trade. Farther north the trade had become substantial by the early seventeenth century, when Huron hunters traded furs to French colonizers and explorers. Though the early-seventeenth-century trade was not sufficient to support large-scale colonization in Canada, profits remained substantial and trade continued. Quebec, under control of the English in 1630, became the scene of extensive trade; the Huron brought approximately thirty thousand skins to the town that year.

Once initiated, the fur trade did not stop until hunters threatened the very survival of fur-bearing animals in eastern North America. The fur trade caught on among northeastern Indians not only in British America but in French Canada and New Netherland. The commerce had a particularly devastating impact on beavers, which the Dutch settler Adriaen van der Donck described in the 1650s as having "the shape of a cucumber which has a short stem, or a duck that has the neck and head cut off." But the trade in beaver skins had ecological implications beyond the decline in the mammal's numbers. In 1492 there might have been as many as sixty million beavers in North America, and virtually every one of them, except for the very young, busily altered the ecosystem; no other species, except for homo sapiens, so changed the North American environment. Yet beavers' modifications of the environment and limited mobility made them relatively easy to find. Beavers tended to remain in the vicinity of their dams throughout the course of the year, with only young beavers leaving the colony to search for new mates. Though their dams proved generally impenetrable to other animals, they were no match for Indian hunters, especially when these hunters had procured metal from traders and attached iron to their axes and spears.

Given the demand for beavers among Europeans, it is not surprising that their numbers dwindled considerably in North America. After all, Europeans had long hunted beavers before they ventured across the ocean, and it was the decline in availability of Old World beavers that provided such an initial enthusiasm for the North American fur trade. The beavers' practice of limiting the size of their colonies further exacerbated the decline in the species; their natural rate of population increase simply could not keep pace with the rate at which they died in the fur trade. As Indians became increasingly bound into trade with colonists, and in the process modified their approach toward their periodic hunts, beavers became the most noticeable victims of the spread of the European market in the western hemisphere.

Beavers began to decline rapidly by the mid seventeenth century. By 1660 the decline was evident throughout the coastal region of Massachusetts and in the Narraganset country, though the trade survived longer in major river valleys, no doubt because these drainage basins had provided beavers with the greatest choice of habitats before the trade became so widespread. The decrease in the trade had a dramatic impact on the economy of towns that had become dependent on the commerce; Springfield, on the Connecticut River, and Chelmsford, Concord, and Lancaster, on the Merrimac, each felt the decline of the trade. In New York the decline in beaver, along with other factors relating to the spread of English colonies, contributed to animosities between the Iroquois and other Indians in the 1640s and after. Along the Susquehanna River, beavers had experienced substantial decline by the early eighteenth century, though traders continued to record beaver pelts in their accounts through the middle of the century. In northern New England and parts of Canada, beavers survived the colonial period, mostly because these areas attracted far less settlement, but here too Indian hunters killed beavers for the European market. Wherever colonists built their settlements, they found more abandoned dams than beavers.

The decline in American beavers had an impact on other forest denizens. Dams on small creeks tended to increase the biological diversity of specific areas. Fish soon lived in the ponds behind the dams, and they attracted animals and birds that fed on them. Further, beaver dams tended to raise the water level in particular areas, often helping to prevent flooding. To serve this function, however, the dams had to remain intact. But as all beavers knew, dams that remained untended soon fell into disrepair, a situation these fastidious mammals did their best to correct whenever possible. Ignored, the dams eventually broke, releasing their water downstream.

Though the destruction of the dams decreased the biological diversity of particular areas, the long-term impact of the loss of the dam and pond was not entirely disastrous for colonists. While the dam existed, the impounded water in the pond killed trees. When the dams broke, microorganisms remained that prevented trees from growing quickly again in the area. Thus while forests might immediately begin to grow again after a forest fire (though often with a different composition of trees), the regrowth could not occur rapidly in former beaver ponds. Instead of trees recapturing the area, grasses tended to grow extremely well. When colonists moved into these areas, often ten to twenty years after the beavers had been removed by hunters, they found ideal pasture for their livestock without having to go through the often arduous procedure of clearing their fields first. Since these meadows could frequently encompass as many as two hundred acres (80 hectares) and could produce perhaps as much as four tons of hay per acre (per hectare), it was no wonder that colonists scrambled to claim lands formerly under water behind beaver dams. The decline of one species, then, could serve the interests of others, though such instances were generally rare in early America.

Yet beavers were not the only animals to decline dramatically as a result of the expansion of the trade system. In the Northeast, traders' records reveal that hunters, most of them Indians seeking trade goods, brought a wide range of other animals to their posts. The skins of bears, panthers, fishers, muskrats, otters, wildcats, raccoons, and foxes all became commodities in the new economy of the eastern woodlands.

Hunting the Southern Deer
In the Southeast, where the climate was less attractive to furbearing animals, the trade in deerskins became a vital economic pursuit for colonists. Indians also became integrated into the transatlantic commerce in skins, especially in the eighteenth century. There too, as in the northern colonies, the decline in deer was a direct consequence of the spread of the European market. Like beavers, southern deer limited the size of their populations. Many were monogamous, and with a seven-month gestation period leading to the birth, in most instances, of only two fawns,

the natural growth rate was sufficient to keep the species numbers high only in times with no great external pressure.

But such sociobiological habits were not designed to replace a quickly declining population. In the southern British colonies, deer populations made a partial recovery only during times when their human hunters were engaged in war and thus were too busy to carry on the hunt. The decline of deer was none too surprising, given the growth in the skin trade and the incorporation of hundreds of southeastern Indians, including Creek, Cherokee, and Choctaw, into the European-based commerce. Decline was especially evident over the course of the eighteenth century. Annual exports from Charles Town, the most important southern port for the trade, increased from approximately seventeen thousand to twenty-four thousand in the late 1710s to eighty thousand by the early 1730s and up to one-hundred and fifty thousand by the middle of the century. But the growth in the trade could not last indefinitely. In contrast to the abundance of skins they were able to take during the early colonial period, by the end of the eighteenth century Indian hunters were unable to find sufficient animals to maintain the trade.

THE NEW ECONOMY OF THE FOREST

The early modern Europeans who migrated across the ocean had come from a world that was, in general, not heavily forested. Centuries of demographic and economic growth had decimated the original forests of Europe, and residents of the continent had responded, as much as possible, by using wood only for vital purposes. Thus when colonists sent reports of the seemingly endless forests of eastern North America, Europeans, particularly those interested in overseas commerce, realized that they had found abundant supplies of a commodity as precious as beaver pelts and a great deal more in demand. Within a few decades of settlement, colonists were busy shipping wood products eastward. Such trade had a dramatic impact on American forests; so did the production of charcoal for the developing pig iron industry in the eighteenth century. The phenomenal growth of the colonial population and the expansion of settlements westward had perhaps an even greater effect on American forests, many of which have never recovered.

Indians, of course, had cleared substantial portions of the forest, a fact many early colonists recognized. English and Dutch colonists benefited from earlier Indian clearing activities, carried out mostly by burning. Thomas Morton noted for New England in the late 1630s that:

The Salvages [sic] are accustomed to set fire of the Country in all places where they come and to burne it twize, in the yeare, viz: as the Spring and the fall of the leafe. The reason that mooves them to doe so, is because it would other wise be so overgrowne with underweedes that it would be all coppice wood, and the people would not be able in any wise to passe through the Country out of a beaten path. (Quoted in Michael Williams. *Americans and Their Forests,* p. 44)

Rather than an endless forest, Morton wrote that some of New England's forests were sufficiently open to remind him of England. "The trees growe here and there as in our parks," he recalled, "and makes the Country very beautifull and commodious." William Wood, surveying Massachusetts in the early seventeenth century, commented on the direct connection between the Indians' burning and access to the forests:

It being the custom of the Indians to burn the wood in November when the grass is withered and leaves dried, it consumes all the underwood and rubbish which otherwise would overgrow the country, making it unpassable, and spoil their much affected hunting; so that by this means in those places where the Indians inhabit there is scarce a bush or bramble or any cumbersome underwood to be seen in the more champion ground. (*New England's Prospect,* p. 38)

Morton and Wood would have been even more impressed if they had been able to travel several hundred miles to the west. There, along the western edge of the forest, in the present-day states stretching from Wisconsin to Texas, Plains Indians periodically used fire to maintain the grasslands vital to their economy, and it seems likely that the extent of their fires was far greater than that of Indians living in the eastern woodlands. Everywhere the overall amount of forest consumed by Indian burning remained beyond the knowledge of colonial observers, since forests had grown again in once burned over regions. Yet seventeenth- and eighteenth-century descriptions of certain types of forests—particularly extensive slash, longleaf, and loblolly pine forest in the Southeast and white pine forest in the Northeast—reveal earlier burning, presumably by Indians, and the regrowth on those tracts of species that fare better after fires than hardwoods.

Yet Indian clearing of forests could not compare with the colonists' depletion of American woods in the pursuit of economic gain. Long before their westward migrations, Europeans had two basic notions about forests. On the one hand, they knew that they needed the wood products available in forests; wood was vital to the construction of dwellings, and it provided the most important source of fuel, though early depletion led some Europeans to rely on other products, such as peat, when they had denuded forests. On the other hand, in addition to their economic promise, forests were places of nightmarish danger: hideous man-beasts patrolled the forests of Ireland; the Greeks feared evil centaurs and satyrs who lived in wooded areas; and everywhere in Europe the popular culture, especially fairy tales, enumerated the dangers, human and nonhuman, one would encounter when traveling in forests. To be sure, there was some basis for fearing a visit to a forest, at least as long as wolves and other predators still prowled there. But the fear of forests was greater than the actual risk of danger, at least by the early modern period.

This cultural baggage came with the colonists to North America and shaped their responses to wooded areas. To many colonists, the accessibility of the forest meant economic promise, especially when commerce in forest products brought profit before farmers could earn much through agriculture. Further, they believed, as Christians in Europe had earlier, that clearing forests reduced the perceived threat of otherworldly beasts (or, in North America, of Indians). Whether motivated by a deeply felt cultural imperative to abolish forest denizens or searching for the commercial products that they thought existed in forests, colonists soon began what became, by the end of the colonial period, an assault on forests that did not ebb until the late nineteenth century and the emergence of a new sensibility regarding wooded areas. Colonists acted on the presumption that American forests were extensive because of the fertility of the soil. "The land also is so natural to produce wood," Dutch settler Adriaen van der Donck wrote in the 1650s, "that in a few years large trees will be grown, which I can say with certainty from my own observation; and that unless there be natural changes or great improvidence, there can be no scarcity of wood in this country."

Lumber and Naval Stores

Faced with apparent opportunity, English colonists were eager to commence the lumber trade in North America, particularly in New England. "The plants in *New England* for the variety, number, beauty, and vertues, may stand in Competition with the plants of any Countrey in Europe," John Josseyln informed the readers of his 1674 travel account. Those already in America were already busy harvesting this resource. Colonists built sawmills in Maine in the 1630s; by 1682 they had built twenty-four sawmills in southern Maine alone, and others dotted the landscape of the eastern colonies. In the mid seventeenth century, the mouth of the Piscataqua River became an important center of lumbering and the focal point of the mast trade, with perhaps twenty sawmills drawing on its water and a host of shipbuilders plying their trade along its banks in the mid 1660s.

Though New England lumber exporters dominated the trade with England, arranging for the shipment of over 60 percent of all lumber products in the late colonial period, virtually every major port along the Atlantic coast took part in the trade. Surviving customs records for the late 1760s and early 1770s indicate that the trade was indeed substantial. Approximately 233 million board feet (6,291,000 meters) of lumber left these ports from 1768 to 1772. Northern lumberers shipped mostly pine, with perhaps one-quarter of their output comprised of oak. In southern ports pine became so important that it was virtually the only species exported.

White pines, to English eyes, were ideal for shipbuilding, particularly for masts. Growing up to two hundred feet (60 meters) and with diameters reaching six feet (2 meters), the trees seemed a perfect replacement for the wood then in use in England. Fearful of depleting such a valuable resource, Crown officials moved to protect American white pines through legislation. The Massachusetts charter of 1691 thus contained a clause that "all [mast] trees of the diameter of twenty-four inches [160 centimeters] and upwards at twelve inches [30 centimeters] from the ground" be reserved for the Royal Navy; soon afterward Crown surveyors marked appropriate trees. The passage of the White Pine Act of 1722 placed even greater restrictions on colonial use of these trees: it ordered that no white pines growing beyond the range of established townships be cut; all were reserved for the navy. Colonists balked at the unworkable act, and many realized that not all of these trees were adequate for masts. Still, such legislation fueled animosity between colonists and the Crown. Though Crown officials sought to save white pines for the navy's sole use, North American trees remained, throughout the colonial period, substantially less important for masts than trees imported to England from the Baltic states.

In the end legislation intended to preserve white pines, which Crown officials continued to pass until the end of the colonial period, generally failed. Colonists everywhere in British America acted toward the forest as the fur traders had acted toward beavers: confronted with an apparently endless supply of a desirable resource, they set about cutting down trees with abandon. If Britons back home had to pay high prices for fuel and could use wood only sparingly for their dwellings, colonists burned wood whenever they desired and used what Europeans deemed valuable hardwoods for any purpose whatsoever. Colonists' unwillingness to preserve trees derived directly from the contradictions between their economic plans and the need for lumber in England. Sir John Wentworth, surveyor general of His Majesty's Woods during the 1770's, wrote,

The acts of Parliament relative to the preservation of pine timber in America, being merely penal and too general, operated so much against the convenience and even necessities of the inhabitants that, had, or could they have been strictly executed, they would have prevented cultivation, and soon put an end to the lumber trade, both to the West Indies and England, though the latter was an object of parliamentary bounty. Hence it became almost a general interest of the country to frustrate laws which comprehend nearly an unlimited reservation. (Quoted in Robert Greenhalgh Albion. *Forests and Sea Power*, p. 268)

In Canada, where indigenous forests had great potential for producing naval stores desperately needed by the French navy, a combination of circumstances prevented the development of a substantial lumber industry when the territory was under the control of the French. Problems in transportation, competition with a short-lived timber industry in Acadia, officials' concerns about the costs of surveying, cutting, and shipping lumber, and reports that trees in the Saint Lawrence Valley were not as good as those that could be obtained in Europe diminished enthusiasm for developing the naval stores industry in Canada, at least before the British acquired the territory after the Seven Years' War. With settlements in Canada receiving only a few ships from France each year and delays in transporting masts causing them to suffer from exposure that limited their utility, lumbering in New France supported colonists' needs more than those of the French navy. Given the obstacles it was not surprising that the French interest in Canadian naval stores waned in the early eighteenth century and that shipments virtually stopped after 1731.

Yet naval stores represented only one potential use of American forests. From the beginning of settlement in British America, colonists looked to forests for their economic potential. Thus William Wood published a rhyme enumerating the types of trees available in New England, believing that such information "may be necessary for mechanical artificers." "Trees both in hills and plains in plenty be," he began,

The long-lived oak and mournful cypress tree,
Sky-towering pines, and chestnuts coated rough,
The lasting cedar, with the walnut tough;
The rosin-dropping fir for masts in use,
The boatmen seek for oars light, neat-grown spruce,
The brittle ash, the ever-trembling asps,
The broad-spread elm whose concave harbors wasps,
The water-spungy alder good for nought,
Small eldern by the Indian fletchers sought,
The knotty maple, pallid birch, hawthorns;
The horn-bound tree that to be cloven scorns,
Which from the tender vine oft take his spouse,
Who twinds embracing arms about his boughs.
Within this Indian orchard fruits be some,
The ruddy cherry and the jetty plumb,
Snake-murthering hazel, with sweet saxifrage,
Whose spurns in beer allays hot fever's rage.

The dyer's sumac, with more trees there be,
That are both good to use, and rare to see.

(*New England's Prospect*, p. 39)

Wood's poem clearly suggests that colonists paid attention to tree species when they engaged in trade. Sugar planters in the West Indies, for example, needed barrels for their product, and they soon set up commercial ties to New Englanders for sufficient shipments of red and white oak for hoops and staves. Cedar, both white and red, proved ideal for clapboards, shingles, and fence posts; around Boston some Indians even became involved in the preparation of cedar products for the market. Further, colonists used conifers, particularly pine, to produce ships and naval stores—tar, turpentine, pitch, and resin—though production of these goods (other than ships), like the maple sugar industry that developed in northern colonies, did not have a substantial impact on American forests, especially compared with lumbering and clearing for fields.

Colonial lumberers soon altered the composition of American forests. Cedar and white pine did not grow well again in once-cleared areas. In general, hardwoods encroached on areas previously dominated by pines; red maple, for example, proved suited to regions formerly containing cedar. The use of various trees for specific economic functions, then, did not so much denude the forests as it altered their composition, which precluded their further use for the same purposes.

Wood for Fuel

But forests did decline in response to the growth of the colonial population. Wood remained, throughout the colonial period, the most important source of fuel for colonists, just as it had been for the Indians inhabiting the eastern woodlands before them. Indeed, when Indians moved their villages every fifteen to thirty years, they did so because they had depleted the fuel supplies within what they considered a reasonable walk from their homes.

Colonists, who took a rather different approach to their settlements, did not move to new supplies of wood after they had denuded nearby lots. Instead, they began to import the fuel they needed from the hinterland. Population growth, particularly in long-settled towns along the eastern seaboard, created the need for massive importation of fuel from the still heavily forested lands further west. During the 1760s colonists burned approximately one hundred million cords of wood (a cord being 128 cubic feet, or a pile of four feet [120 centimeters] by four feet by eight feet [240 centimeters]); during the next decade they used up about 125 million cords. Though the numbers continued to escalate into the nineteenth century, the figures for the late colonial period demonstrate the validity of some observers' fears that the continent's wood supplies were being depleted. Rising demand led to a rise in price, a fact recognized early in New York, Newport, Boston, and Philadelphia. The price increases led them all to appoint officials for inspecting the size of cords to ensure that customers received the amount of wood they ordered.

Further, the development of colonial industry, particularly the production of pig iron, created a need for substantial quantities of charcoal. Though difficult to calculate precisely, a recent analysis suggests that colonists needed tens of thousands of acres of forest to produce the quantities of iron made in North America in the eighteenth century. Iron "plantations," from the middle colonies northward, tended to exhaust nearby forests, sometimes in less than twenty years, after which the enterprises had to be abandoned or moved. Colonists traveling near such works noted the paucity of trees in areas formerly dominated by forests. Since charcoal fires to produce iron also changed the soil nearby, the ecological consequences of this early industrial activity went beyond merely denuding forests. The heavy consumption of wood for charcoal by the iron industry occurred even though iron producers in England had switched to coke for smelting during the eighteenth century; the persistence of wood-wasting technology demonstrated that American ironmongers did not believe depletion of supply to be a problem in the forseeable future.

Field Clearing and Building Needs

Though fuel consumed by far the greatest amount of trees in American forests, colonists were busy clearing for other purposes as well, notably for fields and construction materials. Settlers celebrated the clearing of fields, and they worked assiduously at the task until they had opened sufficient acres to sustain their farms. The importance of field clearing was evident in a rhyme, dating from at least the early 1690s in Pennsylvania, which extolled the process:

> When we began to clear the Land,
> For room to sow our Seed,
> And that our Corn might grow and stand,
> For Food in time of Need,
> Then with the Ax, with Might and Strength,
> The Trees so thick and strong,
> Yet on each side, such strokes at length
> We laid them all along.
> So when the Trees, that grew so high
> Were fallen to the ground
> Which we with Fire, most furiously
> To Ashes did Confound.

(Quoted in Michael Williams. *Americans and Their Forests*, p. 61)

Though estimates of rates of cutting varied, most colonists, in British America at least, could probably clear from ten to fifteen acres (four to six hectares) per year. French *habitants* found it more difficult to clear lands in the Saint Lawrence Valley; one Jesuit missionary noted that a man could clear about one and one-half arpents (one and one-quarter acre or one-half a hectare) each year "if he is not engaged in other work. . . . If they had an interest in the matter, perhaps they would do more."

Colonists used wood for their houses—though some rich colonists, to distinguish their homes from others, built their abodes of brick or stone—and for fences as well. The growth of the colonial livestock population and the need to keep animals out of fields led to substantial fence construction, particularly of so-called Virginia or worm fences. Though these fences—built of such trees as walnut, American chestnut, and oak—used much wood, colonists believed they were the most effective type of barrier they could construct, given the existing resources and time constraints. Without such fences, animals—both the livestock they had imported and indigenous species—would have happily consumed the farmers' crops.

Colonial methods for clearing land had a distinctive impact on American forests. During the early years of field clearing many colonists used girdling, a technique that killed trees where they stood and left them to be removed later. To girdle a tree, one had to cut a ring in the bark, whereupon the tree dried up and died. This allowed more sunlight, vital for crops, to reach the ground below. Some colonists, or the slaves they put to the task, then burnt the trees where they stood; others chopped them down when they felt they could spare the time. In either event girdling led to the distinctive look of eastern fields: crops sown among tree stumps. In the South, planters and their slaves sowed tobacco and other crops in the fields, though soil exhaustion, always associated with tobacco in particular, forced growers to move fields often; in their wake they left barren soil and tree stumps.

Though time effective, girdling did not prove the most popular form of clearing for many farmers, especially in northern areas, where farmers chose to cut trees instead. There they discovered a market for the ash from trees once it was purified into pot and pearl ash. Indeed the ash from trees burned to make way for fields became the first cash crop for many farmers in New York and New England, where land was covered by hardwoods such as sugar maple and oak, the best trees for producing ash. Once processed into lye, potash had a number of uses for colonists: some employed it in the manufacture of saltpeter and for tanning; others used it to make soap. Lye found a market not only in the areas of British America that were dominated by pines—and were thus unsuitable for local ash production—but overseas as well.

The Environmental Impact of Forest Depletion

Whether it was done for lumber or ash, the cutting of trees often had effects beyond the clearing of particular tracts. In order to make their lumbering operations more efficient, colonists at times cut trees right to the edge of particular watercourses; such openings allowed them to drag lumber more easily to rivers and streams and thence downstream to market. This practice increased the amount of runoff in these particular areas due to the destruction of roots that had absorbed water. More runoff meant more soil erosion, which increased the amount of silt flowing into rivers. Once in rivers, silt made watercourses shallower by elevating their beds; in summer, when rivers ran low as a matter of course, colonists found it even more difficult to travel by water.

The ecological consequences of this shift in rivers went beyond inconveniencing colonists. Shifting the levels of the streambeds altered the temperature of water in those channels and thus hampered fish, including trout and perch, that sought cool, deep water. Logjams on rivers, as well as milldams, also impeded the movement of fish, particularly anadromous species that migrated to spawn. By the end of the colonial period, some provincial officials had awakened to this problem, ordering that major channels remain unobstructed by milldams or fishing seines. However, legislation for this purpose stemmed from recognition of a profound, already existing problem and did not prevent substantial decline in fish populations into the mid nineteenth century.

Further, depletion of forests prevented the natural population growth of many animals and birds. Though the skin trades were directly responsible for the greatest decline in animals, the advance of colonial settlements impeded the reestablishment of these species. In particular, the "edge" habitats created and maintained by Indian fires diminished substantially; they either reverted to forest or became incorporated into colonists' fields. The loss of such areas had a dramatic impact on animals whose populations had earlier grown in response to the greater availability of foodstuffs in the edges. Deer, elk, turkey, quail, porcupine, and hare all thrived in these borderlands between fields and forests, and when their numbers increased, so did the numbers of animals who hunted them, especially wolves, foxes, hawks, and eagles. When the edge habitat declined, so too did the species that were dependent on it. Thus the wild turkey had dramatically decreased in number by the close of the colonial period; around 1672 one colonist reported that the bird was so depleted that " 'tis very rare to meet with a wild turkie in the woods" of Massachusetts. Deforestation also led to the drying up of lakes and streams, prompting animals that relied on these watercourses, such as mink, otters, and muskrats, to leave denuded regions.

By the end of the colonial period, the state of the forests throughout eastern North America showed the symptoms of economic development.

Fields replaced forests, and the landscape of the revolutionary generation bore little resemblance, in many places, to what early seventeenth-century travelers had observed. Even would-be developers feared the consequences. William Cooper, father of the novelist James Fenimore Cooper and the founder of Cooperstown, described the problem as it existed in central New York during the early nineteenth century:

Our winters require large supplies of fuel, and we have neither peat nor coal to resort to, when constant consumption in fuel and fencing will have rendered that most necessary article scarce. Nor have we other mountainous lands to resort to for wood, nor stony ground for the construction of stone fences. The soil being all fit for culture, will all be cultivated, and the wood of course wasted. (*Guide In the Wilderness*, p. 28.)

In much of eastern North America, the forests had yielded to the economic, and too often myopic, dreams of farm builders.

THE ECOLOGICAL CONSEQUENCES OF COLONIAL FARMING

To twentieth-century historians the fur trade and the thinning of the forests represent the most dramatic ecological developments of the colonial period. Each had a drastic impact on the environment of North America, and it was not until the twentieth century that some eastern parts of the continent began to recapture the biological diversity of the seventeenth century. Yet farming also altered the ecosystem in far-reaching ways, and with almost as many long-term consequences as the fur and lumber trades. Promoters of colonization circulated tracts proclaiming the fertility of American soils, thereby encouraging, from the very beginning of settlement, the transfer of European agriculture to North America. Some groups, notably Dutch settlers in the New Netherlands, Acadians in Nova Scotia, and English rice growers in South Carolina, modified the environment by diking marshlands, a practice already long-developed in parts of Europe. Other ecological changes associated with farming were more widespread. Most obviously, the clearing of fields out of once-forested areas led to depletion of forests, especially in British colonies. Also, bounties placed on predators and pests contributed to the decline in certain animal species. The spread of European-style farming, with its emphasis on cereals, tobacco, rice, and Old World livestock had other ecological effects as well.

Exterminating Predators

The expansion of European-style farming led colonists to post bounties for indigenous American predators that threatened their livestock and crops. Enterprising farmers and hunters could turn a profit by hunting specific animals in a campaign of deliberate destruction. Foxes, perceived as a threat to fowl, had bounties placed on them; so did squirrels, which attacked crops. But the predators most at risk from bounties were wolves. They had a special place in European folklore, and the threat of these creatures had led to their virtual extinction in Europe by the early modern period. In North America, however, wolves were ubiquitous, according to colonists. "These be killed daily in some place or other, either by the English or Indian, who have a certain rate for every head," William Wood wrote in the early 1630s. Despite this, he added,

there is little hope of their utter destruction, the country being so spacious and they so numerous, travelling in the swamps by kennels. Sometimes ten or twelve are of a company. Late at night and early in the morning they set up their howlings and call their companies together—at night to hunt, at morning to sleep. In a word they be the greatest inconveniency the country hath, both for matter of damage to private men in particular, and the whole country in general. (*New England's Prospect*, p. 46)

But Wood was mistaken. By the end of the colonial period, wolves had been wiped out in all but the northern areas of New England. More of them survived outside of New England only because the pressure of population on land was not yet as great as in that region. These predators survived best in the marshlands of the empire such as West Florida, where a 1770 law declared that hunters' habits of "leaving the carcasses of deer near the plantations" had enticed "wolves to the destruction of cattle."

Altering the Species Mix

Colonists' agricultural practices also changed the composition of species inhabiting farming regions. In essence farmers believed in single-crop fields. The resulting monoculture—in contrast to the mixed-crop fields of eastern woodlands Indians—altered the biological balance of particular tracts. By doing so, monoculture created ideal conditions for certain types of pests that, in the greater diversity of the forests and the Indian fields, had been unable to expand their populations dramatically. When corn or wheat fields replaced forests, thus driving out the insects and birds that had inhabited them, insects and birds that thrived on these cereals found themselves in the midst of a cornucopia. Almost immediately they had as much food as they could eat, while at the same time their traditional predators for the most part fled. Other pests similarly benefited, especially squirrels and crows, whose populations grew in spite of the bounties colonists placed on them. Further, the accidental transportation of European weeds and the persistence of Old World agricultural practices brought the familiar problem of wheat "blast" across the ocean. The disease, black stem rust, destroyed the grain and forced some farmers to plant other crops.

Soil Erosion

Erosion added to the ecological consequences of farming. Colonial farmers, like Indians, knew that the best soil for agriculture was usually in the floodplain of a river; periodic flooding replenished the soil with vital nutrients, and those who were willing to run the risk of having their fields wash away during particularly heavy spring runoffs could stave off soil exhaustion far longer than their neighbors who farmed higher ground. But when farmers cleared trees right to the edge of a particular watercourse, as many did, they soon discovered that those watercourses widened each year because the tree roots that had once helped contain moisture were no longer present. In some places, such as the Susquehanna Valley in northeastern Pennsylvania, colonists watched with dismay when the river progressively swallowed up the land they had struggled hard to clear and plant in the first place.

Farm Animals

The importation of livestock from Europe also had a profound impact on the landscape, though in far different ways than the depletion of forests

741

and erosion. Indians had never domesticated livestock in the way that Europeans had, though some tribes kept dogs long before 1492. The initial appearance of Spaniards on horseback mystified many Indians in Mexico, and Indians, in what was to be New France, became fascinated by the close relationship between colonists and large animals. Europeans had relied for centuries on domesticated livestock, particularly cows, horses, pigs, and fowl. When Dutch, Spanish, French, and English migrants ventured to America, they took these animals with them. The Dutch believed European livestock so vital to their colonization efforts that they forbade colonists from slaughtering any of the animals transported across the ocean, though the offspring of these cattle, sheep, horses, and hogs could be killed; severe penalties awaited anyone who violated the rule, and from their earliest colonizing efforts the Dutch tried to keep careful track of their livestock. Whether used for their labor, milk, eggs, hides, or meat, transported livestock were vital to all European colonists in spite of the increased risk of disease colonists ran because of their close contact with these animals.

European livestock proliferated throughout North America, and became the agents for the most profound ecological changes in the Southwest. In 1598 Spanish colonizers under the direction of Juan de Oñate drove seven thousand cattle to New Mexico from northern Durango, and in the latter half of the seventeenth century cattle ranches appeared in Texas; by the mid 1680s, with Spanish settlements spreading in the Southwest, cattle ranching developed in California, Arizona, and eastern Texas. Other European animals also moved northward from New Spain, at times under the direction of colonizers, at times on their own since there were not enough Spanish ranchers to control the growing herds. Sheep appeared in New Mexico by the early seventeenth century; hardy *churros*, an Iberian breed that yielded little fleece but proved remarkably adept at adapting to dry environments, became especially numerous in New Mexico, outnumbering cattle seven-to-one in the mid eighteenth century. Horses, too, moved northward from New Spain; Santa Fe became the central point for the Spanish distribution of horses for the Southwest, though feral horses also proved numerous. By the late seventeenth cen-

tury feral horses had spread through parts of New Mexico and Texas, and they continued to move northward: to the southern plains by the 1720s, to the upper Missouri by the 1730s, to the northern plains and Canada by the mid eighteenth century. One observer noted that Texas, by 1777, was densely populated by horses: "their trails make the country, utterly uninhabited by people, look as if it were the most populated in the world." The Spanish brought livestock to the Southeast as well; Pedro Menéndez de Avilés brought breeding herds of horses to Saint Augustine, the town he founded, in 1565 and to the Carolinas soon after.

The spread of European livestock throughout the Southwest had far-reaching effects on the environment. In particular, the grazing of cattle, sheep, and horses initiated long-term changes in the ability of soil to maintain water from California to Texas; these animals' hooves compacted soils they trod upon, and their grazing eliminated grasses necessary for preventing erosion. Runoff increased dramatically, forming deep gullies that transported much-needed rain out of desiccated areas rapidly; this gullying lowered water tables, and areas once home to vegetation and the animals drawn to these plants soon diminished; some areas even turned to desert. Wherever animals grazed near rivers, the damage was equally profound, especially when grazing had led to the breakdown of riverbanks and subsequent erosion.

Once in the Western Hemisphere, imported livestock soon altered American fields. North American grasses, at least those east of the Mississippi River, had never had to share fields with cattle, horses, and sheep; soon after the advance of colonial livestock into particular areas the indigenous grasses mostly died out, and they survived thereafter only in more remote areas. Fortunately for the livestock and their owners, some animals had unwittingly transported the seeds for the grasses they ate, the seeds perhaps clinging to hides or carried in hooves or dung. These accidentally transported grasses proved remarkably adaptable to American soil; within a short time, European grasses had even spread beyond the range of colonial settlement, their advance furthered by the fertilizer that often supported their initial growth. Over time the two most important grasses inadvertently imported by migrants, white clover and what is now termed Kentucky bluegrass, spread into trans-Appalachia before settlers turned their sights to that region in the late eighteenth century. Dandelions and daisies, seemingly so ubiquitous today, were also migrants to North America during the colonial period.

Old World Species in the New World Environment

Other European migratory plants also fared remarkably well in North America, including the Old World peach. Initially introduced in Florida by Spanish or perhaps French explorers as early as the sixteenth century, peach trees rapidly spread northward. The trees were so prolific that some colonists complained, in the words of the early-eighteenth-century explorer John Lawson, "that we are forced to take a great deal of care to weed them out, otherwise they make our land a wilderness of peach trees."

Old World livestock often prospered in North America. Pigs, at times left behind by explorers so as to provide a predictable source of meat for later venturers, fared remarkably well. They obtained nourishment from the indigenous roots that were so plentiful in the forests and also from the thousands of peach trees that spread prolifically, especially in the Southeast. Cattle, too, many of them free ranging, eventually fared well in the colonies; in the hinterland of Pennsylvania few households were without at least one cow, and so families could count on a regular supply of much-needed milk. Within a generation of settlement in most places, some of the cattle had become feral and soon inhabited territory from the lower Mississippi Valley to present-day Nova Scotia. Colonists everywhere integrated cattle into their economies and some, particularly in Carolina, even imported African slaves to tend the semidomesticated herds roaming the woods.

Staple Crop Production

In some sense the spread of colonial farming was, for migrants and their descendants, an unquestionable success, at least in material terms. But in places where the production of staple crops led colonists to pursue profits regardless of the far-reaching impact on the environment,

colonists so altered the ecosystem that they brought profound problems upon themselves. Glimmers of the difficulties brought by economic development were evident in the rise of lumber prices, especially in cities. More profound, however, were the consequences specific to plantation agriculture.

Nowhere were the ecological consequences of farming clearer than on staple crop plantations in the South and in the Caribbean. Plantation agriculture had a drastic effect on the mainland, particularly since tobacco farmers depleted fields of their nutrients rapidly and rice growers transformed the Carolina lowlands to irrigate their crops. Tobacco could exhaust soil within four years; rice depleted its soil more slowly because of the nutrients these fields periodically received from the water used to grow the crop. Because of soil exhaustion, planters eager to market the crops had to move their fields and their bound laborers periodically. Further, irrigated rice fields increased the amount of standing water in the Southeast and so provided more breeding opportunities for mosquitoes carrying malaria and, on occasion, yellow fever.

In the West Indies, the ecological consequences of economic development were still clearer. Europeans had developed an enormous demand for sugar by the early modern period, yet the climate appropriate for its production had been found only in places such as Madeira, and even there planting sugarcane proved so difficult that an observer compared the task of building the necessary irrigation system to the construction of the pyramids. But the West Indies, with their tropical temperatures and favorable winds, proved ideal for sugar, and colonists did not hesitate to prepare the ground for the crop and import hundreds of thousands of slaves to produce sugar and its byproducts, particularly molasses and rum. To those who believed that colonies in the periphery should exist to enrich the metropolis, the transformation of the West Indies into plantations made perfect sense.

Yet when migrants set about to produce sugar in massive quantities, beginning in the seventeenth century and continuing for generations, they denuded the islands of their indigenous plants and animals. Colonists stripped Barbados, perhaps the most important of the British colonies in the region, of its trees to make sugar fields. When Sir Henry Colt traveled to Barbados in the early 1630s, he found the island covered with a variety of tropical trees, which he described in his diary. A generation later he would not have been able to do that. By the 1650s colonists on the island had succeeded in virtually denuding the island of its trees, forcing the settlers to look elsewhere for needed lumber; by the 1660s, according to one study, the island "had less woodland than most districts of England." Colonists struggled enthusiastically to clear the indigenous vegetation of the island, apparently believing all the while that the growth of the forest impeded economic progress. By doing so, they deprived themselves of goods they vitally needed: wood for houses and the outbuildings and mills that dotted sugar plantations, wood for barrels, and wood for fuel. In order to make their economy profitable, then, planters had to import a product that had been on the island before the spread of sugar plantations. The pursuit of gain had done more than create the most horrendous labor conditions in the Western Hemisphere; it had also prompted colonists to transform what might have been seen as a paradise into an ecological wasteland devoid of the biological diversity it once boasted.

THE ALTERATION OF THE NATURAL ENVIRONMENT

In the final analysis, then, agriculture, and especially the production of staple crops for the European market, altered the environment of North America in ways as significant as the fur or lumber trade. The development of farming allowed colonists to recreate a beloved landscape, filled with familiar animals, familiar house types, and fences stretching across fields.

Yet in America, as in Europe, the creation of that landscape came at a high cost to the environment. In the end, the wasteful practices of colonists in the Americas, as they pursued economic development, diminished the biological diversity of the Western Hemisphere. Once transformed into commodities, the natural resources of North America did bring profits to those colonists able to take them to market. It remained for later generations of Americans to assess the precise costs of that transformation.

BIBLIOGRAPHY

Primary Sources

Bradford, William. *Of Plymouth Plantation, 1620–1647.* Edited by Samuel Eliot Morison. 1856; New York, 1952.

Cooper, William. *A Guide In The Wilderness.* 1810; repr., Freeport, N.Y., 1970.

Josseyln, John. *John Josselyn, Colonial Traveler: A Critical Edition of Two Voyages to New England.* Edited by Paul J. Lindholdt. Hanover, N.H., 1988.

———. *New Englands Rarities Discovered.* 1672; repr. 1972.

Quinn, David B., ed. *New American World: A Documentary History of North America to 1612.* 5 vols. New York, 1979.

Rea, Robert R., comp. *The Minutes, Journals, and Acts of the General Assembly of British West Florida.* University, Ala., 1979.

Thwaites, Reuben G., ed. *The Jesuit Relations and Allied Documents. Travels and Explorations of the Jesuit Missionaries in New France, 1610–1791.* Vol. 9, Cleveland, Ohio, 1896–1901.

van der Donck, Adriaen. *A Description of New Netherlands.* Edited by Thomas F. O'Donnell. 1655; Syracuse, N.Y., 1968.

van Laer, A. J. F., ed. *Documents Relating to New Netherland, 1624–1626, in the Henry E. Huntington Library.* San Marino, Calif., 1924.

Wood, William. *New England's Prospect.* Edited by Alden Vaughan. 1634; Amherst, Mass., 1977.

Secondary Sources

Albion, Robert Greenhalgh. *Forests and Sea Power: The Timber Problem of the Royal Navy, 1652–1862.* Cambridge, Mass., 1926; repr. Hamden, Conn., 1965.

Bamford, Paul Walden. *Forests and French Sea Power, 1660–1789.* London, 1956.

Bennett, Deb, and Robert S. Hoffman. "Ranching in the New World." In *Seeds of Change: A Quincentennial Commemoration.* Washington, D.C., 1991.

Carroll, Charles F. *The Timber Economy of Puritan New England.* Providence, R.I., 1973.

Clark, Andrew Hill. *Acadia: The Geography of Early Nova Scotia to 1760.* Madison, Wisc., 1968.

Cronon, William. *Changes in The Land: Indians, Colonists, and the Ecology of New England.* New York, 1983.

Crosby, Alfred. *The Columbian Exchange: Biological and Cultural Consequences of 1492.* Westport, Conn., 1972.

———. *Ecological Imperialism: The Biological Expansion of Europe, 900–1900.* New York, 1986.

Day, Gordon M. "The Indian as an Ecological Factor in the Northeastern Forest." *Ecology* 34 (1953):329–346.

Dunn, Richard S. *Sugar and Slaves: The Rise of the Planter Class in the English West Indies, 1624–1713.* Chapel Hill, N.C., 1972.

Harris, Richard Colebrook. *The Seigneurial System in Early Canada: A Geographical Study.* Madison, Wisc., 1966.

Hauptman, Laurence M. "The Dispersal of the River Indians: Frontier Expansion and Indian Dispossession in the Hudson Valley." *Canadian Ethnology Service Papers* 39 (1978):242–260.

Jordan, Terry G., and Natti Kaups. *The American Backwoods Frontier: An Ethnic and Ecological Interpretation.* Baltimore, Md., 1989.

Kozlowski, T. T., and C. E. Ahlgren, eds. *Fire and Ecosystems.* New York, 1974.

Krech, Shepard III, ed. *Indians, Animals, and the Fur Trade: A Critique of Keepers of the Game.* Athens, Ga., 1981.

Lower, Arthur R. M. *Great Britain's Woodyard: British America and the Timber Trade, 1763–1867.* Montreal, 1973.

Mancall, Peter C. *Valley of Opportunity: Economic Culture Along the Upper Susquehanna, 1700–1800.* Ithaca, N.Y., 1991.

Martin, Calvin. *Keepers of the Game: Indian-Animal Relationships and the Fur Trade.* Berkeley, Calif., 1978.

Merchant, Carolyn. *Ecological Revolutions: Nature, Gender, and Science in New England.* Chapel Hill, N.C., 1989.

Norton, Thomas Eliot. *The Fur Trade in Colonial New York, 1686–1776.* Madison, Wisc., 1974.

Pilleri, G., ed. *Investigations on Beavers.* Bern, 1983.

Ray, Arthur J. *Indians in the Fur Trade: Their Role as Trappers, Hunters, and Middlemen in the Lands Southwest of Hudson Bay, 1660–1870.* Toronto, Ontario, 1974.

Rink, Oliver A. *Holland on the Hudson: An Economic and Social History of Dutch New York.* Ithaca, N.Y., 1986.

Silver, Timothy. *A New Face on the Countryside: Indians, Colonists, and Slaves in South Atlantic Forests, 1500–1800.* New York, 1990.

Spurr, Stephen H., and Burton Barnes. *Forest Ecology.* 3rd ed. New York, 1980.

Thomas, Keith. *Man and the Natural World: Changing Attitudes in England, 1500–1800.* London, 1983.

Trigger, Bruce G. *The Children of Aataentsic: A History of the Huron People to 1660.* 2 vols. Montreal, 1976.

Vernon, Howard. "The Dutch, the Indians, and the Fur Trade in the Hudson Valley, 1609–1664." *Canadian Ethnology Service Papers* 39 (1978):197–209.

Weber, David J. *The Spanish Frontier in North America.* New Haven, Conn., 1992.

Williams, Michael. *Americans and Their Forests: A Historical Geography.* New York, 1989.

Wolf, Eric. *Europe and the People Without History.* Berkeley, Calif., 1982.

Wood, Peter H. *Black Majority: Negroes in Colonial South Carolina from 1670 through the Stono Rebellion.* New York, 1974.

Worster, Donald. *Nature's Economy: A History of Ecological Ideas.* 1977; repr. New York, 1985.

Peter C. Mancall

SEE ALSO **The Natural Environment.**